HANDLOADER'S DIGEST

1994/13th EDITION

Edited by
Bob Bell

DBI BOOKS, INC.

ABOUT OUR COVERS

Nosler bullets seemingly have been with us since the dawn of time, at least from a reloader's viewpoint, and we're proud to have them on the front and back covers of the 1994 HANDLOADER'S DIGEST.

Perhaps the best known of the Nosler line is the Partition bullet. The Partition has two cores, the two separated by a wall of copper jacket material. The front core is designed to flatten the jacket and curl it out and to the rear on impact. The rear core remains intact to ensure deep penetration. Because of its stellar performance over the years, the Nosler Partition is arguably the bullet of choice for big game hunting around the world. Partition bullets are available in all popular calibers and styles for today's hunting needs.

Nosler's single core bullets are also highly refined, and available in two styles—the Solid Base softpoint and Ballistic Tip. The Solid Base uses a conventional softpoint design for excellent mushrooming characteristics. The Ballistic Tip has a solid polycarbonate tip in the lead core to protect against tip damage in the magazine and to provide maximum ballistic coefficient. The cavity in the core behind the shank of the tip allows it to compress on impact, rupturing the jacket for reliable, consistent expansion. Ballistic Tip bullets are color coded according to caliber: orange for 22 caliber; purple for 6mm; blue, 25 caliber; brown, 6.5mm; yellow, 270; red, 7mm; green, 30 caliber; maroon, 338.

Nosler's handgun bullets have also gained an excellent reputation, whether they're used for plinking, competition or hunting.

Hunters have a choice of caliber and weight, hollowpoint or softpoint design for use in the game fields. All Nosler handgun hunting bullets utilize a pure lead core and a jacket with tapered interior and thin jacket mouth for expansion. Calibers offered are 9mm/.355-inch; 38/.357-inch;10mm/.400-inch; 41/.410-inch; 44/.429-inch; 45/.451-inch; 45 Colt/.451-inch. In other words, there's a Nosler handgun hunting bullet for nearly every hunting need.

Our covers also feature the popular and excellent Redding handloading tools, the first choice among many discriminating reloaders.

At center stage is Redding's "The Boss", a cast iron O-frame press with 36-degree frame offset for visibility and accessibility. The primer arm is positioned at the bottom of ram travel; there's positive ram travel stop machined to hit exactly top-dead-center; and the linkage provides tremendous mechanical leverage to handle the toughest case sizing chores. The Boss is available in kit form with shellholder and a set of Redding AA dies.

To the left of the press is Redding's new Competition Bullet Seating Die. This straight-line seater has a depth micrometer and a precision-ground seating stem to match bullet diameter. The micrometer is calibrated in .001-inch increments for precise seating depth and has a zero-set feature to zero for a specific rifle.

At far right is the new Redding Competition Model BR-30 powder measure. Designed strictly for the benchrest shooter, the BR-30 limits charge range from 10 to about 50 grains, the most useful for this kind of reloading. The powder baffle is placed above the metering chamber for exceptional charge uniformity. The micrometer uses a special mechanism to take up all minute tolerances in the screw thread, meaning the parts can't work loose and are fully self-adjusting—even compensating for wear over the years. The micrometer setting is guaranteed to be precise and exactly repeatable. Serious shooters need serious equipment, and Redding is more than able to supply it.

Photo by John Hanusin.

Manuscripts, contributions and inquiries, including first class return postage, should be sent to Handloader's Digest Editorial Offices, 4092 Commercial Avenue, Northbrook, IL 60062. All material received will receive reasonable care, but we will not be responsible for its safe return. Material accepted is subject to our requirements for editing and revisions. Author payment covers all rights and title to the accepted material, including photos, drawings and other illustrations. Payment is at our current rates.

Arms and Armour Press, London, G.B., exclusive licensees and distributor in Britain and Europe; New Zealand; Nigeria, South Africa and Zimbabwe; India and Pakistan. Lothian Books, Port Melbourne, Aust., exclusive distributors in Australia.

ISBN 0-87349-140-8

Library of Contress Catalog #62-15069

THIS IS THE 13th edition of HANDLOADER'S DIGEST and its first as an annual. The very first edition of HANDLOADER'S came out in the very early '60s and was followed at several-year intervals by eleven more. The late John T. Amber, renowned and long-time editor of *Gun Digest*, put out the first eight editions, and Ken Warner, who took over the editor's spot on *Gun Digest* after John died, put out HANDLOADER'S 9th through 12th, the last appearing in 1990.

But editing a huge annual like *Gun Digest*, plus annual editions of *Knives*, and being editor for *Cartridges of the World* every three years or so and *Gun Digest Treasury* in addition to writing an occasional book of his own, was a bit much, even for someone of Ken's awesome ability. So he plotted a way to shuffle HANDLOADER'S off onto a naive and unsuspecting friend of many years. Namely me.

I was sort of at loose ends, having recently retired after a 23-year stint as editor of *Pennsylvania Game News*, one of the oldest and largest-circulation state hunting magazines in the country. And I had at least a tenuous relationship with HANDLOADER'S, having been the associate editor of *Gun Digest* back in the mid-'60s, which automatically gave me the same position on HANDLOADER'S. Furthermore, I had been writing for decades as a contributing editor of *Gun Digest* and as a freelancer for HANDLOADER'S. Now, if you have been able to follow all that, maybe you can understand why I was offered the editor's job for HANDLOADER'S DIGEST.

It seems only reasonable to tell you that I'm a handloader, too. Have been since early 1946, when I finished three years in the Army. I mostly load rifle stuff, but also a fair amount of shotgun and handgun fodder. Like Pennsylvania's favorite gun writer, Don Lewis, I, too, had a small commercial handloading shop for some years...until it dawned on me that I was doing all the work and someone else was doing all the shooting. That didn't make a lot of sense, even for a guy who was weird enough to enjoy World War II. (Hell, the ammo was free!) Anyway, I gave up the shop, but I never stopped filling cases for myself. Tens of thousands of handloads have worn out quite a few barrels for me in the decades since.

I mention all this so you'll know I have a nominal acquaintance with the basic procedure of getting a new primer, powder charge and bullet into a case. I do not claim to be an expert. But I do know some experts, which gives me a chance to ask them complex questions about the subject.

A significant number of those experts have contributed to this edition of HANDLOADER'S DIGEST. If you've been reading handloading stuff awhile, as well as stuffing the cases, you'll recognize most of the bylines. Names like Ed Harris, Don Zutz, Ed Matunas, Dean Grennell, Sam Fadala, Dave Corbin, Rod James, Ken Walters...I could go on but it's simpler if you just check the Table of Contents.

They're a good gang, and I think you'll find that reading their articles is almost as good as it would be to personally argue guns and loads with them all night over coffee. (Maybe better; that way the coffee doesn't get cold.)

Now I want to tell you something important. Talking with these men and corresponding with them over a period of months, repeatedly brought one subject to the fore: safety. Taken together, these men have at least 500 years of handloading experience. But still, every time one of them uncapped a can of powder, or loaded a cartridge, he was fully aware that he was dealing with materials that have deadly force.

Many things can go wrong on a loading bench. The most important thing a handloader can do is make certain he is using the correct components for his purposes—cases that fit the rifle's chamber, bullets of the correct diameter, design and weight, the proper powder and the correct weight of powder. It's probably easiest to make a mistake with the powder in one way or another. Many of them look alike but no two of them have identical burning rates, even those with similar identifying numbers. Don't confuse one with another. And make certain your powder measure is set to throw the charge you want. Check it against a good powder scale, and check that the scale is set up properly. It's easy for the sliding weight on a scale beam to be jogged into an adjacent notch. That would normally put your charge 5 grains off, and if on the high side could make things disastrous. Check and recheck—that's what our contributors stress constantly, and they know what they're talking about. Believe them. I don't think you can match their 500 years of experience.

Bob Bell

CAUTION: Technical data presented here, particularly technical data on handloading and on firearm adjustment and alteration, inevitably reflects individual experience with particular equipment and components under specific circumstances the reader cannot duplicate exactly. Such data presentations, therefore, should be used for guidance only, and then only with caution.

Since the author, editor and publisher have no control over the components, assembly of the ammuntion, arms in which it is to be fired, the degree of knowledge involved or how the resulting ammunition may be used, no responsibility, either implied or expressed, is assumed for the use of any of the loading data in this book.

CONTENTS

FEATURES

CONTENTS

FEATURES

CATALOG

by STAN TRZONIEC

When handloading for serious shooting with an autoloader, be it for self-defense or high-level competition, remember this:

After charging cartridge cases with powder, it's a good idea to visually check that there's the same amount of propellant in each case.

Consistency

LET'S PUT OUR cards on the table. No matter how much you cut the deck or gamble on the status quo of today's modern handguns, automatics are the wave of the future. They will beat a full house anytime, especially when new variations and innovations hit the market quicker than you can reach for that extra ace up your sleeve.

I don't recall any firearm doing so much to the marketplace as automatic pistols. Looking back, the 357 Magnum really got folks to their feet, especially for big-game hunting with a large-framed revolver like the Smith & Wesson Model 27. The 44 Magnum came on board later—and, yes, it did raise a few eyebrows as both Smith & Wesson and Ruger vied for customers in a friendly battle that has not ended.

After that, it seemed like time stood still for quite awhile. Then, like a fog, small things started to generate here and there without much notice. With an upswing in crime, revolvers—mainly because of their bulk and limited cartridge capacity—were starting to get the thumbs-down sign within many law enforcement agencies. At the same time, custom makers were showing us they could slim down a large 45-caliber automatic to fit handily in one's belt or purse. Ammunition companies on the high side of technology, like Super-Vel, were loading light bullets at fast velocities to capitalize on expansion for greater knockdown (killing) power. After all, let's be frank: Defensive guns serve one purpose—*defense*!

While guns were getting better and munitions people were working long hours designing ammunition that would function perfectly in autoloading weapons, handloaders were having some related problems. At that time, handloading for autoloading pistols was comparatively new, and there were tricks and techniques to master before "100-percent dependability" could be claimed. And while good ammunition is indispensable to the well-being of a happy autoloader, guns

With today's modern autopistols, excellent accuracy can be obtained if you follow Trzoniec's suggestions in this article.

If the time comes when you have to protect your family or your home from a criminal or terrorists, you may have to depend upon handloaded ammunition.

Reliability

With modern autoloaders that are fine-tuned and carry excellent sights, you owe it to yourself to investigate all the possibilities available in handloaded ammunition.

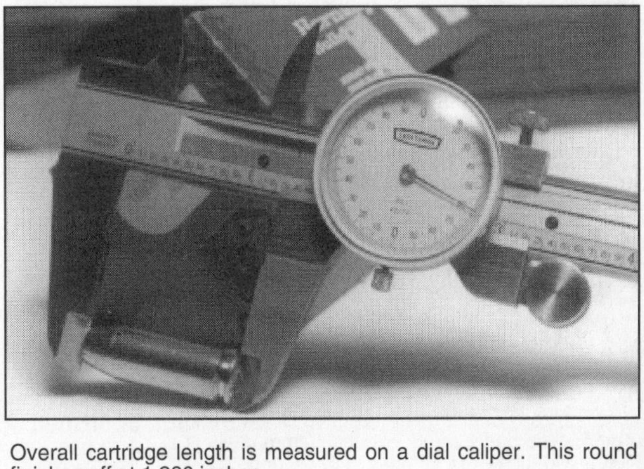

Overall cartridge length is measured on a dial caliper. This round finishes off at 1.280 inches.

Brass—and lots of it! The best way to start on the right track for perfect reloads is to buy new or once-fired American name-brand brass. After sizing, you will be ready to prime, charge with propellant, seat the bullet and taper crimp.

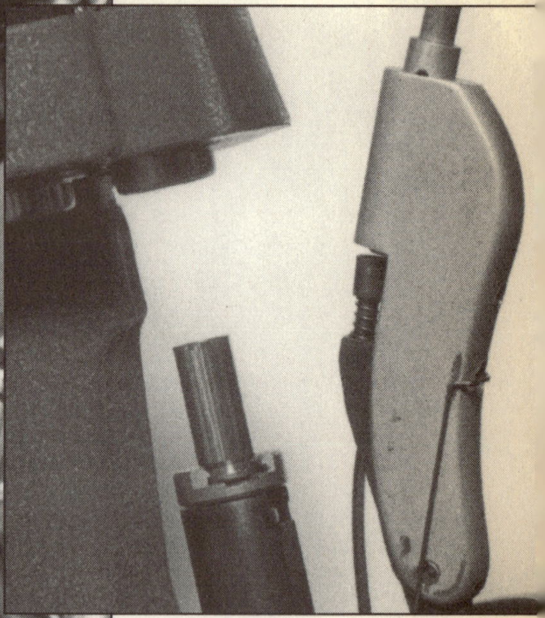

Here is the small but important flare on the case as discussed in the text. The primer arm is ready and waiting, as in the author's procedure this is a two-step operation—flaring and priming the case.

Even if you load large quantities of cartridges, you can turn out excellent ammunition if you follow the author's suggestions.

have also come a long way in the finishing department. This writer can remember all too well that it was almost routine practice to "tune" an automatic when it came from the box to ensure proper feeding and functioning. Barrels and slides were checked for smoothness and fit, feed ramps were polished with Dremel tools and Cratex wheels, and magazines, magazine wells and feed lips were massaged to bring about the ultimate in reliability, especially if involved in serious handgun use.

My education with automatics came from shooting in competitive games like IPSC and regular target matches. How quickly I learned about "stovepipes," "failure to feed," and, worse yet, "failure to eject." To win, you not only had to shoot well, but be armed with a very reliable pistol. Although my experience fell in the fields of 9mm, 38 Super and 45 ACP, my techniques applied to everything from the minute 25 and 380 ACPs to present-day wonders like the 10mm Automatic and 40 Smith & Wesson.

If I had to focus on one word in handloading ammunition for autopistols, it would be consistency. Over the years, many an autoloading pistol has fallen to the wayside simply because it would not work. Period. Many chose the revolver because, if for some reason a round did not fire, just cycling the gun via double action brought another round under the firing pin. The automatic, some thought, was just too chancy. If you had a misfire, you then had to use the other hand to jack the slide back to eject the dud and then let it slam shut into shooting position. Some blamed the gun; most blamed the ammunition. As time marched on, we recognized the pitfalls and corrected them. Today the automatic is the weapon of

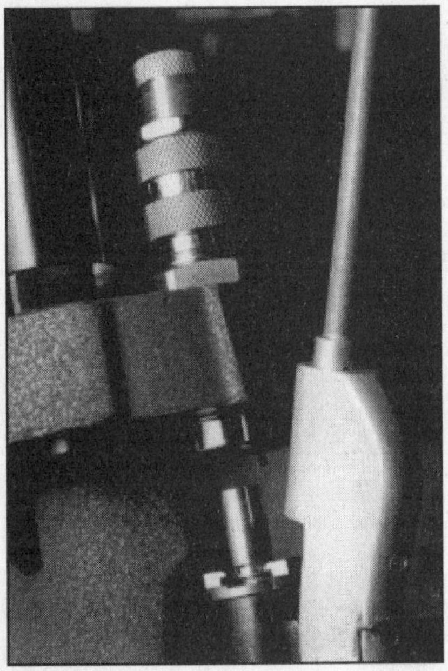

The first step is to size all cases (even the new ones) to factory specifications. Here is the author's setup in one of his vintage Lyman presses.

choice in a vast number of law enforcement departments and for countless individuals concerned about personal protection.

Now, let me explain how you can reap the benefits of shooting your automatic pistol with ammunition of infallible quality in easy-to-understand handloading steps.

First and foremost is brass—lots of it. There's nothing better than starting on the right foot. So with everyone in the business today—Federal, Remington and Winchester—producing better than acceptable brass, there is no excuse for not procuring the finest around. When I purchase brass, no matter the cartridge being loaded, I start with at least 500, often more. Two reasons. One, it's cheaper in the long run, and two, you are assured of getting one lot, or run, of brass, which simply means that all 500 cases were made at the same time and at the same location. Again, when striving for consistency, this is a good place to start.

If the budget is tight and you're into once-fired brass, that's all right, too. All you have to do is separate your brass by headstamp before moving on to cleaning and inspecting. What is not all right is mixing in steel military cases (as in the 45 ACP), bargain basement brass, or cases of foreign manufacture which might be Berdan-primed. Once-fired brass can be purchased locally from many sporting goods shops; in fact, if you are lucky, they might already be sorted out and boxed. One final note: Never depend upon once-fired brass for defensive loads. Always have clean, fresh cases in your gun when your life may depend upon your handloaded ammunition.

In any event, whether utilizing pristine or once-fired brass, there are a few duties to perform before moving on. Pick out any deformed cases (yes, there can be imperfections, even with new brass). Irregularities can include deep scratches, body dents, wall cracks, case mouth damage from ejection or rim problems that could, in the overall picture of things, severely hamper operation. After this primary inspection, throw the whole batch into the tumbler, primer and all in the once-fired cases, for that all-important first-round cleaning session.

Some may ask, "Why not size those cases first, and then clean them?" Good question, and that's OK if they are factory fresh. But if you are looking at once-fired brass, it's better to clean everything first than run the small risk of damaging that expensive tungsten die with something that got stuck on a case wall. After tumbling is complete, shake and check all cases for tumbling media or minor deficiencies that may have slipped by the first time.

Full-length sizing is next, and without hesitation, you do it even to factory brass right out of the box. Why? Because even new brass can include out-of-round cases or case mouths that need some truing up before they are expanded or belled on their way to becoming a finished round. Now, with the press bolted down to your bench, let's talk about dies for a minute.

On our long road toward consistency, the last thing we want to do is scrimp on reloading dies. Don't feed the kids for a week, raid the cookie jar, do whatever it takes, but purchase the best carbide die set you can afford. The days of case lubing are over, especially when it comes to automatic pistol ammunition. Leading manufacturers such as Hornady, Lyman, RCBS and Redding, to name a few, create die sets at a level of precision not even dreamed about a dozen short years ago. One other point—when ordering a die set, if it doesn't already include a taper crimp die, get that, too. I'll have more on that later.

The first die (in your four-die set) should contain a carbide insert and a decapper. This die's purpose is twofold. First, with it we true-up (new) or resize (fired) cases. On the same upstroke we eject the expended primer. Sometime back, one of the major die companies made the decapper part of the expanding/belling die, but as I see it, this increased the work effort. I believe die sets with the decapper incorporated into the sizing die are the best choice in both money spent and time saved.

Both large and small primers are used in semi-automatic cases. The 10mm on the left uses large primers, the new 40 Smith & Wesson on the right takes small primers.

When using the sizing die, it's important to check the *inner* dimensions carefully with regard to *outside* bullet diameter being used. While the sizing die reduces the case to essentially factory dimensions, it still must hold a bullet tightly after the case mouth is expanded slightly to facilitate starting a bullet. As an example, the inside measurement of my 38 Super die is .352-inch, which is right for bullets of that caliber that mike out at .355. In yet another example, my 10mm Automatic die set reads .356 for a 40-caliber bullet. This inside tension combined with the later use of a taper crimping die will keep the bullet from being driven down inside the case during feeding; that could result in a malfunction or, more importantly, high pressure problems upon ignition.

After sizing and subsequent cleaning, run through the cases, making sure primer pockets are free of any lubricant (if you insist on using those outdated conventional dies) or debris in the form of tumbling media. Next, check for overall case length as specified in recent

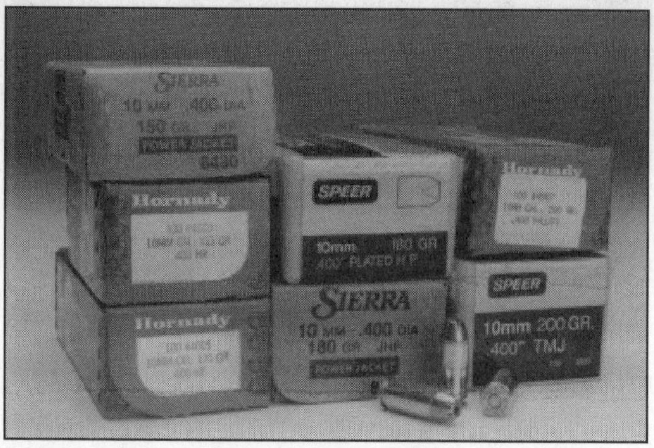

A small selection of the bullets suitable for both the 10mm and 40 Smith & Wesson cartridge.

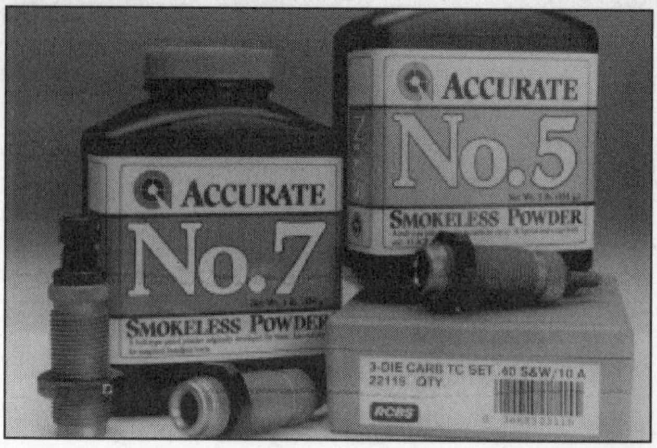

Here are examples of the top quality dies and powders available to today's handloader.

loading manuals. Too long a case will keep the slide from closing; too short a case can lead to misfires. If you are running a bit on the long side, which is common after three to four shootings, shorten the cases on a case trimmer made by RCBS, Lyman, Hornady or one of the other brands on the market today. You are now ready for the next step.

Although expanding the case mouth may be the smallest part of the entire operation, it is one of the most important. Too much flare will lead to premature mouth splitting due to the constant working of the brass; too little will cause crushing of the mouth as there is no clearance for the bullet to enter the case.

The best approach is to work slowly. First, take the expanding die apart and check the outside dimension of the "plug." You will notice that it has a slight taper near the top; this, in effect, is where the taper starts (and ends) and is regulated by the depth of the expander plug downward toward the shellholder. Checking my 9mm expander, for instance, shows that it measures .352-inch, which again is just about perfect for .355 bullets.

Place the outer body of the die in your press and screw it downward until it almost touches the shellholder. Place a case into the shellholder, raise it to the uppermost limit of the press and leave it there. Screw the expander into the die until you feel a slight resistance as it starts to enter the case. Now, alternating movements of the handle and lowering the plug will soon get you to the point where you begin to notice a belling of the case mouth. Stop! Remove the case and place the base of a bullet on the case mouth. If the bullet tilts or tips to one side or the

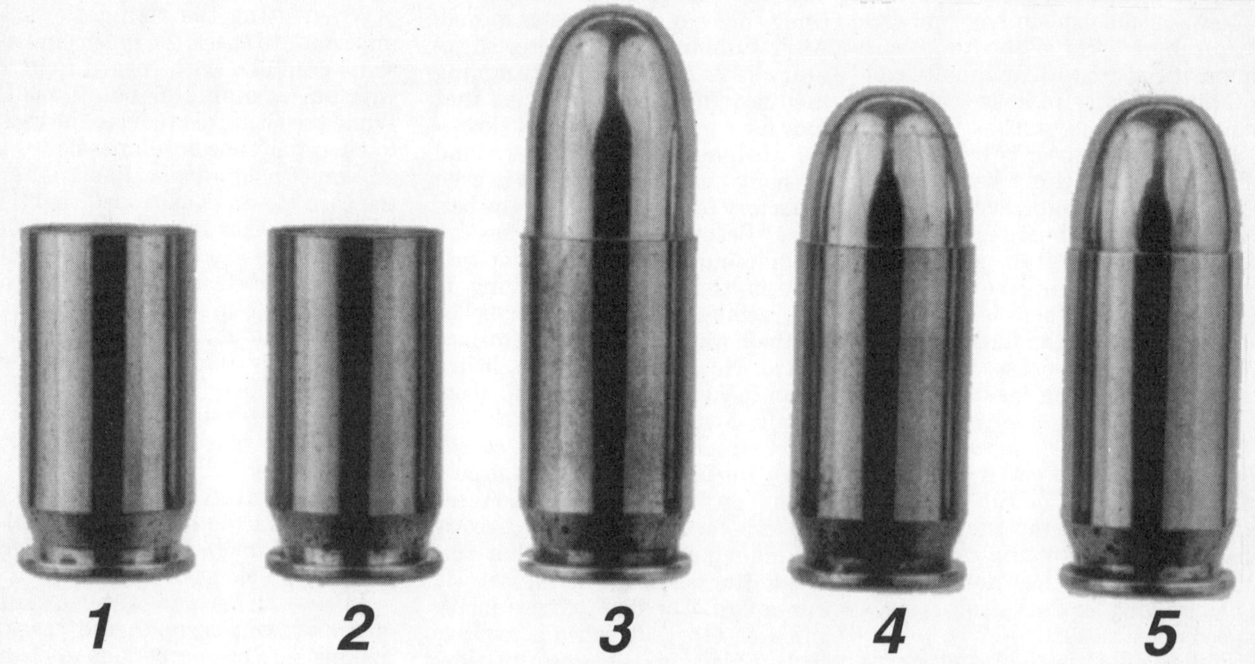

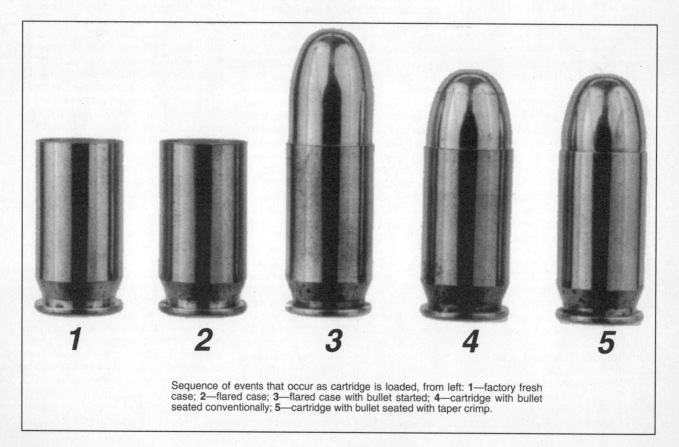

Sequence of events that occur as cartridge is loaded, from left: **1**—factory fresh case; **2**—flared case; **3**—flared case with bullet started; **4**—cartridge with bullet seated conventionally; **5**—cartridge with bullet seated with taper crimp.

An inside view of the taper crimp die discussed in text shows the gradual inside taper which not only removes the flare made on the case mouth during loading, but also helps guide the complete round into the chamber.

other, expand the case mouth a little more by turning the plug downward. When the bullet sits perfectly on the case mouth, *stop* again and tighten everything down. You're now ready for the next operation—priming.

Actual priming of your cases can be accomplished a number of ways. The first is by use of a hand priming tool which simply means that you prime each case separately and away from the press—even while watching television. To me this is labor intensive and gets you away from the mainstream of things happening right at your loading bench. The second option—and in my opinion the best—is to prime the case on the downstroke out of the expanding die. This saves time, and since the case has been centered on the expanding plug, priming is that much truer within the primer pocket, adding yet another dimension to our quest for consistency.

Primers are made in two sizes and two intensities: small and large, regular and magnum. Small primers are used in cases like the 380, 9mm and 38 Super. Large primers go into such notables as the 10mm and 45 ACP. Because our small-capacity automatic cases thrive on faster-burning propellants, regular primers are fine; magnum primers are not needed nor desired.

On propellants, the field is generally open, but I suggest limiting choices to faster-burning products like Bullseye, Olin's excellent 231, Unique, Accurate Arms No.5 or No.7, Red Dot, Herco, and, one that I especially like in the 38 Super, Hodgdon's HS-6. Keep in mind that small cases demand fast powders for a quick recoil impulse to cycle and charge your autopistol.

Bullets are also available in designs and weights that were unavailable in years past. Pick the projectile according to your needs (target, hunting, defense) and match the powder load with data available in the accompanying chart and up-to-date loading manuals. Stay away from maximum loads as they tend to batter both shooter and the gun in short order. If you need something more powerful, go to another cartridge or gun. Don't even think about *magnumizing* autopistol handloads.

After carefully weighing and verifying all charge weights as they come from your powder measure, charge each case in your loading block in succession. Check each case for the proper amount of propellant. Be advised that fast-burning powders don't fill up cartridge cases completely, so there can be space for a double charge—*an extremely dangerous situation*. Inspect all cartridge cases for the proper powder level.

The next step is bullet seating. First, check the manual for the correct overall length with bullet installed (OVAL). While these figures are not carved in stone, variables do exist that can make or break the total operation of your favorite autopistol. Bullet depth can vary, but keep in mind we are talking in *thousandths* of an inch, not in quarters of an inch. If the gun does not feed right, perhaps the bullet is out too far and is hitting the top inside of the chamber on its trip from magazine to breech. Too deep seating can increase pressure to sometimes dangerous levels, or give bad accuracy and erratic velocity readings.

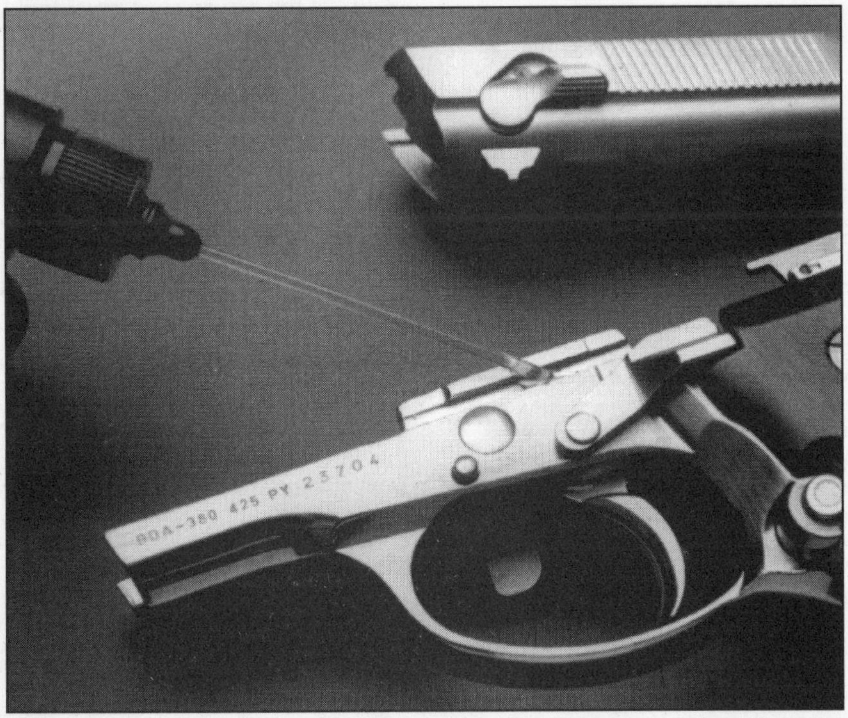

One other step that must be adhered to is the very limited use of lubrication on automatic pistols. Too much will just gum up the works, trapping residue from the spent cartridges and rendering your pistol useless. One or two drops on the slide rails is more than sufficient to keep that pistol running flawlessly.

Now that you have mastered the handloading of fine semi-automatic ammunition, go out and shoot it.

SELECTED SEMI-AUTOMATIC HANDLOADS

Caliber	Bullet (Wgt. Grs.)	Bullet (Type)	Load (Grs./Powder)	MV (fps)
9mm	88	Speer	5.5/Bullseye	1425
9mm	90	Sierra	7.0/Unique	1501
9mm	100	Hornady	6.5/Herco	1300
9mm	115	Hornady	5.7/Unique	1250
9mm	115	Speer	5.0/WW231	1205
9mm	124	Speer	4.5/Bullseye	1096
9mm	130	Sierra	4.7/700X	1186
38 Super	90	Sierra	6.9/WW231	1382
38 Super	100	Speer	7.0/Unique	1323
38 Super	115	Sierra	6.9/Unique	1262
38 Super	124	Hornady	8.7/Blue Dot	1131
38 Super	130	Remington	9.8/HS-7	1264
40 S&W	150	Sierra	7.8/AA5	1168
40 S&W	155	Hornady	10.0/AA7	1025
40 S&W	170	Hornady	6.9/AA5	1028
40 S&W	180	Sierra	6.5/AA5	941
40 S&W	200	Speer	6.0/AA5	887
10mm	150	Sierra	12.6/AA7	1285
10mm	155	Hornady	13.3/AA7	1361
10mm	170	Hornady	12.2/AA7	1255
10mm	180	Sierra	11.5/AA7	1138
10mm	200	Hornady	10.3/AA7	1110
45 ACP	185	Sierra	5.2/Bullseye	900
45 ACP	185	Sierra	7.3/Unique	950
45 ACP	200	Speer	4.0/Bullseye	800
45 ACP	230	Hornady	5.7/WW231	750
45 ACP	230	Hornady	6.5/Unique	850

The above loads are from the author's personal files. When starting out please reduce the above by 5 percent and work up as favorable conditions permit. The author and publisher assume no responsibility for typographical errors, so please check each load by cross-referencing against current reliable reloading manuals.

Finally, after all the parameters have been served, it's time for taper crimping. This, in my opinion, has been the greatest single factor in gaining autopistol reliability over the years. Taper crimping makes each round consistent with the rest of the batch just loaded, and it takes just a short time to do. Taper crimping involves smoothing that expanded mouth of the case inward, essentially streamlining the case so it feeds flawlessly. Since photos sometimes speak better than words, the ones nearby showing the sequence of loading events should help illustrate the point.

A word to cost-conscious shooters. Some die makers now incorporate the taper crimp into the seating die so both can be done at the same time because the bullet is exactly centered in the die for concentricity. An excellent idea.

Today's modern autopistols offer a level of accuracy, reliability and dependability never before seen in the field. While factory ammunition works wonders in new guns, handloading really brings out the best of both worlds. Whether your game is target shooting, hunting at moderate ranges or just plinkin' on the north forty, reloading is the way to go.

And the way to accomplish this 110-percent level rests on one word: *Consistency!* ●

Varmint rounds that the writer is currently loading include, from left: 17 Remington, 22 Hornet, 224 Weatherby, 220 Swift, 223 Remington and 240 Weatherby Magnum.

One-hole accuracy is fascinating as an abstract goal for a cartridge-stuffer, but most back-pasture chuck shooters can go with...

PRACTICAL HANDLOADING FOR VARMINTS

by LONNY WEAVER

VARMINT SHOOTERS reload for accuracy, but can a varminter get carried away with accuracy reloading?

Let me give you a relatively recent practical example of what I am getting at.

My all-time favorite varmint cartridge is the sizzling 220 Swift. Well, a couple of years back, Remington's Custom Shop began putting together a varmint hunting version of their famed 40X target series of bolt actions chambered for the Swift. The rifle, as you may know, wears a Kevlar stock, 27¼-inch heavy stainless steel barrel, and has about the sweetest trigger you'll ever come across on a factory rifle.

Anyway, as soon as I could scrape together the cash (Remington does not give these babies away), I dashed off my order and settled back for a not very patient year-long wait.

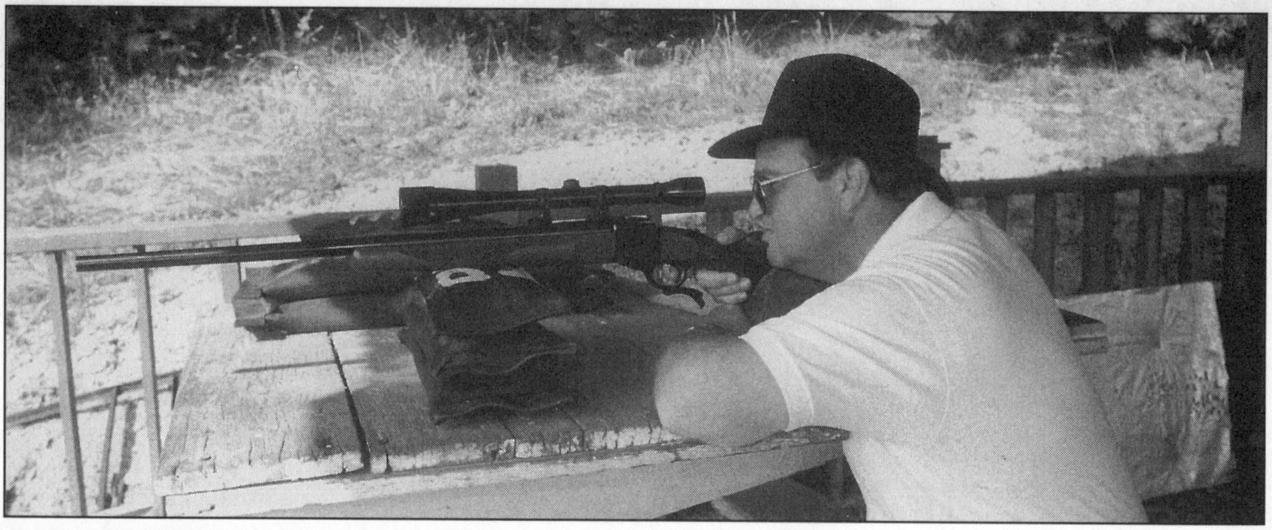

Always test your handloads from a solid shooting position. The writer is trying a batch of loads in a 220 Swift Ruger No. 1V from a benchrest. Note the sandbags under the forearm.

As luck would have it, the rifle came the first week of May. I was so excited I took a day's vacation, mounted a Redfield 6-18x Golden Five-Star scope, grabbed a couple of boxes of reloads consisting of 38.0 grains of IMR-4064 behind a Sierra 52-grain hollowpoint boattail bullet and ignited by a CCI 200 primer in a full-length sized Winchester case, and headed for the range for a morning sight-in session to be followed the rest of the day by chuck busting on a previously scouted farm.

I used the first twenty rounds to gently break in the barrel, settle the action and scope mounts, and to get the scope adjusted to print 1½ inches high at 100 yards. The second box was used for serious paper punching. Four five-shot groups averaged .588, the smallest going into a tight .340-inch.

I used this load all summer to ring up eighty-three chucks out of eighty-six shots.

The following winter I decided to see just what this Remington Swift would do with "proper" handloads.

Starting with new brass sharing the same case lot number, I spent nearly a week's worth of evenings turning necks, weighing cases, and performing an endless list of nitpickings guaranteed to put me in

These two chucks won't be eating more soybeans, thanks to a practical handload in this Sporter-weight Remington 700 BDL chambered for the 223.

This RCBS Posi-Prime tool uses a standard shellholder and allows the handloader to "feel" the primer into place during the separate priming operation.

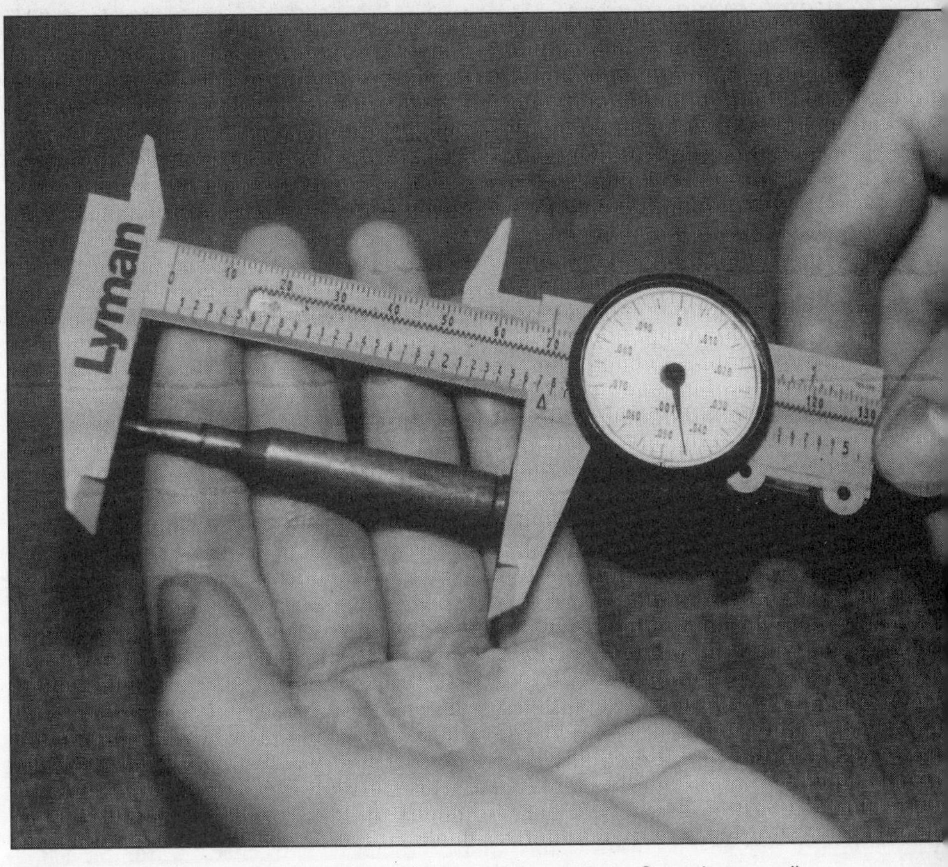

Correct bullet seating depth is a prerequisite to superb accuracy. Once that overall cartridge length is determined, record the information for future loads.

the one-hole class of paper punchers.

It just did not happen.

My best "super" load beat my everyday load by a mere .004-inch.

A case of overkill, in my humble opinion.

The trick to developing a top-notch load for your favorite varmint rifle is to complete the task without burning out the barrel, breaking the family budget, and wearing yourself out.

I've loaded for all of the current commercial varmint rounds, a couple of obsoletes, and a small handful of wildcats over the last quarter-century, and can't recall a single instance when a good, practical handload couldn't be put together with a minimum of fuss.

This is not to imply that all benchrest loading techniques are a waste of the varmint shooter's time, money and effort. Quite the contrary, in fact. But, the bitter truth of the matter is that few, if any, production-grade hunting (and that includes varminting) rifles are capable of significantly benefitting from super loads. For sure, darn few shooters, myself included, are capable of profiting from such loads in a practical hunting sense.

What's a "good practical handload?"

For my purposes it's the one that produces the best combination of speed and accuracy.

One of my favorite rifles is a beautiful little Kimber Model 82 Custom Classic chambered for the mild-mannered 22 Hornet. Mine wears a 24-inch semi-target barrel. Topped with a 3-9x Leupold Compact scope in Kimber mounts and rings, this little honey weighs a scant 8¾ pounds.

For some reason, the Hornet cartridge's famed accuracy had always evaded my efforts. When I got this Kimber, I was also using an old Savage 219 break-action single shot that usually could be counted upon to put five rounds of Winchester Super-X ammo (both the 45-grain softpoint and the 46-grain hollowpoint) into a shade under 2 inches at 100 yards. The Kimber routinely shaded that average by a little more than a quarter-inch. I tried every 45-grain bullet I could lay my hands on and still had a tough time beating the Winchester-made stuff in both rifles.

And talk about problems! For some reason I still haven't figured out, I began getting stuck cases in both rifles with mild charges of IMR-4227. That's when I threw out the book on conventional wisdom relating to loading the Hornet.

Realizing the Hornet is a 150-yard cartridge, I asked myself why I should confine bullet choice to the single selection everyone in the know recommended—the 45-grain slug. Fact was, at the time, the only load I had come up with capable of marginally beating the factory offering barely exceeded the velocity of the rimfire 22 WMR!

I began using 40-grain softpoints from Speer and Sierra and immediately cut group size dramatically, while boosting velocities to between 2700 and 2800 fps with W-680 powder teamed with the Winchester 6½ primer. And guess what—no more stuck cases. So what if the 40-grain pill loses velocity faster than the usually recommended 45-grainer? Started out much faster, the lighter bullet has more than enough punch left to level any 150- to 175-yard chuck in my neighborhood.

About the time I traded the Model 219 away to a buddy, I stumbled upon another unconventional Hornet tip when an acquaintance of my father mentioned that he always used pistol primers when loading the round back in the late '40s. About a year later, Ross Seyfried passed on the same tip received from a *Guns & Ammo* reader.

By substituting a CCI 500 pistol primer for the usual Winchester 6½ I had been using to ignite my load of W-680, I cut average group size from a hair over an inch to a neat .824. This got my attention and I subsequently settled on 13.0 grains of W-680 teamed with the CCI pistol primer. The load generates 40 fps less velocity than with the small rifle primer, but shrinks average group size to a startling .626.

Speed and accuracy.

One other thing before we get down to actual mechanics. I believe in loading my varmint rifles to their potential. Not overloading, of course, but to the level that will give me the highest practical velocities with trouble-free loads. A lot of emphasis is placed by some of the accuracy clan on the importance of loading below maximum in order to obtain top accuracy. Sorry, but I don't buy this line of wisdom. If I wanted a lesser cartridge than say, a 22-250, I would buy a Hornet, 222 or 223. It has been my experience that ½- to ¾-inch groups (and often less) are just as easy to get when loading a given centerfire varmint cartridge to full throttle as it is to underload. Remember, you are loading for practical hunting—to humanely dispatch varmints—not just for shooting the tiniest possible groups off a rock solid rest at known distances with the help of wind flags and other aids.

At the very least, you should begin load development by separating your brass into brands. Naturally, I use only Remington brass for my 17 Remington reloads simply because that's the only source. I began using only Winchester brass for all of my 220 Swift reloads when it became apparent that was more readily available locally than offerings from Norma and Frontier. Likewise, Weatherby is still the only source of 224 WM and 240 WM brass for the varmint hunter. In the instance of the more popular rounds such as the 222, 223, 22-250, 243 and 6mm, which are available from many sources as either factory loaded ammo or new unprimed brass, my advice is to confine yourself to the one that is most available or, perhaps, the most accurate factory offering in your particular rifle.

When the opportunity arises, it's a good idea to latch on to five or six boxes of new, unprimed brass sharing the same lot number. That number is usually found on the inside flap of the box. If your local gun shop doesn't stock an extensive line of reloading supplies, simply ask that they order you "six boxes of ______ (fill in the blank)." More than likely it will be of the same lot.

By the way, I always start with six boxes. I load the first 100 rounds and save the remaining 20 for replacements due to wear, reloading slips, losses in the field, etc.

The idea behind sorting by brand is uniformity. Not all brands of brass are of uniform wall thickness. Chances are, though, that each Federal 22-250 case, for instance, is very close dimensionally to the one before and after it. By buying new brass from the same lot, you are improving your chances in regard to case dimensions as well as chemical properties, annealing, etc.

Some handloaders weigh their cases to ensure even better uniformity. I've done that, but if my purpose is to slay woodchucks in farmer Hale's pasture, consider the task a waste of time. Case weighing doesn't tell you all that much anyway. A better indication of case uniformity, if you simply have to do this in order to sleep, is to check water capacity. Then, separate the cases by capacity.

Unless you have put a few thousand dollars into a super-duper pasture-poodle plasterer, you will also find case head squaring a royal waste of time. I make mention of it only for record.

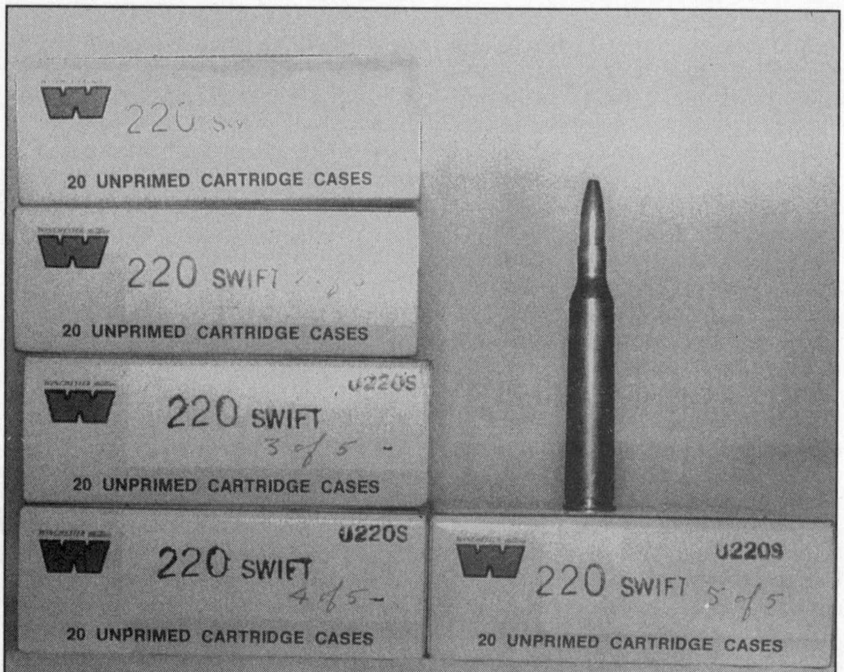

When buying new brass, always order from the same lot number and keep cases separated by lot as was done with these 220 Swift cases.

In the instance of new brass, I always run the cases through a full-length sizing die to square them up (you will be surprised how "unsquare" new brass can be), trim to an even overall case length and do a couple of things to the primer pocket.

Until a few years back, I didn't do much to primer pockets except make sure they had a flash hole and to clean them up after every couple of loadings. Don't laugh about that "flash hole" business. I've got a .224-caliber Weatherby case that slipped by without one.

After reading about reaming flash holes to the same diameter and squaring primer pocket bases, I gave both a try over an extended period of time and do believe they encourage uniform powder ignition and thus improve accuracy in a practical sense. Both jobs are easy and quick, which, in my opinion, adds to their appeal.

American cases have their flash holes punched. Usually left behind on the inside of the case head is a burr of varying degrees; this tends to hinder uniform ignition of the powder charge. I use a K&M Flash Hole Uniformer that, at the twist of the wrist, deburrs the hole and turns it to a uniform diameter. Then I grab a Match Prep from Whitetail Design and Engineering and, with another twist of the wrist, recut the primer pocket to a uniform depth.

Before each reloading of a fired case, I clean the primer pocket. Some experts doubt the usefulness of this, but I figure that if I'm going to the trouble of uniforming flash holes and primer pockets, it would be folly not to clean up the area after each firing.

By the way, you can get away with using a drill bit for flash hole reaming, if you wish. Supposedly, American cases have a hole measuring .080. But if you have a new 22 or 6mm PPC, don't let someone sell you a reamer. These cases have drilled holes that should not require deburring/uniforming.

OK, now for neck turning. I believe Neal Knox was the first to write about neck turning and, my goodness, it seemed like overnight every shooter in America was shopping for the tool. Admittedly, many cases have lopsided necks due to manufacturing processes that leave the case thicker on one side than on the other. Outside neck turning helps this as does, to a lesser degree, inside neck reaming. There are a number of outside neck turners to choose from and most are hand held. All are difficult to adjust and no fun to operate. I don't use them and doubt that you should either, unless you have a rifle that requires it to get the round chambered.

I currently own varmint rifles from Kimber, Ruger, Remington and Weatherby, and can honestly say that neck turning did nothing to dramatically enhance the accuracy of these fine rifles. No difference was apparent in my 17 Remington Kimber 84 Super Varmint, 22-250 Ruger No. 1V, or 224 Weatherby Varmintmaster. As noted at the beginning of this piece, there was a very slight improvement in my 220 Swift Remington 40X KS Varmint Special. The reason, of course, lies in the chamber dimensions of my production rifles. I believe that if you are not already shooting half-inch or better average groups with your varmint rig, neck turning will not show an apparent improvement.

The last step to perform before actually loading the new brass is case mouth chamfering. This is an important step that prevents base deformation when seating the bullet in the case. The trick is not to put a knife-like edge on the case, but rather a smooth, gentle bevel on both the inside and outside of the case mouth. Done properly, this bevel will also encourage square seating of the bullet. I've used a chamfering tool from Lyman for at least twenty years. Just give the tool a gentle twist. That's all.

Since you are only going to load "new" brass once, now is the time to touch on the arguments of full-length sizing versus neck sizing only of fired cases.

When you gently stroke the trigger on your Remington 700 Varmint Special or maybe your tack-driving Winchester 70 Varmint, tremendous gas pressure caused by the burning powder charge expands the flexible walls of the brass cartridge case against the rifle's chamber wall and bolt face. When the bullet rushes out of the case mouth, the elasticity of the brass case makes it instantaneously retract, though it doesn't completely go back to its original dimensions. You now have a "custom fitted" case, so to speak, that very closely matches the dimensions of your rifle's chamber.

If this case is to be used again in only this particular varmint rifle, you do not need to resize the case back to its pre-fired dimensions. All you need to do is resize the neck portion of the case so that it will once again tightly hold the bullet in place. This is known as neck sizing.

Full-length sizing, then, is done by forcing the entire case fully into the resizing die. This essentially returns the entire case to its original unfired dimensions.

Most benchrest shooters neck size only. Reloading experts generally recommend neck sizing only for maximum accuracy and minimum wear and tear on the expensive brass case.

I full-length size all of my cases and have found no loss of practical accuracy or brass longevity compared to neck sizing. Almost without exception, neck-sized cases are harder to chamber smoothly and quickly and in my opinion will, over a number of reloads, likely cause a flexing of the action upon chambering of the round due to uneven bearing on the locking lugs.

This recalls the first real problem I encountered when I began reloading in earnest many years ago. My first true varmint rifle was a Winchester M70 220 Swift. Until I bought it, I had never loaded in quantity and found the superb, hand-held, neck sizing Lee Loader at under $10 to fit my needs perfectly.

All went well until the fourth loading of my Winchester brass. The stuff would not chamber except with great effort. Guessing that the brass was "worn-out," some new was purchased, and on about the third reload, the same chambering problem was encountered.

Having read of the strength of 220 Swift brass from the popular writers at the time, I wrote to the National Rifle Association. for a solution to my problem. I still have the letter that stated, "the 220 Swift is a difficult cartridge to reload and cannot be safely reloaded by the neck sizing method."

I stumbled on the real cure myself when a case length gauge was bought. Case trimming cured the problem. On reflection, I have no idea why that Model 70 did not blow to pieces.

Neck stretching is unpredictable. I remember a particular lot of 223 Remington brass that required trimming every other firing. Later, using the same load but with a different lot of brass from the same source, my records show I got six firings before having to trim. Actually, those cases still hadn't reached maximum length, but they were trimmed for uniformity. Be safe and use a case length gauge or calipers and check for safe length every time following resizing.

I've always made case priming a separate operation. At first, this was done because that was the procedure required by my Lee Loaders. Later, when my budget allowed the

In working up a handload, first pick the weight and style of bullet you wish to use and go from there.

purchase of a benchmounted press—an RCBS Jr. that I'm still using with perfect satisfaction—I had the option of priming in conjunction with case resizing, but just couldn't get used to the idea or feel. "Feel" is what primer seating is all about.

The hand-held tool allows me to actually feel the primer bottoming in the primer pocket, and firm contact is another element of accuracy loading that is essential as well as practical.

Some years back, I began using the beautifully made RCBS Posi-Prime tool when I discovered that a Lee or MRC tool could not be readily had to accommodate the odd-size case head of my 224 Weatherby. The RCBS tool uses the same shellholder employed in the reloading press.

When handling primers, be extra careful not to contaminate them with oil or resizing lube. That's another reason I make priming a separate operation. After lubing and sizing the cases and cleaning the primer pockets, I wipe the excess lube from the resized cases, clean up the loading area, wash my hands and only then begin handling my primers.

For the most part, I use standard primers. Despite some rather lengthy testing on the subject, I can't really detect much difference between them in terms of practical accuracy. The only exception concerns my loading of the 17 Remington. Here, I normally use only the rather thick Remington $7^1/_2$ to protect against pierced primers. The CCI BR4 match-grade primer has also given me excellent service in this 17-caliber.

Of course, brands and types of primers often differ in "hotness." If you change primer brands or types (magnum for standard rifle, for example), always cut the powder charge in your established load by 10 percent and work back up in order to avoid any potential pressure problems.

When I sit down to load a batch of 100 cases for one of my rifles, I fill the powder measure, adjust it to give the desired charge, throw and check-weigh a couple of charges, and then proceed to rhythmically get the job done. I do not weigh individual charges for my varmint rifles.

Done correctly, with a bump of the charging handle at the top and bottom of each stroke, charge weight is, for all practical purposes, as accurate as individual weighing. The only time, in fact, that I individually weigh charges for my varmint rifles is when I get involved with a load development project.

Developing a load can be a bewildering task unless you absorb a little ballistic fact, sit back and look at things logically.

The first step in developing a good, practical varmint load without burning out the barrel in the process is to decide on the bullet weight and type you wish to use. The second step is to go through several handloading manuals and pick out the powders giving the highest velocities for that particular bullet weight. More times than not, these powders and the heaviest listed charges will come very close to filling the case to the base of the neck. Such loads are "balanced" and likely to produce the best accuracy.

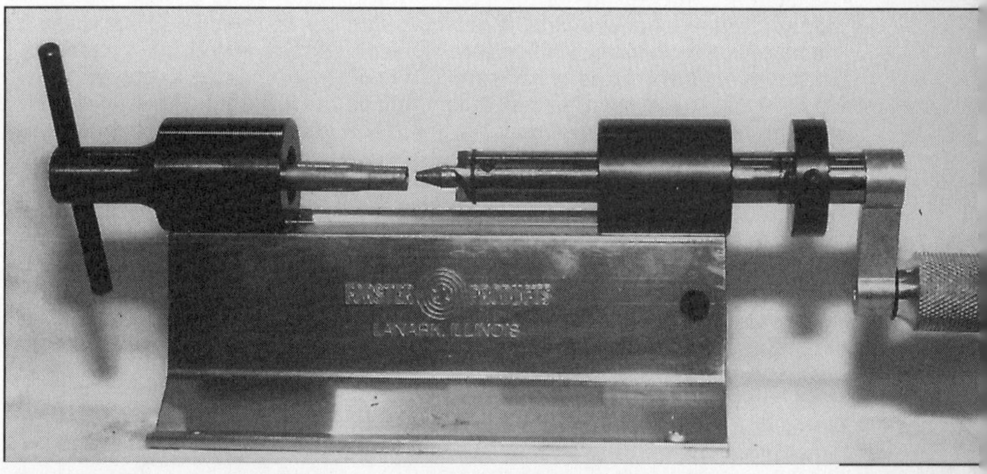

Excessive case length is an invitation to trouble. Trim cases when they approach maximum length and "true up" new unfired cases, such as this 22 Hornet.

For example, let's say you just became the proud owner of a spanking new 22-250 Ruger No. 1V single shot and want to come up with a crackerjack load using the explosive Speer 52-grain hollowpoint bullet.

Grabbing *Nosler Reloading Manual Number Three*, you will find three loads producing the highest velocities with the 52-grain bullet: 34.0 grains of IMR-4895 or 40.0 grains of IMR-4350 will give you an even 3800 fps, while 36.0 grains of IMR-4320 generates 3780 fps.

I'd go for the two heavier loads employing IMR-4350 and IMR-4320, cut the charges by 10 percent and load three rounds each in increasing half-grain increments until reaching the top listed charges. This little task is done to make sure I don't get into excessive pressures and to quickly determine the most potentially accurate load boasting the highest practical velocity (remember: "speed and accuracy").

Next I'd select the two most accurate of these loads, put together twenty rounds of each, return to my benchrest and squeeze off four five-shot 100-yard groups, allowing a full minute between shots to avoid overheating the barrel. That can destroy accuracy in no time flat. The barrel is then given a thorough cleaning, a fouling shot is sent up the barrel, and the next string of five-shot groups is carefully fired.

This done, I'd measure each group, come up with an average, and pick the most accurate as the winner.

Some time should be put into the selection of bullets, but expensive match or custom-grade bullets are not always needed for top-notch accuracy in off-the-shelf varmint rigs. And, some bullets in my experience always seem to turn in superb accuracy and terminal performance. Several that immediately come to mind are the 25-grain Hornady 17-caliber hollowpoint, the Sierra 40-grain softpoint, Nosler 45-grain softpoint, Speer's 52-grain hollowpoint in the 224 calibers and the 75-grain 243/6mm Hornady hollowpoint. Of course, some rifles simply will not shoot a particular bullet worth a darn for no apparent reason.

At present, my "contrary rifle" is a beautiful Kimber Model 84 Super Varmint chambered for the 17 Remington. For example, it simply will not shoot any Remington bullet (factory load or handload) worth a darn. I tried some custom pills in 20-, 22- and 25-grain weights, and still came up short in the accuracy department. Yet, when fed the little Hornady driven to 4018 fps, this

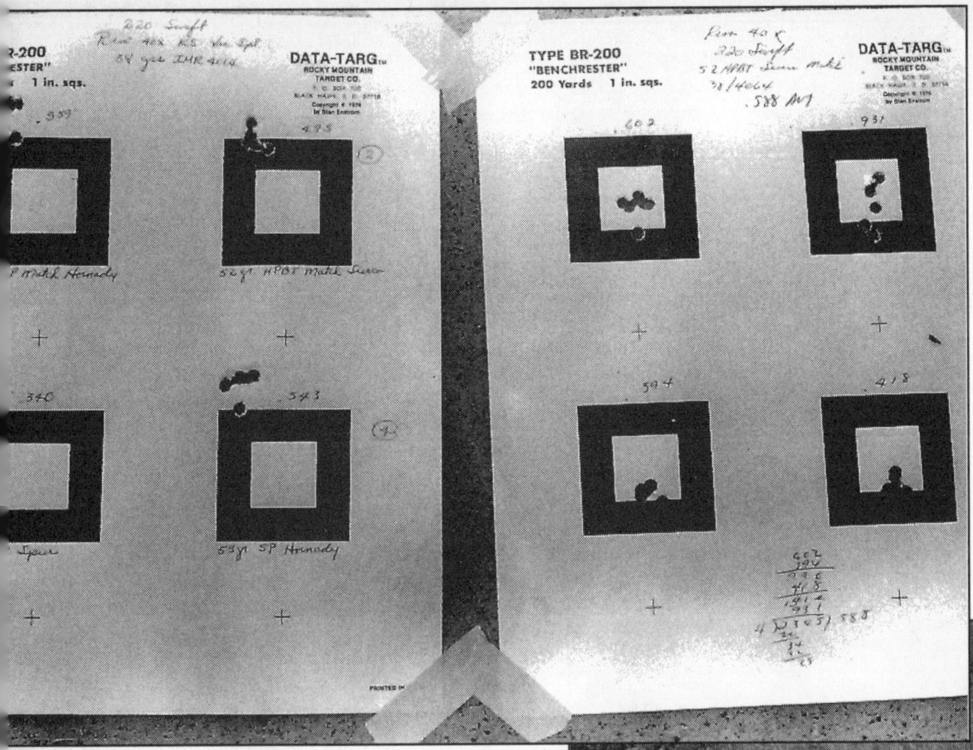

The four groups on the left represent the same charge (38 grains IMR-4064) behind four different bullets—53-grain HP Match Hornady, 52-grain HPBT Match Sierra, 52-grain HP Speer and 55-grain SP Hornady. The four groups on the right, fired from the same 220 Swift Remington 40XB with the same load, used only the 52-grain HPBT Sierra Match bullet.

Writer checks groups fired with 220 Swift handloads from a Remington 40XB KS Varmint Special.

rifle will stay well under minute-of-angle all day, every day, so long as I clean the barrel regularly.

Occasionally I hear or read of match-grade bullets that fail to expand on chuck-size varmints at the longer ranges when driven at moderate velocities. I have never experienced this problem, but confess to confining the more expensive match bullets to the bigger cased 22 centerfires like the 224 WM, 22-250, 220 Swift and a 22-243 wildcat that I played with awhile back.

Once I settle on a specific varmint load, the only refining you will find me doing to it will concern bullet seating depth. Most of my varminters shoot best with the bullet barely "kissing" the rifling. However, not all of my chuck rigs (if they have a magazine that I wish to utilize) will allow me to seat my bullet to that magic overall length. It has been my experience that one of the biggest contributions to accuracy is finding and using the correct bullet seating depth.

By the way, if your varminter has some age on it or an unusual amount of barrel wear, you might be able to restore its formerly superb accuracy by simply going to a heavier, and thus longer, bullet. I did this very thing a few years back with a Ruger 77V 22-250 that was bought new back in the early '70s. My standard load utilized a 52-grain Speer hollowpoint pushed to almost 3800 fps. After nearly 4500 rounds of this load, the throat area was showing wear, which in turn was showing up on targets. I did some experimenting with 55-, 60- and 70-grain bullets, and finally settled on the Speer 70-grain pushed along with 38.0 grains of IMR-4350 to a snappy 3376 fps. In my Ruger this load keeps on drilling neat little five-shot groupings measuring a hair or so beyond a half-inch.

Lastly, always keep good records. I have most of my handloading data on computer disc dating all the way back to that first Winchester Model 70 220 Swift. My loading records are broken down by rifle and contain not only load development and experimentation data, but information on the rifle (serial number, date of purchase, rifle cost, etc.) as well. Just as important, I can account for practically every round sent down a particular rifle's barrel, whether fired at varmint or target, thus allowing me to keep tabs on barrel wear. •

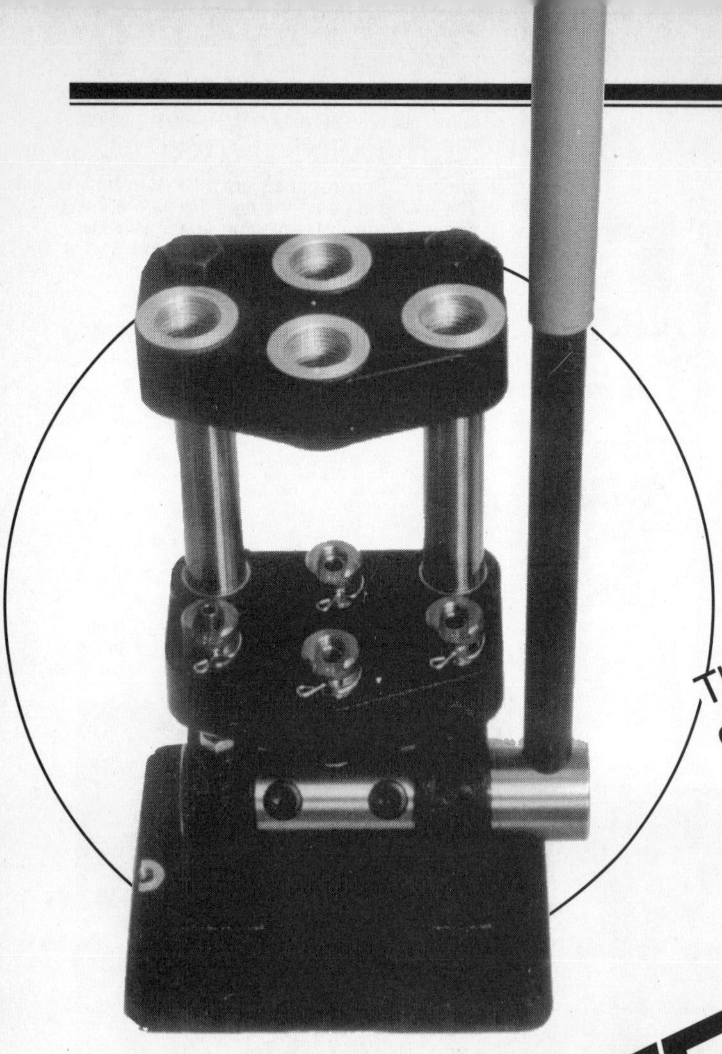

A typical H-press

Though automated reloading tools date back more than a hundred years, today's handloaders want to know what's available today. So here's a rundown on...

THE STATE OF THE PROGRESSIVES

by KENNETH L. WALTERS

OVER THE COURSE of the last ten or so years, hand-operated progressive reloaders have gone from being virtually unknown to dominating the reloading of metallic cartridge ammunition. Here we're going to examine the various models currently available from the major manufacturers.

There has always been some confusion, I think, as to just what is a progressive. Part of the problem is that several terms are used to describe these machines, and the terms have never been all that clearly defined. We'll look at this first. Where I've included a definition, the word is in **bold** type so you can easily find it.

A **progressive** at minimum does all the various reloading functions simultaneously, minimizes case handling and incorporates both automatic priming and powder charging.

Some progressive-like reloaders haven't quite lived up to this minimum list of functions. Usually such machines require manual effort to seat the primer or throw the powder charge. For lack of a better name, I call these machines **pseudo-progressives**. Pseudo, of course, means false. Some of the early Dillon, Hornady and RCBS machines were pseudo-progressives. They were nice machines, mind you, but they weren't true progressives.

Another term you'll occasionally run into is **semi-progressive**. In this design, all the reloading steps were done simultaneously, but each and every case had to be manually advanced between the reloading stations. Semi-progressives were usually just an automated variation of the old H-press idea.

Historically there have also been several progressive designs, but one, in particular, the circular, has dominated. **Circular progressives** have all their reloading stations laid out in a circular pattern. All the machines discussed here are circular progressives.

On many circular progressives, the dies and powder system can be removed as a unit by removing a **tool head**. Caliber conversion by tool head removal considerably speeds up the conversion process.

Circular progressives have another unique feature. All the cases are held in a **shell plate**. The shell plate is the circular progressive's equivalent to the single station's shellholder. This plate may be either manually or automatically advanced, but advancing one case advances them all.

Finally, the progressive design that competed against the circulars from the mid-1930s until just recently was the **straightline**. In these, the dies are laid out in a straight line across the front of the machine.

The departure of the straightline shouldn't be grieved. Though for awhile they were a price-attractive alternative to some of the earlier circulars, they all were rather mechanically complex.

Why did the circular progressives eventually dominate? Because they are easier to use and because they were very aggressively marketed.

The appeal of a progressive is its high reloading rate. This is possible because all reloading functions are done simultaneously and because many of these functions are automated.

Though we tend to think of progressives as a rather recent invention, that's not true. Patent literature clearly indicates that such machines were in use as early as the mid-1880s. Obviously, then, progressives have been around for a very long time.

Star Machine Works

Star Machine Works introduced their first progressive in the late

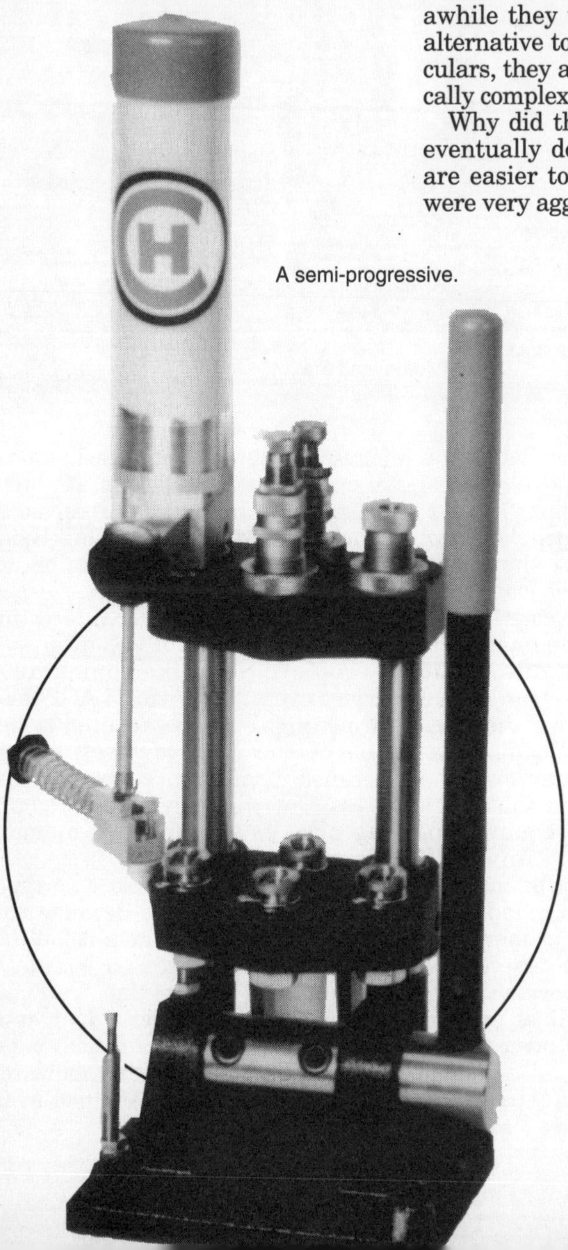

A semi-progressive.

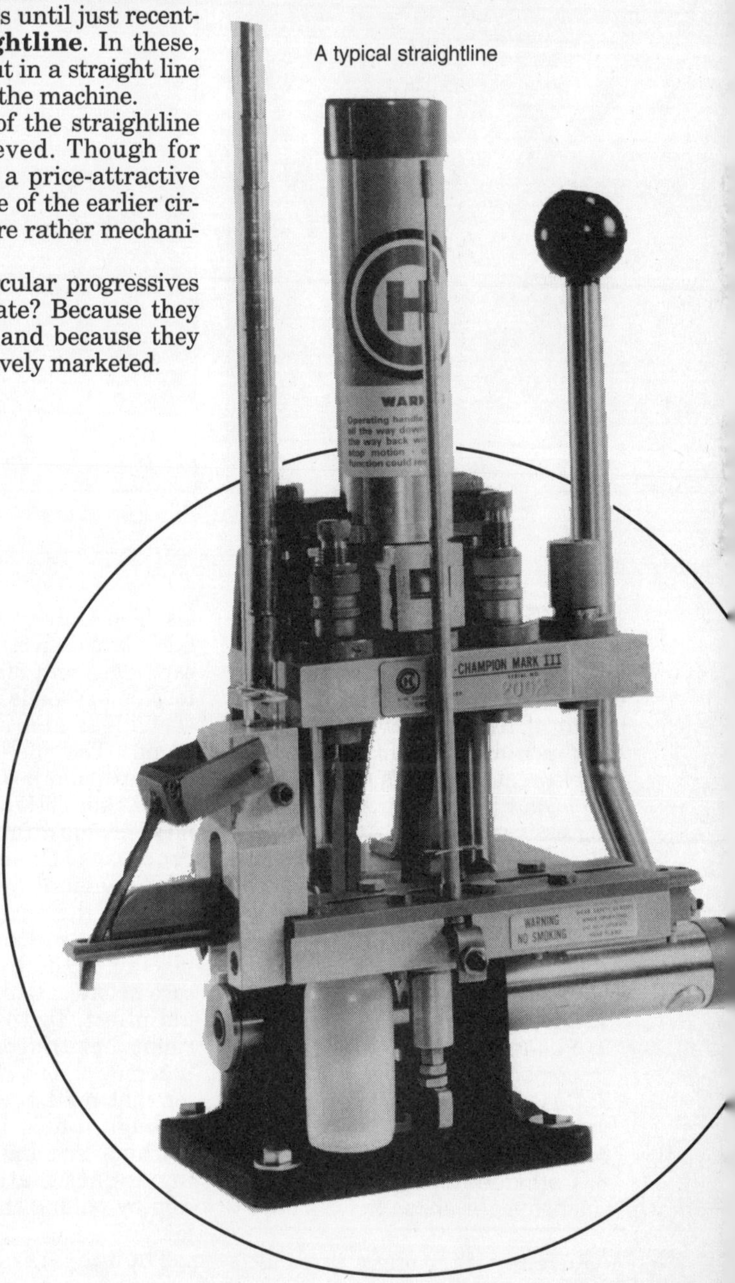

A typical straightline

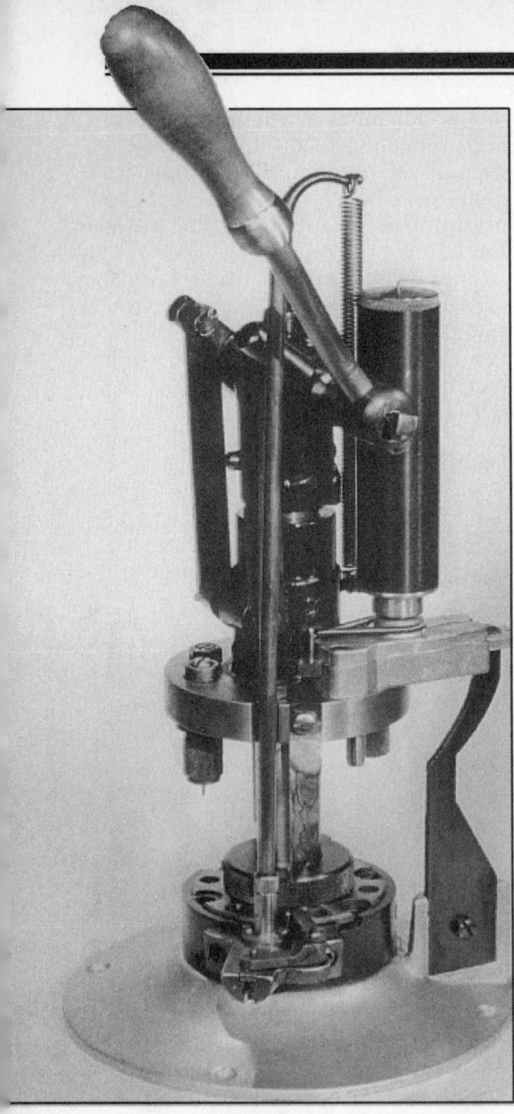

The Star Universal

A totally automated Star

1920s. Though there are design differences between the Star and most of the other models available today, in many ways the Star design set the layout of the reloading stations for the machines that followed. Thus we'll look at the Star's reloading station layout in order to see how most progressives work.

The Star has six reloading stations that perform all of the tasks indicated below. Most other progressives are at least similar.

Reloading Station: Task Performed
1: Case insertion.
2: Full-length resizing and spent primer removal.
3: Case-mouth flaring and priming.
4: Powder charging.
5: Bullet seating and crimping.
6: Cartridge removal and double-charge prevention.

Currently, Star offers three models. The Universal is available in a fairly large selection of popular pistol cartridges and 30 Carbine. The pistol/rifle tool loads most popular pistol cartridges and several short rifle rounds. The rifle machine loads most of the popular large rifle cartridges.

The Star design has an interesting mix of manual and automatic processes. Case insertion, **case advancement** (advancing the cases between the various reloading stations) and **bullet placement** (the placing of the bullet on top of the case before seating) all require manual effort. In the Star Universal, rimmed cartridges must be manually removed, but rimless rounds and, for that matter, spent primers, fall through a hole in the base of the machine. Priming and powder charging are automatic. Caliber conversion by pulling the tool head is trivial.

Though Star has never made accessories to automate their manual operations, others have. No other progressive, in fact, has received so much after-market attention. Using these accessories, a Star can be virtually automated to death.

The Star has another interesting historic distinction. It was extensively copied. Star-like copies have loaded everything from 25 ACP to 50 Browning. I always wanted to see one of the 50 Browning clones because it must have been one *big* press. Unfortunately, it also had one *big* price tag—$6000+, if memory serves.

On the Star Universal, two types of dies are available. Because this Star was introduced long before the industry standardized on $^7/_8$x14s, it has its own unique size. You can, however, special order a Universal with $^7/_8$x14 dies. Some machining of the dies may be necessary, however, to make them fit into the tool head.

Though no longer made, this Star-like progressive loaded the 50 Browning. It was expensive and very large.

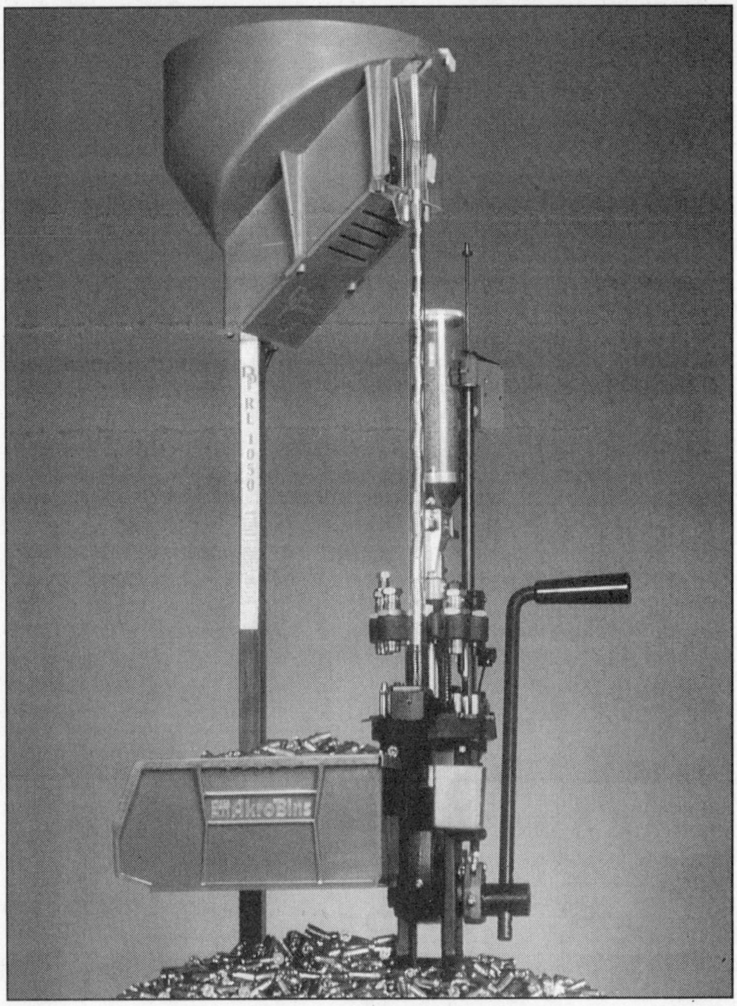

The Dillon RL1050

Star will do this for you. The other two Star models use only 7/8x14 dies.

The Star comes completely assembled and adjusted. On virtually all other progressives, some assembly is required. This assembly can range from truly trivial to quite a bit of work.

The Star has one final distinction. Because they have been made for more than sixty years, if given anything approaching proper care, it is a documentable fact that a Star will last a lifetime. Certainly there are other excellent progressives, but only Star can point to decades of long-term survivability for their quality product.

Dillon Precision

Star Machine Works essentially introduced the progressive, but Dillon Precision popularized it. More than any other company, Dillon understood the power of advertising. There can be no doubt that Dillon's aggressive advertising not only made them the leading progressive manufacturer, but also established the progressive as the dominant metallic cartridge reloader.

Dillon also excels at customer support. Many firms do a fine job here, but Dillon pushes this hard. All Dillon progressives have a lifetime guarantee and, whether your unit is in current production or not, if you need support, you'll get it.

Dillon also aggressively upgrades, improves or replaces their models almost continuously. Many of the improvements Dillon has made over the years were easily retrofitted to their earlier, similar units. Some competitors have suggested that this continuous product refinement is somehow bad. Not true!

The current Dillon line consists of four machines: the RL1050, the RL550, the XL650 and the Square Deal. This isn't quite the right way to refer to them, as some have a B suffix, meaning the second version of, but I've ignored that distinction. All these machines, incidentally, have removable tool heads.

The RL1050 is the current top of the Dillon line. The RL1050 can load pistol rounds and a few short rifle cartridges, as well as incorporate automatic case insertion and advancement, automatic priming and powder charging, and primer pocket swaging.

As good as the RL1050 is, it's the RL550, and its predecessors, that made Dillon what it is today. This design, a Dillon original, is based on a modified single-station O-press. This approach, which many other firms have now adopted, is, I think, the force behind low-cost, reliable progressives. As was true of the Stars, there is an interesting mix of manual and automatic operations in

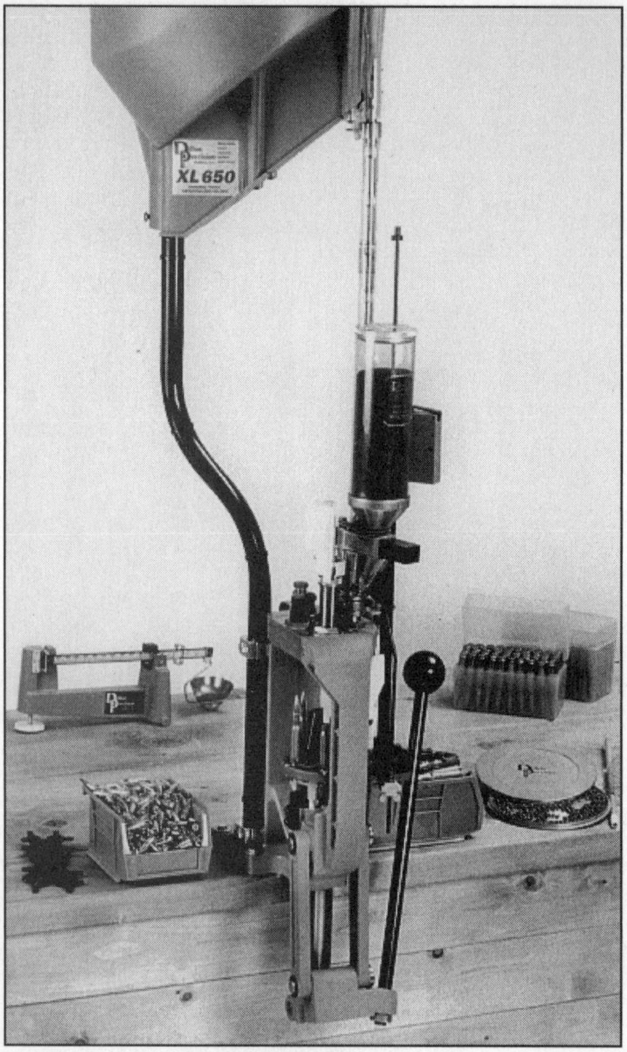

The Dillon XL650

the RL550. Case insertion, case advancement and bullet placement require manual effort. Priming and powder charging are automatic.

Tool head change is particularly easy on the RL550 because the tool head is held in place by only two small pins. Though it may appear that this arrangement isn't all that stout, when the dies come into contact with the shell plate, this pressure forces proper tool head alignment.

The RL550 can handle a very wide variety of both pistol and rifle cartridges, is very reliable and easy to use, and makes caliber conversion trivial.

The newest member of the Dillon lineup is the XL650. As this is being written, the available information consists of only a photograph and a rough-draft instruction manual. Thus, the machine that is eventually available might be a bit different.

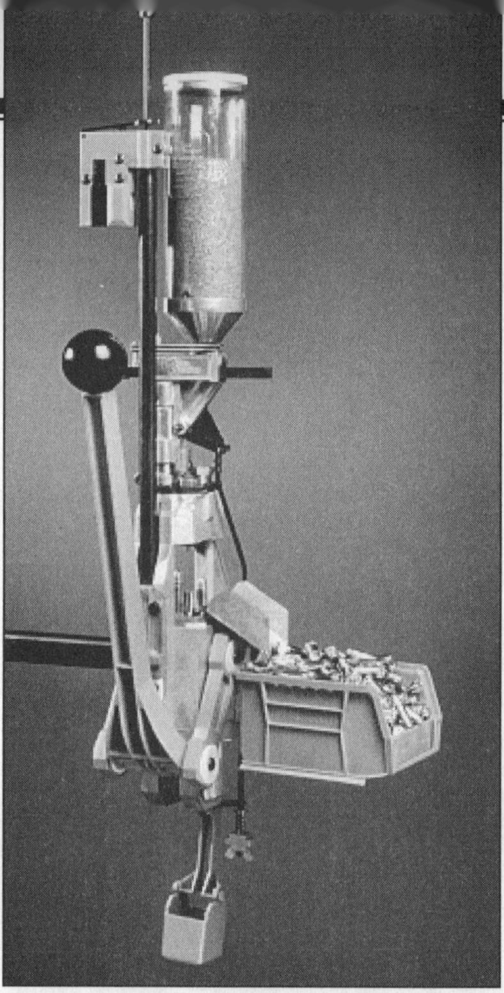

The Dillon Square Deal

The Dillon RL550

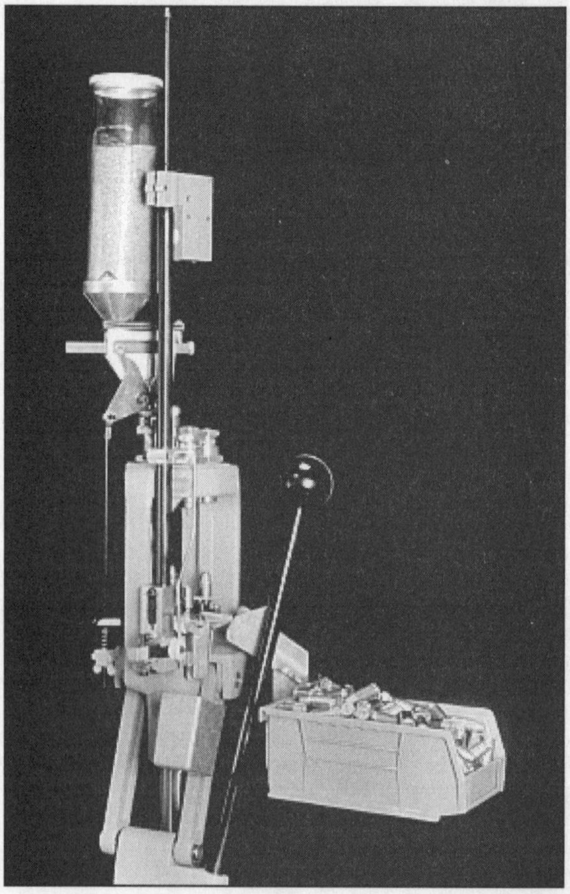

The XL650 is apparently a cross between the RL1050 and the RL550. With the exception of primer pocket swaging, which the XL650 cannot do, the XL650 is an RL1050-like unit set in an RL550-like frame. In addition, there is a double-charge preventing mechanism. This and the case feeding system are options that can be purchased separately. Finally, the XL650 loads a wide selection of both pistol and rifle cartridges.

The final Dillon unit is the Square Deal, the only Dillon progressive that loads only pistol cartridges. Cases are automatically advanced, priming and powder charging are automatic, and, as is true on all current Dillon models, the completed round is automatically ejected. About all you have to manually do is case insertion and bullet placement. Unlike Dillon's other current units, however, this one does not use $^{7}/_{8}$x14 dies.

The Lee Load-Master

Two machines discussed here don't use $^{7}/_{8}$x14 dies—one version of the Star Universal and the Dillon Square Deal. Some potential buyers seem concerned about that. Don't be.

Lee Precision

Lee Precision is the unquestioned master of inexpensive reloading equipment. Thus, you can start out by using Lee gear and find out if you're really interested without investing much money. The Lee Pro 1000 progressive is an excellent case in point.

Derived from their earlier turret press, the Lee Pro 1000 loads most popular pistol cartridges and a few short rifle rounds. It also has just about every automated feature—either built-in or available as an option—that you could possibly want. Case advancement, priming, powder charging, and loaded-round ejection are all automated. Automatic case-inserting gear can be bought as an option.

The more advanced Lee progressive is the Lee Load-Master. At this writing, all I have is the description in Lee's 1992 catalog, so things may change by the time this tool is readily available. The Load-Master can load both rifle and pistol rounds, and has automatic case insertion and advancement, automatic priming and powder charging, automatic cartridge ejection and automatic bullet placement.

The novel feature in the Load-Master is the automatic bullet placement. This is done by an automatic bullet feeder. Automatic bullet feeders have been made before, but, well, they just didn't work. If Lee has a reliable design, and I would certainly assume that they do, this is a real achievement.

RCBS

The current RCBS progressives consist of the Auto 4x4, the Piggyback and the new AmmoMaster.

The Auto 4x4 is the automatic version of an earlier machine called, naturally enough, the 4x4. That unit required manual effort to seat the primers and throw the powder charge. Thus, the 4x4 was a pseudo-progressive.

The Auto 4x4 is a true progressive. It incorporates automatic case advancement, priming, powder charging and loaded-round ejection. Both pistol and rifle cartridges can be loaded. It does not, however, have removable tool heads.

Why would a progressive not have a removable tool head? Because this is an older design introduced before removable tool heads were commonly employed. Since the Auto 4x4 still sells well, it's still available.

The RCBS Piggyback is more a conversion kit than a progressive.

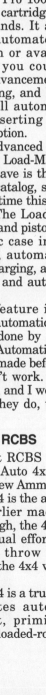

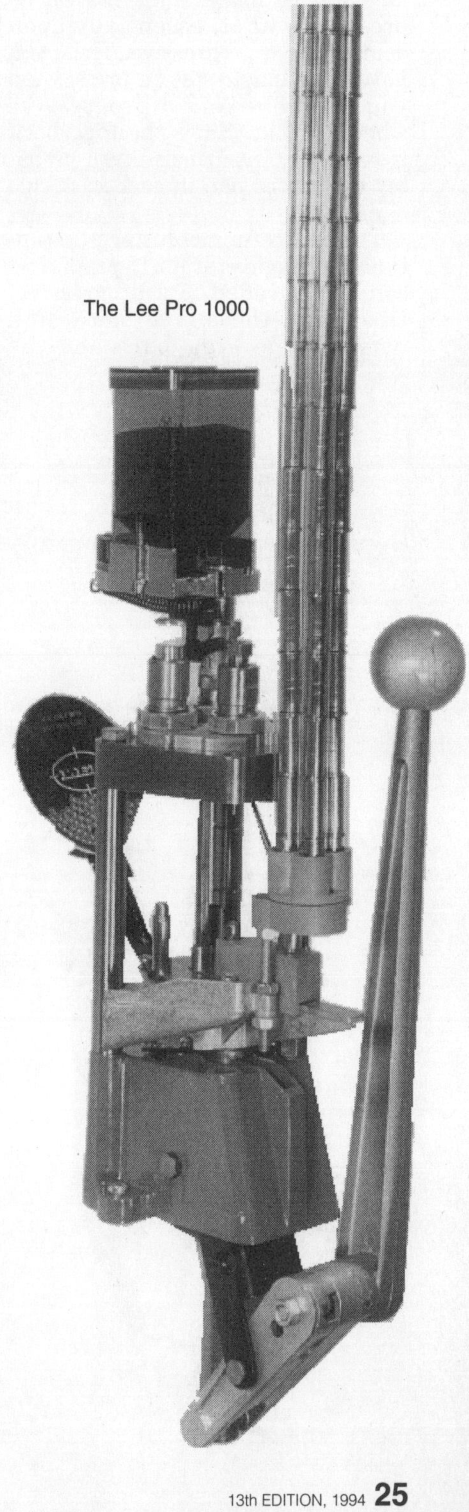

The Lee Pro 1000

Basically this is a set of parts that, when installed on a single-station press, converts that press into a progressive. The automatic features are the same as those found in the Auto 4x4. Tool head change isn't possible here for the simple reason that the kit is, essentially, a tool head. The unit can load most pistol and a few small rifle rounds.

The Piggyback idea, I think, is a fascinating one because it lets almost anyone who has a single-station O-press convert it, essentially upon demand, to a progressive. Thus, you have got a single-station press when you need one and a progressive when you like. Since the Piggyback is relatively inexpensive, you probably can afford one in each cartridge of interest.

The RCBS AmmoMaster is, essentially, a single-station H-press that can be upgraded to a progressive. Obviously, there is a logical link between the Piggyback and the AmmoMaster concepts. The idea here was that a buyer could start out with an RCBS single-station press and upgrade this machine if desired. Clever.

The AmmoMaster has the usual list of circular progressive features. It can do either manual or automatic case advancement, and has automatic priming, powder charging and loaded-round ejection. Though not obvious, caliber conversion by tool head change is possible because the top plate in the AmmoMaster can be unbolted and removed. That's the tool head.

RCBS also offers two dies that are of interest, no matter what progressive you might have. One lubricates cases, the other checks powder levels. Not every progressive has enough stations to use these two dies, but if your machine has an unused station or two at the right places, I'd certainly recommend installing these.

A couple of final points about RCBS. All their equipment comes with a lifetime guarantee, and they excel at customer support. Oddly enough, however, they don't make a big deal out of this. I've never understood that.

Hornady

Hornady, of course, makes excellent reloading equipment. Their progressive, the Pro-Jector, has the normal list of features. It can load rifle and pistol cartridges, and does automatic case advancement, priming, powder charging and loaded-round ejection. Like the RCBS Auto 4x4, however, the Pro-Jector does not employ a removable tool head. Why not? Because it's an older design introduced before this feature became commonly available.

Final Comments

I've come to believe that some facets of progressive design aren't all

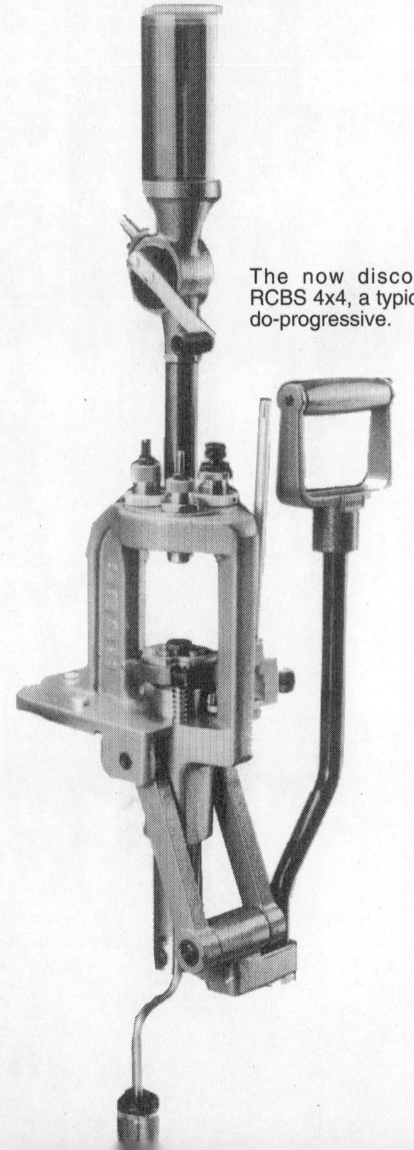

The now discontinued RCBS 4x4, a typical pseudo-progressive.

The RCBS Auto 4x4

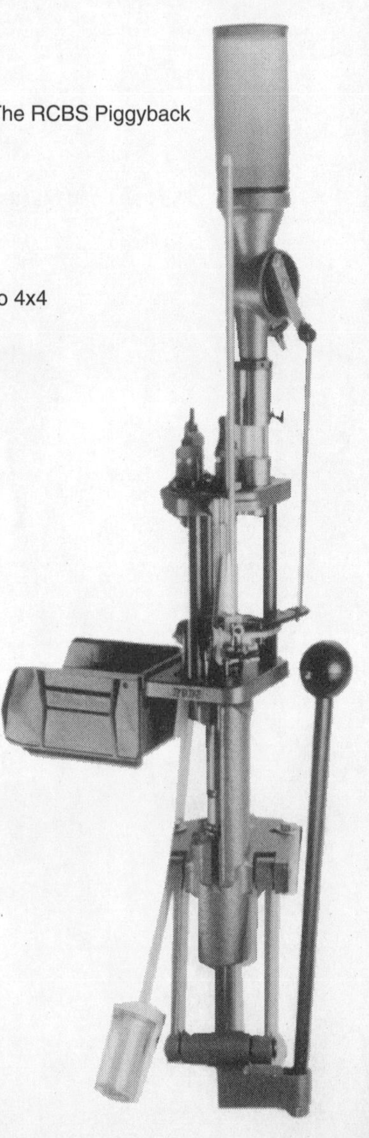

The RCBS Piggyback

that important. One is the number of reloading stations. Whether a machine has four or eight doesn't really matter because it will get the job done with the number it has.

Another aspect of progressive design that I don't think is highly important is the degree of automation. Automatic case insertion, for instance, might be nice, but I don't think it's really necessary. I recommend sticking to the basics and skipping the options, at least initially. You can always add the optional features later if you think they'll help.

If you're seriously considering purchasing a progressive, find a friend who has the model you want and have him show you how to use it. As common as progressives are these days, this really shouldn't be all that hard. Actually I'd try, before purchase, as many different progressives as I could find.

Also, at least for the first-time progressive buyer, I strongly suggest that you buy a new one. You're going to have to learn how your machine works. You don't need the additional potential hassle of trying to figure out what's wrong with the used machine that you have. Then, too, with a new one you have a warranty and the manufacturer is there to help you if you need support.

Where can you get these machines? In the back of this book is a directory listing the addresses of these firms. I'd contact Dillon and Star directly. The rest sell through distributors who advertise in *Shotgun News* or *Gun List*. If you are unfamiliar with these publications, you should be able to buy copies at any large gun store.

One last point: The two greatest safety features inherent in any progressive are the intelligence and the attention of the person using it. Sooner or later any progressive will develop a problem. Most will be due to operator error.

When you get your machine, learn how to use it. Study the manual. Prove to yourself that you know what's going on. When something goes wrong, and this will happen, stop and figure out what's up. Never just try to force one.

Pay particular attention to the primer and powder systems. Some primer systems don't like some brands of primers. Personally, I think that Winchester primers and, for that matter, Winchester brass work best. Also be sure that your powder system is set up correctly. If it is not, some machine will occasionally throw a partial charge or not throw a charge at all.

Check the weight of your powder charge every time you get a new can of powder. Weights thrown volumetrically can vary between lots by as much as 12 percent. I know that may be hard to believe, but it's true.

No one is a greater fan of progressives than I. I want to make one point very clear, however. Progressives work well, but only if you pay attention and know what you're doing. If you cannot give them your undivided, skilled attention, don't buy one. There isn't a progressive out there, new or used, that can compensate for an operator who doesn't know what he's doing. ●

RCBS single station AmmoMaster

RCBS AmmoMaster progressive

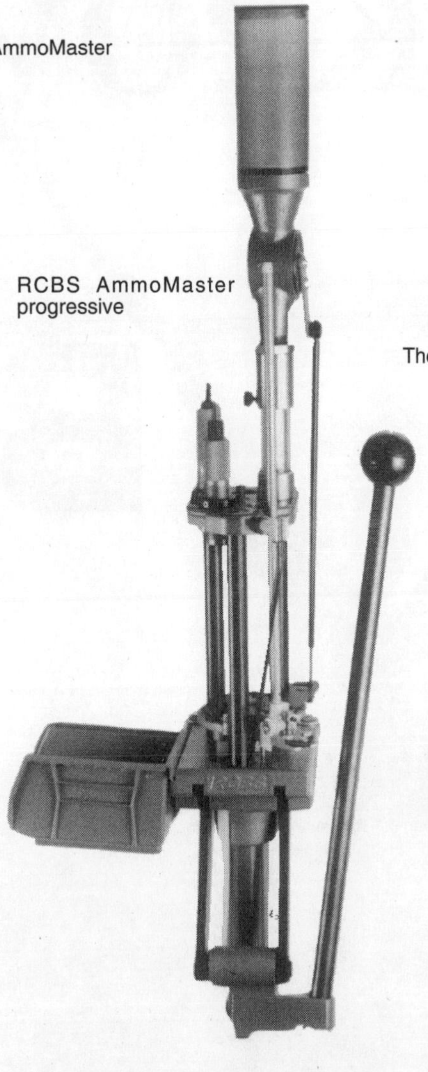

The Hornady Pro-Jector

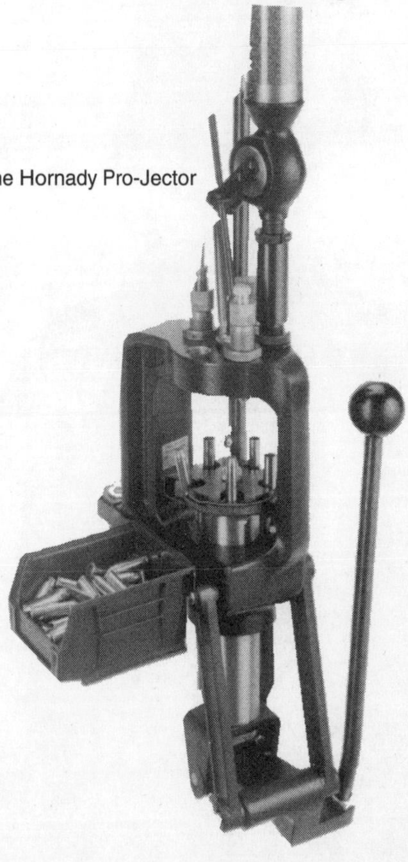

By Sam Fadala

When old-time blackpowder shooters wanted more punch from their muzzle-loaders, they resorted to double charges. But we've found that's not the correct approach to....

The flared base on this Minie ball indicates the skirt was stressed during firing. In extreme cases, the skirt is blown out much more, or ruptured, thereby ruining accuracy. A bullet with a thicker skirt is the obvious cure for this problem.

Loading The BLACKPOWDER BIG BORE

BY POPULAR DEMAND, the Thompson/Center company brought out its Big Boar muzzle-loading rifle. Hunters wanted more authority from a Hawken-like frontloader, and T/C knew how to get it. Early hunters on this and every other continent also knew how to gain more snort from their muzzle-loading round ball rifles. Simple. Increase the caliber. It was the only way to improve the power of the blackpowder longarm.

Of course, a proper powder charge had to be dropped below that big ball. Not too much or the law of diminishing returns would rear its Medusa head. Not too little powder or you would have a popgun. A powder charge that gave the highest safe velocity with the biggest bullet was just right. Most old-time hunters didn't know about the law of diminishing returns, so they "double-charged" when they wanted more punch. That was a waste of good powder. But, there was more smoke and a good deal more recoil, so our forebearers figured the ball had a lot more zing on it.

The old-timer may have been in the dark about efficient blackpowder charges. But as noted above, he knew if he wanted more power the round ball had to get bigger because blackpowder was then, and remains today, a comparatively inefficient fuel. That's why it can be loaded safely by bulk or volumetric charges. Oddball half-grain charges are a joke. No chronograph made can tell the difference between 60.0 grains of FFg and 60.5 grains of FFg in a 45-caliber muzzleloader. Since blackpowder was not efficient enough to gain high velocity as we know it—2000 fps for a round ball was really scooting along—the only way to go was more mass in the projectile.

There was one neat thing, however, about increasing the diameter of a round lead ball. As bore size and ball size increased, missile weight went up way out of proportion. A .350 round ball weighs only 65 grains. But double that diameter to .700 and the resultant ball weighs 516 grains, as shown by the formula:

$$D^3 \times .5236 \times 2873.5$$

This is the volume of a sphere (D to the third power multiplied by .5236) times the weight of one cubic inch of pure lead in grains (2873.5).

Hunters went forth to slay every wild beast on every land with blackpowder rifles shooting round lead balls. In fact, some of the best hunters of the day stayed with the round ball even after the conical gained popularity. Sir Samuel Baker is a prime example of this truth. Sam didn't trust the conical. He liked a big round ball better, even for elephants—no, especially for elephants. The conical, according to Sir Sam, "made too neat a wound," whereas the big lead pill upset more tissue and did more damage. Cotton Oswell believed the same and used a large round ball for his elephant hunting in Africa. Of course, the round balls spoken of here were truly large, up to 4-bore and on rare occasions even bigger. A 4-bore, at four round balls to the pound, weighs $^1/_4$-pound per unit, or 1750 grains, almost ten times more heft than the popular 180-grain 30-caliber bullet of today. After awhile, the conical projectile caught on. After all, here was an easy avenue to more mass without carrying a rifle that had a bore large enough to house a colony of fruit bats.

The comparison demonstrated earlier of a .350 round ball and a .700 round ball showed weights of 65 vs. 516 grains. However, a 70-caliber round ball is closing in on 12-gauge. And as

This new Thompson/Center Big Boar 58-caliber rifle with 26-inch barrel was used to generate the ballistics featured in this report.

(Left) Fadala likes the 54-caliber Knight MK-85. This modern muzzleloader shoots elongated projectiles such as the Minie or Maxi-Ball, and also modern-style lead conicals or jacketed pistol bullets, the latter encased in plastic sabots.

These Buffalo Bullet Co. projectiles show some of the variations possible. Note that bullets on left and right have very thick skirts so that heavy powder charges will neither flare the skirt too far nor split it.

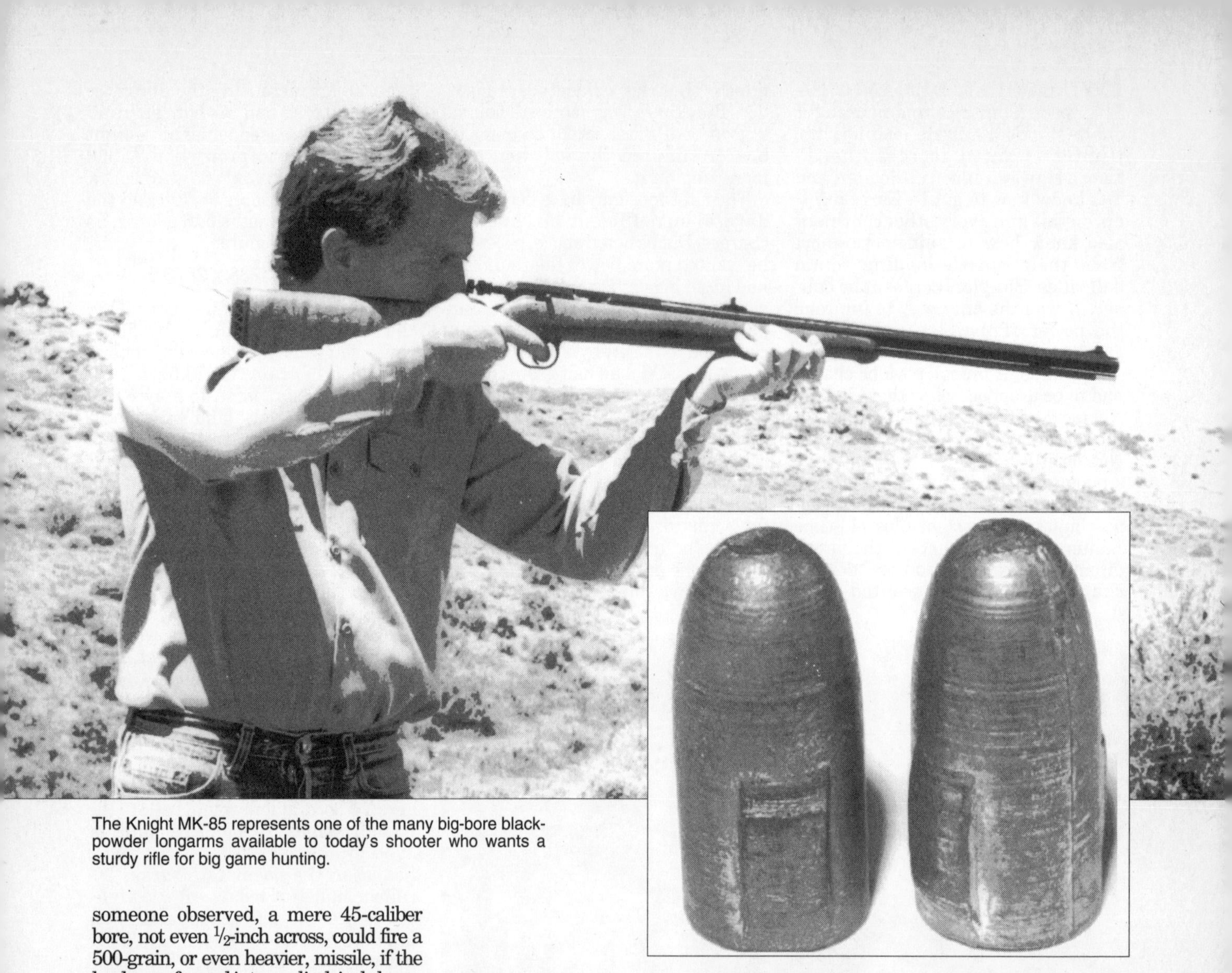

The Knight MK-85 represents one of the many big-bore blackpowder longarms available to today's shooter who wants a sturdy rifle for big game hunting.

These old-style finned bullets weigh over 500 grains each and represent another approach to gaining higher mass per caliber by going to a conical projectile.

someone observed, a mere 45-caliber bore, not even $\frac{1}{2}$-inch across, could fire a 500-grain, or even heavier, missile, if the lead were formed into a cylindrical shape. And the rest is history.

When smokeless powder came along, it allowed even smaller bores because high velocity was possible. The 8mm Lebel, probably the first smokeless powder cartridge to gain a foothold in the world of shooting, propelled a long bullet at some 2000 fps with less than half the powder charge required to drive a 50-caliber round ball at about the same muzzle velocity. The 30-40 Krag followed with similar results. And the 25-35 Winchester and 30-30 Winchester, both appearing in 1895 in the Model 1894 Winchester rifle, continued the trend with sportsmen in mind. (The 8mm Lebel and 30-40 Krag were originally military rounds.)

All of this history would have stayed history except for an odd bipart occurrence. The first part of the event had to do with the fact that blackpowder wouldn't go away and find a bush to hide under. Hunters stuck with blackpowder *cartridges* because they were cheaper than smokeless and they got the job done. That's understandable. But it is less clear why the muzzleloader didn't fade away when the smoke*less*pole came in. But it did not. Old-time guns kept on shooting. Anyone doubting this can turn to *American Rifleman* magazines from the past. Blackpowder articles appeared there regularly over the years.

The second part of the phenomenon was the re-introduction of the wheel. Original blackpowder arms were joined by modern replica muzzleloaders. And that's where we are today—a whole branch of shooting dedicated to the old propellant and its replica fuel, Pyrodex. The branch of shooting is represented by caplock revolvers, single shot pistols, replica Hawkens and in-name-only Hawkens, "rifled muskets," shotguns, even modern muzzleloaders that burn blackpowder but resemble great-granddad's longarm like Pee Wee Herman mirrors Arnold Schwartzenegger.

Aside from the fun and romance of blackpowder shooting, the sport is also kept alive by special hunts. This is where the big bore comes in. Some of these special blackpowder only (called primitive) hunts are for big mountain mule deer and bigger elk. Moose and bear hunting with the smokepole is also possible. And a few of the boys have managed to book a free-roaming bison hunt with smokepoles in mind. For all of these game animals, the key that opens the door to success is the same one that turned the blackpowder lock a century and more ago—a big bullet. That's why Thompson/Center and other companies have their big-bore smokepoles.

But how to load for the large bore? The how is accomplished in two ways: A shooter who owns a chronograph can enjoy a do-it-yourself load-making searchout. The fellow who doesn't own a chronograph has another avenue: the loading manual. *The Gun Digest Black Powder Loading Manual, Revised Edition* (DBI Books, Inc.), for example, lists many recipes for big bores, including a notice on the law of diminishing returns so that shooters aren't pouring in extra fuel for the sake of more noise, flame, smoke and recoil.

All big-bore loads must remain within the confines of the maximum loads recommended by the gun-maker. The maximum is not a starting point for loading; it is an apex to work up to. Blackpowder guns can be overloaded, in spite of information to the contrary. The old hokum about blackpowder never achieving over 25,000 psi (pounds per square inch) pressure in a firearm is just that—nonsense. Even if it were so, 25,000 psi can be way too much pressure for the open system of the frontloader which, after all, has no cartridge case to help contain runaway gases. Even the modern in-line muzzleloader does not have the locking breech system of a bolt-action cartridge rifle. However, blackpowder can engender far more than 25,000 psi. Noble and Abel, two British experimenters, found this out in the 19th century, and our own American Navy verified the findings in a huge study also made in the last century. Pressures in the 100,000 psi domain were registered by test. So the maximum blackpowder/Pyrodex load for a given frontloader is to be obeyed.

The shooter with a chronograph has this goal: to start with about one-half of the recommended maximum powder charge and work up to some safe point not exceeding maximum, all the while analyzing and keeping careful records of results. It's as obvious as a buzzing fly in a bowl of soup that if a maximum load of 120 grains of FFg blackpowder or an equivalent *volume* of Pyrodex RS renders 1600 fps with a particular bullet from a particular frontloader, while 100 grains volume of these propellants turns up 1550 fps, the 100-grain charge makes more sense than the 120-grain charge.

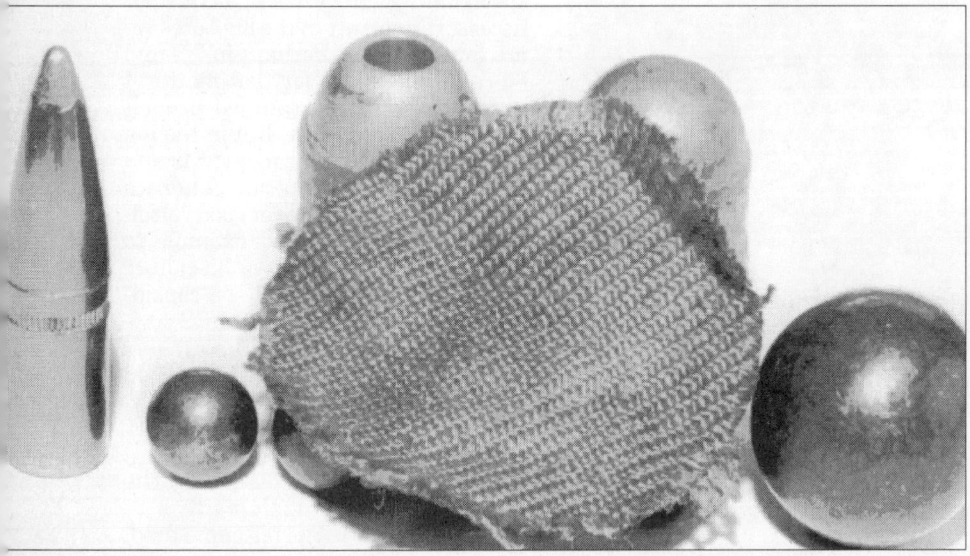

The big 12-gauge round ball on the right indicates how blackpowder authority is generated with a spherical projectile. Compare it to the 180-grain 30-caliber bullet on the far left.

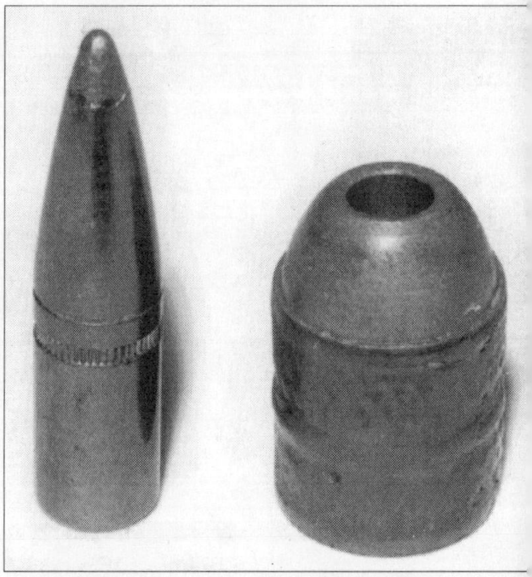

Calibers 54 and 58 represent big bores by modern standards. This 54-caliber 400-grain Buffalo Bullet is compared with a 180-grain 30-caliber projectile as a standard.

Take a look at the nearby ballistic chart for our test rifle, the Thompson/Center Big Boar rifle. This big 58-caliber shooting heavy conicals clearly shows a relationship between how much powder is burned and the results. The recommended maximum 120-grain charge is a powerhouse. But so is the 110-grain charge. The 120-grain load does not improve significantly on the 110-grain load, so 110 grains is optimum in the Big Boar with a conical. The shooter who does not have access to a chronograph should, as advised earlier, turn to a loading manual to gain similar data.

A good example is from *The Gun Digest Black Powder Loading Manual* page 205 of the revised edition. The Zouave rifled musket is treated. With this 58-caliber rifle using a 530-grain conical, 50 grains of FFg propels the bullet at 850 fps. Another 10 grains of the same powder boosts velocity to 971 fps, a meaningful increase. At 70 grains of powder, muzzle velocity jumps to 1035 fps, which is a gain, but one that's significantly less than the previous increase. The next 10-grain increment, however, gives even less increase as an 80-grain charge of FFg pushes the 530-grain bullet to only 1095 fps. In my opinion, this is not enough to merit using the 10 additional grains of fuel.

Aside from waste of powder, an important reason for keeping the law of diminishing returns in mind while loading is recoil. Recoil is in part a condition of powder charge *weight*. Blackpowder is inherently inefficient, so it takes a hefty charge to get the projectile into motion. Therefore, a blackpowder rifle is already leaning toward heavy recoil because of the powder weight factor. There is no reason to add 10 grains of fuel in the above example to realize a gain of only 60 fps. That's not enough additional velocity to markedly increase power nor to improve trajectory.

It can be argued that an increased muzzle velocity of 60 fps with a 530-grain bullet is meaningful in terms of energy. It is...in terms of *muzzle energy*. At the muzzle, the 70-grain charge of FFg with the 530-grain

Recoil can be heavy with a muzzleloader because hunting loads require large powder charges to achieve reasonable velocity, and the powder charge weight is one of the factors that affect recoil.

conical doing 1035 fps delivers 1261 foot-pounds of energy, whereas the same bullet at 1095 fps gives 1411 foot-pounds, an increase of 150 foot-pounds, or roughly 12 percent. But at 100 yards, the remaining energy of the heavier load is only 46 foot-pounds greater than the lighter one's, roughly a 5 percent gain. The shooter has to decide for himself whether that's enough increase to justify the heavier charge. In this instance, I opt for the lighter charge because I know that any difference between them on big game will be negligible.

So these are the two major means of determining the right load for the big bore, the hands-on approach using your own chronograph and pocket calculator, or a fingertip page-turning through a loading manual.

Other factors of consideration in big-bore loading are what type of powder to use, trajectory and sight-in factors, accuracy and caliber.

The right powders for the big bores are FFg blackpowder and Pyrodex RS. The use of FFFg blackpowder in the big bore is not illogical. FFFg is ideal for target work. But the tradeoff for high-power loads with FFFg in the big bore is not a wise one. FFFg improves velocity per charge weight in an extremely meaningful way. A modest dose of FFFg equals or surpasses a heavy charge of FFg. For example, in one test, a particular rifle gained about the same velocity with 40 percent less FFFg as compared with FFg. However, pressure-wise, the FFg load was far superior. In short, FFg, even though it did require quite a lot more fuel for the same amount of work, got the same velocity as FFFg with a much better pressure/velocity ratio.

RS, of course, is the FFg equivalent in Pyrodex and when used in the same *volume* produces similar results. The latest Pyrodex formula is the best ever, by the way, with improved ignition qualities and more "power" per charge weight. It is also lighter per volume than past formulas.

For example, a 100 volume charge of FFg blackpowder from an adjustable powder measure rendered slightly over 99 grains by weight. Leaving the measure set exactly at the 100 mark, Pyrodex RS was poured in. A 100 volumetric setting on the powder measure turned out 71.5 grains Pyrodex RS by weight. Yet resulting velocities were excellent for the Pyrodex load.

On the other end of the granulation spectrum, Fg and Pyrodex CTG are not necessarily correct in the big bores we are familiar with. Perhaps in 70- and 80-caliber rifles, or for that matter 4 bores, these large-granuled propellants would be perfect. But in the big bores that are popular today, 54s and 58s, Fg and CTG do not generate enough pressure to render good velocities. It takes a lot of Fg, for example, to reach a velocity in a 54- or 58-caliber rifle that would normally be considered a target load with FFg or RS powders. Fg and CTG do have their applications, of course. Both are good in the 10-gauge shotgun and ideal in the blackpowder cartridge, especially cartridges of the Sharps clan.

Trajectory of the big bore limits the range of these muzzleloaders to about 125 yards in the big game field. I'm aware of literature to the contrary, but those super long shots of the past belong in the past. Loaded safely and correctly and sighted in a tad high at 50 yards, the 54s and 58s using round or conical bullets drop about a half-foot at 125 yards. That's all the guesswork I feel should be allowed on a big game animal.

So sight-in about an inch high at 50 yards. Real precision may not be possible due to group size, but a "tad high" at 50 yards will do the trick. This puts the 54- or 58-caliber round ball or conical about an inch low at 100 yards and six inches low at 125 yards. The reason these different projectiles follow about the same path over this distance is that the ball, which weighs only about half as much as the conical projectile, starts faster but loses its speed faster. Energy-wise, the heavier conical holds onto its steam much better than the ball, but trajectory-wise they are essentially equal for practical field work.

Accuracy is obviously important in

arriving at the best big-bore load, but it's not as serious a consideration as a shooter may think. Big bores are meant for big game hunting. Therefore, a slightly larger group size with considerably higher delivery of energy is desired over a shred better accuracy with a lot less power. Ideally, however, a shooter should sit at the bench with his muzzleloader compiling careful records of loads vs. accuracy. It may come out that a half-charge of recommended maximum is the most accurate load, although this is in no way a norm. Often, the top end loads are every bit as accurate as the lesser powder charges.

What really matters here is figuring out *why* a load is not accurate. Many factors can be involved, but two obvious problems are round ball patch deterioration and Minie skirt blowout. Avoid the first by installing

The two powders used in these tests were Pyrodex RS and Goex FFg blackpowder, shown here with conical projectiles of 500 grains weight for the Whitworth rifled musket.

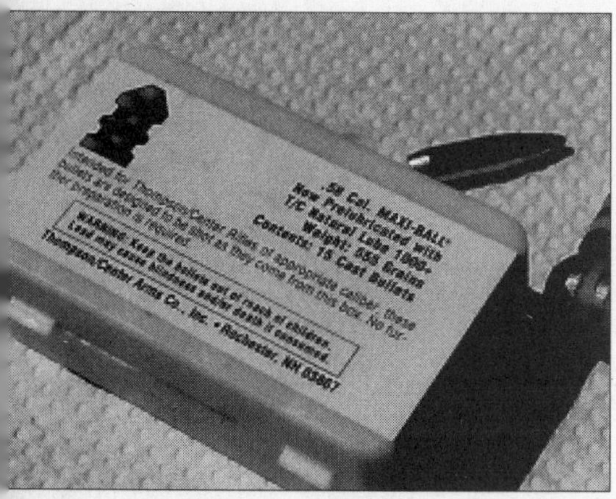

Test bullet used in Thompson/Center Big Boar rifle was the T/C 58-caliber 555-grain Maxi-Ball pre-lubed with T/C 1000+ lube.

several sheets of hornet nesting material on top of the powder charge before the patched ball is seated. This will protect the patch. Even though the stuff blazes at the touch of a match in open air, this insect-made material is like asbestos down in the bore. Solving the Minie ball skirt problem takes more drastic measures. A lower powder charge will preserve the skirt, but velocity/power will drop off. The answer is a Minie ball designed with a thicker skirt, of which there are many.

Caliber choice boils down to two because only two are popular in the above-50 range. These are the 54 and the 58. For round ball shooting I prefer the 54. Beyond this size, the ball demands a lot more powder to generate anything like good velocity and trajectory. I tested a 62-caliber round ball rifle that burned 140 grains of FFg blackpowder for a muzzle velocity under 1600 fps. A 58-caliber tested by Lyman generated less than 1500 fps with a round ball even though 150 grains of FFg was used. Meanwhile, I have a 54-caliber ball-shooter that gains close to 2000 fps with an allowed charge of 120 grains of FFg.

The 54 and 58 both shine with conicals. Neither pushes the lead cylinder very fast, but bullets well over 500 grains serve in both calibers, with 600-grain slugs available in caliber 58. So lack of speed is made up for by mass of missile. Naturally, if the shooter returned to the big bores of the old days, the 54 and 58 would crawl into the shade. Then super power would be the rule with huge powder charges driving equally huge projectiles at modest velocity.

The big-bore muzzleloader is capable of doing a remarkable job on big game within blackpowder range because a lack in delivered energy is somewhat overcome by the fact that the big bore's bullets start out larger than many lesser calibers end up after expansion. Furthermore, the "pure lead" projectile has something going for it. It sticks together. Rarely will a lead round ball or conical fragment. The molecular cohesion of lead is high as long as striking velocity is comparatively low. Consequently, long straight wound channels are the rule. It was no fluke that even the largest game in the world, the elephant, could be dropped in its tracks by lead bullets from the old-time frontloader. It was a matter of a large bore accommodating a large bullet at reasonable velocity. The formula has not changed one decimal point over the ages. Today's blackpowder big bores are powerful for the same reasons their ancestors were. •

LOAD AND BALLISTICS CHART

Test Rifle: Thompson/Center Big Boar 26" Barrel, Caplock
Powders: Pyrodex RS; one test load of Goex FFg*
Maximum T/C Load: 120 grains FFg or equivalent Pyrodex RS with either 58-caliber 555-grain Maxi-Ball or 58-caliber 560-grain Maxi-Hunter conicals.
Test Bullet: The 58-caliber 555-grain Thompson/Center Maxi-Ball, No. 7797, was used for all testing. Velocities with T/C Maxi-Hunter No. 7790 58-caliber 560-grain Maxi-Hunter would be nearly identical. *All test bullets were pre-lubed with T/C Natural Lube 1000+.*

Volume/Wgt. Grs.	MV (fps)
80/57.0	1117
90/64.0	1175
100/71.5	1290
110/79.0	1345
120/82.5	1351

*Only 100 volume (99.5 grains by weight) of Goex FFg blackpowder was used in this test as a cross-reference. Results with FFg were excellent. Velocity was 1201 fps.

DRUDGERY. In spite of all the satisfaction and enjoyment that handloading offers, some tasks within the process are boring, just operations that must be performed in order to get the job done. Personally, I'm not too thrilled with priming cases or casting bullets. Once you get started, they're just dull, repetitive work. Both priming and casting eventually lead to an enjoyable pastime—shooting—but watching bullet number seventy-three drop out of the mould and knowing that I have another seventy-seven to go is about as exciting for me as peeling potatoes.

Worse yet is drudgery that is wasteful too. Fireforming cases tops that list. Perfectly good bullets shot for what seems to be no good purpose, generally at no particular target. I know, I know. Cream of Wheat and some wadding and powder, and you can save the bullets for later. Sometimes. But what a mess, and it's still *boring*.

Sometime back, I was working on a project of converting a perfectly good Remington 700 Classic in 250 Savage to the immensely better 250 Ackley Improved (HANDLOADER'S DIGEST, 12th Edition). It required fireforming a minimum of 200 cases. I looked forward to the process as I would to a root canal. But it had to be done, so I took fifty cases and loaded

Some handloading operations are boring—just drudgery. To make them fun, I started...

LOADING FOR L-O-N-G SHOTS

by DAVID WARD

From a convenient overlook, Ward searches the far side of the cirque for targets of opportunity. Shots are taken up to 1200 yards or so...and make the boring part of handloading fun.

them up with 60-grain bullets and lit out for the hills. Ten shots later, as I had expected, the thrill was gone and the cases were not forming well either. So back to the bench I went. It's only time and mileage; who cares if it's wasted?

Full-power loads were apparently going to be the only way to do this right, but such a waste of hunting bullets. I loaded them anyway, 34 grains of H-335 and 100-grain flat-base bullet, a max load for the 250 Savage. In the improved chamber, pressures should be considerably lower than max because of the larger volume of the case. Would've been a great deer load, but 200 cases

The two rifles used by the author for cross-canyon shooting. Left is M700 Remington Classic in 250 Ackley Improved and right is M700 Remington Varmint Special in 308 Winchester. Both cartridges shoot very well out to 1200 yards or so, even through 20-inch barrels.

(Below) Prone shooting across the valley with the 308 Winchester. The heavy barrel offers outstanding accuracy in long-distance shooting.

require too many seasons (about the year 2185 or so depending on your luck) to fireform.

As I sat at the bench, I had a little idea. One of my family's favorite hiking places is up on Berthoud Pass west of Denver. The area is just above timberline, sporting an elevation of about 11,800 feet above sea level, and is pocked with steep, three-sided, bowl-shaped valleys called cirques. These valleys range from 800 to 1500 yards across around here and are just far enough from the road and require just enough of a climb to be nearly always deserted. The particular one in mind was dotted with several shallow alpine ponds.

What a place to fireform some cases!

I got so excited I loaded another fifty rounds (and didn't even notice the priming), gathered my equipment, and made a beeline up to the pass. Twenty minutes from the car, and I was perched on the side of the bowl, catching my breath for the umpteenth time and overwhelmed, as always, at the panorama that lay before me. To the southeast, 14,000-foot Mt. Evans looked almost subdued. Southwest along the rim of the cirque ran the ridge of the Continental Divide at about 12,500 feet, barren of anything but rock and tundra grasses and snow.

I turned my attention to the bowl below me. Targets of opportunity abounded everywhere from 300 to 1200 yards. A football-size rock beckoned to me from the center of the pond. I eyeballed the distance at

AUTHOR'S LONG-SHOT LOADS

Bullet Weight (Grs.)	Load (Grs./Powder)	MV (fps)
250 ACKLEY IMPROVED		
87	43.5/IMR-4320	3358
	44.0/BL-C2	3316
100	41.5/IMR-4320	3141
	42.0/BL-C2	3134
	42.0/IMR-4895	3155
120	38.3/IMR-4320	2807
	42.5/H-380	2811
308 WINCHESTER		
130	49.0/H-335	3064
150	46.8/IMR-4064	2763
	45.6/H-335	2840
165	47.2/W-748	2619
	46.0/BL-C2	2576
168	45.2/H-335	2676

Rifles—M700; Barrel Length—20 inches; Primers—CCI; Velocity— average of ten shots taken 5 feet from muzzle.

about 450 yards, and dialed in that number on the Redfield 3-9x Accutrac secured to the top of the rifle. Moments later, a geyser of water showed I was high and right about a foot. Can't be, I thought. Then I remembered the breeze blowing from the left, and that I was shooting down on the pond.

The Redfield was dialed back to 350 and I held left a bit. A loud smack echoing back indicated a direct hit. Through the scope I saw debris from the rock showering down on the water. Nailed it!

I searched for another target to test my ability. It showed in the form of a saucer-shaped rock on the other side of the valley—700 yards away, I figured, plus or minus a few. I looked through the scope, adjusted for range and squeezed. Three shots later, the rock was still safe.

Taking a shot with the 250 AI from the sitting position. Light recoil and flexibility make this cartridge an excellent one for the handloader who likes big-game performance from a short-action rifle. Don't forget your ear protection.

Maximum-range shots to the far side of the cirque at perhaps 1200 yards were even more challenging. Various size rocks were scattered everywhere. With the Redfield set on its maximum range of 600 yards, holdover was guesstimated. A puff of dust indicated a miss, a loud smack and no dust a hit. Frankly, it is surprising how good you can get at these distances with just a little practice. The fifty rounds were gone in no time.

Maybe it was time to get serious—well, semi-serious—about this long-range shooting.

Back at the house, I continued with the 250 Ackley project. At the same time, some loads for my M700 Remington Varmint Special in 308 Winchester were in order. Its favorite load is 45.6 grains of H-335 behind the Hornady 150-grain SPBT. The combination generates 2840 fps out of the rifle's 20-inch barrel, and five shots usually leave a hole in the target slightly smaller than $^3/_4$ inch. So what about some 165-grain boattails? Certainly. The rifle thrives on both Speer and Sierra bullets. The Speer 168-grain Match is also a winner. In spite of what military minds and others might think, I feel that anything heavier than 168 grains in the medium-capacity 308 gives up more than it gains, especially in this kind of recreational shooting.

Although not quite so comfortable as the 250 Ackley Improved to shoot for 50 or 100 rounds, the 308 was still great fun at the cirque. Its increased power was noticeable in a louder impact thump. I could not notice much difference in the trajectories of the 150- and 165/168-grain boattail bullets. Both shot plenty flat for me, considering the informal nature of the shooting. However, there was a difference between flat-base bullets and the boattails, especially when dealing in ranges past 600 or 700 yards. The aerodynamic advantage of the boattail really gets into play way out there. At hunting ranges and in hunting situations, the average handloader would be hard pressed to note much difference between the two. The same held true for the 250 AI. The boattails outperformed the flat-bases, with the 100-grainers giving the best performance in the medium-capacity case.

Long-range shooting of this type is an excellent way to field-test both handloads and rifle, be they for varmints or big game hunting. I tried batches of 75- and 87-grain bullets in the 250 AI and some 130-grain bullets in the 308. All performed pretty well considering the distances involved, but the lightweights are really out of their league at extreme distances.

Recently, I was talking about all of this to a friend of mine, going on and on about the great pastime I'd discovered. Then he told me that he and his father had done the same thing thirty years ago with a 30-06, shooting at chunks of limestone across a valley on the family farm in Iowa.

Oh.

(Right) Fireforming cases for the 250 Ackley Improved became a pleasure when shooting at targets at long ranges. The loaded cases are before and the fired ones after.

(Left) What's left from an afternoon of fun: Remington M700, lots of spent cases in 308 Winchester, and the all-important hearing protection.

Marlin's big lever action offers handloaders the chance to assemble 45-70 cartridges with ballistics unavailable from any factory load. Accuracy can be surprising: five-shot 100-yard groups near one inch are not uncommon!

Comparison of new and old. The silver wash and checkering are both about worn off. This octagon-barreled, pistol grip, 5-digit original Model 1895 Marlin is chambered for the 38-56, a bottlenecked—wildcat type—cartridge based on the 45-70 case.

M1895 MARLIN Gives 45-70 New Lease On Life

by M.L. McPHERSON

WITH ITS smooth-operating, short-throw lever-action, Marlin's $7^1/_2$-pound Model 1895 offers the handloader an excellent firearm for hunting large North American game. With the right handloads, one suspects that, within 150 yards, it would be well suited for all but the largest game anywhere in the world.

Featuring true side-ejection, the 1895 easily accommodates a telescopic sight. Mounting is simple, using the holes provided, and this allows one to take better advantage of the 1895's surprising accuracy.

Sling attachments are provided, but I prefer to carry this rifle in my hand. It balances well when my fin-

Plenty of eye relief on the scope is mandatory. Note the warning on the lid of the cartridge box, MARLIN ONLY. This improvised rest, using pipe stands and sand-filled tire tubes, was good enough to get minute-of-angle groups.

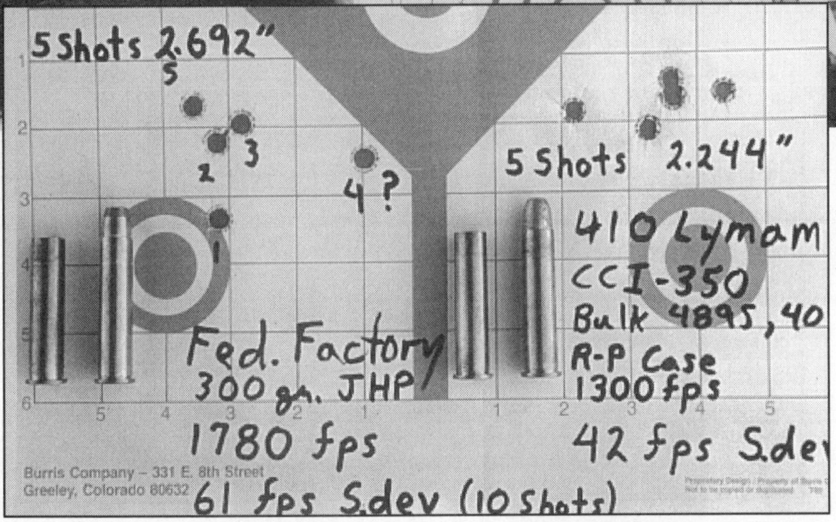

Federal factory, left, shows at least one flier on this 100-yard target. Right, my first and only 45-70 cast bullet test load—good enough for my uses.

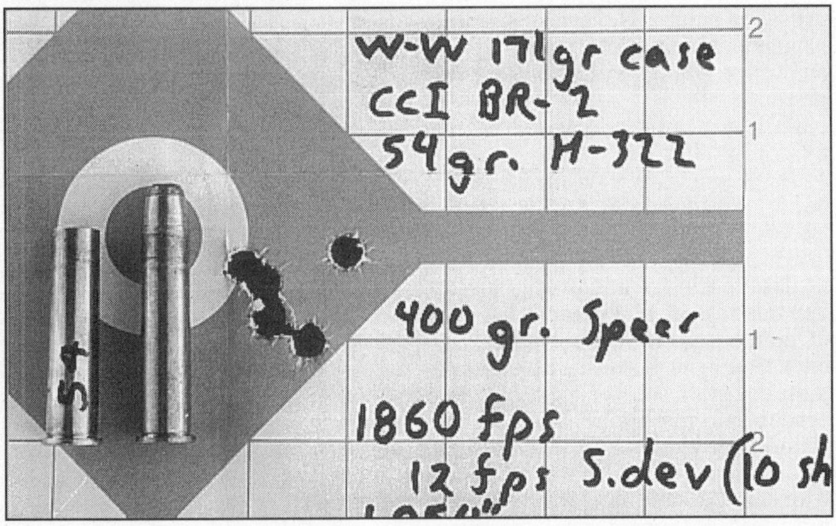

Who says a lever action won't shoot?

gers enclose it just in front of the lever. This is a comfortable method of carry. Further, because the front sling hookup is connected to the barrel, using a sling to steady the aim could influence zero. For these reasons, I do not use a sling with this rifle.

I have done considerable experimenting with various bullets and powders in the 45-70 Marlin 1895, which I, for several reasons, feel should be considered a unique species. First, cartridge overall length is restricted to 2.55 inches. This more or less precludes jacketed loads using bullets heavier than 405 grains. Second, this relatively strong lever action allows one to consider use of cartridges loaded to exceed pressures suitable for the Trapdoor Springfield and other weak rifles of this caliber, for which loads must be held to about 28,000 CUP.

The 1895 is built with the same tough steel as the 444 Marlin, which is based on the same action. Maximum pressure specification for the 444 Marlin is 44,000 CUP. Since the 45-70 case has about 10 percent greater cross-sectional area than the 444, 45-70 loads at *about* 40,000 CUP should generate approximately

TABLE 1: CARTRIDGE CASE DATA

Head Stamp	Source, Date	Mean Wgt. (grs.)	SD (grs.)	Number Weighed
W-W 45-70 Gov't.	Single Lot, '91	167.1	0.4	100
W-W 45-70 Gov't.	'60s-'80s	170.0	0.7	50
F C 45-70 Gov't.	Single Lot, '84	187.4	0.8	30
R-P 45-70 Gov't.	One Box, '80	184.6	1.1	20
WRA 45-70 Gov't.	Unknown	163.9	NA	1

Note: This is remarkable consistency within make. Compare this to 200 W-W 7mm Remington Magnum cases purchased from one lot in 1979; those varied more than 9 grains in weight.

the same bolt-thrust as maximum loads in the 444. Various handloading sources, including the *Hornady Handbook*, 4th ed., confirm the prudence of this pressure limit for the 45-70 Marlin.

As load pressure increases, the amount of thrust transferred to the bolt increases. In any rear-locking action, case stretching and possible separation—with potential for catastrophe—can result from excessive bolt-thrust. Therefore, bolt-thrust is a critical consideration when handloading for the 1895. More on this later.

Without access to pressure-testing equipment, the handloader can only make educated guesses about load pressure. With a cartridge working in the 30,000 to 40,000 CUP range, there are few helpful clues. Nay, none.

Some have claimed sticky extraction will indicate the onset of excessive pressure in a lever-action. *Don't you believe it!* In some rifles this may be a useful indicator, but it was *never* noted in my 1895 Marlin. Even test loads that caused considerable case stretching extracted effortlessly.

For high-pressure rifle cartridges, I prefer to measure the diameter of the case-web before and after firing. The amount of change in diameter is a measure of relative safety margin. However, at *safe* Model 1895 Marlin pressures, web diameter simply does not increase.

Some suggest that primer appearance can be a useful pressure indicator, though I do not trust this method. Perhaps, given an understanding of the great variation in primer cups, one can use the radius of the flattened portion of a fired primer as a comparative indicator for *high-pressure* rifle cartridges.

In the Marlin 45-70, with test loads ranging from about 25,000 to a bit over 40,000 CUP, I could discern absolutely no pattern with any rifle primer tested. Quite simply, they all looked exactly the same to me. This just isn't enough pressure to significantly deform the cup of a rifle primer.

At this pressure level, the softer/thinner cups used in CCI's #350 large pistol primers seem to work well, and I have achieved good ballistic uniformity using these primers in 45-70 loads. These pistol primers do show variations in appearance, when used across this pressure range. Nevertheless, any primer's appearance after firing can only give a suggestion of *relative* pressure.

With a bit of common sense, and by comparing data from various sources, one can now make fairly good guesses about 45-70 Marlin load safety. But when I began experimenting with this rifle, I could find no data to use nor any to compare to. For this reason, and because I am an inveterate experimenter with a good background in both mechanics and metallurgy, I set out to determine actual safe maximum loads in my rifle. Today, the handloader has appropriate data from several sources. All the major reloading manuals list loads using various powders and bullets. Those sources should be referred to for loading data.

For several reasons, I would like to detail my experiments. First, they confirm the prudence of published data: Test loads generating significantly higher pressure than published maximums caused measurable case stretching. Second, this technique is the only one I know which establishes safety of *any* load in a rear-locking action. Third, this process helped me develop several particularly accurate and powerful loads. Finally, it was fun, and I hope you will find it interesting.

While it might be possible to burst or swell the barrel with an extreme overload, a more practical consideration limits one to loads far below the pressure which would result in such violent damage. As noted earlier, this rifle uses what is termed a rear-lockup—its locking bolt is several inches behind the cartridge head. Springing in the action will allow case stretching at some critical pressure level. At higher pressures or

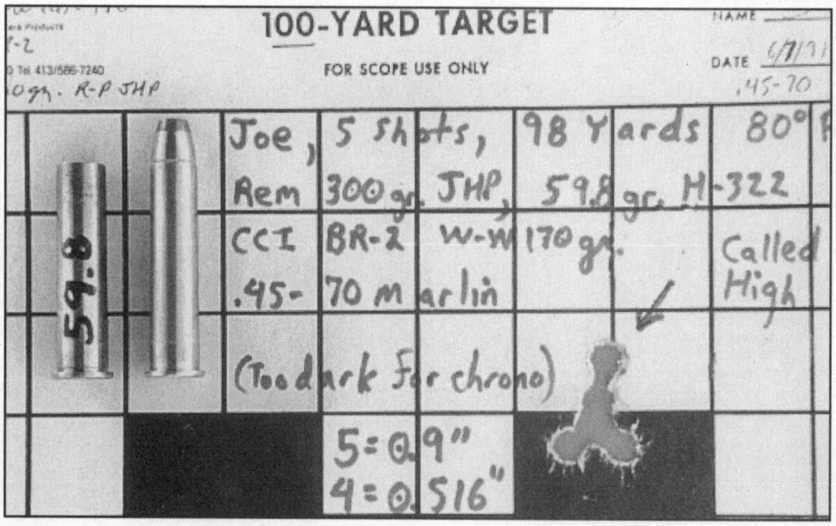

My son holds the record for this rifle. He knew he had touched that one shot off high, even before the bullet got to the paper. Too bad!

TABLE 2: BULLET DIAMETER DATA

—Bullet— (Wgt. Grs.)	(Type)	Diameter (in.)
300	Hornady	.4578-.4580
300	Remington	.4570-.4574
400	Speer	.4568-.4570
405	Remington	.4571-.4575

Notes: All bullets purchased in 1990. Marlin suggests that because of its shallow "Micro-Groove" rifling, the M1895 tends to do better with bullets near the maximum nominal diameter of .458-inch.

TABLE 3: LOAD INFORMATION/BALLISTICS AND UNIFORMITY

Five-Shot, 100-Yard Groups

Load No.	Bullet (Grs./Type)	Case (Grs./Type)	Load (Grs./Powder)	COAL (ins.)	Shots Chrono.	SD (fps)	—Muzzle— (fps)	(fpe)	—100 Yds.— (fps)	(fpe)	Zero Yd.	-3" Range	Best Grp. (ins.)	Avg. Grp. (ins.)	Est. Press. (C.U.P.)
1	300/H	167/W-W	50.0/H-322	2.537	0	(A)	1632	1773	1411	1325	136	159	***	***	<28,000 (E)
2	300/Rem.	187/F C	52.5/H-322	2.532	23	23.0	1796	2148	1558	1617	150	175	1.36	1.65	<28,000
F C	300/Fed.	187.4/F C	—	—	34	85	1767	2080	1521	1542	146	170	1.80	2.65	<28,000 (F)
3	300/H	187/F C	57.0/H-322	2.537	20	11.8	1963	2566	1708	1943	161	189	1.49	1.35(B)	28,000
4	300/Rem.	170/W-W	59.8/H-322	2.532	20	11.5	2032	2750	1770	2087	166	194	0.90	1.34	35,000
5	300/H	167/W-W	60.0/H-322	2.537	10	25.1	2015	2704	1752	2045	165	190	1.01	1.51	35,000 (G)
W-W	405/W-W	170/W-W	—	—	7	74	1160	1210	1050	991	102	120	***	***	<28,000 (H)
6	400/Sp.	167/W-W	54.0/H-322	2.532	10	12.6	1847	3029	1559	2158	150	174	1.054	(C)	35,000
7	405/Rem.	167/W-W	55.5/H-322	2.540	10	18.8	1909	3277	1658	2472	158	184	1.60	2.35(D)	40,000
8	410/Lym.	170/W-W	40.0/4895	2.530	10	35.0	1300	1538	1098	1098	108	127	2.24	(B)	<28,000 (I)

KEY: COAL=Cartridge Overall Length. **Chrono.**=Number of shots chronographed—several targets were fired when it was too late in the day to get chronograph data. **SD**=Standard Deviation (indicates ballistic uniformity). **-3-Inch Range**=With this zero, bullet path is +/-3" of line of sight to the range shown. ***=No accuracy data. **H**=Hornady. **Rem.**=Remington. **Fed.**=Federal. **W-W**=Winchester. **Lym.**=Lyman original 45-70 405-grain bullet cast of pure wheelweights. **Sp.**=Speer.

LOAD NUMBER: F C=Loaded with about 50 grains of a tubular powder that looks and burns similar to IMR-3031. **8**=Considerable unburned powder in the barrel, all other tested loads were very clean. CCI-350, roll crimp—all other handloads CCI BR-2 and a moderate crimp applied with Lee Factory Crimp Die. **3, 4, 5, 6, 7**=Powder installed with a six-inch drop tube. This is critical for consistent powder packing which improves ballistic uniformity. **All loads** had a case length of 2.105 inches. Velocities corrected to standard sea-level conditions.

NOTES: (A) Estimated velocity. **(B)** Each of two groups had one called shot deleted; including those shots, average group 1.74 inches. **(C)** Only one group fired. **(D)** One group: 3.11 inches vertical, 0.58-inch horizontal. Could this be evidence of barrel heating? **(E)** Uniformity suffers in this light load. H-4198 is probably a better choice for lighter loads. **(F)** Published velocity, 1880 fps. Fliers common. **(G)** Note lower velocity than load #4. Remington bullet is harder and longer than Hornady. **(H)** No longer cataloged. **(I)** This load can be approximated with any of several similar burning powders. Leading was not observed.

with continued reloading of cases at this pressure, case separations can occur. Separations can be unpleasant experiences. A case separation occurring while considerable pressure remains in the barrel could be exceedingly dangerous, even fatal.

Loads below the pressure level which cause stretching will result in some flexing of the action and a small amount of case springing. At these lower pressures, cases will return to normal, unharmed. This is typical, even for cartridges fired in strong front-locking bolt actions. A certain amount of case springing, usually non-harmful, always occurs.

To check for onset of stretching, I performed a simple test. After ensuring both rifle chamber and cartridge cases were absolutely free from any form of lubricant, I fired a series of test loads. With each tested powder and bullet, powder charge was increased until case stretching occurred, as noted by any measurable increase in case length after firing.

Clean, dry cases and a clean, dry chamber ensured that the case walls would cling to the rifle chamber. This prevented the entire case from following as the head moved to the rear. Such an eventuality would prevent stretching and invalidate this test.

To ensure my own safety, the gun was tied to an old tire and a long string was used to pull the trigger. *Remember: Safety is the critical point in handloading. Do it safely or don't do it at all!*

Shooting the Speer 400-grain and Remington 405-grain loads this day. With a better setup—using pipe stands and bona-fide sandbags—we expected to shoot better. Maybe we did. Nonetheless the groups were bigger. Evidently this rifle prefers 300-grain bullets. It is possible that, given this better rigging, I was getting the shots off faster and barrel heating may have been a problem.

When measurable stretching was noted, in even one of the three cartridges fired with each charge, I reduced the powder charge by at least 7 percent to arrive at what I considered an absolute maximum load. This reduction was intended to allow for variations in primers, bullets, cases, powder lots, temperature, loading techniques, etc.

As noted earlier, every tested load extracted effortlessly, even those which caused significant case stretching. *Therefore, do not assume sticky extraction will warn you of the existence of too high and dangerous pressure!*

Loads I settled on as maximum caused no case stretching in my rifle and are evidently very easy on the brass. With the sizing die turned out two full turns, I have reloaded one batch five times. Chambering remains effortless. To date, I have experienced no case failures of any kind. However, variations in rifles and components can alter results significantly. For this and other reasons, I make no specific recommendations whatsoever. Loads listed in this article are given only for comparison. For loading data, I suggest the Speer No. 11 or Hornady No. 3 or No. 4 manuals.

No doubt, a safe load using either of Hornady's 500-grain, .458-inch bullets could be assembled to work through this action. However, extreme reduction in usable capacity, resulting from the necessary deep-seating of those bullets, would reduce ballistic potential substantially. Further, recoil would be heavy, and I see no need for such massive bullets on anything but the biggest of bears or large, dangerous African game. Finally, I hesitate to load any round-nose bullet in a high-recoil, tubular-magazine rifle. Chances of a chain reaction in the magazine—caused by a bullet nose crushing and setting off a primer—may be small; nevertheless, I have no interest in testing that possibility nor observing its consequences.

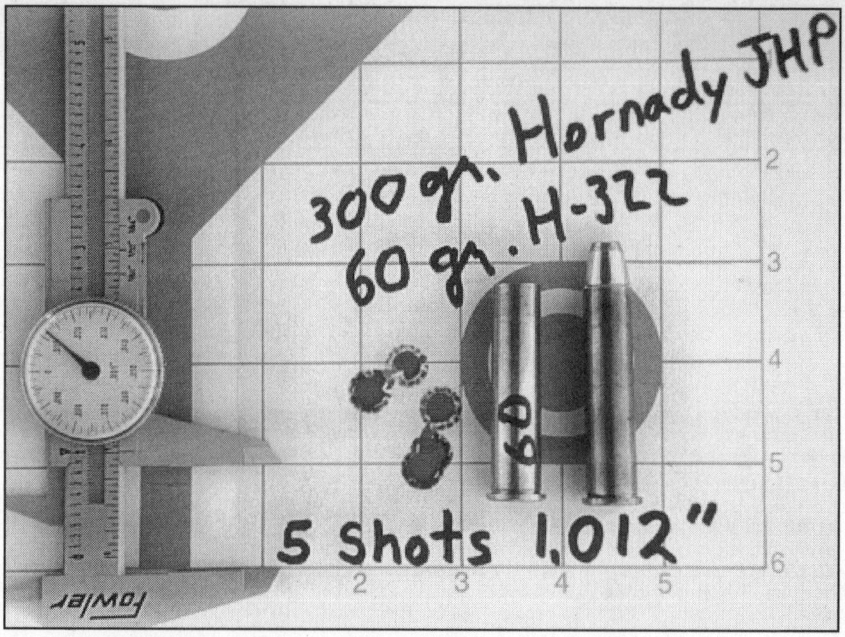

My best groups were with Hornady's 300-grain bullet.

I have not tested the 350-grain Hornady RN. I believe this bullet is designed for proper expansion at higher velocities than are normally achieved in the 1895 Marlin. Speer's recently introduced 350-grain flat-nose spitzer offers an interesting option. (I realize that the term "flat-nose spitzer" is self-contradictory, but that's the best description I can offer. This bullet has a typical spitzer shape, but the nose is sheared off and the jacket opening is larger than normal.) Like Hornady's 350-grain bullet, this Speer is designed for 458 Magnum velocities, but either bullet might offer adequate expansion at top 45-70 Marlin velocity, and could be expected to hold together well.

Before loading the 350-grain Hornady bullet, I would file the round-nose flat, to ensure safety in the tubular magazine.

Speer's 350-grain bullet is longer than I like. If seated to the crimping groove, the cartridge will not function through the Marlin action. One might load this bullet over a compressed charge of H-322, and seat it deeply enough to apply a roll-crimp over the ogive. With its improved ballistic coefficient, this bullet could perform noticeably better at the longer practical ranges on game such as elk.

This is an experiment I intend to undertake soon. For hunting big meanies, I'd likely use one of these 350-grain bullets. When the game can bite back, I want a bullet that will hold together!

While useful loads using 500-grain cast bullets can be assembled, I have not explored that option. Bullets cast from Lyman's original 45-70, 405-grain mould work well, and I suspect any similar bullet would be useful for practice or short-range hunting loads.

The bulk of my experimenting has been with the following bullets: Sierra, Hornady and Remington 300-grain JHP; Speer 400-grain JFP and Remington 405-grain JSP. For hunting non-dangerous game, I am satisfied with these less expensive and more readily available bullets.

All of these bullets feature a pure lead or low-alloy lead core and a thin jacket. The design of the hollowpoint in the lighter bullets varies slightly, and this variation probably has some influence on terminal performance. Nevertheless, the points and jackets are similar, and most of the variation that might affect terminal performance is in the composition of the bullet core.

Comparing hardness of the cores of these bullets is simple—one only has to determine which of two different bullets deforms the other. With the large amount of exposed lead, this is an easy test: simply push the two together by hand.

There are other variables, but I am confident that the bullet with the harder core will give less expansion and will penetrate deeper, on average.

To coin a phrase, "One can learn a lot, just from testing!" Remington's affordable bullets were a pleasant surprise. Priced about one-half what comparable bullets cost, these exceeded my pessimistic expectations in several areas.

The hardest 300-grain bullet tested was Remington's. Its accuracy was comparable to that of Hornady and Sierra bullets.

An even bigger surprise was Remington's 405-grain bullet. It is significantly harder than Speer's 400-grain and shoots almost as well from my rifle. Speer uses a pure-lead core in their 400-grain bullet; this ensures expansion at Trapdoor velocities.

Remington's 405-grain and all of the 300-grain bullets are more streamlined than Speer's blunt-nosed 400-grain. The difference is possibly significant for those needing to stretch usable range to near 200 yards.

With more than 10 percent higher muzzle velocity and similar ballistic coefficients, the lighter bullets can shoot flatter across the useful range. All hunting handloads reported here carry substantial energy to any reasonable range for North American species. Terminal bullet performance and one's ability to place the shot properly are the most important considerations in bullet choice.

When loaded to similar pressures, combinations with the heavier bullets deliver a 25-percent increase in theoretical free recoil energy. My shoulder suggests that this theoretical difference is too modest.

The high recoil of top-velocity, heavy bullet loads may be a factor for some. One should remember, though: On heavy game, especially

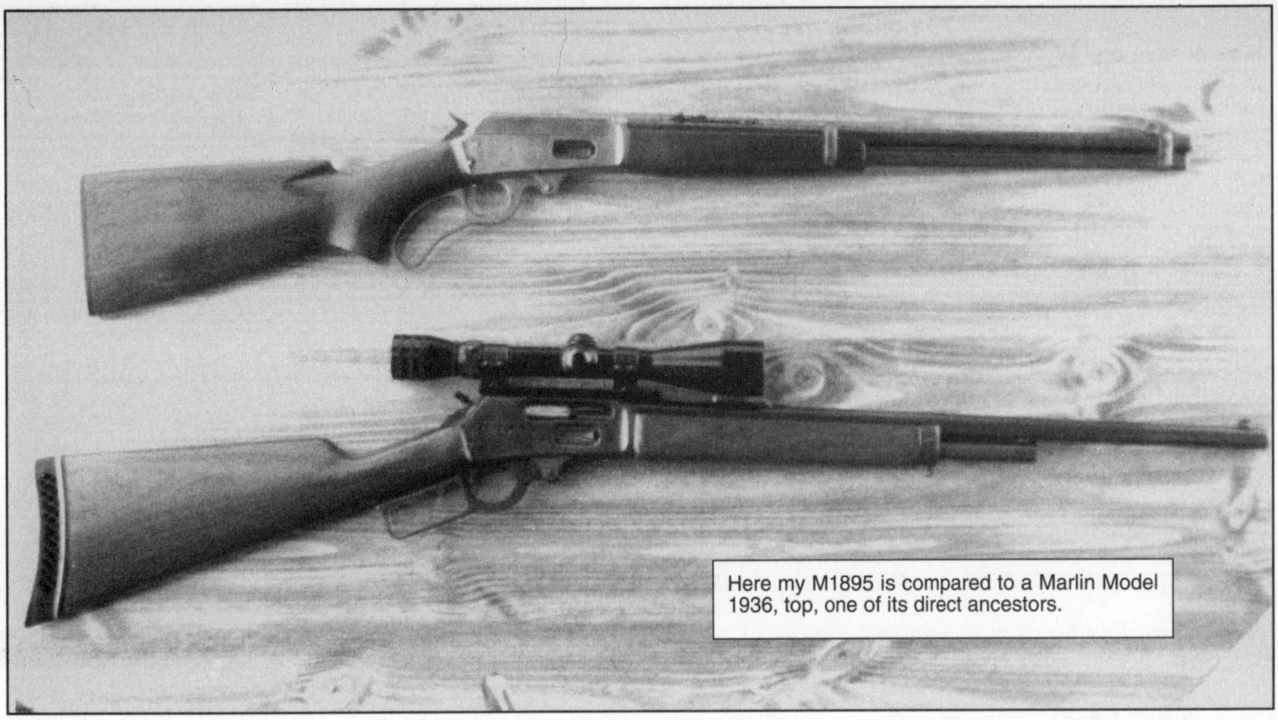

Here my M1895 is compared to a Marlin Model 1936, top, one of its direct ancestors.

big bear, terminal performance may be critical.

For all but the largest North American species, any of these bullets should do the job.

I was surprised to learn that my Marlin gets its best accuracy with 300-grain bullets rather than the heavier ones. After decades of experience with straight-sided pistol cartridges, which almost invariably shoot better with heavier bullets, I had anticipated better accuracy with the heavier ones here, too.

When properly sighted, any of the hunting handloads tabulated here will hit within 3 inches of point of aim to somewhat past 150 yards. Those hunting lighter game in areas which provide longer shots, perhaps to about 200 yards, may prefer the 300-grain bullets. When loaded to top Marlin 45-70 velocities and properly sighted, these shoot within 3 inches of point of aim past 200 yards.

Another factor that must be considered is the cartridge case. As with most rifle cartridges, different makes of cases show significant variations in weight, and thus in volume. Obviously, wide variation in case capacity warrants care in loading. When using R-P or F-C cases with data from loads developed in W-W cases, reduce powder charge by at least one full grain.

Based on my limited sample, uniformity within each make of case is unusually good. For example, 150 W-W cases, spanning at least 30 years of manufacture and from no less than five lots, have less than 5 grains difference between lightest and heaviest. (See Table 1.)

Because of the tremendous battering which occurs in the magazine at the moment of firing, I have adopted a practice which prevents bullets from being driven into the case under recoil stresses. The idea is simplicity itself: I choose a powder which requires considerable compression of the charge. If the bullet is already compressing the powder significantly, it will be impossible for recoil battering to drive it deeper into the case.

When an uncompressed powder charge is used, the bullet can be driven much farther into the case. Normal loading relies on proper crimping in conjunction with high bullet-to-case friction to prevent this from happening.

Hunting loads listed here require enough powder compression to almost certainly eliminate deep seating. If you experiment with faster or denser powders, keep this possible problem firmly in mind. A deep-seated bullet might boost pressure dangerously. Under the wrong circumstances, a graver eventuality exists: A short cartridge might jam the gun, either by binding the feed ramp or by catching the exposed cartridge mouth on the rear face of the barrel.

While a good, heavy crimp helps prevent a bullet from being driven into the case, I am more confident when the powder is already firmly compressed. Because I am relying on powder compression, I can dispense with worrying about getting a *perfect* crimp. I set my Lee Factory Crimp Die to apply a moderate crimp and have experienced no problems with bullet movement.

Before getting into specific details of loads, several cautions must be mentioned. First, as with all handloading, only competent persons should consider using data found in any source. In the case of the 45-70, they should consider handloading only with full knowledge that loads which are perfectly safe in certain modern rifles may be patently unsafe in others.

This cannot be overstated. While the loads given here have caused no problems whatsoever in *my* rifle, they could easily wreck certain older guns and possibly modern replicas of those.

If one chooses to load high-performance 45-70 cartridges for use in the modern Marlin 1895, one must take whatever steps are necessary to ensure those cartridges never end up in the hands of someone who might chamber them in a weaker rifle.

To belabor this point: *These loads are not portrayed as being safe for use in any rifle other than mine and are given here only for comparison purposes. If you choose to consider improved loads for use in your New Model 1895, do so only after you understand what you are doing.*

TABLE 4: LIGHTER VS. HEAVIER BULLETS IN 45-70

Load	Test/Shot	Bullet (Wgt. Grs.)	Bullet (Type)	MV (fps)	Penetration (ins.)	Retained Wgt. (grs./%)	Surface Area (sq. ins.)	Diameter Min./Max.
Federal Factory	1/A	F-C 300	JHP	1913	7.75	160/53	0.52	0.77/0.86
	1/B			1866	7.00	171/57	0.52	0.79/0.83
	1/C			1754	7.25	219/73	0.54	0.73/0.93
Handload	2/A	R-P 300	JHP	1846	8.50	182/61	0.46	0.72/0.81
	2/B			1867	8.75	185/62	0.55	0.81/0.86
	2/C			1798	9.00	186/62	0.46	0.70/0.84
Handload	3/A	Hrn. 300	JHP	1910	10.25	227/76	0.57	0.77/0.94
	3/B			1932	9.25	222/74	0.52	0.78/0.84
	3/C			1945	9.75	217/72	0.61	0.76/0.99
Handload	4/A	R-P 300	JHP	2282	6.38	80/27	0.40	0.64/0.78
	4/B			2300	6.50	98/33	0.46	0.70/0.83
	4/C			2283	6.63	129/43	0.52	0.78/0.85
Handload	5/A	R-P 405	JFP	1497	10.38	402/99	0.56	0.81/0.87
	5/B			1518	10.63	402/99	0.53	0.79/0.86
	5/C			1508	11.63	400/99	0.54	0.80/0.86
Handload	6/A	R-P 405	JFP	2025	11.13	393/97	0.97	1.09/1.14
	6/B			2031	10.13	392/97	1.04	1.08/1.22
	6/C			2067	11.25	397/98	0.98	1.08/1.15

The data clearly show the significant advantage of using the heavier bullet, at least in this medium. The big consideration here is bullet construction. Should one of the lighter bullets fail to hold together, the results could be a wounded and lost animal. Even at the mild factory velocity, the 300-grain bullets are marginal at best. On the other hand, Remington's 405-grain bullet holds together quite well even at shoulder bruising velocities, yet expands nicely at Trapdoor velocities.

I am satisfied with the R-P 405-grain bullet; considering its low cost (about 13 cents each at this time) and impressive accuracy potential, I see no need to seriously consider any other bullet for elk and smaller non-dangerous game. Bullets were fired into water-saturated phone books.

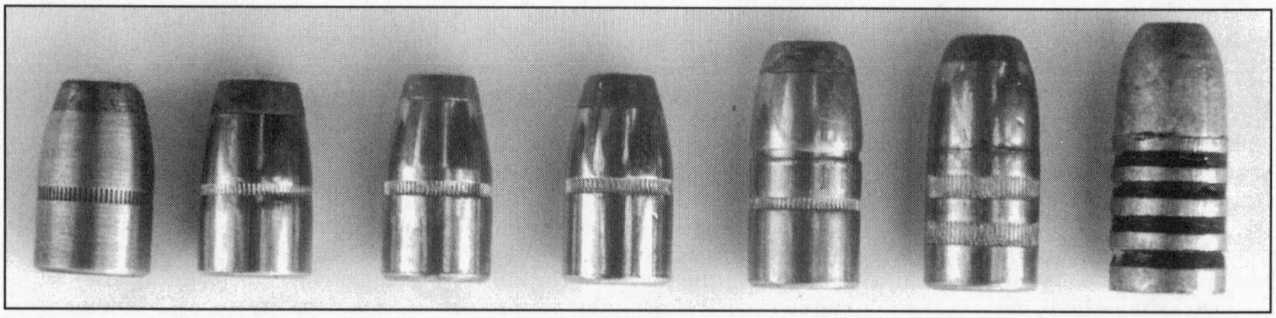

From left, 300-grain bullets: discontinued Sierra JFP, Federal JHP, Hornady JHP, Remington JHP; 400-grain Speer JFP; 405-grain Remington JSP; 410-grain Lyman (nominal 405-FP cast of wheelweights). Note the wide variations in profile and bullet length. The Federal bullet is very similar to Sierra's 300-grain JHP.

Those expecting lever-action rifles to deliver sub-par accuracy may be surprised by the 1895 Marlin. For the purpose of gathering accuracy data for this article, I mounted a 3-9x Redfield on my rifle. We have now fired more than thirty five-shot 100-yard groups from an improvised rest. Center-to-center accuracy is reported in Table 3. I believe every tested handload is capable of better accuracy in my rifle, given a better rest and a better shooter.

Each shot was clocked on an Oehler 35P. Velocities are corrected to the muzzle. External ballistics were computer-generated using PC-BULLET, from Blount, Inc. Ballistic data is calculated for sea level, 59 degrees F, 29.53 inches of barometric pressure and 78 percent humidity (standard conditions). Calculations are based on a scope-sighted rifle with its scope centered 1.63 inches above the bore center.

Data reflect measured and estimated ballistic coefficients, using downrange ballistic data, drag coefficient measurements, and comparisons of actual bullet profiles. Published values are evidently out of date and inaccurate.

As a means of comparison, several boxes of Federal ammunition were tested for velocity, uniformity and accuracy. Federal's 45-70 load uses a 300-grain JHP that is similar in appearance to Sierra's offering. These cartridges are loaded with about 50 grains of a tubular powder that resembles IMR-3031 in both appearance and performance.

Uniformity and accuracy of these 1983-manufacture cartridges, all from one lot, were disappointing. I wrote Federal with details of the results. They responded with a nice letter—possible reasons, an apology, and concern were expressed. Further was the promise of a replacement box of ammo. Evidently, Federal does care about customer satisfaction and product quality. That's a fine attitude.

While I waited for the replacement ammunition, I got to looking at the remaining cartridges from that 1983 lot. A possible explanation for its poor accuracy was observed. One group of nine shots had six in 3 inches, but was spoiled by three fliers that opened it to 9 inches! Some bullets of this early lot were deformed,

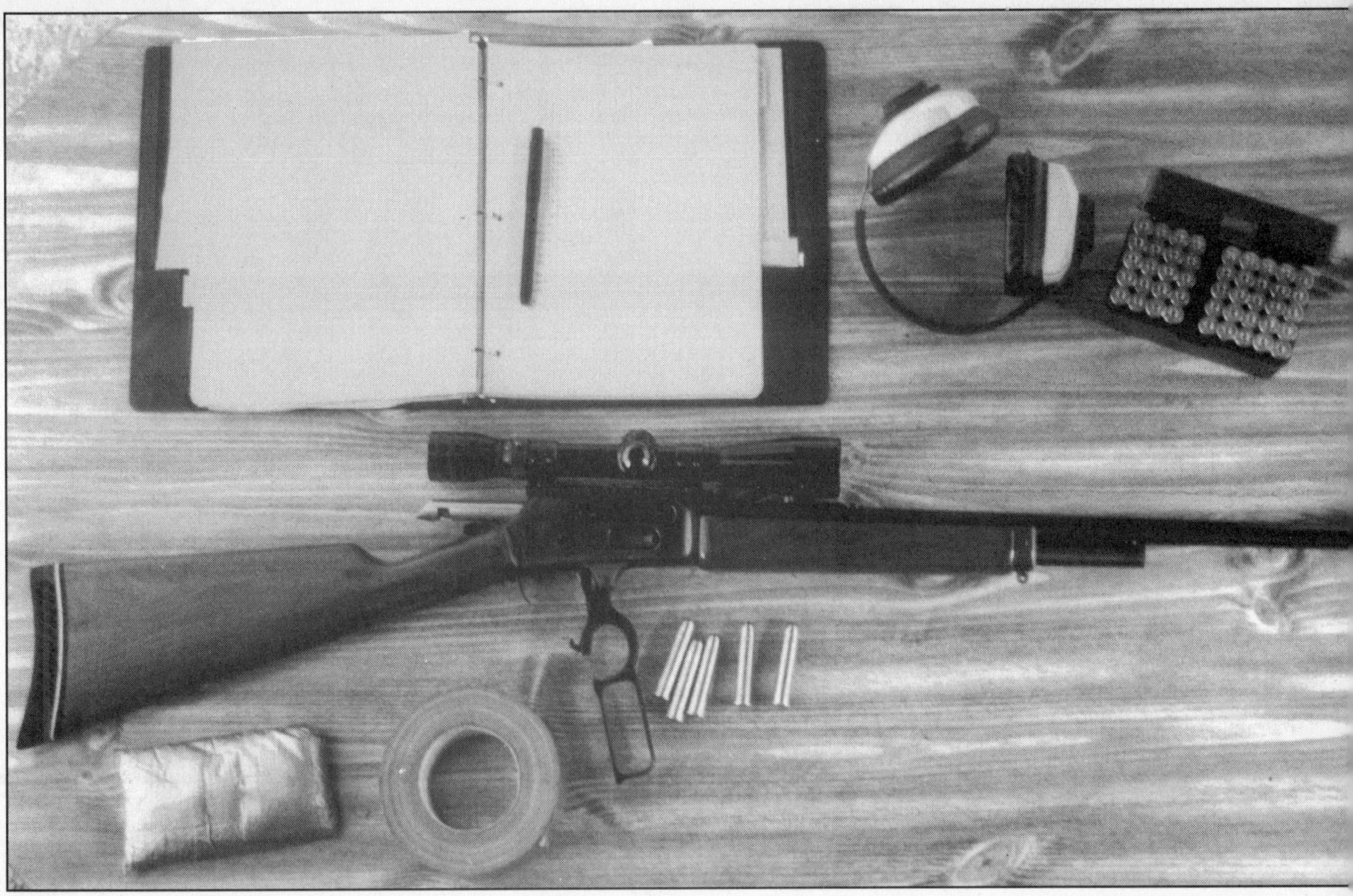

My early edition lacks the pistol grip of later models. I have added a good, thick recoil pad. Note the duct tape and duct-taped object—that 5-pound bag of shot saved my poor shoulder. Without the weight gained by attaching this to the butt-end of the stock, I could never have completed this bench testing.

presumably during the seating operation. They showed an annular ring extending about halfway around the bullet just behind the jacket/core junction. Possibly this was the reason for the fliers. But I cannot understand how the velocity could vary so much.

When the replacement box of ammo arrived, I noted it had been manufactured in 1991. The bullets showed no blemishes. Using it, my son, Joe, fired two five-shot groups at 100 yards from a second, newer M95 Marlin. Muzzle velocity was approximately 1800 fps with a standard deviation of 22 fps, and the groups measured 1.6 and 3.3 inches, on centers. Joe called two fliers in the second group, blaming them mostly on the very heavy trigger pull of this rifle, perhaps 10 pounds. While only ten shots were fired, the results suggest the newer ammo shows significant improvement over the old in ballistic uniformity and accuracy.

As a matter of further interest, expansion tests were run with selected bullets in the 45-70. Terminal performance was tested by using water-saturated telephone books. This technique is not as well understood as it should be. It can be carried out by shooters who lack access to what might be considered a more sophisticated setup. Saturated telephone books do not perfectly duplicate game animals, but neither do "accepted" penetration media such as ballistic gelatin or clay. And unlike those materials, old phone books are easy to obtain and prepare, and they provide consistent and repeatable test results so long as they all come from one production run. To ensure this, I gather mine from local businesses when the new issues come out. One trip to a small mall provides a trunkful.

I prepare the books by first removing all glossy pages and then soaking loosely-bound stacks of them for twenty-four hours before testing. I further ensure that the stacks are of equal thickness for an equal number of pages, since it is primarily the paper and not the water that acts on the bullet.

Based on hundreds of tests involving rifle and handgun cartridges ranging from the 22 LR to 458 bullets at 2050 fps, using both expanding and non-expanding bullets, I can say that this procedure gives very good comparative information. And a good comparison is all we need. This experience leads me to offer this general observation: No expanding bullet, and probably no non-expanding bullet, will penetrate as far in saturated phone books as it will in a game animal. So field results will normally surpass test results.

Results of testing with various factory and handloaded 45-70 ammo are summarized in Table 4. In my opinion, the following factors are most important: maximum penetration, as indicated from the front of the undisturbed stack to the last broken page; expanded bullet frontal area; uniformity of expanded diameter; core-jacket integrity; retained weight; and, finally, the consistency of these factors across several shots.

I feel these tests bear out our earlier contention—that properly handloaded for the Model 1895 Marlin, the ancient 45-70 cartridge is an excellent choice for hunting our largest game at woods ranges. ●

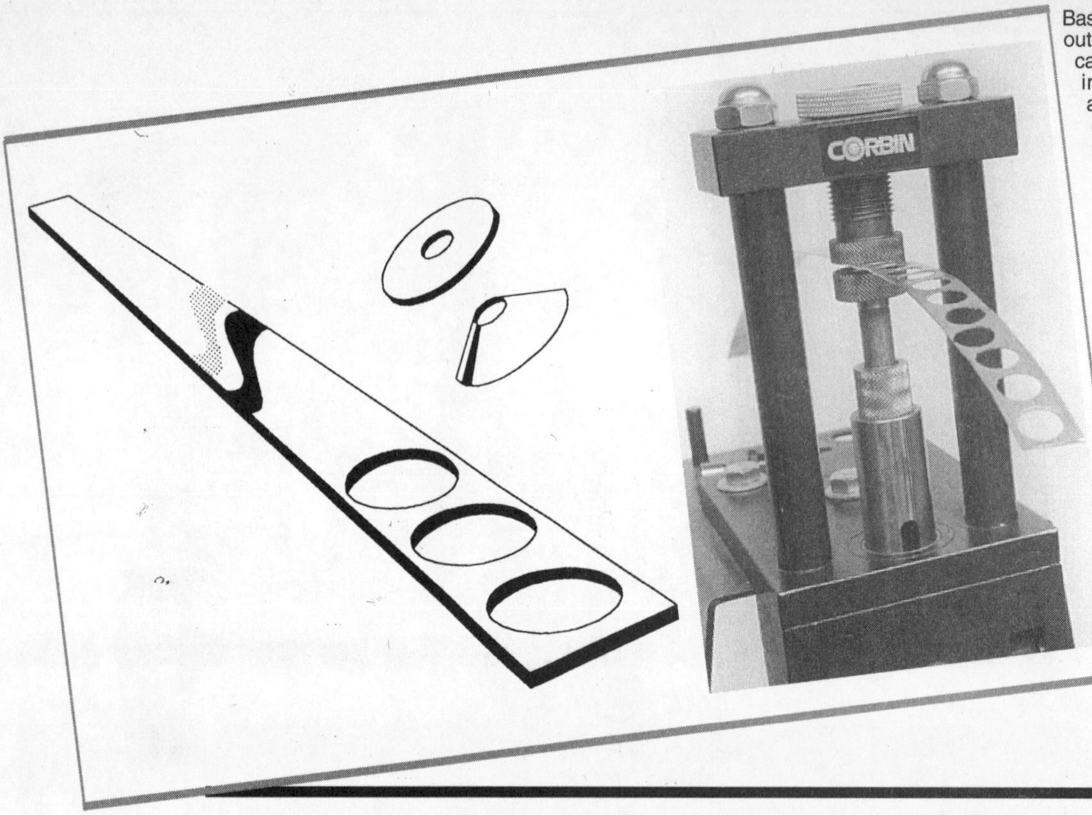

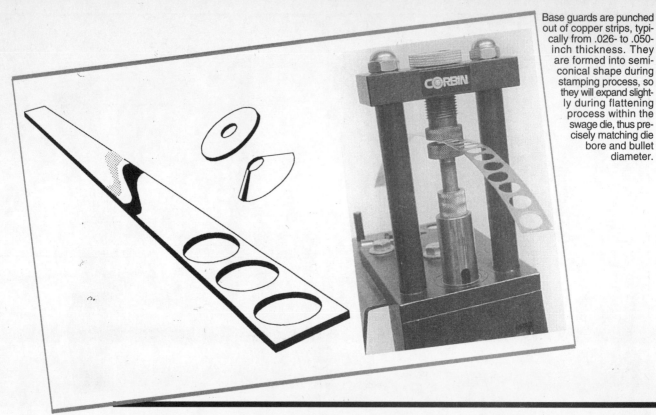

Base guards are punched out of copper strips, typically from .026- to .050-inch thickness. They are formed into semi-conical shape during stamping process, so they will expand slightly during flattening process within the swage die, thus precisely matching die bore and bullet diameter.

Sometimes washer bases have prevented lead fouling at high velocity, but mostly they haven't. Here's what a top researcher learned about them and how he created...

by DAVE CORBIN

This is a complete set of base-guard dies, including the disk maker and the bullet swage.

WHAT WOULD you say if someone told you it was possible to shoot soft lead bullets at speeds over 1400 feet per second without any lubricant and without any fouling? Probably, you'd be too polite to tell him he didn't know much about shooting. I would have thought the same thing, until three years ago, when a serious investigation into the old zinc-washer-based bullets accidentally turned up some startling facts, and led to the development of a new kind of swaged bullet.

If I didn't have a business that depends on new ideas in bullets for its very existence, I probably would never have looked into such a preposterous concept. For the past couple of decades, Corbin Manufacturing & Supply, Inc., has been furnishing nearly all the custom bullet swaging machinery, tools, and product development services in what used to be called the "free world" nations. Around 200 businesses in the United States alone were started with products and tools designed under contract in the die-works in White City, Oregon, and our presses and dies can be found at Sandia National Labs, the Air Force Armaments Research Center, U.S. Army Weapons Center, DuPont Research, and a list of nearly 5000 other clients who need to experiment with unusual bullet designs.

If you haven't heard of our twenty-year-old outfit, it isn't too surprising: we're one of the "behind-the-scenes" kind of operations whose products aren't normally found in your local gunshop and whose services are use-

Base-guard disk is swaged to bottom of lead slug while the bullet is being formed. Disk can be made of copper, brass, sheet iron or zinc.

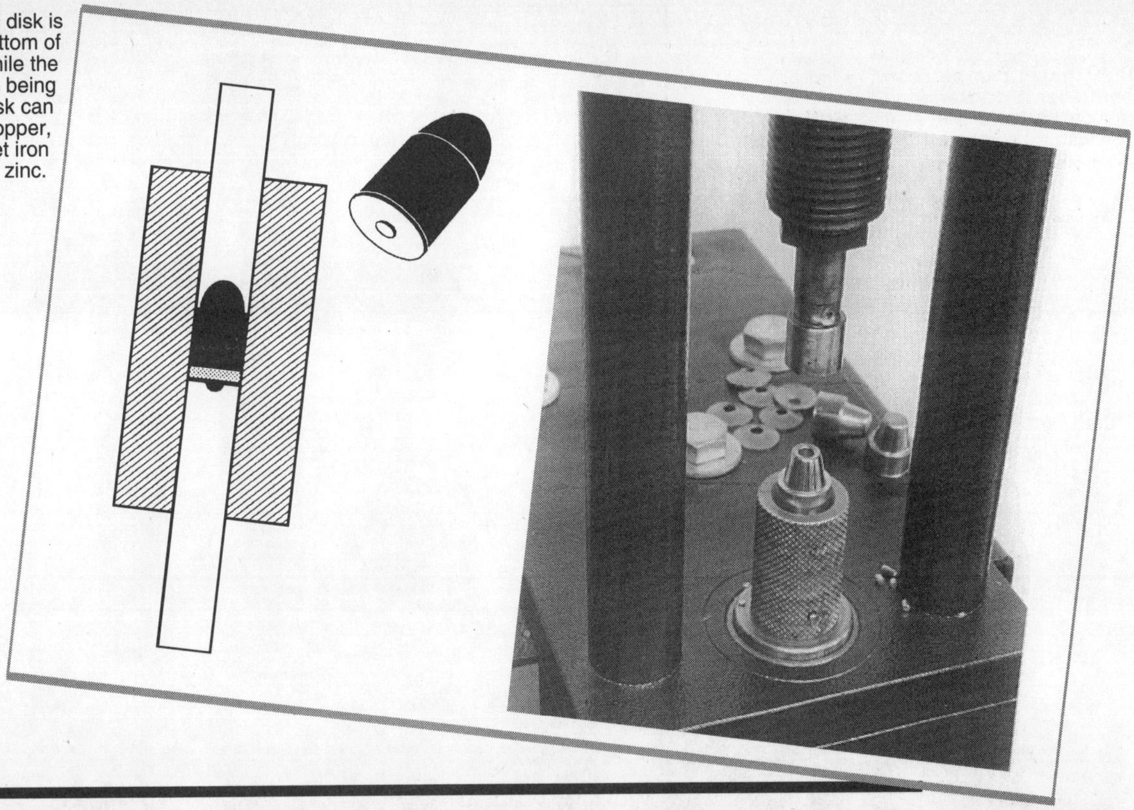

BASE-GUARD BULLETS THAT WORK

ful to people who take the time to seek them out for a specific purpose. In this particular case, someone had asked about the old zinc-washer design and why it still had some devotees, even though the National Rifle Association had printed at least two fairly thorough articles proving the idea didn't work. They found that soft lead bullets fouled the bore with or without a zinc washer swaged to the base.

Yet, when I looked back over the years of records, I saw that quite a few people had asked us to make just such swage dies and to furnish zinc washers. I had no particular enthusiasm one way or the other: We make so many different kinds of tools that zinc-washer dies are just not that big a deal. We're glad to make whatever customers want made. But why would people want them if they really didn't work? There had to be something more to it. And I had the crew and the funds to find out what I had only wondered about years ago. The die-makers were more than happy to take a break and help with the experiments!

To find out, we built several sets of dies for ourselves, loaded up a large number of bullets in various calibers and speeds, and began shooting. The zinc-washer bases had little or no effect on fouling, which was terrible at speeds over about 900 fps in most of our test guns. As you'd expect, harder lead caused a little less fouling. But every so often, we'd notice that a few tests didn't produce as much fouling as others. And we started looking very hard at why this might be.

While measuring the zinc washers, we noticed that most of them had diameter tolerances of up to two thousandths of an inch. Our dies were holding tolerances of less than 100 millionths of an inch in the air-conditioned die-works where we were shooting into ballistic media bullet traps over a chronograph table. And one side of the washers was stamped with a slight curve to the edge, while the other had a slight burr. From years of experience in making bullet swages, we knew that lead will flow easily through a gap of only two thousandths of an inch when the pressure on it reaches 30,000 psi or more. Hmmm....

Here we had zinc washers, stamped out on conventional punch presses, that had typical hardware tolerances. And people had been firing them in guns that could easily develop pressures that required a much tighter seal to prevent lead flow. And finally, there were two ways these washers could have been put on any given bullet base: round side forward or sharp side forward. What if we made some precision washers, ourselves, and made sure they all went on with the sharp side forward?

We built some stamping dies and punched out disks with a small hole in the middle. To ensure that the washer and the bullet would be exactly the same size, with tolerances in the low millionths of an inch, we made the washers slightly conical. With this shape, putting the tip of the cone toward the base of the

Base guard can be seen here after it is inserted in die on top of a piece of soft lead.

A base-guard bullet, 45-caliber, swaged with a hand press.

bullet would ensure that lead would immediately start to flow through the hole while the washer was flattened under pressure. Flattening a cone makes the disk grow larger in diameter, until it hits the die walls. This way, the lead and the disk would both be stopped and controlled by the die in which the bullet was swaged, and not by the tolerances of the stamping dies.

It worked. Bullets fired at up to 1200 fps, with these precision washers fastened to the bottom (by extruding a lead "rivet head" through the center hole in the washer), gave almost *no* fouling, even when used with soft lead and without any lubricant whatsoever. Thinking we'd just solved the world's problems regarding jacketed bullet cost and poor expansion with hard cast bullets, we happily loaded up several more calibers to test.

Two of those guns (a 9mm and a 45 Long Colt) produced unacceptable fouling. But we were doing all the same things with the guns that didn't foul. More head-scratching and measurements of the barrels turned up a sobering fact: The disks on the bullet bases only worked to scrape out all the fouling if the bullet, disk and bore were a very good fit. Loose bores with light loads caused insufficient expansion to seal the bore against powder gas, and lead was melted off. Tight bores sometimes caused the hard washer to bend too far backward and lose the advantage of its sharp, tool-like scraping edge.

Obviously, then, this idea would work well only if the bullet diameter was matched closely to the bore. Except for badly pitted, poorly cut or excessively worn barrels, however, it turned out that most commercial handguns and blackpowder rifles (especially 45-70 caliber barrels) can use bullets and disks (washers) that are industry-standard diameter without fouling. And zinc is not only not necessary for the washer material, but it isn't even the best material to use. We had better results with ordinary roofing copper (.032-inch thick), brass and even sheet iron (tin can metal). Barn siding was even tested with good results (although it is hard on the stamping dies).

International metallic silhouette champion Jim Crane offered to try some 44 Magnum bullets with these "base guards" attached. He loaded his usual hot "Field Class" loads and fired a match, which he won (as usual). His bore was nearly as clean after the match as it was before. Excited by the results, we told several of our clients about the concept and designed tooling so that they could manufacture bullets commercially with a pure copper disk attached to the base. Several of them began offering these designs, which are just now starting to become popular among IPSC competitors.

The point, however, is that you can make the same thing for yourself, if you wish. All it takes is copper sheet or strip, which is available from your local roofing and sheet metal shops (sometimes as scrap) as well as from Corbin, and any brand of bullet swaging die, so long as you

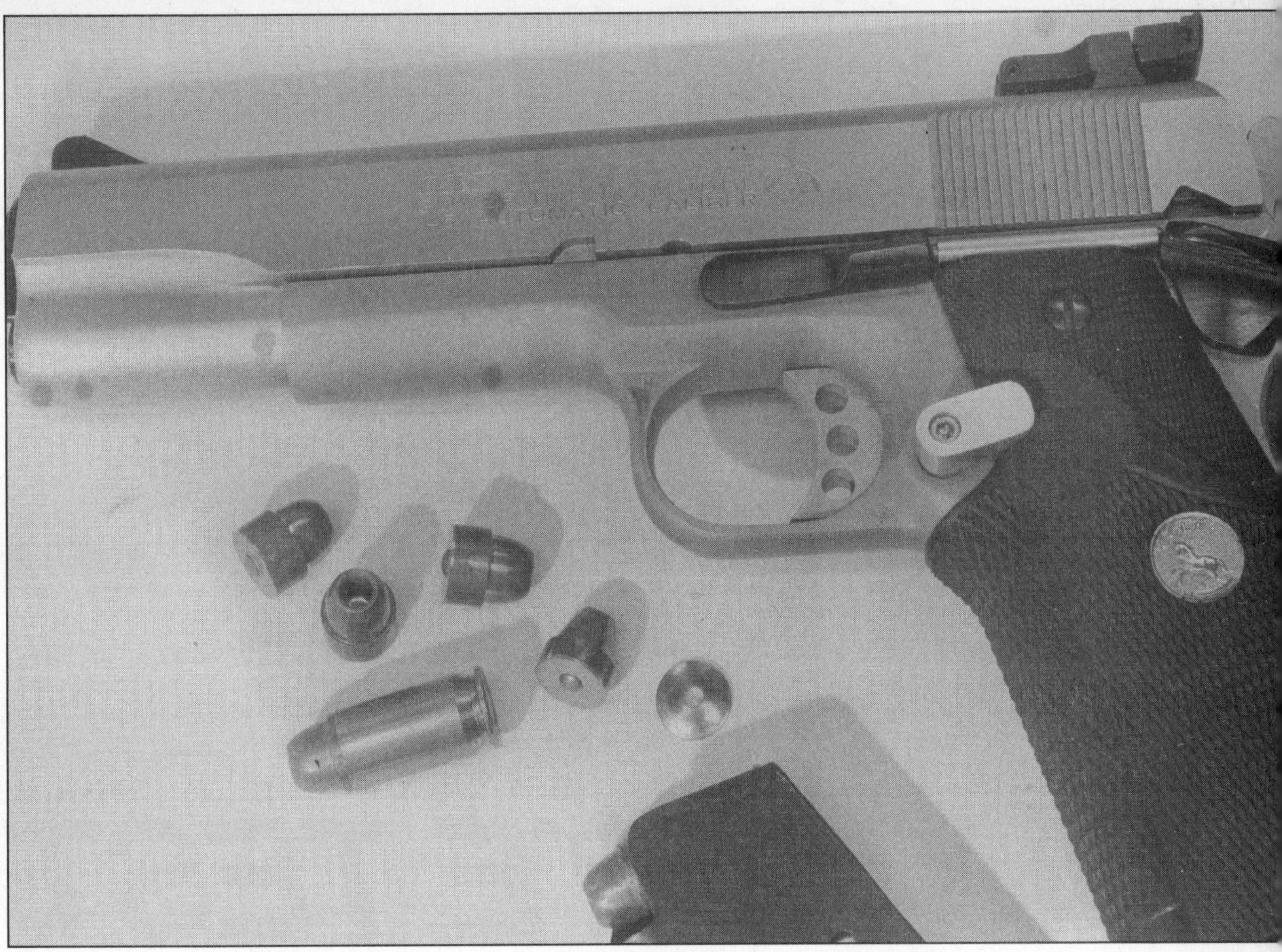

Ultra-lightweight 45-caliber bullets fitted with base guards can give major power factor with 9mm "kick." That makes things easier on the shooter.

can get or modify the base punch to have a small curved depression in the center (to make the rivet head), and a die to cut out the base guards. If you are handy with machine tools, you can turn one out in about four hours. Or, if you want one made from heat-treated die steels, the Corbin die-works makes them in all calibers.

The combination of exact, custom-fitted diameter (created by using a conical stamping that flattens out within the swage die itself) and uniform sharp tooling edge (created by the stamping die and maintained by the need to always put the top of the cone toward the bullet base) turned out to be the main secret behind the old zinc-washer bullet idea. The only trouble was, it was so secret that not even the people who promoted the concept knew what made it work, so it quite often didn't.

The advantage for you is that a soft lead bullet carries more energy (because soft lead is more dense than hard alloys), has a slightly higher ballistic coefficient, expands and holds together better than hard lead, and, if you can prevent bore fouling, has no disadvantages. The base-guard disk, unlike the cup-shaped gas check, actually scrapes out the fouling that is deposited by completely filling the bore, right to the bottom of the rifling, with a material harder than the lead, yet softer than the barrel steel.

The base guard is like a lathe bit: It faces the workpiece, which is the fouling on the barrel surface, and presents a tool edge to the material. With reasonably thick disks (about .026-inch is the minimum that seems to work, whereas even .050-inch is quite acceptable), the fouling cannot bend or push past the disk's edge. Any fouling is presented with two choices: either get pushed out of the bore or bend back the disk and escape under it. The thick disk eliminates the second choice. Fouling harder than the disk could and will cut a groove in it. Thus, severe copper fouling may have been work-hardened to the point where it will cut the disk, and thus create a small gap where powder gas can reach the lead and melt or cut it. A barrel that is already fouled needs to be cleaned before switching to the base-guard bullets.

The upper limit of the base-guard velocity seems to be about 1400 fps, probably because the bullet is being accelerated so fast that it begins to slip and widen the rifling grooves impressed on it. The base guard turns separately from the bullet under those conditions, helping to maintain a gas seal, but eventually the force of the lead fouling ahead of the disk causes it to bend slightly backward and let the lead pass under, where it remains as bore fouling. Within the range of most handgun and factory-loaded 45-70 rifle speeds, the base-guard design eliminates the need for lubrication or jackets. ●

The sheer size, weight and number of so many of the Dark Continent's game species, to say nothing of their toughness and ferocity, easily make...

Africa--THE ULTIMATE TEST FOR RELOADS

by ED MATUNAS

I HAVE been reloading ammunition for almost forty years. During that time, I have been fortunate enough to test, under laboratory controlled conditions, more than a million rounds of reloaded ammunition. Much of this was in conjunction with the development of three *Lyman Handbooks* during the late 1960s (#44, #45, and the first shotshell book). Since then, I have written several reloading handbooks for DBI Books, Inc., as well as more than 500 magazine columns and features on handloading. All in all, more than two million rounds of reloads have been assembled and fired. Additionally, almost all the game I have taken has been with reloads.

It was not until I started to plan my first safari that I realized there had been too little field-testing for me to make unequivocal statements about the absolute suitability of hand-assembled ammunition for all purposes. Indeed, I admit to having formed some new opinions on ammo quality after a number of safaris had been completed.

Of all the decisions that must be made before a safari, the one that often gets the most thought is choice of caliber. However, the near-universal opinion of extensively experienced African hunters is that bullet choice is more important than specific caliber choice. My own experience thoroughly supports this school of thought.

I have been fortunate enough to have the opportunity to assist in the cropping of large numbers of animals. The shooting of so many animals during relatively short time

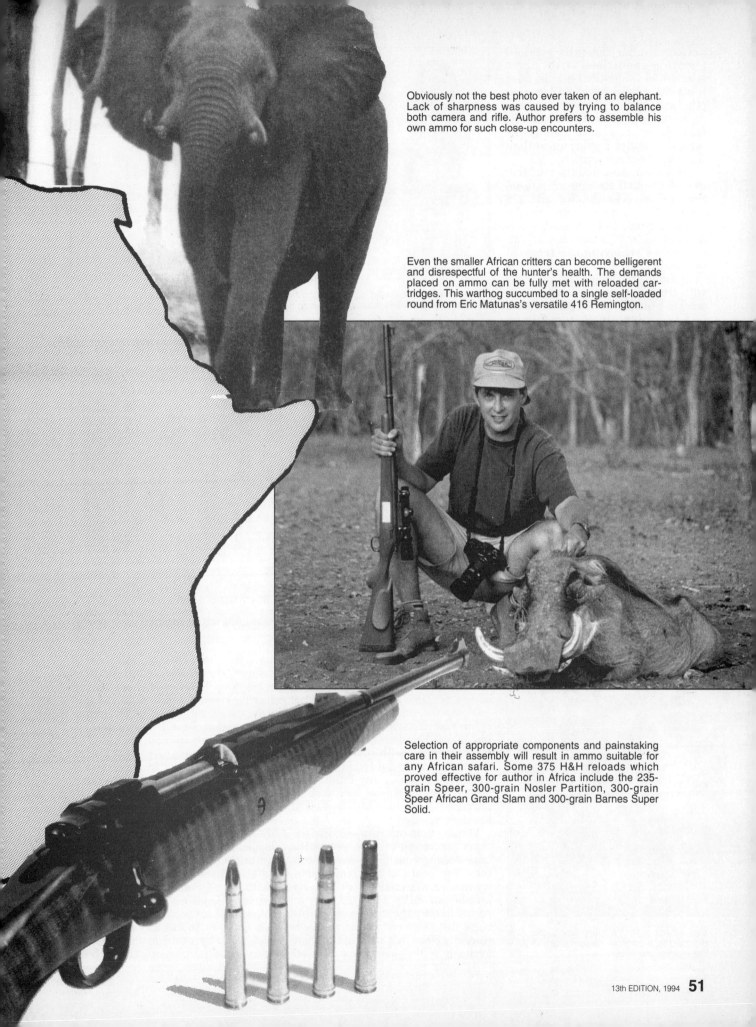

Obviously not the best photo ever taken of an elephant. Lack of sharpness was caused by trying to balance both camera and rifle. Author prefers to assemble his own ammo for such close-up encounters.

Even the smaller African critters can become belligerent and disrespectful of the hunter's health. The demands placed on ammo can be fully met with reloaded cartridges. This warthog succumbed to a single self-loaded round from Eric Matunas's versatile 416 Remington.

Selection of appropriate components and painstaking care in their assembly will result in ammo suitable for any African safari. Some 375 H&H reloads which proved effective for author in Africa include the 235-grain Speer, 300-grain Nosler Partition, 300-grain Speer African Grand Slam and 300-grain Barnes Super Solid.

periods (under carefully selected shooting conditions with ammo selected for evaluation) has provided me a thorough look at bullets that otherwise would not have been used on so many critters. Unfortunately, there have been more disappointments in bullet performance than there has been satisfaction.

I have seen firsthand the total failure of the 280 Remington, 30-06 Springfield, even the 300 and 378 Weatherby Magnums to anchor 120-pound impalas. In every case, it was a matter of "soft" bullets disintegrating before achieving the required penetration.

In some instances, impala, hit with the 378, dropped dead in their tracks. Still the bullet performance had to be interpreted as a failure. The offending bullet, one with a very thick jacket and of very heavy weight, never gave more than 10 inches of penetration; the heaviest bullet fragment that could be recovered weighed only 10 percent of the original bullet's mass. This, of course, is a fault of bullet design and structure, not caliber or cartridge. It occurs because the bullet does not hold together at high impact velocity. In comparison, a 223 with full-metal-cased bullets will often shoot through impala with heart shots taken from a broadside angle. (On broadside shots, if any bullet does not exit the far side of such a small animal, it is invariably because it has disintegrated.)

For the first safari, the considerations for ammo to be used on the largest dangerous game caused concern. Ten years as an ammo industry insider, associations with a large number of folks who had hunted Africa frequently, and years of full-time data development made it painfully clear that none of the then-available factory-loaded solid bullets were free from recorded instances of failure. There were countless documented occurrences of these "solids" having riveted, bent, ruptured and even expanded, often under circumstances that were life-threatening. (Solids that deform cannot be depended upon to penetrate as hoped or to travel in a relatively straight path once entering the quarry.)

None of the sophisticated solids, such as the Barnes Super Solid, a monolithic bronze bullet, were loaded in generally available factory ammo when I planned my first safari. These are now available in Remington's Safari Grade 416 Remington Magnum ammunition. I knew, without soul searching, that I did not care to use any bullet that had a background of failures, no matter how infrequently the problem

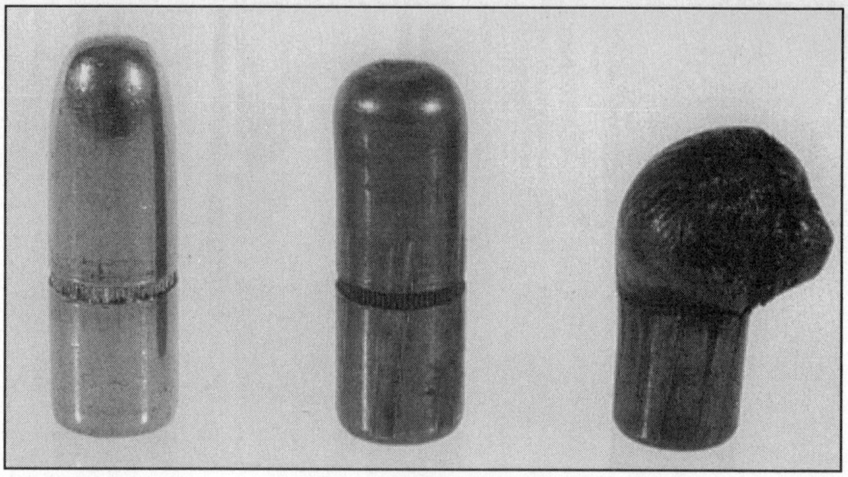

Not all solids are created equal, as can be seen by these examples. Left, unfired bullet. Center bullet riveted slightly, while one on right bent badly and mushroomed, and didn't get the job done.

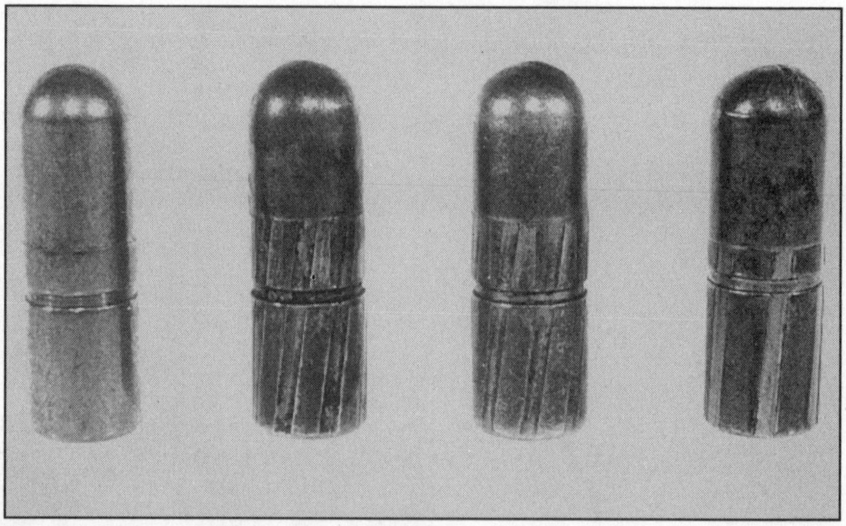

Here are one unfired and three fired monolithic solids (made of solid bronze) as made by Barnes and A-Square. Other than the rifling engraving, the recovered bullets are in all ways as new.

One of the author's many kudu, this one dropped to a carefully assembled 338 Winchester Magnum round.

Author and his first buffalo, taken with a carefully selected and handloaded 416 solid. Note author's bare feet—one of his favorite tactics for getting close to the really tough game of Africa.

Author photographed this buffalo at a range of 20 feet to show just how close dangerous African game is often engaged. Nothing but the very best ammo can be depended upon under such circumstances. Author has proven many times that reloads are up to the task.

was encountered. I did not want to become the means for some belligerent Cape buffalo to vent any pent-up emotions. *Reloads were essential!* I chose 400-grain 416 A-Square Monolithic Solids for my first encounter with critters that could reverse the roles of hunter and hunted.

There is no better way to become convinced about the performance of any solid than to use it on such game as Cape buffalo. On broadside shots you need complete penetration, even when both shoulder bones are pierced. Without this degree of penetration, it is unlikely that sufficient penetration can be had when difficult angle shots must be taken. Also, it is nice to know that a bullet fired at the stern end of a wounded buff has the potential of reaching all the way into the chest cavity. When facing a buff coming full steam straight at you, it is also comforting to know your bullet is up to the task. When you tag him on the tip of the nose—the best shot to reach the brain—you need to know the bullet is not going to deform or veer off course.

My first buffalo was taken at 17 yards; rather, the first shot was fired at that range. The buff, killed with the first shot, was not ready to admit defeat. He angled across in front of me, traveling about 25 yards, while I put in two more shots. All three could have been covered by the palm of your hand and all three exited the far side having traveled a straight-as-an-arrow path through the tough critter, busting up both of the shoulders. Admittedly, the bashed bones did not immediately put the buff down, but they sure did prevent him from considering any but that straightforward final lunge which carried him to our side and on a non-destructive path.

Those who hunt elephant are also in great need of deep penetrating bullets. One solid, made from bronze, penetrated a wounded and retreating elephant from the stern end to the vitals. That bull went but few yards before collapsing. Impressive performance!

If you have read much African literature, you are aware that hunting ranges can be very short; often the distances involved are measured in feet rather than yards. The real thrill of dangerous game comes from up-close-and-personal contact. Typically, such hunting is done at 50 yards or less. Ranges of 50 feet are not uncommon. On one occasion, I photographed a buffalo at a measured 20 feet! When you get this close to game that can be belligerent, you want ammo that can bring a swift and single-round conclusion to any disagreement between hunter and hunted. Lesser performing ammo may find an animal's rush compels the professional hunter to get into the fracas. Worse, the "squirt" from the aggressive beast may end some distance behind a now-prostrate gun-toting would-be nimrod.

Solids that enjoy an unblemished reputation include the previously mentioned Barnes Super Solid, the

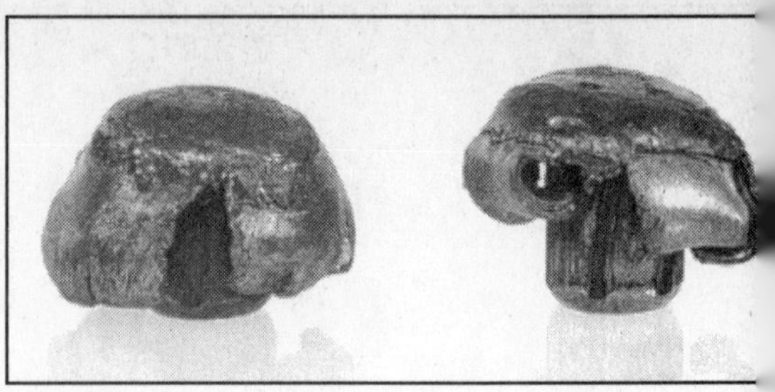

The best softpoint bullets will expand to at least double their original diameter and retain most of their original mass weight.

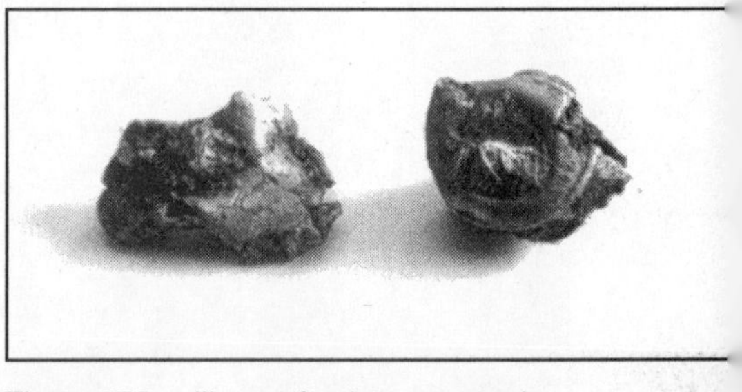

These 375-caliber softpoints gave unimpressive results on African critters. One failed to penetrate a warthog, the other an impala, and both lost most of their weight. The one on the right has no jacket material left.

(Above and left) Difficult angle shots should usually be passed up. However, the African hunter must be ready to take a tough shot when it becomes essential. This is when premium bullets prove their worth.

A-Square Monolithic and the Sledgehammer made by Trophy Bonded Bullets.

My first choice of softpoint bullets for Africa also required some pondering, as hunters of extensive experience had many tales to tell of too-soft expanding bullets that failed to adequately penetrate because of premature expansion and loss of mass. Some bullets not only lost too much weight, but also actually disintegrated before traveling very deep, never reaching the vitals.

I settled on 210-grain 338 Nosler Partitions, in both handloads and factory-loaded ammo (Federal Premium 338 Winchester Magnum). The factory loads were taken because I had heard numerous comments on handloads that did not perform as expected in the extreme African heat. Still, I was convinced I could assemble reloads of expected ballistics without incurring extraction problems due to heat-induced, higher-than-desired pressure. As things worked out, my handloads proved nothing less than perfect and the factory ammo was never used.

Of all the bullets I have used in Africa, I have taken the most game using various Nosler Partitions. These bullets begin expanding upon impact even when the quarry is relatively light. Progressive expansion continues until the entire front end has expanded back to the partition wall which separates the front and rear cores. This often means there will be no front core lead left on recovered bullets, dependent upon impact velocity and if any massive bones are struck. Expansion will go to greater than double diameter and then be reduced somewhat if there is sufficient energy to keep the bullet penetrating after the front end has been fully consumed. With typical loads, using appropriate bullet weights, penetration will exceed two feet at most hunting ranges. Remaining bullet weight will typically be 60 percent, or slightly greater, when there is sufficient energy to fully utilize the front core.

Nosler Partitions are great all-round bullets that work well on tiny antelope that weigh as little as 20 to 30 pounds, as well as being fully satisfactory on animals to 700 pounds or so. I have never experienced, or been made aware of, any confirmed instance when one of these bullets has failed to perform as expected. They are an excellent choice for all cartridges to be used for general plains game. As mentioned, the non-reloader can obtain factory ammo loaded with these bullets in some Federal Premium calibers.

When hunting very large critters, those that weigh up to 1000 or so pounds, I prefer a bullet that will retain more mass weight than typical of the Nosler Partition. If the

The 338 210-grain Nosler Partition bullet has proved up to the task on many safaris. These were recovered from a zebra and two kudu. Each was found just under the skin on the off-side of the quarry, and each broke through at least one shoulder.

Roger Whittall, famed modern hunter and safari operator, with the 6.5x53mmR English-built Mannlicher with which the legendary Frederick Courteney Selous killed countless elephant, proving shot placement and bullet quality are more important than the cartridge used.

quarry weighs even more, perhaps 1500 to 2500 pounds, then I insist on using a bullet that will retain at least 90 percent of mass weight. This is because as a bullet loses weight, it loses the ability to penetrate, and very deep penetration is essential to reach the vitals of truly large animals. One bullet capable of the needed performance is the Swift A-Frame. While these are very expensive, they are worth every dollar.

I have used many Swift A-Frame bullets, in reloads as well as factory loaded Remington Safari grade ammo. I have never recovered one of these bullets that did not retain at least 92 percent of its original weight. Penetration and expansion are almost unbelievable.

The A-Frame bullet is somewhat similar to the Partition type except for the fact that the front core is soldered to the jacket. This helps keep core and jacket intact. Another difference, perhaps non-functional, is a very small connection of the front and rear bullet cores through a narrow opening in the bullet's partition.

Recovered A-Frame bullets in the heavy calibers and weights typically expanded to double diameter or more and penetrated up to 50+ inches. Naturally, penetration will vary dependent upon caliber, weight, impact velocity, and whether heavy bone is pierced. Also, when used on game as light as 30 pounds, I have always been satisfied that the bullets perform well. It is generally impossible to recover an A-Frame bullet unless the game weighs more than 600 pounds. Penetration is most often complete on light animals.

During one hard eland hunt, the A-Frame saved the day. When the shot came, it was at the very last bit of light on the fourth day. The bull was facing directly away. I normally pass up such difficult angle shots, but it seemed that this might be my only chance for an eland. My confidence in my reloads proved well-founded as the bullet easily made it up into the chest cavity, destroying a lot of vital organs before it stopped. When recovered, it weighed 375 grains (more than 90 percent of the original 400 grains) and was beautifully expanded to about 90-caliber.

The newer Speer African Grand Slam bullets also have been used quite successfully in Africa in a 416. All worked perfectly. If the various diameters and weights of this bullet all work equally well, they are sure to become very popular.

I have seen many a report describing performance with Trophy Bonded Bear Claw bullets as perfect, but I have not used enough of these to have formed an opinion.

Tales of heavy game that took repeated solid hits from more than adequate cartridges are too numerous to count. As often as not, the problem is traceable not to super tough animals, but rather bullets that are not up to the task. Stories of lost eland, which typically weigh about 1800 pounds, come most to mind. Even many factory bullets in such suitable calibers as 375 H&H, and larger, fail to get the eland job done properly. Select bullets with extreme care and do not hesitate to spend even a couple of dollars per bullet. For any bullet to securely anchor the really large animals, bullet weight retention cannot be overstressed.

That bullet selection is more important than caliber has been pointed up on many occasions. My son Eric has taken many a nice African trophy with a 30-06 and

The fact that good size game can be taken by modest cartridges is proven here. This zebra weighs about 700 pounds and was dispatched by the author's son Eric, using a 30-06 with selectively loaded ammunition with a premium-grade partition-style bullet.

Professional hunter William Finaughty holds very-high-in-the-record-book-size bushbuck cleanly taken by author with a handload at about 30 feet.

The first of your ammo can be tested on relatively light game such as this impala. Regardless of the angle or range, any load to be later used on heavier game should completely penetrate an animal of this size while still leaving indications of proper expansion.

first-quality 180-grain bullets. Species have included zebra and kudu weighing about 700 pounds. Eric, when using the 30-06, will pass up extremely difficult angle shots if the quarry is beyond the cartridge/bullet capability. Still, with selected shot placement, he has killed many species of African game with this combination.

The extreme example of good bullets and properly placed shots are the many hundreds of elephants killed by the world-famous elephant hunter, Frederick Courteney Selous. One of his favorite rifles was built on a Mannlicher action in England, very near the end of the 1800s. I had a chance to examine this rifle during one of my safaris on the game-rich Humani ranch. The rifle now belongs to Roger Whittall, a hunter and safari operator of extensive experience. Whittall, who well understands the importance of bullet over caliber, is justifiably proud of the rifle. It was given to his grandfather by Selous, in appreciation for his companionship on many hunts. The rifle is chambered for the tiny 6.5x53mmR. It, with full-metal-case bullets, has accounted for more elephants and other game than most hunters would believe.

Naturally, today no one should use such a small cartridge as did Selous. He was undoubtedly one of the finest shots and hunters Africa ever knew. He placed every bullet perfectly at very short range or he did not fire. Today's hunter should choose the biggest possible round he can shoot comfortably. Unlike in Selous' day, the modern hunter may get but a single opportunity to take an elephant. Having every possible edge can be essential not only to bagging the trophy, but also to preserving his life.

Naturally, there is lot more to proving ammo than having bullets work as hoped, though this is the prime consideration. Dimensionally, reloads can give the African hunter unwanted problems. Strive to load ammo that is dimensionally the equivalent of factory ammo. The dust of the Dark Continent has a way of reducing too-tight tolerances into no-go fits. Run each and every round through the magazine and into the chamber to ensure smooth and effortless functioning. Of course, this is done only at the range. But a maximum cartridge gauge is also a valuable tool at the bench. Drop every loaded cartridge into the gauge to make sure it is as hoped.

When testing ammo for accuracy, be certain to load the magazine fully and to shoot groups by functioning the ammo through the magazine and feeding cycles. I have heard a number of stories about jammed guns at crucial moments. This type of problem can be avoided by verifying beforehand that all is as it should be.

And finally, it is not a bad idea to review all that you know about reloading, but may have forgotten. Reading a book such as *Metallic Cartridge Reloading,* 2nd Ed., by DBI Books, Inc., will help ensure that no mistakes will be assembled and later regretted.

Africa is the place where many can gain the ultimate experience in

AUTHOR'S FAVORITE LOADS PROVEN IN AFRICA

Caliber	——Bullet—— (Wgt. Grs.)	(Type)	Load (Grs./Powder)	MV (fps)	Bbl. (ins.)
280 Rem.	160	Nos. Part.	54.0/IMR-4831	2800	22
30-06 Spring.	180	Nos. Part.	57.0/IMR-4350	2750	22
	180	Nos. Part.	57.0/IMR-4350	2850	26
300 H&H Mag.	180	Nos. Part.	60.0/IMR-4350	3050	24
300 Wea. Mag.	200	Nos. Part.	80.0/IMR-7828	2900	24
338 Win. Mag.	210	Nos. Part.	72.0/IMR-4831	2825	24
	210	Nos. Part.	75.0/Reloder 22	2800	24
	210	Nos. Part.	Fed. Prem. Fact.	2825	24
	225	A-Frame	70.0/IMR-4831	2700	24
	250	Nos. Part.	69.0/IMR-4831	2575	22
	250	Nos. Part.	69.0/IMR-4831	2600	24
	250	Nos. Part.	Fed. Prem. Fact.	2575	24
375 H&H Mag.	300	Nos. Part.	78.0/IMR-4831	2475	23
	300	Nos. Part.	Fed. Prem. Fact.	2475	23
	300	Barnes Sld.	77.0/IMR-4831	2450	23
416 Rem. Mag.	400	Speer AGS	80.0/Reloder 15	2375	22
	400	A-Frame	80.0/Reloder 15	2400	22
	400	A-Frame	Rem. Fact.	2400	22
	400	Barnes Sld.	79.0/Reloder 15	2375	22
416 Rigby	400	Speer AGS	97.0/IMR-4831	2425	24
	400	A-Frame	CHAA Custom (H-4350)	2475	24
	410	"Solid"	Fed. Prem. Fact.	2325	24

Nos. Part.:Nosler Partition; Wea.:Weatherby; Win.:Winchester; AGS:African Grand Slam; Sld.:Super Solid; Fed. Prem. Fact.:Federal Premium Factory; A-Frame: Swift A-Frame.

Dropping each handloaded cartridge, as it is completed, into a maximum cartridge gauge is one essential step to ensure that your ammo will chamber easily when fast shooting is required.

Ammo and sights should always be verified before beginning the hunt. If you do not have a free-floated barrel or synthetic stock, it is wise to check point of impact every few days. The extremely variable weather of Africa can cause substantial changes in moisture content of stock and wood pressure against barrel.

Only confidence in truly fine ammunition allowed the difficult shot that resulted in this nice eland. It is 1400 or so pounds of positive proof of the effectiveness of reloads in Africa.

hunting with reloads. Typically, on one safari, a hunter will take more game than in a decade of stateside hunting. For those who wonder about such things, Africa can still be affordable. I arrange all of my safaris through Len Pivar's Safaris Africa (614-848-8449) at very affordable prices. It is still possible to use your ammo on a dozen head of big game during a ten- to fourteen-day hunt for a lot less than the cost of taking one or two animals in Alaska. And, I know that the satisfaction of bagging a wide variety of game with your own ammo will make for a lifetime of memories.

An important caution: Be sure to test all ammo at the first opportunity after arriving in your safari camp. Better to discover that something is amiss here than when the opportunity of a lifetime comes along. If you have done your best in load development and ammo testing, this precaution will give you added confidence that your loads are up to the extreme heat and that your careful sight-in at home has not been altered during the long flight to Africa.

When hunting, if you have chosen the correct bullets along with a good moderate pressure load, you will be up to even the difficult angle shots. However, if you are using a bullet of which you are unsure, it is wise to start with light game, i.e. impala, and easy broadside shots. If the first animals show that the bullet is less efficient than desired, it will be time to look into your kit for something else. ●

HANDLOADING THE 10mm AMT MAGNUM

This is a fairly intimate view of the headstamp on a round of 10mm Magnum ammunition. The cases are produced by Starline, which explains the symbolism of the two stars joined by a short segment of curved line.

There are a number of excellent 10mm (40-caliber) handgun cartridges around these days. This is about Arcadia Machine & Tool's version—and it's impressive!

by DEAN A. GRENNELL

THE TITLE designation includes the AMT to specify the straight-sided cartridge from Arcadia Machine & Tool. For a time, they operated as Irwindale Arms, Inc., but they went back to the AMT designation on a full-time basis. The test autoloader at hand bears the discontinued IAI logo.

There also is or has been a 10mm Wildey Magnum, based upon the 284 Winchester case, introduced by Wildey J. Moore. My only contact

Left to right, cartridges in the following calibers: 10mm AMT Magnum; 10mm Auto and 40 S&W. The first two operate with large pistol primers and the 40 S&W takes small pistol primers. Ruger pistols chambered for the 40 S&W are marked, "40 Auto." Approximate case lengths are, respectively, 1.241, .983, and .841, as measured on fired cases.

This photo shows the author shortly after firing a round of 10mm AMT Magnum in the autoloading pistol of that caliber. It was taken automatically by a paddle-switch of his own design and construction, positioned just ahead of the muzzle to be activated by powder gas.

with that one has been via an engineer's dimensional drawing. Frowning at the drawing with pursed lips, I'd guesstimate it might outperform the 10mm AMT Magnum in barrels of the same length, but there's no ready way of verifying that.

As to test guns on hand, there is the IAI (now AMT) Automag IV with an 8½-inch barrel that juts out of the 7-inch slide. It has one magazine that holds six cartridges, provided you have strong fingers and a solid place upon which to rest the magazine base.

The design of the Automag IV is such that the only way you can coax a cartridge into the chamber is by stripping it off the top of the magazine. That's to say it won't work if you lock the slide to the rear, insert a round in the chamber and mash down on the slide stop to let the slide bang forward. The extractor won't ride over the flange at the cartridge head, and the action will be left some small distance out of battery. If you wish to fare afield with a seven-shooter, you can chamber one via the magazine and either point the muzzle in a harmless direction to lower the hammer with care or press the slide-mounted safety-lever down to cover the red dot and put it in safe mode. After that, you can remove the magazine and put six, maybe even seven more rounds in it. If you can crowd in seven, my response would be the punchline of an ancient joke: "My profound respects to his grace, the Duke!"

When the safety-lever of the Automag IV is down, in safe mode, the firing pin is securely locked against forward movement, even in the event of a brutal impact against the muzzle, and a sturdy stainless steel boss comes up to make sure the hammer can't reach the rear of the firing pin. The design is single action, meaning you must cock the hammer manually to get off the first round, after which it self-cocks until you run out of ammo or cease firing. With the hammer cocked and the safety-lever in the down (safe) position, pulling the trigger drops the hammer but the roll bar of the safety prevents it from hitting the rear of the firing pin.

In addition to the AMT auto, I have two Thompson/Center Contenders in 10mm Magnum. The one with a 10-inch barrel has standard T/C barrel markings as a 10mm Magnum and a remarkably round serial number—444444. The T/CC that carries the 14-inch barrel is marked as a 10mm Auto, but was rechambered by the friendly folks at AMT, and that barrel, curiously enough, is on T/CC receiver number 333333. The 10-incher has adjustable iron sights, and I've fitted the 14-incher with a 2½-7x Simmons scope on Burris base and rings. I tend to view that as an eminently satisfactory sighting system, comparable to the 2½-7x RP (Recoil-Proof) Thompson/Center scope and the 3-9x Burris scope.

The 14-inch Contender barrel was produced without an iron front sight, and there aren't even any holes drilled and tapped at the muzzle. This is much in line with my personal preferences, if I'm planning to scope a Contender barrel.

AMT produces some 10mm Magnum factory loads, put up in neat 50-round plastic boxes with a 180-grain JHP bullet. I fired five rounds apiece of those through all three test guns and got the following averages:

AMT Factory Loads

Handgun	MV (fps)	ME (fpe)
8 1/2-inch IAI/AMT	1713	1173
10-inch T/CC	1801	1297
14-inch T/CC	1868	1395

Back in early 1991, Walt Jones of IAI/AMT worked up some load data in the IAI/AMT brass—made by Starline and the only cases available in 10mm AMT Magnum—using Winchester 296 powder with Winchester magnum large pistol primers. The cartridge overall length (COL) is not available. Chronographed from an 8 1/2-inch barrel in the Automag IV, performance is seen in Table 1.

My first tests with the 8 1/2-inch IAI/AMT test gun were with loads made up with charges of 17.5 grains of Accurate Arms No. 9 powder, henceforth referred to as AA-9, as dispensed from a Jones Micro-Measure at 30.000 on its micrometer adjustment stem. I used the Federal No. 150 primer in the AMT brass and recorded the COL dimensions. Results are seen in Table 2.

If you're already set up to load either 10mm Auto or 40 S&W, there is no need to purchase additional dies or another shellholder to handload the 10mm Magnum. I've done all my loading for the 10mm Mag by using my set of RCBS dies in 40 S&W with carbide sizing die, and they performed just fine. All you have to do is adjust the dies higher in the press head in the usual manner.

Although RCBS now markets a No. 27 shellholder for use with the 10mm Auto, et al, I've found that their No. 6 shellholder works just as well. The No. 6 is the holder customarily used with the 38 Special, 357 Magnum and others with the same head dimensions.

Like the 10mm Auto, the 10mm Magnum takes large pistol primers, while the 40 S&W uses the small pistol size.

It is possible to rechamber several existing guns to the 10mm AMT Magnum, provided their bore dimensions and rate of rifling pitch are suitable. One friend had his Smith & Wesson Model 610 revolver converted to 10mm Mag, using the half-moon clips S&W customarily supplies. Ranch Products can provide full-moon and third-moon clips for the same application.

The Buckeye Sports special run of Ruger Blackhawks with cylinders in both 10mm Auto and 38-40 WCF could have its 10mm Auto cylinder rechambered to the 10mm AMT Magnum. The single-action design would handle the rimless case just fine.

TABLE 1: 10mm AMT MAGNUM LOAD DATA

Load (Grs./Powder)	Bullet (Wgt. Grs.)	Bullet (Type)	MV (fps)	ME (fpe)
23.0/296	180	Sierra JHP	1616	1044
23.0/296	190	Sierra FPJ	1612	1096
23.4/296	190	Sierra FPJ	1628	1118
23.8/296	180	Sierra JHP	1713	1173
23.8/296	190	Sierra FPJ	1725	1255
22.0/296	200	Hornady JHP	1626	1174

TABLE 2: VARIOUS HANDLOADS FOR 10mm AMT MAGNUM

Bullet (Wgt. Grs.)	Bullet (Type)	MV (fps)	ME (fpe)	COL (in.)
Load: 17.5/Accurate Arms No. 9 (AA-9)				
150	Nosler JHP	1575	826	1.521
155	Hornady JHP	1549	826	1.522
150	Sierra JHP	1572	823	1.508
170	Nosler JHP	1533	887	1.522
180	Hornady JHP	1487	884	1.532
190	Sierra FPJ	1482	927	1.516
190	Speer TMJ	1482	927	1.516
200	Speer TMJ	1451	935	1.519
Load: 18.3/Accurate Arms No. 9 (AA-9)				
150	Nosler JHP	1608	861	1.521
170	Nosler JHP	1543	899	1.522
Load: 19.3/Accurate Arms No. 9 (AA-9)				
150	Nosler JHP	1655	913	1.521
170	Nosler JHP	1646	1023	1.522
Load: 21.6/Hodgdon H-110				
170	Nosler JHP	1565	925	1.522
180	Hornady JHP	1598	1021	1.532
200	Hornady JHP	1617	1161	1.541

JHP:Jacketed Hollowpoint; FPJ :Flatpoint Jacketed; TMJ:Totally Metal Jacketed.

Here, photographed by a gas-operated shutter control, Grennell has just fired a round of 10mm AMT Magnum from the Thompson/Center Contender with its original 14-inch 10mm Auto factory barrel converted to 10mm AMT Magnum by AMT. Recoil is not all-out cataclysmic, but it is reasonably substantial. Note that he has positioned two sandbags between his right elbow and the upper surface of the shooting bench to avoid possible trauma from the toggle effect of recoil. He learns slow, but he learns good, that boy.

TABLE 3: JACKETED BULLET 10mm AMT MAGNUM LOADS

Bullet (Wgt. Grs.)	Bullet (Type)	Load (Grs./Powder)	MV (fps)	ME (fpe)
135	Nosler JHP	15.9/AA-7	1605	772
		16.7/AA-7	1698	865
		18.8/AA-9	1666	832
		19.8/AA-9	1763	932
150	Speer JHP	15.0/AA-7	1458	708
		15.8/AA-7	1543	793
		17.7/AA-9	1550	800
		18.6/AA-9	1640	896
155	Hornady JHP	14.7/AA-7	1472	746
		15.5/AA-7	1558	836
		17.1/AA-9	1487	761
		18.0/AA-9	1574	853
170	Nosler JHP	13.8/AA-7	1365	704
		14.5/AA-7	1444	787
		16.2/AA-9	1422	763
		17.0/AA-9	1505	855
180	Speer JHP	14.0/AA-7	1334	711
		14.7/AA-7	1412	797
		15.8/AA-9	1375	756
		16.6/AA-9	1455	846
190	Sierra FPJ	13.5/AA-7	1295	708
		14.2/AA-7	1370	792
		15.5/AA-9	1359	779
		16.3/AA-9	1438	873
200	Speer TMJ	13.1/AA-7	1229	671
		13.8/AA-7	1300	751
		14.9/AA-9	1313	766
		15.7/AA-9	1389	857

Back in August of 1991, Marty Liggins, the ballistician at Accurate Arms, sent out a sheet with numerous loads for the 10mm AMT Magnum. There were two sets of loads. Maximum pressure level for the first group was 38,500 CUP; for the second group, 43,500 CUP, with the stipulation the second group was for use in the IAI (AMT) guns only.

Liggins had obtained a pre-production supply of Nosler's 135-grain JHP bullet and listed data for its use. Within more recent times, Nosler has added this one to their regular line, along with their 150- and 170-grain JHPs.

The data sheet noted the loads had been tested in the Automag IV with an 8½-inch barrel, using the Starline brass and Winchester large pistol primers. Maximum case length was quoted at 1.255, trim length 1.245, maximum cartridge overall length (COL) of 1.555, minimum COL, 1.500. These loads, up to 38,500 CUP, used Accurate Arms No. 7 and No. 9 powders, offering both starting and maximum loads. They covered four cast bullets in weights of 165, 175, 185 and 195 grains, with velocities ranging up to 1401 fps and energies to 805 fp.

The Table 3 loads, also up to a pressure of 38,500, use the same powders, offering both starting and maximum loads. They cover seven jacketed bullets of weights from 135 to 200 grains, with one load giving 1763 fps and an energy of 932 fp. Note that AA-9 showed a slight edge over AA-7.

Getting on to Table 4, with peak pressures kept to 43,500 CUP, all listings were for AA-9.

I did some thoughtful huddling with Liggins' loads and concocted six more test loads to try out in the various guns. I made up fifteen rounds of each with the hopeful intention of clocking five apiece through all three guns. What with one thing and another, time at the range came down a bit short, so I put five through the IAI/AMT pistol and five through the 14-inch Thompson/Center Contender. The extra 5½ inches of barrel made a useful amount of difference, compensating to a consid-

Another gas-operated photo of Grennell firing the 10mm Magnum. The camera body was a Nikon N8008, with no provision for mirror lock-up. As a result, the photo is made about 1/60-second after electrical contact. He is trying to reduce the time-lag, so as to catch the ejected case, if not the actual speeding bullet. The device beneath the upflung muzzle is an Oehler Model 35P chronograph fitted with Grennell's Cordon Bleu tape winder, discussed in his 5th edition of *ABC's of Reloading*.

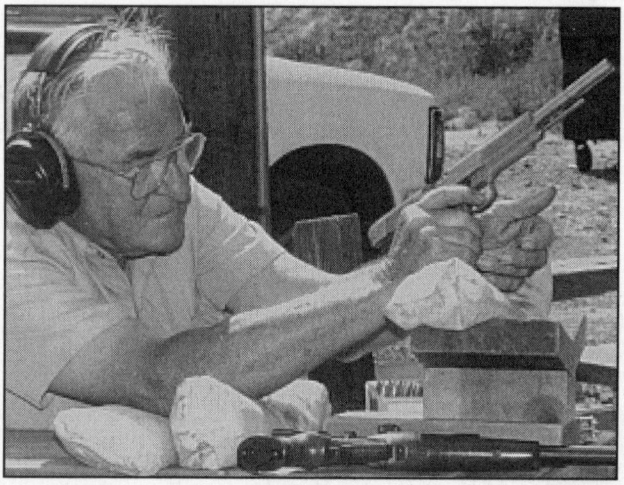

This is yet another shot of firing the 10mm Magnum auto, except it was the last round in the magazine and the slide locked to the rear. The converted T/CC is in the right foreground.

erable extent for its reduced rate of rounds per minute.

I used the AMT/Starline brass and CCI-300 standard large pistol primers for the loads with AA-9, CCI-350 magnum large pistol primers for the loads with Winchester 296 powder, recording the COL for each load because I am convinced it's useful data to have in the logbook for future consideration.

My first load used 19.3 grains of AA-9 behind the 135-grain Nosler JHP, manufacturer's index number 44838, at a COL of 1.522. In the 8½-inch auto, that one averaged 1718/885, and gave 1851/1027 out of the 14-inch Contender.

I inched up the charge weight by half a grain to 19.8 grains of AA-9, other specifications the same as before, and made small gains. The auto averaged 1726/893 and the Contender upped it to 1885/1065.

Dropping back to an even 19.0 grains of AA-9 and substituting the 170-grain Nosler JHP, still at 1.522 inches COL, I got the auto up to 1595/961 and the big single shot to 1819/1249.

Boosting the charge to 22.5 grains of AA-9 and returning to the 135-grain Nosler JHP gave me averages of 1836/1011 from the auto and a thoroughly respectable 2072/1287 from the Contender.

Recognizing that there are other powders besides AA-9, I changed to 23.3 grains of Winchester 296 and the CCI-350 magnum primers, as noted, staying with the 135-grain Nosler JHP, still at 1.522 inches COL. That dropped me back to 1553/723 in the auto and only 1816/989 in the single shot.

Cutting the charge weight of Winchester 296 back a little farther, to an even 21.0 grains, I capped the loads with the 200-grain Speer TMJ at a COL of 1.516 inches. The auto pistol delivered 1561/1082, with 1730/1329 in the Contender.

Summing up, I think the 10mm AMT Magnum is an interesting cartridge that has yet to reach the outer limits of its performance capability. You'll note some of my loads in the Contender were well up into Liggins' second category (Table 4). Contenders routinely cope with pressures at around that level, using cartridges somewhat larger in diameter, such as the 44 Magnum. *I do not suggest that others duplicate these loads. I am merely reporting I assembled these loads, fired them, and observed no alarming symptoms.*

It seems doubtful that Smith & Wesson will produce a revolver in 10mm AMT Magnum, because it's my understanding they dropped the Model 610 stainless revolver in 10mm Auto some while ago. Whether or not Thompson/Center will ever list Contender barrels in 10mm AMT Magnum strikes me as an iffy bet, either way. Their only new caliber offering within recent times has been the 375 Winchester. I've worked with that and can confide it's one steamy rascal. The 10mm AMT Magnum, however, would have access to a vastly greater offering of bullets, and that would make it an interesting offering for the Contender, in my humble opinion.

Existing 10mm Auto guns of suitable credentials can be converted to take 10mm AMT Magnum ammo by AMT or by SSK Industries; quotes for the service are available upon request. ●

TABLE 4: 10mm AMT MAGNUM LOADS FOR IAI (AMT) GUNS

Bullet (Wgt. Grs.)	Bullet (Type)	Load (Grs. Powder)	MV (fps)	ME (fpe)
135	Nosler JHP	19.8/AA-9	1763	932
		22.5/AA-9	1900	1082
150	Nosler JHP	18.6/AA-9	1640	896
		21.0/AA-9	1770	1044
155	Hornady JHP	18.0/AA-9	1574	853
		20.2/AA-9	1712	1009
170	Nosler JHP	17.0/AA-9	1505	855
		19.2/AA-9	1615	985
180	Speer JHP	16.6/AA-9	1455	846
		17.5/AA-9	1503	903
190	Sierra FPJ	16.3/AA-9	1438	873
		17.5/AA-9	1467	908
200	Speer TMJ	15.7/AA-9	1389	857
		17.0/AA-9	1432	911

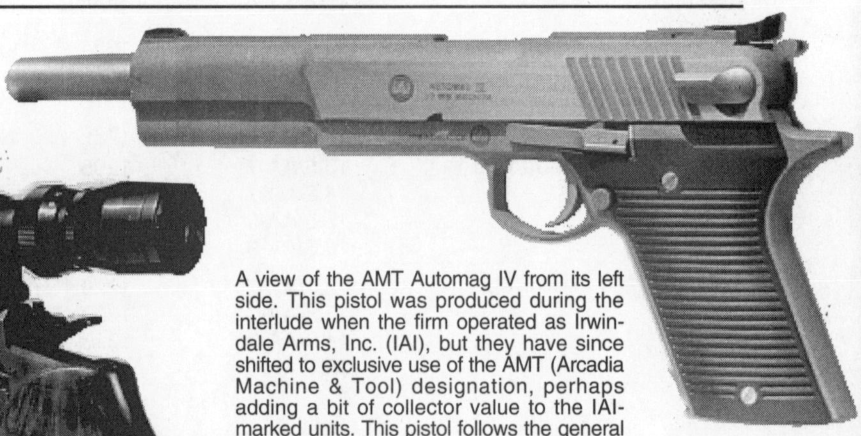

A view of the AMT Automag IV from its left side. This pistol was produced during the interlude when the firm operated as Irwindale Arms, Inc. (IAI), but they have since shifted to exclusive use of the AMT (Arcadia Machine & Tool) designation, perhaps adding a bit of collector value to the IAI-marked units. This pistol follows the general Browning/M1911 design with a 7-inch slide and an 8.5-inch barrel.

This T/C Contender has a 14-inch bull barrel, originally factory-chambered in 10mm Auto and so marked. It was rechambered to 10mm Magnum by AMT and has the Herrett Handgun Hunter stock handle. The scope is a 2.5-7x Simmons on Simmons base and rings. The muzzle is not drilled or tapped for a front sight. The frame serial number is 333333.

An aid to cast bullet shooters, both rifle and handgun...

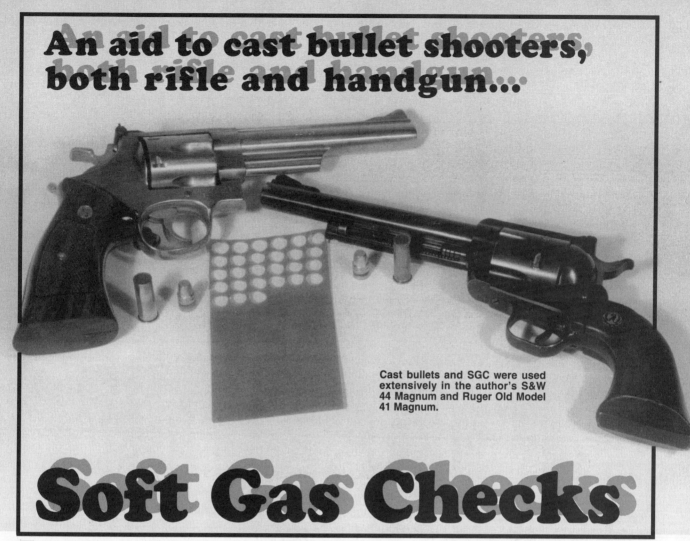

Cast bullets and SGC were used extensively in the author's S&W 44 Magnum and Ruger Old Model 41 Magnum.

Soft Gas Checks

THE BIGGEST CURSE on cast-bullet shooters is barrel leading—the build-up of lead in the grooves of a barrel. As the bullet travels down the bore, friction causes lead deposits to accumulate in the grooves. These unwanted accumulations also occur as hot burning powder gases literally melt away lead from the bullet's base, significantly adding to bore leading. When this problem occurs, accuracy deteriorates immediately. Cleaning a badly leaded bore is a task you will not care to repeat, as leading does not come out easily.

My cast-bullet shooting has been void of leading since I began using Soft Gas Checks (SGC) several years ago. A blend of modern waxes, SGC protects bullet bases, prevents leading and does an excellent job of sealing powder gases.

SGC material comes in sheets. Each sheet measures 3x6 inches, and one sheet services 112 38/357 cases, 78 41s, or 72 44/45 loadings.

After cases are sized, primed, belled and charged, the SGC material is pressed against the mouth of the case, cutting the SGC from the sheet, while ensuring 360-degree contact between the case and the SGC. Being almost transparent, cases and sheets are easy to line up. With the SGC in place, bullets are seated and crimped in the normal manner.

Upon firing, it is theorized that the wax discs vaporize, thereby cooling and slowing the hot powder gases seeking to blow by the bullet. Personally, I find this theory rings true when using heavy loads. On the other hand, I question its validity when lighter loads such as 8.5/Unique, 220-grain SWC in 41 Magnum or the same load with a 250-grain SWC in 44 are used, as I have found fired SGC discs intact in the snow at the shooting range. In reality it probably doesn't matter, because SGC does what it is intended to do, and does it extremely well.

CF Ventures, the company that manufactures and distributes SGC material, cautions users that no air space should exist between the wax gas check and the bullet, as this might cause ringed or damaged cases or chambers. Although CF Ventures says this has never happened, why take the chance? Bullets will still require normal lubrication, as SGC is *not* a substitute for this. Also, there should be no airspace between the SGC and the powder. More on this later.

It is common reloading practice and common sense that one must always watch for pressure signs and approach maximum loads with cau-

by JAMES W. TANK

(Left) Indoor shooting at 50 feet is excellent practice, especially when shooting heavy loads. This particular load fired in the author's 629 S&W 44 Magnum consisted of 20/2400/245 cast SWC and SGC.

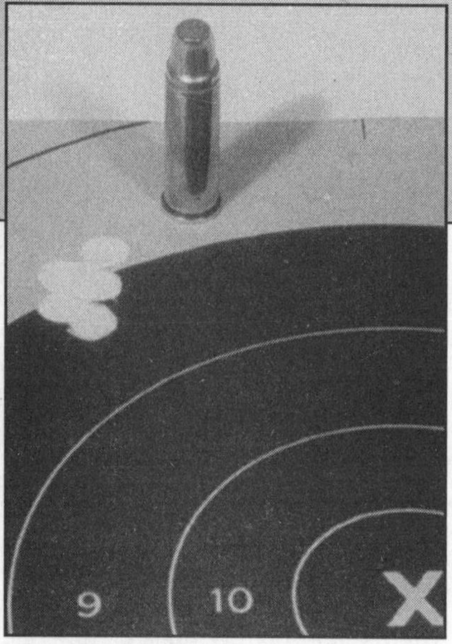

This 25-yard five-shot group was shot with a S&W M657 41 Magnum using SGC and 18.0 H-110/220 SWC.

(Below) Unique, H-110 and Hercules 2400 are excellent powders for cast bullet shooting in 44 and 41 magnums.

tion. I found this to be especially true when using SGC, as the superior gas sealing and the fact that SGC adds to overall bullet weight can and do increase pressures.

My first experience with SGC was with my 41 Magnum. I assembled some 215-grain SWC bullets cast from linotype in an old Ohaus mould, 10 grains of Unique and CCI standard primers, a less-than-max load according to several references.

When the first, and only, shot with that load was fired, the muzzle of my old model Ruger rose straight up and the blast made my ears ring. After pounding the empty case out of the cylinder with a hammer and punch, the primer revealed the story. Pressure had taken off like a rocket, flattening the primer in a way I have never seen before nor since. Were it not for the color difference between primer and the case, it would have been difficult to tell the two apart.

"It sure would be interesting to chronograph one of those," my shooting partner said. "But only one."

The incident taught me to start experimental handloads a minimum of 3 grains under maximum when using SGC, then work up in half-grain increments. This proved a good safety precaution.

Using the above method, I found an accurate, pleasant shooting load for my 41 Magnum: 18 grains of H-110 with a 220-grain SWC cast from my Lyman #410459 mould. Velocities average 1120 fps from the Ruger's $6^1/_2$-inch barrel, according to my Oehler Model 12 chronograph. In my 6-inch S&W 629 44 Magnum, 20 grains of Hercules 2400 with a 245-grain SWC cast from a Lyman #429421 mould gave velocities averaging 1250 fps.

With Lyman #2 alloy, 44-caliber bullets drop out of the mould weighing 250 grains; my 41s weigh 220 grains.

Until SGC came along, there were basically three ways to prevent leading: 1) harden the alloy, 2) lower bullet velocities, or 3) use metal gas checks. While each of these is helpful, I find them lacking for various reasons.

I use Lyman #2 alloy for my bullet casting simply because the compo-

The author's Ruger No.1 chambered for the 450 Ackley, Ruger 41 and S&W 44 perform well with cast bullets and SGC.

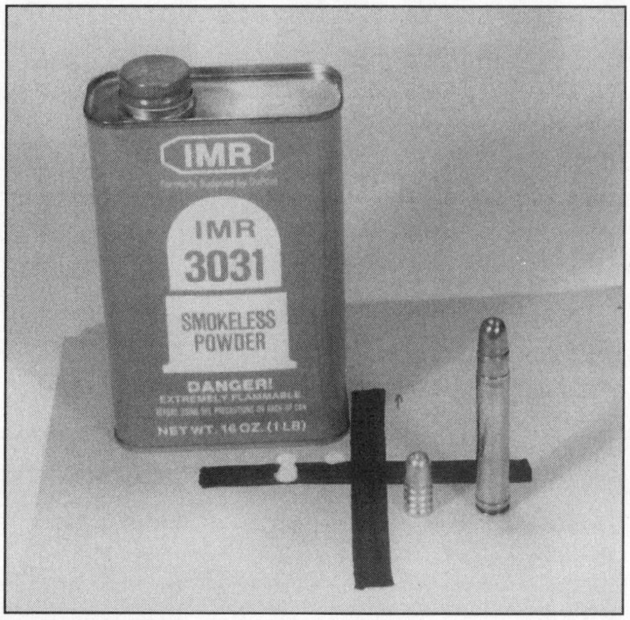

Tumblelube and SGC contribute greatly to accuracy in author's 450 Ackley. Barrel was not cleaned for 37 shots, and when it was, a bore brush was not necessary.

nents (wheelweights and 50/50 bar solder) are readily available and relatively cheap. Yes, one can shoot straight linotype without incurring leading, but linotype is expensive and hard to find.

My 41 and 44 Magnum cast bullets are confined to velocities of 1050 to 1250 fps depending on the load used. My 450 Ackley Magnum throws a 385-grain cast projectile at 2150 fps. I have no desire to lower any of my cast-bullet velocities.

Metal gas checks present distinct problems, at least for me. First, my bullet moulds are of the plain-base design, and to effectively utilize standard gas checks I would have to buy more moulds. Second, metal gas checks cost about twice as much.

Some speculate that SGC melts at a temperature of about 130 degrees. I don't know if that is true, but unless loaded ammunition is kept on the dashboard of a vehicle on an extremely hot sunny day, for example, I can't see how such melting would be a problem. However, I live in Wisconsin. Someone who lives in Arizona might view things differently.

Another advantage of SGC material is a by-product called Tumblelube, an extremely effective bullet lubricant.

To make Tumblelube, simply take leftover scraps of used SGC sheets, roll them into a lump about the size of a golf ball, and put it into a jar. Add enough lacquer thinner to just cover the ball. In about two days the jar will contain a pink substance having a consistency similar to that of thick salad dressing. If the composition seems too fluid, add more scrap; if too thick, add more lacquer thinner. The SGC wax blend has now become Tumblelube. Once given this treatment, the Tumblelube is no longer suitable for use as SGC, as the blend has been chemically altered.

Bullets can now be put in the jar and the jar rotated until their lube grooves are filled with Tumblelube. Bullets should then be placed on a sheet of paper to dry for at least two days. They can then be loaded with or without SGC. As you can see, nothing gets wasted.

Tumblelube is used on cast bullets in my 450 Ackley. These hefty 385-grain slugs drop out of my Lyman #457124 mould ready for lubing and loading. They are not sized. Loaded in front of 67.5 grains of IMR-3031, Cream of Wheat filler and an SGC, and ignited with a Federal 215 primer, velocities average 2150 fps.

The combination of Tumblelube and SGC does such an efficient job of eliminating leading that after 37 shots from my 450, without cleaning the barrel, shot numbers 35, 36 and 37 went into $1^3/_8$ inches. Shooting was done at 60 yards from a bench, using the express sights.

The above load is $^1/_2$-grain below the listed maximum for the 458 Winchester Magnum, necessitating the Cream of Wheat filler between the powder and bullet due to the increased case capacity of the 450. *Remember, there cannot be an airspace between the SGC and the powder or the bullet. Shooters using tapered or bottleneck cases will have to experiment with different ways of eliminating potential airspace.*

Sometimes I shoot so much that I don't have time to cast enough revolver bullets, so I purchase them from the Wisconsin Cartridge Co. In 41 and 44 calibers, they are listed at 210 and 240 grains, respectively. I use SGC with them even though they are very hard, apparently cast from linotype. Although barrel leading isn't a problem, with SGC I am assured of total gas sealing.

I am so impressed with the performance of SGC that I expect they'll always be a part of my cast-bullet shooting. I feel that SGC has lived up to the manufacturer's claims. Their address is CF Ventures, 509 Harvey Drive, Bloomington, Indiana 47401. ●

After 50-plus seasons of deer hunting, this Pennsylvania guncrank has some definite opinions about...

Handloads for WHITETAILS & MULIES

By DON LEWIS • Photos by Helen Lewis

"PUT SIERRA 60-grain hollowpoints in these 243s, and shove the velocity up as high as possible," a constant critic of my reloads stated. "I'm sure you're aware that a lot of speed with the 60-grain hollowpoint bullet makes a top 243 deer load."

"No, I'm not, and I'm not putting 60-grain bullets in your deer loads," I answered. "Your idea of a top 6mm deer load goes against all ballistic common sense."

"I've been using 60-grain slugs on chucks all summer, and the results I've seen have proved to me this bullet weight would be perfect for deer, especially at long ranges."

"There's a heck of a difference between the bone structure of a woodchuck and a deer," I tossed back. "A 60-grain bullet sure does a lot of damage on a 7-pound chuck, but it could literally blow to pieces on the shoulder of a 140-pound buck. The chances would be high that it wouldn't penetrate the heavier bones and muscles of a deer. If you want me to load your deer shells, you'll have to settle for bullet weights in the 100-grain class. Keep in mind the 243 is not my idea of a top deer cartridge even with its heaviest bullet."

The last remark brought an outburst of expletives that nicely seasoned a complete analysis of my total ignorance of ballistics, handloading and deer cartridges. The man claimed that more knowledgeable handloaders had advised him to use lightweight bullets for deer, and he fully intended to take their advice. When the two-minute tirade ended, he left with his empty brass.

That wasn't the first time I had encountered the low-weight/high velocity argument from deer hunters. Most of these hunters had very successfully used lightweight bullets during summer chuck hunts, and felt they would get the same results in the deer woods.

There's no question that any cartridge from the 6mm to the 338 Winchester is usable for deer under certain conditions, assuming the proper load is chosen. But after a half-century of deer hunting in a number of states under all conditions, plus fifteen years of operating a handloading shop, I think a whitetail or mule deer hunter should not only pick the best cartridge for the terrain hunted, but also choose the right primer/powder/bullet combination. What is a good caliber and load for one type of terrain may not be the best for another.

Since deer hunting is done in various types of cover, it's reasonable to assume one caliber or cartridge can't be the complete answer. For

(Opposite page) Lewis is dubious about the 7mm Magnum as a true large game load, but has found it to be excellent for deer at the longer ranges. He dropped this whitetail at about 300 yards with a 140-grain Sierra spitzer and 63 grains of IMR-4350. In his No. 1 Ruger, this load gives about 3000 fps MV and is extremely accurate.

The 348 Winchester, besides being an excellent choice for most American game at woods ranges, has the added advantage of being convenient for southpaws.

instance, in very thick cover or dense stands of timber, I feel deer hunters are better off with slower velocities and heavier bullets. Under these conditions, my pick would be cartridges such as the 348 Winchester, 35 Remington and 30-30 Winchester.

The 348 Winchester and 35 Remington have few peers where brush is thick and shots are close, and the 30-30 Winchester is still the most popular short-range deer cartridge on the market.

I'm sure not too many 348s are still being used in the deer woods. Model 71s have become collector's items. However, since this famous lever action is the epitome of Depression Era craftsmanship and the 348 cartridge is one of the most powerful rimmed cartridges—suitable for elk and moose as well as deer—it deserves mention. My choice whitetail load is 64.5 grains of H-4831 behind a 200-grain Hornady flat-nose bullet. Muzzle velocity is about 2350 fps. It is a deadly woods outfit. Velocity with this bullet can easily be pushed to 2500 fps if bigger critters are the objective.

The 35 Remington cartridge appeared in 1906 in the Model 8 autoloading rifle and was later chambered in the Remington 14, 141 and 760 slide actions, as well as several bolt and lever guns. It has some inherent drawbacks for the handloader, especially in regard to selecting the right powder.

To start with, the 35 Remington case doesn't have a lot of powder capacity and has a very short shoulder. Optimum results usually come from powders such as H-414 and BL-C2. Since the 35 Remington does its best at ranges well under 150 yards, the deer hunter will get excellent results from 38 grains of BL-C2 behind a 200-grain round-nose bullet. Muzzle velocity is a smart 2000 fps and energy touches 1800 foot pounds. This load is basically for brush, but that's what the old 35 is all about.

The 30-30 Winchester has been a popular deer cartridge for almost a century. Unfortunately, the 30-30 doesn't offer the reloader a wide assortment of bullet weights. The 150- or 170-grain should be used for deer. Only flat-nose bullets can safely be used in tubular magazine rifles. Bolt-action fans may opt for pointed bullets, but the 30-30 cartridge does not generate enough velocity to properly benefit from a spitzer design so its absence isn't important. My favorite deer load in the 30-30 is 35 grains of H-4350 behind a 150-grain flat-nose bullet. My Oehler 35P gives this load instrumental velocity readings of 2130 fps 15 feet from the muzzle. True muzzle velocity would be slightly higher.

In post-World War I days, deer hunting in the East was almost exclusively a brush and heavy timber sport. That's not the case today. Large electric power and gasline rights-of-way, timber harvesting, and clear cutting have opened up the once darkened woods. Cartridges designed for medium ranges such as the old 300 Savage and the newer 308 Winchester and 7mm-08 Remington are ideally suited for this kind of shooting.

The 300 Savage came to life in the Savage 99 lever-action rifle in 1921. Some enthusiastic supporters claimed it was equal to the 30-06, but that isn't true. Its smaller case capacity and the strength limitations of the lever action just won't permit the 300 to be loaded equal to the 30-06. But it is a much more efficient cartridge for deer than the 30-30, and many elk and deer have been taken with it, though it really isn't suited for large North American big game. If it were, it wouldn't have lost much of its popularity when the Winchester 308 came along.

Either 150- or 180-grain bullets work well in the 300 Savage for ranges up to 200 yards on deer. Bullets in the 200- to 220-grain category can't be given enough velocity for long shots. I prefer 44 grains of H-414 behind a 180-grain Speer Mag-Tip or round-nose for wooded areas. Velocity in my gun is a snappy 2275 fps.

In open country, the 300 Savage will easily reach the 250-yard mark with 41.2 grains of IMR-4320 behind the 150-grain Sierra spitzer. Chronograph readings of this powder charge/bullet weight combination average just under 2600 fps. I have to point out that 39.9 grains of IMR-4064 driving a 165-grain Sierra hollowpoint boattail shot my tightest three-shot groups in this caliber at 100 yards. Its muzzle velocity of 2500 fps is not far below the 150-grain spitzer load. It might be worth considering.

The 308 Winchester began life as the military 7.62 NATO. When introduced as a sporting cartridge, some rather impressive claims were made for the 308, but like so many fantastic accolades from early enthusiasts, they lack ballistic support. The most common myth, which some riflemen still quote, is that the 308 Winchester stands shoulder to shoulder with the 30-06. This can't be. The 308 can no more equal the '06 than the '06 can equal the 300 Magnum. There's just too much difference in case capacity.

Due to the 308's reduced powder capacity, bullets heavier than 180 grains are not recommended. I prefer somewhat lighter weights. My tests revealed I could easily stay in the 2700 fps velocity range with either 150-grain or 165-grain bullets,

Ray Claypool, below, took this wide-spreading whitetail with an all-time favorite outfit, a M70 Winchester 30-06 carrying a Weaver K4. Load was the 150-grain Sierra spitzer and 48 grains of IMR-4895. Nick Sisley, right, needed only one shot from his 280 for this Alabama trophy. His load was the 150-grain Nosler and 56 grains of AA-3100, which chronographs at almost 2800 fps MV.

so I concentrated on these. Over the years, I have used the 308 to drop eight deer with these weights. My favorite woods load is 47 grains of W-748 behind the Speer 150-grain spitzer. This load leaves the muzzle at over 2700 fps and is extremely accurate. In open terrain, I switched to a 165-grain Hornady spire-point in front of a near-max load of 45.5 grains of Winchester 748 powder. Velocity with this powder charge is just under 2700 fps.

You may wonder why a boattail was not selected for long range. Maybe it's because the 308 is not my idea of a true long-range cartridge. The way I see it, the 308 falls into the 250-yard category. That's not a short shot by any means, but a boattail adds little efficiency here. Distances beyond 250 yards or so require bullets with top aerodynamics and that means a boattail every time.

For comparison's sake, maximum loads of several powders will drive a 190-grain bullet out of an '06 muzzle at 2800 fps. In the 308, maximum powder charges will give a 165-grain spitzer a muzzle velocity just topping 2700 fps. The moral of this is that the '06 can shove a 190-grain bullet out of the muzzle faster than can the 308 with a bullet weighing 25 grains less. The 308 just doesn't give the velocity needed to offer flat trajectory with the heavier bullets over extreme ranges. I think this points out rather emphatically that the 308 is not equal to the 30-06.

The 7mm-08 Remington is an extraordinary deer cartridge. It took Americans a long time to recognize the potential of the 7mm (284) caliber bullet. *Speer Reloading Manual* No. 11 says, "It [the 7mm caliber bullet] has good sectional density in all weights and an excellent ballistic coefficient in any given weight compared to other bullets of the same weight." With bullets from 100 grains to 175 grains readily available, the Remington 7mm-08 is a much better deer cartridge than the 30-30 or any of the 6mms.

Varmint hunters may reload the 100- or 115-grain HP 284 bullets, but deer hunters should stick with the 139- to 154-grain category, I believe. Some years ago, I drove a 175-grain Speer Grand Slam through an antlerless deer's ribcage at about ninety yards. It was a standing shot, and I had a solid rest. When the Model 788 Remington 7mm-08 cracked, the deer bounded away. I found it hard to believe I had missed, but the doe showed no signs of being hit. I found her 122 steps from where she had been standing. The 175-grain Grand Slam had simply driven through her light-boned ribcage without expanding. In all fairness, I must point out that the 175 Grand Slam is designed for elk and other large animals, and the heavily constructed bullet didn't meet enough resistance to properly expand. I would have been far better off with the 145-grain Speer spitzer, say, leaving the a muzzle at around 2850 fps.

In the 7mm-08, I also stick with the medium-weight bullets because the heavier ones must be seated so deep to function in the short-action rifles commonly used for this cartridge that powder capacity is greatly reduced.

It might not be fair to put cartridges in classes such as short range, medium range and long range, since it's possible to make a 300-yard shot with almost any centerfire big game cartridge. Yet, that's the most practical approach for a deer hunter. The 300 Savage, 308 Winchester, 7mm-08 Remington and others obviously have long-range potential, but when distances stretch way out, they can't really compete with the 270 Winchester, 280 Remington, 30-06 or 7mm Remington Magnum. At the same time, it's worth pointing out that these four cartridges can't compete with some of the super magnums either. But from a logical point of view, there are few cases where super magnums are needed for whitetails or mule deer.

It's strange to me that the 277-caliber attracted only two factory entries—the 270 Winchester and the 270 Weatherby Magnum. But .277-

Lewis feels the 338 Magnum has more power than is needed for deer, and he's right. But sometimes—as on an Idaho elk hunt—that's what you're carrying, and with the 275-grain Speer and a compressed charge of H-4831, it gets the job done.

Nowadays, the 30-30 Winchester gets criticized by many high-velocity, bolt-action fans, but Lewis thinks it's a fine woods load—and so does old-timer Hurley Mensinger, who has good reason to feel that way. Five or six million M94 Winchester users can't all be wrong.

Tim Lewis stoked his fast-working M760 Remington 308 with 150-grain Speer spitzers, 46/4064 and 9½ Remington primers for his '92 hunt. One shot through the shoulders dropped this 153-pound (field dressed) 6-point.

(Left) M77 Ruger chambered for high-performance 284 Winchester cartridge was Helen Lewis's choice for anterless season in Pennsylvania. The 150-grain Remington SPCL pushed to 2800 fps by a heavy charge of IMR-4350 penetrated both shoulders for an instant kill.

Mary Ann Workosky with proof that the little 7mm-08 Remington does all that's necessary at conventional ranges. Rifle is Mel Forbes' Ultra Light M20.

diameter bullets have been featured in a fair share of wildcats. Several that come to mind are the 270 Savage, 270-308 and 277 Brooks Short Magnum. The 270 Winchester's popularity stems largely from the fact that it gained a reputation as being a better long-range cartridge than the 30-06. Time has shown this is debatable. The 30-06 can be loaded to achieve superb downrange ballistics. I have to concede that the Hornady 130-grain 270 spitzer, say, has a much higher BC (.409) than their 130-grain 308-caliber spire-point bullet (.295). This gives the 270 a flatter trajectory in this bullet weight than the '06 can produce, when both are max-loaded to about 3100 fps. Zeroed at 200 yards, the 270/130 load is about 38 inches low at 500, while the '06/130 combination is some 46 inches low. But if, instead of matching bullet weights in the two calibers, which isn't too logical, we try to match ballistic coefficients, the 30-caliber Hornady that's closest to the 130-grain 270 is the 165-grain 308, which has a BC of .435. In a heavily loaded '06, this bullet can be given 2900 fps, which with a 200-yard zero is 43 inches low at 500 yards. That's just a few inches more drop than the 270's, but the '06 load has more remaining energy at this range, 1359 fpe vs. 1186, according to the latest *Hornady Handbook,* Vol. 2.

My best results with the 270, both on the range and in the woods, came from 57.5 grains of IMR-4831 behind a 130-grain boattail or spitzer bullet. My other favorite powders for this weight are W-760 and IMR-4064.

Since the 130-grain 277 slug often damages a lot of meat, many deer hunters prefer a 150-grain spitzer in front of either IMR-7828, 4831 or Norma MRP if it can be found. Tighter groups often will be fired with powder charges several grains below maximum. Another excellent choice would be the Hornady 140-grain spire-point pushed by 57 grains of H-450. Velocity is just under 2900 fps, and that's moving a 140-grain 277 bullet.

Maybe I'm old-fashioned, but I still see the 130-grain bullet as the top choice for the 270 Winchester. The Nosler Partition bullet in front of 54 grains of Accurate Arms 3100 ignited by a Federal 210 primer is my pick for a top woods primer/powder/bullet combination. Velocity is around 2800 fps, and that's sufficient velocity to make the Partition bullet very effective.

Ranges beyond 250 yards benefit from bullets with high BCs. For example, a Speer 130-grain boattail with a .411 BC really reaches out when muzzle velocity is in the neighborhood of 3000 fps.

Since I've taken only two deer with Remington's 280 cartridge, my association with it stems mostly from range tests. Remington introduced the 280 in 1957, and eventually chambered several of their models for it, including the M740 autoloader and M760 slide action. In 1979, they changed the name to 7mm Express. It was the same cartridge, but there were suggestions that the newly named load was more powerful than the original factory 280. But having two names for the same cartridge caused an inordinate amount of confusion and Remington went back to the 280 listing about a year later.

The Remington 280 is a little more powerful than the Winchester 270. Also, with new slow-burning powders, another hundred feet per second or so of velocity can be obtained when used in strong bolt-action rifles. Loads which are maximum for bolt actions should be avoided when loading the 280 for slide actions and autoloaders.

My first serious range tests with the 280 were fired shortly after Remington changed the name to 7mm Express. I was torn between the 139-grain Hornady spire-point and the 160-grain Speer spitzer. With 55 grains of IMR-4831, the chronograph reading with the 139-grain Hornady averaged 2875 fps at 15 feet from the muzzle, which meant at least 2900 fps at the muzzle. Sandbox tests showed good expansion with this bullet. With 55.5 grains of N-205 behind the Speer 160-grain spitzer, instrumental velocity was 2785 fps. Muzzle velocity would be over 2800 fps. You can see why I was confused, with less than a 100 fps velocity difference between the two bullet weights.

I used the 139-grain load to drop a walking deer at 117 steps.

Apparently, this Hornady reacted in the deer's chest cavity pretty much the same as it had in the sandbox. It wasn't an instant kill, but the deer collapsed only moments after the shot.

Later, I received a test model Remington 700 Mountain Rifle chambered for the 280. I expected to be hunting in heavy brush, so chose the 162-grain Hornady bullet rather than the 139-grain. The manual indicated that 51 grains of IMR-4350 would give about 2800 fps, so I assembled a box of cases with that load and zeroed-in.

At 4:30 P.M. on the last day of Pennsylvania's antlerless season, a large deer trotted through an opening about eighty yards from me. I got a quick flash of deer in the scope before it melted into the dark heavy brush. There wasn't enough time to make certain it was a legal target. I felt all was lost, but a dozen or so yards farther out, it passed through a spot where the brush had thinned enough for me to see it was a legal doe and to get the crosswires on to her body. An angling shot through the ribcage dropped the deer instantly. The bullet exited in front of the far shoulder. No heavy bones were struck, but the size of the exit hole showed good expansion. It was only one shot, but I'm convinced this is a top brush load.

The venerable 30-06 needs no introduction. Born in the early 1900s as a military cartridge, it derived its common name from its caliber, 30, and the year it came out, 1906. It was a military success for years, and it is still probably the most versatile big game cartridge ever developed. The 30-06 is quite capable of taking all North American big game when the proper bullet is used. Since all bullet weights from a 125-grain spitzer to the 220-grain round-nose can handle deer, the handloader can have his cake and eat it, too.

I've probably tested more 30-06 rifles than any other cartridge, and I've fired hundreds of their slugs into sand, woodpiles and through heavy piles of small limbs into life-size deer targets a few feet beyond. I finally settled on two bullet weights for deer, the 150-grain spitzer and the 165-grain boattail.

When I was developing '06 loads in the early days, I didn't have a chronograph. My 150-grain loads came from the 1950 edition of Lyman's *Handloading—an NRA Manual*. That book's max load of 52 grains of IMR-4895 behind a 150-grain Speer bullet showed a muzzle velocity of 2943 fps at 20 feet, but warned it was "excessive." I dropped down a full grain and loaded thousands of 30-06 empties with 51 grains of 4895 behind a 150-grain bullet.

Interestingly, a somewhat later manual by another publisher gives 55 grains of 4895 as the maximum load and 51 grains as the lowest suggested charge, with a muzzle velocity for the latter of 2816 fps. Why the significant disparity between the two manuals is still a mystery to me, but I never went above 51 grains of the early 4895 ex-military powder.

A word of caution is needed here. Current IMR-4895 apparently is somewhat different than the old military stuff. Suggested maximum loadings with 4895 in the Speer No. 11 manual tops off at 49 grains behind a 150-grain bullet, while the 4th Edition of the *Hornady Handbook* lists 48.7 grains with H-4895. Velocity readings are in the 2900 fps realm from 22-inch barrels.

I believe the 165-grain boattail bullet is unequaled for long-range 30-06 shooting at whitetails and mulies. Many will not agree, claiming the 180-grain boattail is superior, but I tend to think of the 180-grain weight as an elk or grizzly bullet. The 165-grain is more apt to expand better on the light skeletal makeup of a deer. The thick, tough skins and heavy bones of truly big game animals need heavier bullets such as the 180- and 200-grain slugs. The 30-06 will drive a 200-grain spitzer out of the muzzle at 2600 fps, but the same weight slug in the 300 Winchester Magnum can easily top the 2900 fps mark. From many years of shooting, I'm convinced the 150- to 165-grain bulllets are the best in the 30-06 for deer.

The last deer I shot with an '06 was a small "Y" buck. I dropped it at 134 steps with a 150-grain Speer spitzer and 51 grains of 4895. Because the trotting buck never lifted its head while it was in view, I felt it was hot on a doe's track. I didn't have much time, but my hastily fired shot hit just behind the near shoulder and angled into the left one. The buck hit the ground with the crack of the 30-06.

I don't believe magnum big game cartridges are necessary for deer, but doubt that the Remington 7mm Magnum should be classed as a true large game magnum. Bullet weights run to only 175 grains, and that seems light for dangerous animals such as Cape buffalo and Kodiak bears.

While it may not be a true big game magnum, Remington's Big 7 is a heck of a long-range whitetail and mulie cartridge. My favorite all-round whitetail load is the 140-grain Sierra spitzer with 63 grains of IMR-4350. Chronograph tests averaged 2975 fps at 15 feet from the muzzle. The 140-grain Sierra has a high BC of .490. I usually sight-in about 3 inches high at 100 yards. This gives a trajectory arc with a 250-yard zero, falling a couple inches low at 300 and about six inches low at 350. In other words, with this sight-in picture, I have a point-blank range of 350 yards. You might call it a dead-on hold to that distance.

For mule deer hunters, the 160-grain boattail might be a wiser choice, as mulies usually are heavier than whitetails. In my M700, 79 grains of H-870 behind a Speer boattail will produce a muzzle velocity touching the 3000 fps mark. I have also found that Accurate Arms 8700 with the 160-grain Sierra boattail gives superb accuracy. My best groups came from 78 grains of AA-8700 behind the Sierra 160-grain boattail. Muzzle velocity is down a little, to about 2850, but getting tight groups from any magnum cartridge is always impressive.

There's no end to what the handloading deer hunter can have. To me, bullet design is more important than getting the last foot second of velocity. Bullets are designed for specific purposes. I feel a hunting bullet should enlarge its frontal diameter to at least twice the bullet's original caliber. This is only a rule of thumb, but it's important. From my experiences, bullet expansion and killing power go hand in hand. Maybe it's like love and marriage. To get a high degree of expansion in whitetails and mulies without fragmentation, the handloader must choose his bullets carefully. Testing by firing into wet telephone books, sand or even ballistic gelatin isn't conclusive, but does give some idea of how a bullet will perform when it hits.

There's one more factor to consider. Each rifle, regardless of its brand or caliber, handles certain weights, types and makes of bullets better than others. To get optimum results, the handloader must use the process of elimination to find the best load. While that sounds like a lot of work and expense, and to some degree it is, the end results are too significant to overlook. That's one thing I think you can write in stone. ●

Today's new shooters can get started the same way their fathers did. Here's how!

CAST BULLETS ARE BEST IN SURPLUS MILITARY RIFLES

by C.E. HARRIS

German military Mausers are potentially accurate shooters, but the big problem is seeing the sights well enough. Bill Stroud manages OK with this family heirloom brought back from France after WWI, despite its salt and pepper bore.

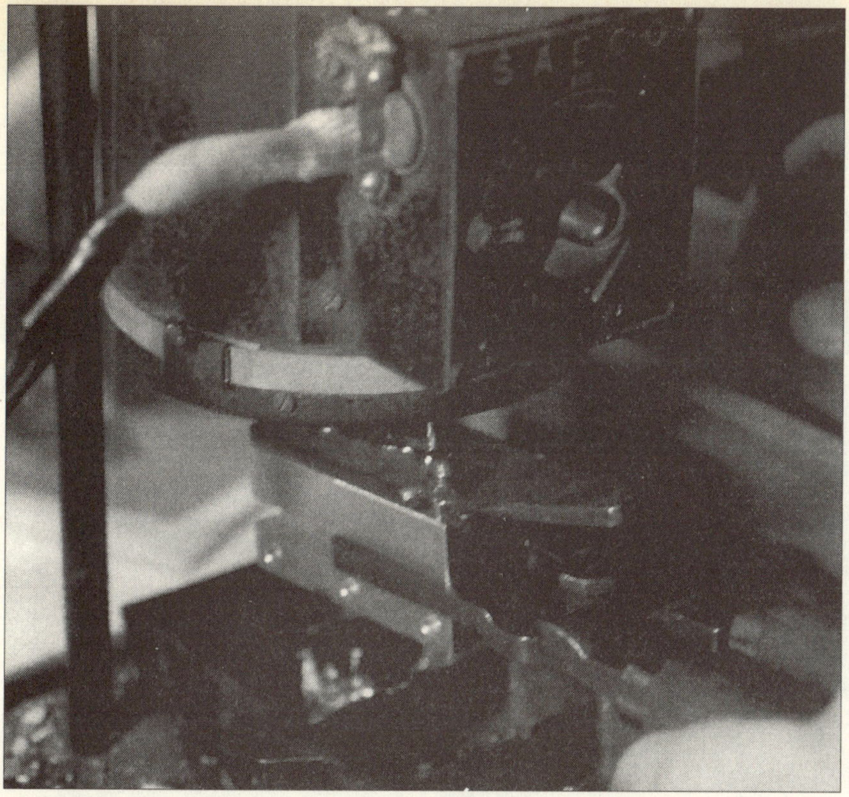

Bottom-pour pots cast more uniform bullets when "drop-poured" right down the center of the sprue hole, rather than holding the mould in contact with the spout, which causes the sprue to solidify too quickly, resulting in solidification shrinkage porosity.

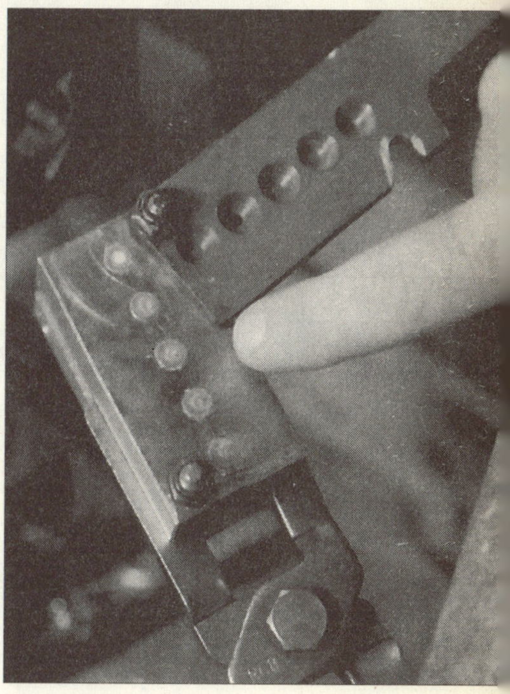

Gang moulds will cast accurate rifle bullets if you are fussy about inspecting the bases. Author likes the aluminum moulds from NEI because they cast good bullets and are less tiring to use than iron.

SURPLUS MILITARY rifles are again available at bargain prices and are still the best way for a new shooter to get started economically. Getting the most accurate shooting for the dollar from a military rifle requires handloading. Surplus ammunition is more expensive and usually less accurate than home-rolled ammunition.

At practical ranges from 50 to 200 yards, cast bullet loads often give a more useful zero with military battle sights than ball ammo. Nothing is more frustrating than a military rifle that shoots a foot high at 100 yards with surplus ammo when the sight is as low as it will go! This is a common event, because the battle sight range for most military rifles is 400 yards or more.

Today's simple and effective equipment, combined with the body of cast bullet knowledge now available, makes it a lot easier for the tyro to get started in bullet casting than when I was a kid. When I got started in high-power competition as a high school student in 1963, I had a DCM Remington 30-06 two-groove M1903A3 I bought for $17. I fired club-issue TW54 Ball M2 ammunition to get brass to reload, then shot bullets cast from wheelweights for practice, as well as at the 200- and 300-yard stages of matches. I tried cast loads a few times at 600 yards, and did OK on the old Army B target with its 20-inch five-ring and 12-inch V-ring, despite the smart remarks from my butt pullers. I devoured the latest cast bullet articles by Col. E.H. Harrison in *American Rifleman* and used this new technology to expand upon the basics I'd already gleaned from J.R. Mattern's summary, which appeared in E.C. Crossman's classic, *The Book of the Springfield* (1932), which I borrowed from the library.

Safety Considerations

Before I get into loading data, I want to emphasize that I recommend only rifle primers, *not* pistol primers. The only place pistol primers should be used with cast bullet loads is in some blackpowder actions, such as Ballards, which have light hammer blows which won't set off modern rifle primers reliably. Pistol primers are dangerous in bolt-action military rifles because their thinner cups may puncture, given the greater striker energy and driven firing pin protrusion of these rifles. More importantly, pistol primers may cause weak ignition, producing hangfires or chamber ringing. Use of magnum rifle primers will not cause a dangerous condition in cast bullet loads which are otherwise safe. Some shooters find magnum primers aid uniformity of reduced loads, and there is some evidence to support this. As for myself, I use mostly Federal 210 or Winchester WLR primers, and find I can interchange them in the same group without noting a difference.

Do not use inert fillers of any kind, such as Dacron or kapok, to take up the excess empty space in the case. This was once common practice, but use of fillers raises chamber pressure and, under certain conditions, contributes to chamber ringing. If a particular load will not work well without a filler, the powder is not suitable for those loading conditions. The loads which follow have worked well in my experience, and, unless stated otherwise, are well under maximum. For any deviation from the stated loads, consult published data.

Author is shown here firing his favorite Smith-Corona Springfield 03A3 from the bench. Spotting scope is held to benchrest pedestal with a camera clamp to facilitate a "quick peek" for conditions without breaking bench position.

Cast Bullet Basics—Circa 1932

Mattern's four load classifications cover all uses for the cast bullet military rifle. I have applied them with great success for many years, and recommend them as starting points for the tyro, as well as prescriptions for the frustrated handloader willing to give cast loads "one more try" in these days of increasing component prices. Mattern's commentary in Crossman's book is based mostly on obsolete powders. Because the information is dated, and its use questionable, even with those powders which are still available, I worked up equivalent charges to obtain the desired velocity ranges with modern powders. Mattern's four categories of 30-06 loads provide a sound basis for loading cast bullets in any post-1898 military rifle from 7mm to 8mm.

These loads are under maximum when used in full-size rifle cases such as the 30-40 Krag, 303 British, 7.65 Argentine, 7.7 Japanese, 7.62x54R or 30-06. They can be used as basic load data in most modern military rifles of 7mm or larger with a standard-weight cast bullet for the caliber, such as 140 to 170 grains in the 7x57, 150 to 180 grains in the 30-calibers and 150 to 190 grains in the 8mm. For bore sizes smaller than 7mm, consult published data.

The Small Game or Gallery Load

I didn't use the small game load much when I was young because the common 110- to 115-grain bullets intended for the 30 M-1 carbine and 32-20 Winchester, such as the Ideal No. 3118, No. 311257 or No. 311316, were not as accurate as heavier ones like the No. 311291. Mattern said bullets lighter than 125 grains were less satisfactory, and he was absolutely right. There isn't a readily available 30-caliber cast small game bullet of this weight. I would like to see a design featuring the driving bands of the Lyman No. 311410 with the nose shape of the No. 311440, or perhaps the No. 311291 in a bevel-based form with two driving bands removed. The closest thing to this I have seen was offered by NEI/Tooldyne. The NEI No. 54A was designed by J. Hansen as a small game bullet for the 303 British and 32 S&W, and weighs about 135 grains in its plain-based version. It has a blunt "bomb" nose which should be perfect. I haven't used it, but would suggest that anybody wanting to seriously pursue the subsonic small game load try it.

The 100-Yard Target and Small Game Load

I still use Mattern's plain-based 100-yard target load to use up my minor visual defect culls for offhand and rapid-fire 100-yard practice. Rather than using a different bullet especially for plain-based loads as Mattern did, I have always substituted my usual gaschecked bullet, but without the gascheck. I started doing this in 1963 with the Lyman No. 311291. Today I do the same thing with the NEI 177-grain No. 43A or 162-grain No. 52A bullets, which I designed especially to fit the throats of typical military 30-caliber and "near-30" rifles. Most of my rifle shooting is done with these two basic designs.

Bullets intended for plain-based loads are blunted using a flat-nosed top punch in my lubricator, providing a 1/8-inch flat which makes them more effective on small game. It also clearly distinguishes them from my heavier gaschecked loads which retain the original spitzer shape. This makes a lot more sense to me than casting different types of bullets.

Bullet preparation is easy. I visually inspect each run of bullets and throw those with gross defects into

These 100-yard targets shot with minor base-defect bullets in a Finn M28/30 with rusty bore showed initial potential, but got wilder as firing continued. Still, with frequent cleaning, this is fine plinking accuracy.

MATTERN'S CAST LOADS FOR THE SPRINGFIELD

Bullet (Wgt. Grs.)	(Type)	Load (Grs./Powder)	MV (fps)	Remarks
125	Plain-based	5.0/Bullseye*	900-1000	Small game or gallery shooting.
150	Plain-based	7.0/Bullseye*	1050-1250	100-yd. target and small game shooting.
170-180	Gaschecked	16.0/Hercules 2400	1500-1600	200-yd. target shooting.
180-200	Gaschecked	26.0/Reloder-7*	1750-1850	Deer or 600-yd. target shooting.

*Or equivalent loads from *Book of the Springfield* by E.C. Crossman, Military Service Publishing Co., 1932, as modified by the author.

my scrap box for remelting. Bullets with minor visual defects are tumble-lubed in Lee Liquid Alox without sizing and used for plain-based plinkers. Perfect bullets are used for 200-yard practice and matches. Gaschecks are pressed onto their bases by hand prior to running into the lubricator-sizer. The NEI bullets facilitate this because the heel is dimensioned so that Hornady gaschecks snap on with firm pressure. The best way for a new shooter to apply gaschecks and size bullets economically is with the Lee sizer die used in a conventional reloading press, using Lee Liquid Alox. This works fine for any of the loads described here. For higher velocity loads, apply a little more lube.

I have loaded gascheck-design bullets without the gascheck for years in almost any 30-caliber rifle using 7 grains of almost any fast-burning pistol powder, including, but not limited to, Bullseye, W-231, Green Dot, Red Dot and Hi-Skor 700-X. I have also had fine results with 8 to 9 grains of medium-burning-rate pistol or shotgun powders such as Unique, PB, Herco, SR-7625 or SR-4756 in any case of 30-40 Krag size or larger. In the 7.62x39 case, use no more than 4 grains of the fast-burning powders mentioned or 5 grains of the shotgun powders. These make accurate 50-yard small game loads which let you operate the action manually and save your precious cases. These plinkers are more accurate than you can hold.

Repeated reloading of rimless cases with these mild loads eventually results in the primer blast shoving the shoulder back, producing a condition akin to excessive headspace unless flash holes are enlarged with a No. 39 drill to 0.099-inch diameter. Cases so modified must *never* be used with full-power loads. Doing so will cause primer leakage and risk of serious personal injury. *Always* identify cases which are so modified by filing a deep groove across the rim, and labeling them clearly to prevent their inadvertent use. For this reason, I prefer to do my plain-based practice shooting with rimmed cases like the 30-40 Krag and 7.62x54R, which maintain positive headspace on the rim and are not subject to this limitation.

This long-barrel Steyr Mauser on a '98 action in 7x57 was made for a South American government. It is one of the better bargains of today's market. It is a tackdriver with the RCBS 7mm-168SP with 20 grains of 4198. The poor sights are the biggest limitation to getting good groups, but with carbide-blacked sights on a hazy day, it will stay under 2 inches at 100 yards.

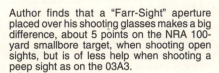

Author finds that a "Farr-Sight" aperture placed over his shooting glasses makes a big difference, about 5 points on the NRA 100-yard smallbore target, when shooting open sights, but is of less help when shooting a peep sight as on the 03A3.

Harris' Subsonic Target Load Is a Compromise

Mattern liked a velocity of about 1250 fps for his 100-yard target load, probably because this was common with the lead-bullet 32-40 target rifles of his era. I have found grouping is best in military rifles with plain-based bullets at somewhat lower velocities approaching match-grade 22 Long Rifle ammunition. I use my subsonic target load at about 1050 to 1100 fps to replace both Mattern's small game and 100-yard target loads, though I have lumped it with the latter since it really serves the same purpose. Its report is a modest pop rather than a crack.

If elongated bullet holes and enlarged groups indicate marginal bullet stability, increase the charge ½-grain and try again. If necessary, for consistent accuracy, try increasing the charge no more than a full grain from the minimum recommended. If this doesn't work, try a blunter and shorter bullet for its weight because it will stabilize easier. If this doesn't do the trick, change to a gaschecked bullet and a heavier load. The *Lyman Cast Bullet Handbook* lists heavier charges for most of these powders, which work

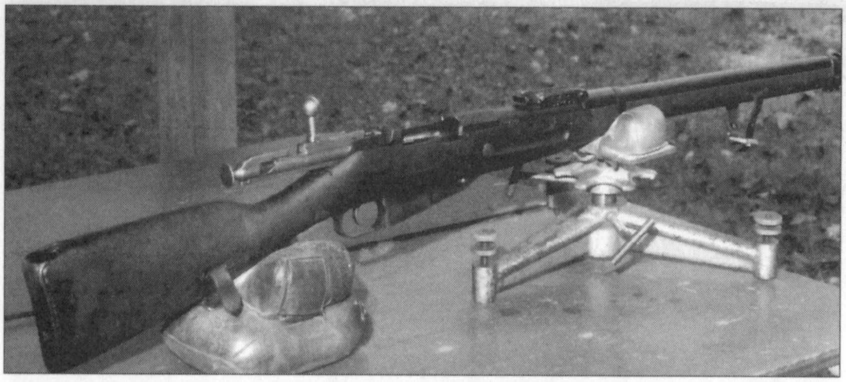

The Finnish M28 has 27-inch barrel which is somewhat heavier than the long Mosin-Nagant M91 from which it derived. The M28/30 is of similar appearance, but has a more rugged rear sight and a front sight which is screw-adjustable for windage.

The Mosin-Nagant M91 is the ugly duckling of the surplus market, but hangs well from a standing position, has a long sight radius to aid older eyes, and is highly accurate when fed proper loads. A bargain when found in good shape.

well with gaschecked bullets. If economy is your goal, save the money you spend on gaschecks and keep velocities below 1300 fps.

My minor visual defect cull bullets loaded as described, without gascheck, using light charges of pistol or shotgun powders, will average 3-inch (or less) ten-shot, iron-sight groups at 100 yards over the long run. This is just fine for practice and casual shooting. Good bullets, of course, do better, but gaschecked bullets are better for serious work.

The Workhorse Load

My favorite load was, and still is, the most accurate—Mattern's so-called 200-yard target load. Back in the 1960s, my No. 311291 cast from wheelweights would hold the 5-inch V-ring of the Army A target from my DCM Remington two-groove 03A3 firing prone rapid with sling. I have also killed a lot of game with this load, including deer. While this has the power of the 32-40, it is inadequate for deer by today's standards. A heavier cast load, over 1800 fps, should be considered the minimum when used by a skilled hunter who gets within 100 yards, chooses his shot carefully and shoots accurately. Deer hit with 30-caliber cast bullets seldom die in their tracks; they are usually recovered a short distance away. The novice cast bullet hunter should use at least a 35-caliber rifle—the 45-70 is ideal.

Today's enlarged forepart NEI military-design cast bullets and improved lubricants enable skilled shooters to clean the NRA A-15 100-yard small-bore target with a high X-count from a good rifle, or fire a comparable score at 200 yards on the military SR-4 reduced target, averaging about 2 MOA *with military iron sights* over the long run.

Mattern's 200-yard target load is easy to assemble. Because it is a mild load, soft scrap alloys usually give better accuracy than harder ones such as linotype. Local military collectors/shooters have standardized with 16 grains of Hercules 2400 as the "universal" prescription. It gives around 1500 fps with a 150- to 180-grain cast bullet in almost any military caliber. We use 16 grains of 2400 as our reference standard, just as high-power competitors use 168-grain Sierra MatchKings and 4895.

The only common military rifle cartridge in which 16 grains of 2400 provides a maximum load which must not be exceeded is the tiny 7.62x39 case. In the 7.62x39, 16 grains of 2400 is a full-power load which functions in the SKS and AK rifles reliably, feeds flawlessly with the 162-grain NEI No. 52A, can be stripper-clip loaded, and provides better accuracy than ball ammunition. Most SKS rifles will function reliably with charges of 2400 as light as 13 to 14 grains with the NEI No. 52A for around 1400 to 1500 fps. I designed this bullet especially for the 7.62x39, but it works very well as a light bullet in any 30- or 303-caliber rifle.

In the 30-06, the NEI No. 43A is usually more accurate because it was designed especially for the Springfield. It is tapered to fit the military chamber and is intended to be shot directly from the mould as-cast without sizing, other than sizing done for attaching the gascheck. The front crimping groove provides

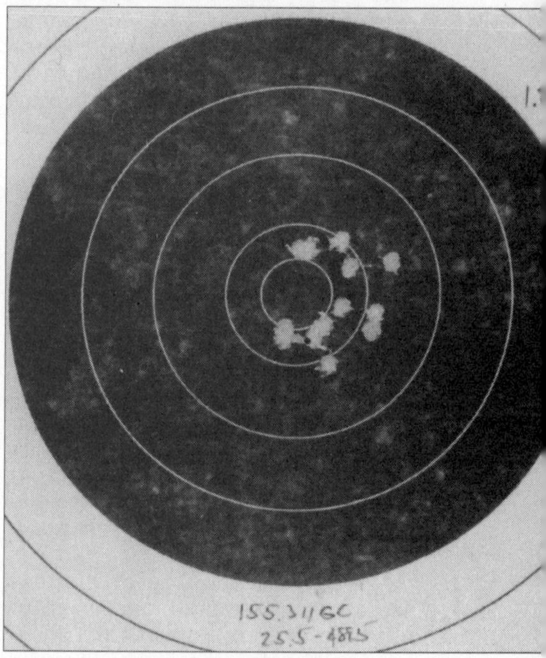

This fifteen-shot target shows the effect of not orienting the powder charge against the primer. Five rounds in the lower part of the group which were not oriented overlapped the main ten-shot group. All fifteen shots are 1.83 inches extreme spread at 100 yards. This target was fired from author's Smith-Corona 03A3 with the NEI No. 52A bullet and 25.5 grains of 4895.

ACCURARY TESTS WITH CAST BULLETS IN MILITARY RIFLES

FIVE TEN-SHOT GROUPS AT 100 YARDS.

	Group 1	2	3	4	5	Avg.
M91 Mosin-Nagant, Finn rebarrel by Tikka, 1940, mint bore, 31.5-inch barrel.						
Norma 146-grain FMJBT	3.71	3.04	3.44	3.49	3.47	3.43
NEI 52A 162-grain quenched, 25.5 IMR-4895	2.73	2.95	2.84	3.35	2.57	2.89
NEI 43A 177-grain quenched, 23 Hi-Vel No. 2*	3.62	2.68	3.70	3.36	2.29	3.10
NEI 43A 177-grain as cast, 23 Hi-Vel No. 2*	3.31	3.71	3.56	3.73	2.17	3.30
NEI 43A 177-grain as cast, no GC, 7.0 B'eye	2.90	2.58	3.37	3.47	3.53	3.17
M28 Finn, Tikka 1934, mint rifle.						
NEI 52A quenched, 25.5 IMR-4895 (elevated)	2.75	2.94	2.04	2.46	2.55	2.55
NEI 52A quenched, 25.5 IMR-4895 (leveled)	2.95	3.08	2.12	3.56	2.55	2.85
NEI 52A as cast, 25.5 IMR-4895	2.69	2.23	2.46	2.42	2.45	2.45
NEI 43A quenched, 23 Hi-Vel No. 2*	2.73	3.34	1.82	2.36	3.32	2.71
NEI 43A as cast, 23 Hi-Vel No. 2*	2.84	2.71	1.88	2.54	2.68	2.53
NEI 43A as cast, no GC, bumped FN, 7.0 B'eye	3.21	3.20	3.59	3.83	2.99	3.36
NEI 43A as cast, no GC, orig. nose, 7.0 B'eye	3.96	3.65	3.66	3.07	3.62	3.59
NEI 52A as cast, no GC, 7.0 B'eye	3.59	3.08	2.62	—	—	3.10
M28/30 Sako, dark pitted bore.						
WCC58 Match pulls 200-grain, 37 Hi-Vel No. 2* (5-shots)	2.33	1.62	2.33	—	—	1.92
NEI 43A as cast, no GC, 7.0 B'eye (5-shot groups)†	4.06	3.16	2.16	1.98	3.20	2.91
NEI 43A as cast, no GC, 7.0 B'eye (10-shot groups)‡	3.00	3.33	4.12	3.49	2.82	3.35
NEI 43A quenched, 23 Hi-Vel No. 2*	2.94	3.30	3.59	3.13	3.25	3.24
NEI 52A quenched, 25.5 IMR-4895	3.12	2.92	2.60	1.93	2.99	2.71
NEI 52A as cast, no GC, 7.0 B'eye	2.76	2.79	2.94	2.83	2.85	2.83
Sierra MK 42 168-grain, Hi-Vel No. 2*	2.49	2.45	2.32	2.72	2.15	2.33
US M1903A3, Smith-Corona, 6-groove, 30-'06, mint bore, 1943						
Ball M2, LC67 lot 42367	2.66	3.43	3.44	3.18	3.58	3.26
Match M72, LC65 Match lot 12015	1.93	1.46	1.62	—	—	1.67
NEI 52A as cast, 21 IMR-4198 (leveled)	2.84	2.21	2.49	—	—	2.51
NEI 43A as cast, 21 IMR-4198 (leveled)	2.95	2.61	3.35	—	—	2.97
NEI 43A quenched, 25.5 IMR-4895 (leveled)	3.27	3.15	2.57	2.74	2.05	2.76
NEI 43A quenched, 22 IMR-4198 (elevated)	1.85	1.83	2.33	2.31	2.12	2.09
NEI 52A as cast, 25.5 IMR-4895 (elevated)	2.28	2.07	1.68	1.91	2.06	2.00
NEI 52A as cast, no GC, 7.0 B'eye	3.03	3.62	2.05	2.42	3.22	2.87

*Hercules Hi-Vel No. 2 has been discontinued for many years and is no longer available. The loads with it are included for historical interest, in order to compare the accuracy produced by Mattern's original data with that for modern powders.

†Cleaned with Sweets, JB paste and GI bore cleaner until no fouling remained.

‡Cleaned with JB Paste and GI bore cleaner—less fouling this time.

the proper seating depth for sporting SAAMI or short-throated pre-1940 30-06 M1903 Springfield chambers; the rear groove is best for worn throats or wartime M1903A3 chambers. It also works well in reworked Finnish 7.62x54R rifles which have tighter bores than the Russian ones. Its large forepart engraves like chambering a round of Eley Tenex 22 LR in your Anschutz 54 or Winchester 52D.

The Universal Load

The same 16-grain charge of Hercules 2400 is universal for all calibers as a starting load. It is mild and accurate in any larger military case from a 30-40 Krag or 303 British through a 30-06 or 7.9x57, with standard-weight bullets of suitable diameter for the caliber. *This is my recommendation for anybody trying cast bullet loads for the first time in a military rifle without prior load development.* I say this because 2400 is not position-sensitive, requires no fiber fillers to ensure uniform ignition, and actually groups better when you just stripper-clip load the rifle and bang them off, rather than tipping the muzzle up to position the charge.

Similar ballistics can be obtained with other powders in any case from 7.62x39 to 30-06 size. If you don't have Hercules 2400, you can freely substitute 17 grains of IMR or H-4227, 18 grains of H-4198, 21 grains of RL-7, 24 grains of IMR-3031, or 25.5 grains of H-4895 for comparable results. However, these other powders may give some vertical stringing in cases larger than the 7.62x39 unless the charge is positioned against the primer by tipping the muzzle up before firing. *Hercules 2400 does not require this precaution.* Don't ask me why. I only know it is true because my experience has been repeated and confirmed by shooters I know and trust who have done so in at least a dozen rifles.

The beauty of the 200-yard target load at about 1500 fps is that it can be assembled with bullets cast from the cheapest scrap alloy, and fired all day without having to clean the bore. It *always* works. Leading is never a problem. Once a uniform bore condition is established, the rifle behaves like a 22 match rifle, perhaps needing a warming shot or two if it has cooled, but otherwise being remarkably consistent. The only thing I do after a day's shoot is to swab the bore with a couple of wet patches of GI bore cleaner or Hoppe's, and let it soak until the next match. I then follow with three dry patches prior to firing. It takes only about three foulers to get the 03A3 to settle into tight little clusters again.

The Deer and Long-Range Target Load

Mattern's deer and 600-yard target load can be assembled in cases of 30-40 Krag capacity or larger up to 30-06 size using 18 to 21 grains of 2400 or 4227, 22 to 25 grains of 4198, 25 to 28 grains of RL-7 or 27 to 30 grains of 4895, which give from 1700 to 1800 fps, depending on case size. *These charges must not be used in cases smaller than the 30-40 Krag without cross-checking against reliable published data!* The minimum charge should *always* be used initially, and the charge adjusted within the specified range only as necessary to get best grouping. I sincerely believe that a "high-velocity cast bullet load" is an oxymoron, sort of like "military intelligence."

Hercules 2400 usually gives tight clusters only within a narrow range of charge weights, and the universal 16-grain load is almost always best. Believe me; a lot of time has been spent trying to improve on this, and you can take my word for it. Some individual rifles produce acceptable groups with charges of 2400 approaching the maximum of 21 grains, while others simply will not tolerate them.

Base defects of this magnitude were the worst included in firing tests. Bullets with major voids larger than these should be remelted. These bullets gave 3-inch groups at 100 yards, which are OK for practice and plinking, but not for matches.

Help for Heavier Loads

If bore leading and/or bigger groups occur as charges are increased much above 16 to 18 grains of Hercules 2400, I recommend use of a cooler powder such as 4198, RL-7 or 4895 for heavier loads. It is far more difficult to achieve consistent grouping with heavier charges. Loads over 1800 fps require stronger alloys of at least 15 BHN, unless bullet fit and lubrication are perfect and you clean frequently. When I want a heavier load for 200-yard matches on windy days, I assemble Mattern's 600-yard load with my usual 177-grain NEI No. 43A gascheck bullet cast from one part linotype to three parts police pistol range scrap. The bullets are then run at a higher temperature and cast more rapidly so they emerge from the mould uniformly frosted. I quench these directly from the mould in a bucket of water to harden them.

Hard-quenched bullets are not acceptable for hunting because they zip right through without expanding. For target work, however, this is cheaper and easier than keeping separate casting pots for scrap and linotype. The bullets I run in getting the mould hot enough to quench are put aside for use in lighter loads. This allows me to run 15 to 20 pounds of bullets from a gang mould in an evening. In reality, I use *a lot* more soft bullets than hard ones.

The main reason I use heavier charges for occasional hunting is to avoid having to use all the elevation on the sights to obtain the desired point of impact for 200-yard competition using the battle sights. Some people like to hunt deer with cast bullets, and for the experienced hunter who is patient and stalks close, they will do the job. I have killed seven deer with 30-caliber cast bullet loads at about 1800 to 1900 fps, and feel they are as effective within 100 yards as a 30-30 factory load.

The caveat is that the bullet must be fairly heavy for the caliber and blunt-nosed like the RCBS 30-180 FN, Lyman No. 31141 or NEI No. 46. For hunting loads, you must be sure the bullet will retain at least 1700 fps at impact and use alloy no harder than 14 BHN to ensure expansion. Be aware that when trying to use softer alloys at over 1800 fps you may have only a half-dozen accurate shots before leading starts to open groups. This is somewhat variable depending upon the individual rifle. To find out, I simulate field conditions by hunting woodchucks during the off-season.

A lot of newcomers to the field might be concerned about the imperfect bore conditions of surplus rifles for sale. If the bore cleans up so it shines even a little, the light "salt and pepper" pits won't hurt. Most surplus militaries on today's market were in service prior to the use of non-corrosive primers, so a perfect bore is more the exception than the rule, particularly if the rifle ever saw combat. If the muzzle is in good shape, even a worn bore will shoot well, given a thorough cleaning.

Popular folklore suggests a rifle barrel must be near-perfect for good results with cast bullets, but this is mostly bunk, though you may have to be persistent. I have a rusty-bore Finnish M28/30 which I have shot extensively to make direct comparisons with the same batches of loads on the same day with a mint M28, and there was no difference.

The secret to getting a worn bore to shoot acceptably is to remove all prior fouling and corrosion. Then you must continue to clean the bore "thoroughly and often" until it maintains a consistent bore condition. You must also keep cast bullet loads under 1800 fps for hunting, and under 1600 for target work.

A cleaned and restored bore will usually give good accuracy with cast bullet loads if the bullet fits the chamber *throat* properly, is well lubricated, and the velocities are kept below 1800 fps. *The distinction between throat diameter and groove diameter in determining proper bullet size is important.* If you are unable to determine throat diameter from a chamber cast, a rule of thumb is to size bullets .002-inch over groove diameter, such as .310-inch for a 30-

EFFECT OF VISUAL DEFECT CAST BULLETS UPON PRACTICAL ACCURACY IN MILITARY RIFLES

TEN-SHOT GROUPS , FIRED FROM BENCHREST AT 100 YARDS WITH ISSUE IRON SIGHTS

Rifle	Bullet Defect Location				No Defects	Row Mean
	Base	Band	Forepart	Ogival Nose		15 Targets
Finn M91, Tikka 1940	4.31	3.40	4.38	3.00	3.36	
7.62x54R, 31.5-inch barrel,	3.14	3.14	3.59	2.85	2.68	
mint bore	3.83	4.21	3.38	3.66	2.29	
Avg. 3 Targets	3.76	3.59	3.78	3.17	2.78	3.415, Sd. 0.60
Finn M28, Tikka 1934	4.69	3.61	3.64	3.46	2.73	
7.62x54R, 27-inch barrel,	1.68	3.51	3.51	3.69	2.36	
mint rifle	5.46	4.51	3.49	2.71	3.32	
Avg. 3 Targets	3.94	3.88	3.55	3.29	2.80	3.49, Sd. 0.93
Finn M28/30, Sako 1932	3.68	3.07	2.75	2.87	2.78	
7.62x54R, 27-inch barrel,	3.07	2.89	2.43	2.69	2.55	
dark bore	2.36	2.81	2.06	2.25	2.46	
Avg. 3 Targets	3.03	2.92	2.41	2.60	2.60	2.715, Sd. 0.40
US M1903A3, SC-43	3.02	2.95	2.11	2.84	1.85	
30-06, 24-inch barrel,	3.17	1.77	2.26	1.64	1.83	
mint bore	3.07	3.25	2.99	2.28	2.33	
Avg. 3 Targets	3.09	2.66	2.45	2.25	2.00	2.491, Sd. 0.57
Column Mean						
12 Targets	3.46	3.26	3.05	2.83	2.56	
Standard Deviation	1.02	0.70	0.73	0.59	0.46	

All test targets fired with NEI No. 43A 177-grain gaschecked bullets cast from the same four-cavity gang mould from an alloy blended of one part salvage linotype and three parts police range backstop scrap, having an average analysis of 3.66 percent antimony, 0.72 percent tin, 0.1 percent arsenic and 0.07 copper. As-cast bullet hardness averaged 13 BHN at 30 days aging prior to firing, Hornady gaschecks were seated using a .311-inch die in an RCBS lubricator, which crimped the gaschecks but left the bullets otherwise unsized. The lubricating grooves were filled with Lee Alox-Beeswax, and the bullets given a light overcoat of Lee Liquid Alox. The powder charge was 23.0 grains of Hi-Vel No. 2, chosen mainly for historical interest because it was Mattern's recommended 200-yard target load in his 1932 writings.

The author wishes to thank Mr. Frank Kurek of Lakeville, Pennsylvania, for furnishing the Hi-Vel No. 2 powder used here.

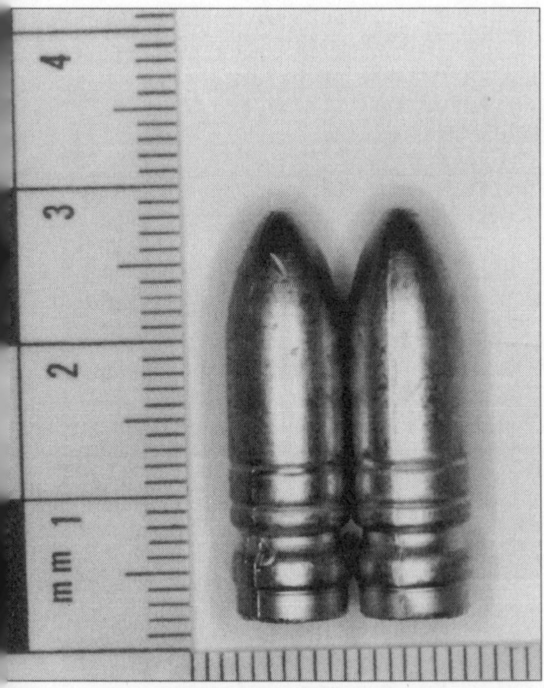

Defects such as these in the driving bands open groups if they prevent the gases from being sealed behind the bullet. If they are no worse than these shown, you can use them for mild loads up to 1600 fps, at some sacrifice in accuracy.

06, .312-inch for a 7.62x54R, and .314-inch for a 303 British.

"Oversized 30s" like the 303 British, 7.7 Japanese, 7.65 Argentine and 7.62x39 Russian frequently give poor accuracy with 30-caliber cast bullets designed for U.S. barrels having .300-inch bore and .308-inch groove dimensions. This is because the part of the bullet ahead of the driving bands receives no guidance from the lands in barrels of larger bore diameters. The quick rule of thumb to checking proper fit of the forepart is to insert the bullet nose first into the muzzle. It it enters clear up to the front driving band without being noticeably engraved, accuracy will seldom be satisfactory.

The forepart is not too large if loaded rounds can be chambered with only slight resistance and the bullet does not telescope back into the case or stick in the throat when extracted without firing. A properly fitting cast bullet should engrave the forepart positively with the lands, and be no more than .001-inch under chamber throat diameter on the driving bands. Cast bullets with a tapered forepart at least .002-inch over bore diameter give the best results. The two 30-caliber NEI bullets mentioned have even larger tapered foreparts and can be used successfully in a greater variety of barrels of various rifling forms and diameters than any other cast bullet. Many pre-WWII Russian rifles of U.S. make, and later Finnish reworks, particularly those with Swiss barrels by SIG, have very snug chamber necks and cannot be used with bullets over .311-inch diameter unless case necks are reamed or outside-turned to .011-inch wall thickness to provide safe clearance.

Bullets with a large forepart like the NEI No. 43A, 52A or Lyman No. 311299 will work best in the 7.62x54R because the forcing cones are large and gradual. Standard 30-caliber gaschecks are correct. Finnish 7.62x54R, Russian 7.62x39 and 7.65 Argentine bores are smaller than Russian 7.62x54R, Chinese 7.62x39, Japanese 7.7 or 303 British, and usually have standard .300-inch bore diameters (Finnish barrels occasionally are as small as .298) and groove diameters of .310- to .3115-inch.

The Lyman No. 311299 is a good all-round heavy bullet designed for the 303 British. It also shoots well in the 7.7 Japanese, 7.62x54R Russian and 303 British if you can find blocks to the original dimensions of .313- to .314-inch on the base and about .303- to .304-inch on the nose, weighing 205 grains in linotype or 215 in wheelweight alloy. Lyman reduced the diameters of this bullet a few years ago to fit ordinary 30-caliber barrels, which is wonderful if you have an 03A3 or a tight-bored Finnish 7.62x54R.

The 7.9x57 military 98 'Mausers work well with cast loads if you can find a suitable bullet. Most common cast bullets supposedly intended for the 8mm are really designed for the 32-40 and 32 Winchester Special. While they will shoot well in the older J-bore (.318- to .320-inch groove diameter) rifles, they are too small for WWII-era 98k rifles which require a .324- to .326-inch bullet. Many Eastern European Mausers have very large bores and need bullets of up to .330! The NEI No. 65 bullet is a good choice for most 8mm rifles. It casts .325-inch diameter, weighs 175 grains from wheelweights, and can be used with any of the cast bullet loads listed in this article.

In getting the best grouping with iron-sighted military rifles, you will soon find that eyesight is the limiting factor. Anybody older than forty who shoots iron sights should equip himself with a Farr-Sight from Gil Hebbard or Brownell's. This adjustable aperture for your eyeglass frame was intended for indoor pistol shooters, but it sure helps my iron sight rifle shooting, adding about five points to my score!

So now you have enough fundamentals to get started. If you want to have fun, give that old military rifle a try. You'll never know what you've been missing until you try it for yourself! ●

CAST BULLETS IN COMPETITION

When the Cast Bullet Association (CBA) initiated postal matches for as-issued military rifles, I thought it looked like fun and started looking for an 03A3 because I wanted to recapture some memories. The mentors of my youth who are still around still get misty-eyed over a good Springfield, and think even a wartime 03A3 is put together better than any sporter produced today.

I was lucky to find a clean Smith-Corona 03A3 in an estate sale, which filled the void in my gun closet. The rifle was a former DCM sale, and apparently had not been touched by its previous owner in more than twenty years. It was like being reintroduced to an old friend. I have also tried and traded a litany of militaries to find the best lead bullet shooters, and have come to the conclusion that a good M1917, Pattern 14 Enfield, Finnish M28 or M28/30, and Swiss K31 are all serious contenders.

Most of my target shooting today is with these old "militaries" because cast bullet loads are far more economical with regard to powder and lead, have less noise and recoil, and are a lot more fun to shoot! The cost advantage is obvious, particularly if you shoot a lot. Jacketed 30-caliber match bullets cost about $18 a box, and new powder is almost the same per pound. I can cast 500 30-caliber bullets from low-cost scrap alloy in an evening, and I get more than 300 rounds from a can of powder vs. 120 rounds with jacketed 30-06 loads. I don't have to worry about replacing an expensive match rifle barrel after a season or two of active competition either!

The CBA conducts a full season schedule of postal matches, many of which are fired using as-issued military rifles, of any caliber, from any country, using cast bullets. The most popular rifles among the winners seem to be the U.S. M1903A3 and M1917, Swedish 6.5x55 Mausers, and the Finnish M28 and M28/30s. The usual courses of fire are either four five-shot groups on the 100-yard small-bore target from the bench, or a ten-shot target for score, either bench or off-hand. A "deer hunter's practical" match on a whitetail target at 100 yards receives a particularly good following, and is fair game for the iron-sight military rifles.

The CBA is affiliated with the NRA and annual dues are $12, which includes six issues of a 32-page bimonthly newsletter *The Fouling Shot*, which is crammed full of technical data. For information, write the Director of Membership, Ralland J. Fortier, 4103 Foxcraft Road, Traverse City, Michigan 49684.

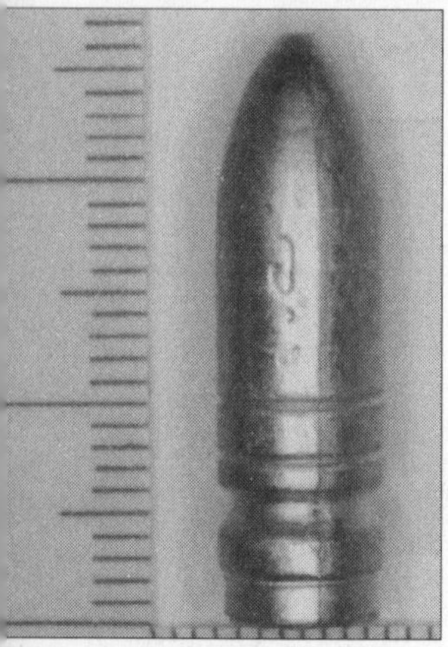

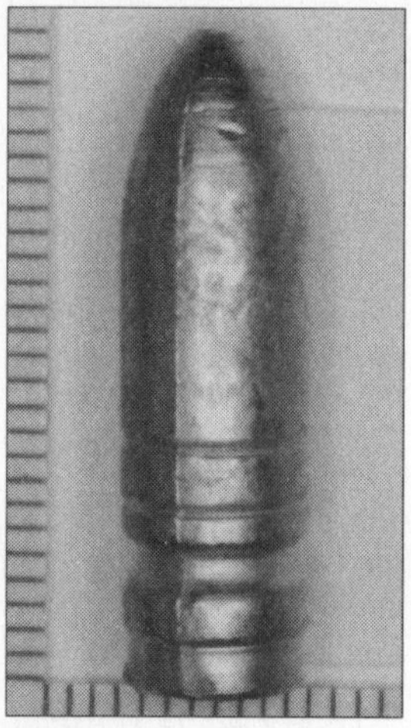

Nose defects are unsightly but have almost no effect upon grouping of iron-sighted military rifles, except for serious competition.

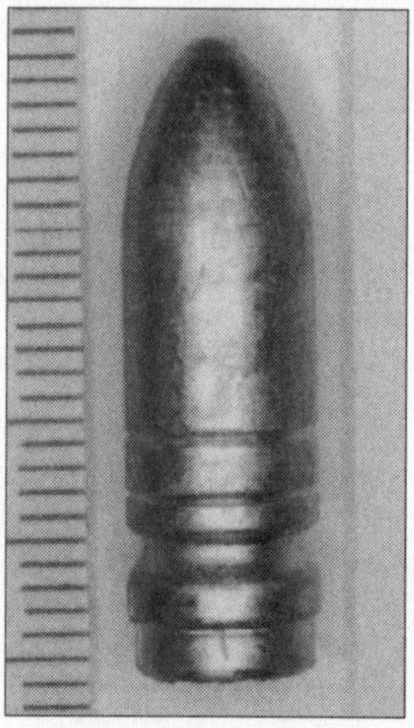

This is a good bullet, well filled and uniformly frosted.

In mid-1992, I was informed by NEI that they were not accepting bullet mould orders at that time, and expected to be out of production for about six months. In case they are still not producing moulds at press time, I have provided the drawings for my No. 43A and No. 52A to the following firms, who have offered to make them available: Donald V. Eagan, P.O. Box 196, Benton, PA 17814/717-925-6134 (single cavity only, nose pour available); LBT, Inc., HCR 62, Box 145, Moyie Springs, ID 83845/208-267-3588 (single or multiple cavity, no nose pour available); Lee Precision, 4275 Hwy. U, Hartford, WI 53027/414-673-3075 (special order moulds for No. 52A). *C.E. Harris*

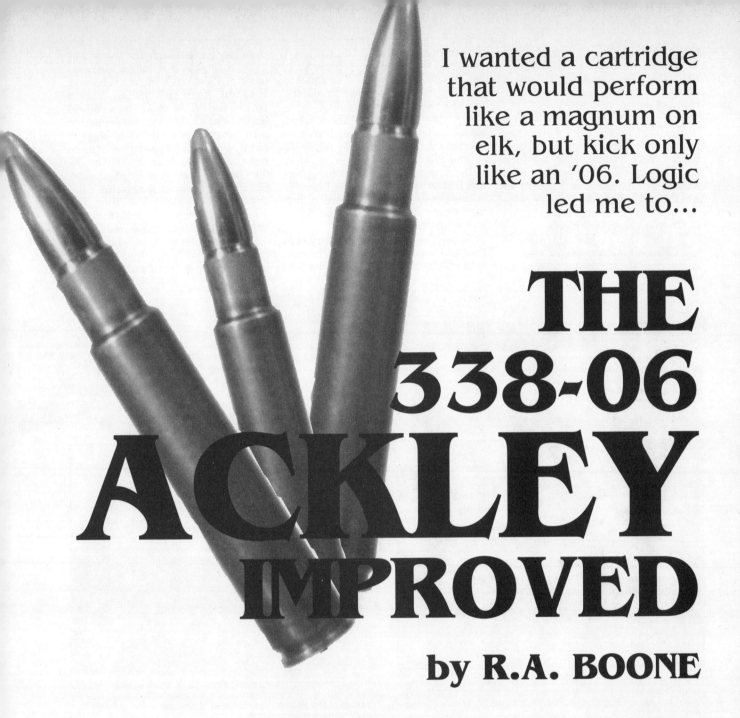

I wanted a cartridge that would perform like a magnum on elk, but kick only like an '06. Logic led me to...

THE 338-06 ACKLEY IMPROVED

by R.A. BOONE

THIS RIFLE'S PURPOSE is hunting elk. I have no intention of ever using it for any other game, let alone competition. The action is a highly modified Winchester Model 54, manufactured in 1930. The trigger, safety, firing pin and bolt handle are modified to Model 70 style. The only outward differences between this gun and a fine pre-war Model 70 are the one-piece trigger guard/floorplate assembly and a flathead screw at the rear of the left side of the receiver. This screw holds the bolt-stop in place. This was necessary since the trigger, which also performs the function of bolt-stop on the Model 54, was replaced with a Model 70 trigger, which works only as a trigger. A subtle difference between my gun and the Model 70 is the location of the front action screw. It attaches to the bottom of the recoil lug instead of between it and the magazine well, so is slightly less than an inch ahead of the Model 70's front action screw.

My rifle's primary sight was a Leupold Vari-X III $2^1/_2$-8x scope. I installed it in a Griffin & Howe double lever side mount so it would be quickly detachable and thus permit use of a Lyman 48 aperture sight mounted on the receiver bridge. The rifle will be used on extended trips to the back country, and knowing that a scope-damaging fall will not end the hunt is reassuring. The Lyman 48 is a pretty decent sight in its own right, of course.

The stock is mildly figured walnut in Reinhart Fajen's Model 70 Super Grade style. The forend is an inch longer than normal, with a 3-inch tip of fancy Bastogne walnut burl added. The benefits are a shift in weight that makes for steadier holding and more area to grasp when firing from awkward positions.

The barrel is by C.P. Donnelly. It is a 22-inch medium-weight sporter. A Burris Patridge is set in a ramp front sight to mesh with the Lyman 48. The weight of the rifle, scope, 1-inch Whelen-type sling, detachable swivels and six rounds of ammunition is 10 pounds, 7 ounces. This was mildly shocking as I had estimated it to be lighter by at least a pound. This is due, in part, to being conditioned by weights of empty rifles. The rifle and mounted scope weigh 9 pounds, 9 ounces. This is 2 pounds heavier than a featherweight rifle/scope and 1 pound heavier than a standard-weight rifle/scope. The additional weight is in the larger and denser stock. This added weight does not impair the handling characteristics, however. For a long hike, I imagine I would prefer a lighter rifle, but when the time comes to squeeze the trigger, I will be glad I paid the price for the extra shootability.

For elk, I wanted to shoot what many consider the premier high-production elk bullet: the 210-grain 338-caliber Nosler Partition. The other bullet I would use is the 200-grain 338 Bitterroot Bonded Core. I consider this the world's best elk bullet, but availability is limited so I use them rather sparingly.

To use these bullets in factory cartridges I am limited to two choices, both of which are magnums: the 338 Winchester and the 340 Weatherby. Both require widening the magazine rails and opening the bolt face. In addition, the Weatherby requires lengthening the magazine by removing metal and strength from the lower locking lug area and in front of the trigger. None of these changes appeal to me.

The terrain and hunting conditions of the areas I hunt in eastern Washington state for the most part limit shooting distance to approximately 300 yards. Under this limitation, the advantage of the magnums would be the increased striking energy within 300 yards, rather than any increase in effective range.

To stay with a standard case yet use the 338-caliber bullets I desired, I opted for the 338-06 Ackley Improved. The case is a 30-06 necked-out to 338 and fireformed to minimum taper and a 40-degree shoulder. Headspace distance remains the same as that of the 30-06. Dies are special order at present, but so many people are getting rifles chambered in either 338-06 or 338-06 Ackley, I believe the 338-06 will soon become a production item.

Tapered case neck expanders are generally available; however, my brother-in-law Geoff custom-made mine out of a machine bolt. It is $1\frac{1}{2}$ inches long, with a $\frac{1}{4}$-inch section of .30-inch diameter at one end, $\frac{1}{4}$-inch of .33 diameter at the other, and 1 linear inch of taper in the middle. The center of the large end is drilled and tapped to fit the expander rod of the die. To form cases, I just remove the regular expander button and screw on the tapered one. This is the same method as the factory-tapered expanders, but mine tapers at less angle.

Initially, I formed cases by running the case over the tapered expander and fireforming. This was done by loading an adequate charge

Much modified M54 Winchester 338-06 Ackley Improved is Boone's top choice for elk in the Pacific Northwest. His reasons, as explained herewith, make much sense.

Though Boone's favorite elk rifle is a M54 Winchester, its trigger, safety, firing pin and bolt handle have been modified to M70 style, as shown here. Trigger guard/floorplate assembly is now the most obvious M54 feature.

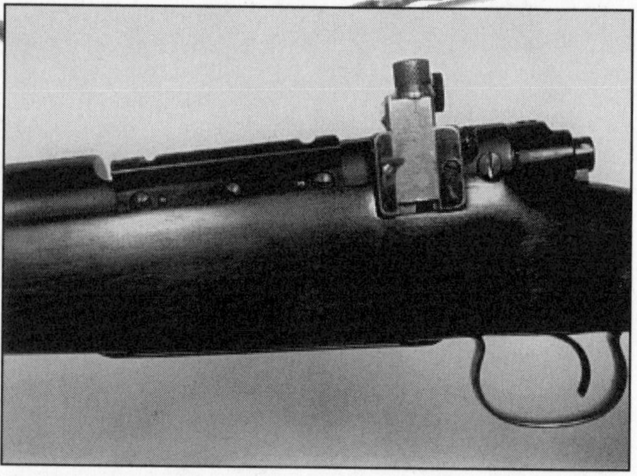

Left side of receiver shows how Lyman 48 aperture sight is installed when scope is removed from Griffin & Howe side mount, leaving the base of the receiver clean. Head of special screw used as bolt stop can be seen behind sight.

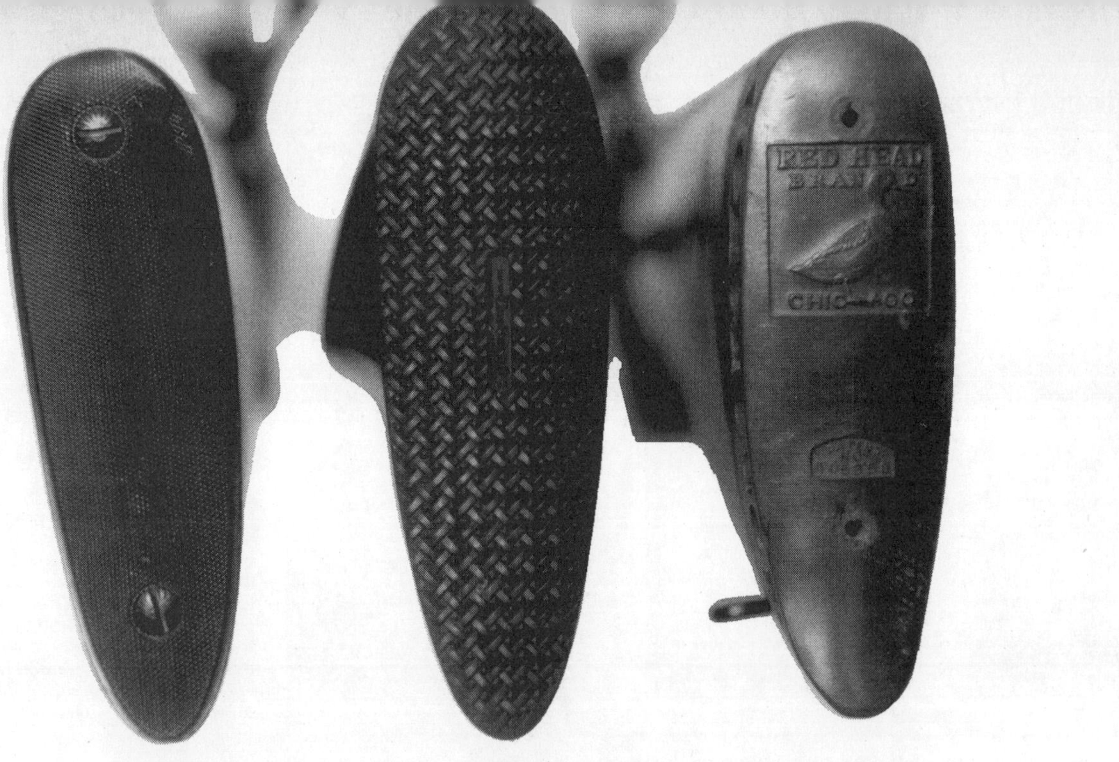

Buttplate of 338-06 Ackley Improved, center, was deliberately made large to distribute recoil over more area. It's compared here to the buttplate of Boone's FN Mauser 257 Ackley, left, and his featherweight pre-'64 M70 Winchester 30-06. Large pad and increased rifle weight make recoil of 338-06 AI similar to '06's.

of powder and a bullet, chambering the cartridge and firing. This uses a lot of powder and a bullet to no avail, so I tried expanding the neck, loading with 7 grains of fast pistol powder (Bullseye, 231, etc.), loosely filling the case with most any standard filler (kapok, dacron, etc.), then chambering and firing. This method has two advantages: It doesn't waste powder and bullets, and it doesn't require a trip to the range.

In most firings, the cases formed correctly; however, in several instances, excess headspace developed. It appeared that the 17½-degree shoulder angle of the case did not have enough purchase on the 40-degree angle of the chamber to prevent it from being driven into the chamber throat when hit by the firing pin.

The problem was corrected by adding another step to the forming process. After the necks were expanded to .338, they were expanded again to .358, turning the cases into 35 Whelens. In fact, if the reloader purchased 35 Whelens instead of 30-06s, he could avoid the tapered expanders. The cases were then sized back down to .338 in the 338-06 Ackley die. The die had been carefully adjusted so that the formed cases would fit tightly in the rifle chamber. This left a 40-degree shoulder on the case between .358-inch and .338-inch, which apparently holds the case securely during the firing process and eliminates the previously mentioned headspace and case-stretch problems.

Some of Donnelly's customers reported velocities of 2800 fps for 210-grain bullets when fired in the improved cartridge. This is only 100 fps slower than several loadings for the same bullet fired in the 338 Winchester Magnum. I have seen only a few sources of loading data for the 338-06 and none for the Ackley Improved. I have two starting points for determining loads: The rule of thumb whereby 5 percent is added to the starting loads of the standard 338-06, and consulting with my trusty Powley computer. This applies to factory cartridges and wildcats alike.

I weighed a few cases, filled them with water to the base of the neck, re-weighed them to determine the water weight and then took the average. Water capacity averaged 66 grains. This relates to 57 grains of IMR-type powder. Working through the computations showed the optimum powder to be IMR-4320. Fired from a barrel with overall length of 22 inches, this load is expected to produce 2560 fps with a 210-grain bullet while generating 46,000 units of pressure. To obtain the desired pressure level of 50,000 units, it would be necessary to either compress more powder into the available space or use a slightly faster powder.

First, I wanted to put the Powley information to the test. I tried several sources for 4320, but to no avail. Both Dupont and IMR had discontinued its manufacture. Unable to get IMR-4320, I tried several other powders, including IMR-4064, IMR- and H-4350, H-414 and W-748. The Powley computer was correct with regard to burning rate, as powders slower than IMR-4320—such as H-414 and the 4350s—ran out of room before they could match the velocities of the faster numbers, while those faster than IMR-4320 could be overloaded to cause high pressure indicators.

Best performance was turned in by IMR-4064 when used with bullets of 200 to 210 grains. A load of 56 grains pushed the 210 Nosler to 2830 fps, measured 12 feet from the muzzle, with spectacular consistency. One series of ten had a maximum/minimum spread of 21 fps and an average deviation of 4 fps.

The velocities indicated I had reached the desired level of pressure. The process of developing loads was two-step. The minimum load for a specific bullet/powder was fired over a chronograph. Velocity was noted and the amount of case expansion at the pressure ring, the portion of the case just ahead of the web, was measured and recorded. The process was repeated to see if pressure indicators

Comparison of, from left, 30-06 with 180-grain bullet; standard 338-06 210-grain; 338-06 Ackley Improved, 210-grain; and 338 Winchester Magnum, 210-grain. Boone's modified M54 338-06 AI gives up some velocity to the magnum case, but accepts six cartridges in magazine/chamber, compared to four in most 338 Magnums.

Boone believes the 338-caliber 210-grain Nosler Partition is the premier high-production elk bullet. It's shown here with the 180-grain Partition bullet which often is used in the present '06 case. The 338 has a sectional density of .263 and a ballistic coefficient of .400, compared to .271 and .361 for the 30-caliber. With essentially identical muzzle velocities, the 338 has a slightly flatter trajectory, 20-percent increase in frontal area, and 30-grain increase in weight.

appeared on the cases. If cases could be fired ten times with the same load and still have tight primer pockets, the load was deemed safe in this rifle. The powder charge was then increased by a grain and the process repeated. When cases showed an increase in pressure ring expansion of .0005-inch over the prior load, or other more common indicators manifested themselves, the load was discontinued because of undesirable high pressure. If the load passed these tests, but the primer pocket loosened prior to the tenth loading, the process was also discontinued. Then, the bullet/powder combination reverted to the previous load in which all criteria were met, and that became the maximum for that bullet/powder in this rifle.

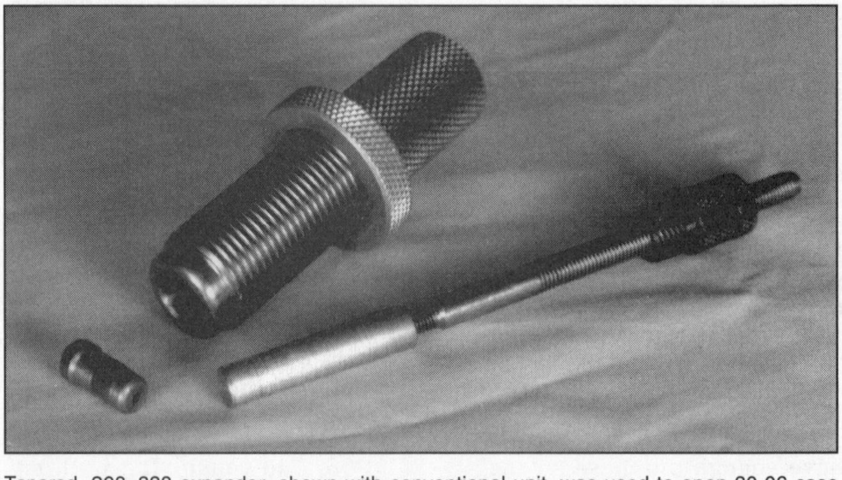

Tapered .308-.338 expander, shown with conventional unit, was used to open 30-06 case necks to accept 338 bullets. An alternative method of obtaining 338-06 cases is to buy commercial 35 Whelens and neck them down to 338.

Ballistic coefficient for the 200-grain Bitterroot is .380. With a velocity of 2850 fps and a 200-yard zero, the bullet is only 8 inches low at 300 yards. That is within an inch of a 200-grain 308-caliber Nosler Partition fired from a 300 Winchester Magnum. The 210-grain 338 Nosler Partition fired from the Ackley is only slightly less flat over 300 yards than the same bullet fired from the Winchester Magnum.

Sighted in as I prefer—3 inches high at 100 yards—the zero is extended to about 225 yards, and either the 200-grain Bitterroot or the 210-grain Nosler will be less than 5 inches low at 300 yards. Thus the reticle can be placed on the middle of an elk's chest with no regard whatsoever for bullet drop at any range up to 300 yards. If conditions require a longer shot, adjustments will be similar to those for a 300 Magnum with 200-grain bullet. That certainly qualifies the 338-06 Ackley as a flat shooting rifle with sufficient punch for elk.

In addition to amazing ballistics, the 338-06 Ackley shows very good accuracy. Most shots at elk are between 100 and 300 yards, so I split the difference and used 200 yards for the accuracy tests. From a solid position at a bench, ten-shot groups approaching 1 MOA (minute of angle) were not uncommon. A representative group put ten 210-grain Noslers into a maximum spread of 2⅝ inches. Seven of that group went into 1⅜ inches. It is quite possible that careful assembly of components with consideration to exact uniformity could reduce ten-shot groups to the seven-shot group dimension. I didn't have enough Bitterroots to fire ten-shot groups with them, but for what they show, three-shot groups indicated 2 MOA could be expected.

LOADS TRIED IN AUTHOR'S 338-06 ACKLEY IMPROVED				
Bullet (Wgt. Grs.)	Bullet (Type)	Load (Grs./Powder)	MV (fps)	Remarks
200	Hornady	57/W-748	2814	Accuracy marginal, velocity erratic.
200	Speer	58/IMR-4064	2860	Accuracy good; Bitterroot may be used.
210	Nosler	56/IMR-4064	2830	Outstanding accuracy.
210	Nosler	65/H-414	2726	Compressed load.
210	Nosler	62/H-4350	2771	Compressed load.

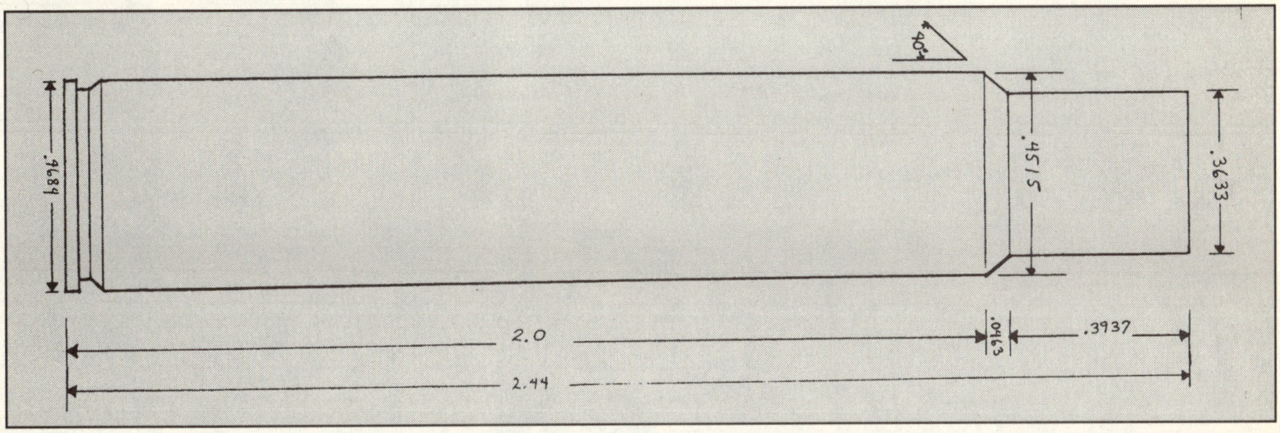

Dimensional drawing of 338-06 AI.

Boone's M54 will accept a handful of 338-06 AI cartridges—five in the magazine and another in the chamber—which he figures is more than he'll fire in any elk hunt. That's understandable—considering that this gunful of ammo supplies some 22,000 foot pounds of energy.

Obviously, both will stay on an elk's chest at 300 yards or more if I do my part. Suddenly, not being able to get IMR-4320 didn't seem as urgent as it once had been.

At one of my range sessions, I also fired two other rifles, a pre-'64 Winchester Model 70 featherweight 30-06 loaded with 150-grain bullets, and a custom FN Mauser chambered in 257 Ackley and loaded with 120-grain bullets. The 257 weighed 7 pounds, 9 ounces; the 30-06 7 pounds, 10 ounces. Felt recoil of the 338-06 Ackley was substantially more than the 257's, but was very comparable to that of the 30-06's. My conclusion is that the increased ballistic performance is offset by the 2 pounds of added weight and the larger surface area of the Model 54's recoil pad.

The benefits of this conversion are most notable when the parent 30-06 using 180-grain bullets is compared to the 338-06 Ackley using 210-grain bullets. Velocity of both bullets is 2800 fps. The advantages of the 338 bullet are clear: 20 percent increase in frontal area, 30-grain increase in weight, and slightly flatter trajectory over all ranges.

Shooting several boxes of 210-grainers exiting at over 2800 fps erased any fear I had that a rifle with such performance would be painful, and in the process I built a great sense of confidence. I am very familiar with the rifle and cartridge. When October arrives, I shall challenge the elk with a cartridge that performs like a magnum, but kicks only like an '06. There is not another rifle in the world I would rather use to hunt elk.

A final thought.The loads mentioned herein were fired hundreds of times in scores of cases, but in only one rifle. Loading data from various bullet and powder manufacturers developed by firing thousands of rounds in hundreds of cases in several rifles would provide a better indication of what most rifles will do. It is possible that when C.P. Donnelly built my barrel, things happened just right, and it's one of those rifles that comfortably digests loads that would be dangerous in another 338-06 Ackley Improved. So if you have, or get, a 338-06, standard or improved, develop your loads for it carefully and with full consideration for signs of high pressure. ●

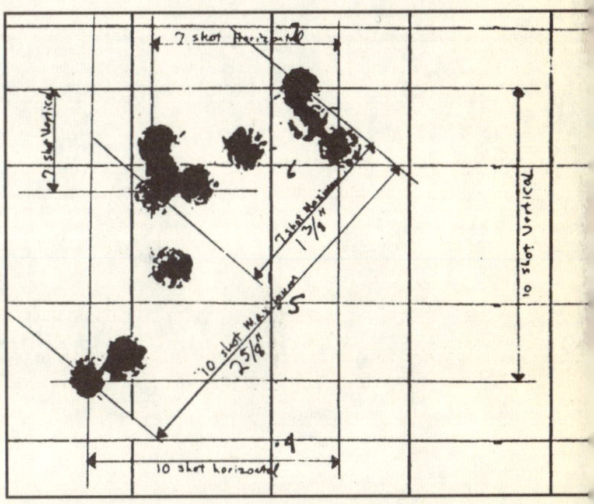
Expecting his elk shots to come between 100 and 300 yards, Boone did most of his testfiring at the midway point, 200 yards. This ten-shot group measured 2.62 inches, with 7 shots in 1.37. Load was the 210-grain Nosler Partition, 56/IMR-4064, velocity 2830 fps.

It might not rate high as entertainment, but a serious shooter can learn a lot from...

PROJECTILESCOPY

(Above) Some are hot and some are not. Though various makes of commercial ammunition and well-finished handloads look fine, results may be less than pleasing at the target. A low-power magnifying glass such as this 7x triplet can reveal important clues to accuracy, or the lack thereof, in the examination of fired bullets.

by C. RODNEY JAMES

PROJECTILESCOPY is a high-class, guilt-inspired term I invented for looking at used bullets. In our youth, it was a private joke between my brother and me that digging for spent bullets to examine was the lowest form of time-wasting, and anyone indulging in this practice was hell-bound for sure. My brother works in the Pentagon and I am a freelance writer. I hope the jury remains out on this issue because I still do this on occasion.

The pioneer ballistician, Dr. Franklin Mann, author of the seminal work *The Bullet's Flight From Powder To Target*, had to be the greatest bullet examiner ever, and his examinations led him to conclusions regarding the fundamentals of ballistics that have since been elevated to the status of scientific laws. His best-known law is that the most critical factor affecting a bullet's accuracy is the quality of its base, which must be perfectly formed and at an absolute right angle to the long axis of the bullet.

What can we learn from similar examinations? The question the beginning shooter wants answered is: Which ammunition—will give me the greatest accuracy and power bang for my buck? Trial and error—targeting various makes of factory ammunition—will eventually sort out those brands, bullet styles and loadings which perform better than others. The advanced shooter, who is almost always a handloader, is more interested in accuracy than power, and in the pursuit of same seeks to answer the question: Why does one particular powder, bullet, lubricant, alloy, primer and cartridge combination group consistently better than another in a particular gun? It has been this author's experience that much can be learned about this by examining fired bullets. That "X" brand of rimfires delivers better accuracy than "Y" brand—or that "X" combination of bullet, alloy and powder shoots more consistently than "Y" combination—can be established by targeting it.

If a shooter wants to know *why* he is getting these results, or why he is *not* getting the results he wants, he can learn a good bit from examining fired bullets. Sometimes *one* is all it takes. He can begin by comparing those that are straight shooters with those that are not and noting the differences. Beyond that, at least one probable cause of fliers and evidence of inaccuracies caused by inadequate lubrication, improper sizing, a poor gas seal, imperfect concentricity of a bullet with the bore, base deformation and fouling incompatibility can be identified. Bullet examination will, of course, yield nothing regarding inaccuracies caused by velocity variations resulting from primer and/or powder problems. These can sometimes be heard, but must be studied with a chronograph.

Lead and lead-alloy bullets, in particular, are delicate and easily damaged. When one which has been moving hundreds of feet a second comes to a sudden stop, it usually resembles a wad of used chewing gum. Such bullets, dug from an earth bank after having first passed through a can or plank, have little value beyond their metal as material for reuse. To learn anything from a fired bullet, it must be, as nearly as possible, in exactly the same condition as when it left the muzzle of the gun. The principal examiners of bullets have been forensic firearms examiners seeking to collect comparison data between test bullets and evidence bullets for legal purposes. Various substances have been used to catch bullets in near-perfect condition. After some eighty years of experimentation, the best recovery material seems to be water and snow, although Dr. Mann reported good results with sawdust, sifted fine and well saturated with light machine oil.

I live in the country and don't recommend trying this in the city. Since I lack a handy pool of deep, clear water, snow has been my medium of choice. Though seasonal, it's free and disposes of itself after use. The method is simple. A long snow loaf, free of ice and debris, about 2 feet by 2 feet on the end, is built along the concrete walk in back of my house. The length is varied according to the power of the ammunition. The gun is held about a foot from the end of the snow loaf to avoid excessive splashback, which can be eliminated by a sheet of newsprint over the snow.

About 4 feet of good-packing fresh snow will stop a Long Rifle bullet from a rifle. A couple more feet will handle a 22 Magnum. By actual measure, 14 feet stopped 500-grain 45-70 bullets with a muzzle velocity in excess of 1600 fps. Behind a long "slowing loaf" is a shorter "recovery loaf" with a sheet of newsprint in front of it to record the point of entry. If things are calculated precisely, which doesn't happen that often, the bullet can be found lying in front of this paper, ready to pick up. Care must be taken to avoid angling shots off-center. One of those 45s once knocked a dent in my pump house.

Bullets should be spaced to avoid collisions and cavities must be closed by repacking the snow after a few shots. Normal recovery is by carefully sweeping down to the probable location of the bullet with a whisk broom. A cardboard carton is placed at the rear of the "recovery loaf" to catch the bullet, or at least verify that one has passed through and more snow is required. Certain bullets such as FMJ 223 rounds at velocities of 3000 fps have, so far, defied capture—boring through more

Text continues on page 90.

WHAT TO LOOK FOR

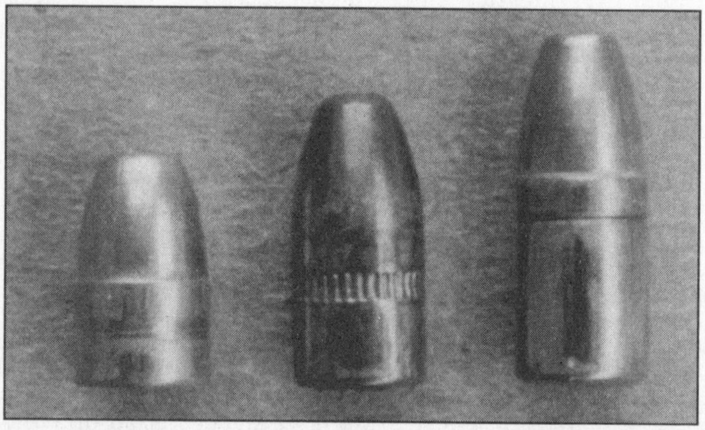

Left, CCI 30.5-grain +V 22 WMR through a clean dry barrel at 2100 fps evidences only a slightly deeper engraving than 40-grain Winchester (center) and 50-grain Federal (right) fired through a fouled barrel. All three copper-jacketed bullets show little distortion and are very accurate, grouping .3- to .5-inch at 35 yards. Absence of distortion shows why jacketed bullets usually produce smaller groups than those of lead alloy.

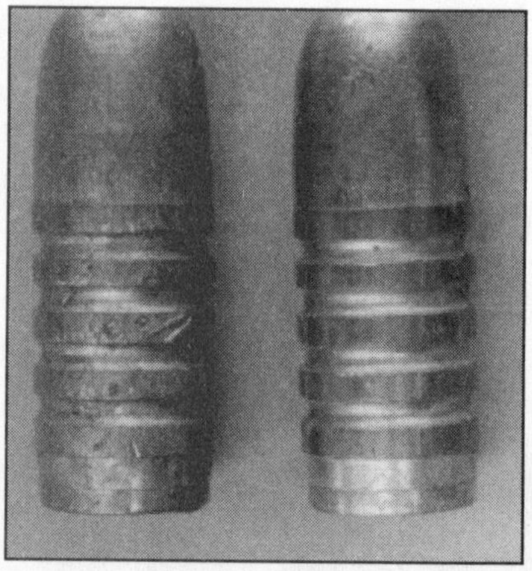

Hard-alloy 480-grain 45-70 (left) backed by 25 grains of IMR-4227 was badly gas-cut on the bottom, in spite of being gas checked. Bullet at right was gas checked with Hornady crimp-on check which obdurated the bore more effectively, preventing gas cutting and improving accuracy.

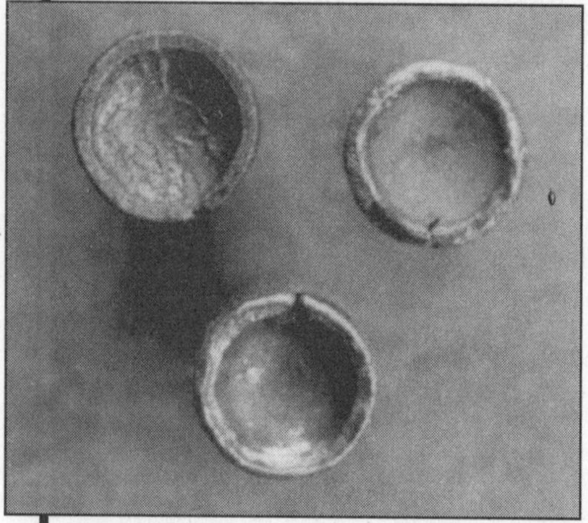

Blowouts at the thin edge of the hollow- or dish-based bullet may well be a cause of fliers, with the escaping gas giving the base of the bullet a lateral slap as it exits the muzzle. Three 22 Long Rifle bullets with base blowouts are, right, Remington Viper, left, CCI +V and CCI SGB, bottom. Neither the Viper nor the +V are exceptional groupers in the author's 52 Winchester. The SGB is, with the exception of the annoying odd flier. (At bottom) Side view of Viper, +V and SGB shows blown bases.

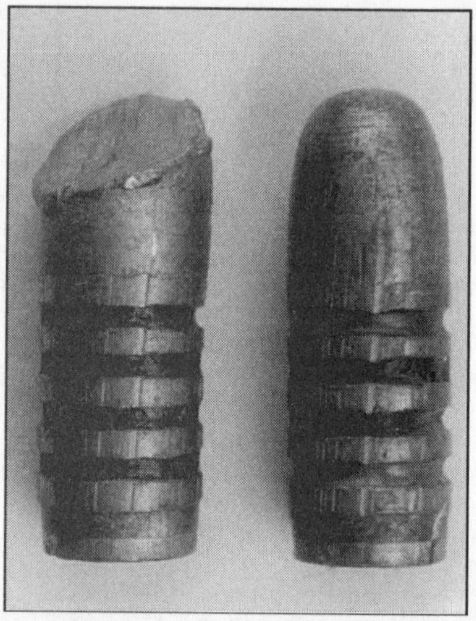

Left, 500-grain 45-70 soft-alloy bullet (wheelweight metal) through a clean barrel of a C. Sharps rifle. Upset resulted from collision with a pebble. Right, same bullet with same load of 40-grain IMR-4320 through 4320 fouling. Unburned grains of powder made multiple striations on the bearing surface. Harder alloy eliminated scoring and improved accuracy, leaving the bearing surface undamaged.

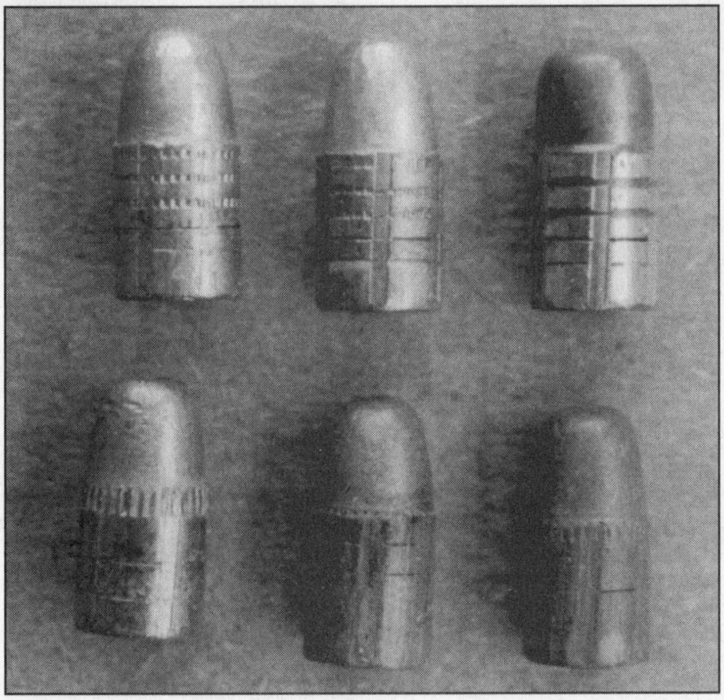

Top row: Left, copper-plated Super-X Long Rifle through a clean, dry barrel is evenly engraved and compressed. CCI Mini-Mag, center, is identically marked. Both are exceptionally accurate for high-speed loads and give no evidence of stripping. On right, clear engraving, even compression and fine accuracy characterized an RWS standard-velocity hollowpoint. Partial expansion was evident in soft snow. Bottom row: Left, Federal HV hollowpoint was stripped of plating. Subsequent fouling shots failed to stop this—compression is excessive, accuracy poor. Center and right are old Western Xpert and Gambels' Stores Revelation HV, possibly loaded by Federal. Both produced severe leading after four shots in the author's M52.

Top left, Eley Tenex shines like polished silver; right, Remington Palma Match evidences equally clean rifling impressions. Cannelures on both are evenly compressed all around. Bases are level with little evidence of flanges. Both group extremely well (.4- to .5-inch at 35 yards) and cost accordingly. Bottom row, two Western Super Silhouette 42-grain Long Rifle bullets evidence excessive and, by comparison, uneven cannelure compression—evidence of a lack of concentricity and oversized bullets for this particular bore (Winchester 52). While no leading was experienced, accuracy was not very good—.9-inch at 35 yards.

Top row: Copper-plated Winchester 22 WRF bullet on left was fired through a clean polygonal-bore HK 300 rifle, producing 35-yard groups as small as .3-inch. Bullet on right was fired after fouling the barrel with copper-jacketed bullets. Plating and lead was stripped from the bullet, and accuracy suffered. Bottom row: Three consecutive shots through a M52 Winchester. Left, lubricated, copper-plated PMC Zapper 22 LR was stripped of much of its plating by a clean dry barrel. Center and right bullets are PMC Zappers shot through their own fouling. They exhibit little stripping and grouped well, as Zapper lubricant coated the barrel. This would certainly justify the importance of fouling shot.

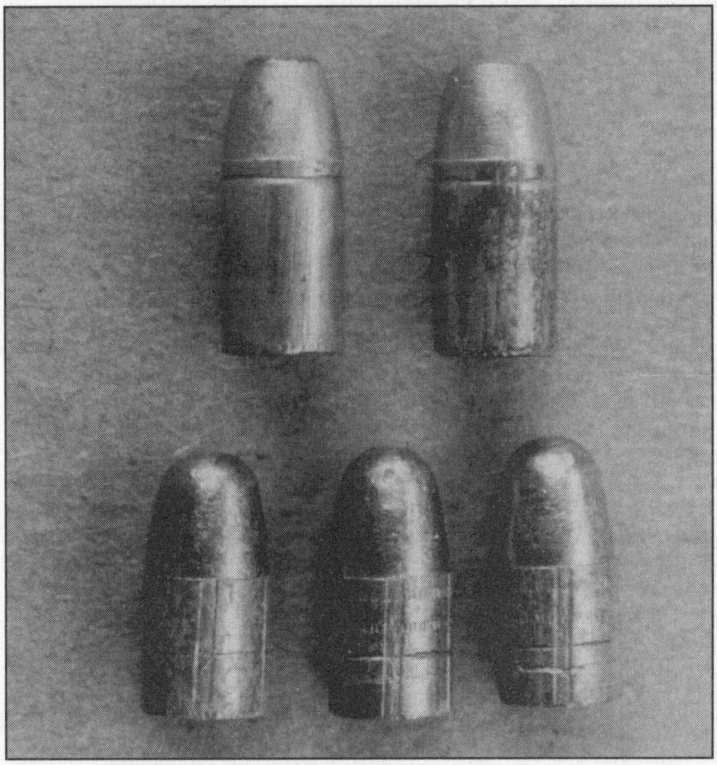

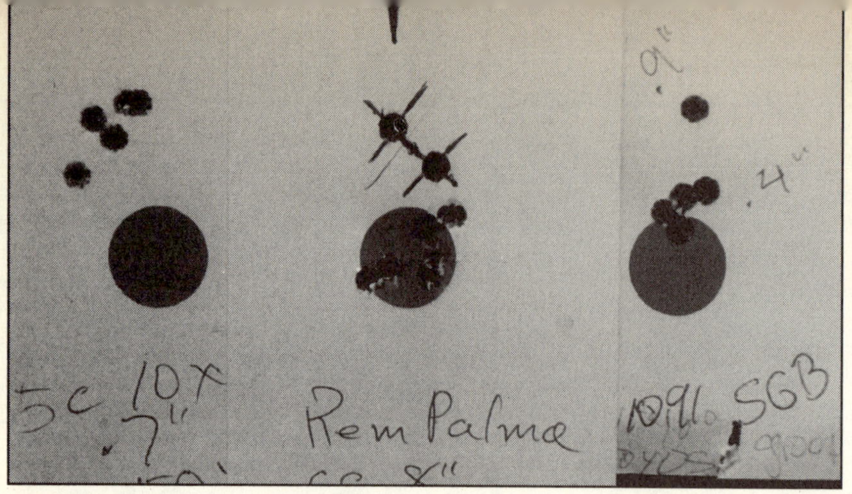

Three 50-yard groups from the Winchester 52, sandbag rest, shot in a light breeze (4-5 mph) in 40-degree F. weather, February 10, 1991. Left, five Eley Tenex through a warmed, fouled barrel in .7-inch. Center, six shots of Remington Palam (ca. 1940s) in .8-inch. The two fouling shots at the top were not counted. Right, five CCI SGB. Flier spread the group from .4- to .9-inch.

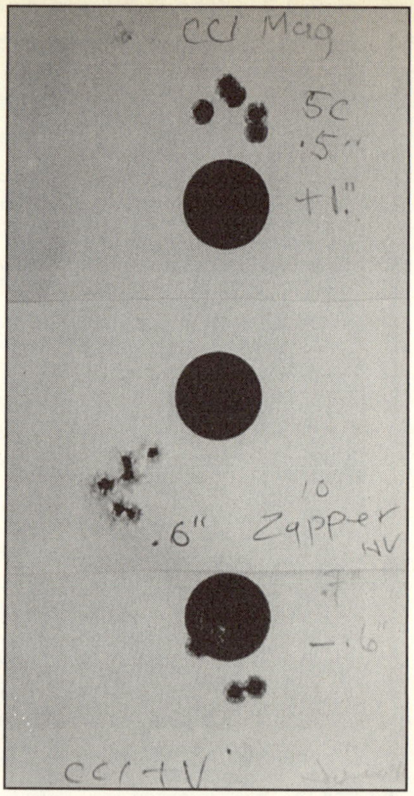

Three 35-yard groups from the Winchester 52, sandbag rest, fired June 16, 1990, in calm air, 70 degrees F. Top, five CCI Mini-Mags in .5-inch. Center, ten PMC Zappers in .6-inch. Bottom, five CCI +Vs in .7-inch. Although not a bad group, I consider the two bottom shots fliers.

Text continued from page 87.

than 30 feet of snow. Bullets of fragile construction such as hyper-velocity 22 hollowpoints and Foster-type shotgun slugs upset to such an extent as to offer little bearing surface for examination.

In an excellent article on rimfire accuracy in the January, 1991, *American Rifleman* ("Rimfire Accuracy for a Song"), C.E. Harris again raised the question of the value, or lack thereof, of plating on lead-alloy bullets. In his investigation, he targeted one box each of Federal HV plated and unplated Long Rifles. The unplated ammunition had a slight, though not statistically significant, accuracy edge. His explanation, new to me, was that the tumbling of the bullets in the plating process caused minute damage to the bases, thus decreasing accuracy. Earlier theories had held that the thin plating stripped off in firing, leaving a scaly fouling in the barrel which thus reduced accuracy. It is a well-known fact that unlubricated plated bullets often lead even good bores. Such ammunition deposited long lines of lead in the author's 52 and his brother's K-22 S&W. My examination of recovered bullets suggests that the lubricant on the bullet is *the* critical factor in keeping that useless plating attached to the bullet and not deposited in the bore.

Stripping of plating is generally bad news in the accuracy department and indicates one of several possible conditions. The first is inadequate lubrication. Visible bore leading is not necessary to open groups. Bullets that continue to strip on their own fouling from a clean barrel are leaving metal fouling behind. Three recovered bullets are about all that are needed for confirmation. A second cause of stripping is oversized bullets. In my experience, these never shoot as straight as those which are exactly bore-size. For this reason, stripping is accompanied by excessive compression of the cannelures on the bearing surface. The third reason is incompatible fouling. Copper fouling left by shooting jacketed bullets has a great affinity for lead, even when copper plated, and will strip lead alloy bullets until it is removed. Other incompatibilities include the deposit of hard fouling such as that left by blackpowder and unburned grains of hard smokeless powder which will score and/or strip the next bullet's bearing surface.

Inadequate lubrication may be less obvious with plain lead bullets, but if a bullet is properly sized and not driven too fast for the type of alloy, lubricant failure will sometimes result in a scuffed or smeared surface, blurring the rifling striae. An oversized bullet will have a similar appearance, but will also exhibit excessive compression of the cannelures, indicating an overly tight fit in the bore.

A lack of concentricity of the bullet with the bore can be either a gun problem or an ammunition problem. If the signs appear on a variety of bullets—both cast and commercial—it's a gun problem. If it occurs only with certain bullets or brands of commercial ammunition, it's a bullet problem. A concentricity problem is visible in the uneven compression of cannelures on the bearing surface. This usually indicates the bullet was tipped in the case.

Imperfections in bullet bases are visible in commercial ammunition only *after* the bullets have been fired. An angled base can be detected by rolling the bullet or standing it on its base on a flat surface beside a straight vertical edge. Tipped and oversized bullets may exhibit uneven fins of lead pulled from the base—bad for accuracy, opening groups. Occasionally, certain bullets, particularly those with hollow-bases featuring thin edges at the outer rim, may rupture at the edge, allowing a jet of gas to escape to the side just as the bullet leaves the muzzle. To offer absolute proof that this is *the main* cause of fliers would require more time, ammunition and snow than I have available. I have noted, however, a positive correlation between this type of base failure and an excess of fliers with certain types of hollow-base Long Rifle ammunition.

Winter is admittedly not the most pleasant time to be outdoors, and considerably less liquid water is needed for bullet recovery than snow. Law enforcement personnel generally use a kind of modified livestock-tank contraption for bullet recovery, and I have heard of backyard swimming pools occasionally being put to this use. I have no recommendations on these methods beyond: "Caveat Shoot-or." ●

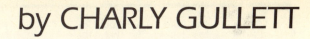

by CHARLY GULLETT

POWER SEARCH

For generations, both hunters and ballisticians have searched for ways to reliably rate a cartridge's true efficiency. Here's the most comprehensive system yet.

SHOOTERS HAVE been aware of the ballistic limitations of common power delivery calculations for some time. While bullet shape and composition are additional parameters of entry (and, to some degree, exit) wound characteristics, they remain a separate study from power delivery ballistics. IPSC Power Factor, widely used for handgun competition, is a simple and straightforward method of determining major and minor power floors for practical shooting events. The Taylor Knockout rating, developed by the famous Mozambique hunter John Taylor, has been the standard for African cartridge comparisons for many decades.

Einstein once said, "Things should be simple, but not too simple." Both IPSC and Taylor compute limited resolution within their respective power calculations in an attempt to maintain simplicity. This is useful only if the shooter desires broad comparisons within certain power bands. IPSC Power Factor was never intended to define firepower for dangerous African game, and Taylor never foresaw the use of his KO rating to separate a 38 Special from a 9mm Auto. One has to believe that some other power algorithm can be found to accurately define all cartridges regardless of application. Exploring the strengths and limitations of IPSC and Taylor reveals the parameters necessary to construct a new universal power algorithm.

IPSC calculates the product of two variable parameters divided by one constant. The parameters are muzzle velocity (MV) and bullet weight (BW); the constant is 1000.

$$\text{IPSC Power Factor} = \frac{(MV)(BW)}{1000}$$

The constant is superfluous except that it reduces the results to three digits. For instance, a 230-grain bullet moving at 850 fps results in a product of 195,500. Although many shooters have a propensity for big-bore firearms, few care for big calculations. Dividing the result by 1000 yields an IPSC Power Factor of 195.5 for this venerable "major" cartridge (a 45 ACP). This computation, in conjunction with a chronograph, allows competitive sporting events to quickly qualify cartridges to be used in a shooting match.

There are two limitations to the IPSC formula. First, bullet diameter is not taken into account. Almost anyone who has hunted dangerous game will say the bigger the hole the better, all else being equal. To illustrate this, consider two bullets of the same weight and velocity (180 grains at 1200 fps), but different diameters (357- and 40-caliber). Even though one bullet would have some finite advantage in having a larger diameter, the IPSC rating would yield an identical power factor for both bullets (IPSC Power Factor = 216). Bullets will normally expand upon impact, although it is difficult to determine how much. Whatever else occurs, it is safe to assume that if the bullet does not expand it will at least demonstrate impact ballistics related to bullet diameter. Therefore, bullet diameter has a useful place in power calculations.

The second IPSC limitation is the abbreviated use of mass and velocity in determining power. Taylor KO ratings have the same limitation. The classic kinetic energy formula (a law of physics) is stated the following way:

$$KE = \frac{\frac{(BW)}{(7000g)}(MV)^2}{2}$$

You will probably recognize everything in this formula except possibly the "g" parameter. Physicists use this to represent acceleration due to gravity. Ever since Galileo dropped two cannonballs off the top of Pisa Tower in the 1630s, acceleration due to gravity has been a recognized force upon ammunition. Sir Isaac Newton used this and other information to develop his universal law of gravitation (1687), demonstrating that gravity varies with altitude. Proof of these effects was demonstrated by an inventor named Benjamin Robins who built the first ballistic pendulum in 1740. There is an enormously boring equation, developed by a scientist named Helmert, used to determine acceleration due to gravity at various latitudes and elevations. Helmert's equation is chock-full of cosines and scientific notations and trigonometric symbols that, for the most part, do not serve our purposes here. Acceleration due to gravity *does not change very much* with different latitudes and elevations. Fortunately,

(Right) Big game load for blackpowder Kodiak 50-caliber double rifle. This 410-grain Buffalo Bullet will launch at about 1500 fps and yield a UPI of 1044. IPSC calculates to a factor of 615 due to large bullet weight. Taylor would rate the KO at 44.8 for this charcoal burner mostly as a result of bore size.

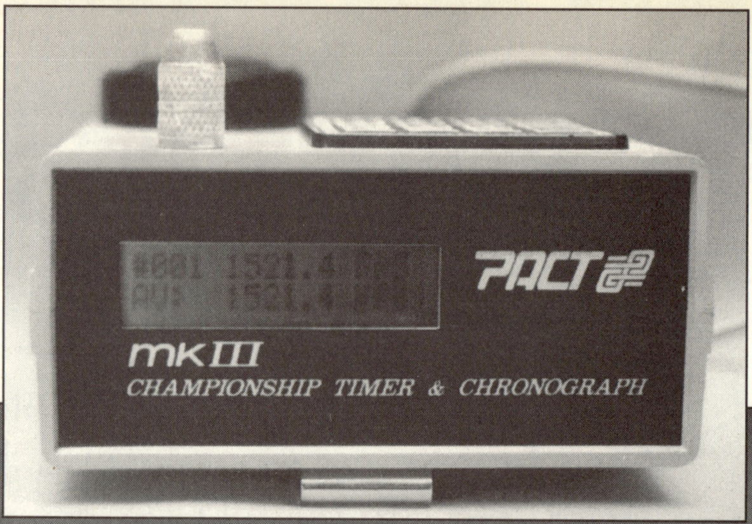

(Below) Some custom work was required to safely fire the 410-grain bullet at 1500 fps for the UPI test. The under-barrel lug securing the forend to the barrel was removed and a solid lug nearly three times the size of the original was welded into place. You will feel twenty rounds of 1000 UPI in your shoulder the next day.

the International Committee on Weights and Measures has adopted an accepted standard for this value:

$$g = 32.174 \text{ ft/sec}^2$$

The "g" factor must be included to accurately represent gravitational bullet mass. This "mass" portion of the energy formula converts bullet weight to pound units (bullet weight in grains divided by 7000 grains in a pound), while factoring in gravitational acceleration. American scientists like to work in pound units. (In fact, when it comes to bullet weights, our scientists prefer the avoirdupois pound, which contains 7000 grains, not the troy pound, which contains 5760 grains.) European shooters convert this to kilograms and meters per second, and it is still correct, the point being that this portion of the formula indicates there is a great deal more to power factors than just bullet weight and simple velocity (note the physics formula squares the velocity). This is the kinetic energy formula used by all American powder, bullet and ammunition manufacturers to specify a given bullet at a given velocity, and the result is stated in "foot pounds" (fp).

Using this KE formula, the 45 ACP discussed earlier would develop 369 foot pounds of energy at the muzzle. A standard 357 Magnum launching a 125-grain bullet at 1300 fps turns in about 469 foot pounds. Just to gain some relativity, a 500-grain 458 Winchester Magnum bullet idling out the bore at 2050 fps churns up a mere 4665 foot pounds!

John Taylor had hunted extensively in Africa with most of the big bores of the day when he developed his now-famous Knockout rating. One of his favorite elephant cartridges was a 3-inch 577 Nitro Express. This little shoulder cannon launched a 750-grain solid at 2050 foot seconds for a skosh under 7000 foot pounds of energy. His formula gives this behemoth a KO value of

(Right) The 10mm Auto. This full-power load consists of a 200-grain FMJ-FP with a muzzle velocity of 1198 fps. IPSC would rate this at 239.6, Taylor at 13.69, and UPI at 254.9.

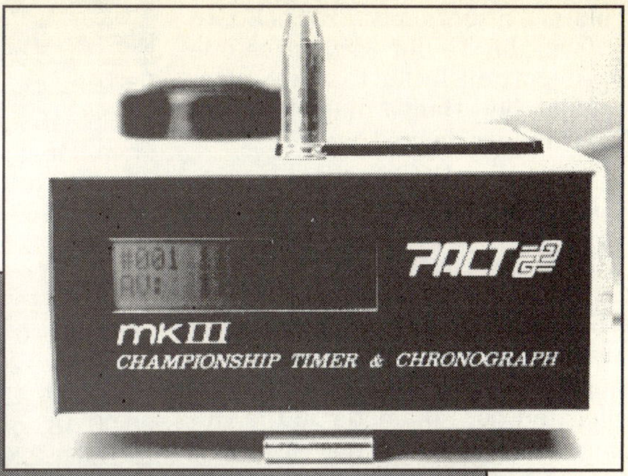

(Below) This Colt 10mm Delta Elite required no additional throating or ramping as the factory designed this modern firearm to handle truncated bullets. Norma factory loads produce 1200 fps for a kinetic rating of 639 foot pounds and a UPI power rating of 255. This places the cartridge power between 357 and 44 Magnum.

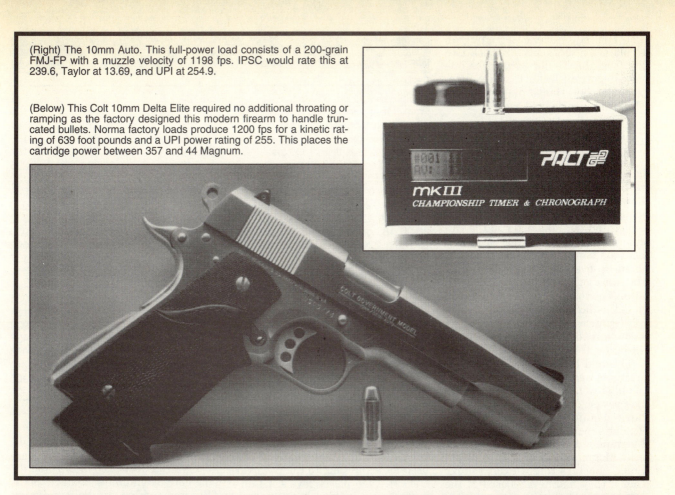

(Right) This 45 ACP produces 848 fps with a 230-grain FMJ-FP and a UPI rating of 165.6 (IPSC 195, Taylor 12.6). Both IPSC and Taylor KO would rate this more powerful than a 125-grain 357 Magnum at 1300 fps. The UPI formula would rate the two very nearly equal in power (see Table).

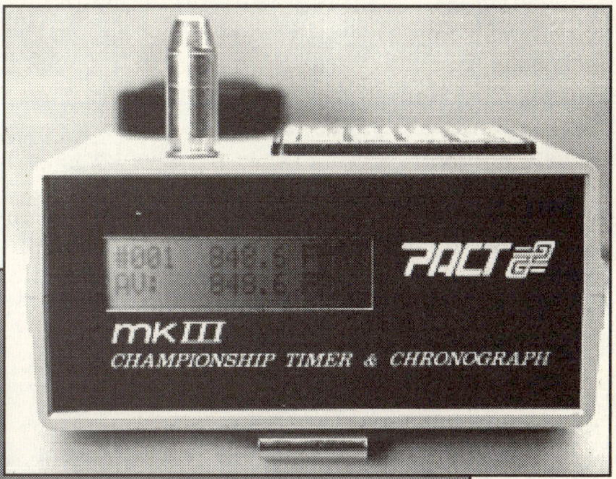

(Below) Series 70 version of John Browning's 1911 Colt Government Model. Designed to cycle .451-inch 230-grain "ball" (round-nose) ammo, throating and barrel ramping improve ability to feed truncated bullets for UPI velocity test. Custom work by Phoenix gunsmith Ted Yost.

127. His requirement for getting an elephant's attention is a KO of 60. In his formula, Taylor recognizes one very important factor that was mentioned earlier—bullet diameter (BD). His formula is defined as:

$$\text{Taylor KO} = \frac{(BW)}{7000} \times MV \times BD$$

I have read accounts which suggest that Taylor used bore diameter rather than bullet diameter in his formula, but the same accounts were using KO ratings based on both the bullet and bore diameter in the calculation. There are minor variations between bores from the same manufacturer, even between bullets from the same lot. There is very little variation between a 45 bore and a 458 bullet as far as it affects the results of Taylor's power ratings. As we know already, IPSC would have no variation at all.

The real limitation of the Taylor rating is again the abbreviated use of bullet weight and velocity to calculate power, even though the bullet or bore diameter is included. By Taylor's method, a 350 Remington Magnum out powers the 300 Weatherby Magnum (KO of 28.1 vs. 23.8). Some shooters might even believe that if they had never looked at the comparative ballistics on a computer. A 180-grain 300 Weatherby Magnum will actually deliver more kinetic energy at 300 yards than the 225-grain 350 Remington Magnum will deliver at 200 yards (2557 vs. 2305 foot pounds).

So why does Taylor's formula run amiss? Good news; bad news. The good news is Taylor includes bullet diameter; the bad news is that it is not included with anything useful. More specifically, the formula is light on energy, *making the bullet diameter more important than it should be* in a conservative analysis. In this case, a bullet of .358-inch diameter is given the edge over a bullet of .308-inch diameter even though careful consideration of overall ballistics would indicate otherwise. If you remove bullet diameter from Taylor's equation, all that's left are the same two variable parameters as the IPSC formula, bullet weight and simple velocity, with a different constant, 7000 instead of 1000. The same anomaly occurs with the 9mm edged out by the 38 Special. Clearly, simply including bullet diameter in the formula is not the final answer.

What may be obvious at this point is the idea of bullet diameter included in a formula utilizing true mass, gravitational acceleration and velocity. Following is a formula I have used for some time to compare various cartridge power levels. I find it useful for everything from my handguns to my high-power double rifles. I call it the Universal Power Index (UPI) and it looks like this:

$$\text{UPI} = \frac{\frac{(BW)}{(7000)(32.174)} x V^2}{2} x BD$$

While not quite as simplistic as IPSC, and a bit more elegant than Taylor, the Universal Power Index nonetheless provides a realistic measure of delivery power. Further, because it takes into account all scientific factors relating to energy (mass, gravitational acceleration, square of velocity and bullet diameter), the formula may be used to determine delivery power at any distance from the muzzle for which you can determine velocity. I have worked out the UPI for a number of common cartridge loadings in a nearby table with both the IPSC and Taylor ratings for comparison. Using the UPI formula, chamberings fall about where I would expect, including the 300 Weatherby and 350 Remington. Note that both IPSC and Taylor ratings show the 357 Magnum loading as less efficient than the 45 ACP and the 40 S&W.

It is easy to see that minor calibers on this index fall at about 100 UPI and below. Major handgun cartridges run about 150 to 250, and the big-bore magnum handguns to 500+. Big game rifles and light magnum rifles index up to about 1500 UPI with the light African magnums indexing at about 2000. At this point we reach Taylor's attention-getting level for elephant.

The big-bore African heavies index from about 2500 up to 7000+. Jeff Cooper's favorite, the 460 G&A Magnum, has demonstrated 3000 UPI to be about optimum for all big African varmints. The 460 Weatherby Magnum goes a bit beyond that and the old Cordite Nitros are obviously real neck snappers. The 8 Bore, with its 1200-grain solid moving at 1700 fps, would develop 7699 foot pounds of kinetic energy at the muzzle for a UPI rating of 7006. Compare that thump with a 9mm Auto!

In conclusion, it can be seen that the use of ammunition manufacturers' kinetic energy ratings, IPSC and Taylor power factors are useful for their intended purpose. They do, however, lack certain physics parameters necessary for high-resolution universal power comparisons. Mixing physics and common sense to combine accurate energy calculation with bullet diameter provides meaningful insight into power delivery ballistics. ●

COMPARATIVE POWER FACTORS

Caliber	IPSC	TKO	UPI
38 Spl., 158-gr. SP, 850 fps	134	6.84	91
9mm, 115-gr. FMJ, 1050 fps	120	6.12	100
40 S&W, 180-gr. FMJ, 950 fps	171	9.77	144
45 ACP, 230-gr. FMJ, 850 fps	195	12.60	166
357 Mag, 125-gr. JHP, 1300 fps	162	8.30	167
10mm, 200-gr. TMJ, 1200 fps	240	13.69	255
41 Mag, 210-gr. JHP, 1500 fps	315	18.50	430
44 Mag, 240-gr. JSP, 1500 fps	360	22.00	526
454 Casull, 260-gr., 1600 fps	416	26.90	670
30-30 Win, 150-gr., 2300 fps	345	15.20	542
30-06, 180-gr. SP, 2750 fps	495	21.80	930
350 Mag, 220-gr., 2500 fps	550	28.10	1092
300 Weatherby, 180-gr., 3000 fps	540	23.80	1107
338 Win. Mag, 250-gr., 2750 fps	688	33.20	1419
375 H&H Mag, 300-gr., 2450 fps	735	39.40	1499
416 Mag, 400-gr., 2375 fps	950	56.50	2083
458 Mag, 500-gr., 2050 fps	1025	67.10	2136
460 G&A, 500-gr., 2400 fps	1200	78.50	2928
460 Weatherby, 500-gr., 2600 fps	1300	85.10	3436
577 Nitro Express, 750-gr., 2050 fps	1537	126.70	4093
600 Nitro Express, 900-gr., 1950 fps	1755	150.40	4710
700 Nitro Express, 1000-gr., 1950 fps	1950	195.00	5909
8-Bore, 1200-gr., 1700 fps	2040	233.00	7006

Revolvers like this Model 57 S&W 41 Magnum easily fire light loads. Only half the weight is needed of Unique or Red Dot to achieve the approximate velocities of slower powders such as 2400. When developing a load for self-loading firearms, make sure the powder charge develops enough pressure to cycle the action.

Sometimes one of the most important considerations in handloading is...

by JOHN HAVILAND

SHOOTING FOR CHEAP

TALK ABOUT sticker shock. After driving to a "sale" at the local sporting goods store, I found factory-loaded ammunition costs at least 50 cents a shot, and the price of reloading supplies has gone the way of my blood pressure. I drove home with a few paltry items. To keep my firearms in forage, I had to come up with a number of ways to get more discharges for the dollar.

I am sure someone has found a way to recharge primers, but for the rest of us, the only way to save money on primers is to buy a lot of them on sale. I use one brand and type for as many firearms as possible. Rifles from 22-250 to 35 Whelen are all loaded with standard large rifle primers. For the 41 and 44 Magnums, standard primers work just as well as magnum primers. Buying standard instead of magnum primers saves ten cents per hundred.

Because of the variety of powders, money can be saved several ways. Instead of filling the case with a maximum of powder, a minimum charge saves around a penny per shot. My 41 Magnum revolver shoots, as a maximum load with a 210-grain bullet, 18

Cast bullet loads in rifles save not only on bullet cost but powder as well. The 7mm Magnum can be shot for pennies a round with a cast bullet and Unique powder.

grains of Hercules 2400 powder. My 30-06 shoots 59 grains of IMR-4350 powder every time the sear trips to eject a 150-grain bullet. For the sake of argument, say powder costs $12 a pound. That works out to 3.09 cents for powder per shot in the 41 and 10.1 cents in the 30-06.

By substituting a minimum load for the 41, a penny per shot is saved. Shooting a minimum, instead of a maximum, charge of IMR-4350 in my 30-06 saves only about half a penny.

But changing to a faster burning powder can cut powder expense by half in a handgun. Switching from 18 grains of 2400 to 8 grains of Red Dot powder saves me 10 grains of powder per shot while only losing 99 fps. By using a faster burning powder in my 30-06, like IMR-4895, I can save 2.3 cents a shot. (See Table 1.)

Allan Jones, of Blount, Inc., which manufactures Speer bullets and RCBS reloading equipment, said when he first started reloading he never considered the cost of powder. "Now that powder is up around $12 to $15 a pound, I think about it a lot," he told me.

Jones said by shooting IMR-4895 in his 30-06 instead of IMR-4831, he saves 10 grains of powder per shot. "If I am not looking for top velocity, but just a load for practice and enjoyment of my gun, I'll even go to a minimum charge of these faster powders to get even more loads per pound," he said.

But performance can suffer when a cartridge case is only partly filled with powder. Douglas Engh, of Hornady Mfg., pointed out that with reduced loads powder shifts to different positions in the case when the gun is raised and lowered. "This often leads to a wide deviation in velocity," he said. "In a handgun, the cost of powder is cheap, so shooting for cheap and shooting well are not necessarily the same."

Engh said he loads his handgun cartridges with a powder that almost fills the case. He shoots the same loads in practice as in competition. "I don't like surprises on the firing line," he said.

TABLE 1: POWDER COMPARISON AND SAVINGS

Load (Grs./Powder)	MV (fps)
41 Magnum, 210-Grain Bullet	
18.0/2400	1258
8.0/Red Dot	1159
30-06, 150-Grain Bullet	
59.0/IMR-4831	2861
49.5/IMR-4895	2865
45.5/IMR-4895	2621

An example of what Engh is talking about is my 25-06. Loaded with 75-grain bullets and a light charge of IMR-4320, and then increasing the charge a grain at a time, the velocity variation noticeably shrinks. Loads that essentially fill the case also tend to shoot tighter groups, although I have shot a few 2-inch groups at 300 yards with the light loads. (See Table 2.)

A chronograph test with a 38 Special and a 41 Magnum showed consistent results with light charges of powder. (See Table 2.)

Jones said a friend of his developed an accurate load for a target handgun and shot it for years. One day, the friend happened to test the load over a chronograph. The load had a wide velocity deviation, but still shot well. "At the short range of a pistol, this high velocity deviation in relation to accuracy is more theory than reality," Jones said.

Self-loading firearms are very particular about powders. Take a 30 Carbine of mine: By loading Unique instead of 2400 in a batch of reloads, I saved enough money to buy a candy bar. What I didn't consider was the Unique load did not build enough pressure to cycle the action. So now I have 300 30 Carbine shells, which I am slowly shooting one at a time.

One thing about lower pressure, though, is cases last much longer. I assembled a batch of mild 6mm Remington practice loads with 70-grain jacketed and 100-grain cast bullets. These cases are still going strong after twelve years and many, many loadings. On the other hand, maximum hunting loads for this rifle with 100-grain jacketed bullets last about eight firings.

Gas checks on cast bullets permit using less desirable alloys, like wheelweights.

Powder selection in rifle cartridges can save a couple of pennies a shot. Eleven grains of powder can be saved by using IMR-4320 instead of 4831 in a 7mm Magnum.

Engh owns a 32 H&R Magnum which is hard to find cases for, and they're expensive when he does. "When I reload them, I treat them like gold," he said.

Engh leaves the cases uncrimped to prolong their life. Constant belling of the mouth to accept the bullet, then crimping the edge to the bullet, chews the case mouths and causes them to split. "You don't need a crimp to hold the bullet tightly if you are just going to put the loaded rounds in a plastic box, then take them out and shoot them," Engh said.

At least one reloading manual states a heavy crimp is needed on handgun cartridges to hold bullets in place during recoil and on firing to retard the start of the bullet and give the powder time to fully burn. Again I took my chronograph and 41 Magnum revolver to the range. I measured the length of one uncrimped cartridge and left it in the cylinder while I shot ten others. The loaded round measured the same 1.63 inches when it came out as when I put it in.

I also recorded the velocity of the heavy and light loads with and without crimps. As Table 3 shows, for some reason, the crimp worked better with the light load, but not as well with the heavy load—which is the opposite of what the theory states.

Because cases are used over and again, their cost per shot is small. A bullet, though, is used only once. Engh said bullet selection is the best way to save money. He shoots swaged lead bullets in his handguns because they are so much cheaper than jacketed bullets. "Lead bullets are shot slower than jacketed bullets," he said, "so I don't have to worry about leading the bore."

Jones said while Blount sells swaged lead bullets, they cannot compete with local one-man operations who make and sell cast bullets with little overhead. "Before you make the initial investment for the equipment to cast your own bullets, you had better ask yourself if the money wouldn't be better spent on someone else's cast bullets or jacketed bullets," Jones told me. "You can buy a lot of jacketed bullets for what the equipment costs."

A look in the back of HANDLOADER'S DIGEST, 12th Ed., showed a retail price of $427 for all the RCBS equipment needed to cast pistol bullets. Half of that cost is for a Pro-Melt furnace. For years, I took a cheaper, yet satisfactory, route and melted my lead in a pot on a Coleman stove. I ladled the molten lead from the pot into the mould with a dipper. The pot and dipper cost only $20. The Pro-Melt furnace is easier and faster to use, of course.

After the equipment has been amortized, Jones said that cast bullet handgun loads cost about the same as 22 rimfire ammo.

For handgun velocities, the copper cup swaged onto the base of a cast bullet is an unneeded expense. "About the only reason to use a gas check on pistol bullets is so you can use softer alloys," Jones said. With linotype becoming scare, a person can add a gas check to bullets cast from softer wheelweights and still keep the bore from leading.

The jacketed bullet load with H-4831 powder in a 6mm Remington costs almost 20 cents a shot. In contrast, a 100-grain cast bullet with 9 grains of Unique costs only 4 cents.

Before Jones went to work for Blount, he worked in a crime lab in Texas. In his work, he recovered and studied bullets shot into a water tank. The water stopped the bullets without distorting them.

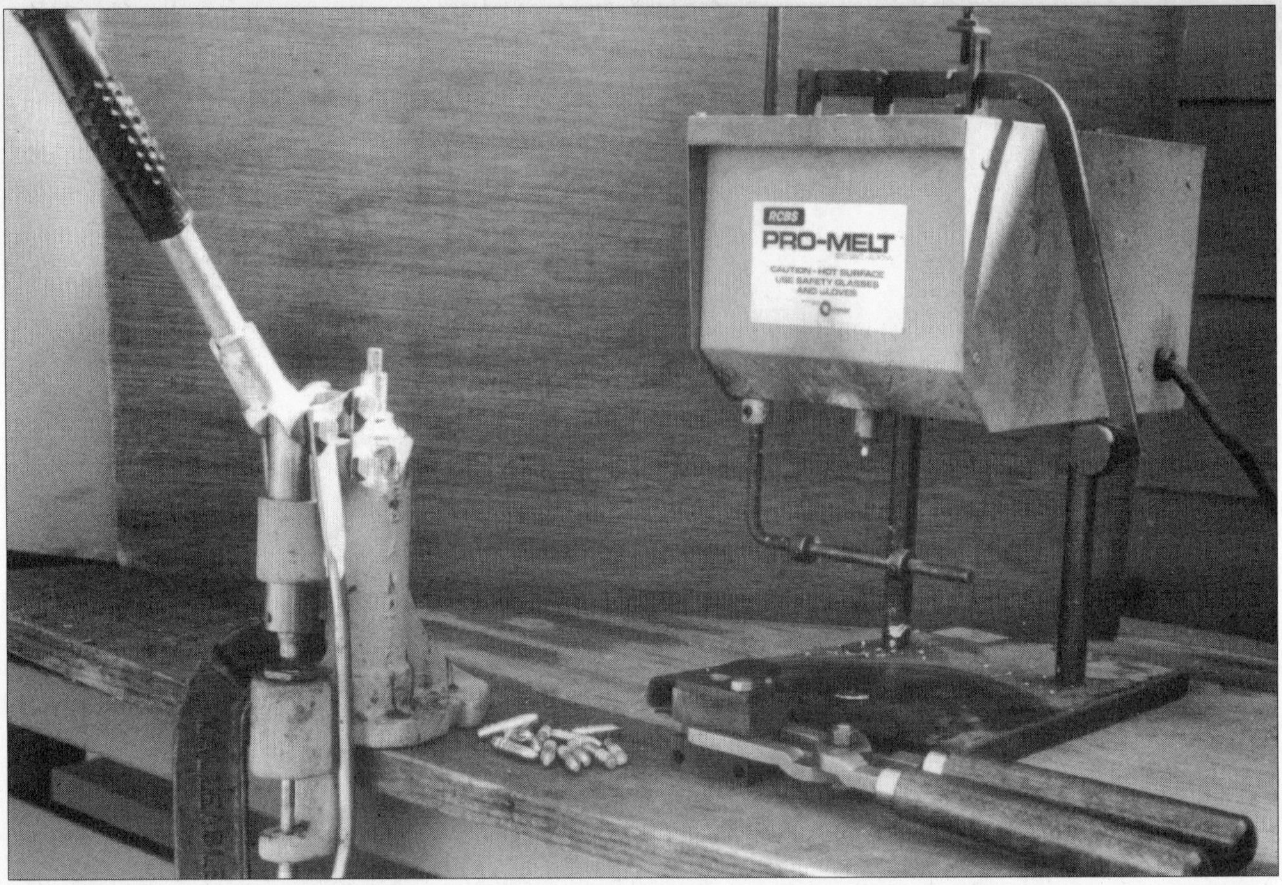

All the equipment you need to cast bullets: an RCBS mould, Pro-Melt furnace and Lub-A-Matic lubricator-sizer.

"I noticed the base of lead bullets did not melt," Jones said. "If anything, the gas cut around the sides of the bullets." He noticed bullets with square bases swelled slightly to fill the bore and kept powder gas from forcing past the bullet.

A square base is essential for cast bullets shot at higher velocity from rifles. "A gas check at the higher velocities keeps the bullet base square. The powder gas hits the gas check and flattens it to seal the bore," Jones said.

Some of the more affluent authorities recommend buying several mould designs to see which bullet design shoots the best in a particular firearm. With the price of a double-cavity mould from $40 to $100, I will take my chances that one mould will produce accurate bullets. Jones recommends trying several different powders instead as a cheaper alternative. "There's one powder out there that is going to work better with a particular bullet design than any of the others," he said.

In my 6mm Remington, Unique shoots 100-grain cast bullets very well. The bullets poke along at 1453 fps, but have an extreme velocity spread of only 8 fps and group well at 50 yards. My son, who has just started shooting big game rifles, shoots these 6mm loads as fast as I can seat the bullets.

Practicing is where I save the money on rifle bullets. When my son wants to take the 6mm or his 7mm-08 to the range to rehearse for the morning when a buck will step out of the forest, I supply him with plenty of cast bullet loads for only pennies apiece. The recoil of these loads is slight. That lets him concentrate on aiming and squeezing.

However, cast bullets have not replaced jacketed bullets for hunting.

TABLE 2: POWDER WEIGHT AND UNIFORM VELOCITY

Bullet (Wgt. Grs.)	Bullet (Type)	Load (Grs./Powder)	MV (fps)	Standard Deviation
25-06 Remington				
Ruger M-77, 24-inch barrel. L.C. military cases necked down.				
75	Hornady	46/IMR-4320	3406	83
75	Hornady	47/IMR-4320	3450	61
75	Hornady	48/IMR-4320	3455	50
75	Hornady	49/IMR-4320	3484	30
38 Special				
Model 19 S&W, 4-inch barrel.				
150	Cast	4.0/Unique	638	16
150	Cast	3.7/W-231	699	22
41 Magnum				
Ruger Blackhawk, 6.5-inch barrel.				
210	Cast	18.0/2400	1258	62
210	Cast	7.0/Red Dot	1032	10

Middle of skyscreens of Oehler Model 33 Chronotach is 15 feet from muzzle.

Jacketed bullets allow much higher velocities and expand better than cast. When opening morning comes and a buck is standing at the far side of a park, a jacketed bullet is worth the dime and a nickel it costs.

Going to a plumbing supply house or junkyard to buy alloys for casting takes some of the fun out of shooting for cheap. I prefer to scrounge my materials.

One of my ancestors must have rubbed the picture off every coin he owned before it passed from his hand. Whoever it was, I have a hunch he is from my maternal side of the family. My mother always finds a deal. Every Saturday, she cruises the garage sales. I usually go along, because the best bargains for shooting components are from people cleaning their attics and basements.

This past spring I read a classified ad for an estate sale at the edge of town. The ad read "50 years of good stuff."

The sale was at an old farmhouse and barn that, over the years, the expanding town had overtaken. Rusted tractor parts and tools for non-existent machinery lined the yard. But in the middle of it all stood tables of bullets, lead shot, powders, cartridge cases, shotgun shells, wads and factory and reloaded rifle and shotgun shells.

Old loading manuals often found at garage sales contain a wealth of cast bullet and obsolete cartridge loading data.

Factory 6mm jacketed bullets cost at least a dime apiece, while cast bullets cost, at most, three pennies.

TABLE 3: CRIMP OR NO CRIMP

	MV (fps)	SD
41 Magnum		
18.5/2400, 210-grain cast bullet		
Crimp	1282	18
No Crimp	1294	18
7.0/Red Dot, 210-grain cast bullet		
Crimp	1032	12
No Crimp	1015	20

I prefer to leave reloaded cartridges alone, because of the possibility of blowing up my gun with someone else's reloading mistake. Unless cartridge cases are new or once fired, I also avoid them. The first time you reload them, they might all separate at the head. About the only way to tell if they have been fired once is if the factory primer is still in place, such as the brass-colored primer in Remington cartridges. Shotgun shells are a different matter. As long as the shell mouths are not ragged, they are fine.

I bought one box of 12-gauge reloads for $1. I bought them primarily for the Herter's plastic box they came in. I also bought wads and bullets at giveaway prices. The best buy of the day was a dollar for a box, missing four shells, of 3-inch magnum Federal 12-gauge shells.

At other yard and estate sales, I have bought linotype bullet metal in 20-pound ingots, factory-loaded 38 Specials, rifle shells in plastic Case-Gard boxes, and old shooting and hunting books and reloading manuals. These old manuals, such as the old Lyman Ideal handbooks numbers 39, 40 and 41, have a wealth of loading information for cast bullets and obsolete cartridges, such as the 348 Winchester, 35 Winchester and 38-40 WCF, and loads for a variety of cast bullet weights.

Yet for all the sweating over the casting pot and penny pinching at the garage sales, I haven't really saved a dime. I have just ended up buying more components and shooting more. But that's what shooting for cheap is all about. •

John Buhmiller with a very nice Cape buffalo taken on his first trip to Tanganyika Territory in 1955. Rifle is a 505 Gibbs which he built on a modified M1917 Enfield action. He also designed and installed the muzzlebrake, which reduced recoil significantly.

Many Americans have distinguished themselves in the gamefields of Africa, but one stands alone at the summit of hunting achievements. This is the story of the old Montana rifle-barrel maker who truly walked a special path....

John Buhmiller— In The Footsteps of Selous

by JACK LOTT

IN MY OPINION, the late John Riley Buhmiller, more than any other American, is the man who followed most closely the hunting tradition of Selous. Frederick Courteney Selous was, of course, generally conceded to be the greatest of all hunter-naturalists in what might be called the golden age of African hunting. He was an Englishman

Another typical crop-raiding elephant that fell to a Buhmiller magnum—probably a cow, as they are often the aggressive leaders of raider-herds. Though a poor "trophy," such elephants are fast and extremely dangerous to those who hunt them.

John R. Buhmiller and one of the many crop-raiding Cape buffalo bulls he took in Tanganyika, East Africa, in the mid-to-late '50s.

whose hunting, natural history fieldwork, exploration, soldiering and writing brought worldwide acclaim. Capt. F.C. Selous, DSO, FRGS, was shot dead as he led an attack on German troops at Beho Beho Ridge, Tanganyika, in 1917 at age 65.

John Buhmiller was born in 1893 in the state of Indiana. When his family moved to California, John worked in the timber country. After moving to Montana, he became a cowboy and acquired many of the outdoor skills which were so useful to him as an amateur naturalist and big game hunter. He was a voracious reader of the best literature on exploration and natural history—books by Selous, Baldwin, Stigand, Theodore Roosevelt, and others of their rank. Buhmiller returned to Indiana, where he learned the trade of railroad telegrapher, and in that capacity later went back to Montana, where he experienced nature on a grand scale and where following game spoor seldom led to a barbed wire fence.

In 1914, Buhmiller joined the Whitefish Rifle Club, which led to his membership on Montana's state rifle team. In 1931, he shot in the 1000-yard Wimbledon match at Camp Perry, and the following year joined forces with Harvey Lovell, the wildcatter-shooting competitor who designed the long-popular 22 Lovell. They bought a lot of barrels which turned out to be of inferior quality, so John bought some barrel-making machinery with the intention of making his own. The machinery was not the best quality either, but by modifying it, making new parts, and paying close attention to countless details, he began producing what many riflemen claimed were the best barrels in America since those of the great Harry Pope. His Kalispell, Montana, shop became a mecca for match shooters and the new breed of wildcatters.

By 1948, Buhmiller was producing 3500 to 4000 barrels annually. That year, Jack O'Connor, *Outdoor Life*'s shooting editor, wrote an article on the remarkable groups he was obtaining from a Buhmiller 257 Roberts barrel. In 1952, the Dewar Cup was won by C.R. Carter of Great Britain with a Buhmiller barrel (I don't know the caliber), and in 1953 Col. Crawford Hollidge, a well-known rifleman of the day, fired a ten-shot .264-inch group at 100 yards with an 18-pound 219 Donaldson Wasp built on a Mauser action with a Buhmiller barrel fitted and chambered by Bob Wallack.

Buhmiller's personal 1000-yard Wimbledon rifle was a bullpup he built on an M1917 Enfield single shot action. It had a 30-inch barrel chambered for the 300 Hoffman, a sharp-shouldered version of the 300 H&H Magnum. The long barrel produced a healthy extra measure of muzzle velocity and reduced muzzle blast and flash with no increase over a normal powder charge.

I believe John is credited with being the originator of the bullpup concept; if not, he was certainly one of the early users. This design is seldom seen nowadays, so I'll say that a bullpup is a rifle of much shorter than normal overall length due to the metal parts being moved backward so that the action is near the buttplate. A 30-inch-barrel bullpup is shorter than a conventionally stocked bolt action with a 24-inch barrel. The idea never became popular, but is sound—if you are like John, in that resting your face essentially atop the action while you touch off a cartridge creating 50,000 psi pressure is not a psychological hazard.

Tanganyika bull elephant crop-raider dropped by Buhmiller with a single shot from one of his 45-caliber wildcats. Fundi, John's tracker, holds the Buhmiller custom Brevex-action Mauser.

In 1940, Buhmiller obtained a U.S. patent for an action, the configuration of which I regret not knowing. Chances are it was a single shot action intended for match use, as such a rifle is pictured in Elmer Keith's classic book, *Keith's Rifles for Large Game* (Standard Publications, Huntington, West Virginia, 1946). Commenting on it, Keith wrote:

> John Buhmiller made by hand the finest and most accurate single shot action I have ever seen or used. It allowed perfect placement of the firing hand, had an adjustable trigger pull, and firing pin travel was very short. The action was large and heavy enough to stand the pressure of any shoulder rifle load now in existence, and gas from a punctured primer had no chance to come back into the shooter's eye...I honestly believe it was the finest single shot action I have ever seen or used.

Having long realized the advantages of large-caliber magnum rifles for dangerous game, John, being no big-bore masochist, undertook experiments to develop an effective muzzlebrake. To test its effectiveness on kick, he devised a mechanical setup to measure free recoil, and eventually developed a brake which reduced recoil a measured 40 percent. Unfortunately, the effectiveness of a muzzlebrake seems measurable by the amount of awful blast its vents jet rearward. Nearly deaf from years of such punishment, John describes himself as having "callused ears."

In 1955, after considerable correspondence with an English farmer in Tanganyika, John accepted an invitation to visit his farm near Arusha. John made up a battery of rifles on Model 1917 Enfield and Brevex magnum Mauser actions, shipped them off by sea, and enplaned for Africa. The battery included a 458 Winchester Magnum, a 378 Weatherby Magnum, a 505 Gibbs, a 416 Rigby, and a straight 450 belted magnum. This 450 used Norma cylindrical H&H belted brass and Barnes copper tubing jacketed 500-grain soft-nose and solid bullets, and Kynoch 480-grain bullets made for their 450 Nitro Express. Also in the battery was another big wildcat which I call the 458 Buhmiller. It was built on the 378 Weatherby case necked up to use 458 bullets—a configuration which many large-bore riflemen will recognize as essentially today's 460 Weatherby Magnum.

In the 458 Buhmiller, John used the 500-grain Barnes solid ahead of 100 grains of IMR-4320 as his working load (velocity unspecified). In the 450 straight belted magnum, he used the 500-grain bullet and 90 grains of 4320, which gave a velocity of 2350 fps. For the big 458 Buhmiller, he developed extra-powerful fodder about which he wrote to P.O. Ackley:

> It can be loaded with a case full of 4350 (115 grains) for 2700 fps with the 480-grain Kynoch, or 2650 fps using the Barnes 500-grain solid. Outside of some special emergency, nothing more is needed than 100 grains of 4320 and a 500-grain bullet. But you can carry a couple of "blockbusters" in your pocket just in case.

The above quote is from a letter in Ackley's *Handbook for Shooters and Reloaders*, where John also wrote:

> The 458 Winchester proved very satisfactory, completely adequate for elephant and rhino. The buffalo is the tough one of the lot, in this area of heavy brush...and we found the 450 Magnum and the 45 Weatherby were undoubtedly slightly better killers on buffalo than the 458...I would be inclined to favor the 450 Magnum using the full-length Norma case...magazine capacity is greater and it will work nicely in an FN Mauser action, which will make into a lighter gun than a Brevex.

Buhmiller had an interesting technique for ensuring ignition of his bigbore magnums. He dropped a second primer into the case along with the powder. Doubtless it helped ignite the large powder charge, but with such magnum primers as today's fine Federal 215, I have found no need for such an ingenious trick.

Buhmiller's farmer host was suffering costly depredations by crop-raiding elephant and Cape buffalo when John arrived, and had appealed to the Game Department for help in controlling the nightly raiders. But the game rangers were snowed under elsewhere, so the farmer had been left to deal with the problem as best he could. When discussing this with Buhmiller, John volunteered to take up the spoor of the crop raiders on a regular basis, providing the Game Department licensed him, which it did after the farmer testified to John's ability. By this time, John had taken a buffalo and an elephant on his general hunting license, starting out before dawn with no breakfast and accompanied only by Fundi, a native tracker, with whom he communicated through the

As well as being an ardent hunter, Buhmiller was also a naturalist and game cinematographer, with a deep interest in all wildlife. Here he faces an alert grizzly in Alaska, with only a loaded camera in hand.

few words and phrases each knew of the other's language.

From that beginning, over at least a half-dozen months-long hunts, Buhmiller spoored down and shot hundreds of destructive elephants and buffalo, plus occasional specimens of other dangerous game species and numerous antelope needed for food. All of this hunting was done on his own, without the guidance and protection of a professional hunter, although he was occasionally accompanied by the farmer or a local friend, and almost always by Fundi. I have no exact account of John's buffalo and elephant kills, and am not sure he did either, although he kept fairly detailed diaries of his African hunts. But there's no doubt that no other American hunter, at least of modern times, can match his tally and the on-his-own way that he took them.

John Buhmiller would be called a big-bore man by those who think in terms of such superficial categorizing. But he is perhaps better termed a pragmatic man in that he didn't enjoy taking heavy recoil or carrying for miles under tropical conditions rifles weighing over 10 pounds. Before arriving in Africa, Buhmiller had seen the results of using small calibers on large and sometimes dangerous game in North America. Yes, a 30-06 with a 220-grain full-jacketed bullet or a solid brass homogeneous slug can kill a Cape buffalo or elephant if quick-stopping is not required, but such calibers, even in overbore magnums, lack the frontal bullet area that gives maximum stopping power. And they often drill heavy bones instead of smashing them as 450 and larger calibers with 480- to 500-grain solids traveling at 2150 to 2350 fps often do. That is why Kenya's Wild Animals Protection Act, Chapter 376 of the laws of Kenya, specified, "Category (1) Elephant, rhino, buffalo, hippo: Do not use a rifle of less than caliber 400. Persons with experience do use the 375 Magnum, but it is on the light side and has caused frequent woundings, especially of buffalo. The buffalo is the hardest animal to kill, and some will try to kill them with too light a rifle. Category (2) Lion, leopard, eland: Do not use a weapon smaller than a 375 Magnum (excluding the 375 Mannlicher-Schoenauer [9.5x57] but including the 9.3 Mauser). In following up wounded lion and leopard in thick bush, an effective weapon is a shotgun (12-bore) loaded with SSG."

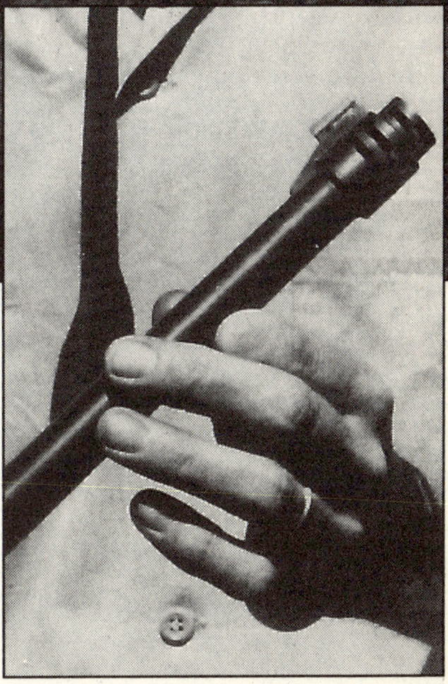

Buhmiller's muzzlebrake design on one of his heavy caliber magnum wildcats. According to Buhmiller's tests, it reduced recoil 40 percent.

The collective experience of generations of African hunters dictated the correctness of these restrictions, and John did not need convincing in order to accept them. He wrote:

> On a regular safari, one will be watched by his professional hunter, and if danger threatens, he will be protected. He can, to a large extent, choose the caliber of rifle he wishes to use. But if he does use a 375 Magnum, most likely his white hunter will do most of his big game killing after the first shot is fired.

As my choice for a general game caliber for antelope, zebra and pigs, I have taken several hundred African animals, mostly for meat, with my 375 Holland-Mauser, using mostly 300-grain bullets. But aside from unwounded lion and leopard, I do not overtax the abilities of this great cartridge by using it on dangerous game. And like Buhmiller, I recommend as minimum a 458 full-length magnum which fires 500-grain bullets at 2300-2350 fps for reliable quick-killing of Cape buffalo and elephant when the shoulder, spine or brain is penetrated.

I am reminded of two near-fatal incidents where experienced hunters used inadequate calibers on lion and buffalo and survived only through luck and good surgery. Frans Harmse of Springs, Transvaal Province, South Africa, had taken several lions using a 30-06, and one day wounded a huge male which went into some thick bush. In the follow-up, it charged Harmse, who was using a 30-06 although he had a 375 Magnum along. Harmse's hands, arms and legs were horribly mangled. He hit the lion two more times at very close range, knocking it down with his first shot and again after it got up. Meanwhile, he was charged by a lioness, which he stopped with a spine shot. Several of his shots on the male were well placed and would have proved fatal, but they had insufficient stopping power. A heavier caliber, or at least his 375 (though a mediocre charge stopper) might have spared Harmse his mauling.

In the second incident, Tony Challis, a professional with Safari South, hit a buffalo bull a client had wounded, just after the client fired. The 300-grain bullet from his 378 clipped the top of a lung, as it was dropping. In the follow-up in thick bush, Challis was charged by a different buffalo after firing into its chest from only a few feet off. The bull hooked Challis, impaling him on a curved horn and lifting him aloft like a rag doll. Challis managed to heave himself up and off of his hook and, covered with both his and the buff's blood, he brained it.

The first buffalo had dropped when it took the client's bullet, but was gone when the spot was reached.

Challis had mistakenly thought his BRNO ZKK-602 would perform better on buffalo, elephant and lion when rechambered to the 378 Weatherby, so he had this done by Ritchie, the famous gunsmith of Florida, Transvaal. But the extra velocity only means more penetration for a solid bullet and, due to its higher striking velocity, less penetration with expanding bullets. As I see it, Challis and others, impressed by higher muzzle energies with identical medium-caliber bullets, draw the wrong conclusions, not realizing that giving a particular weight 30 or 375 bullet a lot more velocity only makes that caliber perform equally to the standard round but at longer range.

I don't know if Challis learned the obvious lesson from this near-fatal encounter since he, George Bates and Boet Dannhauser, all professionals with Safari South, died in a plane crash en route to examine a new hunting area when Bates' light aircraft slammed against the ridge of the Zoutpanberg Mountains, killing all aboard.

This is the Aberdare Forest buffalo bull that ran over Buhmiller and gave him his closest shave in his game-control hunting career before John freed a jammed round, rechambered it and brained the "mbogo."

Buhmiller had declared himself a magazine rifle man, but that changed a bit when he was invited to cull crop-raiding buffalo by a Kenya farmer named Preston who grew wheat in the White Highlands on the edge of the Aberdare Forest. The Aberdares are wet bamboo jungle, the home of the bongo, giant forest hog, buffalo and rhino. The buffalo raid the fields at night, then spend the daylight hours in dense bamboo thickets.

For this Burma-like hunting, John had brought along a 475 No. 2 double rifle and his 450 full-length magnum on the Norma cylindrical H&H belted case. In the latter, he used 85 grains of 4320 and 500-grain Barnes soft-noses with the bases forward. He lent this 450 to Githetu, his Kikuyu hunter-tracker.

Well into the bamboo, John heard the 450 roar three times, then five shots from another's 9.3x62 Mauser. Githetu rushed to him, saying he was out of ammo.

"I have plenty of ammo," John said, "I'll go in and get him!" He exchanged guns with Githetu, who led John to where the buff had last been seen. They had barely reached the spot when the bull charged from pointblank. Only a small bush stood between John and the bull as it came full force. At 15 feet, John planted a reversed 500-grain soft-nose in the shoulder. The bull staggered, then resumed the charge. To gain time and space to continue the fight, John moved backward, working the bolt. With the muzzle all but touching the buff's neck, John pulled the trigger. Only a *click* sounded. A misfire at the moment of truth! Jerking the bolt open, John saw that the reversed soft-nose round had not fed from the magazine. Then he tripped over a small bush and was flat on his back when the bull slid much of his weight onto John's lap. Eyeball to eyeball and mutually unpleasant reactions made it a brief *frente a frente*. Then the bull clambered to his feet and John scrambled away to find his rifle, which had been knocked out of his hands at the collision. With his pocketknife, he pried the stuck case free and slammed the round into the chamber. The buff was standing nearby, very sick, when John fired at its massive head. The unmistakable whine of an exiting or ricocheting bullet sounded and Preston shouted, "Shoot him again!" But the reversed soft-nose had penetrated clear through the skull, horns and all.

John was chagrined at not being able to find out what had caused the failure to feed, as he had previously worked all the reversed-bullet rounds through the action. Perhaps it had been his tentative time to die, but the Red Gods demurred. Had John's first shot killed the buff, its full weight would have come down on his legs and crushed them. Instead, he spent an eternity of seconds eye-to-eye at bad-breath range with the world's most dangerous animal.

Back home in Kalispell, John decided to build another mega-magnum for just such occasions. He decided to open the 378 Weatherby case to accept the 500-grain bullet of the 470 Nitro Express. But later he concluded that nothing more was needed for quick kills and stopping on buffalo (the real tough one) than his 450 Magnum on the full-length basic H&H case using 90 grains of 4320 and a 500-grain bullet at about 2350 fps.

Recognizing the importance of bullet design on the dangerous African game, Buhmiller created many versions and tested them on wood and steel plate. Some were homogeneous copper solids with conical concavities. For others, he melted the cores from WW 510-grain 458 soft-noses and soldered Nosler 375-caliber Partition bullets inside. Other designs included 458 solids made with jackets formed from 45 ACP cases.

One of his last projects was a 423 Magnum on the 378 Weatherby case.

> If one should want a cannon in this caliber, I used the 378 Weatherby shell opened up to 423, most of the taper removed for maximum powder capacity, getting with 125 grains of 4831 and 400-grain bullet, and 120 grains 4320 and 300-grain bullets—just altogether too much velocity. With the 500-grain Barnes and 120 grains of 4831, about 2700 fps velocity.

Elsewhere, Buhmiller, always the compulsive experimenter, wrote:

> Also more work on the 475 using empty 30-06 cases as the jacket...another pretty good idea. The 475 solid in my belted 475 worked so good for me. I killed 80 elephants with the plain factory bullet (Kynoch 500-grain 475 solid), which seemed plenty deadly—must have keyholed on entering.

His biggest wildcat was a 500 Buhmiller on the 378 or 460 Weatherby case, but he never used it in Africa.

By 1965, John's reputation as a top elephant and buffalo control hunter-rifleman had spread to southern Africa, where the Africaners (Boers) called him "Uncle John" or "Oom Janie" as a term of respect. The great Kenya professional Eric Rundgren had a special contract to cull a large number of buffalo in Botswana's Chobe District. John was invited to help and impressed all with his hunting and shooting ability. Rundgren spoke of John's 45-caliber belted wildcat as, "That bloody great cannon with the hotted-up bullets."

In a letter written after his return from his 1965 Botswana buffalo cull, John wrote:

> As things now stand, I feel the load mentioned on the sheet by John Burger (450 straight belted magnum on Norma H&H brass), 90 grains of 4320 and 458 500-grain solid with which I killed 11 buffalo with 13 shots, is the best I've come up with. Will try to make it serve as my high water mark on buffalo loads, although it seems very small chance I will ever hunt buff again. But can I hope?

He also observed:

> The old Mauser "wing" safety is preferred because the tracker will spot it and put it right if it goes off proper position. After doing a lot of experimenting, I settled on an open iron rear sight with a wide shallow V and a straight blade front painted white. On elephant control, I found we came onto them about noon in heaviest timber and I tried a 1/4-inch peep, but my best shooting was with open sights, and when your shots are at short range, the above is the best you can do.

When he wasn't hunting, Buhmiller often fished. if circumstances permitted it. In this photo taken on the banks of the Nile River, John poses with a morning's catch of monstrous Nile perch. He didn't mention whether his bait was "magnum" type.

Written before his Kenya Aberdare bamboo jungle hunt was this:

> I used a magazine rifle always. A double rifle does not suit my requirements for this sort of shooting where one should have five or six shots available without reloading. The above mentioned charge came after I had just dropped two elephants. The third came for me. I was ready and dropped number three without incident. With a double rifle I'd have been hard pressed to get it loaded in time—and there's little use to run!

Despite his high reputation among experienced dangerous-game hunters, John was not admired by a few trophy hunters who sought big tusks. One now deceased wealthy tusk hunter wrote him a number of poison pen letters, commenting caustically about the poor ivory of many of the elephants John had shot on control. Animals taken on such hunting are often cows, of course, and even culled bulls rarely have trophy ivory. But elephants are not cropped for trophies. Hunting crop-raiders is also more dangerous than most trophy ivory hunting. John dismissed this hostile letter writer as follows:

> He is merely a mentally disturbed dilettante and having his own troubles. Whenever a letter comes from him I'll mark it "Return to sender. Suspected pornographic material."

John was proud of the praise Eric Rundgren accorded him when he said: "He's the finest shot we've ever had out here, except for a Chief of Staff whose name I forget."

Despite several mild strokes and obviously failing powers, John in 1974 was homesick for Africa and wrote to me while I was on an extended trip in Rhodesia that year: "If that 600 (double rifle) sells, I'll most likely be on my way again. A fellow hates to quit."

"Quit" in any context did not apply to John Buhmiller. His enthusiasm, intellectual curiosity, and thirst for adventure remained youthful to the end. But age—the wearing out of that organic plumbing known as the cardiovascular system—meant his body could no longer keep pace with the commands of a youthful brain. On July 13, 1975, John Riley Buhmiller died peacefully. No more would the sound of his great rifles echo through the African forests. No more would the whisper of persistent footsteps signal the approach of the Montana hunter of buffalo and elephants. America had lost its greatest hunter of the world's largest and most dangerous game. ●

ACCURACY EXPERIMENTS WITH A RUGER NO. 1 338 MAGNUM

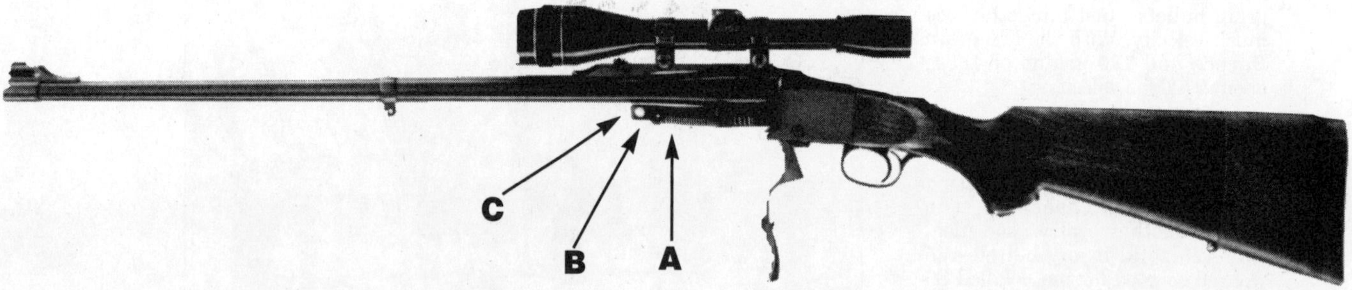

Model 1-S Ruger No. 1, SN132-90528, used for experimenting, sans forearm. For best accuracy, Bosselman says, it is critical that the forearm be properly bedded to the receiver extension at A and free-floated to the barrel. B indicates the primary contact point for the forearm; and C shows the necessary gap between the extension and the barrel (especially important with heavy barreled models) for top accuracy. Scope is a Leupold M8-8x; stock has a Pachmayr Slip-On recoil pad to increase pull length to fit Bosselman.

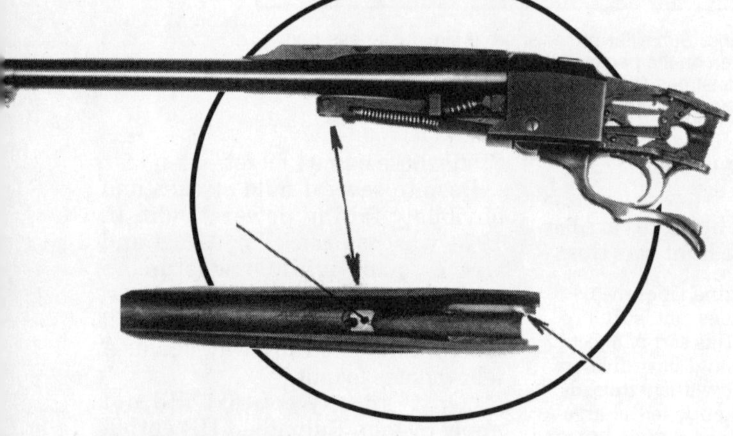

Very important contact points, forearm to receiver extension; forearm must be properly glass-bedded. Double arrow indicates assembly position.

FIREARMS, LIKE virtually everything else, are highly individualistic. One of the prerequisites to obtaining optimum and consistent accuracy levels in production-grade rifles is the touch of a qualified gunsmith for correct bedding of the stocks. In addition to this, while most longarms will shoot okay with many factory loadings, or with some untailored handloads, experimentation with several brands or loads of ammunition with bullet weights and styles conducive to the type(s) of hunting or shooting to be done is usually a requirement for top performance.

To illustrate these points, I obtained a new Ruger No. 1 Single Shot Rifle in 338 Winchester Magnum caliber, a fine-quality production-grade rifle of exceptional design that is indeed capable of producing superb levels of hunting rifle accuracy.

From a benchrest-supported shooting position, I believe a varmint rifle needs an accuracy level of about 1/2-inch at 100 yards; for a stalking rifle (plains and mountains hunting), 3/4-inch to 1 1/4 inches, with my recommendation of 1-inch or smaller, is excellent. For timber and brush hunting of the larger game animals, especially dangerous species animals from the Alaskan big bears to African Cape buffalo, 2 1/2 inches or smaller for 100-yard groups is good. But, since most all of the big-bore and Express-caliber guns can be made to shoot between 1 and 2 inches at that distance, if not even less, while still

Bosselmann has been a No. 1 aficionado for more than twenty years, and regularly uses a baker's dozen of them in the U.S., Canada, Alaska and Africa. Here are the results of some of his work with one of this single shot Ruger's largest calibers...

by KARL BOSSELMANN

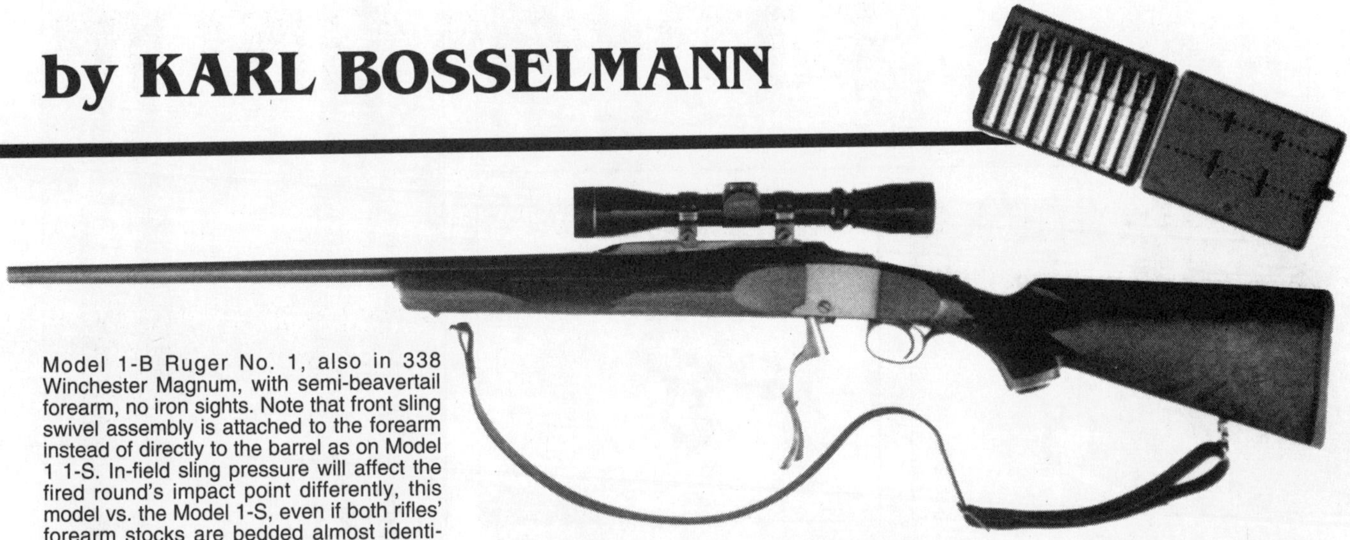

Model 1-B Ruger No. 1, also in 338 Winchester Magnum, with semi-beavertail forearm, no iron sights. Note that front sling swivel assembly is attached to the forearm instead of directly to the barrel as on Model 1 1-S. In-field sling pressure will affect the fired round's impact point differently, this model vs. the Model 1-S, even if both rifles' forearm stocks are bedded almost identically. Even slight manufacturing variations can produce quite different results. MTM ammo wallet in upper right hand corner—an extremely handy item. Scope is a Leupold Vari-X II, 2-7x; carrying strap is by Hunter.

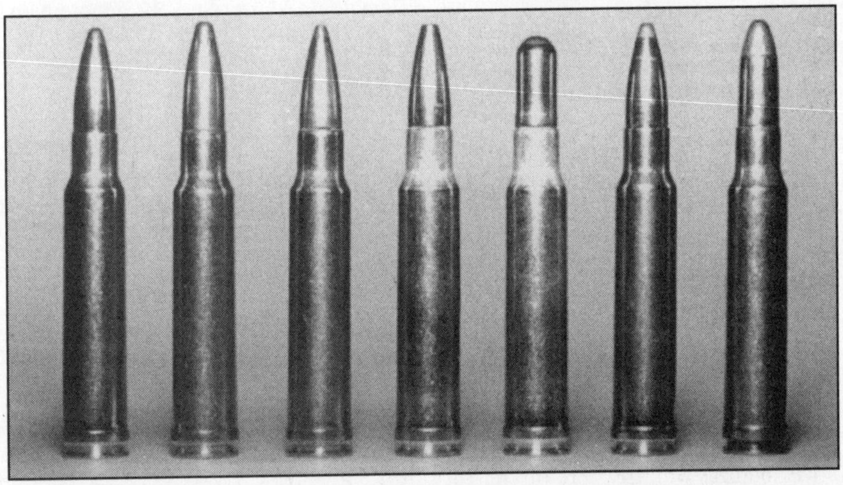

Commercially loaded cartridges Nos. 1 through 7 as accuracy tested by Bosselman. From left: Federal Premium Safari 250-grain NPB, Winchester 200-grain PP, Winchester 225-grain SP, Remington 250-grain PSP, A-Square Dead Tough 250-grain SP, Federal Premium 250-grain NPB, Western 250-grain ST.

retaining optimum functioning reliability, there's no valid reason to not achieve such levels of accuracy. If your rifle produces excellent accuracy afield, this will allow a slight bit more shooter error without reducing the likelihood of a clean kill with the first shot.

In a recent conversation with the customer service manager of Sturm, Ruger & Co., he made the following statements concerning No. 1 Single Shot Rifle accuracy:

•[Here at the factory]...the No. 1s shoot right along with our Model 77 bolt action; they're very accurate.

•Pressure-bed the lightweight barrels; float *or* pressure-bed the varmint barrels and those of the heavy 458s.

•A correctly bedded forearm is described as follows: It does not allow contact of its bottom (rear) radius with the receiver lip—a space of about .003-inch or slightly more is necessary; it has solid contact with the vertical lines of the front of the receiver; it has standard pressure contact at the large diameter portion of the barrel; and it has the middle section floated, but with slight upward pressure at the forearm tip against the barrel of about 3 to 6 pounds.

The chart on page 109 shows:

•Accuracy variations (i.e., group sizes) with an assortment of factory-produced ammunition.

•Some impact (group placement) variations produced by these rounds.

•Accuracy variations and improvements achieved by: Removing the forearm from the new rifle (correct forearm fit is vitally important to top accuracy).

•Group comparison after firing approximately 150 rounds through the barrel.

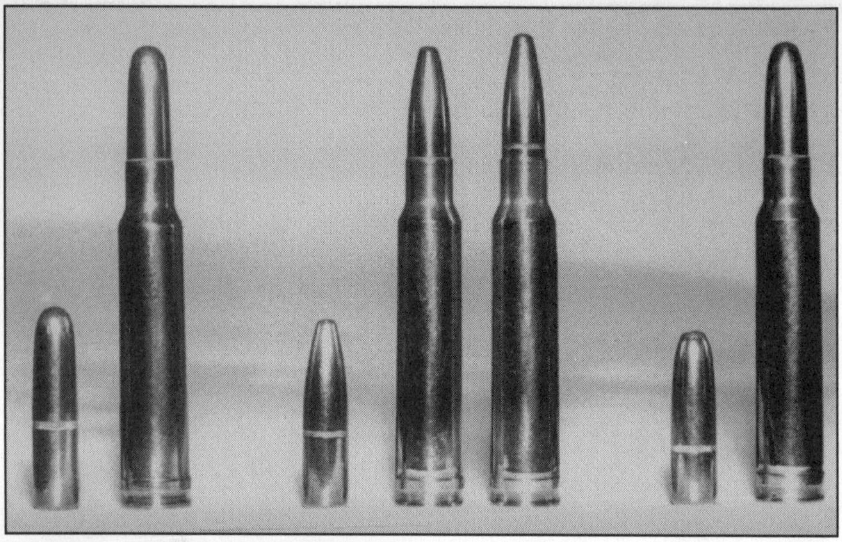

(Left) From left: FACTORY: Cartridge No. 10 and a pulled bullet: Winchester Super-Speed, 300-grain Power Point. HANDLOADS: Cartridge No. 11 and bullet used: New Remington full-length-sized case and 250-grain Speer Grand Slam. Cartridge No. 12: Same but with bullet seated out to contact chamber throat. Cartridge No. 13 and bullet used: New Remington full-length-sized case and 250-grain Hornady round-nose softpoint.

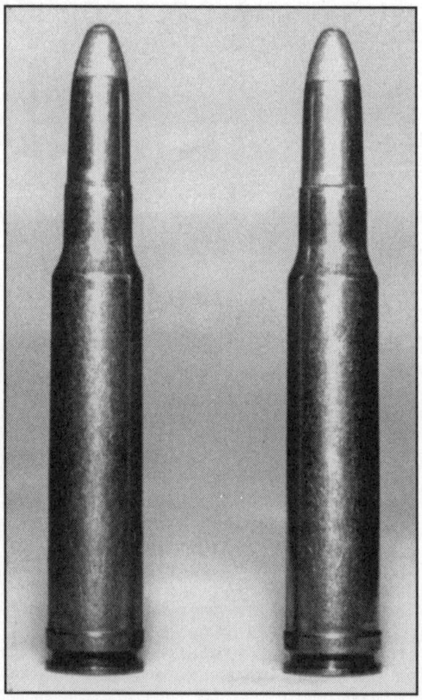

Cartridge No. 7 on left; one of older manufacture on right.

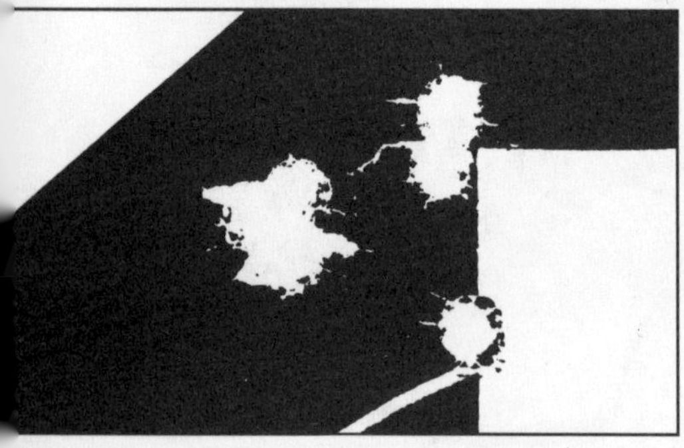

Federal 250-grain NPB Premium Safari ammunition #P338B2. This group was shot after the rifle had been fired 139 rounds and the stocks bedded. This five-shot 100-yard group measures $1^{1}/_{16}$ inches.

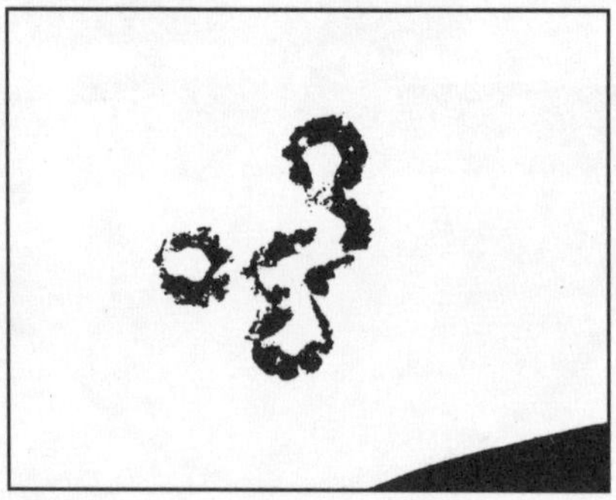

Remington 250-grain PSP ammunition #R338W2; five rounds, $^{11}/_{16}$-inch, 100 yards.

●Group comparison after properly bedding the stocks.

●Improvements after lapping (honing and polishing the rifling which *must* be done by a knowledgeable professional) the barrel bore.

With the initial seven six-round groups fired at a distance of 100 yards, here are the impact centers showing their respective placement. Federal's Premium Safari 250-grain NPB loading was the zero or control group ($1^{15}/_{16}$ inches with factory-fitted forearm, new rifle); extremes were produced by Winchester's 200-grain PP (cartridge #2) to the low, and A-Square's 250-grain Dead Tough softpoint (cartridge #5) to the high. Thus, by the use of different ammunition, the out-of-the-box rifle went from a sub-2-inch group to one exceeding $5^{3}/_{4}$ inches, center-to-center. With this huge overall group being produced at the relatively short distance of 100 yards, such an extreme dictates that ammunition selection be consistent even for close-in hunting.

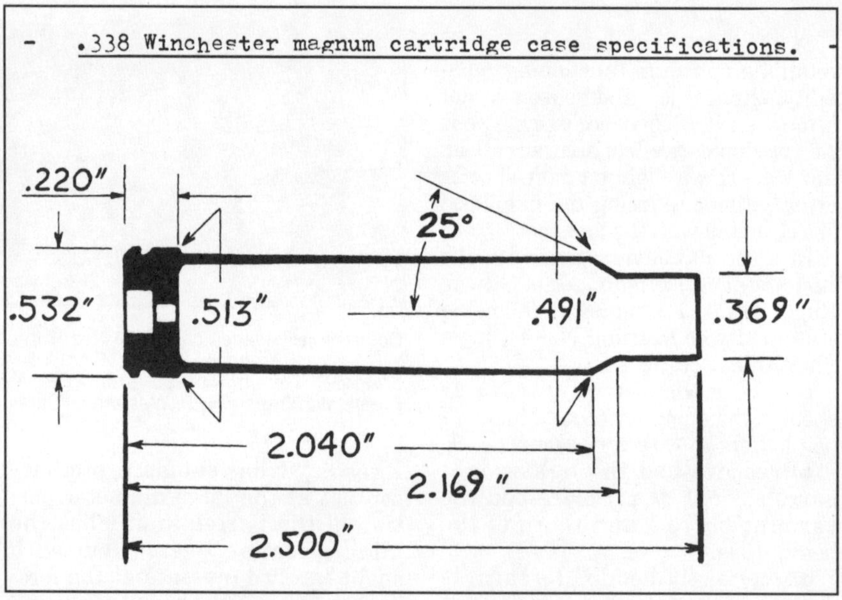

Cartridge case specifications for the 338 Winchester Magnum. (Courtesy Hornady Handbook)

For many years, IMR-4350 and IMR-4831 powders have proven excellent choices when applied to handloading the superbly versatile and effective 338 Winchester

AUTHOR'S ACCURACY EXPERIMENTS WITH RUGER NO. 1 AND FACTORY AMMUNITION

Each group contained six shots; one round fired every minute with a 20-minute time lapse between groups.

No.	Cartridge	Product #/ Bullet Wgt. (grs.)	MV (fps)/ Test Barrel Length (ins.)	Lot #	Center-To-Center Group Size (ins.): Factory-Fitted Forearm, Unlapped Bore	Forearm Removed, Unlapped Bore	Lapped Bore
1	Fed. Prem. Safari*†	P338B2 250 NPB	2660 26	4B-9756	$1\frac{15}{16}$	$1\frac{11}{16}$	$1\frac{1}{4}$
2	Win. Super-X	X3381 200 PP	2960 26	13YK22	$2\frac{1}{2}$	$2\frac{11}{16}$	$1\frac{9}{16}$
3	Win. Super-X	X3383 225 SP	2780 26	68BH20	$2\frac{15}{32}$	$2\frac{3}{8}$	$1\frac{5}{16}$
4	Rem. High Velocity	R338W2 250 PSP	2660 26	K 04C B3623	$2\frac{27}{32}$	$2\frac{13}{16}$	$1\frac{1}{16}$
5	A-Square	Dead Tough® 250 SP	2700 26		$3\frac{1}{8}$	$2\frac{3}{4}$	$1\frac{27}{32}$
6	Fed. Prem.**	P338B 250 NPB	2660 26	4C 8418	$1\frac{31}{32}$	$1\frac{25}{32}$	$1\frac{3}{8}$
7	Western Super-X	3382 250 ST (obsolete)	2660 26	14LE72	$1\frac{9}{16}$	$2\frac{27}{32}$	$1\frac{13}{16}$
						Average Group Size:	$1\frac{13}{32}$
ADDITIONAL FACTORY AMMUNITION							
8	Fed. Prem. Safari	P338A2 210 NPB	2830 26	0400051486			$\frac{7}{8}$
9	Fed. Hi-Power	338C 225 SP	2780 26	4C-0668			$1\frac{1}{16}$
10	Win. Super-Speed	W3383 300 PP (obsolete)	2450 26	32BK91			$1\frac{15}{16}$

RIFLE: Ruger No. 1 Single Shot, Model 1-S, SN132-90528, purchased new for this testing. Buttstock pull length $13\frac{5}{8}$ inches with factory recoil pad. (Fired 19 times prior to testing).
CALIBER: 338 Winchester Magnum (cartridge commercially introduced by Winchester in 1958); bullet diameter, .338-inch.
BARREL: Medium-weight, contoured, 26 inches in length; right-hand square-cut rifling with a groove depth of .004-inch and 1:10 twist. Slugging proved groove diameter to be .3387-inch***
SCOPE: Leupold fixed power M8-8x, SNX148201, with adjustable objective and Duplex reticle, purchased expressly for this testing. New Ruger #S-100RH (high) rings provided the necessary and ideal height clearance for easy chamber access as well as for the scope's large objective lens. Since I require at least a $14\frac{3}{4}$-inch stock pull length with the larger caliber Ruger No. 1s, I added a Pachmayr Slip-On Recoil Pad with a special $\frac{3}{8}$-inch thick foam rubber insert to achieve it. The $12\frac{7}{16}$-inch long scope was then mounted on the rifle's quarter rib to the appropriate and maximum eye relief measurement of $3\frac{7}{8}$ inches. (Had the pull length been any longer, extra-high rings (#S-100RXH) would have been necessary to provide adequate scope clearance to the front of the quarter rib assembly).
CONDITIONS: 3200-foot elevation (about a 13 percent correction factor [higher velocity] than sea level), direct sunlight, southwestern desert U.S.A. location with a mean temperature of 78 degrees F.

*Targeted (control group) ammunition; 100-yard zero.

**This Premium offering in the larger calibers was dropped in 1988, being replaced by the Premium Safari line which was new for the 1989 catalog.

***Measurements taken across the extreme corners of the slug; grooves were a bit flat in contour without the usual pronounced radius. Mid-point measurement across the grooves ran .3375-inch.

†After firing 123 rounds through the rifle with reinstalled factory forearm, center-to-center group size was $1\frac{27}{32}$ inches. After properly glass-bedding the stocks, center-to-center group size was $1\frac{1}{16}$ inches.

NPB=Nosler Partition Bullet; PP=Power Point; SP=Softpoint; PSP=Pointed Softpoint; ST=Silvertip

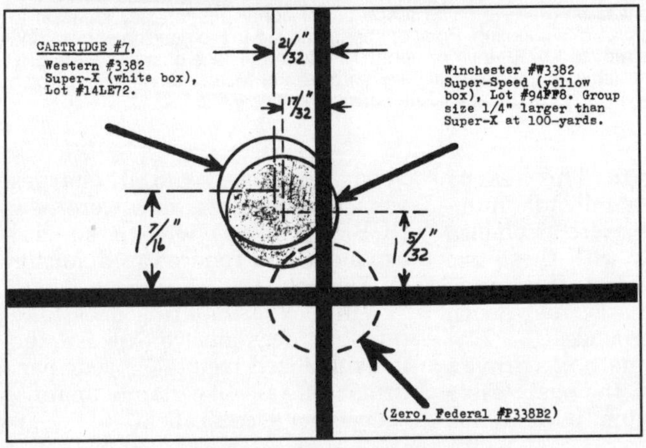

Even with same brand name, weight and bullet type, if dates of manufacture are far apart, or if storage conditions of even the same lot number vary significantly, impact points will probably not be the same and field results can be compromised. These two Winchester 250-grain 338 Winchester Magnum Silvertip cartridges were manufactured about twelve years apart, and storage conditions of each are unknown. Here is the impact difference at 100 yards. It's not a lot; however, at longer distances, game shooting results could suffer.

AUTHOR'S ACCURACY EXPERIMENTS WITH RUGER NO. 1 AND HANDLOADS

No.	Bullet (Wgt. Grs.)	Bullet (Type)	Load (Grs./Powder)	Primer	Crimp	Est. MV (fps)	100-Yard Group Size (ins.)
11	250	Speer Grand Slam #2408	57/IMR-4064* (7 grs. Super Grex case filler)	CCI #200	Medium	2450	1 1/8
			68/IMR-4350	CCI #250	Medium	2650	1 15/16
			68/IMR-4350	CCI #250	None	2650	1 5/8
			69/IMR-4350	CCI #200	Medium	2650	1 19/32
			70.5/IMR-4831	CCI #200	Medium	2600	7/8
			71/IMR-4831	CCI #200	Medium	2600	11/16
12	250	Speer Grand Slam #2408	67/IMR-4350	CCI #200	None	2600	13/16**
13	250	Hornady RNSP #3330	57/IMR-4064* (No case filler)	CCI #200	Medium	2450	2 27/32 (vertical dis.)
			68/IMR-4350	CCI #250	Medium	2650	1 7/16
			69/IMR-4350	CCI #200	Medium	2650	1 1/2 (vertical dis.)
14	250	Sierra Spitzer BT #2600	69/IMR-4350	CCI #200	None	2650	3/4**
			69/IMR-4350	CCI #250	None	2675	1 5/8**
			70/IMR-4831	CCI #200	None	2600	11/16**
15	250	Speer Semi-Spitzer #2411***	69/IMR-4350	CCI #200	None	2650	1 3/16**
			70/IMR-4831	CCI #200	None	2600	1 15/16** (vertical dis.)
16	275	Speer Semi-Spitzer #2411	65/IMR-4350	CCI #250	None	2550	1 3/8**
			66/IMR-4350	CCI #200	None	2550	1 7/32**
			68/IMR-4831	CCI #200	None	2550	1 3/16**

*Reduced loading.
**Bullet seated out to contact chamber throat.
***275-grain bullet faced off in a lathe to a wide flat nose and 250-grain weight.

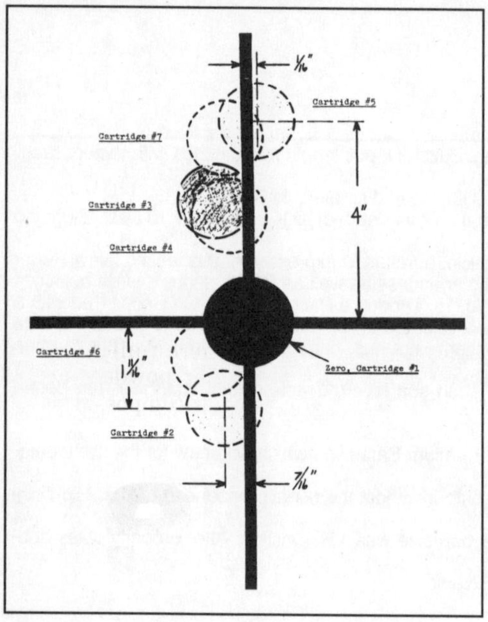

This diagram shows the variation in points of impact given by seven different factory loads in Bosselman's No. 1 338. All individual groups were well under 2 MOA, but vertical spread went to almost 6 inches when the various makes and bullet weights were fired with same sight setting. That is enough to cause problems at almost any hunting range.

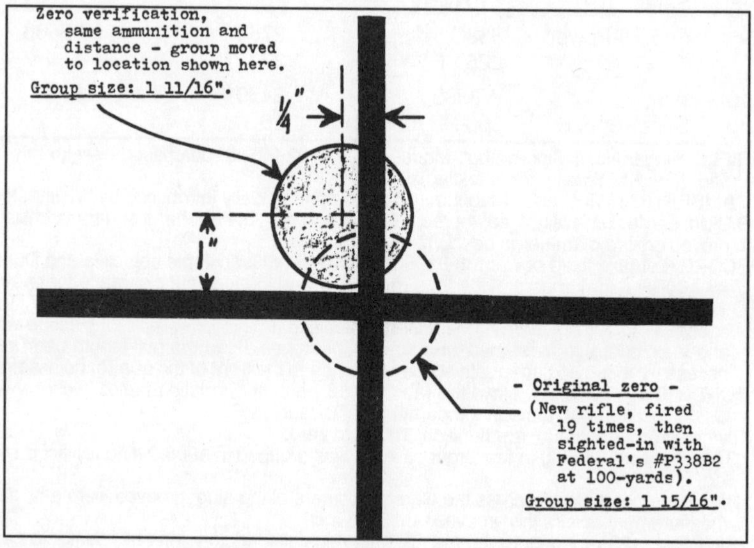

After firing 133 rounds through the rifle, Bosselman decided to verify the established zero (control group impact point). This six-round group (same ammo and lot number) was fired at the same range under conditions virtually identical to those of the previous shooting. Point of impact moved to the position shown, and its size was reduced by 1/4-inch or about 12 percent. These changes were produced by the firing of approximately seven boxes of factory ammunition, which naturally began to lap and break in the barrel of this new rifle.

Magnum cartridge. The nearby table of selected handloads, numbers 11 through 16, were assembled almost exclusively with these two powders and show the efficiency of this cartridge. As previously, each group contains six rounds.

These handloads have proven accurate for me in the past. Cases were new Remington; powder was newly purchased and all charges were handweighed; dies were new RCBS (#16301) with a special expander ball reduced in diameter to .335-inch.

While experimenting does take time and does involve expense, the individualized results for your particular rifle(s) will certainly improve chances for success afield. ●

The Brigadier line.

Another powder supplier for handloaders...

The Scot Brigadier Line

by R.H. VanDenburg Jr.

Editor's Note

In July of 1993, Accurate Arms announced the purchase of Scot Powder Co.

SINCE 1988, handgun and shotgun reloaders around the country have had the opportunity to test the wares of a new entry in the handloading market. The Scot Powder Co. of Wilmington, Delaware, was formed to market smokeless powders manufactured by the Nobel Explosives Co. of Scotland. Nobel, in turn, is a subsidiary of the industrial conglomerate ICI. These new powders—Royal Scot, Pearl Scot and the Solo series (Solo 1000, 1250 and 1500)—have been well received.

Now, at least since 1989, Scot has been marketing several rifle powders: the Brigadier line. As with all Nobel sporting powders, Brigadier powders are manufactured with nitro-cotton instead of nitro-cellulose, the principal ingredient being cotton fiber instead of wood fiber. Purported advantages are that nitro-cotton powders burn cleaner and cooler, and are more uniform from lot to lot. Brigadier powders are of single-base, tubular composition.

At the 1990 NRA Convention in Anaheim, California, when talking with Dr. Spencer "Doc" Watson, Scot's president, I was delighted to discover that the Brigadier line is the old Herter line of powders. Many of today's handloaders have probably never heard of Herter's, so let's look back in time a bit.

From just after World War II to the early 1970s, Herter's, Inc., of Waseca, Minnesota, was one of the nation's premier purveyors of hunting, fishing, shooting and camping equipment. Although several retail

AUTHOR'S LOADS
WITH SCOT'S BRIGADIER POWDERS

Cartridge	Bullet (grs.)	Load (Grs./Powder)	MV (fps)
243 Winchester	70	40.0/4065	3239
	85	42.0/4351	3199
	105	41.0/4351	3004
30 Herrett	135	29.0/4197	2057
30-30 Winchester	170	31.0/3032	2225
	180	30.0/3032	2113
	190	29.0/3032	2050
30-06 Springfield	150	52.0/4065	2859
	165	56.5/4351	2889
	180	55.0/4351	2792

Note: Above loads were developed in author's guns. Some approach maximum. Cut loads 10 percent to start and work up carefully; back off at first sign of excessive pressure.

The Brigadier line with its conventional counterparts. IMR (DuPont) also manufactures an IMR 4198.

stores were opened across the country in later years, Herter's was primarily a mail-order house. Their products were advertised via catalog. It was, in my opinion, the most fascinating catalog ever put out by anyone! Back then, I could, and did, pore over the catalog for hours on end. Apparently, I ordered a few things too. As I look around my modest accumulation of hunting, fishing and shooting accoutrements, I find the Herter's name fairly represented by knives, fishing tackle and reloading equipment. I store my gun cleaning patches, which I prefer to make myself, cutting them from bolts of outing flannel, in still-serviceable Herter's boxes. From where I sit, I count no fewer than seventeen red plastic ammo boxes, each with "Herter's, Inc." embossed on the top. However, I had never used Herter's powders. To do so now would be as close an opportunity to stepping back a quarter-century in time as I am ever likely to get.

After I returned from the convention, I again contacted Dr. Watson. A short time later, I had samples of each of the Scot rifle powders and a copy of their latest reloading manual.

There are four powders in the Brigadier line:

No. 4197 is described as slightly slower than IMR-4198, and formerly sold as "Herter's Perfect Rifle Powder No. 103."

No. 3032 is described as slightly faster than IMR-3031. Formerly "Herter's Perfect Rifle Powder No. 102."

No. 4065 is listed as slightly faster than IMR-4064 and is promoted as similar in some respects to IMR-4320 and IMR-4895. This powder was formally marketed as "Herter's Perfect Rifle Powder No. 101."

No. 4351, the slowest of the series to date, is described as slightly faster than IMR-4350 and H-4350. This one was "Herter's Perfect Rifle Powder No. 100."

At the time the powders arrived, I was busy investigating the use of heavier-than-normal bullets in the 30-30 Winchester. While IMR-3031 is often considered *the* 30-30 powder, I found, depending on case brand and trim length, I often could not get enough 3031 into the case ahead of 180- and 190-grain bullets to obtain maximum performance. Since Scot's Brigadier 3032 is slightly faster and should require a smaller quantity, I had hopes that it might prove more suitable.

As things turned out, 3032 was perfectly suited to the task. With 170-, 180- and 190-grain bullets, Brigadier 3032 exceeded the accuracy and velocity levels attained by other powders and left the cleanest barrel, after firing, I have ever seen. Pressure levels, within my ability to gauge them, appeared to be well within acceptable limits.

In the testing of all the powders, I approached pressure estimating the same way—objectively, by careful case head measurements before and after firing and comparing them to factory ammo, and subjectively, by a visual comparison of primers after firing and by extraction "feel."

In the end, for my 170-grain and heavier bullet loads in the 30-30, Scot's Brigadier 3032 has become *the* powder.

I worked with Brigadier 4197 next, choosing the 30 Herrett cartridge as the vehicle. This was done for several reasons. First, it represents the typical small-capacity case usually associated with IMR-4198-range powders; second, I have had excellent results in the Herrett with other powders and wondered how 4197 would measure up.

After testing the new powder with an exceptionally accurate bullet, Sierra's 135-grain for single shot pistols, two things became apparent. One, Brigadier 4197 is slower than its IMR counterpart, for 29 grains of 4197 produced virtually the identical velocity of 27 grains of 4198. And two, 4197 is also very clean burning. Accuracy was too close to call, with both producing excellent results.

Due to their burning rates, the next two powders in the Brigadier line, 4065 and 4351, were each tested in two different calibers. For the rather large number of calibers occupying the 308 Winchester, or medium, case capacity range, the

Old and new. Scot powders are same as those once sold under the Herter's name.

243 Winchester was chosen. To represent larger capacity calibers, the venerable 30-06 Springfield was selected. For both of these cartridges, many reloaders consider IMR-4350 to be the only powder necessary. However, in both instances, IMR-4064 is quite popular, especially with lighter bullets. How would their Scot Brigadier counterparts perform? That was next on the testing schedule.

To test Brigadier 4065 in the 243 Winchester, I chose the Hornady 70-grain SXSP. This is a fine varmint bullet, designed to disintegrate upon impact. The *Hornady Handbook*, 4th Ed., suggests keeping muzzle velocity below 3400 fps or disintegration may occur before impact.

In prior testing of this bullet, 41 grains of IMR-4064 produced a nifty 1/2-inch group on the 100-yard target. Unfortunately, it included only three holes. The other two bullets never reached the target. This also occurred with 3031, 4895, 4320 and 4350. Push the bullet too fast and—poof! Dropping back to 40 grains of 4064, or even 39.5, produced suitable velocities and assured hits while maintaining MOA-or-better accuracy, if I did my part and it wasn't too windy.

All tests made at measured ranges and from a sturdy bench.

Interestingly, the 40/IMR-4064 load produced a velocity of 3313 fps. The same amount of Brigadier 4065, supposedly a faster powder, gave me somewhat less—3239 fps. However, the 4065 load included a five-shot extreme spread of only 16 fps, a standard deviation of 5, and was the more accurate load of the two. Quite a range of loads using 4065 were tried, but I was most impressed with the 40-grain load. It apparently isn't quite maximum in my rifle, but is well-balanced and very accurate.

In trying Brigadier 4065 in the 30-06, I chose the Speer 150-grain SP bullet. Designed for hunting rather than target work, it is nonetheless quite accurate and suitable for silhouette competition with both rifle and handgun.

While my 30-06 has a definite preference for heavier bullets, one 150-grain load that has served me well for game when this weight was appropriate has been 51 grains of IMR-4064. Velocity has been chronographed at 2740 fps. The same amount of Brigadier 4065 pushed the same bullet to 2791 fps, and accuracy was even better. Scot's listed maximum of 52 grains of 4065

Components used in tests, from left: 30 Herrett case and 135-grain Sierra; 30-30 Winchester case and 170-grain Speer flat-point, 180-grain flat-nose (from 307 Winchester), 180-grain Speer Mag-Tip, 190-grain Silvertip (from 303 Savage); 243 Winchester case and 70-grain Hornady SPSX, 85-grain Sierra, 105-grain Speer; 30-06 Springfield case and 150-grain Speer, 165-grain Nosler Partition and 180-grain Nosler Partition.

turned in 2859 fps and 1-inch groups—exceptional performance for this weight bullet in this rifle.

To test Brigadier 4351 in the 243 Winchester, I began with Sierra's 85-grain flat-base spitzer. A favorite load of many shooters over the years for this combination has been 44 grains of IMR-4350. For my own rifle, I had settled on 43.5 grains. Velocity has been clocked at 3111 fps. This from a 24-inch barrel and at an elevation of 7500 feet. Accuracy is generally as good as I can hold.

The Scot manual's maximum load of 42.5/4351 produced 3216 fps using this bullet, with an extreme spread of 15 fps, and was very accurate. However, I eventually settled on 42.0 grains and 3199 fps. This is a good load in my gun. I also tried 4351 with the Speer 105-grain spitzer, a bullet I have used with success on antelope and deer. Heretofore, my usual load has been 41 grains of IMR-4350 with the CCI 200 primer for 2995 fps and acceptable accuracy. The same amount of Brigadier 4351 produced almost identical velocity (3004), but groups shrank.

Turning to the 30-06, I tested Brigadier 4351 with two bullets, the time-proven 165- and 180-grain Nosler Partitions. For years, my favorite load with the 165-grain bullet has been 57 grains of IMR-4350, which has a load density of 98 percent. The *Nosler Reloading Manual No. 3* lists this load as both maximum and the most accurate. I have clocked it at 2794 fps in my rifle, and groups run from 1-$1^1/_4$ inches. Not bad for a hunting gun with a low-power scope and a fairly heavy trigger pull.

With Brigadier 4351, I was able to work up to 56.5 grains and picked up 95 fps (to 2889) with no loss of accuracy.

Going to the 180-grain Nosler, things got interesting. The load I have used most with it has been 55 grains of IMR-4350. It has been superbly accurate, often producing five-shot, sub-1-inch groups at 100 yards. Velocity out of my 22-inch barrel is 2608 fps. A bit more powder could be called for, but there is no room. The Nosler manual lists this combination as 102 percent loading density—which means it is compressed.

Long-time users of the Powley computer already know this. Until relatively recently, there was no powder ideally suited for the 180-grain bullet in the 30-06. IMR-4350 was too slow, as can be seen above, and 4320 was too fast. Indeed, if you tried to pick the proper powder using the computer, you got "D." Still, we all used 4350 because it was the best available choice. More recently, several powders have been introduced to fill the void. Perhaps the most popular for this combination have been H-414 and W-760. There are others, but most require compressing the powder charge. Now there is another, Brigadier 4351. Scot's manual lists 56 grains as its maximum, producing 2740 fps. My specific combination using 55 grains got me 2792 fps. Groups opened slightly from the 4350 load, but were still in the $1^1/_2$-inch range. That's fine enough accuracy for a hunting gun, in my opinion.

SOME MANUFACTURER'S MAXIMUM LOADS

Cartridge	Bullet (grs.)	Load (Grs./Powder)	MV (fps)
218 Bee	45	15.0/4197	2550
22-250 Remington	50	36.0/4065	3800
223 Remington	50	23.5/4197	3178
6mm PPC	63	28.5/3032	3300
25-06 Remington	117	48.0/4351	3060
7mm Rem. Mag.	160	64.0/4351	3000
270 Winchester	130	55.0/4351	3100
308 Winchester	150	46.0/4065	2800
35 Remington	150	39.0/3032	2235

Caution: Above loads are all manufacturer's suggested "maximums." Begin load development with the Scot manual "starting load" or cut charge by 10 percent and work up carefully, backing off at the first indication of excessive pressure.

In summing up, I have thoroughly enjoyed testing the Brigadier line of powders. They are a most welcome addition to our handloader's world. For my own use, I have been particularly impressed with 3032 and 4351. They fill specific needs of mine exceptionally well. However, a couple of points should be clarified.

Several times throughout the text, I have indicated using the same charge of the purportedly faster Scot powders (3032, 4065 and 4351) as I had with the slower IMR counterpart. I did *not*—nor should you even think about it—blithely substitute components. In each case, I carefully worked up from several grains below. That I could, in some instances, use the same quantity merely indicates that each individual rifle is, to some extent, a law unto itself, and that relative burning rates among powders are not absolutes. Changing cartridges or even bullet weights within the same cartridge often impacted the Scot/IMR burning-rate relationship.

TABLE OF CASE CAPACITIES		
Cartridge	Case Capacity*	Powder
243 Winchester	50	4065,4351
30 Herrett	30	4197
30-30 Winchester	35	3032
30-06 Springfield	61	4065,4351

*Grains of water

Reloads used in testing, from left: 30 Herrett with 135-grain Sierra; 30-30 Winchester with 170-grain Speer flat-nose, 180-grain flat nose (from 307 Winchester), 180-grain Speer Mag-Tip, 190-grain Silvertip (from 303 Savage); 243 Winchester with 70-grain Hornady SPSX, 85-grain Sierra, 105-grain Speer; 30-06 Springfield with 150-grain Speer, 165- and 180-grain Nosler Partitions.

In the 30-06/180-grain situation, the IMR powder limitation was case capacity, not pressure. I simply could not get enough IMR-4350 into the case to make the most of the cartridge. The Scot equivalent made it possible at apparently acceptable pressure.

In some other cases, pressure was the limiting factor, and caution had to be exercised. A good example is with Brigadier 3032 and the 30-30 Winchester. The maximum listed load in the Scot manual for 3032 with the 170-grain bullet is 33 grains. For old 30-30 hands, this is a shock. Brigadier 3032 is supposed to be faster than IMR-3031, yet no other current manual that I'm familiar with comes close to using this much 3031 in the 30-30. Indeed, the maximum IMR-3031 load in *Hornady Handbook No. 4* (28.5 grains) is *lower* than the starting 3032 load in the Scot manual (30.0 grains) with the same 170-grain bullet. Older Hornady manuals, on the other hand, listed 31.5 grains of 3031 as the top load. But, of course, maximum recommendations change over time for various reasons, and the most current references should always be consulted when handloading. In this case, I began with the Scot manual's recommended starting load of 30 grains of Brigadier 3032 and worked up to 31 grains. In my gun, this produced the same velocity, 2225 fps, as the Scot manual listed for 33 grains.

Guns used in tests: Thompson/Center Contender in 30 Herrett (top), Remington 700 heavy barrel in 243 Winchester, Remington 700 in 30-06 Springfield, and Winchester 94 in 30-30 Winchester.

None of this is intended as a criticism, but rather an admonition. Starting loads are in manuals for a reason. Start low and pay attention!

Finally, since I started this project, several changes have occurred at Scot Powder. First, the company was purchased by the Austin Powder Co. of Cleveland, Ohio. All facilities have been moved. The new name and address is Scot Powder Co. of Ohio, Inc., 430 Powder Plant Road, McArthur, OH, 45651.

Recent correspondence from "Doc" Watson indicates that several new powders are under development for handgun/shotgun use and that Royal Scot will be replaced by Royal Scot D. The new powders are all from Czechoslovakia.

Also being considered are eight new rifle powders from Czechoslovakia. Whether all, or any, will make it onto dealer shelves in the U.S. remains to be seen, but Scot powder is an aggressive player on the handloading scene and we are the beneficiaries. ●

"When you wish upon a star—be sure to know its name."

Jeanne Henry shoots this century-old Miller & Val. Greiss under-lever double rifle with confidence because a chamber cast and evidence from the DWM list show that her cartridges are properly formed from DWM case-pattern #41.

MYSTERIOUS METRICS

DWM AND THE FEEDING OF FOREIGN FIREARMS

by DON L. HENRY

IT WAS AN AGE of awe. Cartridges were saints. Supernatural. Names were invoked.

There were luminaries from the far ends of the earth. Bright, but seldom seen. And stars too faint to wish upon. No one knew their names.

Case of the Cartridges

The double rifle was a 416 Rigby, according to the gun show dealer. For it, he accepted three rifles, two handguns and my savings account. Small price to own a star.

A quarter-century ago, I didn't know that an under-lever back-action sidelock hammer double, however lovely, could not hold that cartridge. I wanted to believe that it was a 416 Rigby, the possession of which might send me hunting worldwide. It wasn't. It did.

Another time, a dealer took six long guns and an air rifle in trade for a still new pre-war J.P. Sauer *Bockbuchsflinte*. Its locking leather case came complete with the wrong key. The rifle barrel, proofmarked "8x57," wouldn't accept any version of an 8x57 Mauser cartridge either.

These arms, and many others, were beautifully made, exquisitely engraved and—because cartridges for them were unknown to the owners—priced well below what constituted a good buy.

Amongst the millimeters were unidentified American and English calibers such as the 22 WCF

Speer, of Idaho, offered a line of ammunition assembled from DWM brass and their own components. DWM headstamps were marked with the caliber. Speer made good ammo, but kept poor records. The Speer-DWM connection lasted about a decade; all inventory was gone by 1973.

Don with a Model 1908 Mannlicher-Schoenauer sometimes designated "8x56mm," sometimes marked "8.2mm." Regardless of discrepancies in nomenclature, it fires DWM case #528.

(5.6x35R), 22 High Power (5.6x52R), 25 Remington (6.5x52), 25-35 WCF (6.5x52R), 30-30 WCF (7.62x51R), 30-06 U.S. (7.62x63), 303 British (7.7), 404 Jeffery (10.75x73), and the 500 Jeffery (12.7x70). It was an era of metriarithmophobia.

Elementary Deduction

A carefully measured chamber cast sometimes led to identification of a cartridge case which could be reformed for reloading. That worked for the under-lever double rifle twenty-five years before I had any idea what the proper cartridge for it might be called. Often as not, the odyssey of identification was long and frustrating.

A few DWM sporting cartridge numbers were listed in Stoeger's *Shooter's Bible*. Anti-Germanic sentiment ran strong for three decades, and provincial American shooters didn't much care that additional metric cartridges could be identified in German literature like *Waffen und Munitions*, and that more DWM numbers were listed in the 1911 August Stukenbrok catalog *Moderne Waffen, Munition, Jagdartikel*.

Some DWM numbers were German equivalents of better known British cartridges. When the English loads began to disappear, a lucky shooter might serve the arm by finding DWM brass which could be identified by the headstamp code. This ammo procurement procedure could also be reversed by the few who had access to the limited literature.

Funny Foreign Guns

Following World War II, countless foreign arms in commonly unknown calibers entered this country to be sold as surplus. Besides these, and battlefield souvenirs, victorious servicemen acquired high-grade Continental sporting arms chambered for unknown cartridges. It is not surprising that a soldier would choose the finest specimen available from stacks of surrendered weapons. These exotic arms included many types: *Schutzen* (target rifle); *Doppelbuchse* (double rifle); *Bockdoppelbuchse* (over/under rifle); *Bockbüchsflinte* (over/under shotgun-rifle); *Bergstutzen* (single shot hunting rifle—literally, "mountain carbine"); *Kipplaufbuchse* (break-open single shot rifle); *Drilling*, pronounced "dry-link," (double shotgun over rifle); *Doppelbuchse Drilling* (double rifle over shotgun); and *Repetierbuchse* (repeating rifle), to name just some.

There were enough cartridge variations among the Schuetzen (English spelling) rifles alone to cause a Yankee wildcatter to think he had gone to cartridge heaven. Or hell.

Metric Mystery

That older European ammo was mostly all Berdan-primed seemed less inconvenient when there was no other choice. American-made RCBS standard and automatic priming tools can be used with Berdan caps. Primer rod assemblies are available in sizes 5.5mm (.217), 6.1mm (.240) and in 6.5mm (.255). These require a special shellholder which RCBS also supplies. Berdan primers made by RWS are available from Dave Cumberland (The Old Western Scrounger). Dave also has RWS

Primary sources of rare DWM data. The 1904 catalog is an out-of-print reprint. Small catalog is an undated original. Datig's book, published in 1962, is a numbered limited edition of 1000.

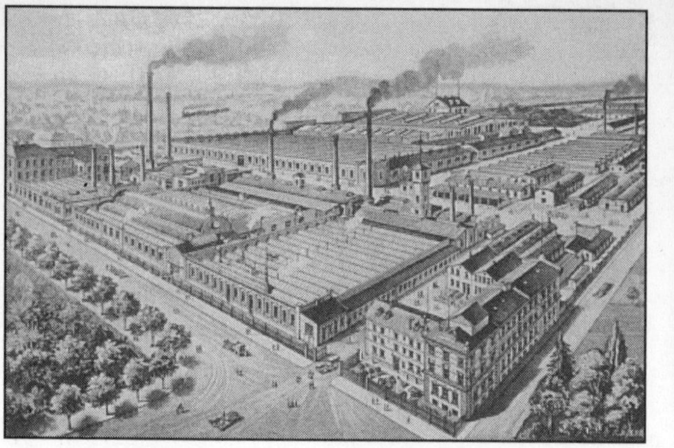

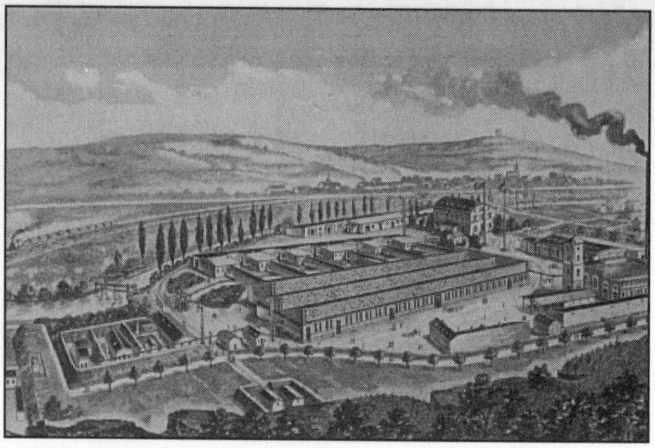

The Deutsche Waffen und Munitionsfabriken (DWM), German Weapons and Ammunitions Factory, in 1904 shipped coded cartridges to the nations of the world. The DWM code is more than a shooter's Rosetta stone; it is nearly a history of European cartridge firearms. Although no longer pivotal to the destiny of civilization, its value is still inestimable. The DWM factory was bombed extensively during WWII. Still, the DWM archive survived in a secret steel vault. If anyone knew what the numbers meant, they weren't telling. It was an era of metriarithmophobia.

Long a fancier of foreign firearms, the author has hunted as hard and far for ammo to shoot in them as he has while hunting with them. He rests here warm in the knowledge that shooters of metric cartridges need no longer be out in the cold.

cases and ammo for Continental calibers among which the lucky heir to an old German rifle may find ammo. Some of these cartridges originated more than a hundred years ago and are not otherwise easily available in the U.S.

A millimeter/caliber designation found among the proofmarks on a firearm might not directly describe the requisite cartridge because some calibers are designated by bore diameter (top of lands) while others are calculated by groove diameter (bottom of grooves).

Doesn't Add Up

The 6.5x54 Mannlicher-Schoenauer, for example, has a nominal bore diameter of .256 and a nominal groove diameter of .264. Those proofmarked "6.7" refer to the .264 grooves while the more common "6.5" designates the .256 bore (top of lands). Some 6.5 Mannlichers have been encountered with barrel groove diameters ranging from .263 to .267.

A true 7mm measures .276, which is closer to the .277 we know from the 270 Winchester than it is to the .284 bullet which the 7mm actually shoots.

The 8x56 Mannlicher-Schoenauer (M-S), at .315 bore diameter, takes a .323 bullet to fit the grooves. These have been encountered marked "8mm" and "8.2mm." Some are marked by bore, others by groove diameter.

The 9mm is properly .354. Some Germanic arms marked 9mm indicate a bore diameter of .354 and take a .357-.358 groove diameter bullet. Others, however, take a .354 groove diameter bullet. Confusing.

The 9.5x57 M-S measures .374 groove-to-groove. It takes a .375 bullet.

It can be seen that European, like American, cartridges are not uniformly designated either by bore or groove dimensions.

Enigmatic designations explain why Continental arms may sell for a fraction of their true value. A cased, bas-relief engraved V. Chr. Schilling Drilling was purchased economically because, although the shot barrels were 12-gauge (uncommon in prewar Germanic arms), the rifle barrel was marked "7.7mm." However, 7.7mm equals .303, and it did not chamber the 303 British round. It was sold, the seller said, "Because nobody makes ammo for it." As it turned out, it takes the 8x57JR (.318 groove) rimmed cartridge. This is DWM case #366. Norma and RWS ammo and cases are still available.

Neither is there uniformity in metric case lengths. Sometimes the length given includes the case rim; sometimes it does not. The 8x57R Sauer (DWM #462) is actually 58mm long including the rim. It is interchangeably designated 8x57R Sauer and 8x58R (rimmed).

No rule can be formulated from which to deduce reliable decimal dimensions for all metric cartridges. When the inconsistencies are compounded by a cartridge which is designated one way, but which fits a chamber defined by the alternate correlative dimensions, it can be easily understood why otherwise calm collectors exhibit a fear of foreign firearms.

Shooter's Rosetta Stone

In 1872, DWM's parent firm, Patronenhuelsenfabrik (Cartridge

Miller & Val. Greiss made this under-lever double rifle a full century ago. It would, and may, bring them pleasure to know that it still works perfectly well with ammo made from the equivalent of DWM case-pattern #41.

Case Manufactory) Henri Ehrmann & Co., was founded in Karlsruhe, Germany. It was destined to become one of the world's largest small arms ammunition manufacturers and to supply cartridges worldwide.

From 1878 to 1889, the company was known as Deutsche Metallpatronenfabrik Lorenz. In 1889, the company was purchased by Ludwig Loewe & Co., and merged with Pulverfabrik (powder factory) Rottweil-Hamburg and Reinische-Westfaelische Pulverfabriken to become Deutsche Metallpatronenfabrik Karlsruhe (DMK). Cartridges marked DMK used the same number codes which were later used by DWM.

Deutsche Waffen und Munitionsfabriken (DWM) was organized on 7 November 1896 as a combination of all Loewe, Mauser and DWM holdings. Additional mergers enlarged the company in 1898. In 1922, the name DWM was dropped in favor of Berlin Karlsruhe Industrie-Werke A.G. In 1935, the old DWM name was restored.

The DWM catalog of cartridges survived persistent bombing during WWII because the plant directors kept it in a specially built solid-steel bomb-proof vault. The directors realized that this bit of intelligence would have been highly valuable to either side. Most archives of German arms and munitions production, if they did survive both World Wars, were lost during the post-war Soviet occupation. The DWM records cover the period from 1896 to 1956.

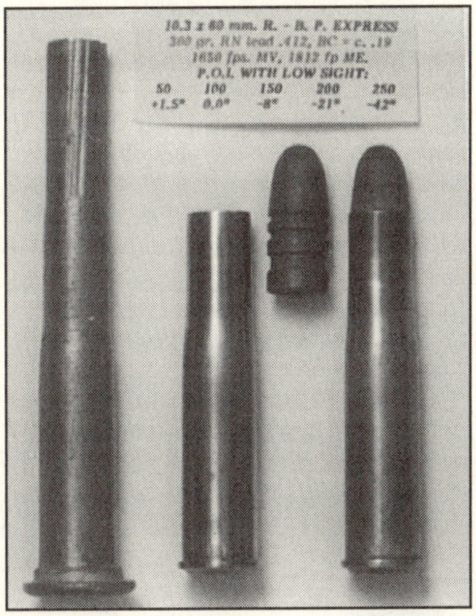

Chamber cast showed that 43 Mauser brass could be sized and fireformed to serve a 100-year old Miller & Val. Greiss double rifle. A single acceptance proofmark gave no clue to the original cartridge specifications.

Industrie-Werke Karlsruhe (IWK) wrote on 27 November 1959, "DWM existed until 1945, i.e. the end of War II. As it was then prohibited to manufacture arms and ammunition, our firm had to adapt its production to the new conditions. Under the name of Industrie-Werke Karlsruhe Aktiengesellschaft we gradually resumed our work..."

Assignment of DWM code numbers ceased in 1945. When ammunition manufacturing recommenced in 1954, some headstamps bore both caliber and code. The code soon fell into disuse.

Caliber-marked DWM brass and loaded ammo were imported into the U.S. by Stoeger and by Speer of Lewiston, Idaho. Some of the early loaded imports were Berdan-primed. Americans demanded Boxer-primed brass and cartridges for reloading. Speer soon offered a line of ammunition assembled from DWM brass and their own components. The Speer-DWM connection was later severed, and Speer's last remaining stocks were sold by 1973.

Datig Delivers Data

The DWM list, first revealed to the outside world in 1956 through the generous offices of Fred Datig, remained the province of advanced cartridge collectors mainly because others failed to recognize its wider value. The DWM list is more than a cartridge collector's and reloader's Rosetta stone. It is nearly a history of European cartridge firearms. The DWM catalog sheds new light on other rare arms as well. DWM #483, for example, is a 6.5x70mm which was made for an experimental weapon built by Spencer and A. Ohlhoff of Portland, Oregon, U.S.A.

During WWII, the Allies would have cheerfully paid 2.5-million U.S. dollars for the DWM archive. It wasn't for sale. Although it is no longer pivotal to the destiny of civilization, the value of the DWM data must still be inestimable because the arms and ammunition referenced in it are increasingly less familiar.

When *Cartridges of the World* was first published in 1965, Frank C. Barnes focused American lights into the dungeon of cartridge designations by providing detailed dimensions for as many DWM numbers as could be found to measure.

In addition to unlocking the identity of firearms, the DWM list may provide the necessary headstamp number so that cartridges can be found. By using the DWM list in conjunction with Barnes' measurements, ammunition can often be crafted to restore old arms to service.

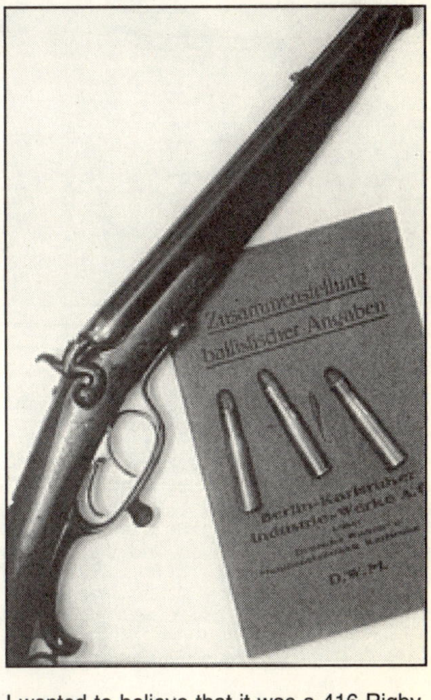

I wanted to believe that it was a 416 Rigby, the possession of which might send me hunting worldwide. It wasn't. It did.

Case numbering began in 1878 when Wilhelm Lorenz founded Deutsche Metallpatronenfabrik Lorenz. All of the company's successors continued the same case numbering system until 1945 through the last numbered case, DWM #605.

For reasons unknown, a few numbers were set aside yet never assigned. Some numbers were found to be attributed twice (#40 and #272). A meaningful taxonomy within a group number, i.e. 294A through 294IX, has not emerged. There are two figures for 294B which, while they might help a reloader seeking cases to shoot, to load or to reform, lend only confusion to an otherwise straightforward system. Information on arms manufacturer, nation of use, and cartridge designer have, when available, been added by the author and several persons mentioned in the bibliography, in order to aid identification. This is especially useful when the make or model of arm is known or when ancillary marks indicate that the arm was adopted by another nation.

Because the DWM catalog is an invaluable cipher to cartridge identification and, therefore, to the safe enjoyment of cartridge firearms, it is presented here with this article, unabridged on pages 124-133.

Shots Fired

A factory cartridge for the underlever double rifle that wasn't a 416 Rigby had not been identified. The barrel rib was marked "Miller & Val. Greiss, Munchen," (Munich, capital of Bavaria). Otherwise, it bore but a single crown over V mark, the V standing for Vorrat or supply. The crowned V, also called a view proof, indicates that the arm was accepted without test and was marked to comply with the proof law of 1891. No cartridge identification here.

Chamber casts were still available from long ago when they were first measured for comparison with data in Barnes' *Cartridges of the World*. It was again clear that the 43 Mauser case was of proper head diameter and rim thickness to be formed to fit.

Eager to shoot it as I had been back then, I had simply necked down Boxer-primed Canadian CIL brass in a 41 Magnum pistol die until it would chamber.

A fireforming load of 60 grains of FFg blackpowder pushed a 220-grain Speer pistol bullet through 5 inches of oak, where it was found expanded to over an inch.

A Lyman #412263 mould for the 405 Winchester dropped 300-grain bullets to shoot as cast. The rifle showed a particular liking for a lightly compressed load of 85 grains of FFg over a 3-grain charge of Red Dot, which facilitated ignition and cleaner burning. It delivered bullets from both barrels into an under-3-inch group at 75 yards. The load chronographed at 1650 fps, and the 300-grain slugs tore through the $7\frac{1}{2}$-inch railroad ties in front of the dirt backstop and how much more I couldn't determine.

Case Reopened

When Datig's *DWM Cartridges 1896-1956* became available, the cartridge search resumed.

Sherlock Holmes' method was to first eliminate what was false in order to give attention to what remained. Elimination of everything that doesn't fit is what makes detective work tedious. Hundreds of cartridges—some promising in one dimension but not in another—were weeded out by Holmes' method. The procedure was complicated by the aforementioned inconsistencies in metric cartridge designation.

Because the rifle was well served with reformed ammo, two new interests emerged: First, what was the identity and nomenclature for the

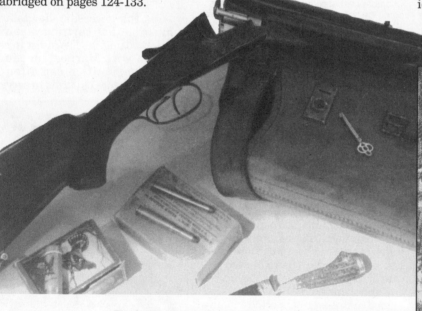

The key to unlock the gun case wouldn't. The 8x57 cartridge indicated by the proofmarks on this J.P. Sauer & Sohn *Bockbücksflinte* didn't fit either. A locksmith opened the gun case. It took a private detective and the catalog of DWM cartridge codes to solve the cartridge case.

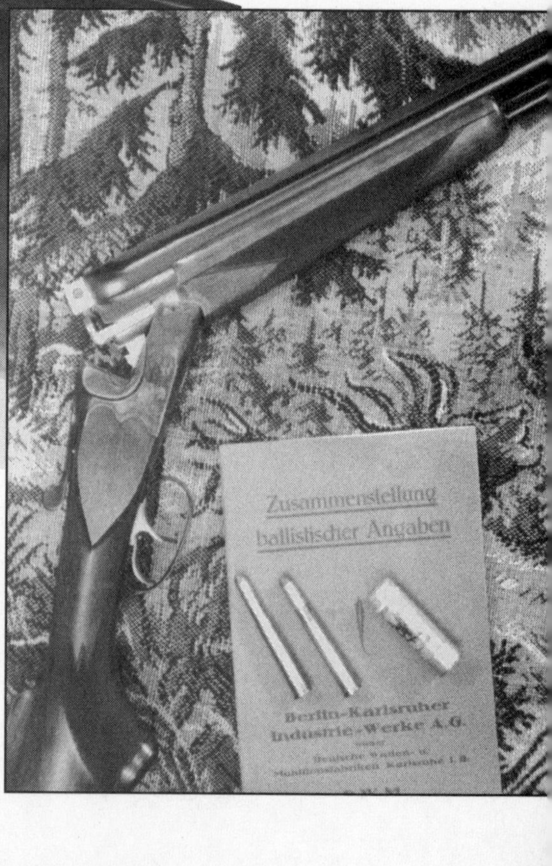

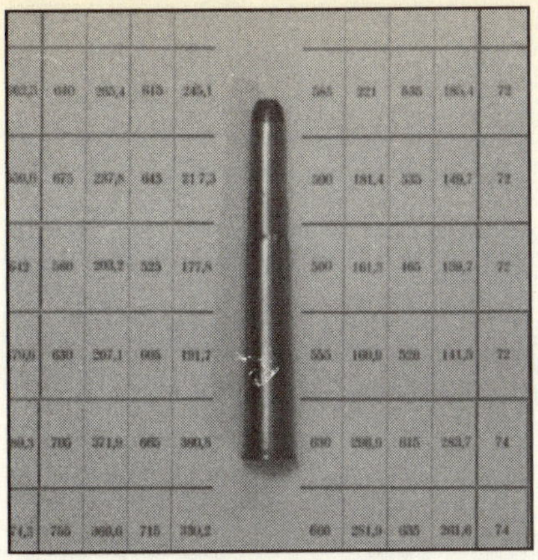

DWM #446 was an 8x57 all right, but the rifle barrel on a combination gun marked 8x57 wouldn't chamber any variation of the 8mm Mauser cartridge. Case #462 is a J.P. Sauer proprietary rimmed cartridge which must now be formed from the DWM #77 family of cartridges, which includes the still available 9.3x72R.

The 360-8x57 cartridges are too valuable to collectors to shoot, even when they can be found. Fortunately, DWM case #77 and its RWS companion the 9.3x72R are common and are easily reformed to provide affordable ammo.

The 6.5x54mm Mannlicher-Schoenauer takes DWM cartridge #477. Thanks to the Catalogue of DWM Cartridge Case Pattern Numbers, knowing the number will tell the caliber—or vice-versa—thus simplifying the search for shootable shells.

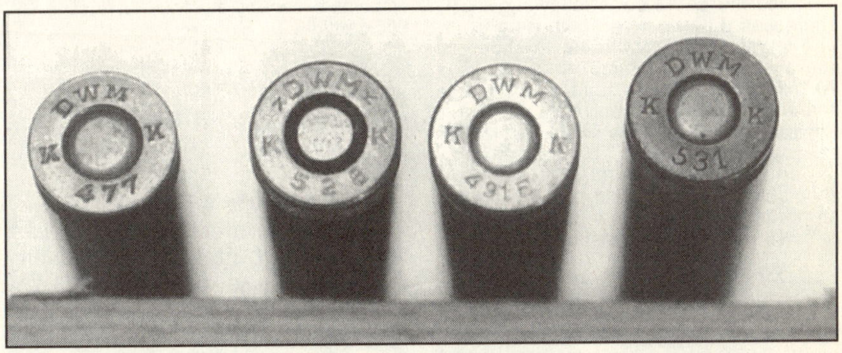

Without the DWM cartridge code catalog, it would be difficult to identify cartridges. All these fit different Mannlicher-Schoenauers: #477 fits the 6.5x54mm, #528 is the 8x56mm, #491E chambers in the 9x56mm, and #531 is the 9.5x56, which is also variously known as the 9.5x56.7, the 9.5 Mannlicher-Schoenauer, and the Brits call it the 375 Nitro Rimless Express. A program helps identify the players.

double rifle's cartridge? Secondly, would the DWM list have provided other cases to serve the rifle had the 43 Mauser case not been found?

There was the 10x42R Mueller & Val. Greiss, DWM #108. The name, a minor spelling variation, matched the rifle, but the case was too short and from a later time. Quite possibly the cartridge is the 10.2x60R Deutsche Schutzen (German Schuetzen), DWM #49; unfortunately, neither drawings nor measurements are available from DWM. Or, perhaps the cartridge was obsolete before DWM records began in 1896. Positive identification remains unestablished.

Cartridges which might be reformed to serve the double rifle were identified from the DWM list. DWM #238 is a Schutzenhulse (Schuetzen case), 11x60R, but its dimensions are unavailable. DWM #259 is another Schuetzen cartridge, 9.3x60R, which might be necked up were it not so rare that even the DWM factory didn't have the dimensions. It would appear that the relatively recent straight case from the 10.75mm B. Stahl, Suhl, Puerschbuechse, DWM #495, could be necked down. Except for caliber, chamber cast dimensions seemed similar to the 9.3x60R Deutsche Schutzen case #35 and to the 10.15x60R Schweden (Swedish) case #36.

The earliest DWM numbers for cases similar in style to the chamber cast were #35 and #36; these were of a period close to the rifle's manufacture. DWM case #41 indicated a 11.15x60R cartridge for the M71 Mauser.

A 43 Mauser!

Going in circles is not necessarily bad. One is truly lost only when he cannot return to from whence he started. I had navigated the metric world, mapped future explorations, and had filed claims on precious metals for which others are now digging on my behalf.

I recently discovered that the 10.3x60R Swiss cartridge is a perfect fit except for a too thin rim. The list doesn't show a DWM number for the 10.3x60R Swiss.

Dies based on the chamber cast and fired cartridges will arrive soon from Bill Keyes, special order supervisor at RCBS, so my wife Jeanne can load her own ammo. She calls the 7½-pound double her "Little Big Bore."

I don't remember wrapping a ribbon around it.

Positive Identification

The Sauer *Bockbuchsflinte* was more directly served by the DWM list. The Sauer's obscure cartridge was identified, and DWM numbers supplied sources of shootable shells.

Though it was marked "8x57," it wouldn't chamber the 8x57JRS or the 8x57JR cartridge. The seller had stated that it would chamber either the 32-40 Winchester or the 32 Winchester Special cartridge. "And I'll bet we could name a dozen others that would fall into the hole," I said.

A chamber cast revealed that the 8x57 marking, which was factory (or

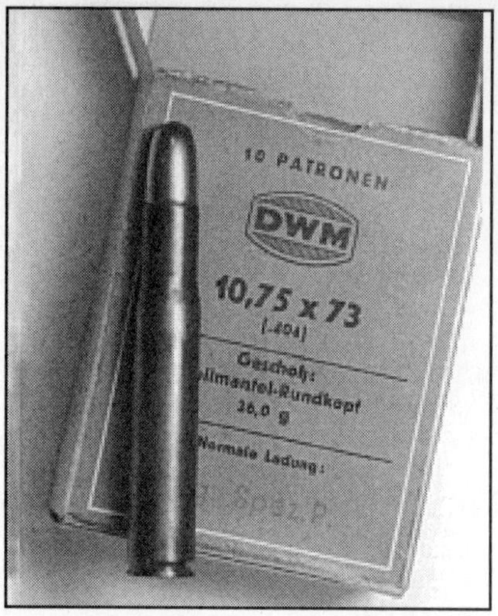

Caliber headstamps, like this "10.75x73," replaced the DWM code following WWII. There was a period when both were used. The DWM code is valuable to shooters seeking hard-to-get ammo. An owner of a 10.75x73, for example, needs to know that it is merely the metric equivalent of the 404 Rimless Nitro Express, which is also known as the 404 Jeffery. This information expands the possibilities of securing shootable ammo. It would be a shame for an owner of a 404 to pass up DWM ammo or brass with a "555" headstamp.

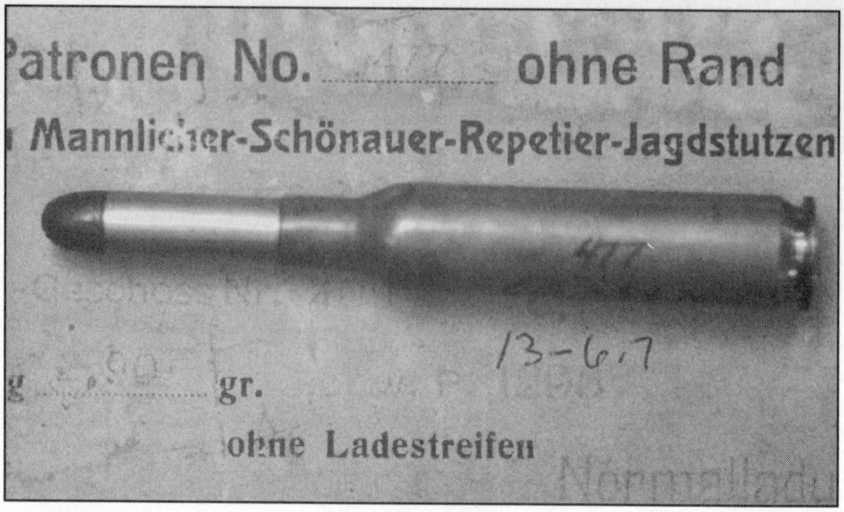

Original DWM cartridge box does not specify which Mannlicher-Schoenauer cartridge it contains except by the code #477. The DWM code catalog is key to identification of some 600 cartridges.

proof-house) stamped onto the barrel, indicated the 8x57R Sauer cartridge. This is the cartridge which both Barnes and DWM refer to as the 8x58R Sauer, DWM #462. The same cartridge is also designated "Kal. 8mm Dornheim Jagdbuchse 8x57R 360/57/8mm" and is listed as DWM #446. It was based on the British 360 case, and specimens of factory ammunition obtained after this search are so marked "360-8x57." The confusion created by such discrepancies of nomenclature is often insurmountable without the DWM catalog's positive identification.

Happily, the DWM list showed that the 360 case is also the basis for a whole family of 9.3 cartridges, which includes the 9.3x48R, the 9.3x57R, the 9.3x70R, the 9.3x72R, the 9.3x80R and the 9.3x82R. All are based on DWM case #77, subscripts A through F. It was no problem obtaining new Boxer-primed RWS 9.3x72R brass from Dave Cumberland and a die set from Bill Keyes. Loading data for available powders was supplied by my good friend Dr. John Stransky and was subsequently published by him in *Handloader* #139 (May-June, 1989), where he reported that the reformed cartridges fired from his antique under-lever *Bockbuchsflinte* resulted in three one-shot kills on Barbados and mouflon sheep.

Advocate's Summary

The identification of a proper cartridge for each firearm is convincing evidence for the value of the DWM archive cartridge catalogue list. Most often, only elementary deduction from the firearm's markings and from the DWM data enables positive identification.

Obtaining ammunition for the Miller & Val. Greiss *Doppelbuchse* required far more time and effort because specifications were found neither on the double rifle nor in the DWM list.

The mistaken identity of two firearms was solved largely through evidence supplied by the DWM list.

The Schilling *Drilling* was rendered serviceable simply by correctly interpreting its misunderstood metric markings and identifying available ammunition.

Cartridges have been crafted for the Sauer *Bockbuchsflinte* based on information supplied by the DWM list.

The correct identities of the rifle's caliber are proven by the cases at

Together again: Mannlicher-Schoenauer sporting carbine, 6.5x54mm cartridges to fit it, DWM data table which helped join them, and an Austrian tapestry. Each item traveled separately and incognito from Europe, identified by code or unpronounceable foreign names.

MILLIMETERS TO INCHES

MM	Inches	MM	Inches
6.00	.236	8.20	.323
6.35	.250	9.00	.354
6.50	.256	9.30	.364
7.00	.276	9.30	.366
7.62	.300	9.50	.374
7.65	.301	10.40	.409
7.70	.303	11.00	.433
7.92	.312	11.70	.460
8.00	.315		

Dimensions above were taken from arms manufactured in Steyr, Austria. Tolerances from time to time and from manufacturer to manufacturer do vary.

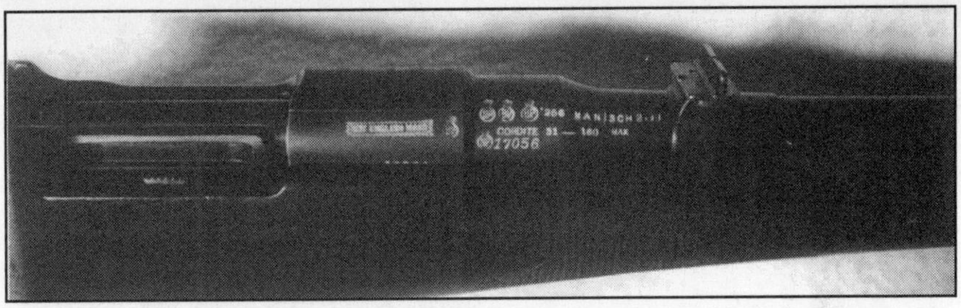

The Brits re-proofed everything foreign. They called the 6.5x54mm M-S the 256. Translation came complete with loading data; 31 grains of Cordite with a 160-grain bullet, thus saving the owner from retaining Sherlock Holmes.

hand. Several of them, actually. Enough to shoot.

The DWM list is a map of cartridge heaven for all who have wished upon an unknown star.

Case Closed

Collectors and shooters of antique arms, and especially of Germanic rifled arms, owe a debt of gratitude to the Directors of DWM and IWK: Herr Director Bauer (DWM) and Herr Director Holl (IWK), and to Herr Stober (DWM), Herr Maldi (IWK), and Herr Walter Gehmann. After sixty years of secrecy, these gentlemen elected to open their archive treasure to a world of interested historians, collectors and shooters.

Aficionados of Continental firearms owe special gratitude to Fred A. Datig who is, quite literally, the private investigator who brought the DWM archive to the English-speaking world, pro bono. Fred Datig thereby blessed not only arms historians, forensic ballisticians, and cartridge collectors, but also collectors and shooters of funny foreign guns as well. ●

Old brass often requires Berdan primers, which have always been available in the U.S. Berdan priming is a minor inconvenience only when there is a choice. They can be loaded with RCBS equipment.

Bibliography

Barnes, Frank C. *Cartridges of the World,* 6th Edition. Northbrook, IL: DBI Books, 1989.

Datig, Fred A. *Cartridges for Collectors,* Vol. 1. Beverly Hills, CA: Fadco Publishing Co., 1956.

Datig, Fred A. *Cartridges for Collectors,* Vol. 2. Beverly Hills, CA: Fadco Publishing Co., 1958.

Datig, Fred A. *Cartridges for Collectors,* Vol. 3. Los Angeles, CA: Borden Publishing Co., 1967.

Datig, Fred A., *DWM Cartridges 1896-1956.* Beverly Hills, CA: Fadco Publishing Co., 1962.

Deutsche Metallpatronenfabrik Lorenz. Export Katalog. Circa 1883.

Deutsche Metallpatronenfabrik Lorenz. Katalog 1. Circa 1885.

Deutsche Metallpatronenfabrik Karlsruhe. Katalog No. 2. April, 1891.

Deutsche Waffen und Munitionsfabriken. Munitionskatalog No. 3. DWM, 1904.

Deutsche Waffen und Munitionsfabriken. Original-Hulsenverzeichnis. 1913.

DWM, *Zusammenstellung Ballistischer Angaben.* Berlin: Berlin-Karlsruhe Industrie-Werke A.G., n.d.

Erlmeier, Hans A., et al. *Handbuch der Pistolen und Revolver Patronen,* Vol. 1. West Germany: 1967.

Erlmeier, Hans A. *DWM Case Pattern Numbers,* n.p., n.d. Errata: In identification of DWM #157 the author has changed "Schweitzer" to "Schweden." To better identify DWM #483, Mr. Muckel has amplified the entry to "Kal. 6.5x70, Spencer & A. Ohlhoff, Portland, Oregon."

Logan, Herschel C., *Cartridges,* New York: Stackpole, 1959.

Muckel, Gary B. Portland, OR: Personal interview 22 December 1990. The author is sincerely grateful to advanced cartridge collector Mr. Muckel for his gracious loan of scarce manuscripts, books, and cartridges without which this article would have been impoverished. A few of these items are visible in the photos which illustrate the text.

Nonte, George C., Jr. *Cartridge Conversions.* Harrisburg, PA: Stackpole, 1961.

Rosenberger, Dr. Manfred R. and Lilla E. Rosenberger. *Cartridge Guide 11/71.* Bremen, West Germany: Sporting Goods GmbH, 1971.

Stukenbrok, August. *Moderne Waffen, Munition, Jagdartikel* (1911). Wurzburg, Germany: Frankonia Jagd, (reprint).

Tikker, Kevin S., San Francisco, CA. Mr. Tikker is Archivist for the Mannlicher Collectors Association, P.O. Box 7144, Salem, OR 97303.

Tonn, Norman G., Oregon. Telephone interview 23 July, 1992. Herr Tonn is an advanced student of reloading in Germany.

Waffen und Munitions. Druckerei E. Schwend GmbH: n.p., 1976 (reprint).

White, H.P. and B.D. Munhall. *Centerfire Metric Pistol and Revolver Cartridges, Volume 1 of Cartridge Identification.* Washington, D.C.: The Infantry Journal Press, 1948.

White, H.P., and B.D. Munhall. *Cartridge Headstamp Guide.* Bel Air, MD: H.P. White Laboratory, 1963.

Woodin, William, Tucson, AZ. Telephone interview 13 January 1991. Mr. Woodin observed, "Oddly enough, there is little interest in metric sporting ammo in Germany from a collector's standpoint."

CATALOG OF DWM CARTRIDGE CASE PATTERN NUMBERS

1 Revolver, Mauser, 11x36.5R
2 Revolver, Mauser, 11.4x28R
3 Revolver, Mauser, 10x27R
4 Revolver, Mauser, 10x20R
5 Revolver, Mauser, Kal. 7.6mm
5A Revolver, Mauser, 7.6x25R
6 Revolver, Mauser, Kal. 9mm
7 Revolver, Mauser, Kal. 10.5mm
8 Teschin, 9x34.5R
9 Hülse 11.5x35R
10 Hülse 9.5x40R
11 Hülse 9.5x42R
12 Hülse 10x45R
13 Schweizer, Beaumont, 9.5x47R
14 Schweizer, Martini, 10.5x47R
15 Schweizer, 10x47R
16 Schweizer, 9x47R
17 Schweden, Remington, 12.7x44R
18 Schweizer, Vetterli M 69/71, 10.5x42R
19 Schweizer, Vetterli, 10.5x38R
20 Schweden, Remington, 12.5x35R
21 Deutsche Schützen, Werder, Kessler, Luck, 11.5x40R
22 Deutsche Schützen, Kern, 9.5x42R
23 Deutsche Schützen, Kessler, Luck, 9.5x47R
23A Deutsche Schützen, Kessler, Lindner, 9.5x47R
24 Deutsche Schützen, Landjäger, 11.15x47R
24A M.71/84 Kurz, Mauser, 11.1x49R
25 Deutsche Schützen, 9x47R
25A
26 Deutsche Schützen, Werder, Kessler, Beaumont, 11.5x50R
26A Deutsche Schützen, P.F. Rottweil, 11.5x50R
27 Deutsche Schützen, Einheitshülse, 10x52R
28 Werndl, 11.5x50R
28A Werndl, 11.5x35.7R
29 Deutsche Schützen, 10.5x47R
30 Deutsche Schützen, 10x47R
31 Deutsche Schützen, 10x47R
31A Deutsche Schützen, Foerster Berlin, 10x47R
32 Deutsche Schützen, 10x45R
33 Deutsche Schützen, 8.1x42R
34 Deutsche Schützen, Bayr, Gendarmerie, 11.5x35R
34A Pistole Mauser M.76
35 Deutsche Schützen, 9.3x60R
35[1] Deutsche Schützen, 9.15x60R
36 Schweden, 10.15x60R
37 M.71 mit hohlem Boden (hollow base)
38 Frankreich, M.74 Kal. 11mm Gras, 11.1x60R
38A Frankreich, M.74 Kal. 11mm Gras, verstärkt
39 Russland, Berdan M.71, 10.8x57.5R
40 Gardner, 11.5x60R
40[1] Rumänien, Henry-Martini M.78, 11.6x60R
40A Nordenfeldt, 11.5x60R

40B Henry-Martini M./III
40C Rumänien
41 Deutschland M.71 Kal. 11mm N./C., 11.15x60R
41[1] Deutschland, Exerzierpatrone M.71/85
41A Deutschland M.71/84 mit Kopf M.88, Kal. 11.2mm
42 Teschin, 10.5x36R
43 Revolver-Kanone, Kal. 25mm
44 Geschütz-Abfeuerungshülse
45 Geschütz-Abfeuerungshülse
46 Geschütz-Abfeuerungshülse
47 Armes-Revolver, Sachsen, 11x20R
48 Deutsche Schützen, Schaffroth
49 Deutsche Schützen, 10.2x60R
50 Werndl, 11x41.75R
51
52 Schweizer, 12.5x50R
53 Deutsche Schützen, Bornmüller, 12.35x50R
54 Teschin, 8x36R
55 Deutsche Grenzaufscher, 11.15x37.5R
56 Berggeschütz, Kal. 5cm
57 Deutsche Schützen, Landjäger, 11.25x32.5R
58 Deutsche Schützen, 11.15x44R
59 Italien, Vetterli, 10.8x48R
59A Italien M.70, Vetterli-Vitali, 10.5x48R
60 Revolver, 11.15x22R
61 Lancaster, Kal. 12
62 Lancaster, Kal. 16
63 Lancaster, Kal. 20
64 Lancaster, Kal. 24
65 Lancaster, Kal. 28
66 Lancaster, Kal. 16 (Kugelpatrone)
67 Lancaster, Kal. 20 (Kugelpatrone)
68 Lancaster, Kal. 24 (Kugelpatrone)
69 Lancaster, Kal. 28 (Kugelpatrone)
70 Express, Kal. .450 lg.
71 Express, Kal. .450 lg.
72 Express, Kal. .500 lg.
72A Express, Kal. .500 lg.
73 Express, Kal. .360 lg.
74 Hülse für Berggeschütz, Kal. 4cm
75 Express, Westley-Richards No. 1, 11.6x70.5R
76 Express, Kal. .450/400 lg.
76A Express, Kal. .450/400 lg.
77 Express, Kal. .360 lg.
77A Express, Kal. .360 lg.
77B Express, Kal. .360 lg.
77C Express, Kal. .360 lg.
77D Express, Kal. 9.3x72R, Normalhülse
77E Express, Kal. 9.3x72R
77F Express, Kal. 9.3x72R
78 Nordamerika M.76, Winchester Centennial, 11.6x47R
79 Lancaster, Kal. 10 (französische Schrothülse)
80 Lancaster, Kal. 10 (englische Schrothülse)
81 Lancaster, Kal. 10 (Kugelpatrone)
82 Lancaster, Kal. 12 (Kugelpatrone)
83 Lancaster, Kal. 14
84 Lancaster, Kal. 14 (Kugelpatrone)
85 Lancaster, Kal. 18
86 Lancaster, Kal. 18 (Kugelpatrone)
87 Lancaster, Kal. 32
88 Lancaster, Kal. 32 (Kugelpatrone)
89 Lancaster, Kal. 36
90 Lancaster, L.A., Kal. 12mm
90A Lancaster, L.A., Kal. 12mm
91 Teschin, G.B., 9.1x40R
92 Teschin, R.B., 9x38R
93 Teschin, R.P., 8x38R
94 Teschin, R.B., 7x38R
95 Teschin, T., 9x36R
96 Express, Kal. .450 kz.
97 Express, Kal. .500 kz.
98 Revolver, L.A. 9x19R
99 Deutsche Schützen, Einheitshülse, 11.15x52R
100 Deutsche Schützen, Einheitshülse, 11x52R
101 Deutsche Schützen, Einheitshülse, 10.15x52R
102 Deutsche Schützen
103 Deutsche Schützen, 10x46R
104 Deutsche Schützen, Mauser, 10x46R
105 Stiegele, 9.5x46R
105 Deutsche Schützen, 9.55x46R
106 Deutsche Schützen, Dieter, 9.5x46R
107 Deutsche Schützen, 9.5x45R
108 Deutsche Schützen, Müller & Greiss, 10x42R
109 Deutsche Schützen, 9.5x42R
110 Deutsche Schützen, Bornmüller, 12.5x42R
111 Deutsche Schützen, 11.25x40R
112 Deutsche Schützen, 10.5x40R
113 Deutsche Schützen, 10.25x40R
114 Deutsche Schützen, 9.5x40R
115 Deutsche Schützen, Werder, Braun, Kost, 10.5x35R
116 Deutsche Schützen, 10.25x35R
117 Deutsche Schützen, 9.5x35R
118 Deutsche Schützen, 9.15x35R
119 Deutsche Schützen, 9x35R
120 Deutsche Schützen, 12.5x30R
121 Deutsche Schützen, 11x28R
122 England M.71, Kal. 11.43mm Henry-Martini-Gatling
123 Schweizer, 10.5x48R
124 Schützen, Eley Bros., 11.5x57.5R
125 Schützen, Eley Bros., 11x57R
126 Schweizer, Vetterli, 12.9x42R
127 Schweizer, Ordonnans (alt). 10.5x42R
128 Schweizer, 10.25x42R
129 Schweizer, Probst, 10.5x42R
130 Schweizer, Vetterli, 10.25x38R
131 Schweizer, Knecht, 10.5x38R
132 Oesterreich M.77, Werndl, 11.15x58R
133 Werndl, 11x41.75R
134 Waenzl, 9.75x40.5R

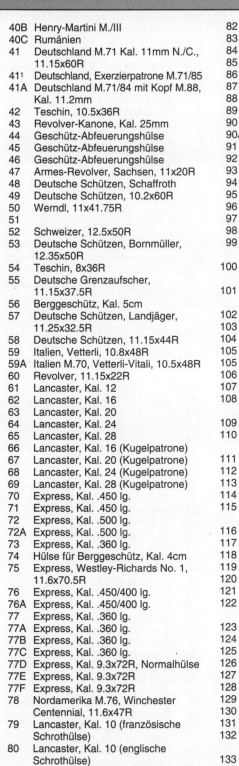

135 Werndl, 11.25x36R
136 Werndl, 11.1x36R
137 Werndl, 9.5x36R
138 Werndl, 11.5x30R
139 Lancaster, Kal. 24 S.B. No. 577, 15.6x50R
140 Niederlands M.71/78, Beaumont
141 Schweizer, Vetterli (alt), 10.1x47.5R
142 Schützen, Eley Bros., 10.75x46.5R
143 Schützen, Norwegen H., 11.1x46.5R
144 Remington, 12.7x44R
145 Schweizer, K, 10.5x47R
146 Deutsche Schützen, M.B., 10.8x47R
147 Dänemark, Remington, 11.7x41.5R
148 Peabody, 15.3x 35R
149 Nordamerika M.73, Winchester
150 Remington, 11.05x57R
151 Schwelzer, 12.5x42R
152 Werndl, 11.5x36R
153 Deutsche Schützen, 11.05x40R
154 Deutsche Schützen, 10.5x50R
155 Schweden, 10.9x57R
156 Deutsche Schützen, 9.75x45R
157 Schweden, Jarmann, 10.15x61R
158 Deutsche Schützen, 10x43R
159 Schweizer, 11x46R
160 Geschütz-Abfeuerungshülse
161 Serbien, Gruson Versuch, 9.95x64.65R
162 Serbien, Gruson Versuch, 9.75x64.65R
163 Deutsche Schützen
164 Lancaster, 10.35x65R
165 Salonstutzen, 4.5x17R
166 Deutsche Schützen, 10.2x53R
167 England, Kal. 11.43mm, Martini-Henry-Boxer, 11.6x59R
167A England, Kal. 11.43mm, Martini-Henry-Boxer, 11.6x59R
167B England, Kal. 11.43mm
167C Henry-Martini, 11.6x59R
167D England, Martini-Henry, Zielübung
168 Schweizer, 10.8x46.5R
169 Schweizer, Knecht, 12.5x50R
170 Schweden
171 Nordenfeldt Revolver-Kanone, Kal. 25mm
171 Lancaster, Kal. 16
171A Lancaster, Kal. 16
171B Lancaster, Kal. 16
172 Hotchkiss Revolver-Kanone, Kal. 3.7mm
173 Schweden, Jarmann, 10.3x61R
173A Schweden, Jarmann
174 Teschin, 9x36R
175 Lancaster, Kal. 12
176 Revolver, 10.53x19.5R
177 Express, 11.35x55R
178 Express, 9.25x36R
179 Deutsche Schützen, Martini, 9.55x47R
180 Deutsche Schützen, Landjäger, 11x42R
181 Schweizer, Vetterli, 10.5x40R
182 Schützen, 11.5x51.5R
183 Oesterreich, Werndl, 9.5x36R
184 Deutsche Schützen, 12.35x40R
185 Schweizer, 12.5x35R
186 Schweden, 12.7x48R
187 Serbien M.78, Mauser, 10.2x62.8R
188 Deutsche Schützen, Landjäger, 11x28R
189 Lancaster, Kal. 24 (Kugelpatrone)
190 Deutsche Schützen, Beaumont, 11.35x50R
191 Express, Kal. .450
192 Revolver Kal. .450
192A Revolver Kal. .450
192B Revolver Kal. 11.5mm, Rohde Copenhagen
192C Revolver Kal. 11.5mm, Rohde Copenhagen
193 Revolver Kal. .380
194 Revolver Kal. .320 kz.
195 Deutsche Schützen, 10.2x54R
196 Express, Kal. .500
197 Schweizer, 10.6x47R
198 Deutsche Schützen, 9.85x47R
199 Schützen, 10.95x46.5R
200 Deutscher Reichs-Revolver M.79/83 n.a., Kal. 10.6mm
200[1] Deutscher Reichs-Revolver, Exerzierpatrone
200A Deutscher Reichs-Revolver M.79/83 n.a., Kal. 10.6mm
200A[1] Deutscher Reichs-Revolver, Exerzierpatrone
200B Deutscher Reichs-Revolver, Schrothülse
201 Deutsche Schützen, 12.3x40R
202 Revolver Kal. .32 S&W
203 Revolver Kal. .38 S&W
204 Revolver Kal. .44 S&W
205 Teschin, 10.9x45R
206 Schweizer, 11.7x47R
207 Deutsche Schützen, 11.5x38.5R
208 Dänemark M.67, Kal. 11mm Remington
208A Dänemark M.67, Kal. 11mm Remington
208B Dänemark M.67, Kal. 11mm Remington
209 Express, Westley-Richards No. 2, 13x72R
210 Krnka, 15.9x40R
211 Deutsche Schützen, 9.2x46R
212 Express, 9.65x57R
213 Schweizer, 11.15x38R
214 Express, 10.25x68.5R
215 Teschin, 9.5x36R
216 Lancaster, Kal. 20
216A Lancaster, Kal. 20
217 Schützenhülse, 11.55x53.5R
218 Revolver, Kal. .380 lg.
218A Revolver, Kal. .380 lg.
219 Revolver, Kal. .320 lg.
219A Revolver, Kal. .320 lg.
220 Schweizer, Knecht, 13.4x40R
221 Revolver, Kal. .442
222 Lancaster, Kal. 28 (Kugelpatrone)
223 Deutsche Schützen, 9.95x44R
224 Lancaster, 14.05x48R
225 Lancaster, 14.05x40R
226 Schützenhülse, 11.6x50R
227
228 Revolver, Kal. .455
229 Revolver, Kal. .442 lg.
230 Deutsche Schützen, 8.85x54R
231 Revolver, Kal. .450 lg.
232 M.71, verlängert, 11.15x67R
233 Revolver, Kal. 320
233A Einsetzülse für Zielübung DWM, M.90, Kal. 7.65mm
233B Einsetzülse für Zielübung DWM, M.88, Kal. 7.9mm
234 Lancaster, Kal. 32
235 Schützenhülse, 9.75x45R
236 Deutsche Schützen, 11.15x50R
237 Schweizer, 10x65R
237A Schweizer, 10.3x65R
238 Schützenhülse, 11x60R
239 Lancaster, Revolver
240 Express, 11.35x45R
241 Express, 9.15x39.5R

242 Russland, Ordonnanz-Revolver, Kal. .44 S&W

243 Schützenhülse, 11.6x56.5R

244 Teschin, 8.1x29.5R

244A Teschin, 7.25x29.5R

245 Revolver, 9.25x22.5R

246 Express, Kal. .360 lg.

247 Lancaster, Kal. 12

247A Hülse, Kal. 12, mit geschlossenem Boden

248 Schweizer, 11x47R

249 Teschin, 8x36R

250 Revolver-Kanone, Kal. 4.7cm

250 Viehtötungs-Apparat, Kal. 8mm (Behr, Hamburg)

251 Teschin, 10.25x30R

251A Teschin, 10.2x30R

252 Deutsche Schützen, 10.5x50R

253 M.71, Kal. 11.15mm, Kopf und Zündung M.90

254 Platzpatrone M.71, 10.2x78R

255 Deutsche Schützen

256 Schweizer

257 Platzpatrone M.71, 12.25x78R

258 Deutsche Schützen, 9.55x46.5R

259 Deutsche Schützen, 9.3x60R

260 Revolver, Kal. .32 S&W

261 Revolver, Kal. .38 S&W

261A Revolver, Kal. .38 S&W

262 Revolver, Kal. .32 lg. Colt

263 Revolver, Kal. .38 lg. Colt

263A Revolver, Kal. .38 lg. Colt

264 Lancaster, Kal. 16

264A Lancaster, Kal. 16

265 Oesterreich, Schützen, Werndl, 10x36R

266 Schützenhülse, 9.75x36.5R

267 Express, Kal. .577 lg.

268 Express, Kal. .450 lg.

269 Deutsche Schützen, 11.10x33R

270 Belgien, Comblain, 11.4x50.5R

271 Egypten, Kal. 11.43mm Remington

271A Egypten, Kal. 11mm Remington

272 Lee, 10.7x57.2R

272 Spanien, Kal. 11mm Remington, 10.9x57.2R

272A Spanien, Kal. 11mm Remington

272B Spanien, Kal. 11mm Remington

272C Spanien, Kal. 11mm Remington

272D Paraguay, Kal. 11mm Remington

273 Revolver, Kal. .500 Constabler

274 Revolver, Kal. .577

275 Lancaster, 14.3x40R

276 Teschin, 8.9x24R

277 Lancaster, Kal. 10

278 Lancaster, Kal. 12

279 Revolver French, Kal. 15mm

280 Revolver French, Kal. 9mm

281 Revolver French, Kal. 12mm

282 Lancaster, Kal. 8

283 Express, 9.45x50.6R

284 Revolver, Kal. .400, 11x24.90

285 Schweizer, 13.7x50R

286 Lancaster, 12.7x46.5R

287 Lancaster, 11.4x36.3R

288 Lancaster, 13.5x49R

289 Schützenhülse, 9x40R

290 M.71, Zielübungs-Patrone, 5.0x77R

291 Beaumont M.71, 11.8x50R

292 Musket W.K1, 9.4x57.5R

293 Comblain No. 1, 12.8x50R

294A Hülse, 9.15x65R

294B Hülse, 9.3x65R

294C Hülse, 9.35x53.5R

294V Hülse, 9.3x60R

294VI Hülse, 9.4x53.5R

294VI Hülse, 11.93x53.5R

294VII Hülse, 9.4x57R

294VIII Hülse, 9.3x59.5R

294IX Hülse, 9x56.5R

295 Deutsche Schützen, Ebecke, 9.9x42.5R

296 Luxemburg, Mannschafts-Revolver, Kal. 9.5mm

297 Revolver French, Kal. 7mm

298 Snider, 14.5x48.5R

299 Bachmann, 10.8x48R

300 Revolver, 7.5x30R

300A Revolver

301 Montigny-Mitraflleuse, 12x58.5R

302 Montigny-Mitraflleuse, 14.7x35R

303 Hebler, zweiteilige Hülse, 7.7x58R

304 Hebler, 7.7x63R

305 Spencer, 12.8x29.5R

306 Revolver, 10.4x27.3R

307 Hotchkiss, 11.5x53.5R

308 Schweizer, Neuhausen, 10.5x38.4R

309 Express, W.R., Kal. .500, 11.6x72.5R

310 Repetier-Pürschbüchse, Mauser, 11.3x50R

311 Revolver, Knecht, 9.35x20R

312 Schützenhülse, 11.15x40R

313 Viehtötungs-Apparat, Kal. 15mm (Behr, Hamburg)

314 Comblain, 9.65x51R

315 Montenegro-Revolver, Kal. 11.3mm

315A Montenegro-Revolver, Kal. 11.3mm

316 Henry-Martini, 11.5x57.5R

316A Henry-Martini

317 England, Enfield-Martini M.85, 10.35x69.35R

318 Schützenhülse, Mauser

319 Portugal, Kal. 8mm Kropatschek, 8.2x59.7R

319A Portugal, Kal. 7.5mm Kropatschek

319B Portugal, Kal. 8mm Kropatschek, 8.2x56.2R

320 Viehtötungs-Apparat (Städt. Schlachtviehhof Karlsruhe), 10.4x14.5R

321 Viehtötungs-Apparat (Städt. Schlachtviehhof Karlsruhe), 10.4x14.5R

322 Schweizer, Peabody

323 Schützenhülse, André, Paris

324 Luxemburg

325 Belgien, Offiziers-Revolver

326 Viehtötungs-Apparat, Kal. 10.5mm (Behr, Hamburg), 10.1x20.75R

326A Viehtötungs-Apparat, Kal. 10.5mm (Behr, Hamburg), 10.2x12.75R

327 Viehtötungs-Apparat, Kal. 6.5 (Behr, Hamburg), 6.55x16.25R

328 Viehtötungs-Apparat, Kal. 9mm (Behr, Hamburg)

328A Viehtötungs-Apparat, Kal. 9mm (Behr, Hamburg), 9.2x18.5R

328B Viehtötungs-Apparat, Kal. 9mm (Behr, Hamburg), 9.2x21.5R

328C Viehtötungs-Apparat, Kal. 9mm (Behr, Hamburg), 9.2x20.5R

329 Repetier-Karabiner, Colt-Lightning, 10.8x33.85R

330 Pürschbüchse, P.F. Rottweil, Mieg

331 Portugal, Nagant

332 Schützenhülse, P.F. Rottweil, 11.35x59.6R

332A Schützenhülse, P.F. Rottweil

333 Portugal. Hebler, Rychner

334 Christiania

335 Christiania

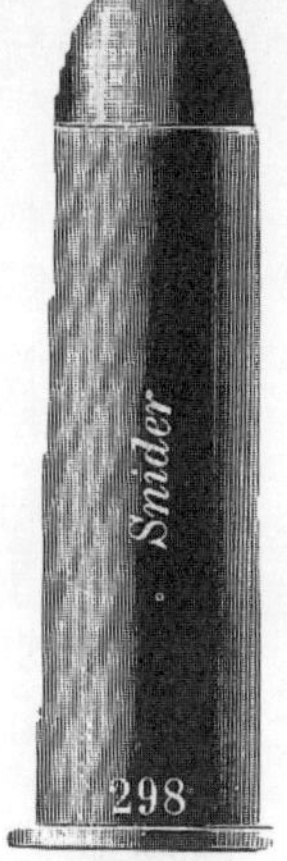

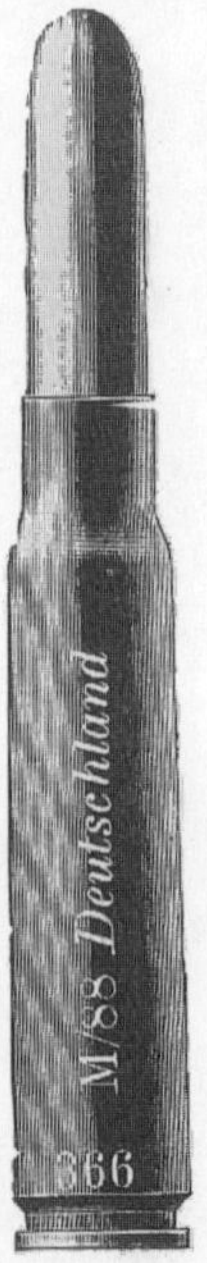

336 Lee Nagant, 8.15x53.35R
337 Lee Nagant
338 Hebler
339 Schützenhülse, 9.75x54.85R
339A Schützenhülse, 9.75x54.85R
340 Radfahrer-Pistole "Bombard", 7.6x16.25R
341 Belgien, Mannlicher
342 Projekt
343 P.F. Rottweil, Rubin
344 Lorenz
345 Daun
346 P.F. Rottweil
347 P.F. Rottweil
348 Friedrich Krupp A.G., Essen
349 Lorenz
350 P.F. Rottweil
351 P.F. Rottweil
352 P.F. Rottweil
353 Daum, Erfurt
354 Schützenhülse, Mauser
355 Schützenhülse, Mauser
356 Deutsche Schützen, Berghaus
357 Deutsche Schützen, Roesl
358 Oesterreich M.88, Kal. 8mm Mannlicher
358 Oesterreich M.88, Exerzierpatrone Mannlicher
358A Oesterreich M.88, verstärkt
358B Oesterreich-Ungarn M.88/90, Kal. 8mm Mannlicher
358B Oesterreich-Ungarn M.88/90, Exerzierpatrone
358C Oesterreich, Bulgarien M.95, Kal. 8mm Mannlicher
358D Oesterreich, Zielübung DWM, 5.15x56R
358E Bulgarien M.93, "S" Kal. 8mm (für Torpedogeschosse), 8.38x54.7R
358F Bulgarien M.93, "S" Kal. 8mm, 8.23x54.7R
359 Spanien, Losada
360 P.F. Rottweil
361 W.F. Mauser
362 Türkei M.87, Kal. 9.5mm Mauser, 9.75x60.35R
362A Türkei M.87, Kal. 9.5mm, verstärkt
362B Türkei M.87, Kal. 9.5mm, 9.75x59.35R
363 Revolver, Kal. 7.5mm Loewe
364 Tempini, Kal. 7.5mm
364A Tempini, Kal. 7.5mm
365 Zündpatronenhülse
366 Deutschland M.88, Kal. 7.9mm
366A M.91, Kal. 8mm
366B M.88A, Kal. 7.9mm Jagd (8x57 R)
366C M.88, mit Boden und Zündung M.92
366D
366D^{1} M.88B, Kal. 7.9mm Jagd, (8x57 JR)
366D^{2} M.88C, Kal. 7.9mm Jagd
366D^{3} M.88D, Kal. 7.9mm Jagd
366D^{4} M.88E, Kal. 7.9mm Jagd
366E Platzpatronenhülse M.88, Kal. 7.9mm, 7.93x82.5
366E^{1} Platzpatronenhülse M.88, "S" Kal. 7.9mm, 7.93x80.5
366F M.88, verstärkt (für Mascninengewehr)
366G M.88, uneingezogen, W.F. Mauser
366H Deutschland M.88, Kal. 7.9mm, Exerzierpatrone mit 3 Querrillen
366H^{1} Deutschland M.88, Kal. 7.9mm, Exerzierpatrone mit 6 Längarillen
366H^{2} Deutschland M.88, Kal. 7.9mm, Exerzierpatrone im Gewicht der scharfen Patrone
366J Deutschland M.88, Kal. 7.9mm, E-Hülse (für Gewehr und Mascninengewehr)
366K M.88, mit verengtem Geschossraum
366L M.88H, Mauser-Pürschbüchse Kal. 7.9mm "K" (8x51)
366L^{1} M.88H1, Mauser-Pürschbüchse Kal. 7.9mm Exerzierpatrone, glatt
366L^{2} M.88H2, Pürschbüchse Kal. 8mm, mit Rand
366M M.88, mit langem Geschossraum
366N Deutschland M.88, "S" Kal. 7.9mm
366N^{1} Deutschland M.88, Revisionspatrone
366N^{2} Deutschland M.98, Kal. 7.9mm, Exerzierpatrone mit 6 Längsrillen
366N^{3} Deutschland M.88, "S" Kal. 7.9mm, Exerzierpatrone mit 3 Querillen
366N^{4} Deutschland M.88, "S" Kal. 7.9mm, Exerzierpatrone mit 3 Querillen
366N^{5} Deutschland M.88, "S" Kal. 7.9mm, Exerzierpatrone im Gewicht der scharfen Patrone
366N^{6} Deutschland M.88, Kal. 7.9mm, Exerzierpatrone mit 3 Querillen, im Gewicht der scharfen Patrone
366N^{7} Exerzierpatrone M.88 "S", mit 3 Querillen
366N^{8} Exerzierpatrone M.88 "S", mit 6 Längsrillen
366N^{9} Exerzierpatrone M.98, mit 6 Längsrillen und schlanker Geschossform
366N^{10} wie 366 N^{9}, nur mit amtlichen Bodenstempel
366N^{11} Exerzierpatrone (schwere Ausführung) mit eingesetzter Feder
366O M.88F, Kal. 7.9mm Jagd, mit verändertem Geschossraum, (W.F. Mauser)
366P M.88GF, Kal. 7.9mm Jagd, mit verändertem Geschossraum, (W.F. Mauser)
366Q M.88, Kal. 7.9mm, Zeilübung
366Q^{1} M.88, Kal. 7.9mm, Zeilübung, 6.5x62.5
366R M.88 "S", mit verlängertem Geschossraum (W.F. Mauser)
366S M.88 "S", mit verlängertem Geschossraum (W.F. Mauser)
366T^{1} Signalpatrone, Kal. 7.9mm, mit 1 Querrille
366T^{2} Signalpatrone, Kal. 7.9mm, mit 2 Querrillen
366T^{3} Signalpatrone, Kal. 7.9mm, mit 3 Querrillen
366U^{1} Signalpatrone, Kal. 7.9mm, für weisses Licht, 1 Längsrille
366U^{2} Signalpatrone, Kal. 7.9mm, für rotes Licht, 2 Längsrillen
366U^{3} Signalpatrone, Kal. 7.9mm, für grünes Licht, 3 Längsrillen
366V Zielübung, Kal. 7.9mm
366W Kal. 7.9mm, DWM Berlin, 8.18x60.6
366X Eiserne Patronenhülse "S" Kal. 7.9mm
366Y Patronenhülse "S" Kal. 7.9mm
366Y1 Patronenhülse M.88 "S" Kal. 7.9mm, für Gewehr und Maschinengewehr
366Z Kupferplattierte eiserne Patronenhülse "S" Kal. 7.9mm für Gewehr und Maschinengewehr
366Z^{1} Kupferplattierte eiserne Patronenhülse "S"
366Z^{2} Kupferplattierte eiserne Patronenhülse M.88 "S" 7.9mm für

Gewehr un Maschinengewehr

367 Belgien, Türkei M.89/M.90, Kal. 7.65mm

367A Türkei M.90 Kal. 7.65mm

367B Argentinien M.91, Kal. 7.65mm

367C Belgien M.89, Kal. 7.65mm

367D Argentinien M.91, Kal. 7.65mm

367E Türkei M.90, Argentinien M.91, Peru M.91, Kal. 7.65mm (Gewehr und Maschinengewehr)

367E^1 Türkei, Argentinien, Peru M.90/91, Exerzierpatrone mit 3 Querrillen

367F M.90 uneingezogen, W.F. Mauser

367G M.90 verlängert, Centralstelle Neubabelsberg

367H M.90 Zielübung, Kal. 7.65mm

367J M.90 Zielübung, Kal. 7.65mm

367J^1 M.90 Zielübung, Kal. 7.65mm (6.5 (6.2)x59)

367K Türkei M.90^S Kal. 7.65mm; mit Firma DWM KK 367K

367L Türkei, Paraguay, Bolivien M.90^S Kal. 7.65mm

367L^1 Türkei, Argentinien, Exerzierpatrone M.90^S/M.91^s Kal. 7.65mm, mit 3 Querrillen

367L^2 Argentinien, Exerzierpatrone Kal. 7.65mm mit 3 Querrillen, im Gew. d. scharfen Patrone

367M Argentinien, Peru, Bolivien, Paraguay M.91S (M/09) Kal. 7.65mm

367M^1 Argentinien, Exerzierpatrone mit 3 Querrillen

367M^2 Exerzierpatrone M.90S/M.91S mit 3 Querrillen, im Gewicht der scharfen Patrone

367N^1 Signalpatrone, Kal. 7.65mm, mit 1 Querrille

367N^2 Signalpatrone, Kal. 7.65mm, mit 2 Querrillen

367N^3 Signalpatrone, Kal. 7.65mm, mit 3 Querrillen

367O Zielübung, Kal. 7.65mm (7.9x53.6 (59.0))

367P Türkei, Kal. 7.65mm, verlängert für Torpedogeschosse

368 Italien, Kal. 6.5mm

368A Italien, Kal. 6.5mm W.F. Mauser

368B Italien, Kal. 6.5mm W.F. Mauser

369 M.91, Kal. 7.65mm Beaumont

370 Dänemark, Revolver M.91, Kal. 9.1mm

371 Großbritannien, Kal. 7.7mm

372 Pistole, Kal. 8mm Meig

373 Kal. 11mm Beaumont

374 Rumänien, Revolver 11.3mm

375 M.91, eingerichtet für Kal. 6.5mm Mieg (6.6x57)

375A Kal. 6.5mm Le Personne & Co., London

376 Revolver, Kal. 6.6mm Mauser

377 Itailien, Kal. 7.65mm

378 Russland M.91, 3 Linien, Kal. 7.62mm Mosin (7.77x53.75 R)

378^1 Russland M.91, Exerzierpatrone mit 3 Querrillen

378A Russland M.91, 3 Linien, Kal. 7.62mm Mosin, im Boden verstärkt

378B Russland M.91, 3 Linien, Kal. 7.62mm "S" (7.80x53.70 R)

378C Russland M.91, Zielübung, 7.77x59R

378D Russland M.91, 3 Linien, Kal. 7.62mm "S"

378E Russland, 3 Linien-Gewehr Kal. 7.62mm "S"

378F Russland, 3 Linien-Gewehr Kal. 7.62mm "S", kupferplatt, Eisenhülse

379 Amerika, Kal. 7.62mm Frankford, 7.75x58.95R

379A Amerika, Kal. 7.62mm Frankford

379B Amerika, Kal. 7.62mm Frankford

379C Amerika M.92, Kal. 7.62mm Krag-Jörgensen

379D Amerika, Kal. 7.62mm (.30) M.03 Magazin, 7.8x65.0

379E Amerika M.06 Kal. 7.62mm "S" (U.S. Mod. 1906 Kal. .30)

379E^1 Amerika Kal. 7.62mm Exerzierpatrone "S"

380 Kal. 7mm W.F. Mauser

380A Kal. 7mm W.F. Mauser

380B Kal. 7mm Fried. Krupp, Essen

380C Kal. 7mm Löwe & Cie., Berlin

380D Spanien M.93, Kal. 7mm W.F. Mauser, 7.22x57.0

380D^1 Spanien M.93, Exerzierpatrone

380E Kal. 7mm W.F. Mauser

380F M.93 Kal. 7mm, verstärkt

380G Chile, Kal. 7mm, verstärkt

380H M.93^A Kal. 7mm, Jagd

380J M.93^B Kal. 7mm, Jagd (7x57 R)

380K Kal. 7mm, Utendoerffer, Nürnberg

380L Spanien, Serbien, Mexiko, Chile, Brasilien, Uruguay M.93, Kal. 7mm

380L^1 Spanien M.93, Exerzierpatrone mit 3 Querrillen, im Gewicht der scharfen Patrone

380L^2 Exerzierpatrone wie 380L1, Jedoch mit S-Geschoss 253E

380M Spanien, Brasilien, San Salvador, Venezuela, Chiles, Columien, Uruguay M.93S Kal. 7mm (Gewehr und Machinengewehr)

380M^1 Barsilien, Exerzierpatrone M.93^S, Kal. 7mm, mit 3 Querrillen

380M^2 Barsilien, Exerzierpatrone M.93^S, Kal. 7mm, mit 3 Querrillen, im Gew. d. scharf. Patr.

380M^3 Spanien, Exerzierpatrone mit 6 Längerillen

380N China, Kal. 7.1mm W.F. Mauser (7.35x57)

380O M.93, Zielübung, Kal. 7mm

380P M.93, Zielübung, Kal. 7mm

380Q Kal. 7mm DWM verlängert für Torpedogeschosse

380R M.93, Zielübung, Kal. 7mm

381 Spanien, Kal. 11.15mm Remington

382 Hülse Kal. 5.5mm

383 Kal. 5.43mm, Louis Mattis

384 Kal. 11mm, Rohde, Kopenhagen

385 Dänemark M.89, Kal. 8mm Krag-Jörgensen

385A Dänemark M.89, Kal. 8mm Krag-Jörgensen, 8.8x58R

385C Dänemark M.89^S, Kal. 8mm, 8.25x58R

386 Hülse Kal. 5mm Mauser

387 Revolver, Kal. 7.5mm, Lotz-Abbot & Co., London

388 Schweiz, Schmidt-Rubin M.90, Kal. 7.5mm

388A Schweiz, Schmidt-Rubin M.90^S, Kal. 7.5mm

388B Schweiz, Schmidt-Rubin M.90^S, Kal. 7.5mm

388C Schweiz, Schmidt-Rubin M.90^S, Kal. 7.5mm

388D Schweiz, Schmidt-Rubin M.08, Kal.

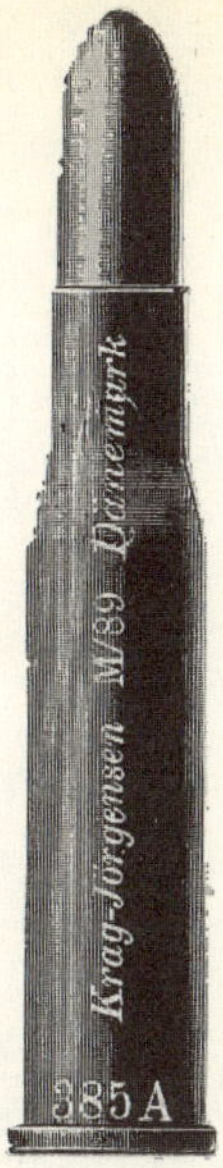

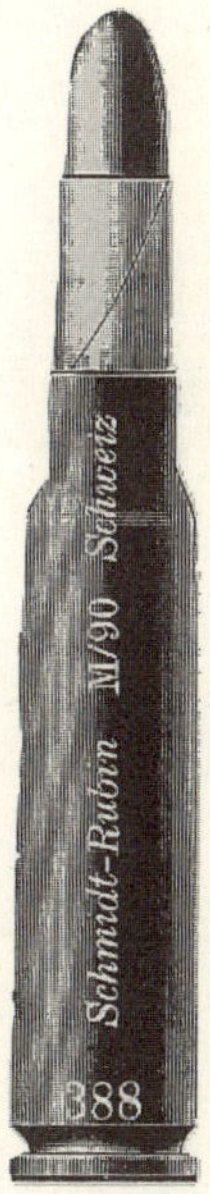

7.5mm (eingeführte Hülse)
389
390 Revolver, Kal. 7.4mm, Grusonwerk
391 Kal. 5.9mm Krohn, Köln
392 Kal. 6.55mm Mauser
392A Kal. 6.5mm Mauser, 6.68x54.0R
392B Kal. 6.5mm Beaumont-Mauser
393 Hülse Kal. 9.4mm (9.55x56.0)
393A Kal 9.4mm Mario Cresta, Hamburg (9.55x50.4)
394 Rumänien M.93, Kal. 6.5mm (Gewehr und Maschinengewehr)
394[1] Rumänien M.93, Kal. 6.5mm Exerzierpatrone mit 3 Querrillen, im Gew. d. scharf. Patr.
394A Rumänien, Kal. 6.5mm (Gewehr und Maschinengewehr)
394B Rumänien M.93, Kal. 6.5mm (für Ogivalgeschosse)
394B[1] Rumänien M.93, Kal. 6.5mm, Exerzierpatrone mit 3 Querrrillen
394C Rumänien M.93, Kal. 6.5mm (für Torpedogeschosse)
394D Rumänien, Kal. 6.5mm (für Torpedogeschosse) 6.70x55.3R
394E Rumänien, Kal. 6.5mm (für Torpedogeschosse) 6.70x57.5R
395 Kal. 6.5mm, P.F. Rottweil
395A Kal. 6.5mm, P.F. Rottweil
395B Holland, Kal. 6.5mm Mannlicher, Francotte & Co., Liège
395C Holland, Kal. 6.5mm, Jagd
395D Holland M.95, Kal. 6.5mm (Gewehr und Machinengewehr)
395D[1] Holland, Kal. 6.5mm, Exerzierpatrone mit 3 Querrillen
395E Holland M.95, Kal. 6.5mm "S"
396 Pistole, Kal. 6.65mm Mieg
397 Schützenhülse, P.F. Rottweil, 10.8x51.4R
398 Hülse Kal. 6.5mm W.F. Mauser
399 Revolver Ed. de Beaumont
400 Hülse Kal. 7.5mm, Löwe & Co., Berlin
401 Lancaster, Casnici Giorami & Co., Verona
402
403 Selbstladepistole M.96, Kal. 7.63mm Mauser (auch für Borchardt-Pistole)
403[1] Selbstladepistole M.96, Kal. 7.63mm, Exerzierpatrone
403A Selbstladepistole M.96, Kal. 7.63mm, Zeilübungspatrone
404 Hülse Kal. 6.5mm Luger, Berlin
404A Hülse Kal. 6.5mm M.88 (6.5x57)
404B Hülse 6.5mm Luger, Berlin
405 Hülse Kal. 6.5mm, uneingezogen, W.F. Mauser
406 Spanien M.71/84 Remington
407 Chile, Kal. 11mm, Einheitshülse Gras-Comblain
408 Hülse Kal. 5mm GR (Georg Roth)
409 Viehtödtung
409A Viehtödtung Heidelberg (9.95x28.75R)
410 Comblain, Frankreich
411 Kal. 11mm, Rohde Kopenhagen (11.6x34.5 R)
412 England Kal. .303", 7.7mm Lee Metford, uneingezogen
413 Pistole, Kal. 6.5mm Bergmann No. 3, ohne Eindrehung
413A Pistole, Kal. 6.5mm Bergmann No. 3
414 Rücklaufpistole, Kal. 6mm W.F. Mauser, uneingezogen
415 Revolver, Kal. 7.7mm W.F. Mauser
416 Pistole, Kal. 5mm Bergmann No. 2, ohne Eindrehung
416A Pistole, Kal. 5mm Bergmann No. 2
416A[1] Pistole, Kal. 5mm Bergmann No. 2, Exerzierpatrone
416B Revolver, Kal. 5mm Pickert, Zella St. Blasi
417
418
419 Hülse Kal. 7.3mm Teschner, Frankfurt a.O.
420 Pistole, Kal. 5mm Reynoso
421 Schweiz, Revolver Kal. 7.5mm
422 Lancaster
423 Pistole, Kal. 7.8mm Reynoso
424 Hülse Kal. 6mm, Versuch W.F. Mauser
425 Nordamerika, Kal. 6mm Marine, U.S. Navy Small Arm
425A Nordamerika, Kal. 6mm Marine, U.S. Navy Small Arm
425B Hülse Kal. 6mm, Versuch W.F. Mauser
425C Hülse Kal. 6mm, Versuch W.F. Mauser "K"
425D Kurze Pürschbüchse Kal. 6mm W.F. Mauser
425E Amerika, Kal. 6mm U.S. Navy Small Arm
426 Amerika, Kal. 6mm Luger, Berlin
426A Amerika, Kal. 6mm Luger, Berlin
426B Amerika, Kal. 6mm Luger, Berlin
426C Amerika, Kal. 6mm Luger, Berlin
427 Amerika, Kal. 6mm Luger, Berlin
428 Schrotpatrone, Dornheim
429 Hülse Kal. 6mm, P.F. Rottweil
430 Hülse Kal. 6.3mm, P.F. Rottweil
431 Norwegen, Kal. 6.5mm Krag-Jörgensen
431A Schweden, Kal. 6.5mm P.F. Rottweil
431B Schweden, Kal. 6.5mm
431C Schweden M.96, Kal. 6.5mm W.F. Mauser (6.65x55.0)
431C[1] Schweden, Kal. 6.5mm, Exerzierpatrone mit 3 Querrillen
431D Luxemburg M.96, Kal. 6.5mm, Gendarmerie- und Freiwilligen-Korps
431D[1] Luxemburg, Exerzierpatrone mit 6 Längarillen
431E Schweden, Kal. 6.5mm Gewehr und Machinengewehr
431F Schweden M.05, Kal. 6.5mm "S" (6.75x55.0)
431G Société Française, Paris (Schweden) Kal. 6.5mm
431H Schweden, Kal. 7.2mm Versuch (7.4x59.0)
431J Schweden, Kal. 7.5mm Versuch (7.7x59.0)
431K Schweden, Kal. 6.5mm Versuch, verlängert für Torpedogeschosse (6.7x58.0)
431L Schweden, Kal. 6.5mm Versuch (6.7x61.0)
431M Schweden, Kal. 6.5mm Versuch (6.7x61.0 R)
431P vom Hofe 5.6mm Super Express (5.76x61.0)
431R vom Hofe 5.6mm Super Express mit Rand (5.76x61.0 R)
432 Hülse Kal. 4mm, Lehmann, Brescia
433 Nord-Amerika, Marine, Kal. 6mm Luger, Berlin
434 Hülse Kal. 7.9mm Fried. Krupp
435 Hülse Kal. 5mm Luger, Berlin

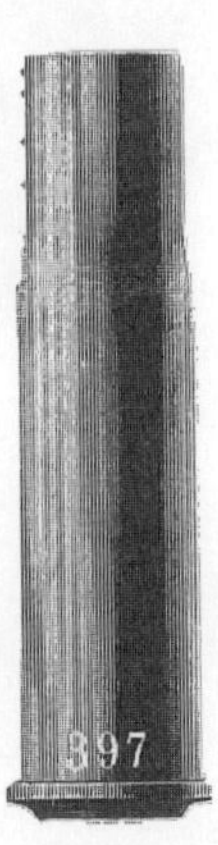

436 Hülse Kal. 5mm Fried. Krupp
437 Hülse Kal. 6.5mm Fried. Krupp
437A Hülse Kal. 6.5mm Fried. Krupp (6.65x54.6)
438 Hülse Kal. 7mm Freid. Krupp
439 Hülse Kal. 8mm Guedes (7.9x59.7 R)
439A Hülse Kal. 8mm Guedes (8.02x59.7 R)
440 Gaggenauer-Hülse
441 M./88D Jagd, Kal. 8mm
442-442D Kal. 6mm und 7mm Mogueira, Versuch
443 Schützen Kal. 11mm, P.F. Düneburg
444 Hülse Kal. 6mm "G", W.F. Mauser, uneingezogen
444A Hülse Kal. 6mm "G", W.F. Mauser
444B Hülse Kal. 6mm "G" (6.16x58.04)
444C Hülse Kal. 6mm "G", W.F. Mauser, verlängert
445 Netzscheren-Pistole "N", Deutsche Marine
446 Kal. 8mm Dornheim (Jagdbüches 8x57 / 360/57/8)
447 Büchse Kal. 11mm, P.F. Düneberg
448 Stockholm, Axel Sjogren
449 Schützen, Rud. Mauser
450
451 Pistole, Kal. 8mm No.4 Bergmann
451A Pistole, Kal. 7.5mm No. 4A Bergmann
452 Revolver, Kal. 9mm Gervais (9.05x17.75R)
453 Großbritannien M.89/95 Kal. 0.303" - 7.7mm Lee-Metford
453A Großbritannien, Zielübung Kal. 7.7mm
453B Großbritannien M.89S/03, Kal. 0.303" - 7.7mm
453B[1] Großbritannien, Exerzierpatrone mit 3 Längerillen
453E Hülse Kal. 303
454
455 Jagd, Normal 8.15x46R
456 Pistole, Kal. 9mm, No. 6 Bergmann
456A Bayard-Bergmann Kal. 9mm, Thieme v. Edler, Eibar (Espana)
456A[1] Exerzierpatrone Kal. 9mm
456B Bayard-Bergmann Kal. 9mm (Star-Pistole)
456C Hülse Kal. 9mm (Eibar)
457 Portugal M.04, Kal. 6.5mm W.F. Mauser (6.65x58.0)
457[1] Portugal M.04, Kal. 6.5mm, Exerzierpatrone mit 3 Querrillen
457[2] Portugal M.04, Kal. 6.5mm, Exerzierpatrone im Gewicht der scharfen Patrone
457A Kal. 6.5mm "K" Mauser (6.5x54)
457A[1] Kal. 6.5mm "K", Exerzierpatrone mit 3 Querrillen und glatte Ausführung
457B Portugal, Kal. 6.5mm S (6.75x58.0)
457C Zielübung Kal. 6.5mm
457D Zielübung Kal. 6.5mm
458 Belgien, Kal. 7.65mm Marga
458A Belgien, Kal. 7.65mm, Zielübung
459 Persien, Kal. 6.5mm
460 Pistole, Kal. 8mm No. 7 Bergmann
460A Pistole, Kal. 7.5mm No. 7A Bergmann
461 Pistole, Kal. 7.5 (7.65)mm No. 5 Bergmann
462 Express Kal. 8mm (S.u.S. 8x58)
462A Express Kal. 8mm (S.u.S. 8x58)
463 Express S.u.S. 6.5x58
463A Express S.u.S. 6.5x48
464 Pistole, Kal. 8.6mm W.F. Mauser
465 Hülse Kal. 7mm W.F. Mauser (7.18x58.0)
465A Kal. 7mm W.F. Mauser kurz
465B Kal. 7mm "S", W.F. Mauser "L"
465C Kal. 7mm "S", W.F. Mauser, Versuch
466 Pistole Mannlicher, Kal. 7.65mm Siber
466A Autom. Pistole, Kal. 7.63mm Sömmerda
467 Dreise-Karabiner, Kal. 5.5mm Sömmerda
468 Dreise-Karabiner, Kal. 5.5mm Sömmerda
469 Hülse Kal. 5mm W.F. Mauser
469A Hülse Kal. 5mm, Sturtevant Engineering Company Ltd., London
470 Hülse Kal. 5.5mm W.F. Mauser
471 Parabellum-Pistole, Kal. 7.65mm Schweiz
471[1] Parabellum Exerzierpatrone Kal. 7.65mm
471[2] Parabellum Exerzierpatrone Kal. 7.65mm
471A Parabellum-Karabiner, Kal. 7.65mm (geschwärzte Hülse)
471B Parabellum, Kal. 7.65mm, Zielübung
471C Parabellum, Kal. 7.65mm, Versuch
472 Frankreich, Kal. 8mm Lebel
473 Italien M.91, Kal. 6.5mm Parravicinio Carcano
473A Italien, Zielübung, Kal. 6.5mm DWM
474 Kal. 9mm Jagd, W. Förster, Berlin (9.0x74.7R)
474A Kal. 9.3mm Jagd, W. Förster, Berlin (9.3x74R)
474B Kal. 9mm Jagd, John Rigby, London (400/360) 9.10x62
474C Kal. 9.3mm Jagd, Dornheim, Suhl/Mauser (9.3x62)
474C[1] Kal. 9.3mm Jagd, Exerzierpatrone
474D Kal. 9.3mm Jagd, Dornheim, Suhl
474E Hülse Kal. 400/360 (9.20x70.0 R)
474F Kal. 9.3mm Jagd, Behrs Waffenwerke Suhl (9.30x86.0R)
475 Pistole, Kal. 7.63mm No. 8 Bergmann
476 Pistole Kal. 6.5mm Ronezewsky (P.27x6.5)
477 Griechenland, Kal. 6.5mm Mannlicher-Schönauer (6.65x53.5) - nur für Armee -
477A Griechenland, Kal. 6.5mm Mannlicher-Schönauer "S" (6.65x58.0)
477 Pürschbüchse Kal. 6.5mm Mannlicher-Schönauer (6.5x53)
478 Pistole, Kal. 10mm Bergmann
479 Autom. Pistole Kal. 7.65mm Browning
479[1] Autom. Pistole Kal. 7.65mm Browning, Exerzierpatrone
479A Selbstlade-Pistole Mauser, Kal. 7.65mm und Automat. Pistole Kal. 7.65mm
479A[1] Exerzierpatrone Kal. 7.65mm
479A[2] Automat. Pistole Kal. 7.65mm, Exerzierpatrone
479B Zielübung, Pistole Mauser, Kal. 7.65mm
479C Winchester, Kal. 7.65mm
480 Parabellum-Pistole Kal. 9mm (M.08)
480C Parabellum-Pistole Kal. 9mm Armes M.08, Marine M.04
480C[1] Parabellum Exerzierpatrone Kal. 9mm
480C[2] Parabellum Exerzierpatrone Kal. 9mm, mit 6 Längerillen

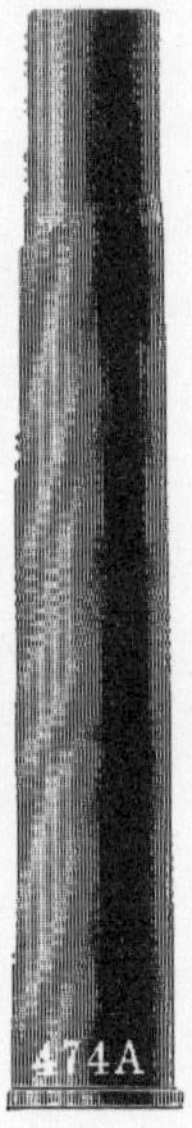

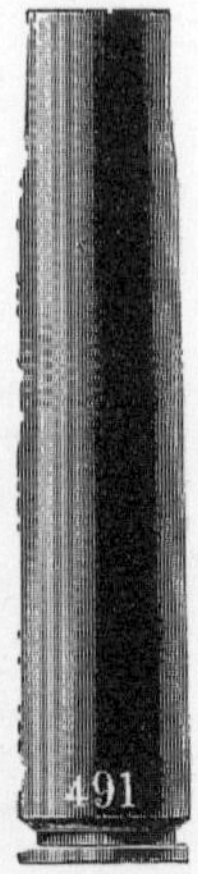

480C^3 Parabellum Exerzierpatrone Kal. 9mm
480C^4 Parabellum Exerzierpatrone Kal. 9mm, im Gewicht der scharfen Patrone
480D Parabellum-Karabiner Kal. 9mm
480E Pist. Patronenhülse 08 (Stahl)
480F^1 Signalpatrone Kal. 9mm, weiss
480F^2 Signalpatrone Kal. 9mm, rot
480F^3 Signalpatrone Kal. 9mm, grün
480F Parabellum Zielübung, Kal. 9mm
480G Parabellum Platzpatrone Kal. 9mm
480H Parabellum Platzpatrone Kal. 9mm
480J Parabellum Zielübung, Kal. 9mm
480K Parabellum, Kal. 9mm
480L Parabellum Platzpatrone Kal. 9mm
481 Japan M.97, Kal. 6.5mm Arisaka
481A Hülse Kal. 6.5mm (6.6x51.0)
482 Luxemburg, Offiziers-Revolver des Gendarmerie- und Freiwilligen Corps, Kal. 8mm
483 Kal. 6.5x70mm, A. Ohlhoff, Portland, Ore.
484 Pistole Kal. 5mm Clement (Behr, Hamburg)
484^1 Pistole Kal. 5mm Clement, Exerzierpatrone
485 Mexico, Revolver-Karabiner Kal. 7.9mm Pieper
486 Mexico, Revolver Kal. 7.9mm Pieper
487 Selbstlade-Pistole Kal. 9mm Mauser
487^1 Selbstlade-Pistole Kal. 9mm Mauser, Exerzierpatrone
487A Selbstlade-Pistole Kal. 9mm Mauser
487B Selbstlade-Pistole Kal. 9mm Mauser
487C Selbstlade-Pistole Kal. 9mm Mauser N.M.
487D Selbstlade-Pistole Kal. 9mm Mauser
487G Selbstlade-Pistole Kal. 9mm Mauser
487J Hülse Kal. 9mm Mauser
487K Pistolenhülse Kal. 9mm
488 Simplex-Pistole Kal. 8mm Bergmann
489 Pürschbüchse Kal. 6mm, W. Förster, Berlin
489A Pürschbüchse Kal. 6mm, W. Förster, Berlin
490 Mars-Pistole Kal. 11mm Bergmann
491 Pürschbüchse Kal. 9mm W.F. Mauser (9.3mm)
491A Pürschbüchse M.88, Kal. 9mm W.F. Mauser (9x57)
491A^1 Pürschbüchse Kal. 9mm, Exerzierpatrone mit 3 Querrillen
491B Pürschbüchse Kal. 9mm W.F. Mauser
491C Pürschbüchse Kal. 9.3mm
491D Pürschbüchse Kal. 9mm, Jul. Hessmer, Berlin (9.03x62.8)
491E Pürschbüchse Kal. 9mm Mannlicher-Schönauer (9.0x56.4)
491F Pürschbüchse Kal. 9mm (9.03x56.5)
491G
491H Pürschbüchse Kal. 9mm, Haenel, Suhl (9.05x62.8)
491J
491K
491L
491M Pürschbüchse Kal. 9mm, W.F. Mauser (9.05x62.8)
492 Pistole, Kal. 10.5mm W.F. Mauser
493 Signal-Apparat, Patent Stritter
494 Pürschbüchse Kal. 6mm (6.20x57.6)
495 Pürschbüchse Kal. 10.75mm, B. Stahl, Suhl
495A Pürschbüchse Kal. 10.75mm, G.C. Dornhein, Lippstadt
495B Pürschbüchse Kal. 10.75mm, H. Leue, Berlin
496 Hülse Kal. 9mm
497 Karabiner und Karabiner-Pistole Kal. 7.65 (7.63)mm Mannlicher M.1901
498 Pürschbüchse Kal. 10.15mm
499 Torpedo-Zündpatrone Deutsche Marine
500 Luxemburg, Kal. 6mm, Gendarmerie und Freiwilligen Corps
501 Pistole Kal. 7mm "Charola y Anitua"
502 Norwegen, Kal. 6.5mm Krag-Jörgensen
502A S-Munition, Kal. 6.5mm, für Schützenvereine nordischer Staaten (6.75x55.0)
503 Pürschbüchse Kal. 11mm, Teschner & Co., Franfurt a.O.
504 Pürschbüchse Kal. 9mm, Teschner & Co., Franfurt a.O.
504A Pürschbüchse Kal. 9mm, Teschner & Co., Franfurt a.O.
505 Pürschbüchse Kal. 8mm, Teschner & Co., Franfurt a.O.
506 Pürschbüchse Kal. 9mm, "Nimrod" Dornheim, Lippstadt
507 Revolver, Kal. 6.5mm
508 Mauser Selbstladepistole, Kal. 6.35mm, Mod. 1910
508A Automat. Pistole, Kal. 6.35mm
508A^1 Automat. Pistole, Kal. 6.35mm, Exerzierpatrone
509 Hülse f.d. Pulverversand. Rh.W.Spr.A.G., Köln-Nürnberg
510 Autom. Glisenti-Pistole Kal. 7.65mm, Tempini, Brescia
511 Hülse Kal. 7mm M.06, W.F. Mauser
511A Hülse Kal. 6.8mm M.07, W.F. Mauser (China)
511A^1 Hülse Kal. 6.8mm M.07, Exerzierpatrone mit 3 Querrillen
511B Hülse Kal. 6.8mm M.08, W.F. Mauser "S"
511B^1 Hülse Kal. 6.8mm M.08, Exerzierpatrone mit 3 Querrillen
511B^2 Hülse Kal. 6.8mm M.08, Exerzierpatrone im Gewicht der scharfen Patrone
511C China M.08, Kal. 6.8mm
511C^1 China M.08, Kal. 6.8mm, Exerzierpatrone mit 3 Querrillen
511D China M.08, Zielbübung
511E China M.08, Zielbübung
512 Pürschbüchse Kal. 8mm, Vierordt & Co., Kehl
513 Automat. Colt-Pistole, Kal. 11.43mm
513A Automat. Colt-Pistole, Kal. 11.43mm, Amerikan. Armee-Mod. .45"
514 Pürschbüchse Kal. 8 (7.9)mm, Behrs Industrie-Gesellschaft
514A Pürschbüchse Kal. 8 (7.9)mm, Berhs Waffenwerke, Suhl
515 Pürschbüchse Kal. 10.75 (10.5)mm, Le Personne & Co., London
515A Pürschbüchse Kal. 10.75 (10.5)mm Mauser, Normalhülse
515A^1 Pürschbüchse, Exerzierpatrone mit 3 Querrillen
516 Patronenhülse, Emil Adolf, Reutlingen
517 Pürschbüchse Kal. 6.5mm "Angier" (6.65x58.7)
517A Pürschbüchse Kal. 6.5mm "Angier"

(6.50x58.7)
518 Siam, Kal. 8mm (8.15x50.5 R)
518A Siam, Kal. 8mm
518B Siam, Kal. 8mm
519 Pürschbüchse Kal. 6.5mm Winchester, engl. Kal. 25/35
519A Pürschbüchse Kal. 6.5mm Remington, "25"
520 Pürschbüchse Kal. 6.5mm Winchester, engl. Kal. 25/25
521
522 Cadet Kal. .310 7.9mm (Greener), Westley Richards & Co. Ltd.
523 Pürschbüchse Kal. 10.5mm, Haenel, Suhl
524 Pürschbüchse Kal. 10.5mm
525 Revolver, Kal. 8mm Lebel
526 Patronenhülse Dir. Castenholz, Köln
527 Kal. 7mm W.F. Mauser, Versuch
527A Kal. 7mm DWM, Berlin
527B Kal. 7mm W.F. Mauser
528 Pürschbüchse Kal. 8 (8.2)mm Mannlicher-Schönauer
529 Hülse Kal. 7mm Luger, Berlin
530 Wurfgranaten-Patrone M. 88s
531 Pürschbüchse Kal. 9.5mm Mannlicher-Schönauer
532 Pistole M.80-82-85 Rohde, Copenhagen
533 Pürschbüchse Kal. 11.5mm, Leue, Berlin
534 Automat. Gewehr, Kal. 7mm W.F. Mauser
534A Automat. Gewehr, Kal. 7mm W.F. Mauser
534B Automat. Gewehr, Kal. 7mm W.F. Mauser
535 Gewehr Kal. 9mm, Karl Puff, Spandau (8.80x62.0)
536 Savage/Karabiner, Kal. 5.6mm/.22 H.P.
537 DWM Berlin, Maschinengewehr Kal. 11mm
538 Automat. Browning-Pist. Kal. 9mm long
539 Winchester Cal. 22/5.6x35, sog. Vierlingshülse
540 Automat. Browning-Pist. Kal. 9mm Kurz
540[1] Exerzierpatrone zur autom. Pistole Kal. 9mm Kurz
541 Gewehr Kal. 8.1mm, W. Brenneke, Leipzig
542 Gewehr Kal. 8x60
543 Winchester Rep. Pürschb. Kal. .30 (Kal. 30/30) (7.62mm)
544 Hülse für Kal. 7.3mm Suomen Osuuskauppojen, Kaskuskunta
545 Hülse 22 H.P. für Winchester u. Savage-Büchse Kal. 5.6mm/5.6x52R
545A Hülse Kal. 5.6x52
546 Pistolenpatronenhülse Kal. 6.35mm, Mauserwerke A.G.
547 Einsteckpatrone für Kal. 7.65mm, Thieme v. Edler, Eibar, Spanien
548 Pistolenpatronenhülse Kal. 6.5mm, Mauserwerke A.G.
549 Patronenhülse z. Viehtötungs-Apparat Karl Schermer, Karlsruhe
550 Pistolenpatronenhülse z. Parabellum-Pistole, Kal. 6.5mm
551 Lancaster-Jagdhülse Kal. 16
552 Lancaster-Jagdhülse Kal. 12
553 Lancaster-Jagdhülse Kal. 12
554 Patronenhülse z. Viehtötungs-Apparat Karl Schermer, Karlsruhe
555 Hülse 404x73, Mauserwerke A.G. (10.7x73.0)
556 Viehschusshülse Kal. 9.2mm
556A Viehschusshülse Kal. 9.2mm
556B Viehschusshülse Kal. 9.2mm Schermer (Hülse mit 1 Zündloch)
557 Hülse z. Patrone 7x64
557A Hülse z. Patrone 7x65R
558 Hülse z. Patrone 8x64
558A Hülse z. Patrone 8x64R
559 Pistolenhülse Kal. 380
559[1] Exerzierpatrone Kal. 380
559A Verlängerte 9mm Pistolen-Hülse
560 Hülse Kal. .315 für Ogivalgeschosse (8x57 J)
560E Hülse Kal. 8mm/8x57 J
561 Hülse Kal. 8mm für Spitzgeschosse (8x57 JS)
562 Hülse 7.65x73
562A Hülse 7.65x70
563 Hülse Kal. 11.35mm
564 Hülse 9.5x73, Kal. .375 Magnum
565 Hülse Kal. 7.3mm, Suomen Osuuskauppojen, Keskuskunta
566 Hülse 7.65x77
567 Hülse 9.3x64
567A Hülse 9.3x65 R (mit Rand)
568 Hülse Kal. .500
569 Hülse 9.3x70
570 Hülse Kal. .318 (Kynoch)
571 Hülse Kal. .315 für S-Gesch.
571E Hülse Kal. .315 (Stahl)
572 Hülse Kal. 7mm
573 Hülse 7x72R
574 Hülse 8x72R
575 Hülse 7x73 Hofmann (7mm Super-Express)
576 Hülse Echolot
577 Hülse für Steyr-Pistole Kal. 9mm
578 Hülse Kal. .22 Hornet
579
580 Pistolenhülse Kal. 8.15mm
581 Bergmann Kal. 7mm
581A Hülse zur Kurzpatrone Kal. 7mm
581B Hülse zur Bergmann-Patrone Kal. 7mm (Stahl)
582 Pist. Hülse Colt, Kal. .38
583 Hülse für Stahlhelmbeschusspatrone
584 Siam, Kal. 8mm
585 Hülse Kal. 7mm (Lübeck)
586 Hülse 6-10
587 Hülse Kal. 8mm (Bulgarien)
588 Hülse Kal. 8mm (™sterreich)
589 Hülse Kal. 8mm (Ungarn)
590
591 Hülse Kal. 8mm
592 Revolver-Patronenhülse Kal. 32 Kurz
593 Revolver-Patronenhülse Kal. 38 lang
594 Lebel-Revolver-Patronenhülse Kal. 8mm
595 S-W-Revolver-Patr. Hülse Kal. 32 Kurz
596 Hülse Kal. 7.9 Mod. 24 sS
597 Hülse Kal. 5.6mm, Schienmann
598 Hülse Kal. 8mm, Brenneke
599 Hülse Kal. 8x73 S
600 Hülse Kal. 9.3x57
601 Hülse Kal. 9.3x70R
602 Hülse Kal. 25/20
603 Hülse Kal. 7.6x66
604 Hülse Kal. 8.15x58R
605 Hülse Kal. 7x75R

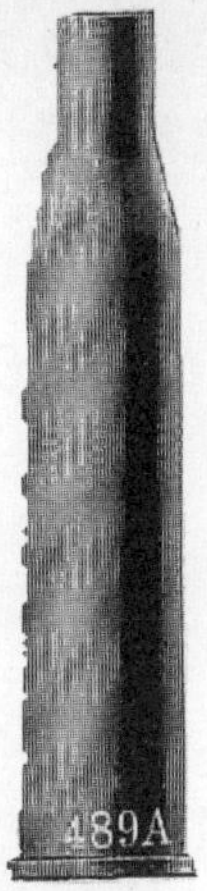

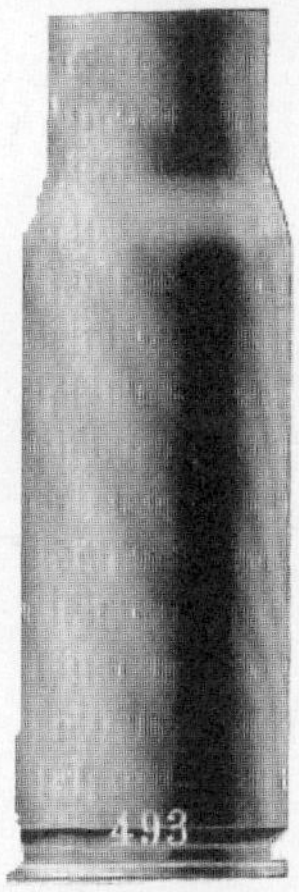

Handloading can be simple... basic...if that's all you need. But when ultimate accuracy is demanded, things are much more complex. Here's....

How The BENCH DO IT

by FRED SINCLAIR

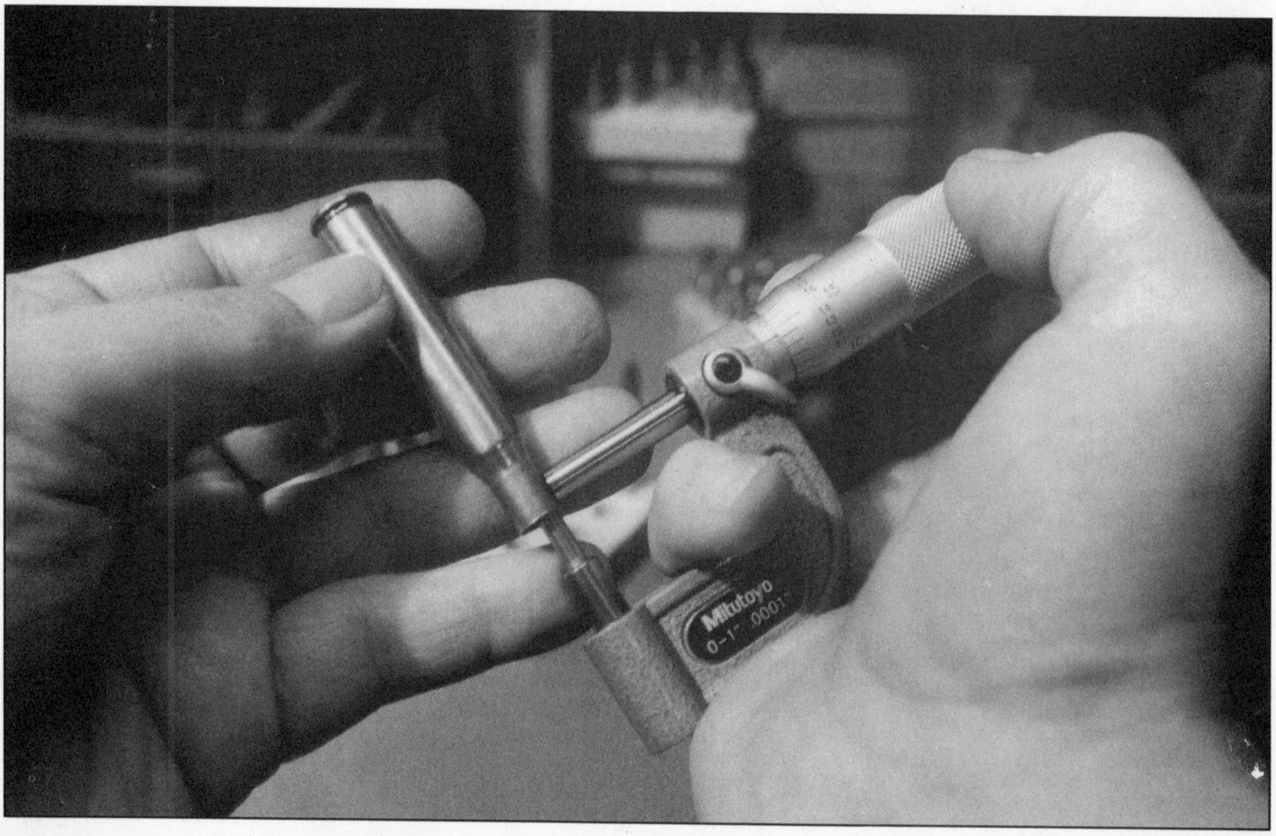

A ball micrometer is a must when working with a benchrest rifle with a close tolerance chamber.

RESTERS

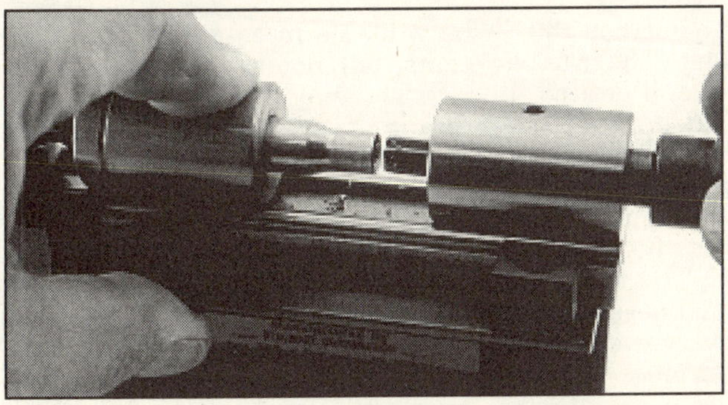

The Wilson neck reamer being used to chamfer a case mouth with an 8-degree angle. It produces a smoother entry than the standard case mouth chamfering tool.

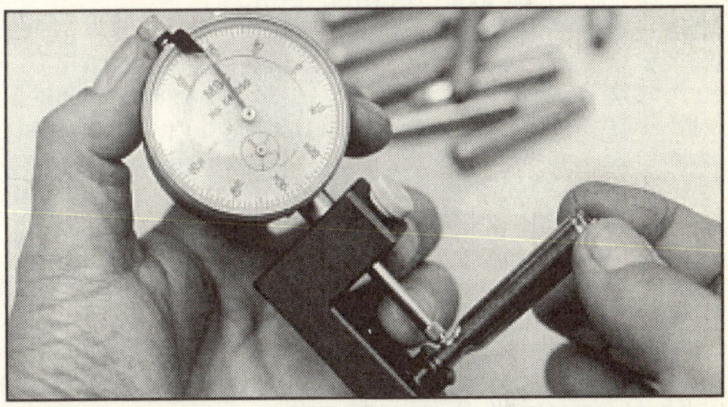

The Sinclair neck wall thickness gauge speeds the case sorting operation. A ball micrometer can be used for the same purpose.

IN THE RIGHT hands, today's state of-the-art benchrest rifle is capable of shooting much less than .200-MOA. For example, at the 1992 International Benchrest Shooters National Championship Matches, the winning shooter, Tony Boyer, fired a total of fifteen five-shot groups at 100 yards and another fifteen five-shot groups at 200 yards, and the total of the 150 rounds fired averaged only .1942-MOA. In doing so, Tony won the prestigious Heavy Varmint Class with an average of .1587-MOA (twenty-five shots at 100 yards and twenty-five more at 200 yards).

Benchrest rifles are built using only the best components and assembled to exacting tolerances. Normally, chambers on these rifles are reamed to "close tolerances." This is to say, headspace is set at the minimum, case body diameters are minimum SAAMI specs, and neck diameters are well below standard chambers. Chambers, reamed to close tolerances, will not accept a standard loaded cartridge. Such chambers will, when the case is properly prepared, limit the expansion of a fired case. Once the case is fireformed, body and headspace dimensions are limited to zero expansion and neck expansion is limited to .002-inch maximum.

Loading for such capable firearms involves much more than working the handle of a reloading press. It requires that the handloader become a cross between a quality-control engineer and a proficient mechanic. If the benchrest shooter expects to shoot well, he must prepare and load each cartridge case to the most exacting standards that his ability will allow.

Precise case preparation is a must. It is tedious and time-consuming, especially in large numbers. Performed separately, you will be hard pressed to see accuracy improvements from some of the prep operations. But as you multiply the steps, the uniformity and efficiency of the cartridge case will be improved, and you will find that each operation enhances the previous one.

Because of the close tolerance chamber specs used for modern B/R rifles, cartridge case life can be extended so that twenty cases will normally outlast the usable life of the rifle barrel. For this reason, plus the fact that most benchrest shooters reload on site, case preparation is normally confined to ten to twenty cases at a time.

Preparation is started with new commercial cases; anything less will be a waste of time and effort. Trying to save a few bucks on cases for a first-rate B/R rifle is foolish, not frugal. Brass that has been fired and reloaded a number of times becomes work-hardened and brittle. This condition will not allow the case to properly respond to some prep operations. Military brass, even the match type, is of a harder alloy and not manufactured with reloading in mind. The life of this brass will be short and the end result will be frequent replacement.

Now that Federal and Norma are no longer offering unprimed brass, our choices are narrowed to Remington, Winchester and PMC. With the availability of bulk Remington and Winchester brass at reasonable prices, there is little reason not to use these brands. I have heard some reloaders comment that bulk brass is inferior to factory-boxed brass, but let me assure you it all comes from the same place.

Quality measuring tools are required for precision reloading. A good pair of stainless steel dial calipers is a must, a 1-inch micrometer comes in quite handy and, when working with a close tolerance chamber, some type of .0001-inch reading ball-end micrometer is mandatory. For case sorting, a neck wall thickness gauge will add speed to the operation. Just remember that dial-type calipers are not the last word in measuring tools and are normally capable of only plus or minus .001-inch accuracy. Your needs will require measuring in the tenths of thousands, so use a standard-style micrometer made for such tolerances.

If I wish to end up with twenty prepared cases, I normally start with twice that number. I know from experience that a few will be discarded and I may ruin a couple during the neck-turning operation.

Most prep operations are influenced by the case neck. More likely than not, the neck and/or mouth are distorted during manufacturing, so the first operation is to resize the neck in some fashion. Use either an expanding mandrel or resizing die that will straighten the full length of the neck.

While resizing, check for any small creases in the case shoulder and neck, and for off-center flash holes. Cases having these imperfections should be discarded.

Most new brass, sized or unsized, has a noticeable burr just inside of the case mouth. Most of us use a standard 60-degree deburring tool to remove this burr. But close inspection will likely reveal that such removal has not been complete. I use a Wilson case trimmer and neck reamer of the correct caliber for inside chamfering. The reamers have about an 8-degree taper for the first .060- to .085-inch. I run the reamer into the case mouth just to where the major diameter of the reamer contacts the case mouth. This produces a nice gradual taper that results in a couple of benefits. It eliminates the "bump" as the bullet is being seated, plus it allows the cartridge case to start over a neck-turning tool mandrel with greater ease. It is a slower method of case mouth chamfering, but it will produce benefits.

I weigh each case when preparing B/R cases. Normally, the weight does not vary much within each lot. I feel that a variance here of 1.5 percent of case weight is a maximum acceptable limit.

Gauging flash hole diameters is an operation I do on a random basis. Most commercial manufacturers aim for an .082-inch diameter flash hole.

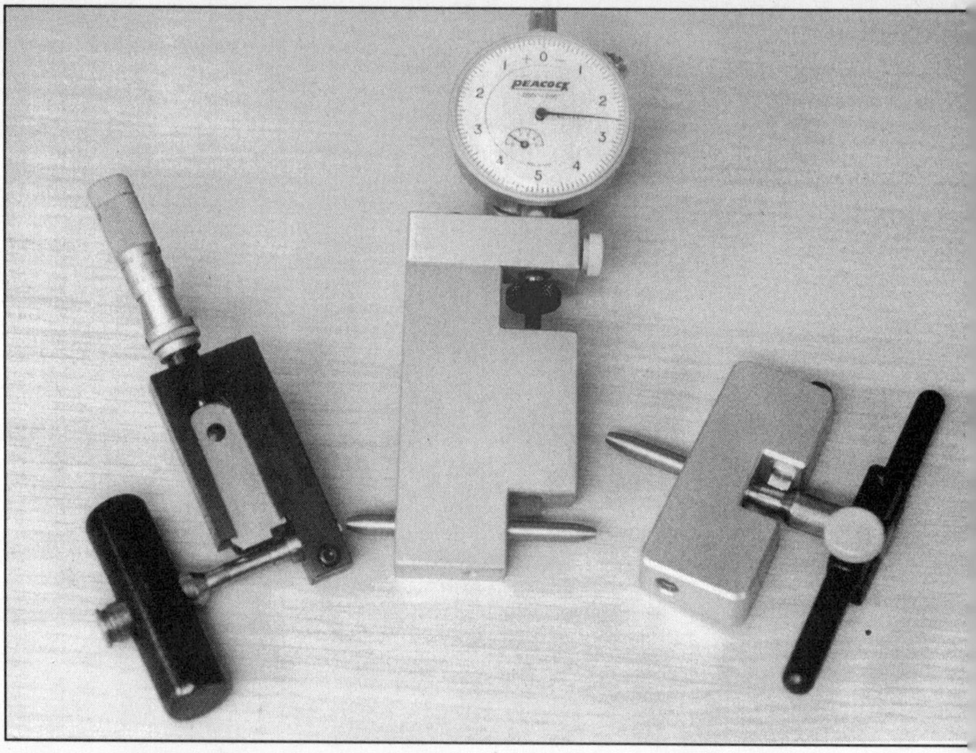

R.W. Hart and Sinclair outside neck turning tools.

There are exceptions, such as PPC. A wire size #45 drill bit (.082) can be used to check hole size, if desired. I do not worry about undersized flash holes, as most flash hole deburring tools, except RCBS, will open the hole to .082.

Next step is to sort the cases by neck wall thickness. The theory is that if neck wall thickness varies, body thickness will vary even more. Extreme body wall variance will create a powder chamber that is off-center with the rifle bore. Knowledgeable B/R reloaders feel this is an undesirable condition.

Using a tool designed for the purpose, check neck wall thickness. You will find it does vary around the circumference. The amount of variance will determine if a case is a "keeper." Discard any with a variance exceeding .0015-inch.

The use of an outside neck-turning tool is mandatory for close-tolerance B/R rifle chambers. Not only is it required to uniform the case neck walls, but it is also needed so the shooter can match the neck diameter of his loaded round to that of the rifle's chamber. Inside neck reamers will not work for neck wall uniforming. The neck reamer is designed to remove excess material. The reamer will only follow the existing hole, unless it is supported—such as in a 7/8-14 ream die. Neck ream dies can be valuable in case-forming operations, but not neck wall uniforming. The major problem with ream dies is that the user has no control over the amount of material being removed. The preferred practice is to outside neck turn.

A number of neck-turning tools are available, but the best for B/R use are the hand-held type. This kind of tool produces the most accurate results. Some are available with micrometers or dial indicators, so the adjustment can be fine tuned to .0001-inch when desired.

Fit of the cartridge case on the neck-turning tool mandrel/pilot is the most important part of the turning operation. A case neck too loose on the mandrel/pilot will sure make for easy turning, but is a waste of time. Any clearance between the mandrel/pilot will be transferred to the finished product. The result will be a neck wall thickness variance equal to the amount of the clearance, the very thing you were trying to correct.

If the resizing performed prior to initial case inspection does not produce the desired fit, you may have to alter or replace the die's expander ball. The expander ball's diameter must be compatible with the neck-turning tool mandrel. An expander ball .001-inch larger than the mandrel will normally obtain an ideal fit.

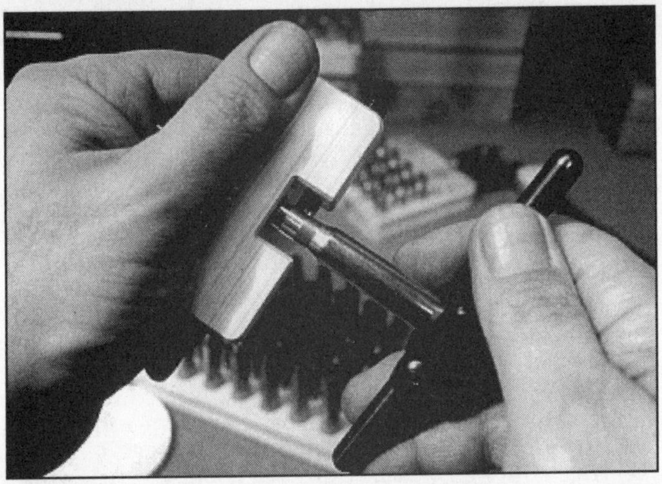

Turn the case neck so that the base of the bullet, when seated, is in the turned portion of the neck. Better yet, turn the full length of the neck.

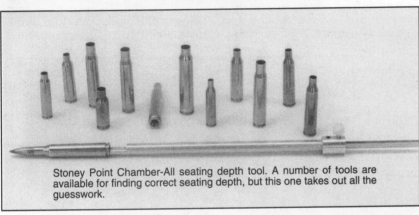

Stoney Point Chamber-All seating depth tool. A number of tools are available for finding correct seating depth, but this one takes out all the guesswork.

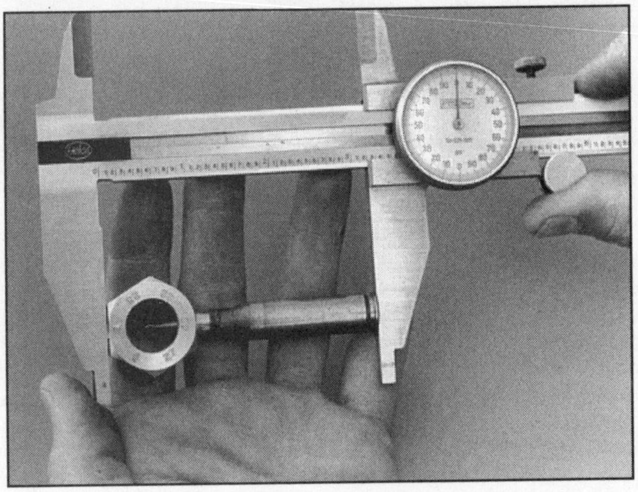

Tools such as this Bullet Comparator are quite beneficial when working with bullet seating depths.

Unfortunately, resizing dies and neck-turning tool mandrels often have incompatible diameters. To correct the problem, the handloader may have to polish either the expander ball or the mandrel to obtain the most desirable fit. This is a fairly simple task that can be done using nothing more than a drill motor and 320-grit emery.

Adjustment of most neck-turning tools can be a little tricky for the beginner. Until you get acquainted with the procedure, use some of those culled cartridge cases when adjusting your tool.

It is best to turn the full length of the neck, but don't go too far into the shoulder. Doing so would cause a weak area at the neck and shoulder junction.

If you are a beginner at turning cases for benchrest-type tight chambers, I suggest turning the case neck so your finished *loaded* round will measure .002-inch smaller than the neck diameter of your rifle's chamber. Once you become acquainted with the tool and the neck-turning operation, you may want to work to a closer neck tolerance, but not the first time around.

At this point, it is time to prime (more on priming will be discussed later) and charge the cases in preparation for fireforming. When selecting a powder charge for fireforming, check one of the current loading manuals. Select a powder that has a mid-range burning rate for the cartridge you are working with, and use a charge that is on the low end of the reloading manual's suggestions.

If you are working with some sort of wildcat that will be blown out considerably during the fireforming operation, use caution not to "over do." If the wildcat has a fairly large case capacity, do not fireform with a slow-burning powder.

Do not use powder XYZ just because you have a lot of it or because it was cheap. And for gosh sakes, *do not* start with somebody's pet load without reducing it first.

Remember that case capacity is at a minimum on new cases. Also keep in mind that when you start with new cases, you may encounter a variation in case volume from manufacturer to manufacturer, and even from lot to lot of the same manufacturer. The load that was right for your last batch of brass may not work as well for the new cases you have just purchased.

I prefer to fireform new cases with the bullets firmly touching the rifling—not jammed against it, but firm. I do so using a reduced load.

Seating against the rifling has several benefits. It forces the case head flush against the bolt face, which helps keep the primer from backing out, and it helps to center the round in the chamber. Results will be an evenly fireformed case, eliminating most of the off-center firing pin indentation and much of the one-sided bulge which can be created by a maximum-size chamber.

Without proper tools, finding the overall length (OAL) that has the bullet just touching the rifling will be trial and error. Smoking a bullet or drawing lines on a cleaning rod shoved down the barrel went out with the hula hoop. Use one of the accurate seating depth tools that are available today. The new Stoney Point Chamber-All gauge is the most versatile tool I have used.

Once you establish that initial seating depth, assemble an unprimed sample round. Assemble samples with other weights and brands of bullets that you might be using. Be sure to mark them accordingly. Such samples should be used as references. They will be used later when you begin fine tuning the seating depth for that ultimate load. They will serve as a gauge for tracking throat wear and initial bullet seater adjustment.

The OAL, when measuring across the bullet's point, is going to vary a little from round to round. Bullets out of the same box will vary as much as .015-inch in length due to the way the bullet swage die works. The use of a Bullet Comparator, Davidson Seating Depth Checker, or the RCBS Precision Mic will allow the handloader to arrive at correct seating depths and eliminate these variations. These tools contact the bullet at the major diameter and, by doing so, offset individual bullet length differences.

Another benefit of using a seating depth tool is that you can, from time to time, remeasure the barrel to analyze the amount of throat wear. As the throat erodes, you must adjust cartridge OAL an equal amount to compensate for the wear, if you expect to maintain peak accuracy.

Once you have arrived at the correct OAL, so the bullet touches the rifling, you are ready to adjust your bullet seater to that measurement. Here is where you can use that sample round. Back off the seater adjustment enough that you are sure it will not contact the sample round. Insert the sample and gently screw the seater stem down until it contacts the bullet of the sample. At this point, seat another bullet in another case and measure it, using a Bullet Comparator or similar tool. The measurement at this stage will likely be a bit longer than your sample round, and the seater will have to be adjusted until the correct OAL is obtained.

For benchrest loading, use hand-type reloading dies. Reasons are simple. Due to the close tolerance chambers, resizing is at a minimum. Neck reduction from a fired case to a resized case should not exceed .002-inch. Such minimum resizing reduces seating effort as well as sizing effort, and either operation can be done by hand if so desired. Normally, a small arbor press is used. The major advantage of hand-type neck dies is that they do not require an expander ball. Actual resizing is done by interchangeable sizing inserts. The handloader is in complete control of the amount of neck reduction and the resultant neck-to-bullet tension. Bullet seaters are designed so that the cartridge case is fully supported in the die body prior to seating the bullet. Portability is another advantage as most benchrest shooters load at the range during practice and when attending a match.

Once the cases are fireformed, clean any powder residue from the outside and inside of the case neck. Use 000 steel wool or a treated brass polishing cloth on the outside and a nylon brush on the inside. At this point, I remove the spent primers, without doing any resizing, and then trim the cases to proper length.

Trimming a case to length is normally one of the first steps a novice handloader will perform. If the cartridge case in question is some sort of shortened wildcat, it may be necessary. If the case is a standard, there is no need to trim until the case has been fireformed, but it should be done before the case is resized.

If you review standard SAAMI chamber and cartridge drawings, you will note that between minimum chamber specs and maximum cartridge specs there is a minimum case-to-chamber average of .024-inch. Unless new brass exceeds this allowance, there is no need to trim prior to initial fireforming. Trimming prior to resizing enhances alignment as the case enters the sizing die.

I suggest that cases not be trimmed to published trim lengths without knowing the actual chamber length of the firearm in which they will be used. Published trim-to dimensions will result in a safe case length, but experience has shown that the actual length of a chamber does not always fall within SAAMI specs. If you have access to a lathe, a simple gauge can be made that will allow you to measure actual chamber length. (See July/August, 1989, *Handloader*.)

Once a case is trimmed, chamfer the mouth in the previously described manner. Case mouth chamfering is crucial and must be performed so that the bullet's base and bearing surface do not become damaged during the seating operation. From an accuracy standpoint, the

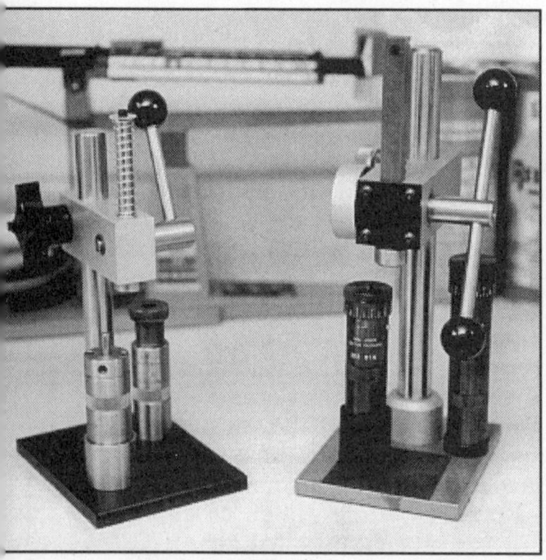

Hand dies put the handloader in control of the sizing and seating operations. Most are used with small arbor presses. Left, Sinclair press with Wilson dies; right, R.W. Hart and Son press with Custom Products dies.

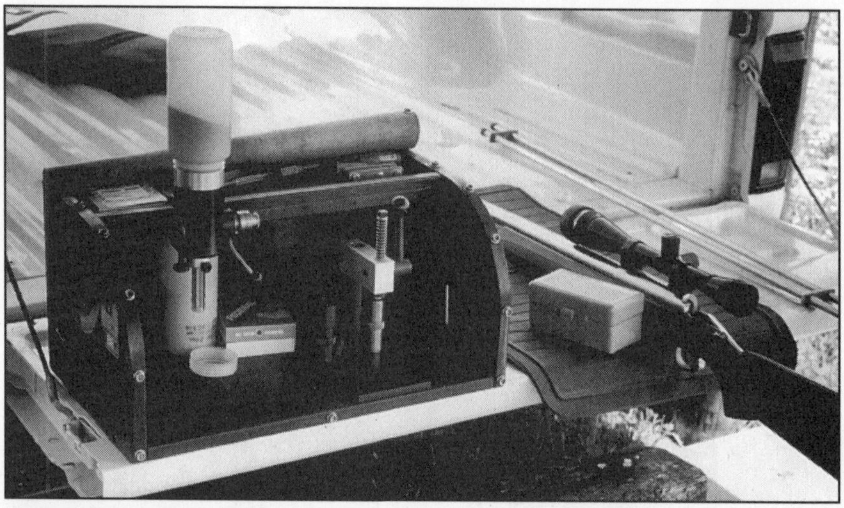

Benchrest shooting requires on-site reloading. Pictured is the author's loading box set up on the tailgate of his pickup.

bearing surface of a bullet—the surface that has actual contact with the barrel—plus the bullet's base are the important areas of the bullet.

Chamber pressures are sealed by the base of the bullet. If the base is deformed, the seal will not be evenly distributed around the circumference of the base as it exits the barrel. This condition can cause a tipping effect on the bullet. If the bullet's bearing surface is damaged, it will more than likely create abnormal jacket wear, or fouling, as the bullet travels through the barrel.

When cases have been trimmed to equal length, their heads are ready to be squared. Case head squaring creates excessive headspace until the case is once again fireformed. This operation should never be performed on unfired cases or full-length resized cases. Due to the manufacturing process, an unfired case is not likely to have its head surface at right angles with the body centerline. Squaring at the unfired state results in removing excessive amounts of material.

Whitetail Design makes a special carbide cutter for the Wilson case trimmer specifically for squaring case heads. This cutter has a .56-inch diameter cutting face, so it will handle case diameters up to and including the standard belted mags.

If the head face does not clean up at .002- to .003-inch after it has been fireformed, you have more problems than just a cartridge case. More than likely there is an alignment problem between the barrel and action which may require major attention.

Once the head squaring is completed, it is time to rework flash holes and primer pockets.

Cartridge cases are manufactured by a series of drawing and punching operations. Primer pockets and flash holes are formed by swaging, punching or both. This is done from the outside of the case, leaving internal problems for the handloader.

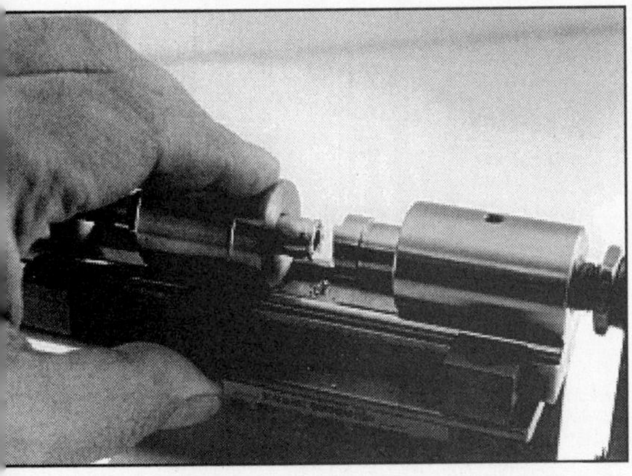

Case head squaring using the Whitetail Engineering cutter in a Wilson case trimmer.

As the flash hole is punched, exit burrs are formed on the inside of the case. This is a major problem. Such burrs cause an uneven dispersion of the primer flash, which, in turn, creates ignition problems.

Removal of this burr and normalizing the length of the flash hole will allow the primer flash to ignite the powder more uniformly. I firmly believe that flash hole deburring is an important operation in any case preparation, perhaps the most important.

Prior to the deburring of any case, *be sure* that the primers are removed. I have never experienced it, but I suspect a live primer could be detonated during this operation. Deburring with a spent primer still in the case will restrict the cutting depth of the tool and defeat the purpose. Fortunately, this is a one-time operation for each case.

Inspection of a new case will also reveal that primer pockets have a radius where the wall meets at the bottom of the pocket. Also note that the bottom is somewhat dished. On the other hand, if you take a good look at a primer, you will see it is constructed so the anvil protrudes from the bottom of the cup. This is necessary so the anvil will rest on the bottom of the primer pocket. When the firing pin strikes the primer, the explosive pellet inside the primer cup is crushed between the anvil and cup, causing the material to detonate. Variations in the depth and configuration of the pocket, not to mention the primer seating operation, can and will alter the effect of the firing pin blow.

If the blow of the firing pin is varied, it will in turn vary the primer ignition and thus result in erratic pressures and velocities. This can create vertical shot dispersion; that is to say, shots will string up and down on the target.

Depending upon the action manufacturer, firing pin protrusion will range from .045- to .060-inch. With this in mind, it is easy to see that a primer seating variance of only .010-inch could alter firing pin influence as much as 20 percent.

Primer pocket uniformers are designed to cut the pockets to uniform depths and, at the same time, square the primer seating surface in relation to the case head. The tools do not alter the primer pocket diameter as the cutters are ground to cut depth only. Alignment is controlled by the pocket walls.

Do not panic if a primer pocket uniformer does not clean up a new case. After a couple of firings, it should. *I do not suggest cutting the pockets deeper* just to get them to clean up. If pockets are that far off specifications, discard the cases.

It must be remembered that not only do cases grow longer with repeated firing, but primer pockets also become shallower, so will require an occasional recutting. For this reason, it is wise to use a carbide tool for the uniforming operation and continue to use the same tool as a primer pocket cleaner. Once the radius has been removed from the bottom of the pocket, some primer pocket cleaners will not clean the pocket completely.

Primer pocket uniforming completes the case preparation operations. It is now time to neck size the finished cases and prepare for load development operations.

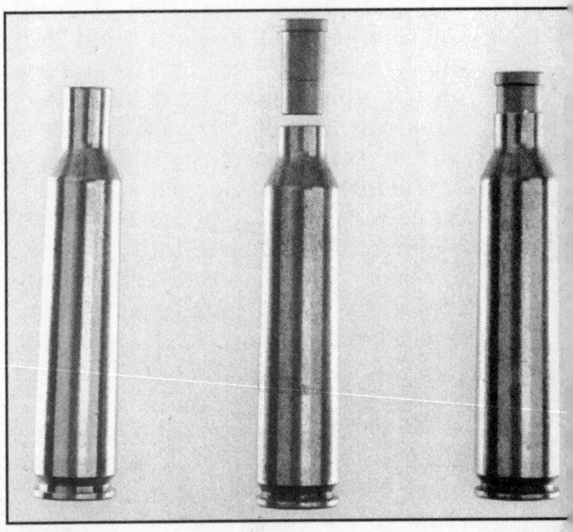

Chamber lengths are not always what they should be. A simple gauge can be made to check the actual length.

Primers are the one component in the reloading process over which we have no control. Their overall height may vary considerably...by as much as .012-inch.

Some years ago, I did a good deal of experimenting with primer variations. I spent hours sorting by overall height, seating by feel, and seating to a predetermined depth. After seating, I lathe-turned the case head so I could reclaim the seated primer for measuring. Hundreds of rounds were also fired using a return to battery rifle. Doing so, I came to the conclusion that the only way to get around the problem inherent with primers is to seat them by feel.

Even with primer pockets of uniform depth and primers sorted by height, I found that most priming tools on the market would not seat primers evenly. For uniform seating, the handloader must use a priming tool that allows him to "feel" the primer as it travels down the primer pocket. When you feel the primer bottom ever so slightly, you have already given it a pre-load of about .005-inch, which, in testing, proved to be the preferred amount of preload. If your present seating method does not allow you to feel the primer as it contacts the bottom of the primer pocket, you are not using the correct tool.

You can spend from $15 to $120 for priming tools. You can buy tools with "bells and whistles." Whatever your preference may be, a good tool can be judged by the way it "feels" and the ease in which it seats the primer. The two do not necessarily go hand in hand.

Regardless of what type of priming tool you use, keep in mind that most tools hold the cartridge case on the upper side of the rim. Case rims can and do vary in thickness and become worn by the rifle's extractor, reloading tool shellholders, and so on.

When priming, give all your cases a visual inspection and discard any that show major damage to the rim. Such damage could result in a "poor feel" and misalignment during primer seating.

Many handloaders, not acquainted with B/R shooting, are a bit shocked when they find out that B/R shooters charge cases right out of the measure. Some mistrust measures for one reason or another and prefer weighing each charge. I have no problem with that. I do feel, however, that measures get shortchanged due to the manufacturer's lack of usage instructions or the user's failure to read instructions.

Granted, most B/R cartridges require charges of 30 grains or less. Most prefer powders which are fine-grained, but the secret to making most measures perform consistently is in the operation technique.

I hasten to point out that every reloader should use a good scale to verify original charge weights. It is *not* a good practice to accept any powder measure setting on faith, even if the information comes from someone with a measure identical to yours.

The operation of a measure is not just a matter of pulling a crank or lever. The reloader must develop a consistent rhythm when using any measure if he desires to throw uniform charges. The name of the game is uniformity, so "play" with your measure, using different techniques and weighing the charges as you go to see which produces the most uniform results.

I find the crank-type measure works best when the operator taps the handle at the top and bottom of the handle's stroke. The tapping helps equally settle the powder in the charge drum and reservoir each time. This procedure produces very uniform charges on most measures of this design.

When filling the reservoir of your measure, do not just dump the powder in and start throwing charges. To do so could create problems. Just after filling the measure, it will normally throw heavier charges for the first few charges. This is caused by the powder being compacted as it is poured into the reservoir. Generally, you will want to cycle about a dozen charges before actually charging your cases. Measures with long reservoirs are bad about this, while those with some type of baffle may not be affected. Regardless, check out this potential problem while you acquaint yourself with the measure.

When using *any* powder measure, be sure it is *always* mounted *solidly*. Make sure your mounting bracket does not flex in any manner. You would be surprised how poorly some measures operate when the mounting is allowed to flex, even to a minor degree. Here again some manufacturers insist on a mount that is nothing more than sheet metal. A cheap mount just will not work.

If you encounter static electricity problems when using a measure, try wiping out the reservoir and affected parts with one of the anti-static sheets your wife uses in the clothes dryer. Works on powder funnels also.

Although it may sound trivial, a measure that has interchangeable drop tubes, of different lengths, is highly desirable. The longer tubes allow the reloader to use "full-density" charges without the fear of compressing the charge.

With a capable benchrest rifle and properly prepared cases, finding a good load combination is normally an easy task. Finding the ultimate load is a matter of fine tuning that good load.

A benchrest shooter is going to know what loads the winning shooters are using, or get some idea of them, by reading the results of recent matches. Use this information as a starting point for the selection of powder and bullet weights. If you do not see a particular powder listed in the winners' column, forget it; use what the winners use. But always keep in mind that a suggested powder charge should be carefully approached from the light side.

Bullets used will most always be custom-made. Obtain two or three different brands. Your rifle will probably have a preference in bullet weights and brands.

Published match results will show you that two or, maybe, three powders are preferred. This simplifies load development. Start with the two most popular powders for your cartridge. Charge only three cases per powder. Using the same brand and

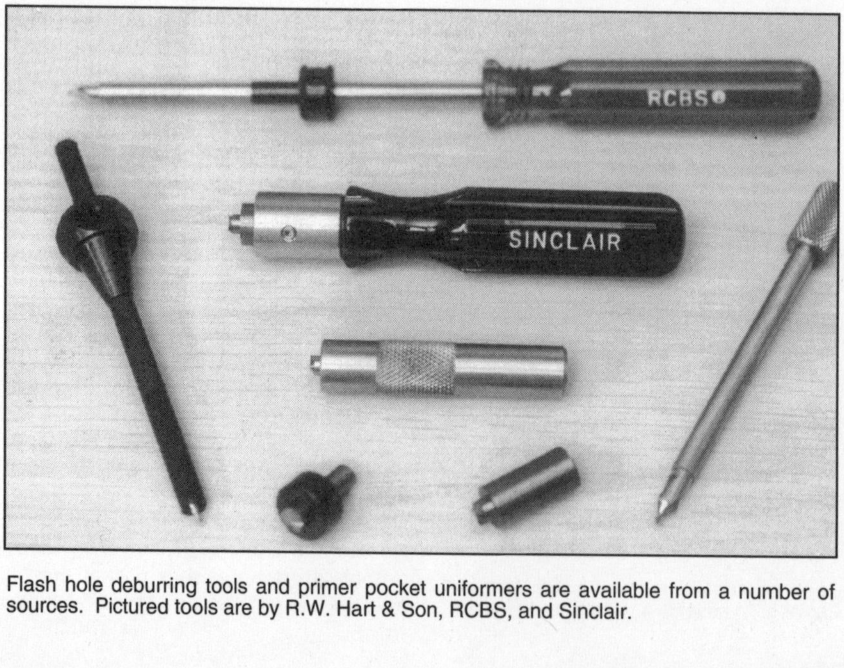

Flash hole deburring tools and primer pocket uniformers are available from a number of sources. Pictured tools are by R.W. Hart & Son, RCBS, and Sinclair.

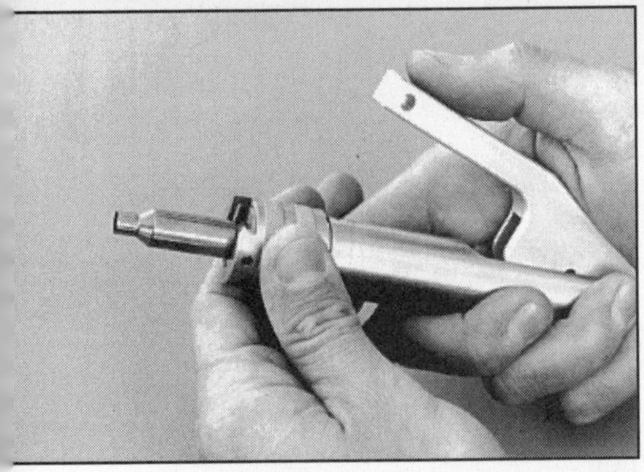

A good priming tool can be judged by the way it "feels" the primer as it is being pressed home. Pictured is the stainless steel Sinclair tool.

weight bullet, seat them to touch the rifling, as described for fireforming.

My experience has been that most 22-caliber rifles perform best with the bullet .010- to .020-inch off the rifling; most 25 and 6mm rifles from just touching to .010-inch off; and larger calibers just touching. This is not a "carved-in-stone" rule, as each rifle is an individual, but generally speaking it has been a reliable guide for my loading. Normally I seat bullets to these beginning settings.

You will note the only variation in my load is the different powders I am going to try. Everything else is the same: bullet, seating depth, primer, etc. Do not try several different things at one time; it will only confuse the process.

Shooting three-shot groups, I fire the different powders and record the results. Usually one of these groups will look better than the others. For example, let's say I used H-4895 and H-322, and the group size ranked in just that order. The next step would be to reload using the H-4895 load. Try it again to just be sure it was not a fluke. If it works well the second time, you are ready to try some load adjustments. If it did not, try the other powder.

Once I settle upon which of the two powders worked best, I inspect the fired primers to see that the load is not too hot. I do not want to see primers all mashed flat around the edges. I prefer a very slight crater around the firing pin dent with the corners of the primer still showing a radius. Look for burnished areas on the case head. Such signs indicate that the load is too hot, a condition normally accompanied by increased resistance when opening and closing the bolt.

If you encounter these high pressure signs, then back your charge down a little bit. If not, continue to increase the charge to the next step shown in the reloading manual you are using, but *always* proceed with caution.

Load another three cartridges and fire them. If the group improves, make another powder charge change in that direction. If it does not, go the other direction with your charge. Continue this procedure until you have settled on the charge that performs best.

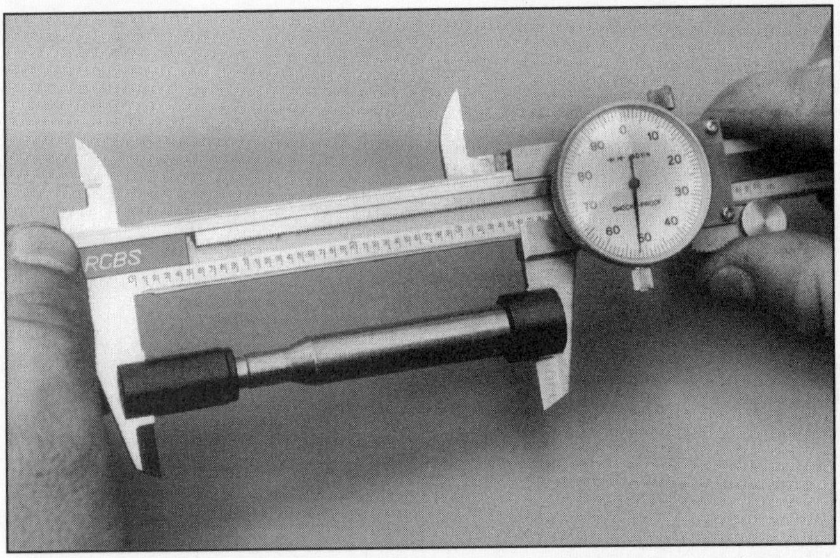

It is mandatory to use a good tool for checking OAL. The Davidson Seating Checker accurately measures the loaded round.

Always bear in mind that changes in brands of powder, and even lots of the same powder, require adjustments in powder charges.

Powders are graded by burning rates that are on a scale. For example, let's say powder #1234 is on a scale from 1 to 10, powder #5678 is on a scale from 10 to 21, etc.

You may have worked up a load with powder #1234 that shoots well for you. When that powder was graded by the manufacturer, it fell in their 1 to 10 scale at 2. You just purchased another can of #1234, but it was from a different manufactured lot, and maybe it was graded at 10 on their scale. You may find, especially if your load is near maximum, that this new can of #1234 may be too hot with your earlier load. You may have to back down on the powder charge. Always use caution when changing lots of powders. Also remember that the super accurate load you worked up in the hot weather of July just might be too mild on a cool October day, or vice versa.

Once you have established a powder preference, it is time to make seating depth changes. Let's say we started with the bullet touching the rifling. Now, load three rounds at this setting and three more at .005-inch off the rifling. Fire both of the groups and then look for an improvement.

If the .005-inch group looks the most promising, load three more at that setting, another three at .010-inch, and try them again. Work the seating depth toward the optimum group. Once you find what looks best, try changes of .002-inch. A good shooting rifle will know the difference. Seating depth is one of the most important factors in obtaining peak accuracy.

It may, at this point, be a good idea to try another bullet. You have already found a working range for the powder charge and a seating depth measurement that performs well. When changing bullets, use a Bullet Comparator to get a correct seating depth measurement of your "pet." Once you have found the correct seating depth for one bullet, these tools will allow you to reset your seating die for different bullets.

Let's say you have worked up a pet load using Smith 65-grain bullets that works well in your custom-built 6PPC B/R rifle. Measure this round with the Comparator and also measure the original dummy for the 65-grain Smith bullet.

For example, assume that the pet measured .005-inch shorter than the original dummy. This tells us that the pet load prefers the bullet to be .005-inch off the rifling. Remember,

Besides being an excellent toolmaker and machinist, Sinclair is a top shooter. Here he's testing a counter-sniper rifle he built for a federal law enforcement agency. Carefully tested handloads bring out the best accuracy in such rifles.

the dummy was assembled from seating depth gauge measurements that had the bullet just touching the rifling.

Now, let us say you are going to try a Jones bullet of a different ogive. Measure your dummy, the one with the Jones bullet, and adjust your seater so that assembled rounds are .005-inch shorter than the dummy. For correct evaluation of the Jones bullet, it must be seated so that the major diameter of the bullet is the same distance from the rifling as the bullet in the "pet" load. Keep in mind that just trying different bullets at the same bullet seater setting will not give you a correct evaluation of each bullet. The ogives would have to be identical to get the same measurement, and that rarely happens.

It is mandatory that the handloader use some type of bullet comparator when making seating depth changes. In the first place, bullets, especially the hollowpoint bullets that generally give best accuracy, will vary by as much as .025-inch in their length. Variations in bullet length may not affect the accuracy of the rifle. They do make it impossible to deal accurately with seating depth in terms of overall cartridge length when measuring across the bullet's point. Secondly, bullets of the same weight from different makers are quite often of different lengths due to variations in the shape of the bullets' ogives. They also will have varying lengths of bearing surfaces (the major diameter).

Since bullets often vary in length, it is important that OAL measurements be made from a fixed reference point, such as that provided by the Bullet Comparator or the Davidson SDC. Based on my experience, I feel that bullet seating depth, when it is measured in terms of the amount of free bullet travel prior to land contact, is a constant for a given rifle.

In other words, while overall cartridge length will vary with bullets of different weights and shapes, for best accuracy, the relationship of the bearing surface of the bullet and the origin of the bore's lands must remain the same regardless of bullet shape or weight.

The OAL figures published in loading manuals are only reference figures to use for correct magazine length. Other than determining whether or not a loaded round will function through a rifle's magazine, published OAL measurements, when measured across the bullet's point, are useless for B/R use.

Remember, however, OAL eventually must be increased to compensate for throat wear in the bore. The frequency with which these changes must be made will depend on the intensity of the cartridge being used and on the number of rounds fired. If you notice that accuracy begins to deteriorate after several hundred rounds, check the seating depth and increase as required.

Summarization of benchrest reloading can be stated by a single sentence: "Nothing is so important as a trifle." Maybe the late L.E. "Sam" Wilson made it even more direct and simple: "Garbage in, garbage out." Either way, if you are not willing to spend the time and effort to become a novice machinist and pay attention to all the details, forget it. ●

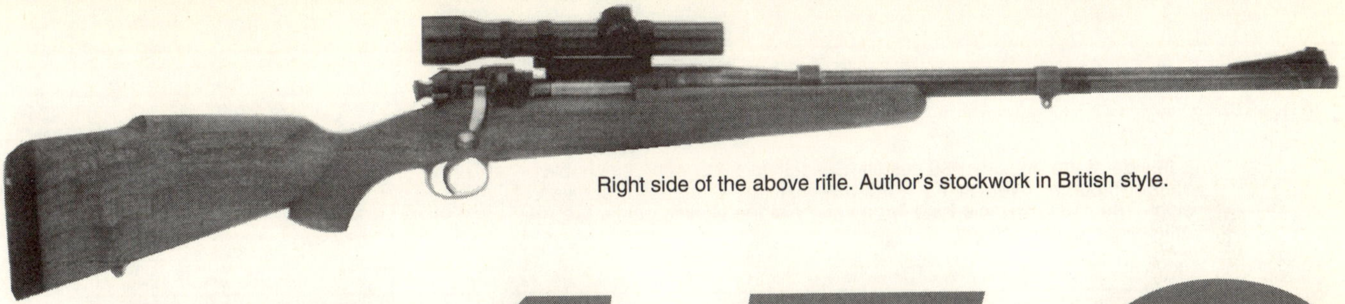

Right side of the above rifle. Author's stockwork in British style.

THE 458 REVISITED

by RAY ORDORICA

ASK ANY SHOOTER to name the first dangerous game cartridge that pops into his mind and chances are he'll say, "The 458 Winchester Magnum." Not a bad answer. The 458 has stood the test of time and has become the standard against which all other heavy rifles are measured. Overlooked by many shooters who think the big cartridge is good only for Africa, the 458 Winchester Magnum is a lot more than just a good elephant cartridge.

Until recently, you had to reload it in order to get something other than rhino-smashing utility out of the chunky, belted 458 cartridge, because the factories gave us only full-power loads that made the 458 live up to its African big game potential. The cartridge companies ignored the possibility that shooters might want to use their 458s on game that is neither large nor dangerous. Federal Cartridge Co. recognized this fact and recently came out with a new 458 load. It features a 350-grain round-nose bullet at 2400 fps at realistic pressures. With this new load, 458 owners can now use their elephant rifles on elk, moose, caribou and even deer without having to listen to too much guff about overkill. The new Federal offering greatly increases the versatility of this fine cartridge.

I'm sure not everyone wants to hunt deer or elk with a 458, but you can bet next week's bingo money that most 458 owners will never hunt elephant. A good 350-grain load expands the usability of the 458 by giving us a flatter trajectory and less recoil than full loads with 500-grain bullets.

Reloaders have, of course, known this all along. The 458 Magnum greatly rewards the reloader. Any reloader would do well to consider the 458 if he's in the market for a versatile big game cartridge with the potential for big horsepower. Cases are easy to get, and with the great variety of bullets and suitable powders available to him, the big game hunter who reloads can make the 458 sing whatever song he wants. He doesn't have to dance to the tune of bone-crushing recoil, not if he doesn't want to.

History

The 458 came into being in 1956, when Winchester brought it out in response to the continued demands of American sportsmen who were going over to Africa and wanted to

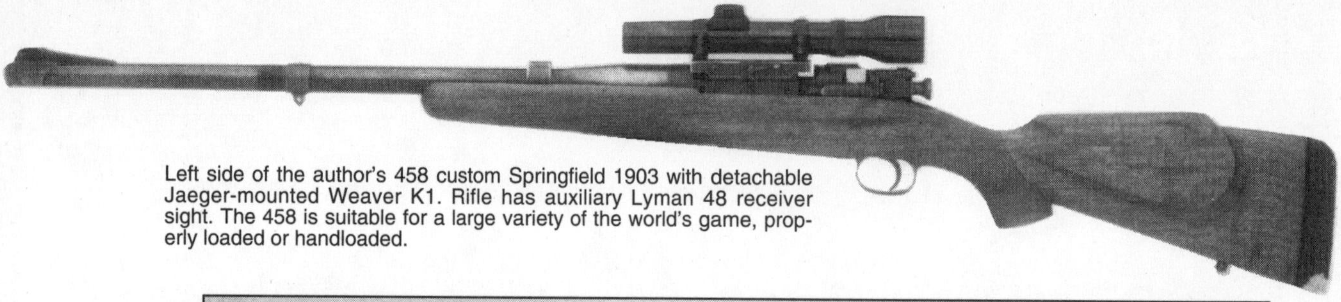

Left side of the author's 458 custom Springfield 1903 with detachable Jaeger-mounted Weaver K1. Rifle has auxiliary Lyman 48 receiver sight. The 458 is suitable for a large variety of the world's game, properly loaded or handloaded.

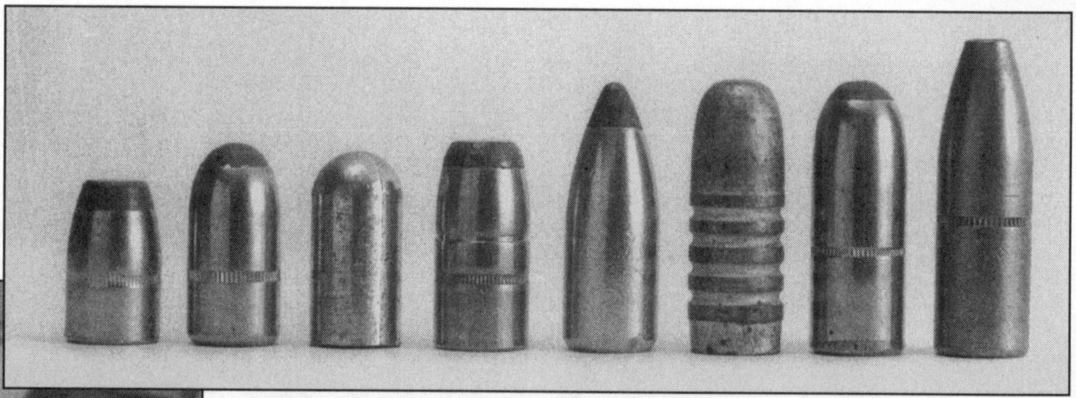

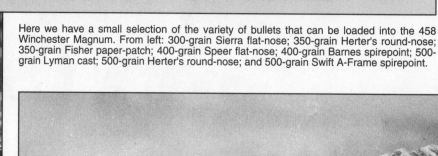

Here we have a small selection of the variety of bullets that can be loaded into the 458 Winchester Magnum. From left: 300-grain Sierra flat-nose; 350-grain Herter's round-nose; 350-grain Fisher paper-patch; 400-grain Speer flat-nose; 400-grain Barnes spirepoint; 500-grain Lyman cast; 500-grain Herter's round-nose; and 500-grain Swift A-Frame spirepoint.

The only critical part of reloading the 458 is to maintain proper case length, most important if you crimp your loads. Heavy loads ought to be crimped.

take a bolt-action rifle to use on the biggest game of that continent.

John "Pondoro" Taylor was at least partly responsible for Winchester bringing out their 458. Taylor's book, *African Rifles and Cartridges*, came out right after WWII (1948) and was targeted at American readers. Taylor said the market was wide open for an American rifle manufacturer to bring out rifles and cartridges for post-war use on African game. Both England and Europe, he reasoned, had been hard hit by the war and would be unable to produce sporting arms and ammo for a long time to come. Winchester obviously listened.

This is Kodiak Island, home of the biggest bears on earth. The hunter here would be well-served with a 458. So, the author believes, would many deer hunters in the lower 48, with a suitably loaded rifle.

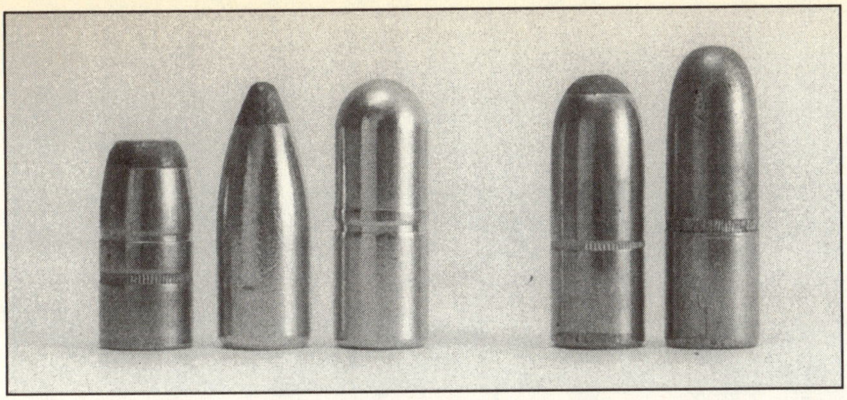

What's the best, 400-grain or 500-grain? Author feels the 400-grain bullets offer much to reloaders. Two types of 400-grain soft-nose and a Barnes Homogeneous solid (left) might be better under some circumstances than the more conventional 500-grain soft-nose and solid (right).

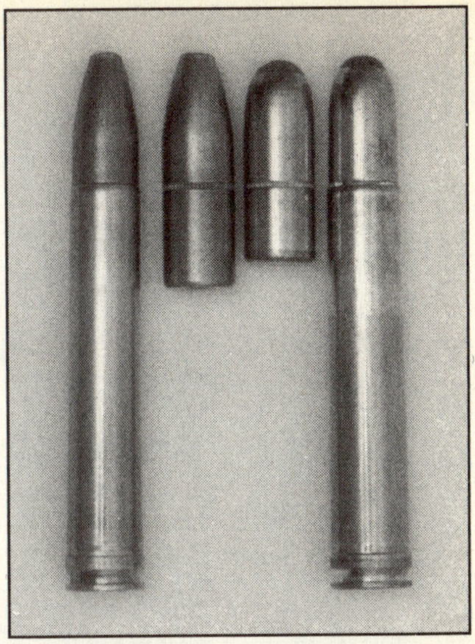

The fine Swift A-Frame 500-grain H-jacket protected-point bullet (left) takes up .150-inch more of the powder capacity of the 458 case than the conventional Herter's 500-grain round-nose when both are seated to crimping cannelure. Reduced powder capacity means reduced velocity—or increased pressure.

The 458 was designed to be the approximate equal of existing elephant rifle cartridges that had already proven their worth in the game fields of Africa. A slew of big rimmed cases had been designed for double rifles, including the 450, 450 No. 2, 500/450, 465 and 470. The model for the 458 was probably the 450 Nitro, although some say it was the 470. These thoroughly reliable cartridges all throw bullets of about 500-grain weight at approximately 2100-2150 fps velocity. All of them operate at significantly lower chamber pressure than does the 458. About two-thirds the pressure, in fact.

Pressure

Although the 458 approximates the ballistics of the big British double rifle cartridges, its relatively high working pressure can lead to problems...at least in the minds of some shooters.

British gunmakers used to define "tropical temperature" as being 120 degrees F and built their rifles and ammo to operate at that temperature. Pressures were low and extraction was easy, even in that extreme heat. The 458 can apparently give extraction problems if ambient temperatures are high and the rifle's chamber is dirty. Launching heavy 458 Winchester Magnum bullets at maximum velocity from an untidy chamber can occasionally lead to sticky extraction. If there is an unhappy elephant nearby, the hunter might find himself in danger of being stomped into another kind of sticky extraction.

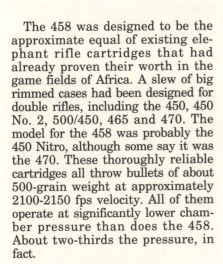

If you think you're risking that kind of termination, the solution is easy. Keep your 458 chamber immaculate and hunt only in cool weather. Failing that, the easiest solution would be for the ammo makers (or you) to load a slightly lighter bullet, thereby reducing chamber pressure while maintaining velocity.

Reduce bullet weight? Won't that make the cartridge unsuitable for dangerous game? Hardly. The first of our modern elephant cartridges was the 450 Nitro Express, introduced in 1898 by John Rigby. It fired a 480-grain bullet of exactly .458-inch diameter at a velocity of 2150 fps. In fact, all the British 45-caliber elephant rifles—the 450 Nitro, the 450 No. 2 and the 500/450—used 480-grain bullets...as does Holland's 465 today. These "light" bullets all work quite well against all manner of dangerous game.

A few years ago, my friend Ross Seyfried shot a 480-grain bullet out of his W-R 450 Nitro through some 11 feet of elephant. That bullet has 5 percent greater velocity and 4 percent less sectional density than the 500-grain 458 solids, which means the performance of these two loads will be essentially identical. Winchester could have used a 480-grain bullet right from the start. Winchester could still do something about it if they thought it was necessary, or if enough people asked.

You can, in fact, today buy 458 ammo loaded with bullets lighter than 500 grains. Art Alphin's A-Square company loads 458 ammo with his 465-grain bullets in three options: his Monolithic solid and two types of soft-nose, the Dead Tough with heavy jacket or the fast-expanding Lion Load. All three have a reported muzzle velocity of 2220 fps. The Australian company, Woodleigh Bullets, markets 480-grain bullets of .458-inch diameter for British double rifle cartridges. They ought to work well in the 458 Winchester Magnum.

Another way to reduce pressure is to increase the volume of the case, which can be done by having your 458 rechambered to 458 Lott. Jack Lott's wildcat will shoot 500-grain bullets at about 2300 fps, or duplicate 458 Winchester Magnum velocities at lower pressure. Best of all, you can still shoot regular 458 ammo in the chamber with no sacrifice of accuracy or velocity, which is nice to know if you run out of Lott fodder some day in deepest Zambia. You don't need to lengthen the magazine either, if you can be content with just one Lott cartridge in the rifle. You can load the chamber with a Lott cartridge and fill the magazine with 458 Winchester Magnum ammo and your rifle will be perfectly happy. (For more on the 458 Lott, see HANDLOADER'S DIGEST, 10th Ed., "The 458-Plus Arrives," by Jack Lott.)

I don't understand why no one else offers alternative loads for this cartridge. Shooters used to complain about a similar lack of loads when the 44 Magnum revolver came out, but take a look now at the vast vari-

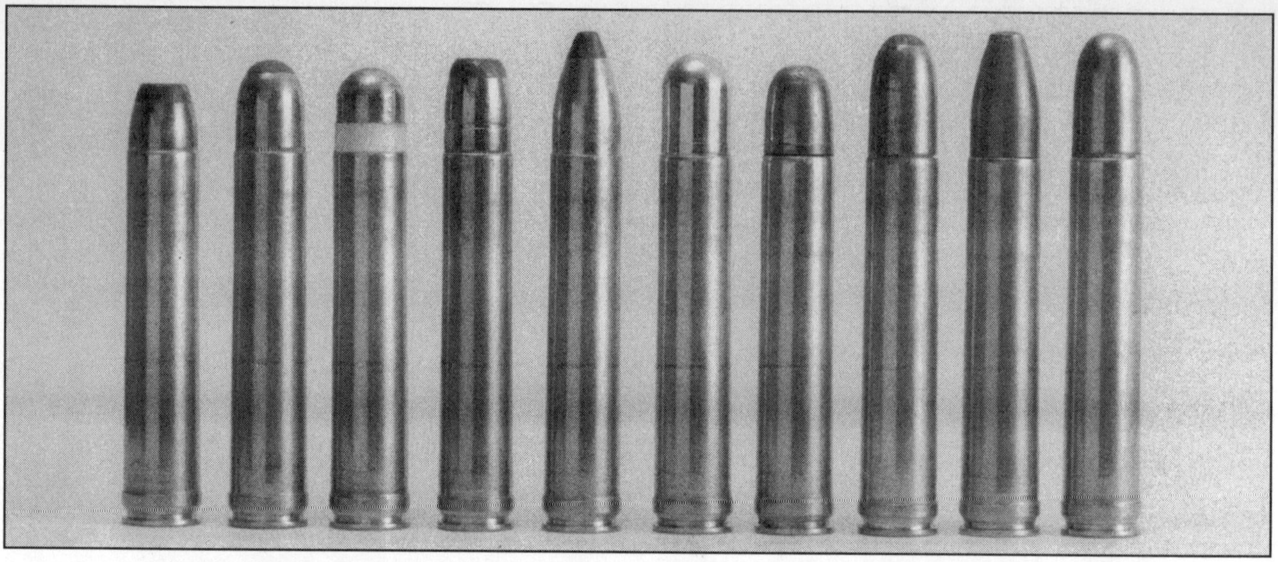

Reloading for the 458 increases its versatility greatly. Here are a selection of useful loads (left to right): 300 Speer; 350 Herter's; 350 Fisher paper-patched; 400 Speer flat-nose; 400 Barnes spirepoint; 400 Barnes solid; 500 cast Lyman; 510 Remington Core-Lokt factory; 500 Swift A-Frame; 500 Hornady solid.

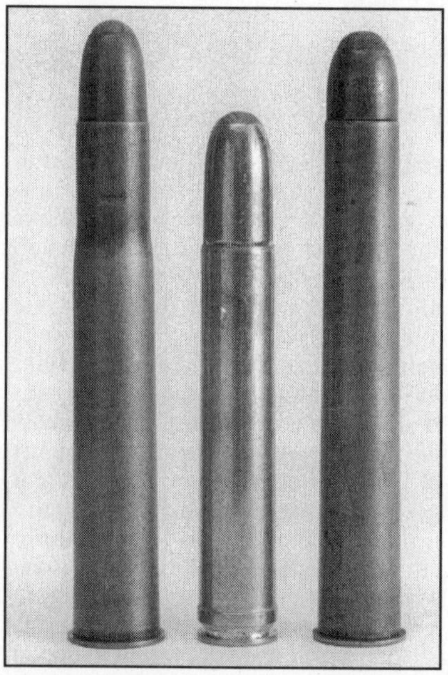

The 458 (center) has its roots in the two British cartridges flanking it. The 500/450 Nitro (left) and the 450 Nitro (right) both use 480-grain bullets of .458-inch diameter. There was another popular 45 British rimmed cartridge, the 450 No. 2, that was a full 3½ inches long, designed for very low pressure. The rimmed British cartridges, originally blackpowder numbers, propelled their nickel-jacket bullets at a full 2150 fps when loaded with Cordite (nitro version). They were successful elephant cartridges. There is no reason why the 458 was not originally loaded with 480-grain bullets like the rimmed cartridges around which it was patterned.

ety of factory loads available for that sixgun cartridge. I feel our cartridge manufacturing companies are missing a good bet with the big Winchester by not giving us a reasonable selection of factory loads featuring *good* bullets lighter than 500 grains.

The 458 has been maligned recently by some gunwriters who complain that its case is too short for best efficiency with the big bullets it was designed to throw. I agree, but heavy bullets are not the whole story. The best bullets for non-life-threatening situations are lighter than those found in most factory loads. To get all the benefits of a good selection of useful loads for the 458, you must reload it.

Reloading

There is something intensely satisfying about reloading for the 458 Winchester Magnum. Maybe it has to do with taming the power of the cartridge. Maybe it is the ease of putting together a great variety of useful loads. Whatever the reason, reloaders will have a very easy time with the big, uncomplicated 458. The lure of the 458 lies in making it do more good things for use than any smaller cartridge can do.

A good variety of 458-caliber bullet weights exist. You can easily find 300- to 500-grain bullets, and you can also use light lead ball muzzleloader bullets or even the big 600-grain Barnes slugs. Cast and jacketed bullets designed for the 45-70 work just fine in many situations.

In my opinion, round-nose bullets are best for the 458. They shoot just as flat as the spirepoints over practical ranges because they can be driven to higher muzzle velocities. (Round-nose bullets take up less of the case's capacity than any pointed bullet of the same weight when both are loaded to the same overall length.) For example, the Swift A-Frame 500-grain bullet is a semi-pointed, premium, best-quality bullet with a partition design. When this long bullet is seated to the cannelure, it takes up .15-inch more of

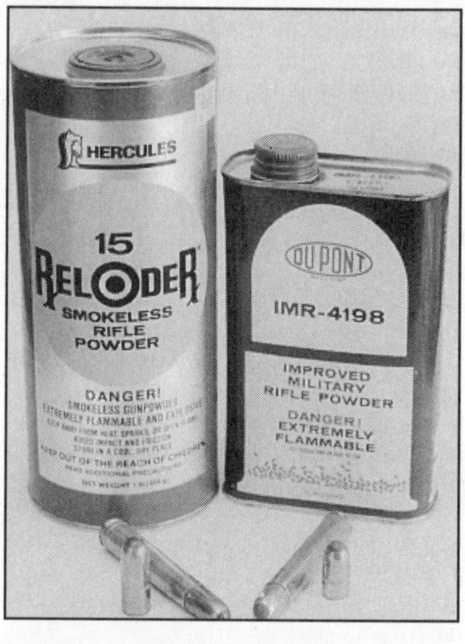

The best powder for loads with 500-grain bullets is Hercules ReLoder 15. The best powder for the 350-grain bullets is DuPont (now IMR) IMR 4198. Author's loads beat factory versions and, are not too hot.

One must use care in selecting a test medium. These recovered bullets may or may not perform well on game, judging from appearances only. From left: the Hornady steel solid ruptured when fired into gravel, yet the bullet has a fine reputation against elephant and other dangerous game. Next, the 350-grain cast bullet shown here is intended to be paper-patched. The recovered bullet was fired into ice; it generally performs very well on everything. Third from left, the Barnes 400-grain spirepoint at 2250 fps shed its core when fired into water-saturated silt. Last, the factory 510-grain Remington Core-Lokt held together well in saturated silt and is a proven performer in the field.

The 458 requires a 3-die set because it is a straight-sided case. The 458 is easy and rewarding to reload. Author's best 500-grain bullet load features RL-15 powder, RP case, and Federal 210 (normal) primers. Any *good* 500-grain bullet will do.

Standing out from the crowd of reloads is the author's favorite 458 load, the 350-grain round-nose at an honest 2500 fps MV. This reload features Herter's bullet with low cannelure, which maximizes the powder volume.

the case's interior length than does a typical round-nose 500-grain bullet. I am told this bullet is popular with owners of rifles chambered for the 458 Lott cartridge.

I had great hopes for the Barnes 400-grain spitzer bullet in the 458. I chronographed it using max loads with numerous powders, and I could get only about 2250 fps with my best load. I got higher velocity out of the flat-nose 400-grain Speer bullet designed for the 45-70 because it took up less of the case volume.

Light Loads

Generally speaking, if you want a light-recoiling load in the 458, use a light bullet, no heavier than 350 grains. I have been having a lot of fun with paper-patched 350-grain bullets in front of 20 grains of Unique, with about 1 grain of Dacron filler loose over the powder to keep it down. These shoot well enough out of my rifle (about 3-inch groups at 50 yards) and have the very nice benefit of putting the final touches of cleaning to the bore. They will actually lap the bore with extended use. In the 458, these light loads give about the equivalent of max loads out of one of John Linebaugh's fine custom 45 revolvers, which is in the neighborhood of 1400 fps with these bullets. Incidentally, paper-patched bullets know no practical velocity limits. You can drive 'em up to at least 3000 fps, and they will perform well on game if not cast too hard.

I can't think of any use for a light load with a heavy bullet out of the 458. However, if you want such a load, try 18-20 grains Unique behind a 500-grain cast bullet such as the Lyman #457406, a gas-check bullet. You don't need gas checks at low speed. The 500-grain cast bullets with gas checks can be driven to any velocity up to full factory specs.

Another way to get really light loads is to use muzzleloader balls. These are available in a size that closely matches groove diameter, or a tad larger. Warning: These are pure lead, intended for use with a cloth patch. When they grate against your bore on their short happy trip to Valhalla, they may leave some of their composition behind. The faster you push them, the more of them will remain in your bore. I'm sure some of our blackpowder specialists can conjure up proper loads utilizing a pure lead round ball and blackpowder, with a gob of grease somewhere

The business end of author's Churchill double 470 is far more imposing than that of 458 custom Springfield, yet the 458 is a more versatile gun in that it can be loaded with a variety of loads. The double only works properly with one load.

in the load, and I leave such load design to them. I haven't tried pure lead balls in my rifle and don't intend to any time soon.

If I were forced to assemble extremely light loads for my 458, I would opt for the "button" bullets. These weigh about the same as a round ball for the same bore size, but this design includes a sizable grease groove. Lyman listed a 458-caliber button bullet mould in a recent catalog. Somebody told me he got "match accuracy" with them out of his 45-70.

Some of the 300- to 350-grain jacketed bullets won't hold together at 458 velocities. If you load any light bullets in your 458, be sure they perform as you want them to. They might blow to flinders if they're fired out of the 458 into any heavy-boned beast. One of my brother gunwriters busted a big African critter with a 350-grain bullet supposedly designed for use in the 458. The bullet failed to penetrate, and he was lucky to recover that animal.

Powders and Loads

The powder for heavy bullets in the 458 Winchester Magnum is Hercules Reloder 15. I was quite happy with IMR-4895 until I read in *American Rifleman* of Finn Aagaard's success with Reloder 15. I tried it with the 500-grain bullet and, as Aagaard reported, it works quite well.

My best 500-grain load with RL-15 beats Remington factory loads a bit. Editor Bob Bell asked me to determine how many reloads I would get out of a case with my loads before the primer pocket loosened, one indication of excessive pressure.

When I develop my loads, I use virgin brass and measure before and after shooting to make sure the belt doesn't expand. When I get the first indication of expansion (about .001-inch), I quit and back up. That is how I determined my best 500-grain load, and also my best 350-grain load.

Once I had good, safe loads, I tested them for case life. I took a case and made sure it was trimmed to length, and then reloaded it with my best 500-grain load, capped it with a 500-grain Hornady solid and crimped it hard. Because I was testing this in Alaska and it was cold out, I kept the rifle hot on top of my heating stove and also made sure the cartridge was good and hot. I then took everything outside and fired the cartridge, then reloaded (and reheated) that same case again, and fired it again.

I loaded that one case ten times with full-velocity 500-grain Hornady steel-jacket solids. Then I loaded and fired that same case five more times with the same powder charge, but with a deep-seated Herter's 500-grain soft-nose bullet (no crimp). Then I loaded that same case with five of my best 350-grain bullet loads (crimped hard), for a total of *twenty full-power reloads on that one case!* The primer seats as firmly now as it did when I started. I had to trim the case when I got to fourteen reloads. There is no sign of cracking or other indication of case failure.

My best 500-grain load: I use either Hornady solids crimped hard on the cannelure or my old stock of Herter's round-nose bullets, which, due to their nose shape and the leade length of my rifle's chamber, need to be seated deeper than their cannelure. I load 74 grains of RL-15 in R-P cases with (note this, please) Federal 210 *regular* (not magnum) primers. This is a compressed load, and I doubt it would work with Barnes Super Solids.

The Herter's bullet chronographs at 2130 instrumental, which my Baltec1 computer program (written by the NRA's Wm. C. Davis, Jr.) corrects to a true muzzle velocity of 2137 fps. This is about 60 fps *faster* than Remington 510-grain factory loads, measured on the same chronograph.

My favorite 458 load of all consists of a 350-grain round-nose softpoint bullet in front of 68 grains IMR-4198, R-P cases, with (again) Federal 210 regular primers. I have had good luck with IMR-4198 powder in both the 300- and 350-grain bullet weights. I crimp the bullet hard in the groove. These big rifles kick hard with any stout load, and the bullets need all the help they can get to stay where they belong as they are battered in the magazine.

I use an old stock of Herter's 350-grain bullets which I believe were made by Norma. Their jackets are .05-inch thick, and they seem to be very good bullets. Their cannelure is 5/16-inch from the bullet base, which maximizes powder volume. Barnes used to make a similar bullet. Hornady still does, but in my opinion their cannelure is too far forward, 7/16-inch from bullet base. These 350-grainers leave my rifle's 22-inch barrel at an honest 2500 fps, and they are a good compromise between trajectory and power.

Author Ray Ordorica prepares to fire his Springfield 458 with 500-grain load. Rifle weighs 9 pounds with quick-detachable scope mounted.

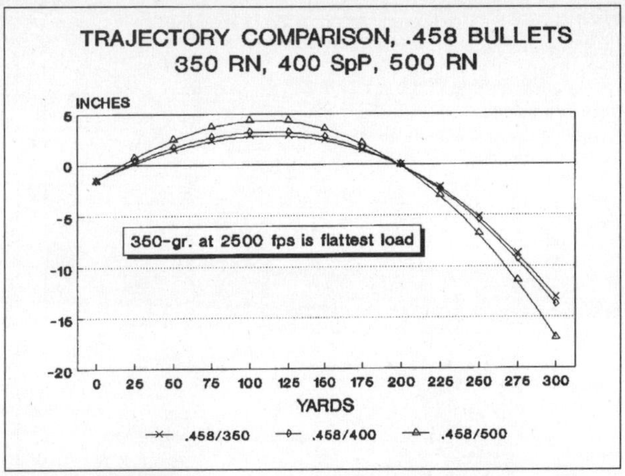

©1991-92, Ray Ordorica

Full recoil with 500-grain loads is not for the uninitiated. Rifle could weigh one or even two ponds more at the cost of handiness, but would be much easier to shoot. Recovery would also be faster, which might be vital if the rifle were used against dangerous game. A comfortable stock that fits the shooter goes a long way toward shooter comfort, as does a soft buttpad.

In my opinion, with one notable exception, the 350-grain bullet weight is the best for American hunters. It is the answer for big bear according to several Alaskan guides, who say the big 500- and 510-grain bullets have a rainbow trajectory that makes longer shots real tough. The 350-grain bullet weight ought to be ideal for elk and moose and not too big for deer. The new Federal load or equivalent handload turns the 458 into an extremely useful cartridge for North American hunting or for non-dangerous African species.

The notable exception is the 300-grain Barnes X-Bullet, a spirepoint made of homogenous material. Even though it starts out 50 grains lighter than the RNs, it will almost certainly weigh more than any 350-grain lead core bullet when it arrives on the far side of a game critter. So you lose nothing giving up a bit of weight.

As we approached deadline for this article, I managed to acquire a supply of 458-caliber X-Bullets in 300-, 350- and 400-grain weights, thanks to Randy Brooks of Barnes Bullets. We did some testing which opened my eyes wide. I found that all three versions opened in almost anything at a wide variety of velocities, yet retained almost 100 percent of their original weight. The velocities of the three are, roughly, 2700, 2500 and 2300 fps for 300-, 350- and 400-grain weights, respectively, with my best loads of IMR-4198 and Federal 210 primers. With these three versions of this remarkable spirepoint design one can tailor loads and penetration to the animal size being hunted. They are *the answer* to my long search for the best 458 bullets. They make the 458 into one of the few rifles available which one can realistically consider for a one-rifle African safari, and a grand all-round for anything, anywhere.

One well-known gunwriter went so far as to say that rebarreling a 458 into 416 Taylor would improve the 458 in every way. I couldn't disagree more, particularly in light of the outstanding bullets available now in the form of these three weights of Barnes X-Bullets. With the other great heavyweights available up to a full 600 grains, the 458 is superior to any 40-caliber rifle for versatility. That gunwriter who favors the 416s is unquestionably one of the world's best shots with anything, and he can "get away" with large, medium-bore rifles. Most of the rest of us will be better served by a true large bore, which the 458 certainly is, particularly when the chips are down.

A charge of 70 grains of IMR-4198 behind the Sierra 300-grain flat-nose zips it along at just under 2600 fps,

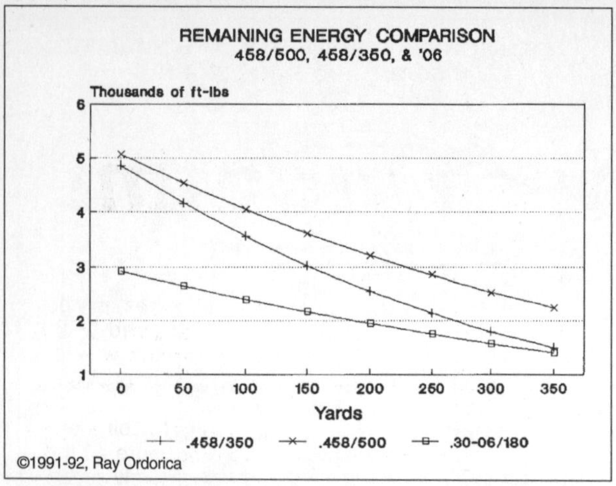

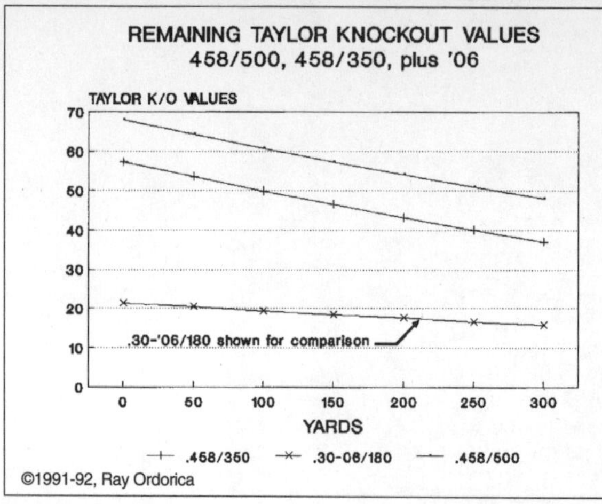

and I could push it a bit faster. A real screamer out of the 458, this bullet is also very accurate out of my rifle. This bullet is also a dandy with reduced loads of IMR-4895, giving in the realm of 2000-2200 fps and very low recoil.

Rifle Fit & Comfort

I have owned three 458s, all good rifles. The first two were a Ruger No. 1 and an FN Browning, both exceptionally accurate. The Browning had a large, soft buttpad that made it more fun to shoot than the Ruger.

My third and present 458 is a custom 1903 Springfield with a 22-inch Douglas Premium tube. I cut down the original stock into an English style of my design, oil-finished and checkered. The rifle weighs $8^1/_4$ pounds with Lyman 48 receiver sight, and just under 9 pounds with the old Weaver K1 locked in place in the quick-detachable Jaeger mount. It fits as if it's a part of me, no small factor in reducing felt recoil. A soft Sorbocoil buttpad really helps.

At 9 pounds, it's delightful to carry, but a bit too light for dangerous-game work because the barrel rises to between 45 and 60 degrees when I shoot 500-grain full-power loads. This means it takes me too long to recover from recoil and work the bolt for succeeding shots. Recoil energy with scope and 500-grain loads is 66.5 fpe, quite a bit for the uninitiated, but tolerable if you are careful.

With my favorite 350-grain load, it has a free recoil energy of 47 fpe. In spite of this, I can easily shoot the rifle forty to fifty rounds from the bench at a sitting, thanks to its fit and balance. It will place as many shots as you'd care to fire inside $1^1/_2$ inches at 100 yards. I have also benched twenty or more full-power 500-grain factory-equivalent loads at a sitting over the chronograph with no problems.

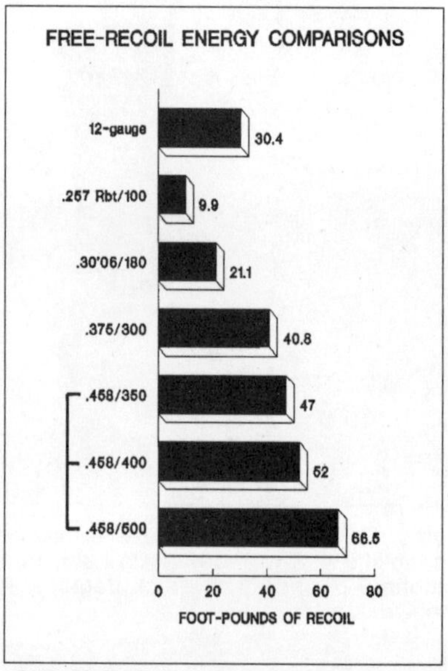

©1991-92, Ray Ordorica

Data on 458 for scoped rifle of $8^7/_8$ pounds, author's best loads.

Left to right: the Herter's .05-inch jacket 350-grain round-nose with cannelure in the right place. This bullet holds together well, but is now unavailable. Next to it is the Hornady 350 RN and its fragments recovered from a snowbank. Author believes the jacket is too thin. On the right are the 300-, 350-, and 400-grain Barnes X-Bullets, with recovered bullets. The Xs expand progressively as they go through more fluids. Maximum expansion is as shown for the 300-grain bullet, which has shed its petals. Author believes this 300-grain bullet lacks sectional density for close shots on very large game, and the 350-grain is best bet for all-around Alaskan use in the 458 Winchester Magnum.

Best Bullet For The 458 Winchester Magnum

Sometime back, I tried to select the very best bullet for the 458 because I carried mine all the time here in bush Alaska, and I wanted to be sure the bullet I used would perform in whatever manner I needed. That included closest-range shots at big bear and mid-range shots at moose or caribou at up to 250 yards. I had no intention of ever packing my 458 after sheep, but I might take a deer with it, and the bullet would have to cover all those bets.

I believe in sighting in my rifles with one bullet and one load, gaining complete familiarity with it, and using just that one load in the rifle for as many uses as seems practical. With the 458, I wanted a 350-grain bullet that I knew I could propel out of the muzzle at about 2500 fps.

I had an old stock of Herter's 350-grain bullets made with a very heavy .05-inch-thick jacket that held together well. They also had the cannelure as close to the base as was reasonable, which permitted maximum powder volume when using a crimp, as I prefer. Only problem with these bullets was they were round-noses, which didn't hold velocity worth a darn at much over 100 yards. And they are also no longer made.

I discovered that Barnes made a good-looking 400-grain spirepoint, but my tests with it were disappointing. I couldn't get the velocity I had hoped for—near 2400 fps. Only a bit over 2200, which gave a trajectory that my 350-grain RN Herter's would beat.

I tried the 350-grain Hornady round-nose, but it didn't perform as I wanted. I got very good accuracy with this bullet, but feel the jacket is too thin. I had them blow to bits and also lose their cores when fired into a snowbank, something I didn't have happen with any other 458 bullet of equal or greater weight. I sectioned them and found the jackets to be very thin and not bonded to the cores. This is not to say they will not work well for certain applications. I, however, live in an area that has honest-to-gosh dangerous game, big things that can hurt me if I don't drop them on the spot when I shoot them. I prefer my bullets to hold together. The 350-grain Hornadys don't, according to my tests, so I have little confidence in them. They also have their cannelures too far forward, which robs the case of powder capacity when they are seated for a good crimp.

Having said all that, I will tell you that I think the 458-caliber Hornady 500-grain steel solids are the best solids going; they are at the top of my list of serious bullets for the biggest game in the world.

So, who makes best-quality 458 bullets of 350-grain weight? As of this writing, in my opinion, just one manufacturer, Barnes. The Barnes X-Bullet, also available in 300- and 400-grain weights, takes a back seat to no one else's bullets in performance. Its ballistic coefficient is given as .402, and the hollowpoint design is sharp enough to retain velocity well. With this bullet, I get 2500 fps, according to my Oehler 35P, and it seems like the very best bullet for me, for the 458.

Yes, a few other manufacturers make 300- and 350-grain bullets, but all I've checked are designed for the 45-70 and modest velocities, generally 2000 fps or less. They don't work well in the 458 Winchester Magnum.

If it seems like an easy task to select the best 350-grain bullet, and it is, try it when you up the ante to 400 grains. When I began my search, I figured I could easily get 2350 to 2400 fps with 400-grain bullets in the 458. I figured wrong. However, I discovered that before Barnes made their X-Bullets, several options existed from other manufacturers. These included Swift, Trophy Bonded, Kodiak Bonded Core (Alaska Bullet Works), and Star "Tough-Bond," as well as both spirepoints and flat-noses from Barnes in their regular copper-tube design. All of these are 400-grain bullets. I tried the Barnes spirepoints first, as mentioned, and found that I could get much better velocity with 350-grain round-noses. That caused me to drop my search for good 400-grainers, and made the search easier once the X-Bullets were in production.

The Xs worked better than anything else in my tests, which included shooting through various amounts of water, and then through a paper "proof sheet," then capturing the bullet in snow. Snow usually catches bullets with no further distortion, but I wanted them to pass through the paper first in order to determine how much expansion took place before they hit the snow. In just about all cases, the bullets did not further expand in the snowbank. (The exception was the 350-grain Hornady RNSP, as already mentioned above.)

The X-Bullets opened a bit just in the snow. They opened more as they passed through progressively greater amounts of water, giving me the impression they would continue to open as they penetrated a game animal. All conventional lead-core bullets opened up rather suddenly to their full expanded diameter in a surprisingly small quantity of water. The copper construction of the Xs seems to permit them to flow as they pass through more resistance, which I believe transmits their energy to the game animal in a more deadly manner, over a longer period of time.

Yes, this is hard to prove, I'll grant you. However, reports from gunwriter friends indicate the Xs perform very well indeed, out of all proportion to their size. They retain their weight and also penetrate extremely well. If they continue to expand as they create their wound channel, I feel that ought to result in a more efficient or perhaps longer time period of transference of energy to the animal. The result should be quicker kills.

Accordingly, I'm sold on the 350-grain Barnes X-Bullet as being the best in the 458 for North American usage. I don't think the velocity gain with the 300-grain Barnes X is applicable to Alaskan conditions, where one might shoot a bear or moose at very close range. The 300-grain seems too light in this caliber. When impact velocity tops 2500 fps, the X-Bullets tend to lose their expanded nose sections, called petals. The resultant slug of copper from the 300-grain bullet will weigh about 225 grains and will be essentially square in profile—a cylinder with length equaling diameter. Such a projectile might not give adequate penetration at close range on a big bear. An experienced bear guide of my acquaintance seconded my opinion, going for the 350-grainers as probably the best of the 458 X-Bullets for Alaska. I would like to try the 400-grainers in Africa. If I could only find someone to pay my way on safari there...

Ray Ordorica

On the left is the Herter's with .05-inch-thick jacket. It is not bonded but holds together very well, unlike the Hornady shown in the middle. Hornady's "Interlock" might work OK at impact velocities below 1800 fps, but in author's opinion, this bullet has no business at 458 Magnum velocities, which exceed 2400 fps. On the right is the Barnes X Bullet in 300-grain weight. There is nothing to separate, the bullet being solid copper with an intricate opening in its front that works extremely well, opening reliably and penetrating very well.

458 WIN. MAG. LOADING DATA

Bullet (Wgt grs.)	Bullet (Type)	Load (Grs./Powder)	MV (fps)	Comments
300	Sierra FN	70/IMR-4198	2570	
300	Sierra FN	64-68/IMR-4895	—	Light load
350	Hornady RN	68/IMR-4198	2502	Fine max load
350	Hornady RN	74/IMR-4895	2249	
350	Hornady RN	71/IMR-4895	2150	
360	Paper-Patch	67/IMR-4895	—	Poor accuracy
400	Speer FN	78/RL-15	—	Max
400	Speer FN	77/IMR-4320	—	Max
400	Speer FN	65/IMR-4198	—	Max
400	Speer FN	70/IMR-3031	—	Max
400	Barnes SpP	77/RL-15	2243	
400	Barnes SpP	76/IMR-4320	2258	
400	Barnes SpP	64/IMR-4198	2246	
400	Barnes SpP	69/IMR-3031	2204	
400	Barnes Solid	66.5/IMR-4895	—	Max compression
400	Barnes Solid	65/IMR-4198	—	Stout load
500	Herter's RN	70/IMR-4895	2079	Compressed
500	Herter's RN	73/IMR-4320	2100	Max
500	Herter's RN	72/RL-15	2069	
500	Herter's RN	74/RL-15	2137	Best 500-gr. load*
510	Rem RN	Factory	2079	

All velocities were measured with a chronograph and corrected to true muzzle velocity with Baltec1, a computer program by Wm. C. Davis, Jr. (Available from Tioga Engineering.)
All loads were assembled in R-P cases. Federal 210 (regular) primers were used in all loads.
The author is not responsible for the misuse of this loading information. Reduce all loads by 10 percent and work up gradually.
*Or Hornady 500 SN, Hornady 500 steel solid, etc.

Happily, my rifle puts my best 350- and 500-grain loads all into the same sub-2-inch group at 50 yards.

Need

Now, then, do you need a 458? Absolutely! Can't do without one! Oughta be the first rifle you buy after your 22 rimfire!...Now that we've got my personal opinion out of the way, let's find out if the 458 is indeed indispensable.

One may not need the potency of the 458 often in big game hunting, but whenever you do need power, you need a lot of it. Any game can be dangerous under certain circumstances. Alaskan game is big and tough, though maybe not as big or tough as the game of Africa. Hunters have been killed by Alaskan game, and by "non-dangerous" North American game as well. A big Colorado bull elk might take it into his head to argue with you about who gets the driver's seat on the way home. The substantial horsepower of a 458 can be mighty comforting.

Most of the big game I've taken in the Lower 48 and Alaska has been taken at relatively close range. I would not have been handicapped by using a 458 on any of my hunts. In fact, my present 458 is a good deal *lighter* than some of the rifles I toted up yonder mountains years ago!

In the Michigan deer woods, or in any similar terrain, I would be very happy to have a 458 loaded with 350-grain bullets as my only rifle for the close-range brush hunting that comes with that kind of country.

I wouldn't choose a 458 for a sheep rifle, but I'd use it if it was all I had. I took my double 470 sheep hunting once, when it was the only rifle available...but that's another story.

Many good 458s are appearing on used gun racks as their former owners trade them in on 416 Remingtons. They can be great bargains. However, if you intend to use your 458 for serious purposes, be sure everything about the rifle works 100 percent, 100 percent of the time. These big rifles have to be smooth and absolutely reliable if they are to be used against anything that can kill us.

Nothing gives such satisfaction to the lone woods wanderer when he is sitting by his evening campfire, the night noises all around, as does a powerful rifle within easy reach. Put that camp deep in dangerous game country and the 458 comes into its own.

Don't have any big bears in your backyard? Neither did I when I got my first 458. I bought it for fun. Shooters across the country and around the world have taken to the 458 Winchester Magnum even though they have no intentions of hunting either Africa or Alaska. They have discovered the potential of using the 458 on non-dangerous big game, and many of them have expanded the usefulness of the big cartridge through handloading. They have found the fun behind the lure of the 458. ●

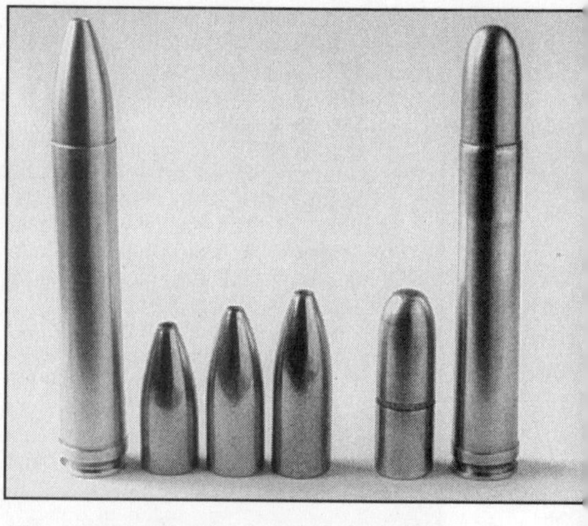

All you need to hunt the world is one rifle, says author Ordorica. Three versions of the Barnes X at 2700, 2500, and 2300 fps in 300-, 350-, and 400-grain weights; plus the Hornady 500-grain steel solid at 2140 fps, from author's handloads.

by DON ZUTZ

NEW AND NOVEL SHOTSHELL CONCEPTS

DON'T LOOK NOW, but American waterfowl and upland game hunting have gone through a lot of changes in the last decade. Take goose hunting, for example. Twenty seasons ago, the 10-gauge was practically obsolete, thanks to the potency of the $1^7/_8$-ounce lead-shot load in the 3-inch 12. But then along came steel shot, and the 10-bore was suddenly the "in" thing. Its huge plastic shot bucket held more of the heavy steel BBBs, Ts and Fs that we found were necessary for positive penetration on geese at the longer ranges, so we reversed gears and went back to the old slugger.

One problem that has cropped up, however, is that the 10-gauge magnum is too much gun for most typical hunters. At 10 pounds or thereabouts, it handles differently than

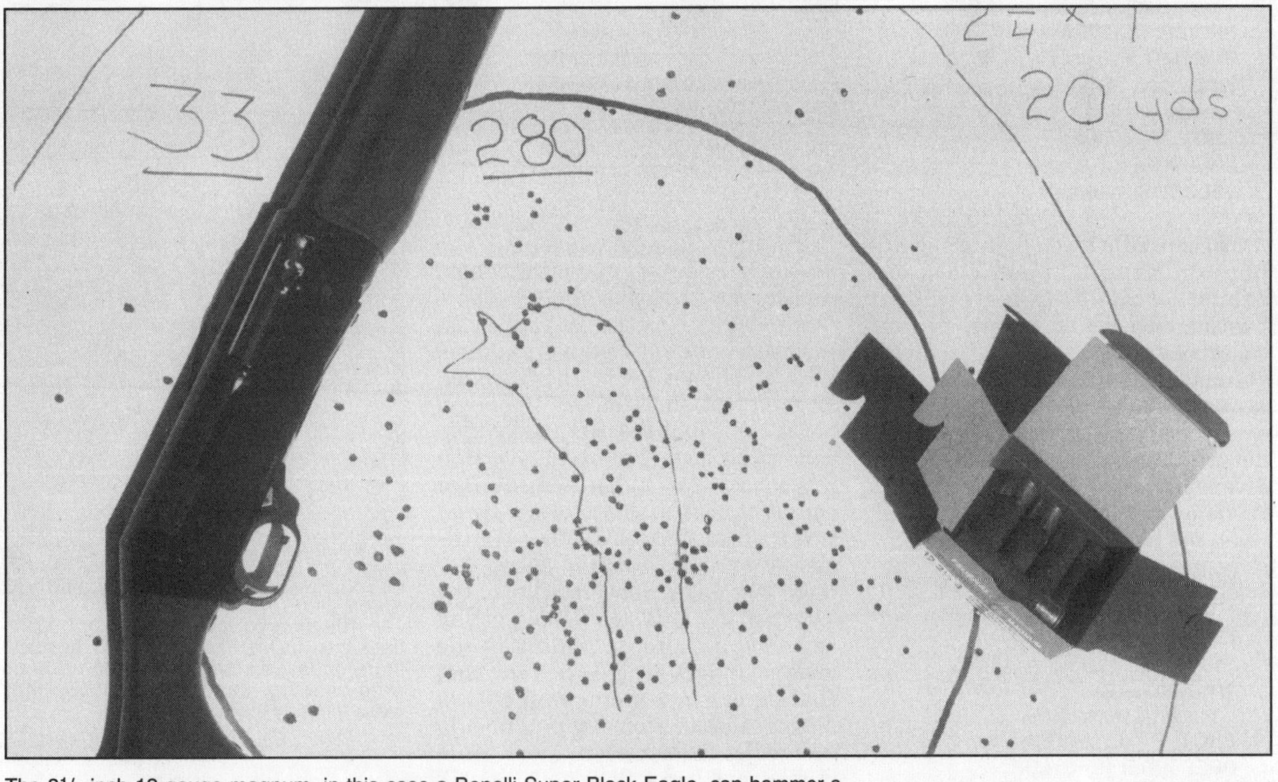

The $3^1/_2$-inch 12-gauge magnum, in this case a Benelli Super Black Eagle, can hammer a turkey target with its $2^1/_4$-ounce reload of lead 4s or 5s.

does a 7 1/2-pound 12-gauge. And that, of course, upsets one's trigger timing. The question is: How does one get meaningful practice with a 10-gauge? As one hunter put it, "I'd like to use my 10-gauge on practice clays, but who can afford it with steel loads? And who wants to try it with 2- or 2 1/4-ounce lead ones kicking your shoulder off?" He does have a point. The 10-gauge loads are tough on your wallet and anatomy.

Unless you reload, that is, for light 10-gauge fodder can indeed be assembled on any press-type equipment. These will not be the cheapest reloads because they require a stack of filler wads to take up space. However, such reloads are still less costly than commercial stuff, and they kick a whole lot less. A couple can be rolled like this:

LOAD

HULL: Rem. plastic SP (3 1/2")
PRIMER: CCI 209 Magnum
POWDER: 28.5 grs. Green Dot
WAD: Rem. SP-10; six 20-ga. .135" cards
SHOT: 1 1/4 oz. lead
PRESSURE: 8800 psi
VELOCITY: 1265 fps
NOTE: Same basic loading can be used in Winchester Polyformed 10-ga. case for nearly identical ballistics.

LOAD

HULL: Fed. plastic 10-ga. (3 1/2") (paper base wad)
PRIMER: CCI 209 Magnum
POWDER: 36.0 grs. Herco
WAD: Rem. SP-10; four 20-ga. .135" cards
SHOT: 1 5/8 oz. lead
PRESSURE: 10,300 psi
VELOCITY: 1285 fps

These will let you swing the 10-bore on hand-trapped clays out behind Uncle Jake's barn without busting either your budget or your collarbone.

Another new use for the 10-gauge magnum is as a duck gun. With husky loads of steel BBs, it can be devastating on high mallards or low divers on the far fringe of the decoys. A snappy performer is:

LOAD

HULL: Fed. plastic 10-ga. (3 1/2") (paper base wad)
PRIMER: Fed. 209
POWDER: 39.5 grs. Blue Dot
WAD: MEC 105; 1/2" MEC filler; 25.0 grs. MEC plastic buffer
SHOT: 1 1/2 oz. steel BBs
PRESSURE: 10,400 LUP
VELOCITY: 1301 fps

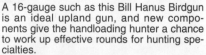

A 16-gauge such as this Bill Hanus Birdgun is an ideal upland gun, and new components give the handloading hunter a chance to work up effective rounds for hunting specialties.

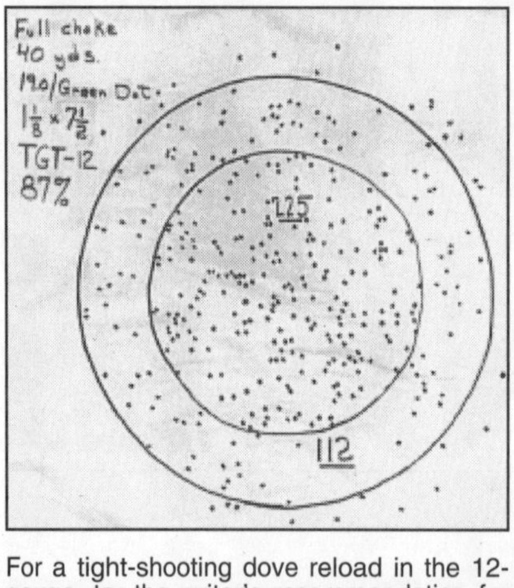

For a tight-shooting dove reload in the 12-gauge, try the writer's recommendation for 1 1/8 ounces of hard lead shot over Green Dot. Patterns like this with No. 7 1/2s are dynamite on long-range shots.

A relatively new concept is the 3 1/2-inch 12-gauge magnum, which was developed to give hunters a shot charge similar to the 10-bore in an easier-to-handle 12-gauge package. With steel shot loads, the 3 1/2-inch 12 falls just short of the 10-gauge, but it can equal the 10's husky 2 1/4-ounce lead load. Unfortunately, that 2 1/4-ouncer hits as hard on the butt end as it does at the muzzle. Great turkey load though it may be, it's simply uncomfortable to shoot. For those who enjoy the versatility of the 3 1/2-inch 12, but don't like getting smashed around, reloading is the answer. In fact, by reducing the shot charge, one can use a wad with a cushioning section for potentially less pellet deformation. Here are a couple that I ran through a Benelli Super Black Eagle with excellent

The 10-gauge is making a brilliant comeback because it can deliver the heaviest loads of large steel shot for long-range wing-gunning. Loads of steel BBs took these formerly high mallards.

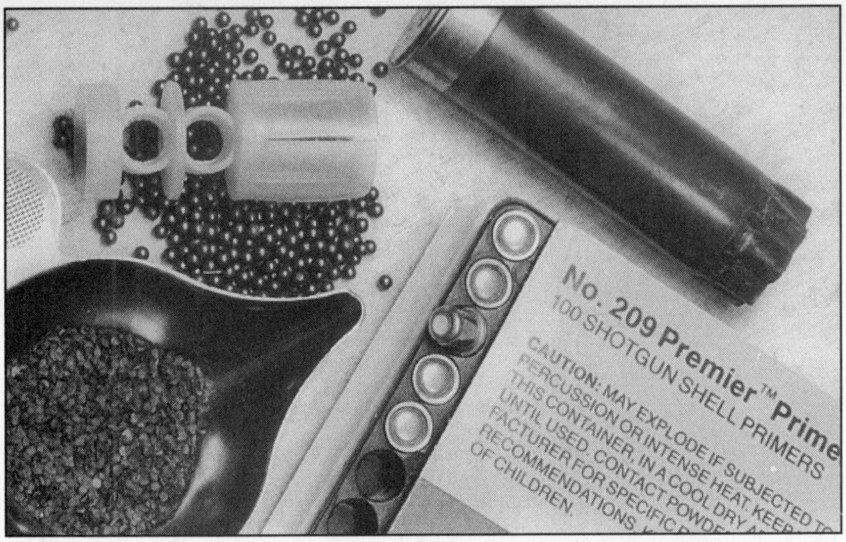

The makings of a tight-patterning dove reload include Green Dot and the Remington 209P primer plus the TGT-12 wad.

tight-patterning results and a more tolerable recoil level.

LOAD
HULL: Fed. plastic 12-ga. ($3^{1}/_{2}$")
PRIMER: Win. 209
POWDER: 40.0 grs. Blue Dot
WAD: Fed. 12S0; one 20-ga. .135" card
SHOT: $1^{7}/_{8}$ oz. lead
PRESSURE: 9000 psi
VELOCITY: 1200 fps

LOAD
HULL: Rem. SP 12-ga. ($3^{1}/_{2}$")
PRIMER: CCI 209 Magnum
POWDER: 39.5 grs. Blue Dot
WAD: Rem. R12L
SHOT: 2 oz. lead
PRESSURE: 11,100 psi
VELOCITY: 1220 fps

For anyone who simply *must* stuff a full 10-gauge magnum shot charge into his new $3^{1}/_{2}$-inch 12-gauge, however, here is a recipe that'll provide any gobbler with Excedrin headache No. 1:

LOAD
HULL: Fed. plastic 12-ga. ($3^{1}/_{2}$")
PRIMER: CCI 209 Magnum
POWDER: 38.5 grs. Blue Dot
WAD: Fed. 12S4; Winchester WAA12F114
SHOT: $2^{1}/_{4}$ oz. lead
PRESSURE: 11,100 psi
VELOCITY: 1150

All these reloads pattern best when given hard, high-antimony lead shot or copper- or nickel-plated pellets. These resist deformation during firing setback and bore travel far better than ordinary chilled shot does. Despite its name, chilled shot isn't very hard, and it normally deforms to such an extent that it patterns 10-25 percent lower than hard, high-antimony or plated shot. Thus, if you're going to use a bigbore for optimum pattern density, be sure to use shot that will deliver rather than deform.

There are already some areas where steel shot must be used in the uplands. One new reload that I've tried seems especially good for this on close-flushing birds with No. 5 steel. It will also be a good steel-shot clay-target reload, in my opinion, especially for Sporting Clays. It's assembled like this, according to Hodgdon Powder Co. data:

LOAD
HULL: Win. AA
PRIMER: Win. 209
POWDER: 31.0 grs. Hodgdon HS-7
WAD: MEC 12-TW steel shot
SHOT: $1^{1}/_{8}$ oz. steel
PRESSURE: 10,700 LUP
VELOCITY: 1264 fps

A lot of hunters are turning to commercial preserves these days, a place where pheasants and chuckars can be almost as challenging as they are on the wing in the wild. An excellent game-preserve 12-gauge load is the old live pigeon round which uses a $3^{1}/_{4}$ drams equivalent powder charge under a $1^{1}/_{4}$-ounce lead shot load for about 1220 fps. This one patterns nicely from Skeet, Improved Cylinder and Modified chokes for target coverage at hunt club ranges, and with hard No. 6 lead shot, it'll account for many positive retrieves. One of the best such reloads that I've found is:

LOAD
HULL: Fed. Gold Medal
PRIMER: Fed. 209
POWDER: 24.0 grs. Unique
WAD: Fed. 12S4
SHOT: $1^{1}/_{4}$ oz. lead
PRESSURE: 10,500 psi
VELOCITY: 1220 fps
NOTE: The Winchester WAA12F114 wad can interchange for the same ballistics.

Accurate Arms Co. makes a powder that should interest hunters because of the way it excels in cold conditions. This is Nitro 100, a flake-type propellant made of nitro-cotton for uniformity. Tests have shown that Nitro 100 loses very little in low temperatures. For example, the following reload was tested in temperatures of 10, 70 and 125 degrees F to determine stability and consistency:

LOAD
HULL: Win. AA
PRIMER: Win. 209
POWDER: 18.0 grs. Nitro 100
WAD: Win. WAA12
SHOT: $1^{1}/_{8}$ oz. lead
PRESSURE: +10F—9400 psi; +70F—9600 psi; +125F—9700 psi
VELOCITY: +10F—1185 fps; +70F—1200; +125F—1208

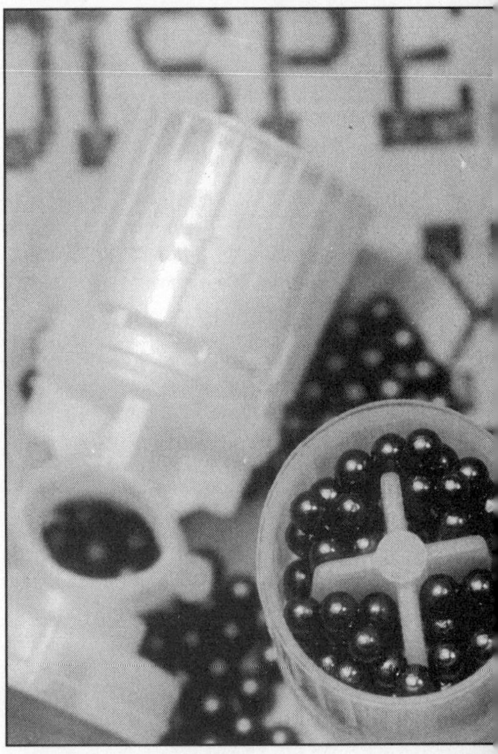

A close-range, scatter-load performance can be had by using the Dispersor-X wad from Ballistic Products, Inc.

All of this makes Nitro 100 look pretty good for those who hunt hard regardless of the weather. And while the above reload is a solid one for much uplanding, this is another with a bit more velocity in it. Accurate Arms has not published the pressure for it, although the velocity is in their manual, but I'm assured that it is indeed within SAAMI parameters:

LOAD

HULL: Win. AA
PRIMER: Win. 209
POWDER: 19.0 grs. Nitro 100
WAD: Rem. RXP-12
SHOT: $1\frac{1}{8}$ oz. lead
VELOCITY: 1255 fps

This is a snappy upland load that patterns nicely and is best stuffed with hard, high-antimony shot or copper-plated pellets.

Bird or cottontail hunters who use open-choked guns do so because they want to take advantage of a wide pattern's effective hitting area on close- or moderate-range targets. However, not all reloads give truly wide, evenly distributed patterns from an open-choked barrel. Many still throw tight center densities with weak outer rims. But a pair of powders with which I've been experimenting have shown a tendency to fill out the fringes of a 30-inch-diameter pattern better than most other powders. These are Solo 1250 from Scot Powder Co. and Super-Lite from Winchester. A pair of exact reloads are:

LOAD

HULL: Win. AA
PRIMER: Win. 209
POWDER: 24.5 grs. Solo 1250
WAD: Windjammer
SHOT: $1\frac{1}{8}$ oz. lead
PRESSURE: 7400 LUP
VELOCITY: 1200 fps
NOTE: Can be taken to 1255 fps with 26.0 grs. Solo 1250 with a pressure of 8400 LUP

LOAD

HULL: Rem. Premier
PRIMER: Fed. 209
POWDER: 20.5 grs. Super-Lite Ball
WAD: Win. WAA12
SHOT: $1\frac{1}{8}$ oz. lead
PRESSURE: 9900 psi
VELOCITY: 1255 fps

Fans of the 16-gauge have long been frustrated by the lack of specialized factory loads and the paucity of reloading components. However, there are now some new and interesting 16-gauge reloading possibilites about. Winchester's Super-Field Ball Powder is a fine match to the 16, especially with Winchester's WAA16 wad. And there are now Gualandi (Italian) wads around for use in the spacious ACTIV all-plastic cases as well as for 1-ounce reloads in some other hulls. Scot's Solo 1250 and 1500 are also good in the 16-gauge case. When using Solo 1500 in the 16—as well as in any other gauge—always follow the company's instructions for wad seating pressures. A couple of hard-hitting 16-gauge field reloads are:

LOAD

HULL: ACTIV all-plastic 16-ga.
PRIMER: Win. 209
POWDER: 28.0 grs. Solo 1500
WAD: Rem. SP-16 seated with 40 lbs. pressure
SHOT: $1\frac{1}{4}$ oz. lead
PRESSURE: 10,800 LUP
VELOCITY: 1220 fps

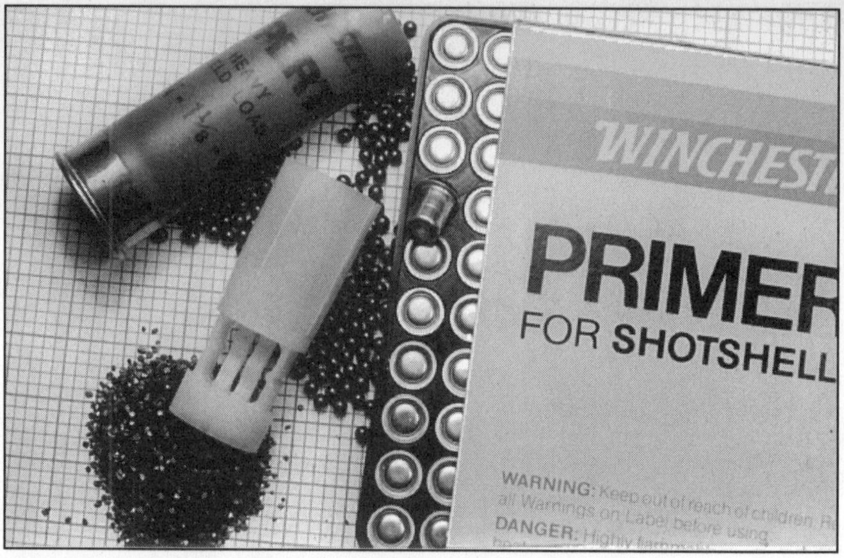

Winchester's relatively new Super-Field Ball Powder and WAA16 wad make up into some excellent upland game and Sporting Clays reload.

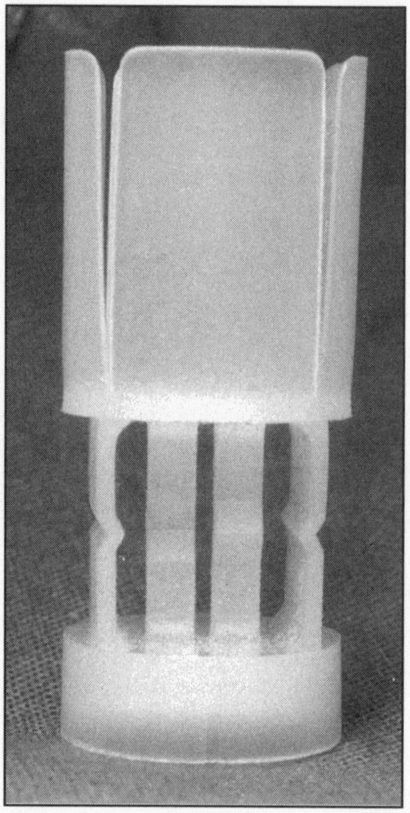

Using the 3-inch 20-gauge hull for $1\frac{1}{8}$-ounce loads makes it possible for the handloader to employ wads with longer cushioning sections, such as the Winchester WAA20.

A novel 20-gauge "plinker" reload with just $\frac{3}{4}$-ounce of lead shot is both economical and light on a beginner's shoulder.

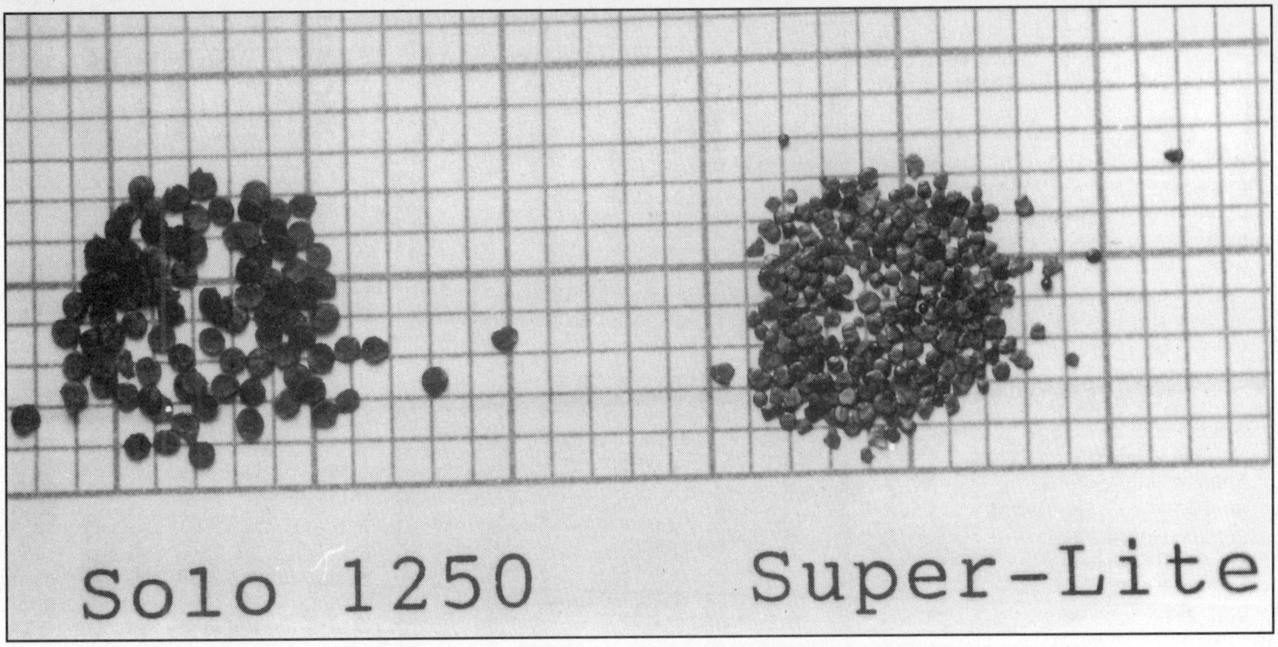

A pair of modern powders that tend to give more even pellet distributions than other propellants which hammer tight center densities are Scot powder Co.'s Solo 1250 and Winchester's Super-Lite.

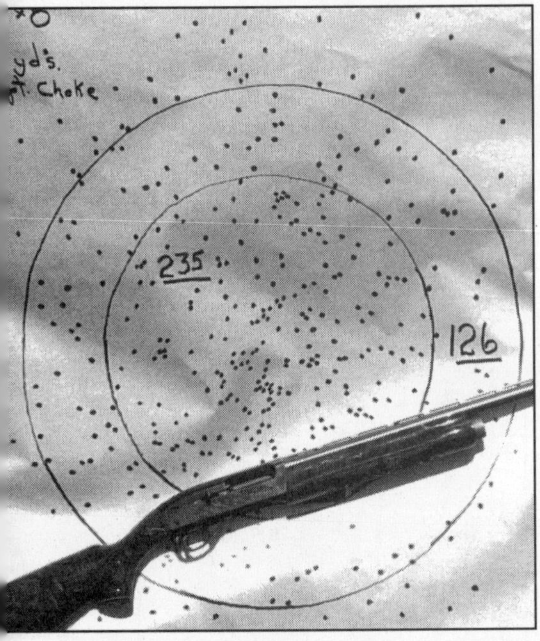

A 12-gauge reload with 22.5 grains of Unique printed this pattern at 25 yards with a light Improved Cylinder choke and hard No. 8s. Not a bad upland cluster.

LOAD

HULL: Win. AA 16-ga.
PRIMER: CCI 209
POWDER: 20.5 grs. Winchester Super-Field
WAD: Win. WAA16
SHOT: $1^1/_8$ oz. lead
PRESSURE: 10,800 psi
VELOCITY: 1185 fps
NOTE: A solid Sporting Clays or Skeet reload for the 16 as well as a light field load

A concept that is quite novel in 16-gauge is the Dispersor-X wad being distributed stateside by Ballistic Products, Inc. A basic one-piece plastic wad, the Dispersor-X has an X-divider moulded into its shotcup to produce a quick-opening pattern from Full-choked guns. (The same is obtainable for the 12-gauge.) The supplier offers some published data for this one, and a good-looking recipe is:

LOAD

HULL: Fiocchi plastic 16-ga.
PRIMER: Fiocchi 616
POWDER: 23.0 grs. Herco
WAD: Dispersor-X
SHOT: $^7/_8$-oz. lead
PRESSURE: 9800 psi
VELOCITY: 1230 fps

The 7/8-ounce load may seem light, but it is needed to keep chamber pressure in line. Also, the $^7/_8$-ouncer is adequate for close-in birds like woodcock.

Through the seasons, we have noted that the 20-gauge is very effective with its heavier charges, but it is often difficult to cram a full $1^1/_8$-ounce baby magnum load into the $2^3/_4$-inch case. Hunters complain of bulged or opened crimps, and in general velocities aren't impressive. So why try? Most 20-gauge guns today have 3-inch chambers, and the $1^1/_8$-ounce loading can be assembled much easier in the magnum-length case. In the 3-inch hull, there is room left for a longer wad with the $1^1/_8$-ounce shot charge; this not only provides somewhat more cushioning, but the added expansion room for early powder gases helps create a more favorable pressure/velocity

Shotguns are individuals, and the only way to learn how a given reload will perform is to shoot it through a specific birdgun and evaluate it.

ratio for higher speeds than the standard-length 20 could cook up with the $1^{1}/_{8}$-ounce load. For example...

LOAD

HULL: Win. C/F 20-ga. (3")
PRIMER: Win. 209
POWDER: 27.0 grs. Win. 571 Ball
WAD: Win. WAA20
SHOT: $1^{1}/_{8}$ oz. lead
PRESSURE: 11,000 LUP
VELOCITY: 1220 fps

LOAD

HULL: Fed. plastic 20-ga. (3") case (paper base wad)
PRIMER: Win. 209
POWDER: 26.0 grs. SR-4756
WAD: Win. WAA20F1
SHOT: $1^{1}/_{8}$ oz. lead
PRESSURE: 10,600 LUP
VELOCITY: 1265 fps

Another interesting use of a 3-inch case is with the .410. This pee-wee bore can use all the pellets it can get into its patterns, but the basic 3-inch 410 load is rather pedestrian and plagued by a long in-flight shot string. A novel approach to 410 field reloads is using the 3-inch hull with an unconventional $^{5}/_{8}$-ounce (273 grains) shot charge. This puts the shot charge near maximum for the 410, while also providing a bit more room in the case for a slightly heavier charge of slow-rate powder for a higher velocity with a shorter shot string.

LOAD

HULL: Win. C/F 410 (3")
PRIMER: Rem. 209P
POWDER: 20.0 grs. IMR-4227
WAD: Trico No. 4
SHOT: 5/8-oz. lead
PRESSURE: 11,900 LUP
VELOCITY: 1230 fps

An important point here is sticking with the Remington 209P primer, which is a mild cap. Hotter primers will send chamber pressures beyond industry parameters. Do not substitute! ●

ADDITIONAL SPECIAL CONCEPT RELOADS

Extra-Heavy 10-ga. Magnum Turkey Load

HULL: Fed. plastic ($3^{1}/_{2}$")
PRIMER: Fed. 209
POWDER: 38.0 grs. SR-4756
WAD: Rem. SP-10
SHOT: $2^{3}/_{8}$ oz. lead
PRESSURE: 10,000 LUP
VELOCITY: 1125 fps

High-Velocity 12-ga. 3" Magnum

HULL: Win. C/F 12-ga. (3")
PRIMER: Fed. 209
POWDER: 36.0 grs. SR-4756
WAD: Win. WAA12F114
SHOT: $1^{3}/_{8}$ oz. lead
PRESSURE: 10,800 LUP
VELOCITY: 1380 fps

Tight-Shooting 12-ga. Dove Load

HULL: Rem. Premier
PRIMER: Rem. 209P
POWDER: 19.0 grs. Green Dot
WAD: Rem. TGT-12
SHOT: $1^{1}/_{8}$ oz. lead
PRESSURE: 7300 psi
VELOCITY: 1145 fps
NOTE: Can be taken to 21.0 grs. Green Dot for 1200 fps and 8800 psi.

Mild-Recoil 12-ga. "Plinker" Load

HULL: Rem. Premier
PRIMER: Rem. 209P
POWDER: 17.6 grs. Clays
WAD: Rem. TGT-12
SHOT: $^{7}/_{8}$-oz. lead
PRESSURE: 6600 LUP
VELOCITY: 1200 fps
NOTE: Can be reduced to 16.5 grs. Clays for about 1150 fps and lower recoil.

Light 16-ga. Reload

HULL: Win. C/F 16-ga.
PRIMER: Win. 209
POWDER: 20.0 grs. Super-Field Ball
WAD: Win. WAA16
SHOT: 1-oz. lead
PRESSURE: 8400 psi
VELOCITY: 1165 fps

Buffered 20-ga. Magnum

HULL: Win. C/F 20-ga. (3")
PRIMER: Win. 209
POWDER: 23.0 grs. 571 Ball Powder
WAD: Win. WAA20F1
SHOT: $1^{3}/_{16}$ oz. lead
BUFFER: 12.0 grs. Win. "Grex" buffer
PRESSURE: 10,900 LUP
VELOCITY: 1115 fps
NOTE: Tight-patterning, close-range load for turkey hunting with 20-ga. gun.

Beginner's 20-ga. Light Load

HULL: Win. AA 20-ga.
PRIMER: Win. 209
POWDER: 15.5 grs. Unique
WAD: Fed. 20S1
SHOT: $^{3}/_{4}$-oz. lead
PRESSURE: 9700 psi
VELOCITY: 1200 fps
NOTE: May not function in autoloaders; can be reduced to 15.0 grs. of Unique for even lighter recoil in single shots.

Solid 28-ga. Field Reload

HULL: Win. AA 28-ga.
PRIMER: Win. 209
POWDER: 20.5 grs. Hodgdon HS-7 Spherical
WAD: Win. WAA28
SHOT: $^{3}/_{4}$-oz. lead
PRESSURE: 11,200 LUP
VELOCITY: 1260 fps

Beginner's Light-Recoil 28-ga. Load

HULL: Win. AA 28-ga.
PRIMER: Fed. 209
POWDER: 12.0 grs. SR-7625
WAD: Win. WAA28
SHOT: $^{3}/_{4}$-oz. lead
PRESSURE: 10,600 LUP
VELOCITY: 1100 fps
NOTE: Not a hunting load; adequate for hand-trap clay shooting and Skeet.

Ultra-High Velocity 410 Reload

HULL: Win. C/F 410 (3")
PRIMER: Win. 209
POWDER: 26.5 grs. IMR-4198
WAD: Fed. 410SC
SHOT: $^{1}/_{2}$-oz. lead
PRESSURE: 10,490 LUP
VELOCITY: 1435 fps

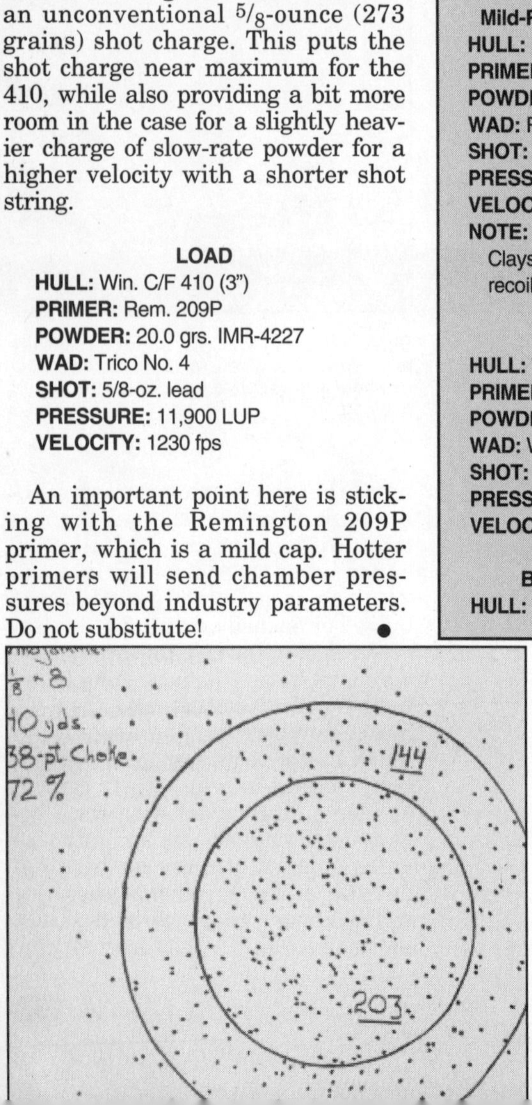

Solo 1250 is a powder that tends to give a more even distribution of pellets rather than bunching them in the center of a Full-choke pattern. Winchester Super-Lite Ball Powder has a similar quality.

Steel in the 16

by JOHN HAVILAND

UNTIL RECENTLY, data and a suitable wad were unavailable for reloading steel shot in the 16-gauge. Ballistics Products now sells a wad, and their manual "How to Load the 16-Gauge" gives information for a 3/4-ounce steel load.

The wad is actually an undersize, longitudinally ribbed, tapered 12-gauge shotcup made for special high-velocity loads in the 12. The base of the BP-12 TUFF shotcup measures .680-inch, while a regular Winchester AA 16 wad measures .625-inch. Although it's a tight fit, the BP-12 TUFF wad fits in the 16-gauge case.

The BP-12 wad is made without slits. Three equidistant scissor cuts down to the base are recommended to make petals that flare once the charge leaves the barrel, allowing the shot to separate from the cup. I found it easier to make two cuts across the the mouth of the shotcup with a knife, to produce four petals.

Seating the shotcups caused a few cases to split about an inch down from the mouth. The cases that split, though, already had cracks in the mouth from previous firings, so it's a good idea to use new or once-fired cases. The wad petals do overlap a bit when seated in the case.

Using a knife to cut slits and form petals in the Ballistics Products shotcup/wad works well.

Ballistic Products recommends inserting a sheet of thin plastic-like material from DuPont, known as Mylar, in the shotcup before adding the shot to further keep the hard steel pellets from contacting the bore. I never used any in my loads.

16-GAUGE STEEL SHOT LOAD FROM BALLISTIC PRODUCTS

Hull: Federal Hi-Power 16-gauge 2 3/4-inch Field
Primer: Winchester 209
Powder: 25.5 grains Hodgdon HS-6
Wad: Two 16-ga. .1-inch nitro cards over powder, plus one BP-12 TUFF shotcup with Mylar wrap inserted into shotcup before shot. (Cut shotcup with three petals to near base of the wad.)
Shot: 3/4-ounce steel shot #4
Pressure: 9000 psi
Velocity: 1280 fps

The spent wads I recovered showed no signs that the shot had grated through. Without the Mylar, though, the shot is loose in the cup. I trimmed the cups down to fit the shot, and that seemed to work well.

Haviland counting pellet holes. This 78 percent pattern was shot with 3/4-ounce of #4 steel at 25 yards. Number 4s patterned tighter than #6s. Both sizes tended to cluster groups of shot pellets.

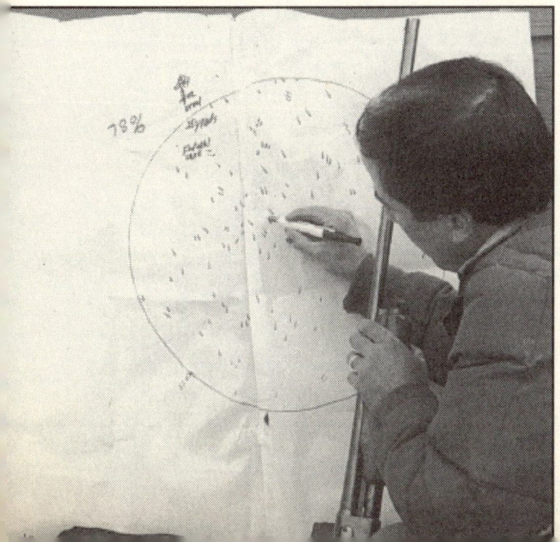

My 16-gauge is a Remington 870. Several years ago, I had the Full choke reamed out to between Improved Cylinder and Modified. Federal and Winchester steel loads shoot Full choke patterns through this degree of choke.

The steel handloads did, too. At 25 yards, the handloads with 3/4-ounce of 4s printed an average of 78 percent in a 19-inch circle. The 6s averaged 71 percent. I didn't pattern these loads in the standard 30-inch circle at 40 yards because they are ineffective on waterfowl at that range. These 3/4-ounce loads have nearly the same number of shot as a 1 1/8-ounce load of lead, so pattern density is fine. Their deficiency is that steel pellets lose significant velocity and penetration at ranges over 35 yards. But many ducks—most of those taken over decoys—are shot within that range.

With a steel load now available for the 16-gauge, reloaders can once again shoot their 16s in the duck blind. •

What's New ON THE LOADING BENCH

by DEAN A. GRENNELL

IN THE INTERIM, since the 12th Edition of HANDLOADER'S DIGEST came off press, quite a few developments of interest to the world's handloaders have come along. I will cover as many of these as possible, with headings for the various categories.

Powders

Accurate Arms introduced their Nitro 100 in 1990, a fast-burning, double-base, extruded-flake powder for target and light field loads in the 12-gauge shotgun, as well as target loads in 38 and 44 Special, 45 ACP and 45 Long Colt. In 1991, they added 2015 BR, 4350, plus 2700, and 2495 BR in 1992.

The 2015 BR is a single-base, small-grained, extruded propellant specifically developed for benchrest cartridges such as the 22 and 6mm PPC. Extremely versatile, it can be used in cartridges as diverse as the 22 Hornet and 458 Winchester Magnum. For example, I've used it to push 210-grain bullets out of a Ruger Model 77 Magnum in 416 Rigby at a little over 3500 fps, with really excellent accuracy.

Accurate Arms powder line.

Accurate Arms 2700 is a ball propellant best suited for comparatively heavy bullets in cartridges such as the 22-250 up through the belted magnums. It is comparable in burning rate to such powders as IMR-4350 and Winchester 760.

Accurate Arms 4350 is a single-base, extruded propellant similar to IMR-4350 and H-4350.

Accurate Arms 2495 BR is a single-base, extruded propellant of medium burning speed, comparable to IMR-4895 or H-4895, developed expressly for use in service rifle cartridges such as the 308 Winchester and 30-06 Springfield. In most applications, it is not position-sensitive and thus tends to perform well with reduced loads.

At press time, Accurate Arms announced the purchase of Scot Powder Company.

Hercules added three new numbers to their Reloder line of rifle powders which previously included R-7 and R-12. The new ones, in fast-to-slow order, are R-15, R-19 and R-22.

Hercules Reloder 19 and 22 rifle powder.

Hodgdon added H-1000, a slow-burning, extruded propellant that performs extremely well with heavy bullets in the big belted magnum cases. Following that, they introduced an extruded-flake powder called Clays and went on to add two more sub-variants called International Clays and Universal Clays.

Clays is intended for target loads in the 12-gauge, with applications for target loads in handgun cartridges such as 38 Special, 40 S&W and 45 ACP.

International Clays is a good choice for target loads in 20-gauge, producing somewhat reduced recoil

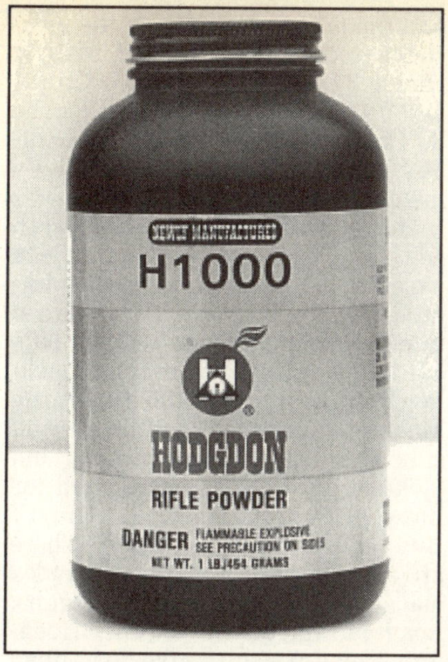

Hodgdon H-1000 rifle powder.

with exceptionally clean-burning properties.

Universal Clays is an extremely small-grained, extruded-flake powder providing consistent charge weights through powder measures. One of the most versatile of the Hodgdon shotgun/pistol propellants, it performs well in nearly all straight-sided handgun cases, as well as 12-gauge 1¼-ounce through 28-gauge ¾-ounce target loads. Both International and Universal Clays can also be used in handloading handgun ammunition. Some handgun load data is printed on the labels, and additional information may be requested from Hodgdon.

Hodgdon's Clays shotgun/handgun powder and safety funnel/pouring spout.

Hodgdon also introduced a plastic funnel/pouring cap for use on all their powder cans. The attached spout cover, when in place, provides an airtight seal to prevent airborne moisture from affecting powder density.

IMR continues to market the line of powders formerly supplied by DuPont, adding no new propellants since their introduction of IMR-7828, a slow-burning rifle powder.

Norma powders, withdrawn from the U.S. market about 1983, were recently reintroduced, imported from Sweden by The Paul Company. The line included R-1 and R-123 handgun powders as well as N-200, N-201, N-202, N-204 and MRP rifle powders, and the same numbers constitute the present offering. Current loading data should be used with the powder of recent production, as Norma says it differs in burning rates from the pre-1983 powders of the same numeric designation.

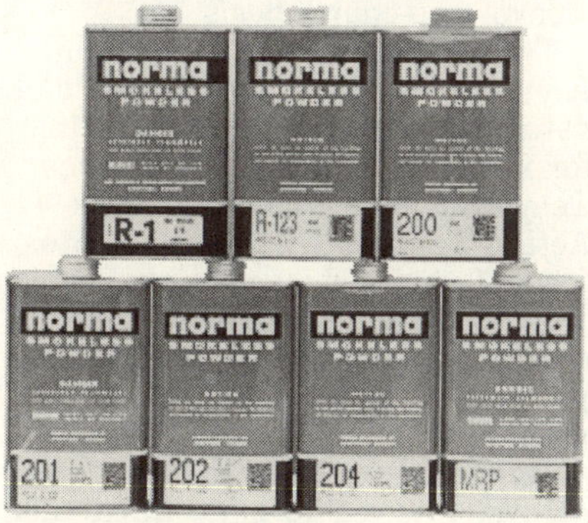

Norma smokeless powder.

Scot powders moved from the East Coast to their present location in Ohio. The firm was purchased by Austin Powder Co. and in mid-1993 was acquired by Accurate Arms. Scot has four rifle powders—Brigadier 4197, 3032, 4065 and 4351, all of which are identical to four rifle powders once marketed by Herter's. The burning rates are similar, but not identical, to comparable numbers in the IMR series. For example, Brigadier 3032, formerly Herter's 102, is a little faster in burning rate than IMR-3031.

Scot Powder Co.'s Brigadier 4065 and DuPont's IMR-4064.

Other Scot powders are for use in shotgun and handgun reloads and include, in fast-to-slow burning order: Royal Scot D, Pearl Scot, Solo 1000, Solo 1250 and Solo 1500. When used in handgun reloads, these Scot powders tend to produce little or no muzzle flash, offering an advantage for defense loads. Royal Scot D replaces the earlier Royal Scot and its density is somewhat greater, requiring bushings with smaller cavities when used in shotshell loading equipment.

At last report, Scot was planning to introduce two additional powders: Red Diamond, similar to Hercules Red Dot, and Scot 453, comparable to the now-discontinued Winchester 452AA.

VihtaVuori powders are produced in a facility operated by the Finnish government and have been distributed in many parts of the world. As of 1992, they became available to reloaders in the United States, being distributed by Kaltron, Inc.

VihtaVuori Oy's N140 "Savutonta Ruutia" and Norma's 204 smokeless powder.

As of early 1993, there are thirteen powders in the VihtaVuori line, five of them principally for use in handguns and eight for use in rifles.

In descending order of burning speed, fast-to-slow, the pistol powders are N310, N320, N340, 3N37 and N350. The rifle powders, in the same ranking, are N110, N120, N133, N135, N140, N150, N160 and N165.

I have been using the VihtaVuori powders, since obtaining some working samples, and have been highly

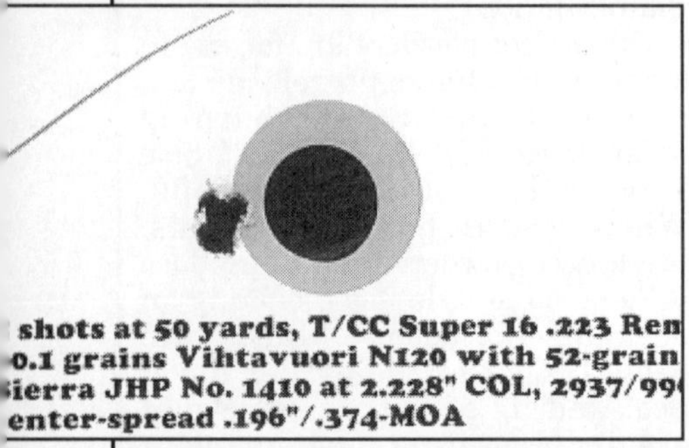

Five shots at 50 yards, T/CC Super 16 223 Remington, 20.1 grains VihtaVuori N120 with 52-grain Sierra JHP No. 1410 at 2.228-inch COL, 2937/996, center spread .196-inch/.374-MOA.

impressed by the performance they deliver, both as to velocity and accuracy.

Winchester has dropped their 452AA powder, replacing it with Winchester Super Trap (WST).

Winchester Super Light (WSL) is the same powder used in the Winchester Super Light AA factory loads, and it is said to produce less recoil while delivering the same pellet velocities.

Winchester WSF1 Ball powder.

Winchester Super Field (WSF) has taken the place of Winchester 473AA, although, as in the example of WST and 452AA, the load data is not necessarily interchangeable.

Winchester has discontinued their 680 powder. Accurate Arms No. 1680 comes pretty close to 680, but the 1680 usually is a little slower in burning speed.

Handbooks & Manuals

Accurate Arms currently has an updated version of their fifth data manual, with listings on their new powders up through 2495 BR. These are 36-page booklets, available free from the firm. They are in the process of producing a sixth version which will be a much larger, hardbound edition. It will not be available on a no-charge basis.

The booklet format has enabled Accurate Arms to keep their load data flexibly up to date, with listings for new cartridges as they appear. They even have a heading for the 41 Action Express (AE), but it notes, "Data for 41 AE is interchangeable with 40 S&W data." My own experience in working with both cartridges puts me in substantial agreement with that.

Barnes Bullets *Reloading Manual, No. 1* is a 356-page hardback book on loading the highly effective Barnes bullets. Tested loads are given for 50-some cartridges from the little 243 to the huge 50-caliber BMG, and for various rifle-size handgun loads. Ballistic tables give full data on the several Barnes lines—the X-Bullet, the Solids, and the Originals.

Unlike some other manuals, this one does not describe reloading procedures. It does tell what should be done, but not how to do it; that information is readily available elsewhere, of course. Price, $24.95.

Hercules continues to issue annually updated versions of their data booklet, usually available free from dealers or upon request from Hercules. The bulk of the book is concerned with reloading shotshells. Listings for rifles and handguns are compressed but comprehensive.

One of the more interesting items in the Hercules book is a discussion of the correlation between crusher and piezo pressures, as quoted in CUP or psi. In most instances, the CUP figure is lower than that for psi, although net pressures are identical and the difference is due to the measuring technique. The 8mm Mauser shows 37,000 CUP and 35,000 psi and both figures are identical for the 30 Carbine and 45-70 Government. Many find this puzzling, definitely including your present typist.

Hodgdon has just issued the 26th edition of their manual—almost 800 pages of up-to-date data. It lists jacketed bullet loads for more than a hundred standard and wildcat rifle cartridges, ranging from the 17 Ackley Bee through the 50 Browning Machine Gun, plus lead bullet and silhouette loads for many. Lead and jacketed bullet loads are listed for handgun cartridges from the 17 BumbleBee to the 454 Casull. There are also shotshell loads and Pyrodex loads for rifles, pistols and shotguns. Loads are given for not only Hodgdon Powders, but also for those assembled with IMR, Winchester and Hercules propellants. They also have a neat little Basic Reloader's Manual that they'll send free on request, so there's no excuse for going without that.

I say that because there are a number of sources for powders with more or less identical numerical designations. For instance, Accurate Arms 4350, IMR-4350, Scot's Brigadier 4351 and Hodgdon's H-4350. And, if you believe all four are identical to sixteen decimals, I have this bridge in Brooklyn upon which I'd like you to make me an offer.

The thing about the Hodgdon manual is that it lists precise data for all the Hodgdon powders and well may be the only source that does so. In addition, they list loads for most of the other powders in the current market. As the old Rogers & Hammerstein lyrics put it, "Everything's up to date in Kansas City"—well, in nearby Shawnee Mission, at least.

Hornady's Handbook is currently in its fourth edition—a two-volume

Two-volume 4th edition *Hornady Handbook of Cartridge Reloading.*

set, with rifle and handgun load data presented in the first volume and downrange trajectory data in the second. That offers convenience, as one can have the first book open to the load data and the second open to review the downrange dope.

I cannot fault HH4 for slighting cartridges. The samples at hand are from the second printing, 1991, and they cover the 41 AE, 40 S&W and even the 44 Auto Mag.

IMR continues to update their reloader's guide in much the same format employed earlier by DuPont, still with the picture of John Lachuk firing a pistol in the upper right-hand corner of the cover illustration. The date of issue appears in the lower RH corner of the back page—October, 1990, on the issue immediately at hand. As with many such booklets from powder makers, free copies may be available from your local dealer of shooting supplies. If you attend the annual NRA meeting, IMR will have a booth on the exhibit floor, and they will not only let you take any reasonable number of copies of the latest version, but will also give you an IMR shopping bag in which to carry other literature you pick up. If all else fails, you can request a copy from IMR by calling or writing.

Somewhat in the manner of the Hodgdon powders, the IMR booklet covers the use of some of their powders listed no more than rarely in other sources, such as SR 4756, SR 7625 and good old PB. In the edition mentioned, they had yet to recognize the .400-inch bullet diameters, nor the 41 Action Express, but they show a load with Hi-Skor 800-X that deals a 170-grain Sierra JHP out of a 10-inch 41 Magnum Contender barrel at a sizzling 1760 fps, and I regard that as smokin'.

Lyman recently brought forth the 47th edition of their reloading handbook. It runs to 480 8$^{1}/_{2}$x11-inch pages. The first 172 pages provide coverage on topics such as procedures and components for reloading, bullet casting and ballistics. The load data is divided into three sections: rifles, handguns, and data for the T/C Contender and Remington XP-100.

As Lyman is a longtime producer of casting equipment, many loads are listed for cast bullets. Loads for jacketed bullets are by no means slighted, however. Many entries carry listings of the pressures developed, given in CUP.

Norma is working up a data book, I'm sure. They do not sanction use of the pre-1983 data sources for contemporary Norma powders. Current data is produced on a copying machine and you may want to keep a jeweler's loupe handy to verify this or that digit in the listing. I'd hope this situation will improve in the closely adjacent future.

Nosler published the third edition of their reloading manual in October, 1989, recently enough to include some of the newer numbers such as the 357 Maximum and 10mm Auto. As a book, it was quite thoughtfully assembled, with the listing for each cartridge prefaced by a comment from one of its major advocates. I, for example, was invited to contribute my comments on the 41 Magnum. The listings, as a whole, tend to be somewhat more energetic than those in most other sources. For example, out of a 10-inch test barrel, they take the 210-grain Nosler JHP bullet to a thoroughly impressive 1650 fps in the 41 Magnum table. For the 10mm Auto, they list a load that puts the 170-grain Nosler JHP out of a 6-inch test barrel at 1200 fps. Originally, that was the only 10mm bullet Nosler had in their catalog; they've since introduced JHPs in 150 and 135 grains. Personally, I'm looking forward to the fourth edition to find out their recommendations for the lighter .400-inchers in both the 10mm Auto and 40 S&W!

Scot has a loading booklet, currently in its 6th edition, providing data for Scot powders in shotshells, handgun and rifle ammunition. Copies are distributed at no cost by dealers who stock these powders, or you may request a copy from Scot if you can't locate a nearby source.

Sierra published the 3rd edition of their manual in 1989 in the form of two volumes in looseleaf binders. One volume lists data for rifles and the other deals with handgun cartridges, with some amount of overlapping to deal with those cartridges that tend to cross party lines.

The staff at Sierra made dedicated efforts to include just about every cartridge that was seeing a reasonable amount of use at the cutoff date for publication. Their dimensional drawings are excellent and include the seated bullet and a dimension for cartridge length overall—helpful information many sources omit. Tables of exterior ballistics are included at the back of both volumes.

Speer brought out their number 11 manual in 1987 and, like all the previous ten, it was purely state of the art. Six years later, it's still one of the first sources I consult when working with the cartridges it covers.

A problem with the big, flossy manuals and handbooks is that they require a staggering amount of research time, effort and expense. For that good and sufficient reason, new editions tend to be few and far between. In the meantime, ammunition and firearms manufacturers keep dreaming up new cartridges and components. That leads me to feel there is something to be said for the updated booklet/annual approach used by some, such as Accurate Arms.

If you're really hard up for the answers when handloading some new miracle cartridge, drop a line to the given firm. Often they can provide a listing of data off the copying machine to get you up and running.

VihtaVuori has a 20-page booklet, 8$^{1}/_{4}$x11$^{11}/_{16}$ (well, 21x30 centimeters), which provides a generous listing of data for use in rifles and handguns. The text is in English with double-gaited data in both metric and inch-speak.

One column gives the breech pressure developed by the given load in MPa, which turns out to stand for megapascal, and one of those is equivalent to 145.0376 psi. If, for example, they list a pressure of 350 MPa, multiply that times 145.0376 to get 50,763.16 psi. Refer back to the comments about CUP/psi in the discussion of the Hercules booklet and you'll see there's no way to convert that to CUP figures.

When working with a particular cartridge, I have found it quite helpful to type up a careful copy from the VihtaVuori booklet of the dope in grains and foot-seconds to pin up over my loading bench. You can request your copy of the VihtaVuori booklet from Vince Tunzi at Kaltron, Inc., and your local dealer can request information about stocking the VihtaVuori powders from the same source.

It should be noted the data listings in the VihtaVuori booklet are absolute maximum, with no suggested starting loads. For that reason, they recommend starting at 10 to 15 percent lower than the charge weights given.

Winchester combines their booklet of loading data with a catalog of reloading components and gets it all into 52 5$^{1}/_{2}$x8$^{3}/_{8}$-inch pages, with quite a bit of the space taken up with listings for shotshells. The twelfth edition, printed in January, 1992, contains listings for use of the nominal shotshell powders in handguns, with pressures listed in psi. You can divide those by 145.0376 to get megapascals, if you like.

Included are loads for both the 10mm Auto and 40 S&W, in bullet weights from 150 to 200 grains, with listings for 231, 540, 571, WST, WSL and WSF powders, with three listings for 296 in the 10mm. Listings for 540 and 571 have been scarce to nonexistent previously, and the WS-powders are additions to the line.

Presses, Dies & Equipment

Blount Sporting Equipment Division is the corporate owner/operator of RCBS, as well as of Speer, CCI, Weaver and Outers. The RCBS division has introduced a great many new items in recent years. Their AmmoMaster loading press is a large and thoroughly engineered single-stage machine, capable of handling cartridges as awesome as the 50 BMG. At any future time, you can buy and install the piggyback adapter to convert it into an equally efficient progressive press, capable of operating manually or auto-indexing. A unique case detection system disengages the powder dispenser if no case is present.

RCBS has a line of bullet moulds, including about thirty designs not shown in the regular catalog. You can request a listing of these from RCBS. Examples include a pair of gas-checked flat-tips for 375s and another GCFT for 416s. Nominal weight of the latter is 350 grains, and it takes a lot of expense out of working with cartridges such as the 416 Rigby.

RCBS was one of the first firms to offer an electronic reloader's scale, with a capacity of 500 grains. It runs on a supplied AC adapter or on batteries, which are not included.

A new RCBS spray lube, called Case Slick, provides convenient aerosol application prior to resizing. The propellant gas is carbon dioxide and it's non-flammable. After resizing, the lube can be removed with a soft, dry cloth or by tumbling in a case cleaner.

New for 1993 is the RCBS CaseMaster, a gauging system which quickly and easily determines several cartridge case dimensions important to getting top accuracy, safety and reliability from handloaded ammunition. It determines case neck concentricity, case neck thickness, case length and bullet run-out. The CaseMaster also makes it quick and easy to detect evidence of an approaching case head separation before the symptoms of this condition become apparent on the case exterior.

RCBS introduced their Powder Checker in 1990 to give a visual indication of the powder level, but it may be difficult to see it on some units. For 1993, they've added the Lock-Out Die, designed to detect a missing or double powder charge and stop the travel of the ram, alerting the

RCBS bullet mould.

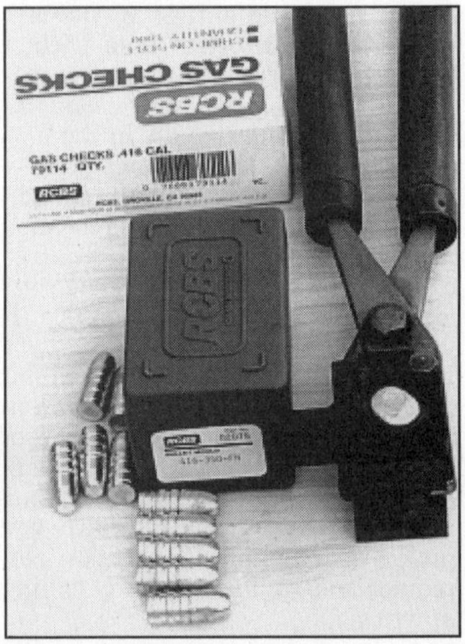

RCBS bullet mould and gas checks.

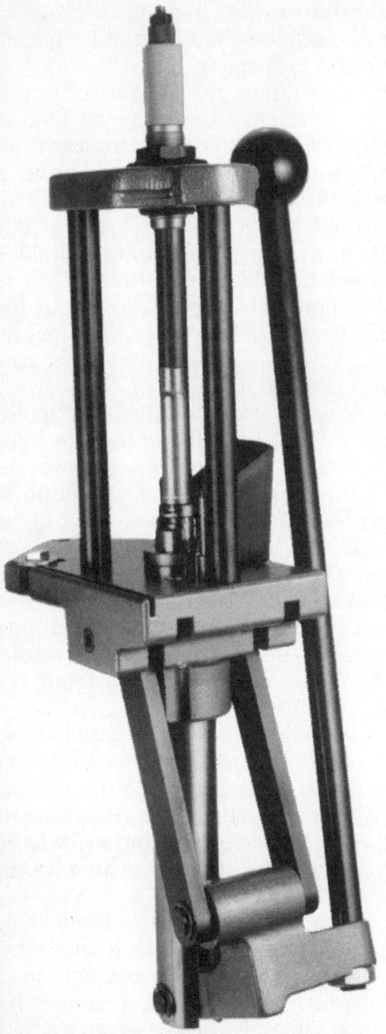
RCBS AmmoMaster single.

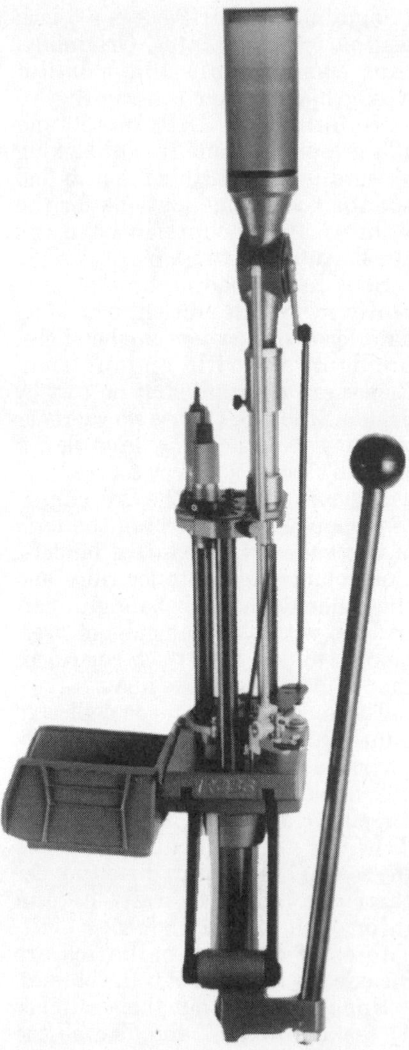
RCBS AmmoMaster auto.

RCBS Case Slick.

operator to the problem. It's installed in the next station after the powder dispenser.

Recently, a large number of surplus pistols for the 9mm Makarov have been imported into this country, and RCBS now has a set of loading dies for it, with a tungsten carbide resizing die and a taper crimp die. Interpolating that information from a release kindly supplied by their Art Peters, I came to a mention that they also can supply a bullet mould which casts a .365-inch, 100-grain bullet for the Makarov, as well as a new .365-inch sizing die and top punch for the RCBS Lub-A-Matic lube/sizer.

RCBS CaseMaster.

Candidly, I rubbed my eyes, looked again, very carefully, and it still read .365-inch. Wot the cotton-pick?!? Finally I called RCBS and got hold of old friend Bill Keyes, who assured me, yes, Dino, there really is a 9mm bullet that measures .365-inch in diameter instead of the usual .355-inch! It still takes the No. 16 shellholder, same as the 9mm Luger and all the rest.

RCBS categorizes their die sets by lettered groups and charges accordingly. The price of a set from Group G, for example, will get your full attention. Supply and demand has led to reclassifying several calibers. For instance, the 9x21mm is now in Group B. Group D now includes the 22 PPC, 6mm PPC, 416 Remington Magnum, 416 Rigby and 224 Weatherby. The 45 Winchester Magnum and 50 Action Express are now down in Group E.

As you may be aware, the fit between case heads and shellholders or shell plates can be either too tight or too sloppy, sometimes depending upon tolerance variations between makes of brass. RCBS has addressed the problem and brought forth six new numbers to designate the same number of shellholders and shell plates.

No. 33 is for the 50 Action Express. No. 34 for the 8x68Smm Magnum. No. 35 for the 38-40 and 44-40 WCF. No. 36 for the 45 Winchester Magnum and/or 451 Detonics Magnum. No. 37 is for the 416 Rigby and the No. 39 is for the 38 Super Auto.

Forster Products offers their new Ultra bullet seater die, which provides full support for the cartridge case and bullet during the seating operation. It features a micrometer stem calibrated in .001-inch graduations, and it is available in no less than 51 different calibers.

Hanned Precision/The Hanned Line produced/produces several items that are handy around the loading bench. They have, for example, something called a Fre-Chek for making your own gas checks out of empty aluminum beverage cans. There is also the Nexpander for putting a slight flare in the mouths of cases from 17 through 475 or so. The SGB (for Small Game Bullet) sleeve makes easy work of flattening the tips of 22 Long Rifle bullets to improve anchoring capability on small game.

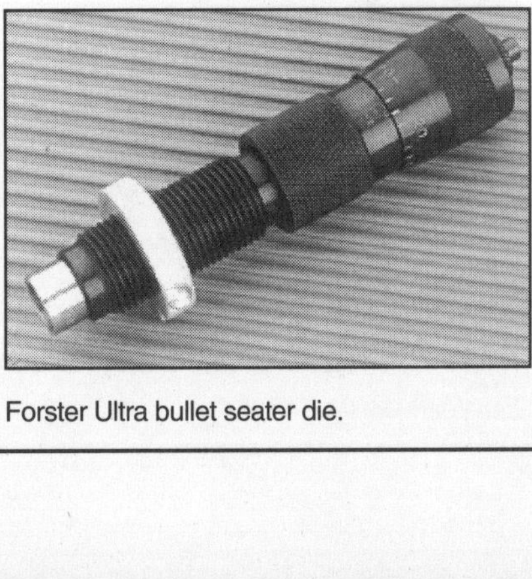

Forster Ultra bullet seater die.

They also have the K-Spinner, a neat little mandrel that can be put in an electric drill or drill press, with a gently tapered area at the business end that engages the inside of the case mouth to spin it for quick, easy and highly efficient cleaning and polishing.

All went well, so long as founder Ed Wosika remained at the helm, but he sold the enterprise to The Hanned Line, and mail addressed to Hanned Precision no longer reaches

K-Spinners from The Hanned Line.

him. That has led about one googolplex of readers to write to me and inquire how they can buy Hanned stuff. (A "googol" is a one followed by 100 zeroes, and a googolplex is a one followed by a googol of zeroes, if the term is unfamiliar. I may be exaggerating, but not much; not by a googol sight!) Literature on items currently available is free on request to The Hanned Line.

Hornady has finally gotten their new Apex shotshell reloaders into production, and they can be had in two versions, Standard or Automatic. You can start out with the Apex Standard and customize it later with any of the features of the Automatic. You can drop shot or powder by hand or automatically, with every pull of the operating lever. Either model lets you stop, back up or take out, examine and replace a shell from any station. You can continue the loading operation with that station empty if you wish.

The Apex Automatic is equipped with many automatic accessories that make reloading more convenient, such as the shell-detect features which prevent shot, powder or primers from dropping when there's no shell in the given station. Both models have swing-out powder and shot drains. The Apex Automatic has an automatic primer feed that holds a whole deck of 100 primers, and the shell-detect feature will keep it from dropping a primer if there is no shell at the station.

Apex loaders are available in 12-, 20- and 28-gauge, as well as in 410 bore. Other handy new items for the hullstuffer include a Stack 'N' Pack shotshell box loader, a Wad & Hull dispenser, and new Hornady shotshell boxes.

Another new item in the Hornady catalog is their Digital Caliper that enables one to perform highly precise measurements up to about six inches. It can measure inside or outside diameters, depth of primer pockets or cases, and case lengths. It comes in a neat, padded wooden storage case, with one battery installed, as well as a spare battery. One battery is good for a year or more of use under normal conditions.

I've been using one of the Hornady Dial Calipers and cannot fault it on any count. I've checked it against the faithful old Swiss 1-inch mike I've

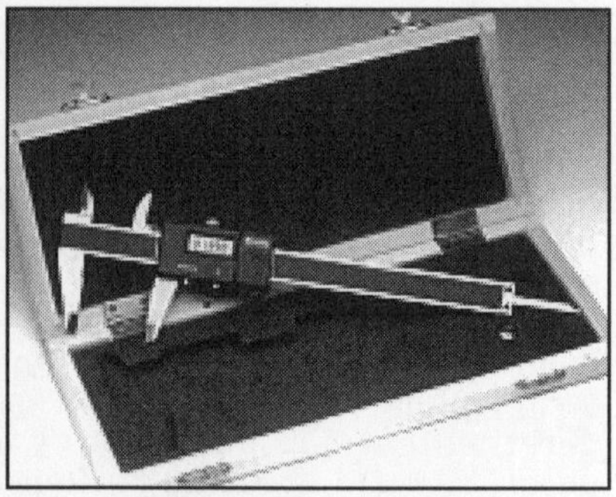

Hornady digital caliper.

been using since about the time Julius Caesar entered the cadet corps, and they agree to the ten-thousandth, which I regard as good enough for who it's for.

I did encounter one slightly vexing thing, but blundered onto a solution. Nominally, the unit turns on when you move the jaw and, if not used for six minutes or so, it turns off to conserve battery life. For some reason, mine would not turn off by itself if I left the jaws apart a little, as one usually does with any caliper when not in use.

Finally, I discovered that if I just pressed the zero button, even with jaws slightly apart, it would turn off the way it was supposed to. Needless to say, when you turn it back on next time, you need to bring the jaws together and re-zero it. Before I discovered that, I got some less-than-credible measurements. There is a separate button for switching from inches to millimeters and back again.

For those who like to keep records of handload performance—or of factory fodder, comes to that—Hornady now has their Shooter's Journal, a looseleaf binder that holds targets with blanks at the bottom on which you enter the pertinent data and particulars.

Lee Precision recently introduced their Load-Master progressive loading tool for rifle or handgun handloading at a base price of $179. Optional equipment includes a case feeder, loaded-round catching box, extra five-hole turrets and case collater, and they are still developing a bullet feeder. The present model requires that the operator place a bullet manually on the mouth of the charged case.

Also new to the Lee line is their

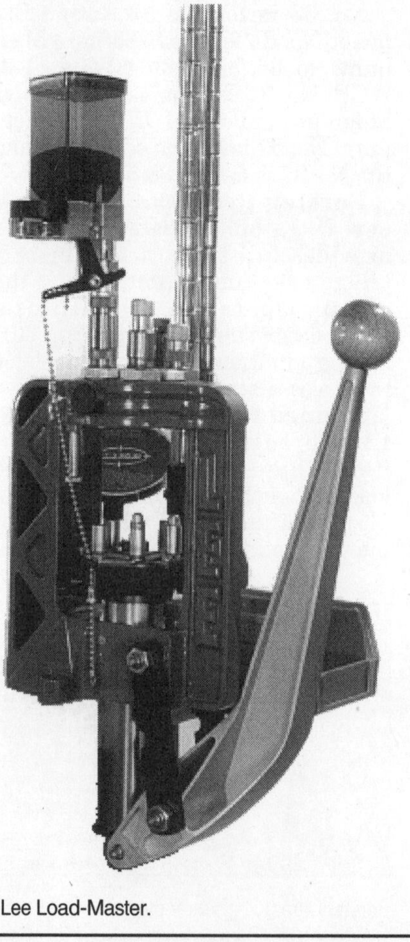

Lee Load-Master.

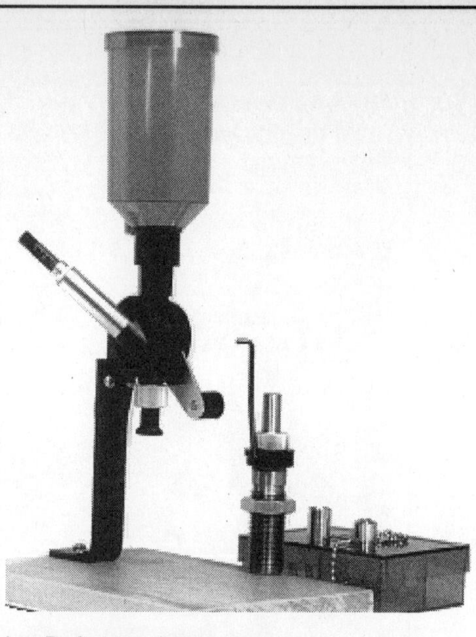

Lee Perfect powder measure.

Perfect powder measure, an adjustable, crank-operated measure with its micrometer-type adjustment rod calibrated in cubic centimeters. A table of powder densities is supplied with the unit, giving the density of each powder in grains per cubic centimeter. By consulting the table and adjusting the stem, it is possible to come quite close to the desired charge weight, requiring only minor adjustment after that.

The Lee Safety Disk powder measure utilizes the little six-cavity disks for use with their progressive and turret presses. It is lever-operated and comes with a steel mounting stand.

Lyman has introduced a new version of their Tubby tumbler with a clear plastic see-through lid and an adjustable tab that allows the user to change from standard to fast tumbling speed.

Lyman also has added a tool for reaming of primer pockets to uniform depth; it's available in both the

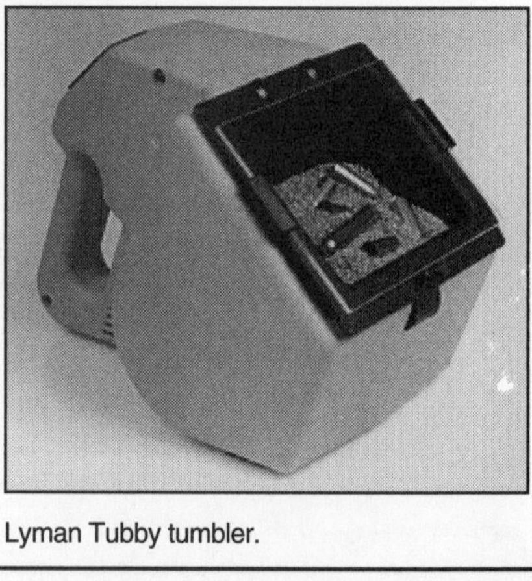

Lyman Tubby tumbler.

.175 and .210 diameters. Each tool has a factory-set stop collar to assure the treated cases will conform to SAAMI specifications. As supplied, the tool comes with Lyman's wooden utility handle, but it also easily adapts to the Lyman trimmers or utility crank.

Another new Lyman offering is a series of cartridge case gauges for

Lyman primer pocket reamer.

checking case length and headspace. Initially, these are available in 223, 243, 308 and 30-06 rifle calibers and 9mm, 10mm, 40 S&W and 45 ACP pistol calibers.

Lyman's four-die sets now combine mouth-expanding and powder

Lyman headspace gauges.

charging in a single die, and they also offer a combination inside/outside case neck deburring tool to perform the two operations simultaneously.

Lyman four-die set with expander and powder charge die.

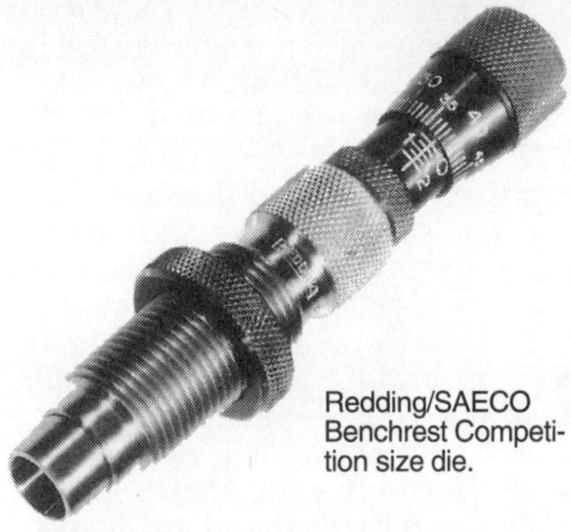

Redding/SAECO Benchrest Competition size die.

Redding/SAECO has a new straightline Benchrest Competition bullet seating die, with a micrometer-type adjustment that can be zeroed at any desired setting. There are no less than twelve new SAECO bullet mould designs, including a 100-grain 9.2mm for handloading the 9mm Makarov, with a .365 sizing die for use with it.

Factory Bullets & Ammo

Alpha LaFranck specializes in 458 bullets that have the same weights and jacket materials as regular factory bullets, customized to reduce drag and boost ballistic coefficients, for single, double or magazine rifles. This results in much higher retained velocity and energy at the longer ranges, as well as flatter trajectories. Alpha also offers hard or soft lead 458 bullets at lower cost, where a jacketed bullet isn't required.

Alpha now conducts all of its business out of the Lincoln, Nebraska, address.

Alpha LaFranck bullets.

Armfield Custom Bullets specializes in 270 and 7mm bullets in what they call Plainsbond for long-range hunting and Fragcore for safe varmint shooting. Bullets can be ordered with a plain flat-base or Very Low Drag (VLD) design in either caliber. You have a choice of pure copper or gilding metal for the jackets.

Ballard Built specializes in caliber 475 and 510 bullets, and they will fairly well tailor them to the customer's wishes in a wide variety of weights, shapes and jacket materials. They invite inquiries for additional information.

Ballard Built bullets.

Bertram Bullet Company is located in Australia and produces a wide variety of bullets, many hardly available elsewhere. They can also furnish many scarce and exotic empty cartridge cases to help out the distraught handloader.

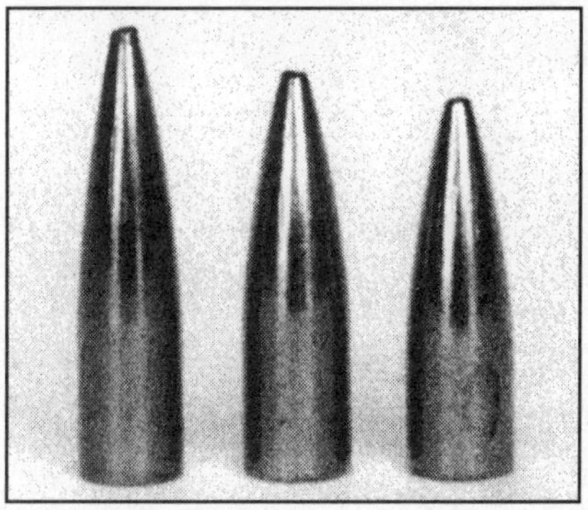

Betram bullets.

Blue Mountain Bullets offers what they term the triple-jacketed "Instant Kill" bullets in 270, 308, 338, 358, 375, 416, 423 and 458 diameters.

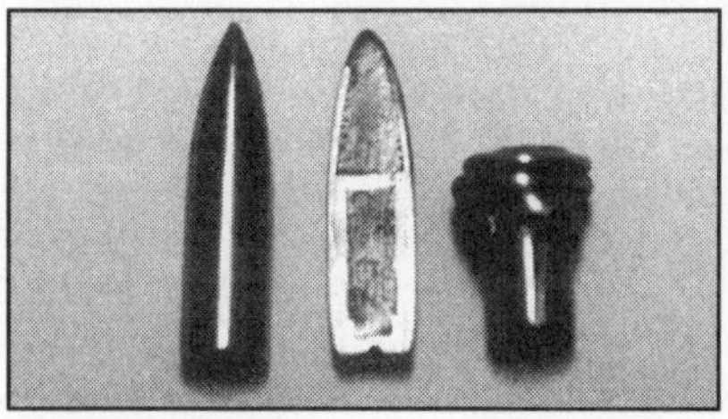

Blue Mountain bullets.

The triple-jacket design incorporates an outer jacket to provide a stable air-frame en route to the target. An internal jacket supports and expands the nose on impact, and a third jacket forms a sort of full wadcutter within the outer bullet shape and comes sliding forward through the wound created by the initial expansion, thus assuring the necessary deep penetration to reach the vital organs, even if the fore-portion of the bullet is destroyed.

Grizzly Bullets currently is producing 308 bullets in weights of 165 and 180 grains, 338 bullets in 225 and 250 grains, and 416 bullets in 350 grains. They have dropped the 358 diameter because of limited demand and need some lead-time to supply 458 bullets, as well as an order for a minimum of 100 bullets in that diameter.

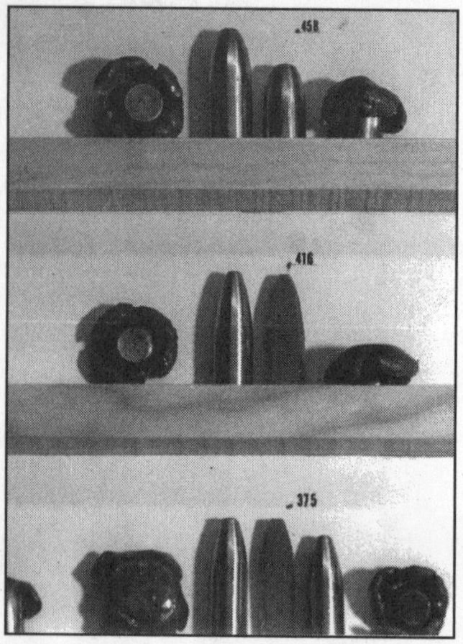

Grizzly bullets.

Harris Enterprises produces custom bullets in 348 Winchester with flat-points for tubular magazines in weights of 190 and 200 grains; these are also available in a bonded-core version. They also offer 264 bullets in 85 and 100 grains for varmint shooting, as well as 120- and 140-grain 264 bullets for deer and elk.

Hornady has added a new bullet design called the XTP, for (e)Xtreme Terminal Performance, which is to say that, like the celebrated ethnic parachute, it opens upon impact. At the lower end of the scale, they have these in .251 diameter for the 25 ACP pistol, at a dainty heft of just 35 grains, and, upon request, they can supply load data to put it out of vest-pocket pistols at velocities up around 1000 fps, at which it is guaranteed to get the target's attention, provided it's aimed properly, of course.

357/180-grain XTP bullets from Hornady.

XTP bullets are available in all popular weights and diameters for handgun cartridges, and the current Hornady catalog, free on request, contains a handsome four-page centerfold you can remove and pin up to serve as a wall chart. Like, eat your heart out, Hugh Hefner, hmm?

New for 1993 are four examples of what Hornady calls their CL-SIL design, and that's the exact, diametrical opposite of the XTP bullets. The term stands for crimp-locked silhouette. Bases of the CL-SIL bullets are entirely enclosed by the jackets and, up front, the jackets are closed in much in the same manner as the crimp in the mouth of a shotgun shell.

The CL-SIL design is currently offered in .357 diameter at weights of 160 and 180 grains, in .410 at 210 grains, and in .430 at 240 grains. Delivered to the suitable point of impact, they should serve as the ram-slammers of all time.

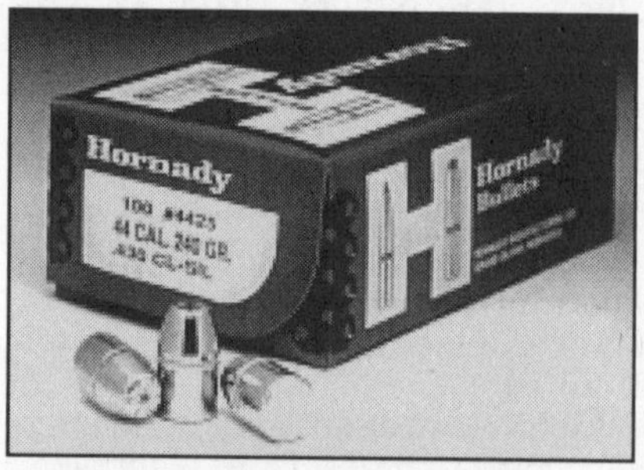

Hornady Crimp Lock Silhouette bullets.

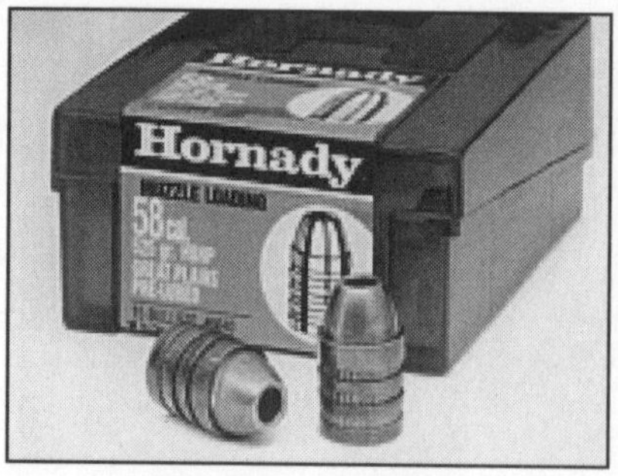

Hornady 58-caliber Great Plains bullet.

MagSafe Ammo customarily markets loaded rounds of handgun ammunition in most popular calibers (including 308 Winchester) that are exceptionally effective. Proprietor Joe Zambone, upon discussing things with a potential customer, may elect to supply their bullets for handloading.

MagSafe bullets are produced by melting the cores out of conventional JHP bullets and replacing them with large shot pellets held in place by a specialized type of epoxy. Unlike some other highly touted ammo with fragmented-core bullets, the MagSafe bullets will deliver accuracy about on a par with conventional solid-core factory loads.

As you might suppose, MagSafe loads and bullets are not cheap, but neither is their performance.

Northern Precision specialized in 416 bullets, offering them in a wide range of weights and designs, from varmint bullets weighing 198 to 250 grains, up through tubing-jacketed spitzers from 375 to 450 grains.

As of 1991, Northern Precision added .458 diameter bullets to their line. Included in the 458 line is a low-cost swaged lead slug with a copper "fouling scraper" attached to the base, termed their Base-Guard design. Owner William Noody adds that jacketed .458 bullets are also available, with a choice of pure copper or gilding metal jackets. More information can be obtained by calling Noody.

Nosler caliber 10mm bullets in 135-, 150- and 170-grain.

Nosler has added a 260-grain Partition bullet in .375 diameter for the sake of big game hunters who favor 375 H&H or 378 Weatherby Magnums, as well as handgun hunters partial to such potent rounds as the 375 JDJ. The bullet is designed to work well on thin-skinned, non-dangerous game such as elk, moose, black bear and deer, as well as numerous African plains species.

Nosler's 135-grain 400 JHP is the lightest generally available for those who handload the 10mm Auto or 40 S&W. It has proved so popular they now offer it in bulk packs of 250 at a saving of 15 percent, compared to the cost of the usual 100-pack. Also newly available in the bulk pack is Nosler's 180-grain 357 silhouette bullet.

Ranier Ballistic Corporation, terming itself the largest independent bullet manufacturer in the United States, recently added six new hollowpoint bullets to their line. They are 9mm at 115 and 124 grains, 38 at 158 grains, 10mm at 180 grains, 44 at 240 grains and 45 at 200 grains. They also have an extensive offering of Totally Copper Jacketed bullets described in a brochure that's free on request by calling Tacoma, WA.

Sierra has not added any new bullets to their 1992 line because they are having minor problems producing bullets fast enough to fill orders for their present line. Several specialty bullets which have been out awhile now deserve some mention, though. Dubbed the Long Range designs, they are hollowpoint spitzer boattail MatchKings of heavier than standard weight, and thus unusual length. Four examples are offered: 338-caliber 300-grain, 30-caliber 240-grain, 6.5mm 155-grain, and 224 80-grain. These are available factory direct only, as they've learned it's necessary to explain about the need for fast rifling twists when using them.

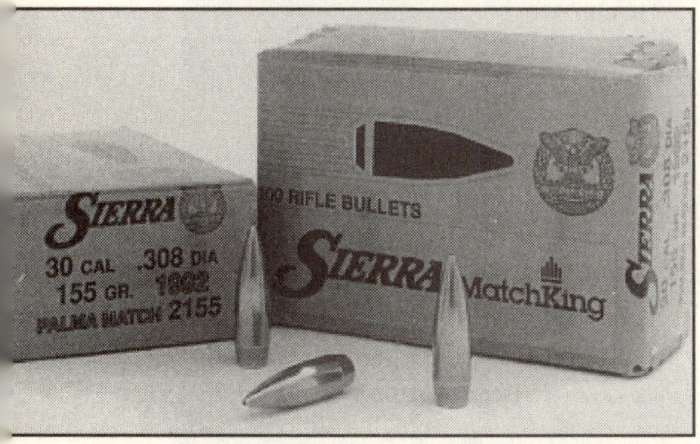

Sierra's new 30-caliber 155-grain HPBT MatchKing.

A couple of years ago, the firm moved from Santa Fe Springs, California, to Sedalia, Missouri, and their Kevin Thomas reports the move has worked out extremely well for them.

Within fairly recent times, I have had uncommonly gratifying results with the Sierra No. 1410 MatchKing bullets. That's a neat little 52-grain HPBT design that seems to display a strong penchant for all to go through the same hole in the paper. If you please, that is a comment, not a complaint.

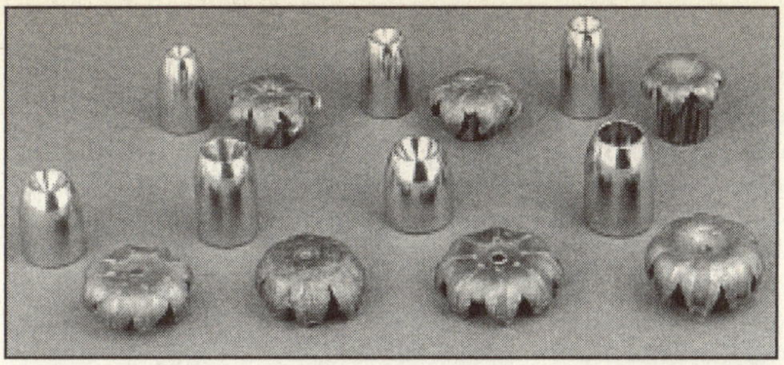

New Gold Dot hollowpoint bullets from Speer.

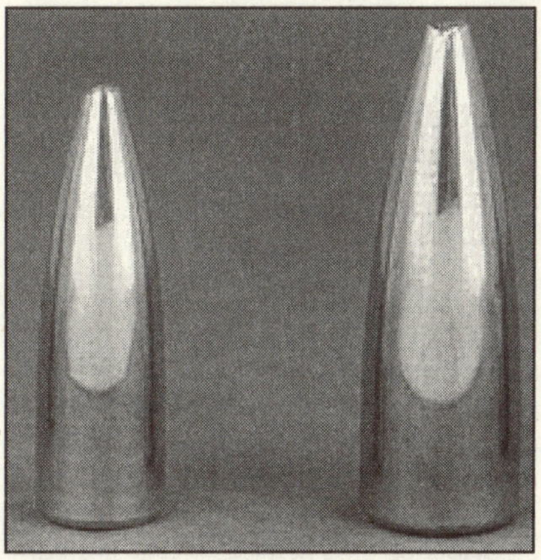

Speer TNT .243-inch/70-grain HP (left) and .308-inch/125-grain HP varmint bullets.

Speer now has what they call their Gold Dot bullets that can only be characterized as having expansive personalities. For the past some years, they have been making bullets by electroplating the jackets onto the cores. Initially, these were termed TMJ, for Totally Metal Jacketed, and their performance has been really outstanding. In 1992, they switched to calling them Uni-Cor, to signify the cores and jackets are so well bonded they perform as one, with core/jacket separations virtually eliminated.

For 1993, Speer has combined Uni-Cor technology with the performance requirements of a major U.S. government law enforcement agency to develop a totally new line of jacketed hollowpoint handgun bullets they are calling Speer Gold Dot.

Tested in calibrated 10-percent ordnance gelatin, with attention given to the effects of clothing and intermediate hard obstacles such as wood, metal or auto glass, the Gold Dot bullets shone brightly in every aspect. Every one proved to be capable of at least 14 inches of penetration in the ordnance gelatin generally regarded as a viable replica of living flesh.

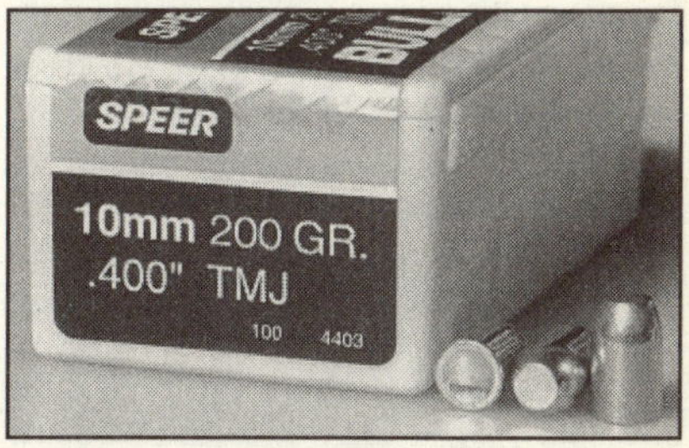

Speer 10mm 200-grain TMJ bullets.

Speer Gold Dot bullets get their name from the dot of jacket material which remains in the center of the expanded bullet. This distinctive dot is an assurance that expansion is complete, with maximum weight retained, and that the bullet has retained sufficient length to deliver deep penetration.

The concept of retained length is seldom considered, but it is of vital importance to adequate penetration. This is especially true of lightweight bullets such as the 9mm 115-grain JHP.

For 1993, Speer will offer the Gold Dot bullets in 115-grain 9mm HP, 124-grain 9mm HP, 147-grain 9mm HP, 155-grain 400 HP, 180-grain 400 HP, 185-grain 451 HP and 230-grain 451 HP. Other variants may be added later.

With some efficient bullets in the catalog for dealing with two-legged varmints, Speer is not neglecting those shooters who continue to strafe the four-legged varieties. Back in 1990, they launched their TNT component bullet for use in 224-caliber centerfire ammunition at a weight of 50 grains. The TNT bullet jackets were internally fluted over nearly 90 percent of their length to provide full expansion, even at comparatively moderate velocities.

Shooter acceptance of the 22 TNT Speer bullet was prompt and enthusiastic; it quickly became one of their best sellers. By popular demand, they are expanding the line with a

70-grain 243 and a 125-grain 308. Like the original 224, the two new ones are intended for varmint hunting when the situation calls for a combination of premium accuracy and explosive expansion.

The two new Speer TNT bullets afford the deer hunter an opportunity to hunt varmints during the spring and summer, with the same rifle, thus maintaining an intimate familiarity with it. That's all to the good when the time comes around for what might be termed venison varminting.

Swift Bullet Company manufactures and markets what they term "A-Frame" bullets with a solid segment of jacket material separating the nose and base portions of the core. Available calibers are 308, 338, 358, 366, 375, 411, 416 and 458, in various suitable weights. The illustrated descriptive brochure is free on request, just call or write.

Bullet Swaging/Casting Equipment

Corbin Manufacturing & Supply has been refining and upgrading their Model CSP-1 bullet swaging presses, which offer the option of conversion to capable, conventional handloading presses by repositioning a cross-pin. They still have their line of hydraulic presses and can furnish tooling to draw your own bullet jackets from scrap copper and similar sources, even with the hand-powered presses. If you don't have access to scrap copper, they can furnish that, cut into convenient strips.

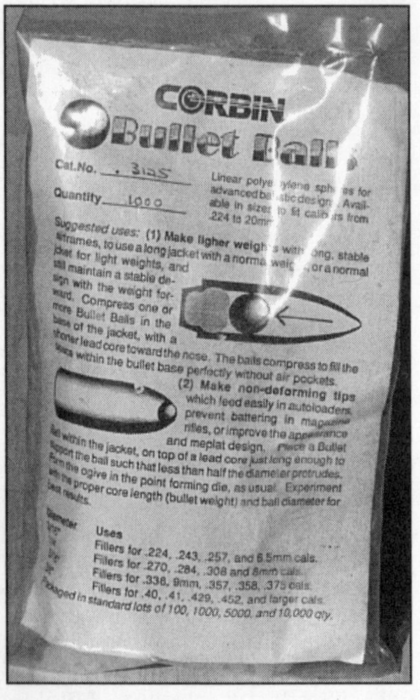

Corbin Bullet Balls.

Corbin can also furnish tooling to make scraper-washers from sheet brass or copper, with dies to rivet such washers to the base of swaged bullets, which can be made of soft lead for maximum expansion. This affords some remarkably interesting possibilities.

Hensley & Gibbs has developed several interesting bullet mould designs within the past few years. They have conicalpoint designs in most of the popular handgun diameters, and these deliver excellent penetration capability, combined with a degree of accuracy that often is highly gratifying.

The No. 352 series offers a number of 44-caliber conicalpoint semi-wadcutter designs in seven different weights; four plain-base and three with gas checks, ranging from superlight to massive maulers better suited for the 445 Gates, 444 Marlin and the like.

Another intriguing H&G concept is what Wayne Gibbs terms the TCFH, which stands for Tuna Can From Hell. These are wadcutters with a single grease groove, only .250 from front to back, with a flat face on either end. They are available in diameters suitable for 38/357, 41 and 44 cartridges. They offer interesting possibilities for multi-projectile loads, and some amount of useful results have been achieved with as many as four TCFH in each cartridge, making it possible for a six-shooter to put 24 holes in a target within a remarkably brief time span.

Lee Precision has an extensive line of bullet moulds, including their innovative Micro Band in weights and calibers popular for target shooting. The MB designs usually require no further sizing and are intended to be tumble-lubed in Lee's Liquid Alox. As Lee now offers a six-cavity mould, at $50, the production of a quantity of load-ready bullets soaks up remarkably little time and effort.

Lyman added six new bullet mould designs to their line in 1992. The 55-grain caliber 22 No. 225646 and the 190-grain 30 No. 311664 follow the popular 270 and 7mm high-velocity designs introduced a year earlier. They feature bore-riding noses and a tapered lead for perfect alignment, and have lube grooves on the nose for total lubrication.

The 150-grain No. 268645 is for the 6.5mm Swedish Mauser and is dimensioned to fit the oversize bores on many military rifles. A new .266 sizing die was added at the same time.

The 400-grain No. 457643 has a short nose to adapt it for use in lever-action 45-70 and 45-90 rifles where the shorter overall length is required for proper feeding.

The 200-grain No. 429303 has been brought back by popular demand. Originally introduced in 1958, it is a conicalpoint SWC with a gas check and unusually deep grease grooves. This is one of the few instances I recall in which Lyman

Lyman MAG tumbler.

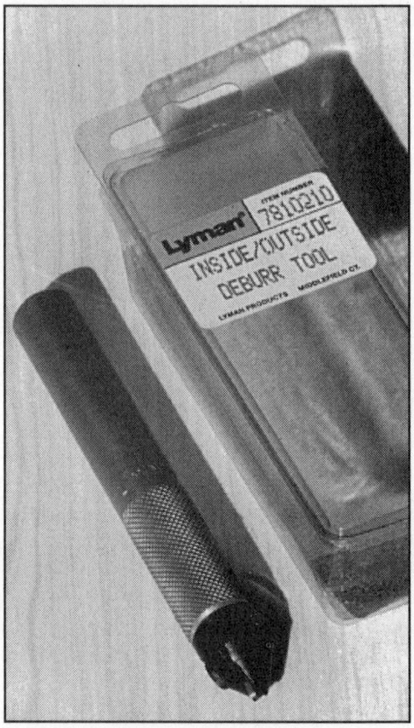

Lyman inside/outside case neck deburring tool.

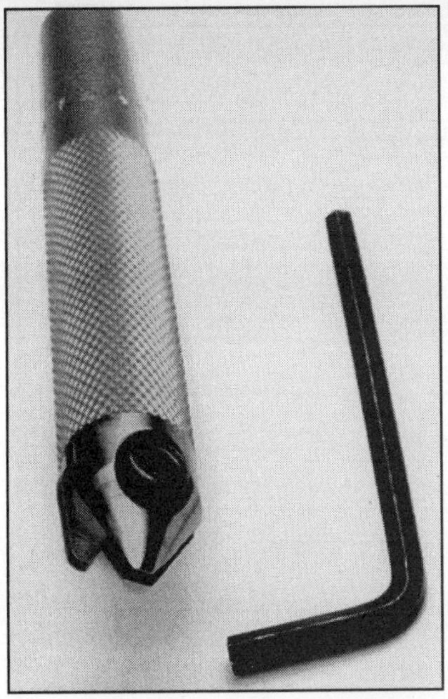

Lyman deburring tool

Lyman Twin tumbler.

reintroduced a mould design previously dropped.

The 285-grain No. 454647 is a gas-check design for the 454 Casull, and it can also be used for the 45 Long Colt in the Ruger Blackhawk or T/C Contender.

Midway has a lubricator heater for use with today's "hard lubes," drilled and tapped for mounting Lyman, RCBS, SAECO and Star lube/sizers. It is thermostatically controlled, and the Midway product number is 252-111. Send your name and address to be placed on the mailing list for Midway's catalog, which offers a great many handloading supplies on a direct basis.

Pressure Testing

Oehler Research recently introduced their Model 43 Personal Ballistics Lab (PBL), which retails for $600 for the basic unit, plus another $170 for a kit of the supplies needed for use with it. Additional options include an acoustic target with three acoustic sensors at $600; a downrange amplifier with 110 yards of cable at $140, a skyscreen mounting kit with 4-foot rails and two adjustable stands at $50, and a package of five extra strain gauges at $35. Shipping and handling costs are added to the quoted prices, which are subject to change without notice.

A personal computer or PC is needed to interpret the output from the PBL. When testing in the field, the PC needs to be a laptop or notebook design operating on rechargeable batteries.

The Model 43 measures chamber pressure using a small strain gauge glued over the chamber area of a rifle or shotgun barrel, or over a single chamber of a revolver cylinder. The Model 43 is adaptable to most single shot pistols, particularly the T/C Contender, but it cannot be used with most auto pistols.

Current particulars on the Model 43 can be obtained by placing a call to Oehler.

New Primers

Winchester now markets the same shotshell primers used in their popular Double A target loads as a component for the handloader.

3-D Remanufactured Ammunition, a pioneer in the production of lead-free ammunition, has introduced Clean-Fire primers in its lead-free rounds to virtually eliminate airborne contaminants at the firing line of indoor ranges. The new Clean-Fire primers are available in all Totally Metal Jacketed rounds manufactured by 3-D. The priming mixture is free of heavy metals and contains no lead, barium or antimony.

It is not clear in the supplied release whether or not 3-D plans to market the Clean-Fire primers as a separate component for handloading, but additional information may be requested from 3-D.

Scales & Powder Measures

RCBS, **Lyman** and **Dillon** now have electronic powder scales. The Lyman has a maximum capacity of 1000 grains and the Dillon goes to 1500 grains. After some decades of coping with the beam balance scales, I can confide the electronic ones are downright addictive when it comes to precision and convenience. •

RCBS electronic scale.

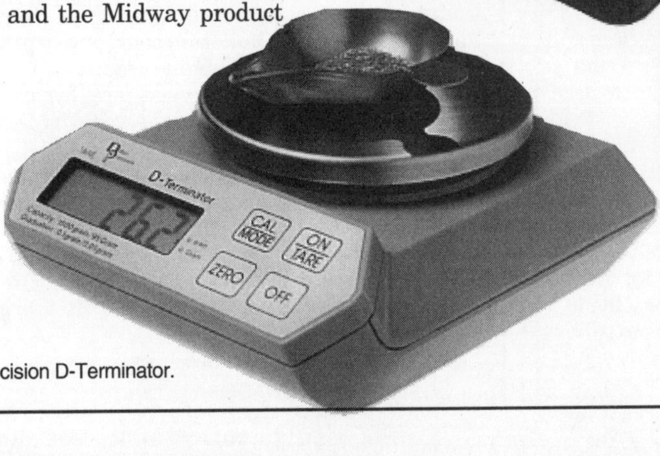

Dillon Precision D-Terminator.

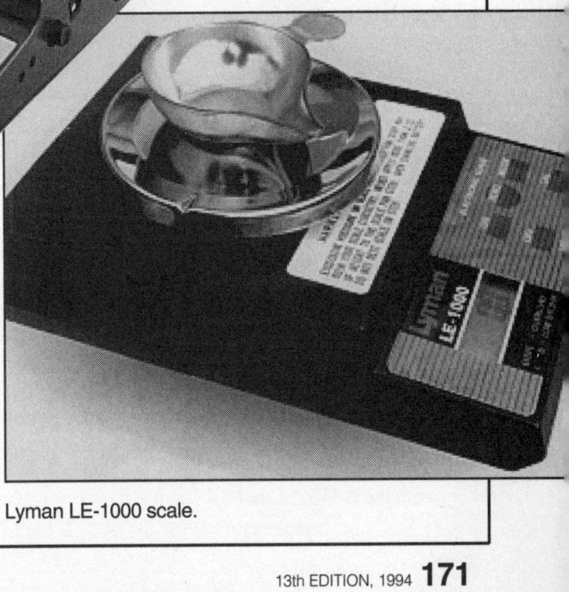

Lyman LE-1000 scale.

HANDLOADER'S MARKETPLACE

SHOWCASING SELECTED PRODUCTS FOR THE RELOADER

SHOOTERS' NEWSPAPER

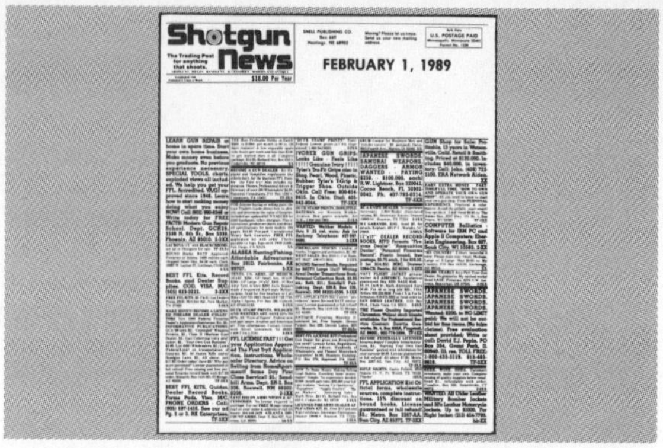
Shotgun News
FEBRUARY 1, 1989

Established in 1946, *The Shotgun News* is a leader in its field.

It offers some of the finest gun buys in the United States. More than 160,000 persons read, enjoy and profit from this newspaper, which is published three times a month.

The Shotgun News has helped thousands of gun enthusiasts locate firearms, both modern and antique—rifles, pistols, shotguns, scopes, etc...all at money-saving prices.

The money saved on the purchase of any of the 10,000 plus listings could more than pay for the $20.00 (36 issue) annual subscription cost.

As it says on the cover, it's "the trading post for anything that shoots."

THE SHOTGUN NEWS

COMPUTER SOFTWARE

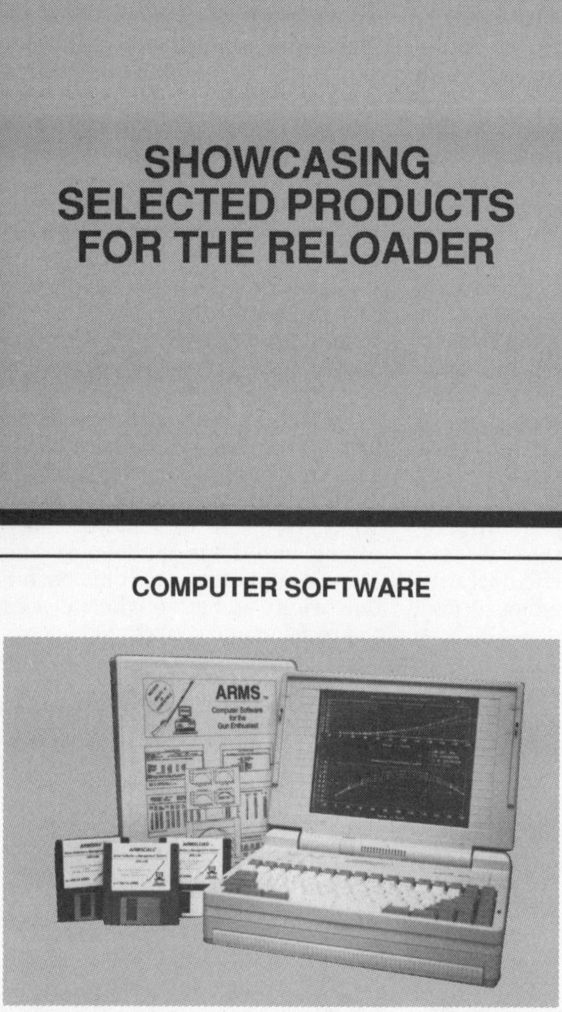

Arms Peripheral Data Systems provides useful computer software for reloaders, shooters and collectors.

ArmsInv easily tracks collections by type, accessories and serial number. It quickly generates a complete audit trail of any firearm sold and can provide net profit/loss as well as a bill of sale.

ArmsCalc is a comprehensive software tool that estimates and graphs how a projectile will behave under predetermined circumstances. It graphically compares loads with different bullet types/weights and charges, and gives energy, trajectory and velocity figures.

ArmsLoad is a comprehensive database for avid and novice reloaders. It tracks and catalogs loads easily and allows consistent, high-quality ammo to be produced. Write or call for more information.

ARMS PERIPHERAL DATA SYSTEMS

QUALITY CUSTOM BULLETS

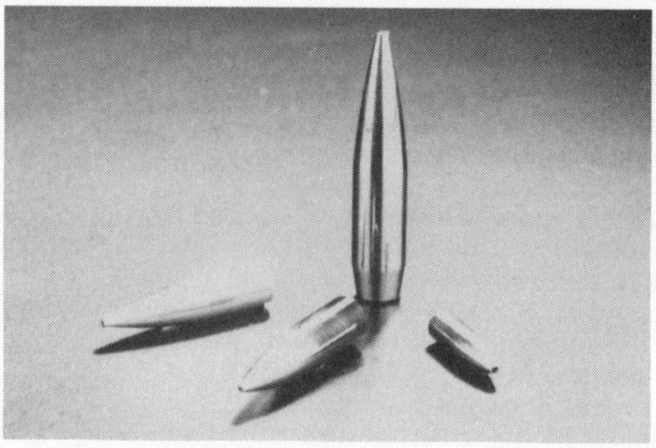

Shot after shot, competition and varmint shooters count on the precision and accuracy of Berger Bullets—match quality bullets at competitive prices that consistently keep shooters on target.

In the custom bullet business for 40 years, Berger makes bullets known around the world for their high-performance standards, standards which include using the J-4 bullet jacket exclusively. The J-4 is recognized industry-wide for its consistent uniformity and concentricity.

Berger Bullets, though a large-volume custom bullet company, operates under the close guidance and supervision of Walt Berger, its founder.

Write today for a free brochure.

BERGER BULLETS, LTD.

See manufacturers' addresses on page 187.

HIGH-PERFORMANCE BULLETS

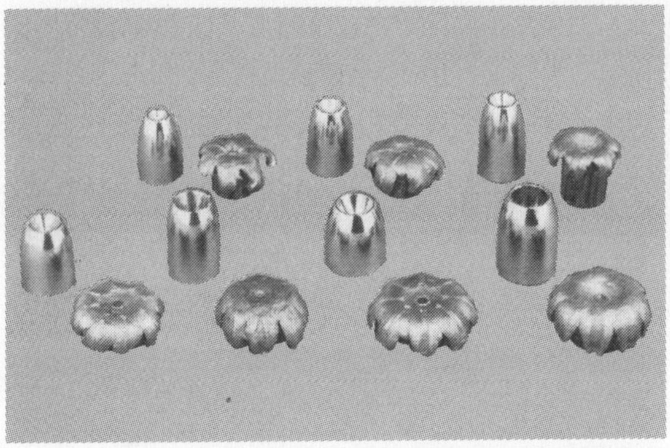

Gold Dot™ bullets from Speer® are unique because the jacket is applied to the core one molecule at a time, making it the only high-performance hollowpoint bullet with a true bonded core/jacket.

Each Gold Dot hollowpoint cavity is individually tuned for maximum expansion and terminal penetration. This delivers optimum wound effectiveness over a range of handgun velocities and through a variety of media. They perform very well in the same performance tests used by many U.S. law enforcement agencies.

Gold Dot bullets are available in 9mm—115, 124, 147 grains; 40-caliber—155, 180 grains; and 45-caliber—185, 230 grains.

Write or call CCI toll-free for more information.

CCI

NEW PRECISION GAUGING TOOL

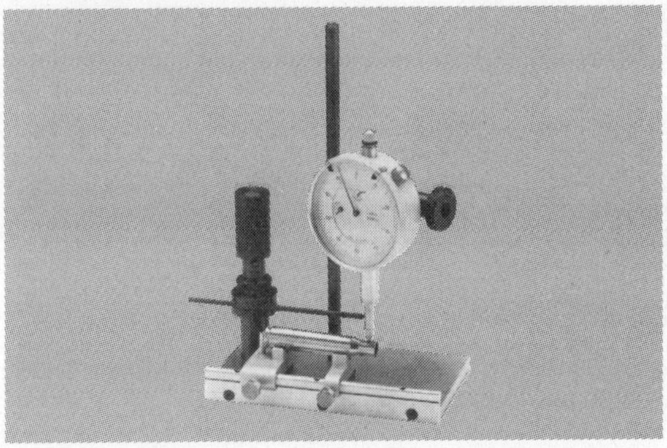

The new RCBS CaseMaster™ gauging system quickly and easily determines the cartridge case dimensions necessary for top accuracy from handloaded ammunition.

The heart of the CaseMaster is a precision dial indicator mounted so that four cartridge measurements can be obtained—case neck concentricity, case neck thickness, case length run-out and bullet run-out. CaseMaster also can detect evidence of case head separation before symptoms become apparent on the case exterior. And CaseMaster can quickly determine if case neck turning or die adjustment is needed.

Write or call RCBS toll-free for more information on the new CaseMaster gauging system.

RCBS

NEW CASE LUBRICANT SPRAY

RCBS Case Slick is an exclusive formula with exceptional lubricating properties for resizing and/or reforming metallic rifle and pistol cases.

The force required to size cases with a variety of case lube sprays was compared. RCBS Case Slick reduced the force required to full-length resize 308 Winchester cases by 35 to 70 percent compared to other sprays, according to the manufacturer. RCBS Case Slick can mean less work and longer case life.

Case Slick is designed to flow evenly across the case surface, providing a thin, even film of lubricant. Case dents due to excessive lubricant are virtually eliminated. RCBS Case Slick is one of the better case lube sprays available.

Write or call RCBS toll-free for more information.

RCBS

HIGH-EXPANSION VARMINT BULLETS

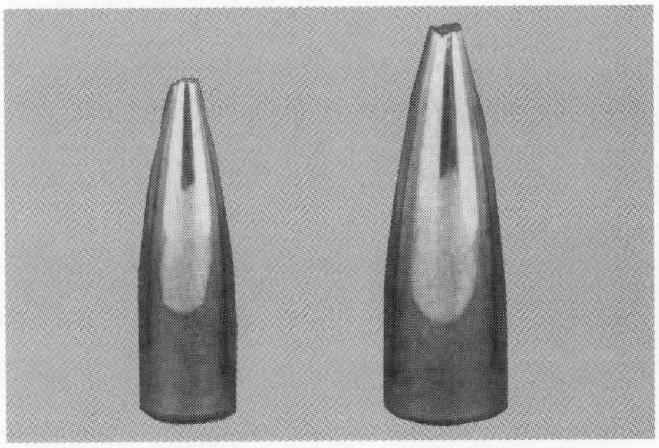

T.N.T.® varmint bullets from Speer® are designed for radical, explosive expansion.

To achieve this, the jackets are internally fluted over 90 percent of their length. This allows full expansion, even at low velocities, where many other varmint bullets fail to expand reliably.

The T.N.T. design delivers a high degree of accuracy for those typical long-range shots common in varmint shooting.

T.N.T. bullets are excellent for serious varmint shooters who are looking for drastic results from their bullets. They are available in 224-caliber, 50 grains; 243-caliber, 70 grains; and 308-caliber, 125 grains.

Write or call CCI toll-free for more information.

CCI

See manufacturers' addresses on page 187.

NEW SIZING AND FORMING LUBE

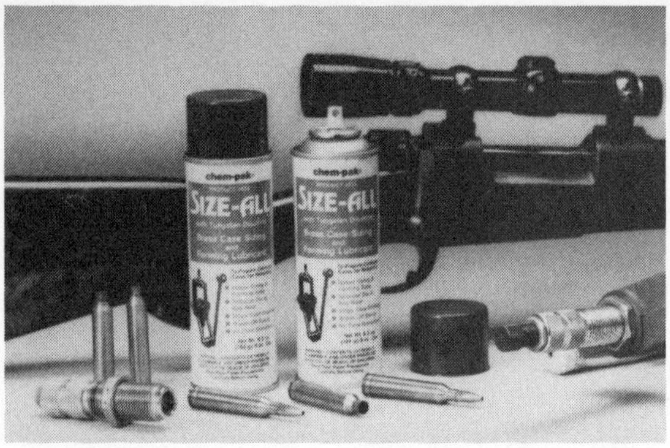

Chem-Pak's #634 Size-All Sizing & Forming Lubricant makes brass and wildcat sizing fast and easy.

Harmless to the ozone, Size-All is non-staining and easy to apply and remove. Used properly, it reduces press pull and expander ball resistance, resizing brass without crushing or distorting. Size-All contains tungsten disulfide, a very slick, heavy-duty outer-space lubricant which helps extend brass life and virtually stops ball and die wear. Tungsten disulfide lubricates to 260,000 psi.

Size-All is available at your favorite gun supply shop. Write, fax or call their toll-free number for free literature. Dealer and distributor inquiries invited.

CHEM-PAK, INC.

PREMIUM SMOKELESS POWDERS

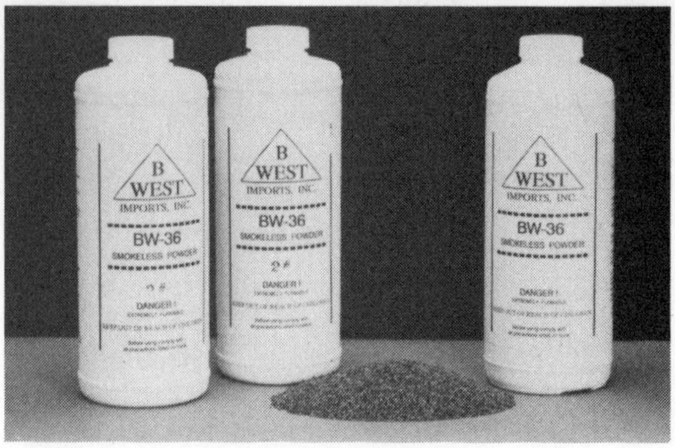

B-West Imports offers a complete line of premium smokeless powders.

BW-36, a single-base extruded powder with superior metering characteristics, is ideal for small- and medium-capacity rifle cartridges with light- to medium-weight bullets.

BW-36 burns slightly faster than IMR-3031, allowing lighter charge weights and greater cost savings for normal velocities. BW-36 is being currently manufactured and is not surplus.

Other new powders in the line include four shotgun/pistol powders, two medium-capacity rifle powders, a fast pistol powder and another extruded powder close to IMR-4064. These powders will be available in late 1993 or early 1994.

B-WEST IMPORTS, INC.

BULLET SWAGING PRESSES

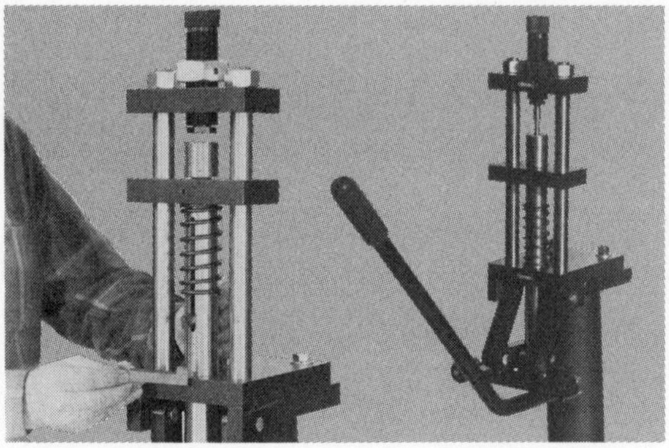

Many of the world's custom bullets are made on Corbin swaging presses. Six press models, ranging from the hand-operated Silver Press to the powerful Hydro-Press, can make any bullet from 14-caliber airgun to partitioned/jacketed 55-caliber Russian Anti-tank.

Corbin's CSP-2 Mega-Mite (above) features heavy-duty roller bearing links and bearing-guided honed alloy-steel rams. It has the ability to load large cases like the 50 BMG, as well as make copper tubing or flat strips into bullet jackets.

The Mega-Mite press comes on a self-supporting floorstand for $850 (other Corbin presses from $189.50). *The Corbin Handbook*, available for $6.00, contains over 200 pages of swaging information.

CORBIN, INC.

AMMO BOXES/ RELOADING ACCESSORIES

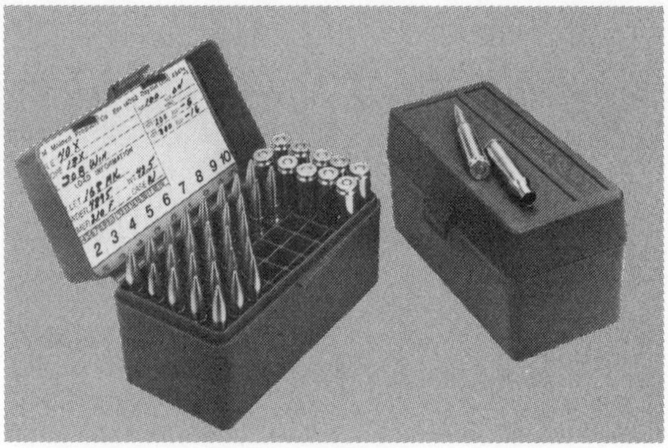

MTM Case Gard manufactures a large selection of ammo boxes and ammunition transport systems. Over the last 25 years, MTM has developed more than 134 different colors and sizes of ammunition containers.

MTM also manufactures reloading items such as loading trays, handloading log books, primer flippers and powder funnels. They also make four sizes of pistol cases and shooter's accessory cases for range equipment. For maintaining firearms, MTM offers a portable Rifle Maintenance Center and bore guides for proper barrel cleaning.

All Case Gard products come with a 10-year replacement guarantee from manufacturer's defect, breakage, or hinge wear. Write for a free copy of their 16-page product catalog.

MTM MOLDED PRODUCTS CO., INC.

 See manufacturers' addresses on page 187.

INDOOR SHOOTING LIGHT FIXTURE

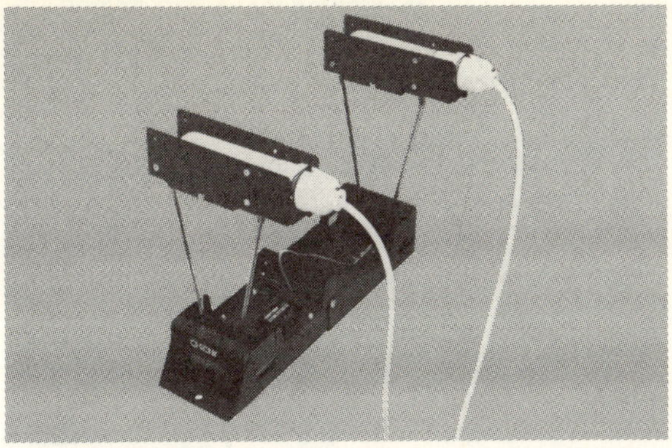

Shooting Chrony recently introduced their unique Indoor Shooting Light Fixture for shooting enthusiasts.

This indoor lighting fixture enables shooters and reloaders to test ammunition in any indoor range setting under all lighting conditions. It should prove to be an invaluable addition for those living in areas where inclement weather can be a constant problem.

The light fixture fits any Chrony-Chronograph equipped with the new "Wire-Rod Aiming System."

Suggested retail price is $29.95; for more information on the Indoor Shooting Light Fixture see your dealer or write Shooting Chrony.

SHOOTING CHRONY, INC.

NEW MODEL CHRONOGRAPH

Chrony-Chronographs from Shooting Chrony are now made with a "Wire-Rod Aiming System." This system replaces the cardboard and plastic diffuser stands of earlier-model Chronys and allows more space for shooting.

The main advantage of the new Chrony is that it is less sensitive to muzzle-blast. It is ideal for measuring velocities of bullets, arrows, shotgun pellets, airgun pellets and paintballs. The Chrony folds up into a 7.5"x 2.5"x 4" package, weighs 2.5 pounds and reports accuracy better than 0.5%.

The suggested U.S. retail price is $99.95. To upgrade earlier-model Chronys to the Wire-Rod Aiming System, send your Chrony and $20.00 (U.S.) plus $4.00 shipping and handling to Shooting Chrony.

SHOOTING CHRONY, INC.

NEW POWDER BAFFLES

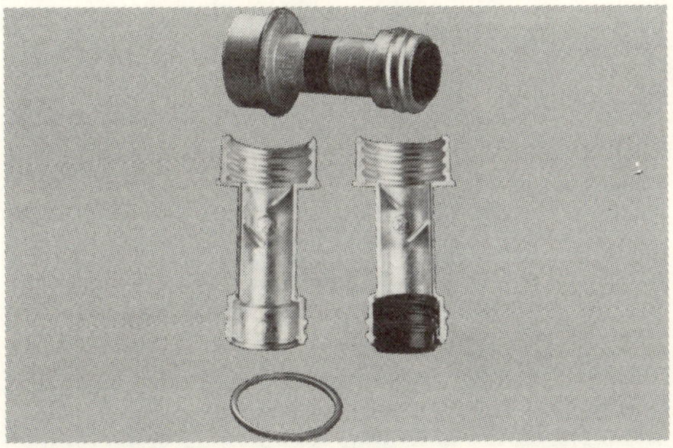

Multi-Scale Charge has introduced a new Powder Baffle.

The Powder Baffle is made of die-cast zinc and has a spring-loaded bushing that presses down on the charge bars. This provides an excellent powder seal when reloading shotshells.

The interior baffles create a uniform powder density inside the powder cavity of the charge bars, resulting in more uniform powder charges from one shotshell to the next.

The Powder Baffle was designed for use on all MEC reloading machines.

Suggested U.S. retail price of the Powder Baffle is $5.95. For more information, see your local dealer or drop Multi-Scale a line.

MULTI-SCALE CHARGE, LTD.

UNIVERSAL CHARGE BARS

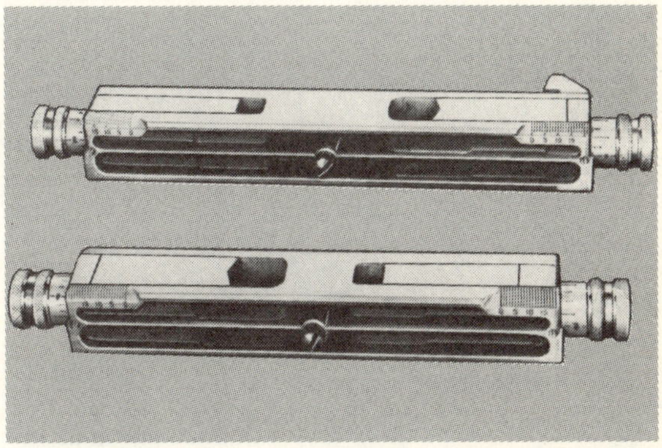

Multi-Scale Charge has been making and selling Universal Charge Bars for almost 20 years.

Designed to work with MEC shotshell reloading machines, they are fully adjustable from $1/2$-ounce to $2^1/_4$ ounces for shot, and from 12 grains to 55 grains for powder. They eliminate the need for nearly all of MEC's 45 powder bushings and standard charge bars.

The Model "C" is for use with MEC single-stage reloading machines, the Model "D" for progressive reloaders, such as the MEC Grabber, and the Models "CS" and "DS" are for reloading steel shot.

Universal Charge Bars are made of precision die-cast zinc and will last a lifetime. Come complete with powder and shot chart. Suggested U.S. retail price $24.95; see your dealer or write Multi-Scale.

MULTI-SCALE CHARGE, LTD.

See manufacturers' addresses on page 187.

ADJUSTABLE BORE SAVER ROD GUIDES

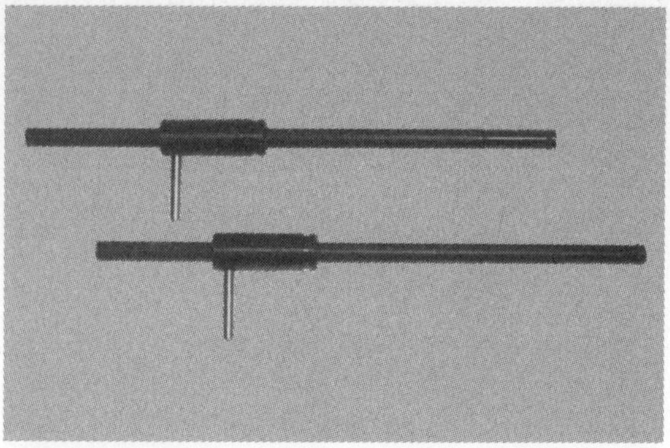

The Dewey Bore Saver cleaning rod guide replaces the bolt in your action while cleaning. The cleaning rod enters the bore straight, without harming the chamber or throat. Made from anodized aluminum in six bore sizes, the Delrin rod guide collar with threaded brass adjustment pin allows for quick adjustment to any bolt length. Chamber-sealing O-rings prohibit solvents from entering the action, trigger and magazine areas. On some rifles, the bolt stop will retain the rod guide by using the groove on the guide collar.

The guide can be used with all cleaning rods; all models fit .695- to .700-inch bolt diameter rifles. All guides allow brush clearance through tube I.D. and come with spare O-rings and O-ring assembly tool. Weatherby models available. Write for information.

J. DEWEY MANUFACTURING CO., INC.

FOLDING BIPODS

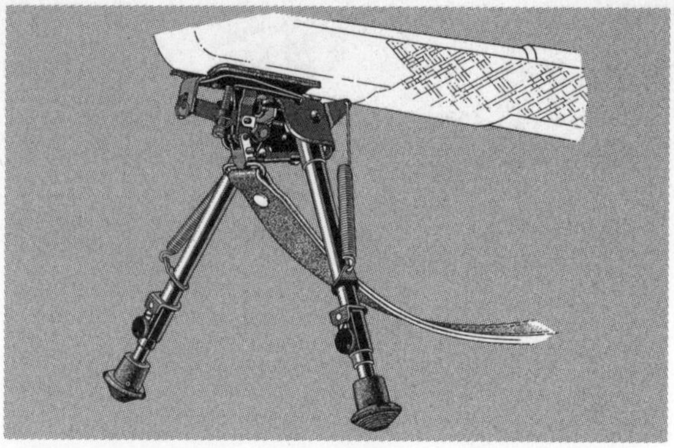

Harris Bipods clamp securely to most stud-equipped bolt-action rifles and are quick-detachable. With adapters, they will fit some other guns. On all models except the Model LM, folding legs have completely adjustable spring-return extensions. The sling swivel attaches to the clamp. This time-proven design is manufactured with heat-treated steel and hard alloys and has a black anodized finish.

Series S Bipods rotate 45° for instant leveling on uneven ground. Hinged base has tension adjustment and buffer springs to eliminate tremor or looseness in crotch area of bipod. They are otherwise similar to non-rotating Series 1A2.

Eleven models are available from Harris Engineering; literature is free.

HARRIS ENGINEERING, INC.

BARREL BEDDING TOOLS

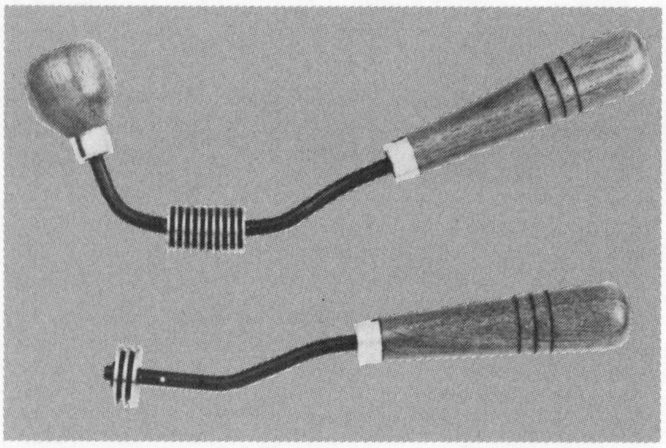

Gunline Barrel Bedding Tools are essential for accurate bedding of rifle to stock, especially when free-floating barrels. With BBT the job is made easy; heavy and light cuts result in a smooth and accurate finish without sanding. The BBT full-size tool has forward and rear handles for full control of cushioned cutters. The single-handled BJ, Barrel Bedder Jr., is suitable for lighter duty. The GS, Groove Shave, is similar to the BJ, but with fewer and larger cutting discs.

The BBT comes in seven sizes from $^{1}/_{2}$ to 1" diameter for \$16.75 and \$18.30; the BJ Tool Set comes with $^{1}/_{2}$, $^{5}/_{8}$ and $^{3}/_{4}$" cutter discs (6 each) for \$24.95; the GS Set has $^{7}/_{8}$, 1 and $1^{1}/_{8}$" sizes (3 each) for \$19.95. Add \$3.00 for shipping. Receive a free brochure for mentioning *Handloader's Marketplace*.

GUNLINE TOOLS

FIREARMS MARKETPLACE

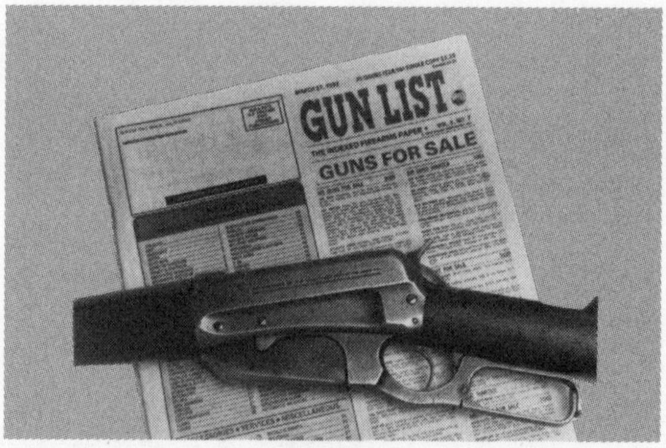

Gun List is a firearms publication for collectors and active shooters. Over 260,000 opportunities for buying, selling and trading nationwide are offered yearly. Each issue features numerous categories of quality firearms and related gun products from dealers, shops and individuals which provide opportunities to compare prices and quality.

Gun List indexes its products alphabetically in an easy-to-read format which allows readers to find their favorite collecting, hunting, reloading or shooting need quickly. Most firearms specialties are covered; nationwide gun show information is included.

A discount sample issue is \$1.00. One-year subscription (26 issues) \$24.95. Write or call for information.

GUN LIST

See manufacturers' addresses on page 187.

CUSTOM RELOADING TOOLS

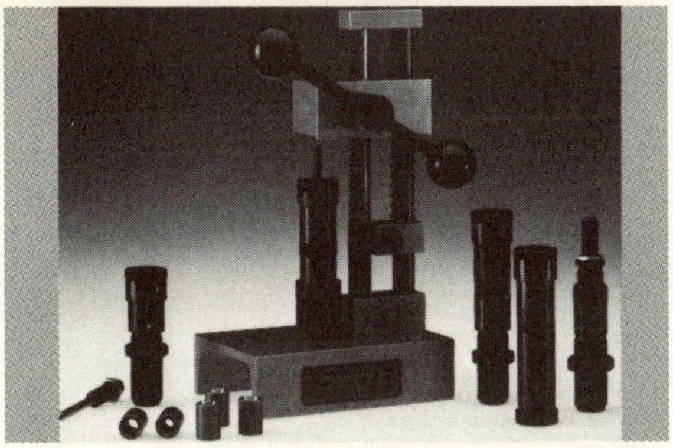

Neil Jones Custom Products offers more than 20 years experience in designing and building the most accurate reloading tools available.

Their designs allow them to custom fit all cartridges including wildcats; they are available in 7/8x14 threaded dies and the straight-line hand dies preferred by benchrest shooters.

Their micro powder measure is second to none in accuracy and repeatability with even the toughest powders. All tools are designed to do the best job possible with improved accuracy as the goal.

Jones will personally assist customers with unusual or difficult handloading problems.

Mention *Handloader's Marketplace* and they'll send you a catalog free.

NEIL JONES CUSTOM PRODUCTS

GUN ACCESSORY CATALOG

In their 1993 product catalog, the B-Square Co. offers more than 200 different no-gunsmithing scope mounting systems for almost every major firearm make and model.

For the competitive shooter, B-Square has a new line of drill and tap mounts and accessories to outfit the ultimate race gun.

B-Square also offers two sizes of laser sights and a variety of interchangeable mounting systems.

Innovative tools for reloading and shooting accessories for most firearms and shooting games are available.

The B-Square catalog is available for $2.00. Be sure to mention *Handloader's Marketplace* when you write or call.

B-SQUARE CO.

PURE ALLOY BULLETS

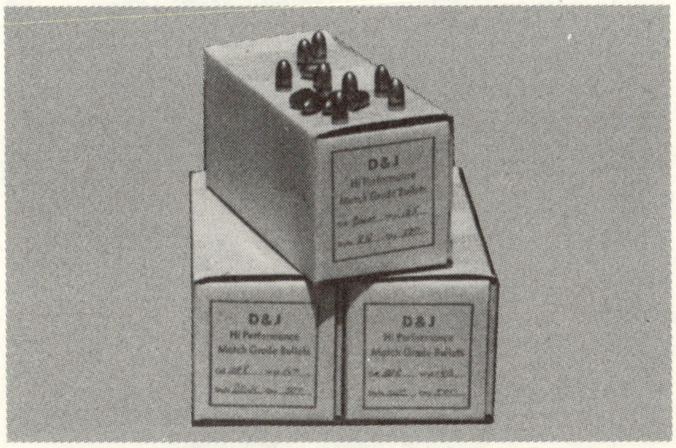

D&J offers bullets constructed of 100% pure lead alloy specifically blended at a high-tech foundry to the proper hardness.

This alloy, when properly cast and loaded, allows the reloader to achieve velocities up to 1350 fps without significant lead buildup, which would affect accuracy. These bullets are cast only on Magma casting machines, which are among the finest in the industry.

D&J bullets are sold per 1,000 and come packaged in two boxes of 500. Calibers available include 9mm, lead and jacketed; 38 Super, lead and jacketed; 38 Revolver; 10mm/40 S&W; 44; and 45 ACP/Long Colt.

D&J offers a money-back guarantee if unsatisfied. Call or write for a catalog.

D&J BULLET CO. & CUSTOM GUN SHOP, INC.

ARBOR PRESS

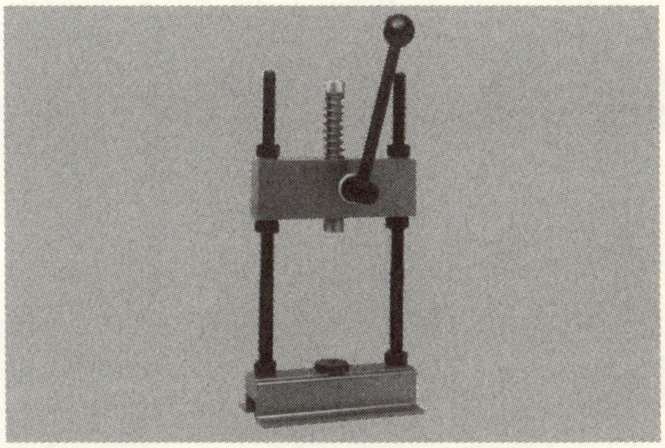

B-Square's Super Mag Arbor Press for precision reloading and industrial use also resizes all calibers of brass easily.

Because the load is placed between twin threaded posts on the press, there is no "spring" when reloading; the press head is fully adjustable up and down for secure positioning.

The ram has replaceable brass caps and spring return, and over a 1-inch keystroke.

The press, with adjustable handle, can be used right- or left-handed. Lightweight and portable for range use, the Arbor Press is rated at approximately 1-ton.

Available for $99.50 at your local dealer; or call B-Square toll-free.

B-SQUARE CO.

See manufacturers' addresses on page 187.

BULLET MOULDS AND SUPPLIES

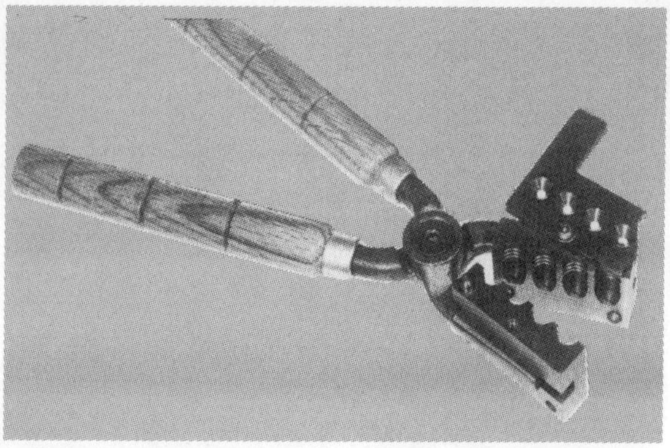

GAR stocks more than 400 bullet mould styles and a variety of products for bullet casters, ready for next-day shipping.

Moulds available include those made by SAECO, Lyman and AMT, plus a broad representation of Schuetzen and other early cartridge moulds. They also offer a full line of Redding and Lyman reloading equipment.

GAR manufactures the Gun Box Magnet and Gun Safe Magnet as well as a line of casting and reloading aids including the well-known Half & Half Bullet Lubes.

GAR is a long-established firm with a great reputation for discount and service. Send $1.00 for their catalog.

GAR

RIGID-BASE SCOPE MOUNTS

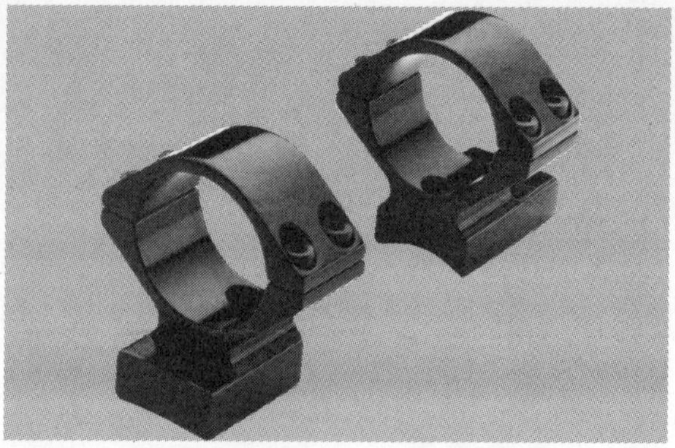

J.B. Holden's most recent scope mount innovation is a line of rigid-base, solid-top scope mounts that was designed to fit most popular hunting rifles.

Like all Holden mounts, the durable PlainsMaster™ line is precision-crafted from the highest strength alloys available.

The base and ring connect points commonly used in a number of older-style mounts have been effectively eliminated in the PlainsMaster.

The result is an uncomplicated, lightweight scope mounting system which offers superior performance and appearance at an economical price.

Write or call for a free catalog on these and other products available.

J.B. HOLDEN CO.

QUICK-CHANGE MUZZLE BRAKE

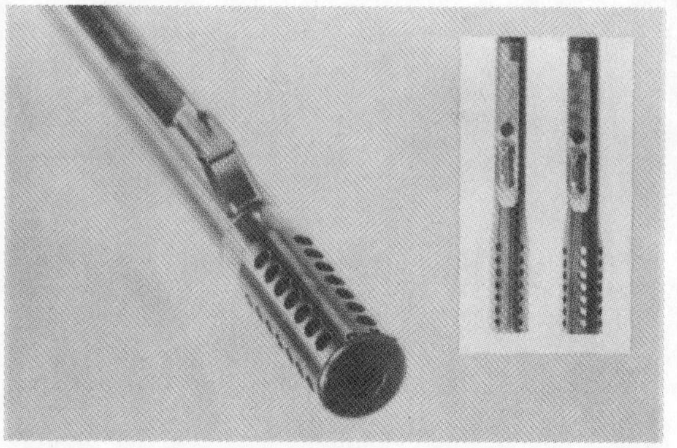

The Hastings Quick-Change Muzzle Brake is right at home on the range or in the woods.

The HQC tames recoil and muzzle jump by deflecting expanding gases perpendicular to the bore. This reduces the pounding taken during extended shooting sessions and helps eliminate flinching.

All effective muzzle brakes do increase noise for the shooter (this is not a problem on the range when ear protection is worn, but can be a problem when hunting). The HQC is unique in that a quick rotation of the outer sleeve seals the gas ports deactivating the brake and returns noise levels to normal.

Hastings installs the HQC on most centerfire rifles. It's available in stainless steel or blued finish. Contact Hastings for complete details.

HASTINGS BARRELS

NEW BORE SCRUBBER

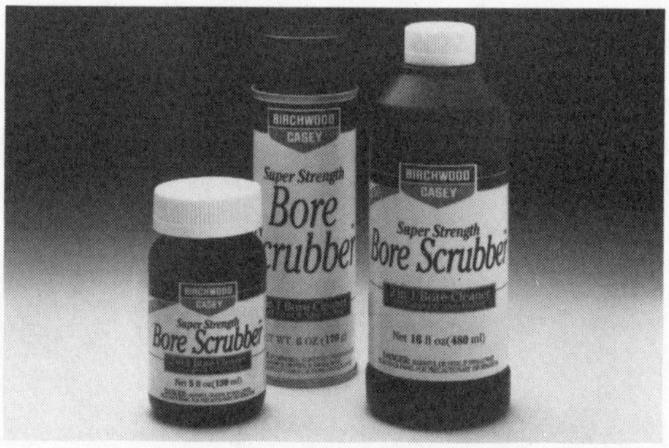

Birchwood Casey has developed a new 2-in-1 formula bore cleaner for copper and nitro fouling. Super Strength Bore Scrubber is great for use on rifles, shotguns and handguns.

Each solvent ingredient was selected for its ability to attack, dissolve and remove all types of barrel fouling—lead, copper, plastic, carbon and powder residue. Superior rust preventive additives were added for long-term protection after cleaning. No nitrobenzene, butyl cellosolve or other highly toxic ingredients were used.

Bore Scrubber is offered in three sizes—5-ounce glass, 6-ounce aerosol and 16-ounce plastic containers. See your dealer or write Birchwood Casey direct for a free catalog.

BIRCHWOOD LABORATORIES, INC.

See manufacturers' addresses on page 187.

PORTABLE GUN REST/CLEANING BOX

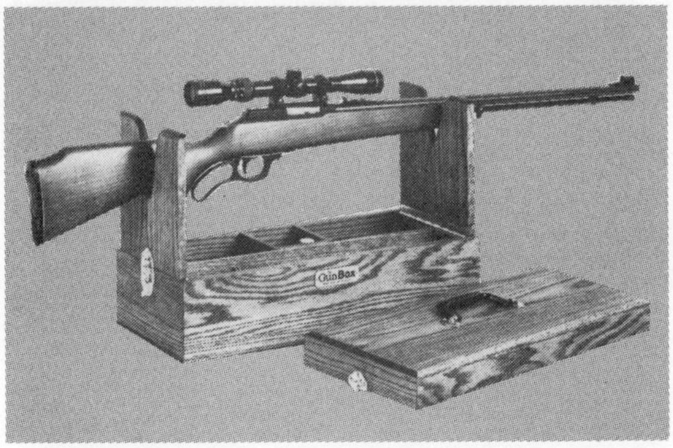

Whether shooting "red-clay," "whitetail" or "black-powder," the Gun-Box from Timber Heirloom Products will last for generations.

This solid oak shooting/cleaning box with protective oil finish has a felt-lined tray and two large storage compartments. A center compartment keeps containers upright, while a hideaway area organizes cleaning equipment.

The fold-out gun rest features full-length piano hinges and heavy-duty tool box catches. This, coupled with the non-marring bumpers, provides the ultimate gun rest for cleaning or shooting.

Send check or money order for $119.95 plus $5.00 shipping/handling to Timber Heirloom Products, or send $1.00 for brochure.

TIMBER HEIRLOOM PRODUCTS

NEW ELECTRONIC CALIPER

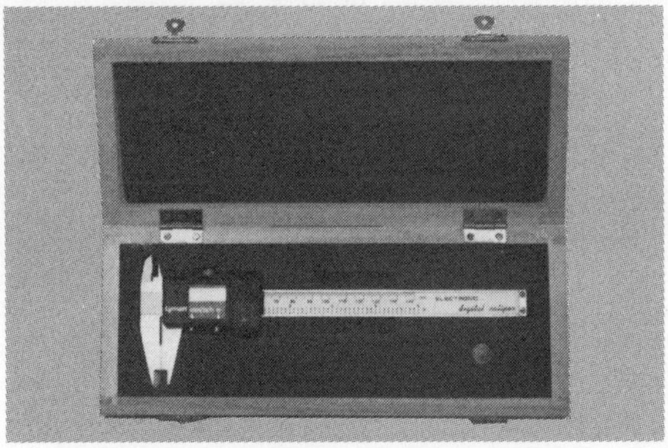

Lyman Products Corp. recently announced the introduction of a new Electronic Digital Caliper for reloaders.

This 6" electronic caliper gives a direct digital readout in inches and millimeters and can measure inside and outside depths.

A special feature of the caliper is a zeroing function that allows the user to select a zeroing dimension and sort parts or cases by their plus or minus variation.

The caliper works on a single standard 1.5 volt silver oxide battery and comes with a fitted wooden storage case.

Retail price for the caliper is $99.95. For more information, write or call Lyman Products Corp.

LYMAN PRODUCTS CORP.

COMPLETE NEW LINE OF TARGETS

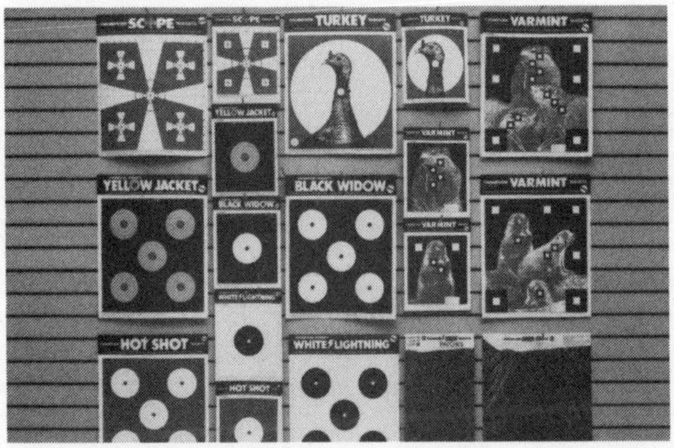

Thompson Target Technology offers a complete target line for the competitor and non-professional, as well as range shooter and hunter/sportsman.

Using a scientific approach to how the eye adjusts to color and light, their targets give shooters the optimum in sight-to-target alignment.

Their line includes scope alignment, conventional bullseye, turkey patterning, varmint, benchrest, deer and animal targets for gun and bow.

The new human silhouette series for police, security and self-defense are used in ranges throughout the country.

See your local dealer or send $5.95 for complete 14-target sample pack and catalog ($2.00 for catalog only).

THOMPSON TARGET TECHNOLOGY

COMPLETE RELOADING KIT

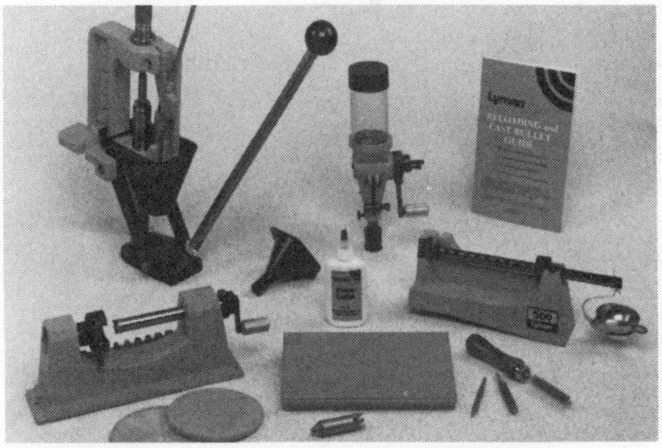

Previously available only with their T-Mag turret press, the Expert Reloading Kit from Lyman Products now comes in a version featuring their Orange Crusher Press.

The Orange Crusher, a powerful single-stage press with a classic "O frame" design, may be used to load rifle and pistol cartridges and converts to either right- or left-hand use.

The Expert Kit, which has a suggested retail price of $329.95, includes all the equipment necessary to start reloading: the press, the 500 scale, universal case trimmer, 55 powder measure and a complete assortment of handy accessories.

For more information, contact Lyman Products Corp.

LYMAN PRODUCTS CORP.

See manufacturers' addresses on page 187.

AMMO/COMPONENTS CATALOG

Old Western Scrounger's 88-page illustrated catalog features hard-to-get ammunition from Eley, RWS, Norma, Geco, Kynoch, Vom Hoffe, Weatherby, Bertram, Woodleigh and others.

Dangerous Dave and his staff offer nine sizes of Berdan primers plus 50-caliber BMG primers, and feature TIG and TUG Brenneke bullets and ammunition.

Their Rock Crusher reloading press will reload ammunition from 50-caliber through 37mm.

Old Western Scrounger specializes in ammunition and components that are not easy to find.

Send $3.00 for a catalog of their products. Old Western Scrounger guarantees satisfaction or your money back. Wholesale/retail.

OLD WESTERN SCROUNGER, INC.

PROGRESSIVE SHOTSHELL RELOADER

Ponsness/Warren has a new fully progressive shotshell reloader for 1993. The L-S-1000 will load lead, steel or bismuth shot progressively. It is equipped with a new patented "Uni-Drop" shot drop system which allows the use of all sizes and types of shot.

All shells are automatically full-length resized and deprimed with the new "Auto-Size and De-Primer" system. Shells drop out of the shellholders when complete. Each shell is precrimped and final crimped with the "Tru-Crimp" system.

The L-S-1000 is available in 10-gauge 3½"; 12-gauge 2¾" and 3"; and 20-gauge 2¾" and 3". Also available is a 12-gauge 3½" conversion kit. For more information contact your nearest Ponsness/Warren dealer or call the company directly.

PONSNESS/WARREN

HIGH-PERFORMANCE CARTRIDGES

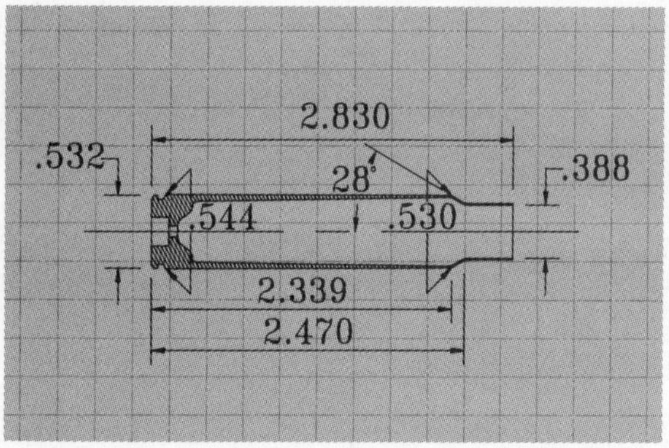

Imperial Magnum Corp. has developed a family of high-performance cartridges specifically for handloaders.

The 7mm, 300, 311, 338 and 360 magnums have a large case capacity and extra brass in the head and side walls which make them especially strong.

These non-belted magnum cartridges were designed for high-velocity performance; and because there is no belt, you'll get more accurate headspacing, smoother feeding and simpler reloading.

Write, phone or fax Imperial for free product information on their line of unprimed cases, loading dies, reamers/gauges and production and custom rifles.

IMPERIAL MAGNUM CORP.

METALLIC RELOADING COMPONENTS

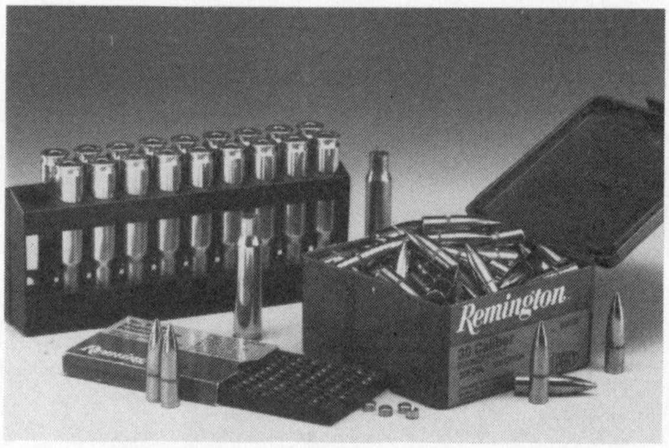

Remington Arms, backed by 178 years of shooting technology, is the only American manufacturer of firearms and ammunition that offers a complete line of factory-tailored ammunition components for metallic and shotshell reloaders.

Famous name brands offered include Kleanbore® Primers; 7030 cartridge brass for rifles and handguns; Targetmaster® wadcutters; semi-jacketed hollowpoint, jacketed hollowpoint, metal case and other popular handgun bullets, along with Core-Lokt®, Power-Lokt® and Bronze Point™ rifle bullets for shooters looking for accuracy and dependability.

All products are American manufactured. See your Remington retailer for these components.

REMINGTON ARMS CO., INC.

See manufacturers' addresses on page 187.

TOLL-FREE BALLISTIC INFO

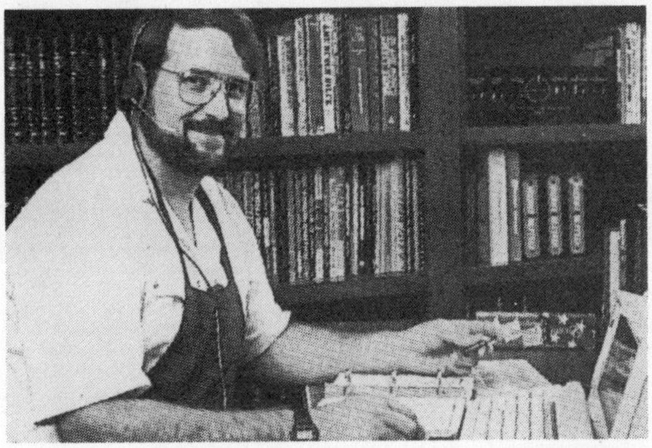

Sierra Bullets has expanded the service hours on their toll-free Tech Line Service to 8 a.m. through 10 p.m. Central Time. Dial their 800 number to talk to one of the many Bulletsmiths® available to answer your reloading questions.

To provide the best service to their customers and distributors, Sierra's Bulletsmiths will answer questions on all bullets, powders and cartridges—regardless of the brand. They want their customers to shoot as safely, competitively and accurately as possible.

In addition to expanding their Tech Line Service, Sierra has improved their tool and die machine shop, upgraded their quality control inspections, redesigned their process for washing and polishing bullets and improved their bullet assembly equipment.

SIERRA BULLETS

COMPETITION SEATING DIE

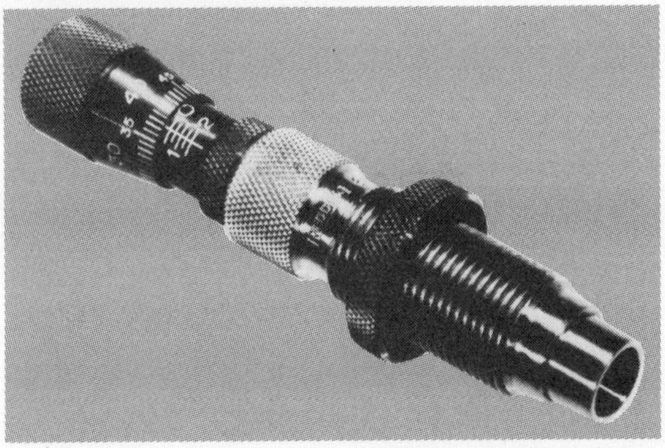

Redding offers a new patented Benchrest Competition Seating Die that was designed to conquer the concentricity problems inherent in many other dies of this type.

Tighter manufacturing tolerances were made possible by the patented seating stem system. The bullet guide and seating stem are precision ground to within .0002" of actual bullet diameter, and internal parts fit so closely they actually "float" on a column of air.

The micrometer is graduated in .001" increments and has a unique "zero" set feature which allows it to be adjusted to any seating depth.

The Benchrest Competition Die is currently available in 31 standard and wildcat calibers. Write or call for their free catalog.

REDDING RELOADING EQUIPMENT

ADVANCED RELOADING VIDEO

You'll gain a competitive edge by consistently reloading accurate rifle ammunition. Sierra Bullets offers a high-power rifle reloading video for seasoned reloaders ready to advance to the next technical level.

Not intended for beginners, the video features champion shooter G. David Tubb, who offers step-by-step instructions, plus techniques and tips to improve a shooter's skill, precision and knowledge.

Whether you are hunting or shooting for competition, target practice, or military/police applications, this video will be a valuable tool for many years to come.

This three-hour video is available in two volumes for $39.95. Call Sierra Bullets toll-free to order. Visa and MasterCard accepted.

SIERRA BULLETS

COMPETITION POWDER MEASURE

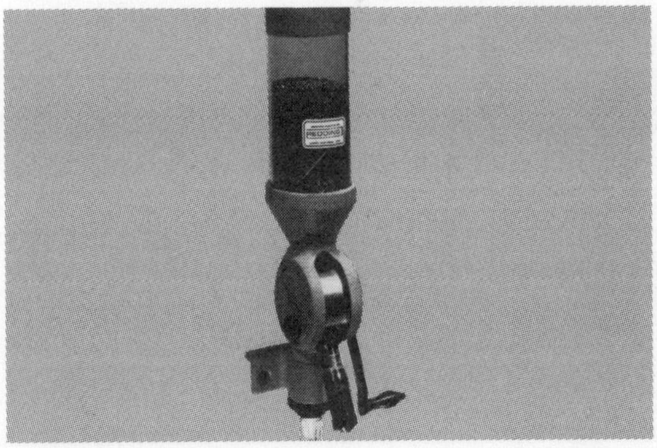

Redding powder measures feature close-tolerance hand-fitted drums and super-accurate micrometers for extreme accuracy.

To obtain the most accurate metering possible, the metering plunger diameter in the newest BR-30 competition model was reduced and given a hemispherical, or "cup," shape. This minimizes irregular powder settling and enhances charge-to-charge uniformity.

The BR-30 has a charging range of approximately 10 to 50 grains and was specifically designed for optimum uniformity at about 30 grains, hence the designation. Although intended for benchrest competition, the BR-30 is also favored by silhouette shooters and varminters.

Write or call for a free catalog.

REDDING RELOADING EQUIPMENT

See manufacturers' addresses on page 187.

ECONOMICAL CLEANING KITS

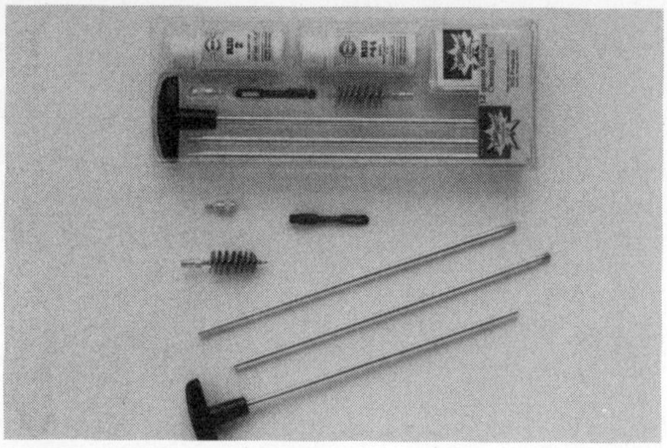

RIG Products, a leading manufacturer of gun cleaning gear since 1936, pays attention to detail and takes pride in their American-made products.

Their stainless steel RIG Rod™ is precision-machined, as are the products in their new Clean-Power™ line.

RIG's new lineup includes economical cleaning kits and aluminum rods. CleanPower patches, among the finest available, are made of densely woven 100% cotton twill fabric. Absorbing up to 10 times more than most patches, they come in six sizes to fit just about any gun.

The RIG Products line is available at sporting goods dealers and gun stores. Call, write or fax for a free brochure.

RIG PRODUCTS

SCOPE RINGS AND BASES

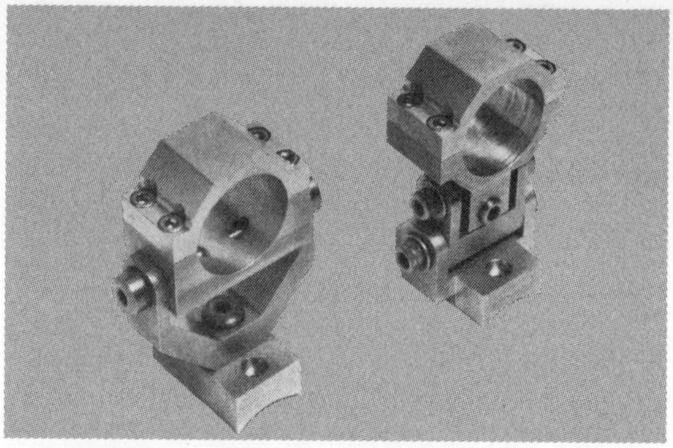

Six Enterprises offers a set of fully adjustable scope rings and bases for the ultimate in scope mounting. With this mounting system, scopes can be optically centered for maximum efficiency.

The adjustable height of the scope above the bore effectively lengthens point-blank range, and allows the shooter with glasses to get behind the scope easier. It also minimizes interference between ear muffs and stock.

Bases are available in flat, radius and dovetail configurations. Windage and elevation adjustments are made with Allen wrenches; everything locks into place.

Scope rings and bases $150.00 a set. Call, write or fax for a free catalog showing their complete product line.

SIX ENTERPRISES

SPECIALIZED TARGET LINE

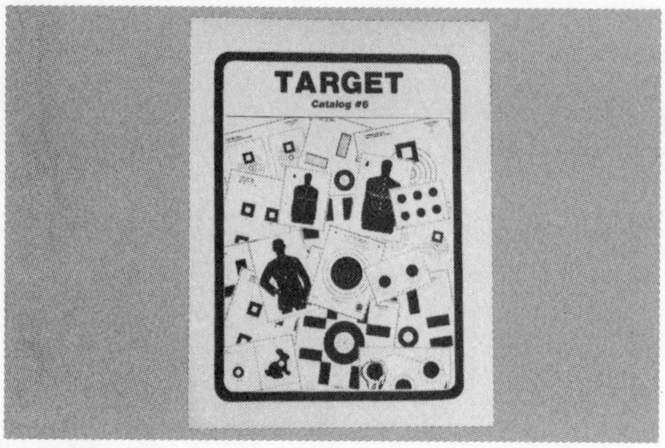

The Rocky Mountain Target Co. offers a specialized line of Data-Targ targets for scope shooters. The targets all have clean, white centers for reticle centering.

Additionally, Rocky Mountain targets are printed on heavy sheet stock that is designed to stay in one piece, and offer enough durability to allow the shooter to save the target as a permanent record of accuracy.

There are 16 types of targets currently available for hunting, varmint and benchrest rifles at ranges from 100 to 200 yards, depending on the power of your telescopic sight.

Contact Rocky Mountain Target for a free target catalog.

ROCKY MOUNTAIN TARGET CO.

PROFESSIONAL CUSTOM BULLETS

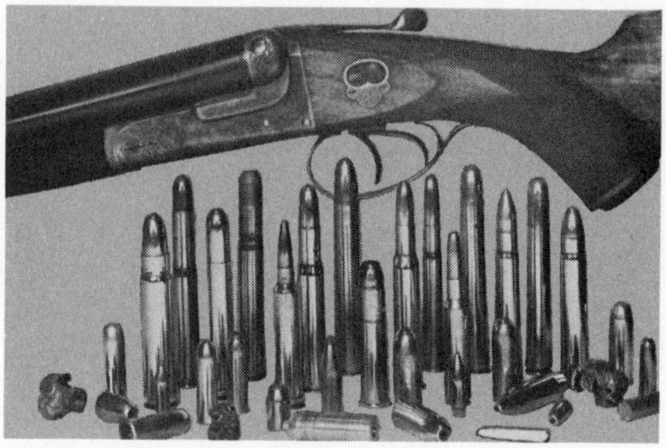

Star Custom Bullets has been making, testing and supplying custom bullets to hunters for 10 years. Made particularly for heavy, dangerous game in Africa and Alaska, these superior bullets have been used successfully on elephant, Cape buffalo, lion and bear by hunters—especially professional hunters guiding and "backing up" clients.

Star incorporates ideas through continuing research of actual testing on dangerous game. They offer various solids and softnose bullets from 22 through 600 N.E. Individual customer specifications may be special-ordered.

To receive their current brochure free of charge, write Star Custom Bullets and mention *Handloader's Marketplace*.

STAR CUSTOM BULLETS

See manufacturers' addresses on page 187.

NEW ADJUSTABLE BORE GUIDE

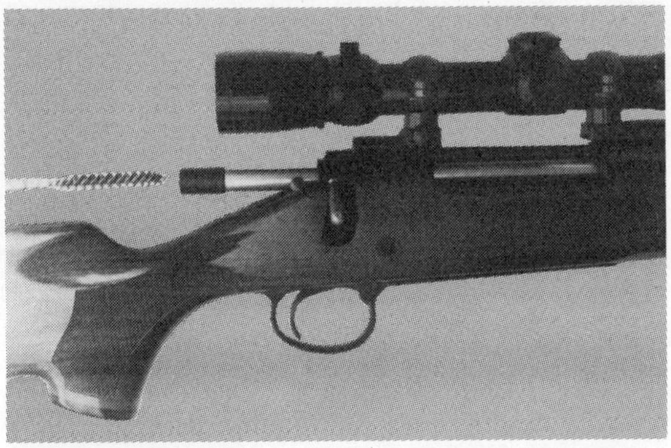

The new precision-machined XL Model Chamber-All™ Bore Guides feature an anodized aluminum tube and special Delrin® fittings. The Bore Guide simply replaces the bolt for cleaning. A slide-adjustable bolt collar with threaded pin locks solidly into any length action. A bore brush or jag will feed easily through the funneled entry guide.

Model XL-101 (.270" I.D.) is suitable for cleaning 17- to 25-caliber barrels, Model XL-202 (.338" I.D.) for 25- to 30-caliber/8mm barrels. Both fit centerfire firearms with .695" to .700" bolt diameters. Optional bolt collars are available to fit Weatherby Vanguard, Tika, and Sako A1 and A2 actions.

Retail: $23.95 each (plus S&H). Ask your dealer, or send for free information.

STONEY POINT PRODUCTS, INC.

NEW BULLET COMPARATOR

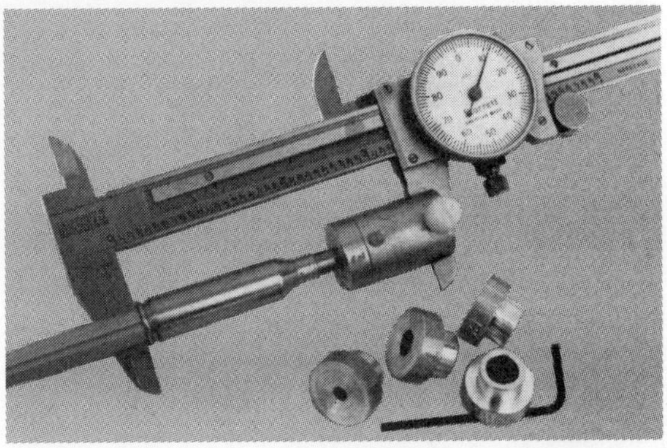

The new Chamber-All™ Bullet Comparator from Stoney Point Products eliminates bullet tip variations to allow precise handloading dimensions from your caliper.

Changes in bullet seating depth can significantly affect accuracy. Since bullet length can vary due to tip variations, bullet and cartridge measurements must be made from the ogive. This is easily accomplished with the comparator and their OAL Gauge.

Machined from tempered aluminum, the Comparator attaches and removes quickly from any caliper with a thumb screw.

Twelve interchangeable bullet inserts range from 17- to 45-caliber. Instructions furnished. Priced at $11.75 for comparator body, $2.65 for each insert size plus shipping and handling. Write for a free brochure.

STONEY POINT PRODUCTS, INC.

RELOADER'S SUPPLY CATALOG

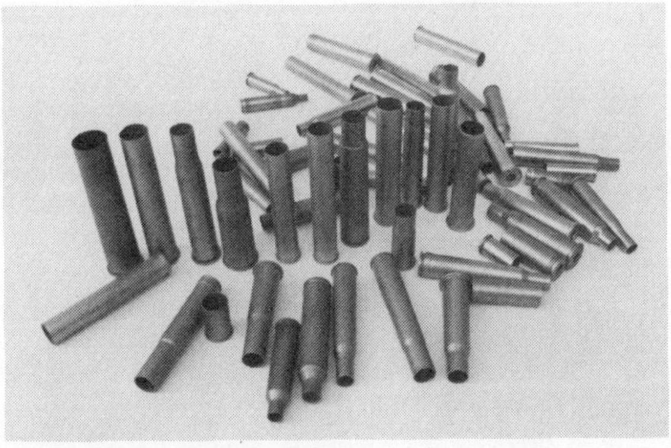

Huntington Die Specialties is one of the foremost suppliers of hard-to-get reloading products, plus standard items from RCBS, CCI, Speer, Bell and Sierra. They also manufacture the Huntington Compac Press.

If you're a serious handloader looking for something unusual, a beginner looking for a place to start, or a dealer trying to fill a customer's needs, the Huntington catalog is a must. It's the type of reloader's "tool" that quickly becomes part of the bench.

Both the retail and dealer catalogs (FFL required) are available from Huntington for $3.00 each.

Don't forget to mention you saw it in *Handloader's Marketplace.*

HUNTINGTON DIE SPECIALTIES

NEW BULLET SEATING GAUGE

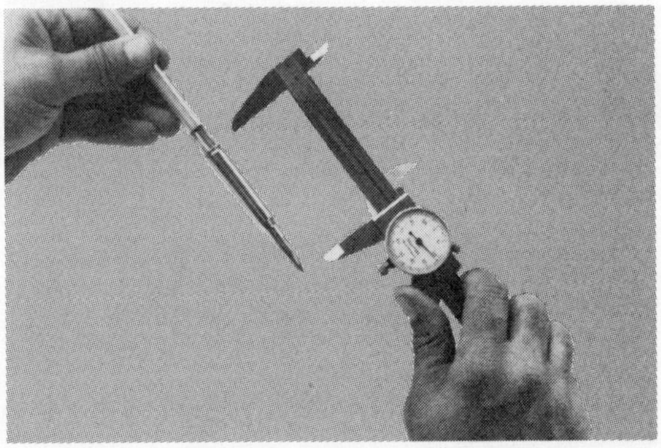

The new Chamber-All™ OAL Gauge can significantly improve shooting accuracy by establishing proper bullet seating depth. After it is removed from the firearm, a special port in the tool allows a caliper to measure from the case's base to bullet tip. This dimension determines proper bullet seating depth.

The precision-machined gauge works with all bolt-actions and single shots and retails for $34.95, complete with choice of Modified Case. Modified Cases are factory altered (neck I.D. .002" oversize and case head threaded) so they may be used interchangeably. Modified Cases are $3.95 each, available in many sizes (SAAMI specifications). Wildcat and improved cartridge brass can be factory-modified for $6.50 each (plus S&H). Ask your dealer, or send for free information.

STONEY POINT PRODUCTS, INC.

See manufacturers' addresses on page 187.

CUSTOM BIG GAME BULLETS

Swift Premium Safari Bullets feature a positive expansion stopper which prevents over expansion and ensures 90% weight retention for maximum penetration.

Their unique A-frame construction causes the bullet to stop expanding abruptly, leaving the shank unchanged.

A special manufacturing process prevents weight loss by bonding the lead to the copper so that it will not separate from the jacket.

The tapered nose of the jacket enables expansion to start on even lighter, thin-skinned game.

For more information, mention *Handloader's Marketplace* and Swift will send you their brochure free.

SWIFT BULLET CO.

NEW SMOKELESS PROPELLANTS

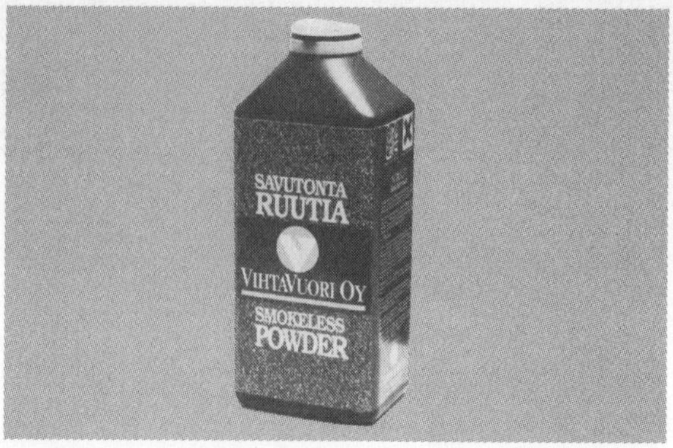

Powders with a purpose are what V-Propellants from Vihtavuori Oy are all about. Ammunition manufacturers such as Sako, Eley, Remington and Federal frequently choose V-Propellants when assembling rimfire ammunition and optimizing specific cartridges. Now, reloaders can obtain these powders to get the best from specific cartridges and bullet weights.

For eye-opening information on pressure, optimized powder charges, case volume, seating depth, ambient temperature effect, accuracy, loading data for the thirteen different V-Powders, and more, the V-Propellant Guide is a must. Reloaders, dealers and master distributors should write or call for a free copy of the guide.

VIHTAVUORI OY

CARBIDE PRIMER POCKET UNIFORMERS

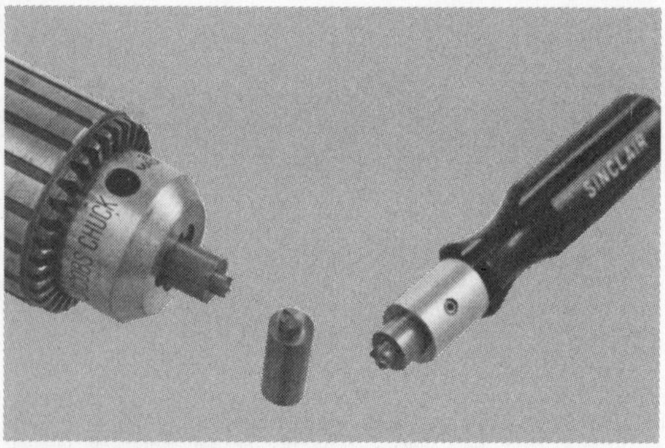

Sinclair International has introduced a new line of primer pocket uniformers designed for the precision handloader.

The 8000 Series Uniformers are designed to cut primer pockets to a uniform depth and square the bottom, allowing for uniform seating of primers. The cutters can be used with power (drill or drill press) or by hand with an optional accessory handle. These uniformers are precision ground from solid tungsten carbide.

Uniformers are available in small rifle, small pistol, large rifle and large pistol for $18.50 each. The optional handle retails for $7.50.

Call or write for a free catalog of other precision reloading equipment.

SINCLAIR INTERNATIONAL, INC.

BLACKPOWDER CAST BULLETS

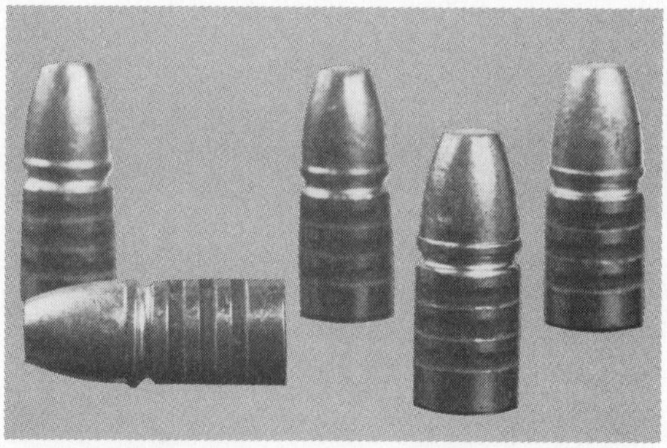

Wyoming Casting Company offers cast bullets in sizes 32-20 through 50-140 for discriminating reloaders. They are one of the few bullet manufacturers to cast bullets for blackpowder cartridge shooters.

Their specialty is a .408" diameter, 40-caliber, 405-grain custom-made bullet designed for the 40-65 cartridge.

All blackpowder bullets are available cast from a 1 to 20 mix and are lubricated specifically for blackpowder shooting.

Wyoming Casting Co. fully guarantees their products. Contact them directly for more information—they should be able to assist you with your special blackpowder cast bullet needs.

WYOMING CASTING CO.

See manufacturers' addresses on page 187.

WINCHESTER 452AA EQUIVALENT

Remember 452AA®? Scot Powder Company of Ohio does...they call it Scot 453™. Scot 453 is an economical, fast-burning, spherical, double-base powder—a near equivalent to Winchester's 452AA.

Small and dense, Scot 453 flows through volumetric measures with superb accuracy. As a 12-gauge trap or Skeet powder, it offers consistent loading shell to shell, which delivers the shot-to-shot consistency needed.

Since it shoots cleaner than most spherical powders, clean-up is easy. Favored by many as a pistol powder, Scot 453 is ideal for accurate pistol target work.

For shotshell and pistol reloading data, call or write Scot Powder Company of Ohio.

SCOT POWDER COMPANY OF OHIO, INC.

SPECIALTY RELOADING DIES

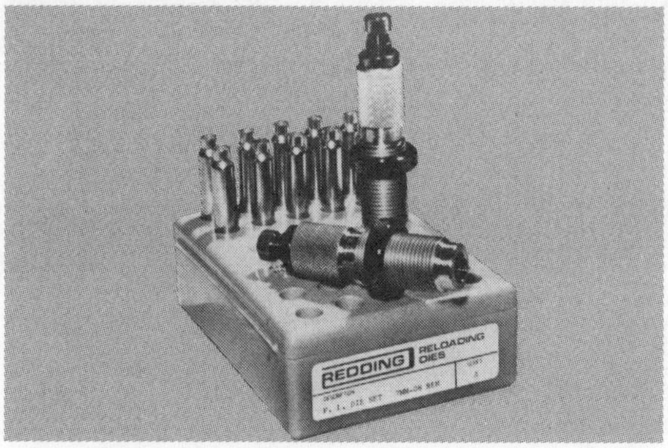

Redding has built a reputation equal to the quality of the reloading gear they produce, and they continue to expand their line of reloading dies that are available from stock.

The latest catalog from Redding lists dies for over 400 different calibers and a whole host of special-purpose dies. There are neck-sizing dies, benchrest competition dies, special-purpose crimping dies, trim dies, custom-made dies and a section on case forming that lists what is needed to form one caliber from another.

If you have something you've always wanted to shoot, or if you're contemplating building up a wildcat, contact Redding Reloading Equipment and they'll be happy to supply the dies.

REDDING RELOADING EQUIPMENT

IMPROVED CLEANER-BURNING POWDER

Some powders can give you a real kick out on the range, but Royal Scot D™ from Scot Powder Company of Ohio takes the sting out of trap and Skeet shells.

Royal Scot D is an improved, higher-density replacement for "Royal Scot" powder. It has the same low recoil performance and charge-weight ballistic efficiency as Royal Scot, but burns cleaner and loads more consistently.

With the improved density of Royal Scot D, a smaller-volume bushing is needed for the appropriate charge weights.

Royal Scot D is a great trap and Skeet powder ideal for 7/8-, 1-, or 1 1/8-ounce 12-gauge target loads. For current reloading data and bushing chart, call or write Scot Powder Company of Ohio.

SCOT POWDER COMPANY OF OHIO, INC.

PREMIUM BULLET MOULDS

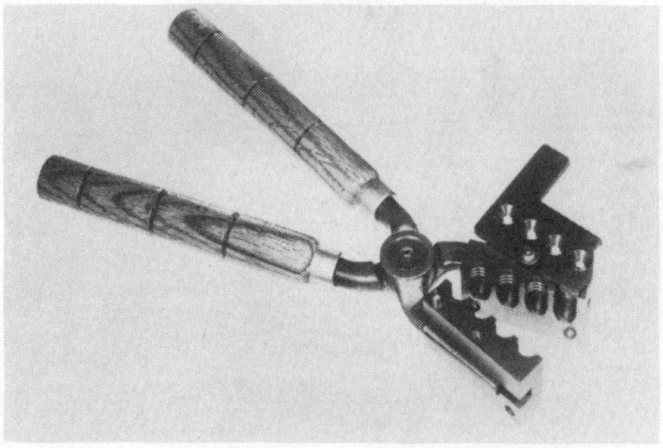

SAECO has long been regarded as one of the premier names in production bullet moulds by knowledgeable casters.

Several years ago, Redding purchased the remains of the old SAECO Reloading Company and is now producing the SAECO bullet mould line.

Redding has been constantly refining and adding to the lineup of sizes and styles to choose from and offers two-cavity and four-cavity blocks as standard items. Single-, three-, six- and eight-cavity moulds are also available on special order.

When you write or call Redding Reloading Equipment for a free catalog of SAECO products, be sure to mention you read about the SAECO lineup in *Handloader's Marketplace*.

REDDING RELOADING EQUIPMENT

See manufacturers' addresses on page 187.

GUN BOOKS & MAGAZINES

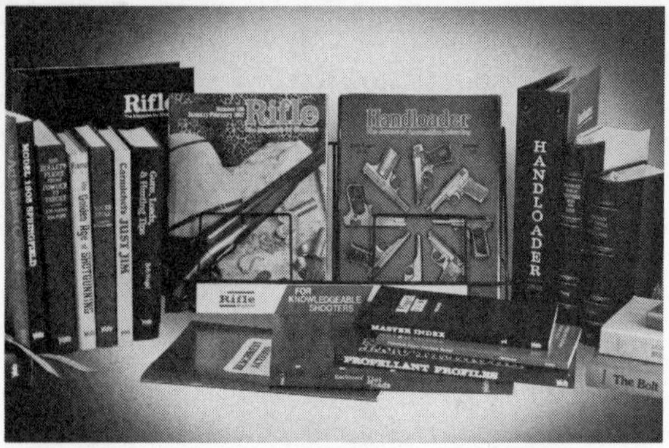

Wolfe Publishing Co. offers a large selection of hunting and firearms books, art prints and magazines for serious outdoor and gun enthusiasts.

They offer three of America's foremost sporting magazines–*Hunting Horizons,* a journal dedicated to the hunt; *Rifle*, an excellent firearms journal; and *Handloader*, the only magazine devoted exclusively to reloading.

If you want to expand your firearms knowledge and want more than mass media gun magazines, Wolfe publications are for you.

The Wolfe catalog lists more than 100 books for the sportsman's library and sells for $1.00—mention *Handloader's Marketplace* and it's free. Contact Wolfe Publishing Co. for more information.

WOLFE PUBLISHING CO.

QUALITY COTTON PATCHES

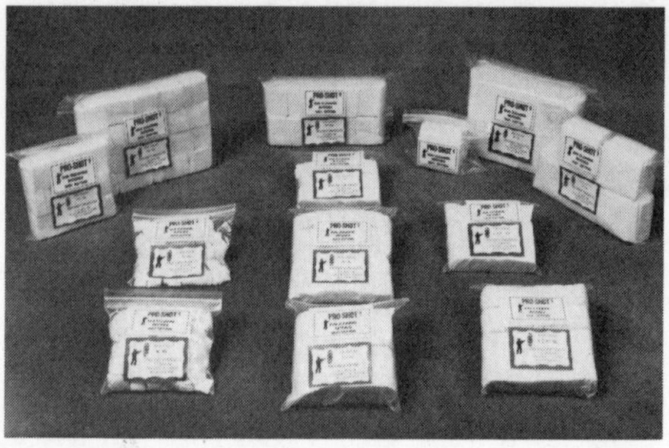

Pro-Shot patches are made of 100% cotton flannel finished on both sides. Cotton patches are absorbent and travel through the bore with a minimum amount of abrasive contact to the barrel's rifling.

They are offered in a variety of sizes including 17-caliber through 12-gauge. Blackpowder patches are also available.

Pro-Shot patches are packaged in a resealable plastic bag with two labels to indicate the caliber and number of patches in each bag. Patches are available in a variety of quantities, including 250, 500, and 1000 count.

Write or call Pro-Shot directly for a free 12-page catalog describing their patches and other accessories.

PRO-SHOT PRODUCTS, INC.

SMOKELESS POWDERS

Accurate Arms offers the handloader a complete line of smokeless powders for handgun, rifle and shotshell reloading.

Depending upon the bulk/density of the propellant, Accurate Arms typically offers their powders in 1-, 4- or 8-pound containers.

Their current lineup includes Nitro 100 for 12-gauge shotshell applications; No. 2, No. 5, No. 7 and No. 9 for handgun applications; and 1680, 2015BR, 2230, 2460, 2495BR, 2520, 2700, 4350, 3100 and 8700 for rifle applications.

Accurate Arms currently offers a complete 32-page loading manual for their propellants free of charge, either through your local gun shop or by contacting Accurate Arms direct.

ACCURATE ARMS CO., INC.

CUSTOM BULLETS

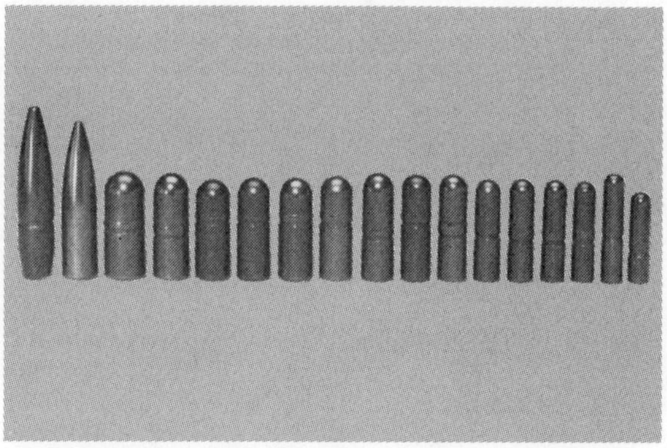

Original Solid™ Bullets, manufactured by Thunderbird Cartridge Co., Inc., are designed to maintain velocity, shape and stability. They offer complete Line-of-Sight™ penetration with virtually no deflection.

Original Solids are made from a homogeneous alloy that provides maximum stability and penetration, and eliminates the riveting, rupturing, base flattening and break-up that sometimes occurs with jacketed bullets because of their lead cores.

According to TCCI, their Original Solid 50-caliber spitzer-type boattail bullets have won more Fifty Caliber Shooters Association National 1,000 Yard Matches than all other bullets combined.

Call or write for a free flyer and loading data.

TCCI

See manufacturers' addresses on page 187.

HANDLOADER'S MARKETPLACE MANUFACTURERS' ADDRESSES

ACCURATE ARMS CO., INC. *(Pg. 186)*
Attn: Dept. HM'94
McEwen, TN 37101 (615-729-4207;
Fax 615-729-4217)

ARMS PERIPHERAL DATA SYSTEMS *(Pg. 172)*
Attn: Dept. HM'94
15110 S.W. Boones Ferry Road, Suite 225
P.O. Box 1526
Lake Oswego, OR 97035 (800-366-5559;
Fax 503-697-3337)

BERGER BULLETS, LTD. *(Pg. 172)*
Attn: Dept. HM'94
4234 N. 63rd Avenue
Phoenix, AZ 85033 (602-846-5791;
Fax 602-848-0780)

BIRCHWOOD LABORATORIES, INC. *(Pg. 178)*
Attn: Dept. HM'94
7900 Fuller Road
Eden Prairie, MN 55344 (612-937-7933)

B-SQUARE CO. *(Pg. 177)*
Attn: Dept. HM'94
P.O. Box 11281
Ft. Worth, TX 76110-0281 (800-433-2909 or
817-923-0964; Fax 817-926-7012)

B-WEST IMPORTS, INC. *(Pg. 174)*
Attn: Dept. HM'94
5132 E. Pima Street
Tucson, AZ 85712 (602-881-3525;
Fax 602-322-5704)

CCI *(Pg. 173)*
(Div. of Blount, Inc.)
Attn: Dept. HM'94
P.O. Box 856
Lewiston, ID 83501 (800-627-3640)

CHEM-PAK, INC. *(Pg. 174)*
Attn: Dept. HM'94
11 Oates Avenue
Winchester, VA 22601-8185 (800-336-9828;
Fax 703-722-3993)

CORBIN, INC. *(Pg. 174)*
Attn: Dept. HM'94
P.O. Box 2659
White City, OR 97503 (503-826-5211;
Fax 503-826-8669)

D&J BULLET CO. & CUSTOM GUN SHOP, INC. *(Pg. 177)*
Attn: Dept. HM'94
Rt. 1, Box 223 A-1
Flatwoods, KY 41139 (Phone/Fax 606-836-2663)

J. DEWEY MANUFACTURING CO., INC. *(Pg. 176)*
Attn: Dept. HM'94
P.O. Box 2014
Southbury, CT 06488 (203-598-7912;
Fax 203-598-3119)

GAR *(Pg. 178)*
Attn: Dept. HM'94
139 Park Lane
Wayne, NJ 07470 (201-256-7641)

GUNLINE TOOLS *(Pg. 176)*
Attn: Dept. HM'94
P.O. Box 478
Placentia, CA 92670 (714-528-5252;
Fax 714-572-4128)

GUN LIST *(Pg. 176)*
(Krause Publications)
Attn: Dept. ABAF8D
700 E. State Street
Iola, WI 54990-0001 (715-445-2214;
Fax 715-445-4087)

HARRIS ENGINEERING, INC. *(Pg. 176)*
Attn: Dept. HM'94
Route 1
Barlow, KY 42024 (502-334-3633;
Fax 502-334-3000)

HASTINGS BARRELS *(Pg. 178)*
Attn: Dept. HM'94
P.O. Box 224
Clay Center, KS 67432 (913-632-3169;
Fax 913-632-6554)

J.B. HOLDEN CO. *(Pg. 178)*
Attn: Dept. HM'94
P.O. Box 320
Plymouth, MI 48170 (313-455-4850;
Fax 313-455-4212)

HUNTINGTON DIE SPECIALTIES *(Pg. 183)*
Attn: Dept. HM'94
601 Oro Dam Blvd.
Oroville, CA 95965 (916-534-1210;
Fax 916-534-1212)

IMPERIAL MAGNUM CORP. *(Pg. 180)*
Attn: Dept. HM'94
1417 Main Street
Oroville, WA 98844 (604-495-3131;
Fax 604-495-2816)

NEIL JONES CUSTOM PRODUCTS *(Pg. 177)*
Attn: Dept. HM'94
RD #1, Box 483A
Saegertown, PA 16433 (814-763-2769;
Fax 814-763-4228)

LYMAN PRODUCTS CORP. *(Pg. 179)*
Route 147, Dept. 445
Middlefield, CT 06455 (800-22-LYMAN;
Fax 203-349-3586)

MTM MOLDED PRODUCTS CO., INC. *(Pg. 174)*
Attn: Dept. HM'94
P.O. Box 14117
Dayton, OH 45414 (513-890-7461;
Fax 513-890-1747)

MULTI-SCALE CHARGE, LTD. *(Pg. 175)*
Attn: Dept. HM'94
3269 Niagara Falls Blvd.
N. Tonawanda, NY 14120 (416-276-6292;
Fax 416-276-6295)

OLD WESTERN SCROUNGER, INC. *(Pg. 180)*
Attn: Dept. HM'94
12924 Hwy. A-12
Montague, CA 96064 (916-459-5445;
Fax 916-459-3944)

PONSNESS/WARREN *(Pg. 180)*
Attn: Dept. HM'94
P.O. Box 8
Rathdrum, ID 83858 (208-687-2231;
Fax 208-687-2233)

PRO-SHOT PRODUCTS, INC. *(Pg. 186)*
Attn: Dept. HM'94
P.O. Box 763
Taylorville, IL 62568 (217-824-9133;
Fax 217-824-8861)

RCBS *(Pg. 173)*
(Div. of Blount, Inc.)
Attn: Dept. HM'94
605 Oro Dam Blvd.
Oroville, CA 95965 (800-533-5000)

REDDING RELOADING EQUIPMENT *(Pg. 181, 185)*
Attn: Dept. HM'94
1089 Starr Road
Cortland, NY 13045 (607-753-3331;
Fax 607-756-8445)

REMINGTON ARMS CO., INC. *(Pg. 180)*
Attn: Dept. HM'94
1007 Market Street, B-6208
Wilmington, DE 19898

RIG PRODUCTS *(Pg. 182)*
Attn: Dept. HM'94
87 Coney Island Drive
Sparks, NV 89431 (702-331-5666;
Fax 702-331-5669)

ROCKY MOUNTAIN TARGET CO. *(Pg. 182)*
Attn: Dept. HM'94
3 Aloe Way
Leesburg, FL 34788-7924 (904-365-9598)

SCOT POWDER COMPANY OF OHIO, INC. *(Pg. 185)*
Attn: Dept. HM'94
Box HD94
Only, TN 37140 (615-729-4207;
Fax 615-729-4217)

SHOOTING CHRONY, INC. *(Pg. 175)*
Attn: Dept. HM'94
3269 Niagara Falls Blvd.
N. Tonawanda, NY 14120 (416-276-6292;
Fax 416-276-6295)

THE SHOTGUN NEWS *(Pg. 172)*
Attn: Dept. HM'94, D. Clark
P.O. Box 669
Hastings, NE 68901

SIERRA BULLETS *(Pg. 181)*
Attn: Dept. HM'94
P.O. Box 818
Sedalia, MO 65301 (816-827-6300;
Fax 816-827-4999)

SINCLAIR INTERNATIONAL, INC. *(Pg. 184)*
Attn: Dept. HM'94
2330 Wayne Haven Street
Ft. Wayne, IN 46803 (219-493-1858;
Fax 219-493-2530)

SIX ENTERPRISES *(Pg. 182)*
Attn: Dept. HM'94
320-D Turtle Creek Court
San Jose, CA 95125 (408-999-0201;
Fax 408-999-0216)

STAR CUSTOM BULLETS *(Pg. 182)*
(Professional Hunter Supplies)
Attn: Dept. HM'94
P.O. Box 608, 468 Main Street
Ferndale, CA 95536 (707-786-4040;
Fax 707-786-9117)

STONEY POINT PRODUCTS, INC. *(Pg. 183)*
Attn: Dept. HM'94
P.O. Box 5
Courtland, MN 56021-0005 (507-354-3360;
Fax 507-354-7236)

SWIFT BULLET CO. *(Pg. 184)*
Attn: Dept. HM'94
201 Main Street
Quinter, KS 67752 (913-754-3959;
Fax 913-754-2359)

TCCI *(Pg. 186)*
(Thunderbird Cartridge Co., Inc.)
Attn: Dept. HM'94
P.O. Box 302
Phoenix, AZ 85001 (602-237-3823;
Fax 602-237-3858)

THOMPSON TARGET TECHNOLOGY *(Pg. 179)*
Attn: Dept. HM'94
618 Roslyn Avenue, S.W.
Canton, OH 44710 (216-453-7707;
Fax 216-478-4723)

TIMBER HEIRLOOM PRODUCTS *(Pg. 179)*
Attn: Dept. HM'94
618 Roslyn Avenue, S.W.
Canton, OH 44710 (216-453-7707;
Fax 216-478-4723)

VIHTAVUORI OY *(Pg. 184)*
(Kaltron-Pettibone)
Attn: Dept. HM'94
1241 Ellis Street
Bensenville, IL 60106 (708-350-1116;
Fax 708-350-1606)

WOLFE PUBLISHING CO. *(Pg. 186)*
Attn: Dept. HM'94
6471 Airpark Drive
Prescott, AZ 86301 (800-899-7810 or
602-445-7810; Fax 602-778-5124)

WYOMING CASTING CO. *(Pg. 184)*
Attn: Dept. HM'94
P.O. Box 1492
Gillette, WY 82717 (307-687-7779 or
800-821-2167)

1994

HANDLOADER'S DIGEST

CATALOG

LOADEX®

An alphabetical listing of all the products in the 1994 HANDLOADER'S DIGEST catalog by manufacturer name and product.

A

B

C

D

E

F

G

H

I

J

K

L

M

N

O

P

Q, R

S

T

V

W

1994 HANDLOADER'S DIGEST

13th EDITION

PART 1 2 3 4 5 6

METALLIC CARTRIDGES

TOOLS & ACCESSORIES

C-H/4-D Heavyweight Champion

Frame: Cast iron
Frame Type: O-frame
Die Thread: $^{7}/_{8}$-14 or 1-14
Avg. Rounds Per Hour: NA
Ram Stroke: $3^{1}/_{4}$"
Weight: 26 lbs.
Features: 1.185" diameter ram with 16 square inches of bearing surface; ram drilled to allow passage of spent primers; solid steel handle; toggle that slightly breaks over top dead center. Includes universal primer arm with large and small punches. From C-H Tool & Die/4-D Custom Die.
Price: **$199.00**
Price: With die set and shellholder **$229.50**

C-H/4-D No. 444

Frame: Aluminum alloy
Frame Type: H-frame
Die Thread: $^{7}/_{8}$-14
Avg. Rounds Per Hour: 200
Ram Stroke: $3^{3}/_{4}$"
Weight: 12 lbs.
Features: Two $^{7}/_{8}$" solid steel shaft "H" supports; platen rides on permanently lubed bronze bushings; loads smallest pistol to largest magnum rifle cases and has strength to full-length resize. Includes four rams, large and small primer arm and primer catcher. From C-H Tool & Die/4-D Custom Die.
Price: **$158.00**
Price: With die set and four shellholders **$185.00**

C-H/4-D No. 444-X Pistol Champ

Frame: Aluminum alloy
Frame Type: H-frame
Die Thread: $^{7}/_{8}$-14
Avg. Rounds Per Hour: 200
Ram Stroke: $3^{3}/_{4}$"
Weight: 12 lbs.
Features: Tungsten carbide sizing die; Speed Seater seating die with tapered entrance to automatically align bullet on case mouth; automatic primer feed for large or small primers; pushbutton powder measure with easily changed bushings for 215 powder/load combinations; taper crimp die. Conversion kit for caliber changeover available. From C-H Tool & Die/4-D Custom Die.
Price: . . . . **(See chart for pricing.)**

FORSTER Co-Ax B-2

Frame: Cast iron
Frame Type: Modified O-frame
Die Thread: $^{7}/_{8}$-14
Avg. Rounds Per Hour: 120
Ram Stroke: 4"
Weight: 18 lbs.
Features: Snap-in/snap-out die change; spent primer catcher with drop tube threaded into carrier below shellholder; automatic, handle-activated, cammed shellholder with opposing spring-loaded jaws to contact extractor groove; floating guide rods for alignment and reduced friction; no torque on the head due to design of linkage and pivots; shellholder jaws that float with die permitting case to center in the die; right- or left-hand operation; priming device for seating to factory specifications. "S" shellholder jaws not included. From Forster Products.
Price: **$248.00**
Price: Shellholder jaws **$21.20**

C-H/4-D 444-X Pistol Champ

C-H/4-D No. 444

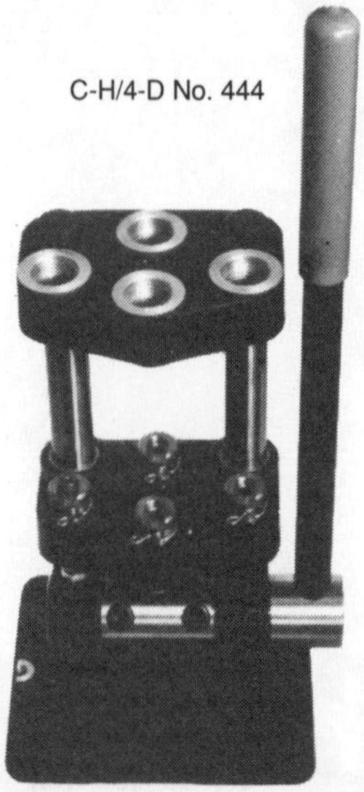

C-H/4-D				
Caliber	No. 444 Pistol Champ Carbide Sizer	Steel Sizer	444-X Conversion Kit Carbide Sizer	Steel Sizer
10mm/40 S&W	$278.90	$260.00	$84.00	$62.00
30 M1 Carbine	286.50	255.00	90.00	57.10
32 S&W/H&R Mag.	273.90	255.00	79.00	57.10
38 Spl/357 Mag.	269.50	255.00	75.00	57.10
41 Magnum	273.90	255.00	79.00	57.10
44 Magnum	269.50	255.00	75.00	57.10
45 ACP	269.50	255.00	75.00	57.10
45 Colt	273.90	255.00	79.00	57.10
9mm Luger	273.90	255.00	79.00	57.10

Forster Co-Ax B-2

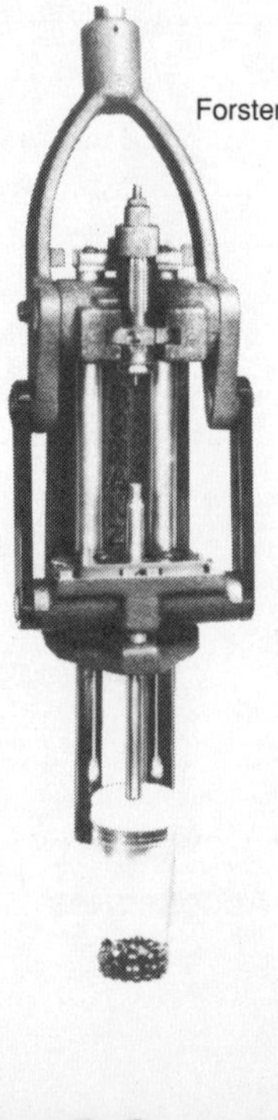

FORSTER Co-Ax "S" and "LS" Shellholder Calibers — PISTOL	
22 Rem. Jet	38 Special
30 Luger	351 Win.
32 Auto	25-20 Win.
32 Colt P	351 Win. S.L.
32 S&W	32-20 Win.
9mm Luger	41 Rem. Mag.
38 Special	44 Rem. (LS)
38 S&W (LS)	44 S&W (LS)
380 Auto	44-40 Win.
32 Short Colt	45 Auto
32 Long Colt	45 Colt
9mm Win. Mag.	45 Win.
32 Rem.	38-40 Win.
30 Rem.	303 Savage
38 Auto	45 Auto Match
38 Short Colt	44 Rem. Mag.
38 Long Colt	10mm
25 Auto	

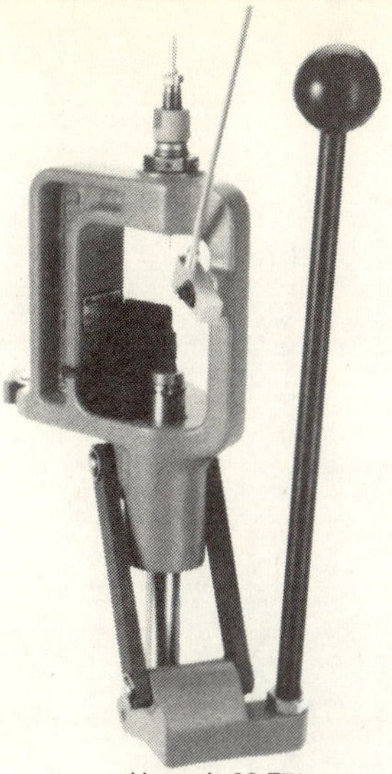

Hornady 00-7™

Hollywood Senior Turret

FORSTER	
Co-Ax "S" and "LS" Shellholder Calibers	
RIFLE	
17 Rem.	284 Win.
218 Bee	300 Savage
22 Hornet (LS)	30-30 Win.
221 Rem.	30-40 Krag
222 Rem.	300 Win. Mag.
222 Rem. Mag.	303 British
223 Rem.	307 Win.
5.6x50	308 Win.
30 Carbine	308 Nat'l M
32-20 Win.	308 Norma
219 Zipper	30-06
22 Savage	300 H&H
224 Wea.	300 Wea.
220 Swift	8mm Rem. Mag.
22-250 Rem.	8mmx57
225 Win.	8mmx68S
240 Wea.	32 Win.
243 Win.	32-20 Win.
6mm Rem.	38-40 Win.
6mm PPC	338 Win.
25-06 Rem.	340 Wea.
250 Savage	348 Win. (LS)
256 Win. Mag. (LS)	35 Rem.
25-35 Win.	350 Rem. Mag.
257 Roberts	356 Win.
257 Wea.	358 Win.
264 Win. Mag.	358 Nor. Mag.
6.5x54 Mann.-Schoe.	375 Wea.
6.5 Rem. Mag.	375 H&H
6.5 Swede	378 Wea. (LS)
270 Win.	38-55 Win.
270 Wea.	444 Marlin
7x64 Brenneke	44-40 Win.
7mm-08	45-70 (LS)
7mmx57	45-90 (LS)
7mm BR	458 Win. Mag.
7mm Rem.	375 Win.
7mm Wea.	32-40 Win.
280 Rem.	416 Rigby (LS)
	416 Rem. (LS)

Hollywood Senior

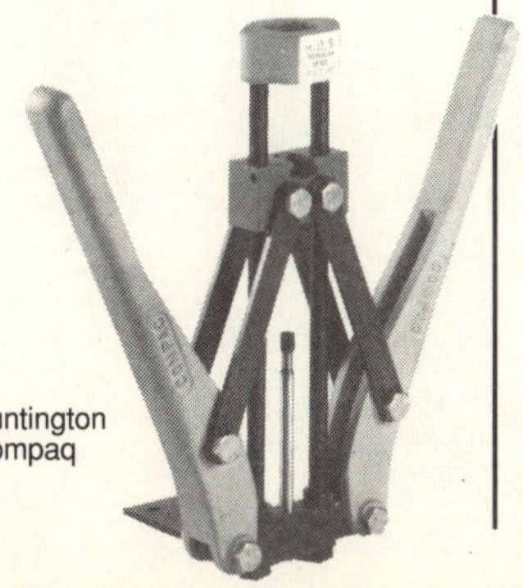

Huntington Compaq

HOLLYWOOD Senior Press

Frame: Ductile iron
Frame Type: O-frame
Die Thread: 7/8-14
Avg. Rounds Per Hour: 50-100
Ram Stroke: 6 1/2"
Weight: 50 lbs.
Features: Leverage and bearing surfaces ample for reloading cartridges or swaging bullets. Precision ground one-piece 2 1/2" pillar with base; operating handle of 3/4" steel and 15" long; 5/8" steel tie-down rod for added strength when swaging; heavy steel toggle and camming arms held by 1/2" steel pins in reamed holes. The 1 1/2" steel die bushing takes standard threaded dies; removed, it allows use of Hollywood shotshell dies. From Hollywood Engineering.
Price: **$475.00**

HOLLYWOOD Senior Turret Press

Frame: Ductile iron
Frame Type: H-frame
Die Thread: 7/8-14
Avg. Rounds Per Hour: 50-100
Ram Stroke: 6 1/2"
Weight: 50 lbs.
Features: Same features as Senior press except has three-position turret head; holes in turret may be tapped 1 1/2" or 7/8" or four of each. Height, 15". Comes complete with one turret indexing handle; one 1 1/2" to 7/8" die hole bushing; one 5/8" tie down bar for swaging. From Hollywood Engineering.
Price: **$500.00**

HORNADY 00-7 Press

Frame: Die cast heat-treated aluminum alloy
Frame Type: O-frame
Die Thread: 7/8-14
Avg. Rounds Per Hour: NA
Ram Stroke: 3 5/8"
Weight: 14 lbs.
Features: Solid steel linkage arms that rotate on steel pins; 30° angled frame design for improved visibility and accessibility; primer arm automatically moves in and out of ram for primer pickup and solid seating; two primer arms for large and small primers; long offset handle for increased leverage and unobstructed reloading; lifetime warranty. Comes with primer catcher. Dies, shellholder and automatic primer feed available separately or as additional package with New Dimension or Titanium Nitride Series III dies and shellholder. From Hornady Mfg. Co.
Price: Press **$105.40**
Price: Press with ND dies **$153.25**
Price: Press with Series III dies **$166.50**

HUNTINGTON Compaq Tool

Frame: Aircraft aluminum
Frame Type: NA
Die Thread: 7/8-14
Avg. Rounds Per Hour: NA
Ram Stroke: NA
Weight: 37 oz.
Features: Small and lightweight for portability; performs all standard reloading operations; sufficient leverage to full-length resize, decap military brass and case-form. Accepts standard shellholders. Is bench mountable. Dimensions: 3 1/2" x 9". From Huntington Die Specialties.
Price: **$64.98**

LEE Challenger Press

Frame: ASTM 380 aluminum
Frame Type: O-frame
Die Thread: $^{7}/_{8}$-14
Avg. Rounds Per Hour: 100
Ram Stroke: $3^{1}/_{2}$"
Weight: 4 lbs., 1 oz.
Features: Larger than average opening with 30° offset for maximum hand clearance; steel connecting pins; spent primer catcher; handle adjustable for start and stop positions; handle repositions for left- or right-hand use; shortened handle travel to prevent springing the frame from alignment. Dies and shellholders not included. From Lee Precision, Inc.
Price: **$43.00**

LEE Hand Press

Frame: ASTM 380 aluminum
Frame Type: NA
Die Thread: $^{7}/_{8}$-14
Avg. Rounds Per Hour: 100
Ram Stroke: $3^{1}/_{4}$"
Weight: 1 lb., 8 oz.
Features: Small and lightweight for portability; compound linkage for handling up to 375 H&H and case forming. Dies and shellholder not included. From Lee Precision, Inc.
Price: **$22.98**

LEE Reloader Press

Frame: ASTM 380 aluminum
Frame Type: C-frame
Die Thread: $^{7}/_{8}$-14
Avg. Rounds Per Hour: 100
Ram Stroke: 3"
Weight: 1 lb., 12 oz.
Features: Balanced lever to prevent pinching fingers; unlimited hand clearance; left- or right-hand use. Dies and shellholders not included. From Lee Precision, Inc.
Price: **$24.98**

LEE Turret Press

Frame: ASTM 380 aluminum
Frame Type: O-frame
Die Thread: $^{7}/_{8}$-14
Avg. Rounds Per Hour: 300
Ram Stroke: 3"
Weight: 7 lbs., 2 oz.
Features: Replaceable turret lifts out by rotating 30°; T-primer arm reverses for large or small primers; built-in primer catcher; adjustable handle for right- or left-hand use or changing angle of down stroke; accessory mounting hole for Lee Auto-Disk powder measure. Optional Auto-Index rotates die turret to next station for semi-progressive use. Safety override prevents overstressing should turret not turn. From Lee Precision, Inc.
Price: **$67.98**
Price: With Auto-Index **$81.98**
Price: Extra turret **$10.98**

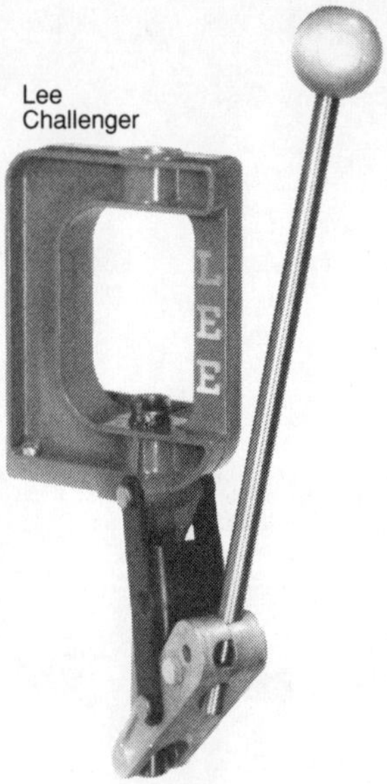

Lee Challenger

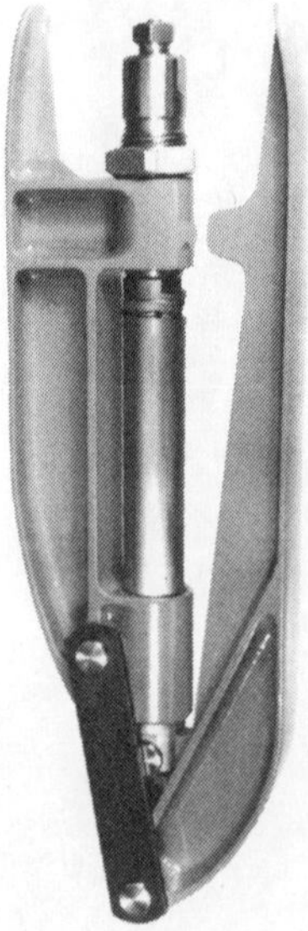

Lee Hand Press

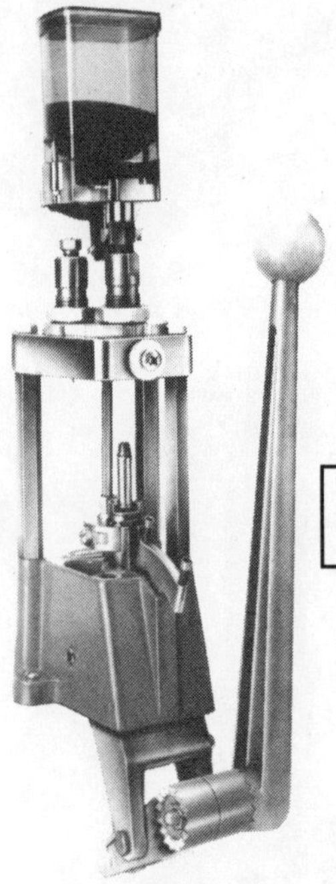

Lee Turret

Consult our Directory pages for the location of firms mentioned.

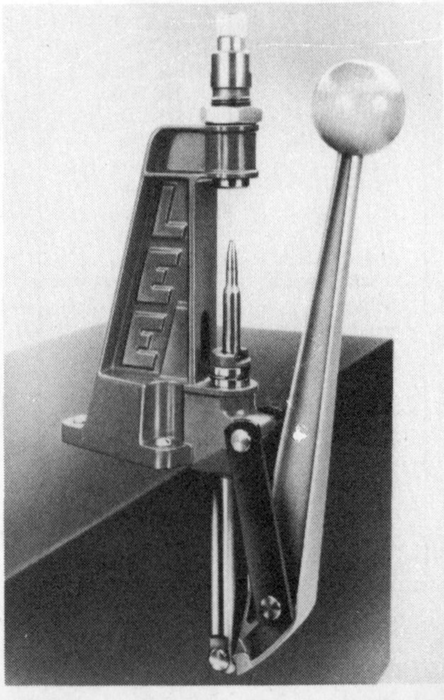

Lee Reloader

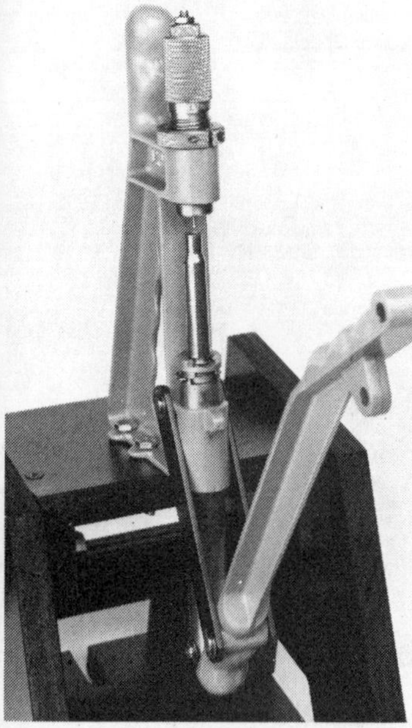

Lyman AccuPress

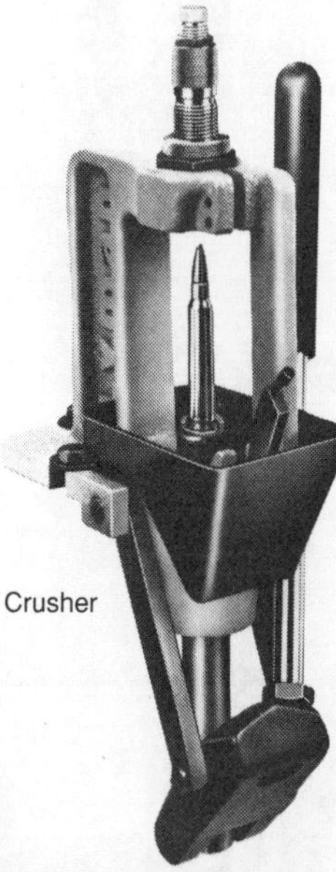

Lyman Orange Crusher

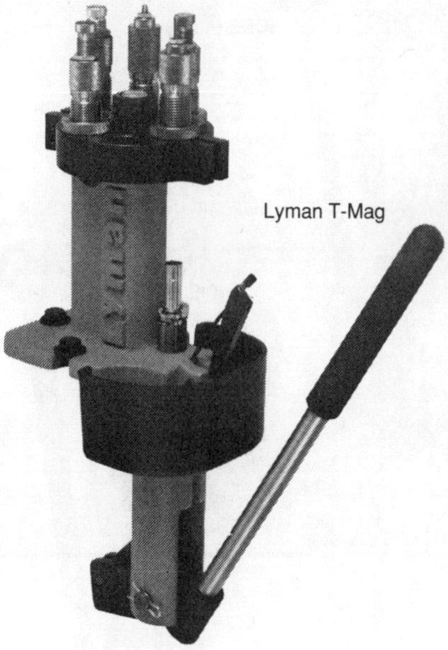

Lyman T-Mag

LYMAN 310 Tool Die Sets	
RIFLE	
Cartridge	Handle Size
222 Rem.	S
223 Rem.	L
222 Rem. Mag.	L
243 Win.	L
6mm Rem.	L
270 Win.	L
30 M1 Carbine	S
30-30 Win.	L
30-06	L
7.62mmx63	L
300 Savage	L
308 Win.	L
38-40	S
44-40	S
45-70 Gov't.	L
PISTOL	
Cartridge	Handle Size
9mm Luger	S
38 Auto	S
38 Spl./357 Mag.	S
44 Rem. Mag.	S
45 ACP	S
45 Colt	S

Lyman 310

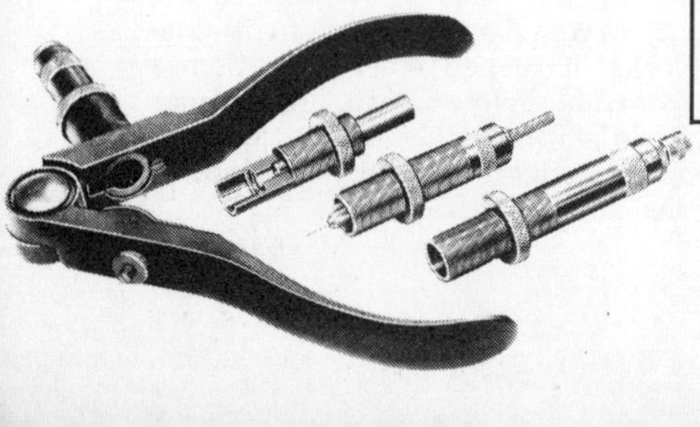

LYMAN 310 Tool

Frame: Stainless steel
Frame Type: NA
Die Thread: $^{7}/_{8}$-14
Avg. Rounds Per Hour: NA
Ram Stroke: NA
Weight: 10 oz.
Features: Compact, portable reloading tool for pistol or rifle cartridges. Adapter allows loading rimmed or rimless cases. Die set includes neck resizing/decapping die, primer seating chamber; neck expanding die; bullet seating die; and case head adapter. From Lyman Products Corporation.
Price: Dies **$35.00**
Price: Press **$35.00**

LYMAN AccuPress

Frame: Die cast
Frame Type: C-frame
Die Thread: $^{7}/_{8}$-14
Avg. Rounds Per Hour: 75
Ram Stroke: 3.4"
Weight: 4 lbs.
Features: Reversible, contoured handle for bench mount or hand-held use; for rifle or pistol; compound leverage; Delta frame design. Accepts all standard powder measures. From Lyman Products Corporation.
Price: **$32.95**

LYMAN Orange Crusher

Frame: Cast iron
Frame Type: O-frame
Die Thread: $^{7}/_{8}$-14
Avg. Rounds Per Hour: 75
Ram Stroke: $3^{7}/_{8}$"
Weight: 19 lbs.
Features: Reloads both pistol and rifle cartridges; $4^{1}/_{2}$" press opening for loading magnum cartridges; direct torque design; right- or left-hand use. Comes with priming arm and catcher. Dies and shellholders not included. From Lyman Products Corporation.
Price: **$109.95**

LYMAN T-Mag

Frame: Cast iron
Frame Type: Turret
Die Thread: $^{7}/_{8}$-14
Avg. Rounds Per Hour: 125
Ram Stroke: $3^{13}/_{16}$"
Weight: 18 lbs.
Features: Detachable turret head for caliber change; new turret head stabilizer to improve precision; right- or left-hand operation; triple mounting holes for stability; handles all rifle or pistol dies. Comes with priming arm and primer catcher. Dies and shellholders not included. From Lyman Products Corporation.
Price: **$149.95**
Price: Extra turret **$19.95**

MCRW Lyman 310 Tool

Frame: Stainless steel
Frame Type: NA
Die Thread: $^{7}/_{8}$-14
Avg. Rounds Per Hour: NA
Ram Stroke: NA
Weight: 10 oz.
Features: Handles completely accurized. Bored, faced, squared, glass beaded and threaded to U.S.A. SAE standard. Stainless steel body and parts use Wilson buttons. Available in 6mm PPC and Brin. Comes complete for one caliber. From MCRW Associates.
Price: **$110.00**

PONSNESS/WARREN Metal-Matic P-200

Frame: Die cast aluminum
Frame Type: Unconventional
Die Thread: $^{7}/_{8}$-14
Avg. Rounds Per Hour: 200+
Weight: 18 lbs.
Features: Designed for straight-wall cartridges; die head with 10 tapped holes for holding dies and accessories for two calibers at one time; removable spent primer box; pivoting arm moves case from station to station. Comes with large and small primer tool. Optional accessories include primer feed, extra die head, primer speed feeder, powder measure extension and dust cover. Dies, powder measure and shellholder not included. From Ponsness/Warren.
Price: **$135.00**
Price: Extra die head **$13.60**
Price: Powder measure extension **$15.70**
Price: Primer feed **$31.45**
Price: Primer speed feed **$10.45**
Price: Dust cover **$20.95**

RCBS AmmoMaster Single

Frame: Aluminum base; cast iron top plate connected by three steel posts.
Frame Type: NA
Die Thread: $1^{1}/_{4}$"-12 bushing; $^{7}/_{8}$-14 threads
Avg. Rounds Per Hour: 50-60
Ram Stroke: $5^{1}/_{4}$"
Weight: 19 lbs.
Features: Single-stage press convertible to progressive. Will form cases or swage bullets. Case detection system to disengage powder measure when no case is present in powder charging station; five-station shellplate; Uniflow Powder measure with clear powder measure adaptor to make bridged powders visible and correctable. 50-cal. conversion kit allows reloading 50 BMG. Kit includes top plate to accommodate either $1^{3}/_{8}$"x12 or $1^{1}/_{2}$"x12 reloading dies. Piggyback die plate for quick caliber change-overs available. Reloading dies not included. From RCBS.
Price: **$177.08**
Price: Single-to-auto kit **$237.44**
Price: 50 conversion kit **$68.76**
Price: Piggyback/AmmoMaster die plate **$21.33**
Price: Piggyback/AmmoMaster shellplate **$26.22**
Price: Press cover **$6.93**

RCBS Partner

Frame: Aluminum
Frame Type: 30° offset O-frame
Die Thread: $^{7}/_{8}$-14
Avg. Rounds Per Hour: 50-60
Ram Stroke: $3^{5}/_{8}$"
Weight: 5 lbs.
Features: Designed for the beginning reloader. Comes with primer arm equipped with interchangeable primer plugs and sleeves for seating large and small primers. Shellholder and dies not included. Available in kit form (see Metallic Presses—Accessories). From RCBS.
Price: **$51.95**

Reloader Special-5

Frame: Aluminum
Frame Type: O-frame
Die Thread: $1^{1}/_{4}$-12 bushing; $^{7}/_{8}$-14 threads
Avg. Rounds Per Hour: 50-60
Ram Stroke: $3^{1}/_{16}$"
Weight: 7.5 lbs.
Features: Single-stage press convertible to progressive with RCBS Piggyback II. Primes cases during resizing operation. Will accept RCBS shotshell dies. From RCBS.
Price: **$102.40**

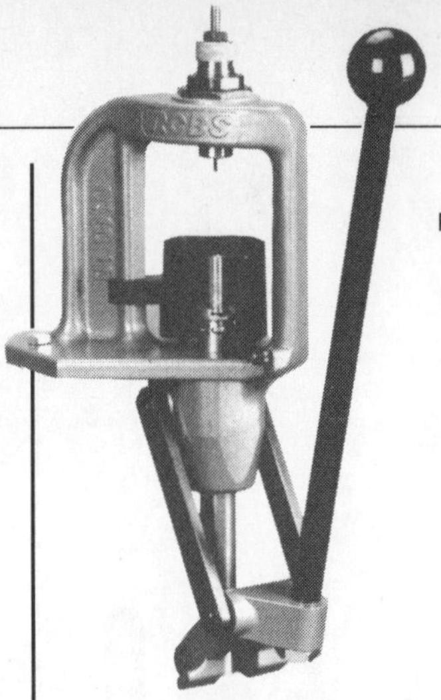

RCBS Reloader Special-5

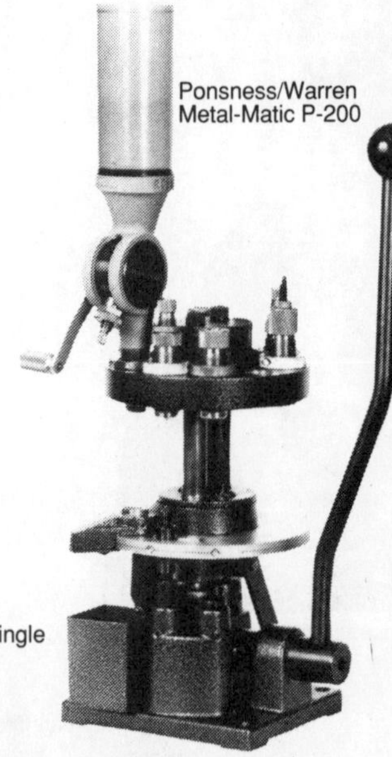

Ponsness/Warren Metal-Matic P-200

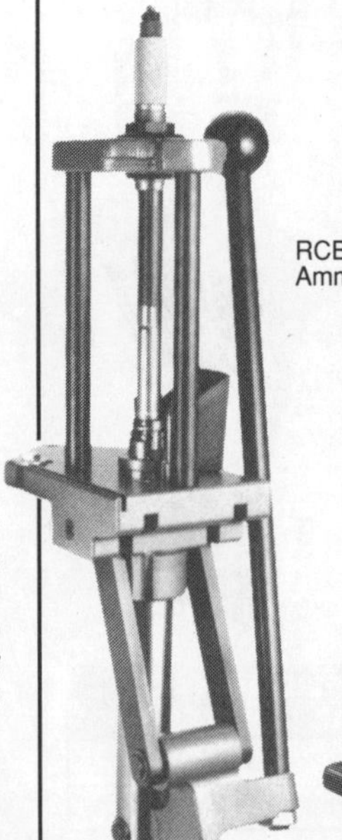

RCBS AmmoMaster Single

RCBS Partner

RCBS Rock Chucker

RCBS Rock Chucker

Frame: Cast iron
Frame Type: O-frame
Die Thread: $1^{1}/_{4}$"-12 bushing; $^{7}/_{8}$-14 threads
Avg. Rounds Per Hour: 50-60
Ram Stroke: $3^{5}/_{16}$"
Weight: 17 lbs.
Features: Designed for heavy-duty reloading, case forming and bullet swaging. Provides 4" of ram-bearing surface to support 1" ram and ensure alignment; ductile iron toggle blocks; hardened steel pins. Comes standard with Universal Primer Arm and primer catcher. Can be converted from single-stage to progressive with Piggyback II conversion unit (see Metallic Presses—Accessories). From RCBS.
Price: **$191.50**

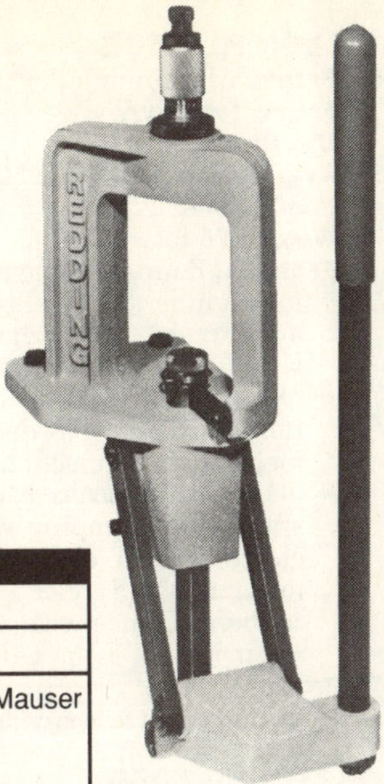

Redding The Boss

REDDING	
Series AA Die Press Kits	
RIFLE	
221 Rem. Fire Ball	7mmx57 Mauser
22 Hornet	280 Rem.
220 Swift	284 Win.
222 Rem.	7.62x39
22-250 Rem.	30-30 Win.
223 Rem.	30-40 Krag
243 Win.	30-06 Sprfld.
6mm Rem.	300 H&H Mag.
250 Savage	300 Savage
25-06 Rem.	300 Win. Mag.
257 Roberts	308/307 Win.
6.5mmx55 Swed. Mauser	303 British
264 Win. Mag.	32 Win. Spl.
270 Win.	8mmx57 Mauser
7mm-08 Rem.	338 Win. Mag.
7mm Rem. Mag.	35 Rem.
	375 H&H Mag.
PISTOL	
30 M1 Carbine	41 Mag.
32 S&W Long	44 Spl.
32 H&R Mag.	44 Mag.
380 Auto	44-40 Win.
38 Spl.	45 ACP & AR
357 Mag.	45 Colt
38 Spl./357 Mag.	

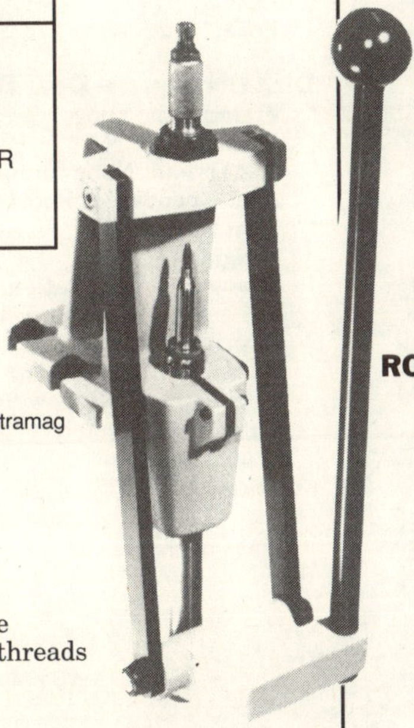

Redding Ultramag

RCBS Reloader Special-5

Frame: Aluminum
Frame Type: 30° offset O-frame
Die Thread: 1¼"-12 with ⅞-14 threads
Avg. Rounds Per Hour: 50-60
Ram Stroke: 3$^{1}/_{16}$"
Weight: 7½ lbs.
Features: Primer arm with primer plugs and sleeves for large and small primers; removable bushing allows use of RCBS shotshell dies for reloading 12-ga. shells and attachment of the Piggyback single-stage to progressive conversion unit; primer catcher. From RCBS.
Price: **$102.40**

REDDING Model 25 Turret Press

Frame: Cast iron
Frame Type: Turret
Die Thread: ⅞-14
Avg. Rounds Per Hour: NA
Ram Stroke: 3.4"
Weight: 23 lbs., 2 oz.
Features: Strength to reload pistol and magnum rifle, case form and bullet swage; linkage pins heat-treated, precision ground and in double shear; hollow ram to collect spent primers; removable turret head for caliber changes; progressive linkage for increased power as ram nears die; slight frame tilt for comfortable operation; rear turret support for stability and precise alignment; six-station turret head; priming arm for both large and small primers. Also available in kit form with shellholder, primer catcher and one die set (see chart). From Redding Reloading Equipment.
Price: **$249.00**
Price: Kit **$279.00**

REDDING The Boss

Frame: Cast iron
Frame Type: O-frame
Die Thread: ⅞-14
Avg. Rounds Per Hour: NA
Ram Stroke: 3.4"
Weight: 11 lbs., 8 oz.
Features: 36° frame offset for visibility and accessibility; primer arm positioned at bottom of ram travel; positive ram travel stop machined to hit exactly top-dead-center. Also available in kit form with shellholder and set of Redding AA dies. From Redding Reloading Equipment.
Price: **$109.50**
Price: Kit **$139.50**

REDDING Ultramag

Frame: Cast iron
Frame Type: Non-conventional
Die Thread: ⅞-14
Avg. Rounds Per Hour: NA
Ram Stroke: 4.25"
Weight: 23 lbs., 6 oz.
Features: Unique compound leverage system connected to top of press for tons of ram pressure; large 4¾" frame opening for loading outsized cartridges; hollow ram for spent primers. Kit available with shellholder and one set Redding AA dies. From Redding Reloading Equipment.
Price: **$244.50**
Price: Kit **$274.50**

ROCK CRUSHER Press

Frame: Cast iron
Frame Type: O-frame
Die Thread: 1½-12
Avg. Rounds Per Hour: NA
Ram Stroke: 5¾"
Weight: 67 lbs.
Features: Designed to load and form ammunition from 50 BMG up to 23x115 Soviet. Frame opening of 8½" x 3½"; 3" diameter hole in tool head available upon request for loading up to 50mm; develops over 20,000 lbs. ram pressure; 40mm diameter ram. Angle block for bench mounting and reduction bushing for RCBS dies available. Rockcrusher powder measure, dies, shellholder, bullet puller, priming tool, case gauge and other accessories found elsewhere in this catalog. From The Old Western Scrounger.
Price: **$695.00**
Price: Angle block **$45.00**
Price: Reduction bushing **$28.00**

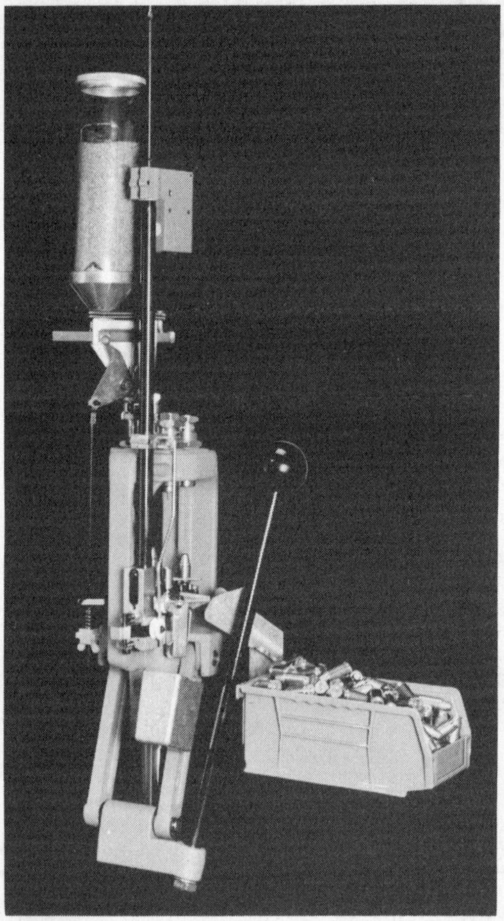

Dillon RL 550B

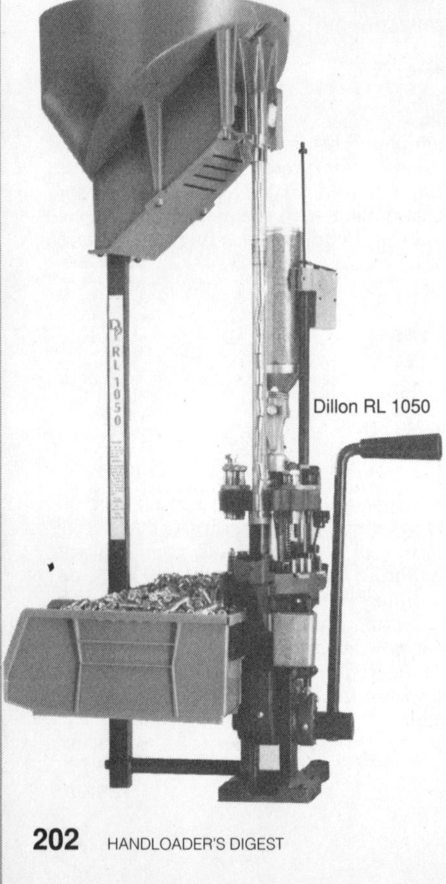

Dillon RL 1050

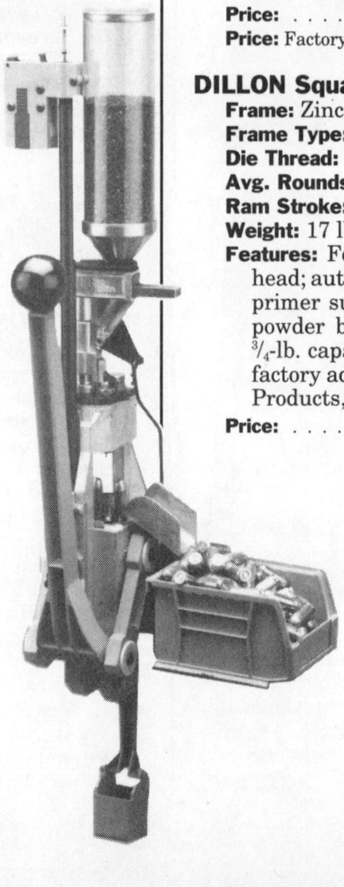

Dillon Square Deal B

DILLON RL 550B

Frame: Aluminum alloy
Frame Type: NA
Die Thread: $^{7}/_{8}$-14
Avg. Rounds Per Hour: 500-600
Ram Stroke: $3^{7}/_{8}$"
Weight: 25 lbs.
Features: Four stations; removable tool head to hold dies in alignment and allow caliber changes without die adjustment; auto priming system that emits audible warning when primer tube is low; a 100-primer capacity magazine contained in DOM steel tube for protection; new auto powder measure system with simple mechanical connection between measure and loading platform for positive powder bar return; a separate station for crimping with star-indexing system; 220 ejected-round capacity bin; $^{3}/_{4}$-lb. capacity powder measure. Will reload 120 different rifle and pistol calibers. Comes with one caliber conversion kit. Dies not included. From Dillon Precision Products, Inc.
Price: **$294.00**
Price: Factory set for one caliber **$333.95**

DILLON RL 1050

Frame: Ductile iron
Frame Type: Platform type
Die Thread: $^{7}/_{8}$-14
Avg. Rounds Per Hour: 1000-1200
Ram Stroke: $2^{5}/_{16}$"
Weight: 62 lbs.
Features: Eight stations; auto case feed; primer pocket swager for military cartridge cases; auto indexing; removable tool head; auto prime system with 100-primer capacity; low primer supply alarm; positive powder bar return; auto powder measure; 515 ejected round bin capacity; 500-600 case feed capacity; $^{3}/_{4}$-lb. capacity powder measure. Loads all pistol rounds as well as 30 M1 Carbine, 223 and 7.62x39 rifle rounds. Dies not included. From Dillon Precision Products, Inc.
Price: **$1,010.95**
Price: Factory set for one caliber **$1,049.95**

DILLON Square Deal B

Frame: Zinc alloy
Frame Type: NA
Die Thread: None (unique Dillon design)
Avg. Rounds Per Hour: 400-500
Ram Stroke: $2^{5}/_{16}$"
Weight: 17 lbs.
Features: Four stations; auto indexing; removable toolhead; auto prime system with 100-primer capacity; low primer supply alarm; auto powder measure; positive powder bar return; 170 ejected round capacity bin; $^{3}/_{4}$-lb. capacity powder measure. Comes complete with factory adjusted carbide die set. From Dillon Precision Products, Inc.
Price: **$208.95**

DILLON XL 650

Frame: Aluminum alloy
Frame Type: NA
Die Thread: $^7/_8$-14
Avg. Rounds Per Hour: 800-1000
Ram Stroke: $4^9/_{16}$"
Weight: 46 lbs.
Features: Five stations; auto indexing; auto case feed; removable tool head; auto prime system with 100-primer capacity; low primer supply alarm; auto powder measure; positive powder bar return; 220 ejected-round capacity bin; $^3/_4$-lb. capacity powder measure; 500-600 case feed capacity with optional auto case feed. Loads all pistol/rifle calibers less than $3^1/_2$" in length. From Dillon Precision Products, Inc.
Price: **$394.95**
Price: Factory set for one caliber **$434.90**

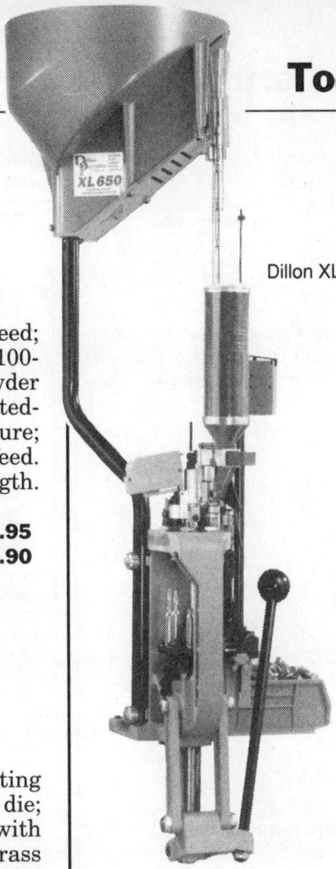
Dillon XL 650

HORNADY Pro-Jector

Frame: Die cast heat-treated aluminum alloy
Frame Type: O-frame
Die Thread: $^7/_8$-14
Avg. Rounds Per Hour: NA
Ram Stroke: $3^3/_4$"
Weight: 26 lbs.
Features: Five-station die platform with option of seating and crimping separately or adding taper-crimp die; auto prime with large and small primer tubes with 100-primer capacity and protective housing; brass kicker to eject loaded rounds into 80-round capacity cartridge catcher; offset operating handle for leverage and unobstructed operation; 2" diameter ram driven by heavy-duty cast linkage arms rotating on steel pins. Comes with Series I or II New Dimension dies, shellplate and auto primer feed and shut-off and brass kicker. Lifetime warranty. From Hornady Mfg. Co.
Price: **$370.20**
Price: With Series II dies **$382.65**

Lee Load-Master

LEE Load-Master

Frame: ASTM 380 aluminum
Frame Type: O-frame
Die Thread: $^7/_8$-14
Avg. Rounds Per Hour: 600
Ram Stroke: $3^1/_4$"
Weight: 8 lbs., 4 oz.
Features: A $1^1/_2$" diameter ram for handling largest magnum cases; loads rifle or pistol rounds; five-station press to factory crimp and post size; auto indexing with wedge lock mechanism that will hold one ton; auto priming; removable turrets; case inserter and optional four-tube case feeder; loaded round ejector with chute to optional loaded round catcher; quick change shell plate; primer catcher. Dies and shellholder not included. From Lee Precision, Inc.
Price: **$189.00**

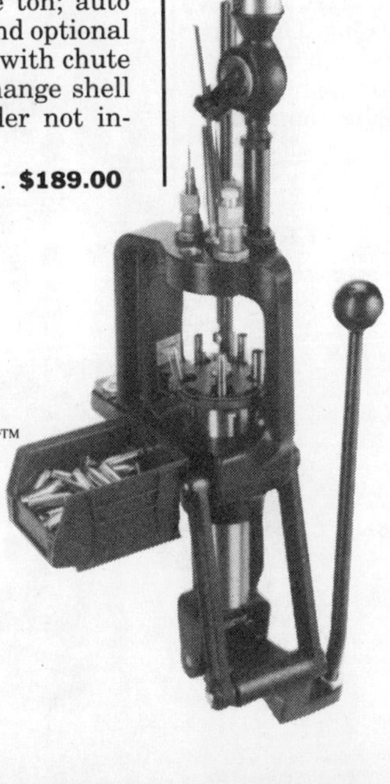
Hornady Pro-Jector™

HORNADY	
Pro-Jector New Dimension Dies	
SERIES I	SERIES II
222 Rem.	7.62x39
223 Rem.	9mm Luger
22-250	38/357/357 Max.
243 Win.	10mm Auto/40 S&W
270 Win.	41 Mag.
7mm Rem. Mag.	44 Spl./44 Mag.
30-30 Win.	45 ACP
308 Win.	45 Wea. Mag.
30-06	45 Auto Rim
300 Win. Mag.	45 Long Colt

LEE Pro 1000

Frame: ASTM 380 aluminum and steel
Frame Type: O-frame
Die Thread: $^7/_8$-14
Avg. Rounds Per Hour: 600
Ram Stroke: $3^1/_4$"
Weight: 8 lbs., 7 oz.
Features: Optional transparent large/small or rifle case feeder; deluxe auto-disk case-activated powder measure; case sensor for primer feed. Comes complete with carbide die set (steel dies for rifle) for one caliber. Optional accessories include: case feeder for large/small pistol cases or rifle cases; shell plate carrier with auto prime, case ejector, auto-index and spare parts; case collator for case feeder. From Lee Precision, Inc.
Price: **$189.98**

PONSNESS/WARREN Metallic II

Frame: Die cast aluminum
Frame Type: H-frame
Die Thread: $^7/_8$-14
Avg. Rounds Per Hour: 150+
Ram Stroke: NA
Weight: 32 lbs.
Features: Die head with five tapped $^7/_8$-14 holes for dies, powder measure or other accessories; pivoting die arm moves case from station to station; depriming tube for removal of spent primers; auto primer feed; interchangeable die head. Optional accessories include additional die heads, powder measure extension tube to accommodate any standard powder measure, primer speed feeder to feed press primer tube without disassembly. Comes with small and large primer seating tools. Dies, powder measure and shellholder not included. From Ponsness/Warren.
Price: **$269.00**
Price: Extra die head **$38.80**
Price: Primer speed feeder **$10.45**
Price: Powder measure extension **$15.70**

RCBS Auto 4x4

Frame: Cast iron
Frame Type: O-frame
Die Thread: $^7/_8$-14
Avg. Rounds Per Hour: 400-450
Ram Stroke: 3"
Weight: 27 lbs.
Features: Four-station press for high volume reloaders. Loads medium-length rifle or pistol cartridges. Can be used as a single-stage tool and has the strength to form wildcat cases or swage bullets. Comes with powder measure adaptor and assembly; depriming tube; large and small automatic primer feed assemblies; ammunition catch box and base; hex key wrenches; cleaning brush; resizing lubricant; primer tray; deprime bottle and cap. From RCBS.
Price: **$385.85**
Price: Shellplate **$28.22**

LEE Pro 1000 Die Sets
32 S&W Long
32 H&R Mag.
380 Auto
38 Spl.
357 Mag.
45 ACP
9mm Luger
40 S&W
10mm Auto
41 Mag.
44 Spl.
44 Mag.
45 Colt
223*

*With steel rifle charge die.
Other calibers not stocked but made to order include: 7.62x39 Russian; 32 Auto; 38 Auto and 38 Super; 222 Rem.; 30 M1 Carbine.

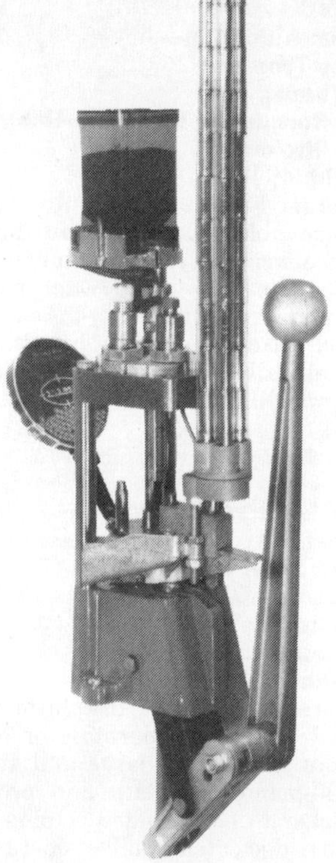

Lee Pro 1000

Ponsness/Warren Metallic II

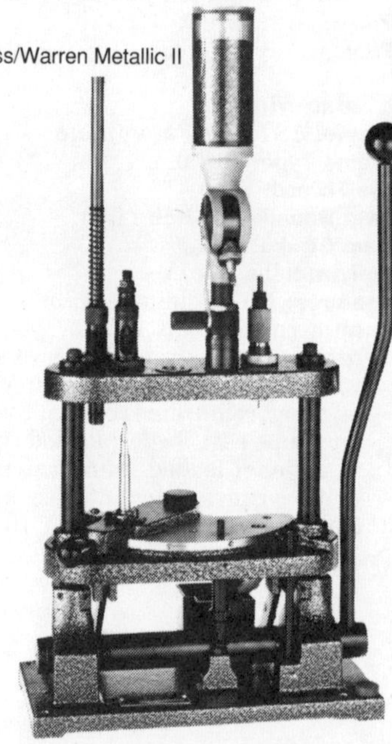

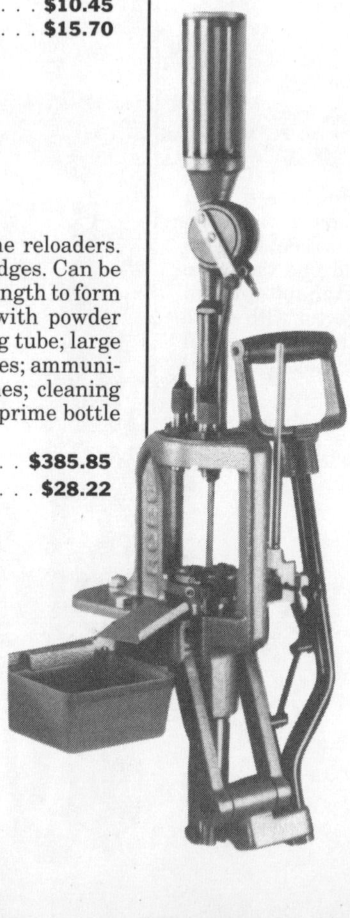

RCBS Auto 4x4

RCBS AmmoMaster-Auto

Frame: Aluminum base; cast iron top plate connected by three steel posts.
Frame Type: NA
Die Thread: $1\frac{1}{4}$"-12 bushing; $\frac{7}{8}$-14 threads
Avg. Rounds Per Hour: 50-60
Ram Stroke: $5\frac{1}{4}$"
Weight: 19 lbs.
Features: Progressive press convertible to single-stage. Features include: automatic indexing, priming, powder charging and loaded round ejection. Case detection system disengages powder measure when no case is present in powder charging station. Comes with five-station shellplate and Uniflow powder measure with clear powder measure adaptor to make bridged powders visible and correctable. Piggyback die plate for quick caliber change-over available. Reloading dies not included. From RCBS.

Price: **$403.64**
Price: Auto-to-single kit **$68.76**
Price: Piggyback/AmmoMaster die plate **$21.33**
Price: Piggyback/AmmoMaster shellplate **$26.22**
Price: Press cover **$6.93**

STAR Universal Pistol Press

Frame: Cast iron with aluminum base
Frame Type: Unconventional
Die Thread: $\frac{11}{16}$-24 or $\frac{7}{8}$-14
Avg. Rounds Per Hour: 300
Ram Stroke: NA
Weight: 27 lbs.
Features: Four or five-station press depending on need to taper crimp; handles all popular handgun calibers from 32 Long to 45 Colt. Comes completely assembled and adjusted with carbide dies (except 30 Carbine) and shellholder to load one caliber. From Star Machine Works.

Price: With taper crimp **$947.00**
Price: Without taper crimp **$925.00**
Price: Extra tool head, taper crimp **$367.00**
Price: Extra tool head, w/o taper crimp **$345.00**

STAR Universal Rifle Press

Frame: Cast iron with aluminum base
Frame Type: Unconventional
Die Thread: $\frac{7}{8}$-14
Avg. Rounds Per Hour: 300
Ram Stroke: NA
Weight: 30 lbs.
Features: Same as pistol press but has length of stroke to handle most popular large rifle calibers. Shellplate and expander plug included, dies not included. Comes completely assembled. From Star Machine Works.

Price: **$1,500.00**

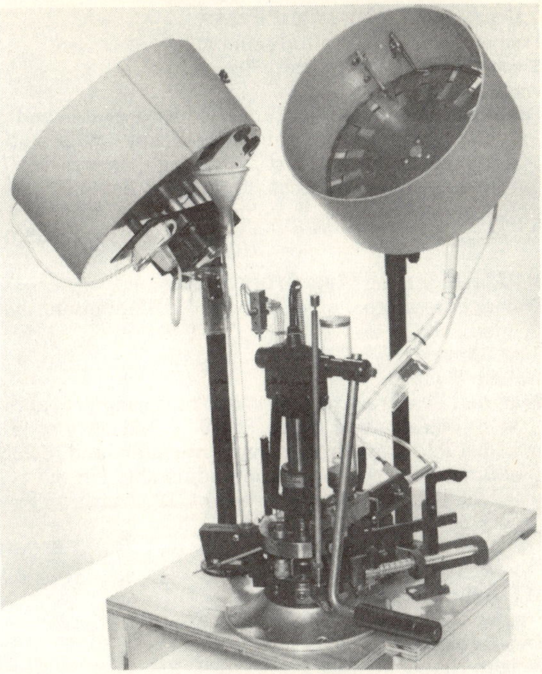

Fully-automated Star Universal

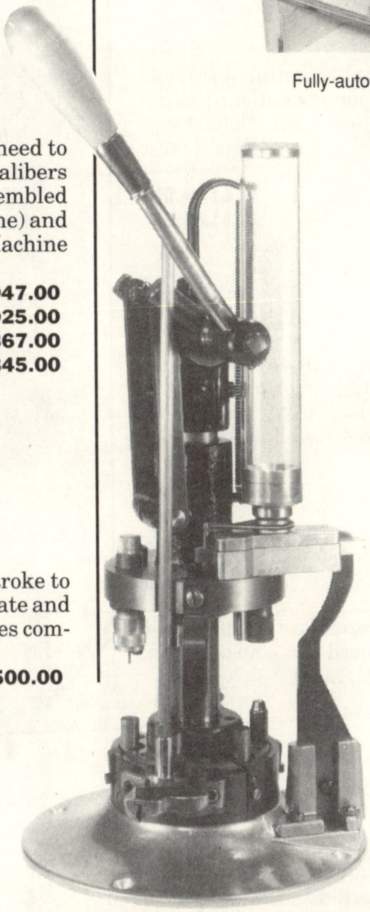

Star Universal

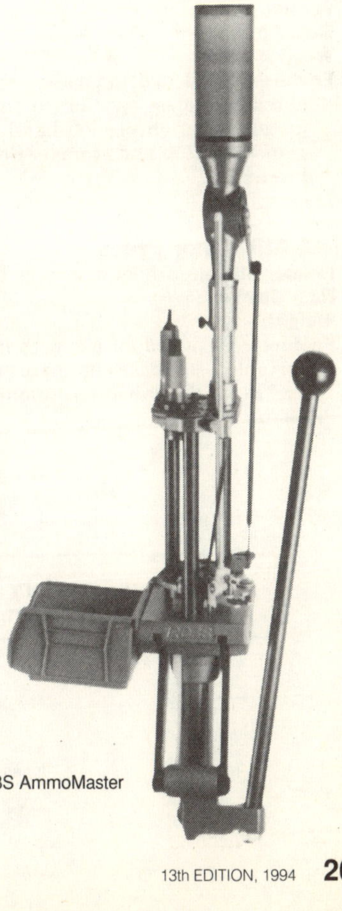

RCBS AmmoMaster

BALD EAGLE Lightweight Press
Frame: 2024-T6 aircraft aluminum
Mechanical Advantage: 1:5
Weight: 1.25 lbs.
Features: Spring-loaded plunger which elevates and returns handle to original position. Uses Wilson-style seater die. Main support is $6\frac{5}{8}$" high; base is 3" x 5". Finish is black hardcoat. From Bald Eagle Precision Machine Co.
Price: **$55.00**

B-SQUARE Super Mag Arbor Press
Frame: Stress-proof steel with 60/61T6 aluminum base and head
Ram Stroke: $1\frac{1}{2}$"
Weight: $8\frac{1}{2}$ lbs.
Features: Features twin posts for "no-spring"; capability to full-length size up to 30-06 in Wilson die; fully adjustable press head; spring return ram and replaceable brass caps; $4\frac{1}{2}$" handle adjustable for right- or left-hand use. Dimensions: height, 12"; width, 4". From B-Square Company.
Price: **$99.50**

HART Arbor Press
Frame: Steel and aluminum
Ram Stroke: 3.5"
Weight: NA
Features: Bronze bushings; vertical adjustment from 1" to 7"; handle offers 2" stroke per revolution; locking handle for securing vertical adjustments. Deluxe version available with spring return on ram. From Robert W. Hart & Son, Inc.
Price: **$108.95**
Price: Deluxe press **$125.95**

JONES Arbor Press
Frame: Aluminum alloy
Ram Stroke: NA
Weight: 4 lbs.
Features: Hardened and polished steel guide post; adjustable head; open base for catching spent primers; adjustable for right- or left-hand use; easy takedown for transportation and storage. From Neil Jones Custom Products.
Price: **$125.00**

SINCLAIR Arbor Press
Frame: Stainless steel with steel base
Ram Stroke: $3\frac{1}{2}$"
Weight: $4\frac{1}{2}$ lbs.
Features: Designed for use with hand dies; compact and portable; steel base eliminates need to clamp down for use. From Sinclair International, Inc.
Price: **$65.00**

Consult our Directory pages for the location of firms mentioned.

Bald Eagle Lightweight

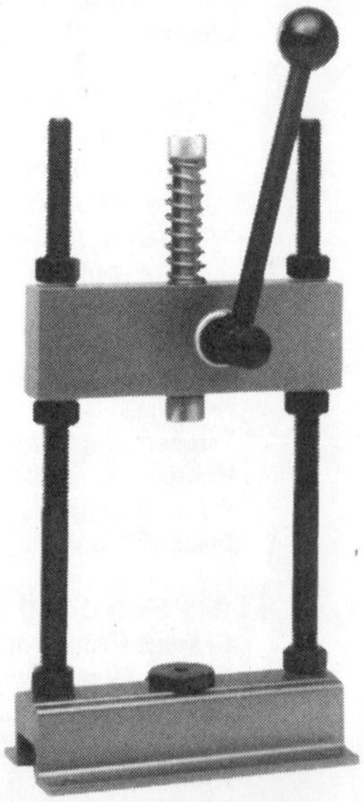
B-Square Super Mag Arbor

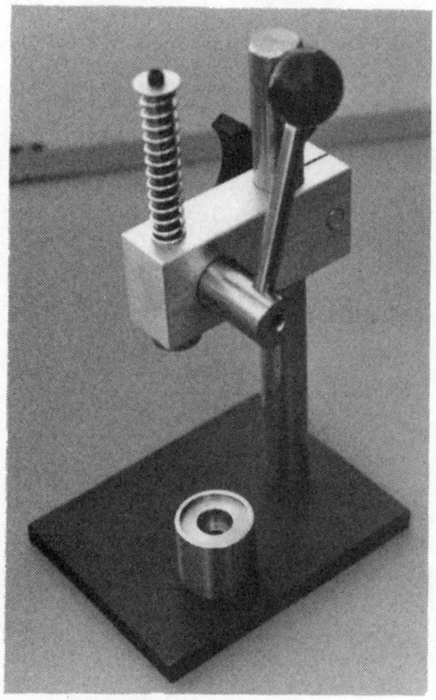
Sinclair Arbor Press

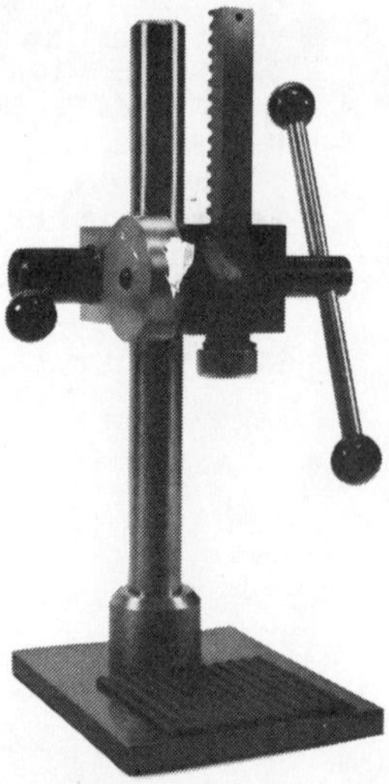
Hart Arbor Press

Jones Arbor Press

BULLET SWAGING SUPPLY

Rock Chucker Conversion Unit

Converts RCBS Rock Chucker into swaging press. Consists of modified ram for swaging, a punch holder and ejector pin. One hole must be drilled in base of press for ejector pin. Includes BSS 3-die set. From Bullet Swaging Supply, Inc.

Price: **$270.00**

C-H/4-D

Auto Champ Conversion Parts

To convert the discontinued Auto Champ progressive press from one caliber to another. From C-H Tool & Die/4-D Custom Die.

Price: . . . . **See chart for pricing.**

Auto Champ Handle

A spade or shovel-type handle for the discontinued C-H Auto Champ progressive press. Made from steel with wooden handle. Adds $2\frac{1}{2}$" length to present handle. Supplied with screw. From C-H Tool & Die/4-D Custom Die.

Price: **$15.00**

"H" Ram

Can be used with any Hollywood or Dunbar press and will accept any universal shellholder head. From C-H Tool & Die/4-D Custom Die.

Price: **$6.95**

Shellholder Adaptor

Fits all Herters and Lachmiller presses which use one or two setscrews to hold shellholder. Adapts them to standard snap-in shellholder. From C-H Tool & Die/4-D Custom Die.

Price: **$12.95**

Shellholder Extension

For use when trimming short cases in file trim die. Extends shellholders $\frac{3}{4}$". From C-H Tool & Die/4-D Custom Die.

Price: **$10.95**

Universal "C" Ram

Features relieved clearance for primer and floating shellholder action for alignment. Shellholder not included. From C-H Tool & Die/4-D Custom Die.

Price: **$14.95**

Universal Shellholders

Detachable shellholders fit all popular presses. From C-H Tool & Die/4-D Custom Die.

Price: **$4.50**

C-H/4-D

Auto Champ Caliber Conversion Parts

Caliber	Die System	Mk III, IV Priming System	Mk Va Priming System	Main Slide	Rails
10mm	$74.00	$18.00	$20.15	$40.00	$37.00
32 S&W	69.00	18.00	20.15	40.00	37.00
38/357	65.00	18.00	20.15	40.00	37.00
40 S&W	74.00	18.00	20.15	40.00	37.00
41 Mag.	69.00	18.00	20.15	40.00	37.00
44 Mag.	65.00	18.00	20.15	40.00	37.00
45 ACP	65.00	18.00	20.15	40.00	37.00
45 Colt	69.00	18.00	20.15	40.00	37.00
9mm Luger	69.00	18.00	20.15	40.00	37.00

C-H/4-D Shellholder Extension

C-H/4-D Shellholders

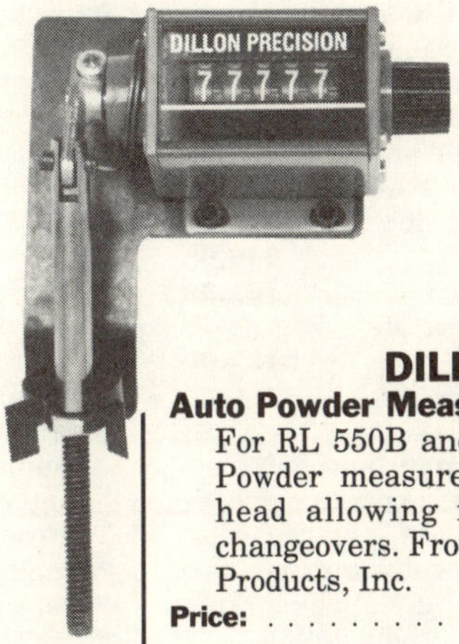

Dillon Cartridge Counter

C-H/4-D Auto Champ Handle

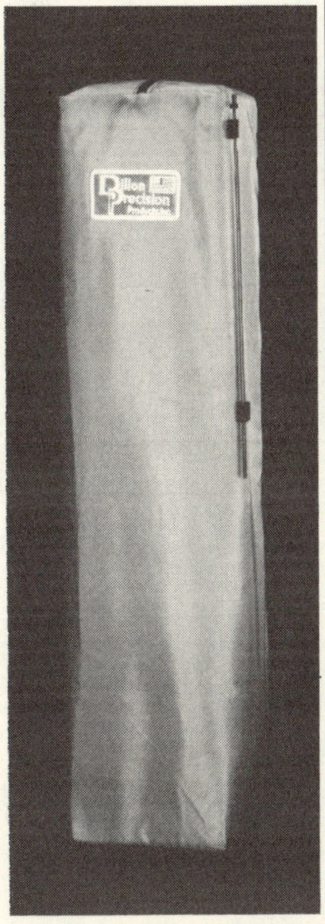

Dillon Press Cover

DILLON

Auto Powder Measure System

For RL 550B and XL 650 presses. Powder measure to fit extra tool head allowing for quick caliber changeovers. From Dillon Precision Products, Inc.

Price: **$43.95**

Bench Wrenches

Has all correct sizes for Dillon dies, powder systems and press adjustments. From Dillon Precision Products, Inc.

Price: **$4.95**

Cartridge Counter

Attaches to all Dillon presses or any "crimp only" crimp die. Counts number of rounds of loaded ammo. From Dillon Precision Products, Inc.

Price: **$15.95**

Powder Dies

Designed for the XL 650 press. Allows moving powder measure from tool head to tool head without changing the "belling" adjustment. From Dillon Precision Products, Inc.

Price: **$4.50**

Press Covers

Packcloth nylon machine cover for all Dillon presses. Features D-ring for locking heavy-duty zipper and optional master lock. From Dillon Precision Products, Inc.

Price: RL 550B/Square Deal B with lock **$22.90**

Price: RL 550B/Square Deal B cover only **$19.95**

Price: RL 1050/XL 650 with lock **$37.90**

Price: RL 1050/XL 650 cover only **$34.95**

DILLON

RL 550B Caliber Conversion Kits

Contains shellplate, powder funnel and locator buttons. See chart for available calibers. From Dillon Precision Products, Inc.

Price: All calibers **$25.50**

RL 1050 and XL 650 Powder Check System

Automatically checks cases for over or under powder charges. From Dillon Precision Products, Inc.

Price: **$49.95**

RL 1050 Caliber Conversion Kits

Includes dies (optional), shellplate, locator buttons, swage backup rod/expander, case feed adapter, case feed plunger and powder funnel. See chart for available calibers. From Dillon Precision Products, Inc.

Price: With dies **$96.95**
Price: No dies **$61.95**
Price: 223, 30M1 with carbide dies **$137.00**

Square Deal B Conversion Kits

Carbide sizer die, expander/powder funnel, seat die, crimp die, shellplate and locator buttons. See chart for available calibers. From Dillon Precision Products, Inc.

Price: **$52.00**

DILLON

Tool Head Conversion Assembly

A separate stand-alone unit used in conjunction with Dillon caliber conversion kit to change calibers easily on Dillon progressive presses. **RL 550B Assembly:** Includes toolhead, powder measure, powder die, cartridge counter and tool head stand; dies optional. **RL 1050 Assembly:** Comes with tool head, powder measure and cartridge counter. **XL 650 Assembly:** Tool head, tool head stand, powder measure and cartridge counter. From Dillon Precision Products, Inc.

Price: RL 550B with dies **$105.90**
Price: RL 550B without dies **$65.95**
Price: RL 1050 . . . . **$154.85**
Price: XL 650 . . . . **$67.95**

Tool Heads

For Dillon RL 550B, Square Deal B and XL 650 progressive presses for caliber changeovers. Keeps dies in alignment to eliminate time-consuming die adjustment when changing calibers. Tool head stand extra. From Dillon Precision Products, Inc.

Price: RL 550B **$9.95**
Price: Square Deal B **$16.50**
Price: XL 650 . . . . **$12.95**
Price: Tool head stand **$5.00**

Dillon
Tool Head Assembly

DILLON RL 550B
Caliber Conversion Kits

RIFLE				PISTOL
17 Rem.	257 Wea. Mag.	32 Rem.	6.5-06	30 Mauser
218 Bee	25 Rem.	32 Win. Special	6.5x52 Carcano	30 Luger
219 Zipper	264 Win. Mag.	33 Win.	6.5x54 Mann.-Sch.	32 S&W Mag.
219 Donaldson	270 Win.	338 Win.	6.5x55 Swedish	32 H&R Mag.
220 Swift	270 Wea. Mag.	340 Wea. Mag.	6.5 Jap.	32 Short Colt
221 Rem. Fireball	280 Rem.	348 Win.	6.5 Rem. Mag.	32 ACP
222 Rem.	284 Win.	350 Rem. Mag.	6mm PPC	380 ACP
22-250	30 M1 Carbine	356 Win.	7mm-08	9mm
222 Rem. Mag.	300 Win. Mag.	357 Herrett	7.62x39 Russian	38 S&W
223 Rem.	30-06	358 Win.	7.65x53 Mauser	38AMU
224 Wea. Mag.	300 H&H	358 Norma Mag.	7.62x54 Russ. Rim.	38 Super
225 Win.	300 Savage	35 Rem.	7mmx57 Mauser	38/357 Mag.
22 Hornet	300 Wea. Mag.	35 Win.	7x64 Brenneke	10mm/40 S&W
22 Rem. Jet	303 British	35 Whelen	7.7 Japanese	41 AE
22 Sav. Hi-Power	30-30 Win.	375 Win.	7mm BR	41 Mag.
240 Wea. Mag.	30-338 Win.	375 H&H Mag.	7mm Express	44 Special
243 Win.	30-40 Krag	375 Super Mag.	7mm Int'l.	44 Mag.
244 Rem.	307 Win.	375 Wea. Mag.	7mm Rem. Mag.	45 ACP
250 Savage	308	38-40 Win.	7mm Merrill	45 Auto Rim
25-06	308 Norma Mag.	38-55 Win.	7mm Int'l Rimmed	455 Webley
25-20 Win.	30 Herrett	416 Rem. Mag.	7mm TCU	45 Long Colt
25-35 Win.	30 Merrill	444 Marlin	7mm Wea. Mag.	45 Win. Mag.
256 Win. Mag.	30 Rem.	45-70 Gov't.	8mm Mauser	454 Casull
257 Roberts	32-20 Win.	458 Win. Mag.	8mm Rem. Mag.	
257 Ackley Imp.	32-40 Win.	6mm Rem.		

DILLON Square Deal B
Caliber Conversion Kits

- 380 ACP
- 38 Special
- 357 Magnum
- 38 Super
- 9mm
- 40 S&W
- 10mm
- 41 Magnum
- 44 Magnum
- 44-40 Win.
- 45 ACP
- 45 Colt

DILLON RL 1050
Caliber Conversion Kits

- 32 S&W
- 380 Auto
- 9mm
- 38 Super
- 38/357 Mag.
- 40 S&W
- 10mm
- 41 Magnum
- 44 Magnum
- 45 ACP
- 45 Long Colt
- 223
- 30M1 Carbine
- 7.62x39

DILLON

XL 650 Caliber Conversion Kits

Comes complete with shellplate, locator buttons, powder funnel and casefeed adapter parts. See chart for available calibers. From Dillon Precision Products, Inc.

Price: **$46.25**

XL 650 Case Feed Assembly

To change to large pistol, small pistol, large rifle or small rifle. Comes with case feed bin, case feed tube and attachment bar. From Dillon Precision Products, Inc.

Price: **$134.95**
Price: Extra case feed plate **$28.50**

FORSTER

Shellholder/Primer Conversion Kit

For Co-Ax presses manufactured prior to 1983. Converts old shellholder/primer system to the current "S" jaw/primer catcher system. From Forster Products.

Price: **$35.00**

Forster Conversion Kit

DILLON XL 650
Caliber Conversion Kits

RIFLE	PISTOL
17 Rem.	30 Luger
22 Rem. Jet	30 Mauser
221 Rem. Fireball	32 ACP-7.65mm
222 Rem.	32 H&R
222 Rem. Mag.	32 Short Colt
22-250	32 S&W
223-5.56mm	9mm
224 Wea. Mag.	380 ACP
243 Win.	38 Super
25-06	38/357 Mag.
256 Win. Mag.	10mm/40S&W
257 Roberts	41 Mag.
257 Ackley Imp.	44 Special
270 Win.	44 Mag.
30M1 Carbine	45 ACP
30-06	454 Casull
303 British	45 Long Colt
30-30 Win.	
308-7.62 Nato	

HOLLYWOOD

Primer Feed

Fits Hollywood Senior Turret press for automatic priming of cases. Available for standard rifle/pistol cases as well as 50-caliber and shotgun primers. From Hollywood Engineering.

Price: Rifle/pistol **$35.00**
Price: 50-cal./shotgun **$45.00**
Price: Primer tube with spring . . . **$15.00**
Price: Tube only **$10.00**
Price: Primer tube spring **$5.00**

Shellholder Extension

Shortens stroke on Hollywood presses. Makes loading small cartridges easier and assists in case forming and heavy press work. Must have special priming rod. From Hollywood Engineering.

Price: **$15.00**

Special Priming Rod

For use with shellholder extension and Universal shellholder and button inserts. Height will depend on combination of use. Specify press model and primer size. For all Hollywood presses. From Hollywood Engineering.

Price: **$25.00**

HORNADY
00-7 Kit New Dimension Dies

SERIES I	SERIES II
222 Rem.	38/357/357 Max.
223 Rem.	41 Rem. Mag.
22-250	44 Spl./44 Mag.
243 Win.	45 ACP
270 Win.	45 Wea. Mag.
7x57 Mauser	45 Auto Rim
7mm Rem. Mag.	45 Long Colt
30-30 Win.	
308 Win.	
30-06	
300 Win. Mag.	
9mm Luger	

Hornady 00-7 Reloading Kit

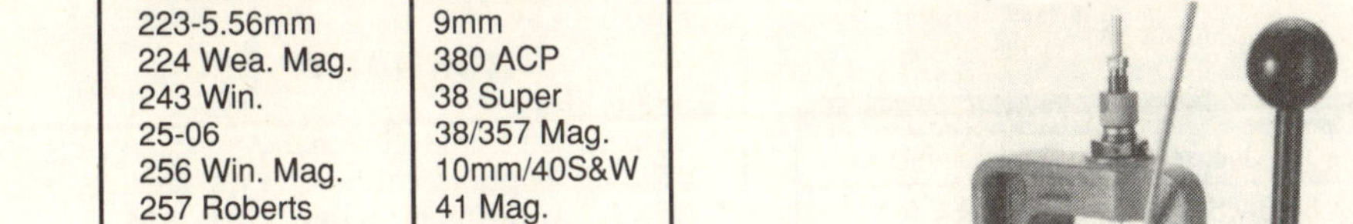

HOLLYWOOD

Senior and Universal Turret Head Plates

Turret head plates for the Hollywood Senior press can be ordered in four configurations: eight, 1 1/2-12 threaded holes for large dies; four 1 1/2-12 threaded holes; four, 7/8-12 holes; or eight, 7/8-14 holes. Turret plates are also available for the old Hollywood Universal press. Available as standard turret or solid aluminum 10-hole turret threaded 1 1/2-12 for use with all large dies. From Hollywood Engineering.

Price: Senior **$80.00**
Price: Universal, standard **$100.00**
Price: Universal, 10-hole **$200.00**

Standard Priming Rod

For use on all Hollywood presses. Specify press, small or large, flat or oval, pistol or rifle. From Hollywood Engineering.

Price: Standard calibers **$20.00**
Price: 50 BMG **$30.00**
Price: 20mm **$40.00**
Price: Shotgun **$30.00**

Universal Shellholder

Will accept all button inserts. Must have special priming rods for use on Hollywood presses. From Hollywood Engineering.

Price: Standard calibers **$10.00**
Price: Shellholder inserts **$6.00**
Price: 50 BMG **$30.00**
Price: 20mm **$40.00**
Price: Shotgun **$25.00**

HORNADY

00-7 Reloading Kit

Includes 00-7 press plus set of New Dimension or Series III dies with shellholder; die wrench; deluxe powder measure; powder scale; Universal reloading block; powder funnel; primer turning tray; case lube; chamfer/debur tool; three case neck brushes; large and small primer pocket cleaners; accessory handle; reloading video. From Hornady Mfg. Co.

Price: With ND dies **$314.95**
Price: With Series III dies **$329.05**

Brass Kicker

Accessory for Hornady Pro-Jector press to automatically eject loaded round with each stroke of the press handle. From Hornady Mfg. Co.

Price: . . . . . **Contact the manufacturer.**

HORNADY

Accessory Pack

Reloading accessories minus the press and shellholder. Includes deluxe powder measure; magnetic scale; nonstatic Universal powder funnel; Universal reloading tray; primer turning plate; Unique case lube; chamfer and debur tool; three case neck brushes; large and small primer pocket cleaners; accessory handle; reloading video. From Hornady Mfg. Co.

Price: **$169.25**

Auto Powder Drop

Progressive press accessory for Hornady, RCBS and Redding powder measures. Allows powder to be dispensed automatically with each pull of the press handle. Includes rod, spindle, powder measure handle, spring and brackets. Weight: 1 lb. From Hornady Mfg. Co.

Price: **$18.75**

Auto Primer Shutoff

Standard on the Hornady Pro-Jector press, primer shutoff also available as accessory. Allows removing primer tubes from auto primer feed without spilling primers. Weight: 4 oz. From Hornady Mfg. Co.

Price: **$9.35**

Automatic Primer Feed

For 00-7 and 0-7 single-stage presses. Comes with large and small primer tubes. Weight: 1 lb. From Hornady Mfg. Co.

Price: **$18.75**

Large Cartridge Catcher

Holds one-third more reloaded cartridges than standard catcher on Pro-Jector press. Capacity for over 100 rounds. Weight: 1 lb. From Hornady Mfg. Co.

Price: **$4.70**

Pro-Jector Reloading Kit

Includes Pro-Jector press, New Dimension dies, shellplate plus deluxe powder measure; magnetic scale; Unique case lube; primer turning plate; Universal reloading block; powder funnel; chamfer/debur tool; large and small primer pocket cleaner; three case neck brushes; accessory handle; and *Hornady Handbook of Cartridge Reloading* video tape. From Hornady Mfg. Co.

Price: With ND dies **$533.10**
Price: With Series II dies **$545.30**

Hornady Shellholder Extension

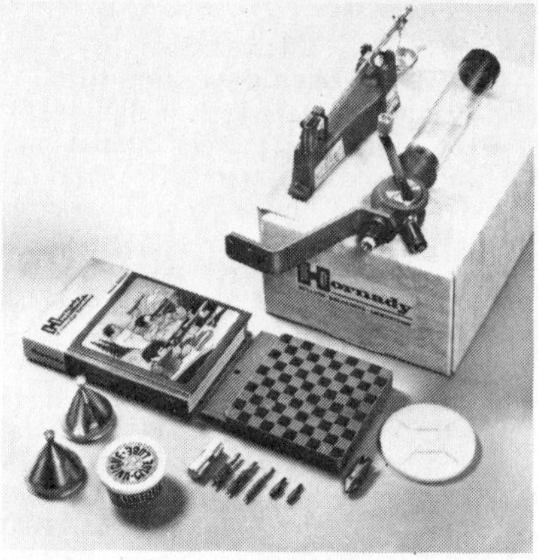

Hornady Accessory Pack

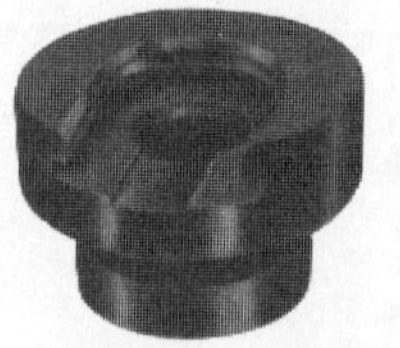

Hornady Shellholder

Hornady Pro-Jector Reloading Kit

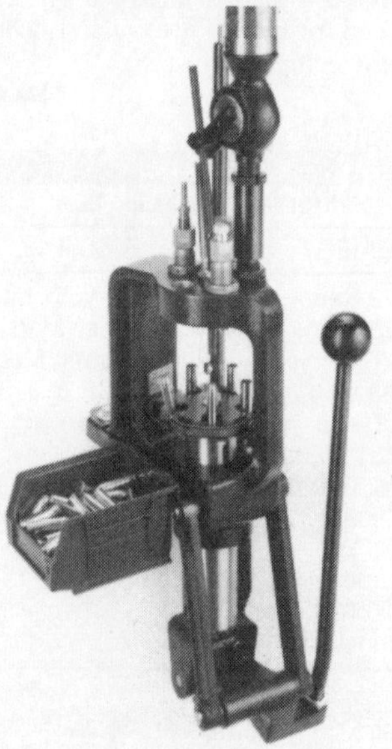

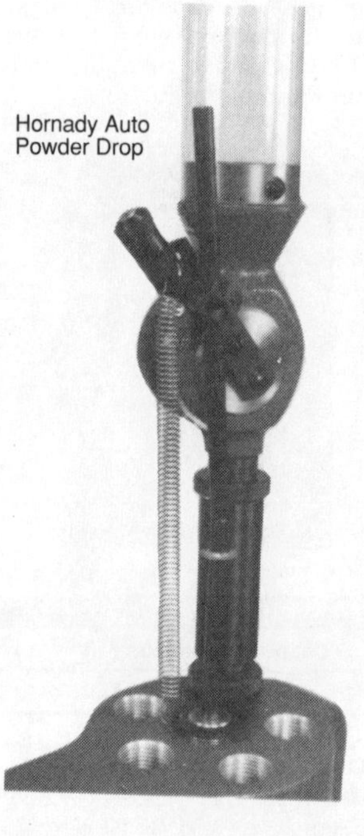

Hornady Auto Powder Drop

HORNADY
Pro-Jector Kit New Dimension Dies

SERIES I	SERIES II
222 Rem.	38/357/357 Max.
223 Rem.	10mm/40 S&W
22-250	41 Mag.
243 Win.	44 Spl./44 Mag.
270 Win.	45 ACP
7x57 Mauser	45 Wea. Mag.
7mm Rem. Mag.	45 Auto Rim
30-30 Win.	45 Long Colt
308 Win.	
30-06	
300 Win. Mag.	
7.62x39	
9mm Luger	

HORNADY

Shellholder

Machined from solid steel. Available for all popular calibers. Fits Hornady and most other standard presses. Weight: 1/4-lb. From Hornady Mfg. Co.

Price: **$4.65**

Shellholder Extension

Fits all rams designed for universal shellholders. Extension shellholder number corresponds with standard, removable-head shellholder number. Available in #1, #2 and #16. Weight: 1/4-lb. From Hornady Mfg. Co.

Price: **$9.40**

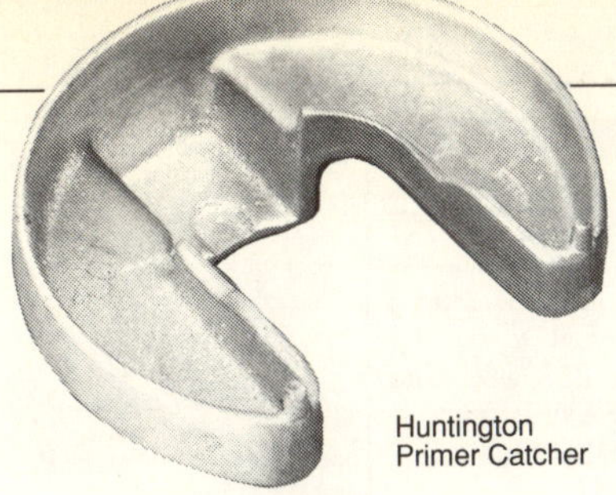

Huntington Primer Catcher

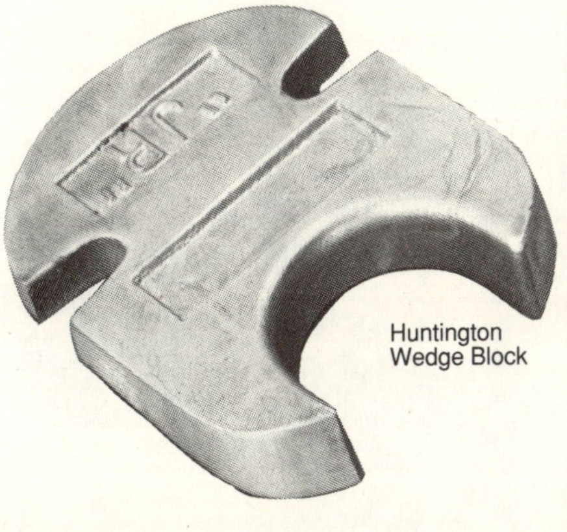

Huntington Wedge Block

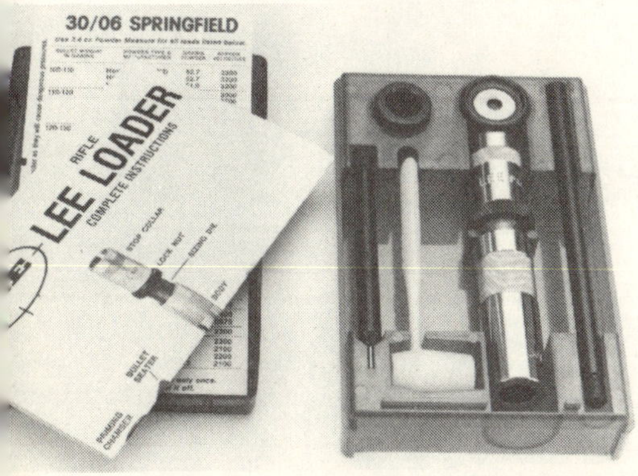

Lee Loader Kit

Lee Case Feeder

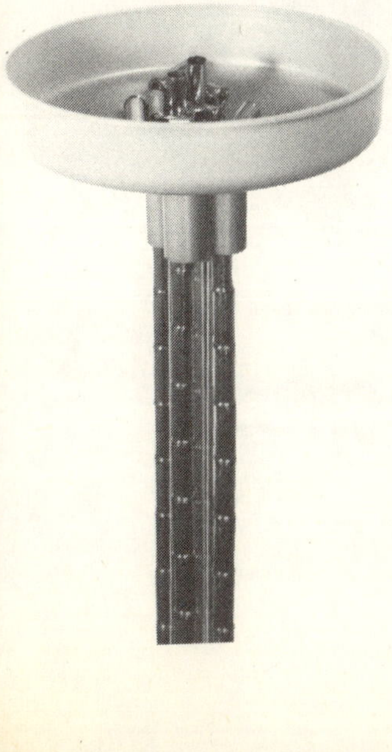

HUNTINGTON

Aluminum Primer Catcher

Designed for RCBS reloading presses to replace plastic primer catcher standard on Rock Chucker, Jr. or Reloader Special-5. Cast from aluminum and designed to attach to press with rubberband. From Huntington Die Specialties.

Price: **$6.98**

Aluminum Wedge Block

For the old RCBS Jr. press. Allows the press to be tipped back at a more comfortable angle. From Huntington Die Specialties.

Price: **$6.98**

KLEINENDORST

Expand-Iron

Smooths and rounds case mouth or, with next larger caliber size mandrel, expands 22 case to 6mm, 6mm to 25 or 7mm to 30. Fits all standard threaded presses. Stop screw at end of plug adjusts to contact inside web of case head to prevent damage to case neck or shoulder. Pilots for 17 through 30 caliber available. Comes complete for one caliber. From Bob Pease Accuracy.

Price: **$20.00**
Price: Extra pilots **$11.00**

LEE
Hand Press Kit Calibers

RIFLE	PISTOL
223	9mm Luger
243	38 Spl.
270	357 Mag.
30-30	44 Spl.
308	44 Mag.
30-06	45 ACP

These are Lee PaceSetter dies with crimp die.

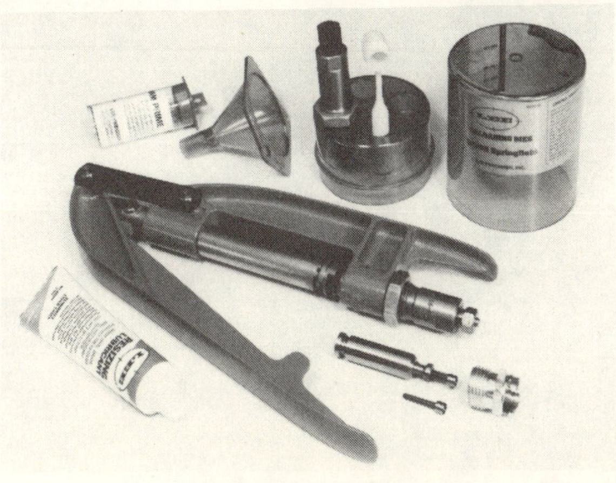

Lee Hand Press Kit

LEE

Anniversary Reloading Kit

Includes Lee Challenger press; Lee Perfect powder measure; Lee Safety scale; powder funnel with powder data manual; case cutter and lock stud for trimming cases; chamfer tool; tube of sizing lube; Lee Auto-Prime tool with shellholders for over 115 cartridges; primer pocket cleaner. From Lee Precision, Inc.

Price: **$99.98**

Case Feeder

For the Lee Pro 1000 and Load-Master presses. Transparent four-tube case feeder for large or small pistol and rifle cases. Large pistol case feeder will handle 38 Special, 357 Magnum, 41 Magnum, 44 Special, 44 Magnum, 45 ACP, 45 Colt, 10mm Auto and 7.62x39 Russian cases. Small feeder handles 9mm Luger, 380 Auto, 32 Auto, 32 S&W Long, 32 H&R Magnum, 38 Auto and 38 Super. Rifle feeder takes 222, 223 and 30 M1 cases. Extra case feeder tubes available. From Lee Precision, Inc.

Price: All sizes **$25.00**
Price: Extra tubes, 7-pack **$4.00**

Challenger Press Kit

Includes Lee Challenger press; ram prime; powder funnel; case sizing lube; dies for one caliber with shellholder; powder dipper and load data. Available in 2-die rifle sets or 3-die carbide pistol sets. Special kit price with purchase of Lee die set. From Lee Precision, Inc.

Price: 2-die kit **$66.98**
Price: 3-die kit **$73.98**
Price: With Lee die set **$39.98**

Hand Press Kit

Includes hand press; ram prime; powder funnel; case sizing lube; dies for one caliber and shellholder; powder dipper; and load data. Available in 2-die rifle sets or 3-die carbide pistol sets. Special kit price with purchase of Lee die set. From Lee Precision, Inc.

Price: 2-die set **$54.98**
Price: 3-die set **$59.98**
Price: With Lee die set **$26.98**

Load-Master Pistol Kit

Comes with Lee Load-Master press, carbide die set for one caliber, Deluxe Auto-Disk powder measure and a case feeder. From Lee Precision, Inc.

Price: **$330.00**

LEE

Load-Master Rifle Kit
Includes Lee Load-Master press, Lee Pace-Setter dies, Perfect powder measure, Universal charge die and case inserter. From Lee Precision, Inc.
Price: **$320.00**

Load-Master Shellplate
Five-station shellplate for Lee Load-Master. From Lee Precision, Inc.
Price: **$29.98**

Load-Master Turret
Five-station turret for Lee Load-Master press with 20 locking lugs for quick caliber changeover. From Lee Precision, Inc.
Price: **$14.98**

Loaded Round Catcher
Accessory for Lee Load-Master. Made of tough plastic. Capacity for 100 45 ACP rounds. From Lee Precision, Inc.
Price: **$14.98**

Loader
Kit consists of reloading dies to be used with mallet or soft hammer. Neck sizes only. Comes with powder charge cup. From Lee Precision, Inc.
Price: **$19.98**

Pro 1000 Shell Plate Carrier
To change calibers entire shellplate carrier can be replaced. Includes shellplate, Auto Prime, case ejector, Auto Index and spare parts. From Lee Precision, Inc.
Price: **$53.98**

Pro 1000 Shellplates
Three-station shellplates for Lee Pro 1000. If converting to caliber of different primer size, Pro 1000 primer attachment must be ordered. From Lee Precision, Inc.
Price: **$20.00**

Ram Prime
Primes on press up-stroke. Includes punches for large and small primers. From Lee Precision, Inc.
Price: **$11.98**

Shellholder Box
Plastic transparent box to hold eleven shellholders. From Lee Precision, Inc.
Price: **$2.60**

Shellholder Set
Eleven shellholders to fit over 115 of the most popular cartridges. From Lee Precision, Inc.
Price: **$19.98**

Turret Press Kit
Includes Lee Turret press; Auto-Index with factory installed and adjusted carbide dies for one caliber; shellholder. From Lee Precision, Inc.
Price: **$102.98**

LEE — Turret Kit Calibers

PISTOL
9mm Luger
38 Spl.
357 Mag.
41 Mag.
44 Spl.
44 Mag.
45 ACP
45 Long Colt
223 (with rifle charge die)

LEE — Shellplate Carrier Calibers

SHELLPLATE #	CALIBER
1	38 Spl., 357 Mag.
2	45 ACP
4	222, 223, 380 Auto, 32 S&W Long, 32 H&R Mag.
7A	30 M1 Carbine
9	41 Mag.
11	44 Spl., 44 Mag., 45 Colt
19	40 S&W, 9mm Luger, 38 Super, 38 Auto, 41 AE
19L	10mm Auto

LEE — Challenger Press Kit Calibers

RIFLE	PISTOL
223	9mm Luger
243	38 Spl.
270	357 Mag.
30-30	44 Spl.
308	44 Mag.
30-06	45 ACP

These are Lee PaceSetter dies with crimp die.

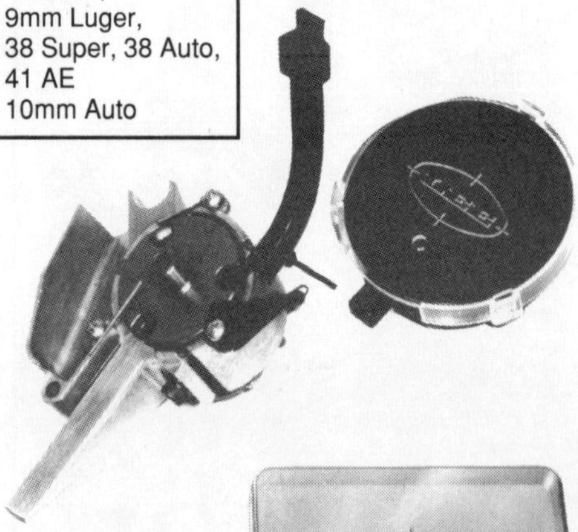
Lee Pro 1000 Shell Plate Carrier

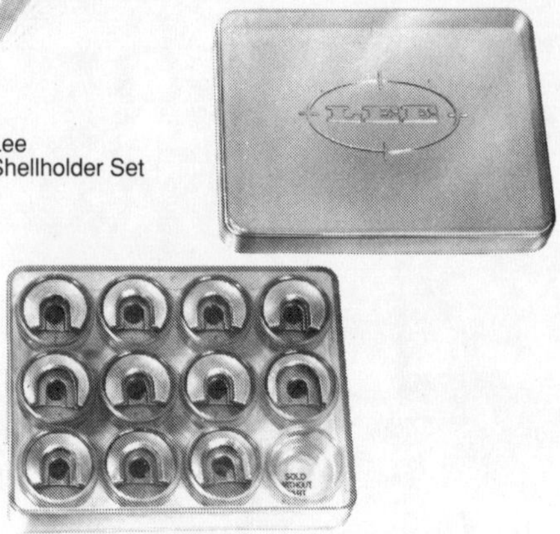
Lee Shellholder Set

Lee Load-Master Turret

Lee Turret Press Kit

Lee Load-Master Shellplate

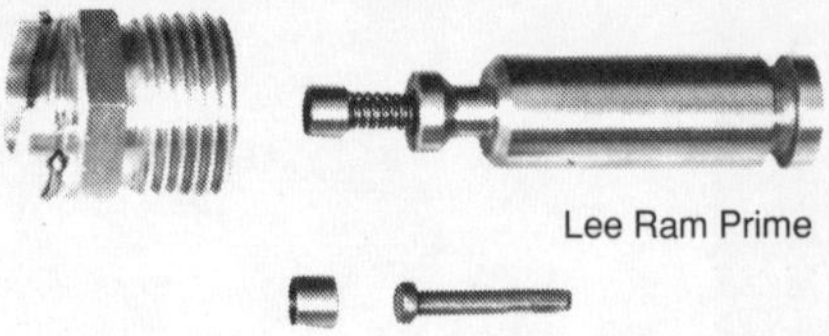
Lee Ram Prime

LYMAN

AccuLine Starter Kit
Includes AccuPress, AccuScale, case lube kit, ram prime die, deburring tool, powder funnel, primer tray, loading block and *Metallic Reloading User's Guide*. From Lyman Products Corporation.
Price: **$99.95**

Ammo Handler Kit
Accessory kit without the press. Comes with No. 55 powder measure; Model 500 scale; case lube kit; powder funnel; deburring tool; primer tray; loading block; *Metallic Reloading User's Guide*; Accurate Arms powder load data booklet. From Lyman Products Corporation.
Price: **$174.95**

Auto-Primer Feed
For T-Mag and Orange Crusher presses. Specify older presses when ordering. Comes with two tubes, large and small. Weight: 3 lbs., 1 oz. From Lyman Proucts Corporation.
Price: **$20.00**

Detachable Shellholder
Precisely machined and hardened for Orange Crusher, O-Mag, T-Mag or Special-T presses. From Lyman Products Corporation.
Price: **$6.40**

Orange Crusher Starter Kit
Kit contains Orange Crusher press; choice of Model 500 powder scale or AccuScale; case lube kit; loading block; powder funnel; primer tray; *Lyman 47th Edition Reloading Handbook*. Weight: 25 lbs. (500 scale); 24 lbs. (AccuScale). From Lyman Products Corporation.
Price: With 500 scale **$199.95**
Price: With AccuScale **$174.95**

Primer Catcher
Heavy-duty plastic. Locks securely to Orange Crusher, T-Mag, Special-T and Spar-T presses. From Lyman Products Corporation.
Price: **$6.00**

Pistol Reloaders Starter Kit
Designed to get the beginner started or for the high-volume reloader to set up separate decap or powder charge station. Includes AccuPress; AccuMeasure rotary powder measure with three rotors; Universal decap die; ram prime die; case lube kit; loading block; powder funnel; primer tray; *Pistol and Revolver Handbook and User's Guide*. From Lyman Products Corporation.
Price: **$109.95**

LYMAN

Expert Kit
Includes choice of T-Mag or Orange Crusher press; Universal case trimmer with expanded pilot multi-pack; M-500 reloading scale; #55 powder measure; Universal priming arm; primer tray; auto primer feed; detachable shellholder; primer catcher; quick-release turret system (T-Mag only); deburring tool; case lube kit; powder funnel; extra decapping pins; $^7/_8$-14 adaptor for mounting powder measure; instructions; and *Lyman Reloading and Cast Bullet Guide*. T-Mag kit available with or without dies and shellholder. T-Mag Rifle Set includes rifle die set (223, 22-250, 243, 270, 308, 30-30, 30-06) and shellholder to load one cartridge, 30 lbs; Carbide Pistol Set includes carbide 3-die set (9mm, 38/357, 10mm/40 S&W, 44 Mag., 45 ACP) and shellholder to load one caliber, 31 lbs. Orange Crusher Expert Kit comes in no-cal version only and does not include dies or shellholder. From Lyman Products Corporation.
Price: T-Mag rifle set **$399.95**
Price: T-Mag pistol set **$409.95**
Price: T-Mag no-cal **$369.95**
Price: Orange Crusher no-cal . . **$329.95**

Shellholder Set
Includes 12 standard shellholders for most popular pistol/rifle cartridges in organizer/storage box. Box also sold separately. From Lyman Products Corporation.
Price: **$24.95**
Price: Storage box **$2.50**

Universal Priming Arm
Seats all sizes and types of primers. Supplied with two priming sleeves, large and small. From Lyman Products Corporation.
Price: **$9.50**

Lyman Expert Kit

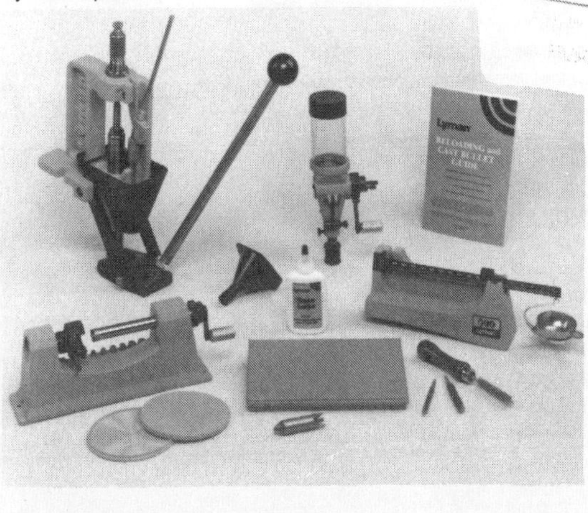

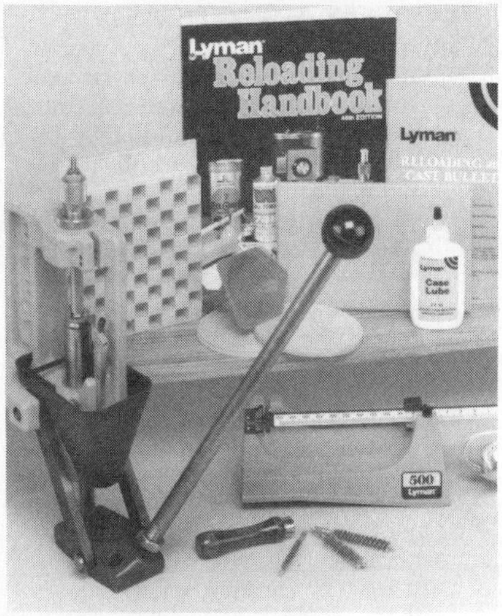

Lyman Orange Crusher Starter Kit

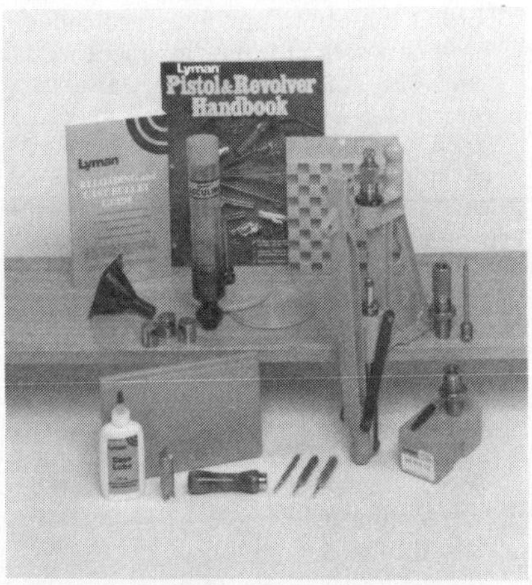

Lyman Pistol Reloaders Starter Kit

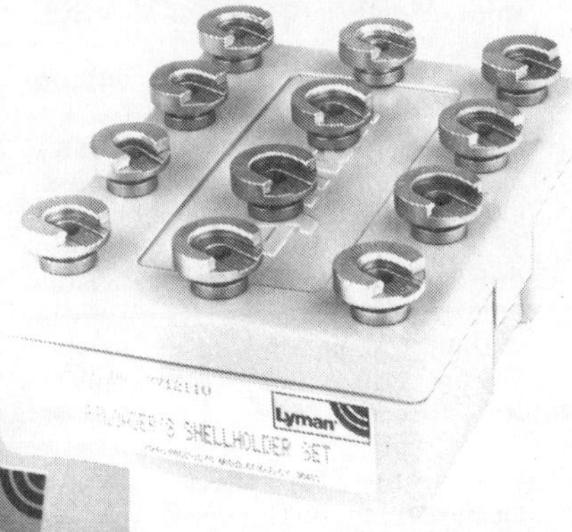

Lyman Shellholder Set

METALLIC PRESSES/ Press Accessories

M-A SYSTEMS

Easy Case Feeder for Star Press

Feeds cases automatically. Adjusts for 9mm through 45 Colt; special feed tube available for 380 Auto. Includes two supply tubes 36" long and will adapt to most case collators. Two push rods stabilize self-lubricating nylon case shuttle bar to reduce operating force and wear. Weight: 2 lbs. From M-A Systems.

Price: **$164.50**

Easy Loader

Mounts to Star, Dillon RL 1000 and C-H/4-D Die Inline to feed bullets base down at rate of 2500 per hour. Operates automatically in sequence with press from regulated 50-60 psi air source. Accepts all flat-based bullets, some hollow base, round-nose, wadcutters and semi-wadcutters. Comes complete for 9mm through 45-caliber with two sizes of bullet supply tubes, four feed tubes and two sets of bullet grippers. 223 and 380 Auto require special grippers; 223-caliber requires special feed tubes. Weight: 4 lbs. From M-A Systems.

Price: Star **$410.00**
Price: Dillon **$465.00**

Eject-Ease for Star Press

Side-ejects loaded 30- through 45-caliber rounds at taper crimp station. Round held securely in shellplate taper crimp pocket eliminating side crimp and case crushing. As tool head moves up, the spring wire ejector moves case out of shellplate and clear of press. No press modification required. Comes complete with installation instructions. Weight: 1-lb. From M-A Systems.

Price: **$45.00**

Roller-Ease Handle for Star Press

Replacement handle for Star press. Operating arm of steel; roller handle 1" diameter aluminum, medium knurled for non-chafing grip surface. Increases effective fulcrum without increasing length of stroke. Weight: 1-lb. From M-A Systems.

Price: **$24.95**

Roto-Ease for Star Press

Designed for the Star press to automatically advance shellplate increasing reload rate from 400 to 800 rounds per hour. Operates with all calibers. Cam operation controls acceleration and deceleration of shellplate. Operating hook pulls in plane with shellplate and mounts to right rear of press. No press modification required. Weight: 2 lbs. From M-A Systems.

Price: **$169.50**

M-A Systems Easy Case Feeder

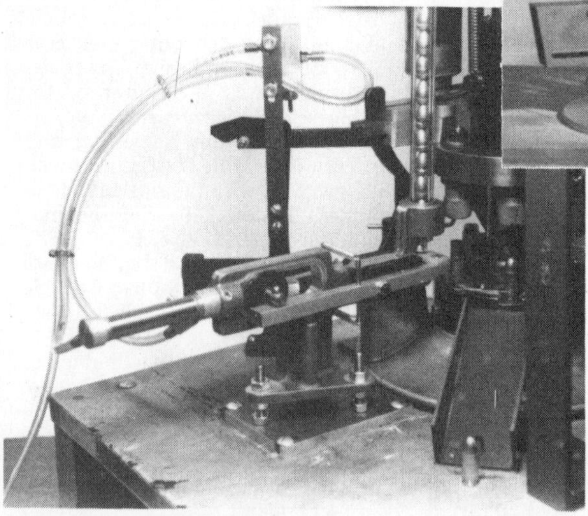

M-A Systems Easy Loader

M-A Systems Eject-Ease

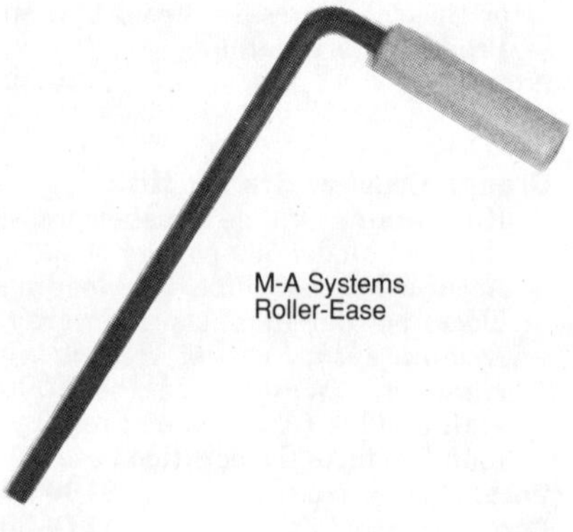

M-A Systems Roller-Ease

M-A Systems Roto-Ease

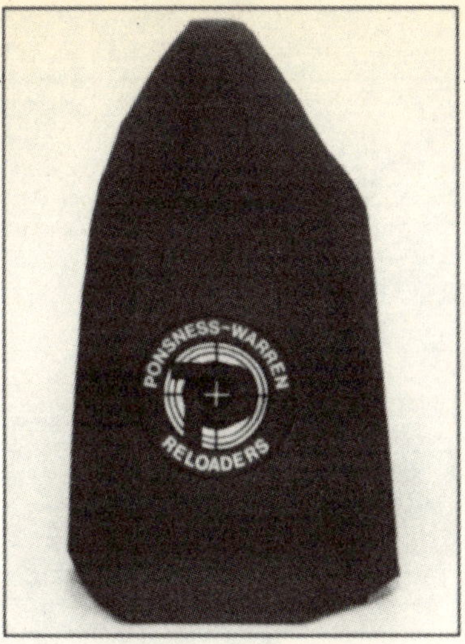

Ponsness/Warren Dust Cover

Ponsness/Warren
Metallic II Die Head

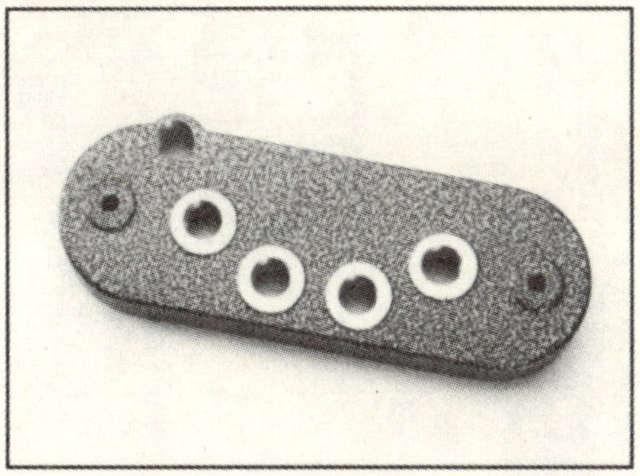

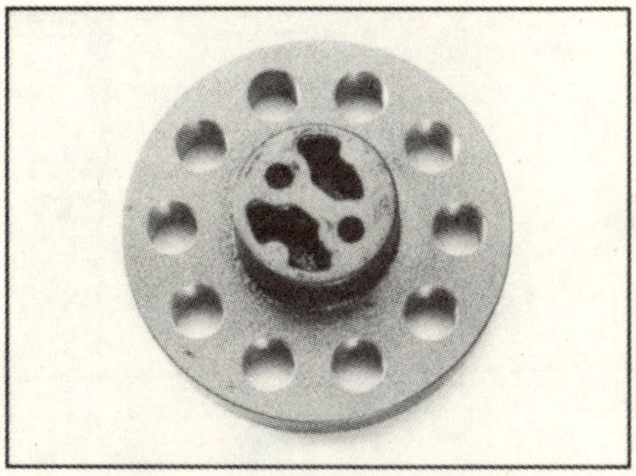

Ponsness/Warren
P-200 Die Head

PONSNESS/WARREN

Dust Covers
Sturdy canvas cover for Metallic II and Metal-Matic presses. From Ponsness/Warren.
Price: **$20.95**

Metallic II Die Head
Extra die heads for changing and mounting a different caliber. From Ponsness/Warren.
Price: **$38.80**

Metallic II Measure Extension
Raises powder measure above dies. Complete with housing, spring and large and small primers. From Ponsness/Warren.
Price: **$15.70**

P-200 Die Head
Extra die heads for changing and mounting a different caliber. From Ponsness/Warren.
Price: **$13.60**

P-200 Primer Feed
Fits all Metal-Matic presses. Includes large and small primer tubes and steel primer tube shield. From Ponsness/Warren.
Price: **$31.45**

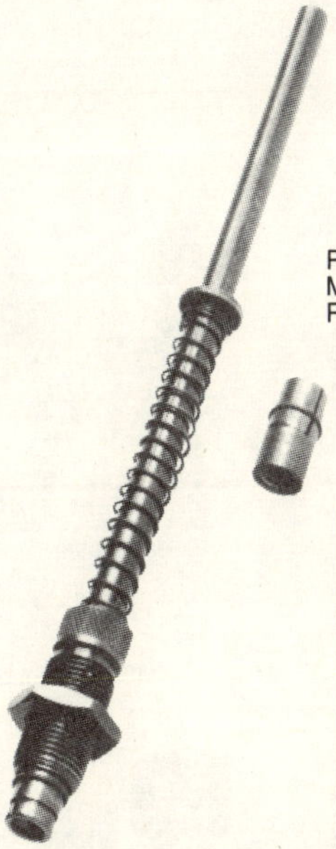

Ponsness/Warren
Metallic II/P-200
Primer Feed

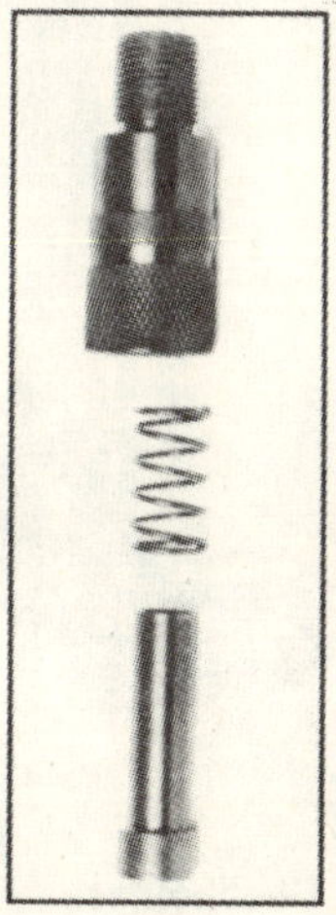

Ponsness/Warren
Metallic II/P-200
Powder Measure
Extension

QUINETICS

Auto Multi-Caliber Shellholder
Adjusts automatically to case size and accommodates 71 different calibers to include popular old-timers. Will also remove stuck cases from die. From Quinetics Corp.
Price: **$13.75**

Quinetics Multi-Caliber Shellholder

RCBS

Accessory Base Plate-2
Heavy .820" thick aluminum casting measuring 9$^{7}/_{8}$" x 5$^{1}/_{2}$" with holes drilled and pre-tapped for mounting reloading tools. For use with RCBS rotary case trimmer, powder measure stand, Lube-a-Matic, Reloader Special-5 press, Rock Chucker, Partner press, auto and standard priming tools. Fasteners included. From RCBS.
Price: **$22.54**

Ammo-Crafter Kit
Accessory kit without press. Includes: Rotary Case Trimmer-2 kit (case trimmer; collet #1, #2 and #3; pilots for 22, 24, 27, 28, 30, 35, 44 and 45 calibers); Primer Tray-2; *Speer Reloading Manual*; 5-0-5 scale; Uniflow powder measure; case loading block; deburring tool; case lube kit; and powder funnel. From RCBS.
Price: **$247.11**

Case Kicker
For use with RCBS Jr., Reloader Special and Rock Chucker presses. An ejector spring assembly that mounts on right side of press and pushes the case out of the shellholder into a box mounted on left side of press. Includes primer deflector to catch decapped primers and direct them to container on floor. From RCBS.
Price: **$20.98**

Lock-Out Die
Detects a no-powder or double charge condition in the progressive reloading process and locks up or halts ram travel at the case mouth. For use with pistol calibers. From RCBS.
Price: **$35.52**

RCBS Lock-Out Die

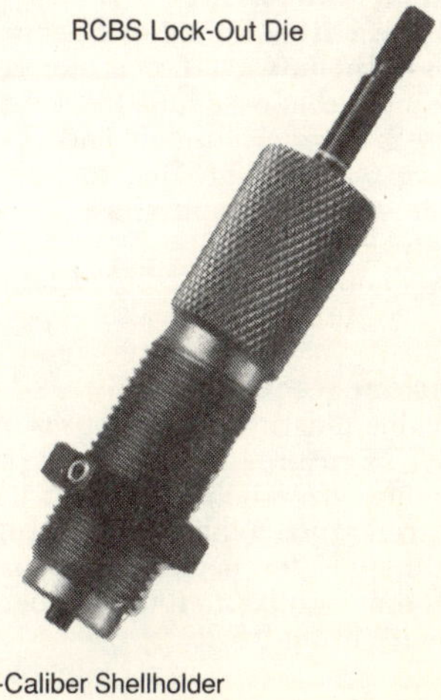

RCBS

Partner Reloading Kit

Comes with Partner press. Includes: 5-0-2 scale; case loading block; case lube kit; Primer Tray-2; deburring tool; powder funnel; and *Speer Reloading Manual*. From RCBS.

Price: **$143.66**

Piggyback II

Converts RCBS Rock Chucker, Reloader Special-3 and Reloader Special-5 single-stage presses to progressive units. Features automatic indexing, priming, powder charging and loaded round ejection. Case detection system disengages powder measure when no case is present in powder charging station. Comes with clear powder measure adaptor to view and correct bridged powders. Five-station shellplate, reloading dies and powder measure not included. From RCBS.

Price: **$158.29**

Powder Checker

For use with progressive presses to confirm each case receives the correct powder charge. A moving rod indicates the presence of powder and provides a quick visual comparison for the amount of powder dropped. Located between the powder charging and bullet seating stations. Black oxide finish. From RCBS.

Price: **$22.76**

Reloading Accessory Kit

Includes: Powder measure/Piggyback stand; powder trickler; primer pocket brushes for large and small pockets; case loading block; stainless steel dial caliper; small and medium case neck brush. From RCBS.

Price: **$86.93**

Reloading Starter Kit

Comes with Reloader Special-5 press. Includes: 5-0-5 scale; case loading block; case lube kit; Primer Tray-2; powder funnel; and *Speer Reloading Manual*. Dies and shellholders must be purchased separately. From RCBS.

Price: **$220.14**

Shellholder Rack

Durable plastic rack measures $5^3/_4$" x $6^7/_8$". Features 32 numbered pegs for each size shellholder and pull-out reference table listing proper shellholder for popular rifle/pistol calibers. Can be mounted on bench or wall. From RCBS.

Price: **$14.45**

RCBS Powder Checker

RCBS Shotshell Die

RCBS Shellholder Rack

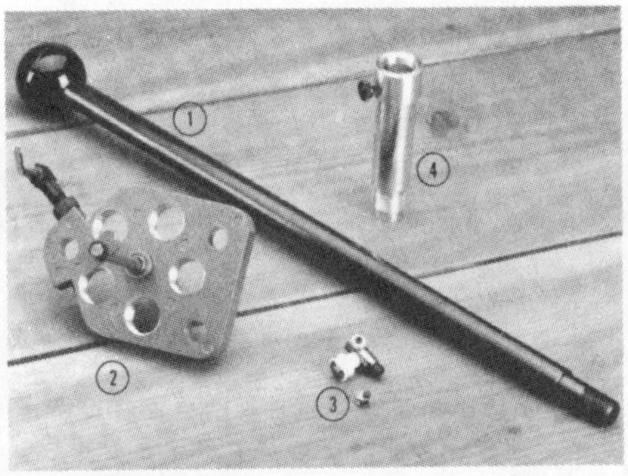

RCBS Piggyback II Kit

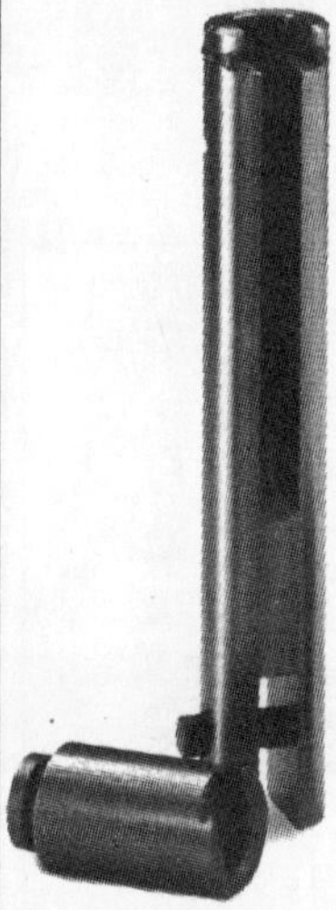

RCBS Shellholder, Ram, Adaptor, Extended Shellholder

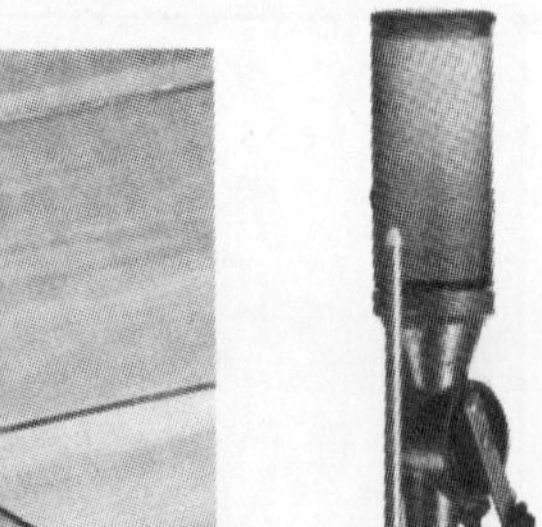

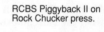

RCBS Piggyback II on Rock Chucker press.

RCBS

Shellholders

Price:	**$6.04**
Price: Extended shellholder	**$8.28**
Price: Shellholder ram, C press . .	**$18.60**
Price: Adaptor, H press	**$12.37**
Price: Adaptor, Herters	**$14.13**

Shotshell Die

Compatible with Rock Chucker and Reloader Special 3/5 and AmmoMaster presses. Transforms metallic press to 10-, 12-, 16- or 20-gauge shotshell press. Designed for compression-formed plastic hulls with appropriate wad column. Can use with high brass hulls and up to 3" magnum loads. Die set includes shot measure, case holder and 6- and 8-point case crimper. From RCBS.

Price: **$55.11**

RCBS

Rock Chucker Reloading Kit

Comes with Rock Chucker press. Includes: 5-0-5 reloading scale; Uniflow powder measure; *Speer Reloading Manual*; Rotary Case Trimmer-2 kit (case trimmer; collets #1, #2 and #3; pilots for 22, 24, 27, 28, 30, 35, 44 and 45 calibers); hex key set; case loading block; case lube kit; automatic primer feed; Primer Tray-2; powder funnel; and deburring tool. From RCBS.

Price: **$349.74**

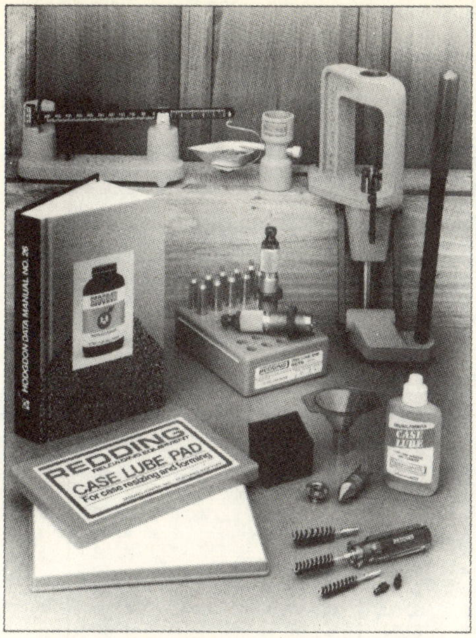

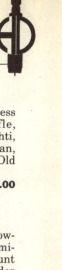

Redding Boss Pro-Pack

REDDING	
Boss Pro-Pak/Press Kit Calibers	
RIFLE	
221 Rem. Fire Ball	7mmx57 Mauser
22 Hornet	280 Rem.
220 Swift	284 Win.
222 Rem.	7.62x39
22-250 Rem.	30-30 Win.
223 Rem.	30-40 Krag
243 Win.	30-06 Spring.
6mm Rem.	300 H&H Mag.
250 Savage	300 Savage
25-06 Rem.	300 Win.Mag.
257 Roberts	308/307 Win.
6.5mmx55 Swedish Mauser	303 British
	32 Win. Spl.
264 Win. Mag.	8mmx57 Mauser
270 Win.	338 Win. Mag.
7mm-08 Rem.	35 Remington
7mm Rem.Mag.	375 H&H Mag.
PISTOL	
30 M1 Carbine	357 Mag.
32 S&W Long	41 Magnum
32 H&R Mag.	44 Special
380 Auto	44 Magnum
9mm Luger	44-40 Win.
38 Special	45 ACP/AR
357 Magnum	45 Colt
38 Spl.	

REDDING

Boss Pro-Pak

Contains Boss reloading press; Model #2 powder/bullet scale; powder trickler; set of Series A reloading dies; pad-style case lube kit; deburring tool for cases from 17- to 45-caliber; Model #18 case preparation kit; powder funnel; and *Hodgdon Loading Data Manual*. See chart for available Series A dies. From Redding Reloading Equipment.

Price: **$288.30**

Model No. 11 Shellholder

Universal snap-in design precision machined and heat-treated. From Redding Reloading Equipment.

Price: **$7.00**

Extended Shellholders

Required when trimming short cases under $1^1/_2$" OAL. From Redding Reloading Equipment.

Price: **$10.00**

Reloading Press Kits

Each Redding press available in kit form to include the press, choice of one set of Series A reloading dies and matching shellholder. See chart for available Series A dies. From Redding Reloading Equipment.

Price: Boss press kit **$139.50**
Price: Turret press kit **$279.00**
Price: Ultramag press kit **$274.50**

ROCK CRUSHER

Shellholders

Shellholders for Rock Crusher press for 50 BMG, 55 Boyes rifle, 12.7mmx107 Russian, 20mm Lahti, 20mm Solothurn, 20mm Vulcan, 23mmx115 Soviet. From The Old Western Scrounger.

Price: **$30.00**

SLAP

Powder Buddy

Simple trip meter fitted to any powder measure or progressive/semi-progressive press to show a count from 1 to 99999 of each powder throw. Helps prevent double charging or no powder charge. All-metal construction. From SLAP Industries.

Price: . . . . **Contact manufacturer.**

VEGA TOOL

Re-Manufactured Shellholders

Shellholders or shellholder adapters to fit obsolete reloading presses. Shellholder adapters for Herters, Lyman, Wells and Hollywood presses accept universal shellholders. Re-manufactured shellholders available in most popular calibers for Lyman J2 type, Hollywood and Herters presses. From Vega Tool Co., Inc.

Price: . . . . **Contact manufacturer.**

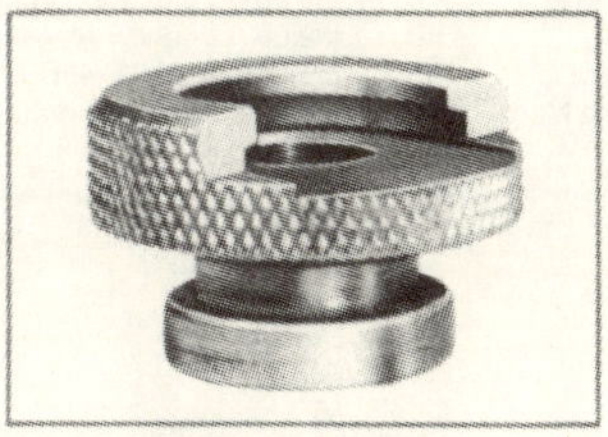

Redding Shellholder

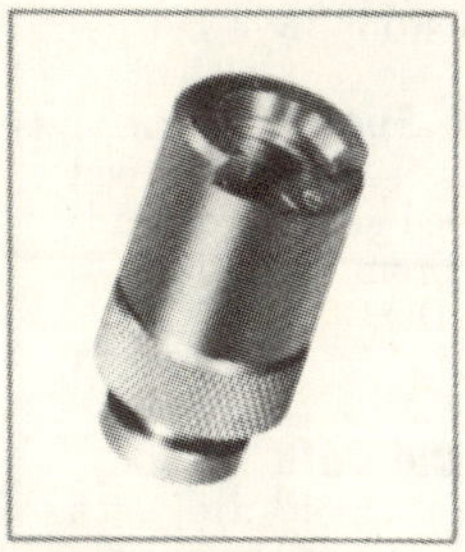

Redding Extended Shellholder

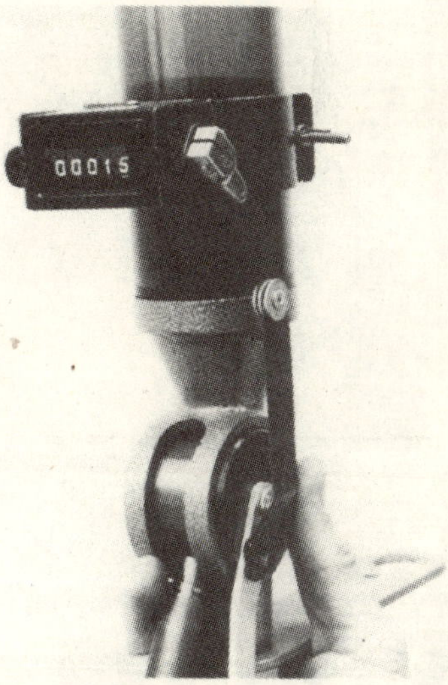

SLAP Powder Buddy

Vega Tool Re-Manufactured Shellholders

A-SQUARE

Rifle Dies

A-Square stocks dies for nine calibers: 338, 375, 460, 495 and 500 A-Square; 425 Express; 450 Ackley; 416 Rigby; 470 NE. Dies in other calibers can be special ordered. From A-Square Co., Inc.

Price: **$111.50**

BULLET SWAGING SUPPLY

22-Caliber Dies

Standard threaded dies designed for RCBS Rock Chucker press with BSS conversion kit. From Bullet Swaging Supply, Inc.

Price: . . . . **Contact manufacturer.**

BALD EAGLE

Unchambered Die Bodies

Stainless steel $^{7}/_{8}$-14 short, medium, long, and tong tool dies. These unchambered sizing dies accept Wilson sizing bushings for adjusting neck tension on loaded rounds. Concentric inside and out. From Bald Eagle Precision Machine Company.

Price: **$55.00**

Bald Eagle
Unchambered Die Bodies

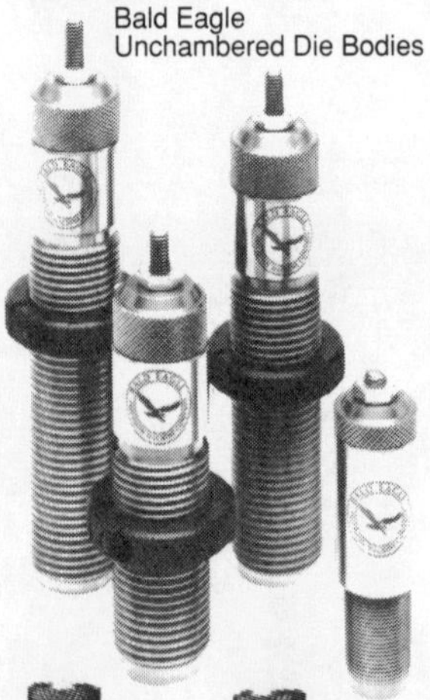

C-H Steel Dies

STEEL DIE SETS

Caliber	Shellholder	Price	Caliber	Shellholder	Price	Caliber	Shellholder	Price
	RIFLE						PISTOL	
17 Rem.	15	$36.00	32 Rem.	5	$40.00	10mm Auto.	28	$34.00
218 Bee	3	32.00	32 Win. Spl.	2	32.00	11.15x58R	43	47.00
219 Zipper	2	36.00	32-40 Win.	2	32.00	11.15x60R	43	47.00
22 Hornet	HT	32.00	33 Win.	47	36.00	30 Carbine	M1	34.00
22 K-Hornet	HT	36.00	338 Win. Mag.	6	32.00	32 ACP (Auto.)	M1	34.00
22 Sav. Hi-Power	2	36.00	348 Win.	34	36.00	32 S&W Long	M1	34.00
22-250	1	32.00	35 Rem.	14	32.00	32 S&W Short	10	34.00
220 Swift	4	32.00	35 Whelen	1	32.00	32-20 Win.	10	34.00
221 Rem.	15	32.00	350 Rem. Mag.	6	32.00	351 SL	5	38.00
222 Rem. Mag.	15	32.00	358 Norma Mag.	6	36.00	357 Mag.	12	34.00
223 Rem.	15	32.00	358 Win.	1	36.00	28 S&W (Short)	12	34.00
224 Wea. Mag.	28	36.00	375 H&H Mag.	6	32.00	38 Spl.	12	34.00
225 Win.	4	32.00	6mm Rem. (244)	1	32.00	38 Super Auto.	3	34.00
240 Wea. Mag.	1	36.00	6mm-284	1	36.00	38-40 Win.	19	38.00
243 Win.	1	32.00	6.5 Rem. Mag.	6	32.00	38-55/375 Win.	2	47.00
25 Rem.	5	40.00	6.5x50 Japanese	65	32.00	38-56 Win.	47	47.00
25-06	1	32.00	6.5x52 Carcano	14	36.00	380 Auto. (Steel)	15	34.00
25-20 Win. Rep.	3	32.00	6.5x54 Mann.-Sch.	14	36.00	40 S&W (Steel)	28	34.00
25-35 Win.	2	32.00	6.5x55 Swedish	2	32.00	40-65 Win.	47	47.00
250 Savage	1	32.00	7mm Express	1	32.00	401 Win. SL	1	47.00
256 Win.	12	32.00	7mm Rem. Mag.	6	32.00	405 Win.	25	47.00
257 Roberts	4	32.00	7mmWea. Mag.	6	36.00	41 Mag.	41	34.00
257 Wea. Mag.	6	36.00	7mm-08	1	32.00	44 Mag.	8	34.00
264 Win.	6	36.00	7x57 Mauser	4	32.00	44 Spl.	8	34.00
270 Wea. Mag.	6	36.00	7x61 S&H	6	40.00	44-40 Win.	19	34.00
270 Win.	1	32.00	7-30 Waters	2	32.00	444 Marlin	27	47.00
284 Win.	1	32.00	7.35x52 Italian	14	36.00	45 Auto.	1A	34.00
30 Rem.	5	36.00	705x55 Swiss	2	36.00	45 Long Colt	LC	34.00
30-60	1	32.00	7.62x39	13	32.00	45-70	47	47.00
30-30	2	32.00	7.62x54R Russian	76	36.00	458 Win.	6	47.00
30-338	6	36.00	7.63x25 (30 Mau.)	LG	40.00	50-70 Gov't	57	47.00
30-40 Krag	8B	32.00	7.65 Lug. (30 Lug.)	LG	40.00	8mm Nambu	26	47.00
300 H&H	6	32.00	7.65x53 Mauser	1	32.00	9mm Steyr	15	47.00
300 Savage	1	32.00	7.7x58 Japanese	1	32.00			
300 Wea. Mag.	6	36.00	8mm-06	1	36.00			
300 Win. Mag.	6	32.00	8x50R Lebel	8L	36.00			
300 British	8B	32.00	8x57 Mauser	1	32.00			
303 Savage	3S	36.00	8.15x46R	2	40.00			
308 Norma Mag.	6	36.00	8.2x53R	76	40.00			
308 Win.	1	32.00	9.3x74R	6	40.00			

C-H

These dies are original offerings from the C-H Tool & Die Company prior to its acquisition by 4-D Custom Die.

Steel Die Set With Speed Seater

Steel pistol 3-die sets with speed seater die to speed seating of wadcutter bullets. From C-H Tool & Die/4-D Custom Die.

Price: **$35.50**

Steel Rifle/Pistol Die Sets

Steel two- and three-die sets threaded $^{7}/_{8}$-14. Sizer and seater die are precision reamed, polished, carbonitrided, tempered and mirror polished inside. All parts steel except nylon ball in lock ring. From C-H Tool & Die/4-D Custom Die.

Price: . . . . **See chart.**

C-H/4-D

20mm Lahti Dies

Dies threaded $1^{1}/_{2}$-12 with expander for use with U.S. 20mm projectiles. Expander for original projectiles available. Shellholder with $^{5}/_{8}$-18 thread and priming tool also offered. From C-H Tool & Die/4-D Custom Die.

Price: **$350.00**
Price: Shellholder **$40.00**
Price: Priming tool **$60.00**

50 BMG Dies

Chrome-plated steel two-die set threaded $1^{1}/_{2}$-12 for reloading 50 BMG caliber. Set includes full-length size and crimp seater. From 4-D Custom Die.

Price: **$275.00**
Price: Shellholder **$15.00**

C-H/4-D Custom Dies

C-H/4-D Carbide Die Sets
10mm Auto
30 Carbine
32 ACP
32 S&W
32 H&R Mag.
32 S&W Short
357 Magnum
38 S&W Short
38 Special
38 Super
380 Auto
40 S&W
41 Magnum
44 Magnum
44 Special
45 Auto
45 Long Colt
9mm Luger

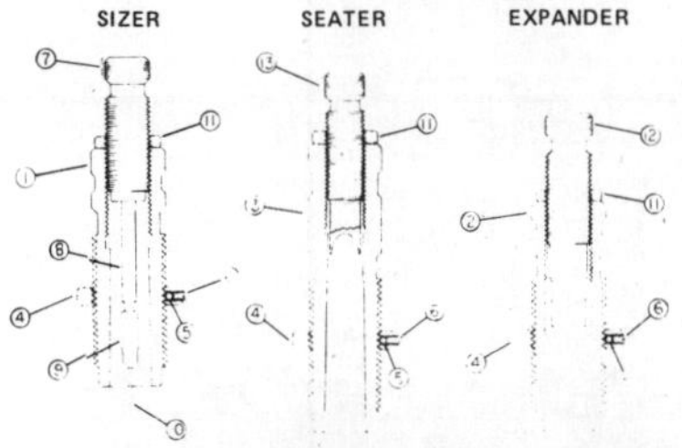

C-H/4-D 3-Die Rifle Set Parts

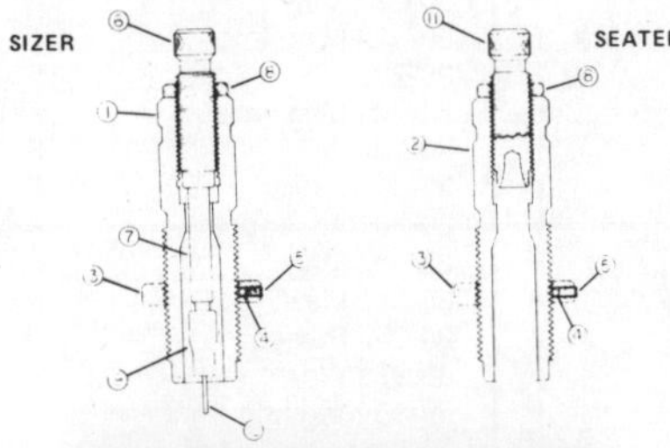

C-H/4-D 2-Die Rifle Set Parts

C-H 3-Die Rifle Set Parts

	DIE/DIE PART	DIE	DIE
	Die Set	$38.00	$47.00
	Sizer Die	18.00	23.00
	Expander Die	13.75	15.00
	Seater Die	16.00	18.00
1	Sizer Body	13.00	18.00
2	Expander (#3) Body	10.00	10.00
3	Seater Body	13.00	15.00
4	Lock Ring Body	1.50	1.50
5	Nylon Ball	.40	.40
6	Set Screw	.60	.60
7	Decapping Rod Head	2.00	2.00
8	Decapping Rod	2.00	2.00
9	Decapping Pin Holder	1.50	1.50
10	Decapping Pin	.40	.40
11	Top Lock Ring	1.00	1.00
12	Expander Unit	3.75	4.50
13	Seating Stem	3.00	3.00

C-H 2-Die Rifle Set Parts

	DIE/DIE PART	DIE	DIE	DIE
	Die Set	$32.00	$36.00	$40.00
	Sizer	19.25	21.50	24.00
	Seater	16.00	18.00	20.00
1	Sizer Body	13.25	15.50	20.00
2	Seater Body	12.50	14.50	16.50
3	Lock Ring	1.50	1.50	1.50
4	Nylon Ball	.40	.40	.40
5	Set Screw	.60	.60	.60
6	Decap Rod Head	2.00	2.00	2.00
7	Decap Rod	2.00	2.00	2.00
8	Top Lock Ring	1.00	1.00	1.00
9	Expander Ball	2.50	2.50	2.50
10	Decap Pin	.40	.40	.40
11	Seat Stem	3.00	3.00	3.00

C-H 3-Die Pistol Set Parts

	DIE/DIE PART	PRICE
	Sizer Die	$13.50
	Carbide Sizer Die	32.00
	Expander Die	15.50
	Seater Die	14.50
	Speed Seater	16.00
1	Sizer Body	12.00
2	Expander (#3) Body	10.00
3	Seater Body	12.50
3	Speed Seater Body	14.00
4	Lock Ring Body	1.50
5	Nylon Ball	.40
6	Set Screw	.60
7	Decapping Rod Head	2.00
8	Decapping Rod	2.00
9	Top Lock Ring	1.00
10	Expander Unit	3.10
11	Decapping Pin	.40
12	Seating Stem	3.00

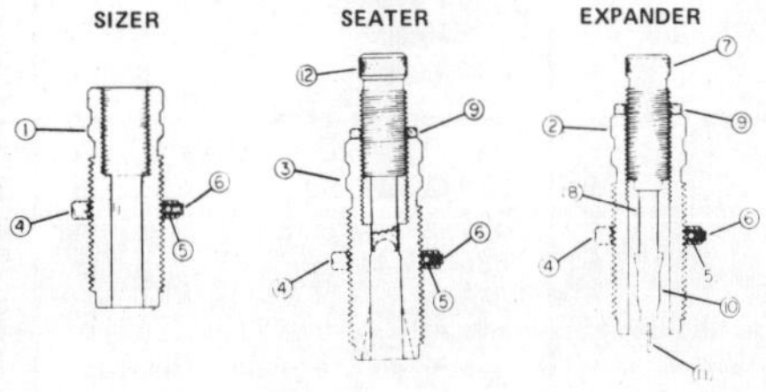

C-H/4-D 3-Die Carbide Pistol Die Parts

C-H/4-D

Blank Crimping Die

Crimp die for loading blank cartridges. Straight-walled cases need only one die. Rimless calibers require shoulder to control headspace thus require shoulder die. Dies available for most popular calibers; odd calibers at extra cost. From C-H Tool & Die/4-D Custom Die.

Price: **$59.00**
Price: Shoulder die, 9mm **$15.00**
Price: Shoulder die, 45 ACP **$20.00**

Carbide Die Sets

Carbide three-die pistol caliber sets. Available for 17 pistol calibers (see chart). From C-H Tool & Die/4-D Custom Die.

Price: **$48.50**
Price: With seater die **$49.50**

Case Head Swage Dies

To swage case base down to required diameter. Each die supplied with solid ram to be used in place of shell-holder for proper case support. Standard 7/8" will accommodate head diameters up to .500"; larger require 1" or larger die diameter. From C-H Tool & Die/4-D Custom Die.

Price: 7/8-14 . . . . **$55.00**
Price: 1-14 . . . . **$65.00**
Price: 1 1/2-12 . . . . **$85.00**

Expander Die Bodies

Available in any length and top thread. Specify length, top thread, body diameter and minimum inside diameter. From C-H Tool & Die/4-D Custom Die.

Price: 7/8-14 O.D. **$10.00**
Price: 1-14 O.D. **$20.00**
Price: 1 1/2-12 O.D. **$40.00**

"M"-Type Expander Plugs

Designed for loading cast bullets or jacketed bullets. Expander has plug .001" smaller than bullet diameter and a taper to bell case mouth slightly to prevent "lead shaving." From C-H Tool & Die/4-D Custom Die.

Price: To 45-cal. **$10.00**
Price: 46-50-cal. **$15.00**
Price: 51-62-cal. **$22.00**

Seater Die

To facilitate seating of wadcutter-type bullets. Die opening is larger in diameter than main body, gradually tapering to seating stem. From C-H Tool & Die/4-D Custom Die.

Price: **$16.00**

CH 4D CUSTOM DIE SETS

Caliber	Die Group
14-17 Rem.	G
14-221	G
14-221 Walker	G
14-222	G
14-222 Imp.	G
14-223	G
14-223 Imp.	G
17 Ackley Imp. Hornet	F
17 Javelina	F
17 Mach IV	F
17-221	F
17-221 Imp.	F
17-222	F
17-222 Imp.	F
17-222 Mag. Imp.	F
17-222 Mag.	F
17-223	F
17-223 Imp.	F
20-221	F
20-221 Imp.	F
20-222	F
20-222 Imp.	F
20-222 Mag.	F
20-222 Mag. Imp.	F
20-223 Imp.	F
218 Mashburn Bee	F
219 Donaldson Wasp	F
219 Zipper Imp.	F
22 Arrow	F
22 Cheetah	F
22 Donaldson Wasp	F
22 Extra Long Maynard	F
22 Gebby Sr.	F
22 ICL Gopher	F
22 Jr. Varminter	F
22 Lindl Chucker	F
22 Lindl Superchucker	F
22 Lovell R-2	F
22 Newton	F
22 PPC	F
22 Rem. BR	F
22 Rem. Jet	F
22 Super Jet	F
22 Varminter	F
22 Vello Dog	F
22 WCF	F
22-06	F
22-06 Imp.	F
22-15-60	F
22-243 Win.	F
22-243 Win. Imp.	F
22-284	F
22-30 Carbine	F
22-3000	F
22-357 Mag.	F
22-6mm Rem.	F
22-6mm Rem Imp.	F
220 Swift Imp.	F
221 Rem. Imp.	F
222 Rem. Imp.	F
222 Rem. Mag. Imp.	F
222 Rem. Imp.	F
223 Rem. Imp.	F
224 Harvey K-Chuck	F
224 Stark	F
228 Ackley	F
240 Cobra	F
240 Flanged Nitro	F
240 Gebby	F
240 Gebby Belted	F
240 Gibbs	F
240 Rhyne	F
243 Win. Imp.	F
244 Gepson	F
244 H&H	F
25 ACP	F
25 Ackley Imp. Hornet	F
25 Ackley Mag.	F
25 Hornet	F
25 ICL Mag.	F
25 Krag Imp.	F
25-06 Gibbs	F
25-06 Imp.	F
25-06 P.M.V.F.	F
25-20 Single Shot	F
25-21 Stevens	F
25-221	F
25-221 Imp.	F
25-222 Copperhead	F
25-222 Imp.	F
25-222 Mag.	F
25-222 Mag. Imp.	F
25-223	F
25-223 Imp.	F
25-240 Wea.	F
25-25 Stevens	F
25-284 Win.	F
25-308 Win.	F
25-35 Win. Imp.	F
25-357 Mag.	F
25-357 Max.	F
25-357 Max. 40°	F
25-36 Marlin	F
250 Cobra	F
250 Donaldson	F
250 Savage Imp.	F
250 Souper	F
25 Souper	F
255 Rook Rifle	F
256 Newton	F
256 Q.T.	F
257 Roberts	F
257 Roberts Imp.	F
270 ICL	G
270 Ingram	F
270 JDJ	F
270 REN	F
270 Win. Imp.	F
270-06 PMVF	F
270-221	F
270-221 Imp.	F
270-222	F
270-222 Imp.	F
270-222 Mag.	F
270-222 Mag. Imp.	F
270-223	F
270-223 Imp.	F
270-250 Savage	F
270-257 Imp.	F
270-284 Win.	F
270-300 PMVF	F
270-308 Win.	F
270-308 Win. Imp.	F
270-357 Mag.	F
275 Rigby Rimless	G
28-30-120 Stevens	F
280 British	G
280 Rem. Imp.	F
280 Ross	F
284-250 Savage	F
285 OKH	F
293-230 Morris Short	F
295 Rook	F
297-230 Morris Long	F
297-250 Rook	F
30 Ackley Mag.	F
30 Belted Newton	F
30 Rem. BR	F
30 Borchart	F
30 Herrett	F
30 Newton	F
30 STW	G
30 Streaker	G
30-06 Imp.	F
30-221	F
30-221 Imp.	F
30-222	F
30-222 Imp.	F
30-222 Mag.	F
30-222 Mag. Imp.	F
30-223	F
30-223 Mag. Imp.	F
30-284	F
30-30 Wesson	F
30-30 Win. Imp.	F
30-357 Mag.	F
30-357 Max .	F
30-357 Paxton	G
30-378 Wea.	F
30-40 Krag Imp.	F
30-8mm Rem. Mag.	G
300 ICL	F
300 Rook	F
300 Sherwood	F
300 Wade Mag.	F
303 Indonesian	F
308x1$^{1}/_{2}$	F
308x1.75	F
309 JDJ	F
310 Cadet	F
318 West. Rich. Rimless	F
32 Extra Long Ballard	F
32 Ideal	F
32 Long CF	F
32 Long Colt	F
32 Short Colt	F
32 Win. SL	F
32-20 for TC	F
32-30 Rem.	G
32-35 Stevens & Maynard	F
32-44 S&W	F
320 Revolver	F
323 Hollis	F
33 Newton	G
33 Poacher's Pet	G
333 Flgd. N.E. (33 Jeffery)	G
333 O.K.H.	F
334 O.K.H.	G
338 O.K.H.	G
338-06	F
338-06 Imp.	F
338-284	F
338-300 H&H	F
338-308 Norma	F
338-308 Win.	F
338-308 Win. Imp.	F
338-378 Wea.	H
340 Wea.	F
35 Ackley Mag.	F
35 Belted Newton	F
35 G&H Mag. (35-375 H&H)	F
35 Newton	F
35 S&W Auto.	F
35 Whelen Imp.	F
35 Win. Self-Loader	F
35 Win.	F
35x30-30 Imp.	F
35-284 Win.	F
35-30 Maynard 1882	F
35-300 Win.	F
35-338 Win.	F
35-348 Win.	F
35-40 Maynard 1882	F
35/30-30 Win.	F
357 Auto. Mag.	F
357 Herrett	F
358 Hess Mag.	G
358 Nitro. Exp.	G
358 Win. Imp.	F
358-444 (35 JDJ)	F
360 #5 Rook	F
360 Black Powder Exp.	H
360 Nitro #2	F
360 Nitro Exp. 2.25"	
375 Flgd. Mag. Nitro Exp.	G
375 Flgd. Nitro Exp. 2$^{1}/_{2}$	G
375 I.C.L	F
375 JDJ	F
375 P.M.V.F	F
375 R.D.S.	H
375 Rimless N.E. 2$^{1}/_{4}$ (9.5x57)	F
375 Wea.	F
375 Whelen (375-06)	F
375 Whelen Imp.	F
375-284	F
375-300 Win.	F
375-308 Win.	F
375-338 (375 Chatfield-Taylor)	F
375-350 Rem. Mag.	F
375-357 Exp.	H
375-358 Norma	F
378 Wea.	F
375 Wea.	F
38 Extra Long Ballard	F
38 Long Center Fire	F
38 Long Colt	F
38 Short Colt	F
38-35 Stevens	F
38-40 Rem.-Hepburn	G
38-45 ACP	G
38-45 Stevens	F
38-50 Ballard	G
38-50 Maynard	G
38-50 Win.	G
38-70 Win.	G
38-72 Win.	G
38-90 Win.	G
38-90 Win.	H
380 Long Rifle	F
380 Revolver	F
40-110 Win. Exp.	H
40-348 Win.	G
40-40 Maynard 1882	F
40-45 ACP	F
40-50 Sharps Necked (Original)	G
40-50 Sharps Necked (Shiloh)	G

See page 222 for prices.

C-H 4D

CUSTOM DIE SETS

Caliber	Die Group
40-50 Sharps St. (Original)	G
40-50 Sharps St. (Shiloh)	G
40-60 Marlin	F
40-60 Maynard 1882	F
40-60 Win.	F
40-63 Ballard	G
40-65 Ballard	G
40-65 Win.	F
40-70 Ballard	G
40-70 Maynard 1882	F
40-70 Rem. (Necked)	G
40-70 Sharps Necked (Orig.)	G
40-70 Sharps Necked (Sharps)	G
40-70 Sharps St. (Orig.)	G
40-70 Sharps St. (Shiloh)	G
40-70 Win.	G
40-72 Win.	G
40-82 Win.	G
40-85 Ballard (40-90 Ballard)	H
40-90 Sharps Necked	H
40-90 Sharps St.	H
400 Black Powder Exp.	H
400 Whelen	F
400 Whelen Imp.	F
401 Herters Powermag	F
404 Jeffery	H
408 Win.	G
41 Auto Mag.	G
41 Avenger	F
41 Long Colt	F
41 Short Colt	F
411 K.D.F	F
411-444 (411 JDJ)	F
416 Rem.	G
416 Rigby	H
416 Taylor	G
416 Wea.	G
416-300 Win.	G
416-338 Win.	G
416-375 H&H	G
416-378 Wea.	G
423 Nitro Exp.	H
425 Wesley Richards	H
430 JDJ	G
44 Auto Mag.	F
44 Ballard Long	F
44 Bulldog	F
44 Colt	F
44 Evans Long	F
44 Evans Short	F
44 Extra Long Ballard	F
44 Extra Long Wesson	F
44 Henry Center Fire	F
44 S&W American	F
44 S&W Russian	F
44 Webley	F
44-100 Ballard	H
44-100 Wesson	H
44-70 Maynard 1882	G
44-75 Ballard	F
44-77 Sharps	H
44-85 Wesson	H
44-90 (44-100) Rem. St.	H
44-90 Sharps Necked (44-100)	
44-90 Shiloh (Necked)	H
445 Super Mag.	F
45 Boxer-Henry Long 1869	H
45 New South Wales	H
45 S&W Schofield Revolver	F
45 Sharps 2 3/4"	H
45 Sharps 2.1"	F
45 Webley Revlover	F
45 Win. Mag.	F
45-100 2.6"	G
45-100 Ballard	H
45-110 2 7/8"	H
45-120 Sharps 3 1/4"	H
45-125 Win. Exp.	H
45-60 Win.	F
45-75 Win.	G
45-80 Sharpshooter	F
45-90 Win. & Sharps 2.4"	F
450 #1 Exp.	H
450 #2 Exp.	H
450 Adams Revolver	F
450 Alaskan	H
450 Black Powder Exp.	H
450 Mashburn Mag.	G
450 Nitro Exp.	H
450 Rigby Match	G
450 Watts Mag.	G
450-348 Imp.	G
450-357 Exp.	H
450-400 Nitro Exp. 3 1/4"	H
450-400 Nitro Exp. 3"	H
454 Casull	F
455 Colt (455 Mk. II)	F
455 Webley (455 Mk. II)	F
455 Webley Auto Pistol	F
458 M.C.W.	H
458x2" American	G
460 Wea.	F
461 Gibbs	H
470 Nitro Exp.	H
475 #2 Nitro Exp.	H
475 A&M Mag.	H
475 Ackley Mag.	H
475 Barnes Supreme	H
475 Nitro Exp.	H
475 Wildey Pistol	G
475-400 #2 Nitro Exp. 3 1/2"	H
476 Eley (476 Enfield Mk. III)	F
476 Nitro Exp.	H
5mm Bergmann	F
506x35 R Vierling	F
5.6x50 (5.5 x 50 R)	F
5.6x52 Rmm	F
5.6x57/5.6 x 57 R	F
5.6x61 Vom Hofe (or 5.6x61R)	G
5.7 M.M.J. (John. Orig. DWG)	F
50 Brn. Machine Gun	N
50 Carbine	G
50 Peabody	F
50 Rem. Pistol	G
50 Sgld. Cadet	G
50-110 Win.	H
50-140 Sharps	H
50-140 Win.	H
50-50 Maynard	G
50-90 Sharps	H
50-95 Win.	G
500 Jeffery	J
500 Jurras	H
500 Nitro Exp. 3 1/4"	H
500 Nitro Exp. 3"	H
500 No. 2 Exp.	K
500-450 #1 Exp.	H
500-450 #2 Musket	H
500-465 Nitro Exp.	H
505 Barnes Supreme	H
505 Gibbs	J
52-70 Sharps	G
55-100 Maynard 1882	G
56-46 Spencer	G
56-50 Spencer	G
56-56 Spencer	G
577 Nitro Exp. 2 3/4"	K
577 Nitro Exp. 3"	K
577 Snider	K
577-500 Mag.	K
58 Berdan	K
58 Berdan Musket	K
58 Gatling 1875	K
58 Rem. Carbine	K
58 Roberts Conversion	K
585 Nyati	K
6mm Cheetah (40 Deg.)	
6mm Ackley Imp. Hornet	F
6mm Benchrest Rem.	F
6mm Cheetah (28 Deg.)	F
6mm I.C.L.	F
6mm Intl. (Original)	F
6mm Lee Navy	F
6mm-06	F
6mm-06 Imp.	F
6mm-221	F
6mm-221 Imp.	F
6mm-222	F
6mm-222 Imp.	F
6mm-222 Mag. (6x47)	F
6mm-222 Mag. Imp.	F
6mm-223 (6x45)	F
6mm-223 Imp.	F
6mm-250 Savage	F
6mm-250 Savage Imp.	F
6mm-284	F
6mm-350 Rem. Mag.	F
6mm-357 Mag.	F
6mm/30-30 Imp.	F
6x29.5 Stahl	G
6x47mm (6-222 Mag.)	F
6x50 (6x50 R)	F
6x50/6x57 R	F
6.5 Bergmann	F
6.5mm BR	F
6.5 Tioga K.C.G.	G
6.5x27 R	G
6.5x30-30 Imp. (40 Deg.)	F
6.5x48R Sauer (6.6x48R)	F
6.5x52R	F
6.5x53R Dutch	F
6.5x53.5R Daudeteau	G
6.5x54 Kurz Mauser	F
6.5x57mm	F
6.5x58R Danish Krag	F
6.5x61/6.5x61R	F
6.5x68/6.5x68R	F
6.5-06	F
6.5-06 Imp.	F
6.5-221	F
6.5-221 Imp.	F
6.5-222	F
6.5-222 Imp.	F
6.5-222 Mag. (6.5x47)	F
6.5-222 Mag. Imp.	F
65-250 Savage	F
6.5-257 Imp.	F
6.5-257 Jap. (Roberts Case)	F
6.5x284 Win.	F
6.5-308 Win. (6.5-243)	F
6.5-308 Win. Imp.	F
6.5-338 Win. Mag.	F
6.5-357 Mag.	F
6.5-357 Max	F
6.5-378 Wea.	H
6.5-7mm Rem. Mag. Imp.	G
600 Nitro Exp.	K
7mm Benchrest Rem.	F
7mm S.T.W.	G
7mm T.C.U.	F
7mmx30-30 Imp. (40 Eg.)	F
7mm-06	F
7mm-06 Imp.	F
7mm-06 P.M.V.F.	F
7mm-08 Imp.	F
7mm-221	F
7mm-221 Imp.	F
7mm-222	F
7mm-222 Imp.	F
7mm-222 Mag. Imp.	F
7mm-222 Mag. (7x47)	F
7mm-223	F
7mm-223 Imp.	F
7mm-250 Savage	F
7mm-30 Waters	F
7mm-30 Waters Imp. (40 Deg.)	F
7mm-300 Wea.	F
7mm-308 Norma	G
7mm-357 Mag.	F
7mm-378 Wea.	H
7mm-8mm Rem. Mag.	G
7mm Nambu	F
7x57 Imp.	F
7x64mm Brenn. (7x65R)	F
7x72 R	G
7.5mm Swed. Nagant Rev.	F
7.5mm Swiss Army Rev.	F
7.5x54 French M.A.S. Rifle	F
7.62mm Nagant Rev.	F
7.62mm Tokarev Pistol	F
7.62x45 Czech M-52	G
7.62x52R	G
7.62x63	F
7.65mm M.A.S. Pistol	F
7.65mm Mann. Pistol	F
7.65mm Roth-Sauer Pistol	F
7.92x33mm Kurz (8mm Kurz)	F
8mm Rast-Gasser Revolver	F
8mm Roth-Steyr Pistol	F
8mm-06 Imp.	F
8mm-284	F
8mm-300 Win.	F
8mm-308 Norma	F
8mm-308 Win.	F
8mm-308 Win. Imp.	F
8mm-338 Win.	F
8mm-378 Wea.	H
8mm Lebel Revolver	F
8x50 Aust. Mann.	F
8x51 Mauser (8x51R)	G
8x52R Siamese T-66	F
8x53R Murata	G

See page 222 for prices.

C-H 4D

CUSTOM DIE SETS (con't.)

Caliber	Die Group
8x54 Krag-Jorg.	F
8x56 Mann.-Schon.	F
8x56R Mann.-Schon.	F
8x57R Kropatchek	F
8x57 Mauser (.318 Bullet)	F
8x57 Imp.	F
8x58R Danish Krag	F
8x60/8x60R	F
8x60R Kropatchek	F
8x64 Brenn. (8x65R)	F
8x68mm	F
8x68R	F
8x72R Sauer	G
8.15x46R	F
9mm Bayard Long	F
9mm Brn. Long Pistol	F
9mm Glisenti Pistol	F
9mm Jap. Rev.	F
9mm Makarov Pistol	F
9mm Mauser Pistol	F
9mm Win. Mag.	F
9x18mm Ultra	F

Caliber	Die Group
9x56 Mann.-Schon.	F
9x57 Mauser	F
9x57 Imp.	F
9x63	G
9x63 Imp. (30 Deg.)	F
9.1x40R	F
9.3x48R	G
9.3x57 Mauser	F
9.3x57R	G
9.3x62 Mauser	F
9.3x65R Collath	H
9.3x70R	G
9.3x72R	F
9.3x74R Imp.	G
9.3x80R	H
9.3x82R	H
9.4 Dutch East Indies	F
9.4 Dutch Revolver M73	F
9.5x56mm Mann.-Schon.	F
9.5x57 Mauser	F
9.5x74R	G
10mm Auto	F

Caliber	Die Group
10.3x65R Baenziger	H
10.4mm Italian Serv. Rev.	F
10.4x38R Swiss Vetterli	G
10.4x42R Swiss Vetterli	G
10.4x47R Italian	G
10.66x57R	H
10.75x57 Mann.	H
10.75x63mm	H
10.75x65R Collath	H
10.75x68 Mauser	H
10.75x70R Collath	H
11mm French Serv. Rev.	F
11mm German Serv. Rev.	F
11x52R Beaumont	H
11x53R Comblain	H
11x59R Gras	H
11x59R Vickers	H
11x60R Murata	H
11x65R	H
11.15x36R Fruthwirth Carbine	H
11.15x36R Werndl Carbine	H

Caliber	Die Group
11.15x37R Grensaufsher	H
11.15x42R Werndl M67	H
11.15x58 Werndl M77	H
11.15x58R9	F
11.15x60R Mauser	F
11.4x50R Comblain	H
11.4x50RWerndl M73	H
11.43x50R Egyptian Rem.	H
11.43x55R	H
11.5x57R Spanish Reformado	G
11.7x41.5R Danish Rem.	H
11.7x45.5R Danish Rem.	H
11.7x51R Danish Rem.	H
11.7x57R Danish Rem.	H
11.7x57R Berdan	H
11.75x36R Montenegrin Short	F
11.75x51R Montenegrin Long	F
12.7x70mm Schuler	H

C-H/4-D Custom Die Prices

DIES	GROUP F	G	H	J,K	N
Die Set	$49.50	$69.00	$98.00	$129.00	$195.00
Neck Size Die	33.00	46.00	65.00	86.50	130.50
Full-Length Size Die	33.00	46.00	65.00	86.50	130.50
Seating Die	25.00	34.50	49.00	64.50	97.50
File Trim Die	25.00	35.00	49.00	65.00	95.00
Case Form Die	25.00	35.00	49.00	65.00	95.00
Taper Crimp Die*	20.00	27.00	38.00	48.00	60.00
Taper Crimp Die**	35.00	45.00	60.00	80.00	115.00
Reamer Die/Reamer	60.00	75.00	85.00	95.00	130.00

*Straight Wall; **Bottleneck/Straight Taper

C-H/4-D

Custom Reloading Dies

Available in any caliber. Die sets, forming dies, trim dies, etc. can be supplied for all listed calibers (see C-H/4-D Die chart). For calibers not listed, dies can be made to order for an additional tooling charge. Die groups F through H are standard $^7/_8$-14 thread; groups J and K are 1-14 thread; group N dies are $1^1/_2$-12 threading. All dies except N are for use with shellholders or shellplates having industry standard dimension of 0.125" from case head to top of shellholder. From C-H Tool & Die/4-D Custom Die.

Price: . . . . **See chart.**

Small Base Die Sets

For reloading cartridges to minimum dimensions. Available for 223 Remington, 30-06 and 308 Winchester. From C-H Tool & Die/4-D Custom Die.

Price: **$32.00**

Taper Crimp Die (Pistol)

Precision-honed, hardened and polished inside with non-glare satin finish outside. For autoloading calibers that headspace off the case mouth. Available in all C-H/4-D calibers. If ordered with C-H/4-D die set, cost of taper crimp die is $10.00. From C-H Tool & Die/4-D Custom Die.

Price: **$14.00**

C-H/4-D

Taper Crimp Die (Rifle)

Available in all C-H/4-D die offerings. Eliminates case trimming and is useful for handloading semi-auto rifle ammo. If ordered with C-H/4-D die set, cost of taper crimp die is $10.00. From C-H Tool & Die/4-D Custom Die.

Price: **$17.00**

Tapered Expanders

Gradual taper for expanding the case neck to larger caliber. Will expand neck .050" to .060". Sizes through 45-caliber, fits any expander body with 9-16 top thread. Larger sizes require special die bodies. From C-H Tool & Die/4-D Custom Die.

Price: To 45-cal. **$10.00**

Price: 46-50-cal. **$15.00**

Price: 51-62-cal. **$22.00**

C-H/4-D

Universal Decapping Die

Comes in two sizes—large and small. Small die decaps calibers 22 Hornet through 6mm-06. Larger die accommodates all calibers from 25-20 to 50-110 Winchester and with $^1/_4$" diameter decap rod and .070" decap rod will decap military 308 and 30-06 cases with crimped-in primers. From C-H Tool & Die/4-D Custom Die.

Price: **$12.95**

FORSTER PRODUCTS

BENCH REST DIE SETS

Cartridge	
17 Remington	270 Winchester
22 Hornet	7 x 64 Brenneke
22 BR Remington	7mm-08
22 P.P.C. Sako	7 x 57 Mauser
221 Fireball	7mm BR Remington
222 Remington	7mm Remington Mag.
222 Remington Magnum	270 Weatherby Mag.
223 Remington	7mm Weatherby Mag.
5.6 x 50 Rimmed	280 Remington
220 Swift	30 Herrett
22/250 Remington	7mm T.C.U.
243 Winchester	30-30 Winchester
6mm BR Remington	300 Winchester Mag.
6mm P.P.C. Sako	300 Weatherby Mag.
6mm Remington (224)	303 British
224 Weatherby Magnum	308 Winchester
240 Weatherby Magnum	308 National Match
25/06 Remington	30-06
250 Savage (250/300)	30-06 Ackley (40)
257 Ackley (40)	8mm Remington Mag.
257 Roberts	8 x 57 Mauser
257 Weatherby Magnum	8 x 68S
264 Winchester	338 Winchester Mag.
6.5 x 57 Mauser	340 Weatherby Mag.
6.5 x 55 Swedish	357 Herrett
6.5 x 55 SKAN	375 H&H

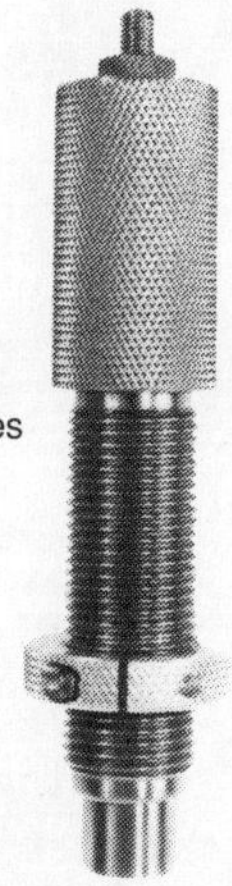

Forster Bench Rest Dies

Forster Ultra Seater Die

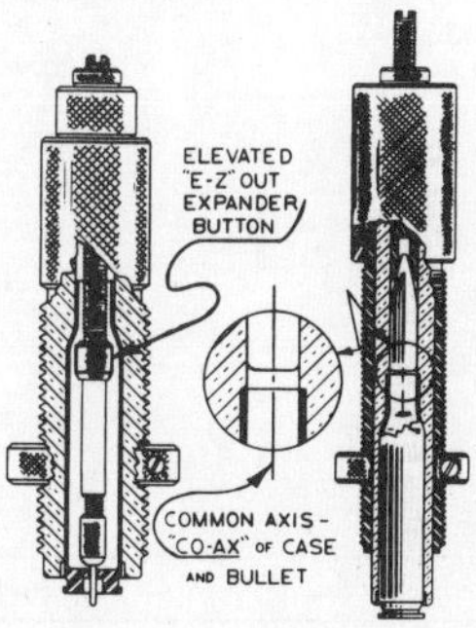

Forster Bench Rest Rifle Dies

FORSTER Ultra Seater Die Calibers	
22 Hornet	7mmx57 Mau.
22 BR Rem.	7mm BR Rem.
22 PPC Sako	7mm Rem. Mag.
221 Fireball	280 Rem.
222 Rem.	30 Herrett
222 Rem. Mag.	7mm TCU
223 Rem.	30-30 Win.
5.6mmx50R	300 Win. Mag.
220 Swift	303 British
22/250 Rem.	308 Win.
243 Win.	30-06
6mm BR Rem.	30-06 Ackley
6mm PPC Sako	8mm Rem. Mag.
6mm Rem.	8mmx57 Mauser
25-06 Rem.	8mmx68S
250 Savage	338 Win. Mag.
257 Ackley	357 Herrett
257 Roberts	375 H&H
264 Win.	224 Wea. Mag.
6.5mmx57 Mau.	240 Wea. Mag.
6.5mmx55 Swed.	257 Wea. Mag.
6.5mmx55 SKAN	270 Wea. Mag.
270 Win.	7mm Wea. Mag.
7mmx64 Brenn.	300 Wea. Mag.
7mm-08	340 Wea. Mag.

DILLON

Carbide Pistol and Rifle Dies

Three-die carbide sets include size/decap, seater and crimp die. Design features include radiused carbide mouth; long tapered carbide ring; heavy headed decap pin; vented seating stem. All have large radiused mouths and wrench hex adjustments. Pistol dies available in 380 Auto, 9mm, 38 Super, 38/357, 10mm/40 S&W, 41 Magnum, 44 Special, 44 Magnum, 45 ACP and 45 Long Colt. Rifle die calibers: 223 Remington and 30M1 Carbine. From Dillon Precision Products, Inc.

Price: Pistol **$39.95**
Price: Rifle **$79.95**

FORSTER

Bench Rest Die Set

Two-die set that includes both the Bench Rest Sizing die and Bench Rest Seater die. From Forster Products.

Price: **$58.00**

Bench Rest Seater Die

Straight-line, chamber-type, non-crimping style die that holds bullet and case in alignment in close fitting channel. From Forster Products.

Price: **$32.00**

Bench Rest Sizing Die

Precision die with polished interior. Special attention given to head-space taper and diameter. Elevated expander button draws through neck of the case at moment of greatest mechanical advantage for better alignment of case and neck. From Forster Products.

Price: **$26.50**

Ultra Bullet Seater Die

Bullet seating die with micrometer seating depth adjustment. Head is graduated in .001" increments with .025" bullet movement per revolution. Available in 51 calibers. Kit to upgrade Forster Bench Rest seater die available. From Forster Products.

Price: Ultra Seater Die **$49.50**
Price: Upgrade kit **$36.00**

Weatherby Bench Rest Die Set

Two-die Bench Rest set, sizer and seater die, for Weatherby magnum calibers from 224 to 340. From Forster Products.

Price: **$65.00**

FREEDOM ARMS

454 Casull Dies

Carbide 3-die set for .452" bullets. From Freedom Arms, Inc.

Price: **$102.75**

FREMONT

Seating Die

A $^7/_8$-14 non-crimping, straight-line bullet seating die using a spring-loaded sliding sleeve to align case neck and shoulder with bullet. Bullet chamber cutaway allows insertion of bullet directly into sliding sleeve. Dies are universal and can seat bullets in any case of same caliber. Short cases require use of Fremont extended shellholder. Available in 17, 224, 6mm, 25, 270, 6.5mm, 7mm, 30, 338 and 35 calibers. From Fremont Tool Works.

Price: **$32.50**
Price: Extended shellholder **$7.50**

GOODWIN

Reloading/Case Form Dies

Precision machined steel reloading and case forming dies made in England by James Goodwin for unusual and hard-to-find calibers. Reloading dies threaded $^7/_8$-14. Special shellholders stocked (see chart). All others use Lyman and RCBS shellholders. Form dies 1"-unthreaded. From Jack First Distributors.

Price: Die set **$100.00**
Price: Form die **$26.50**
Price: Shellholder **$12.00**

HART

Bullet Seater

Stainless steel depth adjustable straight-line bullet seater. Available calibers include: 222, 222$^1/_2$, 222 Mag., 22-250, 6mm Rem. BR, 25-06, 30-338, 6x47, 6mm Rem., 22 Rem. BR, 308 Win., 7mm Mag., 22 PPC, 6mm PPC. From Robert Hart & Son, Inc.

Price: **$96.45**

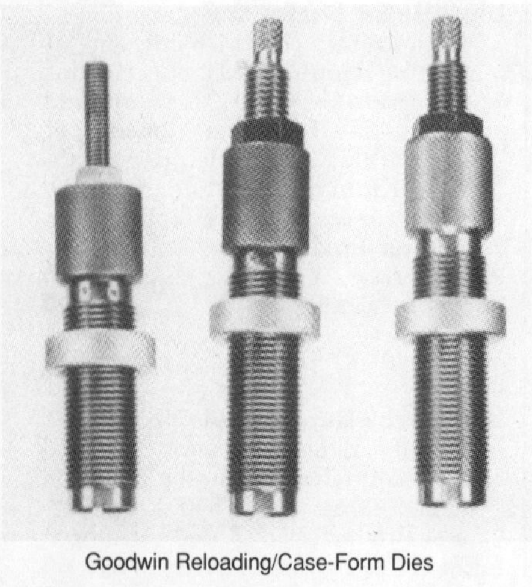

Goodwin Reloading/Case-Form Dies

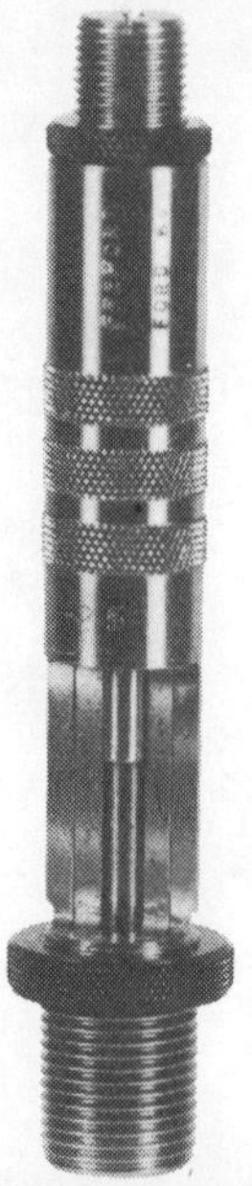

Fremont Seating Die

Hollywood Reloading Dies

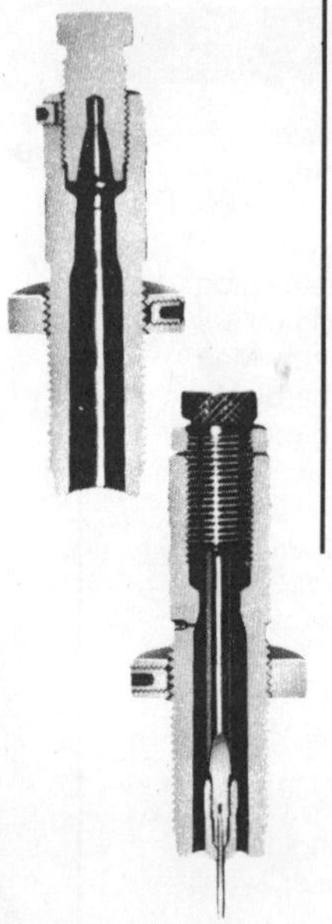

HOLLYWOOD

38-45 Dies

Comes as a complete set for reloading and case-forming or each die separately. A tungsten carbide sizer die is also available. From Hollywood Engineering.

Price: Complete set **$140.00**
Price: Reloading die set **$65.00**
Price: Case-form die set **$75.00**
Price: Carbide size die **$150.00**

50-Caliber Seater/Necksizer Die

Hardened steel and plated die threaded $^7/_8$-14 or $1^1/_2$-12. Comes complete with seater die, necksizer bushing, seater plug, inside lock nut, wrench for lock nut. From Hollywood Engineering.

Price: **$150.00**

HOLLYWOOD
50 BMG Necksizer/Seater Parts

DIE/DIE PART	PRICE
Necksizer/Seater, complete	$150.00
Seater	125.00
Necksizer Bushing	25.00
Seater Plug	18.00
Inside Lock Nut	2.00
Wrench, for lock nut	25.00
$^7/_8$" Thread Nut	2.00
$1^1/_2$" Thread Nut	5.00
Spanner Wrench, medium	15.00
Spanner Wrench, large	20.00

GOODWIN DIES

Die Set	Shellholder Y/N	Form Die# Y/N	Form Dies Final Size
240 Flanged	N	N	2
255 Rook	N	N	2
6.5x68	N	Y	1
26 BSA	N	N	2
280 Ross	Y	Y	1
300 Sherwood	N	N	1
7.62 Nagant Rev.	N	N	1
375-303	N	Y	1
310 Cadet	N	N	1
318 Richards	N	Y	1
7.65 French Long	Y	Y	1
8mm Lebel Rev.	N	N	1
8mm Lebel Rifle	Y	Y	1
8x50R	N	N	1
8x57J	N	Y	1
8x60R Port.	N	N	1
8x68S	N	N	1
8.15x46.5R	N	Y	1
32 Win. Spl.	N	Y	1
33 Win.	Y	Y	2
333 Jeffrey	N	Y	1
9x56	N	Y	1
35 Win.	N	Y	1
400-350	N	N	1
360-$2^1/_2$" NE	Y	N	1
360 #2 NE	Y	Y	2
369 Purdey	Y	Y	2
9.3x74R	N	N	1
375-$2^1/_2$" NE	N	Y	1
375 Flanged	N	Y	1
9.5x56	N	Y	1
38-56	N	Y	1
40-60 Win.	N	Y	1
40-82 Win.	N	Y	1
400 Purdey	N	Y	1
450-400 3"	Y	Y	1

Y = In stock; N = Lyman, RCBS shellholder.

GOODWIN DIES

Die Set	Shellholder Y/N	Form Die# Y/N	Form Dies Final Size
450-400 $3^1/_4$"	Y	Y	1
401 Win. SL	N	Y	1
10.75x68 Mauser	N	Y	1
10.75x73 Jeffery	Y	Y	1
405 Win.	N	Y	1
416 Rigby	Y	Y	2
11mm Mauser	Y	Y	1
425 Wes. Rich.	Y	Y	2
43 Egyptian	N	N	1
45-60 Win.	N	N	1
45-75 Win.	N	N	1
45-90 Win.	N	Y	1
450 $3^1/_4$" NE	Y	Y	1
577-450	Y	Y	2
500-450 $3^3/_4$"	N	Y	1
455 Colt	N	N	1
455 Webley	Y	Y	1
455 Webley Auto	N	N	1
461 Gibbs	N	N	1
500-465	N	Y	1
470 NE	Y	Y	1
475 #2	N	N	1
476 NE	N	N	1
50-95 Win.	N	Y	1
50-110 Win.	N	Y	1
500 Jeffrey	Y	N	2
12.7 Schuller	Y	N	1
500 3" NE	N	N	1
577-500 Mag.	Y	N	1
505 Gibbs	Y	Y	2
577 Snider	Y	Y	1
577 $2^3/_4$" NE	Y	Y	1
577 3" NE	Y	Y	1

Y = In stock; N = Lyman, RCBS shellholder.

HOLLYWOOD

STANDARD PISTOL/RIFLE DIES

—3-DIE SETS—

22 Jet CF	32 S&W	38 Long Colt	44 Webley
221 Rem.	32 S&W Long	38 Spl.	44-40 Rev. Old
25 ACP	32 Short Colt	357 Mag.	44-40 Rev. New
256 Win.	32 Long Colt	38-40 Rev.	45 ACP
30 Mauser	32-20 Rev.	41 Short Colt	45 Long Colt
7.63 Mauser	9mm Short	41 Long Colt	44 Auto Rim
7.65 Mauser	9mm Luger	41 Mag.	455 Webley
7.65 Luger	380 ACP	44 American	45 Colt Blank
7.7 Jap. Nambu	38 Super Auto	44 S&W Spl.	45 Colt Short
31 Jap.	38 S&W	44 Mag.	
32 ACP	38 Short Colt	44 Russian	

—2-DIE SETS—

22 Hornet	25-6mm Donaldson	7x65mm Mauser	340 Wea. Mag.
22 K-Hornet	25-06	7.35mm	348 Win.
218 Bee	25-06 CCC	7.5mm Swiss	348 CCC
218 Bee CCC	25-06 Imp.	7.5mm Schmidt Rubin	348-8mm Alaskan
218 Mashburn	25-20 Repeater	7.7mm Japanese	35 Rem.
22 Lovell	25-20 Single Shot	7.7-06 Case	35 Newton
22 R2 Lovell	25-35 Win.	7.62 NATO	35 Newton
221 Rem.	250-3000 Savage	7.62mm Russian	35 Whelen
222 Rem.	250-3000 CCC	7.92mm German Sht.	35 Whelen Imp.
222 Rem. Mag.	250 Donaldson	30 M1 Carbine	35 Ackley Mag.
219 Zipper	250 Ackley Mag.	30 Rem.	35 Win. S.L.
219 Zipper Imp.	256 Newton	30 Newton	350 K&K
219 Gib. Wasp	256 Japanese	30 Newton Special	350 Rem. Mag.
219 Don. .404	256 Spencer	30 CP Newton Belted	351 Win.
219 Don. .407	256 Win.	30 Ackley Mag.	358 Norma
22 Sav. High-Power	256 Mag. QT	30-30 Win.	358 Win.
22 Sav. High-Power CCC	257 Roberts	30-30 CCC	9x56mm Mann.-Schn.
22 Varminter	257 Roberts CCC	30-30 Krag CCC	9x57mm Rim.
22 Varminter CCC	257 Imp. Roberts	30-40 Krag	9.3x62mm
22 Arrow	257 Wea. Mag.	30-06	9.3x72mm Rim.
22-06 CCC	6.5mm Rem. Mag.	30-06 CCC	9.3x74-357 Rim.
Lindahl Std. Chuck	6.5mm Mann.-Schoen.	30-06 Ackley Imp.	9.3x74-367
Lindahl Super Chuck	6.5mm Japanese	30-06 8mm Ackley Imp.	9.3x74mm Rim. Imp.
22 Gebby Jr. Var.	6.5mm Carcano	30-06 8mm Standard	9.5mm
22 Gebby Sr. Var.	6.5mmx53 Rim.	300 Savage	9.5x57mm Mann.-Schn.
22 Rhetts	6.5mmx55 Krag	300 H&H Mag.	375 Mag. CCC
220 Swift	6.5mmx55 Mauser	300 H&H CCC	375 Mag.
220 Swift CCC	6.5mmx57mm	300 Wea. Mag.	375 Mag. Flanged
220 Wea.	6.5mmx68mm	300 Win. Mag.	375 Mag. Wea.
220 Imp.	264 Win.	303 British	375-06 CCC
22 Mag. CCC	270 Win.	303 Savage	376-357 Imp. Flanged
223 Rem. Mag.	270 CCC	308 Norma	375-9mm Flanged
224 Wea. Mag.	270 Mag. CCC	308 Win.	375-9.3mm Imp. Flngd.
225 Win.	270 Ackley Mag.	32 Win. Spl.	38 WCF
228 Ackley	270 Wea. Mag.	32 Rem.	38-55
240 Gebby Super Var.	280 Ross	32-20 Win.	38-56
240 Gebby Var. Belted	284 Rem.	32-40	401 Win. Auto
240 Cobra	284 Win.	8mm Mauser .318	405 Win.
243 Win.	7mm Mauser	8mm Mauser .323	44 WCF
6mm Rem.	7mm CCC	8mm Lebel	444 Marlin
244 Gibson	7mm Mag. CCC	8x56mm Mann.-Schn.	45-70
244 Rem.	7mm Rem. Mag.	8x57mm Mauser Rim.	45-90
244 H&H	7mm Wea. Mag.	8x57mm Rimless	458 Win. Mag.
25 Rem.	7mm Cradle	8x57mm Jr. Mauser	458 MCW Mag.
25 Souper	7x57mm Mauser	8x60 Rim.	50-110
25 Donaldson Ace	7x57mm Rim.	8x68mm	11mm (43 Mauser)
25 Krag CCC	7x61mm Sharp & Hart	8.15x46mm Rim.	
25 Barr Belted Mag.	7x64mm German	33 Win.	
25 Mag. Belted Cut.	7x64-06 Case	338 Win.	

HOLLYWOOD

Carbide Die Sets

Hollywood offers carbide decap rods, taper crimp dies and neck sizer dies for all their standard die calibers. They also offer full- length carbide sizer dies, full-length bottleneck sizer dies, full-length carbide sets and full-length bottleneck carbide sets for Hollywood, RCBS, Dillon and Star presses. From Hollywood Engineering.

Price: . . . . **See chart.**

Machine Gun Dies

Hardened steel and plated dies to fit any press with $1^1/_2$-12 threaded holes. Available for 50-caliber and 20mm. From Hollywood Engineering.

Price: 50-cal. **$195.00**
Price: 20mm **$290.00**

Standard Pistol/Rifle Die Sets

Two- and 3-die sets in most popular calibers. Dies made of steel and threaded $^7/_8$-14. From Hollywood Engineering.

Price: **$36.00**

Vickerman Seater Die

Steel die for standard and large pistol/rifle calibers and 50 BMG. Threaded $^7/_8$-14 and $1^1/_2$-12. From Hollywood Engineering.

Price: Standard, $^7/_8$" **$60.00**
Price: Large, $1^1/_2$" **$160.00**
Price: 50 BMG **$160.00**

HOLLYWOOD Carbide Pistol/Rifle Dies

Caliber	Die Type	Price
DECAP RODS/TAPER CRIMP/NECK SIZER		
Standard	Decap rod, no carbide ball	$20.00
50	Decap rod, no carbide ball	55.00
Standard	Decap rod, carbide ball to 30-cal.	30.00
50	Decap rod, carbide ball	60.00
Standard	Decap rod, carbide ball 30-cal. and over	POR
22-30	Taper crimp	50.00
30-50	Taper crimp	POR
All	Neck Sizer	92.50
FULL-LENGTH SIZER (HOLLYWOOD, RCBS, DILLON, STAR)		
25 ACP, 32 ACP, 380 ACP, 38 S&W Short		65.00
30 M1, 32 S&W Long, 38/357, 38 Super ACP, 38 Special, 41 Mag., 44 Spl. Mag., 44 Rem. Mag., 45 ACP, 9mm Luger		75.00
10mm, 45 Long Colt		80.00
44 Auto Magnum		120.00
45-70		140.00
FULL-LENGTH BOTTLENECK SIZER (HOLLYWOOD, RCBS, DILLON, STAR)		
223, 308, 22-250, 38-40, 44-40		150.00
25-20 SS, 25-20 WCF, 32-20		130.00
30-06, 25-06, 7mm		155.00
50-caliber		375.00
FULL-LENGTH DIE SET (HOLLYWOOD)		
25 ACP, 32 ACP, 380 ACP, 38 S&W Short		35.00
30 M1,, 32 S&W Long, 38/357, 38 Super ACP, 38 Spl., 41 Mag., 44 Spl. Mag., 44 Rim. Mag., 45 ACP, 9mm		95.00
10mm, 45 Long Colt		100.00
44 Auto Magnum		155.00
45-70		160.00
FULL-LENGTH BOTTLENECK DIE SETS (HOLLYWOOD)		
223, 308, 22-250, 38-40, 44-40		170.00
25-20 SS, 25-20 WCF, 32-20		150.00
30-06, 25-06, 7mm		175.00
50-caliber		470.00

POR = Price on request.

HOLLYWOOD Standard $^7/_8$" Die Parts

DIE/DIE PART	PRICE
Bullet Seater, complete	$35.00
Bullet Seater, stripped	20.00
Seater Stem, with lock ring	5.50
Seater Stem, stripped	4.75
Decap Pins	.75
Decap Rod, complete	9.00
Decap Rod, stripped	6.75
Expander	3.00
Expander, 22-30 cal.	7.50
Expander, 30-06-35 cal.	7.50
Lock Ring, Resizer, Bullet Seat Body	35.00
Bullet Seat Stem, Lock Ring, Decap Rod	15.00
Resize Die, complete	45.00
Full-Length Resizer, stripped	25.00
Set Screw for Lock Ring	.40

HOLLYWOOD $1^1/_2$" Rifle Die Parts

DIE/DIE PART	PRICE
Bullet Seater, complete	$92.50
Bullet Seater, stripped	82.50
Bullet Seat Stem, complete	20.00
Bullet Seat Stem, only	10.00
Decap Pins	.75
Decap Rod, complete	20.00
Decap Rod, stripped	11.50
Expander	12.00
Lock Ring, bullet seat die	5.00
Lock Ring, bullet seat stem/decap rod	2.00
Resizer, complete	92.50
Full-Length Resizer, stripped	82.50
Set Screw for Lock Rings	.40

HOLLYWOOD Special $^7/_8$" Die Parts

DIE/DIE PART	PRICE
Bullet Seater, complete	$50.00
Bullet Seat Stem	45.00
Bullet Seater, stripped	45.00
Bullet Seat Stem, complete	10.00
Bullet Seat Stem, stripped	5.00
Decap Pin	.75
Decap Rod, complete	9.00
Decap Rod, stripped	7.00
Expander	3.00
Lock Ring, bullet seat/ expander unit	22.00
Lock Ring, bullet seat stem/ decap pin	14.00
Resizer, complete	60.00
Full-Length Sizer, stripped	40.00
Set Screw for Lock Ring	.40

HORNADY

Neck-Size Die

Steel die finished in hard satin chrome. Resizes only the case neck. Standard 7/8-14 thread with blued steel lock ring. Interior heat-treated and polished. Weight: 1 lb. From Hornady Mfg. Co.

Price: **$14.80**

New Dimension Series I, II, III, IV Dies

Made of high-quality hand-inspected steel. Dies are lathed to industry-established dimensional tolerances for maximum cartridge size; inside surface hand polished and protective coating applied. Other features include: eliptical expander to reduce friction, case neck stretch and eliminate need for tapered expander; hardened steel decap pin; no-lube Titanium Nitride pistol size die; floating seating stems; and wrench flats. In-line bullet seater has floating alignment sleeve and built-in crimper. Available in most standard rifle/pistol calibers (Series I, II, III). Custom dies (Series IV) also offered on special order. From Hornady Mfg. Co.

Price: . . . . **See chart.**

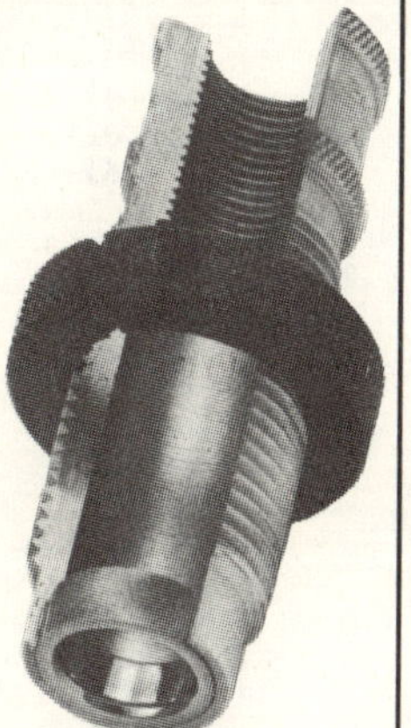

Hornady Titanium Nitride Die

HORNADY
New Dimension Series I, II, III Dies

SERIES I 2-DIE	SERIES I 3-DIE	SERIES III 2-DIE	SERIES II 3-DIE
22 Hornet	30 M1 Carbine	17 Rem.	25 ACP
222 Rem.	375 Win.	218 Bee	32 ACP
223 Rem.	444 Marlin	221 Rem.	32 S&W Long/Short
22/250	45-70 Gov't.	222 Rem. Mag.	H&R Mag.
220 Swift	458 Win.	225 Win.	9mm Luger
243 Win.	458 Win.	240 Wea.	9x21
244/6mm Rem.		6mm/223	380 Auto
6mm PPC		6mm/223	38 Super Auto
25-06		6mm TCU	38/357
257 Roberts		6mm Rem. BR	357 Maximum
6.5x55 Scan.		25-35 Win.	10mm Auto/40 S&W
264 Win. Mag.		250 Savage	41 Mag.
270 Win.		257 Wea.	41 Action Exp.
7x57		6.5mm TCU	44 Spl.
7mm Exp./280		270 Wea.	44 Mag.
7mm-08		284 Win.	45 ACP
7mm Rem. Mag.		7x30 Waters	45 Win. Mag.
7mm TCU		7mm Rem. BR	45 Auto Rim
7mm Wea.		30 Herrett	45 Long Colt
30-30 Win.		7.5 Swiss	
300 Savage		30 Luger	
300 Wea.		30-40 Krag	
308 Win.		300 H&H	
30-06		7.7 Japanese	
300 Win. Mag.		7.65 Belgian	
303 British		32 Win. Spl.	
7.62x39		32/20 Win.	
8mm Maus. (8x57 JS)		8mm Rem. Mag.	
338 Win. Mag.		357 Herrett	
340 Wea.		358 Win.	
35 Rem.			
35 Whelen			
375 H&H			

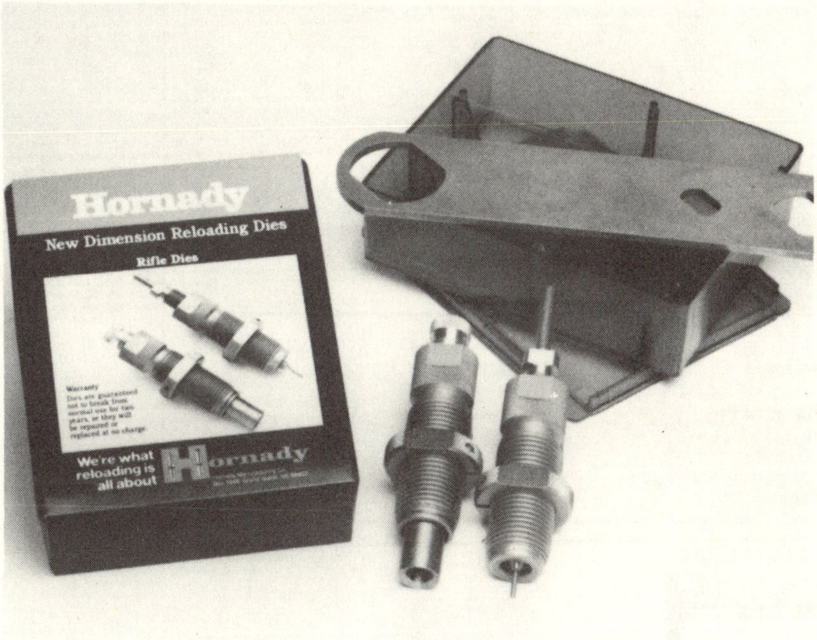

Hornady New Dimension Rifle Dies

HORNADY
New Dimension Die Prices

DIE SERIES	2-DIE RIFLE	3-DIE RIFLE	CUSTOM PISTOL
Series I Set	$22.90	$25.40	$52.65
Full-Length Die	17.05	21.75	
Seat Die	13.50	13.50	
Expander	6.20	7.25	
Series II Set			34.35
Full-Length Die			21.75
Seat Die			13.50
Expander	6.20		7.25
Series III Set	29.85		
Full-Length Die	23.85		
Seat Die	13.50		
Expander	6.20		

Taper Crimp Die

All steel and precision engineered. Add to three-die pistol set to apply crimp to autoloading pistol cases. Available for 9mm, 38, 9x21, 10mm, 40 S&W, 45 ACP, 45 Auto Rim, 45 Winchester Magnum. Weight: 1 lb. From Hornady Mfg. Co.

Price: **$11.05**

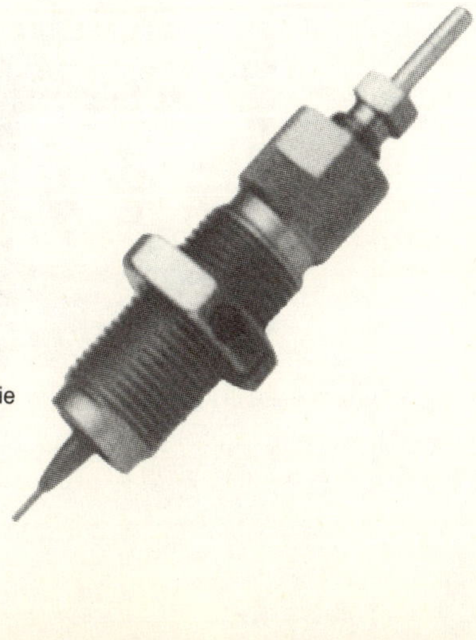

Hornady Neck Size Die

HORNADY
Neck-Size Dies

- 22
- 22 PPC
- 6mm
- 6mm/Short
- 6mm PPC
- 25 Caliber
- 6.5mm/Short
- 6.5mm
- 270 Caliber
- 7mm
- 30 Caliber
- 30 Caliber/Short
- 35 Caliber

Hornady

RIFLE/PISTOL DIES

Cartridge	Die Group	Shellholder	Cartridge	Die Group	Shellholder	Cartridge	Die Group	Shellholder
RIFLE								
17 Rem.	III	16	6.5x55/Scan.	I	19	300 Wea.	I	5
17/222	IV	16	6.5/06	IV	1	308 Norma Mag.	IV	5
17/223	IV	16	6.5mm TCU	III	16	7062 Russian	IV	23
218 Bee	III	7	6.5 Rem. Mag.	IV	5	705 Swiss	III	30
219 Zipper	IV	2	6.5 Mann.	IV	20	32/20 Win.	III	7
221 Rem.	III	16	6.5 Carc.	IV	21	7.62x39	I	6
222 Rem.	I	16	6.5 Japanese	IV	34	7.7 Japanese	III	1
222 Rem. Mag.	III	16	6.5x57	IV	1	303 British	I	11
22 Hornet (.224)	I	3	6.5x68	IV	30	7065 Beig.	III	24
22 K-Hornet (.224)	IV	3	264 Win. Mag.	I	5	32 Win. Spl.	III	2
22 RCFM-Jet (.224)	IV	6	270 Win.	I	1	32/40 Win.	IV	2
22 PPC (.224)	IV	6	270 Wea.	III	5	8mm Mauser	I	1
5.6x50 Mag. (.224)	IV	16	7x30 Waters	III	2	8mm/06	IV	1
5.6x52R (.227)	IV	2	7x57 (7mm Mauser)	I	1	8mm Rem. Mag.	III	5
5.6x57 (.224)	IV	1	7mm/08	I	1	8x60 S	IV	1
223 Rem. (.224)	I	16	7mm Rem. Mag.	I	5	8x68 S	IV	30
22/250	I	1	7mm Rem. BR	III	1	8.15x46 R	IV	2
220 Swift	I	4	7mm TCU	I	16	338 Win. Mag.	I	5
22 Savage HP	IV	2	7mm Merrill	IV	4	33 Win.	IV	14
Wea.	IV	17	7x65 R	IV	13	340 Wea.	I	5
225 Win.	III	4	7mm Wea.	I	5	348 Win.	IV	25
240 Wea.	III	1	7x64	IV	1	35 Rem.	I	26
243 Win.	I	1	7mm/223 Ingram	IV	16	35 Whelen	I	1
244/6mm	I	1	7x47 Helm	IV	16	357/44 B&D	IV	30
6mm Int.	IV	1	7x61 S&H	IV	35	350 Rem. Mag.	IV	5
6mm/223	III	16	7mm Express/280	I	1	357 Herrett	III	2
6mm/PPC	I	6	284 Win.	III	1	358 Win.	III	1
6mm TCU	III	16	7.35 Carc.	IV	21	358 N. Mag.	IV	5
6mm/284	IV	1	30/30 Win.	I	2	375 H&H	III	5
6x47 Rem.	IV	16	300 Savage	I	1	378 Wea.	IV	14
250 Savage	III	1	30 Luger	III	8	9.3x74 R	IV	13
25/06	I	1	30 Merrill	IV	4	9.3x57	IV	1
257 Roberts	I	1	30 Herrett	III	2	9.3x62	IV	1
25/20 Win.	IV	7	303 Savage	IV	33	10.3x60	IV	25
25/35 Win.	III	2	308 Win.	I	1	416 Rem. Mag.	IV	5
256 Win.	IV	6	30/40 Krag	III	11	416 Rigby	IV	38
257 Wea.	III	5	30/06	I	1	416 Wea.	IV	14
25 Rem.	IV	12	300 H&H	III	5	460 Wea.	IV	14
25/284	IV	1	300 Win. Mag.	I	5			
PISTOL								
25 ACP	II	37	38 Smith & Wesson	IV	28	44 Auto. Mag.	IV	1
30 M1 Carbine	I	22	38-357-357 Max.	II	6	44/40 Win.	IV	9
32 ACP	II	22	357 Win.	I	2	444 Marlin	II	27
32 S&W Long/Short H&R Mag.	II	36	10mm Auto.-40 S&W	II	10	45 Auto. Rim	II	31
			38/40 Win.	IV	9	45 ACP/AR/WM	II	1
9mm Kuger/9x21	II	8	41 Action Express	IV	8	45 Long Colt	II	32
380 Automatic	II	16	41 Mag.	II	29	45/70 Gov't	I	14
38 Super Automatic	II	8	44 Spl/44 Mag.	II	30	458 Win.	I	5

Hornady
New Dimension Pistol Dies

JONES

Micro-Adjustable Bullet Seating Hand Die

A straight-line seating die with bushings available in .001" increments to precisely support and align the neck of the case. Adjustable threaded cap and stem allow depth adjustment increments of .00125" and .050" per revolution. Manufactured of steel with black oxide finish. Die and bushings available for all popular calibers including wildcats. State loaded neck dimension of cartridge for proper bushing size. Comes with one bushing. From Neil Jones Custom Products.

Price: **$60.00**
Price: 17-cal. and +30-cal., add . . . **$10.00**

Micro Form Die

Case forming system consisting of micro-adjustable die body and a series of forming bushings. Bushings are manufactured with a larger lead angle than regular sizing bushings to reduce neck diameters and/or move the case shoulder. Number of bushings required depends on the caliber and if the shoulder is moved. Price does not include No. 6 style bushing. From Neil Jones Custom Products.

Price: **$55.00**
Price: Bushing **$8.00**

Micro-Adjustable Neck Sizing Hand Die

A precision neck sizing die that features an adjustable cap threaded to provide .050" of movement per revolution and scribed increments of .00125". Used with Jones neck/shoulder bushings, the case neck is sized and the shoulder moved back in precisely controlled steps as case is forced into die. Shoulder bushings available in all sizes and shoulder angles including wildcats. Made of steel with black oxide finish. Tension adjustable decapping punch suitable for all calibers from 22 on up. For use on arbor press and with Jones bushing style No. 2. Comes with bushing and die base for arbor press use. From Neil Jones Custom Products.

Price: **$60.00**
Price: 17-cal. and +30-cal., add . . . **$10.00**

JONES

Threaded Neck-Sizing Die

Designed for use in conventional reloading press. Manufactured with standard 7/8-14 thread but uses interchangeable hardened steel bushings available in increments of .001" for precision neck-sizing. Single die with proper bushings will accommodate all cartridges with same head diameter. Expansion mandrels to open up case necks to larger caliber also available. Price does not include No. 2 style bushing. From Neil Jones Custom Products.

Price: **$55.00**
Price: 17-cal. and +30-cal., add . . **$10.00**
Price: Bushing **$8.00**
Price: Expansion mandrel **$12.00**
Price: Decap punch **$8.00**

Threaded Seating Die

For use in conventional reloading press. Same design features as Jones micro-adjustable seating die with direct in-line alignment of case neck and floating seating punch adjustable in increments of .001". Available in most calibers and cartridges. Comes with one No. 5 style bushing. From Neil Jones Custom Products.

Price: **$65.00**
Price: 17-cal. and +30-cal., add . . **$10.00**

KING

Used and New Dies

Carries over 200 used and new dies for current, obsolete and wildcat cartridges. Contact King for current listing of available calibers. From King & Company.

Price: . . . . **See chart.**

KING Rifle/Pistol Die Prices

GROUP	PRICE/NEW	PRICE/USED
A	$18.50	$13.44
B	20.35	14.80
C	22.50	16.40
D	24.20	17.60
E	24.20	17.60
F	28.60	20.80
G	35.48	25.80
H	38.50	28.00
I	38.50	28.00
J	72.33	35.00
K	98.63	62.00
L	98.63	62.00
X	156.75	104.50

Jones
Micro-Threaded Neck Sizing Die

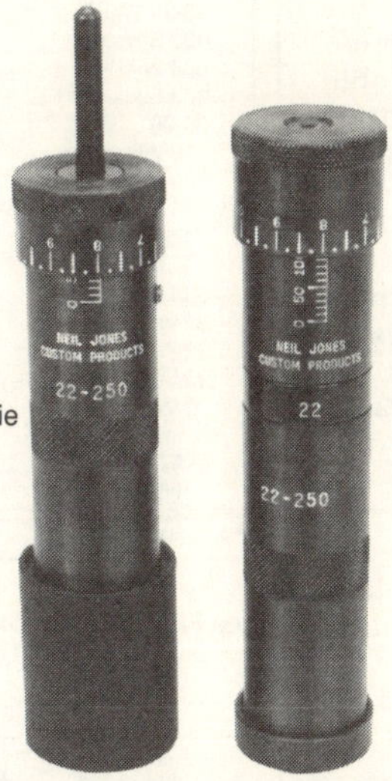

Jones
Micro Bullet Seating Die

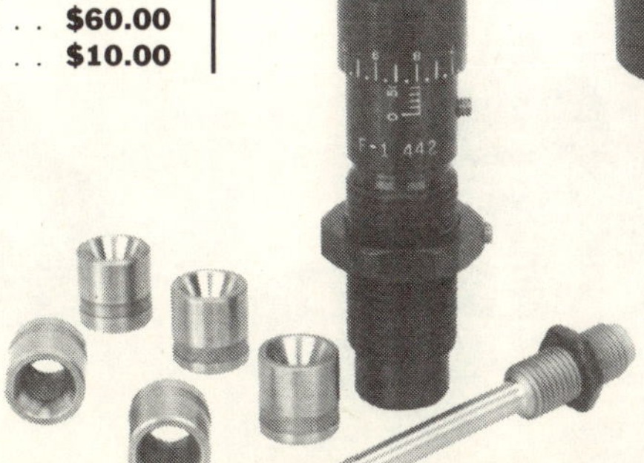

Jones Micro Form Die

LEE

Carbide Factory Crimp Die

For handgun ammunition. Carbide sizer sizes cartridge during crimping operation. Adjusting-screw sets desired amount of crimp. Trim length is not critical. From Lee Precision, Inc.

Price: **$17.98**

Carbide Speed Die

For use in single-station press. Eliminates need to change dies between operations. Comes with shellholder, powder dipper and load data for one cartridge. Available for 9mm Luger, 38 Special, 357 Magnum, 44 Magnum, 45 ACP. From Lee Precision, Inc.

Price: **$19.98**

Carbide/Steel Pistol Dies

Three-die pistol sets. Carbide dies contour ground to provide stepless sizing. Set includes sizer/decapper, powder-through-expander and bullet seater. Each die has enlarged mouth to align with cases, even damaged cases. Steel dies have same features as carbide except case must be lubricated. Come with free shellholder. From Lee Precision, Inc.

Price: Carbide **$35.98**
Price: Steel **$26.98**

Collet Rifle Dies

No-lube necksize-only dies. A collet squeezes case neck against precision mandrel with minimum runout. Not recommended for autoloaders, slide- or lever-action firearms. See chart for available calibers. From Lee Precision, Inc.

Price: **$34.98**

Decapping Die

No-lube decap die removes crimped-in primers on press. One size fits all cases. From Lee Precision, Inc.

Price: **$9.98**

Factory Crimp Die

Standard with Lee PaceSetter die sets. Crimps the bullet in place without possibility of case buckling. From Lee Precision, Inc.

Price: **$11.98**

Limited Production Rifle Dies

Limited Production two-die set includes full-length sizer, bullet seater/roll crimper, shellholder, powder dipper and load data for single cartridge in transparent storage container. This set does not include a factory crimp die. See chart for available calibers. From Lee Precision, Inc.

Price: **$29.98**

LEE

RIFLE/PISTOL DIES

Caliber	RGB Series	—PaceSetter— 3-Die	Ltd.	Limited Production	Collet Necksize	Factory Crimp	Taper Crimp
—RIFLE—							
17 Rem.	NA	NA	NA	A	A	NA	NA
22 Hornet	NA	NA	A	NA	A	A	NA
218 Bee	NA	NA	A	NA	NA	A	NA
22 PPC	NA	NA	NA	A	A	NA	NA
221 Fireball	NA	NA	NA	A	NA	NA	NA
222 Rem.	A	A	NA	NA	A	A	A
223	A	A	NA	NA	A	A	A
22-250	A	A	NA	NA	A	A	NA
220 Swift	NA	NA	NA	A	A	A	NA
243 Win.	A	A	NA	NA	A	A	NA
6mm PPC	NA	NA	NA	A	A	NA	NA
6mm Rem.	NA	NA	A	NA	A	A	NA
25-20	NA	NA	A	NA	NA	A	NA
25-35	NA	NA	NA	A	NA	NA	NA
250 Savage	NA	NA	NA	A	A	A	NA
257 Roberts	NA	NA	A	NA	A	A	NA
25-06	NA	NA	A	NA	A	A	NA
264 Win. Mag.	NA	NA	NA	A	NA	NA	NA
6.5 Carcano	NA	NA	NA	A	NA	NA	NA
6.5 Japanese	NA	NA	NA	A	NA	NA	NA
6.5 Rem. Mag.	NA	NA	NA	A	NA	NA	NA
6.5x55	A	A	NA	NA	A	A	NA
270 Wea..	NA	NA	NA	A	NA	NA	NA
270 Win.	A	A	NA	NA	A	A	NA
7mm BR	NA	NA	NA	A	A	NA	NA
7mm TCU	NA	NA	NA	A	NA	NA	NA
7-30 Waters	NA	NA	NA	A	NA	A	NA
7x57 Mauser	NA	NA	A	NA	A	A	NA
7x64 Brenneke	NA	NA	NA	A	NA	NA	NA
7mm-08	NA	NA	A	NA	A	A	NA
7mm Express	NA	NA	A	NA	A	A	NA
7mm Rem. Mag.	A	A	NA	NA	A	A	NA
284 Win.	NA	NA	NA	A	NA	NA	NA
7mm Wea.	NA	NA	NA	A	NA	NA	NA
7.35 Carcano	NA	NA	NA	A	NA	NA	NA
7.5 Schmidt Rubin	NA	NA	NA	A	NA	NA	NA
7.62x39 Russian	A	A	NA	NA	NA	A	A
7.62x54 Russian	NA	NA	A	NA	NA	A	NA
30 Herrett	NA	NA	NA	A	NA	NA	NA
30/40 Krag	NA	NA	A	NA	NA	A	A
30-30 Win.	A	A	NA	NA	A	A	A
303 Savage	NA	NA	NA	A	NA	NA	A
308 Win.	A	A	NA	NA	A	A	A
300 Savage	NA	NA	A	NA	NA	A	NA
30-06	A	A	NA	NA	A	A	A
300 Win. Mag.	A	A	NA	NA	A	A	NA
300 H&H	NA	NA	NA	A	A	NA	NA
300 Weath. Mag.	NA	NA	A	NA	A	A	NA
7.65 Arg. Mauser	NA	NA	A	NA	NA	A	A
7.7 Japanese	NA	NA	A	NA	NA	A	A
303 British	A	A	NA	NA	A	A	A
32-20	NA	NA	NA	A*	NA	A	NA
32-40	NA	NA	NA	A	NA	NA	NA
32 Win.	NA	NA	NA	A	NA	NA	NA
33 Win.	NA	NA	NA	A	NA	NA	NA
8mm Rem. Mag.	NA	NA	NA	A	NA	NA	NA
8x57 Mauser	A	A	NA	NA	A	A	NA
8mm Lebel	NA	NA	NA	A	NA	NA	NA

A = Available; NA = Not available. *Special Order. **Custom die $30.00.

Lee Factory Crimp Die

Lee Carbide Factory Crimp Die

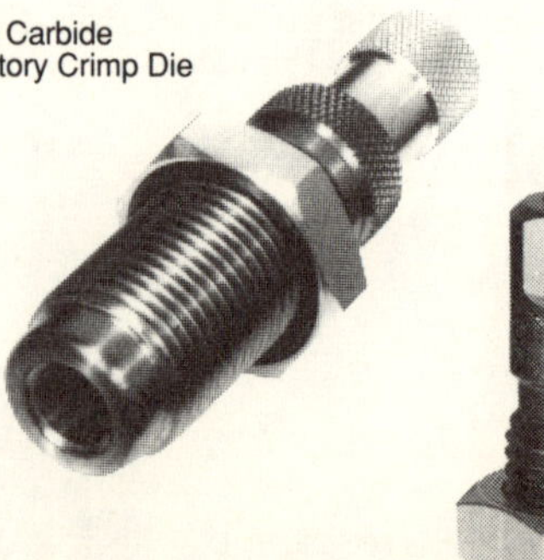

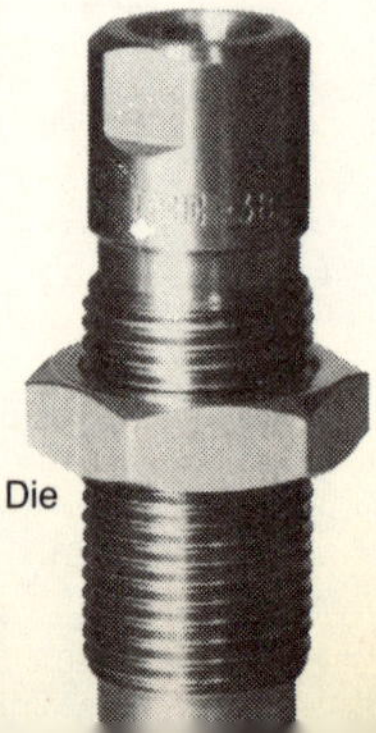

Lee Taper Crimp Die

LEE

RIFLE/PISTOL DIES (con't.)

Caliber	RGB Series	—PaceSetter— 3-Die	—PaceSetter— Ltd.	Limited Production	Collet Necksize	Factory Crimp	Taper Crimp
—RIFLE—							
338 Win.	NA	NA	A	NA	A	A	NA
348 Win.	NA	NA	NA	A	NA	A	NA
350 Rem. Mag.	NA	NA	NA	A	NA	NA	NA
356 Win.	NA	NA	NA	A	NA	A	NA
358 Win.	NA	NA	NA	A	NA	A	NA
35 Rem.	NA	NA	A	NA	A	A	NA
35 Whelen	NA	NA	NA	A	A	NA	NA
38-40	NA	NA	NA	A*	NA	A	NA
38-55	NA	NA	NA	A*	NA	A	NA
38-56	NA	NA	NA	A	NA	NA	NA
375 H&H	NA	NA	A	NA	A	A	NA
375 Win.	NA	NA	NA	A*	NA	A	NA
416 Rem.	NA	NA	NA	A*	NA	A	NA
43 Mauser	NA	NA	NA	A	NA	NA	NA
43 Spanish	NA	NA	NA	A	NA	NA	NA
44-40	NA	NA	NA	A*	NA	A	NA
444 Marlin	NA	NA	NA	A*	NA	A	NA
45-70 Gov't.	NA	NA	NA	A*	NA	A	NA
458 Win. Mag.	NA	NA	NA	A*	NA	A	NA

Cartridge	Carbide 3-Die Set	Steel 3-Die Set	Speed Die	Carbide Size Die	Powder Expand Die	Taper Crimp	Carbide Crimp Die
—PISTOL—							
25 ACP	A	NA	NA	A*	A*	NA	NA
30 M1 Carbine	A	NA	NA	A	A	A	NA
30 Luger	NA	A	NA	NA	A	NA	NA
30 Mauser	NA	A	NA	NA	A*	NA	NA
32 ACP	A	NA	NA	A	A	NA	NA
32 S&W Long	A	NA	NA	A	A	A	NA
32 H&R Magnum	A	NA	NA	A	A*	A	NA
32-20	NA	A	NA	NA	A*	NA	A**
38-40	NA	A	NA	NA	A*	NA	A**
9mm Luger	A	A	A	A	A	A	A
38 Colt N.P.	NA	NA	NA	A	A*	NA	NA
38 Super/38 ACP	A	NA	NA	A	A	A	
380 Auto	A	NA	NA	A	A	A	A
38 S&W	A	NA	NA	A	A*	NA	NA
38 Special	A	A	A	A	A	A	A
357 Magnum	A	A	A	A	A	A	A
40 S&W	A	NA	NA	NA	NA	NA	A
10mm Auto	A	NA	NA	A*	A*	A	A
41 AE	NA	NA	A	A*	NA	NA	NA
41 Magnum	A	NA	NA	A	A	A	NA
44 Special	A	A	NA	A	A	A	A
44 Magnum	A	A	A	A	A	A	A
44-40	NA	A	NA	NA	A*	NA	A**
45 Colt	A	NA	NA	A	A	A	A
45 ACP	A	A	A	A	A	A	A
45 Auto Rim	A	NA	NA	A	A*	A	NA
455 Webley MII	A	NA	NA	A	A*	A	NA
45 Win. Mag.	A	NA	NA	A	A	A	A
454 Casull	A	NA	NA	A	A	A	A
45 HP Italian	A	NA	NA	A	A*	A	A

A = Available; NA = Not available. *Special Order. **Custom die $30.00.

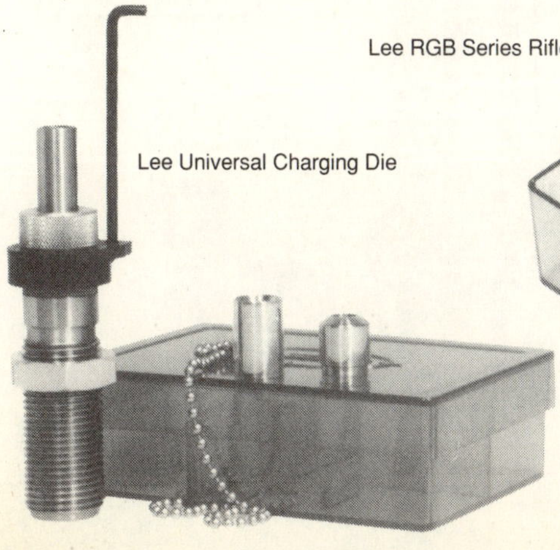
Lee Universal Charging Die

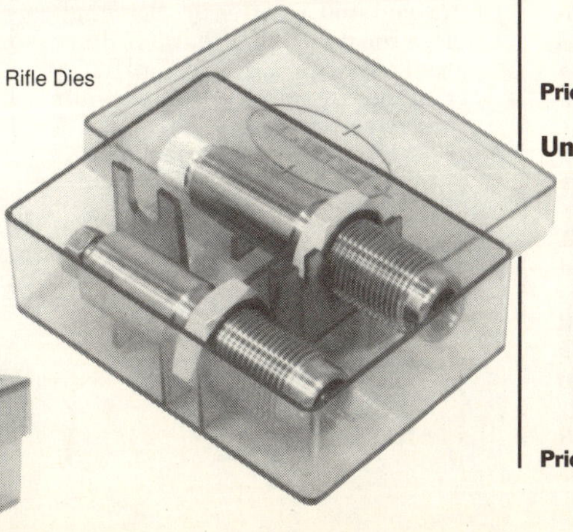
Lee RGB Series Rifle Dies

LEE

PaceSetter Rifle Die Set

Three-die rifle set includes full-length sizer, bullet seater/roll crimper, factory crimp die, shellholder, powder dipper, load data and instructions for single cartridge in transparent storage container. Two price levels—one for standard stocked die sets and another for Ltd. production die sets. See chart for available calibers. From Lee Precision, Inc.

Price: Standard **$26.98**
Price: Limited Production **$29.98**

RGB Series Rifle Die Set

Rifle two-die set with full-length sizer and bullet seater/roll crimper only with load data for one cartridge in transparent plastic storage container. See chart for available calibers. From Lee Precision, Inc.

Price: **$17.98**

Rifle Charging Die

For use on standard threaded presses to charge small-capacity rifle cases using Lee Auto-Disk powder measure. Similar in operation to powder-through-expanding die, except does not expand case mouth. From Lee Precision, Inc.

Price: **$11.98**

Steel Rifle Dies

All Lee dies feature one-piece reaming, wrench flats, collet held decapper, finger adjustable bullet seater, elevated expander, O-ring locks. Dies offer unbreakable decapper, floating bullet seater, heat-treated to maximum hardness and progressively machine-honed inside surface. Lee dies come in five configurations: RGB, PaceSetter, PaceSetter Ltd., Limited Production and Collet dies. From Lee Precision, Inc.

Price: . . . . **See individual listings.**

Taper Crimp Die

Hardened steel die designed to overcome crimp problems caused by incorrect bullet seater dies. See chart for available calibers. From Lee Precision, Inc.

Price: **$9.98**

Universal Charging Die

Charges both rifle and pistol cases. Includes connecting rod and adaptors to actuate measure with the case. Measure positively resets when ram fully lowered. Comes with drop tubes for most cartridges from the 380 ACP to the 300 Winchester Magnum. Does not expand case mouth. From Lee Precision, Inc.

Price: **$24.98**

LYMAN

AA Rifle 2-Die Sets
All steel die set consists of full-length resizing die with decapping stem and neck expanding button and a bullet seating die. Best for reloading jacketed bullets in bottle-necked cases. For reloading cast bullets, add a neck expanding die. From Lyman Products Corporation.

Price: **$26.95**

AA Rifle 3-Die Set
For reloading straight-wall cases. Full-length sizing die with decapping stem, AA two-step neck expanding (M) die and bullet seating die. Also good for loading cast bullets. From Lyman Products Corporation.

Price: **$34.95**

Carbide Pistol 3-Die Set
Tungsten carbide full-length resizing and decapping die, two-step neck expanding die and bullet seating chamber and screw. Comes with extra seating screws for loading all popular bullet designs for given caliber. Two-step expander prevents cast bullet distortion and assures precise case neck tension. Loads both magnum and special length cases. Resizing ring eliminates need for case lubing. From Lyman Products Corporation.

Price: **$41.95**

Carbide Pistol 4-Die Set
Includes separate taper crimp die for reloading semi-auto cartridges; powder charge/expanding die with special hollow expander plugs for two-step neck expansion and powder charging. Top of expand/powder die threaded to accept Lyman #55 powder measure, AccuMeasure or any other brand threaded measure. Neck size die and seating die make up the quartet. From Lyman Products Corporation.

Price: **$49.95**

Metric Rifle 2-Die Set
For reloading metric calibers with jacketed bullets. From Lyman Products Corporation.

Price: **$34.95**

Multi-Expand/Powder Charge Die
Simultaneously expands case mouth and drops powder charge from measure. Includes expander/powder drop tubes for 32, 9mm, 38/357, 10mm/40 S&W, 41, 44 and 45 Auto plus non-expanding universal drop tube. Works with all presses and powder measures with standard die thread. From Lyman Products Corporation.

Price: **$23.95**

LYMAN

Neck Size Rifle 2-Die Set
Works only neck of case to retain fireformed dimensions. Includes special sizing die with decapping stem and expander button and a standard bullet seating die. From Lyman Products Corporation.

Price: **$29.95**

Ram Prime Die System
Designed for primer feeding on top of press. Standard die threading to fit all presses. Includes large and small primer punches. From Lyman Products Corporation.

Price: **$13.95**

Small Base Rifle 2-Die Set
Designed for loading jacketed bullets in cartridges sized to minimum dimensions. Set includes special small base full-length resizing die with decapping stem and expander button and a standard bullet seating die. From Lyman Products Corporation.

Price: **$29.95**

Standard Pistol 3-Die Set
Includes same features as carbide 3-die set except resizing die is steel. From Lyman Products Corporation.

Price: **$29.95**

Taper Crimp Die
Applies proper crimp to pistol and rifle cases. Heat-treated to R50 minimum surface hardness and interior hand polished to 8 rms finish. From Lyman Products Corporation.

Price: **$14.00**

Two-Step Expanding (M) Die
Designed for cast and jacketed bullet loads. Prevents case stretching to extend case life. Expands inside of case neck to just under bullet diameter then expands case mouth to bullet diameter or slightly over. From Lyman Products Corporation.

Price: **$12.50**

Universal Decapping Die
For all calibers 22 through 45 except 378 and 460 Weatherby. Solid one-piece construction of hardened tool steel. Works well for military crimped primers. From Lyman Products Corporation.

Price: **$11.50**

Lyman Carbide 4-Die Pistol Set

Lyman Carbide 3-Die Pistol Set

Lyman Universal Decapper

LYMAN Taper Crimp Die Calibers
32 ACP
32 S&W Long
32 H&R Mag.
380 Auto
38 S&W
38 Super Auto
9mm Luger
38 Spl./357 Mag.
357 Rem. Max.
40 S&W
10mm Auto
41 Magnum
41 Action Exp.
44 Mag./44 Spl.
445 Super Mag.
45 ACP
45 Win. Mag.
45 Colt

Lyman Multi-Expand/Powder Charge Die

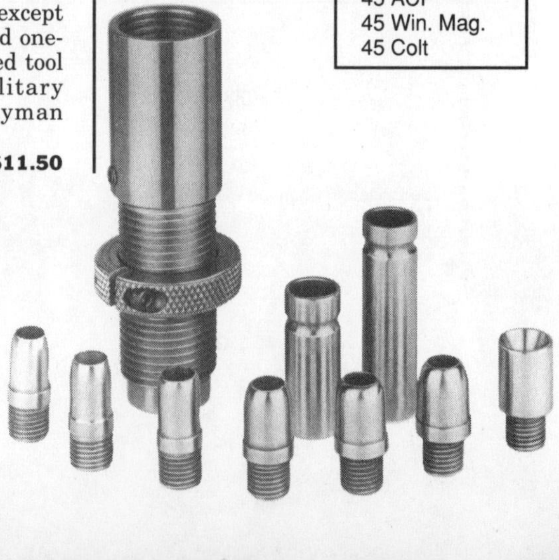

Lyman

RIFLE/PISTOL DIES

Cartridge	Die Group	Shellholder	Cartridge	Die Group	Shellholder	Cartridge	Die Group	Shellholder
	—RIFLE—						—PISTOL—	
17 Rem.	AA-2	26	30-06	AA-2, SB-2	2	25 ACP	S-3	32
22 Hornet	AA-2	4	307 Win.	AA-2, SB-2	6	7mm TCU	S-3	26
222 Rem.	AA-2	26	308 Win.	AA-2, SB-2	2	30 Luger	S-3	12
222 Rem. Mag.	AA-2	26	300 Sav.	AA-2	2	30 Herrett	S-3	6
223 Rem. (5.56mm)	AA-2, SB-2	26	300 Wea. Mag.	AA-2	13	30 Mauser	S-3	12
22-250	AA-2	2	300 Win. Mag.	AA-2, SB-2	13	32 ACP	C-4, C-3, S-3	23
220 Swift	AA-2	5	7.62x39mm	AA-2	3	32 S&W Long	C-4, C-3, S-3	9
5.6mmx50R	MR-2	1	7.62x54 Russian	AA-2	17	32 H&R Mag.	C-4, C-3, S-3	9
243 Win.	AA-2, SB-2	2	7.62x63mm	AA-2, SB-2	2	380 Auto	C-4, C-3, S-3	26
6mm Rem.	AA-2, SB-2	2	303 British	AA-2	7	38 S&W	C-4, C-3, S-3	21
25-06 Rem.	AA-2	2	7.65mm Arg. Maus.	AA-2	2	9mm Luger	C-4, C-3, S-3	12
250 Sav.	AA-2	2	32-20 Win.	AA-3	10	38 Special	C-4, C-3, S-3	1
257 Roberts	AA-2	2, 8	32 Win. Spl.	AA-2	6	357 Mag.	C-4, C-3, S-3	1
25-20 Win.	AA-3	10	8mmx57 Maus.	AA-2	2	357 Rem. Max.	C-4, C-3, S-3	1
6.5mmx55 NK	AA-2		8mm Rem. Mag.	AA-2	13	9mm Makarov	C-3	12
6.5mmx57 Maus.	MR-2	2	338 Win. Mag.	AA-2	13	40 S&W	C-4, C-3	15
6.5mmx57R Maus.	MR-2	14B	35 Rem.	AA-2	8, 2	10mm Auto	C-4, C-3	15
6.5mmx55			35 Whelen	AA-2	2	41 Mag.	C-4, C-3, S-3	30
Swed. Maus.	AA-2	27	358 Win.	AA-2	2	41 Action Exp.	C-4, C-3, S-3	12
270 Win.	AA-2, SB-2	2	9.3mmx62	MR-2		44 Mag.	C-4, C-3, S-3	7
7mm TCU	ND-2		9.3mmx64	MR-2		44 Spl.	C-4, C-3, S-3	7
7mm Rem. Mag.	AA-2, SB-2	13	9.3mmx72R	MR-3		445 Super Mag.	C-4, C-3, S-3	
7mmx57 Maus.	AA-2	2	9.3mmx74R	MR-2		45 ACP	C-4, C-3, S-3	2
280 Rem.	AA-2	2	375 H&H	AA-2	13	45 Win. Mag.	C-4, C-3, S-3	2
7mm-08 Rem.	AA-2	2	375 Win.	AA-3	6	45 Colt	C-4, C-3, S-3	11
7x30 Waters	AA-2	6	38-55 Win.	AA-3	6			
7mm Wea. Mag.	AA-2	13	416 Rigby	AA-2	17			
7mmx64 Brenn.	MR-2	2	44-40 Win.	AA-3	14B			
7mmx65R Brenn.	MR-2	14B	444 Marlin	AA-3	14B			
30 M1 Carbine	AA-3	19	45-70 Gov't	AA-3	17			
30-30 Win.	AA-2	6	50-70 Gov't	AA-3	22			

AA-2 = 2-die set for bottleneck cases; AA-3 = 3-die rifle set for straight-wall cases; MR-2 = Metric rifle 2-die set; MR-3 = Metric rifle 3-die set; SB-2 = Small base 2-die set for jacketed bullets; C-4 = 4-die carbide set; C-3 = 3-die carbide set; S-3 = Standard AA 3-die set.

LYMAN AA Standard Pistol 3-Die Parts

DIE/DIE PARTS	PRICE
AA Standard Pistol 3-Die Set	$29.95
Sizing die body	15.50
Deacapping rod	3.25
Neck expanding die body	10.00
Expanding plug	5.00
Seating die body	13.50
Bullet seating screw	3.95

LYMAN AA Rifle 2-Die/ Small Base Die Parts

DIE/DIE PART	PRICE
2-Die Set	$26.95
Sizing die body	15.50
Decapping rod	2.00
Expanding button	3.95
Seating die body	13.50
Seating screw	3.95
Decapping rod bushing	2.00
Decapping rod nut	.25

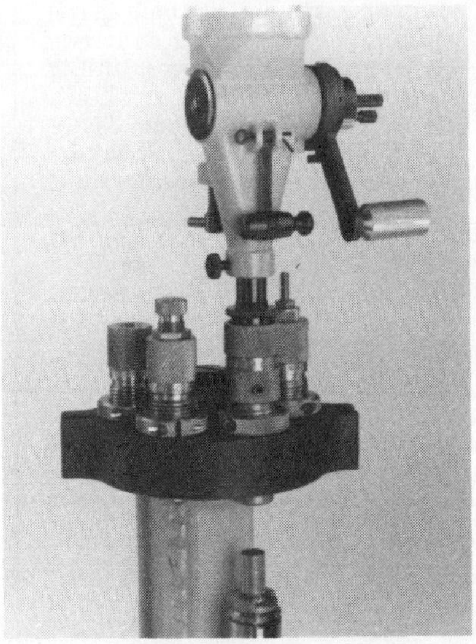

Lyman 4-Die Pistol Set

LYMAN AA Standard Rifle 3-Die Parts

DIE/DIE PART	PRICE
AA Standard 3-Die Set	$34.95
Sizing die body	15.50
Decapping rod	3.25
Neck expanding die body	10.00
Expanding plug	5.00
Seating die body	13.50
Bullet seating screw	3.95

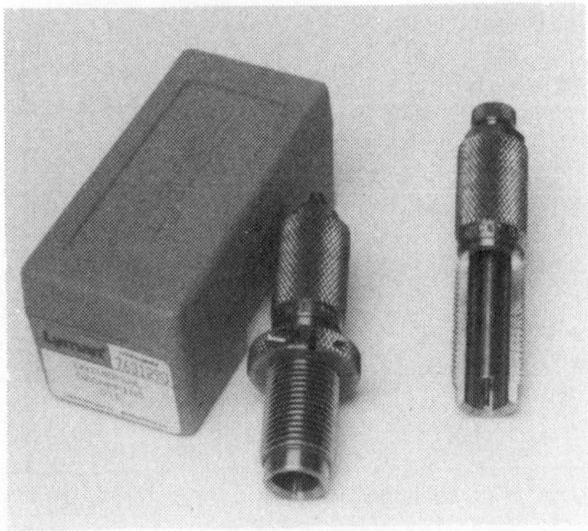

Lyman AA Rifle 2-Die Set

MCRW

Full-Length Resize Die

W-2 hardened steel full-length resize die uses Wilson buttons. Available for standard and wildcat calibers. Specify case and caliber. From MCRW Associates.

Price: **$125.00**

Shoulder Bump Die

Made of W-2 hardened steel. Bump die reforms the neck only. Uses Wilson buttons and fits all standard reloading presses. From MCRW Associates.

Price: **$115.00**

Stainless Decapper/Necksizer

Custom stainless steel decapper/necksizer using Wilson buttons. Specify case and caliber. From MCRW Associates.

Price: **$50.00**

Stainless Steel Bullet Seaters

Custom stainless steel bullet seater with extra tops available for seating a variety of bullets without resetting. Specify case and caliber. From MCRW Associates.

Price: **$50.00**

Price: Extra tops **$15.00**

RCBS

50 BMG Dies

Two-die set contains a full-length sizer and seater die with built-in roll crimper. Dies are produced in two diameters: $1\frac{3}{8}$"-12 for use with Big Max press and AmmoMaster 50 kit; $1\frac{1}{2}$"-12 for use with AmmoMaster 50 kit and other presses. Trim die and neck sizer die also available. From RCBS.

Price: Die set **$365.00**

Price: Trim die **$197.00**

Price: Neck sizer die **$197.00**

Carbide Rifle/Pistol Dies

RCBS **Group B** and **Group C** three-die sets include: carbide sizer die with decapping assembly, expander die, and seater die. Tungsten carbide inner ring resizes without the need for case lubing. From RCBS.

Price: . . . . **See chart.**

Neck Expander Die

For use when reloading cast bullets. Die expands case neck and slightly flares case mouth to prevent lead shearing. From RCBS.

Price: **$19.79**

Price: Die body **$14.35**

Price: Plug **$6.93**

Price: Plug rod **$3.18**

Price: Lock ring $\frac{1}{4}$"-28 . . . . **$1.49**

RCBS

RIFLE/PISTOL DIES

Caliber	Die Group	Shellholder/ Shellplate #
17 Rem.	A	10
218 Bee	D	1
22 Hornet	A, Comp.	12
22K-Hornet	D	12
22 PPC	D	32
22 Rem. Jet	D	6
22 Sav. High-Power	D	2
22-250	A, Comp., RS	3
220 Swift	A	11
221 Rem. Fire Ball	D	10
222 Rem.	A, Comp., RS	10
222 Rem. Mag.	D	10
223 Rem.	A, Comp., RS	10
224 Wea. Mag.	D	27
225 Win.	D	11
5.6x50 Rimmed	D	6
240 Wea. Mag.	D	3
243 Win.	A, Comp., RS	3
6mm PPC	D	32
6mm Rem.	A	3
25 Auto	B	29**
25-06	A	3
25-20 Win.	D	1
25-35 Win.	D	2
250 Sav.	A	3
256 Win. Mag.	D	6
257 Roberts	A	11
257 Roberts Improved	D	11
257 Wea. Mag.	D	4
264 Win. Mag.	A	4/26
6.5 Rem. Mag.	D	4
6.5mm T/CU	D	10
6.5mm-06	D	3
6.5x50 Japanese Arisaka	D	15
6.5x52 Carcano	D	9
6.5x54 Mannlicher-Scho.	D	9
6.5x55 Swedish Mauser	A, Comp., RS	2
6.5x57	D	3
270 Wea. Mag.	A	4
270 Win.	A, Comp., RS	3
280 Rem.	A	3
284 Win.	D	3
7mm BR Rem.	A	3
7mm Rem. Mag.	A, Comp., RS	4/26
7mm T/CU	A	10
7mm Wea. Mag.	A	4
7mm-08 Rem.	A, Comp.	3
7mmx57 Mauser	A	11/3
7mmx64 Brenneke	A, Comp.	3
7mmx65 Rimmed	D	26
7-30 Waters	A	2
30 M-1 Carbine	C	17
30 Herrett	D	2
30 Luger	D	16
30 Mauser	D	16
30 Rem.	D	19
30-06 Springfield	A, Comp., RS	3
30-30 Win.	A, RS	2
30-338 Win. Mag.	D	4
30-40 Krag	A	7
300 H&H Mag.	A	4
300 Sav.	A	3
300 Wea. Mag.	A	4
300 Win. Mag.	A, RS	4/26
303 British	A, RS	7
303 Sav.	D	21
307 Win.	A	2
308 Norma Mag.	D	4
308 Win.	A, Comp., RS	3
7.5mm Schmidt-Rubin	D, Comp.	2
7.62x39	A, RS	32
7.62x54R Russian	A	13*
7.65x53 Belgian Mauser	D	3
7.7x58 Japanese Arisaka	D	3/2
32 Automatic	B	17
32 H&R Mag.	B	23
32 S&W Long	B	23
32 Win. Special	A	2
32-20 Win.	B	1
32-40 Win.	D	2
8mm Rem. Mag.	D	4
8mm-06	D	3
8mmx57 Mauser	A, Comp., RS	3
8mmx68S Mag.	D	34*
33 Win.	D	14*
338 Win. Mag.	A	4
340 Wea. Mag.	D	4
348 Win.	A	5*
35 Rem.	A	9
35 Whelen	A	3
350 Rem. Mag.	D	4
356 Win.	A	2
357 Herrett	D	2
357 Mag.	B	6
357 Rem. Maximum	B	6
358 Norma Mag.	D	4
358 Win.	A	3
9mm Luger	B	16
9mm Makarov	B	16
9mmx21	B	16
9.3x62 Mauser	D	3
9.3x72R	F	30
9.3x74R	D	4
375 H&H Mag.	A	4
375 Win.	C	2
378 Wea. Mag.	D	14*
38 Colt Super Auto	B	39
38 S&W	E	6
38 Special	B	6
380 ACP	B	10
38-40 Win.	E	35*
38-55 Win. & Ballard	F	2
40 S&W	B	27
10mm Auto	B	27
41 Action Express	B	16
41 Mag.	B	30
416 Rem. Mag.	D	4
416 Rigby	D	37*
44 Mag.	B	18
44 Special	B	18
444 Marlin	C	28
44-40 Win.	B	35*
45 ACP	B	3
45 Auto Rim	B	8*
45 Colt	B	20
45 Win. Mag.	E	36*
45-70 Gov't.	C	14*
458 Win. Mag.	C	4
460 Wea. Mag.	D	14*
50 Action Express	E	33*
50-70 U.S. Government	F	31**

Comp. = Competition Dies; RS = Reloader Special Dies.
* Auto 4x4 shellplate not available.
** Auto 4x4 and five-station shellplates not available.
When two shellholder numbers are shown, the most popular is shown first.

RCBS Group A Dies	
DIE/DIE PART	PRICE
Full-Length Die Set	$30.67
Full-Length Sizer Die	23.15
Neck Die Set	30.67
Neck Sizer Die	23.15
Small Base Die Set	30.67
Small Base Sizer Die	30.22
Seater Die	19.57
Expander-Decapping Unit	5.24
Expander Ball	3.36
Expander-Decapping Rod	1.69
Decapping Pin (5)	1.69
Guide Bushing	1.69
Seater Plug	3.98
Trim Die	19.57

RCBS Group B Dies	
DIE/DIE PART	PRICE
3-Die Carbide Set	$41.44
3-Die Set, Roll/Taper Crimp	31.08
Carbide Sizer Die	29.12
Sizer Die	18.52
Expander Die	11.77
Seater Die, Roll/Taper Crimp	15.59
Decapping Unit	5.64
Decapping Pin Holder	2.76
Decapping Rod	1.69
Decapping Pin (5)	1.69
Expander Assembly	5.55
Guide Bushing	1.69
Seater Plug	3.96
Trim Die	19.57

RCBS Group C Dies	
DIE/DIE PART	PRICE
3-Die Carbide Set, Roll or Taper Crimp	$60.36
3-Die Set, Roll/Taper Crimp	40.07
Carbide Sizer Die	43.54
Sizer Die	20.39
Expander Die	14.45
Seater Die, Roll/Taper Crimp	18.60
Decapping Unit	5.64
Decapping Pin Holder	2.76
Decapping Rod	1.69
Decapping Pin (5)	1.69
Expander Assembly	5.55
Guide Bushing	1.69
Seater Plug	3.96

RCBS Group D Dies	
DIE/DIE PART	PRICE
Full-Length Die Set	$52.84
Full-Length Sizer Die	36.22
Neck Die Set	57.78
Neck Sizer Die	41.33
Small Base Die Set	57.78
Small Base Sizer Die	41.33
Seater Die	27.70
Expander Decapping Unit	5.24
Expander Ball	3.38
Expander Decapping Rod	1.69
Decapping Pin (5)	1.69
Guide Bushing	1.69
Seater Plug	3.96
Trim Die	36.71

RCBS
Case-Forming Dies
Contact RCBS for extensive listing of available case-form dies. From RCBS.
Price: . . . . Contact manufacturer.

RCBS Group E Dies	
DIE/DIE PART	PRICE
3-Die Set	$57.28
3-Die Set, Taper Crimp	40.07
Sizer Die	32.05
Expander Die	19.31
Seater Die	25.42
Seater Die, Taper Crimp	18.60
Decapping Unit	28.69
Decap Pin Holder	2.76
Decapping Rod	1.69
Decapping Pin (5)	1.69
Expander Assembly	5.55
Guide Bushing	1.69
Seater Plug	3.96

RCBS Group F Dies	
DIE/DIE PART	PRICE
3-Die Set	$88.08
Sizer Die	44.04
Expander Die	23.15
Seater Die	26.69
Decapping Unit	28.69
Decapping Pin Holder	5.64
Decapping Rod	1.69
Decapping Pin (5)	1.69
Expander Assembly	5.55
Guide Bushing	1.69
Seater Plug	3.96

RCBS Competition Dies	
DIE/DIE PART	PRICE
Full-Length Die Set	$93.60
Full Length Sizer Die	29.78
Seater Die	55.61
Extended Shellholder	8.89
Expander-Decap Assembly	6.63
Guide Bushing	3.18
Expander-Decap Rod	3.18
Expander Ball	3.06
Decapping Pin Holder	1.69
Decapping Pin (5)	1.69
Seater Plug Assembly	7.13
Bullet Guide	4.94

RCBS Reloader Special Dies	
DIE/DIE PART	PRICE
Die Set	$18.88
Sizer Die	15.75
Seater Die	13.44
Expander-Decapper Unit	4.10
Expander Ball	2.73
Expander Decapping Rod	1.37
Decapping Pin (5)	1.84
Collet	1.84
Collet Closer	1.84
Seater Plug	3.96

RCBS
Competition Rifle Dies
Two die sets feature: full-length sizer with raised expander ball for extra leverage and smooth neck expansion; maximum concentricity between die neck and body; seater die with micrometer bullet-seating head with 0.001" click adjustments; side window with sliding guide for bullet insertion and alignment; bullet-seating sleeve for correct alignment; extended shellholder for shorter rounds; and black oxide finish. Sets come with set-screw wrench, hexagonal lock rings. From RCBS.
Price: . . . . See chart.

RCBS
Lube Die
Decaps and lubes cases in one step. Designed for progressive presses but also works in single-stage reloaders. Four sizes for 45 calibers. From RCBS.
Price: $26.22

Powder Checker Die
Confirms powder charge during press operation and provides visual comparison of powder charge from case to case. From RCBS.
Price: $22.76

Precision Dies
RCBS **Group A, E and F** two- or three-die sets featuring: sizing dies with strict tolerances; satin matte finish; fine body knurling for non-slip adjustment; hardened die body; and thread adjustable expander-decapping assembly that locks in place. From RCBS.
Price: . . . . See charts.

Reloader Special Dies
For loading ammunition that exceeds factory specifications. Made with one-piece reamer construction and hardened steel. Features include: non-slip separate collet that holds expander-decapping pin in place and on center; wrench flats and body knurling for easy adjustment; steel hex lock rings with set screws. From RCBS.
Price: . . . . See chart.

Shotshell Die
Designed to load modern compression-formed plastic hulls with appropriate wad column on RCBS metallic presses—Rock Chucker, Reloader Special-3 and -5, and AmmoMaster single. Use with high brass hulls with up to 3" magnum loads. Set includes shot measure, case holder and 6- or 8-point crimper. Available for 10-, 12-, 16-, or 20-gauge. From RCBS.
Price: $55.11

Universal Decap Die
Precision machined die to decap uncleaned, unlubed cases from 22- to 45-caliber. Includes die body, decap assembly with lock nut, die lock ring and plastic storage box. From RCBS.
Price: $11.09

RCBS Reloader Special Dies

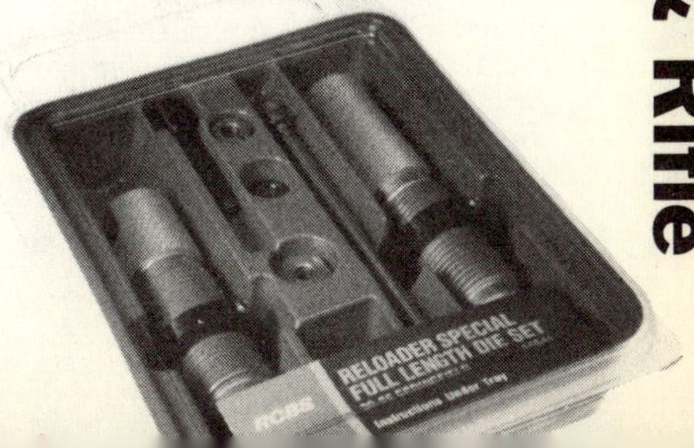

REDDING

Case Forming Dies
Made on a custom basis only to form brass cases from one caliber to another. From Redding Reloading Equipment.
Price: . . . . **Contact manufacturer.**

Competition Bullet Seating Die
Straight-line bullet seater with seating depth micrometer. Seating stem precision ground to exactly match bullet diameter. Micrometer calibrated in .001" increments for precise seating depth and has a "zero" set feature to zero micrometer to specific rifle. From Redding Reloading Equipment.
Price: **$79.50**

Custom Made Dies
All calibers designated "CM" on Redding die chart require Redding custom dies. Die sets for cartridges not listed can be custom made by Redding; send them chamber reamer drawing or dimensions and shoulder angle or cartridge for price quote. From Redding Reloading Equipment.
Price: 2-die set **$79.50**
Price: 2-die set with tapered expander **$84.00**
Price: Full-length sizer or neck sizer **$84.00**
Price: Deluxe die set **$124.50**
Price: Deluxe set with tapered expander **$129.00**
Price: 3-die set **$87.00**
Price: Taper crimp die **$37.50**
Price: Form die **$37.50**
Price: Trim die **$46.50**

Form & Trim Dies
Made to chamber dimensions to eliminate resizing when file trimming. Pistol trim dies require extended shellholder. From Redding Reloading Equipment.
Price: . . . . **See chart.**

Neck Sizing Die
Designed for bottleneck cases to neck size only. Available individually or come standard in Deluxe die set. From Redding Reloading Equipment.
Price: . . . . **See chart.**

Taper Crimp Dies
For handgun cartridges that headspace on case mouth and conventional roll crimp is undesirable. Also available for some revolver cartridges. Rifle calibers include: 223 Remington, 7.62mmx39, 30-30, 308 Winchester and 30-06. From Redding Reloading Equipment.
Price: **$22.50**

REDDING
Competition Die Calibers
221 Rem.
222 Rem.
223 Rem.
22 PPC
22 BR Rem.
22-250 Rem.
22-250 Rem. Imp. 40°
220 Swift
6mm PPC
6mm BR Rem
6mm TCU
243 Win.
6mm Rem.
6mm/284 Win.
250 Savage
257 Roberts
257 Rob. Imp. 40°
25-06 Rem.
270 Win.
7mm IHSMA
7mm TCU
7mm BR Rem.
7mm-08 Rem.
280 Rem.
280 Ackley Imp. 40°
284 Win.
7mm Rem. Mag.
308 Win.
30-06 Spfd.
300 Win. Mag.
30-338 Win. Mag.

Redding Competition Bullet Seating Die

Redding Competition Seating Die Zero Set Feature
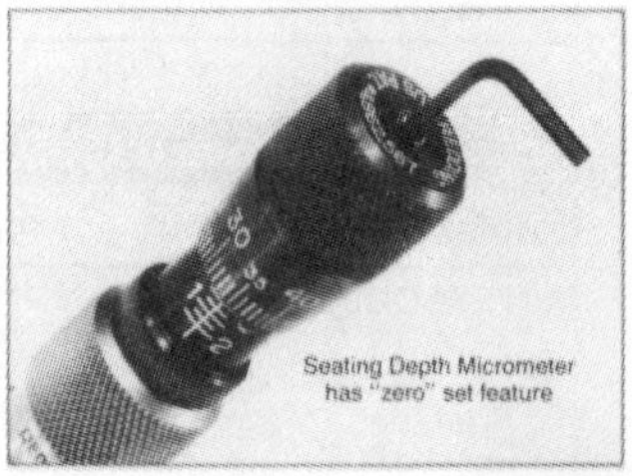

Redding Steel Rifle/Pistol Dies
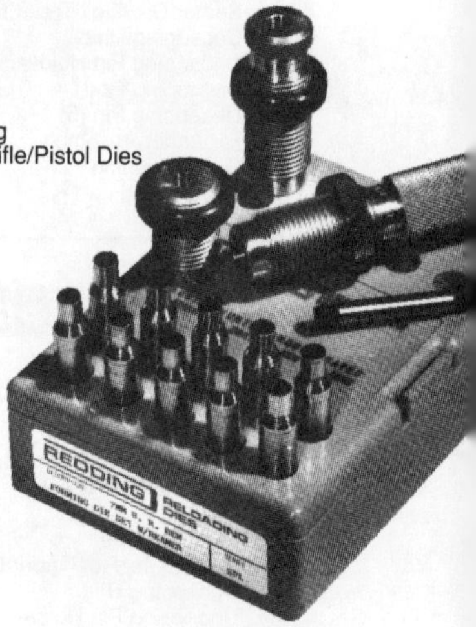

Redding Carbide Size Button

Redding Tapered Size Button

Redding Form & Trim Die

Redding Neck Size Die

Redding Taper Crimp Die

REDDING

RIFLE/PISTOL DIES

—RIFLE—

Caliber	Die Group	Shellholder
17 Rem.	B	10
17 Ackley Hornet	CM	14
17 Bumble Bee	CM	3
17 Ackley Bee	CM	3
17 Mach IV	D	10
17 Javelina	CM	10
17-221 Rem.	CM	10
17-222 Rem.	CM	10
17-222 Rem. Mag.	CM	10
17-223 Rem.	CM	10
218 Bee	B	3
218 Mashburn Bee	CM	3
219 Zipper	C	2
219 Zipper Imp. 28	CM	2
219 Donaldson Wasp	D	2
22 Cheetah Mk. I (40)	CM	1
22 Cheetah Mk. II (28)	CM	1
22 Hornet	A	14
22 K Hornet	B	14
22 Lovell 2R (22-3000 G&H)	CM	10
22 B.R. Rem.	C	1
22 Rem. Jet	C	12
22 P.P.C. USA	CM	12
22 Waldog	CM	12
22 Savage H.P.	C	2
22 Wampus Kitty	CM	1
22 Super PDC	CM	1
22 ULA Honeybee	CM	1
220 Swift	A	4
220 Swift Imp 40	CM	4
220 Swift Imp 32	CM	4
220 Wea. Rocket	CM	4
220 Jaybird	CM	1
220 Coyote #2	CM	2
22-250 Rem.	A	1
22-250 Imp. 40	C	1
22-250 Imp. 28	CM	1
22/243 Win.	CM	1
22/243 Imp. 40	CM	1
22/6MM Rem.	CM	1
22/243 Middlested 30	CM	1
22/30-30 Win.	CM	2
22/30-30 Imp. 40	CM	2
221 Rem.	A	10
222 Rem.	A	10
222 Rem. Mag.	C	10
223 Rem.	A	10
224 Woodchuck	CM	1
224 Clark	CM	1
224 Wea. Mag.	C	12
225 Win.	C	4
5.6x50 R Mag.	D	12
5.6x57 RWS	D	1
5.7MM Johnson (22 Spitfire)	D	22
240 Wea. Mag.	C	1
240 Gibbs	CM	1
240 Cobra	CM	4
240 Coyote #2	CM	2
240 Page Super Pooper	CM	1
243 Win.	A	1
243 Win. Imp. 40°	A	1
243 Imp. 30°	D	1
243 Catbird	CM	1
6mm HLS	CM	1
6mm Bullberry	CM	2
6mm Mashburn Mag.	CM	1
6mm Rem.	A	1

Caliber	Die Group	Shellholder
6mm Rem. Imp. 40°	D	1
6mm Rem. Imp. 30°	CM	1
6mm TCU	B	10
6mm SM Wasp	CM	2
6mm Wasp	CM	2
6mm Olewine	CM	1
6mm BR Rem.	B	1
6mm PPC Rem.	B	12
6mm American (Stekl)	CM	2
6mm American (Tooley)	CM	2
6mm Herrett	CM	2
6mm Cheetah Mark I (40°)	CM	1
6mm Cheetah Mark II (28°)	CM	1
6mm Tomcat (6mm (224 Weaver)	CM	4
6mm/223 Rem.	C	10
6mm-225 Win.	CM	4
6mm-250 (6mm on 22-250 case)	CM	1
6mm-250 Imp. 28° or 40°	CM	1
6mm/284 Win.	C	1
6mm/30-30 Win.	CM	2
6mm/30-30 Win. 40°	CM	2
6mmx44 BR	CM	1
6mmx47 (6mm-222 Rem. Mag.)	C	10
6mmx50 R Mag.	CM	12
6mmx62 Freres	CM	1
6mm-06	CM	1
6mm-06 Imp. 40°	CM	1
25 Rem.	C	5
25 IHMSA	CM	1
25 Bullberry	CM	2
25 TCU	CM	10
25 Herrett	CM	2
25 BR Rem.	CM	1
25 Souper	CM	1
25 Krag	CM	8
25 Gibbs	CM	1
25-06 Rem.	A	1
25-06 Rem. Imp. 40°	D	1
25-20 Win.	B	3
25-20 Single Shot	CM	10
25-35 Win.	B	2
25-35 Ackley Imp. 40°	CM	2
25-36 Marlin	CM	2
25-221 Rem.	CM	10
25-222 Rem.	CM	10
25-222 Rem. Mag.	CM	10
25/223 Rem.	CM	10
25-225 Win.	CM	4
25-243 Imp. 30° or 40°	CM	1
25/284 Win.	D	1
25-308 Win.	CM	1
250 Sav.	A	1
250 Sav. Imp. 40°	D	1
250 Sav. Imp. 28°	CM	1
256 Win. Mag.	B	12
257 Roberts	A	1
Roberts Imp. 40°	B	1
257 Wea. Mag.	B	6
257 Durham Jet	CM	1
257/357 Max.	CM	12
256 (6.5mm) Newton	CM	1
264 Win. Mag.	A	6

Caliber	Die Group	Shellholder
6.5 Bullberry	CM	2
6.5mm IHMSA	CM	1
6.5mm BC	CM	1
6.5mm B.R. Rem.	CM	1
6.55 Rem. Mag.	C	6
6.5mm TCU	C	10
6.5mm-06	C	1
6.5mm-06 Imp. 40°	CM	1
6.5mm-35m (M.O.A.)	CM	1
6.5mmx39 (M.O.A.)	CM	12
6.5mmx50 Japanese	C	4
6.5mmx52 Curano	C	1
6.5mmx54 Mann.	C	24
6.5mmx55 Swed. Mauser	A	1
6.5mmx55 SKAN	CM	1
6.5mmx57 Mauser	C	1
6.5mmx64 Brenn.	CM	1
6.5mmx65 RWS	CM	1
6.5mmx68S	D	19
6.5mm/223 Rem.	CM	10
6.5mm-225 Win.	CM	4
6.5mm-250 Sav.	CM	1
6.5mm Redding	CM	1
6.5mm/257 Roberts	D	1
6.5mm/257 Roberts Imp. 40°	D	1
6.5mm/284 Win.	D	1
6.5mm/300 Wea. Mag.	D	6
6.5mm-308 Win.	CM	1
6.5-308 Imp. 30° or 40°	CM	1
270 Redding (270-243 Imp. Imp. 30°	CM	1
270 Sav.	CM	1
270 Titus Sav.	CM	1
270 Win.	A	1
270 Win. Imp. 40°	D	1
270 Wea. Mag.	B	6
270 Gibbs	CM	1
270 VJ	CM	10
270 IHMSA	CM	1
270-6mm Rem.	CM	1
270-257 Roberts Imp 40°		1
270-284 Win.	C M	1
270-300 Win. Mag.	CM	6
270-300 Wea.	CM	6
270-308 Win.	CM	1
270--308 Imp. 40°	CM	1
270-338 Win.	CM	6
280 Rem.	A	1
280 Rem. Imp. 40°	C	1
280/30 British	CM	8
284 Win.	A	1
7mm Rem. Mag.	A	6
7mm P.P.C.	CM	12
7mm BC	CM	1
7mm Laser	CM	1
7mm Rocket	CM	4
7mm Merrill	CM	4
7mm Herritt	CM	2
7mm B.R. Rem.	B	1
7mm TCU	B	10
7mm ULA	CM	6
7mm INT-R	C	2
7mm INT-X	CM	4
7mm INT-RX	CM	2
7mm Super Mag.	CM	12
7mm E.T. Gates	CM	2

CM = Custom

See page 238 for prices.

Continued page 239.

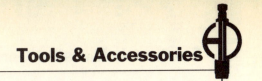

REDDING

Pistol/Rifle Steel Dies

Two- and three-die sets carefully machined to close and uniform tolerances and finish machined on precision lathes. All die parts made of high-grade steel alloy. Knurled outside surface allows hand adjustments. Standard (2-die) and Deluxe (3-die) sets are for bottleneck cases, the Deluxe set containing a separate neck size die. Three-die sets are for straight wall cases and include an expander die. Series A dies are pistol and rifle die sets for most popular calibers; Series B, die sets for slightly less popular calibers; Series C, popular wildcats and less popular rifle/pistol calibers; Series D, represent obsolete calibers and wildcats. Redding will also manufacture custom dies upon request. From Redding Reloading Equipment.

Price: . . . . **See chart.**

Profile Crimp Die

For handgun cartridges that do not headspace on case mouth. Provides tighter more uniform roll-type crimp. From Redding Reloading Equipment.

Price: **$22.50**

Titanium Carbide/Pro Series Pistol Dies

No-lube standard three-die set available also in Pro Series for progressive reloading presses. Pro Series bullet seating die designed for bullet seating only with no crimping. A Profile crimp die is supplied for final crimp except for cartridges that headspace on the case mouth. For these a taper crimp die is substituted. All Pro Series dies have large radius at mouth for easy case entry. From Redding Reloading Equipment.

Price: Titanium carbide die set . . . **$79.50**
Price: Titanium sizer die **$59.50**
Price: Pro Series die set **$79.50**
Price: 9mm, either set add **$10.00**

REDDING Pistol/Rifle 3-Die Prices

DIE SET/DIE PART	SERIES A	SERIES B	SERIES C	SERIES D
Full-Length Set	$37.50	$52.50	$61.50	$69.00
Deluxe Set	60.00	82.50	96.00	108.00
Neck Size Die	26.00	34.50	40.50	45.00
Full-Length Size Die	26.00	34.50	40.50	45.00
Decap Rod Assembly	8.75	8.75	8.75	8.75
Decap Rod	5.50	5.50	5.50	5.50
Size Button	4.50	4.50	4.50	4.50
Seating Die	22.00	30.00	35.50	40.50
Seat Plug	5.00	5.00	5.00	5.00
Form & Trim Die	21.00	28.50	34.50	39.00

REDDING Pistol/Rifle 2-Die Prices

DIE SET/DIE PART	SERIES A	SERIES B	SERIES C	SERIES D
3-Die Set	$37.50	$52.50	$61.50	$69.00
Sizing Die	20.00	27.50	32.00	45.00
Decap Rod Assembly	8.75	8.75	8.75	8.75
Decap Rod	5.50	5.50	5.50	5.50
Seating Die	19.00	26.50	31.00	35.00
Seat Plug	5.00	5.00	5.00	5.00
Expander Die	15.00	20.00	23.00	26.00
Expander	6.00	6.00	6.00	6.00
Trim Die	21.00	28.50	34.50	39.00

Redding Profile Crimp Die

Redding Titanium Carbide Pro Series Pistol Die

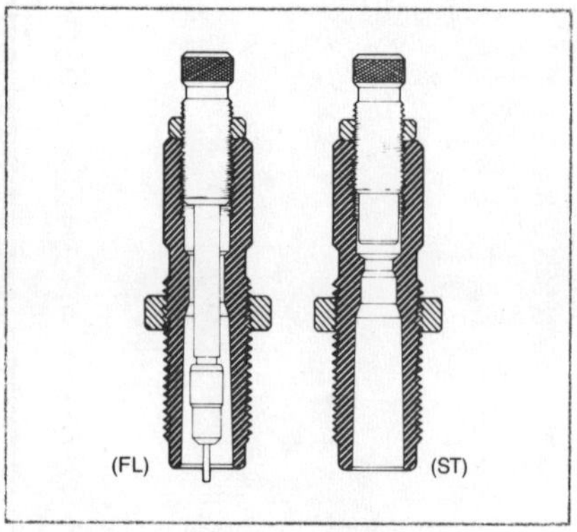

Redding Standard 2-Die Set for Bottleneck Cases

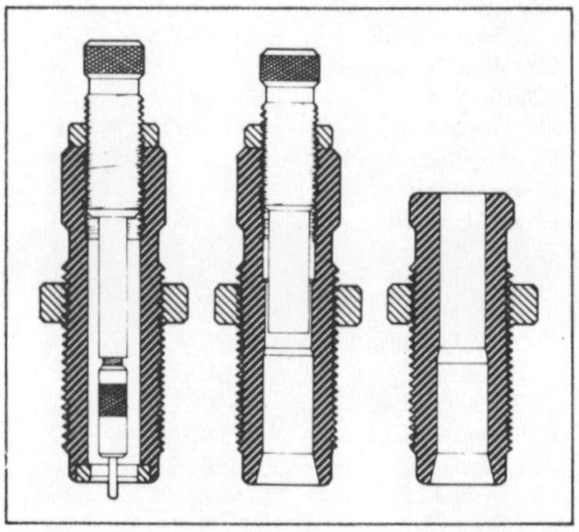

Redding Titanium Carbide Pro Series Die Set

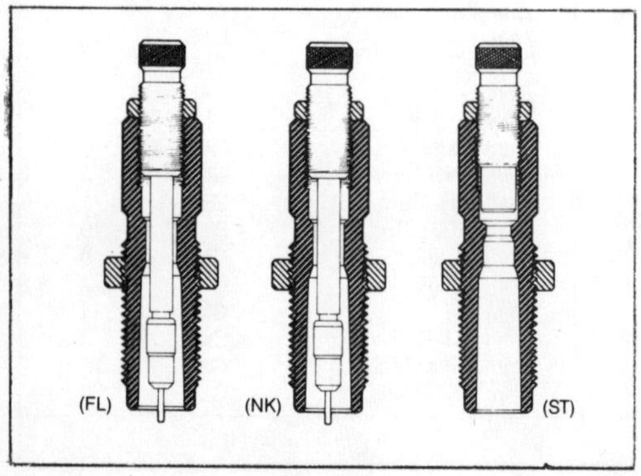

Redding Deluxe 3-Die Set for Bottleneck Cases

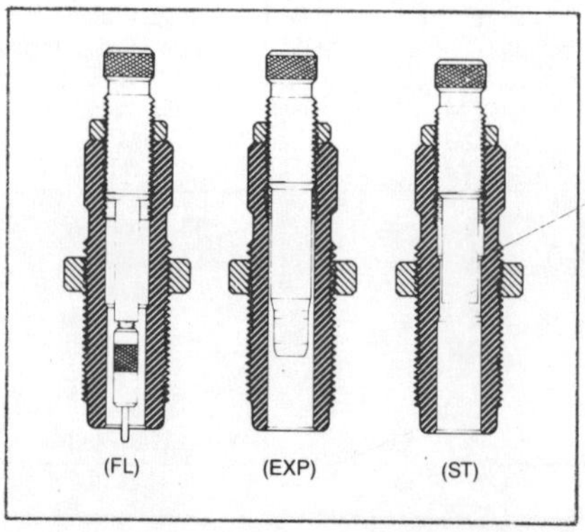

Redding 3-Die Set for Straight Wall Cases

REDDING

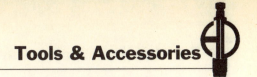

RIFLE/PISTOL DIES (con't.)

Caliber	Die Group	Shellholder
7mm IHMSA	B	1
7mm Wea. Mag.	B	6
7mm Gibbs	CM	1
7mm STE	CM	2
7mm STW	D	6
7mm-06	CM	1
7mm-06 Imp. 40°	CM	1
7mm-08 Rem.	A	1
7mm-08 Imp. 30°	CM	1
7mm-08 Rem. Imp. 40°	D	1
7-30 Waters	B	2
7-30 Imp. 40°	CM	2
7mm-35mm (M.O.A.)	CM	1
7mmx44 B.R.	CM	1
7mmx47 (7mm-222 Rem. Mag.)	D	10
7mmx57 Mauser	A	1
7mmx57 Imp. 40	D	1
7mmx61 Sharp & Hart	D	6
7mmx64 Brenn.	C	1
7mmx66 Vom Hofe S.E.	CM	6
7mm/223 Rem.	CM	10
7mm/250 Sav.	CM	1
7mm/300 Wea. Mag.	C	6
7mm/300 Win.	CM	6
7mm-350 Rem. Mag.	C	6M
7.35mm Carcano	CM	24
7.5 French MAS	CM	7
7.5mm Schmidt Rubin (Swiss)	B	2
7.62x39	A	12
7.62 Russian (7.62x54R)	B	15
30 BC	CM	1
30 B.R. Rem.	CM	1
30 IHMSA	CM	1
30 Herrett	C	2
30 Rem.	C	5
30 Merrill	CM	4
30 Gibbs	CM	1
30 Ace	CM	6
30x44 BR	CM	1
30-06	A	1
30-06 Imp. 40°	C	1
30-20 TC	B	3
30-30 Win.	A	2
30-30 Imp. 40°	D	2
30-40 Krag	A	8
30-223 Rem.	CM	10
30-284 Win.	CM	1
30-338 Win. Mag.	C	6
30-8mm Rem. Mag. (30 Super)	CM	6
30-350 Rem. Mag.	CM	6
30-378 Win. Mag.	CM	18
300 H&H Mag.	A	6
300 Sav.	A	1
300 Win. Mag.	A	6
300 Wea. Mag.	A	6
300 Mashburn Mag.	CM	6
300 Herrett	CM	1
300 Jarrett	CM	6
303 Sav.	B	21
308 Win./307 Win.	A	1, 2
308 Bluebird	CM	1
308 Norma Mag.	B	6
308x1.5 Barnes	CM	1
308x1.75	CM	1
7.65mmx53 Mauser (Belgian)	B	1
7.7mmx58 Japanese	B	1
303 British	A	8
32 Win. Spl.	A	2
32 Rem.	C	5
32-40 Win.	B	2
7.92mmx33 Kurz Mauser	D	1
8mm Gibbs	CM	1
8mm Rem. Mag.	C	6
8mm Lebel	C	26
8mm-06	C	1
8mm-06 Imp. 40°	D	1
8mm-338 Win.	CM	6
8mm-308 Norma Mag.	CM	6
8mm-300 Win. Mag.	CM	6
8mmx52R Siamese	CM	18
8mmx56 Mann.	D	1
8mmx57 Mauser	A	1
8mmx57 Imp.	CM	1
8mmx60S	C	1
8mmx64S Brenn.	D	4
8mmx68S	C	19
8.15x46R	D	2
33 Win.	C	18
330 Dakota	CM	404
338 Win. Mag.	A	6
338 IHMSA	CM	1
338 Gibbs	CM	1
338 Jarrett	CM	6
338 A-Square Mag.	CM	18
338-06	C	1
338-06 Imp. 40°		1
338-270 HGT	CM	1
338/284 Win.	D	1
338-308 Win.	CM	1
338-308 Norma Mag.	CM	6
338-8mm Rem. Mag.	CM	6
338-300 Win. Mag.	CM	6
338-350 Rem. Mag.	CM	6
338-378 Wea. Mag.	CM	18
338/378 Kubla Khan	CM	18
340 Wea. Mag.	B	6
338 Lapua Mag.	CM	18
348 Win.	C	20
35 Rem.	A	1
35 Win.	C	8
35 Whelen	B	1
35 Whelen Imp. 40°	D	1
35 IHMSA	CM	1
35 Brown Whelen	CM	1
35-284 Win.	CM	1
35/30-30 Win.	CM	2
35/300 Wea.	CM	6
35-8mm Rem. Mag.	CM	6
35-338 Win.	CM	6
350 Rem. Mag.	B	6
357 Herritt	C	2
358 Win./356 Win.	B	1,2
358 Norma Mag.	B	6
358 STA	CM	6
9mmx56 Mann.	D	1
9mmx57 Mauser	C	1
9.3x57 Mauser	CM	1
9.3mmx62 Mauser	C	1
9mmx74R	C	6
360 Nitro Exp. #2	CM	6
9.5mmx56 Mann.	CM	1
9.5x57 Mauser	CM	1
375 Whelen	CM	1
375 Whelen Imp. 40°	CM	1
375 H&H Mag.	A	6
375 H&H Mag. Imp. 40°	D	6
375 Washburn Mag.	CM	6
375 Wea. Mag.	D	6
375-284 Win.	CM	1
375-300 Win. Mag.	CM	6
375 JRS (375/8mm Mag.)	CM	6
375-338 Win.	CM	6
375-350 Rem. Mag.	CM	6
375 A-Square	CM	18
378 Win. Mag.	D	18
416 Rem. Mag.	D	6
416 Wea. Mag.	D	18
416 Hoffman	CM	6
416 Taylor	CM	6
416 Jarrett	CM	18
416 Rigby	CM	18
416 R Chapius	CM	31
404 Jeffery	CM	404
425 Exp.	CM	6
450 Ackley Mag.	CM	6
450 Walker	CM	31
460 Wea. Mag.	D	18
460 A-Square Mag.	CM	18
470 Capstick	CM	6

—PISTOL—

Caliber	Die Group	Shellholder
25 ACP (25 Auto)	C	27
25 Hornet	CM	14
270 REN	CM	14
30 M1 Carbine	A	22
7.65mm French MAS Auto.	CM	14
30 Luger	B	13
30 Mauser	B	13
32-20 Win./30-20 TC	C	3
32 Short Colt	D	10
32 Long Colt	D	10
32 ACP	B	22
32 S&W (Short)	D	10
32 S&W (Long)	A	10
32 H&R Mag.	A	10
32 S&W/32 H&R Mag.	A	10
32-20 Win.	B	3
8mm Lebel Revolver	CM	3
8mm Nambu	CM	5
38 Super Auto.	B	5
380 Auto.	A	10
9mm Steyr	CM	13
9mm Luger	A	13
9mmx18 Ultra	CM	10
9mm Makarov	CM	13
351 Win. S.L.	D	5
357 Bobcat	CM	19
357 Auto Mag.	CM	1
357/44 Bain & Davis	D	19
38 S&W	C	12
38-45 ACP	CM	1
38 Spl.	A	12
357 Mag.	A	12
38 Spl./357 Mag.	A	12
357 Maximum	B	12
40 S&W	B	5

CM = Custom

See page 238 for prices.

Continued page 240.

REDDING

RIFLE/PISTOL DIES (con't.)

Caliber	Die Group	Shellholder	Caliber	Die Group	Shellholder	Caliber	Die Group	Shellholder
——PISTOL——								
10mm Auto.	B	5	40-50 Sharps (Bottleneck)	CM	18	444 Marlin	B	19
40 S&W/10mm Auto.	B	5	40-70 Gov't (Sharps Bottleneck 2.1")	CM	18	11mm Mauser	CM	16
10mm Centaur	CM	1	40-70 Sharps (Bottleneck)	CM	18	45 ACP & AR	A	1, 17
38-40 Win.	C	9	40-90 Sharps (Bottleneck)	CM	18	45 Win. Mag.	D	7
40-70 Sharps (Straight)	CM	18	405 Win.	D	8	45 Colt	A	23
375 Win.	B	2	41 Mag.	A	21	454 Casull	CM	23
375 Super Mag.	CM	2	41 Action Exp.	C	13	455 Webley	C	6
375 U.S.A. (Max.)	CM	2	414 Super Mag.	CM	21	45-60 Win.	CM	18
38-55 Win. & Ballard	C	2	44 Russian	C	19	45-70 U.S. Gov't	B	18
38-56 Win.	D	18	44 Special	A	19	45-90 Win.	D	18
41 Long Colt	C	1	44 Mag.	A	19	458x2" American	CM	6
40-65 Win.	D	18	44 Spl./44 Mag.	A	19	458 Win. Mag.	B	6
40-82 Win.	D	18	445 Super Mag.	CM	19	45-100 Sharps (Straight)	CM	18
401 Win. S.L.	D	2	44-40 Win.	A	9	45-110 Sharps (Straight)	CM	18
40-50 Sharps (Straight)	CM	8				45-120 Sharps (Straight)	CM	18

CM = Custom

See page 238 for prices.

PONSNESS/WARREN

Bullet Seating Die

Die body threaded $^{7}/_{8}$-14 to fit all presses. Uses retaining sleeve to seat bullets precisely. Sleeves available in diameters .224 through .358 to handle calibers 22 through 35. From Ponsness/Warren.

Price: Die body **$20.95**
Price: Sleeve **$8.50**

Ponsness/Warren Bullet Seating Die

ROCK CRUSHER

File Trim Die

For the 50 BMG has same features as reloading dies. From The Old Western Scrounger.

Price: **$75.00**

Reloading Dies

Specifically designed for the Rock Crusher press. Precision honed, hardened and mirror finish polished with non-glare outside satin finish. Die sets available for 50 BMG, 55 Boyes rifle, 12.7x107 Russian, 20mm Lahti, 20mm Solothurn, 20mm Vulcan, 23x115 Soviet. From The Old Western Scrounger.

Price: 50 BMG **$250.00**
Price: 55 Boyes **$375.00**
Price: 12.7mm Russian **$375.00**
Price: 20mm Vulcan **$425.00**
Price: 20mm Lahti, Solothurn . . **$400.00**
Price: 23mmx115 Soviet **$575.00**
Price: Shellholder **$30.00**

SKIP'S MACHINE

Custom Steel Die

Shoulder set-back die for benchresters or varmint shooters. From Skip's Machine.

Price: **$75.00**

Rock Crusher Reloading Dies

STAR

Carbide Pistol Dies

Precision machined four and five carbide die sets threaded $^{11}/_{16}$-24 to fit the Universal Star press. Available in most popular calibers. One set standard with press. From Star Machine Works.

Price: . . . . **Contact manufacturer.**

W.B. NIEMI ENGINEERING

Carbide Dies

Custom designed carbide dies with $^{7}/_{8}$-14 thread to produce tangent ogive style benchrest bullets. Three-die sets available for flat base and boattail designs. 17 and 22 calibers, flat base only; 6mm, 25, 6.5, 7mm and 30 calibers, flat base and boattail. Complete flat base die sets include steel core forming die, carbide flat base core seater die, one core seating punch and carbide point-up die. Boattail 22, 6mm and 25 die set comes with steel core form die, carbide boattail core seater, one core seat punch and carbide point up die. 6.5, 7mm and 30 die sets include same three dies plus boattail preform punch and stripper plus boattail ram punch. Available as complete sets or individually. From W.B. Niemi Engineering.

Price: . . . . **See chart.**

W.B. NIEMI ENGINEERING Benchrest Dies

	FLAT BASE	BOATTAIL 22, 6mm, 25	BOATTAIL 6.5, 7mm, 30
Core Form Die	$350.00	$350.00	$425.00
Core Seat Die	425.00	650.00	700.00
Point-Up Die	750.00	750.00	750.00
Extra Punches	35.00	35.00	35.00
Pre-Form Punch/Stripper		110.00	
Boattail Ram Punch			65.00
Complete Die Set	1,550.00	1,750.00	2,050.00

ALEX

Stuck Case Extractor

Removes stuck cases separated above the case head from reloading dies. One extractor will work on nearly all cartridges of the same caliber. Available in calibers 22, 6mm (243), 25, 7mm (270), 30, 338, 35, 375, 44. From Alex, Inc.

Price: **$14.50**

C-H/4-D

Lock Ring

Solid steel lock ring with nylon ball lock for ease of loosening. Fits all makes of dies with $^7/_8$-14 threads. From C-H Tool & Die/4-D Custom Die.

Price: **$2.00**

Stuck Case Remover

Removes stuck cases from sizing dies. From C-H Tool & Die/4-D Custom Die.

Price: **$6.95**

Titanium Nitride Expander Ball

Coated expander ball eliminates need for case neck lubrication. Available in 22, 243/6mm, 270, 284/7mm, 308 and 323/8mm. 7mm and larger have 10-32 inside threads; others have 8-32 threads. Also fits RCBS, Redding, Hornady dies. From C-H Tool & Die/4-D Custom Die.

Price: **$6.50**

Forster Lock Ring

Hornady RCBS-Type Expander

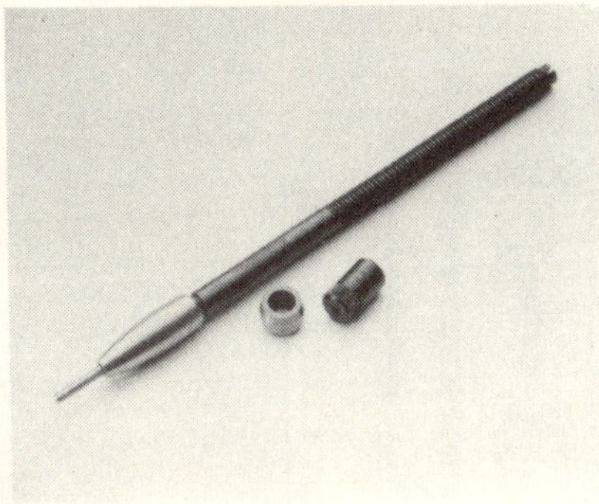

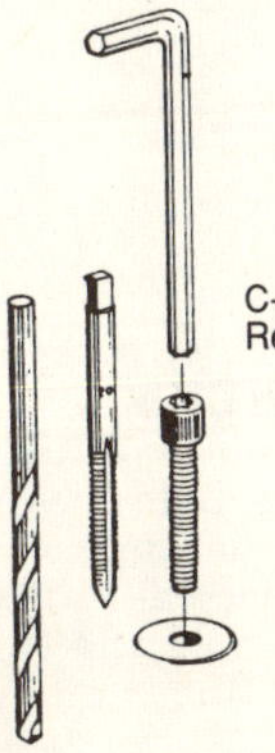

C-H/4-D Stuck Case Remover

FORSTER

Lock Ring

Cross-bolt design for easy tightening and loosening with a screwdriver. From Forster Products.

Price: **$3.00**

Stuck Case Remover

Works on any sizing die and will extract cases which have the decap rod and expander ball stuck in die. Includes two extractor nuts, two punch rods and washer to protect top of die. From Forster Products.

Price: **$16.00**

HORNADY

Die Wrench

Fits flats on New Dimension die spindle assembly, lock rings and die body. From Hornady Mfg. Co.

Price: **$4.95**

RCBS-Type Carbide Expander

Designed to fit RCBS dies. Includes carbide expander, elliptical expander, spindle, deprime pin and collar lock. See chart for die availability. Weight: 1 lb. From Hornady Mfg. Co.

Price: **$21.50**

Stuck Case Remover

Consists of #7 drill and $^1/_4$"-20 tap and remover body that fits shellholder on any standard press. Weight: $^1/_4$-lb. From Hornady Mfg. Co.

Price: **$12.70**

Alex Stuck Case Remover

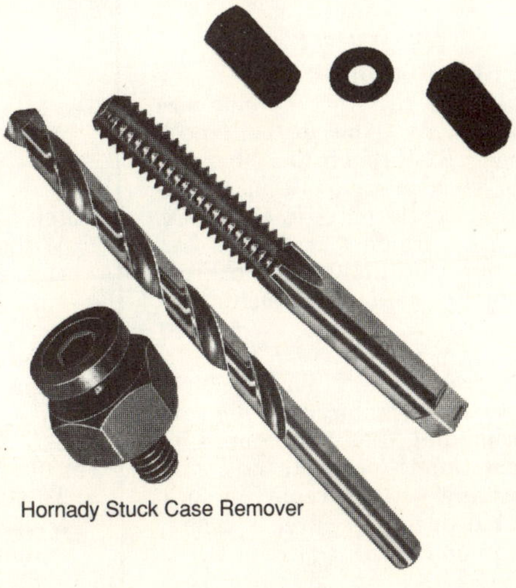

Hornady Stuck Case Remover

HORNADY
RCBS Carbide Expander Assembly

Cartridge	
219 Zipper	6.5 Rem. Mag.
222 Rem.	6.5 Mann.
222 Rem. Mag.	6.5 Carcano
223 Rem.	264 Win. Mag.
225 Win.	270 Win.
22/250	270 Wea.
220 Swift	7x57/7mm Mauser
221 Rem.	7x61 Sharpe & Hart
224 Wea.	7mm Rem. Mag.
243 Win.	7mm Wea.
6mm International	7mm Express
6x47 Rem.	284 Win.
244/6mm Rem.	7mm TCU
6mm/284	30-30 Win.
250 Savage	300 Savage
25 Rem.	303 Savage
25/35 Win.	308 Win.
25-06	30-40 Krag
257 Roberts	7.5 Swiss
257 Wea.	7.62 Russian
25/284	30-06
25/20	308 Norma Mag.
256 Win.	300 H&H Mag.
6.5 Japanese	300 Wea.
6.5x55	300 Win. Mag.
6.5/06	

HORNADY

Sure-Loc Lock Rings

Solid steel rings threaded 7/8-14 lock solid without touching die threads. Weight: 4 oz. From Hornady Mfg. Co.

Price: **$2.15**

LYMAN

7/8-14 Adapter

Used to mount small diameter 310 and obsolete Tru-Line dies to modern presses. From Lyman Products Corporation.

Price: **$5.50**

AA Die Box

Tough plastic box with snap lock hinged cover. From Lyman Products Corporation.

Price: **$2.00**

Hex Nuts

Heavy-duty die check nut. Must be used with other brands of standard threaded dies when used in Spar-T press. From Lyman Products Corporation.

Price: **$1.50**

Split-Lock Ring

Steel split ring fits all standard threaded dies. From Lyman Products Corporation.

Price: **$2.25**

MTM

Multiple Set Die Box

Holds four rifle or pistol die sets with space provided for shellholders and last round loaded with each set of dies. Label on inside of box lid. From MTM Moulded Products Company.

Price: **$10.20**

RCBS

Die Storage Box

Thick plastic box with built-in cradle to hold from one to four dies. From RCBS.

Price: **$3.57**

Stuck Case Remover

Williams-type tool removes stuck cases from sizing dies. Case head is drilled and tapped, stuck case remover placed over die and hex head screw is turned with wrench until case is freed. Comes with drill, tap and wrench. From RCBS.

Price: **$12.85**

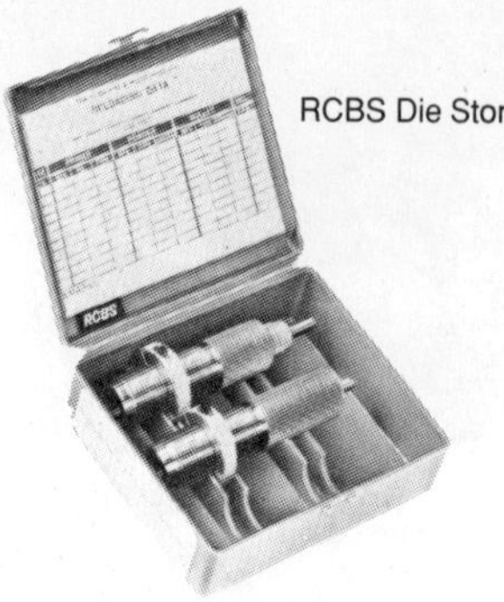

RCBS Die Storage Box

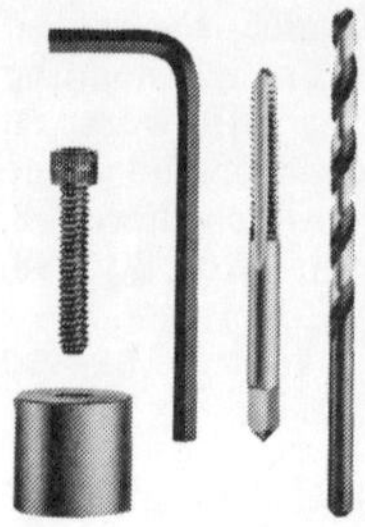

RCBS Stuck Case Remover

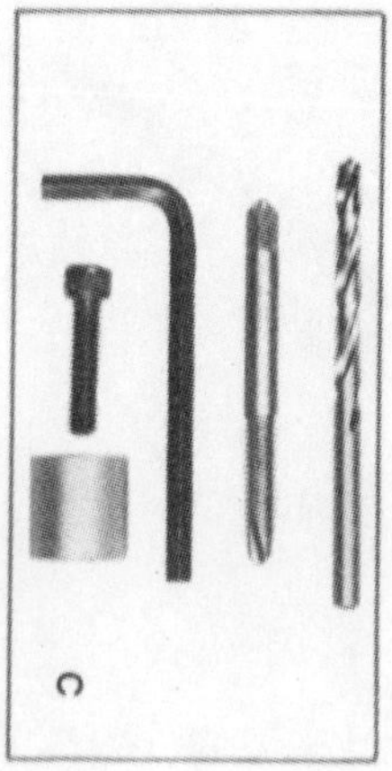

Redding Stuck Case Removal Kit

Lee Die Box

RCBS

Stuck Case Remover-2 Kit

Extracts cases from dies with removable guide bushings or dies with raised expander ball. Kit contains two extractor nuts and two punch rods. From RCBS.

Price: **$5.24**

REDDING

Carbide Size Button Kit

Upgrade die sets with carbide size button kit. Available for bottleneck cartridges 22- through 30-caliber. Die button free floating on decap rod allowing it to self-center in case neck. Includes: carbide size button, retainer and spare decapping pin. From Redding Reloading Equipment.

Price: **$18.00**

Die Spacer Kit

For use with combination die sets and reloading dies to compensate for case length or make no-crimp adjustment without removing lock ring. Kit includes three spacers: .062 for no-crimp or partial resizing; .125, 44 Spl./44 Magnum spacer; .135, 38 Spl./357 Magnum spacer. From Redding Reloading Equipment.

Price: **$7.50**

Redding Die Spacer Kit

REDDING

Stuck Case Removal Kit

Williams-type device to drill and tap case head. Place remover over die, turn hex head screw with wrench until case pulls free from size die. From Redding Reloading Equipment.

Price: **$15.00**

Tapered Size Buttons

To expand necks of bottleneck cartridges up to desired size. Available in 6mm, 25, 6.5, 270, 7mm, 30, 8mm, 338, 35 and 375. From Redding Reloading Equipment.

Price: Button only **$10.50**

Price: Decap rod assembly with tapered button **$15.00**

ASI

Autoscale

Electronic powder scale that uses optoelectronics to sense the position of the balance arm, eliminating friction-caused weighing errors. Powder is dispensed through two barrels. High-speed barrel controls rapid feeding up to 10 grains per second; final load is controlled by the slow barrel with accuracy to +$^{1}/_{20}$-grain. 9-volt transformer fits any household outlet. Designed for large grain rifle powder only. From ASI.

Price: **$289.99**

E. ARTHUR BROWN

Electric Powder Trickler

Will accommodate all powder types—ball, flake, stick. Trickles powder to 1-grain increments at push of a button. Height and position adjustable. Weight: 3 lbs. From E. Arthur Brown Company.

Price: **$17.95**

C-H/4-D

Powder Scale

All metal powder scale. Features chrome-plated all brass beam graduated in 10-grain, 1-grain and .1-grain increments; leveling screw on base; 360-grain capacity. From C-H Tool & Die/4-D Custom Die.

Price: **$37.95**

DEDICATED SYSTEMS

Model 3000S Scale

Electronic scale accurate to 0.05-grain with a capacity of 1000 grains. Features LCD readout, stand-alone or full-auto operation when attached to the 3000D powder dribbler. Comes with battery and AC adapter. From Dedicated Systems.

Price: **$149.00**

Model 3000D Powder Dribbler

Fully automatic powder dribbler attaches to DS Model 3000S powder scale. Required powder weight is input on scale key pad and that amount is dribbled into the powder bowl. Repeat weights dribbled at the push of one button. From Dedicated Systems.

Price: **$70.00**

DENVER INSTRUMENT

Accurate Load III

Electronic scale with 1500-grain capacity and precision weighing to +/-0.1-grain. Response time of 2 seconds. Full range TARE function and flourescent display. Made of cast aluminum. Optional battery pack allows portability. Weight: 12 lbs. From Denver Instrument Co.

Price: **$399.00**

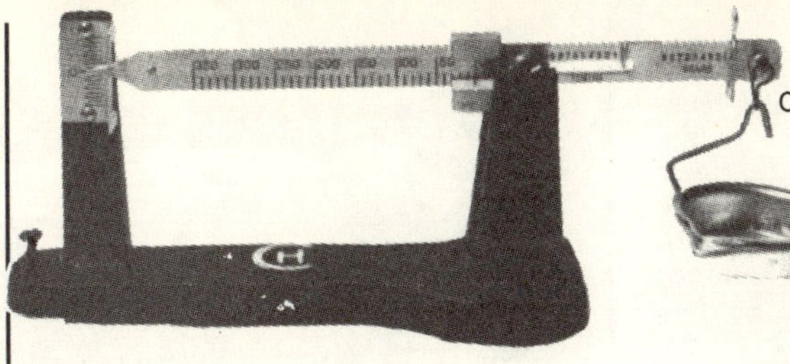

C-H/4-D Powder Scale

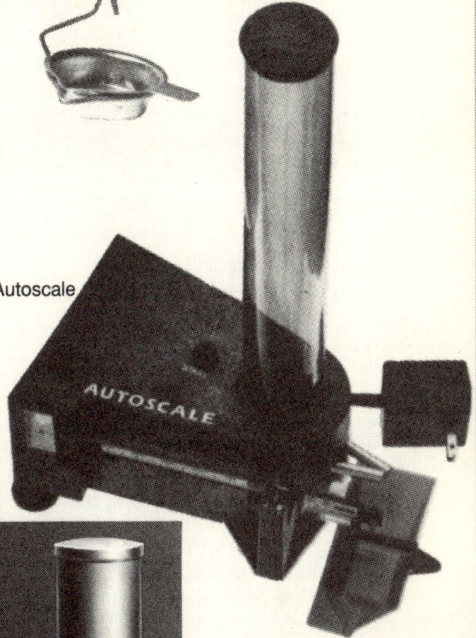

ASI Autoscale

Dedicated Systems Model 3000S

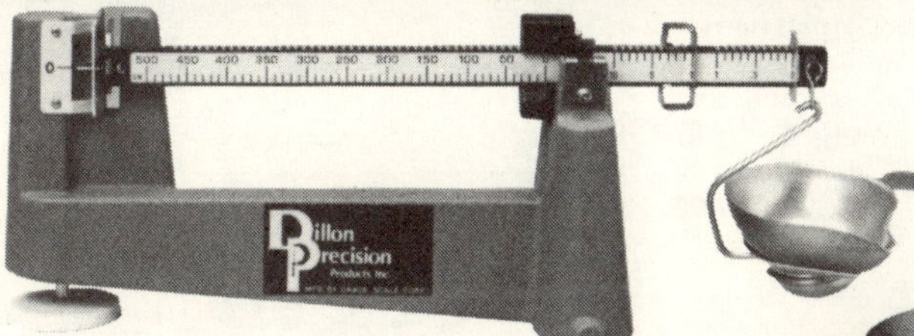

Dillon Eliminator

Dillon D-Terminator

DILLON

D-Terminator Scale

Electronic scale accurate to within 0.1-grain/0.01-grain. Features 1500-grain/9.5-gram capacity and large LCD readout. Uses one 9-volt battery and comes with AC adaptor. From Dillon Precision Products, Inc.

Price: **$219.95**

DILLON

Eliminator Scale

Accurate to 0.1-grain and employs triple-poise balance beam with magnetic damping. From Dillon Precision Products, Inc.

Price: **$43.95**

FORSTER

Blue Ribbon Scale

Features 511-grain capacity; magnetic dampening; three poises; diamond polished agate "V" bearings; Cycolac base, Lexan beam and pan; three-point base suspension with wide stance auxillary leg. Accuracy to $^1/_{10}$-grain; sensitivity to $^1/_{20}$-grain. From Forster Products.

Price: **$70.00**

"Big Red" Powder Trickler

Two-piece construction trickler with ballast for additional stability. From Forster Products.

Price: **$11.00**

"D" Powder/Bullet Scale

Die-cast aluminum base scale with epoxy hardcoat finish. "V" agate bearings at fulcrum reduce friction. Capacity to 330 grains with accuracy to $^1/_{10}$-grain and sensitivity to $^1/_{20}$-grain. From Forster Products.

Price: **$49.50**

HORNADY

Magnetic Scale

Two models available, one to weigh in grains (Model M), the other in grams (Model G). Features magnetic damping; $^1/_{10}$-grain accuracy; 510-grain capacity; conversion table for grains to ounces. Weight: 3 lbs. From Hornady Mfg. Co.

Price: **$50.25**

Powder Trickler

Features large-capacity plastic reservoir with lead counterweight to prevent tipping, brass tube and cushioned knob. Weight: $^1/_2$-lb. From Hornady Mfg. Co.

Price: **$5.65**

Scale Plus Kit

Includes Hornady magnetic scale, powder trickler and powder funnel. Weight: 3$^3/_4$ lbs. From Hornady Mfg. Co.

Price: **$55.50**

LEE

Safety Scale

Features 110-grain capacity; magnetically dampened approach to weight; razor blade pivot for sensitivity; sensitive and readable to $^1/_{20}$-grain; tough phenolic resin beam. From Lee Precision, Inc.

Price: **$29.98**

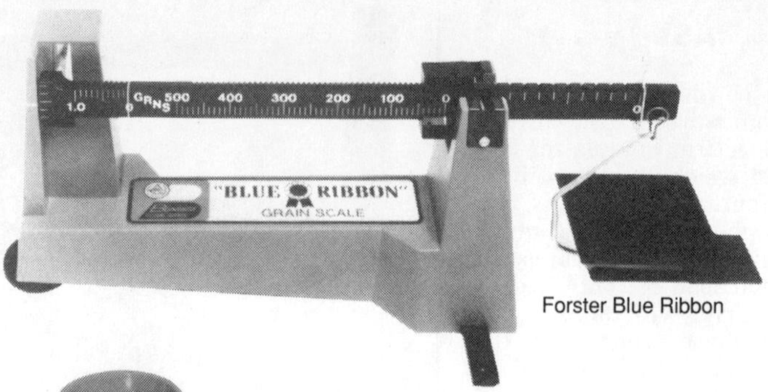

Forster Blue Ribbon

Forster Big Red Trickler

Forster "D"Powder/Bullet Scale

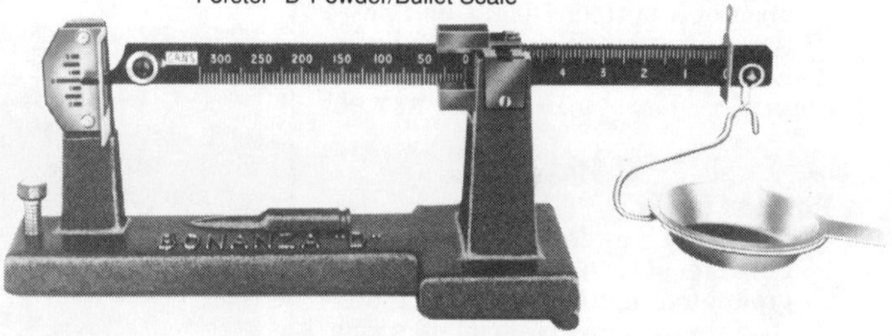

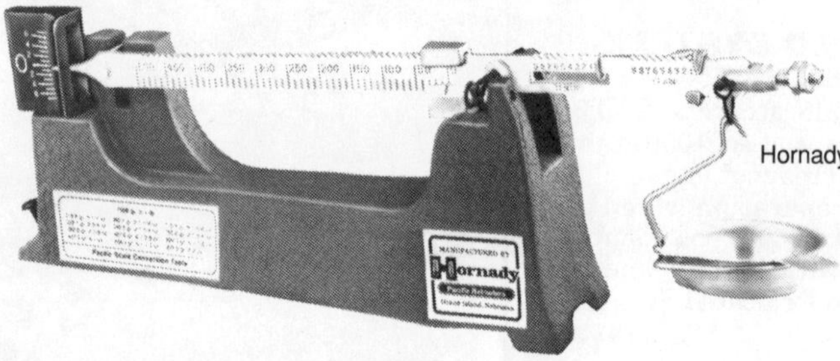

Hornady Magnetic Scale

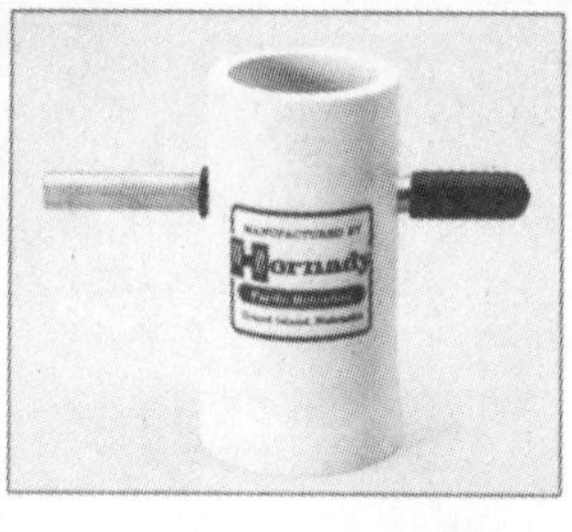

Hornady Powder Trickler

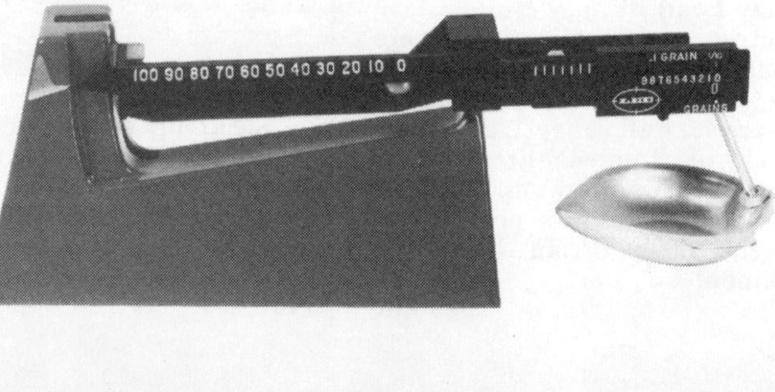

Lee Safety Scale

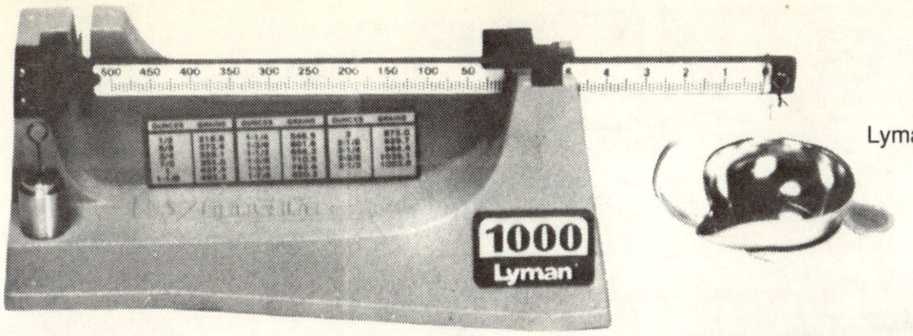

Lyman Model 1000

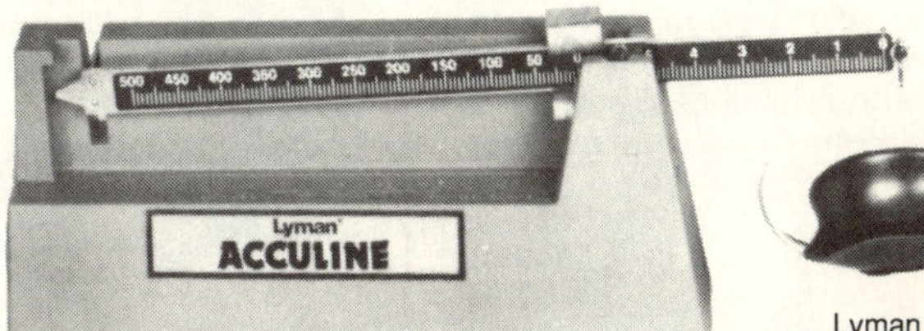

Lyman AccuScale

Lyman Auto Powder Trickler

Lyman LE-1000 Electronic Scale

LYMAN

AccuScale

All-metal beam, magnetic damping and 505-grain capactiy. Accuracy to $^1/_{10}$-grain. Weight: 1 lb. From Lyman Products Corporation.

Price: **$39.95**

Auto Powder Trickler

Push-button operation dispenses powder evenly and consistently. Features built-in vertical and horizontal height adjustments for adapting to various scale designs. Handles all conventional ball, stick or flake powder types. Reservoir removes for cleaning. Comes in 110- and 220-volt. From Lyman Products Corporation.

Price: **$39.95**

Conversion Chart

Ounce-to-grain metal conversion chart with adhesive backing for mounting. From Lyman Products Corporation.

Price: **$1.95**

Electronic Scale Carry Case

Moulded carry case for storing or transporting. Separate compartments for adaptor, powder pan and calibration weight. From Lyman Products Corporation.

Price: **$24.95**

Dust Covers

Nylon dust covers for Lyman 1000, 500 or AccuScale. Hard see-through cover available for LE-1000. From Lyman Products Corporation.

Price: Nylon **$5.95**
Price: Hard **$4.95**

LYMAN

LE-1000 Electronic Scale

Offers 1,000-grain weight capacity with digital display. Converts to metric (gram) mode. Compact frame for storability and transportability. Powered by AC power adaptor or 9-volt battery. Calibration weight included along with power adaptor. Optional carrying case available. 220-volt version for same price. From Lyman Products Corporation.

Price: **$359.95**

Model 500 Powder Scale

Provides 505-grain capacity and accuracy to $^1/_{10}$-grain. Features positive pan positioning and magnetic damping. Also available in 32-gram capacity metric model. Dust cover and conversion chart available separately. Weight: 2 lbs. From Lyman Products Corporation.

Price: **$68.95**
Price: Metric scale **$90.00**

LYMAN

Model 1000 Scale

Large capacity scale holds up to 1,005 grains and is accurate to $^1/_{10}$-grain. Features magnetic damping, precision ground knife edge on agate bearings and postive pan positioning. Comes with conversion table and dust cover. From Lyman Products Corporation.

Price: **$104.00**

Powder Dribbler

Features large powder reservoir and tip-free base. From Lyman Products Corporation.

Price: **$11.50**

Pro 1000 Scale

Capacity to 1,000 grains and accuracy to $^1/_{10}$-grain. Durable moulded frame features built-in storage for 500-grain weight. Conversion table mounted on scale. From Lyman Products Corporation.

Price: **$69.95**

Scale Weight Check Set

To check scale accuracy. Deluxe 10-piece set has 210.5 grains total weight. Shooters weight set totals 60.5 grains. From Lyman Products Corporation.

Price: Deluxe set **$29.95**
Price: Shooters set **$19.95**

RCBS

5-0-2 Scale

505-grain capacity single-beam scale with die cast metal base. Features two-poise design: large poise reads up to 500 grains in 5-grain increments; the small poise to 5 grains in 0.1-grain increments. Magnetic damping system works on force-field principle so beam stops with minimal pointer swing. Weight: $1^1/_2$ lbs. From RCBS.

Price: **$54.42**
Price: Scale cover **$5.94**

RCBS

5-0-5 Powder Scale

The 5-0-5 features a three-poise system. Calibrations on left side of beam are in 10-grain increments; two poises on right side adjust in 1- and 0.1-grain increments. Scale is magnetically damped; self-aligning agate bearings support hardened steel beam pivots with a guaranteed sensitvity of $^{1}/_{10}$-grain. Capacity is 511 grains. Ounce-to-grain conversion table on the base for shotgun reloaders. Available in metric. Weight: $1^{1}/_{2}$ lbs. From RCBS.

Price: **$74.20**
Price: Metric **$89.05**
Price: Scale cover **$5.94**

304 Powder Scale

Direct-dial powder charges to 0.1-grain. Front beam graduated in 10-grain increments to 100 grains; back beam in 100-grain increments to 1,000 grains. Features two poises, hardened steel knives, agate bearings, magnetic damping, oversized aluminum pan and adjustable powder trickler stand. Capacity, 1,110 grains. From RCBS.

Price: **$346.28**
Price: Scale cover **$8.43**

10-10 Powder Scale

Features a lockable micrometer poise for settings of 0.1 to 10 grains; approach-to-weight system to help avoid overloads; magnetic damping; non-stick/non-spill aluminum pan; self-aligning agate bearings; hardened steel pivot knives and plastic cover. Capacity is 1,010 grains. Attachment weight is included. From RCBS.

Price: **$114.33**

Electronic Scale

LCD digital readouts for case, bullet or powder charges in grains, ranging from 0-500. The TARE function allows re-zero for each weight reading. Comes with AC adaptor or can operate on eight AA batteries (not included). From RCBS.

Price: **$395.00**

Scale Check Weights

For testing the accuracy of scale readouts. Comes as standard set of 60.5 grains for powder charges (2x20, 1x10, 1x5, 2x2, 1x1 and 1x.5); or deluxe set of 510.5 grains for bullets, cases and powder (1x200, 2x100, 1x50, 2x20, 1x10, 1x5, 2x2, 1x1, 1x.5, 1 forceps). From RCBS.

Price: Standard **$18.79**
Price: Deluxe **$35.81**

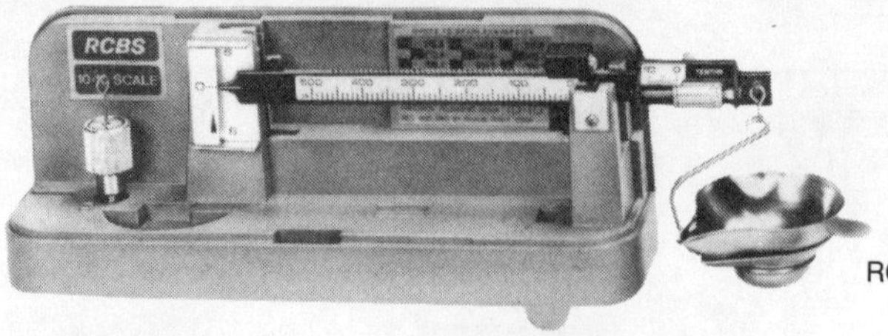

RCBS 10-10 Powder Scale

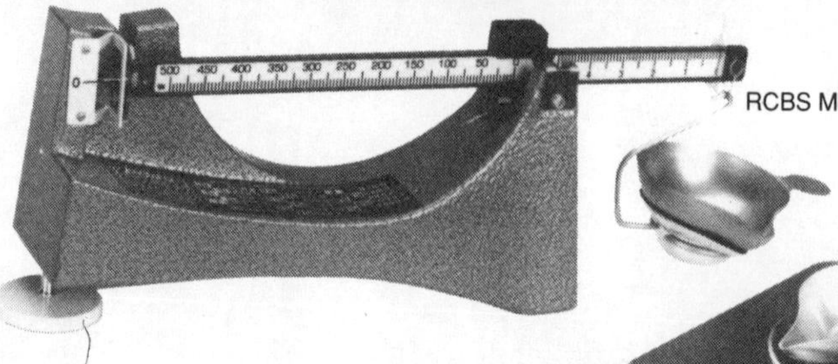

RCBS Model 5-0-2

RCBS Electronic Scale

Redding Model No. RS-1

VibraShine Electric Powder Trickler

RCBS

Powder Trickler

All-metal trickler with knurled plastic knob. Wide base to prevent tipping. From RCBS.

Price: **$11.09**

REDDING

Model No. 2 Powder/Bullet Scale

Features magnetic dampened beam swing; hardened and ground knife edges that ride in milled stainless steel bearing seats; 505-grain capacity; accuracy to $^{1}/_{10}$-grain; pour spout pan; two counterpoise system; $^{1}/_{10}$-grain over/under graduations. From Redding Reloading Equipment.

Price: **$64.50**

No. 5 Powder Trickler

Solid all-metal trickler with metal tube and knurled knob. Features low center of gravity for stability. Weight: 1-lb. From Redding Reloading Equipment.

Price: **$16.50**

REDDING

Model No. RS-1 Powder/Bullet Scale

Two counterpoise system with $^{1}/_{10}$-grain over/under graduations and sensitive to less than $^{1}/_{20}$-grain. Capacity for 380 grains and comes with pour spout pan. From Redding Reloading Equipment.

Price: **$43.50**

VIBRASHINE

Electric Powder Trickler

Features clear dispensing tube; push button switch; adjustable height and position on dispensing tube. Handles all conventional ball, stick or flake powders. From VibraShine, Inc.

Price: **$24.95**

BONANZA

Bench Rest Powder Measure

Features high carbon precision cast body and charge arm. Working surfaces designed to automatically compensate for dimensional changes due to wear. Powder is metered from the charge arm to minimize charge variation and powder shearing. Throws charges of $2^1/_2$ grains Bullseye to 95 grains 4320 without use of extra drums. Vernier scale located on charge arm permits minute changes in capacity. Small outlet in hopper serves as built-in baffle, and hopper cover can serve as primer turner. Two drop tubes for large and small capacity cases supplied with measure. Powder removal from hopper is done directly through charge arm into powder container. Mounts to bench or can be used with measure stand. Long drop tube also available. Weight: $3^1/_2$ lbs. From Forster Products.

Price: **$91.00**
Price: Measure stand **$20.00**
Price: Long drop tube **$14.00**

Bulls-Eye Pistol Powder Measure

Machined steel body with hard brass fixed-charge rotors. Rotors drilled to measure Hercules Bullseye powder in set grain weights (2.5, 2.7, 3.0, 3.5, 4.0, 4.5, 5.0, 5.3, 5.5, 6.0, 6.5, 7.0, 7.5, 8.4). Blank rotors with pre-drilled pilot hole available for customer alteration. Comes with quick detachable bracket for use on bench or as hand-held charger. Rotor not included. Weight: $1^1/_2$ lbs. From Forster Products.

Price: **$24.50**
Price: Rotor **$8.20**

E. ARTHUR BROWN

Auto Charge Bar for Lee Auto Disk

Computer machined from extruded bar stock, Brown's charge bar upgrade allows adjusting powder charges on Lee Auto Disk powder measure with turn of screw. Accuracy to .1-grain. Available for both pistol and rifle measures. Weight: 1 lb. From E. Arthur Brown Company.

Price: **$24.95**

Bonanza
Bench Rest Measure

Bonanza
Bulls-Eye Pistol Measure

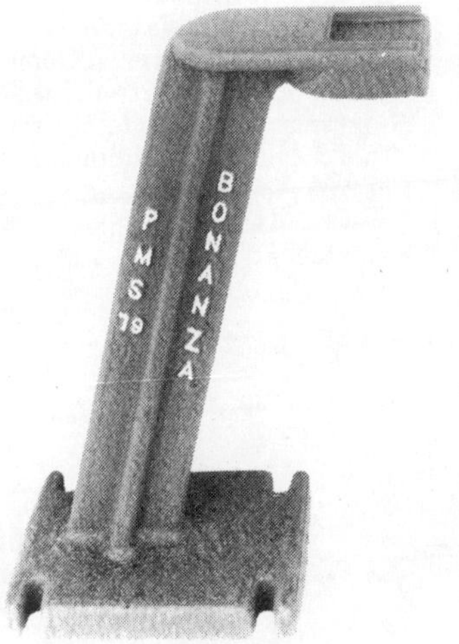

Bonanza Measure Stand

E. Arthur Brown
Auto Charge Bar

E. ARTHUR BROWN AUTO-BAR CHARGE RANGE

Powder	Lee Charge Disks		Pistol Auto-Bar		Rifle Auto-Bar	
	Min.	Max.	Min.	Max.	Min.	Max.
2400	4.0	21.2	2.8	23.6	5.6	47.2
4227	3.9	20.4	2.7	23.7	5.4	47.4
231	3.2	16.9	2.2	19.8	4.4	39.6
296	4.6	24.0	3.4	28.1	6.8	56.2
HS6	4.2	22.0	2.7	25.5	5.4	51.0
Red Dot	2.1	11.1	1.4	13.0	2.8	26.0
Bullseye	2.8	14.8	2.1	16.6	4.2	33.2
AA7	4.6	24.0	3.5	26.7	7.0	53.4
4895	4.1	21.6	3.2	24.0	6.4	48.0
AA9	4.6	23.9	2.9	26.7	5.8	43.4
AA1680	4.6	24.0	2.9	26.9	5.8	53.8
AA2460	4.6	23.9	2.9	26.7	5.8	43.4
AA2520	4.1	21.2	2.6	23.7	5.2	47.4
AA2015BR	4.1	21.5	2.6	24.1	5.2	48.2

C-H/4-D

#502 Micrometer Measure

Aluminium cast non-sparking body; polished steel drum designed for right- or left-hand use; front or back micrometer positioning; up or down stroke powder charge drop. Powder hopper holds approximately ½-lb. powder; optional 10" production hopper holds one pound. Micrometer adjusts up to 25 grains for more dense pistol powders and up to 100 grains for rifle. Base threaded ⅞-14 to fit any standard press or stand. Also available as pistol/rifle combo. From C-H Tool & Die/4-D Custom Die.

Price: **$53.50**
Price: Combo, pistol/rifle **$68.95**
Price: 10" production hopper **$6.50**
Price: Micrometer **$15.95**

Pushbutton Powder Measure

Can be used with any single-station or turret press. Bells and expands case as it dispenses. Seventeen bushings available for over 215 powder/load combinations. Comes with or without hollow expander. Powder bushing not included. From C-H Tool & Die/4-D Custom Die.

Price: With expander **$39.50**
Price: Without expander **$28.50**
Price: Bushing **$2.50**

HOLLYWOOD

50-Caliber Powder Measure

Identical to standard measure except for enlarged drum hole to throw 240-280 grains powder. Threaded ⅞-14 for use in standard presses; spanner lock nut allows attachment to tool head. Comes with one 50-caliber drop tube; 8" transparent cylinder and cylinder cover. From Hollywood Engineering.

Price: **$200.00**

Large 50-Cal. Powder Measure

Features 23" transparent cylinder; 2⅛" adapter for 3½" cylinder; one 50-caliber drop tube and cylinder cover. From Hollywood Engineering.

Price: **$275.00**

Standard Powder Measure

Ductile iron body with ground, hardened steel drum. Adjustable from 2½ grains Bullseye to 93 grains 4350. Disc baffle assures constant powder pressure on metering chamber. Hard-coated conical bearing surfaces for precise cutoff. Threaded ⅞-14 to fit most presses; large lock-spanner ring secures measure to press. Comes with one drop tube (22-270 or 7mm-45), cylinder cover and powder disk. From Hollywood Engineering.

Price: **$100.00**
Price: Drop tube **$12.00**

C-H/4-D Pushbutton Measure

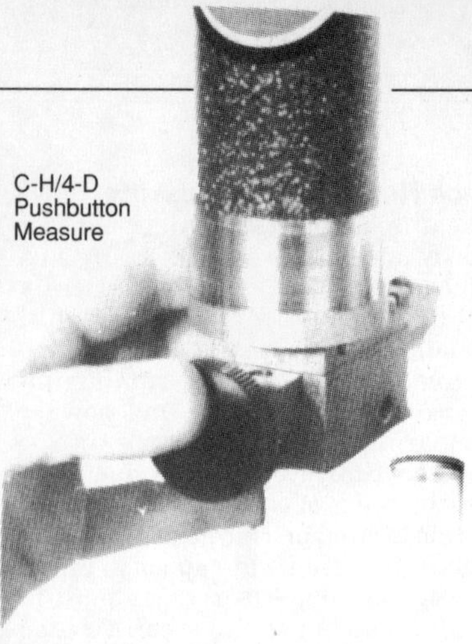

Hollywood Standard Measure

(Left & Right) C-H/4-D #502 Micrometer Measure

Consult our Directory pages for the location of firms mentioned.

C-H/4-D 444-X PUSHBUTTON POWDER MEASURE BUSHING CHART

Bushing	Bullseye	Red Dot	700X	Unique	2400	4227	Herco	H-110	230	630	4756	296	7625	231	HP38
1	2.4	NR	0.9	NR	NR	NR	NR	NR	2.1	4.2	NR	NR	NR	3.2	2.7
2	2.6	NR	1.0	NR	NR	NR	NR	4.0	2.6	4.5	NR	NR	NR	3.5	3.1
3	2.7	1.0	1.1	NR	4.0	NR	NR	4.5	2.9	4.6	NR	NR	NR	3.6	3.2
4	3.0	1.2	1.2	NR	4.4	NR	NR	5.1	3.1	5.0	NR	NR	NR	3.8	NR
5	3.5	1.5	1.5	NR	4.8	NR	NR	5.5	3.6	5.5	3.0	NR	3.2	4.1	3.4
6	3.8	1.8	2.4	NR	5.1	NR	NR	6.0	3.9	5.9	3.3	NR	3.7	4.4	4.0
7	5.0	3.0	3.5	4.0	6.6	6.6	4.2	7.8	5.1	7.8	4.5	NR	4.6	5.4	NR
8	5.9	4.2	4.9	5.5	8.6	8.5	5.4	10.2	6.5	10.2	5.9	10.0	6.3	7.0	NR
9	7.0	5.0	6.2	6.7	10.5	10.2	6.7	12.2	8.0	12.0	7.0	12.0	7.2	8.4	NR
10	8.2	6.2	7.0	7.8	12.5	12.3	7.8	14.2	9.7	14.2	8.1	14.0	8.7	10.0	NR
11	9.3	6.7	7.7	8.9	14.0	13.6	9.0	16.2	11.0	16.3	9.1	15.9	9.8	11.5	NR
12	10.8	7.9	9.0	10.3	16.7	15.6	10.0	18.7	NR	18.7	10.4	18.5	11.4	13.3	NR
13	11.5	8.5	10.0	11.0	17.5	17.0	11.0	20.0	NR	20.0	11.1	19.7	12.0	NR	NR
14	12.3	9.3	10.5	11.7	18.9	18.3	11.9	NR	NR	22.0	12.0	21.3	13.0	NR	NR
15	NR	10.0	11.8	12.7	21.5	20.7	13.5	24.5	NR	24.5	13.8	24.2	14.7	NR	NR
16	NR	10.7	12.5	14.0	22.5	22.1	14.2	26.1	NR	26.3	14.7	25.5	15.6	NR	NR
17	NR	12.9	15.0	16.7	27.2	26.3	16.6	NR	NR	31.0	17.3	30.3	18.5	NR	NR

HORNADY

Deluxe Powder Measure

Micrometer adjustable measure for rifle or pistol powders. Comes complete with two powder-drop tubes (22-30 cal. and 30-45 cal.), large capacity hopper, bench stand and lock ring. Handle can be mounted for right- or left-hand operation. Standard $^7/_8$-14 threads for mounting on bench stand or press. Weight: 5 lbs. From Hornady Mfg. Co.

Price: **$63.95**
Price: 17-cal. drop tube **$3.75**

Pistol Powder Measure

Includes five standard, high-precision, interchangeable bushings, Nos. 7, 8, 9, 11 and 13 for wide load choices. Bushings fit into sliding charge bar. Threaded $^7/_8$-14 for stand or press mounting. Comes complete with stand and lock ring. Weight: 3 lbs. From Hornady Mfg. Co.

Price: **$32.85**
Price: Blank bushing **$4.70**

JONES

Custom Products Micro Measure

Tool steel body 100% machined assuring no rough surfaces. Features micrometer-adjustable brass drum with capacity of 16 to 114 grains and click value of approximately .1-grain; cutting edges designed to slice through most difficult of powders; bottle/adaptor assembly allows changing powders by changing bottles; bottom cutout and plug on reservoir makes it possible to return powder to reservoir without removing bottle from adaptor; baffle assures constant volume of powder on measure drum at all times. Can be mounted directly to bench or attached to powder measure stand. Optional $^7/_8$-14 clamp adaptor or adaptor/baffle for Lyman 55 and other measures available. Comes complete with two 3" drop tubes and one powder bottle. Weight: 5 lbs. From Neil Jones Custom Products.

Price: **$249.00**
Price: Adaptor/baffle Lyman 55 . . **$20.00**
Price: Adaptor/baffle other measures **$20.00**
Price: Powder bottle **$5.00**
Price: Drop tubes, 6" **$8.00**
Price: Powder measure stand . . . **$20.00**
Price: $^7/_8$-14 clamp adaptor **$5.00**

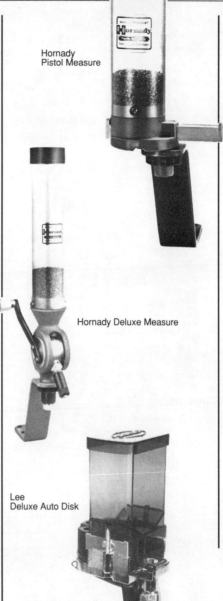

Hornady Pistol Measure

Hornady Deluxe Measure

Lee Deluxe Auto Disk

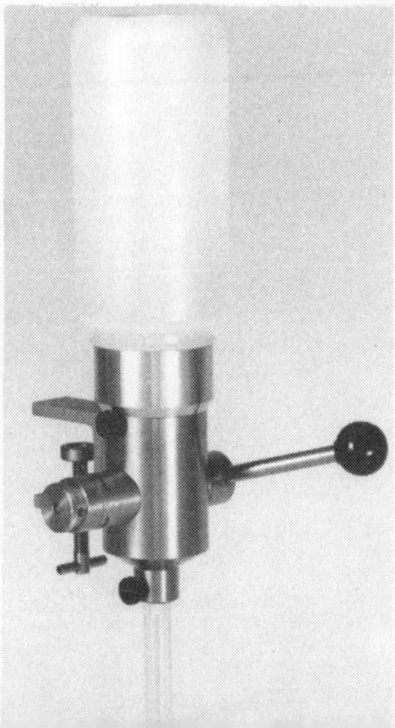
Jones Micro Measure

LEE

Auto-Disk Powder Measure

Fixed-capacity measure. Cast body with polycarbonate see-through hopper. Cartridge case actuates measure while case neck is being flared. Designed for use with Lee powder-through-expanding die. Six-cavity glass-reinforced plastic powder disks. Comes with all four disks for 24 charge weights. From Lee Precision, Inc.

Price: **$26.98**

Auto-Disk Pull Back Lever

For Lee Pro-1000 and Load-Master to eliminate powder binding and reduce chance of missed or double charges. From Lee Precision, Inc.

Price: **$2.98**

Deluxe Auto-Disk Measure

Fixed-capacity measure. Chrome-plated casting with tough polycarbonate hopper and machined metering surfaces. Works best with ball powders. Designed for use with Lee powder- through-expanding die. Comes with all four disks for 24 charge weights. From Lee Precision, Inc.

Price: **$35.98**

Double Disk Kit

Conversion unit designed for standard, deluxe and Safety measures. Allows two disk stacking for fine charge adjustments up or down to .1-grain with different combinations of disks. Complete listing of disk combinations, four extra disks screws and risers included. From Lee Precision, Inc.

Price: **$14.98**

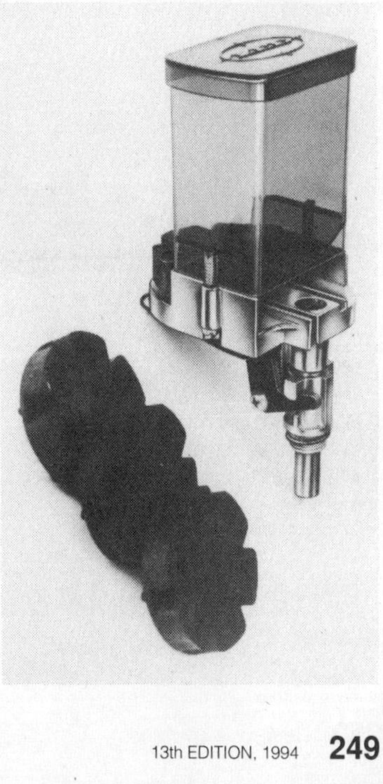
Lee Auto-Disk

LEE

Micro Disk

For Auto-Disk powder measure. Designed to measure small charges below range of standard disks. Six cavities range from 1.1 to 2.5 grains of Bullseye. From Lee Precision, Inc.

Price: **$9.98**

Perfect Powder Measure

Drum-type micro-adjustable measure adaptable to Lee Pro-1000 and Load-Master progressive presses. Features soft elastomer wiper to strike off metering chamber not cut the powder; a self-lubricating nylon cone-shaped drum adjusts to zero clearance; micrometer adjuster in cubic centimeters with O-ring lock; positive powder shutoff for hopper removal or stoppage of flow; tapered drop tube. Charges of from 2 grains to over 100 grains can be thrown. Optional Universal charging die makes measure case-actuated for automation. Adaptors fit most all cartridges. Steel measure stand included. From Lee Precision, Inc.

Price: **$29.98**

Safety Disk Powder Measure

Fixed-capacity measure. Lever-operated with built-in powder baffle and see-through drop tube. Includes measure stand, four, six-cavity disks, and mounting screws. From Lee Precision, Inc.

Price: **$27.98**

Powder Measure Kit

Contains fifteen graduated and proportioned powder dippers. Slide card lists number of grains of every powder type each measure will dispense. From Lee Precision, Inc.

Price: **$7.98**

Lee Micro Disk

Lyman No. 55

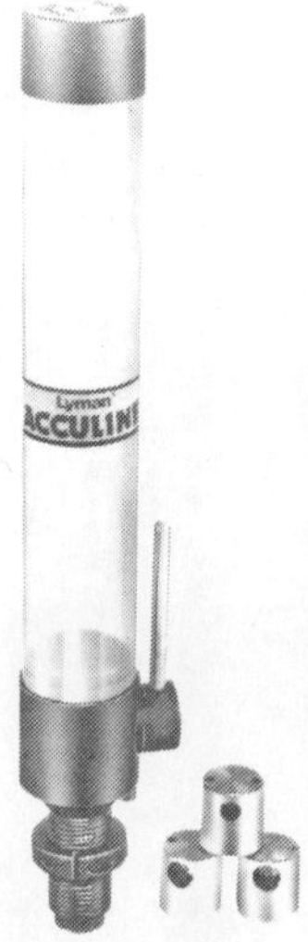

Lyman AccuMeasure

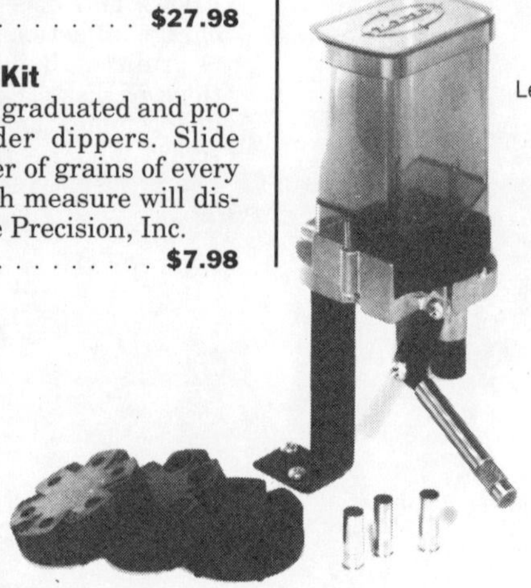

Lee Safety Disk

Lee Powder Measure Kit

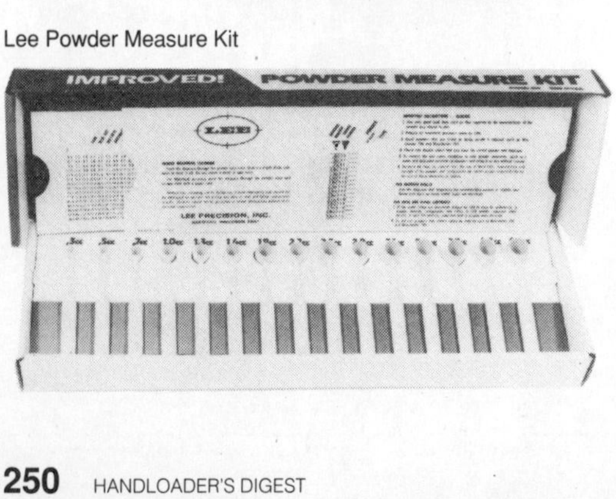

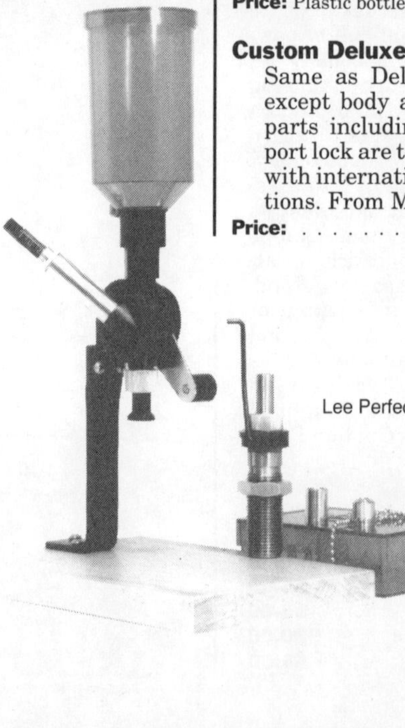

Lee Perfect Measure

LYMAN

AccuMeasure and Rotor Set

Small-capacity measure designed for pistol and small-caliber rifle cases. Features 15 interchangeable brass rotors for over 700 load combinations. Comes with three of the most popular rotors. Additional 12 available separately. From Lyman Products Corporation.

Price: **$33.95**
Price: 12 additional rotors **$49.95**
Price: Single rotor **$8.25**

No. 55 Powder Measure

Features three-slide micrometer adjustable cavity with extra-fine adjustments of width and depth for consistent charges; 2400-grain capacity reservoir; attached knocker to assure complete charge; bench or press mountable. Includes $^7/_8$-14 thread adapter for press or stand mounting. Optional 7,000-grain reservoir available. Weight: 2 lbs., 10 oz. From Lyman Products Corporation.

Price: **$79.95**
Price: 7,000-grain reservoir **$9.95**

Powder Measure Stand

Bench mountable stand threaded $^7/_8$-14 for any standard threaded powder measure. Weight: 3 lbs., 6 oz. From Lyman Products Corporation.

Price: **$19.95**

MCRW

Baffle and Bottle Adapters

For MCRW, Lyman, RCBS and Redding powder measure bodies. From MCRW Associates.

Price: **$18.00**
Price: Plastic bottle **$5.00**

Custom Deluxe Powder Measure

Same as Deluxe powder measure except body and all stainless steel parts including handle and transport lock are teflon coated. Complies with international rules and regulations. From MCRW Associates.

Price: **$250.00**

MCRW

Deluxe Powder Measure

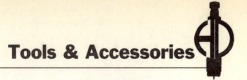

Complete customizing of Lyman Model 55 powder measure for accuracy-minded reloader. Drum, slide and knob made of C-1018 steel hard chrome-plated. Screw, ball, springs and end cap are of stainless steel. Body glass beaded with two layers epoxy paint baked on. Drop tubes also available. From MCRW Associates.

Price: **$199.00**

Drop Tubes

Fit Lyman Model 55 measure or any 9/16" diameter receivers; adapters available for larger receivers. Two inside diameters available: 3/16" for finer powders; 1/4" for coarser. All drop tubes at both ends 60° with 7° transition at apex to help prevent bridging. Come in eight standard lengths. Other custom lengths available. From MCRW Associates.

Price: 3-4" **$7.00**
Price: 5-6" **$7.25**
Price: 7-8" **$7.50**

QUINETICS

Powder Measure

Adjustable plastic hand-held measure with unique spring-action mechanism to prevent powder shearing. From Quinetics Corp.

Price: **$46.25**

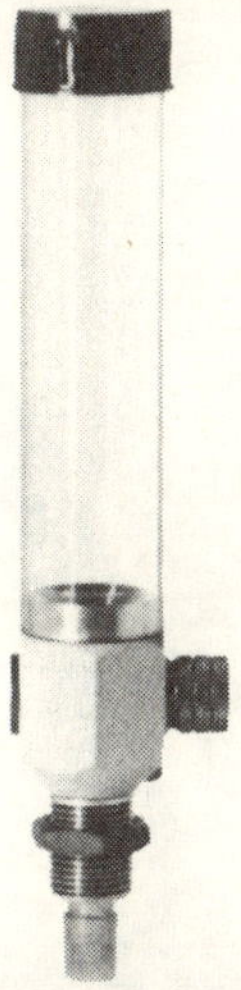

RCBS Little Dandy

RCBS

Little Dandy Pistol Measure

Designed for pistol shooters and small-caliber rifle shooters. Twenty-six interchangeable, fixed-charge powder rotors available to load up to 400 combinations. No re-adjustment after rotor changeover. Can be used hand-held, bench-mounted or mounted to powder measure stand. From RCBS.

Price: **$27.70**
Price: Powder rotor **$7.72**
Price: Measure cover **$6.93**

Quinetics Powder Measure

LITTLE DANDY ROTOR CHARGE TABLE

Rotor #	00	0	01	02	03	04	05	06	07	08	09	10	11	12	13	14	15	16	17	18	19	20	21	22	23	24	25	26
Bullseye	1.7	2.2	2.5	2.7	3.0	3.2	3.5	3.7	4.0	4.5	5.0	5.5	6.0	6.5	7.2	7.8	8.4	9.0	9.7	NR	NR	NR	NR	NR	NR	NR	NR	NR
231	NR	NR	2.7	3.0	3.3	3.6	3.9	4.2	4.5	5.0	5.6	6.2	6.8	7.2	7.9	8.6	9.3	10.0	10.6	11.3	12.1	NR	NR	NR	NR	NR	NR	NR
HP38	NR	NR	2.8	3.0	3.4	3.6	4.0	4.2	4.5	5.1	5.5	6.2	6.8	7.5	7.9	8.8	9.4	10.3	10.9	11.7	12.3	NR	NR	NR	NR	NR	NR	NR
Red Dot	NR	NR	1.7	1.9	2.2	2.3	2.5	2.6	2.9	3.2	3.6	4.0	4.3	4.7	5.1	5.5	6.0	6.5	6.9	7.4	7.8	8.3	8.7	9.1	NR	NR	NR	NR
700-X	NR	NR	2.0	2.2	2.4	2.6	2.8	3.0	3.2	3.6	4.0	4.4	4.8	5.1	5.7	6.2	6.8	7.3	7.7	8.2	8.7	9.2	NR	NR	NR	NR	NR	NR
Green Dot	NR	NR	1.9	2.1	2.3	2.5	2.8	3.0	3.1	3.5	3.9	4.4	4.8	5.1	5.5	6.1	6.6	7.0	7.5	8.0	8.8	8.9	9.6	10.0	10.5	10.7	11.4	NR
SR4756	NR	NR	NR	NR	NR	NR	NR	3.5	3.7	4.2	4.7	5.1	5.6	6.2	6.8	7.3	7.9	8.5	9.1	9.7	10.3	10.9	11.4	12.0	12.4	13.4	13.9	14.5
HS-5	NR	NR	4.2	4.5	5.0	5.3	5.9	6.2	6.6	7.4	8.2	9.0	NR	NR	NR	NR	NR	NR	NR	NR	NR	NR	NR	NR	NR	NR	NR	NR
Unique	NR	NR	2.3	2.5	2.8	3.0	3.3	3.5	3.7	4.2	4.7	5.2	5.7	6.0	6.6	7.2	7.8	8.4	9.0	9.5	10.1	10.7	11.3	11.8	12.4	13.1	NR	NR
SR7625	NR	NR	2.5	2.7	3.0	3.2	3.5	3.8	4.0	4.5	5.0	5.5	6.0	6.5	7.2	7.7	8.3	9.0	9.6	NR	NR	NR	NR	NR	NR	NR	NR	NR
HS-6	NR	NR	NR	NR	NR	NR	5.4	5.7	6.1	6.9	7.6	8.4	9.1	10.1	11.0	12.0	13.0	13.9	14.8	15.7	16.7	17.6	NR	NR	NR	NR	NR	NR
HS-7	NR	NR	NR	NR	NR	4.9	5.4	5.7	6.1	6.8	7.5	8.3	9.1	10.1	11.0	11.9	12.9	13.9	14.8	15.8	16.8	17.7	18.6	NR	NR	NR	NR	NR
Herco	NR	NR	NR	NR	NR	NR	3.1	3.3	3.5	4.0	4.4	4.8	5.3	5.7	6.3	6.7	7.3	7.9	8.4	9.0	9.5	10.1	10.5	11.1	11.7	12.3	13.0	13.6
Blue Dot	NR	NR	NR	NR	NR	NR	NR	NR	NR	NR	5.9	6.5	7.1	7.7	8.4	9.1	9.8	10.6	11.3	12.0	12.8	13.5	14.2	14.9	15.7	16.6	17.5	18.3
630	NR	NR	NR	NR	5.0	5.3	5.8	6.1	6.5	7.3	8.1	8.9	9.7	10.8	11.7	12.7	13.7	14.8	15.8	16.9	17.9	18.8	19.8	20.8	NR	NR	NR	NR
2400	NR	NR	NR	NR	NR	NR	NR	NR	NR	NR	7.0	7.7	8.4	9.3	10.2	11.0	11.9	12.8	13.6	14.6	15.4	16.2	17.0	17.9	18.9	19.8	20.8	21.8
H110	NR	NR	NR	NR	NR	NR	NR	NR	NR	NR	NR	8.9	9.7	10.7	11.7	12.6	13.6	14.6	15.6	16.6	17.6	18.5	19.5	20.5	21.5	22.5	23.7	24.8
296	NR	NR	NR	NR	NR	NR	NR	NR	NR	NR	NR	9.1	9.9	10.9	11.9	12.9	13.9	14.9	15.9	17.0	18.0	19.0	20.0	21.0	22.1	23.2	24.3	25.5
SR4759	NR	NR	NR	NR	NR	NR	NR	NR	NR	NR	NR	NR	NR	NR	NR	NR	NR	NR	10.1	10.7	11.5	12.2	12.8	13.5	14.2	15.0	15.8	16.5
IMR 4227	NR	NR	NR	NR	NR	NR	NR	NR	NR	NR	NR	NR	NR	9.1	9.9	10.8	11.6	12.6	13.3	14.3	15.1	16.0	16.8	17.6	18.6	19.5	20.5	21.5
680	NR	NR	NR	NR	NR	NR	NR	NR	NR	NR	8.2	9.1	9.9	10.9	11.9	12.9	13.9	14.9	15.9	16.9	17.9	18.9	19.9	20.9	21.9	23.1	24.2	25.3
IMR 4198	NR	NR	NR	NR	NR	NR	NR	NR	NR	NR	6.5	7.2	7.9	8.5	9.4	10.2	11.0	12.0	12.7	13.5	14.4	15.2	16.1	16.8	17.8	18.7	19.6	20.4
H-322	NR	NR	NR	NR	NR	NR	NR	NR	NR	NR	NR	NR	NR	NR	NR	NR	NR	13.0	13.8	14.7	15.7	16.6	17.4	18.3	19.3	20.3	21.3	22.3
RL-7	NR	NR	NR	NR	NR	NR	NR	NR	NR	NR	NR	NR	NR	NR	10.4	11.3	12.2	13.2	14.0	14.9	15.9	16.8	17.7	18.5	19.5	20.5	21.6	22.6
AA-2	NR	NR	3.1	3.3	3.9	4.2	4.6	4.8	5.1	5.6	6.2	6.8	7.6	8.4	9.4	10.0	10.5	11.2	12.1	12.9	13.9	15.0	16.0	16.5	16.9	18.3	19.0	19.6
AA-5	NR	NR	4.0	4.3	4.8	5.1	5.6	5.9	6.3	7.1	7.8	8.6	9.3	10.3	11.3	12.2	13.2	14.2	15.2	16.1	17.1	18.0	18.9	19.8	20.8	21.9	23.0	24.3
AA-7	NR	NR	4.2	4.6	5.1	5.4	6.0	6.3	6.6	7.5	8.3	9.1	9.9	11.0	12.0	13.0	14.0	15.0	16.0	17.0	18.0	19.0	20.0	20.9	22.0	23.1	24.3	25.7
AA-9	NR	NR	4.2	4.5	5.0	5.3	5.9	6.2	6.6	7.4	8.1	9.0	9.8	10.8	11.9	12.8	13.8	14.9	15.8	16.8	17.8	18.8	19.8	20.7	21.8	22.9	24.1	25.4
Olin 473AA	NR	NR	2.8	3.1	3.4	3.7	4.0	4.2	4.5	5.0	5.5	6.1	6.6	7.4	8.1	8.7	9.3	9.9	10.9	11.4	12.1	12.8	13.3	14.1	15.0	15.5	16.4	17.0
Olin 452AA	NR	NR	2.4	2.5	2.8	3.0	3.2	3.4	3.7	4.1	4.6	5.0	5.5	6.0	6.6	7.3	7.8	8.2	8.8	9.5	10.0	10.4	11.1	11.6	12.3	12.8	13.3	14.2
Olin 540	NR	NR	3.9	4.3	4.7	5.0	5.6	5.9	6.2	7.0	7.7	8.5	9.2	10.2	11.1	12.1	13.0	14.0	14.9	15.9	16.8	17.8	18.9	19.6	20.7	21.7	22.7	23.9
Olin 571	NR	NR	4.1	4.4	4.9	5.2	5.8	6.1	6.5	7.2	8.0	8.8	9.6	10.7	11.8	12.7	13.7	14.7	15.6	16.8	17.7	18.7	19.7	20.5	21.6	22.8	24.0	25.0

NR=No known recommended load. WARNING: The powder charge weights shown for individual rotors are to be used for general reference only. Lot to lot variations in powder density, temperature, humidity, operating techniques and manufacturing tolerances, all introduce variations in charge weights from the values listed. Each rotor-powder combination used must be checked on accurate scale to determine actual charge weight prior to loading ammunition. From RCBS.

RCBS

Little Dandy Rotor Knob

High-strength aluminum, knurled outer edge knob attaches to Little Dandy rotor with a setscrew. Makes the handle easier to turn. From RCBS.

Price: **$2.67**

Powder Measure Stand

Elevates any powder measure with standard $^{7}/_{8}$-14 thread for positioning powder scale pan or case in a loading block under the drop tube. Bolts to loading bench or table. From RCBS.

Price: **$20.98**

Uniflow Powder Measure

Features large capacity 5" acrylic powder hopper, drop tubes for 22- to 45-caliber, precision-ground measuring cylinder surface and honed main casting. Adjustable cylinder for throwing charges from 0.5-grain Bullseye to 110 grains of 4350. Comes with stand plate for bolting to loading bench. 17-caliber drop tube optional. From RCBS.

Price: **$71.63**
Price: 17-cal. drop tube **$4.46**
Price: Measure cover **$6.93**

UPM Micrometer Adjustment Screw

Install on the RCBS Uniflow Powder Measure and record precise settings for powder charges. Dial in same number for that charge each time. To install, replace the Uniflow's standard metering screw. Available in large or small size. From RCBS.

Price: **$32.64**

REDDING

Bench Stand

For bench-top mounting all Redding powder measures or any other measure with $^{7}/_{8}$-14 threads. Stand is not threaded but fitted with lock ring for rotating measure to any desired position or for dumping of reservoir. From Redding Reloading Equipment.

Price: **$22.50**

BR-30 Zero Backlash Micrometer

RCBS
UPM Micrometer Screw

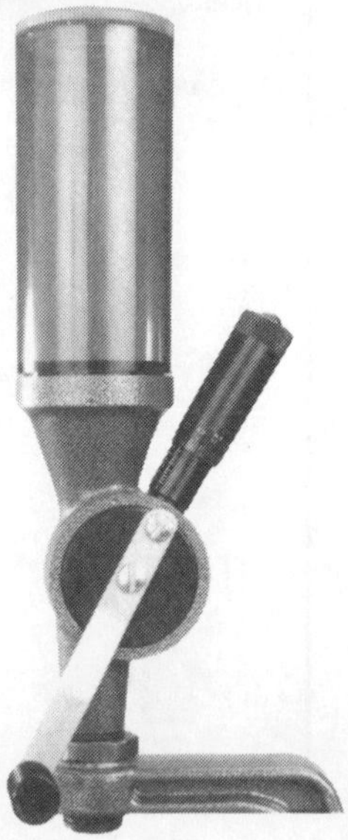

RCBS
UPM on Uniflow Measure

Redding Model 3
on RS-6 Bench Stand

3R Positive Lock System

3R Powder Baffle

Redding Competition
Model BR-30

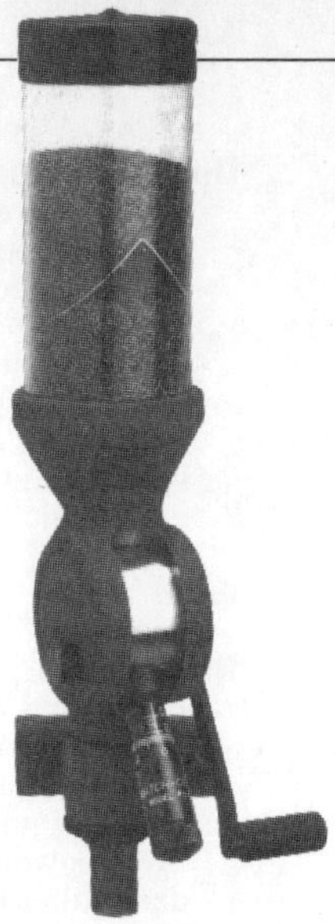

Redding Match-Grade
Model 3BR

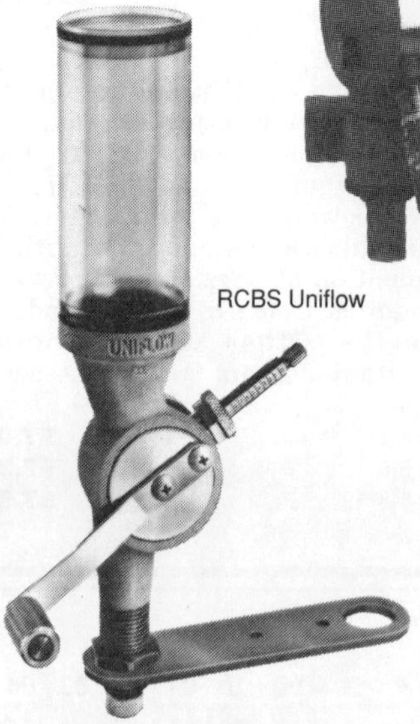

RCBS Uniflow

REDDING

Competition Model BR-30 Powder Measure

Strictly a competition model with specialized drum and micrometer to limit overall charge range from low of 10 grains to maximum of about 50 grains. Has all same features of Redding Match-Grade model plus a reduction in metering cavity diameter and a change in the metering plunger shape to alleviate irregular powder settling and enhance charge uniformity. Unique rotating slightly heavier handle provides more uniform stroke. From Redding Reloading Equipment.

Price: **$148.50**

Master Model 3 Powder Measure

Precision machined cast iron frame with hand-honed fit between frame and hard surfaced drum. Features micrometer metering chamber; cast mounting bracket for shelf or bench attachment; large capacity clear powder reservoir; see-through drop tube for all calibers 22 through 50; threaded to fit measure stand. Comes with Universal metering chamber or with both Universal and pistol chambers. From Redding Reloading Equipment.

Price: With Universal chamber . . . **$94.50**
Price: Both chambers **$24.00**
Price: Measure with both chambers **$115.50**

REDDING

Match-Grade Model 3R Powder Measure

Has all the features of Redding's Master Model 3 measure plus the match-grade conversion features. Match-grade features include micrometer metering chamber; zero backlash micrometer which takes up minute tolerances in screw thread so parts can't work loose and are self-adjusting; powder baffle positioned above metering chamber; positive lock system to allow micrometer setting changes without movement of micrometer body. Two metering chambers available. Universal chamber with charge range of approximately 5 to 100 grains; pistol metering chamber with range of 0 to 10 grains. Measure also offered with both chambers. From Redding Reloading Equipment.

Price: Measure with Universal chamber **$124.50**
Price: Pistol chamber **$36.00**
Price: Measure with both chambers **$156.00**

Powder Measure Reservoirs

Replacement reservoirs available in three sizes with or without caps. Smallest is same size as supplied with any Redding measure. Intermediate is $7^1/_2$" overall length with the largest being 10". Fit any Redding powder measure using $2^1/_8$" OD reservoir. From Redding Reloading Equipment.

Price: Original size, no cap **$5.85**
Price: Original size, with cap **$6.90**
Price: Intermediate, no cap **$8.25**
Price: Intermediate, with cap **$9.30**
Price: Large, no cap **$10.80**
Price: Large, with cap **$11.85**

Supercharger Powder Measuring Kit No. 101

Contains Redding Model RS-1 powder/bullet scale; Model No.3 powder measure; Model No. 5 trickler; and RS-6 bench stand. From Redding Reloading Equipment.

Price: **$159.50**

Supercharger Powder Measuring Kit No. 102

Contains Redding Model No. 2 powder/bullet scale; Model No. 3BR powder measure; Model No. 5 powder trickler; and RS-6 bench stand. From Redding Reloading Equipment.

Price: **$178.50**

Supercharger Powder Measuring Kit No. 102BR

Contains Redding Model No. 2 powder/bullet scale; No. 3BR powder measure; Model No. 5 powder trickler; and RS-6 bench stand. From Redding Reloading Equipment.

Price: **$216.00**

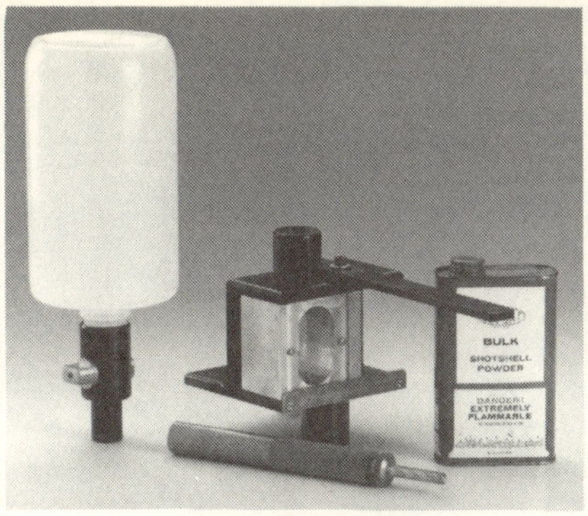

Maxi Measure

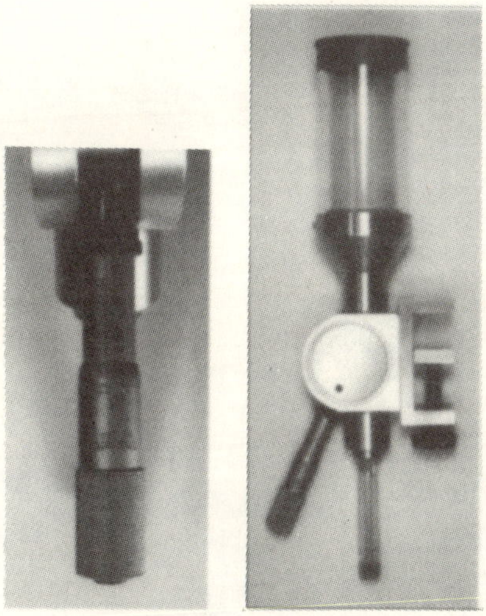

Welsh Precision Measure

MAXI MEASURE

Powder Measure

Designed for loading very large caliber cases, 50 BMG on up. Made of machined steel and aircraft aluminum with solid brass drop tube. Design eliminates charge density variations by connecting hopper to charge reservoir which in turn is transferred to adjustable measuring chamber. Hopper is $^1/_2$-gallon polypropylene bottle with capacity of 11 lbs. Adjustable drop tube is solid brass with adjust range of 0 to 700 grains. Non-adjustable models available on special order. From The Old Western Scrounger.

Price: **$250.00**

SINCLAIR

Bottle Adaptors

Designed for Redding, RCBS Uniflow and Lyman 55 measures to replace the powder hopper with commercial powder bottles and screw them directly onto measure. Requires drilling and tapping small hole in RCBS or Lyman measure casting to attach adaptor; Redding adaptor uses factory screws. From Sinclair International, Inc.

Price: **$18.50**

SINCLAIR

Measure Bracket

Bracket designed for attaching C-clamp type measures to corner of tool box for loading in the field. From Sinclair International, Inc.

Price: **$14.00**

Powder Bottles

16-oz. bottles to use in conjunction with Sinclair bottle adaptors. Helpful when working from larger keg and must keep powder lots separate. From Sinclair International, Inc.

Price: **$3.00**

Powder Drop Tubes

Clear Plexiglass tubes for Redding, RCBS Uniflow and Lyman measures for better visibility and greater powder compression in high density cases. Available in two lengths, 4" and 6" for Lyman and RCBS; or 3" or 5" for Redding. Attachment adaptor required for Redding measure. From Sinclair International, Inc.

Price: Lyman, 4" or 6" **$6.75**
Price: RCBS, 4" **$8.50**
Price: Redding, 3" or 5" **$5.25**
Price: Adaptor for Redding **$8.00**

RCBS Micrometer Insert

Altered Redding 3BR micrometer insert for RCBS small drum Uniflow measure with 15 to 55-grain charge range. From Sinclair International, Inc.

Price: **$39.50**

SLAP

Powder Buddy

Simple trip meter fitted to any powder measure or progressive/semi-progressive press to show a count from 1 to 99999 of each powder throw. Helps prevent double charging or no powder charge. All-metal construction. From SLAP Industries.

Price: . . . . **Contact manufacturer.**

VEGA TOOL

Vega Schuetzen Meter

A remanufacture of the now obsolete Belding & Mull measure with new improvements to include: measure threaded for stand mounting; subreservoir made of brass; operating lever redesigned for more positive and crisp feel. From Vega Tool Company.

Price: **$229.95**

WELSH

Precision Powder Measure

Custom machined aluminum body with stainless steel liner and drum. Powder adjustment via Starrett micrometer. Dimensions: 3.25"x8". Comes with or without powder bottle system. From Bud Welsh.

Price: **$232.00**

FORSTER

"Blue Ribbon" Long Drop Tube Funnel

For use with 4831 and other slow-burning powders where full capacity loads are needed. Long tube adds from 3 to 8 more grains of powder depending on case for a larger volume by weight. From Forster Products.

Price: **$12.00**

"Blue Ribbon" Powder Funnel

Made from Cycolac and designed with four mouth tabs to prevent rolling. One size for 22- to 45-caliber; another for 17 caliber. From Forster Products.

Price: Both sizes **$3.50**

Large Powder/Shot Funnel

Same funnel as used on Bonanza Bench Rest and Bulls-Eye powder measures. Made of tough plastic. From Forster Products.

Price: **$5.00**

HORNADY

Powder Funnel

Tapered tube design to reduce powder spills; fits all cases inclusive of 45-caliber. Anti-static treated transparent plastic. Weight: $^1/_4$-lb. From Hornady Mfg. Co.

Price: **$2.85**

17 Caliber Powder Funnel Adaptor

Aluminum adaptor for Hornady powder funnel seals around mouth of 17-caliber cases to help prevent powder leakage. From Hornady Mfg. Co.

Price: . . . . **Contact manufacturer.**

LEE

Powder Funnel

Large plastic funnel fits all cases from 22- to 45-caliber. Hole in flange permits mounting to Lee turret press, shelf or bench. From Lee Precision, Inc.

Price: **$2.49**

LYMAN

Powder Funnel

Plastic funnel for cases from 22 Hornet through 45-70. From Lyman Products Corporation.

Price: **$3.30**

Forster Large Powder/Shot Funnel

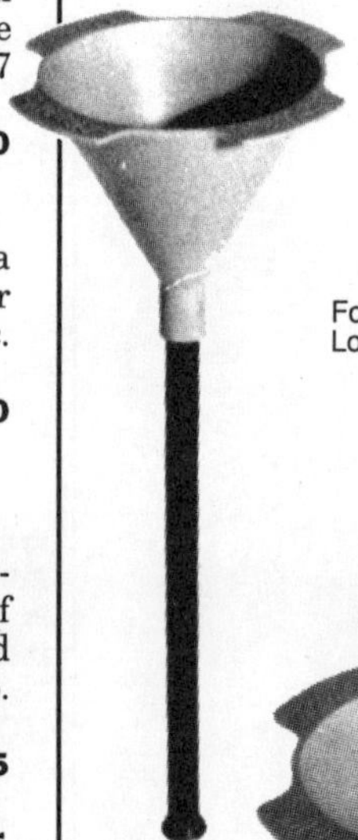

Forster Blue Ribbon Long Drop Tube

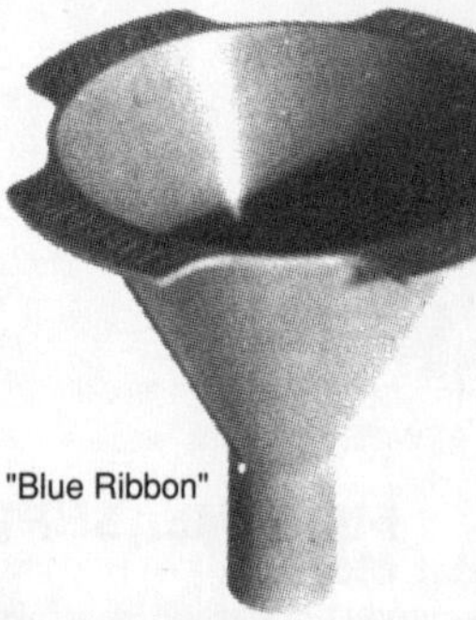

Forster "Blue Ribbon"

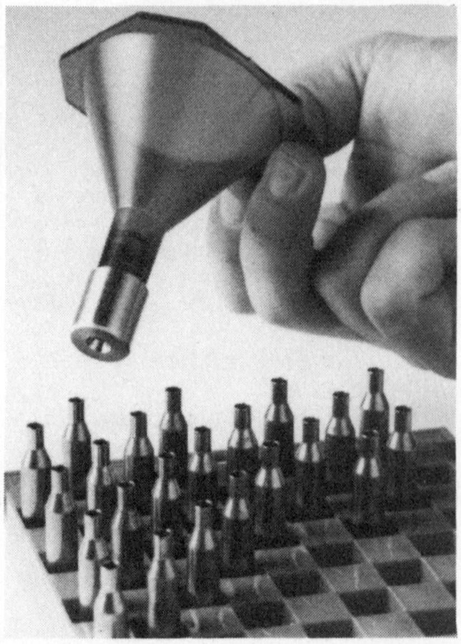

Hornady 17-Caliber Funnel Adaptor

Lee Funnel

MTM

Powder Funnels

Two see-through plastic models available. Universal model fits all calibers from 222 to 45. Adapto 5-in-1 kit includes funnel and standard length adapters for 17 Remington, 222 Remington and 30 through 45 calibers. Long universal drop tube also available. From MTM Moulded Products Company.

Price: Universal **$2.84**

Price: Adaptor kit **$4.09**

PRECISION RELOADING

Aluminum Funnels

All aluminum one-piece construction funnels eliminate static cling of powder and buffer. Available in four sizes: $2^1/_2$-oz. with mouth OD of $2^5/_8$" and spout OD $^7/_{16}$"; $^1/_2$-pint, with mouth OD 4", spout OD $^1/_2$"; $^3/_4$-pint, with mouth OD $4^1/_2$", spout OD $^5/_8$"; and $1^1/_2$-pint, $5^1/_2$" mouth OD, $^3/_4$" spout OD. From Precision Reloading, Inc.

Price: $2^1/_2$ oz. **$1.79**

Price: $^1/_2$-pint **$2.39**

Price: $^3/_4$-pint **$2.79**

Price: $1^1/_2$-pint **$3.49**

RCBS

Powder Funnel

Specially-designed drop tube to avoid powder spills around case mouths, a non-stick, anti-static surface and square lip to prevent rolling. Available in one size for 22- to 45-caliber and another for 17. From RCBS.

Price: **$3.36**

Price: 17-cal. **$4.46**

REDDING

Powder Funnel

Lexan funnel fits all cartridge cases 22- to 45-caliber. Anti-static prevents powder sticking. From Redding Reloading Equipment.

Price: **$3.90**

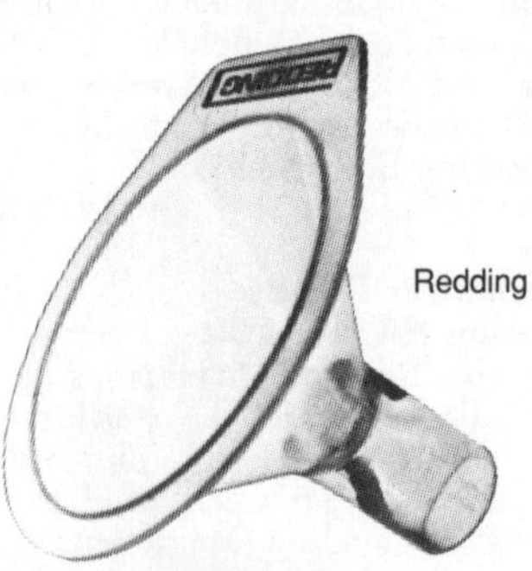

Redding Funnel

RCBS Funnel

C-H/4-D Precision Trimmer

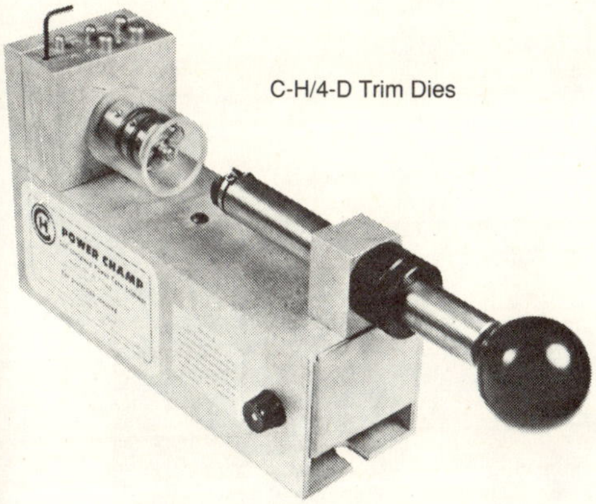

C-H/4-D Trim Dies

C-H/4-D Power Champ

DILLON 1200B Trimmer Calibers
222 Rem.
223 Rem.
220 Swift
22-250
6mm Rem.
243 Win.
25-06
270 Win.
7mm Rem. Mag.
30-30
308
30-06
300 Win. Mag.
300 Wea. Mag.
338 Win. Mag.

C-H Trim Die

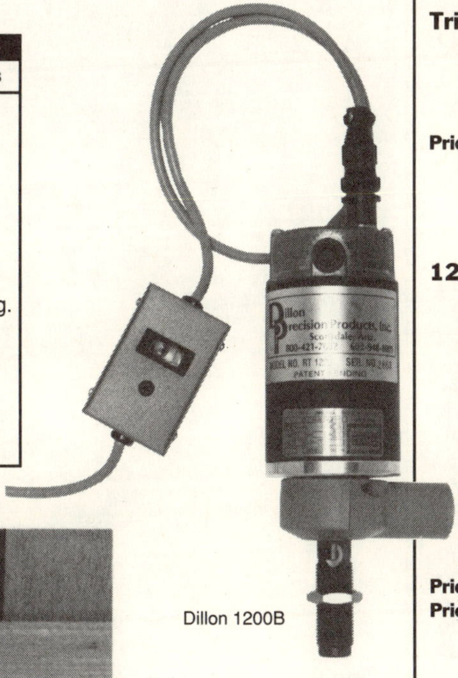

Dillon 1200B

Forster Trimmer

C-H/4-D

Power Champ Case Trimmer

A self-contained power case trimmer that handles any case up to and including 50 BMG. Trims and deburrs outside of case neck in single operation. Tungsten carbide cutter. Comes with one shellholder and pilot. From C-H Tool & Die/4-D Custom Die.

Price: **$179.00**
Price: Pilot **$3.00**
Price: Pilot, 50-cal. **$8.00**
Price: Pilot/shellholder, 50 BMG **$204.00**

Precision Case Trimmer

Hand-operated trimmer with clamping feature that insures uniformity. Comes with one case holder. Custom holders available on request. From C-H Tool & Die/4-D Custom Die.

Price: **$24.95**
Price: Case holder **$5.00**
Price: Custom case holder **$10.00**
Price: Case holder clamp **$2.50**
Price: Cutter assembly **$8.50**

Trimmer Die

Fits any press with 7/8-14 threads. For checking case length or trimming to case length. From C-H Tool & Die/4-D Custom Die.

Price: **$14.00**

DILLON

1200B Case Trimmer

Attach to any standard single station or progressive press to use like a standard sizing die. As case is pushed into die a 1/4-hp electric motor driving a carbide cutter trims the case to length. Chips drawn off through vacuum manifold that clamps to outside of special size/trim die. Vacuum cleaner not included. Comes complete with one steel size/trim die. From Dillon Precision Products, Inc.

Price: **$164.95**
Price: Extra trim die **$23.50**

FORSTER

Case Trimmer

Manual trimmer with hardened, ground cutter shaft. Shaft has four staggered teeth for chatterless cutting. Brown and Sharpe collet holds case without end movement. Stop collar features fine adjustment screws. Collet and pilot not included. Weight: 2 lbs. From Forster Products.

Price: **$48.00**
Price: Collet **$8.00**
Price: Pilot **$2.90**

FORSTER

Case Trimmer Kit

Includes Forster manual case trimmer, three collets (#1, #2, #3) and six pilots (#22, 24, 25, 27, 28, 30). From Forster Products.

Price: **$72.00**

Case Trimmer Power Adaptor

Screws onto cutter shaft of Forster manual case trimmer in place of hand crank. Allows attachment of cordless screwdriver or small power drill. Collet and pilot not included. From Forster Products.

Price: **$12.50**
Price: Collet **$8.00**
Price: Pilot **$2.90**

Power Case Trimmer

Designed for use with drill press. Features line-up bar to align trimmer and drill press spindle; Brown and Sharpe-type collet; sturdy threaded lever for opening and closing collet; cutter shaft with 1/4" shank of hardened steel with four staggered cutting edges. Pilot, collet not included. From Forster Products.

Price: **$48.50**
Price: Collet **$8.00**
Price: Pilot **$2.90**

GACEY

Case Trimmer

Power trimmer for trimming cases to length, deburring and chamfering in single operation. Indexes on resized case shoulder. 500 cases per hour. Comes with one shellholder. From OK Weber, Inc.

Price: **$187.50**

HOLLYWOOD

50 Caliber Case Trimmer

Made of tool steel, this unit can be operated by hand, used in electric drill or drill press. Comes as complete set to trim, ream and chamfer cases. Includes trimmer, pocket reamer, chamfer tool and handle. From Hollywood Engineering.

Price: **$120.00**
Price: Trimmer **$50.00**
Price: Primer pocket reamer **$35.00**
Price: Chamfer tool **$50.00**
Price: Handle **$30.00**

HORNADY

Case Trimmer

Uses standard removable shellholder heads. Adjusts to any case length. Mounts on bench or clamps in vise. Handle removable for electric drill attachment. Includes 10 pilots, Nos. 1, 3, 4, 6, 7, 9, 15, 17, 18, 19. Shellholder not included. From Hornady Mfg. Co.

Price: **$49.95**
Price: Pilot **$2.85**
Price: 17-cal. pilot **$7.75**
Price: Extra cutter **$5.90**

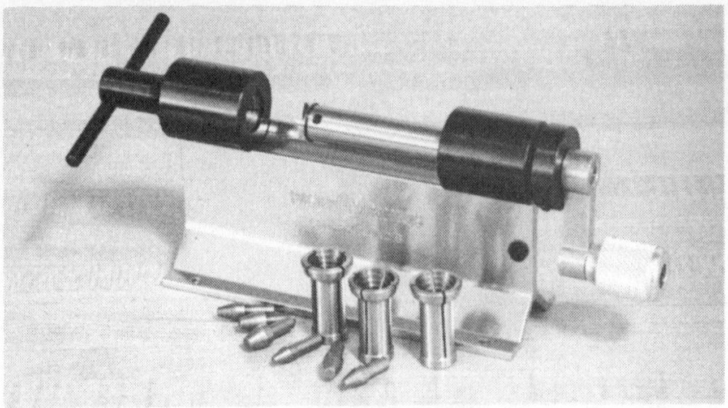

Forster Trimmer Kit

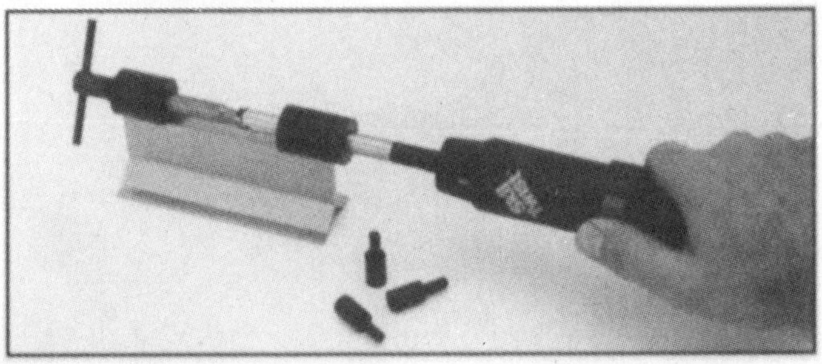

Forster Power Adaptor

Forster Power Case Trimmer

FORSTER Case Trimmer Kit
38 Special
357 Mag.
222 Rem. Mag.
223 Rem.
22-250
243 Win.
244 Rem.
257 Roberts
270 Win.
7x57 Mauser
7mm-08
280 Rem.
308 Win.
30-06
25-06
8x57 Mauser

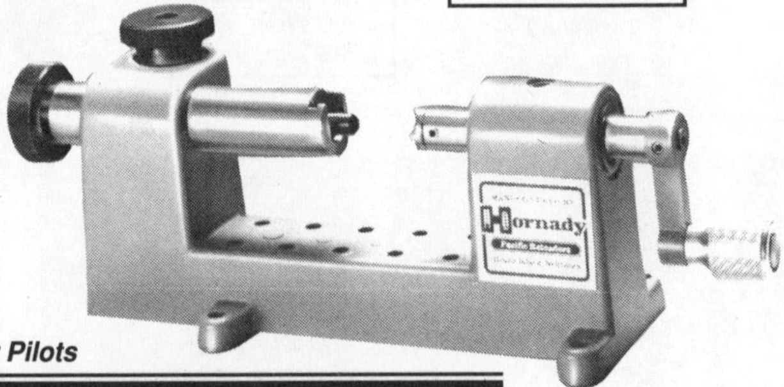

Hornady Trimmer

HORNADY *Case Trimmer Pilots*

Caliber	Bullet Dia.	Pilot #	Caliber	Bullet Dia.	Pilot #
22	.224	1	8mm	.323	11
	.228	2		.333	12
6mm	.243	3		.338	13
25	.257	4		.348	14
6.5mm	.264	5	38	.358	15
270	.277	6		.375	16
7mm	.284	7	41	.410	17
	.300	8	44	.429	18
30	.308	9	45	.452	19
303	.312	10		.361	20
			40	.400	21

FORSTER *Case Trimmers*

Caliber	Bullet Dia.	Trim Pilot Mark	Collet Mark	Min. Neck Dia.	Neck Reamer Mark
17 Remington	.171	17	1	.1730	17
22 Hornet	.223	2	2,3	.2255	223
22 K Hornet	.223	2	2,3	.2255	223
222 Remington	.224	22	1	.2265	224
222 Remington Mag.	.224	22	1	.2265	224
22 Varmint	.224	22	1	.2265	224
223 Remington	.224	22	1	.2265	224
225 Winchester	.224	22	1	.2265	224
5.6mmx50R	.224	22	1	.2265	224
22-250	.224	22	1	.2265	224
220 Swift	.224	22	1	.2265	224
221 Fireball	.224	22	1	.2265	224
22 PPC	.224	22	1	.2265	224
22 BR Remington	.224	22	1	.2265	224
218 Bee & Mashburn	.224	22	2	.2265	224
219 Zipper	.224	22	2	.2265	224
219 Wasp	.224	22	2	.2265	224
22 Savage	.224	22	2	.2265	224
22-30/30	.224	22	2	.2265	224
228 Krag	.224	22	3	.2265	224
22 Jet CF Magnum	.224	22	3	.2265	224
224 Varmint Wea.	.224	22	3	.2265	224
22 PPC	.224	22	3	.2265	224
243 Winchester	.243	24	1	.2455	243
6mm	.243	24	1	.2455	243
6mm Krag Long	.243	24	1	.2455	243
257	.257	256	1	.2595	257
250 Savage	.257	25	1	.2595	257
250 Ackley	.257	25	1	.2595	257
250-3000	.257	25	1	.2595	257
25 Souper	.257	25	1	.2595	257
25-06	.257	25	1	.2595	257
25-20 Repeater	.257	25	2	.2595	257
25-35	.257	25	2	.2595	257
25 Remington	.257	25	2	.2595	257
25 Krag Improved	.257	25	3	.2595	257
256 Winchester	.257	25	3	.2595	257
6.5x57 Mauser	.263	26	1	.2655	263
6.5mm Winchester	.263	26	1	.2655	263
6.5mm Jap.Mauser	.263	26	1	.2655	263
6.5x55 Swede	.263	26	1	.2655	263
6.5x55 SKAN	.263	26	1	.2655	263
6.5x257 Japanese	.263	26	1	.2655	263
256 Newton	.263	26	1	.2655	263
260 AAR	.263	26	1	.2655	263
264 Winchester Mag.	.263	26	1	.2655	263
270 Winchester	.277	27	1	.2795	277
270 Savage	.277	27	1	.2795	277
270 Gibbs	.277	27	1	.2795	277
270 Weatherby	.277	27	1	.2795	277
270 Ackley	.277	27	1	.2795	277
257 H&H	.277	27	1	.2795	277
7mm Mauser	.284	28	1	.2865	284
7x57 Mauser	.277	27	1	.2795	277
7mm Weatherby	.277	27	1	.2795	277
7mmx64	.277	27	1	.2795	277
276	.277	27	1	.2795	277
7mm-08	.277	27	1	.2795	277
7mm TCU	.277	27	1	.2795	277
280 Remington	.284	28	1	.2865	284
284 Winchester	.284	28	1	.2865	284
7mm Rem. Mag.	.284	28	1	.2865	284
7mm BR Rem.	.284	28	1	.2865	284
30-06	.308	30	1	.3110	308
308 Winchester	.308	30	1	.3110	308
300 Magnum	.308	30	1	.3110	308
7.62 NATO	.308	30	1	.3110	308
300 Savage	.308	30	1	.3110	308
30-30	.308	30	2	.3110	308
30 Remington	.308	30	2	.3110	308
30 WCF	.308	30	2	.3110	308
303 Savage	.308	30	2	.3110	308
7.5x55 Swiss	.308	30	2	.3110	308
30-40 Krag	.308	30	3	.3110	308
30 Carbine	.308	30	3	.3110	308
30-40 Improved	.308	30	3	.3110	308
7.62x39	.308	30	3	.3110	308
303 British	.311	31	1	.3135	311
32 S&W Long	.311	31	1	.3135	311
7.65 Mauser	.311	31	1	.3135	311
7.7mm Japanese	.311	31	1	.3135	311
32-20	.311	31	2	.3135	311
8x57	.323	32	1	.3255	323
8x57 JS	.323	32	1	.3255	323
8x57 RS	.323	32	1	.3255	323
8x60	.323	32	1	.3255	323
7.92x57	.323	32	1	.3255	323
8mm-06	.323	32	1	.3255	323
8mm Mauser	.323	32	1	.3255	323
32 Winchester Spl.	.323	32	2	.3255	323
32 Remington	.323	32	2	.3255	323
32-40	.323	32	2	.3255	323
333 Winchester	.333	33	1		
333 OKH	.333	33	1		
333 Ackley	.333	33	1		
33 Winchester	.338	3	4		
338 Winchester	.338	3	1		
338 Winchester Mag.	.338	3	1		
338 Gibbs	.338	3	1		
340 Weatherby Mag.	.338	3	1		
348 Winchester	.348	34	4		
35 Remington	.357, .358	35	1	.3605	358
358 Winchester	.357, .358	35	1	.3605	358
358 Norma Magnum	.357, .358	35	1	.3605	358
38 Colt Super	.357, .358	35	2	.3605	358
38 Special	.357, .358	35	3	.3605	358
357 Magnum	.357, .358	35	3	.3605	358
35 Winchester	.357, .358	35	3	.3605	358
9mm Luger	.355, .356	351	2	.3575	355
380 Auto	.356	351	1		
9.3mmx74R	.365	368	1		
9.3mmx62	.365	368	1		
375 Magnum	.375	375	1	.3780	375
375-06	.375	375	1	.3780	375
375 Barnes	.375	375	1	.3780	375
375 Weatherby	.375	375	1	.3780	375
375 Ackley	.375	375	1	.3780	375
375 H&H	.375	375	1	.3780	375
38-50	.375	375	4		
378 Weatherby	.375	375	4		
375 Winchester	.376	375	2		
41 Colt	.400	400	1		
401 Winchester	.400	400	1		
38-40	.400	400	1		
395-400	.400	400	1		
41 S&W	.400	400	1		
10mm Auto	.400	400	1		
41 Rem. Mag.	.410	410	2	.4125	410
416 Weatherby	.416	416	4		
416 Rigby	.416	416	4		
44 S&W Spl.	.429	432	1	.4340	432
44 Rem. Mag.	.429	432	1	.4340	432
44-40	.429	432	1	.4340	432
444 Marlin Magnum	.429	432	1	.4340	432
45 ACP	.452	452	1		
45 Auto Rim	.452	452	1		
45 Winchester Mag.	.452	452	1		
45-90	.454	452	4		
45 Long Colt	.452, .454	455	1,2		
45-70	.457	458	4		
450 Watts	.459	458	1	.4605	458
458 Winchester	.459	458	1	.4605	458
450 Ackley Magnum	.459	458	1	.4605	458

HORNADY

Case Trimmer/Caliper Kit

Includes Hornady case trimmer, 10 pilots and stainless steel dial caliper. Weight: 4 3/4 lbs. From Hornady Mfg. Co.

Price: **$94.00**

Trim Die

Hardened steel trim die threaded 7/8-14 to fit any standard press. Available in most popular calibers. Weight: 1 lb. From Hornady Mfg. Co.

Price: **$15.98**

LEE

Case Trimmer

Four-piece tool kit includes lock stud and cutter for all calibers and caliber-specific shellholder plus case length gauge. For trimming cases manually or for use with electric drill. From Lee Precision, Inc.

Price: **$4.98**

LYMAN

Accu Trimmer

Trims cases 17-caliber through 458 Winchester. Uses standard shellholders and standard Lyman cutter heads and pilots. Comes with nine pilots. From Lyman Products Corporation.

Price: **$42.95**

Case Trimmer Accessories

Four accessories for Lyman case trimmers. Nine Pilot Multi-Pack for Lyman Universal trimmer or Accu trimmer. Calibers include: 22, 24, 27, 28/7mm, 30, 9mm, 35, 44 and 45A; extra pilots; replacement cutter head; carbide cutter head. From Lyman Products Corporation.

Price: Multi-Pack **$9.95**
Price: Extra pilot **$3.50**
Price: Replacement cutter head . . **$11.00**
Price: Carbide cutter head **$46.95**

Drill Press Trimmer

Universal chuck head eliminates need for collets. Extra cutter head included. Accepts standard Lyman pilots. From Lyman Products Corporation.

Price: **$49.95**

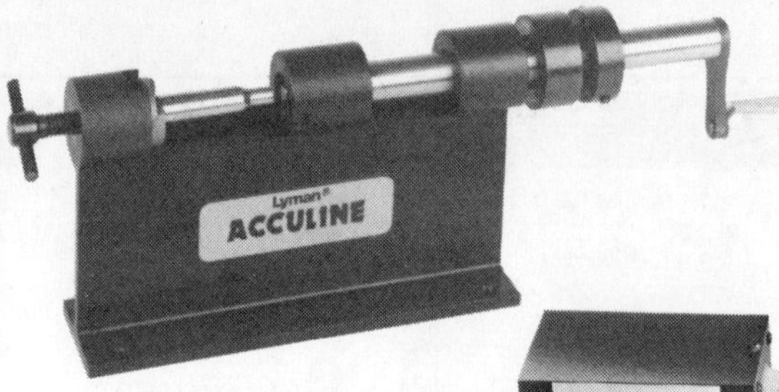

Lyman Accu Trimmer

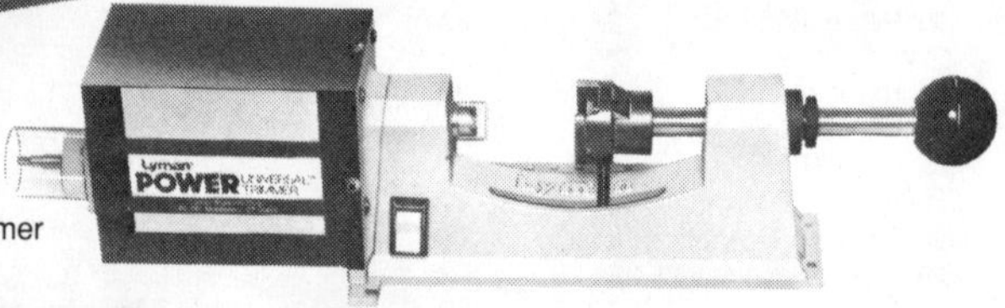

Lyman Power Trimmer

HORNADY
Trim Die Calibers

219 Zipper	7x57/7mm Mauser
17/222	7x61 Sharpe & Hart
222 Rem. Mag.	7mm Rem. Mag.
223 Rem.	7mm Wea.
22/250	7mm Exp./280
220 Swift	284 Win.
243 Win.	30/30 Win.
6mm/284	303 British
25-06	308 Win.
25/35 Win.	30-40 Krag
25/284	308 Norma Mag.
6.5-06	30-06
6.5 Rem. Mag.	300 Win. Mag.
6.5 Mann.	30 Herrett
6.5 Carcano	32 Win.
6.5 Japanese	8mm-06
264 Win. Mag.	35 Rem.
270 Win.	357 Herrett
270 Wea.	

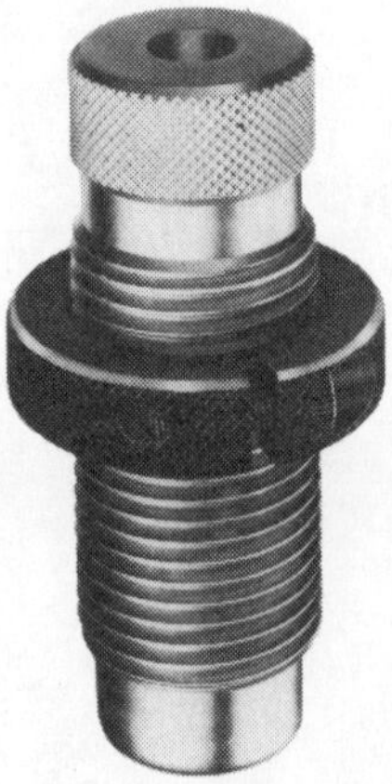

Hornady Trim Die

Lyman Drill Press Trimmer

LYMAN ***Case Trimmer Pilots***

Cartridge	Pilot #	Cartridge	Pilot #	Cartridge	Pilot #
RIFLE					
17 Rem.	17	7mm Rem. Mag.	28	7.62x63mm	31
22 Hornet	22	7mmx57 Mauser	28	303 British	31
222 Rem.	22	7mmx57R Mauser	28	7.65mm Arg. Mauser	31
222 Rem. Mag.	22	280 Rem.	28	32-20 Win.	31
223 Rem. (5.56mm)	22	7mm-08 Rem.	28	32 Win. Spl.	32
22-250	22	7x30 Waters	28	8mmx57 Mauser	8mm
220 Swift	22	7mm Wea. Mag.	28	8mm Rem. Mag.	8mm
5.6mmx50R	22	7mmx64 Brenneke	28	338 Win. Mag.	33
243 Win.	24	7mmx65R Brenneke	28	35 Rem.	35
6mm Rem.	24	30 M1 Carbine	30	35 Whelen	35
25-06 Rem.	25	30-30 Win.	30	358 Win.	35
250 Savage	25	30-06	30	375 H&H	37
257 Roberts	25	307 Win.	30	375 Win.	37
25-20 Win.	25	308 Win.	30	38-55 Win.	37
6.5mmx57 Mauser	26	300 Savage	30	416 Rigby	416
6.5mmx57R Mauser	26	300 Wea. Mag.	30	444 Marlin	44
6.5mmx55 Swed. Mau.	26	300 Win. Mag.	30	45-70 Gov't.	45
270 Win.	27	7.62x39mm	30	50-70 Gov't.	
7mm TCU	28	7.62x54 Russian	31		
PISTOL					
25 ACP	25A	380 Auto	9mm	41 Mag.	41
7mm TCU	28	38 S&W	35	41 Action Exp.	41
30 Luger	30	9mm Luger	9mm	44 Mag.	44
30 Herrett	30	38 Special	35	44 Special	44
30 Mauser	30	357 Mag.	35	44-40 Win.	44A
32 ACP	30	357 Rem. Max.	35	45 ACP	45A
32 S&W Long	31	9mm Makarov	36	45 Colt	45A
32 H&R Mag.	31	40 S&W	39	45 Win. Mag.	45A
38 Super Auto	9mm	10mm Auto	39	45 Colt	

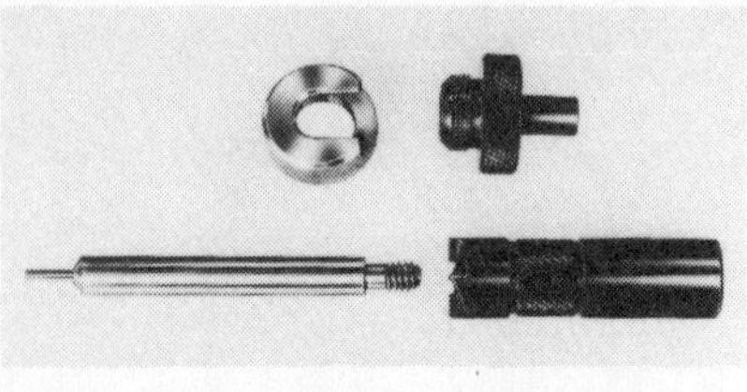

Lee Case Trimmer-2

LYMAN

Power Trimmer

Electric trimmer with 175 rpm motor in 110- or 220-volt. Features adjustable settings for overall trim length; replaceable cutter head; cartridge case lock/unlock. Includes nine pilots, two cutter heads and set of primer pocket brushes. High-speed drive with safety guard. Accessory carbide cutter available. Weight: 12 lbs. From Lyman Products Corporation.

Price: 110-volt **$199.95**
Price: 220-volt **$210.00**

Universal Trimmer

Features coarse and fine adjustments; adjusting ring to dial and lock in approximate setting for repeatability. Comes separately or in Multi-Pack set with nine of most used pilots. From Lyman Products Corporation.

Price: Trimmer **$68.95**
Price: Multi-Pack set **$73.95**

RCBS

Case Trimmer-2 Converter

Converts hand-turned trimmer into a power-driven tool. Works with any standard power drill. From RCBS.

Price: **$4.48**

Rotary Case Trimmer-2

Die-cast metal base trimmer with hardened steel blades for trimming or shortening cases, or correcting uneven case mouths. Cutter assembly has double lock rings, or bushings, to permit a quantity of cases to be trimmed with single adjustment. Interchangeable quick-release, multi-step collets and pilots available for calibers 17 through 45. From RCBS.

Price: **$54.42**
Price: Pilot **$2.97**
Price: Collet **$7.13**

Rotary Case Trimmer-2 Kit

Includes Case Trimmer-2; collets #1, #2, #3; pilot calibers 22, 24, 25, 27, 28, 30, 35, 44 and 45. From RCBS.

Price: **$77.48**

Trim Gauges

A metal collar with adjustable screw and lock nut for caliber changes on rotary case trimmers. Adjust the screw to desired length, lock it to size with nut and use over and over for that same trim length. Fits most 1/2" diameter rotary shafts. Available in six lengths. From RCBS.

Price: . . . . **Contact manufacturer.**

RCBS Case Trimmer-2

RCBS *Case Trimmer-2*

Caliber	Trimmer Collet	Trimmer Pilot	Trim Gauge
17 Rem.	1	17	4
218 Bee	2	22	2
22 Hornet	2	22	2
22K-Hornet	2	22	2
22 PPC	3	22	4
22 Rem. Jet	3	22	2
22 Sav. High-Power	2	22	4
22-250	1	22	4
220 Swift	1	22	4
221 Rem. Fire Ball	1	22	2
222 Rem.	1	22	3
222 Rem. Mag.	1	22	4
223 Rem.	1	22	3
224 Wea. Mag.	3	22	5
225 Win.	1	22	4
5.6mmx50 Rimmed	2	22	4
240 Wea. Mag.	1	24	5
243 Win.	1	24	4
6mm PPC	3	24	4
6mm Rem.	1	24	4
25-06	1	25	5
25-20 Win.	2	25	2
25-35	2	25	4
250 Sav.	1	25	4
256 Win. Mag.	3	25	2
257 Roberts	1	25	4
257 Roberts Imp.	1	25	4
257 Wea. Mag.	1	25	5
264 Win. Mag.	1	26	5
6.5 Rem. Mag.	1	26	4
6.5mm T/CU	1	26	3
6.5mm-06	1	26	5
6.5mmx50 Jap. Ar.	1	26	4
6.5mmx52 Carcano	3	26	4
6.5mmx54 Man.-Scho.	1	26	4
6.5x55 Swedish Mau.	1	26	4
6.5x57	1	26	4
270 Wea. Mag.	1	27	5
270 Win.	1	27	5
280 Rem.	1	28	5
284 Win.	1	28	4
7mm BR Rem.	1	28	3
7mm Rem. Mag.	1	28	5
7mm T/CU	1	28	3
7mm Wea. Mag.	1	28	5
7mm-08 Rem.	1	28	4
7mmx57 Mauser	1	28	4
7mmx64 Brenneke	1	28	4
7mmx65 Rimmed	1	28	5
7-30 Waters	2	28	4
30 M-1 Carb.	3	30	2
30 Herrett	2	30	3
30 Luger	2	30	1
30 Mauser	2	30	1
30 Remington	2	30	4
30-06 Sprngfld.	1	30	5
30-30 Win.	2	30	4
30-338 Win. Mag.	1	30	5
30-40 Krag	3	30	4
300 H&H Mag.	1	30	6
300 Sav.	1	30	4
300 Wea. Mag.	1	30	6
300 Win. Mag.	1	30	5
303 British	1	31	4
303 Savage	2	30	4
307 Win.	2	30	4
308 Norma Mag.	1	30	5
308 Win.	1	30	4
7.5mm Schmidt-Rubin	2	30	4
7.62x39-308/311	3	30/31	3
7.62x54R Russ.	4	30	4
7.65x53 Bel, Mau.	1	31	4
7.7x58 Jap. Arisaka	1	31	4
32 Auto	1	31	1
32 H&R Mag.	1	31	1
32 S&W Long	1	31	1
32 Win. Spcl.	2	32	4
32-20 Win.	2	31	2
32-40 Win.	2	32	4
8mm Rem. Mag.	1	32	6
8mm-06	1	32	5
8mmx57	1	32	4
8mmx68S Mag.	2	32	5
33 Win.	4	33	4
338 Win. Mag.	1	33	5
340 Wea. Mag.	1	33	6
348 Win.	4	34	4
35 Rem.	1	35	4
35 Whelen	1	35	5
350 Rem. Mag.	1	35	4
356 Win.	2	35	4
357 Herrett	2	35	4
357 Mag.	3	35	2
357 Rem. Mag.	3	35	3
358 Norma Mag.	1	35	5
358 Win.	1	35	4
9mm Luger	2	35	1
9mm Makarov	2	35	1
9mmx21	2	35	1
9.3x62 Mauser	1	36	5
9.3x72R	2	36	6
9.3x74R	1	36	6
375 H&H Mag.	1	37	6
375 Win.	2	37	4
378 Wea. Mag.	4	37	6
38 Colt Super	2	35	1
38 S&W	3	35	1
38 Spcl.	3	35	2
380 ACP	1	35	1
38-40 Win.	1	40	2
38-55 Win. & Ballard	2	37	4
40 S&W	3	40	1
10mm Auto	3	40	1
41 AE	2	41	1
41 Mag.	2	41	2
416 Rem. Mag.	1	416	6
416 Rigby	4	416	6
44 Mag.	2	44	2
44 Spcl.	2	44	2
444 Marlin	1	44	4
44-40 Win.	1	44	2
45 ACP	1	45	1
45 Auto Rim	1	45	1
45 Colt	1	45	2
45 Win. Mag.	1	45	4
45-70 U.S. Gov't.	4	45-R	4
458 Win. Mag.	1	45-R	5
460 Wea. Mag.	4	45	6

RCBS

Trim Dies

Standard 7/8"-14 thread file trim die for checking and shortening cases. Available in all calibers with overall case length of 0.875" or more. Cases measuring shorter than 1.70" require an extension on shellholder. From RCBS.

Price: . . . . **Contact manufacturer.**

REDDING

Model No. 1400 Case Trimmer

Unique design featuring stationary cutter for maximum rigidity and stiffness while case is turned. Features cast iron frame; universal collet to fit all popular rifle and pistol cases; adjustable cutter shaft to accommodate longest magnum cases; coarse and fine adjustments for case length to .001" or less. Comes with Universal collet; six pilots, 22, 6mm, 25, 270, 7mm and 30; two neck cleaning brushes, 22- through 30-caliber; large and small primer pocket cleaners. From Redding Reloading Equipment.

Price: **$79.50**

SHERLINE

Power Lathe

Steel bed, precision lathe for trimming large volumes of cases. Features 1/4-hp or 1/2-hp ball bearing motor. Blank collet for boring to caliber size. From Blue Ridge Machinery and Tools, Inc.

Price: 1/4-hp lathe **$360.00**
Price: 1/2-hp lathe **$390.00**

WHITETAIL DESIGN

Cutter for Wilson Case Trimmer

Carbide cutter designed to fit the Wilson case trimmer. From Whitetail Design and Engineering Ltd.

Price: **$30.00**

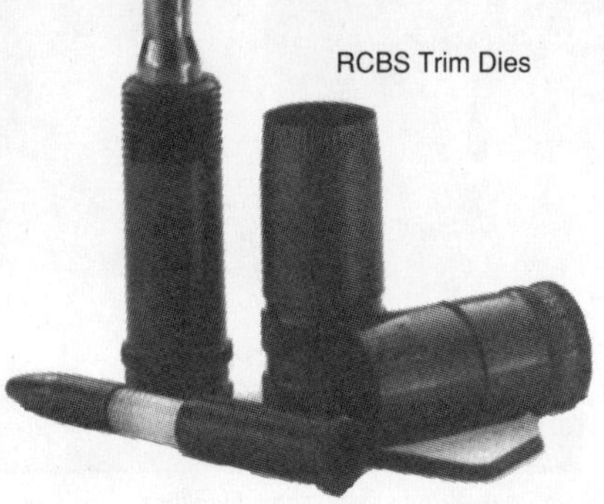

RCBS Trim Dies

No. 1400 Universal Collet

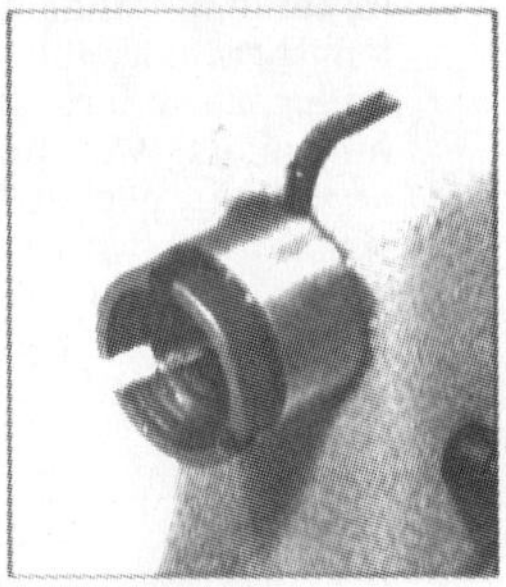

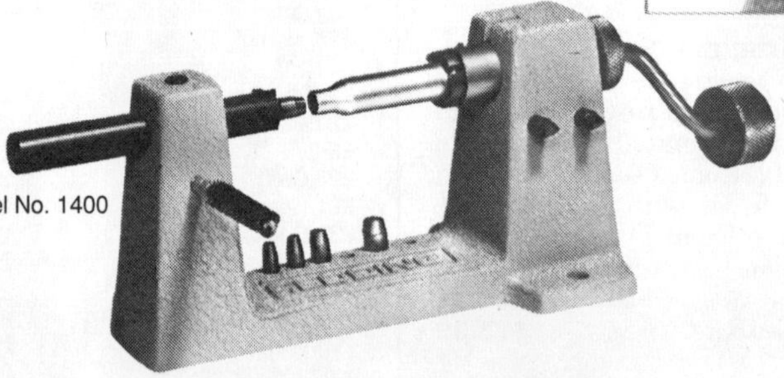

Redding Model No. 1400

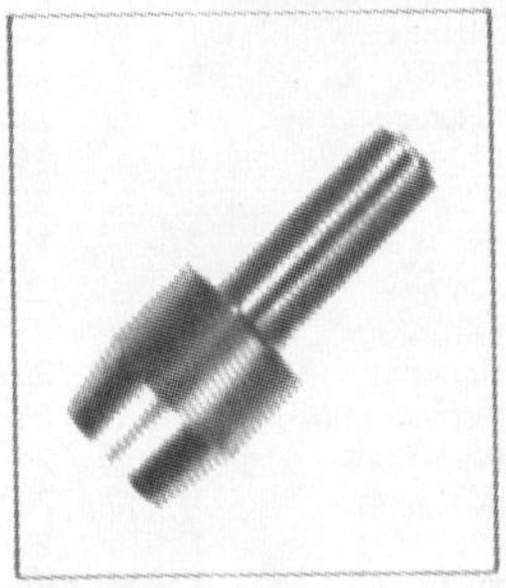

No. 1400 Pilot

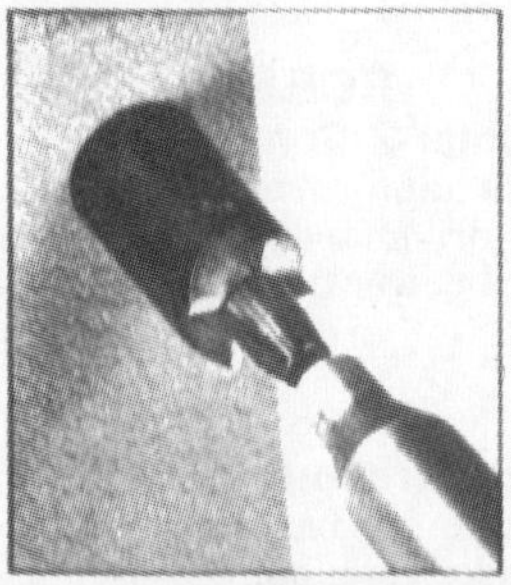

No. 1400 High Speed Cutter Shaft

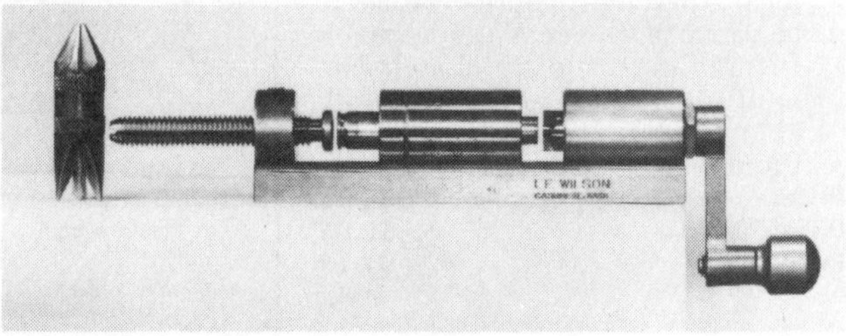

Wilson Case Trimmer

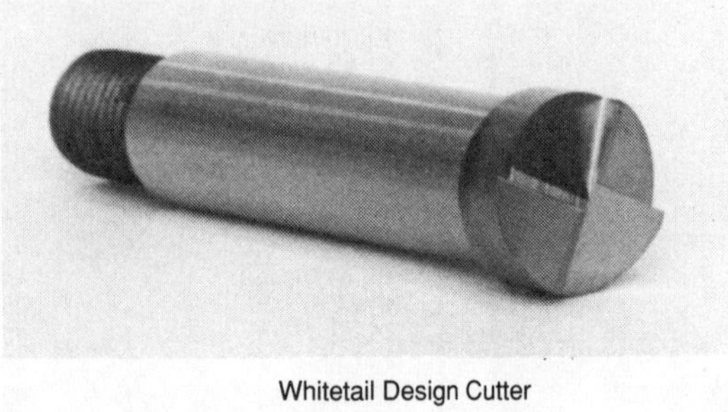

Whitetail Design Cutter

Consult our Directory pages for the location of firms mentioned.

WILSON Trimmer Case Holders	
RIFLE	
17 Rem.	7mm IHMSA
218 Bee	7mm Wea. Mag.
219 Donaldson	30 Herrett
219 Zipper	30 M1 Carbine
22 Hornet	30 Rem.
22 PPC	30-06
22 PPC SAKO	30-30
22 Rem. BR	30-338
22-250	30-40
220 Swift	300 H&H
220 Wilson Arrow	300 Savage
221 Rem. FB	300 Wea. Mag.
222 Rem.	300 Win. Mag.
222 Rem. Mag.	308 Norma
223 Rem.	308 Win.
224 Wea. Mag.	7.62mm Russian
225 Win.	7.62mmx39
240 Wea. Mag.	303 British
243 Win.	7.65mm Belgian Mauser
6mm PPC	32 Rem.
6mm PPC SAKO	32 Win. Special
6mm Rem.	32-20
6mmx47	32-40
6mm Int'l.	8mmx57 Mauser
6mm Rem. BR	8mm Rem. Mag.
25 Rem.	8mm-06
25-06	338 Win. Mag.
25-20	340 Wea. Mag.
25-35	35 Rem.
250 Savage	35 Whelen
257 Roberts	35 Win.
257 Wea. Mag.	350 Rem. Mag.
264 Win. Mag.	358 Norma Mag.
6.5 Rem. Mag.	358 Win.
6.5x55	375 H&H Mag.
270 Wea. Mag.	375 Wea. Mag.
270 Win.	378 Wea. Mag.
280/7mm Express	38-40
284 Win.	38-55
7mm Rem. BR	44-40
7mm Rem. Mag.	444 Marlin
7mm TCU	45-70 Gov't.
7mmx57 Mauser	458 Win. Mag.
7mmx61 S&H	460 Wea. Mag.
7mm-08	
PISTOL	
357 Magnum	44 Magnum
38 Special	44 Special
38 Super Auto	45 Auto (ACP)
9mm Luger	45 Colt
41 Magnum	

WILSON

Case Trimmer

Unique design supports case in chamber-type holder during trim operation to assure correct alignment. Cases trimmed squarely regardless of offset heads or varying neck diameters. Positive stop assures uniform length. Optional tooling allows case head squaring, inside neck reaming and removal of military primer crimp. From L.E. Wilson, Inc.

Price: Trimmer **$35.93**
Price: Rifle case holder **$5.72**
Price: Pistol case holder **$7.63**

WILSON/SINCLAIR

Ultimate Trimmer Kit

Includes L.E. Wilson trimmer, micrometer attachment to replace standard Wilson adjustment screw, mounting bracket with crimp arm to hold down trimmer case holders. Starret 1" travel micrometer head allows accurate setting of trimmer in increments of .001". From Sinclair International, Inc.

Price: **$111.92**

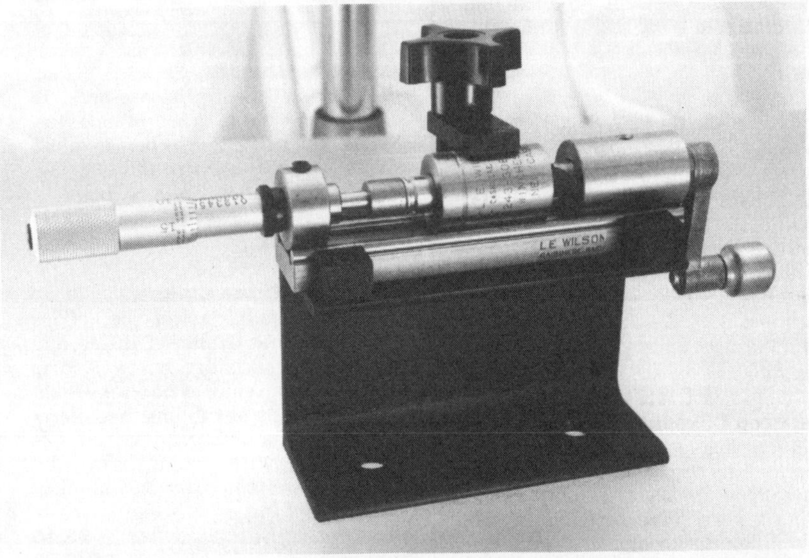

Wilson/Sinclair Ultimate Trimmer

WILSON Q-Type Case Holders
357 Mag.
38 Special
38 Super Auto
41 Mag.
44 Mag.
44 Russian
44 Special
45 Colt

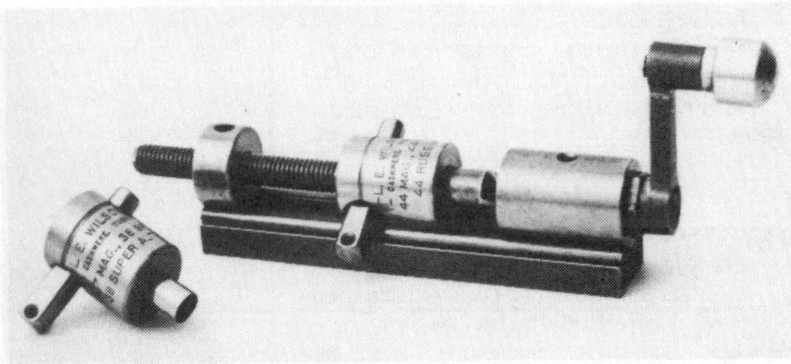

Wilson Trimmer with pistol case holder.

BIRCHWOOD CASEY

Brass Cleaner

Liquid chemical concentrate for cleaning brass. 3-oz. bottle makes 2 qts. of reusable cleaning solution. From Birchwood Laboratories, Inc.

Price: **$3.65**

MIKE DAVIS

Brass Stripper

Ammonia-free liquid brass cleaning concentrate. Comes in 12-oz. bottle. From Mike Davis Products.

Price: **$5.00**

DILLON

Rapid Polish 290

A cartridge case finish. Add to tumbler media. Contains no ammonia. Available in 8-oz. bottle. From Dillon Precision Products, Inc.

Price: **$4.95**

FLITZ

FZ Liquid

Non-toxic, non-abrasive liquid metal polish. Add to tumbler media. Available in three sizes of plastic bottles from 3.4-oz. to 23.6-oz. From Flitz International, Ltd.

Price: 3.4-oz. **$5.15**
Price: 8.5-oz. **$10.35**
Price: 23.6-oz. **$22.39**

FORSTER

Case Prep Cleaning Brush

Cleans inside and outside of case necks. Fits chuck of any power drill. Available for 22, 270/7mm, 30 and 35 calibers. Five brushes in set. From Forster Products.

Price: **$18.00**

Polishing Roll

Silicone carbide impregnated cleaning/polishing material that is washable and reusable. From Forster Products.

Price: **$4.90**

HART

Accessory Tool Handle

Anodized aluminum handle to hold case neck cleaning brushes threaded 8-32. From Robert Hart & Son, Inc.

Price: **$3.25**

HORNADY

Case Neck Brushes

Nine brush sizes for all popular calibers. 17, 22, 6mm, 25/6.5, 270, 7mm, 30, 338-35, 44-45 calibers. Case neck brush handle available. From Hornady Mfg. Co.

Price: **$1.95**

Universal Accessory Handle

Steel, knurled handle fits all Hornady case neck brushes. From Hornady Mfg. Co.

Price: **$2.85**

IOSSO

QuickBrite Case Cleaner

Liquid immersion-type case cleaner. One quart cleans 2,000-5,000 cases. Reusable. Comes in quart, gallon containers or in kit form with strainer bag, pail, lid and quart of QuickBrite. From Iosso Products.

Price: Quart **$7.95**
Price: Gallon **$24.95**
Price: Kit **$15.95**

QuickBrite Case Polish

Liquid additive for tumbling media. Available in quart or gallon containers. From Iosso Products.

Price: Quart **$34.95**
Price: Gallon **$99.95**

RCBS

Case Neck Brushes

Clean and lube inside case necks in one step. Three sizes of brushes: small for 22- to 25-caliber; medium for 270- to 30-caliber; and large for 35- to 45- caliber. From RCBS.

Price: **$1.97**

TSI

400 Ammo Brass Cleaner

A liquid brass cleaner that strips corrosion and oxidation inside and outside of cartridge cases. A drip process that requires no wire-brushing, tumbling or rubbing. Non-flammable, non-staining, non-etching. Is reusable, will last indefinitely. From American Gas & Chemical Company, Ltd.

Price: 16 oz. **$5.40**
Price: 1 gal. **$39.00**
Price: 55 gal. drum **$1,250.00**

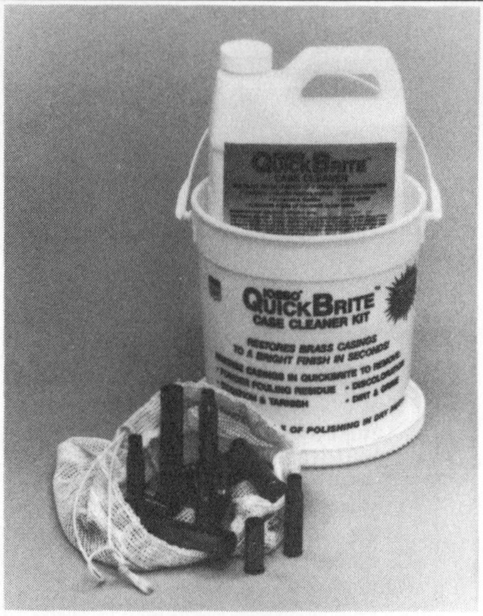

Iosso QuickBrite

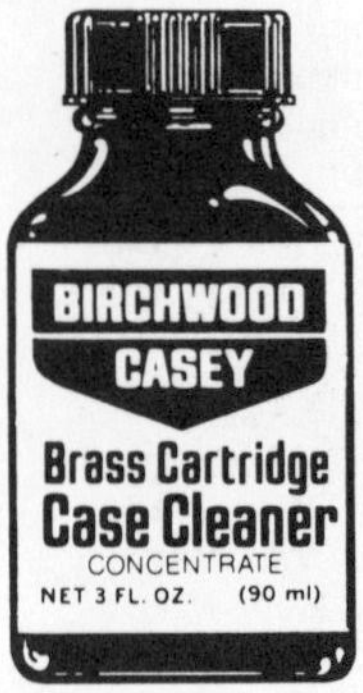

Birchwood Casey Brass Cleaner

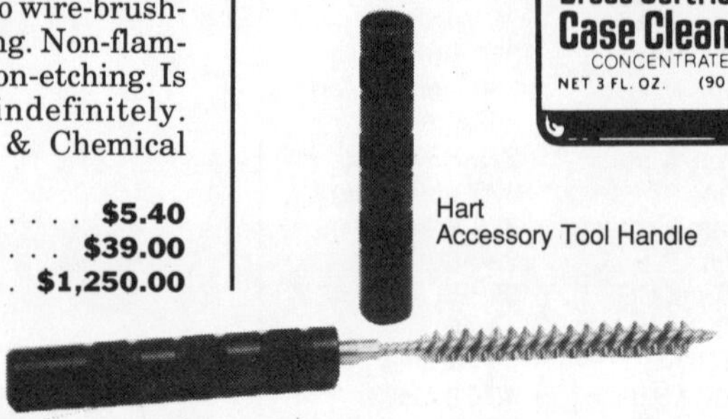
Hart Accessory Tool Handle

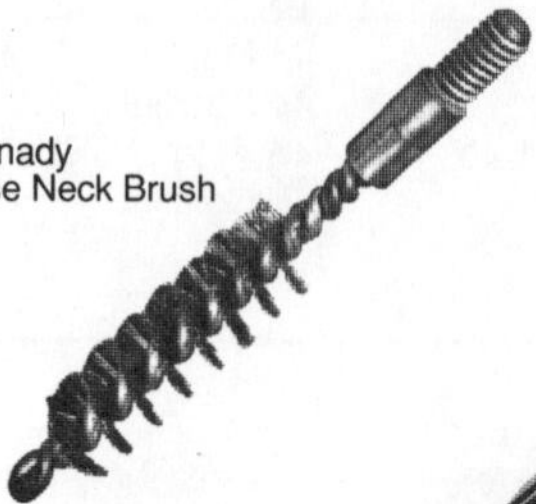
Hornady Case Neck Brush

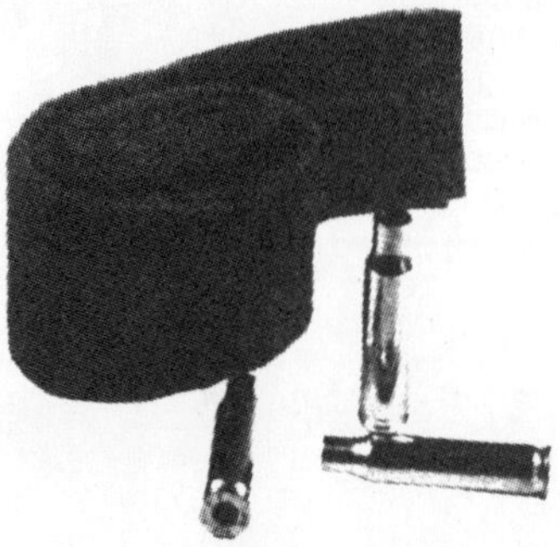
Forster Polishing Roll

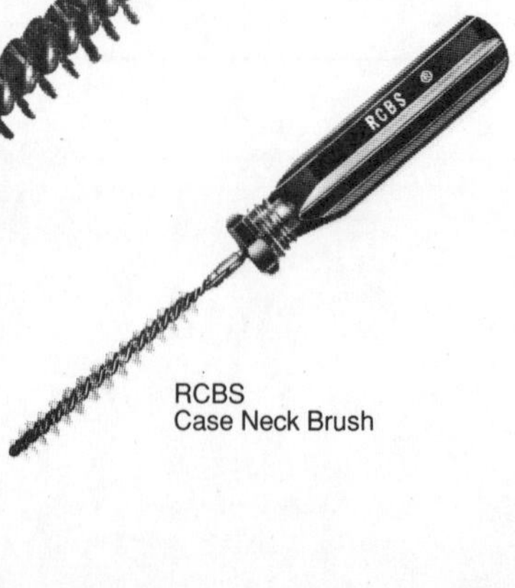

RCBS Case Neck Brush

FORSTER

Case Trim and Conditioning Kit

Includes Forster manual case trimmer with collet, pilot; deburring tool; DBT adapter; case length gauge; neck reamer; primer pocket cleaner; primer pocket center outside neck turner. Weight: 4 lbs. From Forster Products.

Price: **$124.00**

HAYDON

Custom Case Kit

Designed for cleaning, uniforming and deburring primer pockets. Tool ground to uniform pockets to .001" short of max allowed. Includes debur tool, uniformer, case neck brush and handle. From Russ Haydon.

Price: . . . . **Contact manufacturer.**

HORNADY

Case Care Kit

Includes Universal accessory handle, three case neck brushes (6mm, 338-35, and 44-45 caliber), case lube pad/load tray, chamfer/debur tool, large and small primer pocket cleaner heads and case-size lubricant. From Hornady Mfg. Co.

Price: **$22.20**

LYMAN

Case Care Kit

Includes utility crank with adaptor for most Lyman accessories and standard thread; large and small primer pocket reamers and cleaners; inside/outside debur tool; case centering adaptor and ream/clean adaptor for Lyman Universal trimmer. Comes complete in plastic storage box. From Lyman Products Corporation.

Price: **$29.95**

Case Preparation Kit

Large and small primer pocket reamer for military brass; large and small primer pocket cleaner; two hardwood handles; three case neck brushes; case deburring tool. Comes in storage pouch and box. From Lyman Products Corporation.

Price: **$29.95**

PRECISION RELOADING

Micro Case Trimmer Kit

Includes Wilson case trimmer plus shellholder; S-T Micrometer attachment head; Stalwart shellholder bracket clamp and trimmer base; locking micrometer head and ratchet with .0001" division. The 1/2" adjustable anvil stop sleeve is required for cases shorter than 1.720". From Precision Reloading, Inc.

Price: **$109.50**
Price: Micrometer attachment . . . **$62.95**
Price: Stalwart base with shellholder clamp **$24.95**
Price: Adjustable stop sleeve **$14.00**
Price: 1 1/2" stop sleeve for pistol cases **$16.00**

REDDING

Case Preparation Kit

Contains accessory handle, large and small primer pocket cleaners and three case neck brushes to handle all cases from 22 through 45. From Redding Reloading Equipment.

Price: **$15.90**

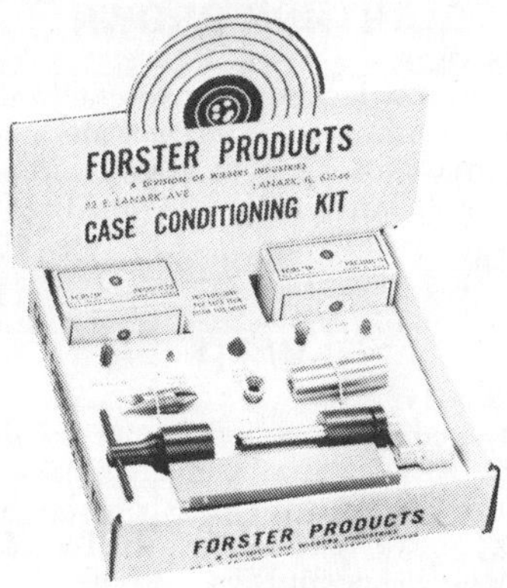

Forster Case Trim and Conditioning Kit

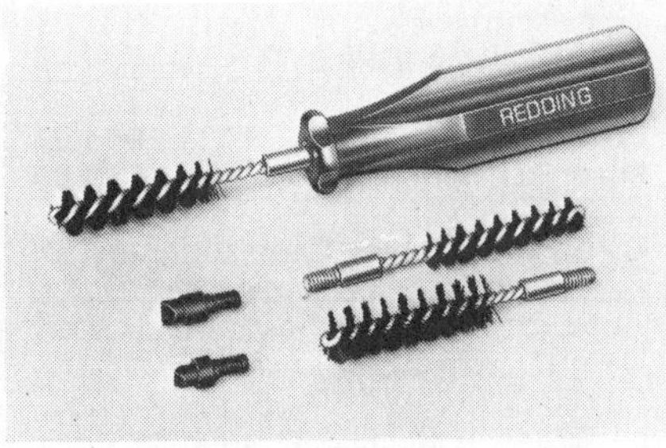

Redding Case Preparation Kit

Lyman Case Preparation Kit

Lyman Case Care Kit

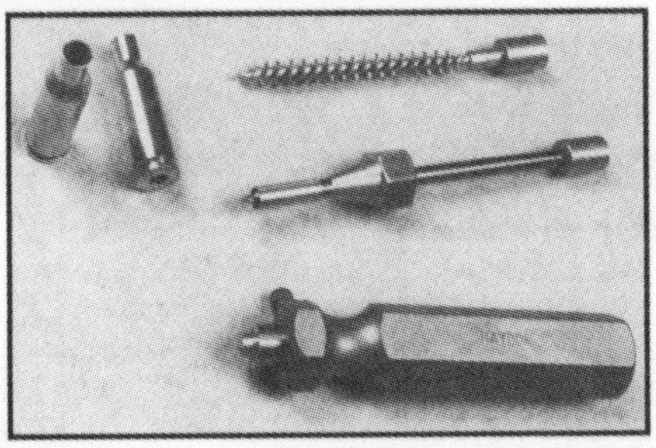
Haydon Custom Case Kit

Precision Reloading Micro Case Trimmer Kit

E. ARTHUR BROWN

EbcoBright

Liquid media additive to protect and polish brass. Does not contain ammonia. Comes in 4 oz. plastic bottle. From E. Arthur Brown Company.

Price: **$4.95**

C-H/4-D

Tumbling Media

Treated or untreated fine grit walnut shell media. Comes in 10-lb. bags treated with polish or 50-lb. bag untreated. From C-H Tool & Die/4-D Custom Die.

Price: Treated **$9.00**
Price: Untreated **$25.00**

Tumbling Media Polish

Dry powder additive for cleaning cases and removing tarnish. Does not give extremely high polish. One-ounce serves 6 lbs. of media. From C-H Tool & Die/4-D Custom Die.

Price: 2 oz. **$2.00**
Price: 1 lb. **$8.00**

CORBIN

Bullet Polisher Kit

Vibratory polishing method that moves the media against cases or bullets versus rolling mixture and knocking components against each other. Includes mounting brackets, vibratory motor with enclosed eccentric weight for vibration, package of media, instructions and hardware. 115-volt operation. From Corbin Manufacturing & Supply, Inc.

Price: **$49.50**

Polishing Media

Walnut shell media for vibratory polishing. Comes in 1-lb. bag. From Corbin Manufacturing & Supply, Inc.

Price: **$2.00**

MIKE DAVIS

Corncob or Walnut Media

Walnut shell media comes fine or medium ground in 5-lb. bags. Corncob available in 3-lb. bags and is fine ground. From Mike Davis Products.

Price: Walnut shell **$2.75**
Price: Corncob **$3.00**

DILLON

Case Media Separators

Large and small case/media separators. Both feature injection moulded rotating "squirrel-cage" hex-shaped basket with wall thickness of $^3/_{16}$". Collection tubs of plastic with integral reliefs for the rotating handle. Large separator basket is 10"x14" with capacity to hold 1600 38 Special cases. Plastic tub measures 18"x 22". Small media separator basket measures $7^3/_4$"x $9^3/_4$" with 13"x 19" tub. From Dillon Precision Products, Inc.

Price: Large separator **$44.95**
Price: Small separator **$29.95**

CV500 Vibratory Case Cleaner

Scaled-down version of the Dillon FL 2000B. Features 11-inch bowl with capacity for 360/30-06, 360/308, 600/44 Magnum, 720/223, 780/45 ACP, 780/357, 1000/38 Super or 1200/9mm; 115V AC electric motor with 1/20-hp; rubber sealed lid and mounts; 5-lb. media capacity. From Dillon Precision Products, Inc.

Price: **$65.95**

DILLON

FL 2000B Vibratory Case Cleaner

Large $12^1/_2$-quart capacity allows polishing 1300 38/357 or 550 30-06 cases. Features 1/20-hp internally cooled and protected motor; thick $^7/_{32}$" injection moulded polypropylene bowl and base. Comes fully assembled. From Dillon Precision Products, Inc.

Price: **$129.95**

Rapid Polish

Ammonia-free liquid additive for tumbling media to shine cases and add protective coating. Comes in 8-oz. plastic bottle. From Dillon Precision Products, Inc.

Price: **$4.95**

Walnut or Corncob Media

Crushed walnut media available in 15-lb. bag; ground corn cob polishing media in 10-pound bag. From Dillon Precision Products, Inc.

Price: Walnut **$15.95**
Price: Corncob **$8.00**

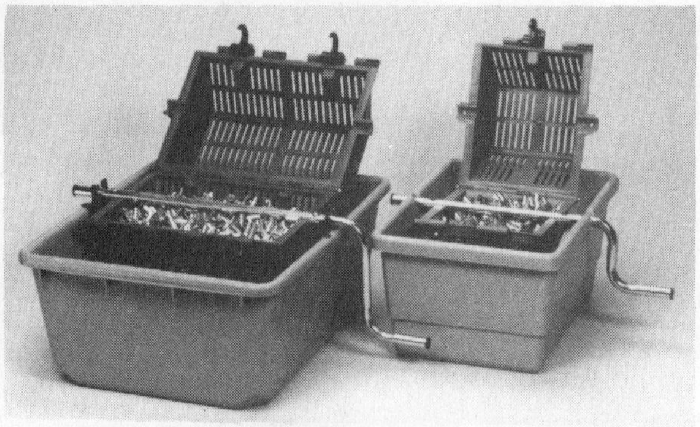

Dillon Case Media Separators

Dillon Rapid Polish

Dillon CV500 and FL 2000B

GAR

Hi-Shine

Tumbling media additive of 100% jewelry grade rouge. From GAR for Reloading.

Price: **$4.50**

HORNADY

M-2 Case Tumbler

Vibratory case cleaner/polisher. Available for 110- or 220-volt. Media not included. Weight: $6^1/_2$ lbs. From Hornady Mfg. Co.

Price: 110-volt **$105.00**
Price: 220-volt **$118.00**

One Shot Tumbler Media

Corncob media impregnated with cleaning solvent. Comes in $^1/_2$-gallon plastic tub. From Hornady Mfg. Co.

Price: **$6.50**

LORTONE

Model 45C Case Tumbler

Compact steel and aluminum frame tumbler with 10-sided solid rubber tumbling barrel. Continuous-duty overload-protected ball bearing motor enclosed in frame. Capacity for 180 38 Special or 75 30-06 cases. UL and CSA listed. Dimensions: $6^1/_4$"x$10^1/_4$". Weight: 7 lbs. From Lortone, Inc.

Price: **$74.50**

Model QT-6, QT-12 and QT-66 Case Tumblers

Heavy-duty, large-capacity tumblers feature 10-sided solid rubber barrel; welded steel frame; fully enclosed drive system and overload-protected ball bearing motor. Capacity of the QT-6 is 260 38 Special cases or 90 30-06 cases; QT-12 can hold 600 38 Specials or 200 30-06. The QT-66 features two barrels with total capacity for 520 38 Special cases or 180 30-06 cases. The two barrel design allows cleaning two different calibers of brass at same time. From Lortone, Inc.

Price: QT-6 . . . . **$110.00**
Price: QT-12 . . . . **$128.00**
Price: QT-66 . . . . **$142.50**

Tumbler Media

Black walnut shell treated with non-toxic industrial cleaning/polishing agents. Comes in 24-oz. plastic pouch. From Lortone, Inc.

Price: **$4.75**

Consult our Directory pages for the location of firms mentioned.

GAR Hi-Shine

Hornady M-2

LYMAN

Auto-Flo Conversion System

For converting Lyman 600, 1200, 2200 and 3200 tumblers to Auto-Flo. Includes bowl, lid, Auto-Flo drain base and media dump pan. From Lyman Products Corporation.

Price: 600/1200 . . . . **$39.95**
Price: 2200 . . . . **$59.95**
Price: 3200 . . . . **$69.95**

Auto-Flo Tumblers

Available in Lyman 1200, 2200, 3200 and Mag models. Features automatic separation of media and cases via exit port in bowl for media removal after cleaning. Conversion kit also available to upgrade standard 600, 1200, 2200 or 3200 tumblers. Either 110- or 220-volt. From Lyman Products Corporation.

Price: 1200, 110-volt **$159.95**
Price: 1200, 220-volt **$160.00**
Price: 2200, 110-volt **$199.95**
Price: 2200, 220-volt **$205.00**
Price: 3200, 110-volt **$249.95**
Price: 3200, 220-volt **$250.00**

Lyman Auto-Flo 2200

Lortone Model 45C

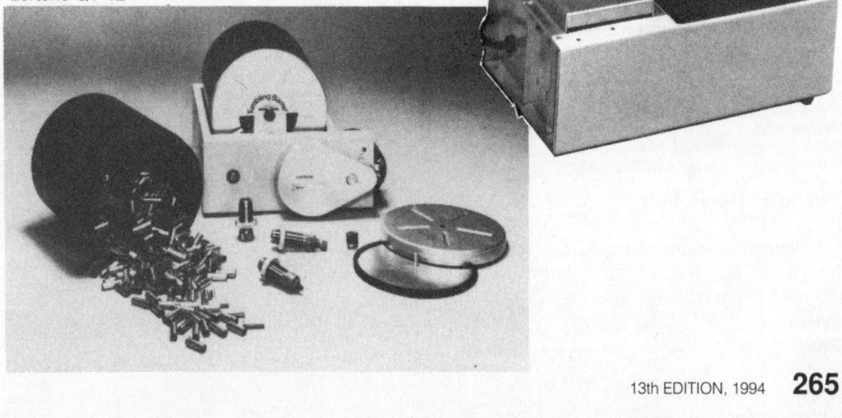

Lortone QT-12

LYMAN

Case Separating Bags
Allows separate cleaning of different calibers or batches of cases during tumbling. Come in packs of 12. From Lyman Products Corporation.
Price: **$4.95**

Easy Pour Media
Large 6-lb. plastic containers of corncob or Tuf-Nut media with flip-top lids. From Lyman Products Corporation.
Price: **$17.95**

Flash Hole Cleaner
Designed to remove bits of media from flash holes and primer pockets. From Lyman Products Corporation.
Price: **$7.95**

Mag Tumbler
High-volume tumbler with capacity of almost 3 gallons or 1,500 cases and media. Features high-strength industrial motor. Available in 110- or 220-volt. From Lyman Products Corporation.
Price: 110-volt **$279.95**
Price: 220-volt **$325.00**

Pop Top Tumbler
Same as the Lyman Model 600 but with see-through plastic lid. Available in 110- or 220-volt. From Lyman Products Corporation.
Price: 110-volt **$124.95**
Price: 220-volt **$125.00**

Tubby Tumbler
Small-capacity vibrating tumbler. Holds 100 38 Spl. pistol cases, 40-50 rifle cases. Features Vibra-Tab for adjustable tumbling speed; built-in handle for easy emptying; see-through lid. Available in 110- or 220-volt. From Lyman Products Corporation.
Price: **$79.95**

Turbo Accessory Bowls
To upgrade tumbler to use with liquid cleaners or double the capacity. 600 bowl for liquid use with 1200 tumbler. 1200 bowl for use with 600 doubles capacity. From Lyman Products Corporation.
Price: 1200 . . . . **$29.95**
Price: 600 . . . . **$24.95**

Turbo Brite Polish
Additive designed for untreated corncob media. Comes in 4-oz. or 16-oz. bottles. From Lyman Products Corporation.
Price: 4-oz. **$3.95**
Price: 16-oz. **$9.95**

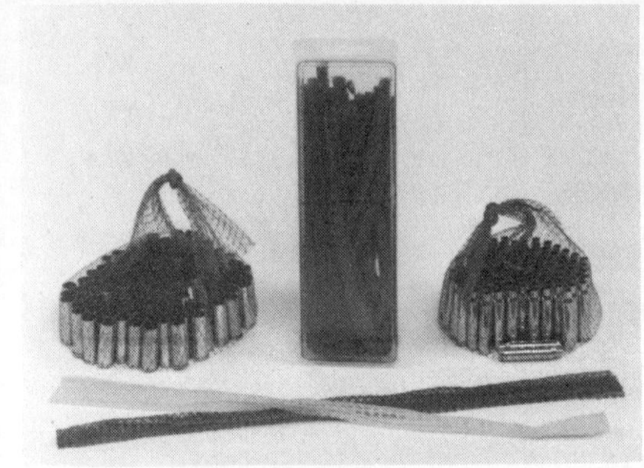

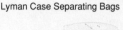

Lyman Case Separating Bags

Lyman
Easy Pour Media

Lyman Mag Tumbler

Lyman Pop Top

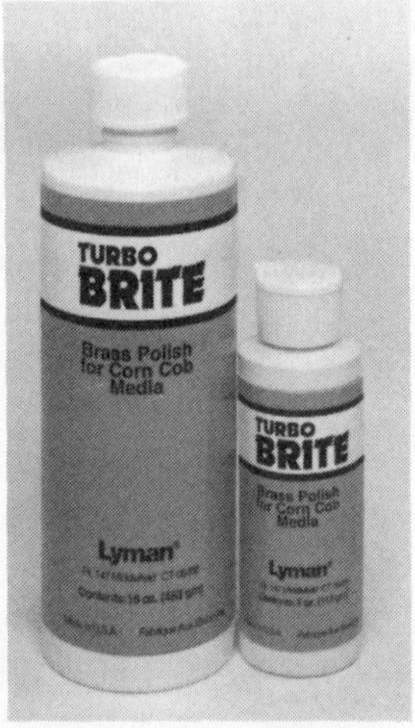

Lyman Turbo Brite

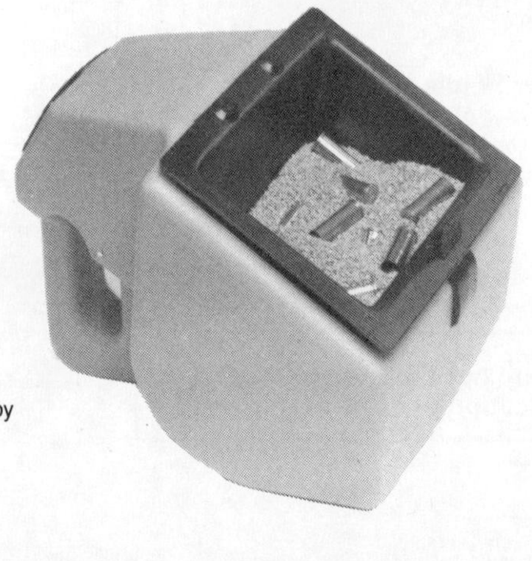

Lyman Tubby

Lyman Turbo Tumblers

LYMAN *Turbo Tumblers*

Model	Media Charge (lbs.)*	# 38 Special Cases	Nominal Capacity	Bowl Size	Media Included	Weight (lbs.)	Price
Tubby	3/4	100	2 pts.	NA	Y		$79.95
600	1	175	3 pts.	8"	Y	7	119.95
1200	2	350	1 gal.	10"	Y	10	149.95
2200	4	750	1.5 gal.	12"	N	12	164.95
3200	5	1000	2.2 gal.	13"	N	13	219.95
Mag	7	1500+	2.75 gal.	14"	N		279.95

*For Auto-Flo models add 1 to 2 lbs. extra.

Lyman Turbo Accessory Bowls

Lyman
Turbo Case Cleaner

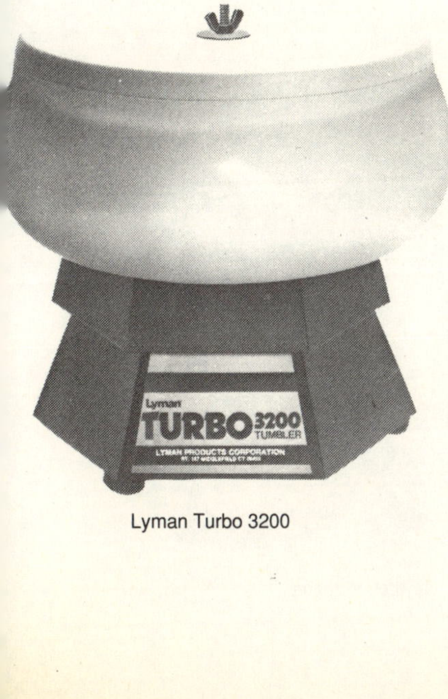

Lyman Turbo 3200

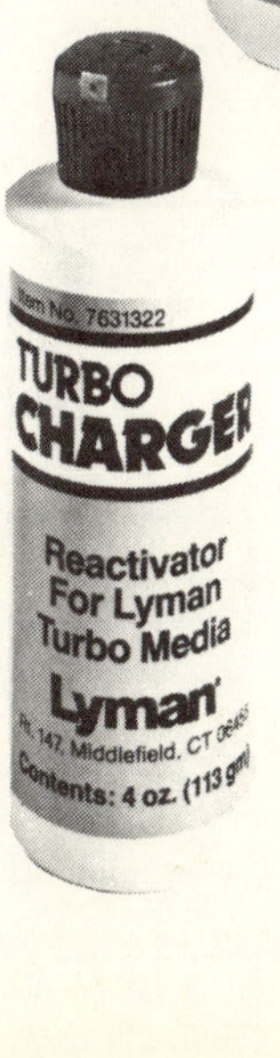

Lyman
Turbo Charger

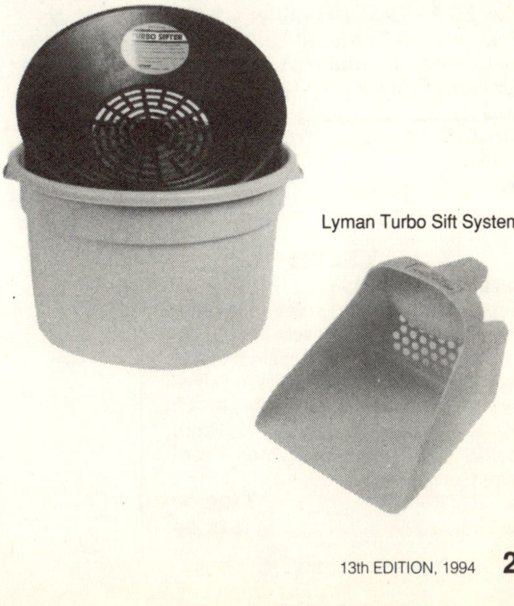
Lyman Turbo Sift Systems

LYMAN

Turbo Charger Media Reactivator

Restores heavily used corn cob media. Available in 4-oz. or 16-oz. bottles. From Lyman Products Corporation.

Price: 4-oz. **$3.95**
Price: 16-oz. **$9.95**

Turbo Liquid Case Cleaner

Non-etching solution for extremely fouled or corroded cases. Use manually or with tumbler. Comes in 16-oz. bottle. From Lyman Products Corporation.

Price: **$5.00**

Turbo Media

Specially treated corncob or Tufnut, rouge bearing crushed nut shell, media. Corncob available in 1-, 2- or 10-lb. quantities; Tuf-Nut in 3- and 12-lb. boxes. From Lyman Products Corporation.

Price: 1-lb. corncob **$5.00**
Price: 2-lb. corncob/3-lb. Tuf-Nut . . **$7.95**
Price: 10-lb. corncob/12-lb. Tuf-Nut . **$19.95**

Turbo Sift Systems

Tub bucket, sifter and scoop for removing and separating cases from tumbler media. From Lyman Products Corporation.

Price: Sifter **$8.50**
Price: Tub bucket **$5.95**
Price: Scoop **$6.95**

Turbo Tumblers

Four basic models, 600, 1200, 2200 and 3200, with varying capacities. All feature high-speed agitation for 2-hour cleaning; top-load design for in-operation inspection; motor screen; on/off switches; ability to handle wet or dry media. From Lyman Products Corporation.

Price: . . . . **See chart.**

MIDWAY

Brass Cleaning Media

Ground corncob or walnut hull media available plain or treated. From Midway Arms, Inc.

Price: Corncob, 15-lb. plain **$16.99**
Price: Corncob, 5-lb. treated **$13.99**
Price: Walnut, 18-lb. plain **$19.99**
Price: Walnut, 7-lb. treated **$15.99**

Brass Polish

Liquid media additive which contains no ammonia or petroleum distillates. Comes in 8-oz. or 32-oz. plastic bottle. From Midway Arms, Inc.

Price: 8-oz. **$4.99**
Price: 32-oz. **$14.99**

Brass Sifter and Plastic Bucket

Designed specifically for brass and media separation. Sifter nests inside bucket top securely with large handles for removal. Bucket available in two sizes, $3^1/_2$-gallon or 5-gallon. From Midway Arms, Inc.

Price: Sifter **$12.99**
Price: $3^1/_2$-gal. **$7.99**
Price: 5-gal. **$8.99**

Clear Tumbler Lid

Designed to fit Midway Model 1292, RCBS or Hornady M2 tumblers. Made of clear polycarbonate (Lexan) for case inspection during tumbler operation. From Midway Arms, Inc.

Price: **$5.99**

Model 1292 Brass Tumbler

All ball bearing motor with lightweight integrated rib bowl. Holds up to 500 38 Special cases or 185 30-06 Springfield cases. From Midway Arms, Inc.

Price: **$54.99**

Model 2094 Brass Tumbler

Features steel encased ball bearing motor and rib reinforced 16" diameter bowl. Capacity for 1,500 38 Special cases or up to 500 30-06 Springfield cases. From Midway Arms, Inc.

Price: **$84.99**

RAYTECH

Separating Screens

Separating tub and screen for separating media from cases. Screen diameter $14^1/_2$"x $2^1/_2$" depth; 1 cubic foot tote container. Five screen sizes avaiable from $^1/_4$" openings to 1". Made of high-impact polymer. From Raytech, Division of Lyman Products Corporation.

Price: Set of five **$120.00**
Price: Each **$21.00**

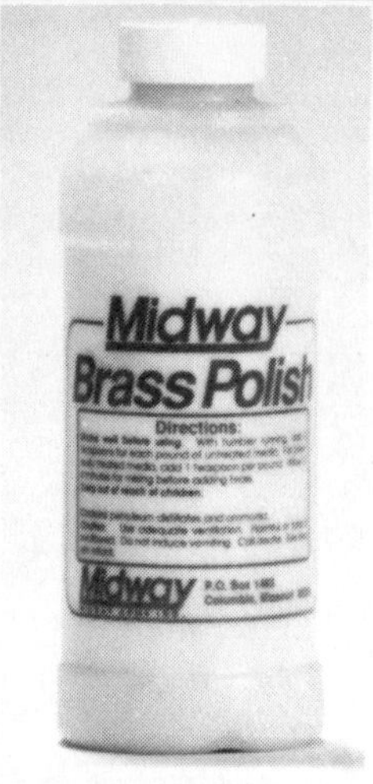

Midway Brass Polish

Midway Model 1292

Midway Model 2094

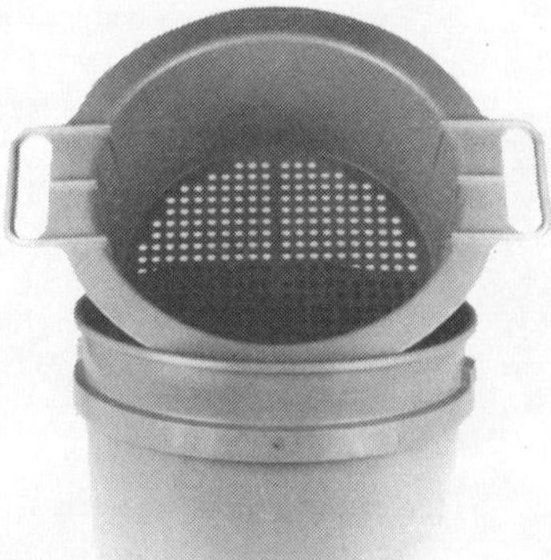
Midway Brass Sifter

Midway Media

Raytech Screens

RCBS Formula 2

RCBS Sidewinder

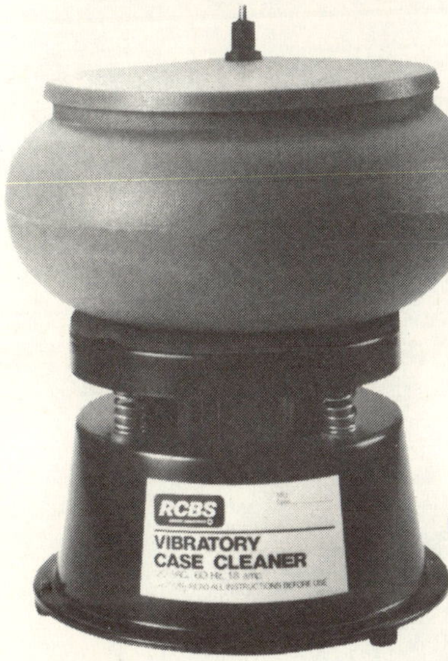

RCBS Vibratory Case Cleaner

Tru-Square Brass Polish

RCBS

Case Cleaning Media

Liquid or dry media. Liquid case cleaner concentrate for use in the Sidewinder tumbler comes in 8-oz. bottle and makes 4 gals. liquid cleaner. Formula 1 walnut shell dry media is ground to a 12/20 sieve size and coated with two cleaning oxides. It comes in 5-lb. box. Formula 2 corncob media combines ground corn cob with a chromium oxide polisher and cleaner. Available in 4-lb. box. From RCBS.

Price: Liquid media **$4.25**
Price: Formula 1 . . . . **$11.57**
Price: Formula 2 . . . . **$13.16**

Sidewinder Case Tumbler

Liquid or dry media tumbler with capacity up to 300 38 Special or 150 30-06 cases. Features tilting drum for easy access; built-in timer for automatic shut-off from 5 minutes to 12 hours; self-aligning rear bearings; industrial-grade timing belt drive system; polyurethane drum; and two covers, one solid cap and one perforated cap that doubles as a media screen separator. Available in 120- or 240-volt models. 8-oz. bottle liquid case cleaner included. From RCBS.

Price: **$237.44**

Vibratory Case Cleaner

Designed for dry-media cleaning and polishing of large quantities of cartridge cases. $3^1/_2$-quart bowl holds up to 400 38 Special or 180 30-06 cases. Thermally protected ball-bearing motor operates on 120/240 VAC. From RCBS.

Price: 120 VAC **$118.54**
Price: 240 VAC **$146.54**
Price: Media sifter **$8.91**

ROOSTER

Brass Polish

Ammonia-free liquid additive to tumbling media. Contains no petroleum distillates or hazardous ingredients. Cleans, polishes and provides protective finish. Comes in 8-oz., 32-oz., 1-, 5- or 55-gallon quantities. From Rooster Laboratories.

Price: 8-oz. **$4.50**
Price: 32-oz. **$12.50**
Price: 1-gal. **$30.00**
Price: 5-gal. **$135.00**
Price: 55-gal. **$1,250.00**

TRU-SQUARE

Brass Bags

Bags to hold brass during tumbling operation. Come six bags to a pack. From Tru-Square Metal Products.

Price: **$2.00**

Brass Polish Corncob Media

Treated crushed corn cob for use in vibratory or rotary tumblers. Comes in 15-lb. bag. From Tru-Square Metal Products.

Price: **$46.75**

Brass Polish Walnut Media

Treated crushed black walnut shell media. Comes in 15-, 30- or 60-oz. containers. From Tru-Square Metal Products.

Price: 15 oz. **$4.76**
Price: 30 oz. **$9.29**
Price: 60 oz. **$18.62**

Brass Media Booster

Additive for walnut or corncob media. Available in 4-oz. bottle. From Tru-Square Metal Products.

Price: **$5.58**

Brass Pack

Includes brass separator, 6 lbs. treated corncob media and 4-oz. bottle media booster. From Tru-Square Metal Products.

Price: **$33.78**

Brass Separator

Plastic 12" diameter sifter to separate brass from media. From Tru-Square Metal Products.

Price: **$8.89**

Liquid Brass Cleaner

Designed for use in rotary tumblers to pre-clean cases. Comes in 8-oz. bottle. From Tru-Square Metal Products.

Price: **$5.11**

TRU-SQUARE

Model AR-6 Rotary Tumbler
Moulded rubber water-tight barrel with 16-sided interior; 3-qt. capacity to hold 400 cases and weight capacity of 9 lbs.; heavy-gauge steel base; 115-volt, 1/75-hp, .67-amp thermally protected motor. Dimensions: 6"x 11"x $10\frac{1}{2}$". Weight: 7.5 lbs. From Tru-Square Metal Products.
Price: **$120.94**

Model AR-12 Rotary Tumbler
Moulded rubber, water tight hexagonal barrel with 1-gal. capacity to hold 150-500 cases and weight capacity to 12 lbs; heavy-gauge steel base; 115-volt thermally protected motor. Dimensions: 11"x 11"x 11". Weight: 10 lbs. From Tru-Square Metal Products.
Price: **$131.41**

Model B Rotary Tumbler
Features water tight steel barrel with heavy rubber liner; $1\frac{1}{4}$-gal. barrel capacity to hold 200-600 cases with weight capacity of 15 lbs; heavy steel base; thermally protected 1/50-hp motor operating on 115-volt, draws .9 amps. Dimensions: 11"x 11"x 11". Weight: 16 lbs. From Tru-Square Metal Products.
Price: **$168.76**

Model UV-10 Vibratory Tumbler
Features removable heavy polyethylene bowl with lid; 3-qt. capacity to hold 125-400 cases and weight capacity to 10 lbs.; overload protected ball bearing motor operating on 115 volts; vibrating action at 3000 vpm. Comes with 3 lbs. media. Dimemsions: 10"x 11". Weight: 8 lbs. From Tru-Square Metal Products.
Price: **$155.94**

Model UV-18 Vibratory Tumbler
Larger than Model UV-10 but with same features. Features $1\frac{1}{2}$-gal. capacity to hold 200-700 cases and weight capacity to 18 lbs. Optional 6 lbs. media. Dimensions: $11\frac{1}{2}$"x $12\frac{1}{2}$". Weight: 11 lbs. From Tru-Square Metal Products.
Price: **$191.60**
Price: With media **$214.67**

Model UV-45 Vibratory Tumbler
Largest of Tru-Square offerings. Features $4\frac{3}{4}$-gal. capacity to hold 1000 30-06 cases and weight capacity to 57 lbs.; variable amplitude for desired finish during deburring. Optional with 15 lbs. media. Dimensions: 17"x 18". Weight: 26 lbs. From Tru-Square Metal Products.
Price: **$522.61**
Price: With media **$571.61**

Tru-Square AR-6

Tru-Square Model UV-18

Tru-Square UV-10

VIBRASHINE

Brass Separator
Plastic separator lid to fit VibraShine VS-20 and VS-30 tumblers and most other popular sizes of tumblers. From VibraShine, Inc.
Price: **$7.95**

Treated Media
Treated processed corncob media for use in vibratory tumblers. Comes in 6-lb. boxes. From VibraShine, Inc.
Price: **$11.87**

VIBRASHINE

VS-10 Brass Polisher
Dual vibrating motor design with no belts or bearings. 3-pint capacity to hold 50 30-06 or 100 45 cases. Features removable see-through bowl with snap-on lid, on/off switch, speed selection, heavy-duty power cord and housing constructed of one-piece injection moulded plastic. Comes with media. From VibraShine, Inc.
Price: **$49.95**

VibraShine VS-30

VIBRASHINE

VS-20 Vibratory Tumbler

Same features as VS-30 with 10" diameter, 3-qt. capacity bowl. From VibraShine, Inc.

Price: **$99.95**

VS-30 Vibratory Tumbler

Designed for high-volume cleaning. Features $1^1/_2$-gal. capacity heavy-duty bowl with removable lid; 1.4 amp thermally protected, fan-cooled, ball bearing motor; on-off switch. From VibraShine, Inc.

Price: **$129.95**

Vibra-Tek Recharge Liquid

VIBRA-TEK

Brass Polishers

Standard and magnum vibrating brass polishers. Capacity for 300 cases for standard model; magnum model holds 5 lbs. media. Features adjustable vibrating action; use with wet or dry media. Comes with polishing media. From Vibra-Tek Company.

Price: Standard with 2 lbs. media . . **$89.95**
Price: Magnum with 5 lbs. media . **$149.00**
Price: 2-oz. recharge liquid **$4.00**

Polishing Media

Fine-ground black walnut shell media impregnated with iron oxide. Available in 2- or 5-lb. quantities. From Vibra-Tek Company.

Price: 2 lbs. **$9.00**
Price: 5 lbs. **$13.95**

WILCOX

All-Pro Scoops

Two scoops for separating media and cases. Sifting Scoop perforated with 217 $^1/_4$" diameter holes; Treasure Scoop has 54 $^3/_4$" holes. From Wilcox.

Price: **$6.49**

VibraShine VS-20

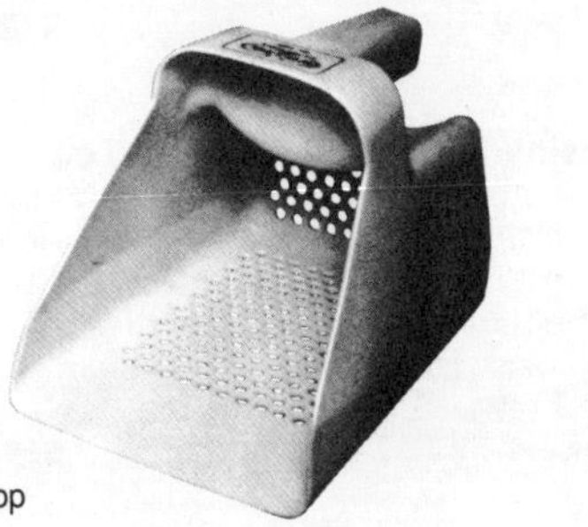

Wilcox Scoop

Vibra-Tek Media

Vibra-Tek Brass Polishers

C-H

Deburring/Chamfering Tool

Standard or magnum size tool for beveling inside and outside of case mouth. Standard tool fits 17- to 45-caliber; magnum tool for 45- to 60-caliber cases. From C-H Tool & Die/4-D Custom Die.

Price: Standard **$8.95**
Price: Magnum **$14.95**

FORSTER

DBT Adapter

Used with Forster deburring tool, this device converts Forster trimmer to deburring tool holder. Mounts on case trimmer cutter shaft and is used with case trimmer collet housing removed. From Forster Products.

Price: **$8.70**

DBT Base

Bench-mountable stand for Forster deburring tool with hand crank for speed of operation. May also be used with Forster power adapter which allows removal of hand crank and functions with cordless screwdriver. Weight: 10 oz. From Forster Products.

Price: **$20.00**
Price: Power adapter **$12.50**

Inside/Outside Deburring Tool

Deburring hand tool. Precision ground cutting edges allow smooth removal of irregularities and burrs at mouth of case. Handles all case sizes from 17- to 45-caliber. From Forster Products.

Price: **$14.00**

Inside Neck Reamer

Removes excess brass from case neck walls. Made from high grade, wear resistant tool steel and ground .002" to .0025" over maximum bullet diameter. Has staggered tooth design for chatterless cutting. For use with Forster case trimmer. Available in standard calibers (17, 223, 224, 243, 257, 263, 277, 284, 308, 311, 323, 338, 355, 358, 375, 400, 410, 432, 452, 458). Weight: 3 oz. From Forster Products.

Price: **$14.50**

Outside Neck Turner Adapter Kit

Adapter kit for RCBS Trimmer II case trimmer. Allows use of Forster outside/inside neck tools, primer pocket and case neck cleaning and chamfering tools plus Forster hollowpointer on RCBS trimmer. Weight: 1 lb. From Forster Products.

Price: **$40.00**

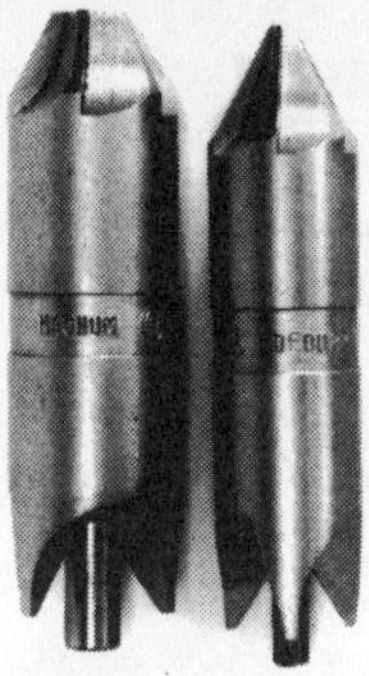

C-H Debur/Chamfer Tool

Forster DBT Adapter

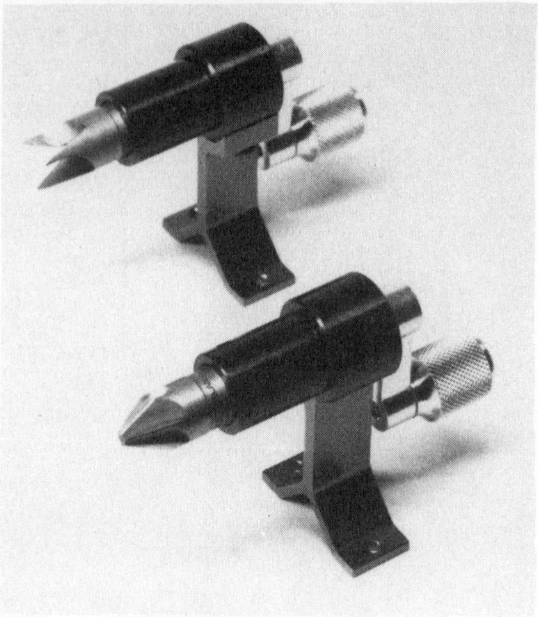

Forster DBT Base

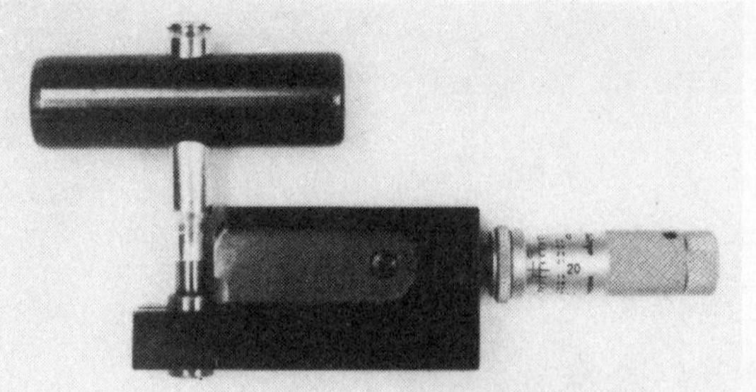

Hart Deluxe Neck Turner

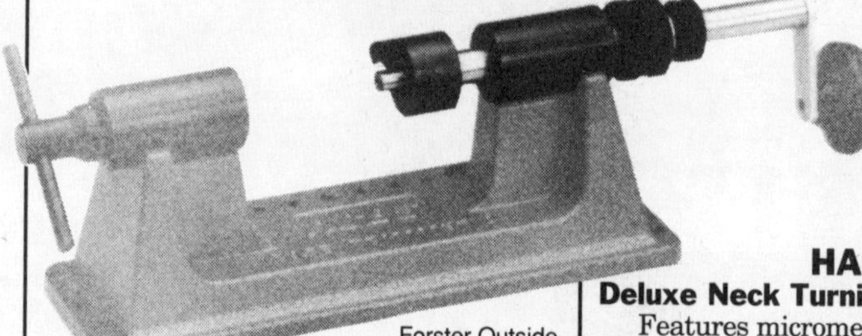

Forster Outside Neck Turner on Case Trimmer

Forster Debur Tool

FORSTER

Outside Neck Turner

Turns any diameter case neck between .170 and .375 concentric to its true axis. For use with Forster case trimmer; replace short pilot with extra long, hardened and ground pilot of desired caliber. Pilot not included. Available in standard calibers (17, 224, 243, 257, 277, 263, 284, 308, 311, 323, 333, 338, 358, 375); custom calibers are additional cost. Long 6½" base for neck turning 375 magnum or longer also available. Weight: 9 oz. From Forster Products.

Price: **$28.00**
Price: Pilot **$6.00**
Price: Long base **$12.00**

HART

Deluxe Neck Turning Tool

Features micrometer dial adjustment for precision cutting. Includes one mandrel, one expansion plug and handle. From Robert Hart & Sons, Inc.

Price: **$129.95**
Price: Extra mandrel and plug . . . **$19.95**
Price: Extra handle **$8.95**

Standard Neck Turning Tool

Designed to turn the outside of case neck to desired wall thickness and depth; will hold a wall thickness of .0003". Mandrel has end stop to assure consistency. Requires handle, mandrel and expansion plug for each caliber from 22 through 30. High speed steel cutter with hardened mandrels. From Robert Hart & Son, Inc.

Price: **$76.95**
Price: Handle **$7.30**
Price: Mandrel and expansion plug . **$16.80**
Price: Replacement cutter **$19.95**

HOEHNS

Carbide Neck Turning Mandrel

Will fit all major manufacturers' neck turners. Available for 17, 22, 6mm, 25, 7mm and 30 calibers. From Hoehns Shooting Supply.

Price: **$30.00**

HORNADY

Chamfer/Debur Tool

Dual-function knurled steel tool to smooth and debur inside and outside of case mouths. From Hornady Mfg. Co.

Price: **$9.90**

K&M

Micro-Adjustable Case Neck Turning Tool

Adjustable outside neck turning tool. Removes desired amount of brass from thick side of case to equal thin side or can be adjusted to cut down case wall thickness to desired dimension. Tolerance to .0001" possible via compound thread equal to 440 turns to the inch. Index marks provided to assist adjustment. Tool is special ground with angles unique to cutting brass. Case holder uses Lee Auto Prime shellholder for various calibers. Power adaptor available for use with low speed drill or cordless screwdriver. Mandrels available in 17, 22, 6mm, 25, 6.5mm, 270, 7mm and 30 calibers. Comes complete for one caliber with pilot and case holder or without case holder. From K&M Services.

Price: Complete tool **$60.00**
Price: Without case holder **$48.00**
Price: Power adaptor **$20.00**
Price: Pilots **$9.00**

Tapered Case Mouth Reamer

Six-fluted reamer features 4" per side taper with adjustable depth stop. For all cases 22- through 30-caliber. Provides consistent chamfer case to case. From K&M Services.

Price: **$18.00**

LEE

Chamfer Tool

Chamfer tool with knurled base to chamfer and debur inside and outside of case neck. Also used to remove crimp from primer pockets of military brass. From Lee Precision, Inc.

Price: **$2.98**

Lyman Universal Debur Tool

K&M Tools

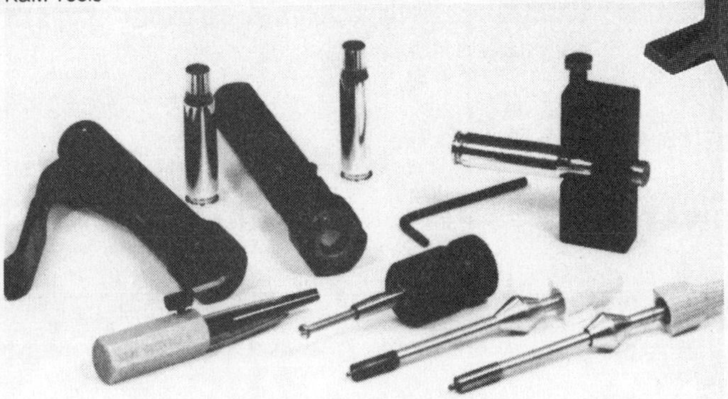

Lyman Outside Neck Turner Accessory Tool

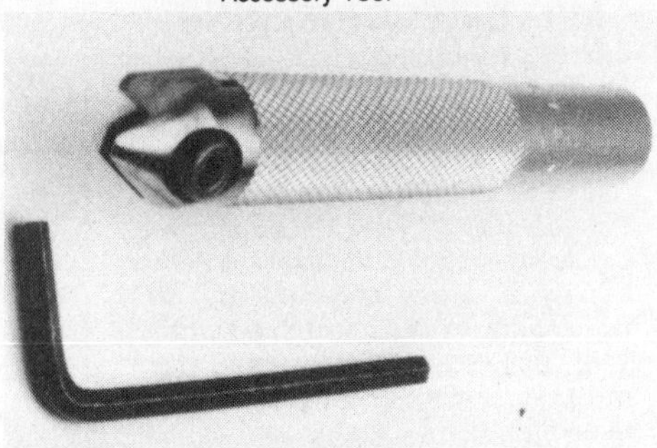

Lee Chamfer Tool

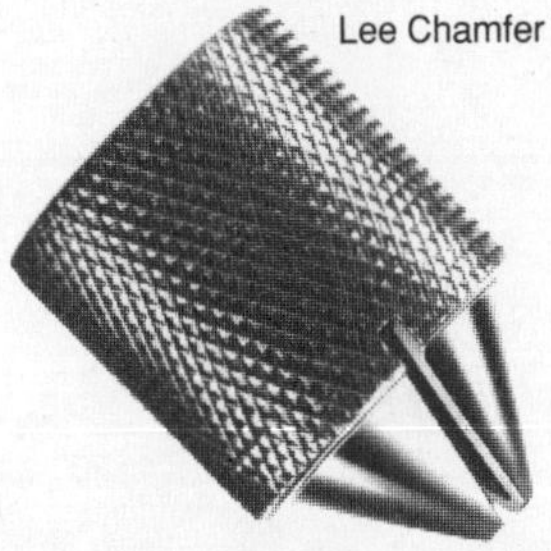

LYMAN

Chamfer/Debur Accessory Tool

For use with Lyman case trimmers and Utility crank. Chamfers and deburs trimmed cases simultaneously. Adjusts to fit case mouths from 17- to 45-caliber. From Lyman Products Corporation.

Price: **$11.50**

Outside Neck Turner Accessory Tool

Designed for use with Lyman's Universal trimmer and Accu trimmer to maintain correct neck wall thickness and outside neck diameter. Features cutter adjustable for length of cut and rate of feed. Cutter blade adjusted to any diameter from .195" to .405". Comes with two extra cutting blades. Mandrels from 22 to 375. Available also with six mandrel Multi-Pack (22, 243, 25, 270, 7mm and 30 calibers). From Lyman Products Corporation.

Price: **$19.25**
Price: With Multi-Pack **$29.95**
Price: Multi-Pack **$12.00**
Price: Replacement cutters (2) **$6.00**

LYMAN

Deburring Tool

Bevels and removes burrs from inside and outside of case mouth. Precision machined and hardened with wood handle; fits all cases 17- to 45-caliber. From Lyman Products Corporation.

Price: **$14.00**

Shell Chamfering Reamer

Chamfers inside case mouth. One size fits all. Precision machined and hardened with wood handle. From Lyman Products Corporation.

Price: **$9.20**

Universal Inside/Outside Debur Tool

All steel tool with anodized aluminum handle machine-knurled for gripping. Features cutting blade which adapts with hex wrench adjustment to any pistol or rifle case. Deburs inside and outside of case in one step. From Lyman Products Corporation.

Price: **$14.95**

MARQUART

Precision Case Neck Turner

Uniformly turns case necks within .0001". "On center" design used for ease of operation. Adjustable cutter with screw threaded 40 threads per inch for .025" increment advancements with each turn. Pilot can be adjusted in frame to govern length of cut. From Marquart Precision Company.

Price: **$48.00**
Price: Holders 222 Rem. to 378 Wea. **$8.00**
Price: Pilots 17- to 30-caliber **$8.00**

MIDWAY

Deburring Tool

Precision machined cutting edges debur and chamfer 17- to 45-caliber cases. Recessed mid-section offers positive gripping. From Midway Arms, Inc.

Price: **$10.99**

MILLER ENGINEERING

Deburring Machine

Electric deburring machine equipped with dual 12-volt motors and two L.E. Wilson deburring tools. Reams bevel on inside and outside of any 17- to 45-caliber case. Press case mouth down on the debur tool with slight pressure and the internal drive unit switch activates. Will also ream primer crimp from military brass. From Miller Engineering.

Price: **$89.95**

RCBS

Case Neck Turning Accessories

Two tools for removal of excessive neck thickness, high spots and case neck out-of-roundness. Guides cutter over sized cartridge case neck and is supported by the pilot. Auto Feed Attachment (Case Trimmer-2 only) advances tool over case neck with each turn of the handle. Pilot/neck reamers available in 17, 223, 6mm/243, 25, 6.5mm, 270, 7mm, 30, 8mm, 338, 35 and 375 calibers. From RCBS.

Price: With Auto Feed **$51.95**
Price: Case Neck Turner **$25.24**
Price: Auto Feed **$33.64**
Price: Pilot/Neck Reamers **$8.63**

Deburring Tool

Case prep tool for beveling inside neck lip and removing interior and exterior case mouth burrs. Features hardened cutting flutes and knurled surface for hand or lathe use. For all cases from 17- to 45-caliber. From RCBS.

Price: **$12.85**

Marquart Case Neck Turner

Midway Deburring Tool

Miller Engineering Debur Machine

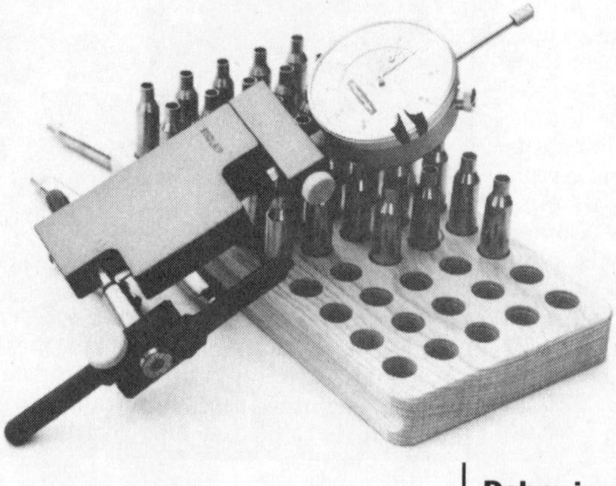

Sinclair Phase II

RCBS	
Debur Tool Calibers	**Pilot Stop Calibers**
22	22
6mm	6mm
25	25
6.5mm	6.5mm
270	270
7mm	7mm
30	30
34	32
375	8mm
45	34
	35
	36
	375
	41
	44
	45

RCBS Debur Tool

REDDING

Deburring Tool

Hardened precision ground flutes for chatter-free cutting. Accepts all cases from 17- to 45-caliber. From Redding Reloading Equipment.

Price: **$16.50**

SINCLAIR

Phase II Neck Turning Tool

Hand-held tool constructed of anodized aluminum and using stainless steel mandrels to remove excess neck thickness, high spots and case neck uniformity. Can be used with .001" dial indicator for setting desired cutting depth. Comes with universal case holder. Mandrels for 17, 22, 6mm, 25, 6.5mm, sold separately by caliber. From Sinclair International, Inc.

Price: **$54.75**
Price: Mandrel **$9.75**

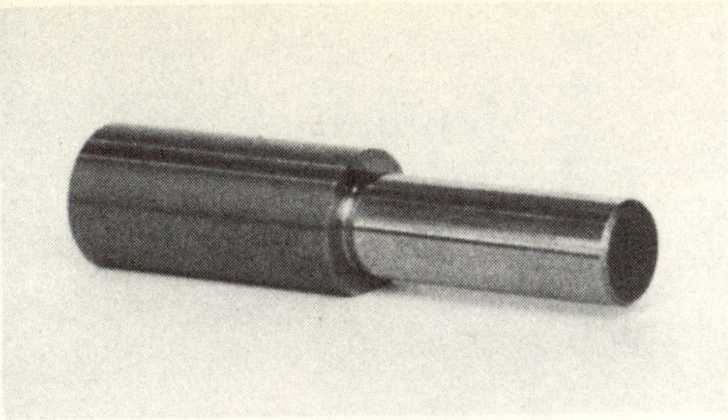

Whitetail Design Mandrel

Wilson Debur Tool

SYNCHRONIZED

Burr Catt™

Attaches to cordless electric screwdriver and accepts any chamfer-debur tool. From Synchronized Shooting Systems.

Price: **$10.00**

WHITETAIL DESIGN

Mandrel for K&M Neck Turner

Carbide mandrel available in 17, 22, 6mm, 25, 7mm and 30 calibers. From Whitetail Design and Engineering Ltd.

Price: **$30.00**

WILSON

Deburring Tool

Knurled tool for deburring outside of case mouth and chamfering the inside. Handles cases from 17- through 45-caliber. From L.E. Wilson, Inc.

Price: **$10.23**

Inside Neck Reamer

To remove excess neck material to guarantee clearance between case and chamber. Reamers replace the Wilson trimmer cutter when in operation. From L.E. Wilson, Inc.

Price: **$23.50**

WILSON

Outside Neck Turning Tool

Similar to Wilson trimmer with chamber-type case holder enclosing case. Case holders will not interchange with trimmer case holders; tool also requires neck pilots. Pilots available only in 22, 6mm, 25, 6.5mm, 270, 7mm and 30 calibers. Optional power adapter for attaching drill motor. Can be converted to case trimmer with optional trimmer cutter and case holders. Wilson case neck reamer and primer pocket reamer work in this tool. Grip tool in vise or mount on Stalwart standard or clamp mount. Pilots and case holders separate. From L.E. Wilson, Inc.

Price: **$97.62**
Price: Pilot **$9.54**
Price: Case holder **$9.54**
Price: Power adapter **$8.48**
Price: Stalwart standard mount . . . **$11.50**
Price: Stalwart clamp mount **$21.00**

WILSON *Neck Turner Pilots & Holders*

Caliber	Pilot	—Holder— Fired	New
219 Donaldson	Y	Y	Y
22 PPC	Y	Y	Y
22 PPC SAKO	Y	Y	Y
22 Rem. BR	Y	Y	Y
22-250	Y	Y	Y
220 Swift	Y	Y	Y
220 Wilson Arrow	Y	Y	Y
222 Rem.	Y	Y	Y
222 Rem. Mag.	Y	Y	Y
223 Rem.	Y	Y	Y
243 Win.	Y	Y	Y
6mm PPC	Y	Y	Y
6mm PPC SAKO	Y	Y	Y
6mm Rem.	Y	Y	Y
6mmx47	Y	Y	Y
6mm Int'l.	Y	N	N
6mm Rem. BR	Y	Y	Y
25-06	Y	Y	Y
250 Savage	Y	Y	Y
257 Roberts	Y	Y	Y
264 Win. Mag.	Y	Y	Y
6.5mmx55	Y	Y	Y
270 Win.	Y	Y	Y
280/7mm Exp.	Y	Y	Y
7mm Rem. BR	Y	Y	Y
7mm Rem. Mag.	Y	Y	Y
7mmx57 Mauser	Y	Y	Y
7mm-08	Y	Y	Y
30-06	Y	Y	Y
30-30	Y	Y	Y
30-338	Y	Y	Y
300 Win. Mag.	Y	Y	Y
308 Win.	Y	Y	Y

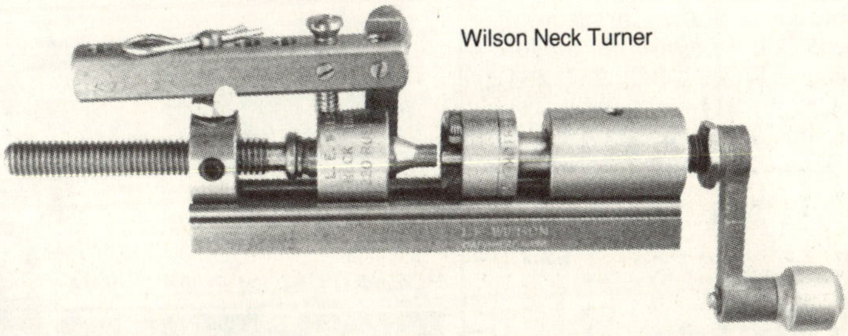

Wilson Neck Turner

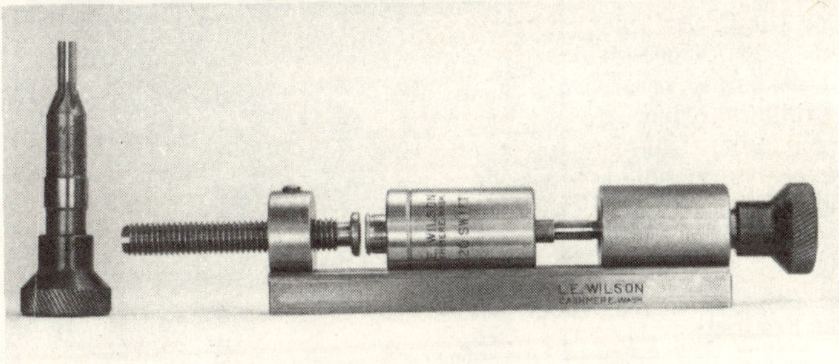

Wilson trimmer set up to ream case necks.

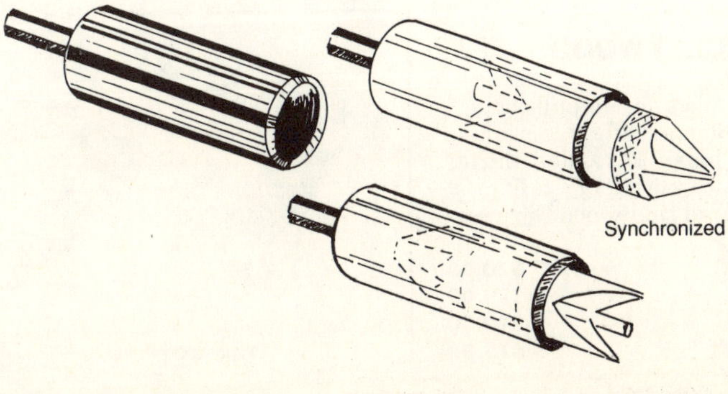

Synchronized Burr Catt™

METALLIC CASES/ Chamfering Tools

C-H

50 BMG Bullet Puller

Breaks down questionable military 50 BMG ammo. Long shank collet fits bullet properly. Ball thrust bearing and spring ejector for ease of operation. Thread size $1^1/_2$x12. Collets for other large calibers available. From C-H Tool & Die/4-D Custom Die.

Price: **$89.95**
Price: Collets **$19.95**

C-H/4-D

Bullet Puller

Positive die-locking action bullet puller for calibers 224 to 45. Comes with or without collet. From C-H Tool & Die/4-D Custom Die.

Price: Without collet **$10.95**
Price: With collet **$14.95**
Price: Extra collet **$5.00**

FORSTER

Collet-Type Bullet Puller

Threaded $^7/_8$-14, this unit will fit any standard reloading press. Hardened steel collet designed to tighten grip on the bullet as pulling pressure is increased. Collets available for following sizes: 17, 224, 243, 257, 264, 277, 284, 308, 311, 323, 333, 338, 348, 357, 358, 375, 410, 432, 452 and 458. Collet not included. Weight: 8 oz. From Forster Products.

Price: **$13.50**
Price: Collet **$7.70**

Super Fast Bullet Puller

Designed for use on the Co-Ax, this puller is threaded $^7/_8$-14 for use on any conventional reloading press. Pulls all jacketed bullets including G.I. armor piercing bullets. Hardened flexible jaw closes on bullet automatically and extracts it from case without bullet damage. Available for the following diameters: .224, .243, .257, .264, .277, .284, .308. From Forster Products.

Price: **$15.00**

HOLLYWOOD

Bullet Puller

Standard collet design pulls bullets from pistol and rifle cases up to 20mm. Comes threaded either standard $^7/_8$" or large $1^1/_2$" to fit most presses. From Hollywood Engineering.

Price: $^7/_8$" **$70.00**
Price: $1^1/_2$" **$125.00**
Price: Collet, $^7/_8$" **$40.00**
Price: Collet, $1^1/_2$" **$75.00**

C-H/4-D Puller

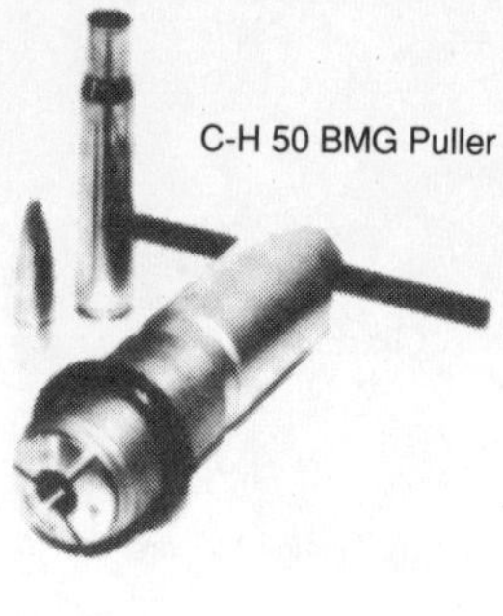

C-H 50 BMG Puller

Forster Super Fast Puller

Forster Collet-Type Puller

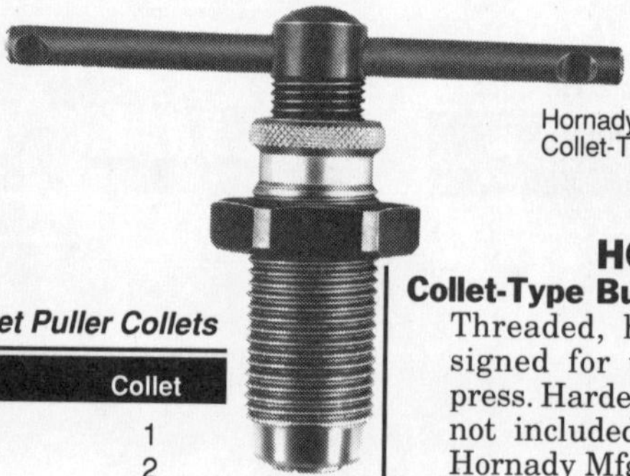

Hornady Collet-Type Puller

HORNADY *Bullet Puller Collets*

Caliber	Collet
17	1
22	2
6mm	3
25	4
6.5	4
270	5
7mm	6
30/303	7
8mm	8
338/38	9
375	10
10mm/41	11
44	12
45	13

Hollywood Puller

HORNADY

Collet-Type Bullet Puller

Threaded, heavy-duty puller designed for use on any standard press. Hardened steel handle. Collet not included. Weight: 1 lb. From Hornady Mfg. Co.

Price: **$13.65**
Price: Collet **$6.10**

Inertia Bullet Puller

For use on rifle or pistol cartridges up to 45-caliber. From Hornady Mfg. Co.

Price: **$22.50**

LYMAN

Inertia Bullet Puller

Three-jaw chuck fits all cartridges from 22 to 45. Made of tough polycarbonate over aluminum handle. From Lyman Products Corporation.

Price: **$27.95**

MIDWAY

Impact Bullet Puller

Inertia-type puller with three collets to fit most centerfire calibers. From Midway Arms, Inc.

Price: **$14.99**

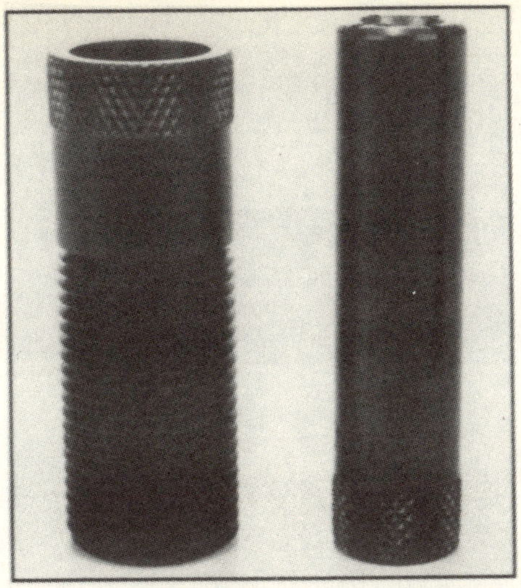

Ponsness/Warren Puller

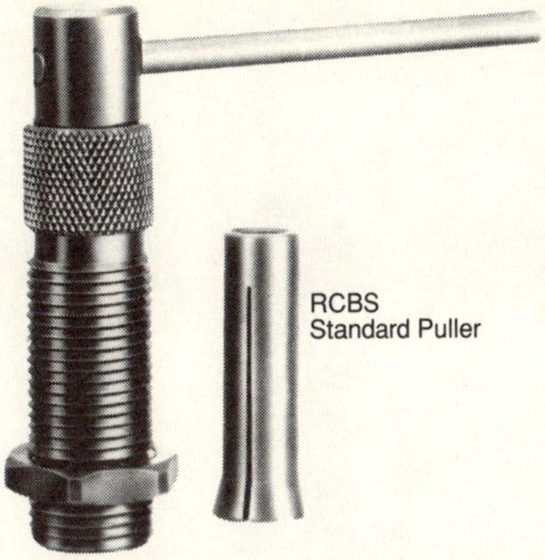

RCBS
Standard Puller

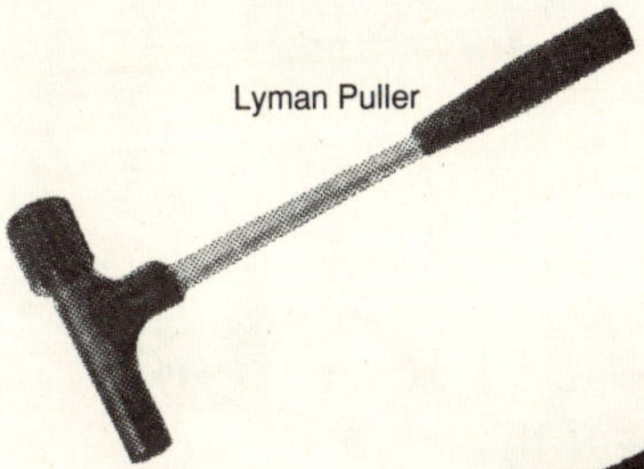

Lyman Puller

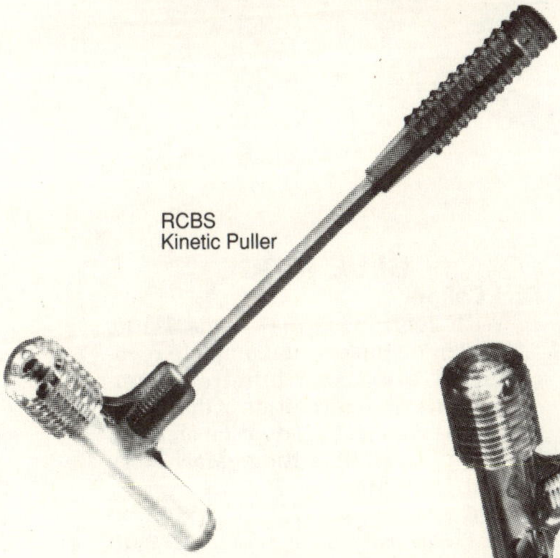

RCBS
Kinetic Puller

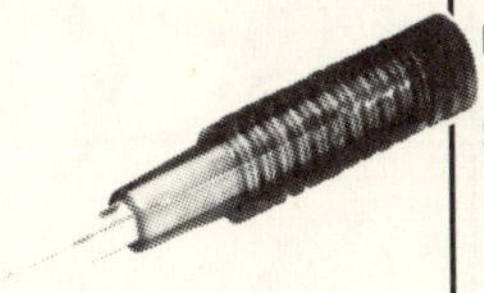

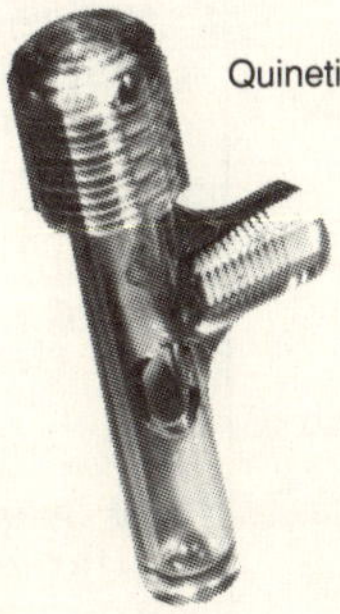

Quinetics Puller

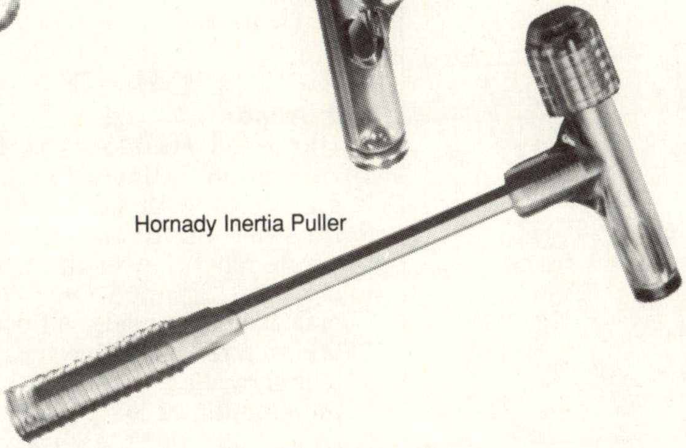

Hornady Inertia Puller

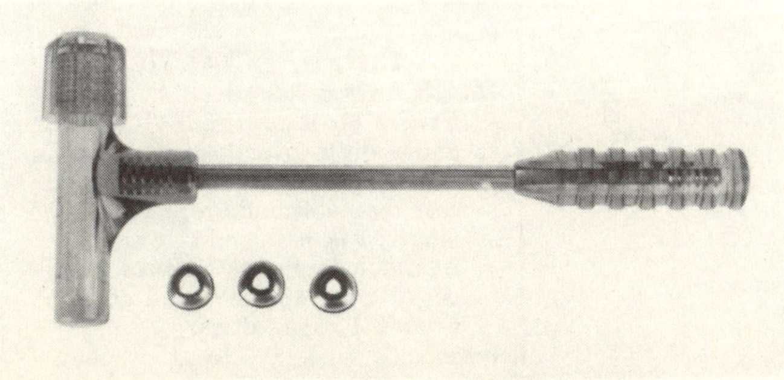

Midway
Impact Puller

PONSNESS/WARREN

Bullet Puller

Tapered die body threaded $^7/_8$-14 and bullet puller collets remove bullets safely. Only one die body needed; collets available in 224, 243, 257, 264, 270, 284, 308, 311, 323, 338, 358, 375 and 429. From Ponsness/Warren.

Price: Die body **$14.95**
Price: Collet **$12.95**

QUINETICS

Kinetic Bullet Puller

For all popular rifle, pistol, rim or rimless centerfire cartridges. Three-jaw chuck grips case with out damage to cannelure or case rim. From Quinetics Corp.

Price: **$18.75**

RCBS

Kinetic Bullet Puller

Features a 3-jaw chuck to grip the case without damage to rim. Made of unbreakable plastic with aluminum handle. Works with most centerfire cartridges from 22- to 45-caliber. Not for use with rimfire cartridges. From RCBS.

Price: **$25.64**

Standard Bullet Puller

Usable in all presses with $^7/_8$"-14 thread. Pulls most lengths or shapes of bullet without damaging or distorting lead. Interchangeable collets lock onto bullet as the case is pulled away. Collets available in 17- to 45-caliber. Collet not included. From RCBS.

Price: **$14.35**
Price: Collet **$8.43**

ROCK CRUSHER

Bullet Puller

Designed for use on very large calibers: 50 BMG, 55 Boyes rifle, 12.7mm Russian, 20mm Lahti, 20mm Solothurn, 23mm Soviet. State caliber when ordering. From The Old Western Scrounger.

Price: **$125.00**

Consult our Directory pages for the location of firms mentioned.

ACCURACY COMPONENTS

Compara-Set

Precise bullet seating measurements. Bullet seating at ogive rifling contact—seating measurement on or off lands; overall loaded round and case length measurements; bullet length from ogive to base and tip to base. Accurate dial indicator. Comes with 14 rifle calibers, 17 to 458. Precision machined components. From Accuracy Components Co.

Price: **$175.00**

ACCURACY DEN

Electronic Thickness Tester

Electronic case wall or bullet thickness tester for precise measurements. Motor-driven readout cuts testing time to 7 seconds. Will look inside a finished bullet ignoring the lead core and reading only jacket construction. Deviation needle 10 to 20 times more sensitive than comparable mechanical units. Uses standard 115 VAC 50/60 cycles. Remote battery operation possible upon request. From The Accuracy Den.

Price: **$495.00**

B&M INDUSTRIES

Multi-Dimensional Case Gauge

Measures wall thickness throughout case body area; concentricity of ID of body to OD of body; wall thickness of the neck area; concentricity of ID of neck to OD of neck; OD at any location along body or neck; overall length of cartridge with Maximum Length master; squareness of body to head; concentricity of body to neck and of body and neck to bullet. With additional accessories will also measure wall thickness of web at the flash hole and primer pocket depth. Heavy plastic carrying case with inside cushions available. Comes with one case gauge master for one caliber. From Precision Reloading, Inc.

Price: With .001 dial indicator . . **$189.95**
Price: With .0005 indicator **$244.95**
Price: Web thickness/primer hull depth accessories **$29.95**
Price: Additional case gauge masters **$8.95**
Price: Set of four masters **$24.95**
Price: Carry case **$29.95**

Accuracy Components Compara-Set

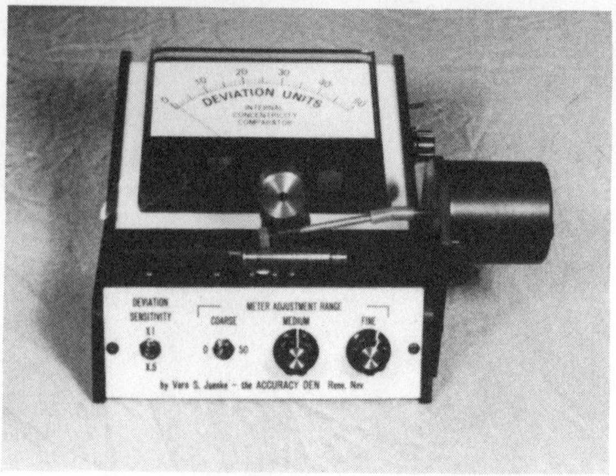

Accuracy Den Thickness Tester

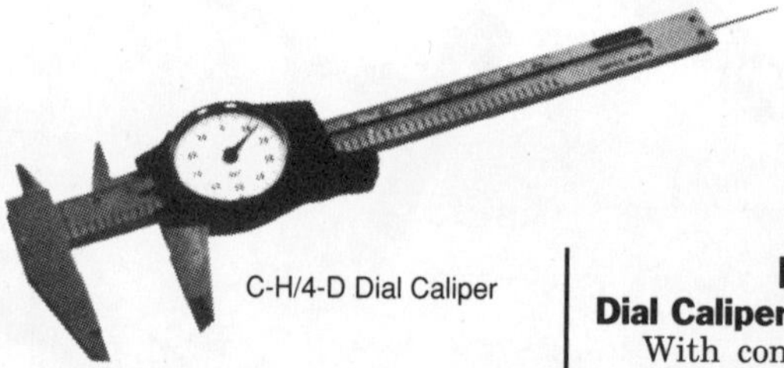

C-H/4-D Dial Caliper

B&M Industries Case Gauge

BLUE RIDGE

Dial Caliper

With continuous dial reads 1-100. Dial hand makes one complete revolution every one hundred thousandths. One revolution of dial hand equals smallest graduation on main beam. From Blue Ridge Machinery and Tools, Inc.

Price: 6" capacity **$42.00**
Price: 8" capacity **$72.00**

C-H/4-D

Dial Caliper

Hardened stainless steel single revolution caliper. Features no-glare dial with adjustable bezel; free-wheeling friction roller for accurate repetitive readings; 6" capacity, .001" graduations; four-way measuring for inside, outside, depth and step readings. Specifications: 0-6" dial reading; graduations in .001" increments, .100" per revolution; resolution, .001"; accuracy, .001". From C-H Tool & Die/4-D Custom Die.

Price: **$45.00**

C.P. SPECIALTIES

Match Ammo Gauge

Precision-machined aluminum gauge drops over loaded round for visual check of correct case length, case diameter and overall cartridge length. 1¼" high and 1" in diameter. Available for 9mm, 9mmx21, 38 Super, 10mm, 40 S&W and 45 ACP. From C.P. Specialties.

Price: **$8.95**

CLYMER ***Headspace Gauge Interchangeability***

Gauge	Calibers Used With
22 LR	22 Short, 22 Long
22 Hornet	Hornet-based wildcats
25-50	32-20, 218 Bee, 218 Mashburn Bee
30-30 WCF	219 Zipper, 219 Zipper Imp., 219 Donaldson Wasp, 25-35 WCF, 7-30 Waters, 7mm Int. R, 30-30 based wildcats, 30 Herrett, 303 Savage, 307 Winchester, 32-40, 32 Winchester Special, 356 Winchester, 357 Herrett, 375 Winchester, 38-55 WCF
30-40 Krag	303 British
32 H&R Magnum	32 S&W Long
357 Magnum	256 Winchester Magnum, 357 Max., 38 S&W Special
44-40 WCF	38-40
45-70 Gov't.	33 Winchester, 348 Winchester
Belted Gauges	.535" base belted calibers
378 Weatherby	30/378 Weatherby, 416 Weatherby, 460 Weatherby, 378 or 460-based wildcats.
223 Remington	6x45
222 Remington Mag.	6x47
PPC Gauges	22 PPC, 6mm PPC
BR Rem. Gauges	22 Remington BR, 6mm Remington BR, 7mm Remington BR
TCU Gauges	6mm TCU, 257 TCU, 6.5 TCU, 7mm TCU
7x57	257 Roberts, 6.5x257 Roberts
284 Winchester	22/284, 6mm/284, 25/284, 6.5/284, 270/284, 30/284, 35/284
308 Winchester	243 Winchester, 7mm-08, 358 Winchester
30-06	25-06, 6.5-06, 270 Winchester, 8mm-06, 338-06, 35 Whelen
32 Remington	32 Remington

Clymer Headspace Gauges for Rimmed Calibers

Clymer Headspace Gauges for Belted Calibers

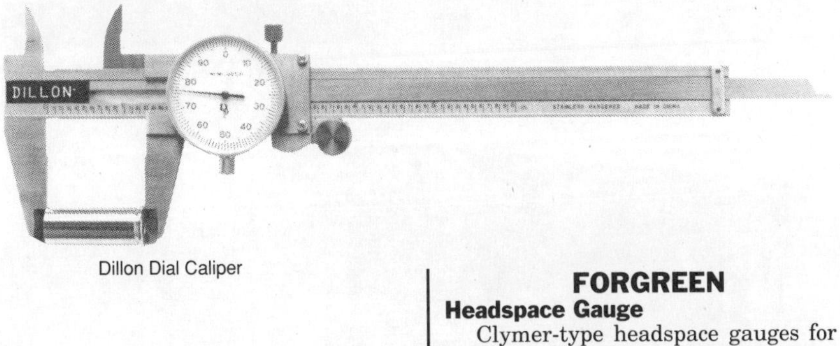

Dillon Dial Caliper

FORGREEN

Headspace Gauge

Clymer-type headspace gauges for rimmed/rimless or 50-caliber and over. From Forgreen Tool Mfg.

Price: Rimmed or rimless **$22.00**
Price: 50-cal. or over **$35.00**

CLYMER

Headspace Gauges

"Go" and "No-Go" headspace gauges for rimmed, rimless or belted rifle and pistol cartridges or shotshell gauges. Rimmed or belted case gauges check headspace from a flange that duplicates the minimum and maximum space allowed in a chamber to secure cartridge rim or belt. Rimless pistol gauges for cartridges that headspace off the case mouth. Rimless gauges for shouldered chambers measure headspace from the breech face to some established point on the shoulder of the chamber. Precision ground within SAAMI specs. Standard or special-order gauges available. From Clymer Manufacturing Co., Inc.

Price: Pistol and rifle **$19.00**
Price: Shotgun **$25.00**
Price: 50-cal. U.S. Ordnance **$40.00**
Price: Special order **$40.00**

DAVIDSON

Seating Depth Checker

Attachment for dial calipers to check seating depth of loaded rounds or ogive to base length of bullet. Nose piece has 6" included angle hole machined .001" smaller than the caliber to represent barrel groove diameter. Available in .224, .243, .257, .277, .284, .308, .338, .35, .375 and .458 diameters. Base piece with three steps machined to accept three different case head diameters. Made of steel with mounting slot width of .140. From Precision Reloading, Inc.

Price: **$17.50**
Price: Nose piece **$8.95**
Price: Base piece **$8.95**

DILLON

Case Gauge

Measures distance from the case head to middle of shoulder. Allows size die adjustment to ensure proper headspace. Also shows maximum case length and trim-to-case length. From Dillon Precision Products, Inc.

Price: **$15.95**

Dial Caliper

Hardened stainless steel caliper with satin chrome finish. Measuring faces hardened, ground and lapped. Features include: .100 per revolution; covered track for longer life; large adjustable dial; complete with fitted case. From Dillon Precision Products, Inc.

Price: **$29.95**

FORSTER/BONANZA

Co-Ax Indicator

Measures degree of concentricity between case and bullet to within .0005". Designed to work with any 2" face dial indicator with back mounting lug. Indicator not included. From Forster Products.

Price: **$46.20**
Price: Indicator dial **$54.60**

FORSTER

Combo Case Length/ Headspace Gauge

Visually check case length and headspace. Proper head to shoulder length is evident when cartridge is placed into the gauge and the rim is even with or lower than maximum step but not below minimum step of gauge. Overall case length is evident when mouth or neck of case is between max and minimum step of neck end of gauge. Weight: 7 oz. From Forster Products.

Price: **$19.30**

Headspace Gauges

Chamber gauges in three lengths, Go (minimum chamber size), No-Go and Field (maximum allowable chamber size). Made to .0003" total tolerance. Available for rimmed or rimless cases and in most popular calibers. Weight: 3 oz. From Forster Products.

Price: **$16.00**
Price: 30 Carbine **$22.00**

HORNADY

Dial Caliper

Stainless steel caliper measures to .001". Measures case length, bullet length, inside and outside diameters, primer pocket depth and overall cartridge length. Comes with carrying case. Available in metric. Weight: 12 oz. From Hornady Mfg. Co.

Price: **$51.70**
Price: Metric **$54.25**

Digital Caliper

LCD display digital caliper reads in either inches or metric; measures inside and outside diameters, lengths, and primer pocket and case depths. Comes in wooden storage case. Installed battery and one spare included. From Hornady Mfg. Co.

Price: **$127.80**

FORSTER *Rimless Caliber Headspace Gauges*

Caliber	Go	No-Go	Field
22-250	1.574	1.579	1.583
220 Swift	1.806	1.810	1.814
222 Remington	1.294	1.297	1.300
222 Remington Magnum	1.493	1.496	1.499
223 Remington	1.464	1.467	1.470
243 Winchester	1.630	1.634	1.638
308 Winchester	1.630	1.634	1.638
7mm-08 Remington	1.630	1.634	1.638
7.62mm NATO	1.630	1.634	1.638
244 Remington	1.777	1.781	1.785
250 Savage	1.579	1.583	1.587
6.5mm SKAN	1.831	1.835	NA
6.5mmx55 Swede	1.779	1.785	1.789
257 Roberts	1.794	1.800	1.804
7mm Mauser	1.794	1.800	1.804
280 Remington	2.100	2.104	2.108
284 Winchester	1.810	1.815	1.817
30-06 Remington	2.049	2.055	2.058
270 Winchester	2.049	2.055	2.058
25-06 Remington	2.049	2.055	2.058
8mmx57 Mauser	1.874	1.880	1.884

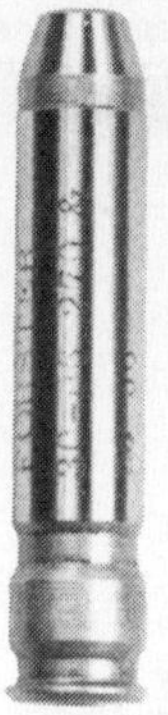

Forster Rimless Gauges

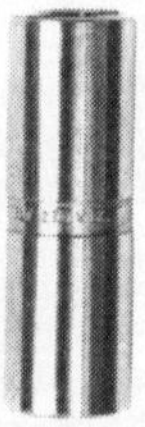

Forster Combo Gauge

FORSTER Combo Case Length/Headspace Gauge Calibers
222 Rem.
222 Rem. Mag.
223 Rem.
22-250
243 Win.
244 Rem.
257 Roberts
270 Win.
7x57 Mauser
7mm-08
280 Rem.
308 Win.
30-06
25-06
8x57 Mauser
38 S&W Spl.
357 Mag.
45 ACP
44 Mag.
9mm

FORSTER *Rimmed & Belted Caliber Headspace Gauges*

Caliber	Go	No Go	Field
219 Wasp	.063	.067	.070
219 Zipper	.063	.067	.070
22 Savage High Power	.063	.067	.070
25-35	.063	.067	.070
30-30	.063	.067	.070
32 Winchester Spl.	.063	.067	.070
32-40	.063	.067	.070
38-55	.063	.067	.070
22 Rimfire	.043	.046	.049
300 Magnum	.220	.223	.226
All belted magnums	.220	.223	.226
303 British	.064	.067	.070
30-40 Krag	.064	.067	.070

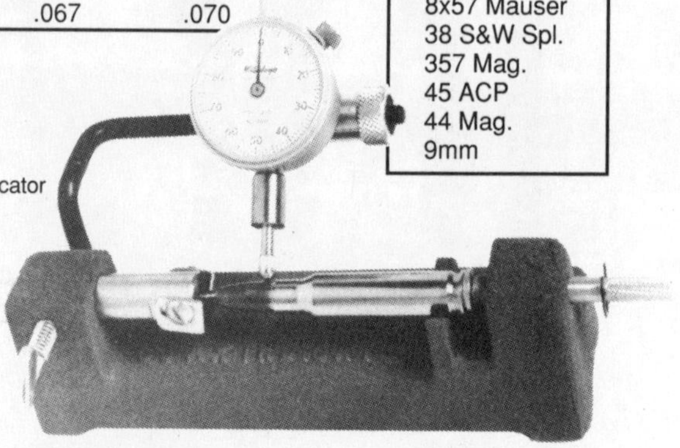

Forster/Bonanza Co-Ax Indicator

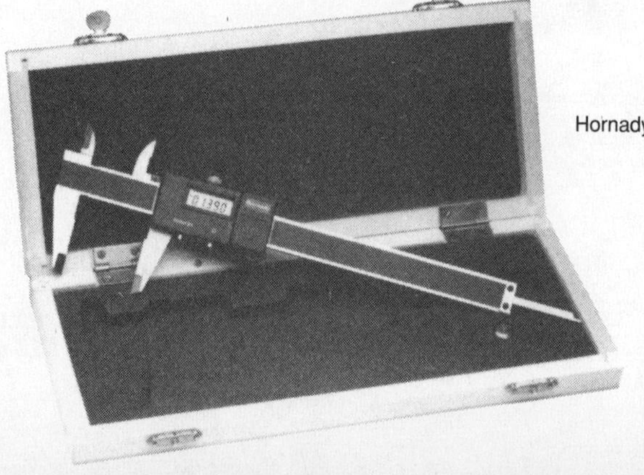

Hornady Digital Caliper

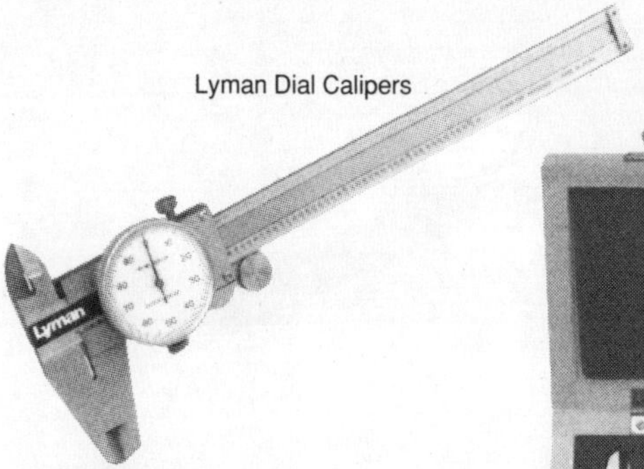

Lyman Dial Calipers

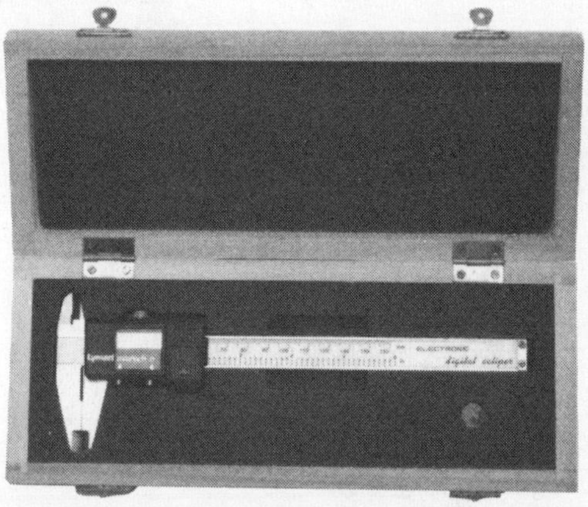

Lyman Digital Dial Calipers

Lyman Pistol/Rifle
Headspace Case Length Gauges

Johnson Case Neck Gauge

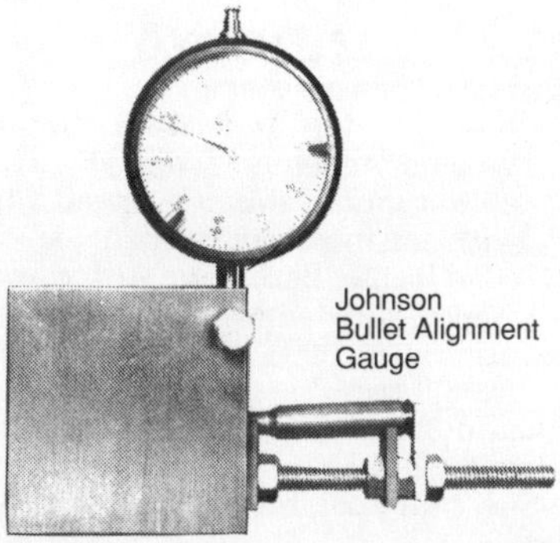

Johnson
Bullet Alignment
Gauge

HORNADY

Micrometer

Accurate to .001" for bullet and case diameter measurements. Includes wrench to adjust zero and carrying case. From Hornady Mfg. Co.

Price: **$46.50**

JOHNSON

Bullet Alignment Gauge

Concentricity gauge for loaded rounds. Uses same dial indicator as Johnson case neck gauge. From Plum City Ballistic Range.

Price: **$59.00**
Price: Without indicator **$24.00**

Case Neck Gauge

Features spring-loaded stabilizing block to press case neck tightly against polished spindle. Measures variation in case wall thickness to .001" or less. Includes dial indicator. From Plum City Ballistic Range.

Price: **$64.00**
Price: Without dial indicator **$29.00**
Price: Both Johnson gauges with one dial indicator **$88.00**

K&M

Spindle Micrometer

Mitutoyo micrometer with modified spindle that has diamond ground 60° angle, leaving 1/8" flat for measuring to within 1/16" of case shoulder. Micrometer features carbide spindle face, large diameter satin-chrome-finished sleeves and thimble, ratchet stop, spindle lock and readings to .0001". Intended for checking concentricity of case necks and jackets, it can be used to check any wall thickness not over one inch with bore not under .190". From K&M Services.

Price: **$83.00**

LYMAN

Case Trim Gauge

Precision made of high strength metal. For measuring case length of both fired and resized cartridge cases. 50 popular rifle and pistol cases represented. From Lyman Products Corporation.

Price: **$13.95**

Dial Caliper

High-strength plastic frame. Includes storage case and case length trim guide. From Lyman Products Corporation.

Price: **$34.95**

Digital Dial Caliper

Electronic 6" caliper with direct digital readout for both inches or millimeters. Powered by standard calculator battery. Features automatic shutoff and push button zeroing to select a zero dimension and sort parts by plus or minus variation. Performs inside, outside and depth measurements. From Lyman Products Corporation.

Price: . . . . **Contact manufacturer.**

Partner Pak Caliper Set

Includes Lyman plastic dial caliper and plastic folding rule. From Lyman Products Corporation.

Price: **$37.95**

Pistol Length/Headspace Gauges

Four pistol gauges, 9mm, 10mm, 40 S&W, 45 ACP, to check all critical dimensions to ensure proper functioning. Checks case length, diameter and overall cartridge length. Other calibers available: 38 Special, 357 Magnum, 44 Magnum. From Lyman Products Corporation.

Price: **$17.95**

Rifle Length/Headspace Gauges

Set of four gauges, 223, 243, 308 and 30-06, to check maximum and minimum allowable headspace and identify cases exceeding maximum allowable case length. Other available calibers include: 22-250, 6.5x55 Swedish, 270 Winchester, 7.62x39. From Lyman Products Corporation.

Price: **$55.00**

Stainless Steel Caliper

Delivers .001" accuracy. Comes with storage case. From Lyman Products Corporation.

Price: **$39.95**

McKILLEN & HEYER

Case Length Gauge

Multiple case length gauge to check overall length. Maximum tolerance of .002" less than maximum for each caliber. Chrome-plated steel gauge. From McKillen & Heyer, Inc.

Price: **$14.95**

MIDWAY

Dial Calipers

Stainless steel caliper to measure case length, bullet diameter, overall case length up to 6". Accurate to .001". From Midway Arms, Inc.

Price: **$29.99**

Max Cartridge Gauges

Automatic pistol and revolver gauges to check mouth diameter, base diameter, rim thickness and diameter, case and cartridge length and bullet diameter. Come in a set of six for auto or revolver or separately. Auto: 380 Auto, 9mm Luger, 38 Super, 40 S&W, 10mm Auto, 45 Auto. Revolver: 38 Special, 357 Magnum, 41 Magnum, 44 Special, 44 Magnum and 45 Long Colt. From Midway Arms, Inc.

Price: **$29.99**

Price: Each **$8.99**

MITUTOYO

Deluxe Test Indicator and Magnetic Base Set

To check case concentricity or runout. Includes dial indicator, base, $^3/_8$" and $^5/_{32}$" diameter posts with dovetail clamp, all in fitted carrying case. Universal mounting clamp fits dovetails on top and bottom of indicator for fast set-ups. Measures anywhere within 240°. Dial indicator comes standard or fine adjustment. From Blue Ridge Machinery and Tools, Inc.

Price: Standard **$94.50**

Price: Fine **$97.95**

Dial Calipers

Feature rigid main beams 3.4mm thick; measuring range from 4" to 12"; extra large dial face; made of hardened stainless steel; measures inside, outside depth and step measurements; supplied with fitted carrying case. From Blue Ridge Machinery and Tools, Inc.

Price: . . . . **See chart.**

Digimatic Caliper

Digital readout caliper with optional SPC output for Mitutoyo Digimatic Processor. Standard measuring jaws with measuring range of 0 to 6" or 0 to 150mm. From Blue Ridge Machinery and Tools, Inc.

Price: **$147.00**

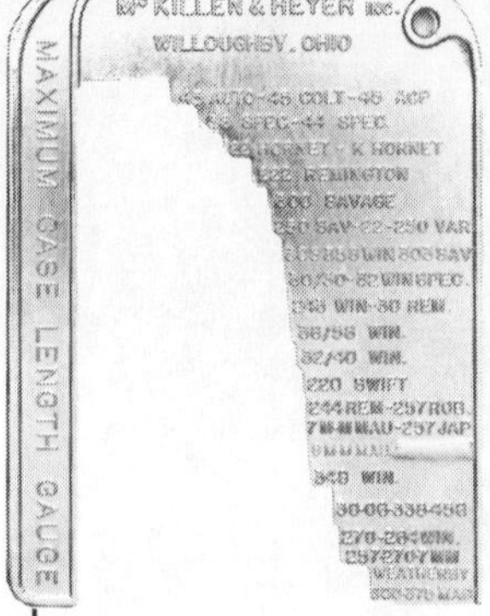

McKillen & Hyer Case Length Gauge

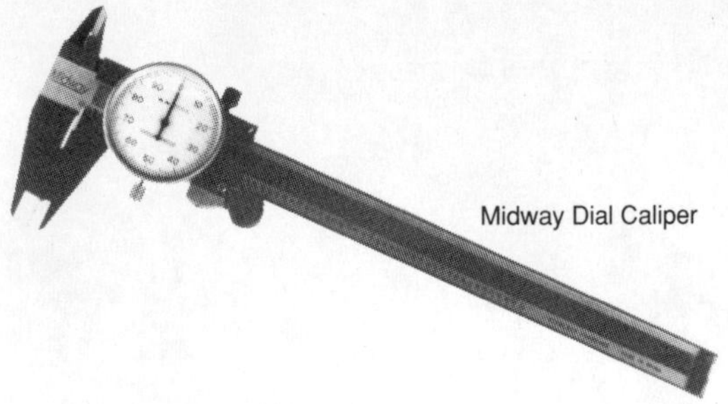

Midway Dial Caliper

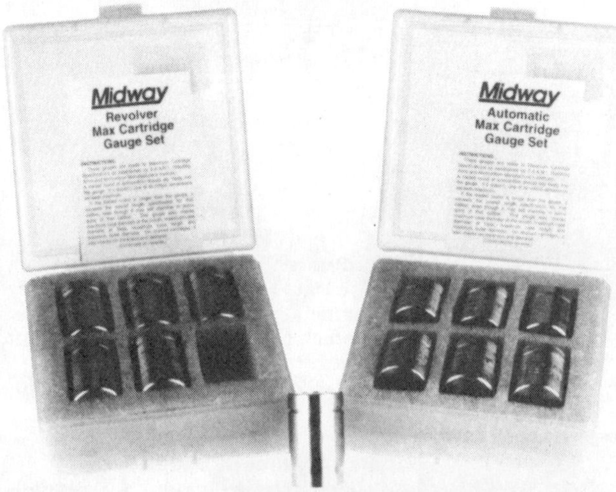

Midway Max Cartridge Gauge

MITUTOYO *Outside Micrometers*

Range (ins.)	Graduation	Type	Price/Ins.	Price/Metric
		STAINLESS		
$0\text{-}^1/_2$	.0001	Rachet	$89.00	
0-1	.0001	Ratchet	72.50	$73.50
0-1	.0001	Friction	72.50	72.50
1-2	.0001	Ratchet	89.00	91.50
1-2	.0001	Friction	89.00	89.00
2-3	.0001	Ratchet	97.00	
3-4	.0001	Ratchet	107.00	
		CAST		
0-1	.0001	Ratchet	65.00	
1-2	.0001	Ratchet	76.50	
2-3	.0001	Ratchet	86.00	
3-4	.0001	Ratchet	97.00	
4-5	.0001	Ratchet	106.00	
5-6	.0001	Ratchet	117.00	

MITUTOYO *Dial Calipers*

Model	Range/ins.	Range*	Price
629	4	.200	$65.50
626	6	.200	76.50
637	6	.100	91.00
627	8	.200	113.00
644	8	.100	123.00
628	12	.200	170.00
645	12	.100	183.00
611	6	.100	101.00

*Per Revolution

MITUTOYO

Outside Micrometers

Ratchet stop or friction thimble-type micrometers. Two styles available: tubular stainless steel frame with satin-chrome finish; or cast solid frame. Both come with carbide tipped anvil and spindle. Graduations in .0001"; measure ranges from 0 to $^1/_2$" to 5" to 6" or 0-25mm and 25mm-50mm. Larger sizes available. From Blue Ridge Machinery and Tool, Inc.

Price: . . . . **See chart.**

MITUTOYO

DP-1HS Portable Digimatic Processor

A data processor to connect directly to dial caliper or micrometer via SPC connecting cables. Offers three separate analysis modes selected via DIP switches on side panel. Connecting cables available to fit most calipers and micrometers. From Blue Ridge Machinery and Tool, Inc.

Price: **$307.00**
Price: Cables, caliper **$24.00**
Price: Cables, micrometer **$31.00**

NECO

Concentricity, Wall Thickness and Runout Gauge

Made of hard anodized aluminum and stainless steel. To measure variation in the cartridge case and loaded round. Comes complete with dial indicator and accessory tools to measure calibers from 22 through 45-70 and instruction manual. From NECO.

Price: **$137.15**

BOB PEASE

Depth Checker

Device fits on 4" or 6" calipers to gauge point at which bullet touches lands and transfer reading to another bullet ogive. Can also be used to check bullet uniformity. Made in .224, .243, .284 and .308 in 1" length for easy calculations. Nickle-plated. Odd calibers available on special order. From Bob Pease Accuracy.

Price: **$10.00**

PRECISION RELOADING

Trim Length Masters

Designed for Wilson case trimmer to eliminate setting trimmer up for proper trim length. Master gauges measure .010" less than maximum case length and are available for all calibers. Two sleeve sizes: 1" small caliber; 1 3/4" mild/magnum calibers. All Masters fit in either sleeve. From Precision Reloading, Inc.

Price: 1 3/4" sleeve **$9.95**
Price: 1" sleeve **$8.95**
Price: Master standard caliber **$7.95**
Price: Master magnum caliber **$8.95**
Price: Custom Master **$12.95**

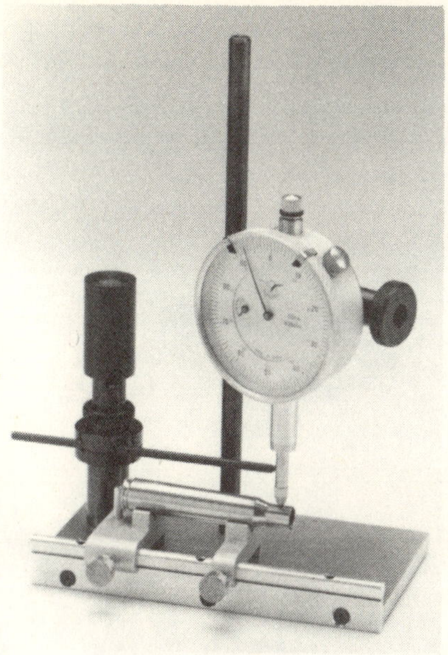

RCBS Case Master

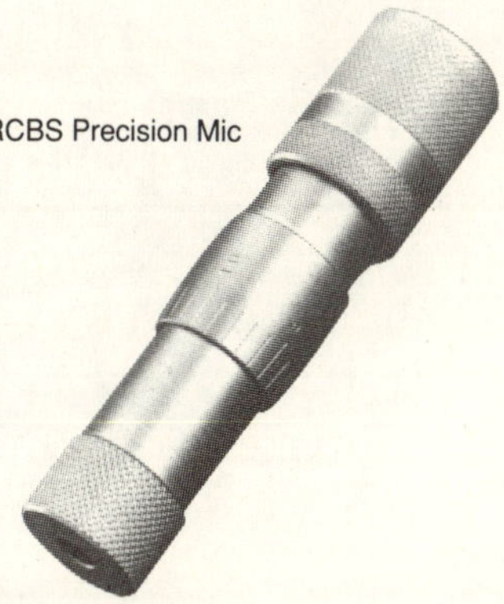

RCBS Precision Mic

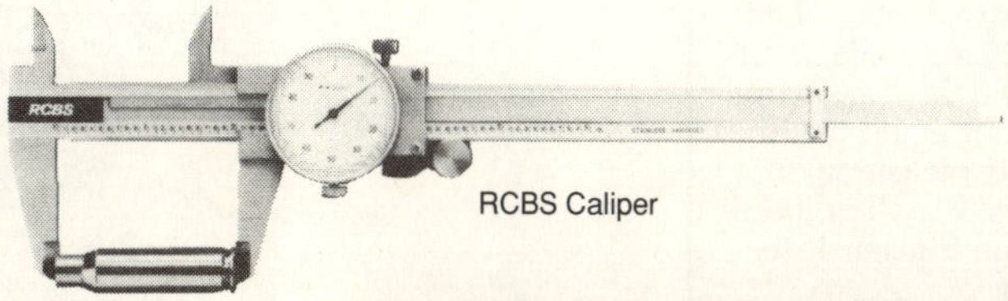

RCBS Caliper

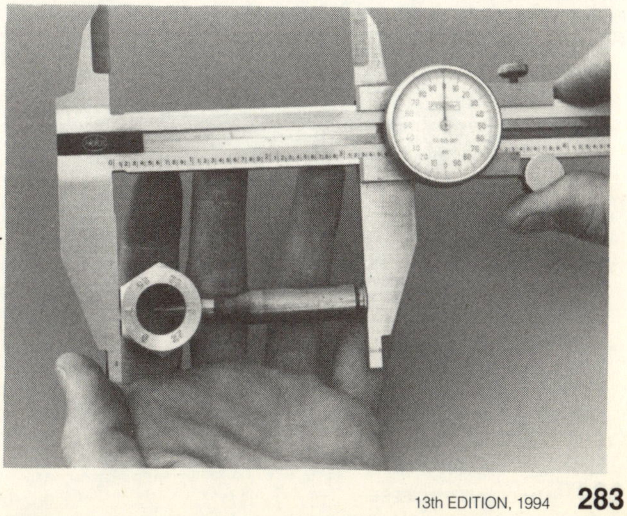

Sinclair
Bullet Comparator

RCBS

Caliper/Case Length Gauge

Features easy-to-read dial; 6" capacity; measurement of four dimensions: outer, inner, depth and step. Dial has .001" gradations for case and bullet measurement. Included are a chart with maximum and trim lengths for all popular calibers and a case with instructions. Stainless steel or plastic versions available. From RCBS.

Price: Stainless steel **$64.11**
Price: Plastic **$38.08**

Case Master Gauging Tool

Precision dial indicator for measuring case neck concentrictiy, case neck thickness, case length and bullet run-out. Also detects case head separation. From RCBS.

Price: **$64.36**

Precision Mic

Provides micrometer reading for chamber headspace and bullet seating depth to 0.001". Measures from the datum point on the case shoulder to the base for comparison to SAAMI tolerance readings. From RCBS.

Price: **$36.60**

SINCLAIR

Bullet Comparator

Stainless steel tool designed to assist in adjusting bullet seater to correct depth from bullet to bullet. Comparator available for 224, 243/6mm, 257, 277, 284/7mm and 308. Use with standard dial calipers. From Sinclair International, Inc.

Price: **$90.00**

SINCLAIR

Case Neck Micrometer

Measures exact thickness of cartridge case neck to .0001". Starrett micrometer head installed on steel base for hands-free operation to rotate cases and use micrometer thimble. Adjustable micrometer and offset anvil plus ratchet control allow measurements up to shoulder and neck junction and dead zero the tool for individual sensitivity. From Sinclair International, Inc.

Price: **$90.00**

Case Neck Thickness Gauge

Pre-sort cases by neck wall thickness. Designed to be used with standard .001" by 1" travel dial indicator. Pilots for calibers 22- through 45-caliber available. One pilot stop comes with tool. From Sinclair International, Inc.

Price: **$18.75**
Price: Dial indicator **$30.00**

Concentricity Gauge

Redesigned with stainless steel V-block to support case. Inspects concentricity of fired and sized cases or loaded rounds up to 460 Weatherby. Features adjustable indicator tower for taking readings any point along case body. Fixture accepts only .001" dial indicators with .375" mounting post and minimum stem/post length of 2.25". Dial indicator sold separately. From Sinclair International, Inc.

Price: **$37.00**
Price: Dial indicator **$30.00**

Seating Depth Tool

Seating depth tool of stainless steel to find distance from case head to rifle lands for individual bullets. Comes with nylon bolt guide to fit most actions, universal measuring rod and two stops of equal length. Stops allow accurate measurements with pair of calipers. For all calibers from 22 on up. From Sinclair International, Inc.

Price: **$17.00**
Price: Extra guides **$5.25**

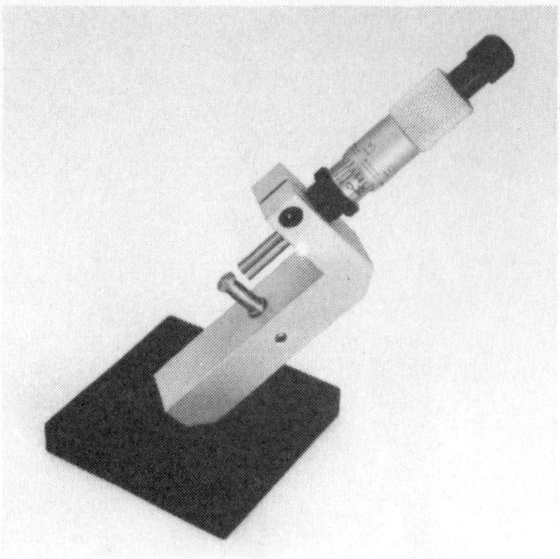

Sinclair Case Neck Micrometer

Sinclair Case Neck Thickness Gauge

Sinclair Concentricity Gauge

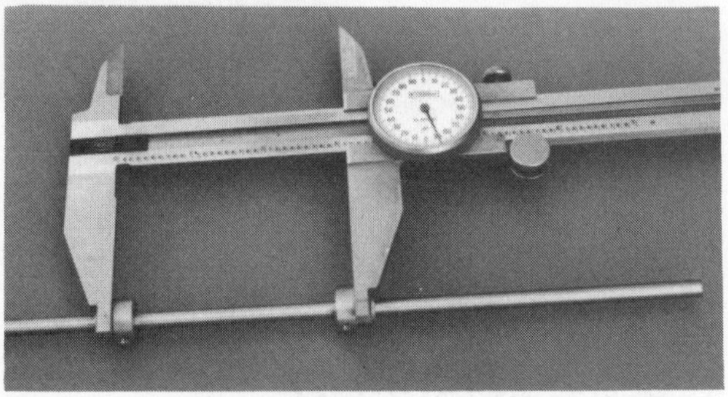

Sinclair Seating Depth Tool

Sinclair Case Gauges

STONEY POINT Chamber-All Modified Cases
17 Rem.
222 Rem.
222 Rem. Mag.
223 Rem.
22-250 Rem.
22 PPC
220 Swift
243 Win.
6mm Rem.
6mm BR
6mm PPC
257 Roberts
250 Savage
25-06 Rem.
264 Win. Mag.
270 Win.
7x57/7mm Mau.
7mm BR
7mm-08 Rem.
280 Rem.
284 Win.
7mm Rem.Mag.
30-30 Win.
300 Savage
308 Win.
30-06 Springfield
300 H&H Mag.
300 Win. Mag.
300 Wea. Mag.
303 British
8x57 Mauser
338 Win. Mag.
340 Wea. Mag.
35 Whelen
375 H&H Mag.
45-70 Gov't.

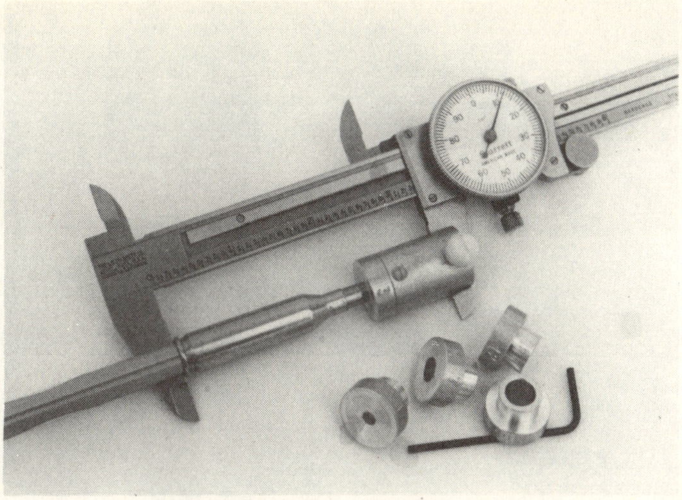

Stoney Point Bullet Comparator

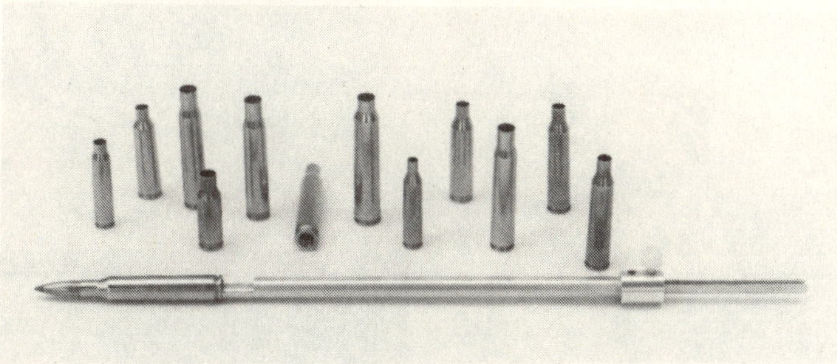

Stoney Point OAL Gauge

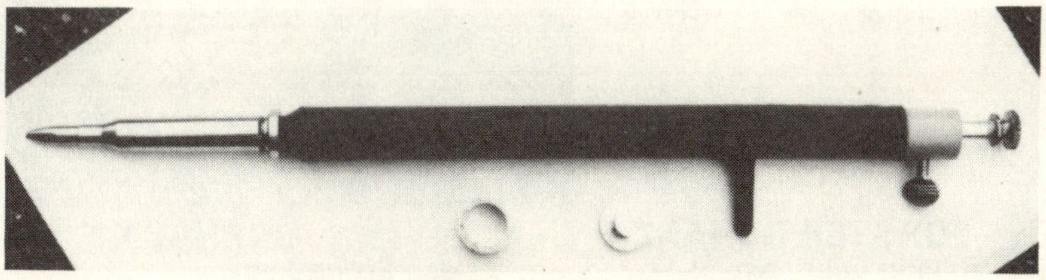

Varner's Bullet Seating Gauge

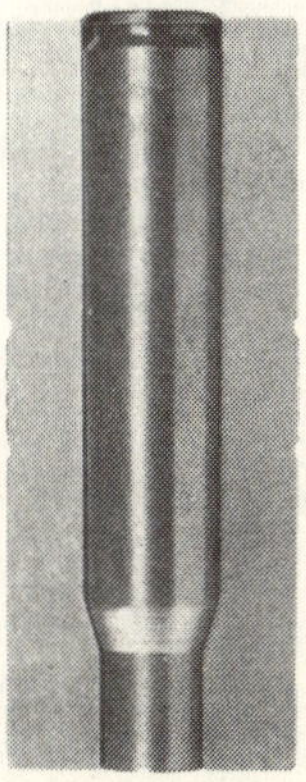

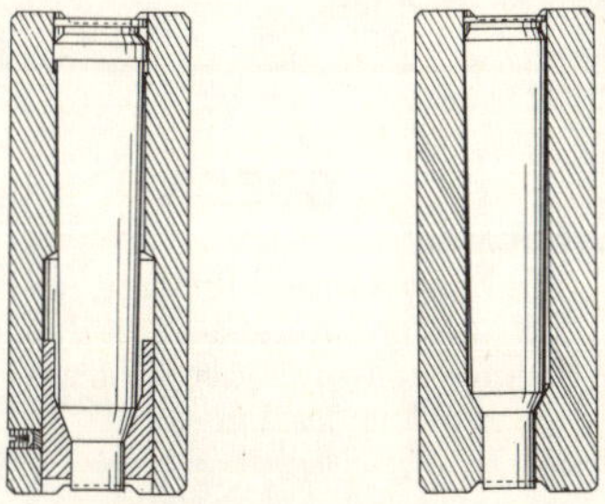

Wilson Adjustable
and Regular Case Gauges

STONEY POINT

Chamber-All Bullet Comparator

Precision machined from tempered alloy aluminum. Measures overall cartridge length from the ogive. Special body design allows proper alignment of caliper in either offset with Stoney OAL gauge or centerline with conventional caliper measurement. Attaches to caliper with thumbscrew. Twelve bullet inserts available: 17, 22, 6mm/24, 25, 6.5mm, 270, 7mm, 30, 33, 35, 37 and 45. From Stoney Point Products, Inc.

Price: **$11.75**
Price: Bullet inserts **$2.65**

Chamber-All OAL Gauge

Designed to accurately determine maximum overall cartridge length, thus establishing proper bullet free run and bullet seating depth dimensions. Gauge, made of anodized tempered alloy aluminum machined to close tolerances, employs modified nickel-plated cases of desired caliber machined to thread onto gauge. Case necks expanded slightly to allow bullets to pass through. Includes one modified case. From Stoney Point Products, Inc.

Price: **$34.95**

VARNER'S

Bullet Seating Gauge

"Lands finder" gauge measuring system to determine correct bullet seating depth. Comes with gauge rod, sleeve spacer, spacer block and case of desired caliber. From Varner's.

Price: **$24.50**
Price: Additional case calibers **$4.00**

WILSON

Cartridge Case Gauges

Available in two configurations, regular and adjustable. The regular gauge checks overall length, cone to head length and is available in most popular rimless calibers. Adjustable gauge available for belted magnums and can be used with different rifles of same caliber. From L.E. Wilson, Inc.

Price: Regular **$19.24**
Price: Adjustable **$26.82**

E. ARTHUR BROWN

Spray-Dry

Non-stick, dry lubricant in a liquid suspension for lubricating cases and dies. Spray it on and the liquid evaporates; the lube remains. Comes in 4-oz. pump plastic bottle. From E. Arthur Brown Company.

Price: **$3.50**

C-H/4-D

Case Die Lube

Oil-base liquid die lube also available in water-soluble formula (#42200). Comes in 2-ounce bottle. From C-H Tool & Die/4-D Custom Die.

Price: **$1.75**

CHEM-PAK

Size-All

Formula includes tungsten disulfide and molybdenum disulfide, industrial performance wear reducing lubricants and other extreme pressure lubricity agents. Conditions die and expander ball for smoother operation. Spray lube wipes off with dry or damp cloth. Comes in 8-oz. aerosol cans. From Chem-Pak, Inc.

Price: **$6.95**

DILLON

Rapid Lube 5000

Non-aerosol cartridge case lube spray. Environmentally safe. Available in 4.5-oz. spray bottle. From Dillon Precision Products, Inc.

Price: **$4.95**

FORSTER

Case Graphiter

Powder graphite lube dispenser constructed of sturdy plastic with three brushes to accommodate all calibers from 22 to 35. Base is drilled for bench mounting. Comes with cover to prevent graphite contamination. From Forster Products.

Price: **$9.40**

Sportlube

Water soluble, 100% animal base lubricant for full-length case sizing operations. Available in 3-oz. and 16-oz. sizes. From Forster Products.

Price: 3-oz. **$3.50**
Price: 16-oz. **$10.00**

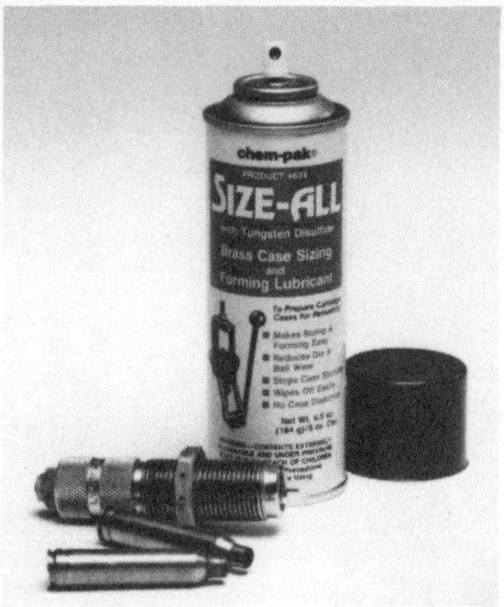

Chem-Pak Size-All

Forster/Bonanza Blue Ribbon

Gozon

Forster Graphiter

Hornady One Shot

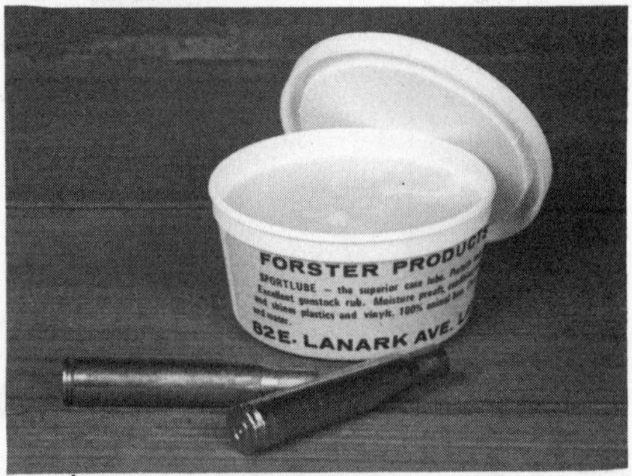

Forster Sportlube

FORSTER/BONANZA

Blue Ribbon Lubricant

High pressure lubricant for full-length case resizing. Available in 2-oz. bottle or case of 12. From Forster Products.

Price: 2-oz. **$3.40**
Price: Case **$28.00**

GOZON

Lubricator

High pressure lubricant designed for use on metal-to-metal actions. Comes in 4-oz. squeeze bottle. From Gozon Corporation.

Price: **$4.95**

HORNADY

Case Lube Pad/Load Tray

Lid of Hornady case lube pad is load tray. Used with Hornady case-size lube, a roll-type lube applicator. From Hornady Mfg. Co.

Price: **$6.60**

HORNADY

Case-Sizing Lube

Liquid lube for use with Hornady pad to lube cases prior to sizing. From Hornady Mfg. Co.

Price: **$2.85**

One Shot Case Lube

Aerosol lube with DynaGlide applies thin non-tacky layer of wax to cases. A non-petroleum product that will not contaminate powder or primers. Weight: 2 lbs. From Hornady Mfg. Co.

Price: **$6.95**

Unique Case Lube

Semi-solid-type lube. Comes in plastic tub. Weight: 1/2-lb. From Hornady Mfg. Co.

Price: **$2.85**

Midway Mica

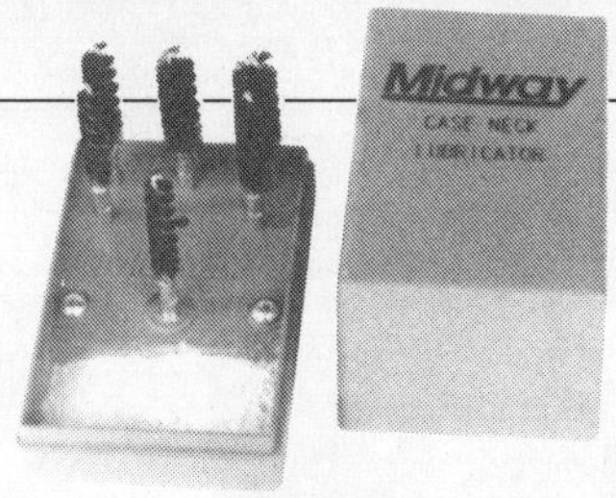

Midway Lubricator

RCBS Case Slick

Redding Case Lube

Lyman Case Lube

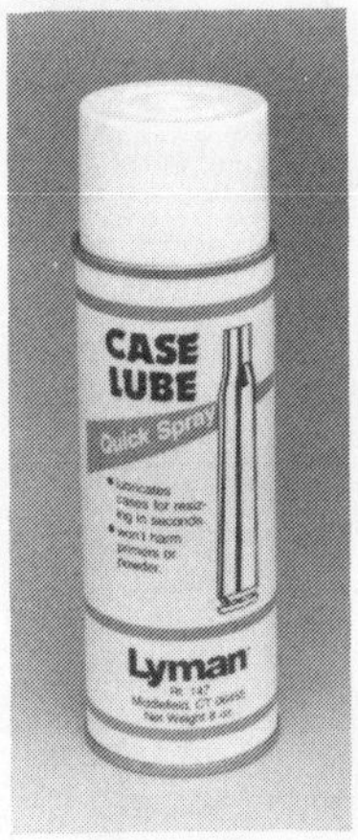

Midway Minute Lube

LYMAN

Case Lube Kit

Complete kit includes cloth lubricating pad, 2 oz. Lyman case lube, three interchangeable neck brushes and wooden handle in plastic case. From Lyman Products Corporation.

Price: **$15.95**
Price: Case lube **$3.50**
Price: Lube pad **$7.50**

Case Neck Dipper

Dry lube to reduce friction from sizing die expander button on interior of bottleneck cases. Includes three brushes and 2 oz. dry mica for all cases from 17- to 45-caliber. From Lyman Products Corporation.

Price: **$9.50**
Price: Mica refill (1 oz.) **$3.00**

LYMAN

Qwik Spray Case Lube

Petroleum based lube in aerosol can with spray trigger gun. From Lyman Products Corporation.

Price: Spray lube **$6.50**
Price: Trigger gun **$3.95**

MIDWAY

Case Neck Lubricator

Designed for use with liquid or dry lube. Includes six nylon brushes for use with most rifle calibers, two mounting screws and Midway mica lube. From Midway Arms, Inc.

Price: **$9.99**

Mica

Dry lubricant for neck sizing without powder contamination. Available in 4-oz., 1-lb. or 10-lb. quantities. From Midway Arms, Inc.

Price: 4-oz. **$4.99**
Price: 1-lb. **$12.99**
Price: 10 lbs. **$42.99**

Minute Lube

Spray-on sizing lubricant that contains no chlorocarbons. Comes in 6-oz. can. From Midway Arms, Inc.

Price: **$5.99**

PONSNESS/WARREN

STOS Lubricant

Moisture resistant non-petroleum lubricant for case sizing. Comes in 2-oz. jar. From Ponsness/Warren.

Price: **$5.20**

RCBS

Case Lube 2

Water soluble non-toxic lube applied to cases using case lube pad or fingers. Available in 2-oz. bottle or 1-gal. size. From RCBS.

Price: 2-oz. **$2.58**
Price: 1-gal. **$97.48**

Case Lube Pad

For lubing cases or bullet jackets before sizing or forming. From RCBS.

Price: **$6.93**

Case Slick Lube

Aerosol spray for lubing cases for resizing or case forming. Reduces the force needed to resize cases and helps prevent possibility of denting the shoulder. Comes in 4.5-oz. can. From RCBS.

Price: **$4.41**

RCBS

Lube Kit

Includes case lube pad, 2-oz. bottle of Case Lube 2, accessory handle with case neck brushes for 22- through 30-caliber. From RCBS.

Price: **$14.84**

REDDING

Case Lube Kit

Case lube pad with non-skid feet and 2-oz. bottle of Redding case lubricant. From Redding Reloading Equipment.

Price: Kit **$12.00**
Price: Pad only **$10.00**

Case Lube Kit (Tong Type)

Tongs conform to body walls of any cartridge case from 22 Hornet up to 458 Magnum for lubing. Includes 2-oz. bottle Redding case lubricant. From Redding Reloading Equipment.

Price: **$12.00**

Original Formula Lube

Formulated for tough resizing and forming operations. Comes in 2-oz. squeeze bottle. From Redding Reloading Equipment.

Price: **$3.60**

Water Soluble Case Lube

Water soluble case lubricant ideal for neck sizing and use with straight-wall pistol cases. Comes in 2-oz. squeeze bottle. From Redding Reloading Equipment.

Price: **$3.60**

ROOSTER

Case-Forming Lubricants

Three lubes for resizing and reforming of cases. CFL-56 designed for radical reforming; slightly softer gel with brass protectant built in. CSL-71 is lighter in body and good for cold weather application; good for resizing and moderate reforming operations. CL-WR-14 liquid lube developed for routine resizing of cases. Available in 2-oz. or 4-oz. jar. From Rooster Laboratories.

Price: CFL-56/CSL-71, 2-oz. **$5.00**
Price: CFL-56/CSL-71, 4-oz. **$9.00**
Price: CL-WR-14, 2-oz. **$4.50**
Price: CL-WR-14, 4-oz. **$8.00**

VIBRASHINE

Case Neck Dipper

Cleans and lubes interior of bottleneck cases. Includes plastic housing with removable cover, three brush sizes and mica lubricant. From VibraShine, Inc.

Price: **$7.95**

BRUNO SHOOTER'S SUPPLY

Delrin Loading Block

White delrin loading block holds 20 cartridges of specified caliber, 308, PPC, 222. From Bruno Shooter's Supply.

Price: **$11.95**

Loading Block

Lucite loading block holds 20 cartridges of specified caliber, 308, PPC or 222. From Bruno Shooter's Supply.

Price: **$13.95**

C-H/4-D

Cartridge Rack

Holds 60 cartridges of varying calibers. Too deep for 38 Special, not large enough for 45-70 or 348 but holds all other sizes up to 375 H&H. Comes in black or white. From C-H Tool & Die/4-D Custom Die.

Price: **$2.00**

FLAMBEAU

Loading Blocks

Two durable plastic loading blocks to hold either 50 or 60 cases. Can accommodate most popular calibers. From Flambeau Products Corporation.

Price: . . . . **Contact manufacturer.**

HORNADY

Universal Reloading Block

Holds 50 cases from calibers 32 ACP through 458 Magnum. Made of high-impact plastic. Weight: 1 lb. From Hornady Mfg. Co.

Price: **$3.75**

LYMAN

Loading Block

Twin heavy-duty plastic loading block holds 50 rifle or pistol cases 22- through 45-caliber. From Lyman Products Corporation.

Price: **$4.75**

MIDWAY

Loading Blocks

Wooden trays made for a single caliber or family of calibers. Made of fine-grain hardwood and lightly varnished. A total of 13 trays available for 25 ACP through 50 Sharps. All hold 50 rounds except #9 which holds 32 rounds. From Midway Arms, Inc.

Price: **$6.79**

MTM

Loading Trays

Hard plastic trays in two models, Universal and Compact. Universal holds rifle cartridges 17- through 45-caliber; 9mm, 38 and 45 pistol cartridges. Compact tray holds all calibers of rifle and pistol. From MTM Moulded Products Company.

Price: . . . . **Contact manufacturer.**

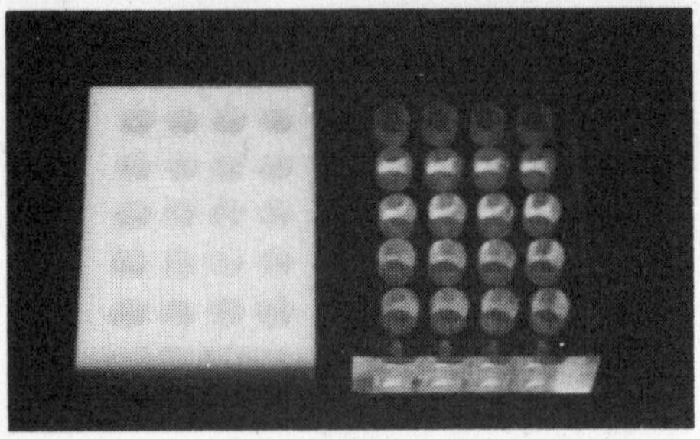

Bruno Delrin and Lucite Blocks

Hornady Universal Block

Midway Blocks

MTM Loading Tray

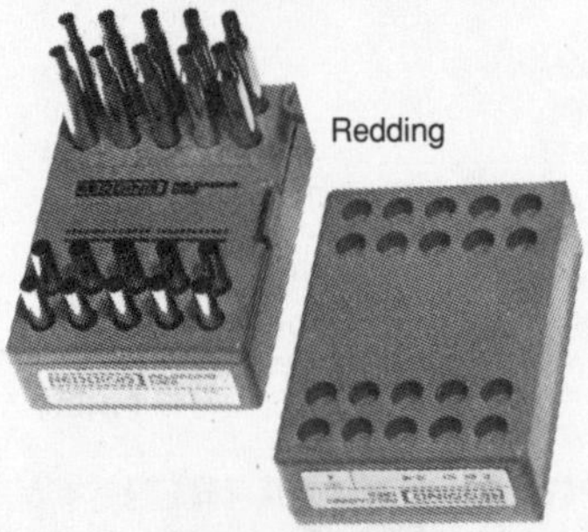

Redding

RCBS Loading Block

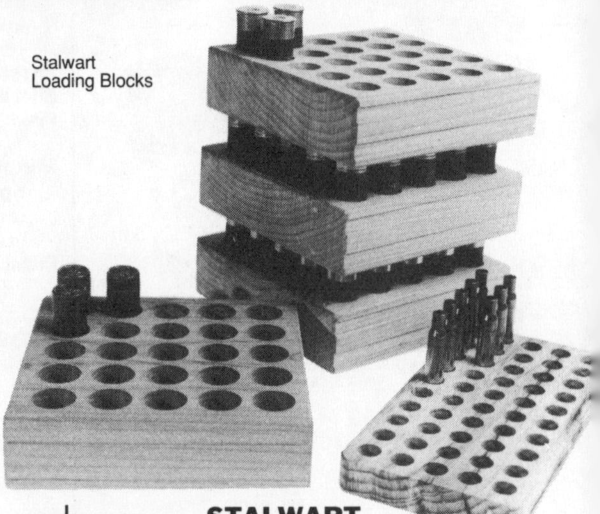

Stalwart Loading Blocks

RCBS

Case Loading Blocks

Heavy plastic blocks hold up to 40 pistol/rifle cases. Features two hole sizes with inside steps to accept most popular calibers. From RCBS.

Price: **$4.75**

REDDING

Combo Die Box/Loading Block

Hard plastic box. Top has provision for 20 cartridges with base size up to 30-06; 20 magnum base size cartridges. From Redding Reloading Equipment.

Price: **$4.50**

STALWART

Loading Blocks

Wooden 25- and 50-hole loading blocks for rifle, handgun calibers and shotshell gauges from 25 ACP through 570 Nitro and 10, 12, 20 and 410 gauges. The 20-ga. block also suitable for 50 BMG. Shotshell blocks stackable for storage. From Stalwart Corporation.

Price: **$5.99**
Price: 25-hole shotshell **$6.99**
Price: 50-hole shotshell **$12.99**

TRICO PLASTICS

Case Holders

Stackable plastic blocks to hold 38- or 45-caliber pistol cases and most rifle cases. Each tray holds up to 150 cases. From Trico Plastics.

Price: **$3.85**

C-H/4-D
Hand/Power Primer Pocket Kit

Electric screwdriver kit for cleaning or reaming primer pockets. Includes both large and small primer pocket brushes, large and small primer pocket reamers, 1/4" hex adapter which fits most battery/electric screwdrivers and a plastic handle for manual operation. All parts have 8-32 threads. From C-H Tool & Die/4-D Custom Die.

Price: **$12.95**
Price: Handle **$2.50**
Price: Adapter **$2.95**
Price: Brush, large or small **$1.95**
Price: Reamer, large or small **$2.95**

FORSTER
"E-Z-Just" Primer Seater

Features automatic 40-primer feed with built-in primer flipper and loading tray. Primer tube has open slot for safely stacking primers sideways. Tool's jaws accommodate most modern Boxer-primed rifle and pistol cartridges with rim thickness of .050" to .072". Comes with small and large primer tubes. Weight: 3 lbs. From Forster Products.

Price: **$56.00**

HART
Heads for Primer Seater

Replacement heads for discontinued Hart primer seater. Available for PPC, Remington BR and 222 Remington. From Robert Hart & Son, Inc.

Price: **$25.45**

JONES
Decapping Tool

For decapping cases as a separate operation to prevent die contamination. Reversible shellholder head takes either .378" or .473" case heads. Decapping mandrels screw off. Mandrels available for 222, 6mm, 7mm and 30 calibers; other calibers available on request. Comes complete for one caliber. Weight: 1 lb. From Neil Jones Custom Products.

Price: **$35.00**
Price: Extra mandrels **$8.00**
Price: Non-standard mandrels . . . **$10.00**
Price: Shellholder **$10.00**

LEE
Auto Prime

Hand tool with auto feed system. Large or small primer tray affixed to hand tool with shellholder. Built-in primer flipper turns primers right side up. From Lee Precision, Inc.

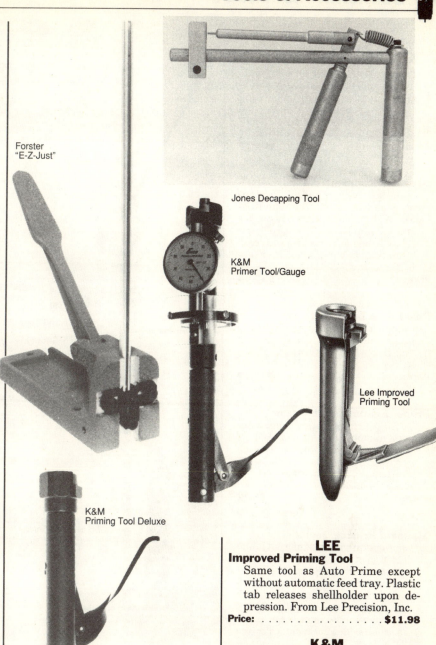

Price: **$16.98**

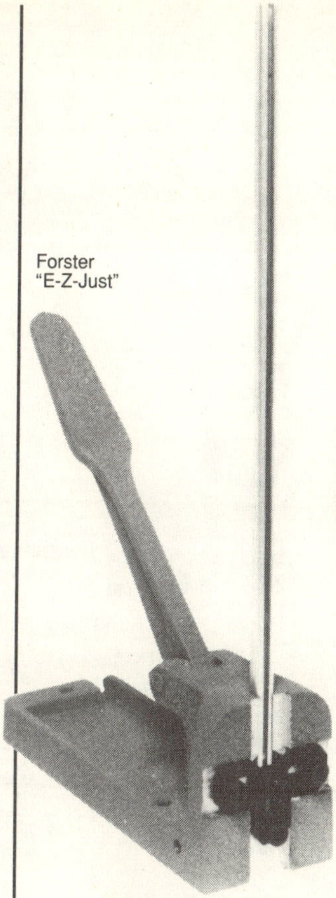

Forster "E-Z-Just"

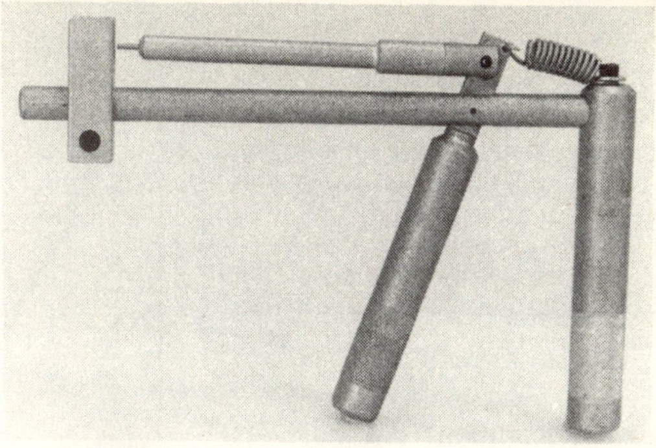

Jones Decapping Tool

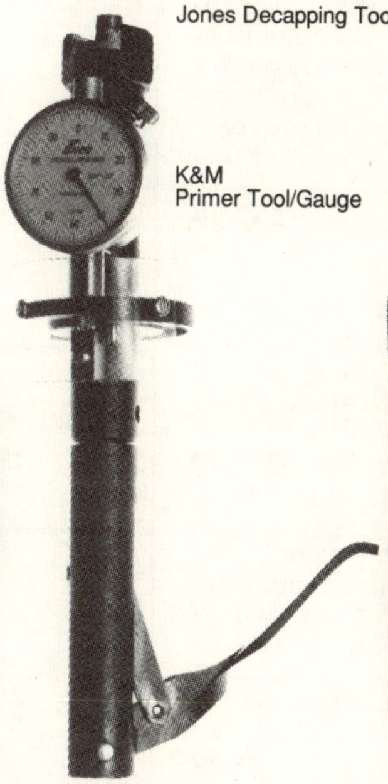

K&M Primer Tool/Gauge

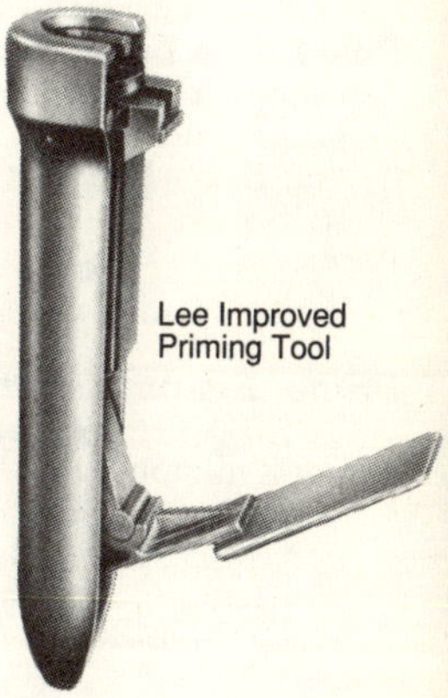

Lee Improved Priming Tool

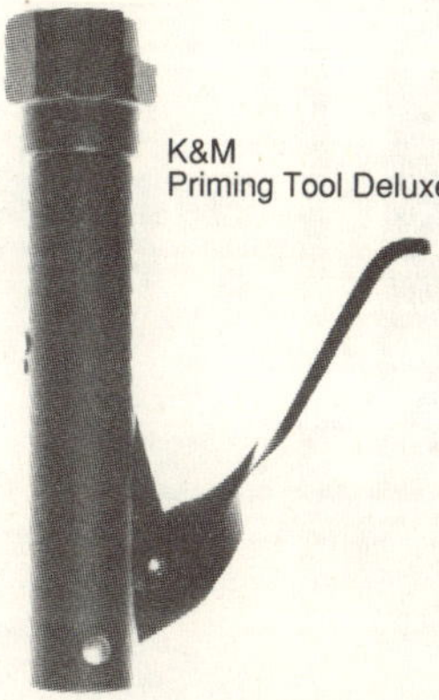

K&M Priming Tool Deluxe

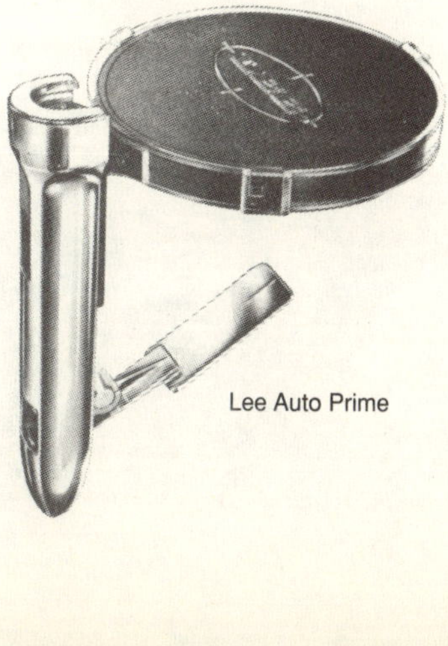

Lee Auto Prime

LEE
Improved Priming Tool

Same tool as Auto Prime except without automatic feed tray. Plastic tab releases shellholder upon depression. From Lee Precision, Inc.

Price: **$11.98**

K&M
Primer Tool/Gauge

Dial indicator attached to K&M priming tool eliminates variables in primer seating and allows primers to be seated to exact same depth. Both large and small primer stations and shellholder for specified caliber are included. From K&M Services.

Price: **$97.50**

Priming Tool Deluxe

In-line primer seater with controlled feel. Primer shroud spring-loaded to push upward squarely on shellholder. Shellholder position adjustable up or down to feel primer seat. Comes complete with shellholder of choice. From K&M Services.

Price: **$39.95**

RCBS

Automatic Priming Tool

One-hand, one-step priming tool. Primers feed through an auto prime feed tube. Single-stage lever system gives sensitive and positive seating feel. Two primer rod assemblies and primer feed tubes included. Shellholder not included. From RCBS.

Price: **$62.93**

Berdan Decapping Tool

Handles wide range of Berdan-primed cases such as the 8mm Rimless, 6.5mm Mannlicher-Schoenauer and 11.7mm Rimmed. Made of heat-treated steel alloy. Comes with case holder and Allen wrench. From RCBS.

Price: **$39.88**

Posi-Prime Hand Tool

Compact, hand-held tool. Primer plugs and sleeves for large and small primers included. From RCBS.

Price: **$16.79**

Primer Seating Depth Gauge

To check primer seating depth without a micrometer. One end of gauge "rocks" on a primer-high case head; opposite end rests flat on primer-low case head. Made of hardened ground steel. From RCBS.

Price: **$5.72**

Standard Priming Tool

Cam-operated for sensitivity and detection of oversized or undersized pockets. Will accept most popular shellholders. Tool attaches to bench with C-clamp or bolts. Comes with two primer rod assemblies for all American-made Boxer-type primers. Shellholder not included. From RCBS.

Price: **$39.18**

SINCLAIR

Priming Tool

Precision machined hand tool with stainless steel body and anodized aluminum handle. Manually "locks" case head flush and at right angle with priming punch to ensure alignment and eliminate influence of case rim on primer seating. Designed for use with Lee Auto-Prime shellholders. Comes complete with instructions and push rods for both large and small primers. From Sinclair International, Inc.

Price: **$75.00**

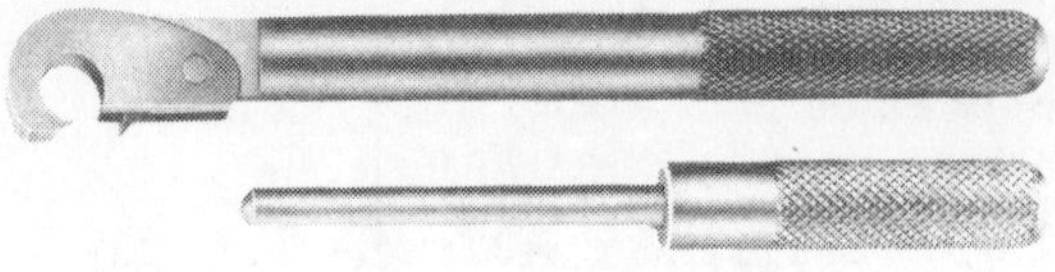

RCBS Berdan Decapper

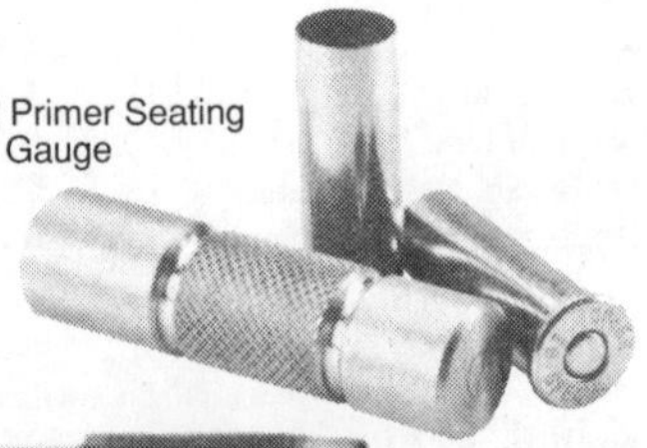

RCBS Primer Seating Depth Gauge

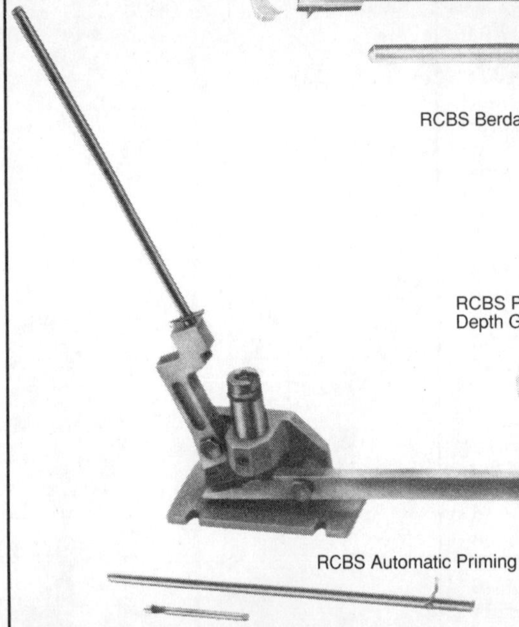

RCBS Automatic Priming Tool

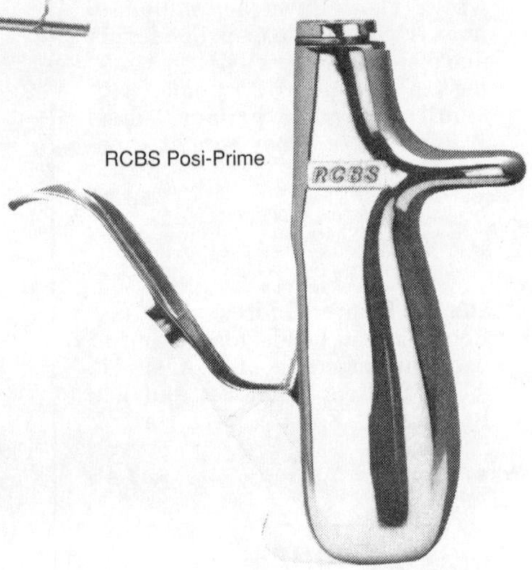

RCBS Posi-Prime

RCBS Standard Tool

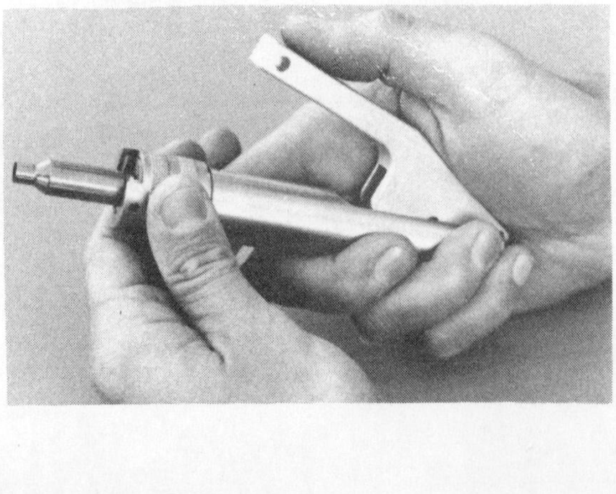

Sinclair Priming Tool

C-H/4-D

50 BMG Priming Accessories

Swage punch, priming post, shellholder and shellholder die with lock ring. Swage punch used with priming tool removes crimp from military primer pockets. Priming post and shellholder can be used with any Hollywood press. With the addition of the shellholder die, these accessories can be used on any press with 7/8" top threads. Sold separately or as complete set. From C-H Tool & Die/4-D Custom Die.

Price: Swage punch **$11.95**
Price: Priming post **$11.95**
Price: Shellholder **$17.95**
Price: Shellholder die **$9.95**
Price: Priming assembly **$39.50**
Price: Primer/swage assembly . . . **$39.50**
Price: Complete set **$49.50**

Automatic Primer Feed

Fits all C-H/4-D "H"-type presses. Available in large, small or conversion for large to small and vise versa. From C-H Tool & Die/4-D Custom Die.

Price: Large or small **$29.95**
Price: Both large and small **$39.95**
Price: Conversion **$12.50**

Magnum H Press Primer Arm

Replacement for original Magnum H-Press primer arm. Will work with all current snap-in shellholders and comes with both large and small primer punches. Replacement parts are available. From C-H Tool & Die/4-D Custom Die.

Price: **$12.00**

Primer Pocket Swage

Removes crimp from any military case. No stripper washers needed; hardened swage punches; use with any reloading press and standard shellholder; large and small primer swage punches furnished. From C-H Tool & Die/4-D Custom Die.

Price: **$16.95**
Price: Shellholder **$4.50**

Priming Tool

All steel priming tool that fits any reloading press with standard snap-in shellholder and 7/8-14 dies. Complete with large and small priming punches and cups. From C-H Tool & Die/4-D Custom Die.

Price: **$14.95**

Swage/Prime Combo

Primer pocket swage complete plus priming tool punch body, base and both large and small punches and cups. From C-H Tool & Die/4-D Custom Die.

Price: **$23.95**

C-H/4-D

Universal Priming Arm

Fits most "C"-type presses. Seats all sizes of primers. Complete with both large and small posts and cups. From C-H Tool & Die/4-D Custom Die.

Price: **$6.95**

DILLON

RL 1050 and XL 650 Priming System

For switching to large or small primer feed. From Dillon Precision Products, Inc.

Price: RL 1050 . . . . **$29.95**
Price: XL 650 . . . . **$49.25**

HUNTINGTON

Berdan Primer Seater

RCBS ram prime unit adapted to take the RCBS Berdan primer assembly to seat Berdan primers using reloading press. Unit fits in the top of press and primer assembly in a holder in the shellholder slot of press ram. Three size assemblies available to accommodate three Berdan primer sizes. From Huntington Die Specialties.

Price: Primer seater **$15.43**
Price: Primer seater assembly, .217, .240, .255 . . . . **$10.06**
Price: Shellholder head drilled to fit **$15.00**

LEE

Auto-Prime II

Uses standard shellholders and will fit any brand loading press with vertical ram. Primes on upstroke. Includes primer feeders and punches for both large and small primers. Primer trap detaches for filling. Primers positioned correctly by shaking tray. From Lee Precision, Inc.

Price: **$16.98**

Ram Prime

Primes on the press up-stroke. Includes punches for both large and small primers. Fits all brands of presses. From Lee Precision, Inc.

Price: **$11.98**

RCBS

Auto Primer Feed Combo

Feeds primers one at a time into primer plug and sleeve. Comes with 100-count primer tube, large or small. Fits most RCBS and C-type presses. Does not fit RS-2, 3, or 5, or Partner press. From RCBS.

Price: Combo **$19.79**
Price: Feed tube, large or small . . . **$8.30**

RCBS

Primer Catcher

Attaches without screws to Reloader Special, Jr. and Rock Chucker presses. From RCBS.

Price: **$5.94**

Primer Pocket Swager Combo

Removes primer-pocket crimp from military cases. Creates primer pocket correct in dimension for Boxer-type primers. Comes with swager heads for large and small pockets; fits nearly all 7/8"-14 presses with removable shellholders. From RCBS.

Price: **$73.15**
Price: AmmoMaster swager **$23.11**

Primer Tray-2

Designed to position primers anvil side up for insertion into primer arm sleeve or anvil down for loading automatic primer feed tubes. Holds 100 primers. From RCBS.

Price: **$3.57**

Ram Priming Unit

Works with any press with 7/8"-14 thread and removable shellholder. Seats the primer at the top of the press stroke. Also allows pre-setting of positive stop for reload speed. Includes primer rod assemblies for all rifle and pistol Boxer-type primers. From RCBS.

Price: **$15.43**

Universal Decapping Die

Removes primers from uncleaned, unlubricated cases prior to tumbling. Handles calibers 22 through 45. Includes die body, decapping assembly with lock nut, die lock ring and plastic storage box. From RCBS.

Price: **$11.09**

Universal Primer Arm

Accessory for Reloader Special, Jr. and Rock Chucker presses. Flat return spring prevents jamming. Plugs and sleeves included. Does not fit RS-2, 3, or 5, or Partner press. From RCBS.

Price: Primer arm **$9.90**
Price: Plugs and sleeves **$2.76**

REDDING

Automatic Primer Feeder

Designed for Model 7 and Model 25 presses to eliminate handling of primers during sizing. Comes complete with individualized tubes for large and small primers. Capacity for approximately 75 primers. From Redding Reloading Equipment.

Price: Model 7 press **$18.00**
Price: Model 25 press **$20.00**

DEWEY

"Baby Crocogator"

Cleans both large and small primer pockets. Tool ends are radiused to conform to pocket contours. Small diamond-shaped teeth assure proper cleaning. Made from hardened steel. From J. Dewey Mfg. Co., Inc.

Price: **$2.95**

DILLON

Super Swage 600

Swages primer pockets of military brass. Case is supported from inside to prevent tearing of the rim. Tool steel hardened swage rod, changeable from large to small primers, rolls crimp away. No reaming necessary. Compound cam leverage system assures alignment. From Dillon Precision Products, Inc.

Price: **$59.95**

FORSTER

Primer Pocket Chamfering Tool

To remove crimp from military brass. Tool fits both small and large primer pockets and can be used on any Forster case trimmer with primer pocket center. Weight: 4 oz. From Forster Products.

Price: **$13.50**
Price: Primer pocket center **$6.00**

Primer Pocket Cleaner

Scraper-type tool that mounts in the cutter shaft of the Forster case trimmer in place of the pilot; the hardened case mouth center mounts in the trimmer collet. Same center cleans both large (.210) and small (.175) primer pockets. Weight: 3 oz. From Forster Products.

Price: **$6.00**

HART

Internal Flash Hole Debur Tool

Hand-held stainless steel tool with steel cutter for removing burrs around primer flash hole. Available in two sizes: standard for U.S. cases and small for PPC cases. From Robert Hart & Son, Inc.

Price: **$13.95**

Primer Pocket Cleaner

Cleans both large and small primer pockets. Knurled body for easy gripping. From Robert Hart & Son, Inc.

Price: **$7.40**

Primer Depth Reamer

Made of tool steel with adjustable cutter to assure uniform primer pocket depth. Comes in either large or small size. From Robert Hart & Son, Inc.

Price: **$14.25**
Price: Replacement cutter **$5.50**

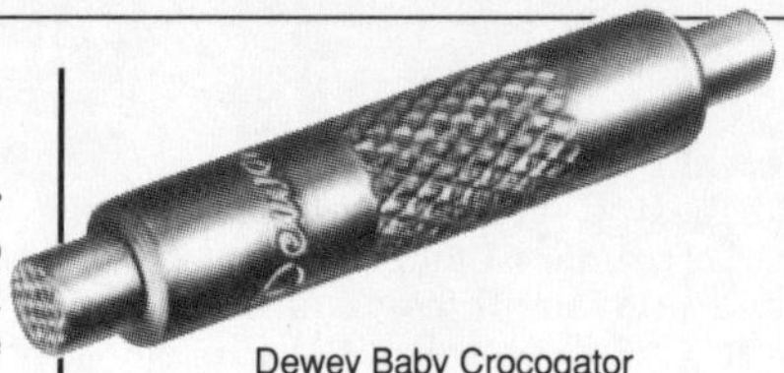

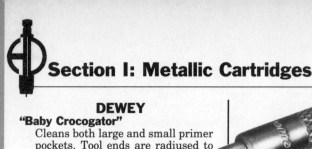

Dewey Baby Crocogator

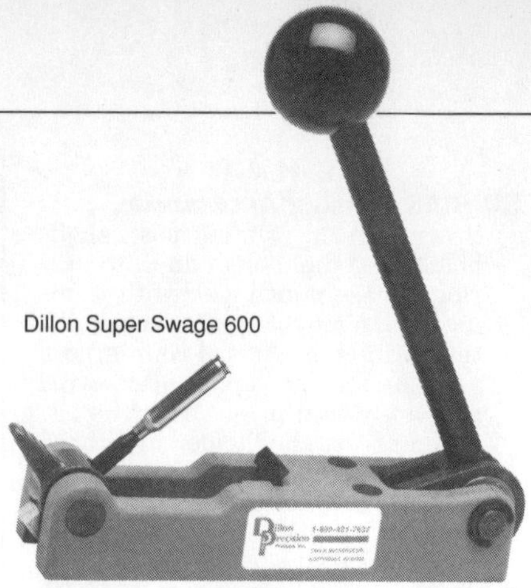

Dillon Super Swage 600

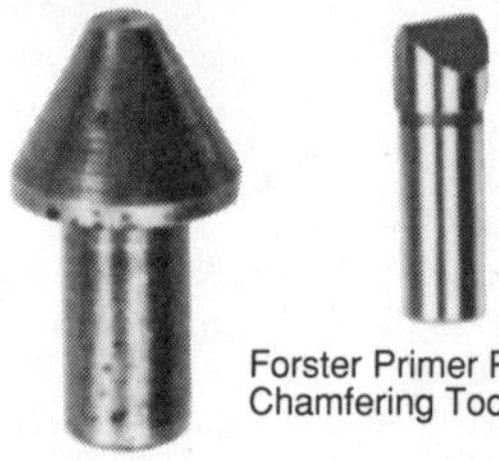

Forster Primer Pocket Chamfering Tool

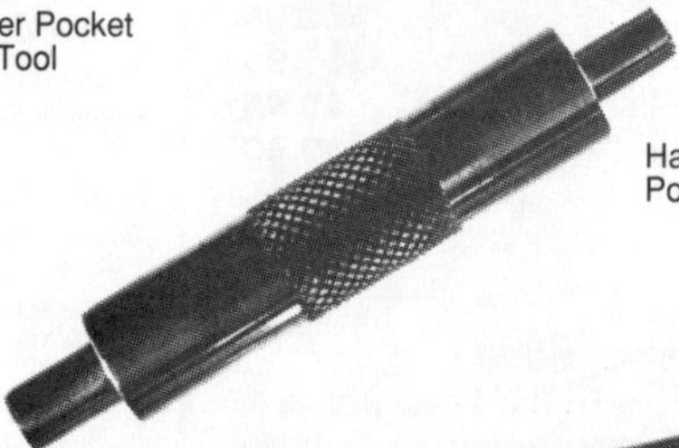

Hart Primer Pocket Cleaner

Forster Primer Pocket Cleaner

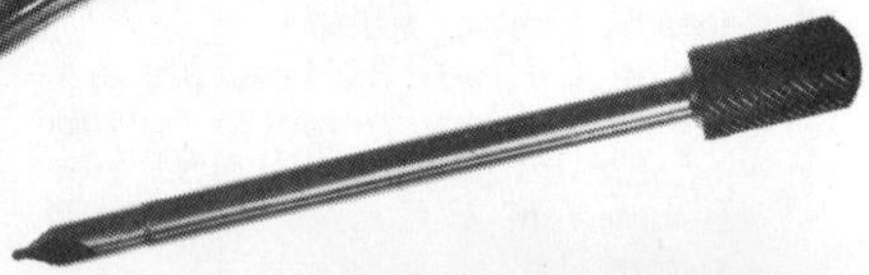

Hart Flash Hole Deburrer

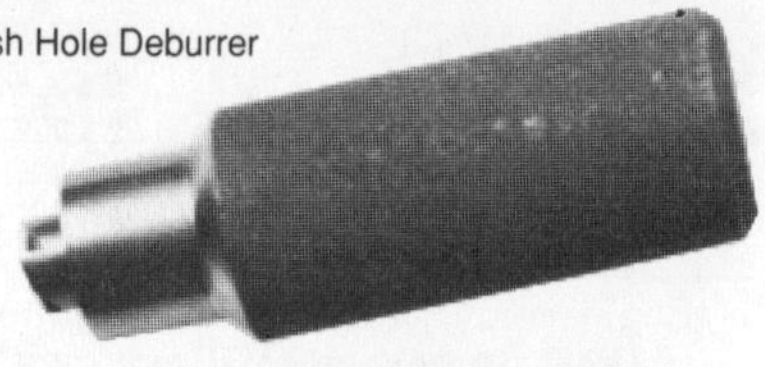

K&M Reamer

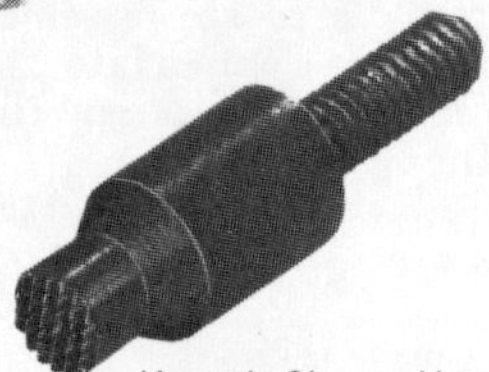

Hornady Cleaner Head

Jones Uniforming Fixture

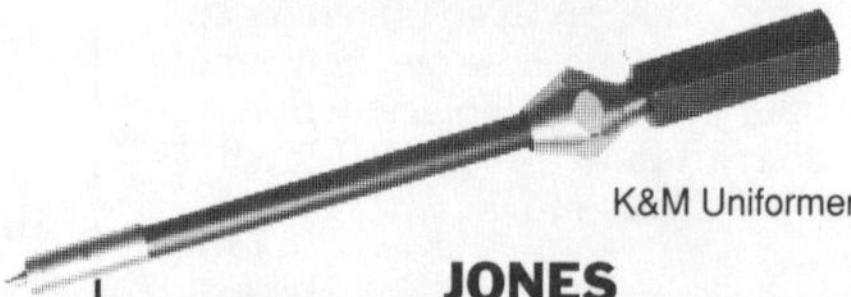

K&M Uniformer

HORNADY

Primer Pocket Cleaners

Metal cleaner heads to remove fouling from large or small primer pockets. Use in conjunction with Universal accessory handle. From Hornady Mfg. Co.

Price: **$3.70**
Price: Handle **$2.85**

Primer Pocket Reamer

Cuts away crimp from military brass. Available for large or small primer pockets. Comes separately or with accessory handle. From Hornady Mfg. Co.

Price: **$5.65**
Price: Complete with handle **$7.05**

JONES

Primer Pocket Uniforming Fixture

Holds cases square to cutter for uniform cutting. Uses Whitetail or Sinclair cutters. Comes with one shellholder. From Neil Jones Custom Products.

Price: **$64.50**
Price: Cutters **$18.00**
Price: Handle **$7.50**

K&M

Flash Hole Uniformer

Patented tool for benchresters to precisely ream, debur and chamfer the inside of flashhole. Features a pre-set depth stop surrounding steel cutter which is referenced to inside-bottom of case not case mouth. Reversible sliding centering cone supplied to keep case aligned and centered during uniforming operation. Accepts all pistol and rifle brass from 22- through 458-caliber. Standard uniformer .080"; PPC/BR .0625". Available in "Master" or "Pro" models. From K&M Services.

Price: Master **$9.50**
Price: Pro **$14.50**
Price: Replacement cutter **$5.00**

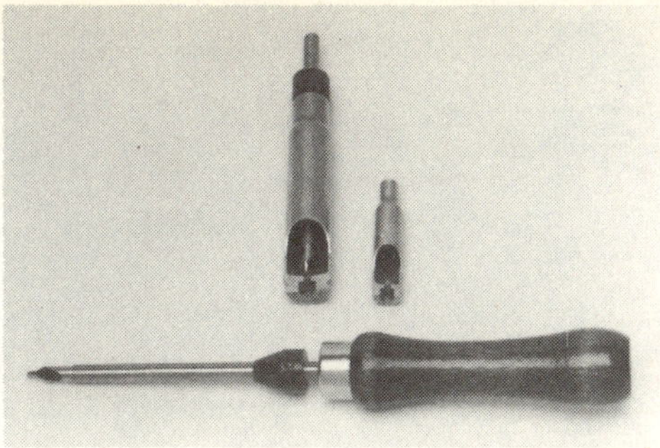

Lyman Flash Hole Tool

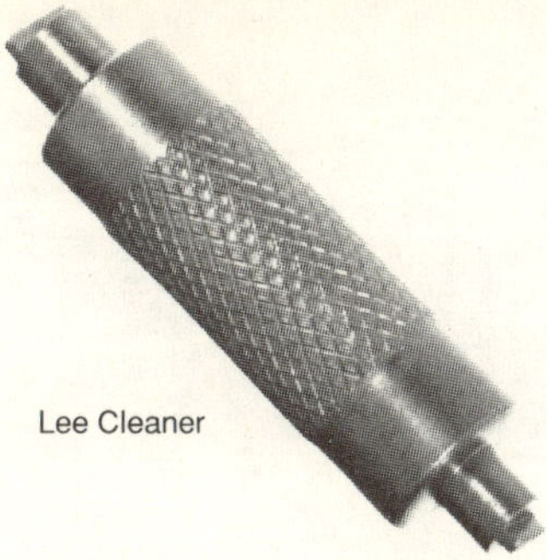

Lee Cleaner

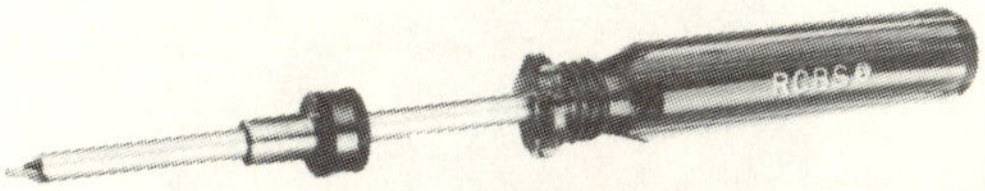

RCBS Flash Hole Debur Tool

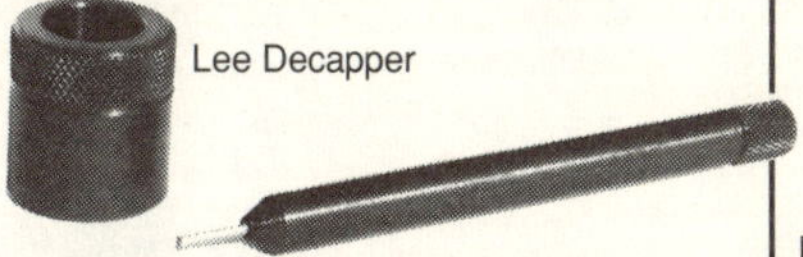

Lee Decapper

Lyman Ream Cleaner

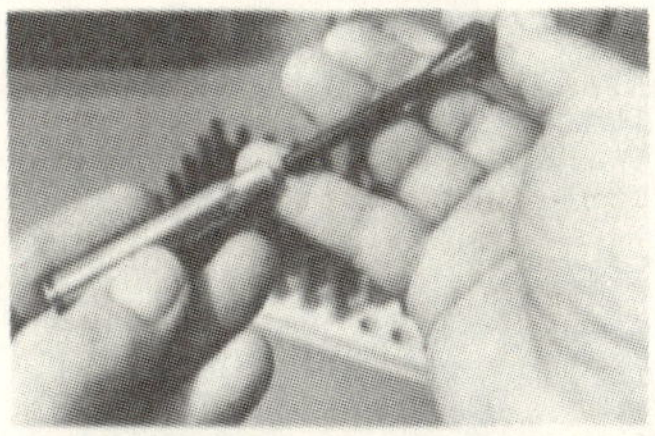

Sinclair Flash Hole Deburrer

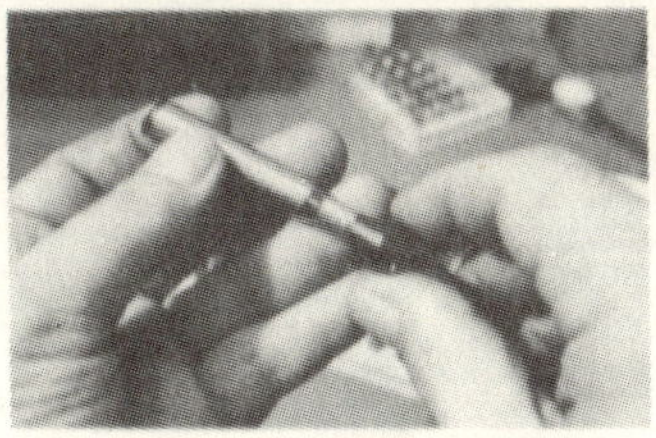

Lyman Primer Pocket Cleaner

LEE

Primer Pocket Cleaner
Double ended design cleans both large and small primer pockets. From Lee Precision, Inc.
Price: **$1.58**

Decapper and Base
Removes crimped-in primers from military cases. From Lee Precision, Inc.
Price: **$3.78**

LYMAN

Flash Hole Uniformer
Removes internal flash hole burrs. Features tool steel cutter with adjustable stop collar for use with any size case. Comes with wood handle. From Lyman Products Corporation.
Price: **$10.50**

Primer Pocket Cleaner
Cleans fouling from primer pocket bottoms. Wooden handle included. Available in large or small sizes. From Lyman Products Corporation.
Price: **$9.20**

Primer Pocket Reamer
Removes military crimps and rough metal edges from primer pocket. Comes with wooden handle. Available in large or small sizes. From Lyman Products Corporation.
Price: **$9.20**

Primer Pocket Uniformer
Assures uniform primer depth with pre-set stop collar set to SAAMI specs. Available in large and small sizes. From Lyman Products Corporation.
Price: **$17.95**

PEM'S

Pedestal Crank
Use with PEM primer pocket cleaner brush for faster operation. Drilled and tapped for bench mounting. From PEM'S Mfg. Co.
Price: **$7.50**

Primer Pocket Cleaner
Fine steel wire brush with metal sleeve. Specify large or small primer pocket. Manual tool or can be used in any motor or hand-driven chuck. From PEM'S Mfg. Co.
Price: **$1.50**

RCBS

Flash Hole Deburring Tool
Removes flash-hole burrs from inside. Features self-locating pilot stop collar to prevent removal of too much brass. Threaded shaft can be chucked into an electric drill. Pilot not included. From RCBS.
Price: **$9.49**
Price: Pilot **$2.58**

Primer Pocket Brush Combo
Removes residue from primer pockets. Brushes have stainless bristles and interchangeable mounts for large and small primer pockets. Comes as combo with accessory handle or as separate components. From RCBS.
Price: Combo **$12.07**
Price: Brush only, large or small . . **$5.24**
Price: Accessory handle **$3.36**

Primer Pocket Hex Adapter
Converts Primer Pocket Brush from manual to power tool. Hex adapter fits most standard power drills or cordless screwdrivers. From RCBS.
Price: **$2.15**

SINCLAIR

Decap Punches and Bases
Removes crimped-in primers on military brass. Case hardened base collects spent primers. Punches and bases ordered separately by cartridge. From Sinclair International, Inc.
Price: Base **$2.28**
Price: Punch **$5.67**

Flash Hole Debur Tool
Cutting depth controlled by hexagon stop tapered to center the cutting shaft during deburring operation. Will work on rifle and pistol cases from 22- through 45-caliber. 50 BMG debur/uniformer tool also available. From Sinclair International, Inc.
Price: **$15.75**
Price: 50 BMG **$39.50**

SINCLAIR

PPC Flash Hole Debur Tool

To accommodate the different internal case head designs of Russian 220 and new PPC cases being imported, this flash hole tool has no preset cutting depth. From Sinclair International, Inc.

Price: **$15.75**

Primer Pocket Uniformer

Precision ground from solid carbide in large rifle, large pistol and small rifle/pistol. Use in drill or drill press ($^3/_8$" chuck) for uniforming primer pockets to correct depth or mount in handle for use as hand tool. Handle is anti-fatigue style with stainless steel insert for holding cutter. From Sinclair International, Inc.

Price: **$18.00**
Price: With handle **$25.50**

VIBRASHINE

Power Brush

Vibratory action cleans fouling from primer pockets or with case neck brush becomes case neck cleaner. Push-button on/off switch. 120-volt AC. From VibraShine, Inc.

Price: **$29.95**

WHITETAIL DESIGN

Match Prep Deluxe

Primer pocket uniformer with anodized aluminum handle and tungsten carbide tipped cutter. Wrench loosens handle to accept cutter; reverse cutter in handle for protection and storage. Available for large rifle, large pistol and small pistol/rifle. From Whitetail Design and Engineering Ltd.

Price: **$25.50**
Price: Extra cutters **$18.00**
Price: Extra handle **$7.50**

Match Prep Tool

Tungsten carbide tipped primer pocket uniformer in three sizes, small rifle and pistol, large rifle and large pistol. Knurled body for gripping. From Whitetail Design and Engineering Ltd.

Price: **$22.50**

Primer Pocket Cleaner

Tungsten carbide tipped tool with knurled end for gripping. Two sizes fit all large and small primer pockets. From Whitetail Design and Engineering Ltd.

Price: **$12.50**

WILSON

Primer Pocket Reamer

Removes crimp on military brass. Specify large or small primer pocket. From L.E. Wilson, Inc.

Price: **$19.50**

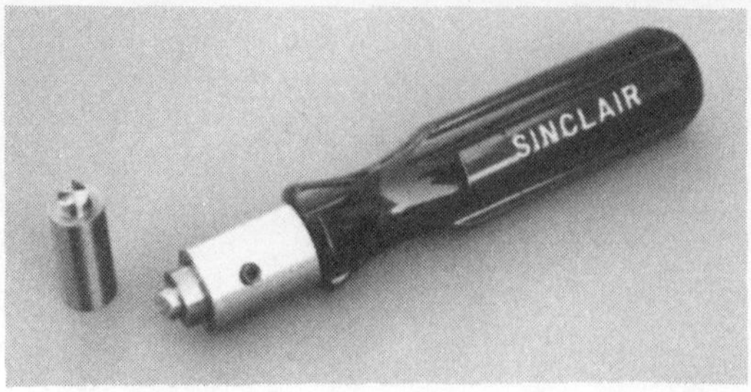

Sinclair Primer Pocket Uniformer

Whitetail Primer Pocket Cleaner

Whitetail Match Prep Tool

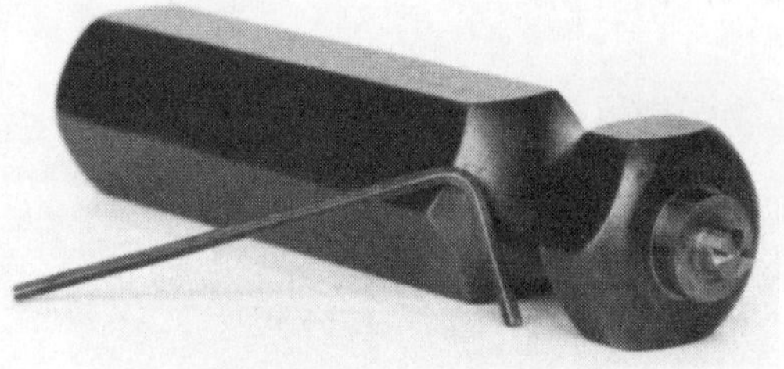

Whitetail Match Prep Deluxe

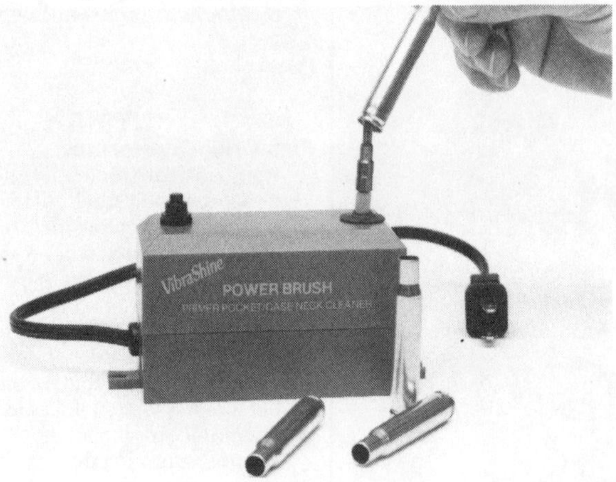

VibraShine Power Pocket Cleaner

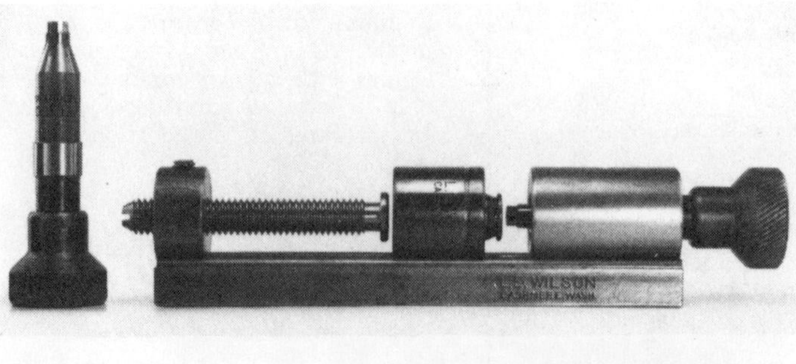

Wilson trimmer set up to ream 45 ACP cases.

BEEMAN

Pena-Dry

Liquid/dry non-sticky lubricant for bearing surfaces of presses and powder measures. Pena-Dry composed of fine particles of molybdenum disulfide suspended in volatile liquid that evaporates and leaves dry lubricant on surface. Comes in 4 oz. bottle. From Beeman.

Price: **$4.95**

C-H/4-D

Cannelure Tool

Solid steel tool for rolling in grooves on bullets prior to crimping or case cannelure on straight-wall cases. Adjustable for depth and height. For bullets from 17- to 45-caliber. Hardened cutting wheel; precision machined. From C-H Tool & Die/4-D Custom Die.

Price: **$34.95**

DILLON

Primer Flip Tray

Heavy tray large enough for new NATO primer package. From Dillon Precision Products, Inc.

Price: **$10.50**

Primer Pickup Tubes

Used to transfer large or small primers from flip tray into 100-primer capacity Dillon auto prime tube. From Dillon Precision Products, Inc.

Price: **$3.50**

DON EAGAN

Bullet Base Chamfering Tool

Designed to bevel bullet base to facilitate full seating of gas checks. Uses scraping action to minimize metal loss. For 22 through 45 calibers. From Donald Eagan.

Price: **$4.00**

FLAMBEAU

Primer Flip Tray

Plastic primer arranger. From Flambeau Products Corporation.

Price: . . . . **Contact manufacturer.**

FORSTER

Hollow Pointer

Use with Forster case trimmers for hollowpointing softpoint jacketed rounds. Available in either 1/8" or 1/16" drill sizes for pistol and rifle cartridges, respectively. Weight: 4 oz. From Forster Products.

Price: **$13.00**

Trimmer Accessory Case

For storing Forster case trimmer collets, pilots, outside neck turner with pilots, neck reamer, primer pocket chamfering tool and cleaner. Double wall construction with positive action latch. Dimensions: 8 1/2 x 5 1/4 x 2. From Forster Products.

Price: **$7.50**

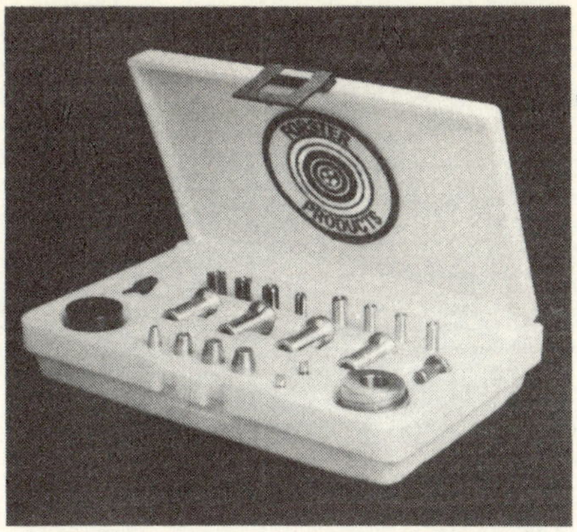

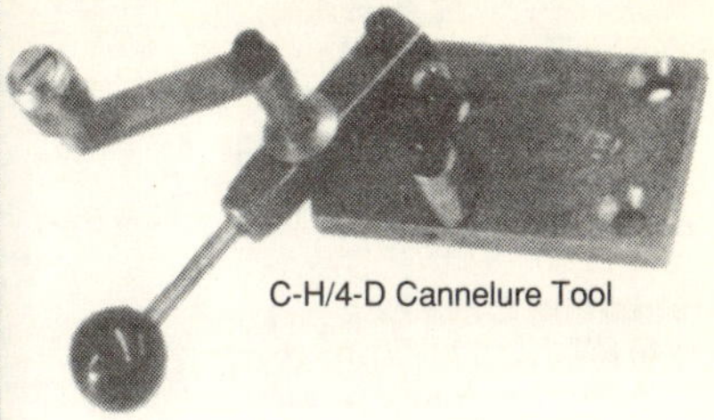

C-H/4-D Cannelure Tool

Forster Case Trimmer Accessory Case

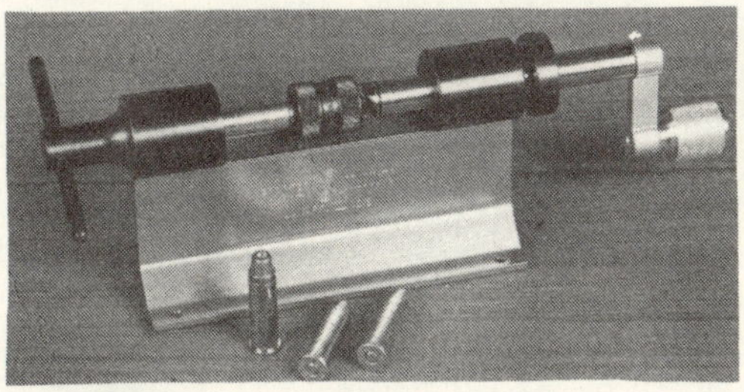

Forster Hollow Pointer

Hornady Primer Turner

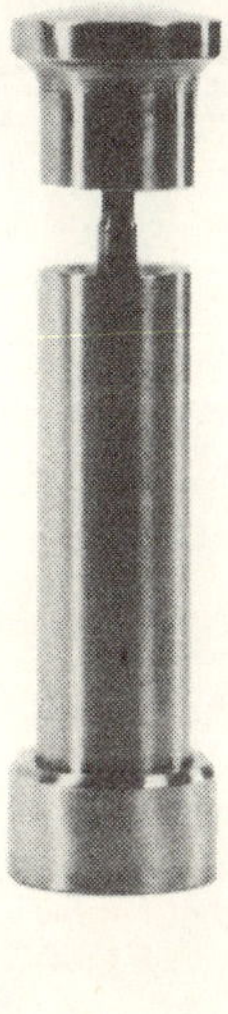

Hart Bullet Seater

Hornady Shooter's Journal

GTM

Hollow Pointer

Hand-operated tool used on loaded cartridges to create hollowpoint bullets. Can also be used in drill press. Available in calibers 22 through 458. From GTM Co.

Price: **$15.95**

HART

Bullet Seater

Depth adjustable straight-line bullet seater with body and head made of stainless steel. From Robert Hart and Son, Inc.

Price: **$96.45**

HORNADY

Shooting Journal

Packaged in weatherproof binder. Contains three styles of sight-in targets with fill-in-the blank load information, preprinted load analysis tables arranged according to firearm and Post-It-Note notepad for recording velocity and trajectory. From Hornady Mfg. Co.

Price: **$19.95**

Primer Turning Tray

Made of sturdy plastic with transparent cover. Weight: 4 oz. From Hornady Mfg. Co.

Price: **$4.25**

LYMAN

Primer Tray

Durable plastic tray flips primers anvil-side up for loading. From Lyman Products Corporation.

Price: **$3.80**

Reloading Data Log

A $8^{1}/_{2}$" x 11" 50-page journal with four large load sections per page to record load data information. Bound in pad and three-hole punched for insertion into binder. From Lyman Products Corporation.

Price: **$4.50**

MA SYSTEMS

Easy Collater Tray

Orients cases or bullets in slotted tray to slide easily into feed tubes. Tray accepts 100 rounds. Dimensions: $8^{1}/_{2}$" x 9". Weight: 12 lbs. From MA Systems.

Price: **$14.95**

MIDWAY

Shooter's Notebook Kit

Notebook with firearms data sheets to record reloading and shooting information plus 100 reloader labels for ammo boxes and five different types of Midway stick-on targets, 100 1" shooting spots, 50 2". From Midway Arms, Inc.

Price: **$25.99**

Price: Notebook only **$19.99**

MTM

Handloaders Log

Space provided for 1000 entries: Date, Range Group Size or Score, Components and Conditions. Reinforced, heavy-duty vinyl three-ring binder. Extra pages available in packs of 50. From MTM Moulded Products Company.

Price: **$9.70**

Primer Flipper Tray

Plastic see-through tray to align primers anvil-side up. From MTM Moulded Products Company.

Price: **$2.28**

RCBS

Hex Key Set

Eight black-oxide heat-treated hex keys in fold-up unit. Fit most Allen screws on RCBS equipment. Case is made of chrome-plated steel. Key sizes: .050, $^{1}/_{16}$", $^{5}/_{64}$", $^{3}/_{32}$", $^{7}/_{64}$", $^{1}/_{8}$", $^{9}/_{64}$" and $^{5}/_{32}$". From RCBS.

Price: **$5.55**

Primer Tray-2

Sturdy plastic tray with 100-primer capacity. Positions primers anvil side up or down . From RCBS.

Price: **$3.47**

MA Systems Easy Collater Tray

Midway Shooter's Notebook Kit

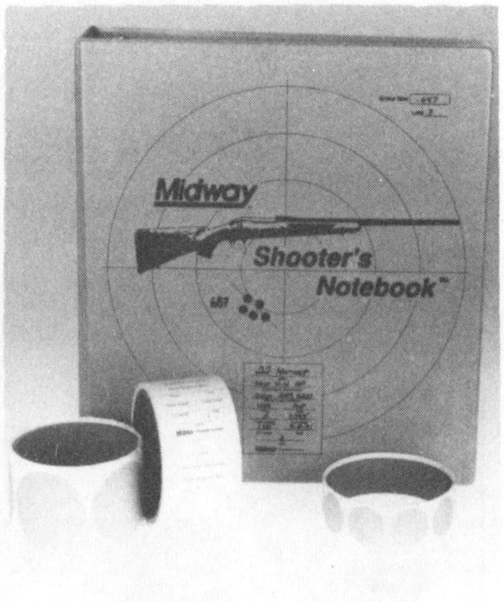

Lyman Reloading Data Log

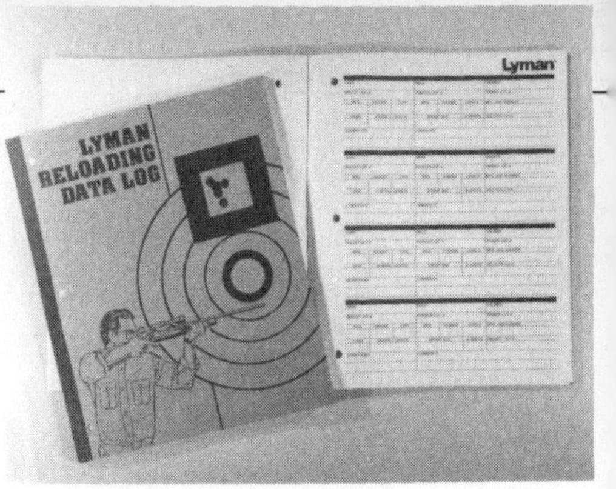

RCBS Primer Flipper Tray

REDDING

Double "C" Clamp

Designed for clamping the Redding powder measure stand and case trimmer to benchtop. Will accommodate bench thickness of up to $2^{1}/_{4}$". From Redding Reloading Equipment.

Price: **$18.00**

RIG

RIG 2 and RIG 3

Aerosol degreaser (RIG 3) and lubricant (RIG 2) for removing sizing and bullet lube from dies and protecting them from rust during storage. Available in 8-oz. spray can or 1-gal. container. From RIG Products.

Price: 8 oz. **$3.00**

Price: 1-gal. **$28.33**

Universal Grease

Semi-solid preservative for storage of dies. Comes in 1-oz., $3^{3}/_{4}$-oz., 15-oz. and 1-gallon jars. From RIG Products.

Price: 1-oz. **$2.58**

Price: $3^{3}/_{4}$-oz. **$4.72**

Price: 15-oz. **$8.84**

Price: 1-gal. **$53.06**

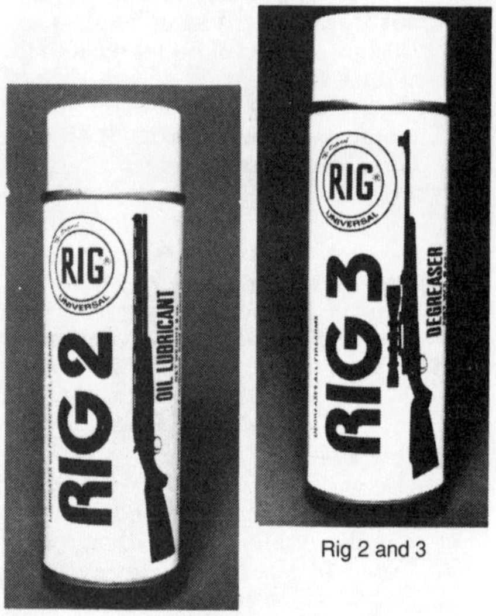

Rig 2 and 3

SINCLAIR

Full-Length Sizing Die

Designed for use on heavy-duty arbor press. Non-adjustable, straight-line die for reforming and resizing cases which have been fired numerous times. Available in most hunting and benchrest calibers. From Sinclair International, Inc.

Price: **$24.00**

TSI 301 Lubricant

TSI

301 Lubricant

A synthetic lubricant/degreaser to clean, protect and lube metal reloading tools. Removes both sizing and bullet lube. Spraying dies prior to storage protects against rust and corrosion. From American Gas & Chemical Co. Ltd.

Price: 6 oz. aerosol **$5.40**
Price: 11 oz. aerosol **$7.60**
Price: 21 oz. pump **$9.45**
Price: 1-gal. can **$35.00**
Price: 5-gal. can **$133.00**
Price: 55-gal. drum **$1,416.00**

WHITETAIL DESIGN

Bushing for L.E. Wilson Neck Size Die

Carbide bushing available in 6mm only. Soon will be offered in 22-caliber. From Whitetail Design and Engineering Ltd.

Price: **$30.00**

Whitetail Bushing for Wilson Neck Size Die

WILSON

Chamber Type Bullet Seater

Positively controls both bullet and case alignment during seating operation. Case pushed firmly into die and bullet pushed straight into case by precision fitting plunger sliding in alignment. Available in most popular calibers. From L.E. Wilson, Inc.

Price: **$45.05**

Neck Sizing Die

Precision hand die used with either small mallet or arbor press to control and/or change incrementally cartridge case neck reduction through a series of interchangeable bushings. Bushings available in increments of .001", from .236 through .343. All neck dies size neck to $^{3}/_{16}$" from mouth end. Available with or without one bushing. From L.E. Wilson, Inc.

Price: With bushing **$55.65**
Price: Without bushing **$44.52**
Price: Bushing **$11.13**

WILSON/SINCLAIR

Micrometer Bullet Seater

Same features as Wilson chamber bullet seater but seating depth precisely controlled by seating micrometer. From Sinclair International, Inc.

Price: **$64.60**

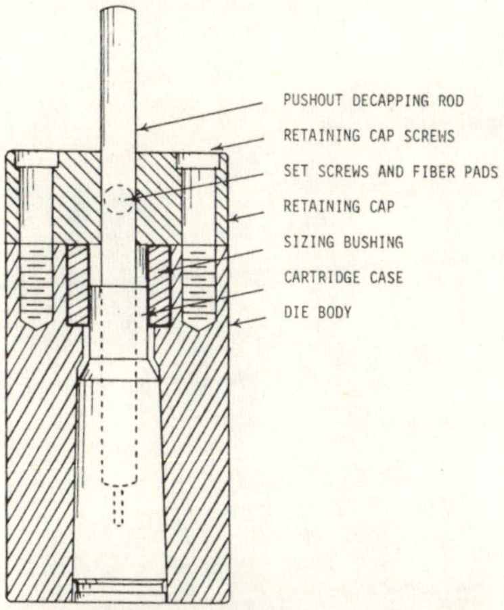

Wilson Neck Sizing Die

WILSON
Neck Sizer Rifle Calibers

218 Bee	250 Savage
219 Donaldson	257 Roberts
22 Hornet	264 Win. Mag.
22 PPC	6.5x55
22 PPC SAKO	270 Win.
22 Remington BR	280/7mm Exp.
22-250	284 Win.
220 Swift	7mm Rem. BR
22 Remington FB	7mm Rem. Mag.
222 Remington	7mm TCU
222 Rem. Mag.	7mmx57 Mauser
223 Remington	7mm-08
243 Winchester	7mm IHMSA
6mm PPC	30-06
6mm PPC SAKO	30-30
6mm Remington	30-338
6mmx47	300 Win. Mag.
6mm Rem. BR	308 Win.
25-06	

WILSON
Bullet Seater Calibers

17 Rem.	25-06
218 Bee	250 Savage
219 Donaldson	257 Roberts
22 Hornet	6.5x55
22 PPC	270 Win.
22 PPC SAKO	280/7mm Express
22 Rem. BR	284 Win.
22-250	7mm Rem. BR
220 Swift	7mm Rem. Mag.
221 Rem. FB	7mm TCU
222 Rem.	7mmx57 Mauser
222 Rem. Mag.	7mm-08
223 Rem.	7mm IHMSA
225 Win.	30-06
243 Win.	30-30
6mm PPC	30-338
6mm PPC SAKO	300 H&H
6mm Rem.	300 Win. Mag.
6mmx47	308 Win.
6mm Rem. BR	338 Win. Mag.

Wilson Chamber Type Bullet Seater

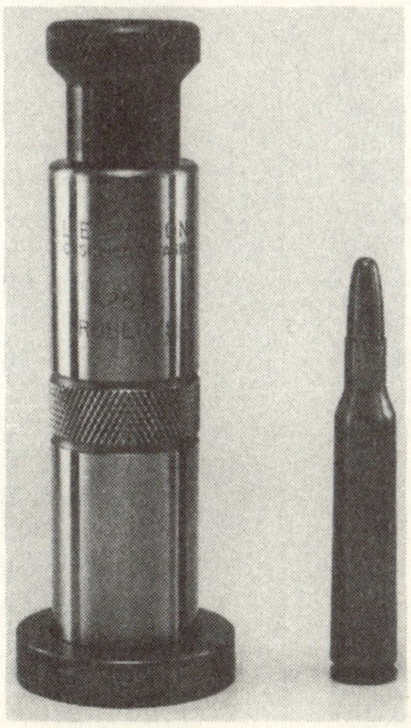

AMMO LOAD Boxing Inspection Table

Boxes loaded ammunition at the rate of 250 rounds per minute in multiples of 30 or 50. For operation on 110-volt, 60 cycles; 220-volt, 50 cycles also available. Same dimensions and weight of standard inspection table. Kit to convert standard Case Vibratory Inspection Table available. From Ammo Load, Inc.

Price: 110v **$2,940.00**
Price: 220v **$3,137.00**
Price: Conversion Kit **$805.00**

AMMO LOAD Case Vibratory Inspection Table

Vibratory inspection table for 38 Special or 357 Magnum cases. Shaking action removes foreign particles from empty cases as they move into position to be inspected and counted. Capacity for over 1,200 cases. For operation on 110-volt, 60 cycles; 220-volt, 50 cycles also available. Dimensions: 38" x 18" x 20". Weight: 127 lbs. From Ammo Load, Inc.

Price: 110v **$2,205.00**
Price: 220v **$2,402.00**
Price: Conversion Kit for 44 Magnum **$392.00**

Ammo Load Mark III

AMMO LOAD Mark III

Calibers: 38 Special, 357 Magnum, 45 ACP, 9mm (standard); 38 S&W, 380 Auto, 44 Magnum, 44 S&W (special order); 25 Auto, 30 Carbine, 32 Auto, 32 S&W Long, 32 S&W Short, 38 Auto, 41 Magnum, 45 Long Colt, 10mm, 40 S&W (custom order)
Rounds Per Hour: 3,600-5,000
Dimensions: 25" x 31$^1/_2$" x 29$^3/_4$"
Weight: 315 lbs.
Features: Foot-switch activated $^1/_2$-hp motor on 110-volt (standard) or 220-volt; automatic case feeder with 500 case capacity; primer magazine; 32-oz. capacity powder flask with removable filter screen; bullet feed tubes with capacity for forty 38- or 45-caliber wadcutters; transparent front guard and slide assembly for automatic case positioning. Safety features added for 1993 include: shut-off switch insulators to keep foreign particles from entering switch; primer filler tube retaining clip to prevent primers coming out top of tube; adjustable bullet knockout to punch out stuck round at top of stroke; powder check rod to eliminate powder spillage at powder check station; powder disk cover to restrict foreign particles entering powder disk; removable flask screen to filter the powder before it is dropped; taller transparent front guard. From Ammo Load, Inc.

Price: **$10,311.00**
Price: Powder Flask Shut-Off **$66.00**
Price: Carbide Final Die **$73.00**
Price: Variable Speed Motor (D.C.) **$588.00**
Price: Special Order Calibers (38 S&W, 380 Auto, 44 Mag., 44 S&W) **$555.00**
Price: Custom Order Calibers . . . . . **Price Varies**
Price: 9mm Double Sizing Set-Up **$411.00**
Price: 220/240v.-50/60 Cycle Transformer **$787.00**
Price: Eight Station Bullet Turret **$283.00**

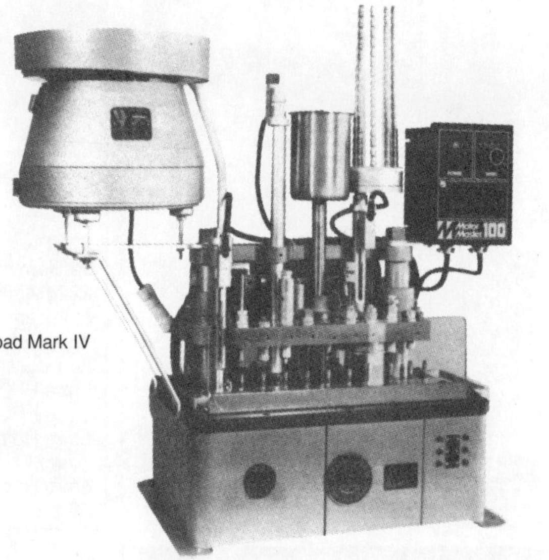

Ammo Load Mark IV

AMMO LOAD Mark IV

Calibers: 38 Special, 357 Magnum, 45 ACP, 9mm (standard); 38 S&W, 380 Auto, 44 Magnum, 44 S&W (special order); 25 Auto, 30 Carbine, 32 Auto, 32 S&W Long, 32 S&W Short, 38 Auto, 41 Magnum, 45 Long Colt, 10mm, 40 S&W (custom order)
Rounds Per Hour: 3,600-5,000
Dimensions: 25" x 34$^3/_4$" x 29$^3/_4$"
Weight: 323 lbs.
Features: Comes with all the features of the Mark III plus: a carbide final sizing die; variable speed DC motor with control box; three auto shut-off switches for low feed at case feed, primer feed and bullet feed; a light panel for low feed signaling; and powder flash shut-off assembly. Safety features added for 1993 include: shut-off switch insulators to keep foreign particles from entering switch; primer filler tube retaining clip to prevent primers coming out top of tube; adjustable bullet knockout to punch out stuck round at top of stroke; powder check rod to eliminate powder spillage at powder check station; powder disk cover to restrict foreign particles entering powder disk; removable flask screen to filter the powder prior to charging; taller transparent front guard. From Ammo Load, Inc.

Price: **$11,673.00**
Price: Special Order Calibers (38 S&W, 380 Auto, 44 Mag, 44 S&W) **$555.00**
Price: Custom Order Calibers . . . . . **Price Varies**
Price: 9mm Double Sizing Set-Up **$411.00**
Price: 220/240v.-50/60 Cyle Transformer **$787.00**
Price: Eight Station Bullet Turret **$283.00**
Price: Electronic Brake **$310.00**

Ammo Load
Boxing Inspection Table

Ammo Load
Primer Tube Filler

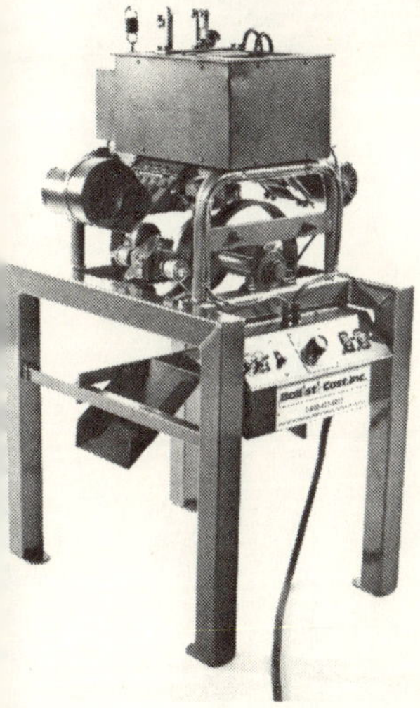

Ballisti-Cast Mark I

Ballisti-Cast Mark II

AMMO LOAD Primer Tube Filler

For use on the Ammo Load Mark III or Mark IV. Features a vibratory bowl to orient the primers and fill the primer tube. The capacity is approximately 5,000 primers per hour. Primer tubes hold 125 primers each. Handles either small or large primers with minor equipment adjustment. For operation on 110- or 220-volt. Dimensions: 6" x $7\frac{1}{4}$" x $17\frac{1}{4}$". Weight: 28 lbs. From Ammo Load, Inc.

Price: **$853.00**

BALLISTI-CAST Mark I Handcaster

Frame: Welded tubular steel.
Calibers: #4 buckshot to 54 Maxi
Moulds: Four 2-cavity.
Avg. Bullets Per Hour: Operator controlled manual lever.
Dimensions: 41" x 19" x 26"
Weight: 240 lbs.
Features: Positive indexing carrier system; quick mould adjustment and replacement; cam-oriented mould closure and spring-loaded opening; timed lead control; 2600-watt, 200-volt, 20-amp thermostatically controlled 100-lb. capacity furnace. Available with Hensley & Gibbs or SAECO moulds. From Ballisti-Cast, Inc.

Price: Hensley & Gibbs moulds **$3,245.00**
Price: Saeco moulds **$3,045.00**

BALLISTI-CAST Mark II Automatic Caster

Frame: Welded tubular steel.
Calibers: #4 buckshot to 54 Maxi
Moulds: Four 2-cavity.
Avg. Bullets Per Hour: 2400+
Dimensions: 41" x 19" x 26"
Weight: 265 lbs.
Features: Gear-driven motor; two heavy-duty air blowers; dust-sealed control panel, indicator working lights, electronic counter; timed lead control; positive indexing carrier system; quick mould adjustment and replacement; cam-oriented mould closure and spring-loaded opening; 2600-watt, 200-volt, 20-amp thermostatically controlled 100-lb. capacity furnace. Available with Hensley & Gibbs or SAECO moulds. From Ballisti-Cast, Inc.

Price: Hensley & Gibbs moulds **$5,070.00**
Price: Saeco moulds **$4,870.00**
Price: Variable speed motor **$325.00**

BALLISTI-CAST Mark V Lube-Sizer and Collator

Lubes and sizes 3500+ bullets per hour using Star and Mercer dies. Lube tube preheater for very hard lubes; auto digital heat controller on base plate; empty lube cylinder auto shutoff; variable speed motor. Bullet collator feeds 9mm through 45 Long Colt bullets base up or down; does not collate full wadcutters; electric stop-start feed control. From Ballisti-Cast, Inc.

Price: **$4,300.00**

Ballisti-Cast Mark V Lube-Sizer and Collator

BEN'S MACHINES Brass Resizer

Automated air-powered brass resizer for 380-9mm, 10mm, 40 S&W and 45 ACP. Cycle rate is 3,000 per hour. Air compressor used must provide 90-100 lbs. constant pressure. Dimensions: 12" x $4\frac{1}{2}$" x 8". Rotors, dies and case collator not included. From Ben's Machines.

Price: **$1,195.00**
Price: Rotors **$150.00**
Price: Dies **$26.00**
Price: MA Systems collator **$475.00**

BEN'S MACHINES Lazy Luber No. 1

Electric/mechanical conversion for a Star lube-sizer available as a complete unit or in component form. Maximum output capacity of 2,400 bullets per hour with realistic capability of 1,750-2,000. Combines conversion table with MA Systems bullet collator and Ben's lube heater and auto feed. From Ben's Machines.

Price: Complete unit **$1,352.50**
Price: Conversion table **$500.00**
Price: Heater (120/240 volt) **$70.00**
Price: Auto-feeder (one bar included) **$75.00**
Price: Additional feed bar **$17.50**
Price: MA Systems collator **$495.00**
Price: Star dies (any caliber) **$26.00**

BEN'S MACHINES Lazy Luber No. 2

Same as above except air-powered version. Mountable unit includes valves, pistons and adapters. Air compressor used must deliver 90 lbs. constant pressure. Available as complete unit or in component form. From Ben's Machines.

Price: Complete unit **$1,552.50**
Price: Air-powered conversion **$695.00**
Price: Heater (120/240 volt) **$70.00**
Price: Auto-feeder (one bar included) **$75.00**
Price: Additional feed bar **$17.50**
Price: MA Systems collator **$495.00**
Price: Star dies (any caliber) **$26.00**

BEN'S MACHINES Sorter Lazy

Automated case sorter by diameter for 22-25 ACP, 380-9mm, 45 ACP, 32 ACP, 38-357-10mm, 44 Spl.-44 Mag. Depending on size of brass, sorts 7,000-10,000 per hour. Will also sort bullets or loaded ammo. From Ben's Machines.

Price: **$1,395.00**

BEN'S MACHINES Sorter Lazy Two

Sorts by case length 380-9mm-38 Super, 40 S&W-10mm-38 Spl.-357 Mag. Cycle rate is approximately 3,000 per hour; production rate, 2,500 per hour. Special feed and rails available for 44 Spl.-44 Mag. Brass collator not included. From Ben's Machines.

Price: **$1,395.00**
Price: MA Systems collator **$495.00**

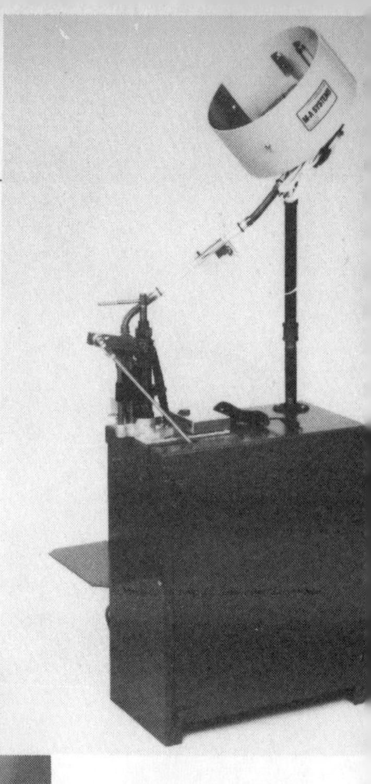

Ben's Machines Lazy Luber No. 1

Ben's Machines Lazy Luber No. 2

Ben's Machines Sorter Lazy

Ben's Machines Sorter Lazy Two

Camdex 2100 Series Loader

CAMDEX 2100 Series Loader

Calibers: Any Nato or commercial handgun caliber.
Avg. Rounds Per Hour: 4400
Dimensions: 32" x 28" x 36"
Weight: 200 lbs.
Features: Comes in three configurations: **Basic Loader** includes case feed, primer pocket, primer feed, primer slide and powder probe monitoring system. Case probe checks for case feeding, foreign particles and live rounds; primer pocket probe mechanically checks the primer pocket for ringers; the primer feed monitors primer feed mechanism; primer slide probe ensures that a jam has not occurred; and powder probe checks for both high and low powder charges. Basic loader also features primer follower rod and weight to maintain primer feed and supply; automatic case feeder with eight-station bullet turret and carbide final size die. **Auto & Continuous Loader** has same features as above plus auto primer feed with air/vacuum system for assisting and monitoring the feed. **2100 Series** has all the features of the A&C loader plus a 14" variable speed auto bullet feeder as standard equipment. All three come with brass powder canister that holds over one pound of powder; die set screws for rapid removal or adjustment; adjustable speed $^3/_4$-hp motor. Conversion units for 9mm, 45 ACP available. From Camdex, Inc.

Price: Basic Loader **$11,900.00**
Price: Automatic & Continuous Loader **$13,210.00**
Price: 2100 Series **$14,500.00**
Price: Auto primer tube filler **$730.00**
Price: Inspection table **$1,750.00**
Price: Conversion units **$2,950.00**
Price: Final size die **$150.00**

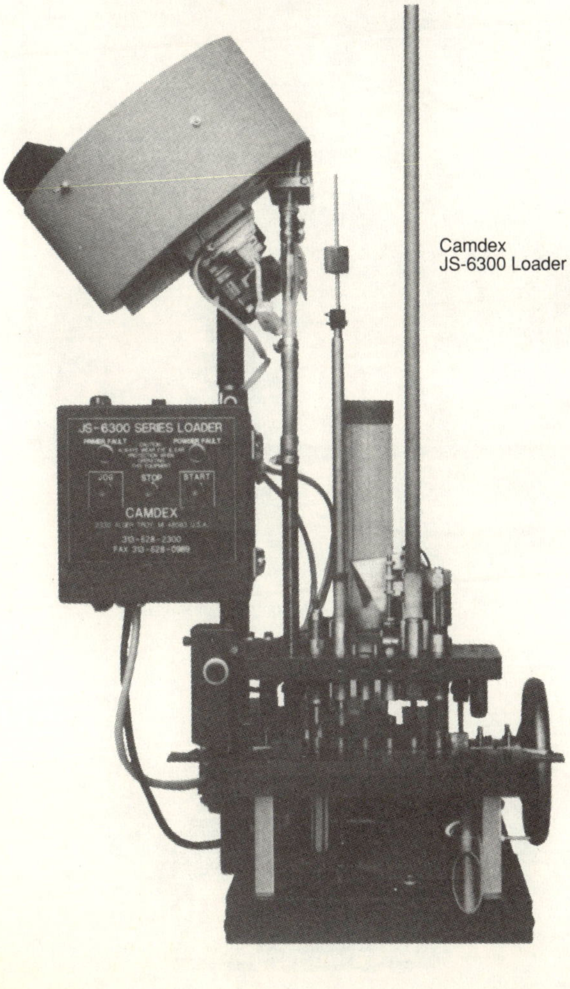

Camdex JS-6300 Loader

CAMDEX JS-6300 Loader

Calibers: Any centerfire pistol caliber.
Avg. Rounds Per Hour: 1800 (auto version)
Dimensions: 20" x 28" x 24"
Weight: 110 lbs.
Features: Hand or auto operation. Cases are tube fed and auto-indexed to each station; size and depriming done by standard $^7/_8$-14 die threaded into upper platen; priming movement by cable operated spring-loaded slide; primer pickup and seating locations adjustable; powder drop station cam activated and synchronized with platen movement; powder slide uses replaceable bushings; fully adjustable case bell function; tube fed bullet slide. The auto model includes same features as above plus control panel and micro switches to monitor powder charge, primer level and primer jamming. Comes with $^1/_4$-hp motor. Optional equipment: auto case feeder; eight-station bullet turret or auto bullet feeder; auto low case level shutoff; final carbide sizing die; caliber conversion units. From Camdex, Inc.

Price: Hand-operated loader **$2,600.00**
Price: Automatic model **$4,500.00**
Price: Caliber conversion kit **$1,150.00**
Price: 8-station bullet turret **$115.00**
Price: Final carbide size die **$150.00**
Price: Extra primer feed tubes **$8.00**
Price: Extra cartridge tubes **$7.95**
Price: Extra bullet tubes **$7.50**
Price: Case feeder **$510.00**
Price: 220/50 HZ electrical **$360.00**

CAMDEX Case Processor

Transforms 9mm cases into "like new" condition. Automatically ejects Berdan primed cases, split and cracked cases and 380 cases. All cases fully resized including base of rimless cases to assure accurate uniform chambering. Military crimp is removed by swaging operation on the primer pocket. Features friction disc clutch, 3750 cycles per hour, two tungsten carbide sizing dies; MA-Systems auto case feeder; one tungsten carbide base size exit die; $^{1}/_{3}$-hp compressor/vacuum pump; $^{1}/_{2}$-hp electric motor. Available in all handgun calibers. Can also be purchased with additional caliber conversions for processing more than one caliber. From Camdex, Inc.

Price: **$9,750.00**
Price: Conversion kit **$1,700.00**

CAMDEX Lube Sizer

Lubes at the rate of 4400 per hour. Vertical feed and horizontal dispensing for bulk or tube packaging. Bullet lube heated by cartridge type element in aluminum block and lube pressure held constant by ratchet and spring assembly inside reservoir. Powered by $^{1}/_{3}$-hp motor. Comes with cartridge heater, foot pedal and forward/reverse switch. From Camdex, Inc.

Price: **$4,850.00**
Price: 45 ACP conversion **$675.00**
Price: 220/50 HZ electrical **$630.00**

CAMDEX Packer

Ammunition packaging machine for the commercial reloader. Capable of boxing over 16,000 rounds per hour. Integral feed hopper holds over 8,000 rounds of 9mm. Operates on 120-volt AC power and draws 4 amps. Available in all popular handgun calibers. Conversion from one caliber to another requires $^{1}/_{2}$-hour. Dimensions: 33" x 15" x 22$^{1}/_{2}$". Weight: 115 lbs. From Camdex, Inc.

Price: **$3,500.00**
Price: Conversion kit **$850.00**

CORBIN CHP-1 Hydro-Press

Die Thread: 1$^{1}/_{2}$-12
Ram Stroke: 6"
Weight: 350 lbs.
Features: Ability to manufacture lead wire, jackets, gas checks, base guards and bullets from 224 to 22mm and reload calibers up to 20mm. Swages hardest lead alloys in calibers from 224 to 512, bullet weights to 1000 grains and lengths to 2.5 inches. Makes lead wire from .120 to .500-inch diameter; draws heavy copper or brass partitioned tubing jackets of .030- to .065-inch walls; and shotgun slugs up to 10-gauge. Uses forced air cooling and 5-gallon hydraulic reservoir to service industrial-grade vertical-drive cylinder. Die pressures exceeding 200,000 psi. Electronic transducers monitor pressure and control ram force. Logic circuits establish stroke length, dwell time and pressure. Color coded control panel; heavy-duty key-lock safety switch; dual-hand control interlock. Press comes standard with 115-120 volt 60 Hz power; 220-240 volt 50-60 Hz conversion optional. From Corbin Manufacturing & Supply, Inc.

Price: **$5,500.00**
Price: 240-volt conversion **$250.00**

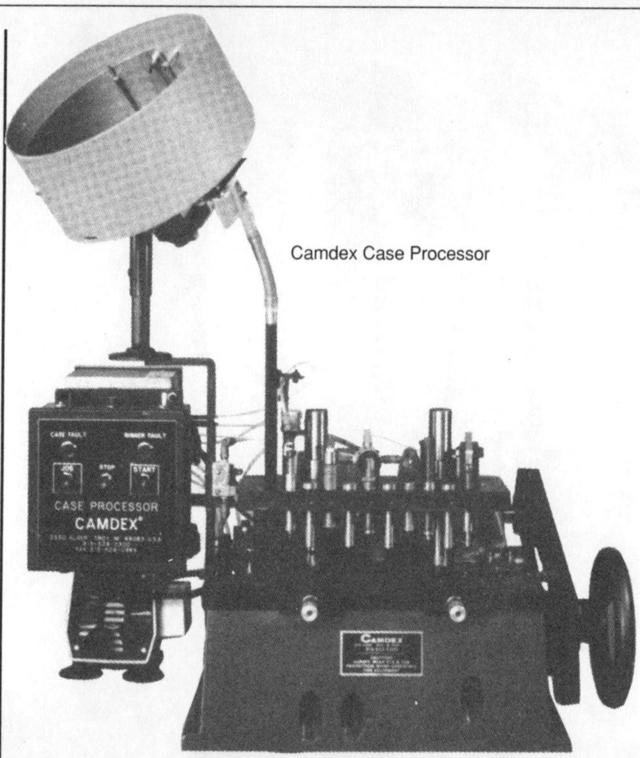

Camdex Case Processor

Camdex Packer

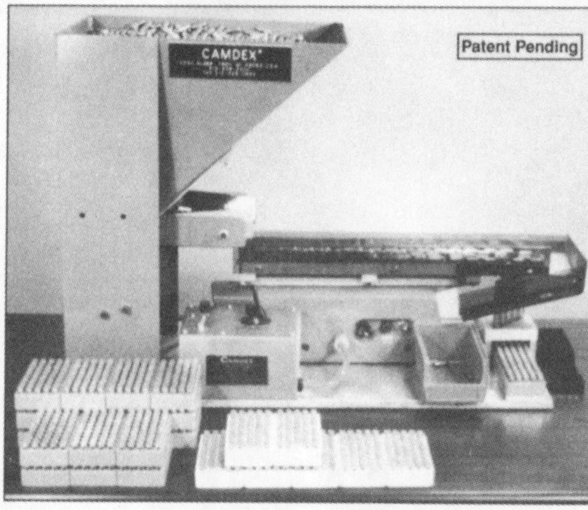

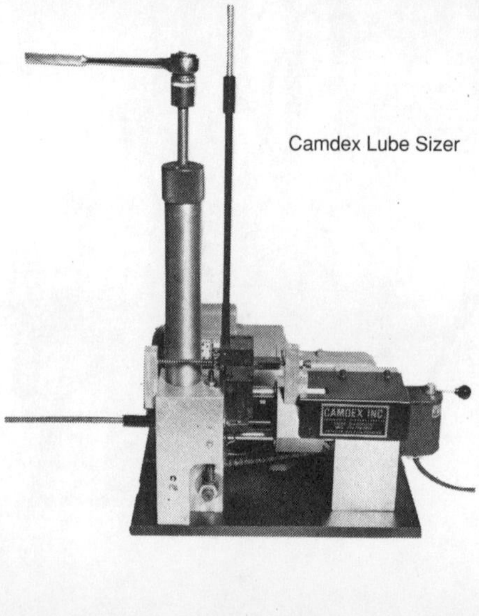

Camdex Lube Sizer

Corbin Power Cannelure

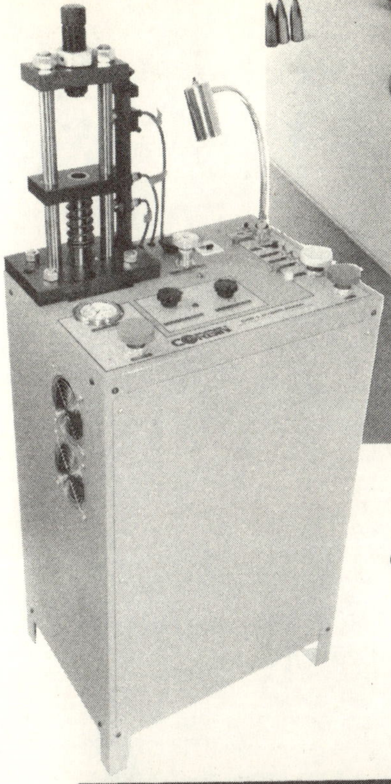

Corbin CHP-1 Hydro-Press

Kapro Hy-Drive
for Dillon RL 1050

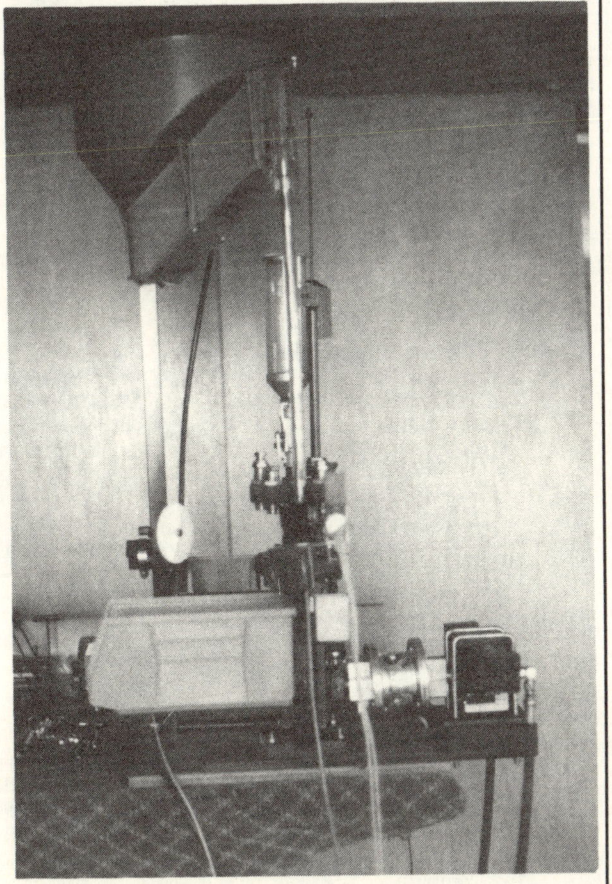

CORBIN Hydro-Mite Swaging Press

Frame: Steel
Frame Type: H-frame
Die Thread: $^7/_8$-14
Ram Stroke: 2" swaging; 4" drawing or jacket making.
Weight: 22 lbs.
Features: Comes on bench stand with separate electric remote control hydraulic pressure system for long production runs, professional pyrotechnic and explosives work. Four precision roller bearings mounted in heavy-duty steel links, bearing on hardened tool steel pins; oil-impregnated bronze bearings surrounding ram; ordnance steel alloy supports and ram; machined frame; electrostatic powder-coated, baked-on finish. Hand-built, hand assembled press. Swages bullets from 14- to 458-caliber. Maximum bullet length, 1.25" in the M dies; 1.35" in S dies; maximum pressure, over 200,000 psi. Comes with floating punch holder for use with external punches of Corbin swage dies. Made for use with Corbin M or S type dies. From Corbin Manufacturing & Supply, Inc.
Price: 120 VAC **$1,950.00**

CORBIN Mega-Mite Hydraulic Swaging Press

Frame: Steel
Frame Type: H-frame
Die Thread: $1^1/_2$-12
Ram Stroke: 3"
Weight: 250 lbs.
Features: Features pressure gauge, panel-mounted direction controls, adjustable ram thrust, self-contained floor stand. Roller bearing linkage; hardened tool steel pivots; precision bronze bushings on polished steel guide rods. Dual stroke operation allows changing from 5.5-inch to 3-inch stroke for reloading up to 50 BMG cases or heavy swaging. Can swage hard lead bullets up to .475 diameter and soft lead to .600. Maximum pressure, 180,000 psi; maximum bullet length, $1^1/_2$"; maximum jacket wall, 0.50" copper. Made for use with Corbin H dies. Comes with thick steel floor stand with 4-inch diameter iron tube and punch holder. Height with floor stand is 66". From Corbin Manufacturing & Supply, Inc.
Price: **$2,950.00**

CORBIN Power Cannelure Machine

High-production machine cannelures 100 lead or jacketed bullets per minute. Cabinet is 10" high with 6" x 8" top work space. Includes one cannelure wheel for all calibers and guide plate for one caliber. Caliber plates available from 22 to 512. From Corbin Manufacturing & Supply, Inc.
Price: **$469.00**
Price: Custom cannelure wheel **$75.00**
Price: Position spacer, .025" or .048" **$10.00**
Price: Spare back plate **$40.00**
Price: Lead knurling back plate **$75.00**

KAPRO Hy-Drive System for Dillon RL 1050

Hydraulic 110-volt power unit and variable speed rotary actuator designed for attachment to the Dillon RL 1050 press. Reloads 1,800 rounds per hour with maximum cycle time 2,100 per hour. Features sealed hydraulics to reduce leaking; adaptable continuous operation for brass processing (adaptable to MA Systems and Howell CNC bullet feeders); no cutting or drilling to fit to press; enclosed pump, motor, valve and rotary actuator; full hydraulic operation; stop and reverse in loading cycle; photo-electric switch for deactivation for manual insertion of bullet. From Kapro Manufacturing Co., Inc.
Price: **$1,895.00**

LORTONE Model R-20 and R-40 Case Tumblers

Commercial-size tumblers engineered to industrial standards. The R-40 tumbler has capacity for 2,400 38 Special cases or 800 30-06 cases. Constructed of heavy gauge welded steel with hexagonal three-point closure steel barrels. Features neoprene rubber liner and gasket; dual rubber-covered drive shafts; heavy-duty bronze bearings and ball-bearing barrel guides. Requires 1/3-hp electric motor. A total of six Model R-40 machines can be coupled and driven by a single 1/3-hp motor. Lortone R-20 is smaller version with capacity for 1,200 38 Special cases and 400 30-06 cases. Dimensions: R-40, 19" x 16"; R-20, 14" x 16". Weights: R-40, 51 lbs.; R-20, 39 lbs. From Lortone, Inc.

Price: R-20 . . . . **$355.00**
Price: R-40 . . . . **$425.00**
Price: Optional 1/3-hp motor with switch and cord . . . **$125.00**

MA SYSTEMS Auto Bullet Collater-14

Designed for high-speed reloading. Feeds round-nose, semi-round-nose or pointed 9mm through 45 Long Colt bullets base down or base up at rates averaging 6,000 bullets per hour. Features 14-lb. capacity; vari-speed, 3 to 7 rpm, rate control for collating or feeding; electric stop/start feed control; adjustable 5/8" O.D. feed tube for varying bullet sizes; standard collating plate to feed 9mm (.550") through 45 (.950"); optional plates available for bullets 1.312" to .400". Adapts easily to any machine accepting tubed bullets. Does not collate full wadcutters. Comes complete with feed tube, flex bends, electric control, mounting column and plastic piping. Also available for 380 Auto and hollow base wadcutter 38-caliber. Weight: 22 lbs. From MA Systems.

Price: **$1,095.00**
Price: 38-cal. hollow base **$1,350.00**
Price: 380 Auto **$1,195.00**
Price: Adapt kit for Camdex or Ammo Load **$33.00**

MA SYSTEMS Conversion Kits

Converts M-A Auto Bullet Collator-14 to 380 Auto collator or 380 collator to ABC-14. Weight: 4 lbs. From MA Systems.

Price: ABC-14 to 380 . . . . **$325.00**
Price: 380 to ABC-14 . . . . **$233.85**

MA SYSTEMS Easy Bullet Collater-12

Collates 9mm (.600") through 45 Long Colt (1.000") bullets at rate of 1,800 to 3,600 per hour depending on bullet size. Special collating plates available for 380 Auto and rifle calibers. Collating bowl holds 7 lbs. Features electric stop/start feed; unique column design to rotate bowl away from machine or remove in five seconds. Adapts easily to any press accepting tubed bullets and feeds base up or down. Comes complete with feed tubes, electric control, mounting column and plastic piping. Weight: 12 lbs. From MA Systems.

Price: **$495.00**

MA SYSTEMS Easy Case Collater-12

Automatically feeds all pistol cartridge cases from 380 Auto to 45 Long Colt base down at a rate of 2,000 or 4,000 per hour depending upon caliber. Collater bowl holds 575 9mm or 360 44 Magnum cases. Unique mounting column allows bowl to rotate away or be removed in five seconds. Will fit Star, Dillon RL-1000, C-H/4-D Die Inline and RCBS Green Machine or adapt to any press utilizing tubed cases. Feed case tube 5/8" O.D. From MA Systems.

Price: For hand-operated presses **$305.00**
Price: For auto presses **$475.00**

MA Systems Auto Bullet Collator

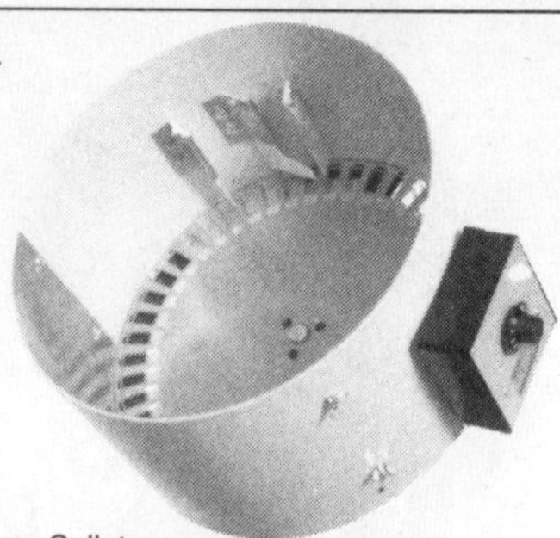

MA Systems Easy Case Collator

MA Systems Easy Loader

MA SYSTEMS Easy Collater Tray

For cases or bullets. Orients either in slotted tray to slide easily into feed tubes. Tray accepts 100 rounds. Dimensions: 8 1/2" x 9". Weight: 12 lbs. From MA Systems.

Price: **$14.95**

MA SYSTEMS Easy Loader

Mounts to Star, Dillon RL 1000 and C-H/4-D Die Inline to feed bullets base down at rate of 2,500 per hour. Operates automatically in sequence with press from regulated 50-60 psi air source. Accepts all flat-based bullets, some hollow base, round-nose, wadcutters and semi-wadcutters. Comes complete for 9mm through 45-caliber with two sizes of bullet supply tubes, four feed tubes and two sets of bullet grippers. 223 and 380 Auto require special grippers; 223-caliber requires special feed tubes. Weight: 4 lbs. From MA Systems.

Price: Star **$410.00**
Price: Dillon **$465.00**

MAGMA Cast Master

Melting furnace with 90-lb. capacity. Features bottom pour with trip lever on right side; four lugs tapped 1/2-13 for mounting to bench or setting caster to preferred height; stainless valve components; removable orifice plate on bottom to increase or decrease metal flow. Comes complete with three-wire cord and one orifice plate installed. Weight: 40 lbs. From Magma Engineering Company.

Price: **$375.00**

Magma
Bullet Master Mk VI

MAGMA Bullet Master Mk VI

High-production bullet casting machine produces 2,400 bullets per hour. Features modular electrical system to ensure proper connections and easy removal; solid-state controllers with LED readouts; temperature control to +/- 7°; stainless steel springs and valves; divided pot for optimum bullet quality; float transfer device for constant lead head pressure; automatically separates bullets and sprues. Moulds available from 32- to 45-caliber. Weight: 225 lbs. From Magma Engineering Company.

Price: **$5,235.00**
Price: Magma mould **$60.00**
Price: Set of eight moulds **$480.00**

MAGMA Lube Master

Sizes and lubes 4,300 bullets per hour. All working parts are hardened steel; parts engaged in sliding contact are ground to precise tolerances. Base block contains cartridge heating element controlled to +/- 5°. Uses Star die. Comes complete for one caliber. Additional sizing dies available in most calibers. Conversion sets for 380- and 32-caliber contain guide bushing and drop tube. 120 or 240 volts. Weight: 125 lbs. From Magma Engineering Company.

Price: **$3,635.00**
Price: Conversion set **$33.00**
Price: Digital heat controller **$378.00**
Price: Counter **$351.00**
Price: Star size die **$27.50**
Price: Mercer/Stillwell size die **$30.00**
Price: Lube Master lube, per pound **$7.00**

Magma Master Caster

MAGMA Master Caster

Produces 800 to 1,000 bullets per hour. Features melting pot, two-cavity mould; automatic sprue cutoff; automatic bullet/sprue sorting; automatic bullet ejection; automatic sprue cutter and mould alignment; single hand operation. Saeco, Lyman, RCBS and H&G moulds can be converted for use on Master Caster at additional charge. 120 or 240 volts, 1350 watts. Weight: 55 lbs. From Magma Engineering Company.

Price: **$595.00**

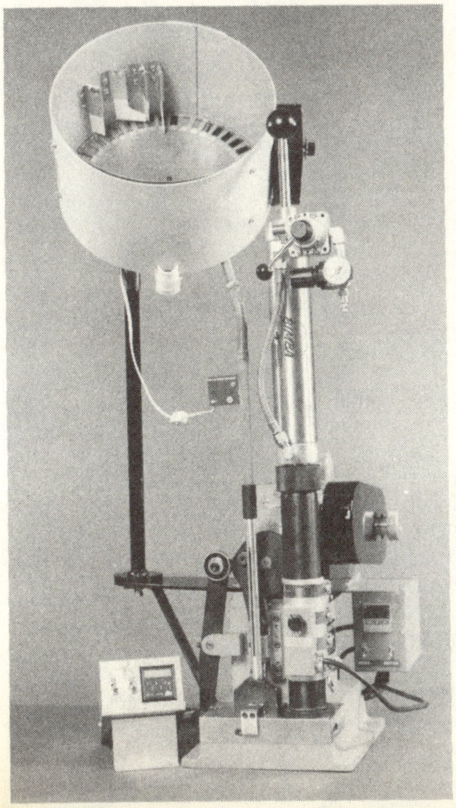

Magma Lube Master

RAYTECH Model 40 and Model 75 Commercial Case Tumblers

Commercial-size tumblers with industrial motor-drive systems to handle heavy loads. Capacity of Model 40 is 2,800 38 Special cases; Model 75 can handle 4,500 38 Special cases. Bowls made of cross-linked polyethylene in $^3/_8$" or $^1/_2$" thicknesses. Features amplitude adjustment, inlet and outlet ports for compound rinsing systems. Both models also offered with Tumble Dump (TD) feature which allows bowl to be disengaged and tipped on hinge point for unloading. For dry or wet media. From Raytech, Division of Lyman Products Company.

Price: Model 40 . . . . **$798.00**
Price: Model 40 TD **$1,050.00**
Price: Model 75 . . . . **$975.00**
Price: Model 75 TD **$1,235.00**
Price: Replacement bowl, M40 . . . . **$160.00**
Price: Replacement bowl, M75 . . . . **$205.00**

RAYTECH MS-75 Media Separator

Variable speed commercial separator with capacity for 4,500 38 Special cases. Automatically separates cases from wet or dry media in two minutes, sending media and cases out two frontal chutes into two 70-lb. capacity tote boxes. A variety of optional quick-change screens available. From Raytech, Division of Lyman Products Company.

Price: **$1,260.00**
Price: Screens, $^9/_{64}$" round to 2" round . . . . **$90.00-$150.00**

SCHARCH Ammunition Boxing Machine

Designed to place rimless ammunition directly into styrofoam or Federal style plastic trays. Will package up to 30,000 rounds per hour. Allows for visual and gauge block inspection. Mounted on solid maple top work bench. 110-volt operation. From Scharch Mfg., Inc.

Price: 9mm, 380, 38 Super **$3,495.00**
Price: 45 ACP, 10mm, 40 S&W **$3,495.00**
Price: 38/357 . . . . **$4,395.00**

SCHARCH Auto Reamer

Same as Case Inspector/Auto Reamer but only reams primer pocket and cuts correct radius at pocket opening. From Scharch Mfg., Inc.

Price: 38/357 . . . . **$9,195.00**
Price: 9mm/380 . . . . **$9,850.00**
Price: 45 ACP **$9,850.00**
Price: 223 . . . . **$10,400.00**
Price: 308 . . . . **$10,400.00**

SCHARCH Range Master Case Inspector Auto Reamer

High-production case inspector for 38/357, 9mm/380 or 45 ACP brass. Processes 5100 cases per hour. Features inspection for bent cases, loaded or foreign objects; pressure check for mouth or sidewall splits; deprimes; inspection of primer pocket for ringers or military crimp; electronic counter for good cases only; electronic memory for rejection of bad cases; chute for good cases, trap for bad cases; primer tube for spent primers; eye shield for operator protection; case feed tube with auto shut-off. Operates on 120 vac 60 Hz. Dimensions: 31" x 23" x 35". Weight: 340 lbs. From Scharch Mfg., Inc.

Price: 38/357 . . . . **$5,895.00**
Price: 9mm/380 . . . . **$6,350.00**
Price: 45 ACP **$6,350.00**

SCHARCH Roller Sizer

Sizes fired cases to proper diameter at rate of 6,000 per hour. Comes complete with case feeder and sturdy steel frame stand. Available in all popular handgun sizes plus 223. Operates on 110 volts. Weight: 180 lbs. From Scharch Mfg., Inc.

Price: **$2,750.00**

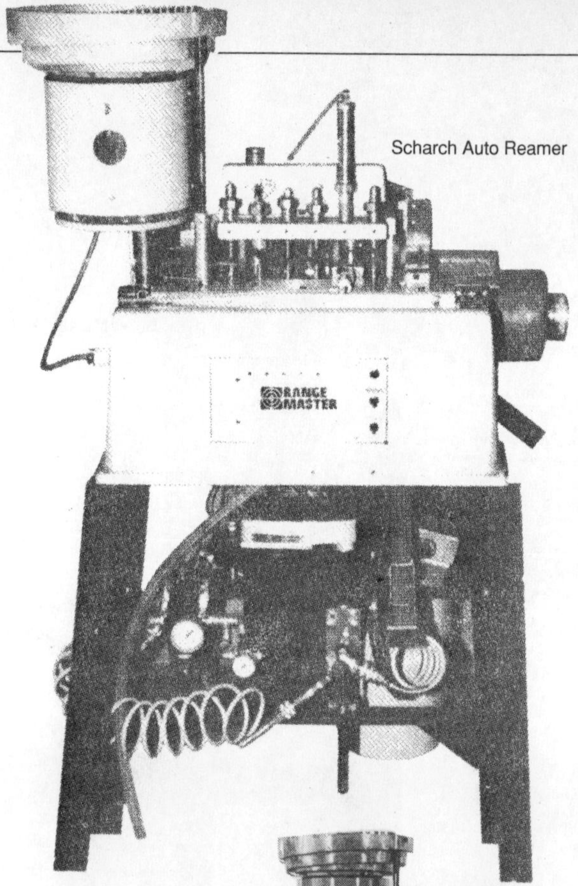

Scharch Auto Reamer

Scharch Case Inspector Auto Reamer

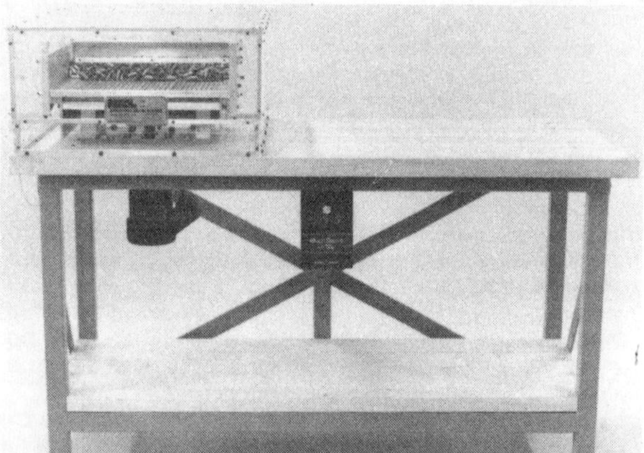

Scharch Ammunition Boxing Machine

Scharch Roller Sizer

PART 1 2 3 4 5 6

SHOTSHELL
TOOLS & ACCESSORIES

HOLLYWOOD Automatic Shotshell Press

Press Type: Progressive
Avg. Rounds Per Hour: 1,800
Weight: 100 lbs.
Features: Ductile iron frame; fully automated press with shell pickup and ejector; comes completely set up for one gauge; one starter crimp; one finish crimp; wad guide for plastic wads; decap and powder dispenser unit; one wrench for inside die lock screw; one medium and one large spanner wrench for spanner nuts; one shellholder; powder and shot measures. Available for 10, 12, 20, 28 or 410. From Hollywood Engineering.
Price: **$3,600.00**
Price: Die set **$195.00**

HOLLYWOOD Senior Press

Press Type: Progressive
Avg. Rounds Per Hour: 200
Weight: 50 lbs.
Features: Made of ductile iron; comes completely equipped to reload one gauge; one starter crimp; one finish crimp; wad guide for plastic wads; decap and powder dispenser unit; one wrench for inside die lock screw; one medium and one large spanner wrench for spanner nuts; one shellholder; powder and shot measures. Available for 10, 12, 16, 20, 28 or 410. From Hollywood Engineering.
Price: **$475.00**

HOLLYWOOD Senior Turret Press

Press Type: Progressive
Avg. Rounds Per Hour: 200
Weight: 50 lbs.
Features: Multi-stage press constructed of ductile iron comes completely equipped to reload one gauge; one starter crimp; one finish crimp; wad guide for plastic wads; decap and powder dispenser unit; one wrench for inside die lock screw; one medium and one large spanner wrench for spanner nuts; one shellholder; powder and shot measures. Available for 10, 12, 16, 20, 28 or 410. From Hollywood Engineering.
Price: **$775.00**
Price: Die set **$195.00**

HOLLYWOOD Shotshell Die Sets

Complete $1^1/_2$" die set for one gauge to include: starter crimp; finish crimp; wad guide for plastic wads; decap and powder dispenser unit; wrench for inside die lock screw; medium and large spanner wrench for spanner nuts; shellholder. Available for 10, 12, 16, 20, 28 and 410. From Hollywood Engineering.
Price: **$195.00**

HORNADY 366 Auto

Press Type: Progressive
Avg. Rounds Per Hour: NA
Weight: 25 lbs.
Features: Heavy-duty die cast and machined steel body and components; auto primer feed system; large capacity shot and powder tubes; adjustable for right- or left-hand use; automatic charge bar with shutoff; swing-out wad guide; primer catcher at base of press; interchangeable shot and powder bushings; life-time warranty. Available for 12, 20, 28 $2^3/_4$" and 410 $2^1/_2$". From Hornady Mfg. Co.
Price: **$435.40**
Price: Die set, 12, 20, 28 . . . . **$86.60**
Price: Magnum conversion dies, 12, 20 . . . . **$19.00**

HOLLYWOOD Shotshell Die Parts

DIE/DIE PART	PRICE
Finish Crimp	$45.00
Crimp Start, w/lock ring, steel star	50.00
Steel Star, 6 & 8 point	15.00
Locking Screw, start crimp die	2.00
Decap/Powder Dispenser Unit	75.00
Decap Powder Pin	20.00
Locking Screw, decap powder pin	2.00
Lock Collar, wad guide spring finger	6.00
Lock Ring	5.00
Set Screw, lock ring	.40
Wad Guide Spring Finger	2.50
Wad Pressure Spring	3.00
Wad Ram	20.00
Wad Receiver, complete	70.00
Wad Receiver, stripped	45.00
Primer Rod Buffer Spring	2.00
Primer Rod Lock Ring, small	2.00
Primer Rod Lock Ring, large	2.50

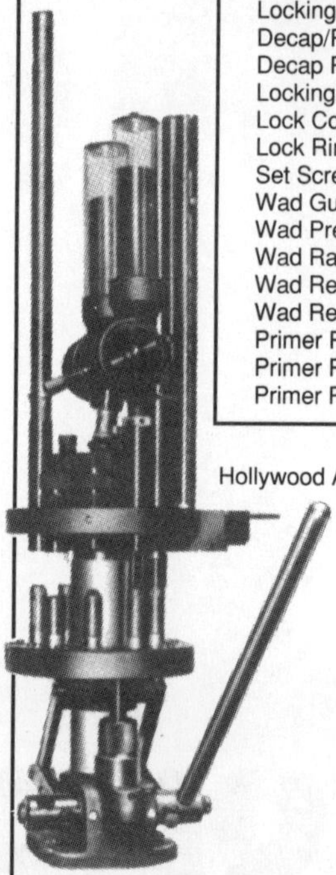

Hollywood Automatic Shotshell Press

Hollywood Senior Turret Press

Hollywood Senior Press

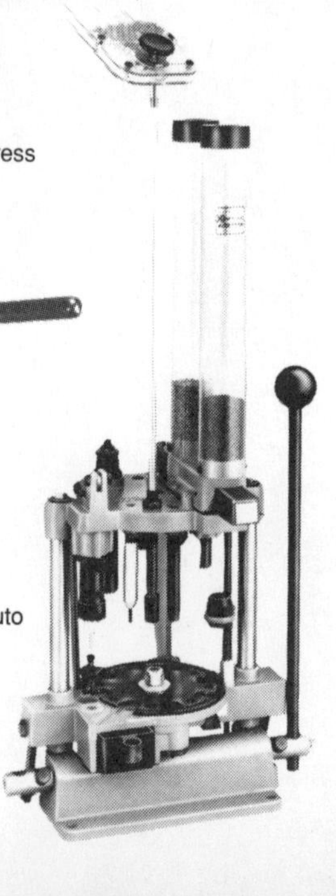

Hornady 366 Auto

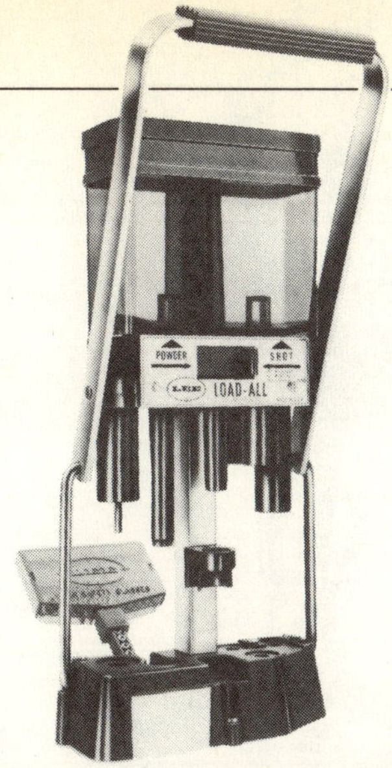

Lee Load-All II

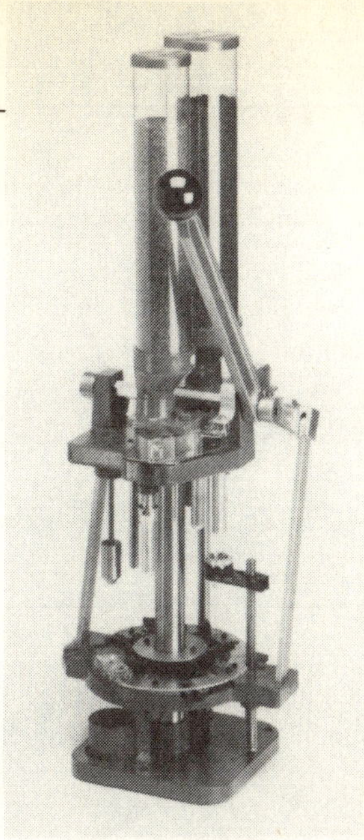
Hornady Apex Standard

Lee Load-Fast 12-Gauge Press

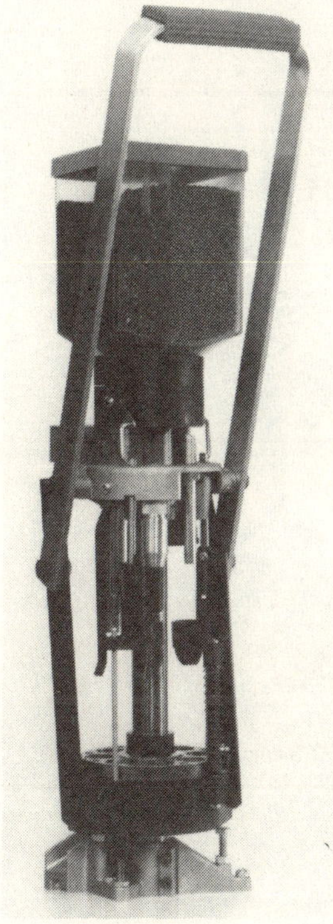

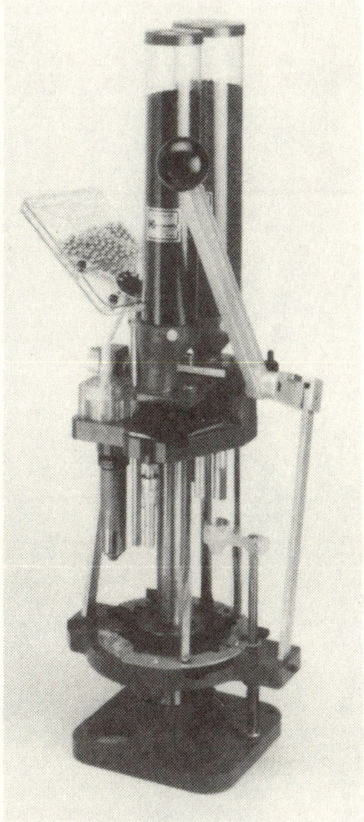
Hornady Apex Auto

HORNADY Apex Auto

Press Type: Auto
Avg. Rounds Per Hour: NA
Weight: 15 lbs.
Features: Includes all the features of the standard model plus: full-length collet size die to automatically size the full length of brass; auto primer feed with shell detect; automatic powder/shot drop with shell detect; cam-activated dual-action crimp/taper die; auto index converts single stage shellplate to progressive. Available for 12, 20, 28 gauges or 410 bore. From Hornady Mfg. Co.

Price: 12, 20 . . . . **$375.00**
Price: 28, 410 . . . . **$414.40**
Price: Die set, 12, 20 . . . . **$140.00**
Price: Die set, 28, 410 . . . . **$179.50**

HORNADY Apex Single Stage-to-Progressive Accessories

Converts Hornady's standard Apex single-stage reloader to a progressive press. The conversion accessories include: collet size die, 2-stage crimp die; auto primer drop with shell detect; auto shot and powder drop with shell detect; and auto index. From Hornady Mfg. Co.

Price: Collet size die, 12, 20 . . . . **$55.00**
Price: Collet size die, 28, 410 . . . . **$70.00**
Price: 2-stage crimp die, 12, 20 . . . . **$25.00**
Price: 2-stage crimp die, 28, 410 . . . . **$32.50**
Price: Auto primer drop **$60.00**
Price: Auto shot/powder drop **$105.00**
Price: Auto index **$25.00**

HORNADY Apex Standard

Press Type: Single stage
Avg. Rounds Per Hour: NA
Weight: 15 lbs.
Features: Auto deprimer drops spent primers into primer catcher at base of press; adjustable primer seater for all base wad heights flares hull mouths; powder/shot charge bars operate together or independently; swing-out wad guide; crimp starter for 8- or 6-point crimps; depth adjustable crimp die; shot and powder hoppers large enough to load up to 200 rounds; high leverage linkage arm; swing-out powder and shot drains; separate shot and powder drop tubes to prevent accidental mixing; shellplate indexes as single stage or progressive. Available for 12, 20, 28 gauges or 410 bore. From Hornady Mfg. Co.

Price: 12, 20 . . . . **$142.00**
Price: 28, 410 . . . . **$159.00**
Price: Die set, 12, 20 . . . . **$60.00**
Price: Die set, 28, 410 . . . . **$77.00**

LEE Load-All II

Press Type: Single stage
Avg. Rounds Per Hour: 100
Weight: 3 lbs., 3 oz.
Features: Loads steel or lead shot; built-in primer catcher at base with door in front for emptying; recesses at each station for shell positioning; optional primer feed. Comes with safety charge bar with 24 shot and powder bushings. Available for 12-, 16- or 20-gauge. From Lee Precision, Inc.

Price: **$47.98**

LEE Load-Fast 12-Gauge Press

Press Type: Progressive
Avg. Rounds Per Hour: 200
Weight: 6 lbs., 7 oz.
Features: Handles seven shells at one time; powder/shot shutoff for emptying or changing hoppers; cases full-length sized including rim; auto-indexing; chute to guide loaded rounds into container or box. Uses same shot/powder bushings as Lee Load-All II. Comes complete with shot and powder bushings for target loads. Options include auto primer feed. From Lee Precision, Inc.

Price: **$154.98**
Price: Primer feed **$19.98**
Price: Set 24 powder/shot bushings **$14.98**

MEC 600 Jr. Mark V
Press Type: Single stage
Avg. Rounds Per Hour: 200
Weight: 10 lbs.
Features: Spindex crimp starter for shell alignment during crimping; a cam-action crimp die; Pro-Check to keep charge bar properly positioned; adjustable for 3" shells. Available in 10, 12, 16, 20 and 28 gauge. Die set not included. From Mayville Engineering Company, Inc.
Price: **$151.81**
Price: Die set **$57.10**

MEC 650
Press Type: Progressive
Avg. Rounds Per Hour: 300
Weight: NA
Features: Six-station press; does not resize except as separate operation; auto primer feed standard; three crimping stations for starting, closing and tapering crimp. Die sets not available. 12, 16, 20, 28 and 410. From Mayville Engineering Company, Inc.
Price: **$298.54**

MEC 8567 Grabber
Press Type: Progressive
Avg. Rounds Per Hour: 500
Weight: 15 lbs.
Features: Ten-station press; auto primer feed; auto-cycle charging; three-stage crimp; power ring resizer returns base to factory specs; resizes high and low base shells; optional kits to reload 3" shells and steel shot. From Mayville Engineering Company, Inc.
Price: **$428.28**
Price: 3" kit, 12-ga. **$36.59**
Price: 3" kit, 20-ga. **$17.74**
Price: Steel shot kit **$13.38**

MEC 9000G
Press Type: Progressive
Avg. Rounds Per Hour: 500
Weight: 18 lbs.
Features: All same features as the MEC Grabber but with auto-indexing and auto-eject. Finished shells automatically ejected from shell carrier to drop chute for boxing. Available in 12, 16, 20, 28 and 410. From Mayville Engineering Company, Inc.
Price: **$520.00**

MEC 9000H
Press Type: Progressive
Avg. Rounds Per Hour: 500
Weight: 23 lbs.
Features: Same features as 9000G with addition of foot pedal operated hydraulic system for complete automation. Operates on standard 110 household current. Comes with bushing type charge bar and three bushings. From Mayville Engineering Company, Inc.
Price: **$1,256.26**

MEC Sizemaster
Press Type: Single stage
Avg. Rounds Per Hour: 250
Weight: 13 lbs.
Features: Power ring eight-fingered collet resizer returns base to factory specs; handles brass or steel, high or low base, heads; auto primer feed; adjustable for 3" shells. Available in 10, 12, 16, 20, 28 gauge and 410 bore. From Mayville Engineering Company, Inc.
Price: **$228.75**
Price: Die set, 12, 16, 20, 28, 410 . . . . **$85.26**
Price: Die set, 10-ga. **$100.06**

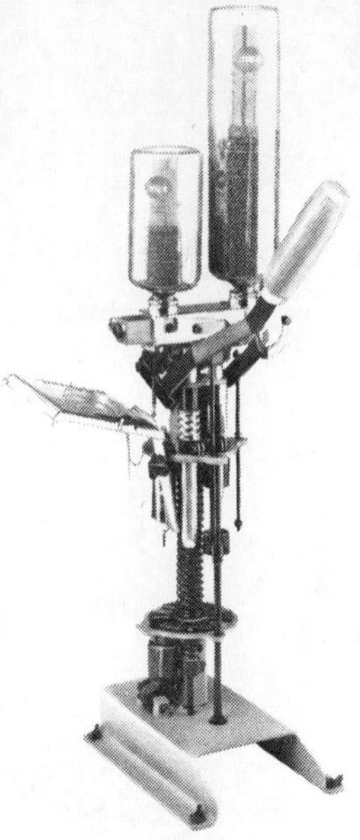
MEC Grabber

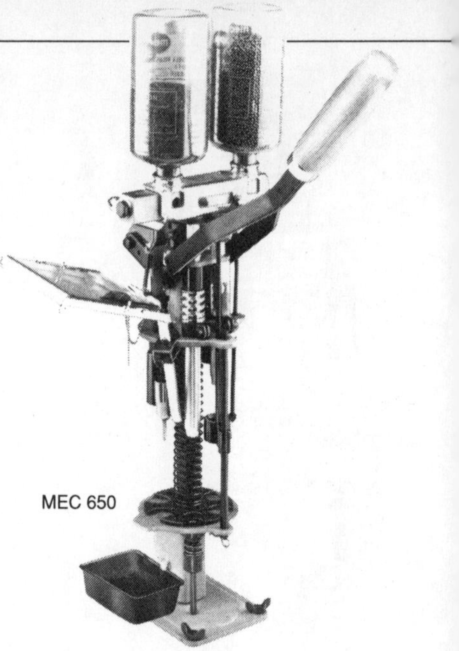
MEC 650

MEC Sizemaster

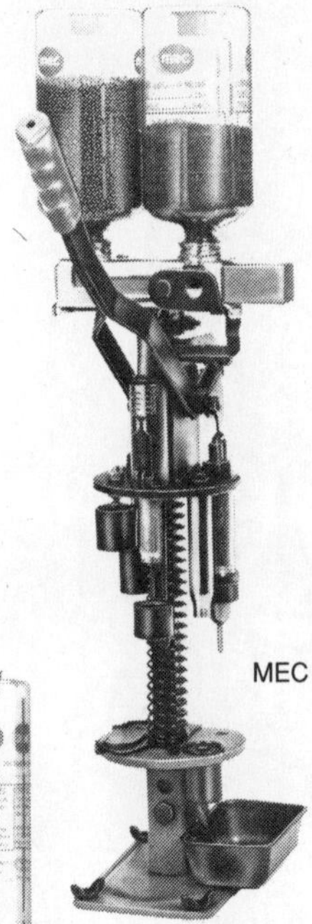
MEC 600 Jr.

MEC 9000G

Ponsness/Warren Hydro-Matic

Ponsness/Warren Du-O-Matic 375C

MEC Steelmaster

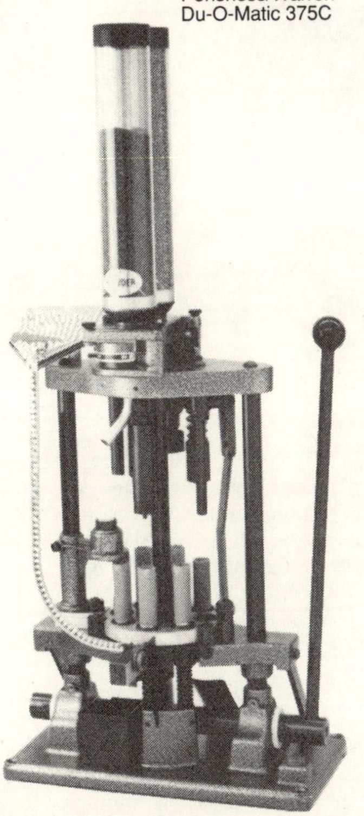

Ponsness/Warren L/S-1000

MEC Steelmaster

Press Type: Single stage
Avg. Rounds Per Hour: 250
Weight: 13 lbs.
Features: Same features as Sizemaster except can load steel shot. Press is available for $3\frac{1}{2}$" 10-ga. and 12-ga. $2\frac{3}{4}$" or 3". For loading lead shot, die sets available in 10, 12, 16, 20, 28 and 410. From Mayville Engineering Company, Inc.
Price: **$238.06**

PONSNESS/WARREN Du-O-Matic 375C

Press Type: Progressive
Avg. Rounds Per Hour: NA
Weight: 31 lbs.
Features: Steel or lead shot reloader; large shot and powder reservoirs; bushing access plug for dropping in shot buffer or buckshot; positive lock charging ring to prevent accidental flow of powder; double post construction for greater leverage; removable spent primer box; spring-loaded ball check for centering size die at each station; tip-out wad guide; two-gauge capacity tool head. Available in 10 (extra charge), 12, 16, 20, 28 and 410 with case lengths of $2\frac{1}{2}$, $2\frac{3}{4}$, 3 and $3\frac{1}{2}$ inches. From Ponsness/Warren.
Price: **$225.00**
Price: 10-ga. press **$249.00**

PONSNESS/WARREN Hydro-Matic

Add-on hydraulic system for Ponsness/Warren 800 or 900 Series presses. Features $\frac{1}{2}$-hp electric motor; $\frac{1}{3}$-gallon reservoir tank; variable speed foot control; dual cylinder system for equal load pressure on press; cycling of 1000 per hour; interchangeablility from press to press. Cylinder kits available for use on second machine. Kits supplied with quick disconnect hose attachments and all mounting hardware. From Ponsness/Warren.
Price: **$849.95**
Price: Cylinder kit **$349.95**

PONSNESS/WARREN L/S-1000

Frame: Die cast aluminum
Avg. Rounds Per Hour: NA
Weight: 55 lbs.
Features: Fully progressive press to reload steel, bismuth or lead shot. Equipped with new Uni-Drop shot measuring and dispensing system which allows the use of all makes of shot in any size. Shells automatically resized and deprimed with new Auto-Size and De-Primer system. Loaded rounds drop out of shellholders when completed. Each shell pre-crimped and final crimped with Tru-Crimp system. Available in 10-gauge $3\frac{1}{2}$" or 12-gauge $2\frac{3}{4}$" and 3". 12-gauge $3\frac{1}{2}$" conversion kit also available. 20-gauge $2\frac{3}{4}$" and 3" special order only. From Ponsness/Warren.
Price: **$769.00**
Price: Conversion kit . . . . **Contact manufacturer.**

PONSNESS/WARREN Size-O-Matic 900 Elite

Press Type: Progressive
Avg. Rounds Per Hour: 500-800
Weight: 49 lbs.
Features: Progressive eight-station press; frame of die cast aluminum; center post design index system ensures positive indexing; timing factory set, drilled and pinned. Automatic features include index, deprime, reprime, powder and shot drop, crimp start, tapered final crimp, finished shell ejection. Available in 12, 20, 28 and 410. 16-ga. special order. From Ponsness/Warren.
Price: **$588.00**

PONSNESS/WARREN Size-O-Matic 900 Elite Grand

Press Type: Progressive
Avg. Rounds Per Hour: 500-800
Weight: 55 lbs.
Features: Same as the Elite but with all the add-on accessoreis. Includes 25-lb. shot tube; shell counter; bushing access top plate; die cleaner bracket and swab; shot and powder bushing kit; shot and powder measure kit; pinpoint applicator; STOS 2-oz. jar; die cleaner brush; dust cover; die cleaner bracket and swab. From Ponsness/Warren.
Price: **$759.50**

BALLISTIC PRODUCTS

Powder Baffle

Now anti-static coated, will fit all MEC presses. Allows powder to flow evenly into bushing. Made of one-piece, high impact plastic. From Ballistic Products, Inc.

Price: **$4.99**

Powder Measure Adaptor

Universally threaded adaptor allows attachment of any threaded powder measuring tool to the Ponsness-Warren loading press. Weight 1-lb. From Ballistic Products, Inc.

Price: **$29.95**

HOLLYWOOD

Standard Shot Measure

Ductile iron body with ground hardened steel drum. Comes complete with one drop tube, 8" transparent cylinder and cylinder cover. From Hollywood Engineering.

Price: **$115.00**

HORNADY

366 Giant Shot/Powder Hoppers

Large 2-foot hoppers hold twice the volume of conventional hoppers. From Hornady Mfg. Co.

Price: Each **$9.90**

366 Primer Tube Filler

Attaches to feed tube of automatic priming system. Holds full box of shotshell primers. Will not drop upsidedown primers into feed tube. Weight: 1 lb. From Hornady Mfg. Co.

Price: **$11.00**

366 Riser Blocks

A set of blocks to raise 366 press above bench and give access to finished shells. From Hornady Mfg. Co.

Price: **$14.00**

366 Wad Guide Spring Fingers

Plastic fingers force case mouth open to prevent wad tipping and tearing. Standard on Hornady press and fit wad guides of most other makes. Available in 10, 12, 16, 20, 28 gauges and 410 bore. From Hornady Mfg. Co.

Price: **$1.50**

Powder and Shot Baffles

Extra set of two plastic baffles for 366 press. From Hornady Mfg. Co.

Price: **$4.75**

Ballistic Products Powder Baffle

Hornady 366 Wad Guide Fingers

Hornady Crimp Starter

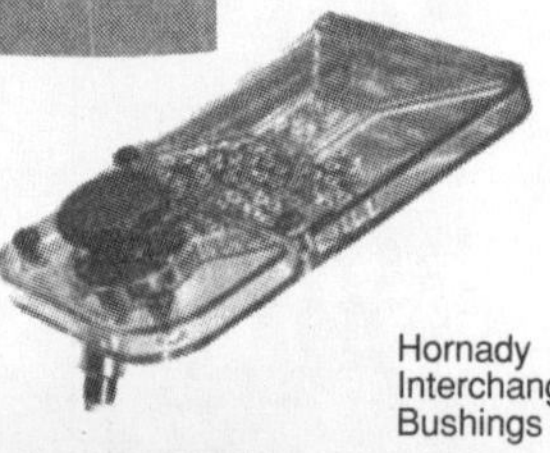

Hornady 366 Primer Tube Filler

Hornady Interchangeable Bushings

HORNADY Field Load Bushings
1/2-oz.
11/16-oz.
5/8-oz.
3/4-oz.
7/8-oz.
1 oz.
1 1/8 oz.
1 1/4 oz.
1 3/8 oz.
1 1/2 oz.
1 5/8 oz.
1 3/4 oz.
1 7/8 oz.
2 oz.
2 1/8 oz.

Hornady 366 Riser Blocks

HORNADY Target Load Bushings

Charge	Bushing
1/2 oz.	9
3/4 oz.	9
7/8 oz.	9
1 oz.	7 1/2
1 oz.	8
1 1/8 oz.	7 1/2
1 1/8 oz.	8 1/2
1 1/8 oz.	8 1/2
1 1/8 oz.	9

Hornady 366 Powder/Shot Baffles

HORNADY

Interchangeable Charge Bushings

Machined from nonferrous metal to assure spark-free operation. Fit all Hornady shot presses. Designed so shot and powder bushings cannot be reversed in charge bar. Made for both powder and lead shot. From Hornady Mfg. Co.

Price: **$2.85**

Lead Shot Field Load Bushings

Bushings for different shot sizes to compensate for tighter packing of small sizes. For all Hornady presses. From Hornady Mfg. Co.

Price: **$2.85**

Steel Shot Charge Bushings

Adapt to Hornady Models 155 and 266 presses for use with steel shot. From Hornady Mfg. Co.

Price: **$4.70**

HORNADY Steel Shot Bushings

Charge	Bushing #	Size
1 oz.	4,6	.712
1 1/8 oz.	4,6	.757
1 1/4 oz.	4,6	.792
1 oz.	1,2	.733
1 1/8 oz.	1,2	.777

HORNADY

Target Load Bushings

Calibrated to measure maximum legal loads for trap and Skeet shooting. From Hornady Mfg. Co.

Price: **$2.85**

Universal Crimp Starter

Engineered for cases with poorly defined memory. Improved radius for tight crimp. Available in 6- and 8-point for 12 and 20 gauges and 6-point only for 10, 28 and 410. From Hornady Mfg. Co.

Price: **$4.00**

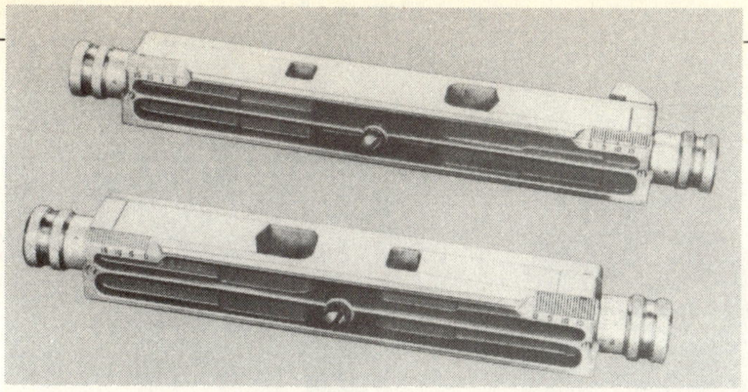

Multi-Scale Charge Bar

Hornady
Steel Shot Bushings

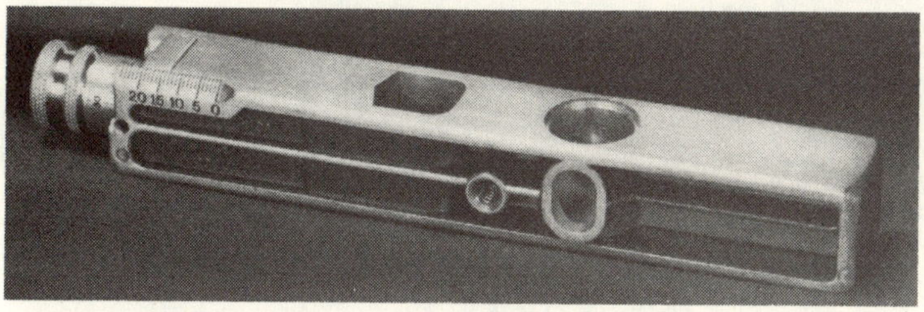

Multi-Scale Shuttle Bar

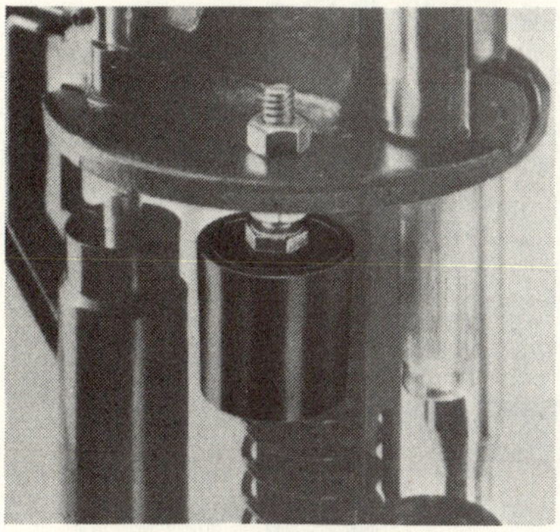

MEC Spindex Crimp Starter

LEE

Load-All II Conversion Kit

For converting Load-All II to another gauge. Includes die carrier, steel sizer, wad guide, shellholder, load data and instructions. Available in 12-, 16- and 20-gauge. From Lee Precision, Inc.

Price: **$19.98**

Load-All II Primer Feed

Optional attachment for Lee Load-All II to automatically feed primers. From Lee Precision, Inc.

Price: **$9.98**

Load-All II Primer Feed Kit

Upgrade kit for the older Lee Load-All presses. Converts press to Load-All II. Includes the new base with primer catcher; column, mounting screws; shellplates for 12-, 16- and 20-gauge; instructions and primer feed. From Lee Precision, Inc.

Price: **$21.98**

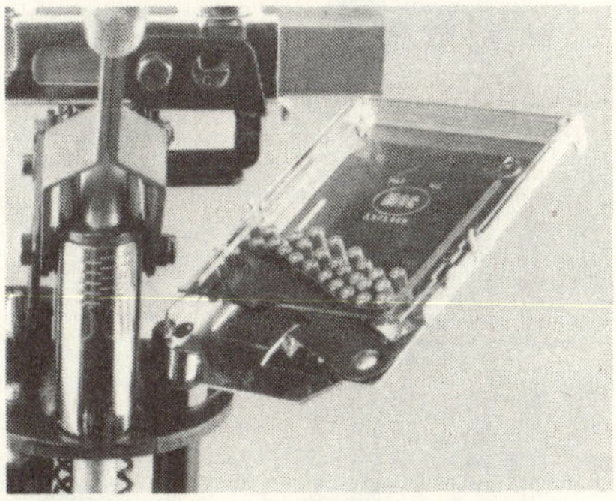

MEC E-Z Prime

MEC

Charge Bars

Quick-change charge bar with removable powder charger bushings. Bars equipped with soft insert to eliminate shearing when using larger shot sizes and hard lead shot. Fits all MEC presses. From Mayville Engineering Company, Inc.

Price: **$10.09**

E-Z Load Handle

Add-on wood handle reduces downward pressure and increases leverage of down stroke. Fits older MEC progressive machines; comes standard on newer presses. From Mayville Engineering Company, Inc.

Price: **$5.60**

E-Z Prime

Standard feature on all MEC presses except 600 Jr. Mark V. Automatically transfers primers to prime station. Not available for 410 single stage presses. From Mayville Engineering Company, Inc.

Price: **$37.07**

MEC

Powder Bushings

MEC offers 47 different bushings to accommodate different powders and loads. From Mayville Engineering Company, Inc.

Price: **$2.04**

Spindex Crimp Starter

Rotates automatically and realigns on orginal crimp of shell. Adjustable for 6- or 8-point crimp. Precision, one-piece Celcon unit standard on MEC reloaders. Adaptable to all MEC presses. From Mayville Engineering Company, Inc.

Price: 12-, 16-, 20-ga. **$4.65**
Price: 10-, 28-, 410 . . . . **$4.08**

Steel Shot Charge Bars

Designed specifically for loading steel shot reloads using MEC presses. Twenty shot charge bars available. From Mayville Engineering Company, Inc.

Price: **$11.06**

MULTI-SCALE CHARGE

Universal Charge Bars

Precision die cast zinc, fully adjustable replacement steel and lead shot charge bars for MEC shotshell presses. Capacity with No. 4 low antimony shot is from $^1/_2$-oz.to $2^1/_4$-oz.; powder capacity 12 to 55 grains. Features bottom guides for powder and shot valves and simplified method for reading and adjusting scales. Four models available: Model D for MEC 650 and Grabber; Model D Steel Shot for MEC 650 and Grabber; Model C for MEC 600 Jr., 700 Versamec, Sizemaster 77, MEC 600, 400, 250 and 250 Super, Mark 5 and the Texan LT, GT and FW; Model C Steel Shot fits same presses as Model C. From Multi-Scale Charge Ltd.

Price: **$24.95**

Powder Baffle

Designed to fit between powder bottle and charge bar of MEC presses for even powder density. Made of die cast zinc. From Multi-Scale Charge Ltd.

Price: **$5.95**

Shuttlebars

Model C and CS steel shot work with same MEC presses as Universal Charge Bar. Made of precision die cast zinc and comes with adjustable shot cavity from $^1/_2$-oz. to $2^1/_4$ oz. and works with all gauges. From Multi-Scale Charge Ltd.

Price: **$24.95**

MULTIPAX

Steel Shot Dispenser

Designed to fit all popular shotshell reloading presses to load steel shot or mount on the bench to load multiple shot sizes in same hull. Five models are available. The Model HMMP111 is for the Hornady Apex-91 with one shot container; Model PMMP201 for the Ponsness/Warren 375 working as a single or double unit for loading single or multiple shot sizes in same hull.; Model LMMP113 mounts on Lee Load-Fast; Model MMMP110 is for the MEC 650 or Grabber and converts the progressive press to a loader that will handle all sizes of steel shot; Model DMP200 is benchmount model with two shot containers or can be used with all single-stage presses. From Multi-Pax, Inc.

Price: HMMP111 . . . . **$32.95**
Price: PMMP201 . . . . **$32.95**
Price: LMMP113 . . . . **$35.95**
Price: MMP110 . . . . **$35.95**
Price: DMP200 . . . . **$42.95**

PATTERN CONTROL

MEC Powder Baffle

Designed for MEC presses to maintain consistent powder charge regardless of powder level in powder hopper. Spring-loaded insert prevents powder leakage between baffle and shot/powder bar. From Pattern Control.

Price: **$5.95**

Pacific Powder Baffle

Designed to fit Pacific No. 155, 266 or 366 presses with shot/powder tubes $1^{1}/_{8}$" in diameter. From Pattern Control.

Price: **$2.95**

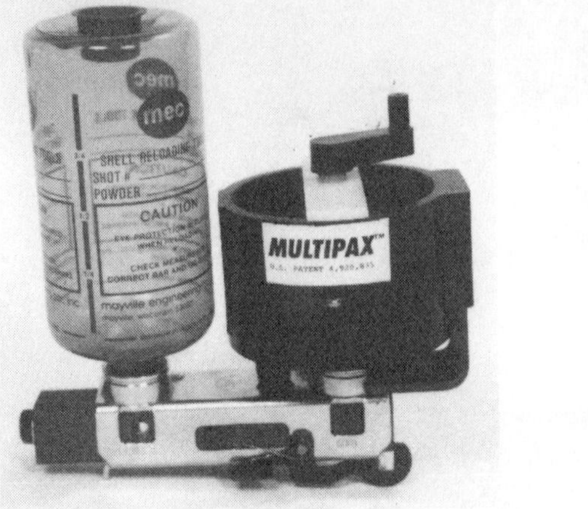

Multipax Model MMMP110

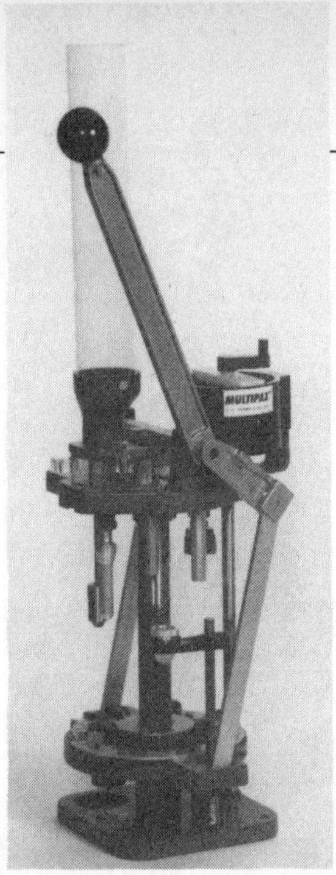

Multipax Model HMMP111

Multipax LMMP113 on Lee Load-Fast

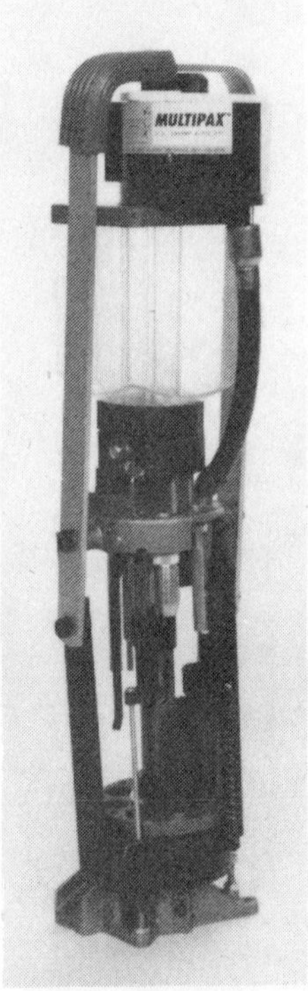

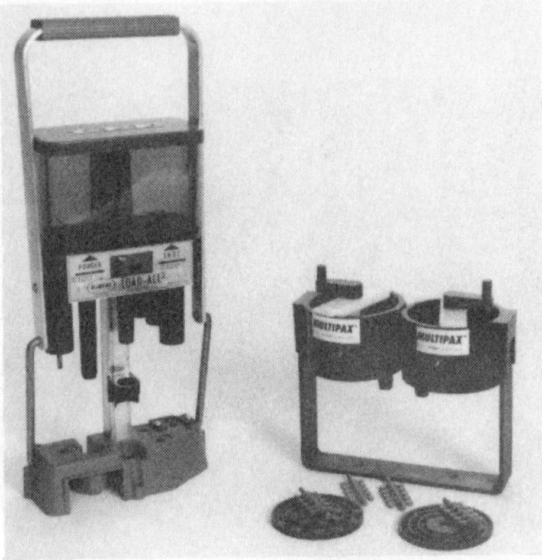

Multipax DMP200

Multipax HMMP111

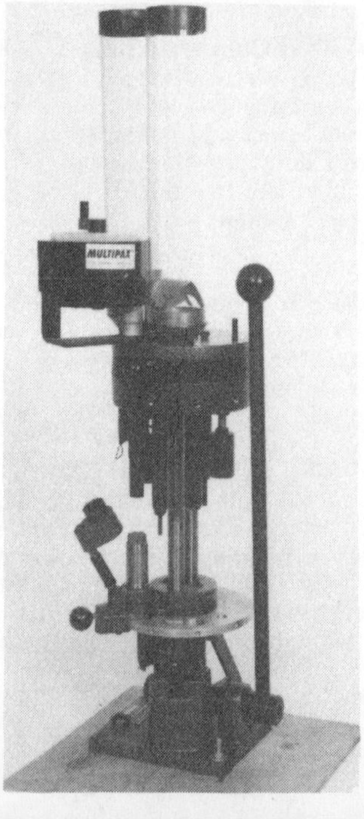

Multipax PMMP201

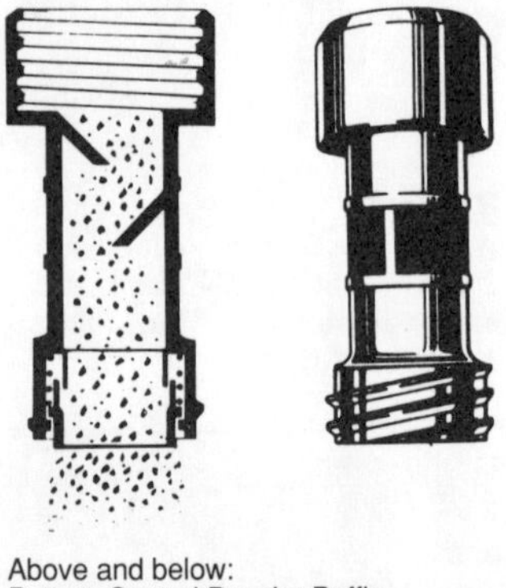

Above and below:
Pattern Control Powder Baffle

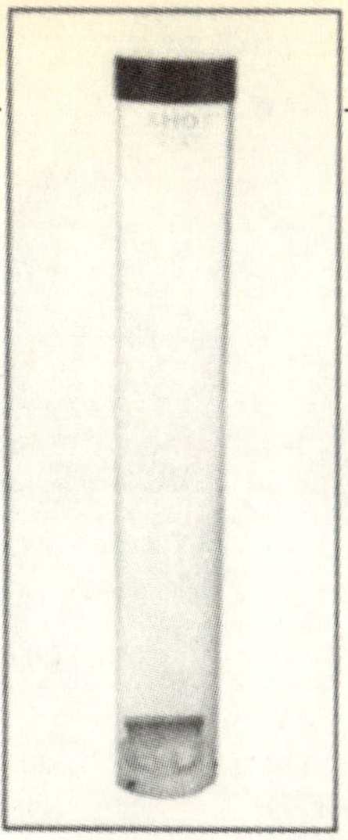

Ponsness/Warren
25-Lb. Shot Tube

PONSNESS/WARREN

25-Pound Shot Tube

Fits any 800 or 900 P/W reloader. Capacity for full bag of shot. Tube is 19" long and 3" in diameter. Includes a baffle. From Ponsness/Warren.

Price: **$18.95**

375 Tool Head

Extra tool head for gauge conversion. From Ponsness/Warren.

Price: **$37.80**

Ponsness/Warren 375 Tool Head

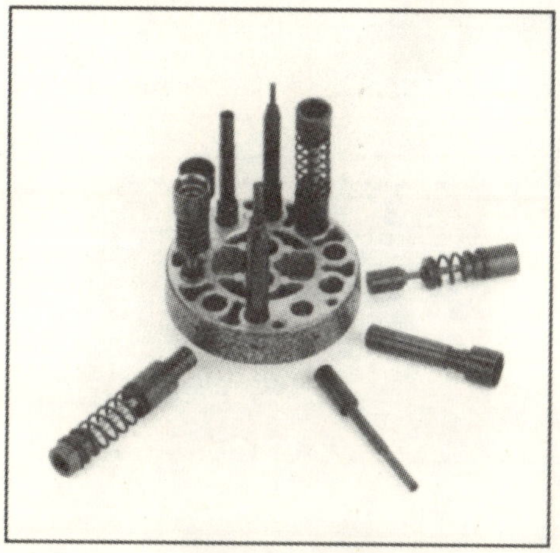

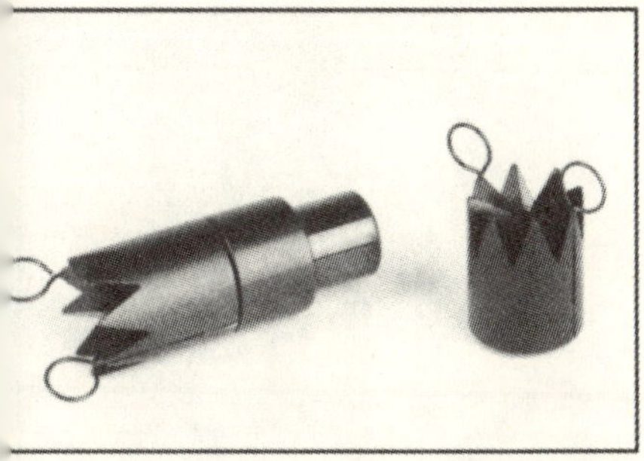

Ponsness/Warren Crimp Starters

Ponsness/Warren Bushing Access Top Plate

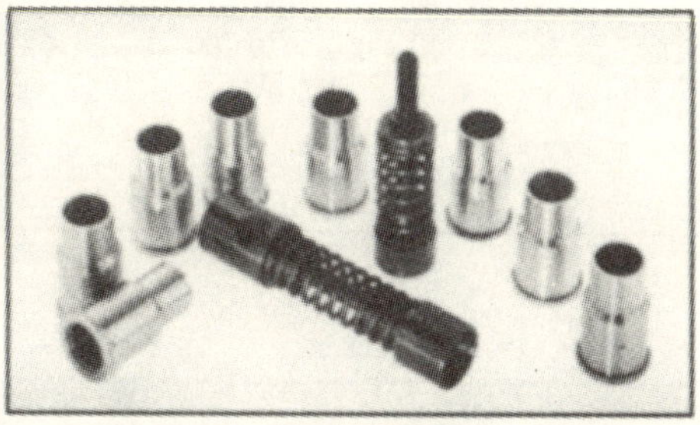

Ponsness/Warren 800B Taper Crimp Kits

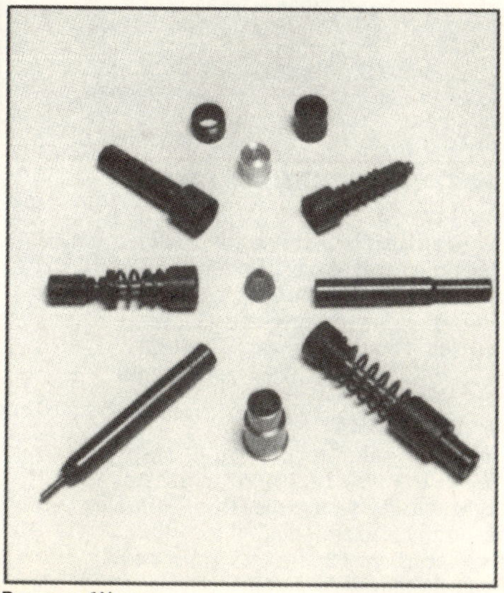

Ponsness/Warren
Du-O-Matic Tool Sets

Ponsness/Warren
375 Conversion Kits

PONSNESS/WARREN

800B Taper Crimp Kits

For P/W 800B press. Includes new sizing dies, final crimp assembly and finish shell knockout. Available in 12, 20, 28 or 410. From Ponsness/Warren.

Price: **$152.25**

Bushing Access Top Plate

Allows access to bushings without removal of shot and powder tubes. Comes with shot and powder bushing pullers. For Size-O-Matic presses. From Ponsness/Warren.

Price: **$49.95**

Crimp Starters

Six- and 8-point crimp starters, ball bearing lined with auto pick-up for perfect alignment and crimp. Comes complete or head only. From Ponsness/Warren.

Price: Complete **$31.45**
Price: Head only **$16.75**

Du-O-Matic 375 Conversion Kits

Allows conversion to 3", 3½" or 2½" shells. Specify B or C machine. From Ponsness/Warren.

Price: 3½", 12 . . . . **$49.95**
Price: 3", 12, 20, 410 . . . . **$31.45**
Price: 3" (B style), 12, 20, 410 . . . . **$34.65**
Price: 2½", 12 . . . . **$34.60**

Du-O-Matic Tool Sets

Tooling comes complete in 12, 16, 20, 28 or 410. Includes sizing die, finish shell knockout, primer knockout, shot and powder drop tube assembly, finish crimp assembly, shell seating cup and assembly, wad cup, wad fingers, shot and powder bushing and a Tru-Start crimp start assembly in 12 and 20 gauge. Metal crimp start assembly in 28 and 410. Special 10-ga. 3½" magnum tooling set available. 10-ga. tooling set also includes tool head, wad guide housing and 6-point crimp starter. Weight: 5 lbs. From Ponsness/Warren.

Price: **$82.95**
Price: 10-ga. Magnum **$103.95**

Dust Cover

Made of sturdy canvas comes in large and small sizes to fit the Size-O-Matic and Du-O-Matic presses. From Ponsness/Warren.

Price: Large **$20.95**
Price: Small **$16.75**

Ex-Er-Matic

Reloading bench for P/W hydraulic set-ups. Welded steel frame with adjustable padded seat and shell and wad hoppers. Adapts to any 800 or 900 Series press. Weight: 75 lbs. From Ponsness/Warren.

Price: **$439.95**

PONSNESS/WARREN

Paper Final Crimp Assembly
For Du-O-Matic and Size-O-Matic presses (C-type tooling only). Crimp conversion kit for reloading paper shells. From Ponsness/Warren.
Price: **$28.60**

Shell and Wad Hopper
Adaptable to any reloading press. Shell hopper holds 500 shells. From Ponsness/Warren.
Price: **$79.95**

Shot and Powder Bushings
Distinctly different diameters to eliminate possibility of being reversed. Powder bushings made of aluminum to assure no sparking. Both clearly etch-marked. From Ponsness/Warren.
Price: **$2.65**

Shot and Powder Measure Kit
For checking shot and powder charges during press operation. Available in single gauge kits or as four gauge kit, 12, 20, 28 and 410. From Ponsness/Warren.
Price: Single gauge kit **$3.95**
Price: Four gauge kit **$13.60**

Sizing Die Cleaner Bracket
Attaches to 800 or 900 series reloaders. Automatically cleans with brush or swab sizing dies during press operation. Available for 12, 20/28 or 410. From Ponsness/Warren.
Price: Bracket **$15.70**
Price: Brush **$1.05**
Price: Swab **$1.35**

Size-O-Matic Primer Tray Extension Kit
Increases primer tray capacity to 300 primers. From Ponsness/Warren.
Price: **$20.95**

Size-O-Matic Shell Counter
Counts shells automatically and attaches to 800 or 900 series presses. From Ponsness/Warren.
Price: **$20.95**

Size-O-Matic Shovel Handle
Made of high-quality aluminum casting with wood grip. Replaces standard ball-type grip that comes standard on the press. From Ponsness/Warren.
Price: **$26.20**

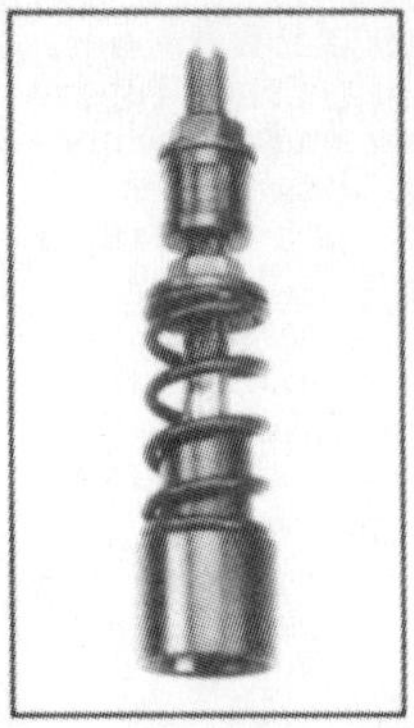

Ponsness/Warren
Paper Final Crimp Assembly

Ponsness/Warren
Canvas Dust Covers

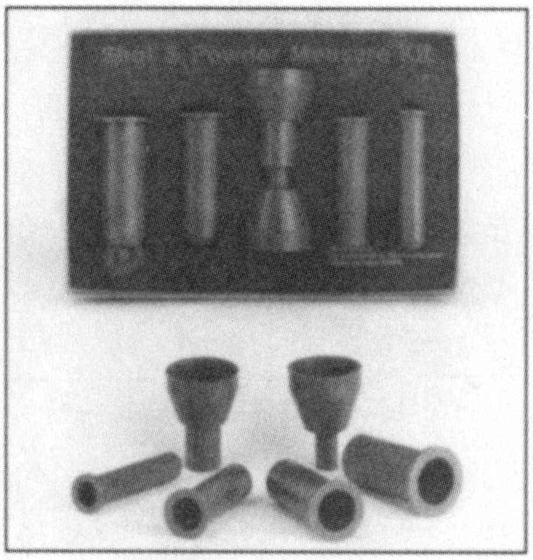

Ponsness/Warren
Shot and Powder Measure Kit

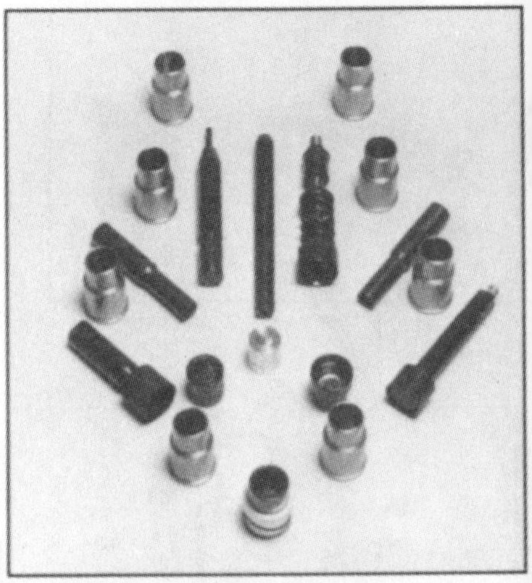

Ponsness/Warren
Size-O-Matic Tool Sets

Ponsness/Warren
Sizing Die Cleaner Bracket

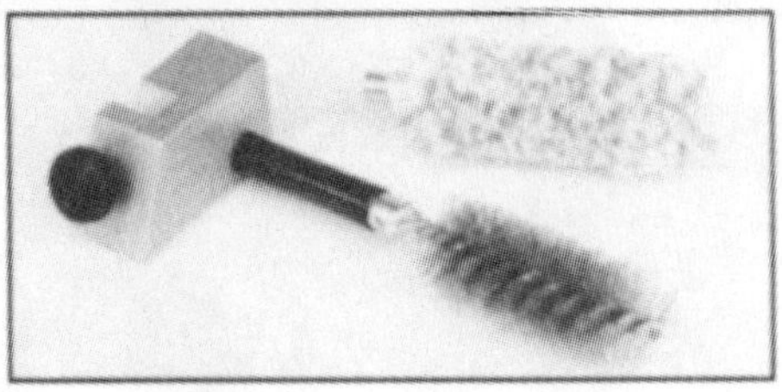

Ponsness/Warren
Size-O-Matic Shell Counter

PONSNESS/WARREN

Size-O-Matic Tool Sets
For all Size-O-Matic convertible models. Comes complete in 12, 16, 20, 28 or 410. Includes sizing dies, finish shell knockout, primer knockout, shot and powder drop tube assembly, final crimp assembly, shell seating cup and assembly, wad cup, wad fingers, shot and powder bushings and Tru-Start crimp start assembly in 12- and 20-gauge. Metal crimp start assembly in 28 and 410. Weight: 7 lbs. From Ponsness/Warren.
Price: **$177.00**

PONSNESS/WARREN

Swing Tray
Allows filling of primer tray without removing tray cover. Cover swings to the left by loosening wing nut for filling. For the Size-O-Matic presses. From Ponsness/Warren.
Price: **$12.95**

Taper Crimp Kits
Converts older model Du-O-Matic 375 to the new taper crimp assembly. Includes sizing die, final crimp assembly and finish shell knockout. Available in 12, 20, 28 and 410. From Ponsness/Warren.
Price: **$52.50**

Ponsness/Warren
Thumb Screws

Ponsness/Warren
Tru-Crimp Package

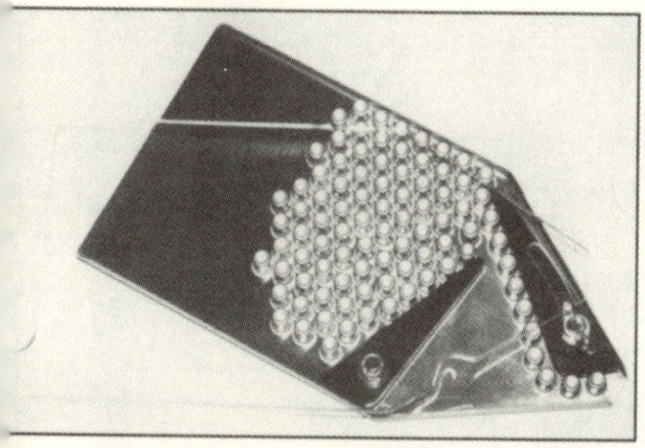

Ponsness/Warren
Swing Tray

Ponsness/Warren
Tru-Crimp Starter

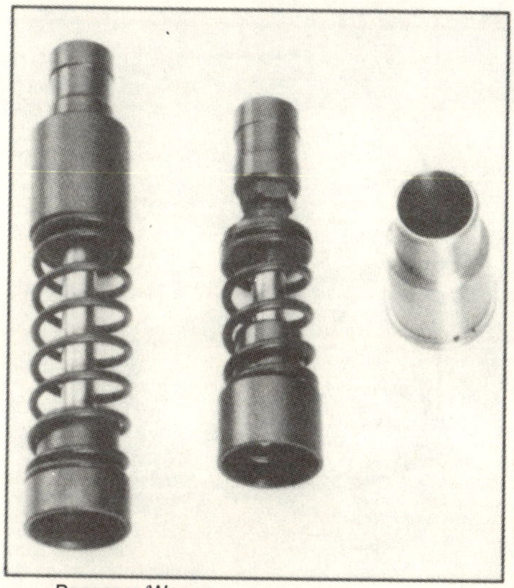

Ponsness/Warren
375 Taper Crimp Kits

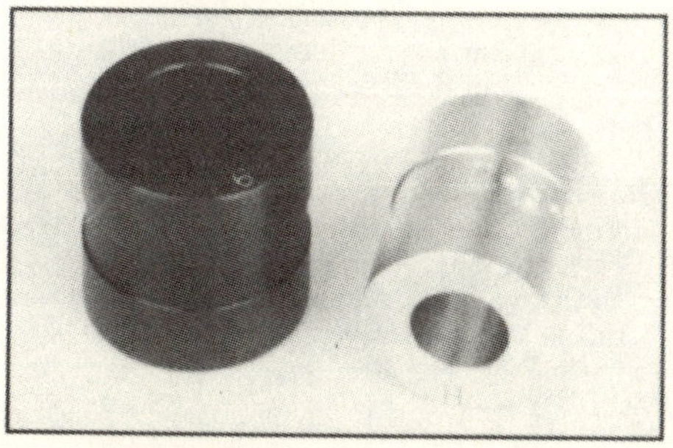

Ponsness/Warren
Shot and Powder Bushings

PONSNESS/WARREN

Thumb Screws

For the top plate on older 800 series presses; standard on the 900 press. These screws allow access to shot and powder bushings and to clean gears. Come in sets of four. From Ponsness/Warren.

Price: **$5.20**

Tru-Crimp Package

Final crimp assembly comes complete with Tru-Start crimp starter and Tru-Crimp final crimp package. For all Ponsness/Warren shot presses. From Ponsness/Warren.

Price: **$34.95**

Tru-Crimp Starter

Specially designed for plastic shotshells. Unique "lead and spin" system ensures shells are pre-crimped in original folds. Available in 6- or 8-point crimps. Available for any P/W shotshell reloader producing a tapered final crimp. From Ponsness/Warren.

Price: **$5.95**

Wad Guide Fingers

Wad guide fingers available in 10, 12, 16, 20, 28 and 410. From Ponsness/Warren.

Price: **$1.05**

PRECISION RELOADING

MEC Powder/Shot Containers

Ten-inch lead or steel shot and powder bottle assemblies for MEC press. Available filled with 10 lbs. PR steel shot. From Precision Reloading, Inc.

Price: **$3.50**
Price: With F, T, BBB, BB, B, #1, #2, #3, #4 . . . . **$19.95**
Price: With #5, #6, #7, #8 . . . . . . **$20.95**

Oak Baseboards

Oak veneer baseboards 16"x19"x$^3/_4$" designed to make MEC presses portable. Bases have polyurethane finish and have rubber feet to prevent sliding. Weight: 7 lbs. From Precision Reloading, Inc.

Price: **$14.95**

Oak Baseboard with Brackets

Same as above with PR aluminum Quick Change brackets installed. Available with either 4" or 7" width brackets. From Precision Reloading, Inc.

Price: **$29.95**

Quick Change Brackets

Solid brass 1"x $^3/_8$"x 8" or aluminum 1"x $^1/_2$"x 8" brackets allow removing and replacing MEC press with another of similar size base. From Precision Reloading, Inc.

Price: Aluminum **$15.95**
Price: Brass **$21.95**

RELOADING SPECIALITIES

12-Ga. Spacer Bushings

Designed for the MEC 600 Jr. and Sizemaster presses to load 3$^1/_2$" or 3" hulls. Eliminates press readjustment when loading shells of shorter length. Brass spacers allow loading 2$^3/_4$" cases with A, D, E spacers; or 3" down from 3$^1/_2$" with B spacers; or 2$^3/_4$" from 3$^1/_2$" with C spacer. A ($^1/_4$"); B ($^1/_2$"); C ($^3/_4$"); D ($^1/_4$"); E ($^1/_4$"). From Reloading Specialties, Inc.

Price: A, B, C **$12.95**
Price: D **$24.95**
Price: E **$29.95**

TRICO PLASTICS

MEC Powder and Shot Bottles

Double-size transparent powder or shot bottles with built-in baffle. Top-loading, fits all MEC reloading presses. From Trico Plastics.

Price: **$5.50**

Wad Guide Fingers

Durable plastic replacement fingers for 12- and 20-ga. Come in packages of two. From Trico Plastics.

Price: . . . . **$.98**

Section 2: Shotshell Reloading

BALLISTIC PRODUCTS

Adjustable Shot Dipper

Tough plastic shot dipper screw-adjusts to measure and drop 1-oz. or $1^7/_8$-oz. lead shot. Also can be used to measure steel shot. From Ballistic Products, Inc.

Price: **$3.95**

Angle Wad Slitter

Aluminum tube with choice of three or four slits and tube base for angle slitting shotcups. Cutting length is adjustable with movable stop. Available for 12-ga. Ranger-Plus, 12-ga. BP12 or BP12-TUFF and 10-ga. BPD or BPD-TUFF wads. Exacto knife and blades extra. From Ballistic Products, Inc.

Price: Angle Cutter **$24.95**
Price: X-Acto knife **$3.95**
Price: X-Acto blades (15) **$4.95**

Buffer Dipper

Use to pour polyethylene shot buffer into shell. From Ballistic Products, Inc.

Price: . . . . **$.50**

D-Loader

Reclaim powder, shot, primer and wad from bad reloads. Made of hard maple with replaceable cutter, D-Loader will also trim the overall length of 10- and 12-ga. TUFF-type wads. From Ballistic Products, Inc.

Price: **$8.95**

Hull Marks

Round self-adhesive labels for load marking. Come in five colors to code loads or mark with pen. Place on side of shell or base. From Ballistic Products, Inc.

Price: 500 . . . . **$3.95**
Price: 1,000 . . . . **$7.50**

Hull Shape-Up Tool

Expands the mouth of 20- to 10-ga. hulls for easier loading and will straighten out most bad crimps for hull re-use. From Ballistic Products, Inc.

Price: **$6.95**

Hull Vise

Firmly grips an empty shell during reloading and crimping process. Adjustable locking action for no spilled loads. Fits all gauges from 10 to 410 bore. From Ballistic Products, Inc.

Price: **$34.95**

Loading Block

Wood reloading block holds 25 or 50 rounds in upright, brass down position. Available in 10-ga. through 410 bore. From Ballistic Products, Inc.

Price: 25-round **$6.50**
Price: 50-round **$10.95**

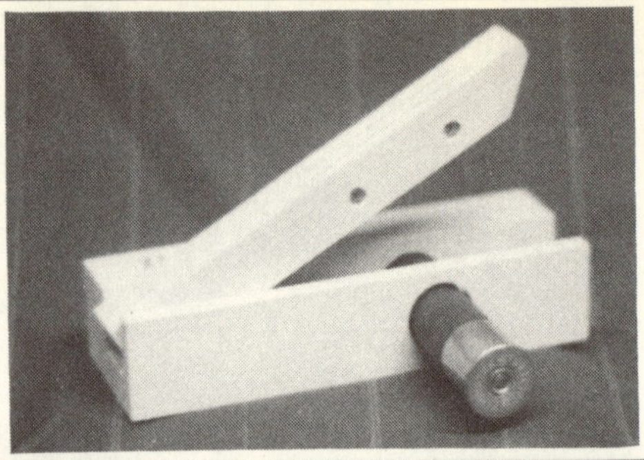

Ballistic Products D-Loader

Ballistic Products Roll Crimpers

Ballistic Products Loading Tray

Ballistic Products Shot Buffer

BALLISTIC PRODUCTS

Loading Tray

Plastic stackable load tray holds 50 shells with brass end up. Can be used in conjunction with MTM 100-rd. or 200-rd. shell cases. Available in 10-, 12-, 16- or 20-ga. From Ballistic Products, Inc.

Price: **$2.95**

Mylar Wrap

For the steel shot reloader. Mylar wraps inside the wad provide barrel protection. Available in either regular thickness (.010") or extra thin (.003"). From Ballistic Products, Inc.

Price: .010"/50 . . . . **$2.50**
Price: .003"/100 . . . . **$3.50**

BALLISTIC PRODUCTS

Roll Crimper

Shell crimping tool available in 10-, 12-, 16-, 20- and 28-gauges. Will fit any $^1/_4$" drill chuck either hand-held or drill press. From Ballistic Products, Inc.

Price: **$19.95**

Shot Buffers

Fine ground polyethylene shot buffer in original mix or special mix #47. Both available in plastic jars with buffer to load 150 shells. From Ballistic Products, Inc.

Price: Original Mix **$3.50**
2 or more **$3.00**
Case of 24 . . . . **$54.00**
Price: Mix #47 . . . . **$3.95**
2 or more **$3.50**
Case of 24 . . . . **$60.00**

Hornady Stack 'N' Pack

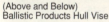

(Above and Below)
Ballistic Products Hull Vise

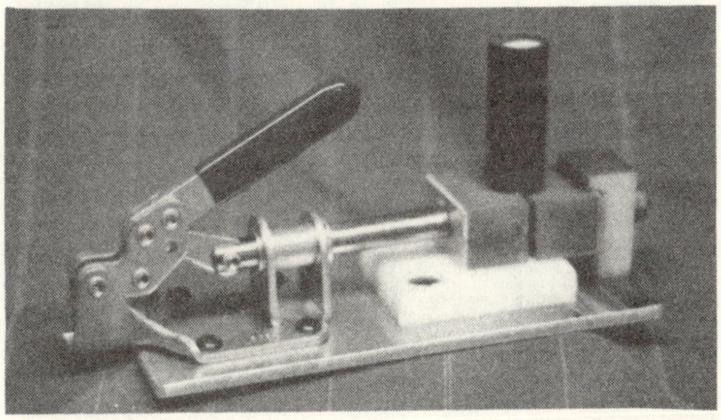

MEC E-Z Pack

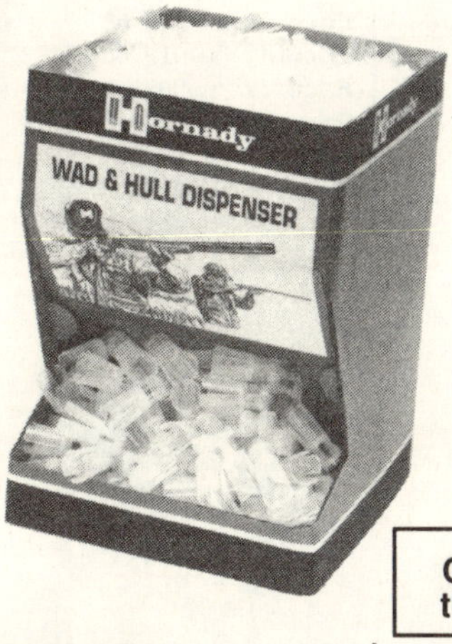

Hornady Wad/Hull Dispenser

BALLISTIC PRODUCTS

Skiver

Reams and tapers the mouth of a new hull for better fold or roll crimps. Made of aluminum oxide abrasive. From Ballistic Products, Inc.

Price: **$6.50**

Super Slick

Liquid silicone treatment applied to hulls and wads for slippery surface for consistent patterns, pressures and increased velocity. Single application lasts the life of the hull. 12-oz. bottle. From Ballistic Products, Inc.

Price: **$12.95**

Teflon Wraps

For use in 10- and 12-ga. low pressure magnum loads, buckshot loads and slug loads. Helps speed up load velocity, protect the shot column or slug from deformation and barrel scrub and reduce slug wandering. Packs of 50. From Ballistic Products, Inc.

Price: **$7.95**

HORNADY

Stack 'N' Pack

Holds 25 shells. Stacks them for packing into boxes. Includes two 12-gauge shotshell boxes. From Hornady Mfg. Co.

Price: **$6.95**

Wad/Hull Dispenser

Cardboard dispenser holds up to 200 wads or hulls. Frees up workspace while reloading. From Hornady Mfg. Co.

Price: **$6.50**

KIRDOC

Shell Dismantler

Lightweight, non-static metal tool designed to precisely cut plastic and paper hulls without destroying the wad. From Precision Reloading, Inc.

Price: **$22.95**

Consult our Directory pages for the location of firms mentioned.

MEC

E-Z Pack

Reloaded shells stack in E-Z Pack as if in box. Slip box over full stacker, turn stacker upsidedown. Available in all gauges. From Mayville Engineering Company, Inc.

Price: **$6.99**

Shotshell Checker

Measure precision of reloaded shells for proper chambering. Precision machined holes labeled "Go" "No-Go" test for size and roundness. Made of durable stainless steel and accommodates 10, 12, 16, 20, 28 and 410. From Mayville Engineering Company, Inc.

Price: **$7.87**

MEC

Steel Shot Adapter Kit

To upgrade MEC 600 Jr. Mark V, Versamec, Sizemaster, 650 and Grabber reloading presses to handle steel shot components. Kits for progressive presses also available. Includes wide-mouthed shot bottle, metal drop tube and large diameter rammer tube. Steel shot charge bar available separately depending on powder and shot size desired. From Mayville Engineering Company, Inc.

Price: **$13.38**
Price: Progressive steel shot kit . . **$21.67**

Steel Shot Buffer

Plastic buffer #520 for loading steel shot. Comes in 8-oz. plastic bag. From Mayville Engineering Company, Inc.

Price: . . . . **Contact manufacturer.**

Super-Sizer

Resizes shotshell base back to factory specifications. Eight steel fingers encircle base and draw it back to original size. Heavy-duty construction with sure grip plastic handle. Available in 10, 12, 16, 20, 28 and 410. From Mayville Engineering Company, Inc.

Price: **$85.16**

PRECISION RELOADING

520 Buffer

Nearly identical to Tru-Square and MEC #520 plastic buffer. Can be subtituted in same charge weight. Comes in 8- or 16-oz. bags. From Precision Reloading, Inc.

Price: 8 oz. **$4.99**
Price: 16 oz. **$8.99**

Motor Mica

Anti-friction dry compound to use as additive to lead and steel shot to avoid bridging; lubricate wads to decrease bore scrub. Comes in 8-oz., 1-lb. or 5 lb. can. From Precision Reloading, Inc.

Price: 8 oz. **$4.49**
Price: 1 lb. **$7.95**
Price: 5 lbs. **$34.95**

Mylar Shot Wrap

Plastic mylar wrap available in two thicknesses .010 or .0075 for 10- or 12-gauge. Come in packages of 50 or 500 or 8$^1/_2$ x 11 sheets. From Precision Reloading, Inc.

Price: 10-ga./.010, 50 . . . . **$2.95**
Price: 10-ga./.010, 500 . . . . **$21.95**
Price: 12-ga./.0075, 50 . . . . **$2.50**
Price: 12-ga./.0075, 500 . . . . **$17.95**
Price: 12-ga./.010, 50 . . . . **$2.75**
Price: 12-ga./.010, 500 . . . . **$18.95**
Price: 12-ga./.0075, 50 . . . . **$2.60**
Price: 12-ga./.0075, 500 . . . . **$18.50**
Price: Sheet, .010 . . . . **$15.00**
Price: Sheet, .0075 . . . . **$12.70**

PRECISION RELOADING

Overshot/Overbuffer Tight Seal

Over shot material conforms to hull shape and eliminates buffer migration; assists in even crimp opening on combustion. Creates no chamber pressure increases. Comes in packs of 500 for 10- and 12-gauge. From Precision Reloading, Inc.

Price: **$5.95**

Spherical Shotshell Buffer

Spherical buffer available with or without C-6 a graphite additive or Motor Mica an anti-friction compound. Comes in plastic storage bottles. From Precision Reloading, Inc.

Price: 12 oz. **$4.99**
Price: 20 oz. **$6.99**
Price: 12 oz. w/C-6 or MM **$5.49**
Price: 20 oz. w/C-6 or MM **$7.69**

RCBS

Shell Loading Block

Heavy plastic block holds up to fifty 12- or 16-gauge shells on one side or fifty 20- or 28-gauge shells on the other. From RCBS.

Price: **$5.84**

RELOADING SPECIALTIES

Super Sam Buffer

Specifically designed for steel shot loads. Granulated plastomers available in 8-oz. bag. From Reloading Specialties, Inc.

Price: **$5.00**

MEC Super Sizer

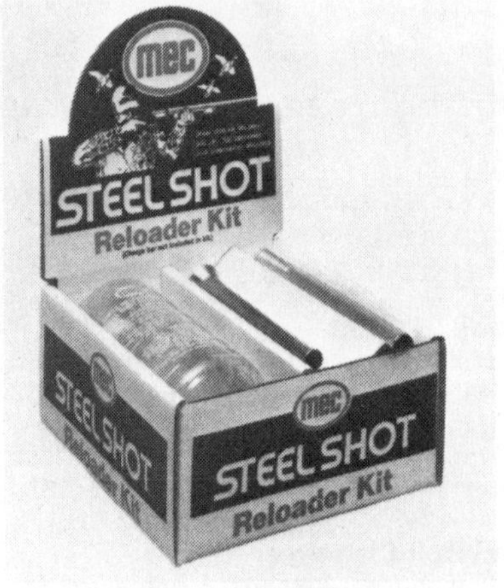

MEC Steel Shot Kit

Consult our Directory pages for the location of firms mentioned.

1994 HANDLOADER'S DIGEST

13th EDITION

PART

1
2
3
4
5
6

BULLET SWAGING

TOOLS & ACCESSORIES

BULLET SWAGING SUPPLY B.S.S.P. Press

Frame: Cast Aluminum
Frame Type: O-Type
Die Thread: $^5/_8$-24
Ram Stroke: $2^1/_{16}$"
Weight: NA
Features: O-frame design allows easy access to working area; horizontally mounted; linkage system engineered to reduce stress on the press frame by 95%, thus eliminating press spring and aiding swaging accuracy; ejects on the up-stroke for swaging speed. Dimensions: $11^1/_2$"x 5"x $2^5/_8$". Will accept dies from the Corbin Mity Mite with no modifications; dies from the SAS Mity Mite need ejection punch replacement in the point form die. Carbide point forming and core seating dies available in 224, 243 and 308 calibers in two configurations: Set #1 includes carbide point forming die, carbide core seating die and steel core swage die; Set #2 includes carbide point forming die, steel core seating die and steel core swage die. From Bullet Swaging Supply, Inc.

Price: Press **$99.00**
Price: Press and steel 3-die set **$300.00**
Price: Press and Set #1 . . . . **$1,049.00**
Price: Press and Set #2 . . . . **$799.00**
Price: 14- and 17-caliber dies, add **$20.00**

CORBIN CSP-1 Series II

Frame: Steel
Frame Type: H-frame
Die Thread: $^7/_8$-14
Ram Stroke: 2" swaging; 4" drawing or jacket making.
Weight: 22 lbs.
Features: Four precision roller bearings mounted in heavy-duty steel links, bearing on hardened tool steel pins; oil-impregnated bronze bearings surrounding ram; dual stroke operation; left- or right-hand handle positioning; ordnance steel alloy supports and ram; machined frame; electrostatic powder-coated, baked-on finish. Hand-built, hand-assembled press. Swages bullets from 14- to 458-caliber. Maximum bullet length, 1.25"; maximum pressure, over 200,000 psi. Comes with floating punch holder for use with external punches of Corbin swage dies. Made for use with Corbin M or S type dies. From Corbin Manufacturing & Supply, Inc.

Price: **$269.50**
Price: Bench stand with storage shelf **$49.50**
Price: Anvil set (ram and head) **$25.00**
Price: Floor stand (150 lbs.) **$239.00**
Price: Extra floating punch holder **$20.00**
Price: Extra reloading adapter for ram **$20.00**
Price: Extra stop pin **$5.00**

CORBIN Series II Press Swaging System

Series II CSP-1 press, 3-die FJFB-3-S swaging set, LW-10 lead wire, CSL-2 swaging lube and PCS-1 core cutter. From Corbin Manufacturing & Supply, Inc.

Price: **$712.50**

CORBIN Hydro-Press CHP-1 Swaging System

Includes Hydro-Press, 3-die FJFB-3-H swaging set, LED-1 lead wire extruder, CSL-2 swaging lube, CTJM-1-H lubing jacketmaker, PCM-1 power cannelure tool, CCB-16 core bond, and HTO-2 heat treatment oven. Any caliber from 224-20mm including 50 BMG and shotgun slug. From Corbin Manufacturing & Supply, Inc.

Price: **$8,634.00**

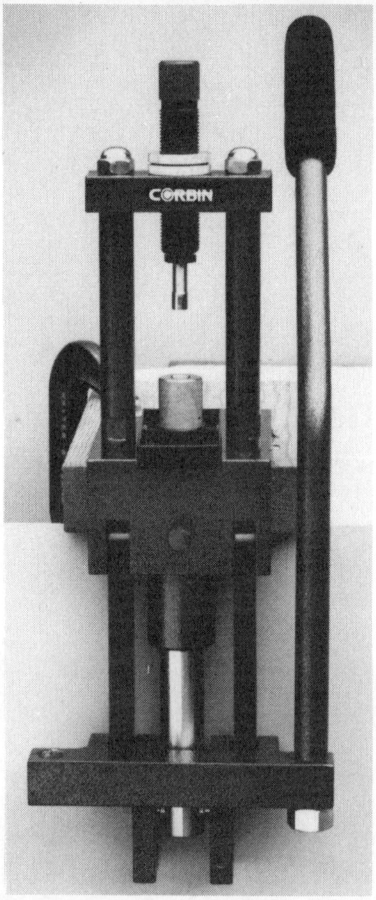

Corbin CSP-1

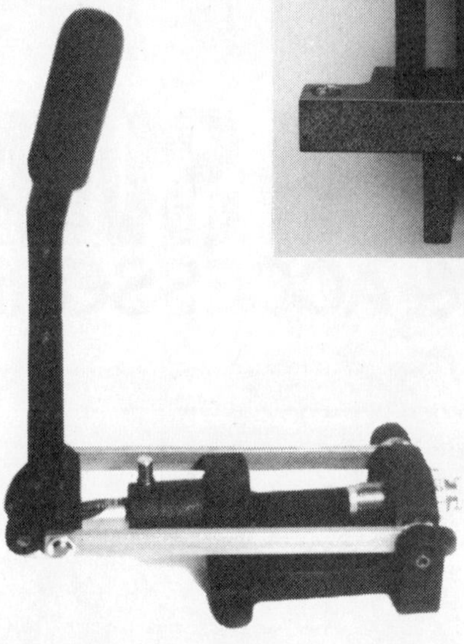

Bullet Swaging Supply B.S.S.P.

CORBIN CSP-2 Mega Mite

Frame: Steel
Frame Type: H-frame
Die Thread: $1^1/_2$-12
Ram Stroke: 3"
Weight: 55 lbs. (press); 160 lbs. (press and floor stand)
Features: Roller bearing linkage; hardened tool steel pivots; precision bronze bushings on polished steel guide rods. Dual stroke operation allows stroke to be changed from 5.5-inch to 3-inch for reloading up to 50 BMG cases or heavy swaging. Can swage hard lead bullets up to .475 diameter and soft lead to .600. Maximum pressure, 180,000 psi; maximum bullet length, $1^1/_2$"; maximum jacket wall, 0.50" copper. Made for use with Corbin H dies. Comes with thick steel floor stand with 4-inch diameter iron tube and punch holder. Height with floor stand is 66". From Corbin Manufacturing & Supply, Inc.

Price: **$850.00**
Price: Without floor stand **$750.00**

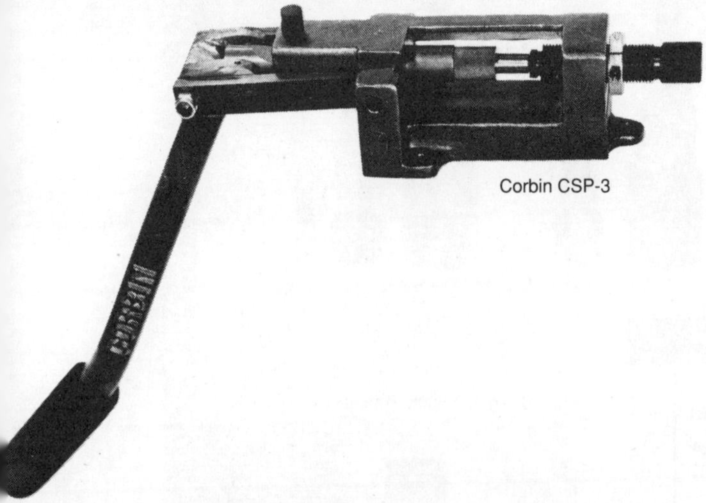

Corbin CSP-3

Corbin Silver Press

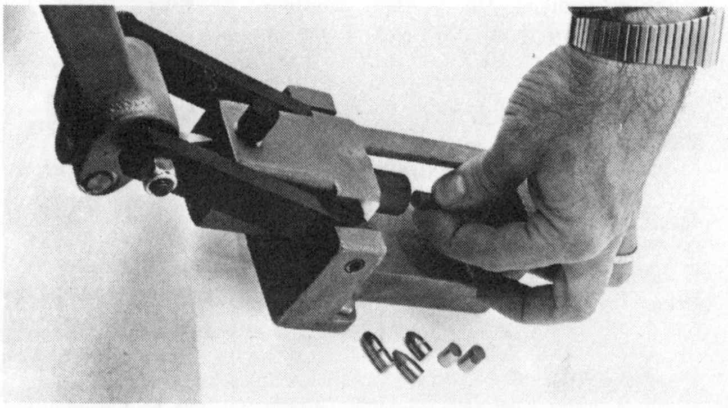

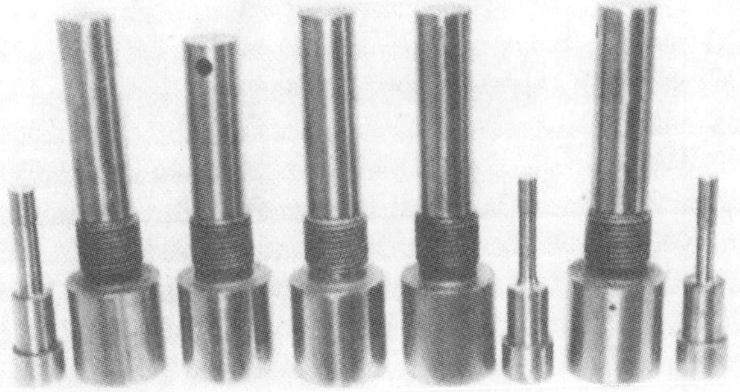

Hydro-Press Swaging System

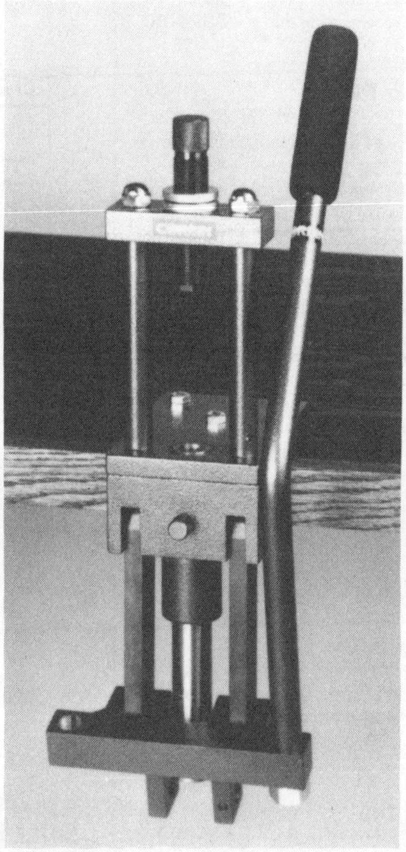

Corbin CSP-2

CORBIN Silver Press

Frame: Cast iron
Frame Type: NA
Die Thread: NA
Ram Stroke: NA
Weight: 13 lbs.
Features: Horizontal stroke, self-ejection and self-alignment. Swages bullets from 14- to 458-caliber; calibers above 308 necessitate use of soft lead. Maximum pressure, 80,000 psi; maximum bullet length, 1.25"; maximum bullet weight depends on ogive shape and caliber but is approximately 450 grains with 1-E ogive .458 copper tubing (.030" wall) bullet. Made for use with Corbin M dies. Comes with spare floating punch holder. From Corbin Manufacturing & Supply, Inc.
Price: **$189.50**

CORBIN Silver Press CSP-3 Swaging System 1

Includes Silver Press CSP-3, 3-die FJFB-3-M swaging set (any caliber from 14 to 458), LW-10 lead wire, CSL-2 swaging lube, and PCS-1 core cutter (calibers from 14 to 458). From Corbin Manufacturing & Supply, Inc.
Price: **$552.50**

CORBIN Silver Press CSP-3 Swaging System 2

Includes CSP-3 press, LSWC-1-M swage die in any caliber (270-458), CSL-2 swaging lube, LW-10 lead wire, and PCS-1 core cutter. From Corbin Manufacturing & Supply, Inc.
Price: **$333.50**

BULLET SWAGING SUPPLY

22 Jacket-Maker Die

Makes 22-caliber jackets out of 22-caliber cases. Designed to remove rims from fired 22 Short, Long or Long Rifle cases. Good jackets if velocity is below 3200 fps. From Bullet Swaging Supply, Inc.

Price: **$40.00**

Boattail Form Die

Point form die with boattail punch. From Bullet Swaging Supply, Inc.

Price: **$100.00**

Carbide Dies

Carbide dies made to exact standards for match-quality bullets. Point form and core seating dies available for 224 and 243 calibers. Three-die set includes carbide point form and core seating die and steel core swage die. Also available as kit with press (see Bullet Swaging/Miscellaneous). From Bullet Swaging Supply, Inc.

Price: 3-die set **$950.00**
Price: Carbide point form die . . . **$625.00**
Price: Carbide core seating die . . **$325.00**

Core Seating Die

Offered in steel or carbide, threaded $^5/_8$-24 and available for both rifle and pistol calibers 14 through 458. Used to seat the lead core in the jacket. Most calibers in stock; custom dies made to order. Send sample jacket so external punch can be machined to fit and specify bullet weight. From Bullet Swaging Supply, Inc.

Price: Steel **$60.00**
Price: Carbide **$325.00**

Core Swage Die

Steel swage die, threaded $^5/_8$-24 and available for both rifle and pistol calibers 14 through 458. Most calibers in stock; custom dies made to order. From Bullet Swaging Supply, Inc.

Price: **$60.00**

Lead Tip Form Die

Steel die designed for spire point or spitzer rifle bullets to form lead bullet tip. From Bullet Swaging Supply, Inc.

Price: **$80.00**

Point Form Die

Gives bullet its final shape and diameter. Offered in steel or carbide, threaded $^5/_8$-24 and available for both rifle and pistol calibers 14 through 458. Most calibers in stock; custom dies made to order. From Bullet Swaging Supply, Inc.

Price: Steel **$90.00**
Price: Carbide **$625.00**

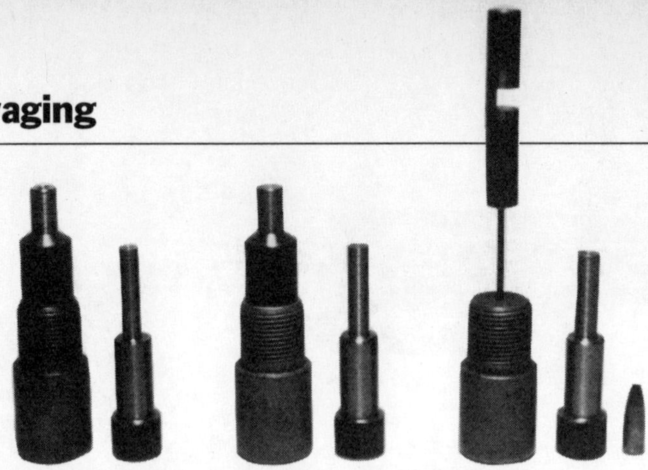

Bullet Swaging Supply 3-Die Set

BULLET SWAGING SUPPLY

RIFLE DIES

CALIBER	DIAMETER
22	.223/.224
	.224
6mm	.243
25	.257
270	.277
7mm	.284
30	.308
	.308
338	.338
358	.358
375	.375
416	.416

PISTOL DIES

CALIBER	DIAMETER
32	
9mm	
38	.357
400	
41	.410
44	.429
45	.4515

Bullet Swaging Supply Tubing Die

C-H/4-D Swage Die

Bullet Swaging Supply Jacket Draw Die

BULLET SWAGING SUPPLY

Ring Die

Designed to reduce jacket diameter from 22-caliber, for example, to 17-caliber. Maximum reduction per die is .0010 to .0020. From Bullet Swaging Supply, Inc.

Price: **$15.00**
Price: Ring die with holder **$30.00**

C-H/4-D

105-Z Zinc Base Swage Die

Swage 38/357 bullets with zinc bases to prevent leading and to preserve bore life. Semi-wadcutter nose punch and washers extra. Can be used with any standard loading press. From C-H Tool & Die/4-D Custom Die.

Price: Die **$29.95**
Price: Nose punch **$9.50**
Price: Zinc base washers/1000 . . . . **$23.20**

C-H/4-D Zinc Base Swage Die

C-H/4-D Swage Die

Corbin Bullet Swage Dies

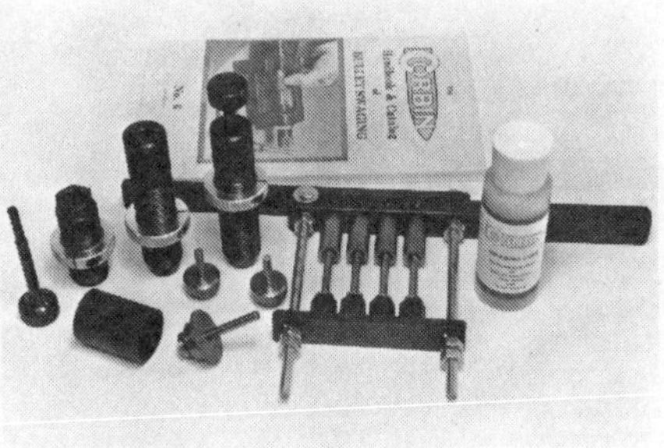

Corbin 224 Kit

CORBIN H-Type Swage Dies

DIE	DESCRIPTION	PRICE
CSW-1-H	Core swage die and punch	$160.00
SC-1-H	Core seating die and punch	160.00
PF-1-H	Point forming die and punch	229.00
LT-1-H	Lead tip forming die and punch	160.00
RBT-2-H	Rebated boattail add-on set	508.00
LSWC-1-H	Lead SWC pistol bullet set	160.00
JSWC-2-H	2-die SWC pistol bullet set	320.00
FJFB-3-H	3-die flat base open tip	549.00
LTFB-4-H	4-die flat base lead tip or open tip	709.00
RBTO-4-H	4-die rebated boattail open tip set	897.00
RBTL-5-H	5-die rebated boattail, lead tip or open tip set	1,057.00
FRBO-5-H	5-die flat base, or rebated boattail open tip	1,057.00
FRBL-6-H	6-die all-style package	1,217.00
DDS-1-H	Dual diameter bullet sizer	229.00
CTJM-1-H	Tubing jacketmaker	649.00
CTJM-2-H	Partitioned jacketmaker	649.00
CTJM-P-H	Partition add-on for CTJM-1-H	250.00
PUNCH-H	Standard punch for any H-die	50.00
DCD-1-H	Disk cutter die for copper sheet	149.00
BGK-1-H	Base guard kit	198.00
JRD-1-H	Jacket reducing die	139.00
BRD-1-H	Bullet reducing die	149.00
LED-1	Lead wire extruder die set	469.00

C-H/4-D

Half-Jacket Bullet Swage Die

Forms and swages bullet with half jacket, automatically bleeds off excess lead. Available in .308, .355, .357, .429 and .451 diameters with either round-nose or semi-wadcutter nose punches. Can be used in any loading press that accepts snap-in type shellholder and standard 7/8-14 threads. From C-H Tool & Die/4-D Custom Die.

Price: **$27.50**
Price: Nose punch **$9.50**

Jacket Reducing Die

Only way to form 41-caliber jackets. Reduces 44-caliber jackets down to .406" diameter to be used with 41-caliber swage dies. Fits any loading press with 7/8-14 threads. From C-H Tool & Die/4-D Custom Die.

Price: **$21.95**

Jacketed Softpoint/Hollowpoint Swage Dies

Forms any full-jacketed pistol bullet from 110 to 250 grains weight. Jacket is swaged up over ogive of bullet. Dies threaded 7/8-14 for use on any press capable of full-length sizing. Punches for solid or hollow-point. Available in 38/357, 41 S&W, 44 Magnum and 45 ACP. From C-H Tool & Die/4-D Custom Die.

Price: **$48.50**
Price: Extra punch **$5.00**

CORBIN

224 Kit

For making 224 bullets from fired 22 cases and scrap lead. Includes BSD-224R, RFJM-22R, CM-4 and CSL-2 dies plus instructions. From Corbin Manufacturing & Supply, Inc.

Price: **$349.50**
Price: For 6mm **$349.50**
Price: Upgrade 224 kit to 6mm . . **$239.00**

Base Guard Bullet Swage Die Kit

To make copper base guard swaged bullets with base-guard design that utilizes precision of 0.001-inch to ensure good seal. Includes Econo-Swage die, Base Guard die, lead wire (70,000-grain spool), magnum core cutter with die and 2-ounce bottle Corbin swage lube. From Corbin Manufacturing & Supply, Inc.

Price: **$372.50**

H-Type Swaging Dies

Designed to fit only Corbin Hydro-Press or Mega-Mite CSP-2 press. Type-H dies are 1 1/2" in diameter. From Corbin Manufacturing & Supply, Inc.

Price: . . . . **See chart for pricing.**

CORBIN

M-Type Swage Dies

For use with Corbin Silver Press or Series II press for any caliber 14 to 458. Only soft lead (Bhn 5) can be used to avoid die breakage. Max bullet length is 1.25"; max bullet weight depends on ogive shape and caliber but is approximately 450 grains with 1E ogive .458 copper tubing (.030" wall) bullet. From Corbin Manufacturing & Supply, Inc.

Price: . . . . **See chart for pricing.**

R-Type Swage Dies

Corbin R-type dies fit a standard 7/8-14 threaded reloading press head and the external punch fits into a standard RCBS-style shellholder slot in the ram. Ejection is either by tapping the knock-out rod with mallet or using the Corbin PE-1 power ejector. Jacket makers are designed to fit presses with round 1-1/8" or smaller diameter ram. Optional oversize ejection tubes are available to fit larger rams. Not for use on light-duty turret presses, or those with universal shellholders instead of T-slot ram. From Corbin Manufacturing & Supply, Inc.

Price: . . . . **See chart for pricing.**

S-Type Swaging Dies

Available in calibers from 308 to 458. Warrantied for use with lead hardness between 5.0 and 8.5 Bhn with up to 0.035" jackets. Recommended for 429- to 458-caliber. From Corbin Manufacturing & Supply, Inc.

Price: . . . . **See chart for pricing.**

CORBIN R-Type Swage Dies

DIE	DESCRIPTION	PRICE
RFJM-22R	Turns 22 cases into 224 bullet jackets	$69.50
RFJM-6MR	Turns 22 cases into 6mm bullet jackets	79.50
SPJM-25R	Turns shotgun primers into 25 ACP jackets	79.50
JRD-1-R	Jacket reducing die	79.50
BRD-1-R	Bullet reducing die	89.50
DCD-1-R	Disk cutter die (copper sheet)	89.50
BGK-1-R	Base guard bullet kit	149.50
EC-1	Econo swage for lead, gas check, or base guard bullets from 224-caliber to 512	149.00
CSW-1-R	Core swage die	89.50
CS-1-R	Core seating die	89.50
PF-1-R	Point forming die	129.50
LT-1-R	Lead tip shaping die	89.50
BSD-xxxR	Core seat and point form die set for rifle 6-S ogive flat base bullets in 224, 243 and 257 calibers; pistol 3/4-E ogive flat base in 251, 308, 312, 355 and 357 calibers	219.00
Punch-R	Optional or spare punches	20.00

CORBIN M-Type Swage Dies

DIE	DESCRIPTION	PRICE
CSW-1-M	Core swage die and punch	$89.50
CS-1-M	Core seating die and punch	89.50
PF-1-M	Point forming die and punch	129.50
LT-1-M	Lead tip forming die and punch	89.50
RBT-2-M	Rebated boattail add-on set	279.00
LSWC-1-M	Lead SWC pistol bullet set	89.50
JSWC-2-M	2-die SWC pistol bullet set	179.00
FJFB-3-M	3-die flat base open tip	308.50
LTFB-4-M	4-die flat base lead tip or open tip	398.00
RBTO-4-M	4-die rebated boattail open tip set	498.00
RBTL-5-M	5-die rebated boattail lead tip or open tip set	587.50
FRBO-5-M	5-die flat base or rebated boattail open tip set	587.50
FRBL-6-M	6-die all-style package	677.00
DDS-1-M	Dual diameter bullet sizer	
CTJM-1-M	Tubing jacketmaker (.030 wall)	338.50
PUNCH-M	Standard punch for any M-die	20.00
LED-2	Lead extruder die set, sub-calibers	169.00
DCD-1-M	Disk cutter die, for copper sheet	89.50
BGK-1-M	Base guard kit	149.00
JRD-1-M	Jacket reducing die	79.50
BRD-1-M	Bullet reducing die	89.50
Rfjm-22M	224 rimfire case jacketmaker	69.50
Rfjm-6MM	6mm rimfire case jacketmaker	79.50
Spjm-25M	25 ACP shotbun primer jacketmaker	79.50
Rfjm-D	224 ring die insert (spare)	30.00
Rfjm-KO	Knock-out rod for jacketmaker	5.00
Rfjm-P-M	Punch for jacketmaker	20.00
Rfjm-ROD	224 screw-in hardened rod	2.00

Corbin Core Swage Die

CORBIN S-Type Swage Dies

DIE	DESCRIPTION	PRICE
CSW-1-S	Core swage die and punch	$119.50
CS-1-S	Core seating die and punch	119.50
PF-1-S	Point forming die and punch	149.50
LT-1-S	Lead tip forming die and punch	119.50
RBT-2-S	Rebated boattail add-on set	319.50
LSWC-1-S	Lead SWC pistol bullet set	119.50
JSWC-2-S	2-die SWC pistol bullet set	239.00
FJFB-3-S	3-die flat base open tip	388.50
LTFB-4-S	4-die flat base lead tip or open tip	508.00
RBTO-4-S	4-die rebated boattail open tip set	558.00
RBTLO-5-S	5-die rebated boattail lead tip or open tip set	707.50
FRBO-5-S	5-die flat base or rebated boattail open tip set	707.50
FRBL-6-S	6-die all-style package	827.00
DDS-1-S	Dual diameter bullet sizer	149.50
CTJM-1-S	Tubing jacketmaker (.030 wall)	398.50
PUNCH-S	Internal punch for any S-die	20.00

Corbin Draw Dies

BULLET SWAGING/ Dies

HOLLYWOOD

Swaging Dies

Rifle and pistol swaging dies for lead and alloy bullets or jacketed rifle bullets. Also available for 50 BMG. For use on Hollywood presses only. From Hollywood Engineering.

Price: Lead, pistol/rifle **$130.00**
Price: Jacketed, rifle **$160.00**
Price: Special calibers, lead . . . **$150.00**
Price: Special calibers, jacketed **$180.00**
Price: 50 BMG **$275.00**

RORSCHACH

Carbide Bullet Swage Dies

High precision tungsten carbide swage dies made to gaugemaster tolerances. Available for flat base and boattail bullets. Flat base core form die to convert random length and weight lead wire slugs into formed cores of uniform size and weight possesses less than .000020" clearance between parts. Core seater designed to permit seating of lead core in copper jacket is diamond honed to within .0003" final size, then lapped to size and mirror finished. Bullet swage die forms standard benchrest bullet 7S or 8S ogive or any custom ogive desired. Boattail swage dies have same features as flat base dies. VLD swage dies also available. From Rorschach.

Price: . . . . **See chart for pricing.**

Sport Flite Derim Die

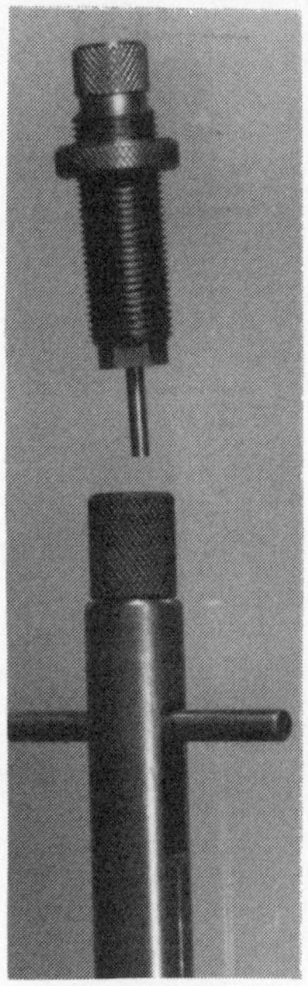

Sport Flite Jacket Bullet Die

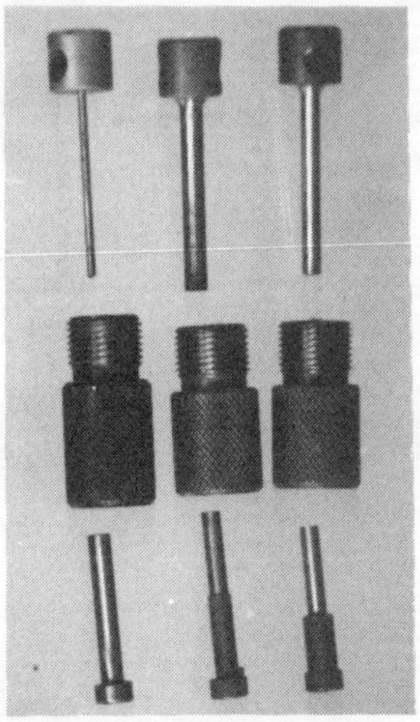

Sport Flite 3-Die Set

RORSCHACH Carbide Swage Dies

DIE	PRICE
FLAT BASE DIES	
Bullet Swage	$1,050.00
Core Seater	562.50
Core Form	460.00
Punch Holder RCBS Rock Chucker	90.00
Punch Holder RCBS A-2	90.00
Auto-Ejector Assembly	90.00
Set of 10 Core Seat Punches in .0005" steps	200.00
Master Gauge	20.00
BOATTAIL DIES	
Bullet Swage	1,250.00
Core Seater	850.00
Jacket Forming	750.00
Core Form	550.00
Punch Holder RCBS Rock Chucker	90.00
Punch Holder A-2	90.00
VLD DIES	
Bullet Swage	1,500.00
Core Seater	850.00
Jacket Forming	750.00
Core Form	550.00
Punch Holder RCBS Rock Chucker	90.00
Punch Holder RCBS A-2	90.00

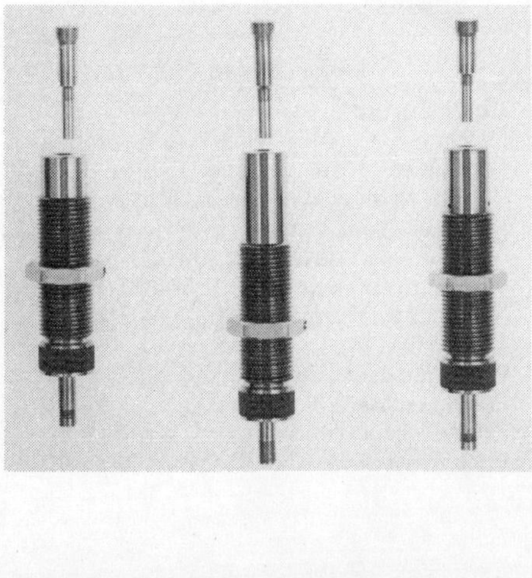

Rorschach Swage Dies

SPORT FLITE

22 or 6mm Die Set

Jacketed bullet three-die 22- and 6mm caliber set made of hardened tool steel. Consists of form die to form lead core to proper diameter, length and weight; core seat die to secure core in copper jacket; and finish die to give bullet final shape. Unique automatic ejection feature with special 1" diameter ram, ejector pin, top punch holder, lock ring and lock nut available only for RCBS Rock Chucker and Lyman Orange Crusher. 22-caliber bullet has nose of 6-caliber ogive; 6mm with 7-caliber ogive. From Sport Flite Manufacturing Co.

Price: **$106.00**
Price: Auto ejection kit **$19.00**

Derim Jacket Form Die

For producing 22 or 6mm bullet jackets from 22 Long, Long Rifle or Short cartridge cases. Threaded 7/8-14 to fit any standard reloading press. Available in two configurations: with ram adaptor for threaded support for bottom punch when using 1" diameter special ram for Sport Flite jacketed bullet die set; or bottom punch to fit universal shellholder. From Sport Flite Manufacturing Co.

Price: 22 die **$25.00**
Price: 6mm die **$16.00**

Pistol Swage Die

Hardened to 52 Rockwell "C" and adjustable to full range of bullet weights and types, round-nose, semi-wadcutter, wadcutter or spitzer. Form zinc base or jacketed bullets. Jackets cannot be formed into ogive or nose of bullet. Dies fit any standard 7/8-14 thread reloading press. Die sets for 30 (.308-.310), 9mm (.355-.357), 38/357 (.357-.358), 44 (.429-.431) and 45 (.452-.454) available. From Sport Flite Manufacturing Co.

Price: **$21.95**
Price: Extra base punch **$4.95**
Price: Extra nose punch **$6.95**

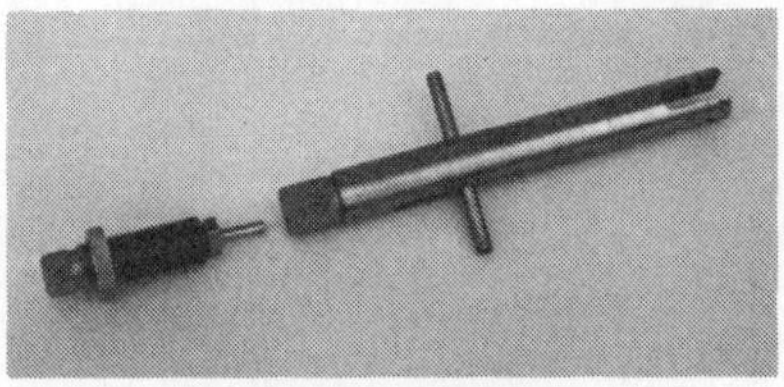

Sport Flite 22-Caliber Die Set

BULLET SWAGING SUPPLY

Carbide Kit #1
Includes BSSP press, carbide point form die, carbide core seating die and steel core swage die. From Bullet Swaging Supply, Inc.
Price: **$1,049.00**

Carbide Kit #2
Includes BSSP press, carbide point form die, steel core seating die and steel core swage die. From Bullet Swaging Supply, Inc.
Price: **$799.00**

Core and Bullet Lube
Contains 50% lanolin and 50% castor oil. Comes in $1^{1}/_{2}$-oz. container. From Bullet Swaging Supply, Inc.
Price: **$2.00**

Core Cutter
Designed to cut any core wire with cutting die for each diameter. Adjustable for desired core weight. Includes one set of dies. From Bullet Swaging Supply, Inc.
Price: **$40.00**
Price: Extra cutters **$8.00**

Core Moulds
Adjustable weight 4-cavity moulds for turning out lead cores. Made in $^{1}/_{32}$" steps from $^{5}/_{32}$" to $^{3}/_{8}$" From Bullet Swaging Supply, Inc..
Price: $^{3}/_{16}$, $^{1}/_{4}$, $^{5}/_{16}$ **$60.00**
Price: $^{5}/_{32}$, $^{7}/_{32}$, $^{3}/_{8}$ **$70.00**

CORBIN

Bullet Balls
Linear polyethylene spheres of precise weight for insertion into bullet jacket as shock-absorbing tip or to make lightweight projectiles. Available in sizes for calibers 224 to 50. Come 1,000 to a box. From Corbin Manufacturing & Supply, Inc.
Price: $^{3}/_{16}$", 224- to 284-cal. **$30.00**
Price: $^{1}/_{4}$", 30- to 35-cal. **$35.00**
Price: $^{5}/_{16}$", 351- to 40-cal. **$40.00**
Price: $^{3}/_{8}$", 41- to 50-cal. **$45.00**

Bullet Dip Lube
Liquid lube that dries to clear hard wax finish. Available in 4-, 16-oz. and 1-gallon containers. From Corbin Manufacturing & Supply, Inc.
Price: 4-oz. **$6.00**
Price: 16-oz. **$20.00**
Price: 1-gallon **$125.00**

Core-Bond
Liquid flux used to bond lead core to jacket. Comes in 2-oz., 16-oz. or gallon sizes. From Corbin Manufacturing & Supply, Inc.
Price: 2-oz. **$4.00**
Price: 16-oz. **$18.00**
Price: 1-gal. **$80.00**

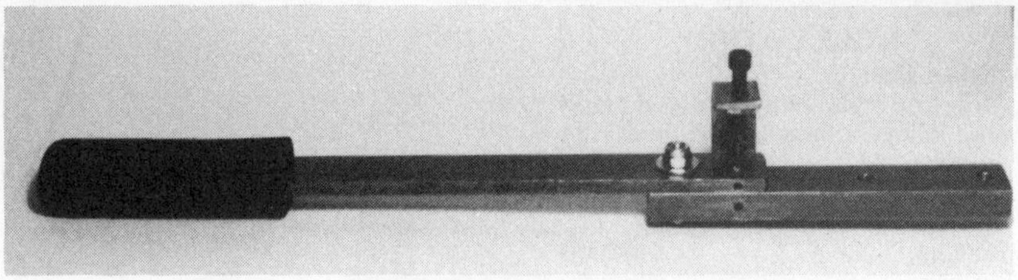
Bullet Swaging Supply Core Cutter

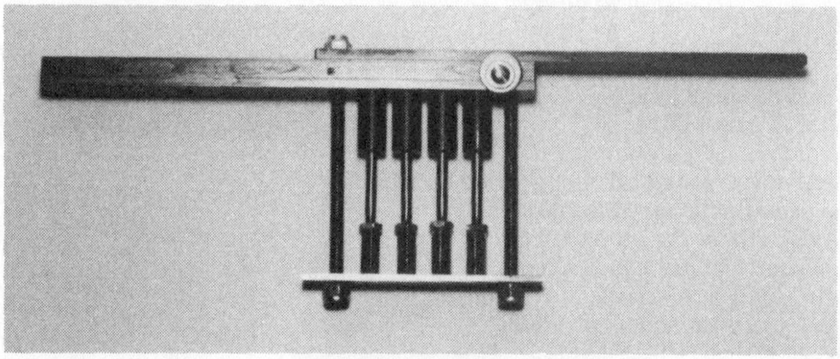
Bullet Swaging Supply Core Mould

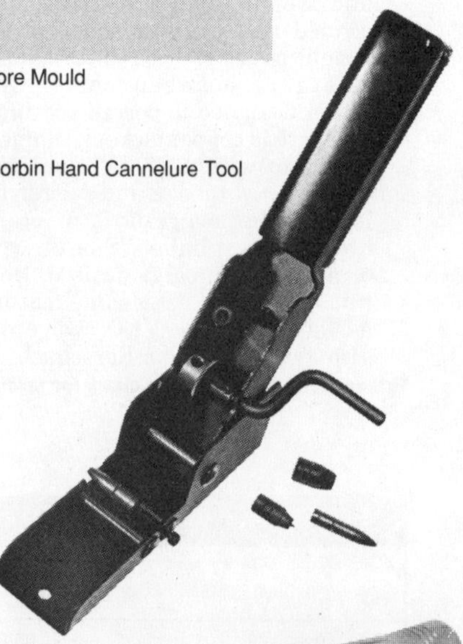
Corbin Hand Cannelure Tool

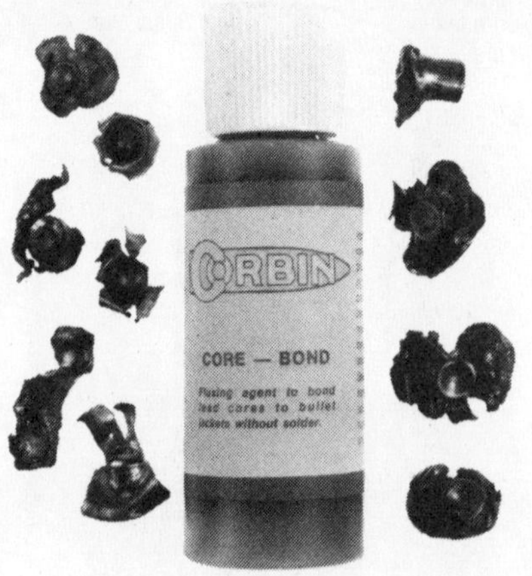

Corbin Core Bond

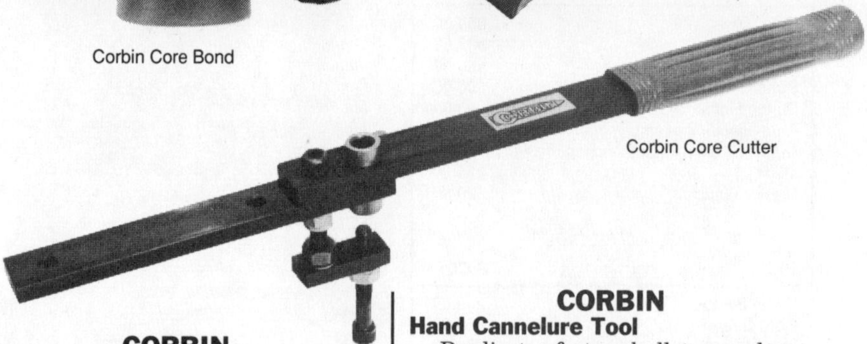
Corbin Core Cutter

CORBIN

Core Cutter
Die-type cutter with two hardened tool steel dies in steel frame with fine thread stop screw. Cutting accuracy to 0.1-grain. Two sizes available: standard tool for .185-.365; magnum cutter for .185-.500. From Corbin Manufacturing & Supply, Inc.
Price: Standard cutter **$29.50**
Price: Die inserts **$5.00**
Price: Magnum cutter **$49.50**
Price: Die inserts **$20.00**

CORBIN

Hand Cannelure Tool
Duplicates factory bullet cannelure on calibers 224 to 460. Depth and position are adjustable. Features padded handle; positive depth stop; horizontal V-way rollers to prevent bullet creep; positive position stop; heavy-duty crankshaft bearings. Works with lead or jacketed bullets. From Corbin Manufacturing & Supply, Inc.
Price: **$39.50**
Price: .05" cannelure wheel **$10.00**
Price: Lead bullet knurling tool . . . **$39.50**
Price: Lead knurling roller set **$25.00**

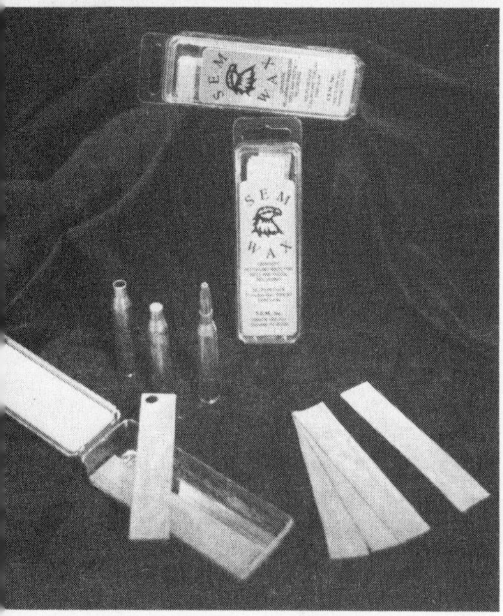

Silver Eagle Sem Wax

Corbin Power Cannelure

CORBIN

HTO-2 Heat Treatment Furnace

Electronically controlled furnace for heat-treating steel and copper, making bonded-core bullets and other metallurgical heating jobs. Features include fast heat up time, temperature range of 2 to 2000° F., forced-air cooling, dual meters to read both absolute temperature and deviation from selected set-point. Cavity size is 4.5" x 4.5" x 6". Available in 115-volt or 220-volt. From Corbin Manufacturing & Supply, Inc.

Price: **$995.00**

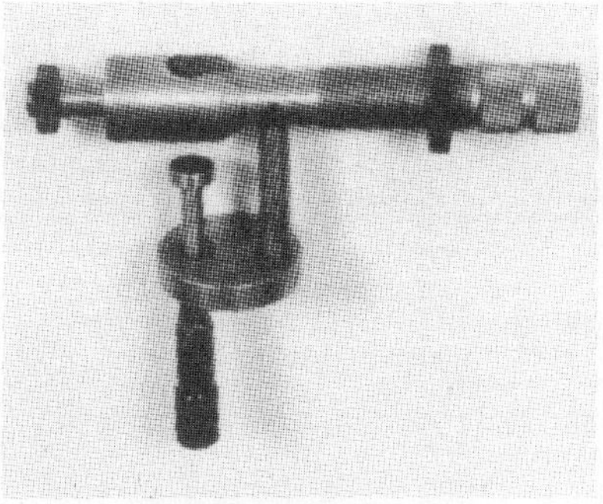

Hollywood Lead Core Cutter

Corbin Core Mould

CORBIN

Core Mould

Four-cavity standard caliber and 3-cavity magnum caliber core moulds. Fully adjustable, bench mountable moulds that require no handles or mallets to eject lead cores from precision honed tool steel die cavities. Available in all calibers. From Corbin Manufacturing & Supply, Inc.

Price: 4-cavity **$59.00**
Price: 3-cavity magnum **$89.00**

Power Cannelure Machine

Cannelures 100 lead or jacketed bullets per minute. Cabinet is 10 " high with 6"x 8" top work space. Includes one cannelure wheel for all calibers and guide plate for one caliber. Caliber plates available from 22 to 512. From Corbin Manufacturing & Supply, Inc.

Price: **$469.00**
Price: Custom cannelure wheel . . **$75.00**
Price: Position spacer, .025" or .048" **$10.00**
Price: Spare back plate **$40.00**
Price: Lead knurling back plate . . **$75.00**

Swage Lube

Liquid lubricant for bullet swage dies. Reduces force needed to swage and provides film between die and components to prolong die life. Also works as case size and jacket-making lubricant. Apply by hand or by rolling on impregnated pad. Available in 2- or 16-oz. bottles. From Corbin Manufacturing & Supply, Inc.

Price: 2-oz. **$5.00**
Price: 16-oz. **$29.50**

HOLLYWOOD

Lead Core Cutter

Comes with or without micrometer. Accurately cuts lead cores from 22- to 45-caliber. For use on the Hollywood Senior press. Micrometer thimble allows lengths and weight referencing. From Hollywood Engineering.

Price: **$85.00**
Price: With micrometer **$100.00**

ROOSTER

Bullet Film Lube

Emulsified liquid lube bonds tightly to cast or swaged bullets. Designed for low velocity pistol loads. Apply by dipping, tumbling or flood-coating. Lubes 100,000 bullets. Available in 16-oz., $^1/_2$-oz. or 1-gallon quantities. From Rooster Laboratories.

Price: 16-oz. **$7.50**
Price: $^1/_2$-gal. **$18.50**
Price: 1-gal. **$30.00**

RORSCHACH

Lubricant

Gives same high film strength as anhydrous lanolin but applies very thin coat and uniform film for more uniform bullets. From Rorschach.

Price: **$25.00**

SILVER EAGLE

Sem Wax

Over powder graphite impregnated wax wad for cast and jacketed bullets to reduce chamber throat erosion, copper fouling and lengthen barrel life. Comes in 4" long, $^3/_4$" wide strips, 10 strips per box. From Silver Eagle Machining.

Price: **$7.50**

SPORT FLITE

Adjustable Core Mould

For casting 30-, 38- and 44/45-caliber cores. Adjustable to provide cores of desired length and weight. From Sport Flite Manufacturing Co.

Price: **$12.75**

Lead Core Cutter

Hardened steel body and shears cut lead wire of 30 (.250); 9mm, 38, 357 (.300) and 44, 45 (.365) to length. Length regulated by adjustable stop. Weight: 4$^3/_4$ lbs. From Sport Flite Manufacturing Co.

Price: **$20.95**

BALLARD

Copper Tubing Jackets

Copper tubing jackets in 1", 1$\frac{1}{8}$", 1$\frac{1}{4}$", and 1$\frac{1}{2}$" lengths in .030 or .050 wall thickness for .475 and .510 calibers. From Ballard Built Custom Bullets.

Price: .475 . . . . **$25.00**
Price: .510 . . . . **$23.00**

BERGER

Rifle Jackets

Berger offers a complete range of J-4 rifle bullet jackets from .172-.308 diameter. From Berger Bullets.

Price: . . . . **See chart for pricing.**

BULLET SWAGING SUPPLY

Gas Check

BSS supplies gas checks for 50-caliber bullets from NEI mould. Price is for 1,000. From Bullet Swaging Supply.

Price: **$34.00**

Rifle Jackets

Rifle bullet jackets from 17- to 45-caliber. From Bullet Swaging Supply, Inc.

Price: . . . . **See chart for pricing.**

C-H/4-D

Pistol Copper Jackets

Copper jackets inspected to ensure concentricity of .0000 to .0003 at a point .110 from base and .0000 to .0005 at a point .125 from mouth. From C-H Tool & Die/4-D Custom Die.

Price: . . . . **See chart for pricing.**

CORBIN

Base Guard Disks

Conical shaped disks available from 30- to 458-caliber. Hole in center lets lead extrude into rivet and secures disk in place. Available in boxes of 1,000. From Corbin Manufacturing & Supply, Inc.

Price: 30-cal. to 9.3mm **$20.00**
Price: 38-40 to 45-70 . . . . **$24.00**

Copper, Steel and Brass Bullet Jackets

Cut to length, deburred copper, brass and steel jackets. Wall thickness of .030, .050 and .065. Come 250 per box. From Corbin Manufacturing & Supply, Inc.

Price: **$20.00**

Copper Tubing

Cut and trimmed tubing to standard lengths. Custom cutting available. Standard diameters are $\frac{3}{8}$" for 378-caliber down to 338 caliber and $\frac{1}{2}$" for 50-caliber down to 379-caliber; wall thicknesses available, .032", .049", .065". Minimum run, 500 pieces. From Corbin Manufacturing & Supply, Inc.

Price: Depending on length and thickness . . **See chart for pricing.**

BERGER PISTOL JACKETS

Caliber	Length	Price/1000
9mm*	.465	$49.46
	.505	
	.530	
	.580	
38	.437	49.46
	.500	
	.500, control H.S.	
	.580	
	.700	
	.700, scored expan.	
44	.550	51.72
	.550, control H.S.	
	.700	
45	.550	51.72
	.580	
	.700	

*Thin wall FMJ

Berger J-4 Jackets

BERGER RIFLE JACKETS

Caliber	Length	Price/1000
.172	.460	$42.35
	.500	
	.560	
	.635	
.224	.600	45.10
	.640	
	.705	
	.800	
	.930	
	1.000	
	1.060	
	1.120	
.243	.750	47.30
	.790	
	.825	
	.900	
	1.400	
.257	.780	53.55
	.850	
	.920	
	.940	
	1.020	
	1.125	
.284	1.000	59.10
	1.400	
	1.500	
.308	.925	59.10
	1.080	
	1.150	
	1.200	
	1.300	
	1.400	

C-H/4-D PISTOL COPPER JACKETS

Caliber	Length	Price
22	.705	$52.00
25	.920	63.00
30/32	.375	48.00
30	.925	63.00
	1.080	63.00
	1.200	63.00
38	.250	48.00
	.437	53.00
	.500	53.00
	.700	67.00
44	.250	48.00
	.550	69.00
	.700	69.00
	.250	48.00
45	.550	69.00
	.700	74.00

BULLET SWAGING JACKETS

Caliber	Length	Price/1000
17	.560	$42.35
22	.705	45.10
	.800	45.10
243	.740	42.00
	.900	47.30
	.925	28.60
25	.940	48.70
284	.940	54.00
30	.925	55.00
	1.150	59.10
	1.225	55.00
38	.500	45.50
	.700	50.00
44	.550	60.00
	.700	60.00
45	.550	60.00
	.700	60.00
	.650	55.00

CORBIN COPPER TUBING

	Price			
Wall Thickness	500 Pieces	Custom	24" Section	Custom
.030	$150.00	$5.00	$200.00	$175.00
.050	175.00	6.00	225.00	200.00
.065	200.00	7.00	250.00	225.00

HORNADY

Crimp-On Gas Checks

Open edge thicker than side wall for more sure crimp. Come in bags of 1,000. From Hornady Mfg. Co.

Price: 22, 25, 35, 6mm, 6.5 . . . . . . **$9.64**
Price: 270, 7mm, 30, 32, 338, 348, 375 **$10.91**
Price: 44, 45 . . . . **$13.87**

LYMAN

Gas Checks

Guilding metal cups for 22- through 45-caliber. Come in boxes of 1,000. Weight: 1 1/2 lbs. From Lyman Products Corporation.

Price: 22- through 35-caliber **$25.95**
Price: 375- through 45-caliber . . . **$29.95**

R.I.S.

Copper Tubing

Copper tubing for swaging bullet jackets. From R.I.S. Co., Inc.

Price: . . . . **Contact manufacturer.**

SPORT FLITE

Copper Jackets

Copper jackets .705" available for 30-, 38-, 44- and 45-caliber. All are half jackets except for the three-quarter 45. Come in quantities of 1,000. From Sport Flite Manufacturing Co.

Price: **$45.00**

Zinc Bases

For 30-, 9mm, 38-, 357-, 44- and 45-caliber bullets. Come in quantities of 1,000. From Sport Flite Manufacturing, Co.

Price: 30, 9mm, 38, 357 . . . . **$14.00**
Price: 44, 45 . . . . **$15.50**

HORNADY GAS CHECKS

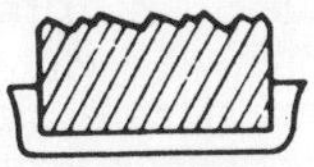

Before sizing on bullets

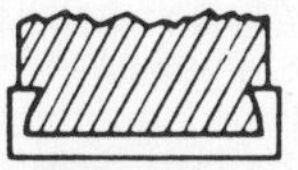

After sizing on bullets

22 cal. . . . . #7010	7mm cal. . . . . . . #7060	35 cal. . . . . #7110
6mm cal. . . . . . . #7020	30 cal. . . . . #7070	375 cal. . . . . #7120
25 cal. . . . . #7030	32 cal. (8mm) #7080	44 cal. . . . . #7130
6.5mm cal . . . . #7040	338 cal. . . . . #7090	45 cal. . . . . #7140
270 cal. . . . . #7050	348 cal. . . . . #7100	

RCBS GAS CHECKS

Caliber	Qty.	Price
22	1000	$24.04
6mm	1000	24.04
25	1000	24.04
270	1000	26.51
7mm	1000	26.51
30	1000	26.51
32-8mm	1000	26.51
35	1000	26.51
375	1000	26.51
416	1000	29.58
44	1000	31.36
45	1000	31.36

Lyman Gas Checks

Corbin Copper, Steel and Brass Jackets

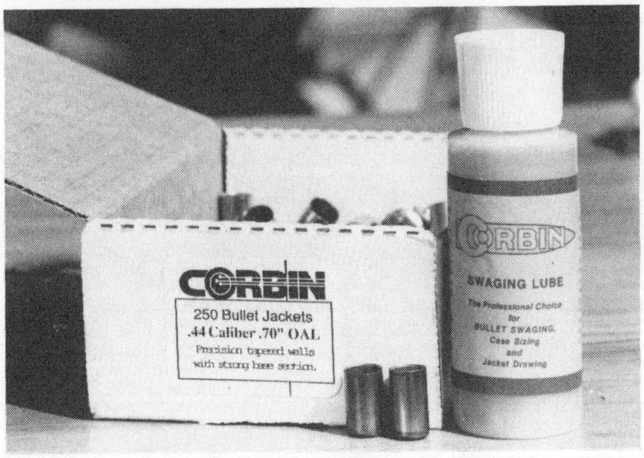

Corbin 44-Caliber Bullet Jackets

Corbin Copper Tubing

BALLARD

Lead Wire

Produced in 17" to 20" sticks and packaged in 10-lb. quantities. Available sizes: .185, .250, .300, .305, .360 and .390. From Ballard Built Custom Bullets.

Price: **$20.00**

BERGER

Lead Wire

Rifle bullet lead wire, laboratory certified and 99 percent pure lead with .5 percent antimony. From Berger Bullets.

Price: Per lb. **$1.15**

BULLET SWAGING SUPPLY

Lead Wire

Available in .187, .218, .250, and .312 diameters. Price for 25 lbs. From Bullet Swaging Supply, Inc.

Price: **$29.00**

C-H/4-D

Lead Wire

Diameters: .250 for 30-32 caliber; .312 for 35-38 caliber; .365 for 44-45 caliber. Available in 10-pound roll or 50-pound spool. From C-H Tool & Die/4-D Custom Die.

Price: Roll **$17.50**
Price: Spool **$60.00**

CORBIN

Lead Wire

Diameters: .125", .185", .218", .250", .275", .312", .340", .365" or .390" diameters. Available in 10-pound spools. From Corbin Manufacturing & Supply, Inc.

Price: **$20.00**

CORBIN

LED-1 Lead Wire Extruder Kit

For the CHP-1 Hydro-Press to extrude wire in any diameter from $^1/_8$" to $^1/_2$". Includes package of four sample lead billets ($^3/_4$" diameter x 4" long), billet mould with extra tubes, extruder body, floating alignment punch, retainer for dies and package of four heat-treated dies for 22-, 30-, 38-, 44/45-caliber wire. From Corbin Manufacturing & Supply, Inc.

Price: **$469.00**
Price: Die insert **$25.00**
Price: Extra billet mould tube . . . **$10.00**

LED-2 Lead Wire Extruder Kit

Sub-caliber (14-20) lead extrusion kit. Includes four-cavity adjustable-weight mould to make $^3/_8$" billets, a punch, die body, retainer bushing and set of extruder dies. From Corbin Manufacturing & Supply, Inc.

Price: **$169.00**

EICHELBERGER

Lead Wire

Lead wire for sub-caliber 14 in .100 diameter. Price is per pound. From Eichelberger.

Price: **$3.50**

R.I.S

Lead Wire

Lead wire for swaging 223- to 704-caliber bullets. From R.I.S. Co., Inc.

Price: . . . . **Contact manufacturer.**

SPORT FLITE

Lead Wire

Lead wire .177" diameter for 30, 38, 44/45 calibers. Available in 10- or 25-lb. quantities. From Sport Flite Manufacturing Co.

Price: 5 lbs. **$10.00**

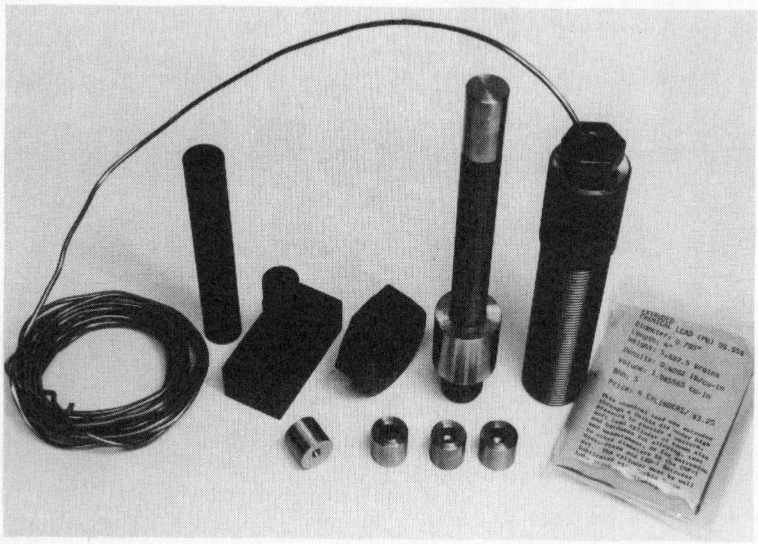

Corbin LED-1 Lead Wire Extruder Kit

PART 1 2 3 4 5 6

BULLET CASTING
TOOLS & ACCESSORIES

LEE

Lead Pot

Drawn steel pot with capacity for 4 lbs. lead. Flat bottom for stability and good contact with heat supply. From Lee Precision, Inc.

Price: **$2.98**

Precision Melter

High speed melter for ingot moulds with infinite heat control. Pot capacity of 4 lbs. 500 watts, AC only. From Lee Precision, Inc.

Price: 110-volt **$29.98**
Price: 220-volt **$33.98**

Production Pot

Capacity for 10-lbs. lead. Melt time is less than 20 minutes using 500 watts power and less to maintain heat level. Large stable base with 2" clearance between up-front spout and base. Features infinite heat control thermostat mounted away from melt pot. Also available in 220-volt export model. From Lee Precision, Inc.

Price: 110-volt **$50.98**
Price: 220-volt **$55.98**

Production Pot IV

Has same features as Lee Production Pot except for 4" clearance between base and spout. From Lee Precision, Inc.

Price: 110-volt **$54.98**
Price: 220-volt **$58.98**

LYMAN

Casting Starter Kit

Includes Lyman Mini-Mag 8-lb. capacity furnace; Model 450 sizer/lubricator; long-handled casting dipper; ingot mould; and *The Lyman Cast Bullet Handbook*. Weight: 8 lbs., 4 oz. Furnace, dipper and ingot mould also available as less expensive set. From Lyman Products Corporation.

Price: Starter kit **$159.95**
Price: Furnace, dipper and ingot mould, 110-volt **$49.95**
Price: Same as above, 220-volt . . . **$50.00**

Mag 20 Electric Furnace

Capacity for 20 lbs. lead. Features bottom pour valve system; adjustable mould guide for single or multiple cavity moulds; warming shelf for pre-heating blocks; industrial grade thermostat with indicator light; 800-watt heating system melts metal in 20 minutes. Weight: 15 lbs. 110- or 220-volt. From Lyman Products Corporation.

Price: 110 . . . . **$269.95**
Price: 220 . . . . **$270.00**

Lee Production Pot IV

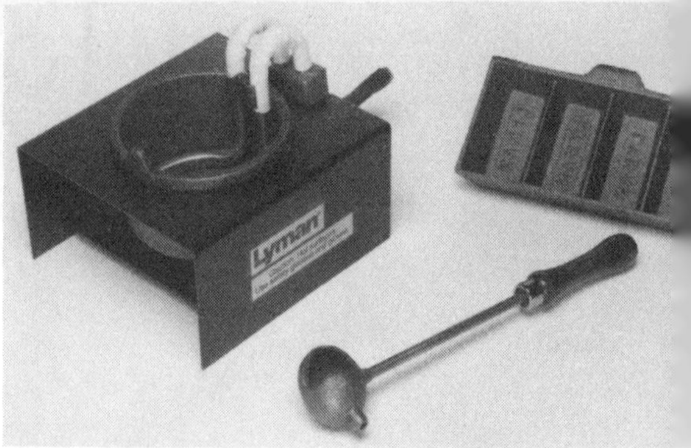

Lyman Casting Starter Kit

Lee Precision Melter

RCBS Pro-Melt Furnace

Rapine RSS20 Lead Pot

LYMAN

Lead Pot

Cast iron pot with 10-lb. capacity and flat bottom to prevent tipping. Weight: 1-lb. From Lyman Products Corporation.

Price: **$14.00**

Magdipper Furnace

Designed for ladle caster with $4^{3}/_{8}$" diameter pot and 20-lb. capacity. Has same body construction, heating system and tip-resistant base of Lyman Mag 20. Weight: 10 lbs. 110-volt only. From Lyman Products Corporation.

Price: **$224.95**

Mini-Mag Furnace

Electric 8-lb. capacity casting furnace. Melts full load in 30 minutes. Weight: 4 lbs., 4 oz. 110- or 220-volt. From Lyman Products Corporation.

Price: 110 . . . . **$49.95**
Price: 220 . . . . **$50.00**

RCBS

Lead Pot

Heavy-duty cast iron pot holds up to 10 pounds of molten metal. Features a flat bottom, bail handle, pouring spout and tab lifter for gripping with tongs. From RCBS.

Price: **$13.26**

Pro-Melt Furnace

Features 22-lb. capacity melting pot with temperature range of 450° to 850° controlled by industrial-grade thermostat. Pot is made of steel with stainless steel liner and bottom pour valve. Fully adjustable mould guide. Can be set up for right- or left-hand use. 800 watts. From RCBS.

Price: 120 VAC **$249.71**
Price: 240 VAC **$266.33**

RAPINE

RSS20 Lead Pot

Stainless steel 20-lb. capacity thermostatically controlled lead pot. From Rapine Bullet Mould Mfg. Co.

Price: **$179.95**

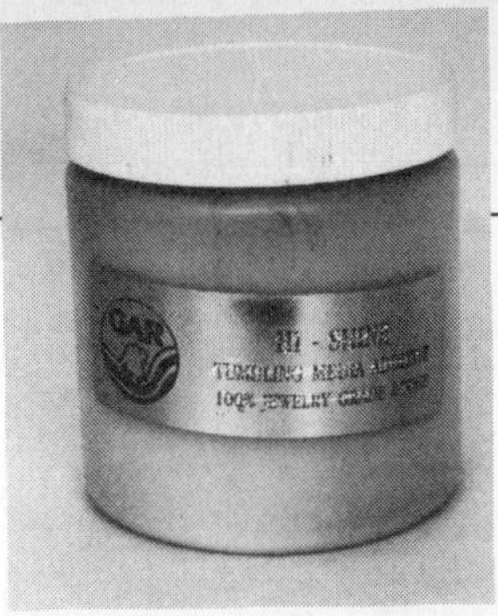

GAR #4 Casting Flux

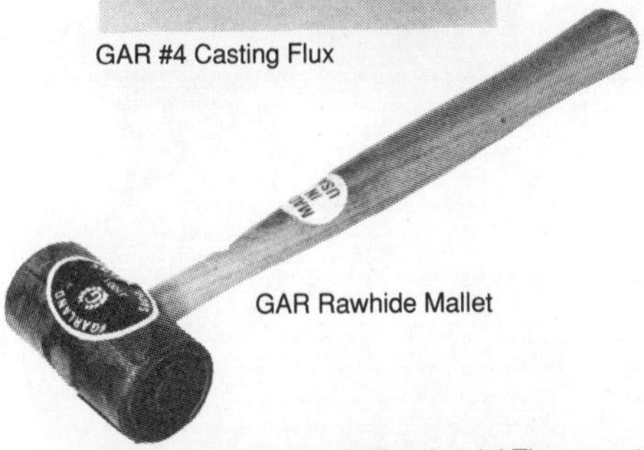

GAR Rawhide Mallet

GAR Industrial Thermometer

Brownells Marvelux

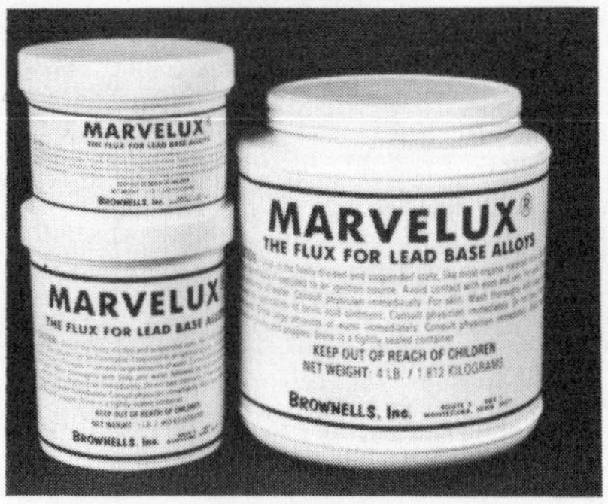

BROWNELLS

Marvelux

Lead alloy fluxing agent non-corrosive to iron and steel. Reduces dross formation and increases fluidity of bullet alloys. Non-smoking, flameless and odorless. From Brownells, Inc.

Price: $\frac{1}{2}$-lb. **$4.10**
Price: 1-lb. **$7.77**
Price: 4 lbs. **$17.29**

GAR

Industrial Thermometer

Constructed of 304 stainless steel, all welded construction. Bi-metallic element dampened with silicone for minimum pointer vibration and maximum heat transfer. Extra heavy glass window standard. From GAR for Reloading.

Price: **$24.95**

GAR

#4 Casting Flux

All organic flux containing no chemicals, no petroleums and no parafins. From GAR for Reloading.

Price: **$3.50**

Rawhide Mallet

Made of buffalo rawhide and designed for long wear. Overall length 10"; length of head $3\frac{1}{4}$"; diameter of face $1\frac{5}{8}$". From GAR for Reloading.

Price: **$8.95**

LBT

Hardness Tester

Rugged all-steel welded construction. Tests hardness of any cast bullet $\frac{1}{2}$" to 1" long. Hardness scale runs from 6 BHN (pure lead) to 40 BHN (copper). Features direct scale readout and guaranteed accuracy to 1 BHN. From Lead Bullets Technology.

Price: **$69.00**

Mould Lube

Colloidial graphite in beeswax carrier extruded into $\frac{1}{4}$" diameter sticks for application to friction points on mould. Eliminates wear and keeps mould working smoothly. One stick supplied with each LBT mould. Comes in packages of four. From Lead Bullets Technology.

Price: **$4.00**

LEE

Ingot Mould

Lightweight aluminum body with wood handles and cavities for two $\frac{1}{2}$-lb. and two 1-lb. ingots. From Lee Precision, Inc.

Price: **$12.98**

Lead Ladle

Convenient size ladle with wooden handle for bullet casting. Pour spout on either side for left- or right-hand use. From Lee Precision, Inc.

Price: **$2.98**

LYMAN

Casting Dipper

Features cast iron head, long stem and wooden handle. Weight: 6 oz. From Lyman Products Corporation.

Price: **$14.00**

Casting Thermometer

Stainless steel thermometer with measuring range from 200° Fahrenheit to 1000° F. Features 6" stem and scale on face showing proper casting ranges for most popular alloys and pure lead. From Lyman Products Corporation.

Price: **$35.00**

SOURCES OF BULLET CASTING METAL

Ames Metal Co.
4324 South Western Blvd.
Chicago, IL
312-523-3230

Roger Busch Metal Merchants
48765 West Road
Wixon, MI 48393
800-876-5337

Essex Metals
1000 Brighton St.
Union, NJ 07083
800-282-8369

Federated-Fry
6th Ave. 41st Street
Altuna, PA 16602
814-946-1611

Art Green
485 South Robertson Blvd.
Beverly Hills, CA 90211
310-274-1283

Liberty Metals
2233 East 16th
Los Angeles, CA 90021
213-581-9171/FAX: 213-581-9351

R.P. Miller Enterprises, Inc.
1557 East Main St.
Brwonburg, IN 46112

Peerless Metals
1445 Osage St.
Denver, CO 80204
303-825-6394

RSR
720 South 7th Ave.
City of Industry, CA 91746-3124
818-330-2294

RSR (Dallas)
1111 West Mockingbird Lane
Dallas, TX 75247
214-631-6070

Signet Metal Corp.
551 Stewart Ave.
Brooklyn, NY 11222
718-384-5400/FAX: 718-388-7488

TCSR
3998 Hoffman Rd.
White Bear Lake, MN 55110-4626
800-328-5323

Tejas Resource
105 Tejas Drive
Terrell, TX 75160
214-563-1220

Wheel Weights Corp.
2611 Hwy. 40 East
Inglis, FL 34449

LYMAN

Ingot Mould

Forms four ingots weighing 1-lb. each. Sides of mould have 30° draft for easy ingot ejection. Weight: 1-lb. From Lyman Products Corporation.

Price: **$14.00**

Mould Guide

For use with bottom pour furnaces. Provides precise set-screw adjustments to hold and align moulds. Compatible with Lyman moulds and those of similar design. Weight: 1-lb. From Lyman Products Corporation.

Price: **$19.95**

MAGMA

Master Lubricant

Protects moulds from rust. Comes in 4-oz., 8-oz. or 16-oz. containers. Smaller containers have spray nozzle. From Magma Engineering Co.

Price: 4-oz. **$16.50**
Price: 8-oz. **$22.50**
Price: 16-oz. **$40.00**

MIDWAY

Drop Out Mould Release

Lubricant and rust prohibitor for bullet casters. Comes in 6-oz. aerosol can. From Midway Arms, Inc.

Price: **$6.99**

RCBS

Bullet Mould Handles

Solid steel frames with extra-long hardwood handles. One size fits all RCBS bullet moulds. From RCBS.

Price: **$25.72**

Ingot Mould

Heavy-duty iron mould to form four ingots. From RCBS.

Price: **$13.26**

Lead Dipper

Large-capacity bowl with tapered pouring spout and hardwood grip. Convertible for left-hand use. From RCBS.

Price: **$13.26**

Lead Thermometer

A 1000° range and ±1% accuracy thermometer. Features 6" probe and 1½" glass-covered face. Comes with an adjustable 6" handle. From RCBS.

Price: **$33.05**

Mould Mallet

For use when opening and closing mould blocks and cutting sprues. Made of birch hardwood. From RCBS.

Price: **$9.21**

REDDING

Ingot Mould

Cast iron ingot mould with capacity to cast four ingots. From Redding Reloading Equipment.

Price: **$15.00**

RCBS Ingot Mould

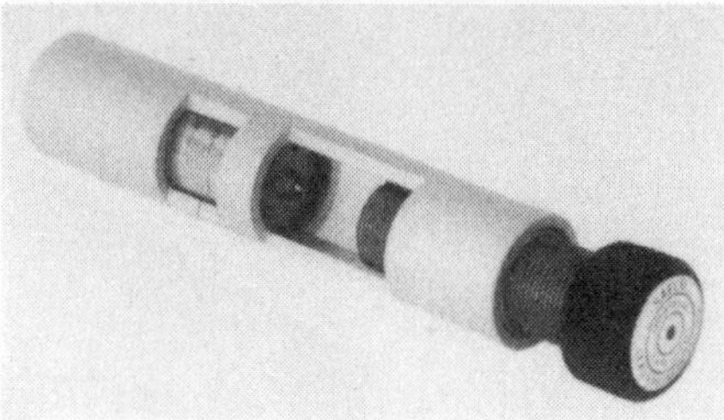

Saeco Hardness Tester

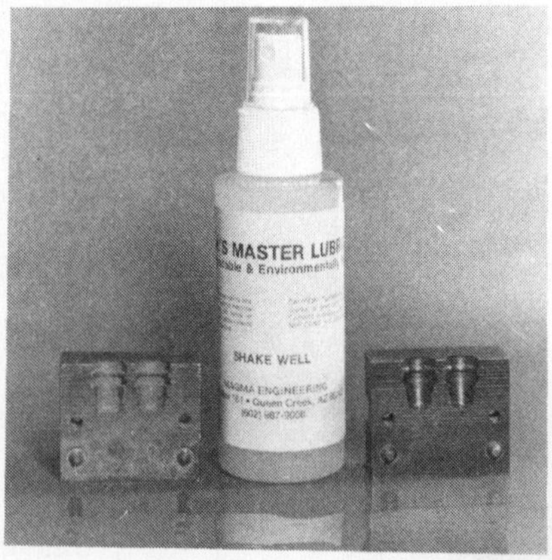

Magma Master Lube

Rowell Bottom Pour Ladle

ROWELL LADLES

Ladle No.	Capacity (lbs.)	Bowl Dia. (ins.)	Bowl Depth (ins.)	Handle (ins.)	Ladle (ins.)	Weight (lbs.)	Price
1	1	2¼	1	9	16	¾	$14.50
2	2	2½	1½	10	17¼	1	15.80
3	4	3	2¼	12	15½	2	20.10
4	4½	4	2	16	20	4	25.15
5	9	5	2½	24	31	5	28.45
6	18	6	3	29	35	9	36.20
7	25	7	4½	29	36	10	41.10
8	40	8	4½	29	37	13	46.10
9	60	9	5	29	38	20	62.10
10	90	10	5¼	29	39	23	70.85

No. 9 and No. 10 can be equipped with two handles for $19.75.

ROWELL

Bottom Pour Ladle

Clean pouring ladle eliminates skimming and wasted metal by delivering lead from the bottom of the ladle bowl. Internal trough inside bowl brings metal from the bottom to the side-pouring spout. Made of durable cast iron with flat base to prevent tipping when set down. Comes in ten sizes. Sizes 1 and 2 have steel bar handle with wood hand grip. Sliding iron sleeve on sizes 4 and up stays cool, protecting user from burns. From Advance Car Mover, Co.

Price: . . . . **See chart for pricing.**

SAECO

Lead Hardness Tester

Precision instrument to accurately determine hardness of bullet casting alloy. Measures hardness by determining depth of penetration of hardened steel indenter into bullet. Vernier scale calibrated in arbitrary units from 0 for pure lead to Saeco hardness of 10. From Redding Reloading Equipment.

Price: **$118.50**

ANDELA

Bullet Moulds

Single-cavity moulds in 14 basic bullet styles. Cherries cut from 11L17 steel. Mould number designates as-cast bullet diameter (cylindrical bullets); large rear band, small front band (two-diameter bullets); or rear band diameter tapering to smaller front band diameter (tapered bullets). Andela will also design bullet mould to specifications.

Style A: Cylindrical: Similar to originial blackpowder factory bullets; front band same as base band; rounded lube grooves.

Style B: Cylindrical: Same as A without front wiper band. Rounded lube grooves.

Style C: Two Diameter: Rear bands slightly larger than bore diameter; front band is groove diameter.

Style D: Two Diameter: Same as C, except without front wiper band; rounded lube grooves.

Style E: Tapered: Front band near groove diameter, tapering to slightly larger than groove diameter.

Style F: Hudson Bullet: Two diameter; front bands near base diameter; two rear bands slightly larger.

Style G: Two Diameter: Same as D, except with beveled band.

Style H, I: Cylindrical: Shorter nose and larger lube grooves than A. For 40-cal. and larger.

Style J: Lightweight bullet.

Style K: Round Nose: Similar to French designs in Lyman catalog.

Style L: Pointed bullet.

Style M, N: Paper patch bullet.

From Andela Tool & Machine, Inc.

Price: **$65.00**

Price: Custom mould **$115.00**

Andela Single-Cavity Mould

ANDELA TOOL & MACHINE, INC.

ANDELA Bullet Moulds

Caliber	Mould #/Dia.	Style	Type	Wgt. Grs.	Comments
22	.224A	A		55	
	.224B	B		60	
	.228B	B		65	
25	.256B	B		90	Copy of factory 25-25.
	.257B	B		95	Similar to original factory 25-20ss.
	.260-.250E	E		100	Popular Pope style.
	.264-.254				2-groove GC
28	.285B	B		130	28-30 bullet
	.287A	A		175	Lyman 287221
	.287-.276C	C		130	Pope-style 20-30
	.288B	B		135	
	.288K	K	RN	125	
30	.308L	L	P		Similar to Lyman 311334
	.308L	L			
	.309B	B		155	
	.309B	B		170	
	.309L	L	P		
	.309-.300E	E	Tapered		Thick Band
	.309-.300L	L		160	Base band bullet.
	.309L	L	PBT		
	.310-.302L	L			Two diameter bullet.
	.310-.304L	L			
	.310-.308				Former NEI 43A
	.311A	A		165	Lyman 31157
	.311B	B		170	Similar to German Schuetzen.
	.311L	L			Lyman 311414
	.311-.310L	L			Former NEI 52A.
	.312-.304D	D	FN	180	GC, 4 groove
	.315B	B		180	Similar to German Schuetzen.
	.316-.301D	D	FN	190	GC, 1 groove.
32	.319-.314B	B		180	Base band bullet.
	.319-.314F	F		185	
	.319-.314F	F		185	
	.321				Heeled bullet, .339 band
	.321B	B		190	
	.322K	K	RN	185	
	.322L	L	SPBT		
	.322L	L	P	180	
	.322-.314				Copy heeled German Schuetzen.
	.322-.314E	E	SPBT		
	.323B	B		190	
	.323L	L		180	
	.323-.313D	D		195	Two diameter bullet.
	.323-.313E	E		190	Pope-style tapered.
	.323-.321L	P			Tapered
	.323-.317L	L	P		Tapered
	.324B	B		190	
	.324-.314E	E			Pope-style Paul Clark.
	.325B	B		190	
	.325-.322D	D		190	Pope-style two diameter.
	.326-.317C	C		175	Pope-style two diameter.
33	.330-.320E	E		170	Tapered
	.331B	B		195	
	.335B	B		215	
	.335-.327E	E			Pope-style two diameter.
	.338A	A		220	Pope-style cylindrical.
	.338B	B		220	
	.338L	L	P	220	
	.338-.329D	D		220	Two diameter.
	.338-.332C	C		225	Pope-style
	.339-.330D	D		220	Two diameter.
	.339-.330E	E		220	Pope-style tapered.
	.339-.331C	C		220	Two diameter.
	.343-.330C	C		220	Copy original Pope bullet.
35	.350A	A		220	Pope-style.
	.354B	B		260	Cylindrical.
	.357		WC		Pistol bullet.
	.358-70J	J			Copy Lyman bullet.

Continued page 338

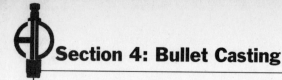

ANDELA Bullet Moulds

Caliber	Mould #/Dia.	Style	Type	Wgt. Grs.	Comments
35	.358A				Pistol bullet.
	.358K	K	RN	180	Pistol bullet.
	.358L	L	SWC		Pistol bullet.
	.360		WC		Pistol bullet.
	.360B	B		360	Cylindrical.
	.360-.351D	D		260	Cylindrical.
	.360-.352		BT		Base band bullet.
	.363-.354D	D		280	Two diameter.
	.364B	B		200	Two diameter.
38	.372-.368D	D			Two diameter.
	.375B	B		330	Copy of Lyman 375166.
	.376B	B		280	
	.377B	B		220	Cylindrical.
	.377-.367D	D		280	
	.378L	L	PBT		
	.378-.372D	D		320	Tapered.
	.378-.373F	F		290	38-55 Schuetzen.
	.379-.366C	C	BT		Two diameter.
	.380A	A		280	Pope-style cylindrical.
	.380B	B		280	
	.380L	L	P		Three-groove.
	.380-.372E	E		285	Pope-style.
	.380-.375C	C			Pope-style two diameter.
	.381L	L	P		Schuetzen.
	.382B	B		285	
	.383A	A		310	Pope-style.
	.383B	B		320	
	.383-.377F				
	.387K	K	RN		
40	.402A	A		325	Cylindrical.
	.403L	L	PBT		
	.404-.398C	C		325	Pope-style.
	.405A	A		300	Pope-style cylindrical.
	.410-.400D	D		330	Two diameter.
	.413B	B		330	
	.413-.406D	D		330	Two diameter.
	.415-.407L	L	P	325	Two diameter.
	.417B	B		330	
44	.429A	A		380	GC
	.431-.425F	F		275	Two-groove.
	.437K	K			43 Spanish bullet.
	.440N	N		495	Paper patch.
	.440-.413D	D		350	Similar to Lyman 441267.
	.445A	A		380	For 44-77, 44-90 Pope-style.
	.445B	B		380	Cylindrical.
	.448A	A		380	Cylindrical.
45	.450B	B		450	For slug gun.
	.455B	B		470	
	.455B	B		500	Cylindrical.
	.457A	A		300	Copy Lyman 457191.
	.457A	A			Similar to Lyman 457122 w/o HP.
	.457B	B		300	Pistol bullet.
	.457-.451D	D		425	Two dia. similar to Lyman 451114.
	.457K	K		450	Heeled bullet.
	.458A	A		470	
	.458B	B	SPBT	450	
	.458-.451C	C		425	Two dia. similar to Lyman 45111K.
	.459K	K	RN	500	Cylindrical.
	.464A	A			Woodworth Pope style.
	.471A	A		550	
	.472L	L	P	620	
	.480A	A			Pope-style cylindrical.
50	.505-.500C	C		470	50-70.
	.510B	B		600	
	.520			350	Three-groove.
	.525B	B		340	For 52 Maynard.
Slugs	.500				One-oz. for recycled 12-ga. sabots.
	.720		SWC	800	Two-groove. For 12-ga. rifled barrels.
	.500				12-ga. sabot slug-Reno bullet.

C-H/4-D

Bullet Moulds

Single- and double-cavity moulds made of special aluminum alloy that is harder than steel. Handles are included. From C-H Tool & Die/4-D Custom Die.

Price: **$49.50**

COLORADO SHOOTER'S SUPPLY

Hoch Pistol Bullet Moulds

Custom and standard base-pour, lathe-bored 2-, 3- and 4-cavity moulds. Standard design moulds fitted with $^3/_{16}$" sprue plate and $^1/_4$" dowel pins. Driving bands and grease grooves can be added or lengthened to increase weight of any design. Any gas-check design can be made plain base and vice versa. Custom pistol moulds made to customer design and specifications. Maximum bullet length: .950"; Maximum bullet diameter: .510"; Minimum bullet diameter: 38-cal. (.350"). Mould handles available. From Colorado Shooter's Supply.

Price: Standard, 2-cavity **$65.00**
Price: Standard, 3-cavity **$80.00**
Price: Standard, 4-cavity **$95.00**
Price: Handles **$18.00**
Price: Custom, 2-cavity **$90.00**
Price: Custom, 3-cavity **$110.00**
Price: Custom, 4-cavity **$130.00**
Price: Handles **$18.00**

Hoch Rifle Bullet Moulds

Custom-made 1-, 2-, 3- and 4-cavity rifle, paper patch bullet moulds. Lathe-bored from fine-grain cast iron (meehanite) in nose-pour only design. Machining tolerances 0 to +.001". Hoch handles and push-type breech seat bullet starters available. From Colorado Shooter's Supply.

Price: Single, 22- to 51-cal. **$70.00**
Price: Single, 52- to 75-cal. **$80.00**
Price: Single, adjustable **$125.00**
Price: Single, hollow-base **$125.00**
Price: 2-cavity, 22- to 50-cal. **$120.00**
Price: 3-cavity, 22- to 50-cal. **$170.00**
Price: 4-cavity, 45-cal. only **$220.00**
Price: Hoch handles **$18.00**
Price: Bullet starter **$45.00**

CORBIN

Core Moulds

Four-cavity and three-cavity moulds for standard and magnum cast cores. Mount to bench; requires no handles or mallets; eject fully-adjustable weight cores from precision honed cavities in tool steel dies. All calibers available. From Corbin Manufacturing & Supply, Inc.

Price: 4-cavity **$59.00**
Price: Insert, 4-cavity **$10.00**
Price: 3-cavity **$89.00**
Price: Insert, 3-cavity **$25.00**

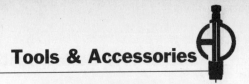

C-H/4-D Bullet Moulds

Caliber	Bullet Dia.	Bullet Wgt. Grs.	Caliber	Bullet Dia.	Bullet Wgt. Grs.
257	.257	75	44 Sil. Ack.	.429	170
	.257	95		.429	215
30 Carbine/Luger	.311	95	44 Sil. Ack.	.429	250
32/20	.311	115		.429	300
30 U.S.	.311	175	11mm Mauser	.446	355
30	.311	180	44 Colt Conv.	.451	210
303 British	.311	205	Paper Patch	.451	420
30-06	.311	210		.451	501
32/40	.319	125	45	.451	365
	.319	145		.451	430
32/40	.319	135		.451	500
	.319	155	45 Auto	.452	251
	.319	175	45 Auto	.452	230
	.319	195	45 Auto	.452	220
8mm	.321	135	45 Auto	.452	200
	.321	155	44 M/L Rev.	.454	215
	.321	175	45 Long Colt	.454	250
	.321	195	45	.454	252
8mm	.323	160	45	.454	220
	.323	185		.454	290
	.323	205	45-70	.457	150
	.323	230		.460	150
	.323	245	45-70	.460	210
Pope Style	.325	135	45-70	.457	250
	.325	155		.460	250
	.325	175	45-70	.457	280
	.325	195		.460	280
8mm	.327	155		.457	311
	.327	175		.460	311
	.327	200	45-70	.460	350
	.327	225		.460	405
	.327	240		.460	450
33 Win.	.338	200		.460	510
348 Win.	.350	215	45-70	.457	350
	.350	235		.457	405
348 Win.	.350	225		.457	450
	.350	250		.457	510
9mm	.357	125	45-70	.461	260
9mm	.357	130		.461	315
38 Super	.357	160		.461	375
38 S&W	.358	150		.461	435
	.358	150		.461	485
35 Rem.	.358	200	45-70	.463	225
	.358	204		.463	280
	.359	180		.463	355
35 Whelen	.360	240	45-70 Gov't.1881	.457	500
9.3	.366	200		.460	500
9.3	.366	195	Paper Patch	.500	500
	.366	250	50-70 Gov't.&May.	.515	320
36 May.	.366	158		.515	385
38/55	.375	250		.515	450
	.375	250	Smith May.	.520	300
36 M/L Rev.	.380	125		.520	350
36 Conv.	.380	100	Smith	.525	300
41 Long Colt	.386	185	Orig. Style Smith	.525	300
40 Dixie	.400	250	Orig. Style May.	.520	357
38/40	.401	180	Spencer	.520	375
Paper Patch	.400	360		.520	435
40/60	.403	185	Spencer	.535	370
	.403	225		.535	400
	.403	250	Spencer	.546	375
	.403	290		.546	440
40 Single Shot	.403	280	Sharps	.544	475
10mm	.403	170		.557	475
10mm	.403	200		.560	500
	.408	336	Sharps	.544	475
41 Action Auto	.412	170		.557	475
41 Action Auto	.412	200		.560	500
40/70	.413	300	Sharps	.544	415
43 Spanish	.439	385	Sharps	.544	500
44/40	.427	210		.557	510
	.429	210	Sharps	.544	440
44	.429	240		.557	476
44	.429	215	Gallagher	.540	300
	.429	260	Spencer Sharps	.544	390
	.429	300	Burnside	.556	360

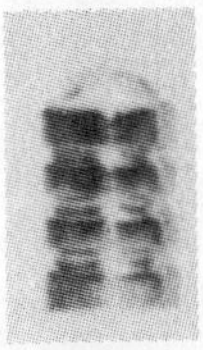

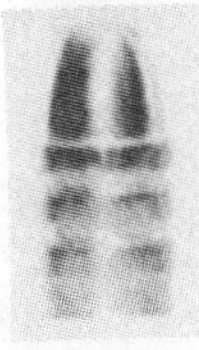

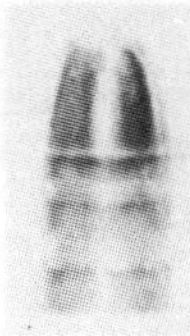

COLORADO SHOOTER'S SUPPLY Standard Pistol Moulds

Caliber	Wgt. Grs.	Type
355	120	SWC
	125	RN
358	160	SWC
	150	SWC
	158	Speed Loader
	165	SWC GC
	148	WC
410	210	Speed Loader
	225	TC Silhouette
	220	SWC
431	250	TC Silhouette
	255	RNFN
	250	SWC GC
	250	SWC
	235	Speed Loader
	225	WC
454	255	RNFN
	255	SWC
452	200	SWC
	230	T/C
	230	RNFN

SWC = Semi-Wadcutter; RN = Round Nose; GC = Gas Check; FN = Flat Nose; WC = Wadcutter.

Colorado Shooter's Supply Hoch Mould

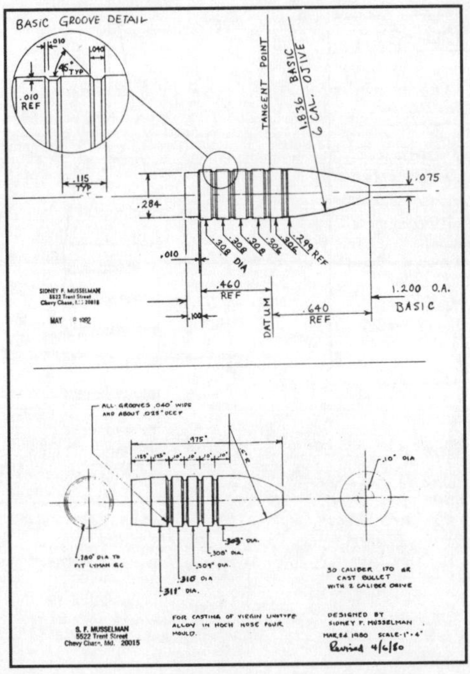

DONALD EAGAN

MX Mould

Nose-pour benchrest bullet moulds available in conventional and tapered designs. Cavity is machined in the block including the base. There is no bottom plate or plug. Base is at true perpendicular to the axis of the bullet. Features brass block and 1/4" steel sprue plate that swings on eccentric bushing for sprue hole to nose gate adjustment. Optional stainless steel plate available. Cut to fit Lyman handles. Dimensions: 1.4"x 1.5"x 1.5". Send $2.00 for detailed sketches of bullet designs. From Donald Eagan.

Price: **$66.00**
Price: Stainless steel plate **$20.00**

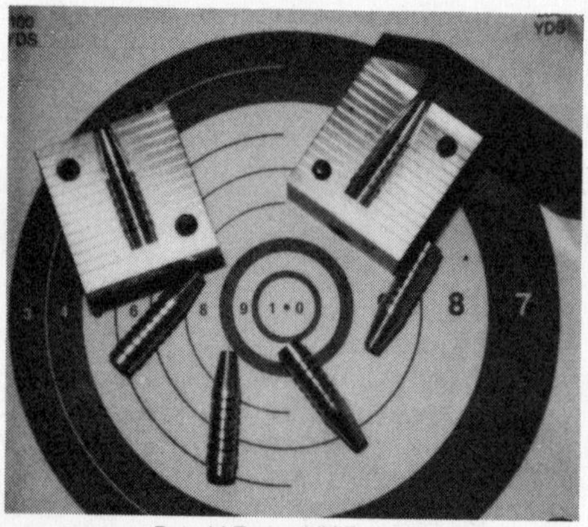

Donald Eagan MX Bullet Mould

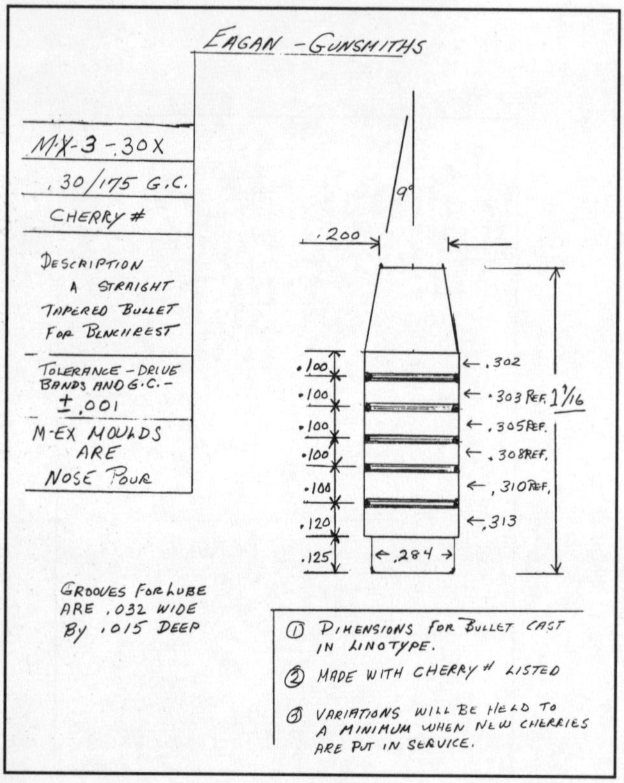

DONALD EAGAN Bullet Moulds

Caliber	As Cast Diameter	As Cast Wgt. Grs	Type	Mould
22	.225	43	GC	MX-2-22
	.225	55	GC	MX-2-22Z
	.221-.227	55	Straight Tapered, GC	MX-3-22
6mm	.238-.246	65	Tapered, GC	MX-3-24X
	.244	80	GC	MX-2-243
	.250-.260	100	Straight Tapered, GC	MX-3-25X
7mm	.276-.287	145	Straight Tapered, GC	MX-3-28X
30	.300-.310	155	For short drive band bullets, GC	MX-2-30W
	.301-.310	160	Taper nose for all 30/30 and 30 WCF, GC	MX-2-30C
	.311	175	GC	MX-2-308
	.310	180	GC	MX-2-30
	.310	185	For 30-06 and 30-40, GC	MX-2-30H
	.304-.315	165	Straight tapered, GC	MX-3-30BR
	.3062-.312	165	Straight tapered, GC	MX-3-30KBR
	.302-.313	175	Straight tapered, GC	MX-3-30X
	.304-.312	155	Straight tapered, GC	MX-3-30J
	.304-.313	172	Straight tapered, GC	MX-3-30V
	.301-.313	190	Straight tapered, GC	MX-3-30G
	.299-.313	196	Straight tapered, GC	MX-3-30US
	.310	120	GC	MX-2-30CAR
	.304-.313	155	Straight tapered, GC	MX-3-30RJ
	.311	166	Tapered, GC	MX-3-30AR
	.313	188	Tapered	MX-3-30ARD
	.302-.312	190	Tapered, GC	MX-4-30A
	.302-.313	180	Tapered, plain base	MX-3-30S
	.304-.319	180	Tapered, plain base	MX-2-32C
32	.314-.324	190	Straight tapered, plain base	MX-3-32S
	.315-.325	210	GC	MX-4-32A
33	.329-.340	250	Straight tapered, GC	MX-3-338
35	.359-.364	220	Straight tapered, GC	MX-3-35M

Hensley & Gibbs 6-Cavity Mould

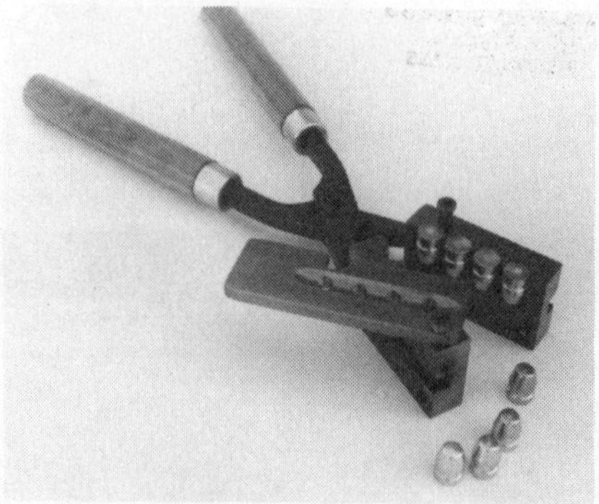

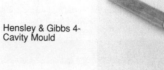

Hensley & Gibbs 4-Cavity Mould

HENSLEY & GIBBS

Bullet Moulds

Handcast moulds in 2-, 4-, 6-, 8- or 10-cavity designs. Standard moulds cut .001" to .002" over sizing diameter in alloy specified. Custom moulds closer to sizing diameter or over .002" larger than specified alloy. Standard matched moulds are cut consecutively with 1/2-grain maximum variance between the two. Custom matched moulds are same as standard match but will resurface-grind and recherry as needed. All custom moulds an additional $20.00. Moulds can be ordered complete with handles or without. From Hensley & Gibbs.

Price: . . . . **See chart for pricing.**

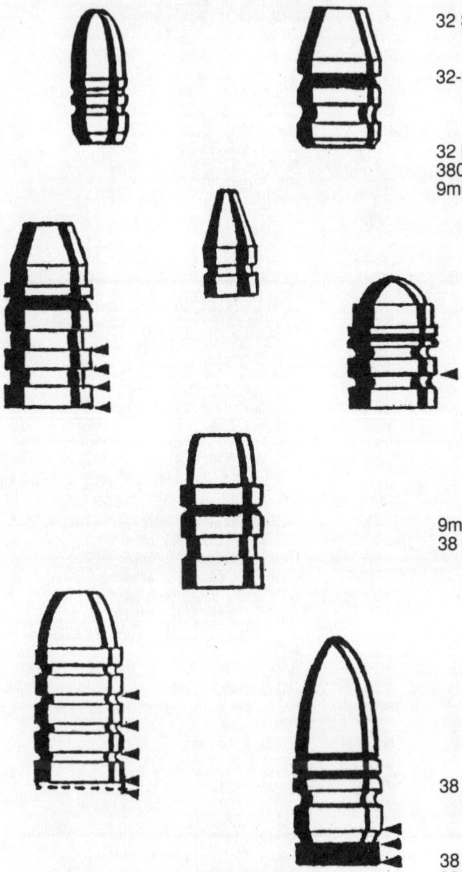

Hensley & Gibbs 10-Cavity Mould

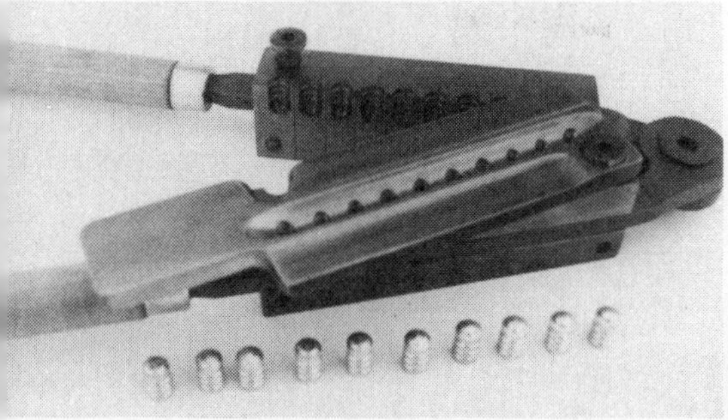

HENSLEY & GIBBS Bullet Moulds

	——Bullet——			——Mould——	
Caliber	Dia.	Wgt. Grs.	Type	#	Comments
25 ACP	.252	50	PB	117	RGG
	.252	55	PB	306	RGG; SM
25-20	.257	58		32GC	SGG; OCG; MM; GC
	.257	65		32GC	SGG; OCG; MM; GC
7mm Nambu	.280	60	PB	134	RGG; OCG
8mm Nambu	.323, .321	100	PB	116	RGG
8mm Lebel Rev.	.323	125	PB	226	RGG; OCG; NDB; SM
30 Luger	.310	90	PB	93	SGG; MM
	.310	92	PB	113	RGG
30 M1 Carbine	.308	113			RGG; GC base
	.308	115	BB	254	RGG
32 Auto	.309	83	PB		RGG
32 Revolver	.312, .313	40	PB	354	RGG; LM
	.312, .313	90	PB	299	RGG; SM
	.312, .313	85	PB	26-4	RGG; OCG; 4DB
	.312, .313	98	PB	26-5	RGG; OCG; 5DB
	.312, .313	98	PB	65	RGG; OCG; BB; SWS; MM
	.312, .313	98	PB	252	RGG; OCG; BB
	.312, .313	90	PB	S216	RGG; OCG; MM; RSWS
	.312, .313	100	PB	216	RGG; OCG; MM; RSWS
	.312, .313	200	PB	220	RGG; OCG; MM; RSWS
	.312, .313	115	PB	361	RGG; OCG; SM
32 S&W Long	.312	100	PB	66	RGG; OCG; LM; SWS BB
	.312	100	BB	353	SGG; LEEF; LM
	.312	105			RGG; square corners, no bevels.
32-20	.312	105	PB	89	RGG; OCG; LM
	.312	115		89	RGG; OCG; LM
	.312	115	PB	67	RGG; MM
	.312	115	BB	388	RGG; OCG; MM
32 H&R Mag.	.313	106	PB		SGG; OCG; SWS; LM
380 Auto	.356	100	PB	S55	RGG; BB
9mm Luger	.356	98	BB	279	RGG; SM
	.356	115	PB	307	SGG
	.356	115	PB	308	RGG
	.356	125	PB	7	RGG
	.356	125	BB	115	RGG
	.356	125	BB	264	RGG; SWS; SM
	.356	125	BB	275	RGG; SWS; MM
	.356	125	PB	309	RGG; LM; BB
	.356	125	PB	310	RGG; BB
	.356	125	PB	318	RGG; RSWS; LM
	.356	125	BB	331	RGG
	.356	128	BB	317	RGG; LM
	.356	135	BB	286	RGG; MM
	.356	135	BB	314	RGG; German army Ogival.
	.356	140		313	RGG; OCG; also for revolver; SM
	.356	147	PB	378	RGG; SM
	.356	150	PB	363	SGG; LM
	.356	150	PB	377	RGG
9mm Makarov	.364	105	PB	375	RGG
38 Super	.356	115	BB	262	RGG; SWS; LM
	.356	130	PB	81	RGG; SWS; LM
	.356	130	PB	157	RGG; MM; RSWS
	.356	130	PB	583	RGG; OCG; SWS; MM
	.356	135	PB	55	BB
	.356	135	PB	161	RGG; MM; RSWS
	.356	145	PB	73	BB; SGG; OCG; SWS; SM
	.356	145	PB	123	RGG; SWS
	.356	150	PB	355	SGG; SWS; SM
	.356	152	BB	335	SGG; SWS; MM
	.356	155	BB	370	SGG; MM
	.356	158	BB	39BB	RGG; OCG
	.356	158	BB	316BB	SGG; OCG; MM
38 Special	.356	145	PB	219	RGG; LEEF; LM
	.356	145	BB	259	RGG; SWS
	.356	146	PB	244	BB; RGG; OCG; LM
	.356	150	PB	248	RGG; OCG; SWS; LM
38 Gold Cup	.356	148	BB		BB; RGG; OCG; SWS; LM
38 Spl./357 Mag.	.358	62	PB		RGG; LM
	.356	148	BB	251	RGG; LM
	.356	148	BB	334	SGG; LEEF; LM
	.358	100		234	GC base; RGG; OCG; SWS; MM
	.358	110	PB	41	BB; RGG; OCG; SWS; LM
	.358	130	PB	246	SGG; SWS; MM
	.358	135	PB	272	SGG; OCG

RGG = Round Grease Groove; SGG = Square Grease Groove; SM = Small Meplat; MM = Medium Meplat; LM = Large Meplat; OCG = One Crimp Groove; TCG = Two Crimp Grooves; PB = Plain Flat Base; BB = Bevel Base; GC = Gas Check; SWS = Semi- or Wadcutter Shoulder; 1DB = One Driving Band; 2DB = Two Driving Bands; 3DB = Three Driving Bands; 4DB = Four Driving Bands; 5DB = Five Driving Bands; RSWS = Rounded Semi-Wadcutter Shoulder; SBB = Short Bevel Base; LBB = Long Bevel Base; EB = Extended Base; OD = Oversize Diameter; NDB = No Driving Band in front of Crimp Groove; LEEF = Loaded Either End Forward; BRN = Bore Riding Nose. *Extra fee for special cross-venting for this design.

#236 160gr

(3)(8)(9)(26)(73)

#290 160gr

(2)(4)(7)(9)(26)(73)

#801BB 160gr

NEW

(1)(7)(9)(26)(73)

#64 163gr*

(2)(7)(9)(26)(72)

#37 165gr*

(2)(4)(8)(9)(26)(73)

#56 165gr*

(2)(8)(9)(10)(26)(39)(73)

#268*

165gr at #268BB length, 156gr at #268PB length.

(8)(9)(26)(73)

#30 170gr*

(3)(8)

HENSLEY & GIBBS Bullet Moulds

Caliber	Bullet Dia.	Bullet Wgt. Grs.	Bullet Type	Mould #	Mould Comments
38 Spl./357 Mag.	.358	140	BB	392	RGG; OCG; NDB
	.358	140	BB	313BB	RGG; OCG; also for rev. bullet; SM
	.358	125	PB	313PB	RGG; OCG; also for rev. bullet; SM
	.358	140		393	GC; RGG; OCG; LM
	.358	140	BB	511	SGG; OCG; MM
	.358	145	PB	63	BB; RGG; OCG
	.358	145	PB	73	BB; SGG; OCG; SM
	.358	146		159	RGG; OCG; SWS; tapered boattail; LM
	.358	148	PB	50	BB; RGG; OCG; SWS; LM
	.358	150	PB	9	BB; RGG; OCG; SWS; LM
	.358	130	PB	12C	GC; RGG; MM
	.358	140	PB	12B	GC; RGG; MM
	.358	150	PB	12A	GC; RGG; MM
	.358	150	PB	27	BB; RGG; OCG
	.358	150	PB	61	SGG; SWS; LM
	.358	150	PB	527	BB; RGG; SWS; LM
	.358	156		135	GC; RGG; TCG; SWS; LM
	.358	156	PB	218	RGG; OCG; SWS; LM
	.358	158	PB	28	BB; RGG; OCG
	.358	158	PB	36	RGG; OCG; SWS; LM
	.358	158	PB	39	BB and GC base; RGG; OCG
	.358	158	PB	48	BB; RGG; OCG; LM
	.358	158	PB	49	BB; RGG; OCG; MM
	.358	158	PB	52	RGG
	.358	158	PB	260	RGG; SM
	.358	158	PB	316	BB; SGG; OCG; MM
	.358	160	PB	51	BB and GC base; SGG; OCG; LM
	.358	160		236	GC; RGG; OCG; SWS; LM
	.358	160	PB	290	BB; SGG; OCG; SWS; LM
	.358	160	BB	801BB	SGG; OCG; SWS; LM
	.358	163*	PB	64	SGG; OCG; SWS; MM
	.358	165*	PB	37	BB; RGG; OCG; SWS; LM
	.358	165*	PB	56	RGG; OCG; TCG; SWS; LM
	.358	165*		268	RGG; OCG; SWS; LM
	.358	170*		30	GC; RGG
	.358	170*		394	GC; RGG; OCG; LM
	.358	173*	PB	43	SGG; OCG; SWS; LM
	.358	185*		376	RGG; OCG; LM
	.358	190*	PB	395	RGG; OCG; LM
	.358	125*		322-3	RGG; OCG; 3DB; SM
	.358	158*		322-4	RGG; OCG; 4DB; SM
	.358	190*		322-4GC	RGG; OCG; 3DB; SM; GC
	.358	175*	PB	57-3	RGG; OCG; 3DB; LM
	.358	200*	PB	57-4	RGG; OCG; 4DB; SM
	.358	200*	PB	138	RGG; OCG
	.358	215*	PB	257	
	.358	230*	BB	127	SGG; OCG; LM
357 Maximum	.357/.358	200*		319	SGG; OCG; SWS; LM
	.357/.358	200*		320	GC; OCG; MM
	.357/.358	200*		321	SGG; OCG; boattail bevel base; MM
375 Super Mag.	.376	165*		380-3	SGG; OCG; 3DB; MM
	.376	185*		380-3GC	SGG; OCG; 3DB; MM; GC
	.376	210*		380-4	SGG; OCG; 4DB; MM
	.376	235*		380-4GC	SGG; OCG; 4DB; MM; GC
	.376	270*		380-5	SGG; OCG; 5DB; MM
38-40	.401	180		6	BB; RGG; OCG
41 Long Colt	.401	185	PB	121	RGG
40 S&W/10mm	.401	125	PB	365	SGG
	.401	135	BB	374	RGG; SWS; SM
	.401	145	PB	360	SGG; revolvers/single shots only.
	.401	155	PB	373	RGG; SM
	.401	155	BB	S359BB	RGG; MM
	.401	175	PB	332	BB; RGG; SWS; MM
	.401	155	PB	S359PB	RGG; MM
	.401	180	BB	359BB	RGG; MM
	.401	190	BB	324	SGG; LM
	.401	200	PB	315	RGG; LM
	.401	200*	PB	396	RGG; OCG; LM
	.401	220*	PB	397	RGG; OCG; LM
41 AE	.410	180	BB	342BB	RGG; SWS; medium shoulder
41 Magnum	.410	79	PB	368	RGG; SWS; LM
	.410	175	PB	255	RGG; OCG; SWS; LM
	.410	175	PB	291	SGG; OCG
	.410	210	PB	253	RGG; LM
	.410	210	PB	256	BB and GC; RGG; OCG; SWS; LM
	.410	210*	PB	261	RGG; OCG; SWS; MM
	.410	210*	PB	263	RGG; OCG

RGG = Round Grease Groove; SGG = Square Grease Groove; SM = Small Meplat; MM = Medium Meplat; LM = Large Meplat; OCG = One Crimp Groove; TCG = Two Crimp Grooves; PB = Plain Flat Base; BB = Bevel Base; GC = Gas Check; SWS = Semi- or Wadcutter Shoulder; 1DB = One Driving Band; 2DB = Two Driving Bands; 3DB = Three Driving Bands; 4DB = Four Driving Bands; 5DB = Five Driving Bands; RSWS = Rounded Semi-Wadcutter Shoulder; SBB = Short Bevel Base; LBB = Long Bevel Base; EB = Extended Base; OD = Oversize Diameter; NDB = No Driving Band in front of Crimp Groove; LEEF = Loaded Either End Forward; BRN = Bore Riding Nose. *Extra fee for special cross-venting for this design.

See page 344 for prices.

HENSLEY & GIBBS Bullet Moulds

Caliber	Bullet Dia.	Bullet Wgt. Grs.	Bullet Type	Mould #	Mould Comments
41 Magnum	.410	220*	PB	258	SGG; OCG; SWS; LM
44-40	.427	210	PB	44	RGG; OCG; NDB; LM
	.427	250	PB	44GC	RGG; OCG; NDB; LM
	.427	210	PB	44BB	RGG; OCG; NDB; LM
44	.429/.431	85	BB	443	RGG; LM
	.429/.431	87	PB	350	RGG; LM
	.429/.431	180	PB	180	RGG; LM; RSWS
	.429/.431	180	PB	273	SGG; OCG
	.429/.431	185	PB	245	RGG; SWS; MM
	.429/.431	185	BB	366	SGG; LEEF; LM
	.429/.431	195	PB	340	SGG; OCG; SM
	.429/.431	200		237	GC; RGG; OCG; SWS; LM
	.429/.431	200	PB	239	RGG; OCG; LM
	.429/.431	200		240	GC; RGG; OCG
	.429/.431	200	PB	241	RGG; OCG; SWS; LM
	.429/.431	205	PB	23	RGG; LM
	.429/.431	205	BB	330	RGG; OCG; SWS; LM
	.429/.431	210	BB	271	RGG; SWS
	.429/.431	220	PB	247	RGG; SWS
	.429/.431	225	BB	341	SGG; OCG; LM
	.429/.431	190	PB	142PB	RGG; SWS; LM
	.429/.431	230		142GC	RGG; SWS
	.429/.431	240	PB	15	GC; RGG; OCG
	.429/.431	240	PB	35	RGG; OCG; SWS; LM
	.429/.431	240	PB	45	BB and GC; RGG; OCG; SWS; LM
	.429/.431	240*		235	GC; RGG; SWS; LM
	.429/.431	135*	PB	107C	RGG; OCG; SWS; LM
	.429/.431	185*	PB	107B	RGG; OCG; SWS; LM
	.429/.431	245	PB	107A	RGG; OCG; SWS; LM
	.429/.431	225	PB	140PB	SGG; OCG; SWS; LM
	.429/.431	250		140GC	SGG; OCG; SWS; LM
	.429/.431	225*	PB	521PB	RGG; OCG; SWS; LM
	.429/.431	250*		521GC	RGG; OCG; SWS; LM
	.429/.431	270*	PB	326	SGG; OCG; SWS; LM
	.429/.431	280*	PB	367	RGG; OCG; LM
	.429/.431	280*	PB	503S	SGG; OCG; SWS; EB band; LM
	.429/.431	300*	BB	327	RGG; OCG; MM
	.429/.431	300*	PB	328	SGG; OCG; SWS; LM
	.429/.431	300*	BB	343	SGG; OCG; LM
	.429/.431	300*	BB	369	SGG; OCG; LM
	.429/.431	320*	PB	356	RGG; OCG; LM
	.429/.431	95*		352-2	SGG; 2DB; LM
	.429/.431	130*		352-2GC	SGG; 2DB; LM
	.429/.431	155*		352-3	SGG; 3DB; LM
	.429/.431	195*		352-3GC	SGG; 3DB; LM
	.429/.431	240*		352-4	SGG; 4DB; LM
	.429/.431	280*		352-4GC	SGG; 4DB; LM
	.429/.431	335*		352-5	SGG; 5DB; LM
	.429/.431	255*	BB	379-3GC	SGG; 3DB; OCG; LM
	.429/.431	300*	BB	379-4GC	SGG; 4DB; OCG; LM
	.429/.431	335*	BB	379-5	SGG; 5DB; OCG; LM
45 Auto	.452	155*	PB	358PB	RGG; SWS; SM
	.452	155*	BB	358BB	RGG; SWS; SM
	.452		PB	S242	RGG; SWS; MM
	.452	170	PB	938	SGG
	.452	172	PB	229	RGG; SWS
	.452	180	PB	293	RGG; SWS; LM
	.452	180	PB	337	RGG; SWS; MM
	.452	185	PB	130	BB; RGG; LM; RSWS
	.452	185	PB	163	2RGG; LM; RSWS
	.452	185	PB	242	RGG; SWS; MM
	.452	200	PB	68	BB; RGG; SWS; MM
	.452	200	PB	249	RGG
	.452	200	BB	265	SGG; SWS
	.452	200	BB	519	Available with PB; RGG
	.452	215	PB	78	BB; RGG; SWS; LM
	.452	215	PB	118	BB; RGG; SWS
	.452	215	BB	351	RGG; SWS; long tapered boattail; MM
	.452	220	BB	294	RGG; SWS; long tapered boattail; MM
	.452	230	PB	34	BB; RGG
	.452	230	PB	292	BB; SGG
	.452	240	PB	329	RGG; SWS; LM
	.452	219	BB	68BBA	SBB; 207-gr. lino; RGG; EB; SWS; MM
	.452	232	BB	68BBB	LBB; 219-gr. lino; RGG; EB; SWS; MM
	.452	231	PB	68S	218-gr. lino; RGG; EB; SWS; MM
	.452	239	BB	68BBS	LBB; 226-gr. lino; RGG; EB; SWS; MM

RGG = Round Grease Groove; SGG = Square Grease Groove; SM = Small Meplat; MM = Medium Meplat; LM = Large Meplat; OCG = One Crimp Groove; TCG = Two Crimp Grooves; PB = Plain Flat Base; BB = Bevel Base; GC = Gas Check; SWS = Semi- or Wadcutter Shoulder; 1DB = One Driving Band; 2DB = Two Driving Bands; 3DB = Three Driving Bands; 4DB = Four Driving Bands; 5DB = Five Driving Bands; RSWS = Rounded Semi-Wadcutter Shoulder; SBB = Short Bevel Base; LBB = Long Bevel Base; EB = Extended Base; OD = Oversize Diameter; NDB = No Driving Band in front of Crimp Groove; LEEF = Loaded Either End Forward; BRN = Bore Riding Nose. *Extra fee for special cross-venting for this design.

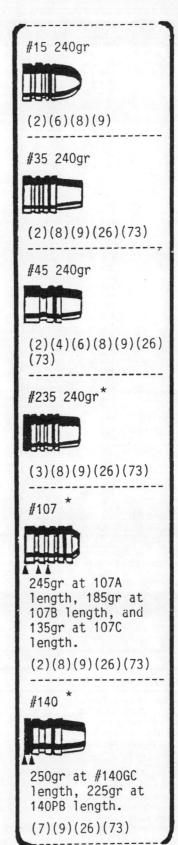

See page 344 for prices.

#15 240gr

(2)(6)(8)(9)

#35 240gr

(2)(8)(9)(26)(73)

#45 240gr

(2)(4)(6)(8)(9)(26)(73)

#235 240gr*

(3)(8)(9)(26)(73)

#107 *

245gr at 107A length, 185gr at 107B length, and 135gr at 107C length.

(2)(8)(9)(26)(73)

#140 *

250gr at #140GC length, 225gr at 140PB length.

(7)(9)(26)(73)

HENSLEY & GIBBS Bullet Moulds

Caliber	Bullet Dia.	Bullet Wgt. Grs.	Type	Mould #	Mould Comments
45 L.C./45 A.R.	.454/.452	160	PB	193	RGG; OCG; LM
	.454/.452	195	PB	312	SGG; OCG
	.454/.452	200	PB	21	RGG; OCG; MM
	.454/.452	200	PB	155	RGG; OCG; SWS; LM
	.454/.452	215	BB	529	RGG; OCG; SWS; LM
	.454/.452	230	PB	16	RGG; OCG
	.454/.452	230	PB	371	RGG; OCG; SWS
	.454/.452	240	PB	46	BB and GC; RGG; OCG; SWS; LM
	.454/.452	240	PB	502	SGG; OCG; SWS; LM
	.454/.452	250*	PB	22	RGG; MM
	.454/.452	255*	BB	387	RGG; OCG; LM
	.454/.452	260*	PB	501	SGG; OCG; SWS; LM
	.454/.452	265*	BB	339	RGG; OCG; LM
454 Casull	.4515	300*	PB	338	SGG; OCG; SWS; LM
	.4515	219*	PB	372-2GC	SGG; 2DB; LM
	.4515	257*	PB	372-3	SGG; 3DB; LM
	.4515	290*	PB	372-3GC	SGG; 3DB; LM
	.4515	340*	PB	372-4	SGG; 4DB; LM
45-70	.458	350*	PB	389	RGG; MM
	.458	355*	PB	348GC	RGG; OCG; SM
	.458	280*	PB	348	RGG; OCG; SM
	.458	300*	BB	348BB	RGG; OCG; SM
	.458	355*	PB	348GC	RGG; OCG; SM
	.458	275*	PB	345-3	SGG; 3DB; MM
	.458	325*	PB	345-4	SGG; 4DB; MM
	.458	395*	PB	345-5	SGG; 5DB; MM
	.458	285*	PB	344-3	SGG; 3DB; MM
	.458	340*	PB	344-4	SGG; 4DB; MM
	.458	405*	PB	344-5	SGG; 5DB; MM
	.458	360*	PB	346	RGG; TCG
	.458	380*	BB	346	RGG; TCG
	.458	405*		346GC	RGG; TCG
	.458	250*	PB	349-2	SGG; 2DB; OD; MM
	.458	300*	PB	349-3	SGG; 3DB; OD; MM
	.458	355*	PB	349-4	SGG; 4DB; OD; MM
	.458	405*	PB	349-5	SGG; 5DB; OD; MM
	.458	350*	PB	390-4	RGG; 4DB; BRN; SM
	.458	410*	PB	390-5	RGG; 5DB; BRN; SM
	.458	320*	PB	364-3GC	SGG; 3DB; MM
	.458	345*	PB	364-4	SGG; 4DB; MM
	.458	375*	PB	364-4GC	SGG; 4DB; MM
	.458	410*	PB	364-5	SGG; 5DB; MM
	.458	195*	PB	347-2	RGG; 2DB; MM
	.458	260*	PB	347-3	RGG; 3DB; MM
	.458	335*	PB	347-4	RGG; 4DB; MM
	.458	400*	PB	347-5	RGG; 5DB; MM
	.458	415*	PB	X347-5	RGG; 5DB; MM
	.458	400*	PB	391-5	RGG; 5DB; MM
	.458	425*	PB	X391-5	RGG; 5DB; MM

RGG = Round Grease Groove; SGG = Square Grease Groove; SM = Small Meplat; MM = Medium Meplat; LM = Large Meplat; OCG = One Crimp Groove; TCG = Two Crimp Grooves; PB = Plain Flat Base; BB = Bevel Base; GC = Gas Check; SWS = Semi- or Wadcutter Shoulder; 1DB = One Driving Band; 2DB = Two Driving Bands; 3DB = Three Driving Bands; 4DB = Four Driving Bands; 5DB = Five Driving Bands; RSWS = Rounded Semi-Wadcutter Shoulder; SBB = Short Bevel Base; LBB = Long Bevel Base; EB = Extended Base; OD = Oversize Diameter; NDB = No Driving Band in front of Crimp Groove; LEEF = Loaded Either End Forward; BRN = Bore Riding Nose. *Extra fee for special cross-venting for this design.

HENSLEY & GIBBS
Price Structure

Mould/Mould Part	2	4	6	8-10
Complete, light/short bullets	$101.00	$135.00	$175.00	$280.00
Complete, heavy/long bullets	111.00	145.00	190.00	280.00
Mould, no handles	85.00	122.00	148.00	244.00
Sprue cutter w/screws, trough-style	18.00	30.00	31.00	57.00
Sprue cutter w/screws, individual hole		40.00	41.00	
Handles	34.00	34.00	52.00	56.00
Blocks, only	68.00	93.00	118.00	188.00
Sprue cutter hinge or stop screw	2.00	2.00	2.00	2.50
Front/rear lock screws (2)	1.50	1.50	1.50	1.50
Handle retainer screws (2)	4.00	4.00	4.00	4.00
Handle pivot bolt/nut	1.50	1.50	2.00	2.00
Complete set of screws	9.50	9.50	10.50	10.50
Complete set of screws plus handle pivot bolt/nut	10.50	10.50	11.50	12.00
Wood Grips	5.00	5.00	6.00	6.00

LBT

Bullet Moulds

Custom 1-, 2- and 4-cavity mould blocks made of hard, stress-relieved 2024-T-351 aluminum with blued machine steel sprue plate. Blocks are larger than necessary to provide more heat radiating surface, higher caloric content and more precise block alignment. Pins are large and spaced further apart. Scientifically designed dual spring tension sprue plate and four-way venting eliminates bullet porosity and base out of squareness. A 60° shoulder angle on pivot screw bears side thrust of knocking sprues without loosening. Available in most popular handgun and rifle calibers. From Lead Bullets Technology.

Price: 1- or 2-cavity **$55.00**
Price: 4-cavity **$95.00**

LOWETH

Webley Mark II Mould

Mould to produce Webley Mark II .455" 265-grain round-nose hollow base bullets. Moulds made to original British government drawings of bullet. From Richard H. A. Loweth Firearms.

Price: . . . . **Contact manufacturer.**

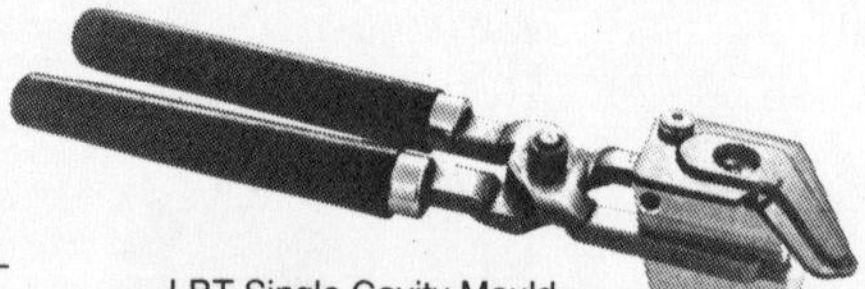

LBT Single Cavity Mould

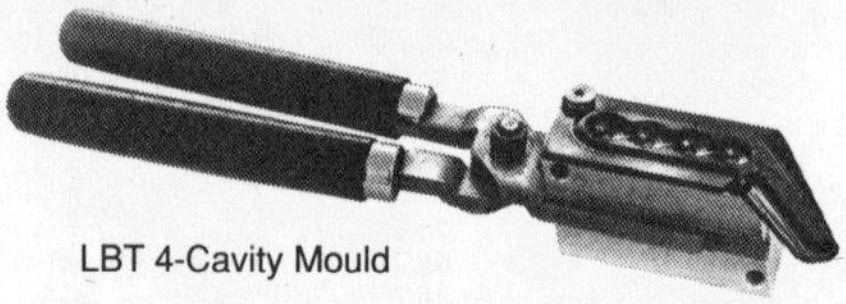

LBT 4-Cavity Mould

Loweth Webley Mark II Mould

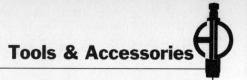

LBT Bullet Moulds

HANDGUN / AUTO PISTOL

Caliber	Wgt. Grs.	Type	Ogive*	Meplat	Length
25 Auto	50	FN	SA	.200	
32 ACP	75	FN	SA	.200	
380 Auto	100	FN	SA	.200	
	100	RN	SA	.200	
	110	FN	SA	.200	
	120	FN	SA	.200	
9MM	90	FN	SA	.200	
	95	TC	SA	.200	
	110	TC	SA	.200	
	125	TC	SA	.200	
	140	BR	SA	.200	
	120	FNBR	SA	.200	
10mm Auto	180	TC	SA	.200	
	185	FNB	SA	.200	
	165	SWC	SA	.200	
45 Auto	200	SWC	SA	.200	
	190	FNB	SA	.200	
	220	FNB	SA	.200	
	230	B	SA	.200	

HANDGUN / REVOLVER / WADCUTTERS

Caliber	Wgt. Grs.	Type	Ogive*	Meplat	Length
32	100	WC	NA	NA	
38	150	WC	NA	NA	
375	170	WC	NA	NA	
41	200	WC	NA	NA	
44	230	WC	NA	NA	
45	260	WC	NA	NA	

HANDGUN / REVOLVER / SFN SERIES

Caliber	Wgt. Grs.	Type	Ogive*	Meplat	Length
32	90	SFN	.160	.080	
	90	FN	.250	.090	
	100	SFN	.160	.080	
	115	FN	.250	.090	
	140	FN	.250	.090	
38	140	FN	.250	.090	
	160	FN	.250	.090	
	180	FN	.250	.090	
	200	FN	.250	.090	Crimp to nose .350 & .400
375	240	WFN	.250	.090	
41	200	WFN	.250	.090	
	220	WFN	.250	.090	
	250	WFN	.250	.090	
	300	WFN	.250	.090	
44	230	WFN	.250	.090	
	260	WFN	.250	.090	
	280	WFN	.250	.090	
	300	WFN	.250	.090	
45	250	WFN	.250	.090	
	280	WFN	.250	.090	
	325	WFN	.250	.090	
475	400	WFN	.250	.090	
500	400	WFN	.250	.090	

HANDGUN / REVOLVER / WLN SERIES

Caliber	Wgt. Grs.	Type	Ogive*	Meplat	Length
38	180	WLN	.400	.090	
41	230	WLN	.400	.090	
44	300	WLN	.400	.090	
45	320	WLN	.400	.090	

HANDGUN / REVOLVER / LFN SERIES

Caliber	Wgt. Grs.	Type	Ogive*	Meplat	Length
358	180	LFN	.130	.340	.725
	210	LFN	.130	.340	.840
375	210	LFN	.130	.340	.770
	225	LFN	.130	.340	.818
	240	LFN	.130	.340	.240
41	210	LFN	.130	.340	.660
	230	LFN	.130	.340	.715
	250	LFN	.130	.340	.774
44	250	LFN	.130	.340	.675
	280	LFN	.130	.340	.775
	300	LFN	.130	.340	.820
	320	LFN	.130	.340	.860
	350	LFN	.130	.340	.920
45	260	LFN	.130	.340	.675
	300	LFN	.130	.340	.775
	320	LFN	.130	.340	.820
	340	LFN	.130	.340	.870
475	380	LFN	.130	.340	.855
	400	LFN	.130	.340	.940
	420	LFN	.130	.340	.955
	440	LFN	.130	.340	.970
500	400	LFN	.130	.340	.820
	420	LFN	.130	.340	.820
	450	LFN	.130	.340	.855

HANDGUN / REVOLVER / K SERIES

Caliber	Wgt. Grs.	Type	Ogive*	Meplat	Length
44	250	K		.340	
45	260	K		.340	
	315	K		.340	

RIFLE & SINGLE SHOT HANDGUN / LFN SERIES

Caliber	Wgt. Grs.	Type	Ogive*	Meplat	Length
257	90	LFN	.130	.340	.745
	100	LFN	.130	.340	.820
	117	LFN	.130	.340	.950
270	120	LFN	.130	.340	.840
	140	LFN	.130	.340	.950
	150	LFN	.130	.340	1.010
7mm	130	LFN	.130	.340	.835
	150	LFN	.130	.340	.955
	170	LFN	.130	.340	1.070
310	150	LFN	.130	.340	.820
	170	LFN	.130	.340	.940
	180	LFN	.130	.340	.955
	200	LFN	.130	.340	1.010
323	150	LFN	.130	.340	.754
	170	LFN	.130	.340	.840
	200	LFN	.130	.340	.971
338	200	LFN	.130	.340	.990
	225	LFN	.130	.340	.880
	250	LFN	.130	.340	1.090
348	200	LFN	.130	.340	.850
	250	LFN	.130	.340	1.035
358	210	LFN	.130	.340	.840
	225	LFN	.130	.340	.880
	250	LFN	.130	.340	.965
375	225	LFN	.130	.340	.880
	240	LFN	.130	.340	.865
	275	LFN	.130	.340	.978
	300	LFN	.130	.340	1.057
40/416	350	LFN	.130	.340	1.025
	375	LFN	.130	.340	1.070
	400	LFN	.130	.340	1.155
458	300	LFN	.130	.340	.775
	340	LFN	.130	.340	.870
	450	LFN	.130	.340	1.072
	500	LFN	.130	.340	1.192

RIFLE & SINGLE SHOT / SPITZER

Caliber	Wgt. Grs.	Type	Ogive*	Meplat	Length
223	50	SP	.264		.300
	55	SP	.264		.350
	60	SP	.264		.400
	66	SP	.264		.450
227	65	SP	.275		.410
	75	SP	.275		.410
243	75	SP	.295		.420
	90	SP	.295		.530
	100	SP	.295		.610
257	80	SP	.303		.370
	90	SP	.303		.440
	100	SP	.303		.510
	120	SP	.303		.650
264	100	SP	.310		.500
	120	SP	.310		.620
	130	SP	.310		.680
	150	SP	.310		.800
270	90	SP	.317		.380
	100	SP	.317		.440
	110	SP	.317		.500
	130	SP	.317		.600
7mm	110	SP	.322		.435
	120	SP	.322		.500
	140	SP	.322		.550
	150	SP	.322		.670
7.35/302	150	SP	.335		.565
	170	SP	.335		.670
	194	SP	.335		.800
310	140	SP	.341		.620
	160	SP	.341		.675
	180	SP	.341		.730
	206	SP	.341		.800
323	150	SP	.350		.480
	150	SP	.350		.480
	175	SP	.350		.590
	200	SP	.350		.700
	220	SP	.350		.800
338	200	SP	.360		.610
	225	SP	.360		.710
	246	SP	.360		.800
358	200	SP	.375		.500
	250	SP	.375		.730
375	275	SP	.385		.700
	310	SP	.385		.800
405-410		SP	.400		.500
	300	SP	.400		.600
	370	SP	.400		.800
458	350	SP	.425		.535
	400	SP	.425		.640
	500	SP	.425		.850
475	400	SP	.430		.550
	510	SP	.430		.800
512	500	SP	.450		.600
	600	SP	.450		.800

SA = Small Auto; FN = Flat Nose; RN = Round Nose; LFN = Long Flat Base; WFN = Wide Flat Nose; FNB = Flat Nose Ball; SP = Spitzer; K = Keith-style

LEE

Bullet Moulds

Aluminum 1- and 2-cavity mould blocks lathe bored to roundness of .001" or less. Most bullets from Lee moulds can be used as cast without sizing. Lee single-cavity, double-cavity, hollowpoint and hollow base single-cavity moulds come with sprue plate and wood handles. Hollowpoint and hollow base moulds have self-centering automatic core pins. From Lee Precision, Inc.

Price: 1-cavity **$19.98**
Price: 2-cavity **$23.98**
Price: Hollowpoint/hollow base . . . **$23.98**

Mould Handles

Precision steel mould handles fit all Lee moulds as well as most other brands of one- and two-cavity moulds. From Lee Precision, Inc.

Price: **$14.98**

Six-Cavity Commercial Moulds

Designed for heavy-duty volume production. Mould and blocks have steel bushing and alignment pins. Cam-operated sprue plate is hard anodized and held with wave washers at each end. Handles not included. From Lee Precision, Inc.

Price: **$50.00**

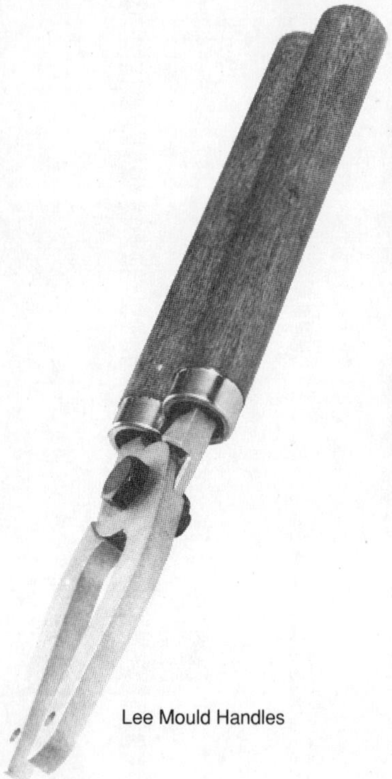

Lee Mould Handles

LEE Rifle Bullet Moulds

Dia.	Wgt. Grs.	Type	Ogive	Gas Check (C) Micro Bands (M)	Mould
270-CALIBER					
.277	125	R	1	C	1-cavity
7MM CALIBER					
.285	130	R	1	C	1-cavity
30-CALIBER					
.309	113	F		C	2-cavity
.309	120	R	1	C	2-cavity
.309	130	R	1	C	1-cavity
.309	150	F		C	1-cavity
.309	160	R	1	C	1-cavity
.309	170	F		C	1-cavity
.309	180	R	1	C	1-cavity
.309	200	R	1	C	1-cavity
.309	200	R	1	C	1-cavity
7.62x39 CALIBER					
.312	155	R	2		1-cavity
.312	160	R	2	M	1-cavity
7.65MM, 7.7MM, 303 BRITISH CALIBERS					
.312	185	R	1		1-cavity
338-CALIBER					
.338	220	R	1	C	1-cavity
45-70 CALIBER					
.457	340	F			1-cavity
.457	405	F			1-cavity*
.457	450	F			1-cavity
.457	500	F			1-cavity

R = Round Nose; F = Flat. *Hollow Point

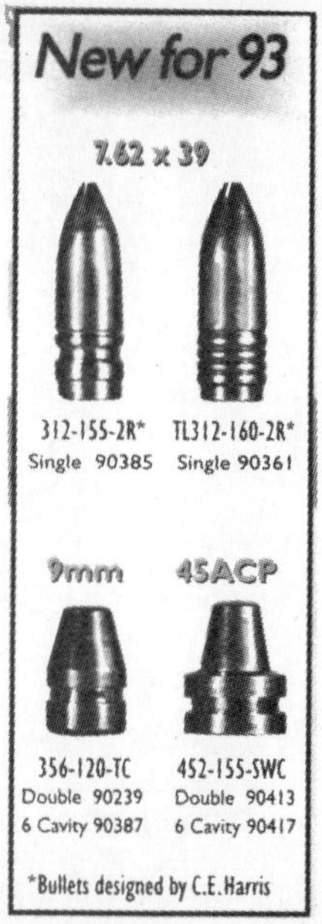

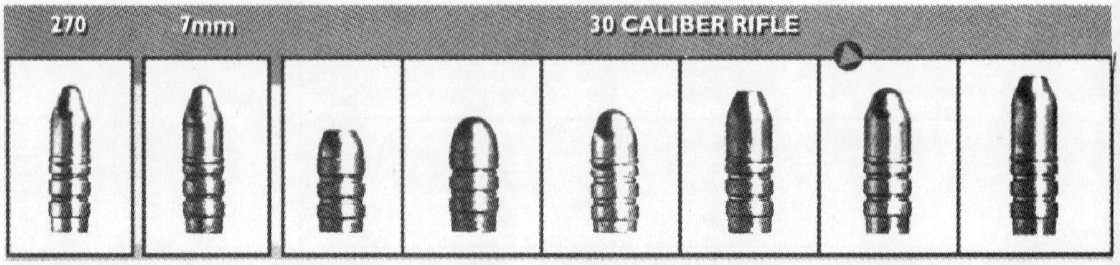

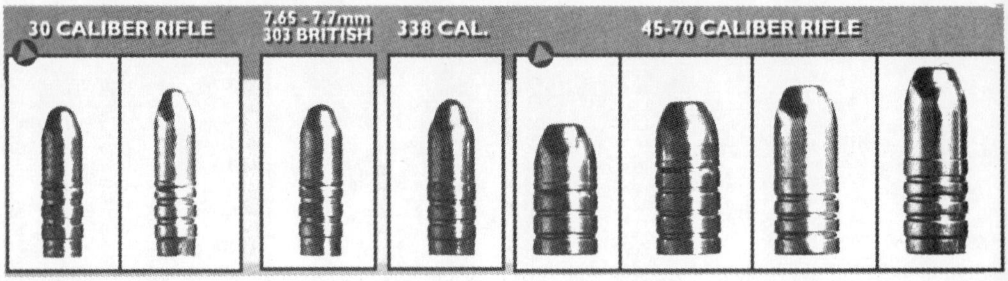

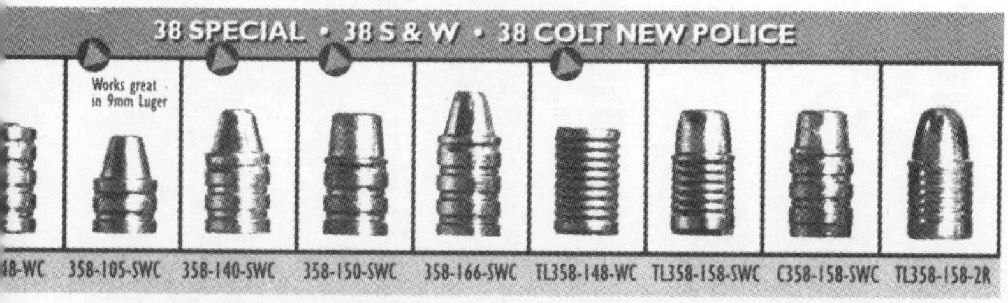

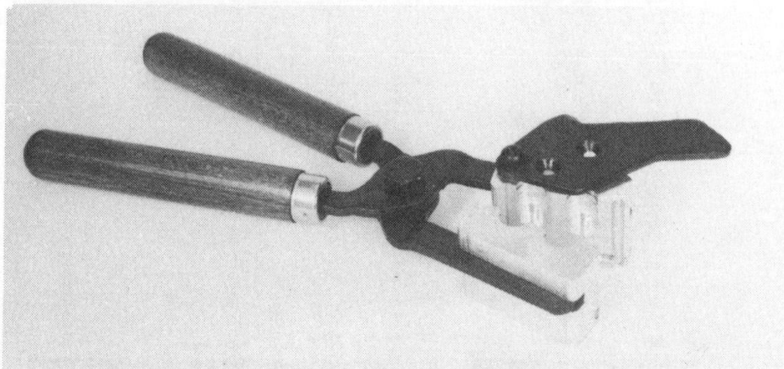

Lee 2-Cavity Mould

LEE Pistol Bullet Moulds

Dia.	Wgt. Grs.	Type	Ogive	Micro Bands (M) Gas Check(C)	Mould
32-20, 32 S&W LONG, 32 COLT NEW POLICE					
.311	93	R	1		2-, 6-cavity
.311	100	R	2		2-cavity
.314	85	WC		M	2-, 6-cavity
.314	90	SWC		M	2-, 6-cavity
38 SPECIAL, 38 S&W, 38 COLT NEW POLICE					
.358	148	WC			2-, 6-cavity
.358	105	SWC			2-, 6-cavity
.358	140	SWC			2-, 6-cavity
.358	150	SWC			2-, 6-cavity*
.358	166	SWC			2-, 6-cavity
.358	148	WC		M	2-, 6-cavity
.358	158	SWC		M	2-, 6-cavity
.358	158	SWC		C	2-, 6-cavity*
.358	158	R	2	M	2-, 6-cavity
.358	150	R	1		2-, 6-cavity
.358	150	WC	1		2-, 6-cavity
9MM LUGER, 38 SUPER AUTO, 380 AUTO					
.356	102	R	1		2-, 6-cavity
.356	111	R	1		2-, 6-cavity
.356	124	R	2	M	2-, 6-cavity
.356	124	TC		M	2-, 6-cavity
.356	120	TC			2-, 6-cavity
.356	125	R	2		2-, 6-cavity
10MM AUTO					
.401	175	SWC		M	2-, 6-cavity
41 MAGNUM, 41 ACTION EXPRESS					
.410	195	SWC		M	2-, 6-cavity
.410	240	SWC			2-, 6-cavity
.410	210	SWC		M	2-, 6-cavity
.410	175	SWC		M	2-, 6-cavity
45 ACP, 45 AUTO RIM					
.452	200	SWC			2-, 6-cavity
44 SPECIAL, 44 MAGNUM, 44-40 (.427)					
.429	208	WC			2-, 6-cavity
.429	214	SWC			2-, 6-cavity*
.429	240	SWC		C	2-, 6-cavity*
.429	255	SWC			2-, 6-cavity
.429	214	R	1		2-, 6-cavity
.429	240	R	2		2-, 6-cavity
.429	240	SWC		M	2-, 6-cavity
45 ACP, 45 AUTO RIM					
.452	155	SWC			2-, 6-cavity
.452	190	SWC			2-, 6-cavity
.452	200	SWC		M	2-, 6-cavity
.452	228	R	1		2-, 6-cavity*
.452	230	R	2		2-, 6-cavity
45 COLT REVOLVER, 45 AUTO RIM					
.452	252	SWC			2-, 6-cavity
.452	255	RF			2-, 6-cavity

WC = Wadcutter; SWC = Semi-wadcutter; RF = Round with flat; RN = Round Nose; TC = Truncated Cone; M = Micro Bands Radius; C = Gas Check. *Hollow Point.

LYMAN

Ideal Moulds

Machined from high-grade steel, blocks are hand fit for precision alignment. Pistol bullet moulds available for all popular bullet designs and come in 2- or 4-cavity blocks. Rifle moulds available in 2-cavity only except where bullet size necessitates single cavity. From Lyman Products Corporation.

Price: Pistol, 2-cavity **$51.95**
Price: Pistol, 4-cavity **$79.95**
Price: Rifle **$51.95**

Shotgun Slug Moulds

Available for 12- or 20-gauge slugs. Mould casts hollow-base slugs which require no rifling. Single-cavity only and cut into the larger double cavity block. Require double cavity handles. From Lyman Products Corporation.

Price: **$51.95**

Mould Rebuild Kit

Includes sprue cutter, washer, all screws for mould block and handle. From Lyman Products Corporation.

Price: 1- and 2-cavity **$4.95**
Price: 4-cavity **$6.95**

Mould Box

Made of tough plastic with snap-lock cover. Impervious to moisture, bore cleaner or oil. Fits single and double cavity moulds only. From Lyman Products Corporation.

Price: **$2.00**

Mould Handles

Solid metal frame with hardwood handles designed to provide uniform grip. Three sizes available: small, for single cavity moulds; large, for double-cavity moulds; and four-cavity for Lyman four-cavity moulds. From Lyman Products Corporation.

Price: 1- and 2-cavity **$24.95**
Price: 4-cavity **$28.95**

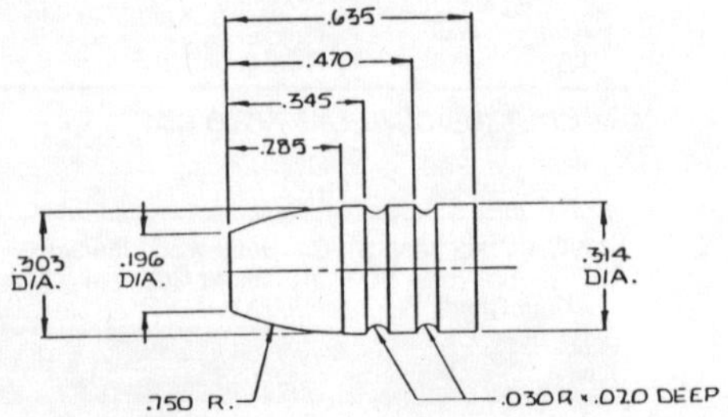

Lyman 32-20 Bullet

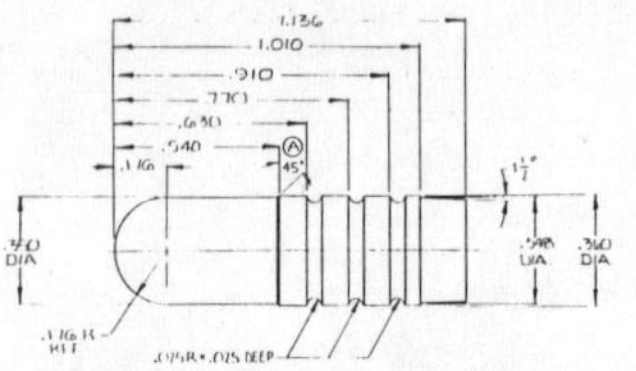

Lyman 35 Whelen Bullet

LYMAN Pistol Bullet Moulds

Bullet #	Caliber	Dia.	Wgt. Grs.	Top Punch #	Gas Check	# Cavity Mould
1	25	.252	50	203		2
2	30	.311	75	465		2
3	32	.313	85	226		2
4		.313	100	8	GC	2
5	9mm	.356	90	311		2
6		.356	100	402		2, 4
7		.356	120	402		2, 4
8		.356	120	311		2, 4
9		.356	130	402		2, 4
10		.356	147	429		2, 4
11	38/357	.358	115	429		2
12		.358	125	93		2
13		.358	140	495		2, 4
14		.358	145	311		2
15		.358	150	495		2, 4
16		.358	150	429		2, 4
17		.358	155	429	GC	2, 4
18		.358	160	311		2, 4
19		.357	165	429		2, 4
20		.358	170	429		2, 4
21		.358	195	430		2
22	357 Max.	.358	215	429	GC	2
23	9mm Mak.	.364	95	226		2
24	10mm/38-40	.401	150	43		2
25		.401	175	43		2, 4
26		.401	175	43		2
27		.401	200	43		2
28	41	.410	215	43	GC	2
29	44-40	.427	205	43		2
30	44/44 Mag.	.429	180	348		2
31		.429	200	303	GC	2
32		.429	210	421	GC	2, 4
33		.429	235	360		2
34		.429	245	421		2, 4
35		.429	255	421	GC	2, 4
36		.429	275	421	GC	2
37		.429	300	421	GC	2
38		.429	325	360	GC	2
39	45	.452	200	460		2, 4
40		.452	200	460		2, 4
41		.452	225	374		2, 4
42	45 Colt	.454	250	190		2
43		.452	255	424		2
44		.452	255	424	GC	2
45		.452	325	424	GC	2

LYMAN Rifle Bullet Moulds

Bullet #	Caliber	Dia.	Wgt. Grs.	Top Punch #	Gas Check #	# Cavity Mould
1	22	.225	44	438	GC	2
2		.225	55	415	GC	2
3		.225	55	415	GC	2
4	6mm	.245	84	203	GC	2
5	25	.257	65	420	GC	2
6	6.5	.266	140	463	GC	2
7		.268	150	463	GC	2
8	270 Win.	.280	150	359		2
9	7mm	.287	135	346	GC	2
10		.287	160	359	GC	2
11	30 M1/7.62x39	.311	115	359	GC	2
12		.311	130	467		2
13	30	.311	152	467	GC	2
14		.311	170	465	GC	2
15		.311	173	8	GC	2
16		.311	180	413	GC	2
17		.311	190	359	GC	2
18		.311	210	467	GC	2
19	32-20	.311	112	8	GC	2
20		.311	115	8		2
21	314	.314	200	467	GC	2
22	8mm	.323	165	470	GC	2
23	35	.358	204	311	GC	2
24		.358	280	430	GC	2
25	375/38-55	.375	249	449		2
26		.375	264	449	GC	2
27	40	.410	400	449		2
28	44-40	.429	250	43	GC	2
29	45	.457	292	191		2
30	45 HP	.457	330	191		2
31		.457	385	374		2
32		.457	400	191		2
33		.457	405	191		2
34		.457	475	374	GC	2
35		.457	500	374		2
36	50	.515	425	141		2

MAGMA Bullet Moulds

Caliber	Wgt. Grs.	Type	Caliber	Wgt. Grs.	Type
32	78	RN BB			
	100	SGG BB	10mm	155	SWC BB
	98	WC BB		170	SWC BB
380	95	RN BB		175	SWC BB
9mm	115	RN BB		180	FP BB
	122	FP BB		200	FP BB
	125	CN BB	38-40	180	RN FP
	135	RN BB	41	215	SWC BB
	147	FP BB	44	180	FP BB
38	160	SWC BB		215	SWC BB
	150	SWC BB		240	SWC BB
	160	RN BB		240	RN BB
	150	RN FB		300	FP BB
	145	RN FB	44-40	200	RN FP
	105	WCD BB	45	155	SWC BB&FB
	125	FP BB		160	SWC FB
	125	FP BB		185	SWC BB
	148	WC DBB SSG		175	SWC BB
	148	WC DBB		180	SWC BB
	148	WC BB		185	SWC BB
	158	SWC BB		200	SWC BB
	150	SWC BB		225	FP BB
	158	RN BB		230	RN BB
	180	FP BB		250	RN FP
10mm	140	RN FP BB		255	SWC BB
	155	RN SWC		300	FP BB

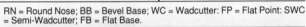

RN = Round Nose; BB = Bevel Base; WC = Wadcutter: FP = Flat Point: SWC = Semi-Wadcutter; FB = Flat Base.

Magma Cast Bullets

OLD WEST Bullet Moulds

Caliber	Cast Size	Wgt. Grs.	Type	OAL	Caliber	Cast Size	Wgt. Grs.	Type	OAL
25	.253	56	PB	.460	40	.402	170	PB	.570
	.259	75	PB	.610		.402	205	GC	.680
	.259	82	GC	.610	41	.405	190	PB	.710
	.259	95	PB	.770		.407	250	PB	.810
	.259	106	GC	.860		.407	280	GC	.930
6mm	.266	130	PB	1.10	40/41	.405	160		.530
	.266	145	GC	1.10		.411	210	PB	.680
270	.279	140	PB	1.10		.411	218	PB	.950
	.279	155	GC	1.10		.411	240	GC	.760
7mm	.286	145	PB	1.04		.411	275	PB	.950
	.286	160	GC	1.04		.411	310	GC	.950
	.287	160	PB	1.10		.413	240	PB	.750
	.287	176	GC	1.10		.413	280	PB	.860
30	.310	180	PB	1.00		.413	310	GC	.980
	.310	198	GC	1.10	416	.419	360	PB	1.190
	.311	114	PB	1.015		.419	400	GC	1.190
	.311	130	GC	1.015	44	.429	215	PB	.670
	.311	140	PB	1.015		.429	270	PB	.810
	.311	170	PB	1.015		.430	240	PB	.700
	.311	190	GC	1.015		.430	275	GC	.810
32	.313	100	PB			.430	315	GC	.830
	.313	118	GC			.431	220	PB	.680
	.314	85	PB	.490		.431	280	PB	.820
	.314	100	GC	.570		.431	320	GC	.910
303	.316	195	PB	1.10		.432	180	PB	.670
	.316	210	GC	1.10		.432	215	PB	.650
32-44	.323	114	PB	.575		.432	230	PB	.670
	.323	144	PB	.575		.432	255	GC	.740
	.323	172	PB	.575		.432	270	GC	.670
	.323	189	GC	.575	45	.454	210	GC	
8mm	.326	190	PB	1.10		.454	239	PB	
	.326	215	GC	1.10		.454	251	PB	
33	.340	215	PB	.950		.454	281	GC	
	.340	230	GC	1.04		.454	310	PB	.770
348	.350	220	PB	.960		.454	390	PB	.970
	.350	245	GC	1.020		.454	490	GC	1.20
	.360	150	PB	.660	45-70	.459	295	PB	.770
	.360	170	GC	.760		.459	350	GC	.890
35	.360	195	PB	.890		.460	326	PB	1.050
	.360	220	GC	.890		.460	405	PB	1.050
	.360	240	PB	1.00		.460	450	GC	1.050
	.360	270	GC	1.10		.462	255	PB	.650
375	.377	220	PB	1.072		.462	320	PB	.850
	.377	260	PB	1.072		.462	360	GC	.950
	.377	294	GC	1.072	50	.515	325	PB	.660
38	.381	220	PB	1.025		.515	385	PB	.830
	.381	255	PB	1.025		.515	470	PB	1.070
	.381	286	GC	1.025		.515	525	PB	1.180

PB = Plain Base; GC = Gas Check.

MAGMA

Bullet Moulds

For use with the Magma Master Caster automatic casting machine and manual Bullet Master. Over 40 bullet styles available. From Magma Engineering Co.

Price: **$60.00**

OLD WEST

Bullet Moulds

Custom lathe or cherry cut single-, double- or triple-cavity moulds for obsolete and modern rifles and handguns in claibers from 22- to 54-caliber. Nose pour or base pour styles available. Cherry cut moulds are base pour and made of brass. Lathe bored nose pour moulds have minimum bullet length, .950"; maximum length, 1.4". Lathe bored base pour moulds, any length up to 1.4". Max number driving bands is six; minimum diameter meplat .1". Sprue plate of $^{1}/_{8}$" thick steel but $^{3}/_{16}$" thick plates available. Single and double cavity moulds fit RCBS or Lyman handles; for three-cavity only RCBS handles. Economy moulds with each cavity a different caliber or bullet weight also offered. From Old West Bullet Moulds.

Price: Cherry cut single, 25 to 50 cal. **$52.00**

Price: Lathe bored single, nose pour **$65.00**

Price: Lathe bored single, base pour **$57.00**

Price: 2-cavity, 25 to 50 cal. **$62.00**

Price: 2-cavity economy, 25 to 45 cal. **$68.00**

Price: 3-cavity, 25 to 50 cal. **$74.00**

RAPINE

Bullet Moulds

Single- and double-cavity moulds machined from high-strength aluminum alloy to precise caliber with highly-polished finish. Come with long wooden handles placed close together to reduce fatigue. From Rapine Bullet Mould Mfg. Co.

Price: **$55.95**

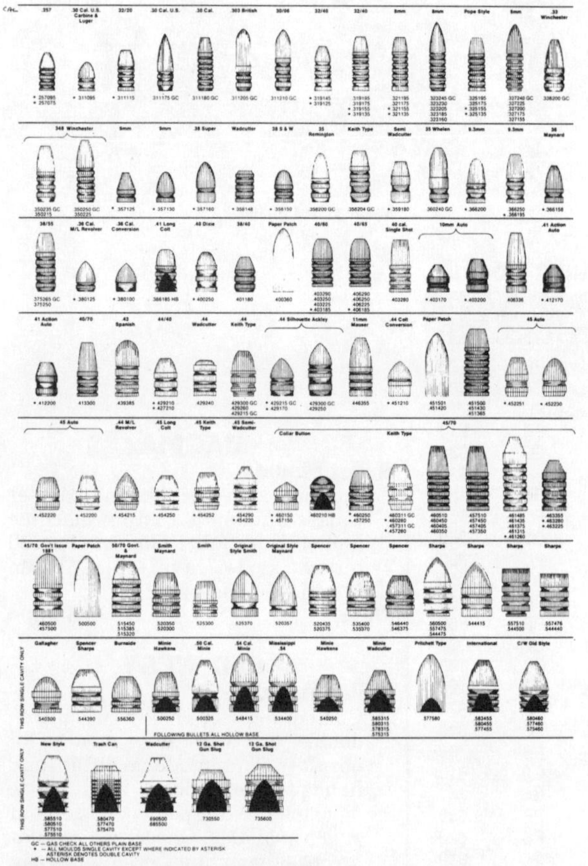

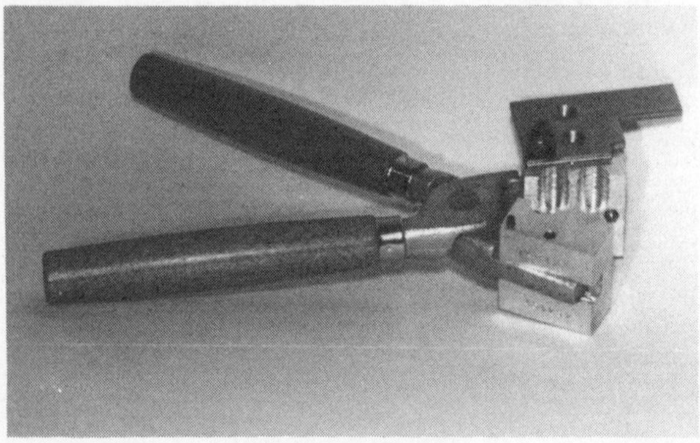

Rapine 2-Cavity Mould

RAPINE Bullet Moulds

Bullet	Caliber	Dia.	Wgt. Grs.
1	257	.257	95
		.257	75
2	30	.311	95
3		.311	115
4		.311	175
5		.311	180
6	303 Brit.	.311	205
7	30-06	.311	210
8	32-40	.319	145
		.319	125
9		.319	135
		.319	155
		.319	175
		.319	195
10	8mm	.321	135
		.321	155
		.321	175
		.321	195
11		.323	160
		.323	185
		.323	205
		.323	230
		.323	245
12		.325	135
		.325	155
		.325	175
		.325	195
13		.327	155
		.327	175
		.327	200
		.327	225
		.327	240
14	33	.338	200
15	348	.350	215
		.350	235
16		.350	225
		.350	250
17	9mm	.357	125
18		.357	130
19	38	.357	160
20		.358	148
21		.358	150
22	35	.358	200
23		.358	204
24		.359	180
25		.360	240
26	9.3mm	.366	200
27		.366	195
		.366	250
28	36 Maynard	.366	158
29	38-55	.375	250
		.375	265
30	36	.380	125
31	36 Conv.	.380	100
32	41 LC	.386	185
33	40 Dixie	.400	250
34	38-40	.401	180
35	Paper Patch	.400	360
36	40-60	.403	185
		.403	225
		.403	250
		.403	290
37	40-65	.406	185
		.496	225
		.406	250
		.406	290
38	40 SS	.403	280
39	10mm	.403	170
40		.403	200
41		.408	336
42	41 Action Auto	.412	170
43		.412	200
44	40-70	.413	300
45	43 Spanish	.439	385
46	44-40	.427	210
		.429	210
47	44	.429	240

Bullet	Caliber	Dia.	Wgt. Grs.
48		.429	125
		.429	260
		.429	300
49	44 Sil. Ack.	.429	170
		.429	215
50		.429	250
		.429	300
51	11mm Mauser	.446	355
52	44 Colt Conv.	.451	210
53	Paper Patch	.451	420
		.452	501
54		.451	365
		.451	430
		.451	500
55	45 Auto	.452	251
56		.452	230
57		.452	220
58		.452	200
59	44 Rev.	.454	215
60	45 LC	.454	250
61	45	.454	252
62		.454	220
		.454	290
63	45-70	.457	150
		.460	150
64		.460	210
65		.457	250
		.460	250
66		.457	280
		.457	311
		.460	280
		.460	311
67		.460	350
		.460	405
		.460	450
		.460	510
68		.457	350
		.457	405
		.457	450
		.457	510
69		.461	260
		.461	315
		.461	375
		.461	435
		.461	485
70		.463	225
		.463	280
		.463	355
71	45-70 1881	.457	500
		.460	500
72	Paper Patch	.500	500
73	50-70 Gov't.&May.	.515	320
		.515	385
		.515	450
74	Smith May.	.520	300
		.520	350
75	Smith	.525	300
76	Orig. Smith	.525	370
77	Orig. May.	.520	357
78	Spencer	.520	375
		.520	435
79		.535	370
		.535	400
80		.546	375
		.546	440
81	Sharps	.544	475
		.577	475
		.560	500
82		.544	415
83		.544	500
		.557	510
84		.544	440
		.557	476
85	Gallagher	.540	300
86	Spencer Sharps	.544	390
87	Burnside	.556	360

RCBS

Bullet Moulds

Hand-machined from blocks of precision-cast, malleable iron. Hardened pins ensure permanent alignment. The sprue cutter is solid carbon steel, locked in place with Allen setscrew. Bullet roundness tolerance to .001". 200 different moulds available. From RCBS.

Price: Pistol or round ball **$49.67**
Price: Rifle or silhouette **$51.45**

Caliber	32	32	32	38	9mm
Size	.311"	.314"	.314"	.356"	.356"
Mould	32-77-RN Part 82021	32-098-WC Part 82060	32-098-SWC Part 82061	38-90-RN Part 82057	09-115-RN Part 82026
Sizer Die	.311" dia. Part 82214	.314" dia. Part 82216	.314" dia. Part 82216	.356" dia. Part 82221	.356" dia. Part 82221
Top Punch	#465 Part 82536	#445 Part 82513	#444 Part 82542	#311 Part 82513	#115 Part 82504

38/357	38/357	38/357	40/10mm	10mm	10mm	41	44	44	44	44	44	44	45 Auto
.358"	.358	.358"	.401"	.400"	.400"	.410"	.430"	.430"	.430"	.430"	.430"	.430"	.452"
38-150-SWC Part 82032	38-158-RN Part 82064	38-158-SWC Part 82065	40-180-FN Part 82066	10mm-170-SWC Part 82067	10mm-200-SWC Part 82068	41-210-SWC Part 82039	44-225-SWC Part 82041	44-240-SWC Part 82042	44-245-SWC Part 82043	44-250-K Part 82080	44-250-SWC Part 82044	44-300-SWC Part 82079	45-185-BB SWC Part 82052
.358" dia. Part 82223	.358" dia. Part 82223	.358" dia. Part 82223	.401" dia. Part 82245	.400" dia. Part 82243	.400" dia. Part 82243	.410" dia. Part 82226	.430" dia Part 82229	.430" dia. Part 82229	.430" dia. Part 82229	.430" dia Part 82229	.430" dia. Part 82229	.430" dia Part 82229	.452" dia. Part 82233
#429 Part 82529	#311 Part 82513	#429 Part 82529	#558 Part 85558	#518 Part 85518	#518 Part 85518	#420 Part 82541	#421 Part 82527	#421 Part 82527	#421 Part 82527	#421 Part 82527	#421 Part 82527	#421 Part 82527	#680 Part 82545

9mm	9mm	9mm	9mm	9mm Makarov	38/357	38/357
.356"	.356"	.356"	.356"	.365"	.358"	.358"
9mm-124-RN Part 82062	09-124-RN-TC Part 82063	09-124-CN Part 82027	9mm-147-FN Part 82077	9mm-100-RN Part 82084	38-148-WC DE Part 82030	38-148-WC Part 82031
.356" dia. Part 82221	.356" dia. Part 82221	.356" dia. Part 82221	.356" dia. Part 82221	.365" dia. Part 82248	.358" dia. Part 82223	.358" dia. Part 82223
#401 Part 82521	#115 Part 82504	#402 Part 82522	#556 Part 85556	#551 Part 82551	#344 Part 82515	#429 Part 82529

45 Auto	45 Auto	45	45 Auto	45 Colt	45 Colt	45
.452"	.452"	.454"	.452"	.454"	.454"	.452"
45-200-SWC Part 82046	45-201-SWC Part 82047	44-225-CAV Part 82081	45-230-RN Part 82048	45-250-FN Part 82049	45-255-SWC Part 82050	45-300-SWC Part 82083
.452" dia. Part 82233	.452" dia Part 82233	.454" dia Part 82234	.452" dia Part 82233	.454" dia Part 82234	.454" dia. Part 82234	.452" dia Part 82233
#460 Part 82534	#680 Part 82545	#552 Part 85552	#374 Part 82519	#190 Part 82506	#424 Part 82528	#424 Part 82528

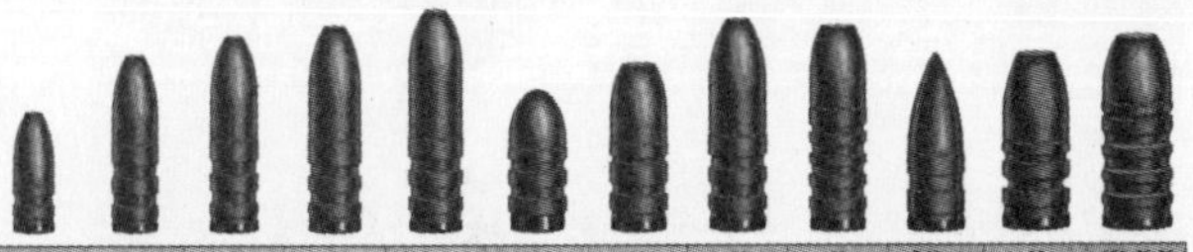

Caliber	22	6mm	25	270	7mm	30	30	30	30	7.62mm	35	375, 38-55
Size	.225"	.244"	.258"	.278"	.285"	.309"	.309"	.309"	.309"	.309"	.358"	.376"
Mould	22-055-SP Part 82007	243-095-SP Part 82015	257-120-SP Part 82016	270-150-SP Part 82017	7mm-168-SP Part 82018	30-115-SP Part 82009	30-150-FN Part 82019	30-180-SP Part 82020	30-180-FN Part 82014	7.62-130-SPL Part 82022	35-200-FN Part 82028	37-250-FN Part 82029
Sizer Die	.225" dia. Part 82240	.244" dia. Part 82202	.258" dia. Part 82204	.278" dia. Part 82206	.285" dia. Part 82209	.309" dia. Part 82212	.309" dia Part 82212	.309" dia Part 82212	.309" dia Part 82212	.309" dia. Part 82212	.358" dia. Part 82223	.376" dia. Part 82225
Top Punch	#506 Part 85506	#509 Part 85509	#515 Part 85515	#529 Part 85529	#531 Part 85531	#535 Part 85535	#546 Part 85546	#541 Part 85541	#546 Part 85546	#554 Part 85554	#565 Part 85565	#570 Part 85570

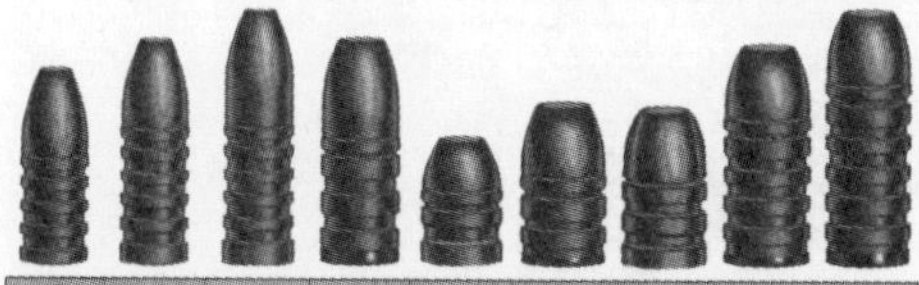

40	40	40	416	44-40	45	45	45	45
.410"	.410"	.410"	.417"	.428"	.458"	.458"	.458"	.458"
40-300-SP-CSA Part 82070	40-350-SP-CSA Part 82072	40-400-SP-CSA Part 82074	416-350-FN Part 82075	44-200-FN Part 82036	45-300-FN Part 82051	45-325-FN-U Part 82045	45-405-FN+ Part 82053	45-500-FN+ Part 82054
.410" dia. Part 82226	.410" dia Part 82226	.410" dia Part 82226	.417" Part 82246	.428" dia. Part 82244	.458" dia. Part 82236	.458" dia Part 82236	.458" dia. Part 82236	.458" dia. Part 82236
#378 Part 82520	#378 Part 82520	#378 Part 82520	#562 Part 85562	#595 Part 85595	#600 Part 85600	#383 Part 85583	#600 Part 85600	#600 Part 85600

Silhouette

Caliber	7mm	308	308	357	44
Size	.285"	.309"	.309"	.358"	.430"
Mould	7mm-145-SIL Part 82150	308-165-SIL Part 82152	308-200-SIL Part 82153	357-180-SIL Part 82154	429-240-SIL Part 82156
Sizer Die	.285" dia. Part 82209	.309" dia. Part 82212	.309" dia. Part 82212	.358" dia. Part 82223	.430" dia Part 82229
Top Punch	#531 Part 85531	#541 Part 85541	#541 Part 85541	#430 Part 82530	#422 Part 82526
Seater Plug	7mm SIL Part 09696	308 SIL Part 09697	308 SIL Part 09697	357 SIL Part 09698	44 SIL Part 09699

RCBS Cast Bullets *Alternate Sizes*

Caliber	Size
22	.244
6mm	.243
25	.257
270	.277
7mm	.284
30	.308
	.310
	.311
32	.312
	.313
	.314
38/357	.354
	.355
38	.356
357	.357
375/38-55	.375
44-40	.427
44	.429
	.431
45	.450
	.451
45 Colt	.454
45	.457

RCBS Bullet Moulds

Caliber	Size	Mould #/Grs./Bullet Type	Top Punch #
PISTOL MOULDS			
32	.311	32-77-RN	465
	.314	32-098-WC	444
	.314	32-098-WC	444
38	.356	38-90-RN	311
9mm	.356	09-115-RN	115
	.356	9mm-124-RN	401
	.356	09-124-RN-TG	115
	.356	09-124-CN	402
	.356	9mm-147-FN	556
	.365	9mm-100-RN	551
38/357	.358	38-148-WC	344
	.358	38-148-WC	429
	.358	38-150-SWC	429
	.358	38-158-RN	311
	.358	38-158-SWC	429
40/10mm	.401	40-180-FN	558
10mm	.400	10mm-170-SWC	518
	.400	10mm-200-SWC	518
41	.410	41-210-SWC	420
44	.430	44-225-SWC	421
	.430	44-240-SWC	421
	.430	44-245-SWC	421
	.430	44-250-K	421
	.430	44-250-SWC	421
	.430	44-300-SWC	421
45	.452	45-185-BB-SWC	680
	.452	45-200-SWC	460
	.452	45-201-SWC	680
	.454	45-225-CAV	552
	.452	45-230-RN	374
45 Colt	.454	45-250-FN	190
	.454	45-255-SWC	424
	.452	45-300-SWC	424
RIFLE MOULDS			
22	.225	22-055-SP	506
6mm	.244	243-095-SP	509
25	.258	257-120-SP	515
270	.278	270-150-SP	529
7mm	.285	7mm-168-SP	531
30	.309	30-115-SP	535
	.309	30-150-FN	546
	.309	30-180-SP	541
	.309	30-180-FN	546
7.62mm	.309	7.62-130-SPL	554
35	.358	35-200-FN	565
375,38-55	.376	37-250-FN	570
40	.410	40-300-SP	378
	.410	40-350-SP-CSA	378
	.410	40-400-SP-CSA	378
416	.417	416-350-FN	562
44-40	.428	44-200-FN	595
45	.458	45-300-FN	600
	.458	45-325-FN-U	383
	.458	45-405-FN+	600
	.458	45-500-FN+	600
SILHOUETTE MOULDS			
7mm	.285	7mm-145-SIL	7mm SIL
308	.309	308-165-SIL	308 SIL
	.309	308-200-SIL	308 SIL
357	.358	357-180-SIL	357 SIL
44	.430	429-240-SIL	44 SIL

RN = Round Nose; WC = Wadcutter; SWC = Semi-Wadcutter; FN = Flat Nose; K = Keith Type; BB = Bevel Base; CAV = Cavalry; SP = Semi-Point; SPL = Special; CSA = C Sharps Arms; U = Universal; SIL = Silhouette; TG = Target; DE = Double End; CN = Conical Nose; PT = Pointed.

SAECO

Bullet Moulds

Two- and 4-cavity moulds machined from blocks of copper alloyed pearlitic cast iron for dimensional stability. Cavities cut using same cherrie on digital equipment for uniformity. Steel sprue plate held against mould blocks by high-temperature Inconel spring washers. Mould handles are ductile iron castings with oak grips. Handles ordered separately. From Redding Reloading Equipment.

Price: 2-cavity **$60.00**
Price: 4-cavity **$105.00**
Price: Mould handles **$31.50**

Special Order Moulds

Three-, 6- and 8-cavity and "magnum" moulds made on special order basis. From Redding Reloading Equipment.

Price: 1-cavity magnum **$60.00**
Price: 2-cavity magnum **$75.00**
Price: 3-cavity **$84.00**
Price: 6-cavity **$174.00**
Price: 8-cavity **$246.00**

Bullet Moulds for Obsolete Cal.

Special order moulds available in single cavity magnum only. Six different bullet styles.

Style A: Cylindrical bullet similar to original factory bullets for most blackpowder cartridges. Diameter at front band is same diameter at base band. Rounded grease grooves.

Style B: Cylindrical bullet with front wiper band deleted. Rounded grease grooves.

Style C: Two diameter bullet with front three bands slightly larger than bore diameter and rear three at groove diameter. Rounded grease grooves.

Style D: Two diameter bullet same as Style C but without front wiper band. Rounded grease grooves.

Style E: Tapered bullet with front band near bore diameter tapering to slightly larger than groove diameter. Rounded grease grooves.

Style F: Hudson bullet. Two diameter with front bands near bore diameter with two rear bands slightly larger than groove diameter. From Redding Reloading Equipment.

Price: . . . . **Contact manufacturer.**

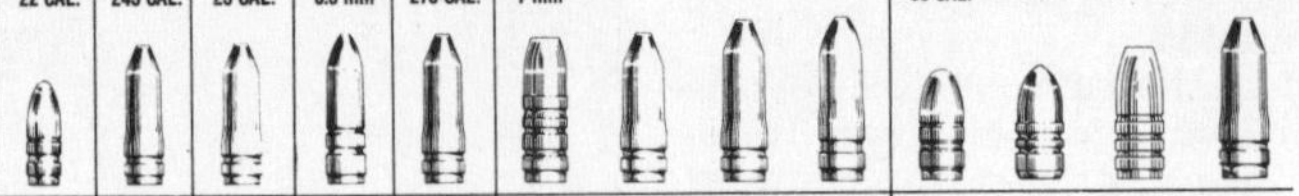

	22 CAL.	243 CAL.	25 CAL.	6.5 mm	270 CAL.	7 mm				30 CAL.			
No.	221	243	257	264	270	281	070	071	073	302	254	316	311
Designation	60gr. SPGC	85gr. TCGC	100gr. TCGC	140 gr. SPGC	140gr. TCGC	145gr. FPGC	145gr. TCGC	160gr. TCGC	165gr. SPGC	120gr. RNGC	115gr. RNBB	150gr. FPGC	165gr. TCGC
Sizing Die	.225	.244	.258	.265	.278	.285	.285	.285	.285	.309	.309	.309	.309
Top Punch	22498	24243	25258	26264	27270	28311	28520	28520	28520	30467	30467	30530	30301
Description	Works Well in .223 Semi Autos	For all .243 & .244 Cal.	.25 Cal. Silhouette		Two perfect 60's shot at Reg. 6 IHMSA	Standard for 7mm	Silhouette	200 meters Silhouette	Heavy 7mm Bullet	For 30 MI, GC	For 30 MI	For 30-30	

	30 CAL. (cont.)			31 CAL. NEW	32 CAL.			NEW		NEW	8 mm	9 mm/38 SUPER	
No.	307	315	301	305	327	323	325	326	321	322A	081	380	922
Designation	180gr. FPGC	175gr. TCGC	196gr. TCGC	180gr. FPGC	75gr. RN	95 gr. WC	95 gr. SWC	100gr. SWCBB	95gr. RN	118gr. FP	190gr. RNGC	95gr. RNBB	115gr. RNBB
Sizing Die	.309	.309	.309	.311	.313	.313	.313	.313	.313	.313	.323/.324	.356	.356
Top Punch	30301	30329	30301	30301	32465	32323	32467	32467	32465	30254	30530	35465	35311
Description		Bench Rest Style "E" Taper	Duplicates Original RG4	303 British	.32 ACP	Good .32 Long Target Bullet			.32 S&W Long	.32-20 Bullet	8 mm Rifle	Good .380 bullet	

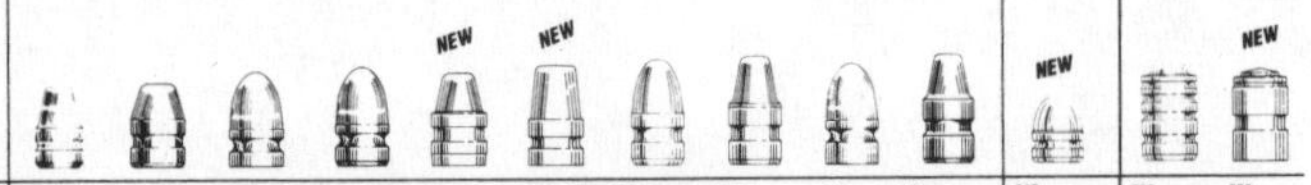

	9 mm/38 SUPER (cont.)				NEW	NEW					9.2 mm NEW	38/357-35 CAL.	NEW
No.	925	377	384	115	924	383	928	929	910	930	940	052	053
Designation	115gr. SWBB	122gr. TCBB	122gr. RN	122 gr. RNBB	124gr. SWCGC	140gr. SWC	145gr. RNBB	145gr. SWCBB	150gr. RN	154gr. SWCBB	100gr. RNBB	148gr. WCBB	148gr. WC
Sizing Die	.356	.356	.356	.356	.356	.356/.357	.356/.357	.356/.357	.356	.356/.357	.365	.358	.358
Top Punch	35925	35375	35311	35311	35925	35429	35311	35925	35311	35925	35465	35550	35381
Description		Good Ballistics for 9mm	Good Feeding 9mm		Good Feeding SWC		38 Super	38 Super		38 Super Wilson Design	9mm Makarov	Target Bullet	GAR Design

BB–Bevel Base, DBB–Bevel Base Both Ends, FB–Flat Base, FP–Flat Point, GC–Gas Check, RN–Round Nose, SP–Spitzer Point, SWC–Semi Wad Cutter, TC–Truncated Cone Point, WC–Wad Cutter.

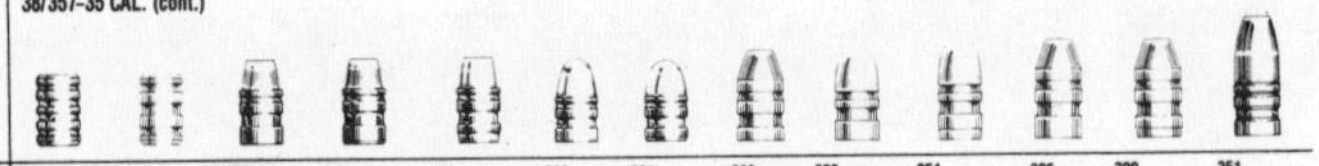

	38/357-35 CAL. (cont.)												
No.	397	348	382	388	393	390	391	398	353	354	396	399	351
Designation	148gr. WCDBB	148gr. DBBWC	158gr. SWC	158gr. SWCBB	162gr. SWCGC	158gr. RN	158gr. RNBB	158gr. TC	180gr. FP	180gr. FPGC	180gr. TC	180gr. TCGC	200 gr. FP
Sizing Die	.358	.358	.358	.358	.358	.358	.358	.358	.358	.358	.358	.358	.358
Top Punch	35344	35344	35429	35429	35429	35311	35311	35399	35353	35353	35399	35399	35311
Description	148gr. Double Bevel Base WC	Single Groove DBB	Kejth Design	Most Popular		Standard .38 Bullet			Super Long Range Bullet	GC Version of Popular 353			Heavy .357 Bullet

	41 CAL. (cont.)							416 CAL. NEW	44 CAL. NEW			
No.	412	417	409	413	415	410	418	*916	944	420	444	446-A
Designation	185gr. SWC	210gr. SWC	190gr. TC	210gr. TCBB	220gr. TCGC	220gr. FP	220gr. SWCBB	365gr. RNGC	200gr. WC	200 gr. TC	200gr. FPSWC	200gr. SWC
Sizing Die	.411	.411	.411	.411	.411	.411	.411	.417	.430	.430	.428	.430
Top Punch	41610	41610	41415	41415	41415	41415	41610	41916	44944	44428	44191	44191
Description						Pistol Silhouette	Bevel Base Keith Style	416 Rifles	GAR Design	Jim Hubert Design	44-40	

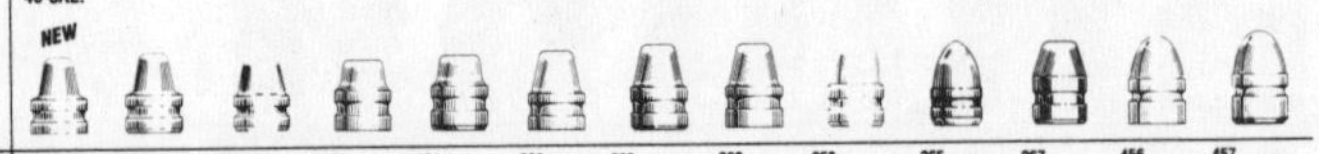

	45 CAL. NEW												
No.	062-B	062	065	130	131	066	068	069	058	265	067	456	457
Designation	160gr. SPL	170gr. SPLBB	180gr. SWCBB	185gr. SWC	185gr. SWCBB	180gr. SWC	200gr. SWCBB	200gr. SWC	215gr. SWCBB	210gr. RNWC	225gr. TCBB	225gr. RN	225gr. RNBB
Sizing Die	.452	.452	452	.452	.452	.452	.452	.452	.452	.452	.452	.452	.452
Top Punch	45452	45452	45429	45421	45421	45429	-45429	45429	45424	45265	45375	45701	45701
Description	Behn Design	-V-MAXX .45 Behn Design	Lt. Wt. IPSC	Most Popular Lt. Target			Most Popular Combat Bullet		Bowling Pin Bullet	Best Feeding .45 ACP		Standard Round Nose	

BB–Bevel Base, DBB–Bevel Base Both Ends, FB–Flat Base, FP–Flat Point, GC–Gas Check, RN–Round Nose, SP–Spitzer Point, SWC–Semi Wad Cutter, TC–Trunated Cone Point, WC–Wad Cutter.

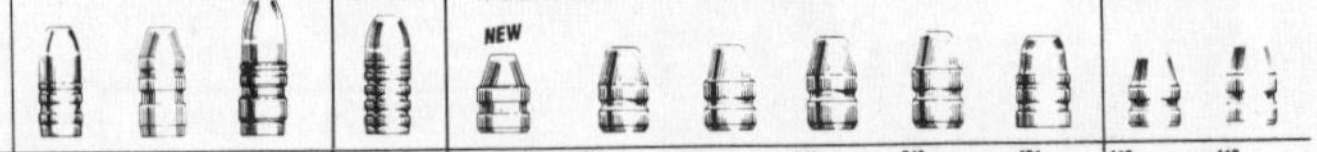

				375 CAL.	40 CAL./10 mm NEW						41 CAL.	
No.	356	395	352	373	040	043	045	047	048	401	416	419
Designation	200 gr. FPGC	200gr. TCGC	245gr. FPGC	265gr. FPGC	155gr. SWCBB	170gr. TCBB	170gr. SWCBB	200gr. TCBB	200gr. SWCBB	190gr.	170gr. SWCBB	200gr. SWCBB
Sizing Die	.358	.358	.358	.376	.401	.401	.401	.401	.401	.401	.411	.411
Top Punch	35311	35399	35311	37570	40048	40047	40048	40047	40048	40101	41447	41447
Description	Handgun Silhouette	Silhouette		Rifle	10mm Auto	10mm Auto	10mm Auto	10mm Auto	10mm Auto	.38-40	41 Auto Petty Design	41 Auto Petty Design

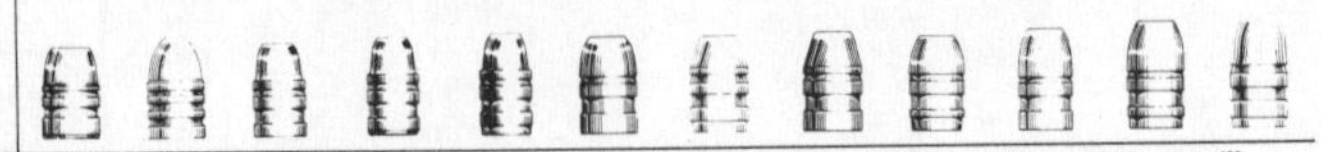

No.	445	442	441	440	439	429	424	428	431	430	432	433
Designation	220gr. SWCBB	246gr. RN	240gr. SWC	240gr. SWCBB	240gr. SWCGC	240gr. FP	240gr. TCGC	240gr. TC	250gr. FPGC	265gr. FP	265gr. FPGC	300gr. FPGC
Sizing Die	.430	.430	.430	.430	.430	.430	.430	.430	.430	.430	.430	.430
Top Punch	44191	44374	44421	44421	44421	44191	44428	44428	44191	44191	44191	44191
Description		Standard 44 Spec. Bullet	Standard Wt.44 Mag Keith Style			Superb Long Range Bullet	GC Version of Popular 428	Most Popular Silhouette	444 Marlin	Superb Long Range Bullet		Silhouette

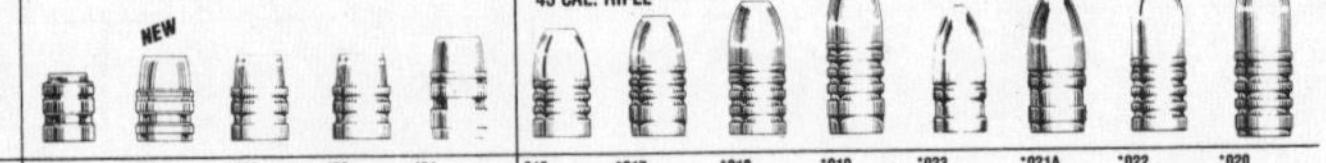

		NEW				45 CAL. RIFLE							
No.	453	945	458	452	454	015	*017	*018	*019	*023	*021A	*022	*020
Designation	225gr. WC	255gr. SWCGC	255gr. SWC	255gr. SWC	300gr. SWCGC	300gr. FP	350gr. FPGC	405gr. FP	450gr. FPGC	375gr. SP	405gr. SPGC	500gr. FP	540gr. FPGC
Sizing Die	.452	.452	.452	.455	.452	.458	.458	.458	.458	.458	.458	.458	.458
Top Punch	45424	45424	45424	45452	45424	45015	45015	45015	45015	45702	45702	45610	45610
Description	Jan Libourel Design	For 45 Colt	For .45 Colt w/.452 Bore	For .45 Colt w/.454 Bore	Heavy .45 Colt & .454 Casull								

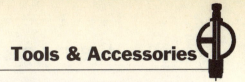

SAECO Bullet Moulds

Caliber	——Bullet—— Grs. Wgt.	Type	Gas Check	Sizing Die	Top Punch
22	60	SP	GC	.225	22498
243	85	TC	GC	.244	24243
25	100	TC	GC	.258	25258
6.5mm	140	SP	GC	.265	26264
270	140	TC	GC	.278	27270
7mm	145	FP	GC	.285	28311
	145	TC	GC	.285	28520
	160	TC	GC	.285	28520
	165	SP	GC	.285	28520
30	120	RN	GC	.309	30467
	115	RNBB		.309	30467
	150	FP	GC	.309	30530
	165	TC	GC	.309	30301
	180	FP	GC	.309	30301
	175	TC	GC	.309	30329
	196	TC	GC	.309	30301
31	180	FP	GC	.311	30301
32	75	RN		.313	32465
	95	WC		.313	32323
	95	SWC		.313	32467
	100	SWCBB		.313	32467
	95	RN		.313	32465
	118	FP		.313	30254
9mm	190	RN	GC	.323/.324	30530
9mm/38 Super	95	RNBB		.356	35465
	115	RNBB		.356	35311
	115	SWBB		.356	35925
	122	TCBB		.356	35375
	122	RN		.356	35311
	122	RNBB		.356	35311
	124	SWC	GC	.356	35925
	140	SWC		.356/.357	35429
	145	RNBB		.356/.357	35311
	145	SWCBB		.356/.357	35925
	150	RN		.356	35311
	154	SWCBB		.356/.357	35925
9.2mm	100	RNBB		.365	35465
38/357	148	WCBB		.358	35550
	148	WC		.358	35381
	148	WCDBD		.358	35344
	148	DBBWC		.358	35344
	158	SWC		.358	35429
	158	SWCBB		.358	35429
	162	SWC	GC	.358	35429
	158	RN		.358	35311
	158	RNBB		.358	35311
	158	TC		.358	35399
	180	FP		.358	35353
	180	FP	GC	.358	35353
	180	TC		.358	35399
	180	TC	GC	.358	35399
	200	FP		.358	35311
	200	FP	GC	.358	35311
	200	TC	GC	.358	35399
	245	FP	GC	.358	35311
375	265	FP	GC	.376	37570
40/10mm	155	SWCBB		.401	40048
	179	TCBB		.401	40047
40/10mm	170	SWCBB		.401	40048
	200	TCBB		.401	40047
	200	SWCBB		.401	40048
	190	SWC		.401	40101
41	170	SWCBB		.411	41447
	200	SWCBB		.411	41447
	185	SWC		.411	41610
	210	SWC		.411	41610
	190	TC		.411	41415
	210	TCBB		.411	41415
	220	TC	GC	.411	41415
	220	FP		.411	41415
	220	SWCBB		.411	41610
416	365	RN	GC	.417	41916
44	200	WC		.430	44944
	200	TC		.430	44428
	200	FPSWC		.428	44191
	200	SWC		.430	44191
	220	SWCBB		.430	44191
	246	RN		.430	44374
	240	SWC		.430	44421
	240	SWCBB		.430	44421
	240	SWCGC		.430	44421
	240	FP		.430	44191
	240	TC	GC	.430	44428
	240	TC		.430	44428
	250	FP	GC	.430	44191
	265	FP		.430	44191
	265	FP	GC	.430	44191
	300	FP	GC	.430	44191
45	160	SPL		.452	45452
	170	SPLBB		.452	45452
	180	SWCBB		.452	45429
	185	SWC		.452	45421
	185	SWCBB		.452	45421
	180	SWC		.452	45429
	200	SWCBB		.452	45429
	200	SWC		.452	45429
	215	SWCBB		.452	45424
	210	RNWC		.452	45265
	225	TCBB		.452	45375
	225	RN		.452	45701
	225	RNBB		.452	45701
	225	WC		.452	45424
	255	SWC	GC	.452	45424
	255	SWC		.452	45424
	255	SWC		.455	45452
	300	SWC	GC	.452	54524
45 Rifle	300	FP		.458	45015
	350	FP	GC	.458	45015
	405	FP		.458	45015
	450	FP	GC	.458	45015
	375	SP		.458	45702
	405	SP	GC	.458	45702
	500	FP		.458	45610
	540	FP	GC	.458	45610

BB = Bevel Base; DBB = Double End Bevel Base; FB = Flat Base; FP = Flat Point; GC = Gas Check; RN = Round Nose; SP = Spitzer Point; SWC = Semi-Wadcutter; TC = Truncated Cone; WC = Wadcutter.

Style A

This a cylindrical bullet, similar to original factory bullets for most black powder cartridges. The diameter at the front band is the same diameter at base band. Rounded lube grooves.

Style B

This also is a cylindrical bullet similar to Style A, except the front wiper band has been deleted. This is an extremely accurate bullet with some single shot rifles. Rounded lube grooves.

Style C

This is a two diameter bullet, having the front 3 bands slightly larger than bore diameter of barrel. Rear 3 bands are groove diameter. Rounded lube grooves.

Style D

Two diameter bullet, same as Style 'C' but without front wiper band. Rounded lube grooves.

Style E

This is a tapered bullet with the front band near bore diameter tapering to slightly larger than groove diameter. This style bullet was furnished by most of the old time barrel makers such as Harry Pope. Rounded lube grooves. This is a very popular schuetzen bullet.

Style F

This is a Hudson bullet. This two diameter bullet has front bands near bore diameter with the two rear bands slightly larger than groove diameter. It carries plenty of lube and is a popular style.

Bullet styles for SAECO obsolete caliber moulds.

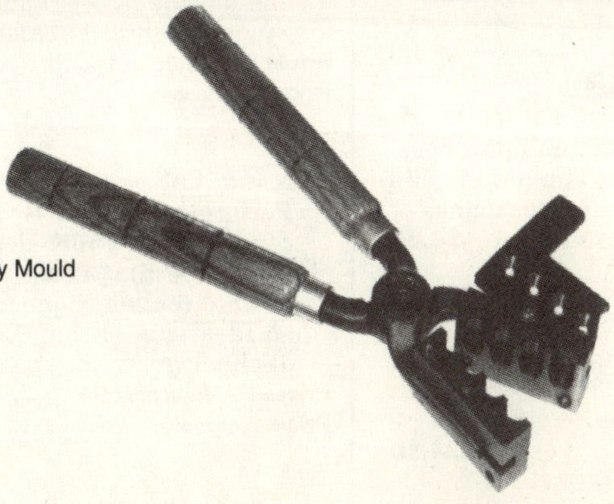
SAECO 4-Cavity Mould

Section 4: Bullet Casting

ANDELA

Bullet Lubricator

Lubricates but does not size bullets for cast bullet accuracy. Accepts hollow stick lubricants and Lyman dies if applicable. Custom made to lubricate cylindrical bullets inserted base first or tapered and two diameter bullets nose first. Comes with brass blank die for bullet fitting. Send casting and Andela will fit a die to bullet. From Andela Tool & Machinery.

Price: **$150.00**
Price: Die fitting **$25.00**

E. ARTHUR BROWN

EbcoJacket Lube

Dry lube puts hard coating on cast bullets. Dip, tumble or flood coat bullets. Comes in 4 oz. plastic bottle. From E. Arthur Brown Company.

Price: **$3.50**

BROWNELLS

Acra-Eez

Aerosol spray mould lubricant to prevent sticking when casting and rust/corrosion protection for storage. Non-flammable, non-toxic. From Brownells, Inc.

Price: 16-oz. **$10.31**
Price: Pint **$9.54**

DONALD EAGAN

MX Lube Die

Designed for Donald Eagan MX bullets and can be used with Lyman 450 or RCBS lube-sizers. Avaliable for all MX tapered bullets. From Donald Eagan.

Price: **$30.00**

Sizing T-Dies

Sizing dies designed for use with Donald Eagan MX3 bullets. Can be used with Lyman and RCBS lube-sizers. From Donald Eagan.

Price: 30T, 28T, 32T, 30TS **$12.00**
Price: 24T, 26T **$18.00**
Price: 22T **$24.00**

GAR

Bullet Lube

Half alox 2138F and half pure beeswax lube in 1" x 4" hollow or solid sticks. From GAR for Reloading.

Price: **$6.90**

Sizer Heater

Lube-sizer heater with magnetic bottom heats to 400°. 120-volt. From GAR for Reloading.

Price: **$24.50**

LBT

Blue Lube

Non-toxic lubricant that flows at room temperature into bullet grooves .015 or deeper. Comes in hollow or solid sticks. From Lead Bullets Technology.

Price: 1 to 4 sticks, each **$4.00**
Price: 5 or more, each **$3.75**

Blue Soft Lube

Semi-soft lube designed to flow at lower temperatures down to 60° Fahrenheit. Has higher melting temperature but gives good performance in extreme cold. Comes in hollow or solid sticks. From Lead Bullets Technology.

Price: 1 to 4 sticks, each **$4.00**
Price: 5 or more, each **$3.75**

Commercial Lube

LBT Blue lube but firmer formula. Lubri-sizers need be warmed to about 100° for good flow. Comes in hollow or solid sticks. From Lead Bullets Technology.

Price: 1 to 4 sticks, each **$4.00**
Price: 5 or more, each **$3.75**

Lubricator Heater

Works with all non-commercial lubricators, Lyman, RCBS, Star, Saeco, Pitzer. Rugged aluminum block 1"x 1½" containing heavy-duty industrial cartridge heater designed for use in plastic injection dies. Suitable for up to 240 volts, AC or DC with use of dimmer switch. From Lead Bullets Technology.

Price: **$30.00**

Lubricator Nose Punches

Two styles available. Lyman and RCBS sizer lubricator nose punches. Flat face works well with 20 BHN and harder flat-nosed handgun bullets. Fitted punches for LBT bullets only for use with soft bullets under 20 BHN and all rifle bullets under 35-caliber. From Lead Bullets Technology.

Price: Lyman, RCBS punch **$5.00**
Price: LBT custom **$8.00**

Magnum Lube

Performance limit to 2600 fps on conventional bullet designs. Semi-solid lube that flows well down to 45° Fahrenheit. Comes in hollow or solid sticks. From Lead Bullets Technology.

Price: 1 to 4 sticks, each **$4.00**
Price: 5 or more, each **$3.75**

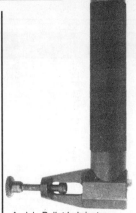

Andela Bullet Lubricator

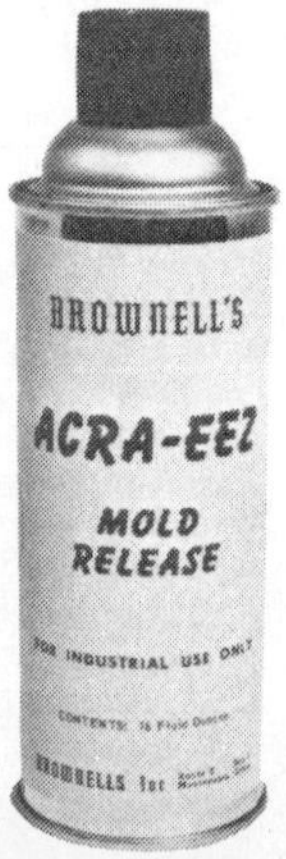

Brownell's Acra-Eez

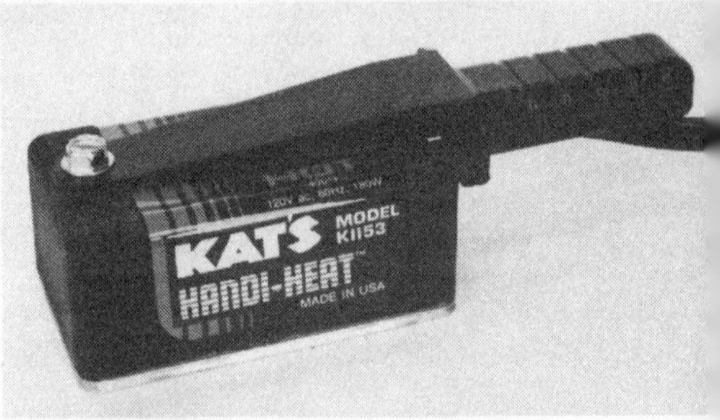

GAR Sizer Heater

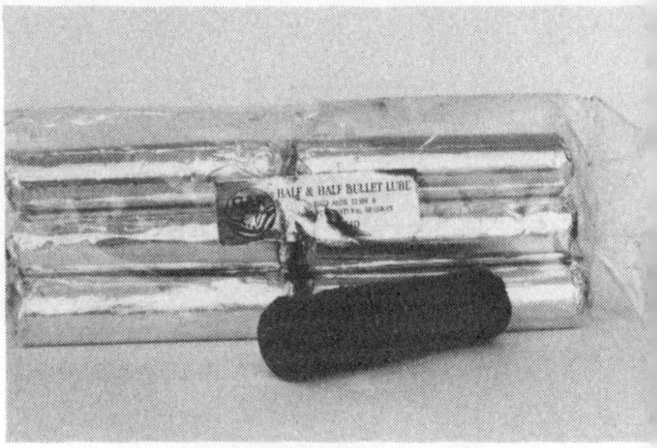

GAR Bullet Lube

LBT Blue Lube

Lee Liquid Alox

Lithi Bee Bullet Lube

Lyman Liquid Alox

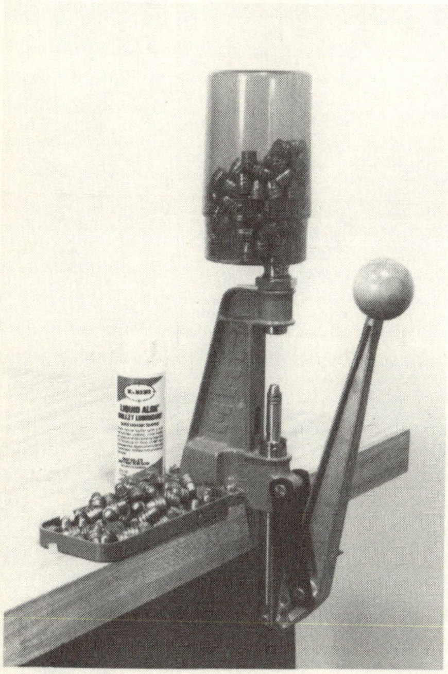

Lee Lube and Sizing Kit

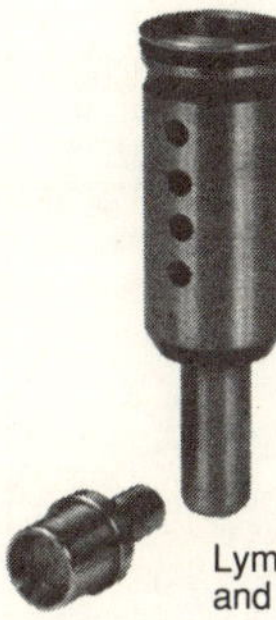

Lyman Size Die and Top Punch

Lyman #450 Bullet Sizer/Lubricator

Lyman Lube/Sizer Heater

Lyman Orange Magic Bullet Lube

LEE

Lube and Sizing Kit

Standard threaded size die with integral container. Bullets pushed through sizing die nose first. Gas checks automatically seated and crimped. Sized bullets are captured in special container. Comes complete with lube for single bullet size. From Lee Precision, Inc.

Price: **$15.98**

Liquid Alox

Liquid lube coats entire bullet and dries to varnish-like finish. Eliminates need for sizing of most cast bullets. Comes in 4-oz. bottle—enough to lube 1,000 bullets. From Lee Precision, Inc.

Price: **$2.75**

NRA Formula Alox

Contains 50% alox 2138F and 50% commercial A-1 beeswax. Hollow stick fits most lubricators. Packed in tubes. From Lee Precision, Inc.

Price: **$3.50**

Price: 12 sticks **$36.00**

LITHI BEE

Bullet Lube

Lithium-based grease blended with pure beeswax. Requires no heating of lube-sizer and will fill bullet lube grooves at temperatures to 58° Fahrenheit. Remains solid at 150° Fahrenheit. Available in 1"x 4" hollow or solid sticks. From Lithi Bee Bullet Lube.

Price: Each **$2.75**

Price: 3-5 boxes (24 per box) **$61.00**

Price: 6 or more boxes **$52.00**

LYMAN

#450 Bullet Sizer/Lubricator

Short stroke, power link leverage system sizes, lubes and seats gas checks. C-type iron-steel cast frame is line bored for die alignment. Comes with gas check seater and Alox lubricant. Adaptable to all bullets by change of size die. Weight: $7^3/_4$ lbs. From Lyman Products Corporation.

Price: **$134.95**

Alox Lube

Comes in tubular form and fits all standard lube sizers. Best for rifle bullets. Weight: 1-oz. From Lyman Products Corporation.

Price: **$3.70**

LYMAN

Ideal Lubricant

Designed to increase accuracy and eliminate barrel leading. Available in solid or hollow sticks and will fit Lyman 40 sizer/lubricator and other similar tools. From Lyman Products Corporation.

Price: **$3.70**

Liquid Alox

For both cast and swaged bullets. Coat bullets and allow to dry overnight. Comes in 4-oz. bottle. From Lyman Products Corporation.

Price: **$3.00**

Lube/Sizer Heater

Aluminum mounting plate/heating block drilled to accept Lyman, RCBS, Saeco and Star lubrisizers. 110-volt. From Lyman Products Corporation.

Price: **$39.95**

Orange Magic Bullet Lube

High temperature lube designed to allow higher cast bullet velocities without leading. From Lyman Products Corporation.

Price: **$4.50**

LYMAN

Lube/Size Dies and Top Punch

Precisely machined top punch fits bullet nose shape exactly (refer to chart in bullet mould section for correct bullet top punch). Tapered mouth and hardened interior of size die forms and lubes bullets. Interior dimension of size die corresponds to suggested diameters for all popular rifle and pistol calibers. From Lyman Products Corporation.

Price: Top Punch **$7.00**
Price: Sizing die **$17.50**

MAGMA

Star Helper

Accessories for the Star Auto Lubricator/Sizer. Heated base for new hard wax bullet lubes; bullet feeder to automatically feed bullets from plastic tube; hard wax bullet lube. Bullet feeder includes setup for one caliber: small, 38-9mm; large, 10mm, 41, 44, 45. Special transfer bars and feed tubes required for short bullets, e.g. 25, 32, 380. From Magma Engineering Company.

Price: Heated base **$85.00**
Price: Bullet feeder **$95.00**
Price: Star lube, per pound **$10.00**

MIDWAY

Lubricator Heater

Thermostatically controlled baseplate heater precisely drilled and tapped for Lyman, RCBS, Saeco and Star lubrisizers. Features industrial-grade heating element and precision thermostat to control lube temperature to within 5°. Mounted on high aluminum plate with cork insulation pad on bottom. Designed to melt hardest lubes. From Midway Arms, Inc.

Price: **$49.99**

LYMAN Lube Size Dies

PISTOL CALIBER	PISTOL DIAMETER	RIFLE CALIBER	RIFLE DIAMETER
22 Jet	.224, .225	22	.224, .225
221 Fireball	.224, .225	243	.243, .244
25 ACP	.251	244	.243, .244
30 Luger	.310	6mm	.243, .244
30 Herrett	.310	25	.257, .258
30 Mauser	.310	264 Win. Mag.	.264, .266
32 ACP	.311, .312, .313, .314	6.5mm	.264, .266
32-20	.311, .312, .313, .314	270 Win.	.277, .278
32 S&W	.311, .312, .313, .314	7mm	.284, .285
32 H&R Mag.	.311, .312, .313, .314	280 Rem.	.284, .285
9mm Luger	.354, .355, .356	284 Win.	.284, .285
38	.354, .355, .356	30	.308, .309, .310
38 Super Auto	.354, .355, .356	7.62 Russian	.310
380 Auto	.354, .355, .356	32-20 Win.	.310
38 S&W	.357, .358, .359, .360	7.65mm Mauser	.311
38 Spl.	.357, .358, .359, .360	303 British	.313, .314
357 Mag.	.357, .358, .359, .360	32 Win. Spl.	.321
357 Max.	.357, .358, .359, .360	32 Win. SL	.321
38-40	.400, .401	32 Rem.	.321
10mm Auto	.400, .401	8mm Mauser	.323, .325
40 S&W	.400, .401	338 Win.	.338
41 S&W Mag.	.410	9mmx56	.354, .355, .356
41 AE	.410	9mmx57	.354, .355, .356
44 S&W Spl.	.429, .430, .431	35	.357, .358, .359
44 Mag.	.429, .430, .431	375 H&H Mag.	.375, .377, .378
45 ACP	.450, .451, .452	375 Win.	.375, .377, .378
45 Auto Rim	.450, .451, .452	38-55	.379
45 Colt	.450, .451, .452	38-40	.400, .401
45 Win. Mag.	.450, .451, .452	44-40	.427, .428
45 Colt	.454	44 Spl.	.429, .430
445 Webley	.454	44 Mag.	.429, .430
		444 Marlin	.430, .431
		45-70	.457, .458, .459
		458 Winchester	.457, .458, .459
		50	.509, .512

Magma Star Helper

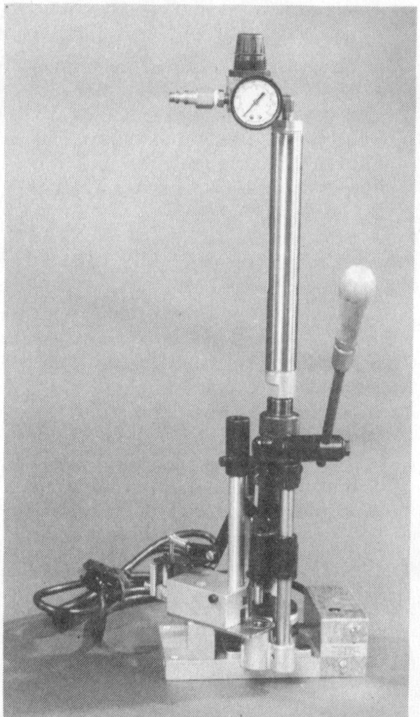

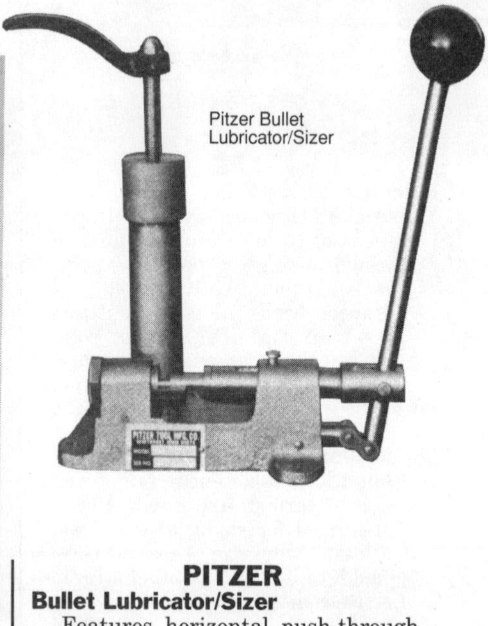

Pitzer Bullet Lubricator/Sizer

Midway Lubricator Heater

PITZER

Bullet Lubricator/Sizer

Features horizontal push-through design; O-ring seals on die; locknut for holding die firmly in tool. Dies available for 9mm to 45. Comes complete with one die and nose punch. From Pitzer Tool Co.

Price: **$154.00**
Price: Die **$22.00**
Price: Nose punch **$8.25**

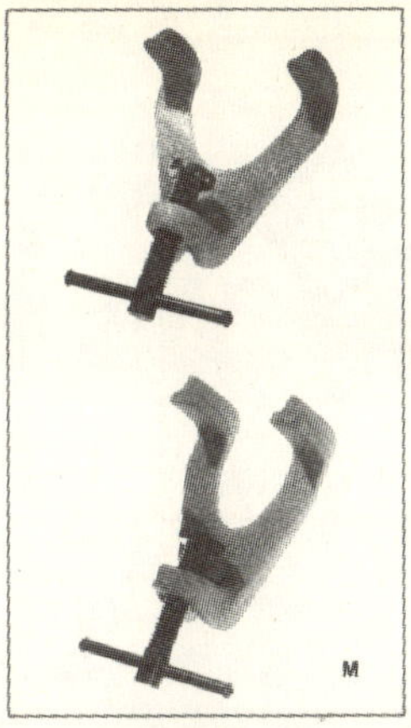

Redding Double "C" Clamps

REDDING Lube Size Dies	
.224	.357
.225	.358
.244	.359
.251	.360
.258	.364
.265	.365
.266	.366
.278	.375
.285	.376
.286	.377
.308	.378
.309	.401
.310	.408
.311	.409
.312	.410
.313	.411
.314	.417
.321	.427
.322	.428
.323	.429
.324	.430
.325	.431
.338	.451
.339	.452
.349	.454
.354	.455
.355	.458
.356	.460

Rooster Bullet Lubes

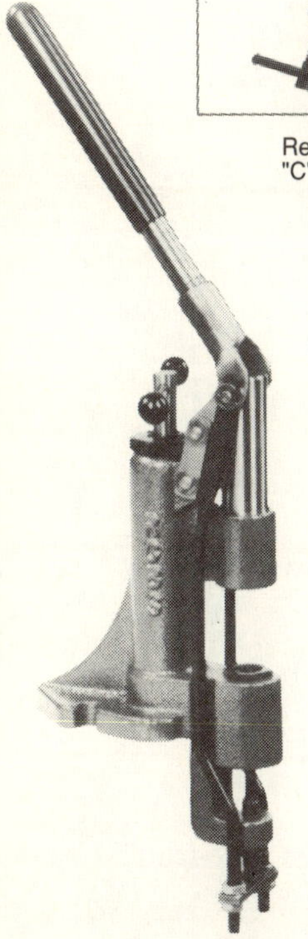

RCBS Lube-A-Matic-2

RCBS Bullet Lube

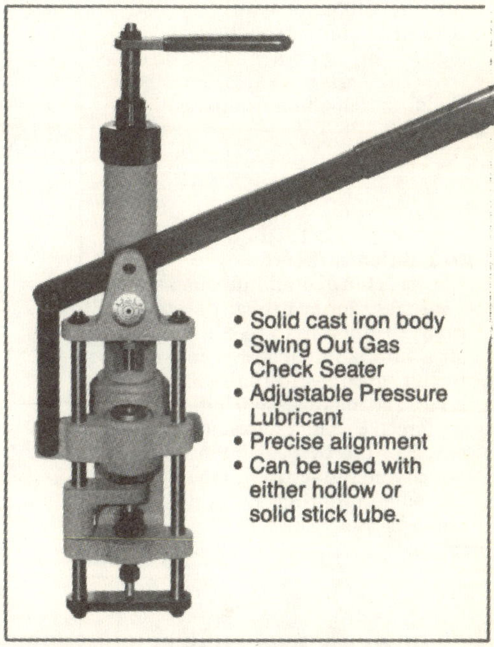

• Solid cast iron body
• Swing Out Gas Check Seater
• Adjustable Pressure Lubricant
• Precise alignment
• Can be used with either hollow or solid stick lube.

Saeco Lubri-Sizer

RCBS

Bullet Lube

Designed for RCBS Lube-A-Matic and other lube-sizers that use hollow-stick lubricant. Non-toxic, temperature-resistant blend of Alox and beeswax to NRA specifications. From RCBS.

Price: **$3.36**

Lube-A-Matic-2

Auto pressure control with finger tip adjustments for depth of sizing. Uses either Lube-A-Matic or Lyman dies. Will also seat gas checks. Sizer die and top punch not included. From RCBS.

Price: **$127.24**
Price: Bullet sizer die **$16.82**
Price: Top punch **$6.33**

REDDING

Double "C" Clamps

Designed for clamping the Saeco lubrisizer to benchtop. Will accommodate bench thickness of up to 2¼". From Redding Reloading Equipment.

Price: **$18.00**

ROOSTER

Bullet Film Lube

Emulsified liquid lube bonds tightly to cast or swaged bullets. Designed for low velocity pistol loads. Apply by dipping, tumbling or flood-coating. Lubes 100,000 bullets. Available in 16-oz., ½-gal. or 1-gallon quantities. From Rooster Laboratories.

Price: 16-oz. **$7.50**
Price: ½-gal. **$18.50**
Price: 1-gal. **$30.00**

Bullet Lubes

Lubri-sizer high-melt cannelure lubes in choice of hardnesses. Zambini is hard tough lube intended for pistol bullets; melting point of 220° Fahrenheit. Comes in 2"x 6" commercial-size sticks and 1"x 4" hollow or solid sticks. HVR is soft but firm and designed for high-velocity rifle bullets; melting point of 220° Fahrenheit. Available in 1"x 4" sticks only. From Rooster Laboratories.

Price: Zambini 2x6, each **$4.00**
Price: Zambini 1x4, each **$3.00**
Price: HVR, each **$3.00**

SAECO

Bullet Lubes

Saeco Gold is alox free formula to reduce leading to a minimum. Saeco Traditional rifle lube is NRA formula with alox and natural beeswax mixture. Saeco Green for both pistol and rifle bullets contains no alox and is slightly harder than the other two lubes. All available in solid or hollow sticks. From Redding Reloading Equipment.

Price: Each **$3.75**

Lubri-Sizer

Features solid cast iron body; swing-out gas check seater for seating gas checks without sizing; adjustable pressure lubricant; two guide rods for alignment of top punch and sizing die; compound leverage; use with hollow or solid stick lube. Top punches and sizing dies not included. From Redding Reloading Equipment.

Price: **$165.00**

SAECO

Sizing Dies

Made with unique prelead that fits "as cast" bullet diameter for depth of approximately .3-inch to ensure straight bullet feed alignment in die. Gentle taper constriction between the two diameters eliminates lead shearing. Dies are internally micro-honed. From Redding Reloading Equipment.

Price: **$28.50**

Top Punches

Tapered shoulder punch assures positive alignment with die body. Straight shank-type punches designed for Lyman and RCBS lubrisizers also available. From Redding Reloading Equipment.

Price: **$10.50**

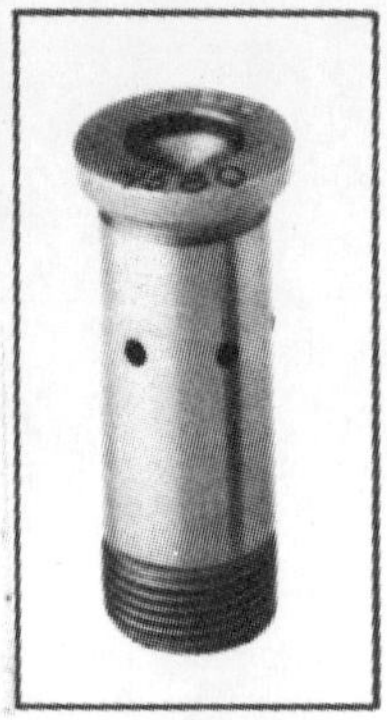

SAECO Sizing Dies

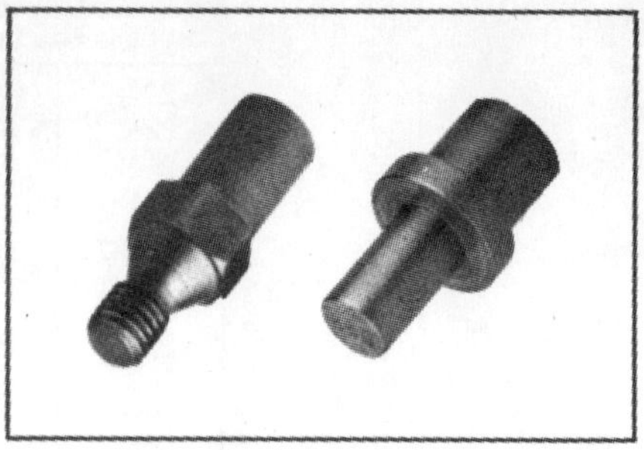

SAECO Top Punches

STAR

Auto Lubricator/Sizer

Constructed of aluminum and steel. Features storage pressure system in grease reservoir to feed high pressure pump which forces lube onto bullet grooves. Single pressure screw setting lubes 200 bullets. Bullet forced through hardened universal sizer die by next bullet in line. Specify manufacturer's mould number when ordering. From Star Machine Works.

Price: **$157.00**

Star Auto Lubricator/Sizer

ROBERT STILLWELL

Lube/Size Dies

Custom-made 257 through 530 dies for Star lubricator/sizer. Heat-treated to 60-62 C. From Robert Stillwell.

Price: . . . . **Contact manufacturer.**

TAMARACK

Hi Temp Bullet Lube

Lube 50% alox 2138-F and 50% hi-temp A-1 beeswax for pistol and rifle bullets with same hardness as NRA formula but melts 40° higher temperature. Both hollow and solid sticks 1"x 5" available. Contact manufacturer for bulk prices. From Tamarack Products, Inc.

Price: Each **$2.85**
Price: 20, each **$1.40**
Price: 50, each **$1.25**
Price: 200+, each **$1.15**

Tamarack Hi Temp Bullet Lube

THOMPSON

Bullet Lubes

Four wax-based lube offerings. Bear Lube Cold soft, non-sticky and requires 90° to flow; Bear Lube Heat is medium hard lube flows at 110°; Lazy Lube same as Bear Lube Heat but designed to flow through automated Star Luber; dry, non-sticky Blue Angel for the commercial caster and requires 125° to 140° flow temperature with melt point of 165°; Red Angel melts at 240° and will flow at 180° or lower. Available in 1"x 4", 1"x 8" or 2"x 6" sticks. For case and partial case prices contact manufacturer. From Thompson Bullet Lube Co.

Price: Bear, Blue Angel, each **$2.25**
Price: Red Angel, each **$2.55**

1994 HANDLOADER'S DIGEST

13th EDITION

PART

1
2
3
4
5
6

COMPONENTS

ACCURATE ARMS

Accurate smokeless powders are listed here in approximate burning order from fastest to slowest. All propellants are double base ball propellants unless described otherwise.

SHOTSHELL

Nitro 100 Fast burning, double base flake propellant for 1 and $1^1/_8$-ounce shot loads in 12-gauge for trap, Skeet and light field. Also applicable in 38 Special, 44 Special, 45 ACP and 45 Long Colt.

HANDGUN

No. 2 Fast burning propellant for use in 38 Special target loads. Also suited to 25 ACP, 32 S&W Long, 32 H&R Magnum, 32/20 Winchester, 380 Auto, 9mm Luger, 38 Super Auto, 357 Magnum, 40 S&W, 41 AE, 10mm Auto, 41 Magnum, 44 Special, 44 Magnum, 45 ACP and 20-gauge shotshell.

No. 5 Relatively fast burning propellant for use in the 45 ACP. Also suitable for 38 Special, 38 Special +P and 9mm sub-sonic loads. Good for target velocity cast bullet loads in magnum handgun cartridges and for IPSC shooters using the 40 S&W or 41 AE.

No. 7 Originally developed for 9mm NATO carbine ammo. Best suited to full-power 10mm Auto ammunition. Also good in magnum handgun cartridges such as 357, 41 and 44 Magnum when less than full power loads are preferred.

No. 9 Popular ball-type 44 Magnum powder. Intended for use in large capacity handgun cartridges (357, 41, 44 Magnum and 454 Casull) but also suited to some small rifle cases (22 Hornet, 30 Carbine) as well as the 410 shotgun. Requires heavy crimp for consistent performance.

RIFLE

1680 Developed specifically for the 7.62x39 and the 30 Herrett. Excellent in the 22 Hornet. Also suitable for small capacity cases such as the T/CU series and the 222 Remington.

2015BR Single base, small-grained, extruded propellant developed specifically for benchrest cartridges such as the PPC and BR series. Serves well in other cartridges from the 22 Hornet to 458 Winchester Magnum.

POWDER SPECIFICATIONS

	%NG*	Avg. Length	Avg. Grain Dia.	Bulk Density**	Comparative Powders***
Nitro 100	27.0	N/A	N/A	0.510	700X, Red Dot
No. 2	24.0	N/A	N/A	0.750	Bullseye, HP38, 231
No. 5	17.0	N/A	0.027	0.950	Unique, 540, 800X
No. 7	10.5	N/A	0.012	0.985	Blue Dot, HS7, 630
No. 9	10.0	N/A	0.015	0.975	2400, H110, 296
1680	10.0	N/A	0.014	0.950	680, 4227, 4198
2015BR	—	0.068	0.029	0.900	4064, 4895
2520	10.0	N/A	0.022	0.970	4895, 4064, 760
2700	10.0	N/A	0.022	0.960	4350, 760, 4320
4350	—	0.083	0.038	0.950	IMR 4350
3100	—	0.083	0.038	0.945	4831, 4350, 785
8700	10.0	N/A	0.030	0.960	870, 5010

*NG=Nitroglycerin (glyceryl trinitrate); **g/cc; ***For comparison only, not a loading recommendation.

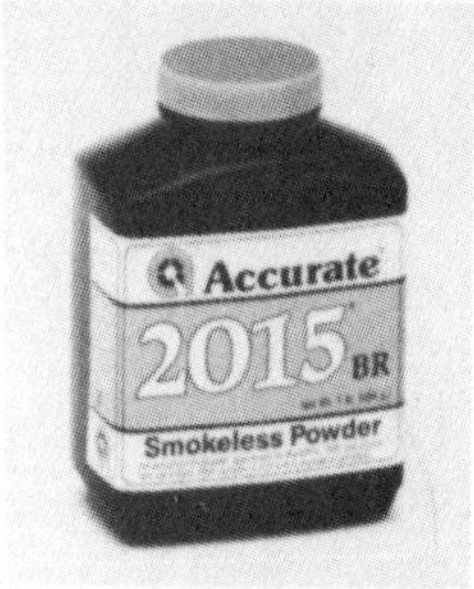

2230 (Formerly MR-223) A medium-burning propellant developed for the 223 Remington (5.56 NATO). Also suitable to 7mm T/CU, 22/250 Remington, 30/30 Winchester and similar cartridges.

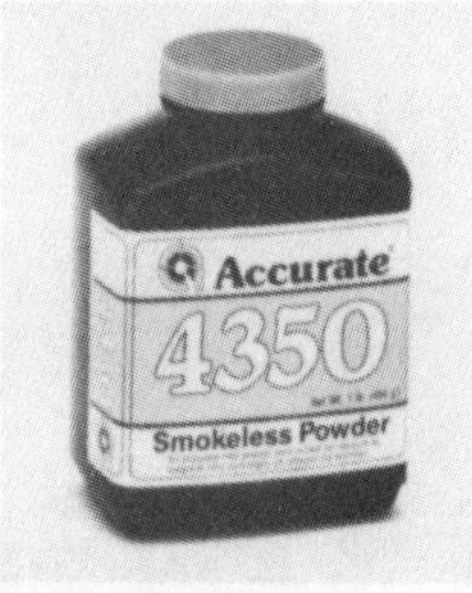

2460 Medium-burning ball propellant popular with NRA, IHMSA and benchrest shooters. Useful in cartridges from 223 Remington to the 30-06 and good in the 30/30 Winchester. Slightly slower than 2230 and shows a pressure advantage over 2230 in bores 7mm and over. Good choice in 308 Winchester and appropriate with M1 and M14 service rifles.

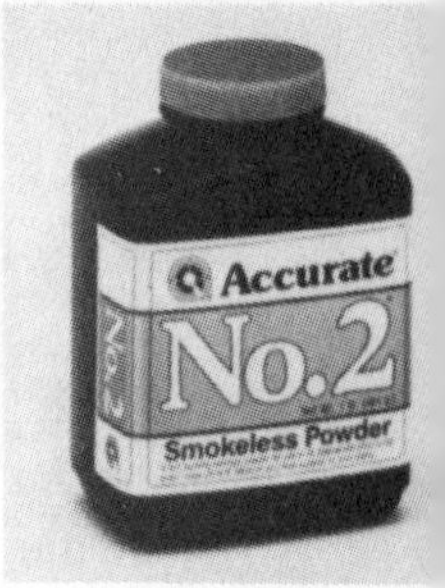

2520 Medium-slow burning propellant that gives excellent results in medium-capacity cases (308 class) and has certain applications in large bore cartridges. 2520 has a pressure curve appropriate for use with M1 and M14 service rifles.

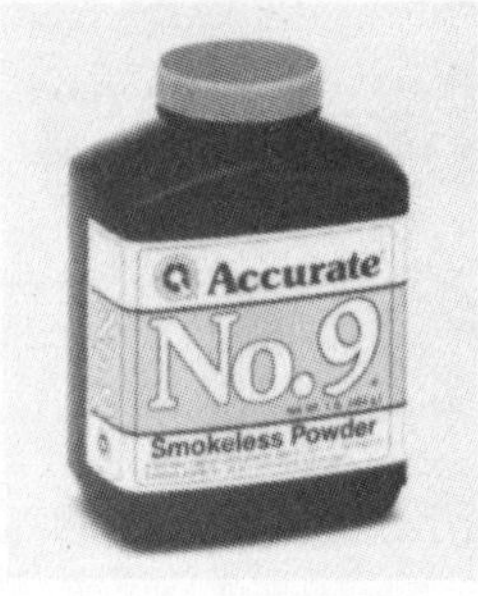

2700 Recent ball propellant that fills the gap between 2520 and 4350. Intended for use as a heavy bullet powder in cartridges from 22-250 Remington to the belted magnums.

4350 Single base, extruded propellent very similar IMR 4350.

3100 Single base extruded propellant for cartridges from the 243 Winchester to the big magnums. 3100 burn rate is between IMR-4831 and H-4831.

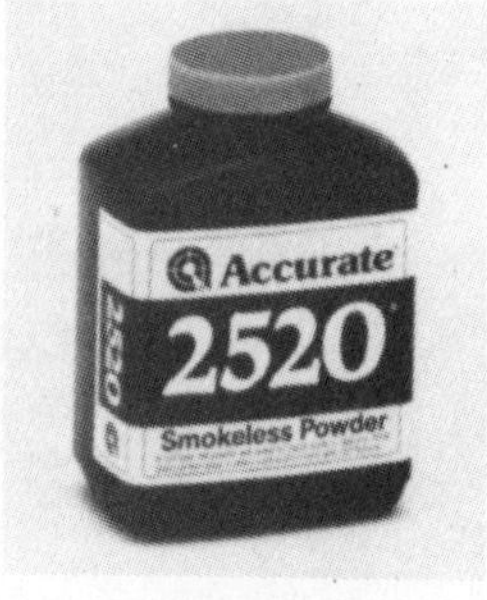

8700 Slowest powder available. Best suited to magnum rifle cases such as the 264 Winchester Magnum, 7mm Remington Magnum, 257 Weatherby Magnum, 270 Weatherby Magnum and 300 Weatherby Magnum. May also be used in cartridges such as the 25/06 Remington and 270 Winchester.

Accurate® Smokeless Powders

SELECTED RIFLE LOADS

Cartridge	—Bullet— Wgt. Grs.	Type	Barrel Length	—Load— Grs.	Powder	MV (fps)	Pressure (psi)	Listed Factory MV (fps)
17 Remington	25	HP	24	22.7	2520	3973	NA	4040
22 Hornet	45	SP	22	12.3	1680	2493	NA	2690
218 Bee	46	HP	19	14.0	1680	2658	NA	2760
222 Remington	50	SP	24	24.5	2230	3227	NA	3140
	55	SP	24	22.5	2015	3047	NA	3020
223 Remington	45	HP	24	26.0	2015	3546	NA	NA
	55	SP	24	26.5	2460	3231	NA	3240
22/250 Remington	45	HP	25	35.5	2230	3745	NA	NA
	55	SP	25	35.5	2460	3480	NA	3680
220 Swift	50	SP	26	44.0	4350	3778	NA	3780
	55	SP	26	42.0	4350	3610	NA	NA
243 Winchester	80	SP	23	42.5	4350	3137	NA	3350
	100	SP	23	39.0	4350	2796	NA	2960
6mm Remington	80	SP	24	49.5	4350	3406	NA	3470
	100	SP	24	45.6	4350	3041	NA	3100
250 Savage	87		22	33.5	2015	3096	NA	NA
	100		22	32.0	2520	2760	NA	2820
257 Roberts	85	SPX	24	46.0	4350	3102	NA	NA
	100	SP	24	33.8	2520	2640	NA	2650
6.5 x 55mm Swedish	140	SP	29	44.0	4350	2643	NA	2850
	160	RN	29	42.0	4350	2454	NA	NA
264 Win. Magnum	125	SP	26	77.0	8700	3142	NA	NA
	140	SP	26	71.5	8700	2890	NA	3030
270 Winchester	130	SP	22	61.0	3100	3024	NA	3060
	150	SP	22	57.0	3100	2827	NA	2850
7mm Mauser	140	SP	22	50.0	3100	2656	NA	2660
	175	SP	22	47.0	3100	2304	NA	2440
7mm-08 Remington	140	SP	24	39.5	2520	2702	NA	2860
	160	SP	24	38.0	2520	2455	NA	2715
284 Winchester	139	SP	22	54.0	4350	2845	NA	NA
	150	SP	22	52.0	4350	2764	NA	NA
280 Remington	145	SP	22	55.0	3100	2840	NA	NA
	175	SP	22	53.0	3100	2602	NA	NA
7mm Rem. Magnum	140	SP	24	67.0	3100	3082	NA	3175
	175	SP	24	75.0	8700	2754	NA	2860

CAUTION: Some of these loads are maximum loads. Start low and work up slowly, being alert for signs of excessive pressure.

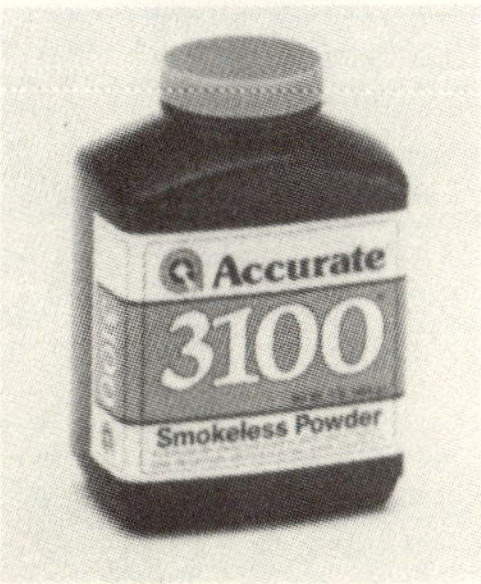

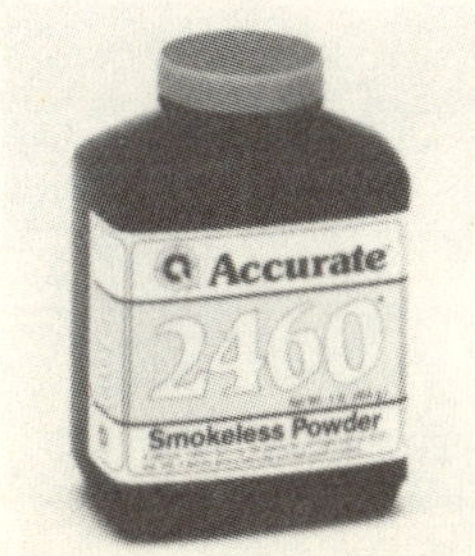

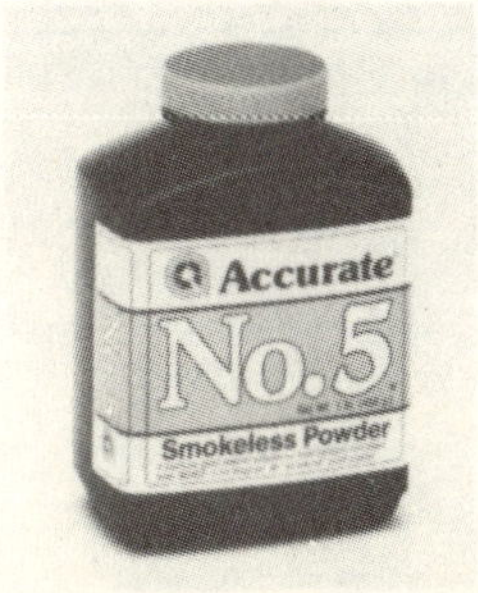

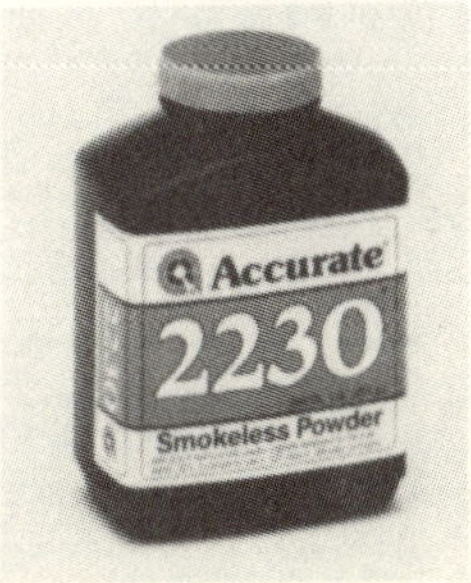

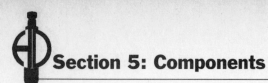

Accurate® Smokeless Powders

SELECTED RIFLE LOADS

Cartridge	—Bullet— Wgt. Grs.	Type	Barrel Length	—Load— Grs.	Powder	MV (fps)	Pressure (psi)	Listed Factory MV (fps)
7.62 x 39mm	123	SP	24	26.5	1680	2350	NA	2300
	135	SP	24	26.5	1680	2332	NA	NA
30/30 Winchester	150	FP	20	33.5	2520	2225	NA	2390
	170	FP	20	31.5	2520	2029	NA	2200
300 Savage	150	SP	22	38.0	2460	2421	NA	2630
	180	RN	22	36.0	2460	2300	NA	2350
308 Winchester	150	SP	22	44.0	2015	2839	NA	2820
	180	SP	22	44.0	2520	2601	NA	2620
7.62 x 54 Russian	150	SP	27	54.0	4350	2656	NA	NA
	180	SP	27	52.0	4350	2544	NA	NA
30/06 Spr.	150	SP	22	48.0	2015	2881	NA	2910
	180	SP	22	57.0	4350	2715	NA	2700
300 Win. Magnum	150	SP	24	73.0	4350	3144	NA	3290
	180	SP	24	72.0	3100	2899	NA	2960
303 British	150	SP	23	39.5	2460	2524	NA	2690
	180	SP	23	45.0	4350	2251	NA	2460
8 x 57mm Mauser	170	RN	23½	48.0	4350	2262	NA	2360
	220	SP	23½	42.0	4350	1906	NA	NA
338 Win. Magnum	225	SP	24	70.5	4350	2785	NA	2780
	250	SP	24	65.0	4350	2586	NA	2660
35 Remington	170	SP	20	39.5	2460	2233	NA	NA
	200	SP	20	39.0	2520	2040	NA	2080
358 Winchester	200	SP	18½	49.0	2520	2393	NA	2490
	250	SP	18½	44.0	2015	2256	NA	NA
35 Whelen	200	SP	22	57.0	2460	2641	NA	2675
	250	SP	22	52.0	2015	2443	NA	2400
350 Rem. Magnum	200	NA	22	54.0	2015	2668	NA	2710
	250	NA	22	51.0	2015	2500	NA	NA
375 Winchester	200	NA	20	40.0	2015	2084	NA	2200
	220	NA	20	40.0	2015	2107	NA	NA
375 H&H Magnum	270	NA	24	81.0	4350	2654	NA	2690
	300	NA	24	75.0	4350	2461	NA	2530
444 Marlin	265	NA	24	52.0	2015	2139	NA	NA
45/70 Government	300	NA	24	70.0	4350	1815	NA	1810
	400	NA	24	49.0	2015	1761	NA	NA
458 Win. Magnum	350	SP	24	77.5	2520	2364	NA	2470
	500	SP	24	70.0	2520	2034	NA	2090

CAUTION: Some of these loads are maximum loads. Start low and work up slowly, being alert for signs of excessive pressure.

Accurate® Smokeless Powders

SELECTED HANDGUN LOADS

Cartridge	—Bullet— Wgt. Grs.	Type	Barrel Length	—Load— Grs.	Powder	MV (fps)	Pressure (psi)	Listed Factory MV (fps)
22 Hornet	45	SP	10	12.3	1680	2169	NA	NA
222 Remington	45	SP	14	27.0	2230	3170	NA	NA
223 Remington	45	SP	14	26.0	2015	3546	NA	NA
25 ACP	50	FMJ	2	1.4	No. 2	660	NA	760
7mm BR Rem.	120	SP	15	30.5	2230	2280	NA	NA
	139	SP	15	29.0	2015	2183	NA	NA
7mm-08 Rem.	120	SP	14½	41.5	2015	2735	NA	NA
	139	SP	14½	40.0	2015	2561	NA	NA
30/30 Winchester	130	SP	14	35.0	2460	2161	NA	NA
	150	SP	14	33.5	2520	1992	NA	NA
32 Smith & Wesson L	90	L	6	2.8	No. 2	840	NA	NA
32 H & R Mag.	85	SP	6	5.3	No. 5	921	NA	1100
380 Automatic	95	SP	3	5.3	No. 5	1011	NA	955
9mm Luger	115	FMJ	4.72	6.9	No. 5	1212	NA	1160
	147	SP	4.72	7.2	No. 7	998	NA	1010
38 Super Automatic	130	FMJ	5	11.9	No. 9	1233	NA	1215
9mm Steyr	115	FMJ	5	8.4	No. 7	1145	NA	NA
38 Special	125	JHP	4	4.6	N100	925	NA	NA
	158	L	4	6.6	No. 5	971	NA	755
357 Magnum	125	JHP	6	14.3	No. 7	1430	NA	1450
	158	JHP	6	15.8	No .9	1331	NA	1235
35 Remington	200	SP	14	37.0	2460	1754	NA	NA
40 Smith & Wesson	150	SP	4	8.5	No. 5	1182	NA	NA
	180	SP	4	7.0	No. 5	992	NA	985
10mm Automatic	155	SP	5	12.7	No. 7	1379	NA	1325
	180	SP	5	11.4	No. 7	1232	NA	1030
41 Magnum	170	SP	6½	19.7	No. 9	1705	NA	NA
	210	SP	6½	14.2	No. 7	1379	NA	1300
44 Special	215	L	6	7.8	No. 5	959	NA	NA
44 Magnum	180	SP	7½	20.5	No. 7	1707	NA	1610
	240	SP	7½	21.5	No. 9	1500	NA	1180
45 ACP	185	SP	5	9.8	No. 5	1022	NA	950
	230	SP	5	8.5	No. 5	869	NA	850
45 Colt	225	L	6	12.1	No. 5	1033	NA	960
45 Win. Magnum	230	FMJ	8	27.5	No. 9	1738	NA	1400

CAUTION: Some of these loads are maximum loads. Start low and work up slowly, being alert for signs of excessive pressure.

HERCULES

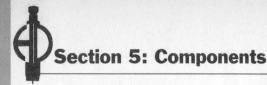

Hercules offers 12 powders for reloading. Within categories, they are listed here in the manufacturer's order of decreasing burning rates. From Hercules Incorporated.

SHOTSHELL

Blue Dot: Designed for magnum shotshell loads 10, 12, 16, 20 and 28 gauges. Also for use in magnum handgun loads. Available in 1- and 5-lb. cannisters.

Red Dot: For light to medium shotshells; designed for 12-ga. target loads. Also can be used for handgun loads. Available in 1-, 4- and 8-lb. cannisters.

Green Dot: For 12-ga. medium shotshell loads and 20-ga. Skeet loads. Available in 1-, 4- and 8-lb. cannisters.

Herco: For high-velocity shotshell loads in heavy and magnum 10-, 12-, 16-, 20-gauge. Also for high performance handgun loads. Available in 1-, 4- and 8-lb. cannisters.

Unique: Broad application from light to heavy shotshell loads and medium to light handgun loads. Available in 1-, 4- and 8-lb. cannisters.

HANDGUN

Bullseye: High energy, quick burning powder designed for pistol and revolver. Also for use in 12-ga. 1-oz. target loads. Available in 1-, 4- and 8-lb. cannisters.

Hercules 2400: For magnum handguns loads, small-capacity rifle cartridges and 410-bore shotshells. Available in 1-, 4- and 8-lb. cannisters.

RIFLE

Reloder 7: Designed for light rifle loads and also applicable to silhouette loads. Available in 1- and 5-lb. cannisters.

Reloader 12, 15: Versatile powders for medium-caliber rifle loads and also usable in silhouette loads.

Reloader 19, 22: Powder designed for magnum rifle loads.

SELECTED RIFLE LOADS

Cartridge	—Bullet— Wgt. Grs.	Type	Barrel Length	—Load— Grs.	Powder	MV (fps)	Pressure (psi)	Listed Factory MV (fps)
17 Remington	25	HP	24	22.8	RL15	3915	50,200*	4040
22 Hornet	45	SP	24	9.0	2400	2552		2690
22/250 Remington	45	SP	24	35.5	RL12	3760	59,400	NA
	55	SP	24	35.3	RL15	3625	59,400	3680
220 Swift	45	SP	24	39.0	RL15	4010	50,300*	NA
	50	SP	24	38.6	RL15	3850	49,800*	3780
222 Remington	45	SP	24	25.0	RL12	3290	46,200	NA
	50	SP	24	24.0	RL12	3120	44,300	3140
223 Remington	55	FMJ	24	27.5	RL12	3255	52,200	3240
	60	SP	24	25.5	RL12	3070	53,300	3100
243 Winchester	80	SP	24	44.5	RL19	3270	57,500	3350
	100	SP	24	41.7	RL22	2950	57,500	2960
6mm Remington	80	SP	24	51.5	RL22	3450	60,900	3470
	100	SP	24	46.0	RL19	3145	62,500	3100
25-06 Remington	100	SP	24	54.3	RL19	3220	61,000	3230
	120	HP	24	50.5	RL19	3025	60,400	2990
250 Savage	87	SP	24	41.0	RL19	2940	42,800*	2820
	100	SP	24	40.0	RL19	2855	43,400*	NA
257 Roberts	87	SP	24	41.0	RL15	3185	43,200*	NA
	100	SP	24	44.7	RL19	2930	43,100*	NA
6.5 x 55 Swed.Maus.	140	SP	24	48.1	RL22	2700	44,400*	2850
	160	RN	24	47.0	RL22	2535	44,000*	NA
264 Win. Mag.	140	SP	24	57.0	RL22	2960	51,300*	3030
	160	RN	24	57.0	RL22	2780	51,800*	NA
270 Winchester	130	SP	24	60.0	RL22	3160	61,500	3060
	150	SP	24	59.5	RL22	2845	60,300	2850
7mm-08 Remington	120	SP	24	45.5	RL15	3070	58,700	3000
	139	SP	24	52.0	RL19	2850	57,900	2860
7 x 57mm Mauser	120	SP	24	54.0	RL19	3030	48,000	NA
	139	SP	24	40.5	RL12	2660	48,800	2060
280 Remington	120	SP	24	58.0	RL19	3115	57,600	3150
	139	SP	24	59.5	RL22	3000	57,500	3000

*CUP

CAUTION: Some of these loads are maximum loads. Start low and work up slowly, being alert for signs of excessive pressure.

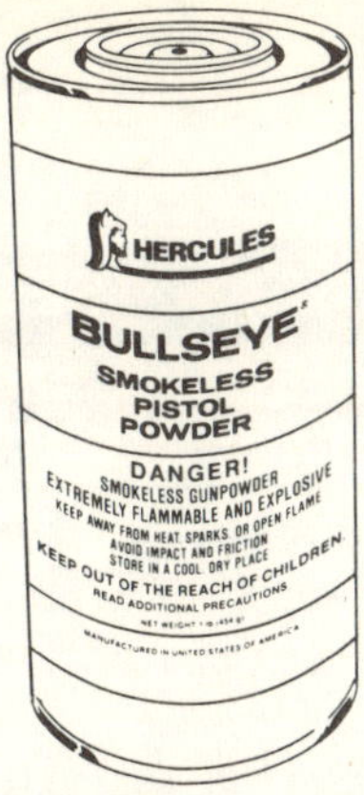

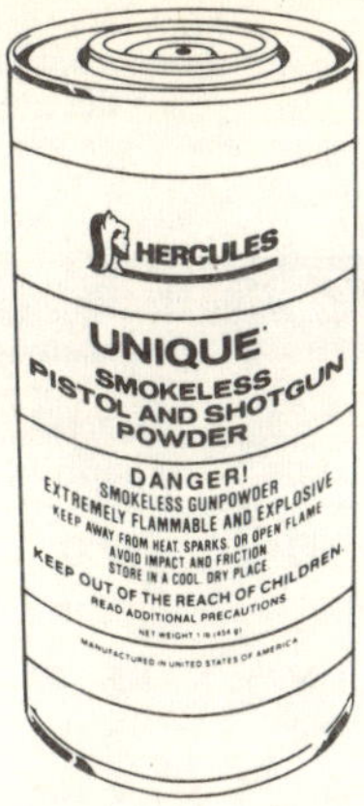

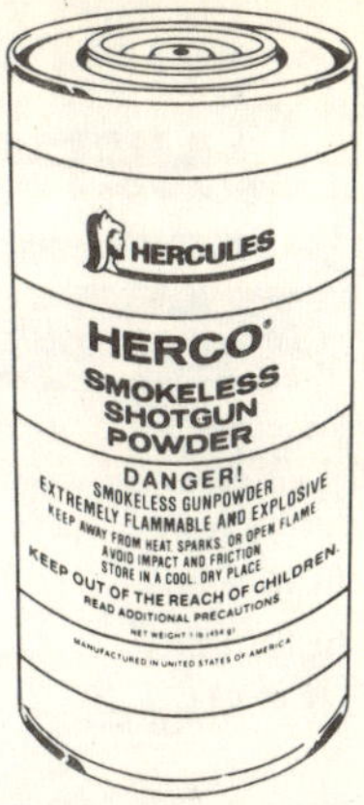

HERCULES

SELECTED RIFLE LOADS

Cartridge	—Bullet— Wgt. Grs.	Type	Barrel Length	—Load— Grs.	Powder	MV (fps)	Pressure (psi)	Listed Factory MV (fps)
7mm Rem. Mag.	139	SP	24	70.0	RL22	3295	58,000	3175
	175	SP	24	61.3	RL22	2900	58,400	2860
30-06 Springfield	150	SP	24	52.0	RL15	2925	57,400	2910
	180	SP	24	58.3	RL19	2740	57,300	2700
30-30 Winchester	150	FP	24	36.0	RL15	2450	40,600	2390
	170	FP	24	32.0	RL12	2160	40,100	2200
300 Savage	150	SP	24	43.0	RL12	2635	41,400*	2630
	165	SP	24	41.0	RL12	2485	40,800*	NA
300 Win. Magnum	150	SP	24	81.5	RL22	3275	60,400	3290
	180	SP	24	76.9	RL22	3030	60,300	2960
303 British	150	SP	24	45.0	RL12	2700	42,900*	2690
	180	RN	24	50.0	RL19	2415	39,800*	2460
7.62 x 39mm	123	SP	20	25.5	RL7	2330	45,000*	2300
	150	SP	20	24.8	RL7	2145	44,600*	NA
308 Winchester	150	SP	24	46.3	RL15	2880	57,300	2820
	180	SP	24	44.0	RL15	2645	57,500	2620
8mm Mauser	150	SP	24	44.0	RL15	2560	36,000*	NA
	170	SP	24	41.4	RL15	2400	36,000*	2360
338 Win. Mag.	225	SP	24	77.0	RL22	2790	46,200*	2780
	250	SP	24	73.0	RL22	2620	45,300*	2660
35 Remington	150	SP	24	32.0	RL7	2290	30,700	2300
	200	SP	24	31.0	RL7	2115	30,700	2080
358 Winchester	200	SP	24	50.0	RL12	2455	44,100	2490
	250	ST	24	34.5	RL7	2075	44,700	NA
35 Whelen	200	SP	24	60.0	RL15	2675	44,800	2675
	250	RN	24	60.0	RL12	2505	49,700	2400
375 H&H Magnum	270	SP	24	73.4	RL15	2685	49,500	2690
	300	SP	24	79.0	RL19	2540	49,600	2530
444 Marlin	240	SP	24	51.0	RL7	2400	38,100	2350
45/70 Government	300	HP	24	50.0	RL7	2075	24,700	1810
	400	FN	24	54.0	RL12	1710	26,100	NA
458 Win. Mag.	300	HP	24	70.0	RL7	2555	41,400	NA
	500	FMJ	24	64.0	RL7	2000	47,000	2040

*CUP

CAUTION: Some of these loads are maximum loads. Start low and work up slowly, being alert for signs of excessive pressure.

HERCULES

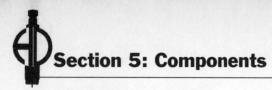

SELECTED PISTOL LOADS

Cartridge	—Bullet— Wgt. Grs.	Type	Barrel Length	—Load— Grs.	Powder	MV (fps)	Pressure (psi)	Listed Factory MV (fps)
25 Automatic	50	FMC	2.0	1.3	Bullseye	760	15,000	760
32 Automatic	71	FMC	4.0	3.2	Herco	880	13,500	905
32 H&R Magnum	85	JHP	5.0	6.6	Blue Dot	1100	19,000	1100
	98	LRN	5.0	3.4	Bullseye	1020	19,500	NA
9mm Luger	115	FMC	4.0	4.5	Red Dot	1150	32,600	1160
	147	HP	4.0	4.4	Unique	1010	32,700	1010
357 Magnum	125	SP	5.6	7.0	Red Dot	1410	34,000	1450
	158	SP	5.6	6.8	Bullseye	1250	33,100	1235
38 Special	110	SP	5.6	4.0	Red Dot	1000	15,800	945
	158	LSWC	5.6	3.1	Red Dot	835	15,800	755
380 Automatic	90	JHP	3.7	6.0	Blue Dot	980	14,800	1000
	95	FMC	3.7	4.2	Unique	910	14,600	955
40 Smith & Wesson	150	HP	4.0	5.9	Red Dot	1155	34,000	NA
	180	HP	4.0	5.0	Red Dot	980	34,000	985
10mm Automatic	155	HP	5.5	11.5	Blue Dot	1340	34,100	1325
	180	HP	5.5	7.0	Unique	1125	35,700	1030
41 Rem. Mag.	210	SP	5.8	10.3	Herco	1320	34,800	1300
	220	HP	5.8	16.4	2400	1365	34,300	NA
44 S&W Special	180	HP	5.6	16.0	2400	950	11,400	NA
	246	LRN	5.6	4.5	Bullseye	765	11,700	755
44 Rem. Mag.	180	HP	5.7	13.0	Unique	1550	35,000	1610
	240	SP	5.7	8.7	Green Dot	1190	35,000	1180
45 ACP	185	HP	5.0	6.5	Green Dot	1030	16,200	1000
	230	FMC	5.0	6.0	Unique	895	16,000	835
45 Colt	250	L	7.3	8.0	Unique	850	11,800	860
	300	HP	7.3	12.5	2400	735	12,200	NA

CAUTION: Some of these loads are maximum loads. Start low and work up slowly, being alert for signs of excessive pressure.

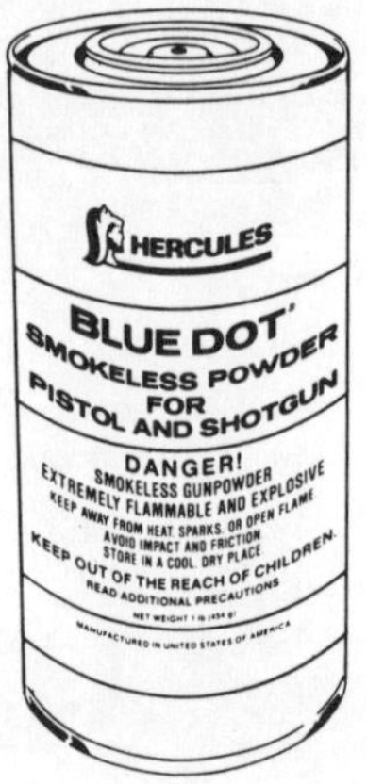

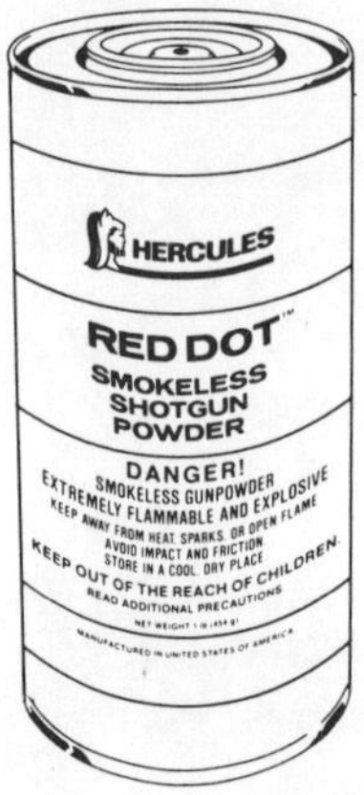

HODGDON

Powders are listed in Hodgdon's approximate order of burn rate from fastest to slowest within categories.

RIFLE

H4227 Fastest burning of Hodgdon extruded powders. Well adapted to the 22 Hornet and specialized loading in the 45-70. Excellent in magnum pistol.

H4198 An extruded powder that's excellent in the 222 and 7.62x39 Russian and some large straight cases including the 45-70, 444 Marlin and 458 Winchester Magnum.

H322 Short-grained extruded powder good in all small and medium capacity cases such as the 223 and 222 as well as the 22 and 6mm PPC. Also works well in many TCU and IHMSA cartridges.

BL-C2 A spherical propellant best suited for the 308. Performs well in most cases smaller than 30-06.

H335 Used by the military for the 223 or 5.56 NATO. Works well in most cases from 30-06 down.

H4895 Versatile extruded powder for the 17 Remington, 22-250, 308 and 458 Winchester. Performance similar to IMR-4895.

H380 Excellent in the 22-250, 220 Swift, 6mm Remington, 257 Roberts and 30-06. Spherical powder.

H414 Spherical powder with wide range of use from the 17 Remington to 375 H&H. Designed to be equivalent of 4350 and produces similar results.

H4350 Designed for use with heavier bullets from the 22-250 through the 375 H&H. Good performer in 243 Winchester. Similar to IMR-4350.

H450 Relatively slow burning spherical powder designed to be similar in performance to 4831. Works well in 25-06, 7mm Magnum, 30-06, 270, 300 Winchester Magnum and 300 Weatherby Magnum.

H4831 This slow burning extruded powder is excellent with heavy bullets in many cases including 25-06, 270, 280, 257 Weatherby and 338 Winchester.

H1000 Extremely slow burning extruded powder with a narrow range of use. Excellent in the 7mm Remington Magnum, it also does well in the 270, 30-06, 300 Winchester Magnum and 300 Weatherby Magnum.

H870 For large capacity big overbore magnum loads. Also used for the 50 BMG.

SHOTGUN/HANDGUN

HP38 Fastest burning powder in Hodgdon line. Spherical propellant for low velocity and mid-range target loads in 38 Special, 44 Special, 9mm and 45 ACP.

CLAYS New powder for 12-gauge clay target shooters using $1\frac{1}{8}$- and 1-ounce loads. Also performs well in handgun calibers, 38 Special, 40 S&W and 45 ACP.

International Clays For reduced recoil target loads in 12- and 20-gauge.

Universal Clays Extremely small grain extruded flake powder. For most all straight-wall pistol cartridges as well as 12-gauge $1\frac{1}{4}$-oz. through 28-gauge $\frac{3}{4}$-oz. target loads.

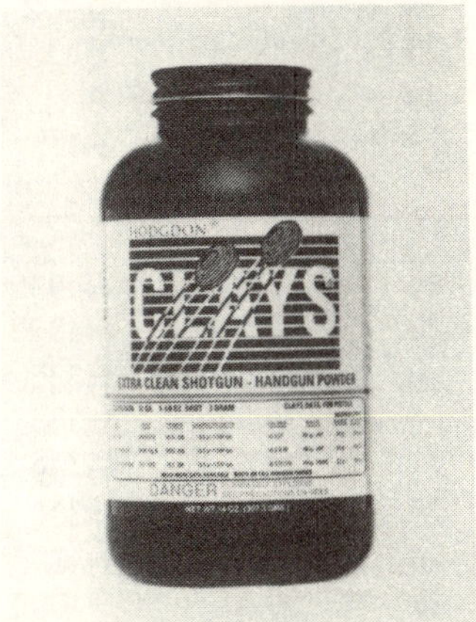

HS6 Good for all bullet weights in the 9mm. Also performs well in most straight-wall pistol cartridges and is well suited to the 45 ACP. A dual purpose spherical powder that is also applicable to 12-gauge $1\frac{1}{4}$-$1\frac{1}{2}$-ounce shot loads and 20-gauge 1-oz.

HS7 Primarily a shotgun propellant for heavy field loads. Also can be used to reload steel shot. Will work in some pistol cartridges including the 357 Magnum, 41 Magnum, 44 Magnum and 45 Winchester Magnum.

H110 Develops high operating pressures and velocities. Recommended for the 30 Carbine and 410-gauge.

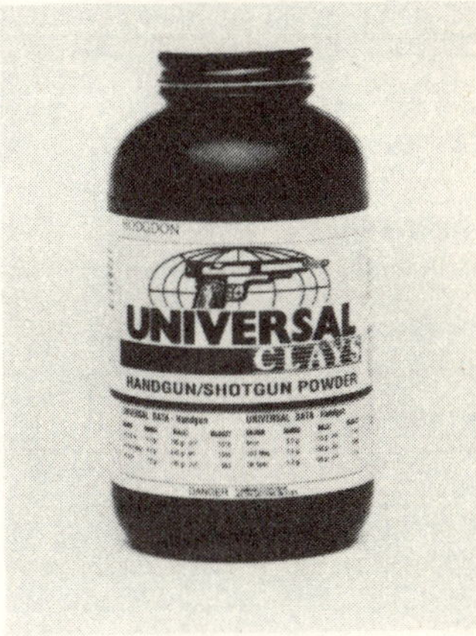

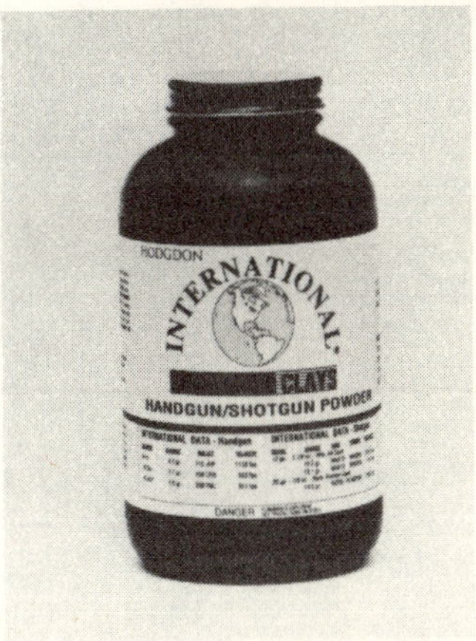

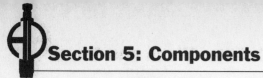

HODGDON POWDER CO.

SELECTED RIFLE LOADS

Cartridge	—Bullet— Wgt. Grs.	Type	Barrel Length	—Load— Grs.	Powder	MV (fps)	Pressure (psi)	Listed Factory MV (fps)
17 Remington	25	HP	24	25.0	H414	3816	NA	4040
	25	HP	24	21.0	H335	3720	NA	4040
22 Hornet	40	SP	20	11.0	H110	2845	NA	NA
	45	SP	20	10.0	H110	2623	NA	2690
218 Bee	40	HP	26	14.0	H4198	2792	NA	NA
	45	HP	26	14.0	H4198	2779	NA	2760
222 Remington	50	SP	26	23.0	H335	3072	45,600	3140
	55	SP	26	23.5	BLC2	3075	47,600	3020
222 Rem. Mag.	50	SP	26	27.0	H335	3476	48,200	NA
	55	SP	26	26.0	BLC2	3221	46,000	3240
223 Remington	52	SP	26	28.0	BLC2	3228	47,600	NA
	55	SP	26	25.3	H335	3203	49,300	3240
224 Weatherby	50	SP	23	31.0	BLC2	3647	NA	NA
	55	SP	23	34.0	H414	3451	NA	3560
225 Winchester	50	SP	26	34.0	BL-C2	3711	48,000	NA
	55	SP	26	33.0	BL-C2	3576	49,000	3570
22-250 Remington	50	SP	26	34.0	H4895	3709	47,600	NA
	55	SP	26	33.0	H4895	3562	47,900	3680
220 Swift	50	SP	26	37.0	H335	3792	49,700	3780
	55	SP	26	36.0	H335	3633	48,700	NA
243 Winchester	75	SP	26	39.0	H4895	3369	48,200	NA
	100	SP	26	38.0	H380	2963	50,500	2960
244/6mm Rem.	75	SP	26	47.0	H4350	3410	49,200	NA
	100	SP	26	50.0	H1000	3073	47,000	3100
240 Weatherby	75	SP	24	51.0	H414	3409	NA	NA
	100	SP	24	51.0	H4831	3111	NA	3395
250 Savage	87	SP	24	40.0	H4350	2910	NA	NA
	100	SP	24	38.0	H4350	2789	NA	2820
257 Roberts	87	SP	26	42.0	H335	3189	42,800	NA
	117	SP	26	35.0	H4895	2663	43,200	2650
257 Weatherby	87	SP	26	63.0	H4350	3550	NA	3825
	117	SP	26	74.0	H870	3069	49,400	NA
6.5x55 Swedish	140	SP	28	45.0	H4831	2392	NA	2850
	150	SP	28	44.0	H4831	2279	NA	NA
6.5 Rem. Mag.	100	SP	26	57.0	H450	3282	49,400	NA
	120	SP	26	57.0	H4831	3114	47,400	NA
264 Win. Mag.	140	SP	26	68.0	H1000	3019	NA	3030
	160	RN	26	54.0	H4831	2732	48,900	NA
270 Winchester	130	SP	26	58.0	H450	3054	46,900	3060
	150	SP	26	63.0	H1000	2783	45,8000	2850

CAUTION: Some of these loads are maximum loads. Start low and work up slowly, being alert for signs of excessive pressure.

HODGDON POWDER CO.

SELECTED RIFLE LOADS

Cartridge	—Bullet— Wgt. Grs.	Type	Barrel Length	—Load— Grs.	Powder	MV Pressure (fps)	Listed Factory (psi)	MV (fps)
280 Remington	130	SP	24	55.0	H4350	3007	NA	NA
	154	SP	24	52.0	H4350	2772	NA	NA
7x57mm Mauser	139	SP	23	48.0	H414	2805	48,800	2660
	175	RN	23	49.0	H4350	2449	48,400	2440
7mm-08 Remington	120	SP	$18\frac{1}{2}$	41.0	H4895	2808	NA	3000
	140	SP	$18\frac{1}{2}$	47.0	H414	2712	NA	2860
7mm Rem. Mag.	139	SP	26	75.0	H1000	3139	50,500	3175
	175	SP	26	77.0	H870	2918	48,600	2860
30 Carbine	100	NA	18	14.5	H110	2013	NA	NA
	110	NA	18	14.0	H110	1906	NA	1990
30/30 Win.	150	FP	20	31.0	H335	2246	NA	2390
	170	FP	20	38.0	H4350	2030	NA	2200
300 Savage	150	SP	22	36.0	BL-C2	2321	NA	2630
	180	RN	22	35.0	H335	2074	NA	2350
308 Winchester	150	SP	26	45.0	H335	2818	49,400	2820
	180	SP	26	46.0	H414	2501	48,000	2620
30/06 Spr	150	SP	26	56.0	H414	2910	46,900	2910
	180	SP	26	56.0	H4350	2733	48,800	2700
300 Win. Mag.	150	SP	26	85.0	H1000	3240	45,300	3290
	180	SP	26	75.0	H4831	2969	49,900	2960
7.62x39 Russian	123	SP	24	31.5	H335	2408	NA	2365
303 British	150	SP	24	45.0	BL-C2	2604	NA	2690
	180	SP	24	46.0	H4350	2349	NA	2460
7.65 Mauser	150	SP	29	49.0	H4350	2614	NA	NA
	175	SP	29	47.0	H4350	2454	NA	NA
8x57mm Mauser .323"	150	SP	23	54.0	H4350	2552	NA	NA
	170	SP	23	45.0	H380	2387	NA	2360
338 Win. Mag.	200	SP	24	70.0	H4350	2884	NA	2960
	250	SP	24	74.0	H4831	2679	53,000	2660
35 Remington	180	SP	20	32.0	H4198	2017	NA	NA
	200	SP	20	36.0	H4895	1781	NA	2080
375 H&H Magnum	270	SP	26	77.0	H4350	2624	NA	2690
	300	SP	26	82.0	H4831	2467	NA	2530
444 Marlin	240	SP	24	60.0	BL-C2	2302	31,000	2350
	265	SP	24	54.0	H322	2248	35,300	NA
45/70 Government	300	SP	$32\frac{1}{2}$	33.0	H4198	1542	NA	1880
	405	SP	$32\frac{1}{2}$	40.0	H4895	1312	NA	NA
458 Win. Mag.	350	SP	22	64.0	H4198	2321	NA	NA
	500	SP	22	70.0	H4895	2048	NA	2040

CAUTION: Some of these loads are maximum loads. Start low and work up slowly, being alert for signs of excessive pressure.

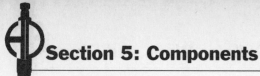

HODGDON POWDER CO.

SELECTED PISTOL LOADS

Cartridge	—Bullet— Wgt. Grs.	Type	Barrel Length	—Load— Grs.	Powder	MV (fps)	Pressure (psi)	Listed Factory MV (fps)
221 Rem. Fireball	45	SP	$10\frac{3}{4}$	15.0	H4227	2592	NA	NA
	50	SP	$10\frac{3}{4}$	15.0	H4227	2582	NA	2650
32/20	80	FP	$7\frac{1}{2}$	4.3	HP38	1175	NA	NA
	115	SP	$7\frac{1}{2}$	3.3	HP38	875	NA	NA
32 H&R Magnum	85	HP	$5\frac{1}{2}$	6.6	HS7	1095	20,900	1100
	95	LSWC	$5\frac{1}{2}$	9.0	H4227	1043	20,900	1030
380 ACP	95	FMJ	$3\frac{7}{16}$	3.2	Trap 100	944	NA	955
38 Super Automatic	125	HP	4	6.6	HS6	1146	NA	1120
	130	MC	$4\frac{7}{8}$	7.0	HS6	1189	NA	NA
9mm Luger	115	FMJ	4	5.0	Trap 100	1144	NA	1160
38 Special	125	HP	$7\frac{1}{2}$	4.8	Trap 100	981	15,500	945
	158	SWC	$7\frac{1}{2}$	3.3	Trap 100	832	14,400	755
357 Magnum	125	HP	$7\frac{1}{2}$	6.8	HP38	1342	28,900	1450
	158	HP	$7\frac{1}{2}$	10.0	HS7	1304	29,300	1235
10mm Auto	155	HP	5	11.4	HS7	1307	28,000	1325
	180	HP	5	6.5	H38	1065	26,900	1030
41 Magnum	170	HP	$6\frac{1}{2}$	23.0	H4227	1437	NA	1250
	210	HP	$6\frac{1}{2}$	21.0	H4227	1319	NA	1300
44 Special	200	HP	$7\frac{1}{2}$	10.5	HS6	1086	15,600	900
	240	HP	$7\frac{1}{2}$	5.0	Trap 100	794	15,900	755
44 Magnum	210	HP	$7\frac{1}{2}$	27.0	H4227	1604	29,400	1610
	240	HP	$7\frac{1}{2}$	12.0	HS6	1176	24,000	1180
45 ACP	185	HP	5	5.2	HP38	884	15,500	950
	230	FMJ	5	5.1	Trap 100	828	15,800	850
45 Colt	250	L	$7\frac{1}{2}$	6.4	Trap 100	847	NA	860

CAUTION: Some of these loads are maximum loads. Start low and work up slowly, being alert for signs of excessive pressure.

IMR POWDER COMPANY

RIFLE

IMR-4227 Originally intended for small cartridges such as the Hornet and Bee but has proved useful in a wide spread of high performance handgun loads.

IMR-4198 The powder that showed early 222 shooters, including the benchresters, how good that cartridge was. Also very useful in large caliber, non-bottleneck cases like the 444 Marlin and 45-70.

IMR-4895 Countless tons of this propellant were used by the U.S. government to load 30-06 ammo during WWII. Probably the most versatile powder ever made. Excellent results with certain bullets in cases from the 17 Rem. to the 458 Magnum.

IMR-4064 Medium-burning powder well suited for a wide range of calibers. Long a favorite of Jack O'Connor in the 220 Swift.

IMR-4320 Like most medium-burning powders, this one is versatile, giving good results in cases as large as the 460 Weatherby. Meters well.

SR-4759 Single base powder ideally suited to cast bullet rifle loads.

IMR-4350 An early slow-burning powder specifically designed for bottlenecked magnum cartridges. Consistent results.

IMR-4831 Another WWII powder, this slow burner made most of today's high velocity magnum cartridges practical. Excellent in 264 Win., 7mm Rem. and 338 Magnums.

IMR-3031 Recommended for medium-size cases such as the 30-30 and 358, it is also useful for mid-range loads and delivers fine results in cases as large as the 460 Weatherby.

IMR 7828 Slowest burning of the IMR rifle powders, this is at its best with bottlenecked large-capacity cases and heavy bullets.

SHOTGUN/HANDGUN

PB Named for the porous base structure of its grains, by which the burning rate is controlled, this powder is used for many handgun loads though it was developed for shotshells.

SR 7625 For use in 12-gauge high-velocity shotshell loads; also suitable for wide variety of handgun cartridges.

SR 4756 Designed for magnum shotshells. Good producer in 410-bore target ammo and heavy centerfire handgun ammuntion.

Hi-Skor 700X Shotgun double-base powder developed for 12-ga. components but has found recent applications in high-volume handgun rounds such as the 38 Special, 9mm Luger and 45 ACP.

Hi-Skor 800X Slower burning than 700X, it has applications in smaller gauges, target loads, 12-gauge field and heavier handgun loads.

SR 7625 Clean burning powder with applications in 12-gauge down to 28-gauge target and field loads. Also viable for handgun loads.

IMR™

SELECTED HANDGUN LOADS

Cartridge	—Bullet— Wgt. Grs.	Type	Barrel Length	—Load— Grs.	Powder	MV (fps)	Pressure (psi)	Listed Factory MV (fps)
22 Rem. Jet	40	SP	10.0	13.5	4227	2290	32,900	NA
221 Rem. Fireball	45	SP	10.75	17.7	4198	2575	44,500	NA
	50	SP	10.75	14.7	4227	2390	51,400	2650
25 ACP	50	FMJ	2.0	1.2	SR7625	755	19,900	760
380 ACP	90	HP	3.75	2.9	700X	895	15,900	NA
38 ACP	115	HP	5.0	5.9	800X	1015	21,900	NA
9mm Luger	115	HP	4.0	6.5	800X	1150	30,300	1155
	124	MC	4.0	4.8	700X	1110	32,600	1110
38 Special	110	HP	6.0	4.2	700X	970	15,400	950
	158	LSWC	6.0	5.0	800X	750	11,600	755
357 Magnum	125	HP	6.0	10.2	800X	1360	35,300	1450
	158	LSWC	6.0	8.9	800X	1215	36,000	1235
41 Rem. Mag.	170	SP	10.0	11.3	PB	1460	40,000	1420
	210	SP	10.0	9.7	PB	1265	40,000	1300
44 S&W Special	240	LSWC	6.5	14.3	4227	790	13,700	NA
	246	LRN	6.5	5.6	PB	745	13,600	755
44 Rem. Magnum	200	HP	8.25	15.5	800X	1600	39,800	NA
	240	HP	8.25	10.3	700X	1205	39,400	1180
45 ACP	185	HP	5.0	8.6	800X	975	18,000	1000
	230	MC	5.0	7.3	800X	840	17,800	835

CAUTION: Some of these loads are maximum loads. Start low and work up slowly, being alert for signs of excessive pressure.

IMR™

SELECTED RIFLE LOADS

Cartridge	—Bullet— Wgt. Grs.	Type	Barrel Length	—Load— Grs.	Powder	MV (fps)	Pressure (psi)	Listed Factory MV (fps)
17 Remington	25	HP	24	22.5	3031	4015	57,700	4040
	45	HP	25	11.5	4227	2515	38,900	2690
222 Remington	45	HP	25	21.5	4198	3315	45,000	NA
	50	SP	25	20.5	4198	3130	44,500	3140
223 Remington	45	SP	24	22.0	4198	3360	50,300	NA
	55	SP	24	25.0	3031	3165	50,900	3240
22-250 Remington	50	SP	24	35.0	3031	3785	52,700	NA
	55	SP	24	34.0	3031	3640	53,000	3680
220 Swift	50	SP	24	43.5	4350	3740	49,100	3780
	60	SP	24	42.5	4831	3555	53,000	NA
243 Winchester	80	SP	22	42.5	4064	3360	52,000	3350
	100	SP	22	43.5	4350	2980	51,300	2960
6mm Remington	80	SP	22	46.0	4350	3310	52,000	3470
	100	SP	22	45.5	4831	3095	52,000	3100
250 Savage	87	SP	24	34.5	4895	3000	44,900	NA
	100	SP	24	34.0	4895	2845	45,000	2820
257 Roberts	100	SP	24	46.5	4831	2950	44,300	NA
	120	SP	24	44.0	4831	2810	45,000	NA
25-06 Remington	100	SP	24	47.5	4064	3240	52,800	3230
	120	SP	24	48.5	4350	2950	51,500	2990
264 Win. Mag.	100	HP	24	60.0	4350	3385	53,900	NA
	140	SP	24	65.0	7828	3115	53,600	3030
270 Winchester	130	SP	23	55.0	4350	3035	53,100	3060
	150	SP	23	56.5	7828	2860	50,600	2850
7mm-08 Remington	139	SP	24	42.5	4064	2835	51,300	NA
	168	HP	24	38.0	4895	2535	51,400	NA
7x57mm Mauser	130		24	50.0	4831	2750	46,000	NA
	160		24	47.5	4831	2540	45,600	NA
280 Remington	150	SP	24	55.0	4350	2895	50,000	2890
	165	SP	24	55.5	4831	2775	50,000	2820
284 Winchester	160	SP	24	47.0	4064	2760	53,700	NA

CAUTION: Some of these loads are maximum loads. Start low and work up slowly, being alert for signs of excessive pressure.

IMR™

SELECTED RIFLE LOADS

Cartridge	—Bullet— Wgt. Grs.	Type	Barrel Length	—Load— Grs.	Powder	MV (fps)	Pressure (psi)	Listed Factory MV (fps)
7mm Rem. Mag.	150	SP	24	66.5	4831	3055	52,000	3110
	175	SP	24	66.0	7828	2910	52,000	2860
30-30 Winchester	150	FP	20	35.5	3031	2370	37,700	2390
	170	FP	20	32.0	3031	2120	37,700	2200
300 Savage	150	SP	24	40.0	4895	2570	45,900	2630
	180	RN	24	44.0	4350	2350	41,900	2350
30-40 Krag	150	NA	25.5	44.0	4064	2695	39,000	NA
	180	NA	25.5	41.0	4064	2435	39,000	2430
308 Winchester	150	SP	23	45.0	3031	2830	52,000	2820
	180	SP	23	43.5	4064	2580	51,700	2620
30-06 Spr.	150	SP	23	52.0	4064	2885	50,000	2910
	180	SP	23	59.0	4831	2700	44,200	2700
300 H&H Magnum	150	SP	24	73.0	4350	3215	53,600	NA
	180	SP	24	60	4064	2875	53,400	2880
300 Win. Mag.	150	SP	24	76.0	4350	3335	53900	3290
	180	SP	24	59.5	4895	2950	53,900	2960
8x57mm Mauser	150	SP	25	47.0	4831	2325	36,800	NA
	170	RN	25	46.0	4831	2255	37,000	2360
8mm Rem. Mag.	185	SP	24	77.5	4350	3090	53,100	3080
	220	SP	24	76.0	4831	2845	53,800	2830
338 Win. Mag.	200	SP	24	73.0	4350	3030	53,900	2960
	250	SP	24	74.0	7828	2565	44,400	2660
35 Remington	150	SP	23	43.0	4064	2320	33,000	2300
	200	RN	23	39.5	4064	2080	34,200	2080
358 Winchester	200	SP	25	40.0	4198	2495	52,000	2495
	250	SP	25	44.0	4064	2270	52,000	NA
350 Rem. Mag.	200	SP	20	62.0	4895	2815	52,300	2710
	250	SP	20	56.0	4895	2485	52,500	NA
375 H&H Magnum	270	SP	25	82.5	4831	2690	50,700	2690
	300	SP	25	67.0	4064	2525	52,500	2530
444 Marlin	240	SP	25	47.0	4198	2335	44,000	2350
458 Win. Mag.	510	SP	25	69.0	3031	2030	43,900	2040

CAUTION: Some of these loads are maximum loads. Start low and work up slowly, being alert for signs of excessive pressure.

SCOT POWDER

RIFLE

BRIGADIER 4197: Quick but cooler burning single base tubular rifle powder. Very similar in burn rate to Reloder 7. Good for varmint loads. Formerly Herter's Rifle Powder No. 103.

BRIGADIER 3032: Medium rate cool burning single base tubular rifle powder. Similar to H322. Good for benchrest applications. Formerly Herter's Rifle Powder No. 102.

BRIGADIER 4065: Medium-slow but cool burning single base tubular rifle powder. Similar to IMR-4895 and H4895. Works well in 257, 264, 7mm and 308. Formerly Herter's Rifle Powder No. 101.

BRIGADIER 4351: Slow but cool burning single base tubular rifle powder. Good for medium to heavy bullet loads in 270, 30-06 and larger calibers. Formerly Herter's Rifle Powder No. 100.

BRIGADIER 322: Medium rate cool burning, short-grained extruded nitrocotton powder. Designed for 223, 222 and 22 and 6mm PPC.

BRIGADIER 4831: Slow and cool burning. The classic magnum rifle powder.

SHOTGUN/HANDGUN

SCOT 453: Spherical, double base powder ideal for 12-ga. target and light target handgun applications. Performs almost identical to Winchester 452AA Ball Powder.

ROYAL SCOT D: Higher density replacement for Royal Scot. Cleaner burning and more consistent.

PEARL SCOT: Medium burning double base flake 12- and 20-ga. powder. Similar to Hercules Unique for $1^1/_8$ and light $1^1/_4$ upland game loads. Also applicable to pistol loads.

SOLO 1000: Fast clean burning single base disc powder for all automatic pistol and shotguns. Uniform grain size. Similar to Hercules Bullseye for light pistol target shooting and to IMR-700-X or PB for shotshells.

SOLO 1250: Medium rate clean burning single base, disc powder for 12-ga. hunting loads or 20 and 28 ga. Skeet. Similar to IMR SR-7625 and Hercules Unique. Also good for pistol loads in 9mm, 40 S&W and 10mm IPSC.

SOLO 1500: Slow clean burning single base disc powder for 357 Magnum, 41 Magnum, 44 Magnum and 10mm silhouette loads with heavier bullets. Similar to IMR SR-4756. Good also for 10, 12, 16 and 20 gauge hunting loads with lead. Some application for 12-ga. steel.

SELECTED HANDGUN LOADS

Cartridge	—Bullet— Wgt. Grs.	Type	Barrel Length	—Load— Grs.	Powder	MV (fps)	Pressure (psi)	Listed Factory MV (fps)
32 Smith & Wesson	71	FMJ	3	1.9	Solo 1000	740	11,100	NA
32 Automatic	71	FMJ	4	1.5	Solo 1000	860	11,800	905
32 S&W Long	90	LSWC	4	2.0	Royal Scot	810	12,700	NA
32 H&R Magnum	90	LSWC	4	3.9	Solo 1250	1045	18,600	NA
380 Automatic	88	HP	$3^3/_4$	5.0	Solo 1500	973	14,500	990
	115	HP	$3^3/_4$	3.1	Solo 1250	876	15,900	NA
9mm Luger	115	FMJ	4	6.4	Solo 1500	1139	30,600	1135
	124	FMJ	4	6.0	Solo 1500	1112	31,000	1110
38 Special	110	HP	6	5.0	Solo 1000	1038	14,900	950
	158	LSWC	6	3.6	Solo 1000	884	16,700	755
357 Magnum	125	FP	$8^3/_8$	8.7	Solo 1250	1448	40,300	1450
	158	SWC	$8^3/_8$	7.0	Solo 1250	1263	40,700	1235
40 Smith & Wesson	155	HP	4	7.8	Solo 1500	1030	26,400	1140
	180	HP	4	5.2	Solo 1250	985	28,600	985
10mm Automatic	180	HP	5	8.4	Solo 1500	1170	31,100	1240
	200	FMJ	5	7.7	Solo 1500	1057	30,500	1160
41 Magnum	170	HP	$8^3/_8$	9.7	Solo 1250	1491	37,800	1420
	210	HP	$8^3/_8$	10.7	Solo 1500	1366	38,300	1300
44 Magnum	180	HP	$6^1/_2$	15.7	Solo 1500	1617	37,300	1610
	240	MC	$6^1/_2$	9.9	Solo 1000	1231	35,800	1180
45 ACP	185	HP	5	9.1	Solo 1500	974	17,000	1000
	230	FMJ	5	8.2	Solo 1500	885	17,100	835
45 Colt	255	LSWC	6	11.0	Solo 1500	900	11,800	NA

CAUTION: Some of these loads are maximum loads. Start low and work up slowly, being alert for signs of excessive pressure.

SCOT POWDER COMPANY

SELECTED RIFLE LOADS

Cartridge	—Bullet— Wgt. Grs.	Type	Barrel Length	—Load— Grs.	Powder	MV (fps)	Pressure (psi)	Listed Factory MV (fps)
222 Remington	40	FMJ	NA	22.5	4197	3500	NA	NA
	50	FMJ	NA	21.5	4197	3300	NA	NA
223 Remington	45	FMJ	NA	27.0	3032	3330	NA	NA
	55	FMJ	NA	25.5	3032	3140	NA	3240
22-250 Rem.	45	FMJ	NA	37.0	4065	3880	NA	NA
	55	FMJ	NA	35.0	4065	3650	NA	3680
220 Swift	50	SP	NA	38.0	3032	3930	NA	3780
	55	HP	NA	36.0	3032	3710	NA	NA
243 Winchester	80	FMJ	NA	43.5	4351	3300	NA	3350
	100	FMJ	NA	41.5	4351	3050	NA	2960
244 Remington	80	FMJ	NA	47.0	4351	3390	NA	3470
	100	FMJ	NA	43.5	4351	3080	NA	3100
25-06 Remington	85	HP	NA	53.0	4351	3515	NA	NA
	100	SP	NA	50.0	4351	3200	NA	3230
6.5x64 Mann.-Scho.	140	FMJ	NA	34.0	3032	2400	NA	NA
	160	FMJ	NA	34.5	4065	2300	NA	NA
264 Win. Mag.	120	FMJ	NA	59.0	4351	3240	NA	NA
	140	FMJ	NA	57.0	4351	2920	NA	3030
270 Winchester	130	FMJ	NA	55.0	4351	3100	NA	3060
	150	FMJ	NA	52.0	4351	2845	NA	2850
7x57mm Mauser	120	FMJ	NA	45.0	4065	3050	NA	NA
	140	FMJ	NA	40.0	3032	2715	NA	2660
7mm Rem. Mag.	140	FMJ	NA	67.0	4351	3250	NA	3175
	175	FMJ	NA	62.0	4351	2880	NA	2860
30-30 Winchester	150	FP	NA	31.0	4197	2350	NA	2390
	170	FP	NA	34.0	4065	2200	NA	2200
308 Winchester	150	FMJ	NA	44.0	3032	2820	NA	2820
	180	FMJ	NA	43.0	4065	2530	NA	2620
30-06 Springfield	150	FMJ	NA	52.0	4065	2900	NA	2910
	180	FMJ	NA	56.0	4351	2740	NA	2700
300 Win. Mag.	180	SP	NA	66.0	4351	2920	NA	2960
303 British	150	FMJ	NA	42.0	4197	2790	NA	NA
	174	FMJ	NA	40.0	3032	2500	NA	NA
8x57mm Mauser	154	FMJ	NA	58.0	4351	2780	NA	NA
	198	FMJ	NA	47.0	4065	2600	NA	NA
338 Win. Mag.	200	FMJ	NA	74.0	4351	3000	NA	NA
	250	FMJ	NA	71.0	4351	2710	NA	2660
35 Remington	150	FMJ	NA	35.0	4197	2270	NA	2300
	200	FMJ	NA	39.0	4065	2060	NA	2080
358 Winchester	200	FMJ	NA	44.0	3032	2430	NA	2490
	250	FMJ	NA	40.0	3032	2220	NA	NA
30 Remington	170	FMJ	NA	32.0	4065	2100	NA	2120
350 Rem. Mag.	200	FMJ	NA	58.0	4065	2540	NA	2710
	250	FMJ	NA	56.0	4065	2400	NA	NA
375 H&H Magnum	270	FMJ	NA	79.0	4351	2660	NA	2690
	300	FMJ	NA	70.0	4065	2495	NA	2530

CAUTION: Some of these loads are maximum loads. Start low and work up slowly, being alert for signs of excessive pressure.

VIHTAVUORI OY

Cylindrical or flaked powders with 94-98% nitrocellulose content. The powders are presented here in burn rate order from the fastest burning to the slowest burning.

SHOTGUN/HANDGUN

N310: Designed for revolvers and smaller pistols.

N320: Shotgun powder for sports cartridges with shot charges of 30-32 grams (about 1$^1/_8$ oz.). Suitable for revolvers.

N340: Shotgun powder especially for hunting cartridges with shot of 34-35 grams (about 1$^1/_4$ oz.).

3N37: For 22-caliber cartridges. Good powder for pistols.

N350: Slowest burning porous propellant suitable for heavy pistol bullets.

RIFLE

N110: Mainly for small and medium sized cases when light bullets are used.

N120: Universal propellant for different 5.6mm calibers. Burns more slowly than N110 and requires higher pressure.

N133: Special propellant for 5.6x45 ball.

N135: Designed for 7.62x51 ball. Versatile powder that can be used from 5.6 caliber up to 8mm.

N140: Slower burning than N135 so good for 30-caliber with heavy bullets.

N150: Rifle powder with burn rate between N140 and N160.

N160: Magnum caliber powder also suitable for 30-06 and 6.5x55.

N165: Magnum powder that burns more slowly than N160.

VIHTAVUORI OY

SELECTED HANDGUN LOADS

Cartridge	—Bullet— Wgt. Grs.	Type	Barrel Length	—Load— Grs.	Powder	MV (fps)	Pressure (psi)	Listed Factory MV (fps)
25 Automatic	50	FMJ	2	1.1	N310	804	18,855	760
30 Luger	93	FMJ	NA	5.4	N340	1280	37,710	1220
32 Automatic	71	FMJ	NA	2.2	N310	1001	26,107	905
32 S&W Long	99	WC	NA	1.7	N310	771	14,504	705
9mm Luger	115	FMJ	NA	7.5	N350	1444	36,549	1135
	124	FMJ	NA	5.5	N331	1110	29,007	1110
380 Automatic	96	FMJ	NA	2.9	N310	919	23,206	955
38 Special	110	JHP	NA	5.8	N320	1147	15,954	950
	158	SWC	NA	6.8	3N37	1050	17,114	755
357 Magnum	125	JHP	NA	10.0	3N37	1469	31,908	1450
	158	JHP	NA	7.5	N320	1245	44,962	1235
38 Super Auto	124	FMJ	NA	8.4	N350	1559	35,534	NA
	147	HP	NA	6.7	N350	1358	35,534	NA
38 Smith & Wesson	147	RNL	NA	3.5	N340	755	13,779	685
44 Magnum	180	JHP	NA	17.7	N350	1671	39,160	1610
	240	JHP	NA	9.9	N320	1181	39,160	1180
45 Automatic	185	SP	NA	7.9	N340	1041	15,954	1000
	230	FMJ	NA	4.0	N310	853	19,580	835
45 Colt	185	HP	NA	9.3	N320	1198	10,153	NA
	230	LRN	NA	9.7	N340	1083	12,328	NA
45 Win. Magnum	185	SWC	NA	19.1	3N37	1873	42,061	NA
	230	FMJ	NA	14.7	3N37	1460	34,374	1400

CAUTION: Some of these loads are maximum loads. Start low and work up slowly, being alert for signs of excessive pressure.

VIHTAVUORI OY

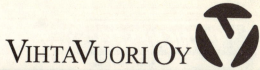

SELECTED RIFLE LOADS

Cartridge	—Bullet— Wgt. Grs.	Type	Barrel Length	—Load— Grs.	Powder	MV (fps)	Pressure (psi)	Listed Factory MV (fps)
17 Remington	25	FMJ	NA	22.8	N135	4040	50,760	4040
22 Hornet	45	SP	NA	9.6	N110	2530	37,709	2690
222 Remington	45	SP	NA	23.9	N133	3284	44,236	NA
	50	FMJ	NA	19.3	N120	3250	46,412	3140
223 Remington	55	SP	NA	24.8	N133	3220	52,214	3240
	60	SP	NA	24.5	N133	3050	53,664	3100
22-250 Remington	50	SP	NA	35.8	N135	3840	53,664	NA
	55	SP	NA	36.4	N140	3630	53,664	3680
220 Swift	50	HP	NA	38.6	N140	3900	53,664	3780
	55	SP	NA	43.1	N160	3710	44,962	NA
243 Winchester	80	SP	NA	38.4	N140	3200	52,214	3350
	100	SP	NA	42.3	N160	2840	52,214	2960
25-20 Winchester	70	SP	NA	10.2	N110	2030	37,710	NA
25-35 Winchester	70	SP	NA	23.5	N120	2950	38,435	NA
	117	SP	NA	27.2	N140	2360	39,160	2230
25-06 Remington	86	HP	NA	56.3	N160	3360	50,760	NA
	120	SP	NA	49.2	N160	2890	50,760	2990
6.5x55mm	140	HP	NA	34.8	N150	2362	46,412	2850
	160	RN	NA	44.9	N160	2510	44,962	NA
6.5x57mm	140	SP	NA	40.7	N140	2690	48,588	NA
	160	RN	NA	44.0	N160	2400	49,313	NA
6.5x68mm	105	SP	NA	67.0	N160	3350	47,862	NA
	125	SP	NA	64.0	N160	3130	47,862	NA
264 Win. Magnum	140	SP	NA	47.8	N140	3020	56,565	3030
	160	SP	NA	56.3	N160	2690	56,565	NA
270 Winchester	130	SP	NA	54.8	N160	3030	52,214	3060
	150	SP	NA	51.1	N160	2710	52,214	2850
7x57mm Mauser	120	SP	NA	47.4	N140	3050	49,313	NA
	175	SP	NA	47.5	N160	2530	49,313	NA
7x64mm	139	SP	NA	48.6	N140	2890	49,313	NA
	175	SP	NA	56.8	N160	2760	52,214	NA

CAUTION: Some of these loads are maximum loads. Start low and work up slowly, being alert for signs of excessive pressure.

WINCHESTER AMMUNITION

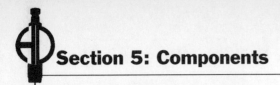

SELECTED RIFLE LOADS

Cartridge	—Bullet— Wgt. Grs.	Type	Barrel Length	—Load— Grs.	Powder	MV (fps)	Pressure (psi)	Listed Factory MV (fps)
7mm Rem. Mag.	150	SP	NA	68.5	N160	3130	59,939	3110
	175	SP	NA	60.2	N160	2810	55,114	2860
7.62x39mm	123	SP	NA	26.7	N120	2360	43,511	2300
30-30 Winchester	155	SP	NA	31.9	N140	2130	39,160	NA
	170	FP	NA	31.5	N140	2020	39,160	2200
308 Winchester	150	SP	NA	46.3	N140	2840	52,214	2820
	180	SP	NA	44.4	N150	2620	52,214	2620
308 Norma Magnum	155	SP	NA	72.8	N160	3100	55,114	NA
	180	SP	NA	70.7	N160	3050	55,114	3019
7.62x54 Remington	150	SP	NA	48.0	N140	2810	49,313	2953
	180	SP	NA	44.8	N140	2610	49,313	2576
30-06 Springfield	150	SP	NA	50.9	N140	2900	50,760	2910
	180	SP	NA	57.1	N160	2710	50,760	2700
300 H&H Magnum	150	SP	NA	75.6	N160	3180	56,565	NA
	180	SP	NA	68.2	N160	2920	56,565	2880
300 Win. Magnum	150	SP	NA	75.3	N160	3310	56,565	3290
	180	SP	NA	73.0	N160	2990	55,114	2960
303 British	180	SP	NA	41.7	N140	2540	46,412	2460
8x57 JS Mauser	127	FMJ	NA	54.8	N135	3180	49,313	NA
	175	SP	NA	49.7	N140	2670	49,313	NA
8x68 S	187	SP	NA	77.9	N160	3070	55,114	NA
	200	SP	NA	72.2	N160	2890	55,114	NA
338 Win. Magnum	225	SP	NA	70.2	N160	2760	55,114	2780
	250	SP	NA	67.9	N160	2670	55,114	2660
375 H&H Magnum	270	SP	NA	73.3	N140	2760	55,114	2690
	300	SP	NA	81.8	N160	2560	55,114	2530
358 Norma Magnum	250	SP	NA	80.2	N160	2790	55,114	2799
9.3x57mm	255	SP	NA	50.9	N140	2260	37,710	NA
9.3x62mm	258	SP	NA	57.6	N135	2510	49,313	NA
	285	SP	NA	54.5	N135	2330	49,313	NA
9.3x64mm	258	SP	NA	67.9	N140	2670	53,664	NA
	285	SP	NA	67.0	N140	2530	53,664	NA
458 Win. Magnum	350	SP	NA	73.7	N130	2518	52,214	2470
	500	SP	NA	74.5	N140	2100	52,214	2090

CAUTION: Some of these loads are maximum loads. Start low and work up slowly, being alert for signs of excessive pressure.

WINCHESTER

Olin Corp., of which Winchester has long been a division, has been producing Smokeless Ball powder commercially since 1933. These nine powders are currently available.

RIFLE

748 Rifle powder suitable for 222 Remington and 458 Winchester Magnum. Popular benchrest propellant.

760 For medium to large cartridges. Broad range of application in medium to large cases.

SHOTGUN/HANDGUN

231 Fast, high energy, clean burning powder for target and standard velocity loads in handguns.

296 For 410-bore, magnum pistol and 30 Carbine. Requires heavy bullets and heavy crimps in magnum pistol cartridges.

540 For heavy shot charges in 12- and 20-gauge. Excellent powder for 28-gauge. Higher density permits easier crimping of heavy loads.

571 For 12-gauge 3" magnum shotshells. Also gives good performance in 20- and 28-gauge.

WSL Winchester Super-Lite For target and standard velocity shotshell loads and reloads with reduced recoil.

WST Winchester Super-Target Replacement shotshell powder for 452AA. Formulated to produce uniform velocity and pressure.

WSF Winchester Super-Field For 20-gauge Skeet and field. Same powder as used in factory 20-ga. AA but can also be used for 12- and 16-gauge.

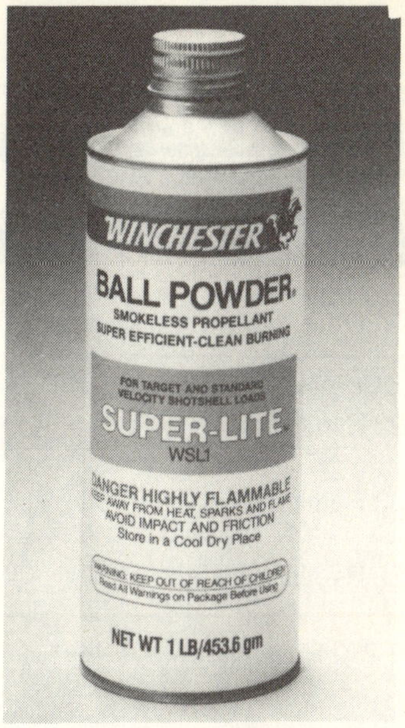

WINCHESTER
AMMUNITION

SELECTED PISTOL LOADS

Cartridge	—Bullet— Wgt. Grs.	Type	Barrel Length	—Load— Grs.	Powder	MV (fps)	Pressure (psi)	Listed Factory MV (fps)
30 Luger	93	FMJ	$4\frac{1}{2}$	4.2	231	1085	25,500	1220
32 Smith & Wesson	85	L	3	1.4	231	595	9,500	680
32 ACP	71	FMJ	4	2.5	231	865	14,000	905
32 S&W Long	98	L	4	2.4	231	765	11,000	NA
38 S&W	145	L	4	2.6	231	675	11,500	685
380 ACP	95	FMJ	$3\frac{3}{4}$	3.2	231	860	15,000	955
38 ACP	130	FMJ	5	4.4	231	875	20,000	NA
38 Special	158	L	6	4.3	231	865	15,500	755
	200	L	6	3.8	231	770	15,500	NA
38 Super Auto	130	FMJ	5	5.4	231	1075	30,500	1215
9mm Luger	115	FMJ	4	7.1	540	1185	33,300	1155
	147	FMJ	4	5.6	540	970	33,000	990
357 Magnum	125	JHP	$8\frac{3}{8}$	18.5	296*	1800	32,500	1450
	158	JHP	$8\frac{3}{8}$	16.6	296*	1610	39,500	1235
40 S&W	155	JHP	4	8.8	540	1160	33,200	1205
	180	JHP	4	4.8	WSL	950	33,200	990
10mm Automatic	155	JHP	5	11.0	540	1350	35,600	1125
	180	JHP	5	5.6	WSL	1060	35,600	1240
41 Magnum	210	SP	$8\frac{3}{8}$	20.4	296*	1460	24,000	1300
44 Special	246	L	$6\frac{1}{2}$	5.4	231	795	12,500	755
44 Magnum	210	JHP	$6\frac{1}{2}$	11.7	231	1385	38,000	1250
	240	SP	$6\frac{1}{2}$	24.0	296*	1430	38,000	1180
45 ACP	185	JHP	5	10.4	540	1030	19,400	1000
	230	JHP	5	8.1	540	840	20,100	835

* Do not reduce powder charges with 296. Magnum primer and very heavy crimp recommended.

CAUTION: Some of these loads are maximum loads. Start low and work up slowly, being alert for signs of excessive pressure.

WINCHESTER AMMUNITION

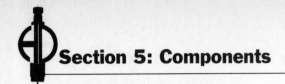

SELECTED RIFLE LOADS

Cartridge	—Bullet— Wgt. Grs.	Type	Barrel Length	—Load— Grs.	Powder	MV (fps)	Pressure (psi)	Listed Factory MV (fps)
22 Hornet	45	SP	24	11.8	680	2650	41,000	2690
222 Remington	50	SP	24	24.0	748	2980	38,000	3140
	55	SP	24	24.0	748	2900	38,000	3020
223 Remington	50	SP	24	26.0	748	3200	40,000	NA
	55	SP	24	26.3	748	3150	39,000	3240
222 Remington Mag.	50	SP	24	27.2	748	3220	43,000	NA
	55	SP	24	27.2	748	3215	42,500	3240
22-250 Remington	46	HP	24	36.8	748	3815	50,000	NA
	55	SP	24	39.0	760	3675	49,000	3680
243 Winchester	80	SP	24	43.5	760	3280	51,000	3350
250/3000 Savage	87	SP	24	39.5	760	2985	43,500	NA
	100	SP	24	38.8	760	2820	42,000	2820
270 Winchester	130	SP	24	52.0	760	2990	49,500	3060
	150	SP	24	49.0	760	2725	48,500	2850
7mm/7x57mm	150	SP	24	46.5	760	2660	43,500	NA
Mauser	175	SP	24	44.0	760	2400	44,500	2440
284 Winchester	125	SP	24	57.0	760	3180	50,000	NA
	150	SP	24	54.0	760	2890	49,000	2860
30 M1 Carbine	110	HP	24	16.0	680	1970	37,500	1990
30 Remington	170	SP	24	35.0	760	2095	35,000	2120
303 Savage	170	SP	24	33.5	748	2090	32,000	NA
30/30 Winchester	150	FP	24	34.5	748	2310	36,000	2390
	170	FP	24	32.0	748	2145	36,000	2200
300 Savage	150	SP	24	42.0	748	2600	41,000	2630
	180	SP	24	44.5	760	2410	41,000	2350
307 Winchester	150	SP	24	44.0	748	2625	44,500	NA
	170	SP	24	41.2	748	2455	44,000	NA
308 Winchester	150	SP	24	48.5	748	2865	48,000	2820
	180	SP	24	46.5	748	2610	48,500	2620
30/40 Krag	180	SP	24	44.5	760	2380	37,000	2430
	220	SP	24	40.5	760	2070	36,000	NA
30/06 Springfield	150	SP	24	54.0	760	2900	48,000	2910
	180	SP	24	53.0	760	2725	50,000	2700
32 Win. Special	170	FP	24	36.2	748	2240	32,500	2250
8mm Mauser	170	SP	24	46.0	748	2410	37,500	2360
338 Win. Mag.	200	SP	24	70.0	760	2900	51,000	2960
	250	SP	24	63.2	760	2545	50,500	2660
35 Remington	200	SP	24	39.0	748	2130	33,000	2080
356 Winchester	220	SP	24	42.1	760	1805	27,500	NA
358 Winchester	200	SP	24	50.6	748	2500	50,000	2490
	250	SP	24	46.2	748	2250	50,500	NA
375 H&H Magnum	270	SP	24	77.5	760	2660	51,000	2690
	300	SP	24	77.5	760	2560	51,500	2530
458 Win. Mag.	500	FMJ	24	73.0	748	2040	39,000	2040

CAUTION: Some of these loads are maximum loads. Start low and work up slowly, being alert for signs of excessive pressure.

B-WEST

Importers of manufactured, not surplus, smokeless powders. BW-36 is a single-base extruded powder ideal for small- and medium-capacity rifle cartridges with light- to medium-weight bullets. Slightly faster burning than IMR-3031. Soon to be available are four shotgun/pistol powders and two medium-capacity rifle powders, a fast pistol powder and an extruded powder similar to IMR-4064.

NORMA

N-201 Primarily for small-bore centerfire competition in cartridges such as 222, 223 or 6mm.

N-202 Typically for 30-caliber hunting or competition as in the 308 or 30-06.

N-204 Intended for use in bottleneck cases with unusually large ratios of powder volume to bullet diameter.

MRP For use in the largest of the big-bore magnum rifles.

R-1 Suitable powder for non-magnum handgun cartridges.

R-123 Designed for magnum handgun cartridges and certain specialized rifle cartridge applications.

THUNDERBIRD CARTRIDGE CO.

Thunderbird offers six powders for reloading use. They are listed here in order of decreasing burning rates. Each powder listed is slower burning than those preceding it and faster than those following it. From Thunderbird Cartridge Co.

T-680: Ball powder designed for 30 M1 Carbine, 7.62x39 and also applicable to 357 and 44 Magnum.

IMR-8208: Short extruded powder that meters well. Applicable to 223, 308, 30-06 and similar cartridges.

BW-36: Clean burning extruded powder with burn rate between IMR-4198 and IMR-3031. Good for 30-30, 308, 30-06, 303 British and 8mm.

T-5020, T-870, T-5070: Slow burning ball powders for belted magnums, over bore capacity rounds with T-5070 for the 50-calibers.

THUNDERBIRD

SELECTED LOADS

Cartridge	Bullet Wgt. Grs.	—Load— Grs.	Powder	MV (fps)	Pressure CUP
50 BMG	700 FB	240	T-5020	3011	48,900
		243	T-5020	3022	49,800
		246	T-5020	3078	52,700
50 BMG	700 FB	230	T-870	2884	45,300
		235	T-870	2949	48,100
		240	T-870	2980	48,900
50 BMG	700 FB	238	T-5070	2919	45,400
		243	T-5070	2970	47,500
		248	T-5070	3012	49,200
		250	T-5070	3046	51,200
50 BMG	750 BT	200	T-5020	2582	39,300
		210	T-5020	2693	43,625
		220	T-5020	2819	45,600
		225	T-5020	2882	48,980
50 BMG	750 BT	220	T-870	2746	43,800
		225	T-870	2837	46,000
		230	T-870	2897	50,280
50 BMG	750 BT	225	T-5070	2774	43,500
		230	T-5070	2880	45,600
		235	T-5070	2900	49,320

FB = Flat Base; BT = Boattail.

CAUTION: Some of these loads are maximum loads. Start low and work up slowly, being alert for signs of excessive pressure.

BOXER PRIMER PRICES												
Primer	CCI	Price	Federal	Price	Fiocchi	Price	Rem.	Price	RWS	Price	Winchester	Price
Large Rifle	200	$19.15/1000	210	$15.98/1000	210	NA	$9^1/_2$	$16.40/1000	5341		WLR	$15.70/1000
Magnum Large Rifle	250	20.15/1000	215	17.98/1000			$9^1/_2$	16.20/1000	5333	$13.25/250	WLRM	16.30/1000
Benchrest Large Rifle	BR2	32.15/1000	210M	22.50/1000								
Small Rifle	400	18.55/1000	200	15.98/1000	200	NA	$6^1/_2$	15.00/1000	4033	13.25/250	WSR	15.00/1000
Magnum Small Rifle	450	20.15/1000	205	17.98/1000								
Benchrest Small Rifle	BR4	30.60/1000	205M	22.50/1000			$7^1/_2$	16.20/1000				
Small Pistol	500	18.55/1000	100	15.98/1000	100	NA	$1^1/_2$	15.00/1000	4031	13.25/250	WSP	15.00/1000
Magnum Small Pistol	550	20.15/1000							4047	13.25/250	WSPM	16.30/1000
Large Pistol	300	19.15/1000	150	15.98/1000	150	NA	$2^1/_2$	16.40/1000	5337	13.25/250	WLP	15.70/1000
Magnum Large Pistol	350	20.15/1000	155	17.98/1000								
50 BMG	35	20.50/100							8212	10.45/50		
Shotshell	209	NA	209A	NA	209	NA	209	NA			W209	25.80/1000
	209M	NA			410	NA					AATP	28.00/1000
Percussion Caps	11	28.85/1000					10, 11	24.00/1000				

DYNAMIT NOBEL Berdan Primers								
Primer #	Min. Dia.		Max. Hgt.		Base Thickness		Description	Price/Per
	mm	in.	mm	in.	mm	in.		
4506	4,50	.177	2,20	.09	0,40	.0157	25 ACP, 32, 380 ACP, some 9mm	$8.40/250
4520	4,50	.177	2,10	.08	0,55	.0217	Small rifle, 22 Hornet, 222 Rem., 5.6	8.40/250
4521	4,50	.177	2,20	.09	0,40	.0151	9mm Luger (9x19), Steyr	8.40/250
5005	5,00	.197	2,20	.09	0,40	.0157	Non-standard, large caliber pistol	8.40/250
5608	5,50	.217	2,80	.11	0,70	.0276	7.62 NATO	9.35/250
5620	5,50	.217	2,65	.10	0,60	.0236		9.35/250
6000	6,34	.250	2,95	.11	0,79	.031	Large dia. for 303 British	9.35/150
6504	6,45	.254	2,35	.09	0,45	.0177	Fits most .254 dia. primed rounds; 577/450, 11.15x58R, etc.	9.35/150
6507	6,45	.254	3,40	.133	0,33	.013	Exact replacement for Eley No. 172 for 500 3", 577 Nitro, etc.	5.00/150

DYNAMIT NOBEL

Berdan Primers

Berdan primers available for small and large pistol; small and large rifle. See chart for specifications and prices. Come in boxes of 250 and 150. From The Old Western Scrounger.

M&D MUNITIONS

Lead Free Primers

M&D offers lead free small pistol primers for reloading. Come in boxes of 1,000. From M&D Munitions, Ltd.

Price: **$17.50**

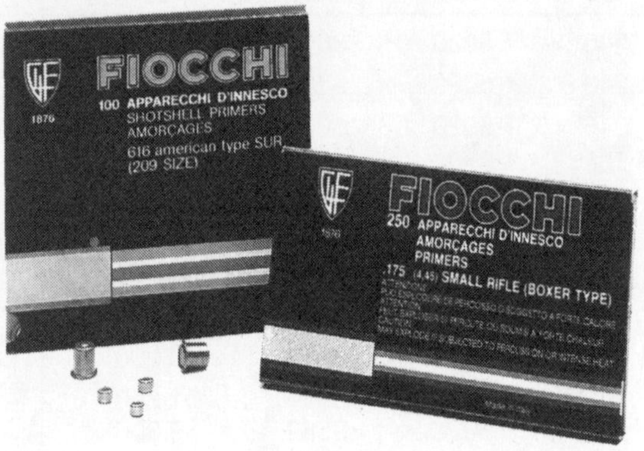

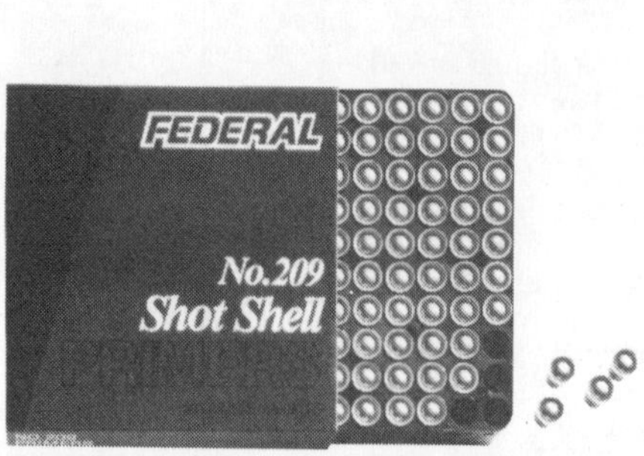

E. ARTHUR BROWN

445 SuperMag Brass

Made from new 30-40 Krag brass trimmed to 1.610"; expanded to slightly under chamber dimensions; neck-reamed to .430 inside diameter; rims turned to .058 thickness; rim diameter reduced to .510; primer pockets reamed to proper depth. From E. Arthur Brown Company.

Price: 50 . . . . **$54.95**
Price: 250 . . . . **$209.95**

BRUNO SHOOTER'S SUPPLY

Lapua and PPC Brass

Bruno supplies Sako PPC and Lapua brass. From Bruno Shooter's Supply.

Price: PPC, per case . . . . **$.79**
Price: Lapua, 1-449 cases, ea. **$1.10**
Price: Lapua, 450-999, ea. **$1.04**
Price: Lapua, 1000+, ea. **$1.00**

BULL-X

Processed, commercial or military once-fired brass in 9mm, 38 Special, 45 ACP or 308 calibers. From Bull-X, Inc.

Price: . . . . **See chart.**

BUZZTAIL BRASS

Pre-formed cases using new factory brass. All cases 90% formed to chamber specifications. From Buzztail Brass.

Price: . . . . **See chart.**

A-SQUARE *Unprimed Brass*

Caliber	Packaging	Price
280 Ross	B	$46.00
7mm STW	W	32.00
338 A-Square	B	27.50
375 NE 2 1/2"	B	40.00
375 Weath.	B	35.00
375 JRS	B	35.00
375 A-Square	W	27.50
375 Flanged	B	48.00
378 Weatherby	W	26.00
45 Basic	B	43.00
450/400 (3")	W	45.00
416 Chapius	W	47.00
416 Taylor	B	37.50
416 Remington	B	34.50
416 Hoffman	B	34.50
416 Rigby	W	42.00
416 Weatherby	W	26.00
404 Jeffery	W	42.00
405 Basic	B	44.00
425 Express	B	37.50
43 Spanish	B	44.00
11mm Beaumont	B	44.00
11mm Mauser	B	44.00
450 NE(3 1/4")	W	47.00
450 #2	W	48.00
458 Lott	B	34.50
450 Ackley	B	34.00
458 Winchester	B	12.00
460 Short A-Square	W	28.50
460 Weatherby	W	27.00
470 NE	W	47.00
470 Capstick	B	34.00
475 #2	W	50.00
495 A-Square	W	28.50
50 Basic	B	44.00
500/465 NE	W	48.00
505 Gibbs	W	59.00
500 NE (3")	B	49.00
500 A-Square	W	28.50
577 NE	W	58.00
600 NE	W	70.00
H&H Cylindrical	B	32.50

B= Plastic box of 20 rounds; W = Plastic wallet of 10 rounds.

BUZZTAIL *Pre-Formed Factory Cases*

Caliber	Price/20	Caliber	Price/20
17 Mach IV	$18.00	7mm STW	20.00
219 Donaldson Wasp	20.00	7mm JRS	20.00
219 Zipper	20.00	7-30 Waters	20.00
219 Zipper Ackley Imp.	20.00	7mm TCU	20.00
22 BR	22.00	7mm Gibbs	20.00
22 Cheetah MkI Lg. Primer	20.00	7x57 Ackley Imp.	18.00
22 Cheetah MkI Sm. Primer	25.00	7mmx300 Weatherby	20.00
22-250 Ackley Imp.	18.00	7mm-08 Ackley Imp.	18.00
243 Ackley Imp.	18.00	7mm-300 Winchester	20.00
6mm-284	20.00	7-45mm	18.00
6mm TCU	18.00	7-47mm	18.00
6mm-257 Ackley Imp.	20.00	300 Jarrett	20.00
240 Page Super Pooper	20.00	30 Gibbs	20.00
240 Gibbs	20.00	30-30 Ackley Imp.	20.00
6mm Int'l. Walker	20.00	30 Herrett	20.00
6mm-45mm	18.00	308 Ackley Imp.	18.00
6mm-47mm	18.00	30-06 Ackley Imp.	18.00
6mm-250	18.00	30-284	20.00
6mm-250 Ackley Imp.	18.00	30-257R	18.00
6mm-222	18.00	30-257 Ackley Imp.	20.00
6mm Ackley Imp.	18.00	30-378 Weatherby	42.00
243 Super Rockchucker	18.00	30x338	20.20
257 Weatherby (Rem)	20.00	8mm-06	18.00
25 Gibbs	20.00	8mm-06 Ackley Imp.	18.00
257 Ackley Imp.	20.00	8mm Gibbs	18.00
25-06 Ackley Imp.	18.00	8mm-300 Winchester	20.00
25-45mm	18.00	8mm-300 Weatherby	30.00
25-47mm	18.00	8mm-7 Magnum	20.00
6.5mm Gibbs	20.00	8mm Ackley Imp.	18.00
6.5-06	18.00	338-06	18.00
6.5-06 Ackley Imp.	18.00	338-06 Ackley Imp.	18.00
6.5-284	20.00	338-08 Ackley Imp.	18.00
6.5 TCU	18.00	338-300 Winchester	20.00
6.5-257R	18.00	338-378 Weatherby	42.00
6.5-257 Ackley Imp.	20.00	338-378 KT	42.00
6.5-308	18.00	338 Gibbs	20.00
6.5-308 Ackley Imp.	18.00	338-378 Kubla Kahn	42.00
6.5-45mm	18.00	35 Gibbs	20.00
6.5-47mm	18.00	35 Whelen	18.00
270 Ackley Imp.	18.00	35 Whelen Ackley Imp.	18.00
270-284	18.00	357 Herrett	20.00
270-257R	18.00	375 Weatherby	28.00
270-257 Ackley Imp.	20.00	375 ICL	20.00
270-308	18.00	375-06	18.00
270-45mm	18.00	375-06 Ackley Imp.	18.00
270-47mm	18.00	416 Rigby	48.00
270 Gibbs	20.00	416 Taylor	20.00
280 Ackley Imp.	18.00	445 Super Magnum	24.00

A-Square Brass and Ammo

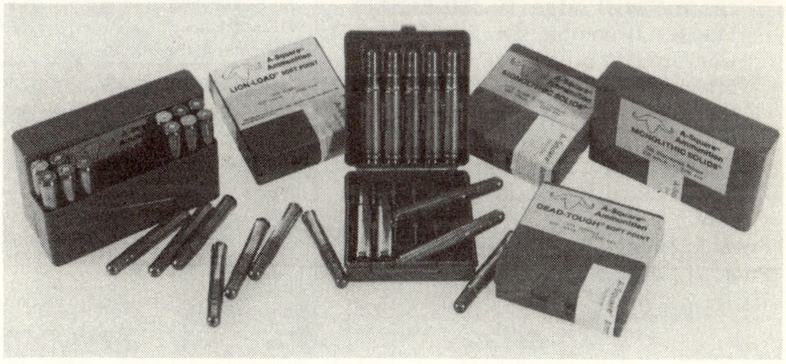

BULL-X *Once Fired Pistol Brass*

Caliber	Price 500	Price 1000	Comments
9mm Military	$25.00	$49.00	Inspected, deprimed, crimp removed, polished
38 Special	$16.00	$30.00	Polished, inspected
45 ACP Military	$35.00	$68.00	Inspected, deprimed, crimp removed, polished
308 Military	$25.00	$45.00	Polished, inspected

CANYON CARTRIDGE

9mm Brass

9mm American-made brass made to Nato and SAAMI specifications. From Canyon Cartridge Corporation.

Price: . . . . **Contact manufacturer.**

CLASSIC BRASS

6mm Classic

American-made 6mm brass similar in dimension to 220 Russian. Available in any quantity. From Classic Brass.

Price: 100 cases **$135.00**

DKT

Brass

New, fully formed brass ready for fire-forming. From DKT, Inc.

Price: . . . . **See chart.**

FREEDOM ARMS

454 Casull Brass

Alloyed unprimed brass cases for 454 Casull with small primer pockets. Come in packages of 50. From Freedom Arms, Inc.

Price: **$25.75**

GOODWIN

New Cases for Obsolete Calibers

Solid head cases turned from bar stock and adapted for U.S. Boxer primers. From Jack First Distributors, Inc.

Price: Each **$2.60**

HARDIN

7.62mm and 44 AutoMag Cases

Primarily manufacturers of casings for ChiCim Tokarev 7.62mm and 44-caliber AutoMag pistols. 7.62mm casing will also fit 30-caliber Mauser Broomhandle. Hand-made from surplus military or commercial brass. All cases full-length sized, have military primer crimp removed and tumble cleaned. Packed fifty to a box and priced per 100. From Hardin Specialty Distributors.

Price: 7.62mm/30 Mauser **$12.50**
Price: 44 AutoMag **$14.50**

BERTRAM *Obsolete Rifle Cases*

Case	Price/20	Case	Price/20
—RIFLE—			
222 Rimmed	$27.50	375 Flanged	$56.98
22-15-60	27.50	38-56 WCF	31.98
5.6x33R Rook	27.50	38-72 WCF Basic	29.98
5.6 Von Hofe Rimmed	38.98	400-375 Belted	38.98
240 Flanged	38.98	400 N.E. 3"	38.98
240 Belted	38.98	400-350	38.98
28-30 Stevens	38.98	400-360 Purdy	38.98
25-25 Stevens	38.98	400-360 Westley Richards	38.98
25-21 Stevens	38.98	40-65 WCF	31.98
25-20 Single Shot	27.50	40-72 WCF	29.98
6.5x58R	38.98	40-82 WCF	31.98
6.5x70R	38.98	405 WCF	29.98
7x33 Sako	38.98	405 Basic 3¹/₄"	29.98
7mm Rigby Thick	38.98	40-90 3¹/₄"	29.98
7mm H&H Thin	38.98	43 Spanish	29.98
7x72R	38.98	11mm 43 Mauser	29.98
30-30 Basic 3¹/₄"	29.98	9.5x47R	29.98
310 Cadet	15.98	10.3x65R Baenziger	29.98
300 Sherwood	27.98	45-90 WCF	29.98
318 Rimless	38.98	45 Basic 2.6"	29.98
300 Rook	27.98	45 Basic 3¹/₄"	56.98
32 Ideal	38.98	450 N.E. Thin	56.98
8x64 Brenneke	38.98	450 N.E. Thick	56.98
8x56R Hungarian	31.98	500 N.E. Basic	56.98
8x58R Danish	31.98	50 Sharps Basic	56.98
33 WCF	31.98	50-110 WCF	56.98
360 Nitro	38.98	577 N.E.	74.98
35 WCF	31.98	577-450 MH	92.98
350 Rigby	60.98	577-500 NE	74.98
375 Flanged 2¹/₂"	38.98	600 NE	109.48/10

From Huntington Die Specialties.

BERTRAM *Pistol Cases*

Case	Price/20
PISTOL	
310 Cattle Killer	$15.98
7.5mm Swedish Nagant	15.98
7.62mm Russian Nagant	15.98
30 Mauser	17.50
9mm Browning	15.98
41 Long Colt	17.50
11.75mm Montenegrin	17.50

From Huntington Die Specialties.

Bertram Brass

WALTER GEHMANN *Obsolete Rifle Brass*

Case	Price/20
5.6x61 Vom Hofe	$31.98
7x66 Vom Hofe	33.98
7x75R	31.98

From Huntington Die Specialties.

GOODWIN Cases

- 450-400 2³/₄"
- 11mm Gras
- 11mm Mauser
- 43 Egyptian
- 43 Spanish
- 11.43x55R Turkish
- 577-450 Martini Henry
- #2 Musket
- 461-#1-Gibbs
- 50-70 Government
- 50-110 WCF
- 577 Snider

EICHELBERGER *14-Caliber Formed Cases*

Case	Price/50
14 Dart	$21.50
14 Hornet	24.50
14 Bee	24.50
14 Carbine	22.75
14/221	24.50
14/222	24.50
14/222	24.50

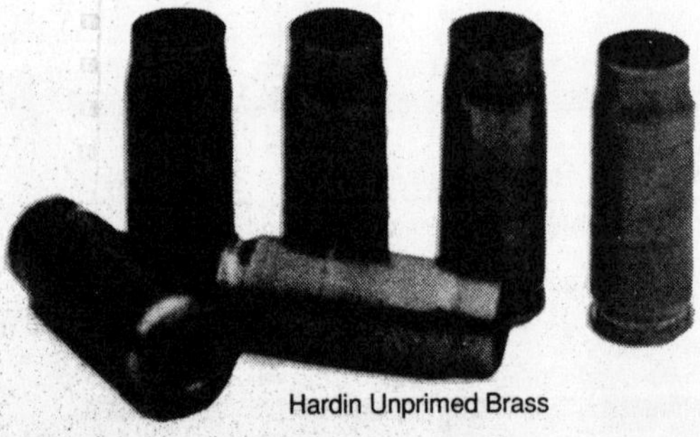

Hardin Unprimed Brass

DKT, INC. *New Formed Brass*

Caliber	Price/20
14 Flea	$30.00
14 Walker Hornet	26.25
14-221	26.25
17 Ackley Hornet	15.00
17 K-Hornet	15.00
17 Bumble Bee	18.75
17 Ackley Bee	18.75
17-221	15.00
17 Mach IV	15.00
17-222 Magnum	18.75
17-223	15.00
17-225 Ackley	18.75
20-222	18.75
20-223	18.75
22 WCF	18.75
5.6x35R Vierling	18.75
5.7mm Spitfire	15.00
22-15-60	45.00
22-3000	33.75
2R Lovell	33.75
22 Jet	26.25
219 Donaldson Wasp	18.75
219 Zipper	16.50
219 Ackley Zipper	16.50
219 Improved Zipper	16.50
22-454 Casull	26.25
22 Cheetah Mach I	30.00
22-284	18.75
5.6x50mm	24.00
5.6x50R Magnum	24.00
5.6x57mm	30.00
5.6x57R	30.00
5.6x61mm SE Vom Hofe	45.00
5.6x61R SE Vom Hofe	48.75
6mm TCU	13.13
6x47mm	13.13
6mmx30-30 Ackley	15.00
6mm Lee Navy	18.75
244 Krag	18.75
240 Page Super Pooper	18.75
244 Ackley Improved	13.13
6mm Mashburn Improved	13.13
6mm-284	15.00
6mm-06	13.13
240 Apex	22.50
240 Cobra	15.00
6x61mm Sharpe & Hart	37.50
256 Winchester	26.25
8x58R Danish Krag	26.25
8x60J	22.50
8x60JR	26.25
8x60S	24.75
8x60RS	26.25
8mm Kropatchek	26.25
8mm-06	15.00
8mm-06 Improved	15.00
8mm Gibbs	18.75
8x64S	26.25
8x68S Magnum	30.00
8x72R	45.00
8.15x46R	26.25
8.15x53R Finnish	26.25
333 OKH	15.00
33 WCF	26.25
338 Woodswalker	22.50
338-350 Remington	26.25
338-378 KT	45.00
8.63x56R	56.25
35 S&W Auto	18.75
35 WSL	18.75
351 WSL	18.75
9mm Bergmann/Bayard	26.25
9mm Browning Long	26.25
9mm Japanese Revolver	30.00
9x56mm Mannlicher	22.50
9x57mm Mauser	18.75
9x57R Mauser	22.50
357/44 Bain & Davis	18.75
357 Auto Mag	41.25
357 Peterbuilt	22.50
357 Herrett	15.00
358 JDJ	15.00
35 Winchester	33.75
35-284	22.50
35 Whelen Improved	15.00
35 Ackley Short Magnum	26.25
35 Newton	48.75
9.3x64mm	33.75
9.3x72R	26.25
360 NE No. 2	93.75
9.5x57mm	22.50
375 Super Magnum	15.00
375 JDJ	15.00
375 JRS	15.00
375-284 Winchester	18.75
375 Flanged H&H Mag	56.25
375 Weatherby	37.50
297/250 Rook	22.50
25-20 Single Shot	30.00
25-21 Stevens	45.00
25-25 Stevens	45.00
25 Remington	18.75
25-25 Ackley	15.00
25-36 Marlin	18.75
25 Souper	15.00
257 Ackley Improved	15.00
25-284	15.00
25-06 Mashburn	13.13
6.5mm TCU	13.13
6.5x53R Dutch	18.75
6.5x53.5 Daudeteau	30.00
6.5x54mm Mannlicher	26.25
6.5 JDJ	15.00
6.5x57mm	24.75
6.5x57R	24.75
6.5x58R	45.00
6.5x444	15.00
256 Newton	22.50
6.5x257	15.00
6.5x284	15.00
6.5-06	15.00
6.5-06 Ackley Improved	15.00
6.5x68mm	30.00
6.5x68R	30.00
270 Ren	18.75
270 JDJ	15.00
270-284	15.00
7mm TCU	11.25
7x45 Ingram	13.13
7mm Super Mag	15.00
7R (7mm IHMSA)	13.13
7-30 JDJ	15.00
7mmx444	15.00
7x57R	22.50
7x57 Improved	15.00
7mm-06	15.00
7mm-06 Improved	15.00
7x64mm	22.50
7x65R	26.25
7x72R	30.00
7x75mm Vom Hofe SE	45.00
7x75R Vom Hofe SE	37.50
276 Dubiel	26.25
7mm-300 Weatherby	22.50
275 H&H Magnum	26.25
28-30-120	45.00
280 Ross Rimmed	75.00
280 Ross	75.00
7.35 Carcano	18.75
7.65mm MAS	22.50
30 Herrett	15.00
375 H&H Ackley Imp	22.50
38/56 WCF	26.25
38/70 WCF	33.75
38/72	37.50
401 Herter Power-Mag	63.75
401 WSL	30.00
40-60 WCF	22.50
40-60 Marlin	22.50
40-65 WCF	26.25
40-70 WCF	33.75
40-70 Sharps Straight	30.00
40-70 Sharps BN	33.75
40-72 WCF	37.50
40-82 WCF	33.75
40-90 Sharps BN	33.75
10mm Wildey Magnum	22.50
405 WCF	33.75
400 Nitro 3"	30.00
450/400 Nitro 3"	93.75
450/400 Nitro 3 1/4"	93.75
411 JDJ	15.00
411 KDF	30.00
416 JDJ	18.75
416/338	26.25
416 Taylor	48.75
416 Remington	37.50
416 Hoffman	45.00
416 Rigby	56.25
404 Jeffrey	48.75
425 Wesley-Richards	56.25
11mm French Ord. Revolver	15.00
11mm German Service Rev.	15.00
11mm Wildey Magnum	22.50
43 Berdan	37.50
44 Evans Short	22.50
44 Evans Long	22.50
44 American	37.50
44 Auto Mag	37.50
445 Super Magnum	22.50
10.75x65R Collath	33.75
43 Spanish	22.75
11x59R Gras	45.00
43 Egyptian	63.75
43 Mauser	33.75
11x50R	33.75
11x52R Beaumont	63.75
44-77 Sharps & Remington	33.75
11.15x65R	37.50
11.2x60mm Mauser	67.50
11.2x72mm Schuler	67.50
454 Casull	33.75
455 Colt	15.00
455 Webley Auto	15.00
45/60 WCF	26.25
30 Wildey Magnum	22.50
7.63mm Mannlicher	26.25
30-223	15.00
30-30 Ackley Improved	13.13
7.5x54mm MAS	18.75
309 JDJ	15.00
30-284 Winchester	15.00
30 Gibbs	18.75
30-338	15.00
30 Newton	48.75
310 Cadet	18.75
303 British Improved	15.00
32 Ideal	45.00
32-40 WCF	15.00
32-40 Remington	26.25
32 Remington	15.00
8mm Roth-Steyr	15.00
8mm Nambu	26.25
7.92x33 Kurz	18.75
8x48R Sauer	33.75
8x50R	18.75
8x50R Siamese	18.75
8x51 Level Rifle	22.50
8x51 Mauser	18.75
8x51R Mauser	18.75
8x52R Siamese	22.50
8x53R Murata	30.00
8x54 Krag	26.25
8x56mm Mannlicher	22.50
8x56R Hungarian	26.25
8mm JDJ	15.00
8x57J	18.75
8x57JR	26.25
8x57JRS	24.00
8x57R/360	33.75
8x58R Sauer	33.75
45/70 WCF Group I/II	11.25
45/70 Group III	15.00
45/75 WCF	30.00
45/90 WCF	33.75
45/120 3 1/4" Sharps	63.75
577/450 Martini-Henry	63.75
450/348	30.00
450 Alaskan	30.00
458x2" American	26.25
450 Watts	37.50
450 NE 3 1/4	60.00
450 NE No.2	105.00
500-450 NE 3 1/4"	105.00
450 Ackley Magnum	37.50
470 Nitro Express	67.50
475 Nitro Express	105.00
475 Wildey	22.50
475 JDJ	18.75
475 Magnum	22.50
50 Special	37.50
500 Magnum	37.50
50 Carbine	28.13
50-70 Springfield/Sharps	28.13
50-90 Sharps	28.13
50-95 WCF	30.00
50-110 WCF	30.00
50-140 3 1/4"	56.25
500 NE 3"	67.50
500 NE 3 1/4"	67.50
505 Gibbs	67.50
577/500 Magnum 3"	90.00
577 Snider	56.25
577 Jurras	63.75
577 NE	105.00
600 NE	150.00
70-150 Winchester Express	15.00

IMPERIAL

Unprimed Brass

Unprimed brass for reloading Imperial magnum cartridges: 7mm Imperial Magnum, 300 Imperial Magnum; 311 Imperial Magnum, 338 Imperial Magnum and 360 Imperial Magnum. Load data supplied with purchase. RCBS dies for these cartridges available from Imperial. From Imperial Magnum Corporation.

Price: . . . . **Contact manufacturer.**

O'CONNOR

Steel Head Cases

High performance cartridge cases with stainless steel heads and brass bodies. Fine-pitch pipe threads on the brass bodies screw into the tempered steel heads. Both 30-06 and magnum heads machined with large rifle primer pockets. Bodies are 2.35" ('06) and 2.45" (magnum) long and annealed for case forming. Available as formed cases in 30-06, 270 Win., 280 Rem., 300 Win. Mag., 8mm Rem. Mag., 338 Win. Mag., 375 H&H Mag., 458 Win. Mag. or straight-sided in .469" diameter rimless and belted magnum .530" at belt. Come in 5-case pack. From O'Connor Rifle Products Co., Ltd.

Price: Formed cases, 30-06, 270 Win., 280 Rem. **$16.95**
Price: Formed cases, 300 Win. Mag., 8mm Rem. Mag., 338 Win. Mag., 375 H&H Mag., 458 Win. Mag. . **$18.95**
Price: .469" **$14.95**
Price: .530" **$16.95**
Price: Replacement brass, formed standard cals. **$6.95**
Price: Replacement brass, formed magnum **$8.95**
Price: Replacement brass, unformed standard cals. **$4.95**
Price: Replacement brass, unformed magnum **$6.95**

RED WILLOW

Obsolete Cartridge Cases

Full line of obsolete and European cases. Will custom headstamp up to twelve letters and make custom cases, initial run 200. From Red Willow Tool & Armory.

Price: Custom headstamp **$150.00**
Price: Cases . . . . **See chart.**

Imperial Brass

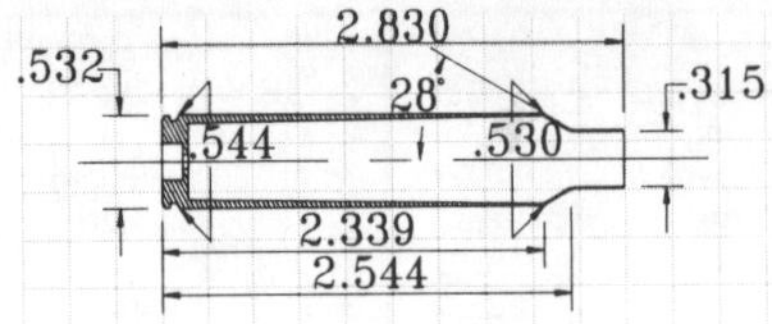

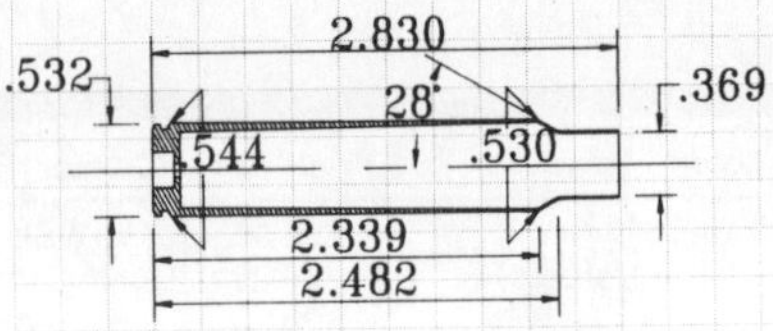

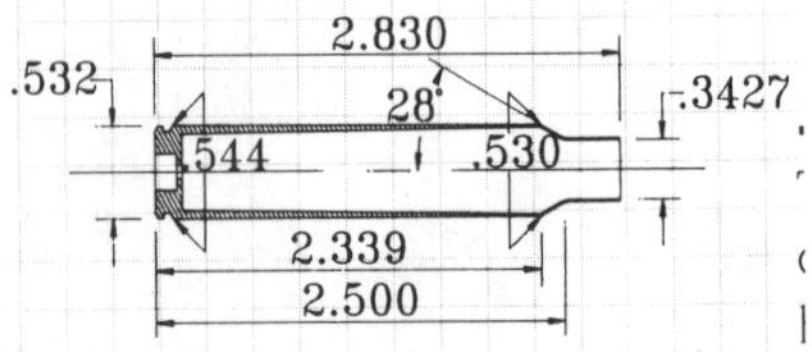

O'Connor Steelhead Cases

HUNTINGTON

Case	Price/20
280 Ross	$46.98
280 Ross Basic	46.98
375 Flanged	46.98
404 Jeffrey	46.98
404 Jeffrey Basic	46.98
405 Winchester Basic	46.98
460 Weatherby Basic	46.98
11mm Beaumont	46.98
450 Basic .040" Rim	46.98
450 Basic .060"	46.98
450-400 3 1/4"	49.98

From Huntington Die Specialties.

RED WILLOW TOOL & ARMORY *Obsolete and European Brass*

Case	Price/20	Case	Price/20
25-20 Single Shot	$29.00	44-90/44-100 Remington	40.00
25-21	29.00	45-60 Winchester	33.00
6.5x72R	33.00	45-70 Government	31.00
32-40 Winchester	33.00	45-75 Winchester	33.00
33 Winchester	33.00	45-100 Sharps Straight	44.00
35 Winchester	33.00	45-90 Winchester	44.00
38-56 Winchester	33.00	45-120 3 1/4 Sharps	44.00
38-70 Winchester	33.00	45-125/300 Winchester	50.00
38-72 Winchester	33.00	50-70 Government	33.00
41 Long Colt	20.00	50-95 Winchester	34.00
40-50 Sharps	33.00	50-90 Sharps	41.50
40-50 Sharps Necked	33.00	11mm Beaumont	41.50
40-60 Winchester	33.00	50-110 Winchester	41.50
40-63 (40-70) Ballard	38.00	50-140 Sharps	47.00
40-65 Winchester	33.00	58 U.S. Musket	50.00
40-70 Maynard (1873)	50.65	375 H&H Flanged	44.00
40-70 Winchester	38.00	9.3x72R	48.00
40-70 Sharps Necked	38.00	404 Jeffrey	55.00
40-70 Sharps Straight	38.00	450 Nitro Express 3 1/4	48.00
40-72 Winchester	38.00	577-450	43.00
40-82 Winchester	38.00	500 Nitro Express 3"	53.00
40-90 Sharps Necked	40.00	500 Nitro 3 1/4	56.00
11.15x60R Mauser	33.00	500/450 No. 1 Express	53.00
40-90 Sharps Straight	40.00	505 Gibbs	60.00
40-85 Ballard	40.00	577 Snider	40.00
401 Winchester	23.00	577 Basic	60.00
405 Winchester	33.00	12-Bore	100.00*
405 Basic	40.00	775 Express	200.00
43 Basic	33.00	8-Bore Rifel	100.00*
44-77 Sharps & Remington	33.00	4-Bore Rifle	140.00*
44-90 Sharps	33.00	4-Bore Shotgun	140.00*

* Price for 10.

Norma Brass

NORMA *Unprimed Rifle Brass*

Case	Price/100
22 Savage High Power	$68.98
6.5x50 Japanese	54.98
6.5x52 Carcano	55.98
6.5x55	54.98
7x57R	63.98
7x61 Sharp & Hart	67.98
7.5x55 Swiss	61.98
7.62x54R Russian	59.98
308 Norma Magnum	70.98
7.65x53 Argentine	54.98
7.7x58 Japanese	52.98
358 Norma	67.98
9.3x62	52.98
9.3x74R	59.98
416 Rigby	134.95
375 Cylinderical	31.98/20

From Huntington Die Specialties.

NORMA *Brass*

Case	Price/20
220 Swift	$13.98
222 Remington	9.98
22-250 Savage	12.98
243 Winchester	12.98
5.6mmx52R	15.75
6.5mm Japanese	14.75
6.5mm Carcano	14.75
6.5mm Swedish	14.75
270 Winchester	13.00
7mm Remington Magnum	17.60
7mmx57R	16.35
7.5mm Swiss	16.25
7x61 Sharpe & Hart	17.85
7x64 Brenneke	14.75
308 Winchester	13.20
308 Norma Magnum	18.95
7.62x54R Russian	15.98
30-06	13.60
300 Winchester Magnum	18.98
303 British	18.98
7.65 Argentine	14.50
7.7 Japanese	14.50
338 Winchester Magnum	16.60
358 Norma Magnum	17.98
9.3x62 Mauser	14.25
9.3x74R	15.75
375 H&H Magnum	16.60
416 Rigby	45.00

From The Old Western Scrounger.

HUNTINGTON *Miscellaneous Brass*

ase	Price/Per	Manufacturer
40 Belted Rimless N.E.	$19.98/20	Kynoch, Boxer primed
0.3x60	60.98	B.E.L.L., basic formed cases
25 Westley Richards Basic	56.98	B.E.L.L.
01 Winchester SL	34.98/50	B.E.L.L., formed cases
2 Gauge	24.98	B.E.L.L.
0 Mauser	28.98/50	Fiocchi
x21	8.50/50	Tanfoglio
45 Super Magnum	16.98/50	Starline
23 Remington	20.50/100	IMI, unprimed
08 Winchester	30.65/100	IMI, unprimed
0-06	30.65/100	IMI, unprimed
.62x39	23.50/100	IMI, unprimed
0 BMG	89.15/50	IMI, unprimed

rom Huntington Die Specialties.

REMINGTON/WINCHESTER *Unprimed Brass*

Case	Price/Per	Case	Price/Per
17 Rem.	$8.00/20	30 Rem.	$8.00/20
22 Hornet	11.50/50	30-30 Win.	5.70/20
222 Rem.	5.00/20	30-40 Krag	5.70/20
222 Rem. Mag.	7.00/20	300 Savage	8.00/20
223 Rem.	6.00/20	308 Win.	7.65/20
225 Win.	7.65/20	30-06 Spfld.	7.65/20
22-250 Rem.	7.65/20	300 Win. Mag.	7.65/20
243 Win.	7.65/20	300 Wea. Mag.	9.00/20
6mm Rem.	7.65/20	303 British	8.00/20
6mm BR	8.25/20	32-20 Win.	9.30/50
257 Roberts	7.65/20	32-40 Win.	19.00/20
250 Savage	8.00/20	32 Win. Spl.	8.40/20
25-06 Rem.	7.95/20	8mm Mauser	8.00/20
25-20 Win.	8.25/50	8mm Rem. Mag.	7.25/20
25-35 Win.	9.20/20	338 Win. Mag.	10.00/20
6.5mm Rem. Mag.	9.20/20	348 Win.	9.25/20
264 Win. Mag.	6.60/20	38-55 Win.	8.40/20
270 Win.	8.00/20	35 Rem.	8.00/20
7mm Mauser	8.00/20	35 Whelen	8.00/20
7mm BR	11.00/20	350 Rem. Mag.	10.00/20
7mm-08 Rem.	8.00/20	375 H&H Mag.	11.00/20
7.62x39	5.25/20	416 Rem. Mag.	10.45/20
280 Rem.	8.00/20	444 Marlin	10.00/20
7mm Rem. Mag.	10.00/20	45-70 Gov't	9.25/20
30 M1 Carbine	10.00/50		

From The Old Western Scrounger.

THE OLD WESTERN SCROUNGER *Miscellaneous Brass*

Case	Description	Price/Per
38 Special	TRounds	$12.50/20
40 S&W	One fired.	7.00/50
401 Winchester S.L.		55.00/50
450 N.E.	Thin rim.	61.00/20
475 #2 N.E.		85.00/20
470 Capstick		48.75/20
50-70 Gov't.		17.25/20
50 BMG	New IMI	26.50/20
50	Basic 3.25" Eldorado	65.00/20
7mmx66 Vom Hoffe	Once fired	20.00/20
7mmx75 Vom Hoffe	Once fired	20.00/20
14 ga. Greener	Primed brass	2.50/1
14.5 Russian		5.00/1
20mmx103	Electric primed	3.00/1

From The Old Western Scrounger.

THUNDERBIRD CARTRIDGE

50-Caliber Brass

Thunderbird offers 50-caliber cleaned military brass, ready to load military brass and primed 50-caliber military brass. Come 100 cases to a bag. From Thunderbird Cartridge Co., Inc.

Price: Cleaned **$22.00**
Price: Ready to load **$49.00**
Price: Primed **$69.00**

VOM HOFE

Brass

Brass cases for 5.6mmx61, 7mmx66 and 7mmx75R Vom Hofe. Come 20 to a box. From The Old Western Scrounger.

Price: 5.6x61, 7mmx75R **$31.65**
Price: 7mmx66 . . . . **$36.00**

RWS *Formed Cases*

Case	Price/20
—RIFLE—	
22 Hornet	$19.10
222 Remington	19.95
223 Remington	20.45
5.6x50 Magnum	18.50
5.6x50R Magnum	18.50
5.6x52R	22.00
5.6x57	26.20
5.6x57R	26.20
243 Winchester	24.65
6.5x54 MS	22.30
6.5x55 Swedish	20.15
6.5x57	20.15
6.5x57R	20.15
6.5x65	25.00
6.5x65R	25.00
6.5x68S	29.40
6.5x68R	29.40
270 Winchester	24.25
7x57	20.15
7x57R	20.15
7x64	20.15
7x65R	20.15
280 Remington	33.00
7mm Remington Magnum	35.50
308 Winchester	21.85
300 Winchester Magnum	33.00
7.5x55 Swiss	30.25
8x57JS	21.00
8x57JR (.318")	21.00
8x57JRS	21.00
8x60S	32.70
8x68S	31.05
9.3x62	23.85
9.3x64	26.00
9.3x72R (.364")	22.70
9.3x74R	26.00
375 H&H	31.70
—PISTOL—	
30 Luger	18.85
9x18 Ultra	18.85
9x21 Police	20.00

From Huntington Die Specialties.

REMINGTON *Nickel-Plated Rifle Brass*

Case	TOWS Price/Per	——HDS—— Price/100	Price/250	Price/500
17 Rem.	17.50/50	21.70	49.98	92.85
22 Hornet	13.50/50	11.70	26.98	49.98
220 Swift		21.70	49.98	92.85
222 Rem.	7.00/20	13.35	30.80	57.15
222 Rem. Mag.		18.35	42.30	78.60
223 Rem.	7.00/20	13.35	30.80	57.15
22-250 Rem.	9.65/20	18.35	42.30	78.60
243 Win.	9.65/20	19.98	46.15	85.75
6mm Rem.	9.65/20	19.98	46.15	85.75
25-20 Win.	11.90/50	13.35	30.80	57.15
257 Roberts	9.65/20	21.70	49.98	92.98
6.5 Rem. Mag.		29.98	69.25	128.98
264 Win. Mag.		29.98	69.25	128.98
250 Savage	10.00/20	24.98	57.98	107.15
25-06 Rem.	10.00/20	24.98	57.98	107.15
270 Win.	10.00/20	19.98	46.15	85.75
7x57 Mauser	10.00/20	24.98	56.98	104.98
7mm BR	13.00/20	31.98	71.98	133.98
7mm-08 Rem.	10.00/20	23.98	53.98	99.98
280 Rem.	10.00/20	23.98	53.98	99.98
7mm Rem. Mag.	12.00/20	29.98	67.98	125.98
7mm Wea. Mag.		36.98	84.98	157.98
30 M1 Carbine	12.00/50	10.98	23.98	44.98
30 Rem.		19.98	45.98	84.98
30-30 Win.	7.70/20	14.98	34.98	63.98
300 Savage	10.00/20			
308 Win.	9.65/20	20.98	48.98	89.98
30-06	9.65/20	20.98	47.98	88.98
300 H&H		32.98	74.98	138.98
300 Win. Mag.	9.65/20	30.98	70.98	130.98
300 Wea. Mag.	13.00/20	36.98	84.98	157.98
303 British	10.00/20	21.98	48.98	90.98
32-20 Win.	11.30/50	13.98	31.98	57.98
8mmx57 Mauser	10.00/20	23.98	55.98	102.98
8mm Rem. Mag.		32.98	74.98	139.98
338 Win. Mag.	13.00/20	30.98	70.98	130.98
35 Rem.	10.00/20	23.98	55.98	102.98
350 Mag.		30.98	70.98	130.98
35 Whelen	10.00/20	24.98	56.98	104.98
375 H&H Mag.		35.98	82.98	153.98
416 Rem. Mag.	13.95/20	39.98	94.98	175.98
444 Marlin	12.00/20	29.98	67.98	125.98
44-40 WCF		14.98	32.98	60.98
45-70 Gov't	12.00/20	32.98	75.98	140.98
458 Win. Mag.		35.98	82.98	153.98

TOWS = The Old Western Scrounger; HDS = Huntington Die Specialties.

THUNDERBIRD *Once-Fired Brass*

Case	Price/M
357 Magnum	$85.00
10mm	115.00
44 Magnum	109.00
45 ACP	107.00
22-250	129.00
30 Carbine	99.00

PRECISION RELOADING *Once-Fired Brass*

Caliber	Price/100
218 Bee	$14.00
22 Hornet	9.00
25-20	9.00
223 Remington	5.00
22/250 Remington	15.00
243 Winchester	11.00
270 Winchester	7.00
7mm Remington Magnum	12.00
300 Winchester Magnum	16.00
30-30 Winchester	5.00
307 Winchester	20.00
308 Winchester	12.00
30-06	9.00
32-20	9.00
35 Remington	10.00
38 Special	3.50
9mm (polished)	5.00
10mm	9.00
444 Marlin	15.00
45-70	21.00

From Precision Reloading Specialties, Inc.

REMINGTON/WINCHESTER *Unprimed Pistol Brass*

Case	TOWS	HDS		
	Price/50	Price/100	Price/250	Price/500
22 Rem. Jet	$8.75	$12.98	$39.98	$55.98
221 Fireball	12.85	18.98	43.98	80.98
25 Auto.	6.00	8.98	20.98	38.98
32 S&W Long		9.98	20.98	39.98
32 Auto.	6.25	9.98	20.98	39.98
32 Short Colt	9.30			
32 Long Colt	9.30			
9mm Luger	6.50	9.98	21.98	40.98
9mm Win. Mag.	8.75			
380 Auto.	6.00	9.98	21.98	39.98
38 ACP +P		9.98	21.98	40.98
38 S&W		9.98	21.98	40.98
38 Special	6.25	8.98	20.98	38.98
40 S&W		13.98	30.98	57.98
10mm Auto		13.98	31.98	57.98
357 Mag.	7.25	9.98	22.98	42.98
357 Max.		11.98	26.98	49.98
41 Mag.	8.25	12.98	29.98	55.98
44 Mag.		12.98	29.98	55.98
44 Special		12.98	29.98	55.98
45 Colt		13.98	31.98	58.98
45 Auto.	7.80	12.98	28.98	52.50
45 Long Colt	8.25			
45 Auto Rim	13.35	12.98	28.98	52.50

TOWS = The Old Western Scrounger; HDS = Huntington Die Specialities.

Winchester Cases

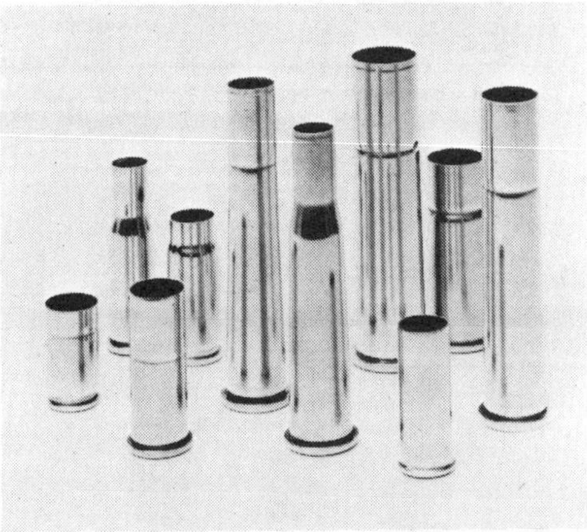

WEATHERBY *Rifle Cases*

Case	Price/20
224 Wea.	$21.65
240 Wea.	21.65
257 Wea.	21.65
270 Wea.	21.65
7mm Wea.	21.65
300 Wea.	21.65
340 Wea.	23.98
378 Wea.	36.00
416 Wea.	40.00
460 Wea.	43.25

From Huntington Die Specialties.

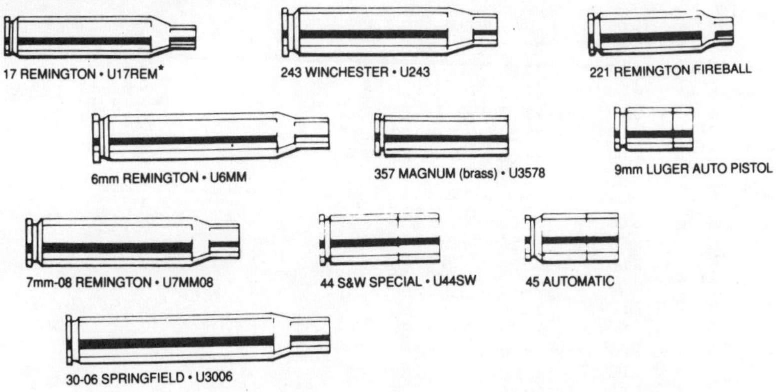

WINCHESTER *Unprimed Handgun Cases*

Case	Price/50
357 Magnum	$8.67
357 Remington Maximum	11.20
9mm Luger	8.00
9mm Winchester Magnum	12.00
38 Special	8.00
41 Remington Magnum	11.36
44 S&W Special	12.00
44 Remington Magnum	11.36
45 Colt	11.36
45 Automatic	10.08
45 Winchester Magnum	12.80

WINCHESTER *Unprimed Rifle Cases*

Case	Price/50
218 Bee	$14.80
22 Hornet	11.84
22-250 Remington	8.00
220 Swift	9.66
222 Remington	5.71
223 Remington	4.80
225 Winchester	8.96
243 Winchester	8.00
6mm Remington	8.00
25-06 Remington	8.72
25-20 Winchester	16.80
257 Roberts +P	10.88
264 Winchester Magnum	9.38
270 Winchester	8.32
280 Remington Magnum	8.32
284 Winchester	11.52
7mm Mauser	8.54
7mm Remington Magnum	10.66
30 Carbine	12.00
30-30 Winchester	7.36
30-06 Springfield	8.32
30-40 Krag	11.52
300 Winchester Magnum	10.66
300 H&H Magnum	13.60
303 British	11.52
307 Winchester	10.56
308 Winchester	8.00
300 Savage	10.88
32-20 Winchester	16.80
338 Winchester Magnum	12.42
348 Winchester	14.40
356 Winchester	11.84
358 Winchester	11.52
375 Winchester	13.44
375 H&H Magnum	12.80
44-40 Winchester	16.80
45-70 Government	8.19
458 Winchester Magnum	12.96

ACTIV

Hulls

Brass-free hull with steel encasement lining to reinforce the head, rim and primer pocket. Steel primer pocket does not expand after repeated firing and hull does not need to be resized when reloading. Mouths are skived for perfect 8-point crimp. Available in 12-, 16-, 20-gauge. From ACTIV Industries, Inc.

Price: . . . . **Contact manufacturer.**

Starter Kit

For the first-time reloader or those who would like to test the ACTIV brass-free hull. Kits come with a choice of 25 hulls in 12-, 16- or 20-gauge, 25 wads, ACTIV Reloading Booklet and patch. From ACTIV Industries, Inc.

Price: Per kit **$3.60**
Price: Case of four **$11.75**

ACTIV *Hull Specifications*

Model	Gauge	Color
UH-12	12 2 3/4"	Red
UH-123	12 3"	Red
UH-20	20 2 3/4"	Yellow
UH-203	20 3"	Yellow
UH-16	16 2 3/4"	Red

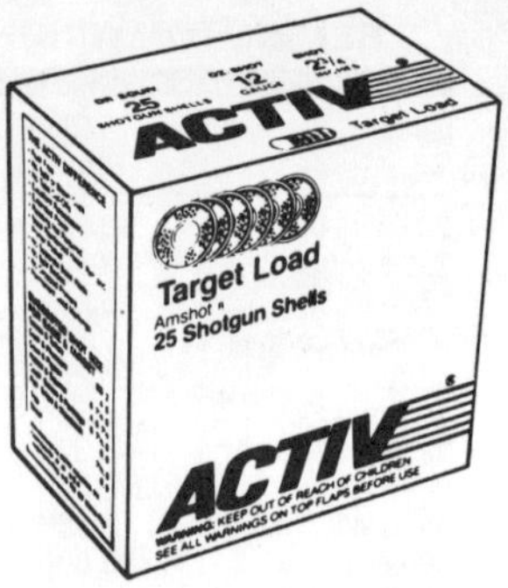

PRECISION RELOADING *New Unfired Hulls*

Gauge	Size	Primed	Description	Price/100
REMINGTON				
10	3 1/2	Y	HMH, plastic base wad	$22.00
12	2 3/4	Y	LBH, RTL, 1-piece plastic	10.75
20	2 3/4	Y	LBH, RTL, plastic base wad	10.75
28	2 3/4	Y	LBH, SP, plastic base wad	11.75
410	2 1/2	Y	HMH, SP, plastic base wad	11.75
FEDERAL				
10	3 1/2	Y	HBH, paper base wad	29.95
ACTIV				
12	3	N	All plastic	9.95
12	2 3/4	N	All plastic	8.95
16	2 3/4	N	All plastic	8.95
20	3	N	All plastic	8.95
20	2 3/4	N	All plastic	8.95

HMH = High Metal Head; LBH = Low Metal Head. From Reloading Specialties.

PRECISION RELOADING *Once-Fired Hulls*

Gauge	Size	Description	Crimp	Price/100	Price/500	Price/1000
FEDERAL						
12	3 1/2	HMH, all plastic	6	$12.00	$55.00	$95.00
12	23/4	HMH, all plastic, 1-piece	6	5.00	23.00	40.00
12	2 3/4	MBH, Gold Medal, 1-piece	8	8.00	36.00	64.00
12	2 3/4	LMH, all plastic, 1-piece	6	4.00	18.00	32.00
20	2 3/4	HMH, paper base wad	8	6.00	28.00	52.00
REMINGTON						
10	3 1/2	HMH, plastic base wad	6	18.00		
12	3	HMH, 2-piece, plastic base wad	6	8.00	36.00	68.00
12	3	HMH, duplex 2-piece, plastic base wad	6	9.00	41.00	72.00
12	2 3/4	LBH, premier target, 1-piece	8	6.00	27.00	44.00
12	2 3/4	LMH, black unibody, 1-piece	6	5.00	23.00	35.00
12	2 3/4	HMH, 2-piece, plastic base wad	6	4.00	18.00	32.00
12	2 3/4	MMH, unibody, 1-piece	6	6.00	28.00	52.00
WINCHESTER						
10	3 1/2	HBH, paper base wad	6	16.00	72.00	
10	3 1/2	HBH, plastic base wad	6	18.00	82.00	
12	3	HMH, CF, magnum	6	9.00	41.00	72.00
12	2 3/4	LBH, CF, AA trap/Sheet	8	8.00	36.00	55.00
12	2 3/4	HMH, CF, SuperX	8	7.00	32.00	50.00
12	2 3/4	HMH, CF, SuperX	6	5.00	23.00	40.00
12	2 3/4	LMH, PF, 2-piece	6	2.00	8.00	12.00
20	3	HMH, CF, magnum	8	10.00	45.00	85.00
20	2 3/4	LMH, 2-piece, polyformed	6	5.00	20.00	35.00

HMH = High Metal Head; MMH = Medium Metal Head; LMH = Low Metal Head; CF = Compression formed; HBH = High Brass Head; MBH = Medium Brass Head; LBH = Low Brass Head; PF = Polyformed. From Precision Reloading, Inc.

BALLISTIC PRODUCTS *Shotshell Hulls*

Manufacturer	Gauge	Lgth.	Price 50	Price 100	Price 500	Comments
Fiocchi	10	3½"	$15.95	$30.90	$139.00	New, unprimed.
Remington	10	3½"	10.95	17.90	82.00	Type IV, disc base, once-fired, Class A
Winchester	10	3½"	8.95	13.90	64.00	Once-fired, polyformed.
Winchester	10	3½"	12.95	20.95	96.00	Steel head, plastic disc base hull.
ACTIV	12	2¾"		9.90	44.90	New, unprimed, brass-free, skived, hi-capacity.
Federal	12	2¾"	3.75	6.90	29.90	Gold Medal, once-fired.
Federal	12	2¾"	5.95	10.70	49.90	Fiber base, once fired.
Fiocchi	12	2¾"	6.95	13.00	59.90	New, primed, disc base, skived.
Remington "RXP"	12	2¾"		5.95	26.90	Once fired.
Remington	12	2¾"	2.95	4.95	22.90	Unibody, once fired.
Winchester "AA"	12	2¾"		6.95	31.90	Once fired.
Winchester	12	2¾"	5.95	10.90	49.90	Hi-brass.
Winchester	12	2¾"	2.95	4.90	22.90	Plastic disc base.
ACTIV	12	3"		10.95	49.90	New, unprimed.
Federal	12	3"	10.95	19.90	92.90	Gold Medal type base, once fired, Class A, hi-brass.
Federal	12	3"	8.95	17.50	92.90	Fiber base, once fired.
Fiocchi	12	3"	10.95	19.90	91.90	New, primed disc base.
Remington Type VI	12	3"	5.95	8.90	40.90	Once fired, black plastic base, hi-brass.
Remington Type II	12	3"	9.95	19.00	88.90	Fiber base.
Winchester	12	3"	7.95	15.00	69.90	Polyformed, once fired.
ACTIV	16	2¾"		9.90	44.90	New, unprimed.
Fiocchi	16	2¾"	6.95	13.00	59.90	New, unprimed.
ACTIV	20	2¾"		9.95	44.90	New, unprimed.
Federal	20	2¾"	3.95	5.90	26.90	Fiber base, once fired.
Fiocchi	20	2¾"	6.95	13.00	59.90	New, unprimed.
Winchester	20	2¾"	4.95	8.90	39.90	Once fired, compressions formed, Class A.
ACTIV	20	3"		10.95	49.90	New, unprimed, brass-free.
Fiocchi	20	3"	6.95	13.00	59.90	New, primed.
Remington Type V	20	3"	5.95	11.00	51.90	Disc base, once-fired, hi-brass.
Remington	20	3"	4.95	8.90	39.90	Fiber base, once fired.
Remington	20	3"	4.95	8.90	39.90	Disc base, once fired.
Fiocchi	28	2½"	7.95	15.00	69.90	New, primed.
Federal	28	2¾"	4.95	8.90	42.90	Fiber base, once fired.
Remington	410	3"	3.95	6.90	31.90	Once fired.

New = Never fired; Class A = very clean, once fired.

Fiocchi Reifenhauser Three-Piece Hull

ACTION

Hard cast pistol bullets in many calibers. Minimum order of 1000. From Action Bullets, Inc.

Price: . . . . **Contact manufacturer.**

ALLRED

Allred specializes in custom, heavy-duty 224 and 308 jacketed bullets designed for hunting, silhouette or target shooting. All have a solid lead core and guilding metal jackets. The 308s feature a copper inner tubing to control penetration and expansion, and provide better weight retention. From Allred Bullet Company.

Price: . . . . **See chart.**

ALPHA LAFRANCK

Heavyweight 430, 452 and 458 swaged lead bullets available jacketed or non-jacketed. The 430 bullets are designed for 44 Magnum and 430 JDJ loads in weights from 240 to 370 grs. Two basic jackets, a short .550" and long .700", and in three nose designs, wadcutter, semi-wadcutter and round-nose. Ten jacket and weight combinations are standard. Alpha's 452 bullets are designed for revolvers, specifically the 454 Casull and strong 45 Colts in weights from 250 to 400 grs. Three jacket types are available, short .550", medium .700" and copper tubing 1.00" lengths. Fifteen jacket and weight combinations standard. The 458 bullets are offered in over 200 weight, jacket and point form combinations. Seven jacket styles available. "PJ" bullet uses thin .550" and .700" jackets for good expansion at low to medium 45/70 velocities. "RJ" jacket available in two lengths, .700" for 300-gr. and .910" for 405-gr. bullets. The "SJ" jacket comes in one length, .850" for 400-gr. "HJ" bullet is offered in 350-gr. with .890" jacket and 500-gr. 1.285" jacket. "TJ" bullet has copper tubing jacket of .032" wall thickness and 1.05" length. From Alpha LaFranck Enterprises.

Price: . . . . **See chart.**

AMERICAN BULLETS

American Bullets offers a line of precision target hard-lead bullets in all popular pistol calibers. Designed for reduced leading at higher velocities, bullets will perform in both standard and polygon rifled barrels. Available in packs of 100 or bulk boxes of 500. From American Bullets.

Price: . . . . **See chart.**

ALLRED

Wgt. Grs.	——Type——	Price/Per
	CALIBER: 224	
50	TJ-OT, TC-OT	$12.00/25
52	TM-OT	14.00/100
	DJ-OT, DC-OT	11.00/25
55	TJ-SF, TC-SF	12.00/25
60	DC-OT	11.00/25
	TJ-LT, TC-LT	12.00/25
65	DC-OT, DJ-OT	11.00/25
70	DC-OT, DJ-OT	11.00/25
	DJ-LT, DC-OT	11.00/25
75	DC-OT, DJ-LT	11.00/25
	DC-LT, DJ-SF	11.00/25
	DC-SF, DJ-OT	11.00/25
80	DC-OT, DC-LT	11.00/25
	DJ-OT, DJ-SF	11.00/25
	DJ-LT	11.00/25
85	DC-OT, DJ-OT	11.00/25
	DC-SF, DJ-SF	11.00/25
90	DC-LT, DJ-LT	11.00/25
	CALIBER: 308	
135	SB-OT	$18.00/25
140	SB-OT	18.00/25
145	SB-SF	18.00/25
150	SB-OT	18.00/25
	TSD-OT	20.00/25
	TSB-OT	24.00/25
	TDC-OT	26.00/25
155	SB-LT	18.00/25
	TSD-LT	20.00/25
	TSB-LT	24.00/25
	TDC-LT	26.00/25
165	SB-OT	18.00/25
180	DC-LT	18.50/25
	CL-SF, CL-OT	20.50/25
	TM-OT	17.50/100
	TDC-LT, TDC-OT	26.00/25
	TCL-OT, TCL-SF	25.00/25
	TSB-OT, TSB-LT	24.00/25
	DC-LT	18.50/25
185	SR-LT	21.50/25
	CL-LT	20.50/25
	TCL-SF	25.00/25
	TDC-SF	26.00/25
190	CL-LT	20.50/25
	TCL-SF	25.00/25
195	DC-LT	18.50/25
	DJ-LT	00.00/00
	CL-SF	20.50/25
200	SR-LT	21.50/25
	CL-LT	20.50/25
	TSD-LT	20.00/25
	TCL-LT	25.00/25
205	DC-LT	18.50/25
	DJ-LT	00.00/25
	TSB-LT	24.00/25
	TDC-LT	26.00/25

Bullet Construction: TM = Single metal jacket; DC = Dual metal jackets, dual core (224); Outer metal jacket, inner copper jacket, dual core (308); DJ = Dual metal jacket, single core (224); Outer metal jacket, inner copper jacket, single core (308); TJ = Triple metal jacket; TC = Triple metal jacket, dual core; SB, CL, SR = Outer metal jacket, inner copper jacket; TSD = Single copper jacket; TDC = Dual copper jacket, dual core; TSB, TCL = Dual copper jacket; LT = Lead tip; OT = Open tip; SF = Small flat tip.

ALPHA LAFRANCK Jacketed Bullets

Jacket	Wgt. Grs.	Type	Price/50
		CALIBER: 430	
S	240	WC	$11.00
	250	WC	11.00
	275	SWC	13.00
	300	SWC,RN	15.00
	325	SWC,RN	15.00
	350	SWC,RN	15.00
	370	SWC,RN	15.00
L	300	SWC,RN	15.00
	325	SWC,RN	15.00
	350	SWC,RN	15.00
	370	SWC,RN	15.00
		CALIBER: 452	
S,L	250	RNF	$15.00
	275	RNF	15.00
	300	RNF	15.00
	325	RNF	17.00
	350	RNF	18.00
	375	RNF	19.00
	400	RNF	20.00
TJ	350	RNF	20.00
	375	RNF	20.00
	400	RNF	20.00
		CALIBER: 458	
RJ	300	FP,HP,SP	$14.00
	400	FP,SP	18.00
SJ	400	FP,SP	20.00
HJ	350	FP,SP	20.00
	500	SP	20.00
TJ	400	SP	20.00/25
	437	SP	20.00/25
	450	SP	22.00/25
	500	SP	22.00/25
	550	SP	22.00/25
PJ	325	FP,HP,SP	15.00
	350	FP,HP,SP	16.00
	375	FP,HP,SP	17.00

FP = Flat Point; HP = Hollowpoint; SP=Spitzer.

ALPHA LAFRANCK Swaged Lead Bullets

Caliber	Wgt. Grs.	Price/50
430	240-370	$12.50
452	250-400	12.50
458	250-400	12.50
458	401-500	15.00
458	501-600	17.50
458	601-650	22.00

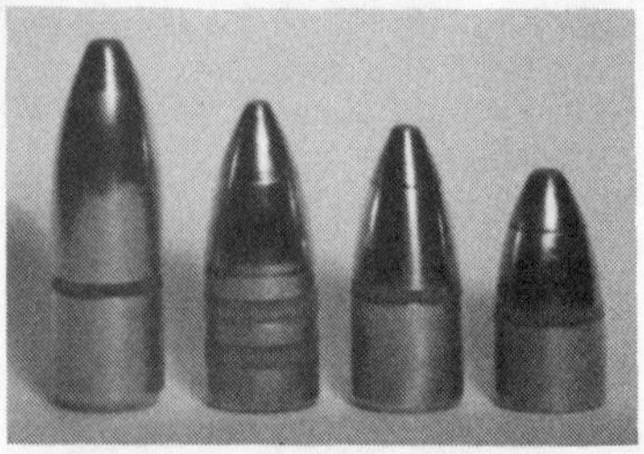

Alpha LaFranck 458 Spitzers

AMERICAN

Caliber	Wgt. Grs.	Type	Price 100	Price 500
380	95	RN	$6.25	$22.50
9mm	125	RN	6.25	22.50
38/357	148	DEWC	6.25	22.50
	148	BBWC	6.25	22.50
	158	RN	6.70	24.50
	160	SWC	6.70	24.50
32 Mag.	100	SWC	6.25	22.50
40 S&W/10mm	175	SWC	7.25	29.75
41 Mag.	220	SWC	7.25	29.75
44 Mag.	240	SWC	7.75	30.75
	290	SWC	8.75	35.00
45 ACP	185	SWC	7.75	29.75
	200	SWC	7.25	22.50
	230	SWC	7.25	22.50
	230	RN	7.25	22.50
	230	FN	7.50	30.50
45 Long Colt	225	SWC	7.25	29.75

RN = Round Nose; SWC = Semi-Wadcutter; DEWC = Double End Wadcutter; BBWC = Bevel Base Wadcutter; FN = Flat Nose.

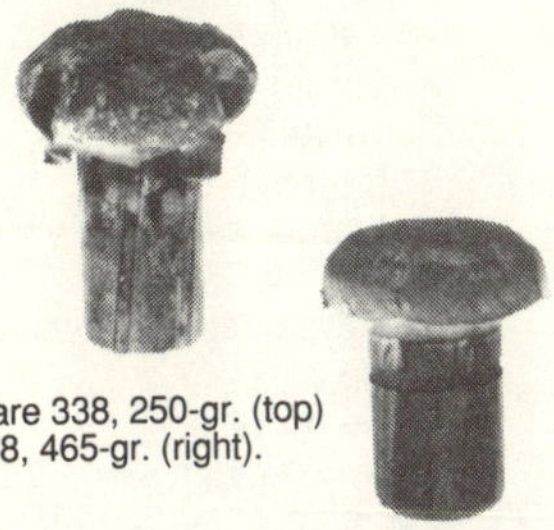

A-Square 338, 250-gr. (top) and 458, 465-gr. (right).

ARMFIELD

Armfield offers 270 and 7mm bonded core (Plainsbond) for large game, pre-fragmented core (Fragcore) for medium to small game or standard solid lead core bullets. Plainsbond available in standard flat-base or Very Low Drag (VLD) and with pure copper or guilding metal jacket. Copper jackets are from copper sheet stock. The 270 jacket has a .020" thick wall forward section and .030" thick wall rear section. The 7mm wall thickness is .025/.035. Fragcore jackets come scored or unscored. Guilding metal jackets can be had in either light or heavy styles. From Armfield Custom Bullets.

Price: . . . . **See chart.**

A-SQUARE

A triad of medium to heavy game bullets either loaded (prices not shown) or component form. Monolithic Solids are nonexpanding, made from a single metal with no lead core for the heaviest of game. Dead Tough Soft Points are expanding general purpose bullets for close-range shots. Lion Load Soft Points are designed for less penetration, 18-24 inches, and more expansion. From A-Square Co., Inc.

Price: . . . . **See chart.**

ARMFIELD

Caliber	Wgt. Grs.	Type	Price/Per
		Plainsbond	
270/7mm	130,140,160,180	FB-OT,SP,RN	$18.95/25
		RBT(VLD)-OT,SP,RN	24.95/25
		Fragcore	
270/7mm	130,140,160,180	FB-OT	$11.95/25
		RBT(VLD)-OT	13.95/25
		RBT Poly Tip(VLD)	18.95/25
		Standard Solid Lead Core	
270/7mm	130,140,160,180	FB-OT,SP,RN	$24.95/100
		RBT(VLD)-OT,SP,RN	26.95/100

FB=Flat Base; OT=Open Tip; RN=Round Nose; RBT=Rebated Boattail; VLD=Very Low Drag; SP=Spitzer; Poly Tip= Polymer (Plastic) Tip.

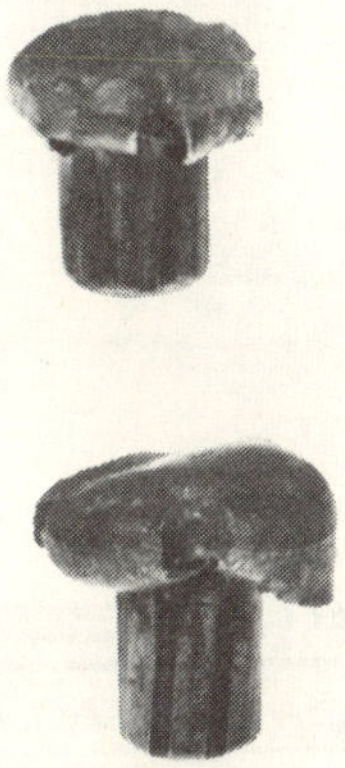

A-Square 475, 500-gr. (top) and 375, 300-gr. (above).

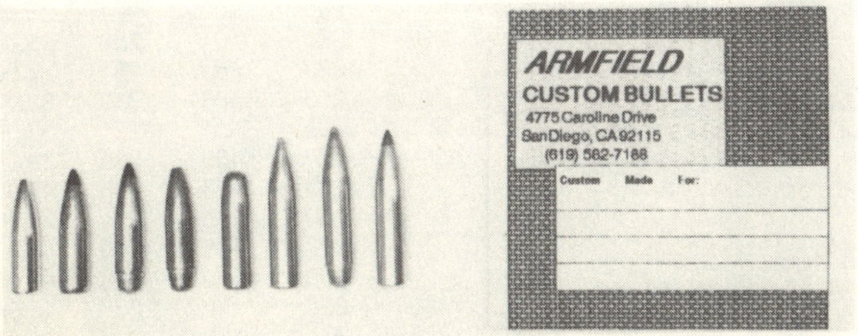

Armfield Bullets

A-SQUARE

Dia.*	Wgt. Grs.	Type	Pric
284	175	Monolithic Solid	$39.5
308	180	Monolithic Solid	39.50
308	220	Monolithic Solid	41.00
323	220	Monolithic Solid	51.00
338	220	Monolithic Solid	52.00
338	250	Dead Tough Soft Point	78.00
338	250	Lion Load Soft Point	51.00
358	275	Dead Tough Soft Point	82.00
	275	Lion Load Soft Point	58.00
366	286	Monolithic Solid	55.00
	286	Dead Tough Soft Point	79.00
	286	Lion Load Soft Point	55.00
375	300	Monolithic Solid	58.00
	300	Dead Tough Soft Point	79.00
	300	Lion Load Soft Point	58.00
409	400	Monolithic Solid	38.00
	400	Dead Tough Soft Point	45.00
	400	Lion Load Soft Point	38.00
416	400	Monolithic Solid	36.00
	400	Dead Tough Soft Point	44.00
	400	Lion Load Soft Point	36.00
423	400	Monolithic Solid	37.00
	400	Dead Tough Soft Point	45.00
	400	Lion Load Soft Point	37.00
458	465	Monolithic Solid	37.00
	465	Dead Tough Solid Point	47.00
	465	Lion Load Soft Point	36.00
	500	Monolithic Solid	38.00
	500	Dead Tough Solid Point	48.00
	500	Lion Load Soft Point	38.00
468	480	Monolithic Solid	41.00
	480	Dead Tough Soft Point	52.00
	480	Lion Load Soft Point	38.00
475	500	Monolithic Solid	40.00
	500	Dead Tough Soft Point	48.00
	500	Lion Load Soft Point	38.00
488	500	Monolithic Solid	46.00
	500	Dead Tough Soft Point	53.00
	500	Lion Load Soft Point	48.00
505	525	Monolithic Solid	46.00
	525	Dead Tough Soft Point	56.00
	525	Lion Load Soft Point	46.00
510	570	Monolithic Solid	45.00
	570	Dead Tough Soft Point	55.00
	570	Lion Load Soft Point	45.00
	600	Monolithic Solid	45.00
	600	Dead Tough Soft Point	57.00
	600	Lion Load Soft Point	45.00
585	750	Monolithic Solid	58.00
	750	Dead Tough Soft Point	90.00
	750	Lion Load Soft Point	56.00
620	900	Monolithic Solid	90.00
	900	Dead Tough Soft Point	100.00
	900	Lion Load Soft Point	88.00

*inches.
**375 and smaller packed 50 per box; 409 and larger packed 25 per box.

...RD

... pistol and rifle ... and 510 calibers. ...ullets are bonded core. ... have 1E ogive and come ... tip or lead tip depending on ...ht. Flat-nose and hollowpoints ...o available. Ogive for 510s is ...4E with flat-nose and hollowpoint variations. Custom jackets are swaged and come in .030 or .050 thickness. Optional cannelure $2.00 per box. From Ballard Built Custom Bullets.

Price: . . . . **See chart.**

BERGER

Match-grade lead core jacketed bullets made to very close tolerances from Rorschach and Simonson carbide dies. Jackets drawn from single set of dies using copper strip the width of a single jacket with tolerance of .0003-inch; $^{3}/_{16}$-inch up from the base. Lead core wire contains .5 percent antimony with dimensional control held to .002-inch. Roundness at the pressure ring held to a standard .001-inch to .00005-inch. From Berger Bullets.

Price: . . . . **See chart.**

BITTERROOT

Bonded core hunting bullets for heavy game in eight calibers from .277 to .423. From Bitterroot Bullet Co.

Price: . . . . **See chart.**

BLUE MOUNTAIN

Multi-stage, tri-jacketed hunting bullets with laminated outer skin for instant expansion upon contact and triple supported shank and base for penetration. Any bullet weight within the range specified for each caliber is available. Spitzer (tangential ogive), open tip or hollowpoint styles are offered as well as lead tips. From Blue Mountain Bullets.

Price: . . . . **See chart.**

BLUE POINT

Offers premium-grade hunting bullets of bonded core construction in standard and non-standard weights and designs. All bullets from 224-7mm in 55-160 grain weights are spitzer flat-base; 165 and up grain weights in same calibers available as rebated boattail. 357-, 430-, 41- and 454-caliber bullets are truncated cone design and for use primarily in handguns, but can be used in rifles chambered for them. The 45-caliber bullets were designed with tough cores for the 454 Casull. From Blue Point Mfg. Co.

Price: . . . . **See chart.**

Ballard Bullets

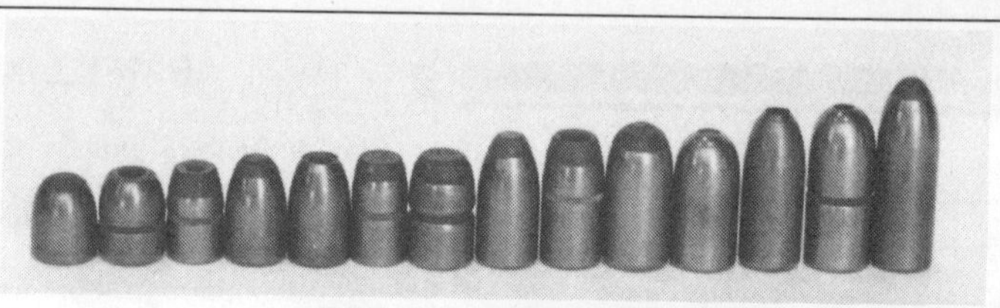

Berger Bullets

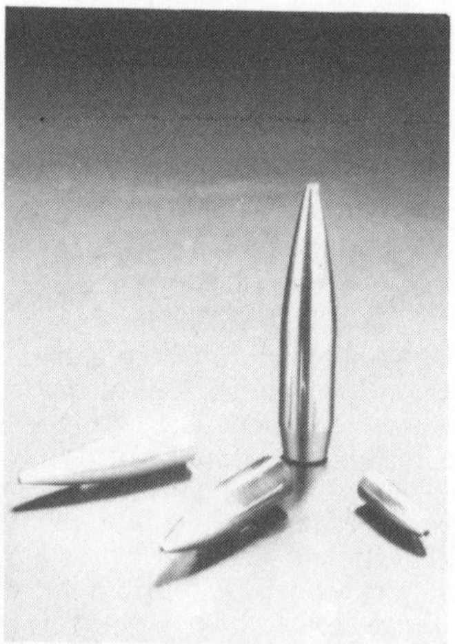

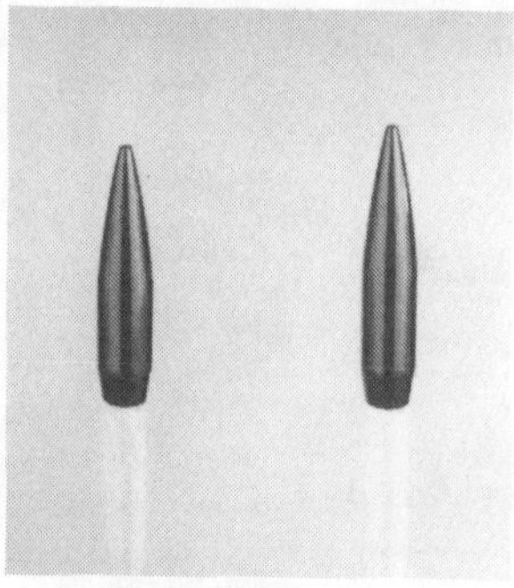

Berger Bullets

BERGER

Caliber	Wgt. Grs.	——Description——	Price/Per
17	20	Small case 17s	$22.00/200
	25	All CF 17s	22.00/200
	30	Larger case 17s	22.00/200
22	45	Small case 22s	11.00/100
	52	All CF 22 cases	11.00/100
	55	Same as 52-gr.	11.00/100
	60	Larger CF 22 cases	11.00/100
	62	Same as 62-gr.	11.00/100
	65	Same as 62-gr.	11.00/100
6mm	60	Small capacity cases	11.55/100
	62	Same as 60-gr.	11.55/100
	65	6mm PPC; 6mm BR	11.55/100
	68	6mm PPC; 6mm BR; 243, 6mm Rem.	11.55/100
	69*	6mm PPC; 6mm BR; 243, 6mm Rem. and large capacity cases	11.55/100
	70	Same as 69-gr.	11.55/100
	71	243; 6mm Rem. and larger cases	11.55/100
	74	243; 6mm Rem. and large capacity cases	11.55/100
	80	Same as 74-gr.	11.55/100
	88*	Same as 74-gr.	11.55/100
	95 VLD	Same as 74-gr.	10.55/80
	105 VLD	Same as 74-gr.; 300-1000 yds.	10.55/80
25	82	All 25 cases	14.30/80
	85	Same as 82-gr.	14.30/100
	87	Same as 82-gr.	14.30/100
	110		14.30/100
30	185 VLD	308 or larger cases	16.00/100
	190 VLD	Same as 185-gr.	16.00/100
	210 VLD	Magnum size cases	16.00/100

*15 Ogive

BALLARD

Caliber	Wgt. Grs.	Ogive	Type	Price/25
475	300	1E	OT/LT	$25.00
	500	1E	OT/LT	25.00
510	300	$^{3}/_{4}$E	FN/HP	25.00
	500	$^{3}/_{4}$E	FN/HP	25.00
44	200		JHP	18.50
	250		JHP	18.50
	300		JHP	18.50
475	400	1E	OT/LT	27.50
	400	1E	BC	40.00
510	400	1E	OT/LT	27.50
	600	1E	BC	40.00

OT = Open Tip; LT = Lead Tip; FN = Flat Nose; HP = Hollowpoint; JHP = Jacketed Hollowpoint; BC = Bonded Core.

BITTERROOT

Caliber	Wgt. Grs.	S.D.	B.C.	Price/20
277	130	.242	.385	$33.00
	150	.279	.450	33.00
7mm	140	.395	.248	33.00
	160	.460	.283	33.00
	175	.495	.310	33.00
308	165	.402	.247	33.00
	180	.440	.272	33.00
	200	.500	.301	35.00
338	200	.407	.250	35.00
	225	.452	.281	37.00
	250	.508	.312	39.00
358	225	.411	.251	37.00
	250	.455	.280	39.00
	275	.490	.308	41.00
375	250	.352	.254	39.00
	275	.395	.280	41.00
	300	.430	.306	43.00
416	335	.390	.277	45.00
423	335	.385	.267	45.00

S.D. = Standard Deviation; B.C. = Ballistic Coefficient

BULL-X

Caliber	Bullet Diameter	Bullet Wgt. Grs.	Bullet Type	Price 500	Price 1000
30	.309	115	RN	$19.25	$37.25
32	.314	100	SW	19.00	36.25
9mm	.355	115	FMJ	28.25	53.50
	.356	122	FP	19.50	38.25
	.356	125	RN	19.50	38.25
	.356	140	SW	21.25	41.00
	.356	147	FP	21.25	41.00
38	.357	125	JHP	28.25	63.50
	.357	140	SW	21.25	41.00
	.358	140	SW	21.25	41.00
	.357	147	FP	21.25	41.00
	.358	147	FP	21.25	41.00
	.358	148	HBSW	20.00	37.28
	.358	148	DEWC	21.25	41.00
	.358	148	BN	21.25	41.00
	.356/.357	150	SW	21.25	41.00
	.357	158	RN	22.00	42.25
	.358	158	SW	22.00	42.25
	.358	180	FP	23.75	45.75
40 S&W	.401	140	FP	21.25	41.00
	.401	175	SW	23.25	45.00
	.401	180	FP	23.25	45.25
10mm	.401	140	FP	21.25	41.00
	.401	175	SW	23.25	45.00
	.401	180	FP	23.25	45.25
	.401	200	FP	25.00	48.75
41	.411	215	SW	26.25	51.00
44	.430	190	SW	25.50	49.50
	.429	215	SW	25.50	49.50
	.429	240	SW	27.75	54.50
	.430	300	FP	30.50*	60.00**
45	.452	150	RN, SW	22.00	42.45
	.452	185	SW	24.25	46.50
	.452	200	SW	25.00	48.75
	.452	230	RN	27.25	53.25
	.452	230	FP	27.25	53.25
	.452	255	SW	29.50	67.25
	.430	300	FP	30.50*	60.00**

* = Price for 400.
** = Price for 800.
FP = Flat Point; RN = Round Nose; DEWC = Double End Wadcutter; BN = Button Nose; SW = Semi-Wadcutter.

BRUNO SHOOTER'S SUPPLY

Caliber	Bullet Wgt. Grs.	Bullet Type	Price/M
22	52, 57, 63	HPBT	$125.00
	52, 57, 63	FB	109.50
6mm	63, 65, 68, 70	HPFB	125.00
	63, 65, 68, 70	BT	129.95
6mm (9/S)	63, 65, 68	FB	139.95
	63, 65, 68	BT	139.95
25	75, 78, 80, 83	FB	159.95
	168, 200	FB	179.50

Bruno Shooter's Supply

BRP

High performance cast handgun bullets from 32- to 50-caliber. Hard alloy in heavy weights and gas checked. Designed for magnum velocities without leading. From BRP Inc.

Price: . . . . **Contact manufacturer.**

BRUNO SHOOTER'S SUPPLY

Benchrest bullets hand-swaged in carbide dies. All are of hollowpoint design. From Bruno Shooter's Supply.

Price: . . . . **See chart.**

BULLSEYE

Bullseye produces hard cast bullets made from virgin alloy with a 8% tin and anitmony content. From Bullseye Bullets.

Price: . . . . **See chart.**

BULL-X

Hard cast match-grade bullets using virgin alloy with high content of tin and antimony. Bullets are sized to exact diameter required and lubed. Come in boxes of 500. From Bull-X, Incorporated.

Price: . . . . **See chart.**

BLUE POINT

Caliber	Bullet Wgt. Grs.	Price/50*	Caliber	Bullet Wgt. Grs.	Price/50*
224	55, 60, 65, 70, 75	$28.00	30	140, 150, 160, 165, 175	$45.00
	80	30.00		180, 185, 190, 200	45.00
228	70, 75, 80, 85, 90	30.00		200+	50.00
6mm	75, 80, 85, 90, 100	35.00	357	130, 140, 150, 160, 170	40.00
6mm**	90, 95, 100, 105, 115	37.50	41	185, 200, 220, 235	48.00
257	85, 90, 95, 100, 115	37.50	44	185, 200, 220, 235, 265	48.00
270	145, 150, 160	45.00	45	250, 260, 275	55.00
7mm	120, 140, 145, 165, 175	45.00			
	180, 185	45.00			

*Add $7.00 per box for rebated boattail. **Halgar rifle.

BLUE MOUNTAIN

Cal.	Bullet Wgt. Grs.	Bullet Type	Price/20
244	75-105	Bonded, triple jacket	$25.00
257	75-125	Bonded, triple jacket	25.00
270	130-170	Bonded, triple jacket	30.00
284	150-180	Bonded, triple jacket	30.00
308	150-220	Bonded, triple jacket	30.00
323	200-240	Copper, heavy wall, triple jacket	30.00
338	200-275	Copper, heavy wall, triple jacket	30.00
358	200-285	Copper, heavy wall, triple jacket	30.00
375	240-350	Copper, heavy wall, triple jacket	30.00
429	250-300	Copper, heavy wall, triple jacket	30.00

BULLSEYE

Caliber	Bullet Diameter	Bullet Wgt. Grs.	Bullet Type	Price 500	Price 1000
380	.356	95	RN-BB	$17.00	$32.00
9mm	.356	125	RN-BB	17.00	32.00
9mm/38 Super	.356	147	FP-BB	18.00	33.00
38/357	.357	148	DE-WC	18.00	33.00
	.357	158	SWC-BB	19.00	34.00
	.357	158	RN-BB	19.00	34.00
10mm	.401	175	SWC-BB	22.00	42.00
40	.401	155	RNSWC-BB	21.00	41.00
41	.411	215	SWC-BB	23.00	44.00
44	.430	240	SWC-BB	24.00	45.00
45	.452	155	SWC-BB	20.00	36.00
	.452	180	SWC-BB	22.00	42.00
	.452	185	SWC-BB	22.00	42.00
	.452	200	SWC-BB	22.00	42.00
	.452	230	RN-BB	24.00	45.00
	.452	255	SWC-BB	22.00*	40.00**
45/70	.458	300	FP-BC	25.00*	48.00**

* = Price for 400. ** = Price for 800. BB = Bevel Base; RN = Round Nose; FP = Flat Point; DE = Double End; WC = Wadcutter; SWC = Semi-Wadcutter; FB = Flat Base.

C.W. CARTRIDGE

Designed for paper Nitro combustible cartridges. Cast of pure lead, three calibers and bullet styles available: 54-, 50- and 45-caliber; solid, hollow-base and hollow-base Minie. From C.W. Cartridge Company.

Price: . . . . **See chart.**

C.W. CARTRIDGE Paper Cartridge Form Kit

Kit includes 200 precut, nitrated paper sheets, glue stick and 7" plastic forming dowel to produce combustible cartridge tubes in .542" diameter for use in 54-caliber Sharps rifles. Refill kit with 500 nitrated sheets and two glue sticks available. From C.W. Cartridge Company.

Price: Kit **$15.00**
Price: Kit refill **$24.00**

JAMES CALHOON

Makers of specialized varmint bullets featuring double hollowpoint and thin jacket construction for expansion; rebated boattail for improved gas seal; and "silver bullet" coating for reduced fouling. From James Calhoon Bullets.

Price: . . . . **See chart.**

CARROLL Bullets

Cast rifle and pistol bullets made from custom blend of virgin metals. All bullets come sized and lubed. Lube is non-toxic and alox free. From Precision Reloading, Inc.

Price: . . . . **See chart.**

COOK BULLETS

Match-grade flat-base or hollow-point 22-caliber and 6mm bullets for the competition target shooter or varmint hunter. Swaged in carbide dies. From Cook Bullets.

Price: . . . . **See chart.**

COR-BON

Premium handgun hunting bullets. Expanding bonded core, full metal jacket and hard cast bullets in four calibers: 357 Magnum, 44 Magnum, 454 Casull and 45 Winchester Magnum. From Cor-Bon Custom Bullet Company.

Price: . . . . **See chart.**

C.W. CARTRIDGE

	Bullet		
Caliber	**Wgt. Grs.**	**Type**	**Price/20**
54	425	Solid	$5.40
	415	Minie	5.40
	380	HB	5.40
50	380	Solid	5.40
	355	HB	5.40
45	300	Solid	5.40
	280	HB	5.40

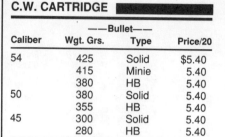

CARROLL

Caliber	Wgt. Grs.	Type	Price/Per
LEAD CAST PISTOL			
380 Auto	95	RNBB	$15.75/500
9mm Luger	125	RNBB	16.50/500
	147	FNBB	17.75/500
38	148	WCBB	16.85/500
357	160	SWCBB	18.00/500
10mm	175	SWCBB	20.25/500
41	215	SWCBB	21.00/500
44	240	SWCBB	21.95/500
45	185	SWCFB	20.50/500
	200	SWCBB	20.50/500
	225	FNBB	21.50/500
	230	RNBB	21.75/500
	255	SWCBB	22.50/500
LEAD CAST RIFLE			
30	190	FNGC	8.55/100
35	210	FNGC	8.70/100
45	405	FNPB	5.63/50
SWAGED HOLLOW BASE			
38	148	HBWC	18.75/500
COPPER JACKETED PLATED			
9mm	125	RN	23.95/500
38/357	158	FP	26.50/500
10mm/40 S&W	180	FP	35.45/500
44	240	FP	41.50/500
45	200	SWC	34.45/500
	230	RN	37.15/500

RNBB = Round Nose Bevel Base; FNBB = Flat Nose Bevel Base; WCBB = Wadcutter Bevel Base; SWCBB = Semi-Wadcutter Bevel Base; FNGC = Flat Nose Gas Check; FP = Flat Point.

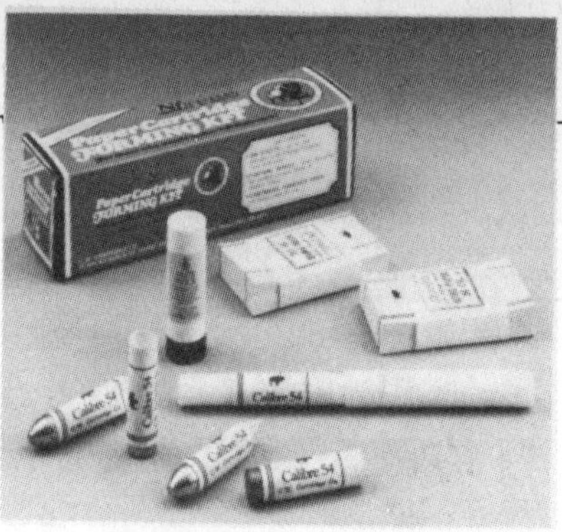

C.W. Cartridge
Paper Cartridge Form Kit

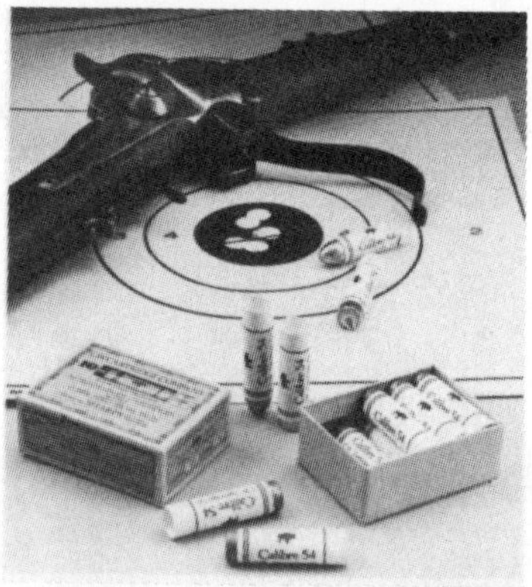

C.W. Cartridge 54-Caliber Cartridges

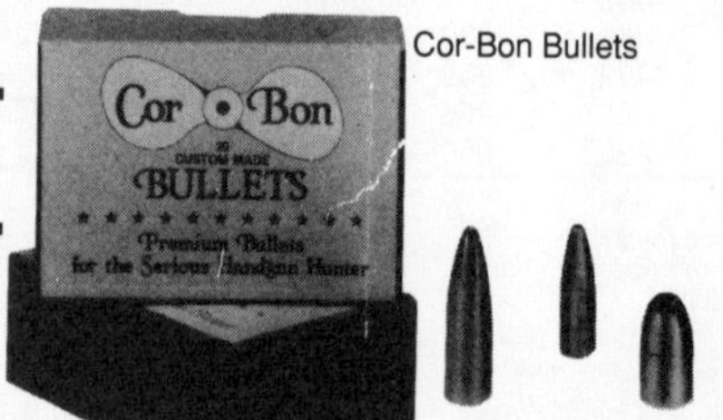

Cor-Bon Bullets

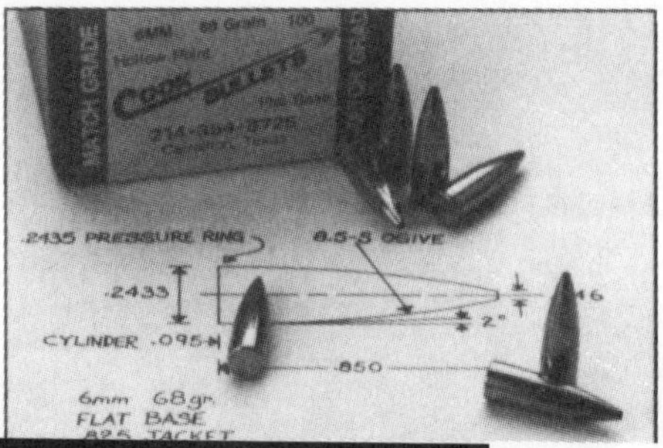

Cook Bullets

COR-BON

Diameter	Wgt. Grs.	Type	Price/Per
EXPANDING BONDED CORE			
.357	180	SP	$29.95/20
.264	120	Spitzer	34.95/40
.308	165	Spitzer	34.95/40
.375	280	Spitzer	24.95/20
.429	260	SP	34.95/50
	280	SP	34.95/50
.452	265	SP	34.95/50
	300	SP	34.95/50
FULL METAL JACKET			
.357	200	FP	29.95/50
.429	305	RN	34.95/50
	305	FP	34.95/50
.452	320	RN	34.95/50
	360	FP	39.95/50
HARD CAST			
.358	205	JDJ	17.95/50
.411	275	JDJ	19.95/50
.430	320	JDJ	19.95/50
.452	350	JDJ	19.95/50

SP = Softpoint; FP = Flat Point; RN = Round Nose.

COOK

				Price	
Caliber	**Wgt. Grs.**	**Ogive**	**Jacket**	**100**	**1000**
22	52	7-S	.705	$10.95	$102.00
6mm	65	7-S	.750	11.75	108.00
	68	8.5-S	.825	11.95	110.00

JAMES CALHOON

Wgt. Grs.	Bullet Type	Bullet For	Price 250	Price 1000
CALIBER: 224				
37	DHP	Hornet to 223	$18.75	$70.25
42	DHP	Hornet to 223	18.90	70.45
45	HP	Hornet to 223	18.45	67.15
50	DHP	221 to 22-250	19.35	72.15
52	DHPRBT	221 to 22-250	19.75	74.25
55	HPRBT	221 to 22-250	19.10	69.90
62	PPRBT	221 to 22-250	19.65	72.50

HP = Hollowpoint; DHP = Double Hollowpoint; RBT = Rebated Boattail; PP = Power Point.

D&J

Wgt. Grs.	Type	Price/1000
CALIBER: 9mm		
115	FMJ	$59.37
124/125	FMJ	60.93
125	LRN	34.82
135	FMJ	60.93
147	LSWC	36.41
147/150	JSP/BTHP	75.00
150	FMJ	75.00
160	LRN	37.50
CALIBER: 38 Super		
115	FMJ	$59.37
124/125	FMJ	60.93
125	LRN	34.82
135	FMJ	60.93
140	LRN	36.41
147/150	JSP/BTHP	75.00
150	LSWC	36.41
150	FMJ	75.00
160	LRN	38.00
160	LSWC	38.00
CALIBER: 38 Revolver		
125	LRN	$34.82
148	LDWC	36.41
148	LSWC	36.41
158	LRN	38.00
158	LSWC	38.00
CALIBER: 10mm/40S&W		
155	LRN	$38.00
175	LSWC	39.58
180	FMJ	84.38
CALIBER: 44		
240	LSWC	$46.88
300	TFP	53.13
CALIBER: 45 ACP		
175	LSWC	$39.58
200	LSWC	41.16
230	LRN	44.32
230	FMJ	93.75
230	JHP	106.25
255	LSWC	49.08
300	TFP	53.13

LRN = Lead Round Nose; LSWC = Lead Semi-Wadcutter; JSP = Jacketed Softpoint; FMJ = Full Metal Jacket; BTHP = Boattail Hollowpoint; LDWC = Lead Dou-

DKT Bullets

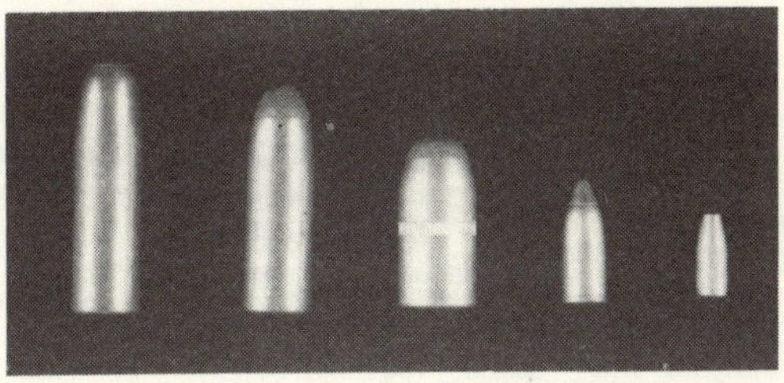

D&J Bullets

D&J BULLET CO.

Competition cast bullets from specially blended 100% pure, virgin alloy with hardness factor rating of 10 and above on the Saeco scale. Designed with longer driving bands for greater accuracy and reduced leading. Velocities of 1350 fps can be achieved without significant lead build-up. Each bullet sized and lubed. Contact D&J for dealer information. From D&J Bullet Co.

Price: . . . . **See chart.**

DKT

Suppliers of cast and jacketed bullets in a variety of calibers and bullet weights. Cast bullets are made from pure linotype and come sized and lubed. Rooster Red lubricant standard, but LBT may be substitued on request. From DKT, Inc.

Price: . . . . **See chart.**

DKT JACKETED BULLETS

Caliber	Diameter	Wgt. Grs.	Type	Price/50
14	.145	12	HP	$20.00
20	.204	35/45	SP	15.00
6.5x58R	.260	120	RN-SP	15.00
280 Ross	.287	140/150	SSP	15.00
7.35mm	.300	128	SSP	16.00
	.300	150	HP	15.00
8mm	.318	150	SSP	15.00
	.318	196	RN-SP	15.00
8.15mm	.324	151	FN-SP	15.00
8mm	.329	210	SSP	15.00
	.330	225	RNSP	15.00
351 WSL	.351	180	SSP	15.00
9mm	.356	200	SSP	15.00
9.3x72R	.364	193	FNSP	15.00
401 WSL	.406	200/250	RNSP	16.00
40-65/82	.406	260	FNSP	16.00
405 WCF	.412	300	RNSP	17.50
11.2x72mm	.440	400	RNSP	35.00*
45	.454	250/300	RNSP	17.50

* = Price for 20. HP = Hollowpoint; SP = Softpoint; SSP = Spitzer Softpoint; FN = Flat Nose.

DKT CAST BULLETS

Bullet	Mould	Nom. Wgt.	Std. Dia.	Opt. Dia.	Price/100
600	LBT	600	.477	.475	$25.00
500	Custom	500	.458	.457 .459	25.00
450	NEI	450	.512	.509 .515	25.00
480	LBT	450	.477	.475	25.00
400	LBT	400	.475	.477	25.00
385	NEI	385	.417		15.00
345	NEI-SSK	345	.451	.450 .452	15.00
340	Custom	340	.452	.450 .451	15.00
311	NEI-SSK	310	.431	.429 .430	15.00
310	NEI-SSK	310	.431	.429 .430	15.00
285	NEI-SSK	285	.431	.429 .430	15.00
275	NEI-SSK	275	.410	.412	15.00
270	NEI-SSK	270	.451	.450 .452	15.00
260	NEI-SSK	260	.431	.429 .430	15.00
182	NEI-SSK	180	.358	.357 .359	15.00
115	Custom	115	*		20.00

*For 310 Cadet.

BULLETS/ Custom

EAGLE FLIGHT

Premium bonded core hunting bullets in wide range of calibers including handguns. From Eagle Flight Bullet Company.

Price: . . . . **Contact manufacturer.**

EICHELBERGER

Swaged 14-caliber bullets in Spitzer flat-base, 12 and 15 grains, or Spitzer boattail leaded copper in 12.7-grain weight. From Eichelberger.

Price: 14-cal. flat-base, per 100 . . . **$45.00**
Price: 14-cal. boattail, per 100 . . . **$19.60**
Price: 14-cal. boattail, per 1000 . **$185.00**

FOWLER BULLETS

Match-grade benchrest/varmint bullets formed in Rorschach and Simonson carbide dies. All are flat-base hollowpoint design. The 22 and 6mm bullets have a 7-caliber ogive and the 25 caliber a 9-caliber ogive with .045" point. From Fowler Bullets.

Price: . . . . **See chart.**

FREEDOM ARMS

Jacketed hollowpoint and flatpoint 240- and 260-grain bullets in 45-caliber. Jacket is .032" thick; core 10.75% tin and antimony mixture. Come in packages of 50. From Freedom Arms, Inc.

Price: **$21.75**

FUSILIER BULLETS

Cast bullets with hardness factors of 30-35 BHN for Imperial Fusiliers and 18-30 BHN for Premium. From Fusilier Bullets.

Price: . . . . **See chart.**

GREEN BAY BULLETS

Rifle and pistol bullets produced using specially purchased lead alloy for consistency. Custom lead hardness and sizing available. All bullets come pre-lubed. From Green Bay Bullets.

Price: . . . . **See chart.**

GRIZZLY BULLETS

Bonded core, large caliber hunting bullets. Copper jackets are bonded to pure lead core using a chemical-metallurgical fusion technique. From Grizzly Bullets.

Price: . . . . **See chart.**

GRIZZLY

Caliber	Wgt. Grs.	Price/20
308	165	$29.00
	180	30.00
338	225	32.00
	250	33.00
375	250	33.00
	300	34.00
416	350	39.00
458	350	39.00*
	400	39.00*
	500	39.00*

*Minimum order of 100 bullets.

FOWLER

Caliber	Diameter	Wgt. Grs.	Price/100
22	.224	52	$11.50
		60	12.00
6mm	.243	63	12.00
		66	12.00
		68	12.00
		70	12.00
		80	13.00
25	.257	79	14.50
		82	14.50
		85	14.50
		110	15.50

FUSILIER

	Bullet			Price	
Caliber	Diameter	Wgt. Grs.	Type	Premium	Imperial
30	.307, .308	170	FP, GC	$9.50	$11.00
9mm	.355, .358	105	TC, FB	7.50	9.00
		147	TC, BB	7.50	9.00
35	.357, .358	148	WC, BB	7.95	9.45
		158	SWCHP, GC	8.25	9.75
		158	SWC, GC	8.25	9.75
		180	TC, GC	8.50	10.00
		180	Hornady-style, TCBB	8.50	10.00
		200	FP, GC	8.95	10.45
37	.375	250	FP, GC	9.50	11.00
10mm	.401	180	Hornady-style, TCBB	8.50	10.00
		200	Hornady-style, TCBB	8.95	10.45
44	.429, .430	208	WCFB	8.95	10.45
		240	SWCFB, GC	9.50	11.00
		250	SWCFB	9.50	11.00
		275	FP, GC	9.95	11.45
		300	Hornady-style, TCBB	9.95	11.45
45	.451, .452	201	SWCFB	8.95	10.45
		225	Hornady-style, TCBB	8.95	10.45
		300	Hornady-style, TCBB	9.95	11.45
45	.457, .458	300	FP, GC	10.25	11.75
		405	FP, GC	11.95	13.45
		500	FP, GC	12.95	14.95

FP = Flat Point; GC = Gas Check; TC = Truncated Cone; FB = Flat Base; BB = Bevel Base; WC = Wadcutter; SWC = Semi-Wadcutter.

Grizzly Bullets

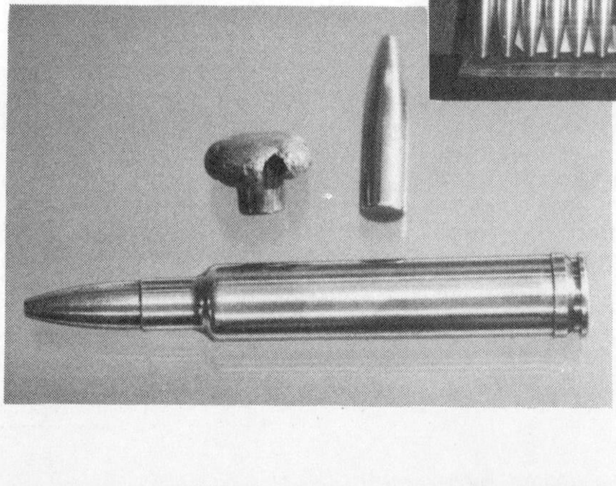
Grizzly 308-caliber 180-gr.

GREENBAY

Caliber	Diameter	Wgt. Grs.	Style	Type	Price/Per
		——RIFLE——			
22	.223	45	RN	GC	$8.95/100
	.223	55	RN	GC	8.95/100
22	.228	59	PT	GC	8.95/100
6mm	.243	85	RN	GC	7.95/100
25	.257	90	RN	GC	7.75/100
	.257	90	FP	GC	7.75/100
	.257	115	RN	GC	7.75/100
6.5mm	.266	125	RN	GC	8.40/100
	.266	140	RN	GC	8.50/100
7mm	.287	140	RN	GC	8.50/100
7.35mm	.298		RN	GC	8.95/100
32/20	.311		RN		5.75/100
	.311	85	FP	GC	7.75/100
	.311	95	SWC		5.75/100
	.311	175	RN	GC	8.25/100
30	.311	120	FP		6.25/100
	.311	115	FP	GC	8.40/100
	.311	115	PT	GC	7.25/100
	.311	130	RN		6.25/100
	.311	155	RN	GC	8.50/100
	.311	170	RN	GC	8.95/100
	.311	180	FP	GC	8.95/100
303	.311	190	OP	GC	9.25/100
32/40	.321	180	FP	GC	8.95/100
	.321	165	FP		7.95/100
8mm	.323	170	RN	GC	8.95/100
	.323	220	RN	GC	8.95/100
33	.338	200	FP	GC	8.95/100
348	.348	185	FP	GC	8.95/100
	.348	250	FP	GC	9.25/100
351	.352	170	RN	GC	9.25/100
35	.358	200	RN	GC	9.25/100
38/55	.379		FP		7.75/100
375	.375	250	FP	GC	7.95/100
38/40	.401	175	FP		6.50/100
	.401	175	FP	GC	6.45/100
40/65	.406	245	FP		7.95/100
405	.412	290	RN		4.95/50
44/40	.427	210	FP		7.75/100
45/70	.457	305	FP		4.75/50
	.457	345	FP		4.95/50
	.457	395	RN		5.25/50
	.457	505	RN		6.25/50
	.457	505	RN	GC	8.75/50
50/70	.515	450	FP		6.95/50
	.515	505	RN		7.50/50
43 Spanish	.439	335	FP		5.25/50

Caliber	Diameter	Wgt. Grs.	Style	Type	Price/Per
		——PISTOL——			
25	.257	65	FP	GC	$7.95/100
8mm Nambu	.323	100	RN		6.25/100
380 Auto	.355		RN		5.25/100
9mm-38 Auto	.356	95	FP		5.25/100
	.356	125	PFP		5.25/100
	.356	125	RN		5.50/100
	.356	125	FP		5.50/100
357	.357	160	SWC		5.95/100
	.357	160	SWC		5.95/100
	.357	160	SWC	GC	8.95/100
38	.358	90	RN		5.50/100
	.358	125	RN		5.75/100
	.358	127	WC		5.75/100
	.358	140	WC		5.95/100
	.358	148	WC		5.95/100
	.358	148	WC		5.95/100
	.358	148	WCBB		5.95/100
	.358	148	PFP		5.95/100
	.358	158	RN		6.25/100
	.358	160	SWC		6.25/100
	.358	195	RN		6.75/100
	.358	200	SWC		6.75/100
38/40	.401	175	FP		6.50/100
	.401	175	FP		6.45/100
41 Mag.	.410	200	WC		6.95/100
	.410	210	FP		6.95/100
44 Mag. & Spl.	.410	210	FP	GC	11.25/100
	.429	225	FP	GC	10.25/100
	.429	245	RN		7.75/100
	.429	245	SWC	GC	10.25/100
	.429	250	WC		7.75/100
	.429	250	SWC		7.75/100
	.429	255	SWC		7.95/100
45 Auto	.452	185	SWC		6.95/100
	.452	185	SWC		6.95/100
	.452	200	SWC		6.95/100
	.452	220	SWC		7.25/100
	.452	225	RN		7.25/100
	.452	240	RN		7.50/100
	.452	240	RN		7.50/100
45 Colt	.454	255	SWC		7.75/100
	.454	260	FP		7.95/100
41 Long Colt		190	Heel		6.50/100

RN = Round Nose; PT = Pointed; FP = Flat Point; SWC = Semi-Wadcutter; OP = Open Point; PFP = Pointed Flat Point; WC = Wadcutter; BB = Bevel Base.

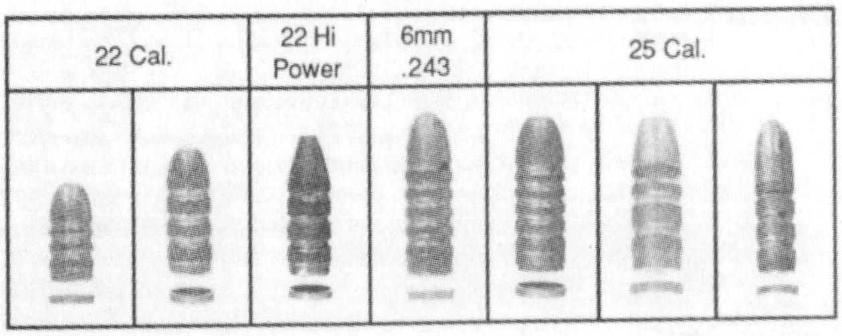

Green Bay Bullets

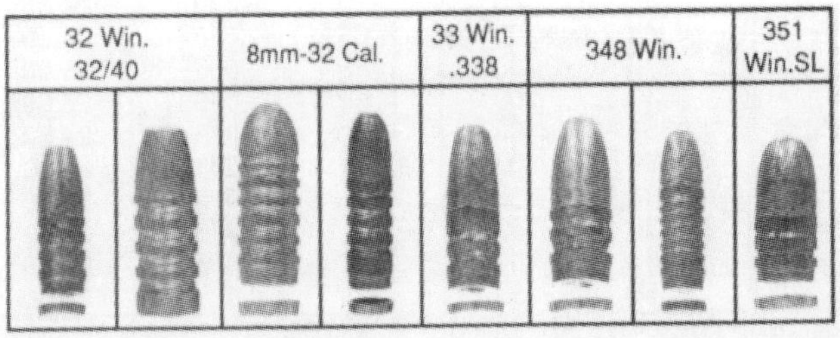

GROUP TIGHT BULLETS

Benchrest bullets hand-made from hand-extruded wire. Flat-base design and jacketed. From Group Tight Bullets.

Price: . . . . **See chart.**

HAMMETT'S VLDS

Very low drag 17- and 6mm caliber target and hunting rifle bullets made with Simonson carbide dies and match-grade jackets. All bullets have a pressure ring at the base of bearing surface for accuracy. From Hammett's VLD Bullets.

Price: . . . . **See chart.**

HART

Benchrest quality bullets in 22-caliber and 6mm from 52 grs. to 70 grs. From Robert W. Hart & Son, Inc.

Price: . . . . **See chart.**

HAWK LABS, INC.

Precision hunting bullets in calibers 270 to 510 with annealed copper jackets. All bullets are double swaged for uniformity and tighter core, weighed twice and cleaned in five separate operations. Hawk draws their own tubing, lead wire and makes their jackets for uniformity of components. From Hawk Labs, Inc.

Price: . . . . **See chart.**

HOBSON

Hard cast and super-hard base bullets with soft-nose cone. Cast from Hensley & Gibbs or Sako moulds from top-quality lead with tin and antimony; BHN hardness reading of 18-20. All bullets come lubed with LBT blue magnum lube. From Hobson Precision Mfg. Co.

Price: . . . . **See chart.**

HART

Caliber	Wgt. Grs.	Type	Price/100
22	52	FB	$10.65
	52	BT	9.95
243/6mm	62	BT	11.75
	68	BT	11.75
	68	FB	11.75
	70	BT	11.75

FB = Flat Base; BT = Boattail.
From Robert Hart & Son.

HAWK LABS

Caliber	Diameter	Wgt. Grs.	Ogive	Jacket Diameter	Price/50
270	.277	80	2	.025	$22.50
	.277	130	2	.025	23.50
	.277	130	8	.030	23.50
	.277	150	8	.035	24.50
	.277	165	8	.035	25.00
7mm	.284	130	8	.025	23.50
	.284	140	8	.025	23.50
	.284	140	8	.030	23.50
	.284	160	8	.030	24.00
	.284	160	8	.035	24.50
	.284	175	8	.035	25.00
308	.308	100	8	.025	23.00
	.308	165	8	.035	24.00
	.308	180	8	.035	24.50
	.308	200	8	.035	25.00
	.308	220	8	.035	26.00
	.308	250	8	.035	27.00
8mm	.318	180	6	.030	24.50
	.318	220	6	.030	25.50
	.323	180	6	.025	24.00
	.323	180	6	.030	24.50
	.323	180	6	.035	25.00
	.323	220	6	.030	25.50
	.323	220	6	.035	26.00
	.323	250	6	.035	27.00
33 Win.	.338	180	FP	.030	24.00
	.338	200	FP	.030	24.50
338	.338	200	7	.035	24.50
	.338	230	7	.035	25.50
	.338	250	7	.035	26.00
	.338	275	7	.035	27.00
348	.348	165	FP	.030	24.00
	.348	180	FP	.030	24.50
	.348	200	FP	.030	24.50
	.348	200	FP	.035	25.00
	.348	250	FP	.035	25.50
351	.351	180	RN	.025	24.50
9mm	.356	200	6	.030	24.50
	.356	250	6	.030	25.00
358	.358	180	2	.025	23.50
	.358	200	2	.025	23.50
	.358	250	2	.025	24.50

Caliber	Diameter	Wgt. Grs.	Ogive	Jacket Diameter	Price/50
358	.358	200	8	.030	23.50
	.358	250	8	.030	24.50
	.358	250	8	.035	25.00
	.358	250	8	.050	29.00
	.358	275	8	.035	26.50
	.358	300	8	.030	26.00
	.358	300	8	.035	27.00
9.3mm	.365	200	6	.030	24.50
	.365	235	6	.035	25.00
	.365	250	6	.030	25.50
	.365	250	6	.035	26.00
	.365	285	6	.035	26.50
	.365	285	6	.050	29.00
	.365	300	6	.030	26.50
	.365	320	6	.030	27.00
375	.375	180	2	.025	23.50
	.375	200	2	.025	24.00
	.375	250	2	.025	24.50
	.375	250	2	.035	26.00
	.375	270	2	.050	28.50
	.375	235	6	.025	24.00
	.375	235	6	.035	24.50
	.375	250	6	.035	25.50
	.375	270	6	.035	26.00
	.375	270	6	.050	28.50
	.375	300	6	.050	29.00
406	.406	235	FP	.025	24.50
	.406	270	FP	.025	25.50
	.406	300	FP	.025	25.50
408	.408	235	FP	.025	24.50
	.408	270	FP	.025	25.50
	.408	300	FP	.025	25.50
406	.406	300	6	.025	24.50
	.406	300	6	.050	29.00
	.406	350	6	.025	25.00
	.406	350	6	.035	28.00
	.406	400	6	.025	25.50
	.406	400	6	.050	29.00
408	.408	300	6	.025	24.50
	.408	300	6	.050	29.00
	.408	350	6	.025	25.00
	.408	350	6	.035	28.00

RN = Round Nose; FP = Flat Point; HP = Hollowpoint.

HAMMET'S VLDS

Caliber	Diameter	Wgt. Grs.	B.C.	Price 100	Price 250	Price 1000
17	.172	17.0	.131	$12.60	$31.00	$120.00
	.172	19.8	.148	12.60	31.00	120.00
	.172	21.9	.198	12.60	31.00	120.00
	.172	25.0	.219	13.00	32.00	126.00
	.172	30.0	.246	13.00	32.00	126.00
6mm	.244	95.0	.547	16.00		155.00
	.244	106.0	.592	16.00		155.00
	.244	110.0	.602	16.00		155.00
	.244	120.0	.659	17.00		165.00

GROUP TIGHT

Caliber	Wgt. Grs.	Type	Price/100
224	52	FB	NA
243	68	FB	$13.00
7mm	120	FB	18.50
30	125	FB	18.50
	135	FB	18.50
	150	FB	NA

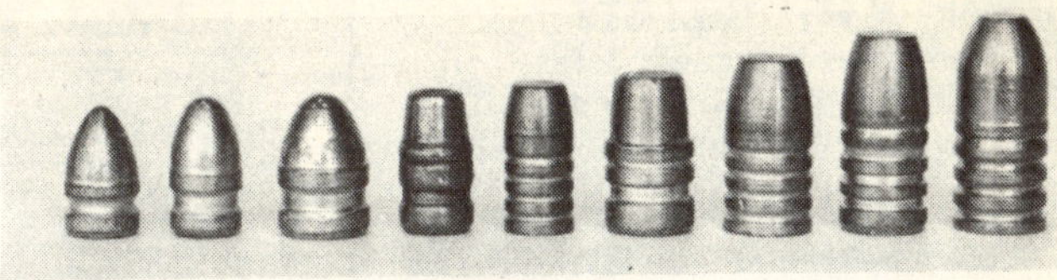

Hobson Bullets

HOBSON

Caliber	Diameter	Wgt. Grs.	Type	Number	Price/1000
9mm	.356	115	SWBB	925	$32.00
35	.356/.357	145	RNBB	928	36.00
38	.358	158	SWC	382	36.00
45 ACP	.452	225	RNBB	457	40.00
44/44 Magnum	.430	240	TC	428	42.00
	.430	344	SHB		42.00
	.430	307	SHB		42.00
357 T/C		185	TC		38.00
		185	SHB		38.00
44 Magnum		307	TC		53.00
45-70		418	SHB		

SWBB = Semi-Wadcutter Bevel Base; RNBB = Round-Nose Bevel Base; TC = Truncated Cone; SHB = Super Hard Base.

HAWK LABS

Caliber	Diameter	Wgt. Grs.	Ogive	Jacket Diameter	Price/50
408	.408	400	6	.025	$25.50
	.408	400	6	.050	29.00
410	.410	300	6	.025	24.50
	.410	300	6	.050	29.00
	.410	350	6	.025	25.00
	.410	350	6	.035	28.00
	.410	400	6	.025	25.50
	.410	400	6	.050	29.00
411	.411	300	6	.025	24.50
	.411	300	6	.050	29.00
	.411	350	6	.025	25.00
	.411	350	6	.035	28.00
	.411	400	6	.025	25.50
	.411	400	6	.050	29.00
416	.416	300	6	.025	25.00
	.416	300	6	.035	26.00
	.416	300	6	.050	29.00
	.416	350	6	.025	26.00
	.416	350	6	.035	28.00
	.416	350	6	.050	30.00
	.416	400	6	.035	28.50
	.416	400	6	.050	30.00
	.416	450	6	.050	32.00
423	.423	300	6	.035	27.00
	.423	350	6	.035	28.00
	.423	350	6	.050	30.00
	.423	400	6	.050	32.00
44/444	.430	250	HP	.025	23.50
	.430	250	FP	.035	24.50
	.430	275	HP	.025	24.50
	.430	275	FP	.035	25.00
	.430	300	HP	.025	25.00
	.430	300	FP	.035	25.50
425	.435	300	6	.035	27.00
	.435	350	6	.035	28.00
	.435	350	6	.050	30.00
	.435	400	6	.050	32.00
	.435	450	6	.050	34.00
458	.458	300	HP	.025	25.50
	.458	350	FP	.025	26.00
	.458	350	4	.035	26.50

Caliber	Diameter	Wgt. Grs.	Ogive	Jacket Diameter	Price/50
458	.458	400	FP, HP	.025	$27.00
	.458	400	RN, FP	.035	28.50
	.458	400	4	.050	30.00
	.458	500	4	.035	31.00
465	.468	400	4	.035	30.00
	.468	400	4	.050	32.00
	.468	500	4	.050	34.00
475	.475	300	1.5, HP	.025	26.50
	.475	350	1.5, HP	.025	27.00
	.475	350	1.5, FP	.035	27.50
	.475	400	1.5, FP	.035	28.50
	.475	400	4	.035	29.50
	.475	400	4	.050	30.00
	.475	500	4	.035	31.50
	.475	500	4	.050	34.50
	.475	600	4	.050	36.00
482	.482	400	4	.035	33.00
	.482	400	4	.050	34.50
	.482	500	4	.035	36.00
	.482	500	4	.050	38.50
488	.488	400	4	.035	33.00
	.488	400	4	.050	34.50
	.488	500	4	.035	36.00
	.488	500	4	.050	38.50
50	.500	300		.025	27.00
	.500	350		.025	28.50
505	.505	400	2	.035	31.00
	.505	400	2	.050	33.00
	.505	500	2	.035	34.50
	.505	500	2	.050	36.00
	.505	600	2	.050	38.00
510	.510	350	2	.025	28.00
	.510	350	2	.035	29.00
	.510	400	2	.035	30.50
	.510	400	2	.050	31.50
	.510	500	2	.035	32.00
	.510	500	2	.050	35.00
	.510	600	2	.035	36.50
	.510	600	2	.050	38.00
577	.585				

RN = Round Nose; FP = Flat Point; HP = Hollowpoint.

HT BULLETS

Computer-designed, lathe-turned solid copper hunting bullets. Grooved bearing surface reduces bullet contact area by over 85%. Radial ridges align the bullet and seal the bore. Bullet nose is "reverse radial design" meaning the ogive out toward the tip is concave. Three annealing processes for varied levels of expansion. From HT Bullets.

Price: . . . . **See chart.**

IDAHO BULLETS

Paper patch pure lead bullets in 45-caliber (.452) only. Sold not patched to allow matching rifle throat and groove diameter. Two styles offered: flat-nose and spitzer. Both are cup-based for the tail of the patch. Spitzer is 4S ogive. Standard bullets weights: Flat-nose, 325, 350, 44, 450, 500, 550; Spitzer, 450, 500, 525, 550. Custom weights between 325 and 550 grains available for additional $2.00/100. Come 50 to a box. From Idaho Bullets.

Price: 50 . . . . **$12.00**
Price: 100 . . . . **$24.00**

J&L SUPERIOR BULLETS

Lead bullets dip-lubed with Space Age lube that dries hard and covers bullets completely. From Huntington Die Specialties, Inc.

Price: . . . . **See chart.**

JENSEN BULLETS

Nylon-tipped, bonded core, jacketed bullets for varminting or big game hunting. Lead core is high temperature flux-bonded to jacket for high weight retention. Jacket is precision machined from pure copper and tapers from thin walls at front to heavy walls where core stops and solid rear shaft begins. Available from 243- to 416-caliber. From Jensen Bullets.

Price: . . . . **See chart.**

JLK BULLETS

Competition and varmint 22-caliber, 6mm and 7mm low and very low drag jacketed bullets. Cut lead cores run through squirt die for +/- .1-grain uniformity in weight from bullet to bullet. Bullets swaged in Simonson carbide dies and jacketed using J-4 jackets. From JLK Bullets.

Price: 22, 6mm per 100 . . . . **$14.00**
Price: 7mm per 100 . . . . **$16.00**
Price: 500 and over 22 VLD, per 100 . . . . **$12.00**

HT

					Price	
Caliber	Diameter	Wgt. Grs.	S.D.	B.C.	20	Solids
6mm	0.243	80	0.209	0.394	$40.00	$24.00
25	.0257	100	0.234	0.442	40.00	24.00
6.5mm	0.264	120	0.266	0.502	40.00	24.00
270	0.277	120	0.240	0.453	40.00	24.00
	0.277	126	0.252	0.475	40.00	24.00
	0.277	130	0.261	0.492	40.00	24.00
7mm	0.284	120	0.230	0.434	40.00	24.00
	0.284	130	0.249	0.470	40.00	24.00
	0.284	140	0.268	0.506	40.00	24.00
	0.284	150	0.288	0.543	40.00	24.00
30	0.308	140	0.227	0.428	40.00	24.00
	0.308	150	0.243	0.458	40.00	24.00
	0.308	160	0.259	0.489	40.00	24.00
	0.308	170	0.275	0.519	40.00	24.00
311	0.311	180	0.284	0.516	40.00	24.00
338	0.338	200	0.270	0.509	40.00	24.00
	0.338	225	0.304	0.574	40.00	24.00
375	0.375	235	0.252	0.450	44.00	26.00
	0.375	250	0.268	0.479	44.00	26.00
	0.375	270	0.290	0.518	44.00	26.00
416	0.416	320	0.277	0.495	44.00	26.00
	0.416	390	0.338	0.398		30.00

S.D. = Standard Deviation; B.C. = Ballistic Coefficient

HT Bullets

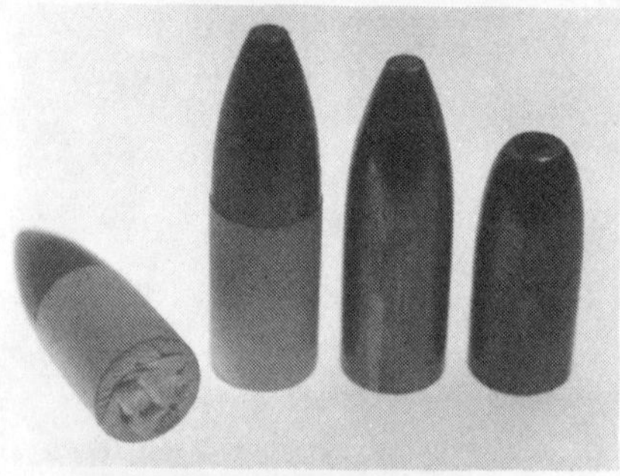

Idaho 500-, 550- and 400-gr. bullets

Jensen Big Game Bullets

J&L SUPERIOR

Caliber	Diameter	Wgt. Grs.	Type	Price/50
		RIFLE		
22	.224	54	FN	$7.98
30	.308	130	RN	7.98
	.308	150	FN	7.98
	.308	180	FN	8.98
32	.308	115	FN	7.98
	.321	170	FN	7.98
	.323	170	FN	7.98
33	.338	200	FN	8.98
348	.348	200	FN	8.98
375	.376	250	FN	8.98
40	.408	260	FN	8.98
	.408	300	CSA	10.98
	.408	350	CSA	10.98
	.408	400	CSA	11.98
38/40	.401	170		8.98
416	.416	350	FN	10.98
43 Spanish	.439	370	FN	10.98
43 Mauser	.446	370		10.98
45	.458	300	FN	10.98
	.458	325	FN	10.98
	.458	405	FN	11.98
	.458	500	FN	11.98
50	.512	450	FN	11.98
	.512	515	FN	11.98
		PISTOL		
9mm Makarov	.364	110	RN	8.98
455 Webley	.455	265	HB	11.98
44-40	.428	200	FN	8.98

FN = Flat Nose; CSA = C. Sharps Arms Design; RN = Round Nose; HB = Hollow Base.

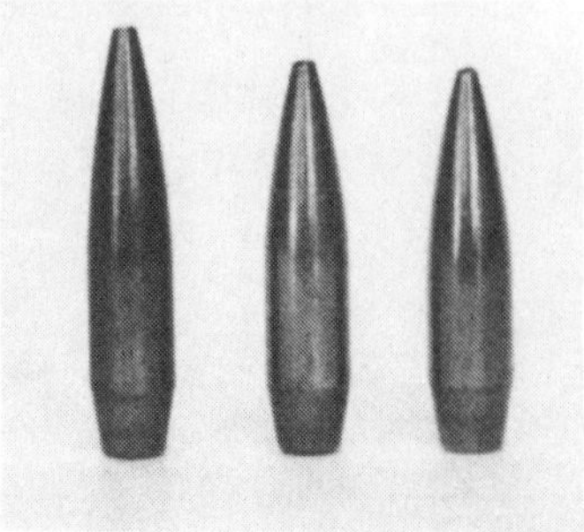

JLK Competition and Varmint Bullets

JLK

Bullet	55	60	65	70	75	80	168	180
Weight	55	60	65	70	75	80	168	180
Length OL	.765	.805	.940	.980	1.050	1.120	1.420	1.520
Bearing Length	.265	.305	.340	.300	.370	.340	.420	.520
Boattail Length	—	—	—	.180	.180	.180	230	.230
Boattail Angle	—	—	—	9.0°	9.0°	9.0°	7.5°	7.5°
Meplat Dia.	.046	.046	.046	.046	.046	.046	.046	.046
Ogive Radius	12	12	15	12	12	15	18	18
Ogive Axial Length	.500	.500	.600	.500	.500	.600	.770	.770
Optimum Twist	14	12	10	1-9	1-8½	1-8	9.5	9
B.C.	.309	.339	.397	.410	.425	.510	.690	.738

Kawser Pin Grabbers

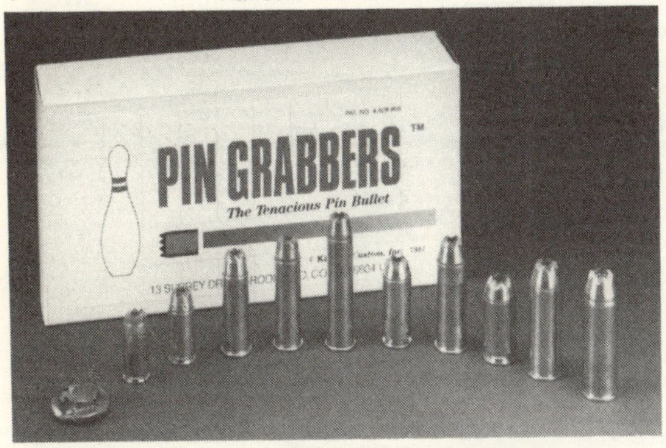

KAWSER Pin-Grabber Bullets

Cartridge	Wgt. Grs.	Type	Price/100
380 Auto	110	JHP	$20.00
9mm Luger	125	JHP	20.00
	150	JHP	24.25
38 Super	125	JHP	20.00
	150	JHP	24.25
38 Special	158	JHP	24.25
357 Magnum	125	JHP	20.00
	150	JHP	24.25
	158	JHP	22.00
357 Maximum	158	JHP	22.00
	180	JHP	24.25
40 S&W	170	JHP	27.25
10mm	170	JHP	37.75
	210	JHP	38.25
41 AE	170	JHP	27.25
	210	JHP	27.25
41 Magnum	170	JHP	27.25
	210	JHP	27.25
44 Special	180	JHP	27.75
44 Magnum	180	JHP	27.75
	210	JHP	31.75
	240	JHP	28.00
	265	JHP	36.25
45 ACP	185	JHP	29.50
	200	JHP	28.25
	225	Lead	16.75
	225	JHP	29.50
	250	JHP	29.50
	260	JHP	29.50
45 Auto Rim	225	JHP	31.50
45 Win. Magnum	260	JHP	31.50
	300	JHP	33.50*
45 Long Colt	260	JHP	31.50
454 Casull	260	JHP	32.25
	300	JHP	33.50*

* = Price for 50. JHP = Jacketed Hollowpoint.

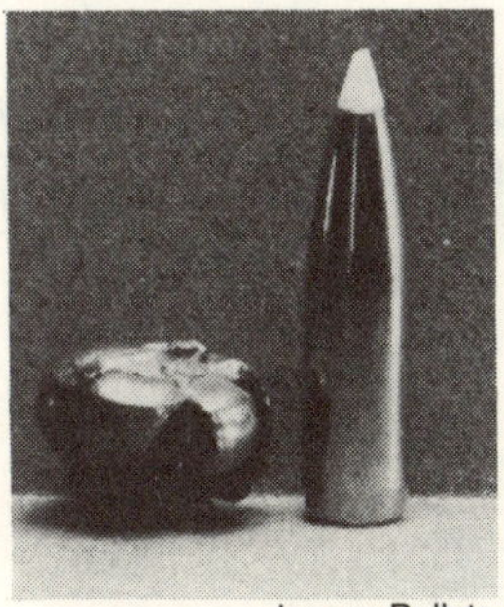

Jensen Bullets

KAWSER CUSTOM

Pistol bullets utilizing unique sawtooth nose design. Kawser's Pin-Grabber bullets are designed specifically for bowling pin competition. Pin-Grabbers require special seater plugs for use in Dillon, Lyman, RCBS and Lee presses. Kawser supplies seater/crimper dies in all Pin-Grabber calibers. Perfect Circle bullets come in two bullet styles, jacketed softpoint and jacketed hollowpoint, and three grain weights for the 50 AE Desert Eagle—230-, 300-, 350-grain. Kawser Custom, Inc.

Price: Bullets . . . . **See chart.**
Price: Seater/crimper die **$18.00**
Price: Seater plug **$12.00**

KEN'S

Custom swaged hunting bullets in any caliber and bullet type. From Ken's Kustom Kartridges.

Price: . . . . **Contact manufacturer.**

JENSEN

Caliber	Wgt. Grs.	S.D.	B.C.	Price/20
243	80	.193	.379	$43.60
	100	.242	.465	44.00
257	100	.216	.434	44.60
	120	.260	.508	45.00
264	125	.256	.539	45.20
277	130	.242	.487	45.20
	150	.279	.563	45.60
284	140	.248	.538	45.60
	154	.272	.590	45.00
	175	.310	.673	46.00
308	165	.248	.532	46.20
	180	.271	.579	47.00
	200	.301	.640	48.00
323	210	.288	.559	48.80
338	200	.250	.483	48.60
	225	.281	.545	49.00
	250	.313	.606	49.40
358	225	.250	.524	49.00
	250	.279	.554	49.40
375	225	.220	.407	54.00
	250	.254	.451	54.00
	300	.305	.621	54.60
416	335	.276	.475	58.00
458	400	.272	.463	62.00

Jensen 375-, 308- and 284-Caliber Bullets.

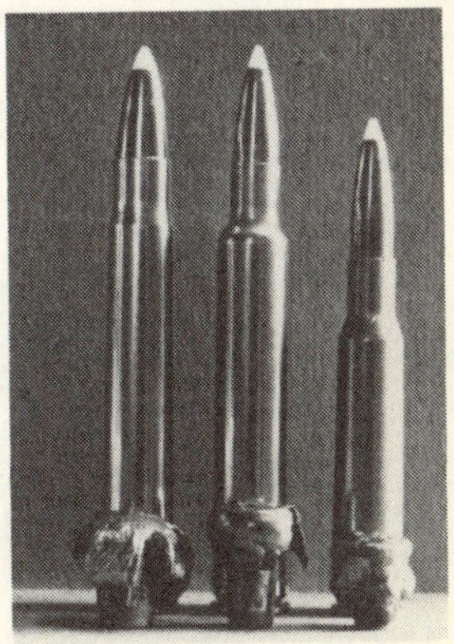

KASWER Perfect Circle Bullets

Wgt. Grs.	Type	Price/100
	Caliber: 50 AE	
230	JSP	$28.00
230	JHP	34.30
300	JSP	45.00
300	JHP	51.30
350	JSP	30.00
350	JHP	33.15

JSP = Jacketed Softpoint; JHP = Jacketed Hollowpoint.

LANE BULLETS

Cast bullets for the target shooter from 30-caliber up to 45-70. Lead/tin/antimony alloy hard enough to prevent base distortion under high pressure. From Lane Bullets, Inc.

Price: . . . . **See chart.**

M&D MUNITIONS

Swaged lead pistol bullets plain, plated and jacketed. Lead bullets double dry-lubed for less leading. Copper plating .0001" thickness and will not separate but will flatten upon impact. Jackets are of guilding metal. From M&D Munitions, Ltd.

Price: . . . . **See chart.**

MAGNUS BULLET CO.

Competition pistol bullets from 32- to 45-caliber. From Magnus Bullet Co.

Price: . . . . **See chart.**

MOLOC BULLETS

Cast lead bullets dry-lubed and sized in calibers 32 through 45. From MoLoc Bullets.

Price: . . . . **See chart.**

MONTANA PRECISION SWAGING

Cast rifle and pistol bullets and swaged paper patch bullets. Cast bullets come lubed and sized. From Montanta Precision Swaging.

Price: . . . . **See chart.**

RICK MULHERN BULLETS

Match 30-caliber bullets in popular weights. Standard or rebated 9° boattail design. Made in Simonson carbide dies. From Rick Mulhern.

Price: . . . . **Contact manufacturer.**

LANE

Caliber	Wgt. Grs.	Type	Price/1000
30	115	RN	$26.22
32	78	RN	25.50
380	95	DEWC	25.60
9mm	115	SWC	26.22
	125	RN	26.70
	147	FP	28.13
10mm	155	RN	29.08
	175	SWC	30.98
38	148	DEWC	28.13
	150	SWC	28.63
	158	SWC	29.08
	158	RN	29.08
41	215	SWC	32.40
44	240	SWC	34.77
45	155	SWC	29.08
	185	SWC	31.45
	200	SWC	31.93
	230	RN	34.30
	255	SWC	35.25
45-70	405	FP	31.93*

* = Price for 500. RN = Round Nose; DEWC = Dead End Wadcutter; SWC = Semi-Wadcutter; FP = Flat Point.

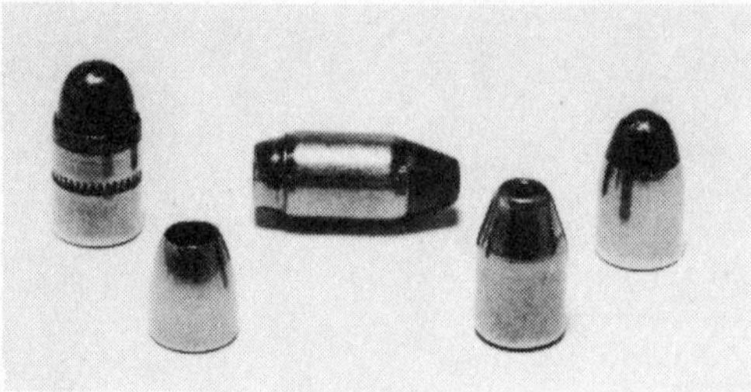

Mo-Loc Bullets

MOLOC

Caliber	Wgt. Grs.	Type	Price/500
32	98	SWC	$18.25
380 ACP	95	RN	18.25
9mm	125	RN	18.25
	125	TC	18.25
9mm/38 Super	147	HTC	18.90
38 Super	160	RN	18.90
38	125	SWC	18.25
	148	BBWC	18.90
	158	SWC	18.90
	158	RN	18.90
	180	FP	23.60
10mm	155	SWC	20.90
	180	SWC	23.60
	180	FP	23.60
41 Mag	210	SWC	24.30
44-40	200	FP	24.30
44 Mag	240	SWC	26.35
	265	FP	29.55
45 ACP	155	SWC	20.90
	185	SWC	23.60
	200	SWC	24.30
	230	RN	24.95
	255	SWC	27.00
45 Long Colt	250	RNFP	27.00

SWC = Semi-Wadcutter; RN = Round Nose; TC = Truncated Cone; BBWC = Bevel Base Wadcutter; FP = Flat Point; RNFP = Round Nose Flat Point.

MAGNUS

Bullet No.	Caliber	Wgt. Grs.	Type	Dia.	Price/500	Price/1000
203	30	115	RNBB	.309	$15.00	$28.00
201	32	100	SWCBB	.313	15.00	28.00
202	32-20	118	FP	.313	15.00	28.00
401	9mm	122	FPBB	.355	15.00	28.00
402		125	RNBB	.355	15.00	28.00
403		147	FPBB	.356	16.00	30.00
301	380	95	RNBB	.355	15.00	28.00
302		100	TCBB	.356	15.00	28.00
502	38/357	148	WCBB	.357	15.00	28.00
503		158	SWCBB	.357	17.00	31.50
504		158	RNBB	.357	17.00	31.50
501		148	DEWC	.358	15.00	28.00
101	40/10mm	180		.401	18.00	34.00
601	41	215	SWCBB	.410	21.00	40.50
702	44	215	SWCBB	.430	21.00	40.00
701		240	SWCBB	.430	19.00	35.50
801	45	185	SWCBB	.452	19.00	35.50
802		200	SWCBB	.452	20.00	38.50
803		225	FPBB	.452	22.00	42.00
804		230	RNBB	.452	22.00	42.00
901		255	SWCBB	.452	20.00	37.50
805		155	SWCBB	.452	17.00	32.00
807		215	SWCBB	.452	21.00	40.00
806		170	SPLBB	.452	18.00	34.00

RNBB = Round Nose Bevel Base; FPBB = Flat Point Bevel Base; DEWC = Dead End Wadcutter; WCBB = Wadcutter Bevel Base; SWCBB = Semi-Wadcutter Bevel Base; FPBB = Flat Point Bevel Base; FP = Flat Point.

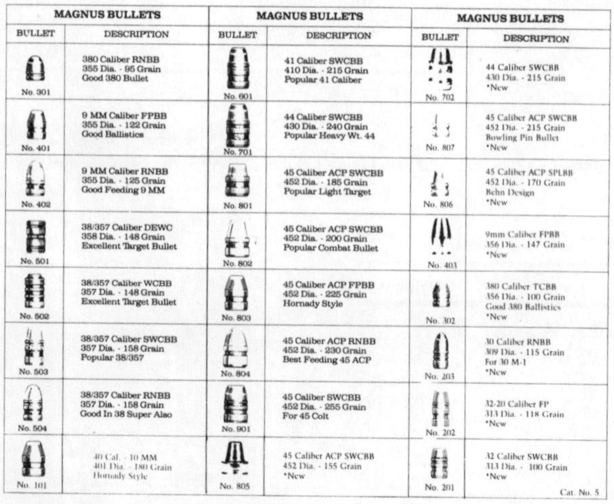

MAGNUS BULLETS		MAGNUS BULLETS		MAGNUS BULLETS	
BULLET	DESCRIPTION	BULLET	DESCRIPTION	BULLET	DESCRIPTION
No. 301	380 Caliber RNBB 355 Dia. - 95 Grain Good 380 Bullet	No. 601	41 Caliber SWCBB 410 Dia. - 215 Grain Popular 41 Caliber	No. 702	44 Caliber SWCBB 430 Dia. - 215 Grain *New
No. 401	9 MM Caliber FPBB 355 Dia. - 122 Grain Good Ballistics	No. 701	44 Caliber SWCBB 430 Dia. - 240 Grain Popular Heavy Wt. 44	No. 807	45 Caliber ACP SWCBB 452 Dia. - 215 Grain Bowling Pin Bullet *New
No. 402	9 MM Caliber RNBB 355 Dia. - 125 Grain Good Feeding 9 MM	No. 801	45 Caliber ACP SWCBB 452 Dia. - 185 Grain Popular Light Target	No. 806	45 Caliber ACP SPLBB 452 Dia. - 170 Grain Behn Design *New
No. 501	38/357 Caliber DEWC 358 Dia. - 148 Grain Excellent Target Bullet	No. 802	45 Caliber ACP SWCBB 452 Dia. - 200 Grain Popular Combat Bullet	No. 403	9mm Caliber FPBB 356 Dia. - 147 Grain *New
No. 502	38/357 Caliber WCBB 357 Dia. - 148 Grain Excellent Target Bullet	No. 803	45 Caliber ACP FPBB 452 Dia. - 225 Grain Hornady Style	No. 302	380 Caliber TCBB 356 Dia. - 100 Grain Good 380 Ballistics *New
No. 503	38/357 Caliber SWCBB 357 Dia. - 158 Grain Popular 38/357	No. 804	45 Caliber ACP RNBB 452 Dia. - 230 Grain Best Feeding 45 ACP	No. 203	30 Caliber RNBB 309 Dia. - 115 Grain For 30 M-1 *New
No. 504	38/357 Caliber RNBB 357 Dia. - 158 Grain Good In 38 Super Also	No. 901	45 Caliber SWCBB 452 Dia. - 255 Grain For 45 Colt	No. 202	32-20 Caliber FP 313 Dia. - 118 Grain *New
No. 101	40 Cal. - 10 MM 401 Dia. - 180 Grain Hornady Style	No. 805	45 Caliber ACP SWCBB 452 Dia. - 155 Grain *New	No. 201	32 Caliber SWCBB 313 Dia. - 100 Grain *New

Cat. No. 5

Magnus Bullets

M&D MUNITIONS

Caliber	Wgt. Grs.	Type	Price/1000
38/357	125	FMJ	$43.50
	125	JHP	43.50
	148	LDEW	22.00
	148	LHBWC	24.50
	158	FMJ	55.75
	158	JHP	55.75
	158	JSP	55.75
	158	LSWC	24.50
	158	LSWHP	25.50
	158	LRN	24.50
9mm	115	FMJ	42.25
	115	JHP	49.50
	124	FMJ	42.25
	125	LRN	24.50
	147	FMJ	51.50
	147	JHP	55.50
380 ACP	95	FMJ	36.00
	95	LRN	20.50
45 ACP	200	MFMJ	72.70
	200	LSWC	29.50
	230	FMJ	69.50
	230	LRN	34.50
44	240	JHP	73.80
	240	SWC	35.50
10mm	180	PHP	60.50
	200	FMJ	65.00

FMJ = Full Metal Jacket; JHP = Jacketed Hollowpoint; JSP = Jacketed Softpoint; LDEW = Lead Double End Wadcutter; HBWC = Hollow Base Wadcutter; SWC = Semi-Wadcutter; SWCHP = Semi-Wadcutter Hollowpoint; LRN = Lead Round Nose; MFMJ = Match Full Metal Jacket; PHP = Plated Hollowpoint.

IMI

Caliber	Wgt. Grs.	Type	Price 500	Price 1000
22	55	FMJ BT	$32.80	$51.81
	62	FMJ BT	74.87	118.40
30	110	FMJ BT	63.52	100.47
	150	FMJ BT	76.42	120.98
311	123	FMJ	73.32	116.04
50	647	FMJ BT	79.27*	731.59**

FMJ = Full Metal Jacket; BT = Boattail. * = Price for 50; ** = Price for 500. From Huntington Die Specialties.

Magnus Bullets

MONTANA PRECISION SWAGING
Paper Patch Bullets

Caliber	Wgt. Grs.	Diameter	Type	Base	Price/100
SWAGED STRAIGHT SIDED UNPATCHED					
38	250	.365	RN	Cup	$24.00
	300	.365	RN	Cup	24.00
40	330	.395	RN	Cup	24.00
	370	.395	RN	Cup	24.00
	400	.395	RN	Cup	24.00
	330	.399	RN	Cup	24.00
	370	.399	RN	Cup	24.00
	400	.399	RN	Cup	24.00
43 Span.	350	.439	RN	Flat, cup	24.00
	400	.439	RN	Flat, cup	24.00
44	380*	.440	FN	Cup	24.00
45	400	.450	RN	Cup	24.00
	500	.450	RN	Cup	24.00
	510	.450	RN	Cup	24.00
	540	.450	RN	Cup	24.00
50	450	.505	RN	Cup	24.00
	500	.505	RN	Cup	24.00
	550	.505	RN	Cup	24.00
SWAGED TAPER UNPATCHED					
45	510	.450	SP		24.00
	540	.450	SP		24.00
CAST TAPER UNPATCHED					
40	330	.402	RN		24.00
	370	.402	RN		24.00
	400	.402	RN		24.00
45	540	.453	RN		24.00
50	385	.500	FN		24.00
	550	.500	FN		24.00
	560	.505	RN		24.00

*380 to 550; RN = Round Nose; FN = Flat Nose.

MONTANA PRECISION SWAGING
Cast Bullets

Caliber	Wgt. Grs.	Sized	Tip	Price/100	Price/500
PISTOL					
32 Colt	93	.311	1R	$7.35	$36.75
38/357	162	.357	SWC	7.35	36.75
41 Mag.	195	.410	SWC	7.35	36.75
44-40 WCF	210	.428	RN	7.35	36.75
45 Colt	250	.454	FN	7.35	36.75
	255	.452	1R	7.35	36.75
	300	.452	GCSWC	8.40	42.00
	300	.452	GCSWC	8.40	42.00
RIFLE					
38	255	.376	FN	14.20	
	255	.379	FN	14.20	
40	300	.408	SP	14.20	
	350	.408	SP	17.85	
	400	.408	SP	17.85	
43	380	.440	FN	16.80	
44	380	.446	FN	16.80	
45	405	.468	FN	16.80	
	500	.458	FN	17.85	
	550	.458	FN	18.90	
50	450	.510	FN	17.85	

SWC = Semi-Wadcutter; RN = Round Nose; GCSWC = Gas Check Semi-Wadcutter; FN = Flat Nose; SP = Spire Point.

NATIONAL BULLET CO.

Cast bullets from alloy mix containing 7% antimony and 2% tin. All bullets come sized and lubed with Thompson bullet lube. From National Bullet Co.

Price: . . . . **See chart.**

NORTHERN PRECISION

Varmint to dangerous game bullets in 416-, 458- and 429-caliber. 416 bullets come in five styles: Varminter Special—ultra lightweight, thin jacketed, high velocity, high fragmentation bullets; Polly Ball Tip—easy expanding with smooth surface tip either bonded core or matching nonbonded; Long Range Open Country—double-jacket design with easy expansion tip with tough backup slug behind it; Brush Country Big Game—blunt softpoint nose design with tough copper tubing jacket and bonded core; Large and Dangerous Game—spitzer bullets with copper tubing jacket, bonded core and thickened ogive for penetration. Three styles of 458 bullets available: thin jacket round-nose; pure lead base guard; and roundnose with .035" jacket. The 429s are in four basic styles: thin jacket non-bonded; thin jacket bonded core; pure lead base guard; and tubing jacketed with .025" or .035" jacket. From Northern Precision.

Price: . . . . **See chart.**

THE OLD WESTERN SCROUNGER

Cast lead bullets from .258 to .512 for obsolete blackpowder cartridges. From The Old Western Scrounger.

Price: . . . . **See chart.**

PRECISION BULLET

Cast pistol bullets coated with special dry lube formula that eliminates need for jackets or wax lubricant. Available in calibers from 9mm to 45 Colt. Come in boxes of 1,000. From Precision Bullet Co.

Price: . . . . **Contact manufacturer.**

PRECISION CAST BULLETS

Made of an alloy approximating Lyman No. 2 in hardness. Bullets lubricated with either BPLC (Black Powder Cartridge Lube) or SPG. From Precision Cast Bullets.

Price: . . . . **See chart.**

NATIONAL BULLET CO.

Caliber	——Bullet——			——Price——	
	Dia.	Wgt. Grs.	Type	Hard Cast	Copper Plate
25	.250	50	RN	$22.50	$35.50
32	.312	77	RN	22.00	35.50
	.312	95	SWC	22.00	35.50
	.312	95	WC	22.00	——
	.312	118	FP	24.00	38.50
30	.308	120	RN	24.00	38.50
380	.355	95	RN	22.00	35.50
9mm	.356	120	TC	24.00	38.50
	.356	125	RN	24.00	38.50
	.356	147	RN	26.00	40.50
38	.357	141	SWC	25.00	39.50
	.357	141	BBWC	25.00	——
	.357	141	DEWC	25.00	——
	.357	148	HBWC	25.00	——
	.357	148	DEWC	25.00	39.50
	.357	158	SWC	26.00	40.50
	.357	158	RN	26.00	40.50
	.357	158	TC	26.00	40.50
	.357	180	TC	30.00	44.50
	.357	200	TC	32.00	46.50
	.357	200	FP	32.00	46.50
10mm	.401	140	FP	28.00	42.50
	.401	155	SWC	29.00	43.50
	.401	170	SWC	30.00	44.50
	.401	170	TC	30.00	44.50
	.401	200	SWC	32.00	46.50
	.401	200	TC	32.00	46.50
41	.410	210	FP	35.00	48.50
	.410	225	SWC	35.00	48.50
44-40	.427	205	SWC	35.00	48.50
44	.429	205	SWC	35.00	48.50
	.429	240	SWC	36.00	49.50
	.429	265	SWC	39.00	52.50
	.429	300	FP	26.00*	40.50*
45	.452	152	SWC	31.00	44.50
	.452	185	SWC	31.00	44.50
	.452	200	SWC	31.00	44.50
	.452	215	SWC	33.00	46.50
	.452	230	RN	34.00	47.50
	.452	230	FP	34.00	47.50
	.452	255	SWC	38.00	50.50
45-70	.458	——	FP	30.00*	44.50*
	.458	——	FP	37.00*	51.50*

RN = Round Nose; SWC = Semi-Wadcutter; WC = Wadcutter; FP = Flat Point; TC = Truncated Cone; BB = Bevel Base; DE = Double End; HB = Hollow Base. * = Price for 500.

Precision Cast Bullets

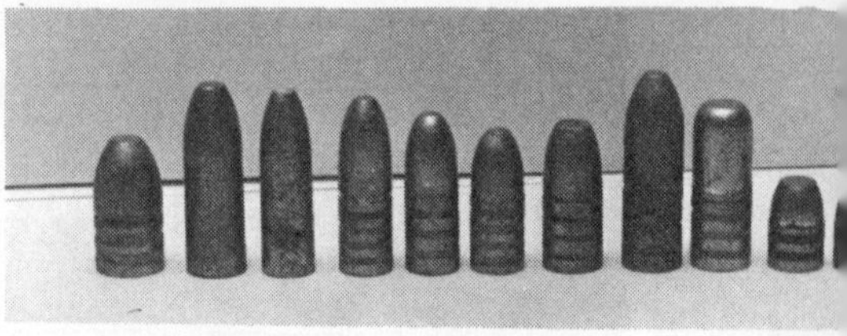

PRECISION CAST BULLETS

Caliber	Diameter	Wgt. Grs.	Price/100
CAST GREASE GROOVE			
40	.408	300	$24.50
	.408	350	26.00
	.408	400	27.00
45	.457	410	27.50
	.457	500	29.50
	.457	550	31.00
50	.512	450	29.00
38-40	.401	175	18.00
44-40	.427	205	19.00
CAST TAPERED PAPER PATCH			
40	.400-.394	395	17.00
45	.449-.440	520	20.00

Northern Precision 416-Caliber 200-450-Gr. Bullets.

REMINGTON

Caliber	Wgt. Grs.	Type	Price/Per
		PISTOL	
25	60	MC	$11.33/100
9mm	115	JHP	9.26/100
	124	MC	8.70/100
357	125	SJHP	9.74/100
	158	SJHP	10.05/100
	158	Lead SWC	6.14/100
38	95	SJHP	9.34/100
	148	LDWC	29.63/600
41 Mag.	210	SP	12.21/100
	210	LD	8.46/100
44 Mag.	180	SJHP	13.33/100
	240	SP	13.33/100
	240	SJHP	11.89/100
45	185	JHP	12.69/100
	230	MC	13.17/100
		RIFLE	
17	25	PLHP	$10.05/100
22	50	PLHP	8.86/100
	55	PLHP	9.02/100
6mm	80	PLHP	11.67/100
	100	PSPCL	11.65/100
25	87	PLHP	13.67/100
270	130	PSPCL	10.93/100
	130	BP	16.08/100
7mm	150	PSPCL	14.20/100
	175	PSPCL	16.08/100
30	150	BP	16.16/100
	150	PSPCL	12.77/100
	180	BP	16.44/100
	180	PSPCL	14.04/100

MC = Metal Case; JHP = Jacketed Hollow Point; SJHP = Semi-Jacketed Hollowpoint; SWC = Semi-Wadcutter; LDWC = Lead Wadcutter; SP = Spire Point; LD = Lead; PLHP = Power Lokt Hollowpoint; PSPCL = Pointed Soft Point Core Lokt; BP = Bronze Point.

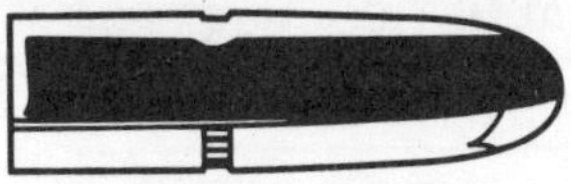
CORE-LOKT® SOFT POINT

POWER-LOKT® HOLLOW POINT

CORE-LOKT® POINTED SOFT POINT

BRONZE POINT™

SOFT POINT

SEMI-JACKETED HOLLOW POINT

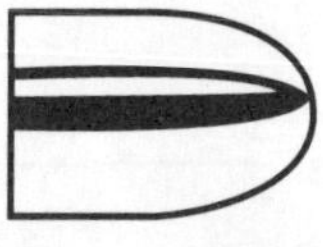
METAL CASE

WADCUTTER

NORTHERN PRECISION

Bullet	Wgt. Grs.	Type	Description	Price/Per
			CALIBER: 416	
Varminter	198-250	HP	Thin jacket	$12.00/50
Polly Ball	300-375	SRN	Bonded	25.00/25
	300-375	SRN	Non-bonded	18.00/25
Long Range	300-450		Double jacket	14.00/25
Brush Country	300-450		Jacket, bonded core	25.00/25
Large Game	375-450	SP	Jacket, thick ogive, bonded core	25.00/25
			CALIBER: 458	
	300-380	RN, FT	Thin jacket	12.00/50
	250-400		Pure lead base guard	10.00/50
	300-500	RN	.035" jacket, bonded/non-bonded	14.00/25
			CALIBER: 429	
	150-330		Thin jacket, non-bonded	12.00/50
	200		Thin jacket, bonded core	25.00/25
	255		Thin jacket, bonded core	25.00/25
	150-330		Pure lead, base guard	12.00/25
	275-330		.025/.035 jacket, non-bonded	12.00/25
	275-330		.025/.035 jacket, bonded	25.00/25

HP = Hollowpoint; SRN = Semi-Round Nose; SP = Spitzer; FT = Flat Tip.

RUBRIGHT

Caliber	Wgt. Grs.	Type	Price/100
224	52	FB	$11.50
	57	FB	11.50
6mm	63	FB, BT	12.00
	65	FB, BT	12.00
	66	FB, BT	12.00
	68	FB, BT	12.00
308	125	FB	17.00
	135	FB	17.00
	150	FB	17.00

FB = Flat Base; BT = Boattail.

OLD WESTERN SCROUNGER

Diameter	Wgt. Grs.	Type	Price/100
.258	87	RN	$13.00
.265	140	SPGC	13.00
.285	145	TCGC	13.00
.309	115	RNBB	13.00
	120	RNGC	13.00
	150	FPGC	13.00
	165	TCGC	13.00
	175	TCGC	13.00
	180	FPGC	13.00
.313	95	SWC	13.00
	118	FP	13.00
.320	160	RN	15.00
.349	185	FPGC	16.50
	220	FP	16.50
.358	230	FP	16.50
.376	250	FP	16.50
	250	FPGC	16.50
.401	172	FP	16.50
	190	FP	16.50
	200	TCBB	16.50
.406	260	FP	16.50
.410	215	SWC	13.00
	210	SWCBB	13.00
.416	350	FNGC	17.50
.428	210	FP	13.00
.430	195	FP	13.00
	240	SWCBB	13.00
	240	SWCGC	13.00
	300	FPGC	16.50
.439	370	FP	18.50
.446	370	FP	18.50
.452	250	RN	13.00
	325	FPGC	17.50
	340	FPGC	17.50
.458	300	FP	18.50
	375	SP	18.50
	405	FP	18.50
	405	SPGC	18.50
	425	FPGC	18.50
	500	FP	18.50
	500	FPGC	18.50
	535	SPBB	18.50
.476	430	FP	18.50
	440	FP	18.50
	450	SP	18.50
.512	350	FP	18.50
	400	FP	18.50
	450	FP	18.50
	600	FPGC	18.50
	655	FP	18.50

BB = Bevel Base; RN = Round Nose; TC = Truncated Cone; GC = Gas Check; SWC = Semi-Wadcutter; SP = Spitzer; FP = Flat Point; BT = Boattail.

RAINIER BALLISTICS

LeadSafe electroplated virgin and lead alloy pistol bullets. Pure copper jacket encloses lead core including base to reduce lead vapor levels and prevent barrel fouling. From Rainier Ballistics Corporation.

Price: . . . . **Contact manufacturer.**

R.I.S.

Specialize in match and varmint quality 50 BMG standard and VLD bullets. In 750-gr., tangent 10S ogive, standard; secant 15S ogive, 855-gr. VLD. Come in boxes of 20. From R.I.S. Co. Inc.

Price: Match **$33.00**
Price: Varmint **$22.00**

R.J. Renner

Rubber "X-Ring" bullets powered by primer only. In 38, 44 and 45 calibers. 50 per bag. From R.J. Renner Co.

Price: 38 . . . . **$7.95**
Price: 44, 45 . . . . **$9.95**

RUBRIGHT BULLETS

Bullets hand-manufactured using carbide dies and available in 22, 6mm and 30 calibers on 8 ogive configuration. From Brian J. Rubright.

Price: . . . . **Contact manufacturer.**

SCHNEIDER

Swaged 22-, 6mm and 30-caliber bullets made in carbide dies on selected jackets. From Roger Schneider.

Price: 38 . . . . **$7.95**
Price: 44, 45 . . . . **$9.95**

SMALL GROUP BULLETS

Swaged 308-caliber bullets handmade one at a time for the benchrest shooter. Four grain weights available: 110, 125, 135 and 150. Come in boxes of 100 bullets. From Small Group Bullets.

Price: **$18.50**

STAR

Custom swaged, bonded core heavy game bullets with solid brass or copper jackets. Closed base bullets to ensure core retention. From Star Custom Bullets.

Price: . . . . **See chart.**

SWIFT

Core-bonded safari bullets designed for use on African game. H-frame construction with .055" copper jacket. From Swift Bullet Co.

Price: . . . . **See chart.**

3-D AMMUNITION & BULLETS

Swaged pistol bullets from 38 Special to 45 ACP with hardness equal to 5% antimony. Produced in carbide dies and come sized and lubed. From 3-D Ammunition & Bullets.

Price: . . . . **Contact manufacturer.**

RAINIER BALLISTICS

Caliber	Wgt. Grs.	Type
9mm	95	RN
	115	RN
	124	FP
	124	RN
	147	RN
38 Super Auto	130	RN
	151	RN
38	125	FP
	148	DEWC
	158	FP
	158	RN
	158	HP
40/10mm	155	FP
	180	FP
	180	HP
41	220	FP
44	240	FP
	240	HP
45	185	FP
	200	SWC
	200	FP
	200	HP
	230	RN
45 LC	250	FP

RN = Round Nose; FP = Flat Point; DEWC = Double End Wadcutter; HP = Hollowpoint; SWC = Semi-Wadcutter.

SCHNEIDER

Caliber	Wgt. Grs.	Price/100
22	52	$9.50
6mm	63, 65, 68, 70	10.50
30	110-150	15.50

SWIFT

Caliber	Wgt. Grs.	Type	Price/50
308	165	SP	$65.00
	180	SP	65.00
	200	SP	65.00
338	225	SP	65.00
	250	SP	65.00
	275	SP	65.00
358	225	SP	75.00
	250	SP	75.00
	300	SP	75.00
366	250	SP	75.00
	300	SP	75.00
375	250	SP	75.00
	300	SP	75.00
411	350	SP	95.00
	400	SP	95.00
416	350	SP	95.00
	400	SP	95.00
458	400	SP	95.00
	500	SP	95.00

From The Old Western Scrounger.

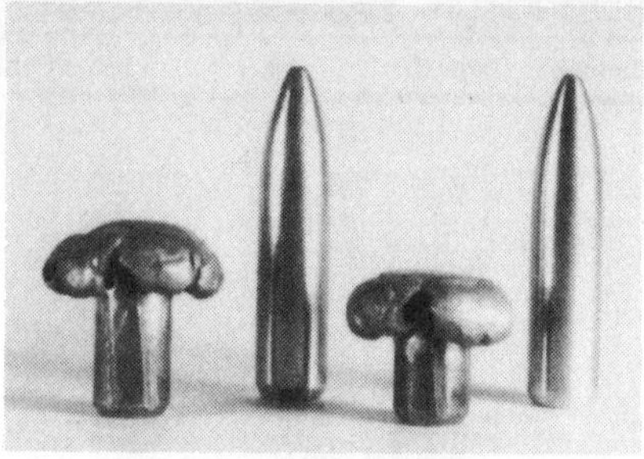

3-D Swaged Bullets

3-D AMMUNITION

Caliber	Diameter	Wgt. Grs.	Type
38 Spl.	.358	158	SWC
	.358	158	RN
	.358	125	SWC
	.357	148	HBWC
	.357	148	DEWC
	.357	100	DEWC
357 Mag.	.358	158	SWC
44 Mag.	.430	240	SWC
9mm Luger	.356	125	RN
38 Auto	.356	115	RN
40 S&W	.452	180	SWC
45 ACP	.452	230	RN
	.452	200	SWC

RN = Round Nose; SWC = Semi-Wadcutter; HBSW = Hollow Base Semi-Wadcutter; DEWC = Double End Wadcutter.

Small Group Bullets

3-D Swaged Bullets

BULLETS/ Custom

STAR

Caliber	Dia.	Wgt. Grs.	—Jacket—	C/B	Price/25
7mm	.284, .288	139	.032, .049	C	$35.00
	.284, .288	160	.032, .049	C	35.00
	.284, .288	175	.032, .049	C	35.00
30	.308	180	.032, .049	C, B	35.00
	.308	200	.032, .049	C, B	35.00
	.308	220	.032, .049	C, B	35.00
	.308	250	.032, .049	C, B	35.00
8mm	.323, .318	185	.032, .049	C, B	35.00
	.323, .318	200	.032, .049	C, B	35.00
	.323, .318	225	.032, .049	C, B	35.00
	.323, .318	250	.032, .049	C, B	35.00
318	.330	SO	.032, .049	C	SO
338		200	.032, .049, .065	C, B	35.00
		250	.032, .049, .065	C, B	35.00
		275	.032, .049, .065	C, B	35.00
		300	.032, .049, .065	C, B	35.00
35	.358	180	.032, .049, .065	C, B	41.00
	.358	250	.032, .049, .065	C, B	41.00
	.358	275	.032, .049, .065	C, B	41.00
	.358	300	.032, .049, .065	C, B	41.00
9.3mm	.366	SO	.049, .065	C, B	SO
375	.375	270	.049, .065	C, B	41.00
	.375	300	.049, .065	C, B	41.00
	.375	350	.049, .065	C, B	41.00
40	.411	SO	.049, .065	C, B	52.00
416	.416	300	.049, .065	C, B	52.00
	.416	410	.049, .065	C, B	52.00
404	.423	300	.049, .065	C, B	52.00
	.423	410	.049, .065	C, B	52.00
444	.429	SO	.049, .065	C, B	SO
425		SO	.049, .065	C, B	SO
11.2mm	.440	409	.049, .065	C, B	52.00
458	.458	365	.032, .049, .065	C, B	52.00
	.458	400	.032, .049, .065	C, B	52.00
	.458	480	.032, .049, .065	C, B	52.00
	.458	500	.032, .049, .065	C, B	52.00
	.458	600	.032, .049, .065	C, B	52.00
465	.468	SO	.049, .065	C, B	SO
470	.475	480	.049, .065	C, B	52.00
	.475	500	.049, .065	C, B	52.00
	.475	520	.049, .065	C, B	52.00
475	.488, .483	SO	.049, .065	C, B	SO
500	.505, .510	400	.049, .065	C, B	52.00
	.505, .510	500	.049, .065	C, B	52.00
	.505, .510	535	.049, .065	C, B	52.00
	.505, .510	600	.049, .065	C, B	52.00
50 BMG	.510	SO	.049, .065	C	SO
577	.585	.049, .065	650	C, B	52.00
	.585	.049, .065	750	C, B	52.00
600	.622	SO	.032, .065	C, B	SO

C = Copper; B = Brass.; SO = Special Order

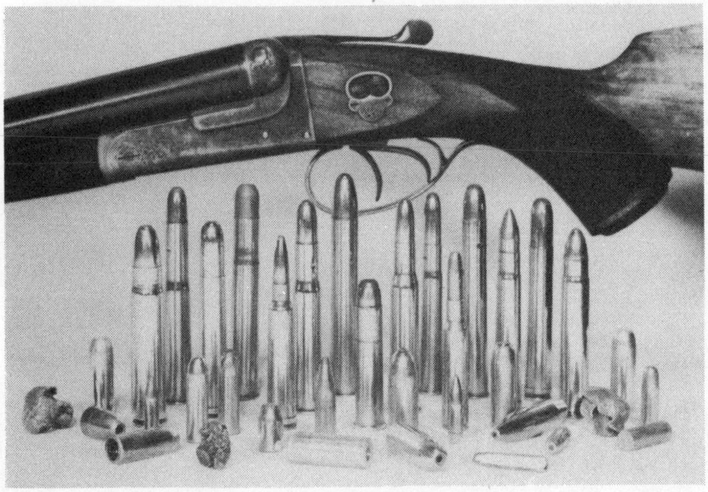

Star "Tough Bond" Bullets

RWS

Caliber	Dia.	Wgt. Grs.	Type	Price/Per
22	.224	45	TG	$50.00/100
	.224	46	SP	45.15/100
	.224	50	TG	50.00/100
	.224	50	SP	45.15/100
	.224	74	CP	26.15/50
22	.228	71	PSP	26.15/50
243	.243	70	TG	50.00/100
	.243	96	CP	34.70/50
264	.264	93	TG	50.00/100
	.264	93	SP	32.95/50
	.264	93	FMJ	31.20/50
	.264	108	CP	36.85/50
	.264	127	CP	36.85/50
	.264	159	SP	32.95/50
270	.277	130	H-Mantel,HP	54.25/50
	.277	150	CP	45.37/50
7mm	.284	123	CP	45.37/50
	.284	139	TG	50.00/100
	.284	139	SP	35.25/50
	.284	162	CP	45.37/50
	.284	162	TIG	39.95/50
	.284	173	H-Mantel,HP	59.20/20
	.284	177	TIG	39.95/50
30	.308	110	SP	35.25/50
	.308	150	TIG	39.95/50
	.308	150	CP	45.45/50
	.308	165	CP	45.45/50
	.308	181	H-Mantel,HP	52.60/50
	.308	181	TUG	39.95/50
30	.309	93	FMJ	13.20/100
8mm	.318	196	SP	32.65/50
8mm	.323	181	CP	39.95/50
	.323	187	H-Mantel,HP	55.90/50
	.323	196	SP	31.00/50
	.323	198	TIG	36.80/50
	.323	224	CP	39.95/50
9.3mm	.364	193	FNSP	41.80/50
9.3mm	.366	247	CP	49.75/50
	.366	258	H-Mantel,HP	61.40/50
	.366	285	SP	37.10/50
	.366	293	TUG	45.70/50
375	.375	300	CP	51.50/50
	.375	300	FMJ	36.40/50
	.375	300	TUG	51.50/50
10.75mm	.423	347	FMJ	41.85/50
	.423	401	FMJ	22.55/20

TG = Target; SP = Soft Point; CP = Cone Point; PSP = Pointed Soft Point; FMJ = Full Metal Jacket; HP = Hollow Point; TIG = Brenneke TIG; TUG = Brenneke TUG; FNSP = Flat Nose Softpoint. From The Old Western Scrounger.

THUNDERBIRD

Big game and 50-caliber competition solids with patented exterior design. Made from an homogenous alloy, big game bullets range in caliber from 308 to 585 and 180-grain weight to 750; competition 50-caliber spitzer boattail and flatbase bullets available in 700- and 750-grain weights. From Thunderbird Cartridge Co., Inc.

Price: . . . . **See chart.**

TRU-FLIGHT

Super hard cast match-grade bullets manufactured from 100% virgin alloy and lubed with 110v lube. Bullets totally encased in copper. From Tru-Flight Bullet Company.

Price: . . . . **See chart.**

VINCENT'S SHOP

Soft-nose, bonded core, dual core and solid pistol bullets in calibers 308 to 416. From Vincent's Shop.

Price: . . . . **See chart.**

WATSON

Match 22-caliber bullets made in Rorschach dies and 30-caliber bullets produced in Pindell bullet dies. From Watson Trophy Match Bullets.

Price: . . . . **Contact manufacturer.**

WOODLEIGH

Big game bullets produced by deep drawing copper and steel bullet jackets to proper taper, then jackets are heat-treated. The solids are steel jackets that have been copper-plated; the weld-core soft-nose bullets are made with pure lead cores welded to jacket for maximum retained weight. From Huntington Die Specialties.

Price: . . . . **See chart.**

WYOMING BONDED

Handgun hunting bullets with bonded cores and annealed jackets for weight retention. Specialize in 358-caliber; other calibers available soon. From Wyoming Bonded Bullets.

Price: . . . . **Contact manufacturer.**

WYOMING CASTING

Cast bullets from 32-20 through 50-140 for blackpowder cartridge shooters. Specialize in .408" diameter, 40-caliber, 405-gr. bullets for the 40-65 cartridge. Bullets come lubed. From Wyoming Casting Co.

Price: . . . . **See chart.**

TRU-FLIGHT

Caliber	Wgt. Grs.	Type	Price/500
TRU-FLIGHT PLUS			
380	95	RN	$23.00
9mm	115	RN	23.00
	125	RN	25.00
38 Super/9mm	147	RN	28.00
38	125	FP	25.00
	148	DEWC	27.00
	158	SWC	28.00
10mm	155	TC	34.00
	180	TC	36.00
41	220	SWC	38.00
44	240	FP	42.00
45	185	TC	36.00
	200	SWC	38.00
	230	RN	38.00
45 LC	250		42.00
HARD CAST MATCH QUALITY			
32	95	WC	$17.00
380	90	RN	17.00
9mm	125	BBTC	17.00
38 Super	140	FBSWC	18.00
	155	BBSWC	18.00
38 Super/9mm	145	BBRN	18.00
38	148	DEWC	18.00
	148	HBWC	18.00
	155	BBSWC	18.00
	180	FP	20.00
	200	FP	22.00
10mm/40	155	BBSWC	20.00
	175	BBSWC	20.00
41	210	BBTC	22.00
44	225	BBTC	22.00
45	225	BBTC	22.00
	225	WC	22.00
	165	FBSWC	20.00
	180	FBSWC	20.00
	185	FBSWC	20.00
	200	BBSWC	20.00
	225	BBSWC	25.00
TRU-FLIGHT ROYALS			
38 Super	115	FMJ	$53.00/1000
	125	FMJ	53.00/1000
	130	FMJ	53.00/1000
	135	FMJ	55.00/1000
9mm	115	FMJ	53.00/1000
	125	FMJ	53.00/1000
	130	FMJ	53.00/1000
	135	FMJ	55.00/1000

RN = Round Nose; FP = Flat Point; DEWC = Double End Wadcutter; SWC = Semi-Wadcutter; TC = Truncated Cone; WC = Wadcutter; BBTC = Bevel Base Truncated Cone; FBSWC = Flat Base Semi-Wadcutter; BBRN = Bevel Base Round Nose; HBWC = Hollow Base Wadcutter; BBTC = Bevel Base Truncated Cone; BBSWC = Bevel Base Semi-Wadcutter.

THUNDERBIRD

Caliber	Wgt. Grs.	Type	Price/50
308	180	RN	$39.00
	220	RN	40.00
323	220	RN	43.00
338	250	RN	44.00
9.3mm	286	RN	48.00
375	300	RN	49.00
416	400	RN	55.00
423	400	RN	56.00
458	465	RN	60.00
468	480	RN	61.00
475	500	RN	62.00
488	500	RN	64.00
505	525	RN	66.00
510	570	RN	68.00
585	750	RN	77.00

Wyoming Bonded Bullets

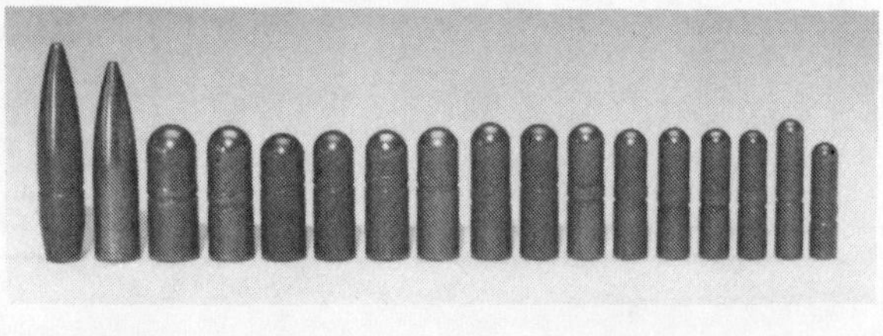

Thunderbird Big Game Bullets

WYOMING CASTING COMPANY

Caliber	Wgt. Grs.	Type	Price/500	Price/1000
32	95	SWC	$16.00	$30.00
9mm	122	FP	16.00	30.00
	125	RN	16.00	30.00
38 Super	147	FP	16.00	30.00
	150	RN	16.00	30.00
38	148	DEWC	16.00	30.00
	158	SWC	18.00	32.00
	158	RN	18.00	32.00
	180	FP	18.00	34.00
40	140	RNFP	16.00	30.00
	155	SWC	18.00	32.00
	175	SWC	18.00	34.00
41	215	SWC	20.00	36.00
44	240	SWC	20.00	37.00
	300	FP	17.00*	30.00*
45	155	SWC	18.00	32.00
	175	SWC	18.00	34.00
	200	SWC	18.00	34.00
	230	RN	20.00	36.00
	300	FP	17.00*	30.00*
270	140	FP	8.50**	15.00**
7mm	155	FP	7.50**	14.00**
30	130	PT	12.00*	22.00*
	145	FP	7.00**	14.00**
	165	FP	8.00**	15.00**
44-40	200	RNFP	12.50*	22.00*
375	249	FP	10.00**	24.00**
38-40	180	RNFP	12.50*	22.00*
40	405	RN	12.50**	30.00**
32-20	115	SWC	12.00*	22.00*
45-70	400	FP	12.00**	30.00**
	500	RN	14.00**	34.00**
50	515	FN	14.00**	34.00**

* = Price for 250/500. ** = Price for 100/250. SWC = Semi-Wadcutter; FP = Flat Point; RN = Round Nose; DEWC = Double End Wadcutter; PT = Pointed Tip; FN = Flat Nose.

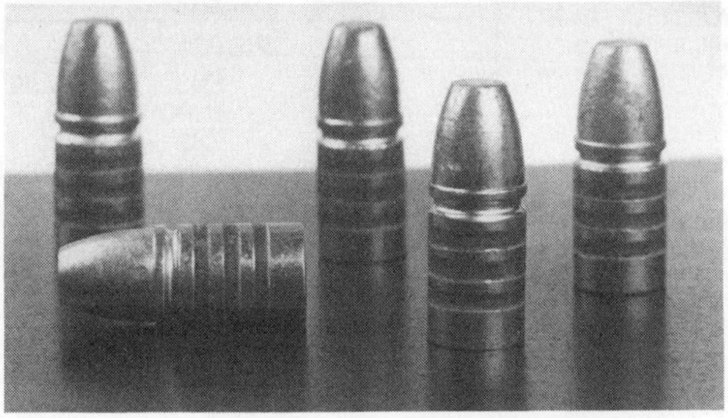

Wyoming Casting Company Bullets

VINCENT'S SHOP

Caliber	Soft Nose	Bonded Core	Dual Core	Solids
308	$.35	$.70	$.60	$.50
323	.40	.75	.65	.55
328	.40	.75	.65	.55
338	.45	.80	.70	.60
358	.45	.80	.70	.60
366	.50	.85	.75	.65
375	.55	.90	.80	.70
408	.60	.95	.85	.75
411	.60	.95	.85	.75
416	.60	.95	.85	.75

WOODLEIGH

Cartridge	Diameter	Wgt. Grs.	Type	Price/Per
700 Nitro		1000	SN	$95.98/25
		1000	FMJ	95.98/25
600 Nitro	.620	900	SN	49.95/25
		900	FMJ	58.98/25
577 Nitro	.585	750	SN	47.50/25
	.585	750	FMJ	58.98/25
	.585	650	SN	39.98/25
500 Nitro	.510	570	SN	35.50/25
	.510	570	SMJ	44.98/25
	.510	535	SN	35.50/25
	.510	535	FMJ	44.98/25
500 BP Express	.510	440	SN	33.50/25
505 Gibbs	.505	525	SN	35.50/25
	.505	525	FMJ	44.98/25
475 N.E.	.483	480	SN	57.98/50
	.483	480	FMJ	77.98/50
475 N.E.	.488	500	SN	57.98/50
	.488	500	FMJ	77.98/50
475 Nitro	.476	480	SN	57.98/50
476 W.R.	.476	520	SN	57.98/50
	.476	520	FMJ	72.98/50
470 Nitro	.474	500	SN	57.98/50
	.474	500	FMJ	77.98/50
465 Nitro	.468	480	SN	77.98/50
	.468	480	FMJ	77.98/50
450	.458	480	SN	57.98/50
	.458	480	FMJ	77.98/50
458 Magnum	.458	550	SN	57.98/50
	.458	550	FMJ	77.98/50
	.458	500	SN	57.98/50
	.458	500	FMJ	77.98/50
425 W.R.	.435	410	SN	54.98/50
	.435	410	FMJ	72.98/50
404 Jeffrey	.423	400	SN	54.98/50
	.423	400	FMJ	72.98/50
416 Rigby	.416	410	SN	54.98/50
	.416	410	FMJ	72.98/50
450/400 Nitro	.411	400	SN	54.98/50
	.411	400	FMJ	72.98/50
375 Magnum	.375	300	SNRN	54.98/50
	.375	300	SPSN	54.98/50
	.375	300	FMJ	72.98/50
	.375	270	RNSN	54.98/50
	.375	270	SPSN	54.98/50
9.3mm	.366	320	SN	54.98/50
	.366	320	FMJ	72.98/50
	.366	286	SN	54.98/50
	.366	286	FMJ	72.98/50
35	.358	310	SN	54.98/50
	.358	310	FMJ	72.98/50
	.358	250	SN	54.98/50
	.358	225	SN	54.98/50
	.358	225	FMJ	72.98/50
338	.358	300	SN	54.98/50
	.358	300	FMJ	72.98/50
	.358	250	SN	54.98/50
	.358	250	FMJ	72.98/50
333 Jeffrey	.330	300	SN	54.98/50
	.330	300	FMJ	72.98/50
	.330	250	FMJ	72.98/50
318 W.R.	.330	250	SN	54.98/50
	.330	250	FMJ	72.98/50
30		220	FMJ	72.98/50

SN = Soft Nose; SP = Semi-Point; FMJ = Full Metal Jacket. From Huntington Die Specialties.

BULLETS/ Custom

BARNES BULLETS

Caliber	Wgt. Grs.	Type	Price/50
RIFLE			
22	60	SPTO	$15.99
	70	SPTO	16.49
6mm	75	SPTX	17.29
	75	SPTS	17.29
	85	SPTS	17.29
	90	SPTX	17.49
	100	SPTX	18.29
	115	RNO	17.99
25	75	SPTX	17.29
	75	SPTS	17.29
	85	SPTX	17.99
	90	SPTS	17.99
	100	SPTX	17.99
	115	SPTX	18.99
	125	SPTO	18.59
6.5	120	SPTX	20.99
	130	SPTS	19.99
	140	SPTX	20.99
270	100	SPTX	19.99
	120	SPTX	20.99
	130	SPTX	20.99
	130	SPTS	19.29
	140	SPTX	20.99
	150	SPTX	20.99
	150	RNS	20.99
	180	RNO	19.99
7mm	100	SPTX	20.99
	120	SPTX	21.99
	140	SPTX	22.99
	140	SPTS	20.99
	150	SPTX	22.99
	160	SPTS	21.99
	160	SPTX	22.99
	175	SPTX	23.99
	175	RNS	21.99
	195	SPTO	20.99
30	110	SPTX	21.99
	125	SPTX	22.99
	150	SPTX	22.99
	165	SPTS	21.99
	165	SPTX	23.99
	180	SPTX	23.99
	200	SPTX	23.99
	220	RNS	27.99
	225	SPTO	$20.99
	250	RNO	21.99
8mm	180	SPTX	23.99
	220	SPTX	24.99
	220	RNS	32.99
9.3mm	250	SPTX	31.99
	286	SPTX	31.99
	286	RNS	43.99
338	175	SPTX	28.99
	200	SPTX	28.99
	225	SPTX	29.99
	225	SPTS	37.99
	250	RNS	38.99
	250	SPTX	29.99
	300	RNO	29.99
348	220	FPO	19.99
	250	FPO	20.99
35	180	SPTX	28.99
	200	SPTX	29.99
	225	SPTX	30.99
	250	RNS	40.99
	250	SPTX	31.99
38/55	255	FPO(.375)	20.99
	255	FPO(.377)	20.99
375	235	SPTX	31.99
	250	SPTX	31.99
	250	SPTS	40.99
	275	SPTX	31.99
	270	RNS	41.99
	300	RNS	43.99
	300	SPTX	32.99
	350	RNO	31.99
411	300	SPTX	33.99
	325	SPTX	33.99
	350	SPTX	34.99
	350	RNS	$47.99
	400	SPTX	34.99
	400	RNS	49.99
416	300	SPTX	33.99
	325	SPTX	33.99
	350	SPTX	34.99
	350	RNS	47.99
	400	RNS	48.99
	400	SPTX	34.99
423	350	SPTX	33.99
	350	RNS	47.99
	400	RNS	49.99
	400	SPTX	34.99
45/70	300	SSPTO	20.99
	300	FPO	20.99
	400	SSPTO	27.99
	400	FPO	27.99
458	300	SPTX	14.29/20
	350	SPTX	14.99/20
	400	SPTX	15.99/20
	400	RNS	20.99/20
	500	RNS	21.99/20
	500	SPTX	16.49/20
50/110 Win.	300	FPO	8.79/20
	450	FPO	10.49/20
50	750	SPTS	27.99/25
	800	SPTS	29.99/25
PISTOL			
44	240	FNS	$27.99
	250	JHPO	19.99
	265	FNS	26.99
	275	JHPO	20.99
	300	JHPO	20.99
45	260	JHPO	20.99
	300	JHPO	21.99
	325	JHPO	22.99

SPT = Spitzer; SSPT = Semi-Spitzer; RN = Round Nose; FP = Flat Point; JHP = Jacketed Hollowpoint; O = Original Bullet; S = Barnes Solid; X = X-Bullet.

Barnes X-Bullets™

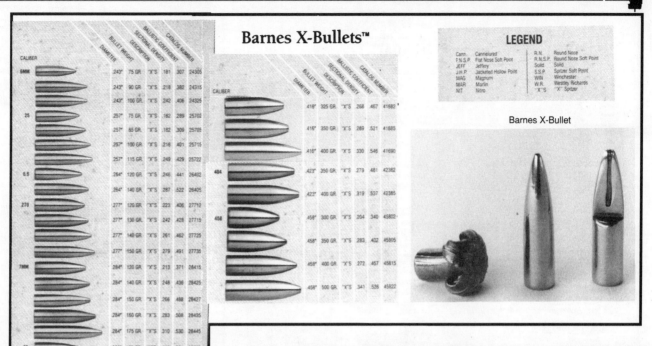

Caliber	Diameter	Bullet Weight	Description	Sectional Density	Ballistic Coefficient	Catalog Number
6MM	.243"	75 GR.	"X"S	.181	.307	24305
	.243"	90 GR.	"X"S	.218	.382	24315
	.243"	100 GR.	"X"S	.242	.406	24325
25	.257"	75 GR.	"X"S	.162	.289	25702
	.257"	85 GR.	"X"S	.182	.309	25705
	.257"	100 GR.	"X"S	.216	.401	25715
	.257"	115 GR.	"X"S	.249	.429	25722
6.5	.264"	120 GR.	"X"S	.246	.441	26402
	.264"	140 GR.	"X"S	.287	.522	26405
270	.277"	120 GR.	"X"S	.223	.406	27712
	.277"	130 GR.	"X"S	.242	.428	27715
	.277"	140 GR.	"X"S	.261	.462	27725
	.277"	150 GR.	"X"S	.279	.491	27735
7MM	.284"	120 GR.	"X"S	.213	.371	28415
	.284"	140 GR.	"X"S	.248	.436	28425
	.284"	150 GR.	"X"S	.266	.488	28427
	.284"	160 GR.	"X"S	.283	.508	28435
	.284"	175 GR.	"X"S	.310	.530	28445
30	.308"	125 GR.	"X"S	.118	.351	30805
	.308"	150 GR.	"X"S	.226	.386	30815
	.308"	165 GR.	"X"S	.247	.456	30825
	.308"	180 GR.	"X"S	.271	.511	30835
	.308"	200 GR.	"X"S	.301	.550	30845
8MM	.323"	180 GR.	"X"S	.246	.382	32305
	.323"	220 GR.	"X"S	.301	.462	32315
338	.338"	175 GR.	"X"S	.218	.392	33880
	.338"	200 GR.	"X"S	.250	.440	33882
	.338"	225 GR.	"X"S	.281	.482	33885
	.338"	250 GR.	"X"S	.313	.521	33890
35	.358"	200 GR.	"X"S	.223	.346	35815
	.358"	225 GR.	"X"S	.250	.455	35825
	.358"	250 GR.	"X"S	.279	.458	35835
9.3	.366"	250 GR.	"X"S	.267	.428	36605
	.366"	286 GR.	"X"S	.305	.468	36615
375	.375"	235 GR.	"X"S	.239	.400	37580
	.375"	250 GR.	"X"S	.254	.450	37582
	.375"	270 GR.	"X"S	.275	.503	37585
	.375"	300 GR.	"X"S	.305	.555	37590
411	.411"	300 GR.	"X"S	.254	.401	41180
	.411"	325 GR.	"X"S	.275	.475	41182
	.411"	350 GR.	"X"S	.296	.536	41185
	.411"	400 GR.	"X"S	.338	.562	41190
416	.416"	300 GR.	"X"S	.247	.394	41680

Caliber	Diameter	Bullet Weight	Description	Sectional Density	Ballistic Coefficient	Catalog Number
	.416"	325 GR.	"X"S	.268	.467	41682
	.416"	350 GR.	"X"S	.289	.521	41685
	.416"	400 GR.	"X"S	.330	.546	41690
404	.423"	350 GR.	"X"S	.279	.481	42382
	.423"	400 GR.	"X"S	.319	.537	42385
458	.458"	300 GR.	"X"S	.204	.340	45802
	.458"	350 GR.	"X"S	.283	.402	45805
	.458"	400 GR.	"X"S	.272	.457	45815
	.458"	500 GR.	"X"S	.341	.526	45822

LEGEND

Cann.	Cannelured	R.N.	Round Nose
F.N.S.P.	Flat Nose Soft Point	R.N.S.P.	Round Nose Soft Point
JEFF	Jeffery	Solid	Solid
J.H.P.	Jacketed Hollow Point	S.S.P.	Spitzer Soft Point
MAG	Magnum	WIN	Winchester
MAR	Marlin	W.R.	Westley Richards
NIT	Nitro	"X"S	"X" Spitzer

Barnes X-Bullet

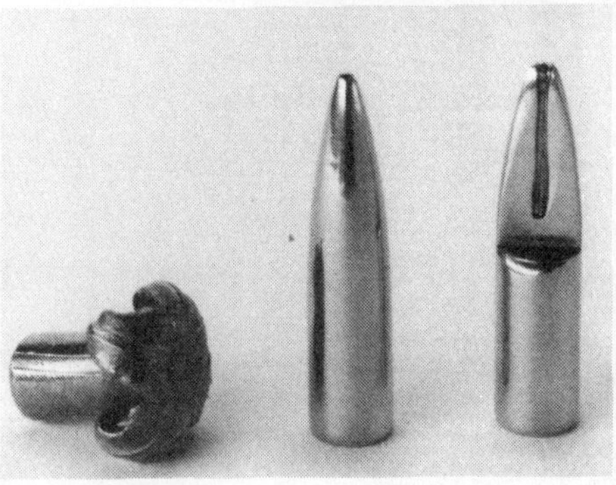

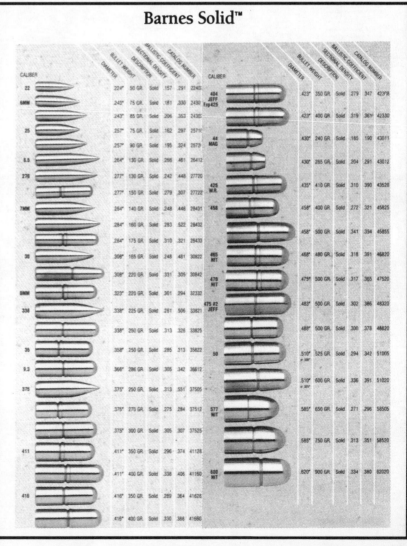

Barnes Solid™

Caliber	Diameter	Bullet Weight	Description	Sectional Density	Ballistic Coefficient	Catalog Number
22	.224"	50 GR.	Solid	.157	.291	2240
6MM	.243"	75 GR.	Solid	.181	.330	2430
	.243"	85 GR.	Solid	.206	.353	2430
25	.257"	75 GR.	Solid	.162	.297	2571
	.257"	90 GR.	Solid	.195	.324	2572
6.5	.264"	130 GR.	Solid	.266	.461	26412
270	.277"	130 GR.	Solid	.242	.448	27720
	.277"	150 GR.	Solid	.279	.307	27722
7MM	.284"	140 GR.	Solid	.248	.448	28431
	.284"	160 GR.	Solid	.283	.522	28432
	.284"	175 GR.	Solid	.310	.321	28433
30	.308"	165 GR.	Solid	.248	.481	30822
	.308"	220 GR.	Solid	.331	.305	30842
8MM	.323"	220 GR.	Solid	.301	.294	32332
338	.338"	225 GR.	Solid	.281	.506	33821
	.338"	250 GR.	Solid	.313	.326	33825
35	.358"	250 GR.	Solid	.285	.313	35822
9.3	.366"	286 GR.	Solid	.305	.342	36612
375	.375"	250 GR.	Solid	.313	.551	37505
	.375"	270 GR.	Solid	.275	.284	37512
	.375"	300 GR.	Solid	.305	.307	37525
411	.411"	350 GR.	Solid	.296	.374	41128
	.411"	400 GR.	Solid	.338	.406	41160
416	.416"	350 GR.	Solid	.289	.364	41628
	.416"	400 GR.	Solid	.330	.388	41660

Caliber	Diameter	Bullet Weight	Description	Sectional Density	Ballistic Coefficient	Catalog Number
404 JEFF Exp425	.423"	350 GR.	Solid	.279	.347	42308
	.423"	400 GR.	Solid	.319	.361	42330
44 MAG	.430"	240 GR.	Solid	.185	.190	43011
	.430"	265 GR.	Solid	.204	.291	43012
425 W.R.	.435"	410 GR.	Solid	.310	.390	43520
458	.458"	400 GR.	Solid	.272	.321	45825
	.458"	500 GR.	Solid	.341	.394	45855
465 NIT	.468"	480 GR.	Solid	.318	.391	46820
470 NIT	.475"	500 GR.	Solid	.317	.365	47520
475 #2 JEFF	.483"	500 GR.	Solid	.302	.386	48320
	.488"	500 GR.	Solid	.300	.378	48820
50	.510" or .500"	525 GR.	Solid	.294	.342	51005
	.510" or .500"	600 GR.	Solid	.336	.391	51020
577 NIT	.585"	650 GR.	Solid	.271	.296	58505
	.585"	750 GR.	Solid	.313	.351	58520
600 NIT	.620"	900 GR.	Solid	.334	.380	62020

BULLETS/ Barnes

Barnes Original™

Caliber	Diameter	Bullet Weight	Description	Sectional Density	Ballistic Coefficient	Catalog Number
22	.224"	60 GR.	S.S.P. .030"	.171	.244	22410
	.224"	70 GR.	S.S.P. .030"	.199	.284	22430
6MM	.243"	115 GR.	R.N.S.P. .030"	.290	.322	24330
25	.257"	115 GR.	S.S.P. .032"	.249	.371	25725
	.257"	125 GR.	S.S.P. .032"	.270	.422	25730
6.5	.264"	165 GR.	S.S.P. .032"	.338	.483	26430
270	.277"	180 GR.	R.N.S.P. .032"	.335	.372	27750
7MM	.284"	195 GR.	S.S.P. .032"	.345	.570	28450
30	.308"	225 GR.	S.S.P. .032"	.339	.595	30850
	.308"	250 GR.	R.N.S.P. .032"	.376	.417	30860
	.323" or .318"	250 GR.	S.S.P. .049"	.342	.512	32350
338	.338"	250 GR.	S.S.P. .049"	.313	.526	33820
	.338"	300 GR.	R.N.S.P. .049"	.375	.416	33830
348 WIN	.348"	220 GR.	F.N.S.P. .032"	.260	.301	34805
	.348"	250 GR.	F.N.S.P. .032"	.295	.327	34810
	.358"	275 GR.	S.S.P. .049"	.307	.470	35830
	.358"	300 GR.	R.N.S.P. .049"	.334	.371	35850
375 WIN	.375"	220 GR.	F.N.S.P. .032"	.223	.246	375W10
	.375"	255 GR.	F.N.S.P. .032"	.259	.290	375W20
38/55	.375"	255 GR.	F.N.S.P. .032"	.259	.290	38/5510
	.377"	255 GR.	F.N.S.P. .032"	.259	.290	38/5520
	.375"	300 GR.	S.S.P. .049"	.305	.546	37520
	.375"	350 GR.	R.N.S.P. .049"	.356	.370	37530
401 WIN	.406"	250 GR.	R.N.S.P. .032"	.217	.241	40610
411	.411" or .408"	400 GR.	R.N.S.P. .049"	.338	.391	41140
416	.416"	400 GR.	R.N.S.P. .049"	.330	.366	41640
	.423"	400 GR.	R.N.S.P. .049"	.319	.354	42320
444 MAR	.430"	250 GR.	H.P. .032"	.193	.214	43010
	.430"	275 GR.	H.P. .032"	.212	.239	43015
	.430"	300 GR.	H.P. .032"	.232	.258	43020
425 W.R.	.435"	410 GR.	R.N.S.P. .049"	.310	.344	43510
45/70	.458"	400 GR.	S.S.P. .032"	.272	.389	457030
	.458"	400 GR.	F.N.S.P. .032"	.272	.302	457040
458 MAG	.458"	400 GR.	S.S.P. .049"	.272	.389	45810
	.458"	400 GR.	R.N.S.P. .049"	.272	.312	45820
	.458"	500 GR.	R.N.S.P. .049"	.341	.379	45840
	.458"	500 GR.	S.S.P. .049"	.341	.487	45830
	.458"	600 GR.	R.N.S.P. .049"	.409	.454	45860
465 NIT	.468"	480 GR.	R.N.S.P. .049"	.318	.362	46810
470 NIT	.475"	500 GR.	R.N.S.P. .049"	.317	.352	47510
	.475"	600 GR.	R.N.S.P. .049"	.380	.422	47530
475 #2 JEFF	.488" or .483"	500 GR.	R.N.S.P. .049"	.300	.333	48810
50/110 WIN	.510"	300 GR.	F.N.S.P. .032"	.165	.183	5011010
	.510"	450 GR.	F.N.S.P. .032"	.247	.274	5011020
50	.510" or .505"	600 GR.	R.N.S.P. .049"	.336	.365	51010
	.510" or .505"	700 GR.	R.N.S.P. .049"	.392	.436	51030
577 NIT	.577"	750 GR.	R.N.S.P. .049"	.313	.346	58510
600 NIT	.620"	900 GR.	R.N.S.P. .049"	.334	.371	62010
PISTOL BULLETS						
44 MAG	.430"	250 GR.	H.P. .032"	.193	.214	43010
	.430"	275 GR.	H.P. .032"	.212	.239	43015
	.430"	300 GR.	H.P. .032"	.232	.258	43020
45 MAG	.451"	260 GR.	H.P. .032"	.182	.187	45201
	.451"	300 GR.	H.P. .032"	.211	.221	45203
	.451"	325 GR.	H.P. .032"	.228	.246	45205
475 MAG	.475"	250 GR.	H.P. .032"	.158	.178	47501
	.475"	300 GR.	H.P. .032"	.190	.216	47505

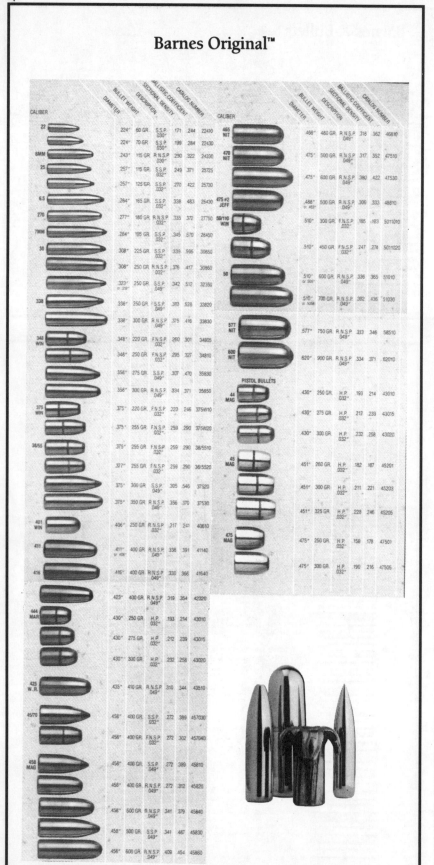

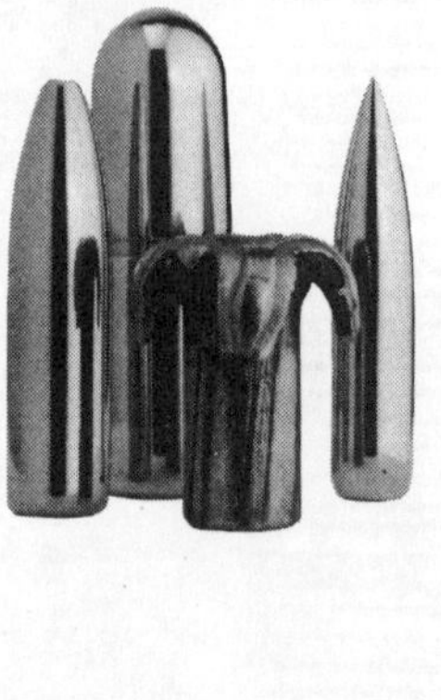

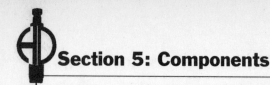

Hornady

BULLETS · RELOADERS · AMMUNITION

RIIFLE

Caliber	Wgt. Grs.	Type	Price/100
17	25	HP	$9.59
22	40	Jet	8.79
	45	Bee	8.79
	45	Hornet (.223)	8.99
	45	Hornet (.224)	8.79
	50	SXSP	9.99
	50	SP	8.79
	52	BTHP Match	10.59
	53	HP Match	10.29
	55	SXSP	9.99
	55	SP	8.99
	55	SP w/c	9.59
	55	FMJBT	9.59
	60	SP	9.59
	60	HP	9.59
	68	BTHP Match	11.59
	70	SP (.227)	12.79
6mm/243	70	SP	11.29
	70	SXSP	11.79
	75	HP	11.29
	80	FMJ	12.49
	80	SP Single Shot	11.49
	87	SP	11.79
	87	BTHP	12.79
	100	SP	12.49
	100	BTSP	12.79
	100	RN	12.49
25	60	FP	11.29
	75	HP	11.49
	87	SP	12.29
	100	SP	12.79
	117	RN	12.79
	117	BTSP	14.99
	120	HP	13.79
6.5mm	100	SP	14.49
	129	SP	14.79
	140	SP	14.99
	140	BTHP Match	18.99
	160	RN	18.99
270	100	SP	13.49
	110	HP	13.99
	130	SP	12.99
	140	BTSP	15.99
	150	SP	14.49
	150	RN	15.99
7mm	100	HP	13.49
	120	SP	13.99
	120	SP Single Shot	13.99
	120	HP	13.99
	139	SP	14.29
	139	FP	15.99
	139	BTSP	15.99
	154	SP	15.99
	154	RN	15.99
	162	BTSP	17.99
	175	SP	17.99
	175	RN	17.99
30	100	SJ	9.29
30	110	SP	$11.99
	110	RN	11.29
	110	FMJ	11.29
	130	SP	14.29
	130	SP Single Shot	13.29
	150	SP	13.99
	150	BTSP	15.99
	150	RN (30-30)	13.99
	150	FMJBT	15.99
	165	SP	15.99
	165	BTSP	16.99
	168	BTHP Match	18.99
	170	FP (30-30)	14.49
	180	SP	15.99
	180	BTSP	17.99
	180	RN	15.99
	190	BTHP Match	18.99
	190	BTSP	18.99
	220	RN	18.99
7.62x39	123	SP	14.29
	123	FMJ	14.29
303 7.7	150	SP	15.99
	174	RN	16.99
32 Spl.	170	FP	15.99
8mm	125	SP	14.99
	150	SP	15.99
	170	RN	15.99
	220	SP	19.99
338	200	SP	19.99
	200	FP	21.99
	225	SP	20.99
	250	RN	21.99
	250	SP	21.99
348	200	FP	20.99
35	180	SP Single Shot	18.99
	200	SP	19.99
	200	RN	18.99
	250	SP	21.99
	250	RN	21.99
375	220	FP	21.99
	270	SP	14.49/50
	270	RN	14.49/50
	300	RN	14.99/50
	300	BTSP	17.99/50
416	400	RN	24.99/50
	400	FMJ	32.99/50
44	265	FP	20.99
45	300	HP	12.99/50
	350	RN	16.99/50
	500	RN	23.99/50
	500	FMJRN	32.99/50

JACKETED PISTOL

Caliber	Wgt. Grs.	Type	Price/100
25	50	FMJRN	$8.99
32	71	FMJRN	9.59
9mm	100	FMJ	10.29
	115	FMJRN	10.29
	124	FMJFP	10.99
	124	FMJRN	10.29
38	160	CL Sil.	$12.99
	180	CL Sil.	13.29
10mm	180	FMJFP	13.79
	200	FMJFP	14.59
41	210	CL Sil.	15.49
44	240	CL Sil.	15.79
45	185	SWC Match	14.79
	200	FMJ C/T	14.79
	230	FMJRN	14.59
	230	FMJFP	14.59

XTP PISTOL

Caliber	Wgt. Grs.	Type	Price/100
25	35	HP	$8.99
32	85	HP	9.99
	100	HP	10.29
9mm	90	HP	9.99
	115	HP	9.29
	124	HP	10.29
	147	HP	10.79
38/357	110	HP	10.49
	125	HP	10.49
	125	FP	10.49
	140	HP	10.99
	158	HP	10.99
	158	FP	10.99
	180	HP	13.49
10mm	155	HP	13.29
	180	HP	13.79
	200	HP	14.59
41	210	HP	14.59
44 Mag.	180	HP	14.29
	200	HP	14.59
	240	HP	15.29
	300	HP	9.99/50
45	185	HP	14.29
	200	HP	14.49
	230	HP	14.79
	Colt 250	HP	15.99
	Colt 300	HP	9.99/50

LEAD PISTOL

Caliber	Wgt. Grs.	Type	Price/100
32	90	SWC	$19.49/500
	90	HBWC	19.49/500
9mm	124	LRN	22.99/500
38	148	BBWC	25.99/500
	148	HBWC	25.99/500
	148	DEWC	29.99/500
	158	RN	27.99/500
	158	SWC	27.99/500
	158	SWCHP	27.99/500
10mm	180	SWC	31.99/500
44	240	SWC	29.99/400
	240	SWCHP	29.99/400
45	200	SWC	32.99/500
	200	L C/T	32.99/500
	230	LRN	28.99/400

SP = Spire Point; BT = Boattail; FP = Flatpoint; HP = Hollowpoint; JFP = Jacketed Hollowpoint; JTC = Jacketed Truncated Cone; RN = Round Nose; LRN = Lead Round Nose; Sil. = Silhouette; SJ = Short Jacket; FMJ = Full Metal Jacket; SX = Super Explosive; SWC = Semi Wad Cutter; HBWC = Hollow Base Wad Cutter; BBWC = Bevel Base Wad Cutter; DEWC = Double End Wad Cutter; w/c = with cannelure; C/T = Combat Target.

Hornady
BULLETS · RELOADERS · AMMUNITION

Rifle Bullets

17 CALIBER (.172)
25 gr. HP #1710

22 CALIBER (.222)
40 gr. Jet #2210

22 CALIBER (.223)
45 gr. Hornet #2220

22 CALIBER (.224)
45 gr. BEE #2229
45 gr. Hornet #2230
50 gr. SXSP #2240
50 gr. SP #2245

22 CALIBER MATCH
52 gr. BTHP #2249

22 CALIBER MATCH
53 gr. HP #2250

55 gr. SXSP #2260
55 gr. SP #2265
55 gr. SP w/c #2266
55 gr. FMJ-BT w/c #2267
60 gr. SP #2270
60 gr. HP #2275

22 CALIBER MATCH
68 gr. BTHP #2278

22 CALIBER (.227)
70 gr. SP #2280

6MM CALIBER (.243)
70 gr. SP #2410
70 gr. SXSP #2415
75 gr. HP #2420
80 gr. FMJ #2430
80 gr. SP Single Shot Pistol #2435
87 gr. SP #2440
87 gr. BTHP #2442
100 gr. SP #2450 InterLock
100 gr. BTSP #2453 InterLock
100 gr. RN #2455 InterLock

25 CALIBER (.257)
60 gr. FP #2510
75 gr. HP #2520
87 gr. SP #2530
100 gr. SP #2540 InterLock
117 gr. RN #2550 InterLock
117 gr. BTSP #2552 InterLock
120 gr. HP #2560 InterLock

6.5MM CALIBER (.264)
100 gr. SP #2610
129 gr. SP #2620 InterLock
140 gr. SP #2630 InterLock

6.5MM CALIBER MATCH
140 gr. BTHP #2633

160 gr. RN #2640 InterLock

270 CALIBER (.277)
100 gr. SP #2710
110 gr. HP #2720
130 gr. SP #2730 InterLock
140 gr. BTSP #2735 InterLock
150 gr. SP #2740 InterLock
150 gr. RN #2745 InterLock

7MM CALIBER (.284)
100 gr. HP #2800
120 gr. SP #2810
120 gr. SP Single Shot Pistol #2811
120 gr. HP #2815
139 gr. SP #2820 InterLock
139 gr. FP #2822 InterLock
139 gr. BTSP #2825 InterLock
154 gr. SP #2830 InterLock
154 gr. RN #2835 InterLock

7MM MATCH
162 gr. BTHP #2840

162 gr. BTSP #2845 InterLock
175 gr. SP #2850 InterLock
175 gr. RN #2855 InterLock

30 CALIBER (.308)
100 gr. SJ #3005
110 gr. SP #3010
110 gr. RN #3015
110 gr. FMJ #3017
130 gr. SP #3020
130 gr. SP Single Shot Pistol #3021
150 gr. SP #3031 InterLock
150 gr. BTSP #3033 InterLock
150 gr. RN (30-30) #3035 InterLock
150 gr. FMJ-BT #3037
165 gr. SP #3040 InterLock
165 gr. BTSP #3045 InterLock

30 CALIBER NATIONAL MATCH
168 gr. BTHP #30501

170 gr. FP (30-30) #3060 InterLock
180 gr. SP #3070 InterLock
180 gr. BTSP #3072 InterLock
180 gr. RN #3075 InterLock

30 CALIBER MATCH
190 gr. BTHP #3080

190 gr. BTSP #3085 InterLock
220 gr. RN #3090 InterLock

7.62 x 39 (.311)
123 gr. SP #3140
123 gr. FMJ #3147

303 CAL. and 7.7 JAP (.312)
150 gr. SP #3120 InterLock
174 gr. RN #3130 InterLock

32 SPECIAL (.321)
170 gr. FP #3210 InterLock

8MM CALIBER (.323)
125 gr. SP #3230
150 gr. SP #3232 InterLock
170 gr. RN #3235 InterLock
220 gr. SP #3238 InterLock

BULLETS/ Hornady

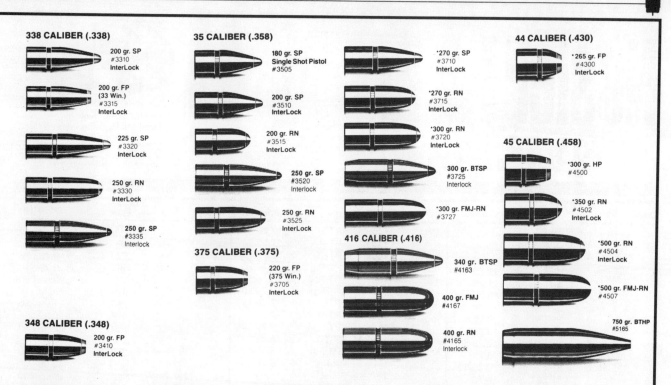

338 CALIBER (.338)

200 gr. SP
#3310
InterLock

200 gr. FP
(33 Win.)
#3315
InterLock

225 gr. SP
#3320
InterLock

250 gr. RN
#3330
InterLock

250 gr. SP
#3335
Interlock

348 CALIBER (.348)

200 gr. FP
#3410
InterLock

35 CALIBER (.358)

180 gr. SP
Single Shot Pistol
#3505

200 gr. SP
#3510
InterLock

200 gr. RN
#3515
InterLock

250 gr. SP
#3520
Interlock

250 gr. RN
#3525
InterLock

*270 gr. SP
#3710
InterLock

*270 gr. RN
#3715
InterLock

*300 gr. RN
#3720
InterLock

300 gr. BTSP
#3725
Interlock

*300 gr. FMJ-RN
#3727

375 CALIBER (.375)

220 gr. FP
(375 Win.)
#3705
InterLock

416 CALIBER (.416)

340 gr. BTSP
#4163

400 gr. FMJ
#4167

400 gr. RN
#4165
Interlock

44 CALIBER (.430)

*265 gr. FP
#4300
InterLock

45 CALIBER (.458)

*300 gr. HP
#4500

*350 gr. RN
#4502
InterLock

*500 gr. RN
#4504
InterLock

*500 gr. FMJ-RN
#4507

750 gr. BTHP
#5165

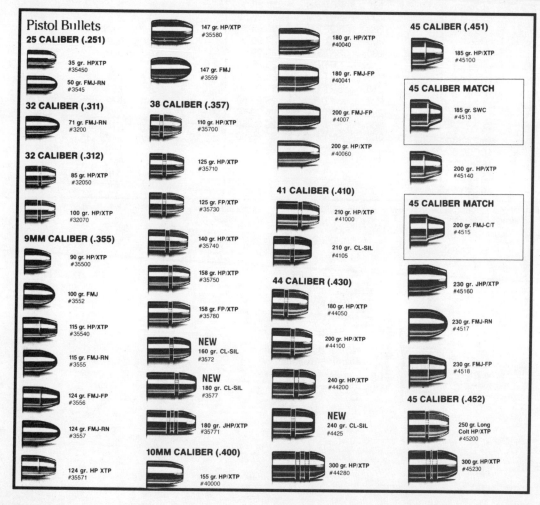

Pistol Bullets

25 CALIBER (.251)

35 gr. HPXTP
#35450

50 gr. FMJ-RN
#3545

32 CALIBER (.311)

71 gr. FMJ-RN
#3200

32 CALIBER (.312)

85 gr. HP/XTP
#32050

100 gr. HP/XTP
#32070

9MM CALIBER (.355)

90 gr. HP/XTP
#35500

100 gr. FMJ
#3552

115 gr. HP/XTP
#35540

115 gr. FMJ-RN
#3555

124 gr. FMJ-FP
#3556

124 gr. FMJ-RN
#3557

124 gr. HP XTP
#35571

147 gr. HP/XTP
#35580

147 gr. FMJ
#3559

38 CALIBER (.357)

110 gr. HP/XTP
#35700

125 gr. HP/XTP
#35710

125 gr. FP/XTP
#35730

140 gr. HP/XTP
#35740

158 gr. HP/XTP
#35750

158 gr. FP/XTP
#35780

NEW
160 gr. CL-SIL
#3572

NEW
180 gr. CL-SIL
#3577

180 gr. JHP/XTP
#35771

10MM CALIBER (.400)

155 gr. HP/XTP
#40000

180 gr. HP/XTP
#40040

180 gr. FMJ-FP
#40041

200 gr. FMJ-FP
#4007

200 gr. HP/XTP
#40060

41 CALIBER (.410)

210 gr. HP/XTP
#41000

210 gr. CL-SIL
#4105

44 CALIBER (.430)

180 gr. HP/XTP
#44050

200 gr. HP/XTP
#44100

240 gr. HP/XTP
#44200

NEW
240 gr. CL-SIL
#4425

300 gr. HP/XTP
#44280

45 CALIBER (.451)

185 gr. HP/XTP
#45100

45 CALIBER MATCH

185 gr. SWC
#4513

200 gr. HP/XTP
#45140

45 CALIBER MATCH

200 gr. FMJ-C/T
#4515

230 gr. JHP/XTP
#45160

230 gr. FMJ-RN
#4517

230 gr. FMJ-FP
#4518

45 CALIBER (.452)

250 gr. Long
Colt HP/XTP
#45200

300 gr. HP/XTP
#45230

Nosler® BULLETS

NOSLER®

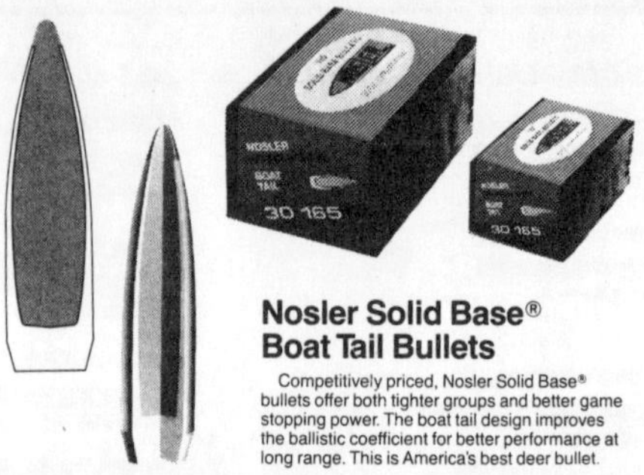

Nosler Solid Base® Boat Tail Bullets

Competitively priced, Nosler Solid Base® bullets offer both tighter groups and better game stopping power. The boat tail design improves the ballistic coefficient for better performance at long range. This is America's best deer bullet.

RIFLE

Caliber	Wgt. Grs.	Type	Price/100
22	45	Hornet SB	$10.99
	50	SPTBT	11.79
	52	HPSB Match	11.79
	55	SPTSB N/C	11.29
	55	SPTSB	10.29
	60	SPTSB	11.79
243/6mm	70	SPTBT	13.79
	85	SPT Par.	15.99/50
	95	SPT Par.	16.29/50
	95	SPTBT	14.79
	100	SPT Par.	16.29/50
25	85	SPTBT	14.79
	100	SPTBT	14.99
	100	SPT Par.	16.29/50
	115	SPT Par.	16.79/50
	120	SPT Par.	17.29/50
6.5mm	100	SPTBT	16.29
	120	SPTBT	16.79
	125	SPT Par.	17.79/50
	140	SPT Par.	17.99/50
270	130	SPTBT	17.79
	130	SPT Par.	17.79/50
	140	SPTBT	18.29
	150	SPTBT	18.79
	150	SPT Par.	18.79/50
	160	SSPT Par.	18.79/50
7mm	120	SPTBT	16.99
	120	FPSB	15.29
	140	SPTSB	16.29

Caliber	Wgt. Grs.	Type	Price/100
7mm	140	SPTBT	$17.79
	140	SPT Par.	17.99/50
	150	SPTBT	18.79
	150	SPT Par.	18.79/50
	160	SPT Par.	18.79/50
	175	SPT Par.	19.79/50
30	125	SPTBT	17.79
	150	SPTBT	17.99
	150	SPT Par.	18.79/50
	165	SPTBT	18.99
	165	SPT Par.	18.99/50
	170	RN Par.	19.79/50
	180	SPTBT	19.99
	180	SPT Par.	19.99/50
	180	PPT Par.	19.99/50
	200	SPT Par.	19.99/50
	220	SSPT Par.	20.99/50
8mm	200	SPT Par.	22.99/50
338	200	SPTBT	20.99
	210	SPT Par.	25.99/50
	225	SPT Par.	25.99/50
	250	SPT Par.	26.99/50
35	225	SPT Par.	25.99/50
	250	SPT Par.	26.99/50
375	260	SPT Par.	26.99/50
	300	SPT Par.	30.99/50

PISTOL

Caliber	Wgt. Grs.	Type	Price/100
9mm	90	HP	$9.79
	115	FMJ	9.79
	115	HP	9.79
	115	HP	20.99/250
38/357	125	JHP	10.29
	125	JHP	21.99/250
	150	JSP	10.99
	150	IPSC	22.99/250
	158	JHP	10.99
	158	JHP	22.99/250
	180	N/EXP SP	12.99
	180	Sil.	26.99/250
10mm	135	HP	10.79
	135	JHP	27.99/250
	150	JHP	10.99
	170	JHP	12.79
	180	JHP	12.99
41	210	JHP	13.79
44	200	JHP	14.79
	200	JHP	27.99/250
	240	JHP	14.79
	240	JHP	30.99/250
	240	JSP	14.99
	300	JHP	15.79
45	185	JHP	14.29
	185	JHP	28.99/250
	230	FMJ	14.79
	250	JHP	14.99

BT = Ballistic Tip; FMJ = Full Metal Jacket; HP = Hollowpoint; JHP = Jacketed Hollowpoint; JSP = Jacketed Softpoint; N/EXP SP = Non-Expanding Softpoint; SB = Solid Base Bullet; SPT = Spitzer; SSPT = Semi-Spitzer

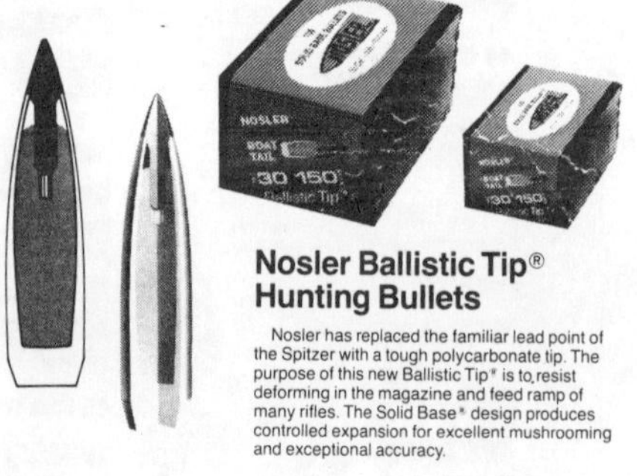

Nosler Ballistic Tip® Hunting Bullets

Nosler has replaced the familiar lead point of the Spitzer with a tough polycarbonate tip. The purpose of this new Ballistic Tip® is to resist deforming in the magazine and feed ramp of many rifles. The Solid Base® design produces controlled expansion for excellent mushrooming and exceptional accuracy.

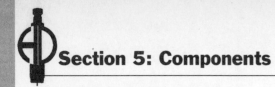

Nosler Partition® Bullets

Caliber/ Diameter	PARTITION	Bullet Weight and Style	Sectional Density	Ballistic Coefficient	Part Number
6mm/ .243"		85 Gr. Spitzer	.206	.315	16314
		95 Gr. Spitzer	.230	.365	16315
		100 Gr. Spitzer	.242	.384	35642
25/ .257"		100 Gr. Spitzer	.216	.377	16317
		115 Gr. Spitzer	.249	.389	16318
		120 Gr. Spitzer	.260	.391	35643
6.5mm/ .264"		125 Gr. Spitzer	.256	.449	16320
		140 Gr. Spitzer	.287	.490	16321

Caliber/ Diameter	PARTITION	Bullet Weight and Style	Sectional Density	Ballistic Coefficient	Part Number
270/ .277"		130 Gr. Spitzer	.242	.416	16322
		150 Gr. Spitzer	.279	.465	16323
		160 Gr. Semi Spitzer	.298	.434	16324
7mm/ .284"		140 Gr. Spitzer	.248	.434	16325
		150 Gr. Spitzer	.266	.456	16326
		160 Gr. Spitzer	.283	.475	16327
		175 Gr. Spitzer	.310	.519	35645
30/ .308"		150 Gr. Spitzer	.226	.387	16329
		165 Gr. Spitzer	.248	.410	16330
		170 Gr. Round Nose	.256	.252	16333
		180 Gr. Spitzer	.271	.474	16331
		180 Gr. Protected Point	.271	.361	25396
		200 Gr. Spitzer	.301	.481	35626
		220 Gr. Semi Spitzer	.331	.351	16332
8mm/ .323"		200 Gr. Spitzer	.274	.426	35277
338/ .338"		210 Gr. Spitzer	.263	.400	16337
		225 Gr. Spitzer	.281	.454	16336
		250 Gr. Spitzer	.313	.473	35644
35/ .358"		225 Gr. Spitzer	.251	.430	44800
		250 Gr. Spitzer	.279	.446	44801
375/ .375"		260 Gr. Spitzer	.264	.314	44850
		300 Gr. Spitzer	.305	.398	44845

Nosler Solid Base® Boat Tail Bullets

Caliber/ Diameter	SOLID BASE	Bullet Weight and Style	Sectional Density	Ballistic Coefficient	Part Number
22/ .224"		45 Gr. Hornet	.128	.144	35487
		52 Gr. Hollow Point Match	.148	.224	25857
		55 Gr. Spitzer w/cannelure	.157	.261	16339
		60 Gr. Spitzer	.171	.266	30323
6mm/ .243"		100 Gr. Spitzer	.242	.388	30390
25/ .257"		120 Gr. Spitzer	.260	.446	30404
270/ .277"		130 Gr. Spitzer	.242	.420	30394
7mm/ .284"		NEW 120 Gr. Flat Point	.213	.195	41722
		140 Gr. Spitzer	.248	.461	29599
30/ .308"		150 Gr. Spitzer	.226	.393	27583
		165 Gr. Spitzer	.248	.428	27585
		180 Gr. Spitzer	.271	.491	27587

Nosler Ballistic Tip® Bullets

Caliber/ Diameter	BALLISTIC TIP	Bullet Weight and Style	Sectional Density	Ballistic Coefficient	Part Number
22/ .224"		50 Gr. Spitzer (Orange Tip)	.142	.238	39522
		55 Gr. Spitzer (Orange Tip)	.157	.267	39526
6mm/ .243"		70 Gr. Spitzer (Purple Tip)	.169	.310	39532
		95 Gr. Spitzer (Purple Tip)	.230	.379	39534
25/ .257"		85 Gr. Spitzer (Blue Tip)	.183	.331	43004
		100 Gr. Spitzer (Blue Tip)	.216	.393	43005
6.5mm/ .264"		100 Gr. Spitzer (Brown Tip)	.205	.350	43008
		120 Gr. Spitzer (Brown Tip)	.246	.458	43007
270/ .277"		130 Gr. Spitzer (Yellow Tip)	.242	.433	39589
		140 Gr. Spitzer (Yellow Tip)	.261	.456	43983
		150 Gr. Spitzer (Yellow Tip)	.279	.496	39588
7mm/ .284"		120 Gr. Spitzer (Red Tip)	.213	.417	39550
		140 Gr. Spitzer (Red Tip)	.248	.485	39587
		150 Gr. Spitzer (Red Tip)	.266	.493	39586
30/ .308"		125 Gr. Spitzer (Green Tip)	.188	.366	43980
		150 Gr. Spitzer (Green Tip)	.226	.435	39585
		165 Gr. Spitzer (Green Tip)	.248	.475	39584
		180 Gr. Spitzer (Green Tip)	.271	.507	39583
338/ .338"		200 Gr. Spitzer (Maroon Tip)	.250	.414	39595

Nosler Handgun Bullets

Caliber/ Diameter	HANDGUN	Bullet Weight and Style	Sectional Density	Ballistic Coefficient	Part Number
9mm/ .355"		90 Gr. Hollow Point	.102	.086	42050
		115 Gr. Full Metal Jacket	.130	.103	42059
		115 Gr. Hollow Point 250 Quantity Bulk Pack	.130	.110	43009 44848
38/ .357"		125 Gr. Hollow Point 250 Quantity Bulk Pack	.140	.143	42055 44840
		150 Gr. Soft Point	.168	.153	42056
		150 Gr. IPSC 250 Quantity Bulk Pack	.168	.157	44839
		158 Gr. Hollow Point 250 Quantity Bulk Pack	.177	.182	42057 44841
		180 Gr. Silhouette NEW 250 Quantity Bulk Pack	.202	.210	42058 44851
10mm/ .400"		135 Gr. Hollow Point NEW 250 Quantity Bulk Pack	.121	.093	44838 44852
		150 Gr. Hollow Point	.134	.106	44849
		170 Gr. Hollow Point	.152	.137	44844
		180 Gr. Hollow Point	.161	.147	44837
41/ .410"		210 Gr. Hollow Point	.178	.170	43012
44/ .429"		200 Gr. Hollow Point 250 Quantity Bulk Pack	.155	.151	42060 44846
		240 Gr. Soft Point	.186	.177	42068
		240 Gr. Hollow Point 250 Quantity Bulk Pack	.186	.173	42061 44842
		300 Gr. Hollow Point	.233	.206	42069
45/ .451"		185 Gr. Hollow Point 250 Quantity Bulk Pack	.130	.142	42062 44847
		230 Gr. Full Metal Jacket	.162	.183	42064
45 Colt/ .451"		250 Gr. Hollow Point	.176	.177	43013

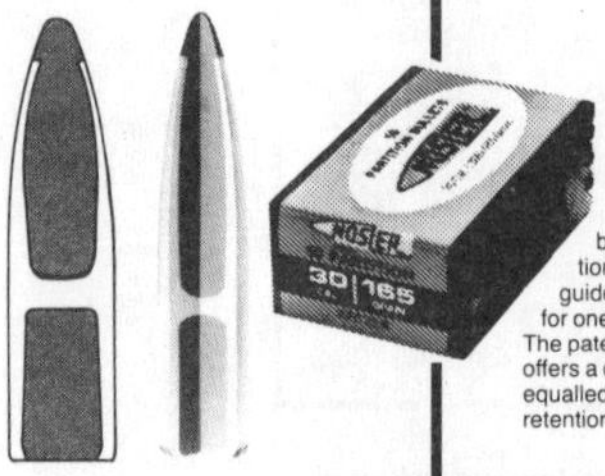

Nosler Partition® Bullets

The Nosler Partition® bullet earned its reputation among professional guides and serious hunters for one reason: it doesn't fail. The patented Partition® design offers a dual core that is unequalled in mushrooming, weight retention and hydrostatic shock.

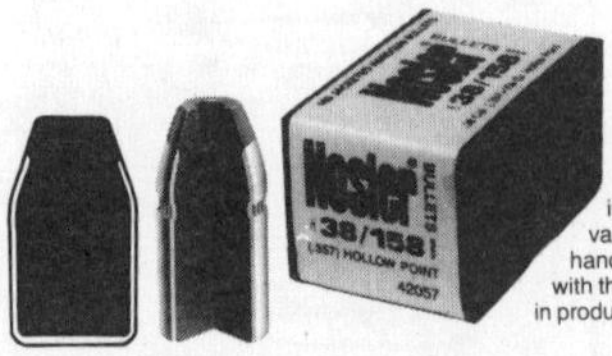

Nosler Handgun Bullets

Manufactured by the industry's most advanced equipment, Nosler handgun bullets are made with the same care exercised in producing rifle bullets.

SIERRA

The Bulletsmiths®

Caliber	Wgt. Grs.	Type	Price/100
RIFLE			
22	40	Hornet	$9.49
	40	HP	9.29
	45	Hornet	9.49
	45	SMP	9.79
	45	SPT	9.79
	50	SMP	9.79
	50	SPT	9.29
	50	Blitz	9.79
	52	HPBT Match	11.49
	53	HP Match	11.29
	55	Blitz	9.79
	55	SMP	9.99
	55	FMJBT	9.79
	55	SPT	9.79
	55	SBT	10.79
	55	HPBT	10.79
	60	HP	9.79
	63	SMP	10.29
	*69	HPBT Match	12.79
243/6mm	60	HP	11.99
	70	HPBT Match	14.29
	75	HP	12.29
	85	SPT	12.79
	85	HPBT	13.99
	90	FMJBT	13.29
	100	SPT	12.79
	100	SMP	13.49
	100	SBT	14.29
	**107	HPBT	17.49
25	75	HP	12.79
	87	SPT	13.29
	90	HPBT	14.49
	100	SPT	13.29
	100	SBT	13.49
	117	SBT	15.79
	117	SPT	14.49
	120	HPBT	16.29
6.5mm	85	HP	14.49
	100	HP	14.99
	120	SPT	15.49
	120	HPBT Match	16.79
	140	SBT	17.99
	140	HPBT Match	19.29
	160	SMP	16.49
270	90	HP	14.29
	110	SPT	14.29
	130	SBT	16.29
	130	SPT	14.49
	140	HPBT	16.29
	140	SBT	$16.79

Caliber	Wgt. Grs.	Type	Price/100
	150	SBT	18.29
	150	RN	15.49
7mm	100	HP	13.79
	120	SPT	14.49
	140	SBT	17.29
	140	SPT	14.99
	150	SBT	17.79
	150	HPBT Match	19.79
	160	SBT	18.29
	160	HPBT	18.29
	168	HPBT Match	19.99
	170	RN	16.99
	175	SBT	20.29
30-30	125	HP/FN	14.79
	150	FN	14.79
	170	FN	15.79
30	110	FMJ	11.79
	110	RN	11.79
	110	HP	13.79
	125	SPT	14.79
	150	FMJBT	15.79
	150	SPT	14.49
	150	SBT	16.79
	150	HPBT Match	19.79
	150	RN	14.79
	155	HPBT Palma	19.79
	165	SBT	17.79
	165	HPBT	17.79
	168	HPBT Match	19.99
	180	SPT	16.29
	180	SBT	18.29
	180	HPBT Match	21.99
	180	RN	15.99
	190	HPBT Match	22.99
	200	SBT	21.99
	200	HPBT Match	22.99
	220	HPBT Match	25.99
	220	RN	17.99
303	150	SPT	16.29
	180	SPT	17.49
8mm	150	SPT	16.29
	175	SPT	17.49
	220	SBT	13.49/50
338	250	SBT	13.49/50
35	200	RN	9.79/50
	225	SBT	12.79/50
375	200	FN	11.79/50
	250	SBT	17.59/50
	300	SBT	18.79/50
45/70	300	HP/FN	14.29/50

Caliber	Wgt. Grs.	Type	Price/100
PISTOL			
25	50	FMJ	$9.29
32	71	FMJ	9.99
	90	JHC	9.99
9mm	90	JHP	9.99
	95	FMJ	10.29
	115	JHP	10.79
	115	FMJ	10.79
	125	FMJ	11.29
	130	FMJ	12.79
38 Spl./	110	JHC Blitz	10.79
357 Mag.	125	JSP	10.99
	125	JHC	10.99
	140	JHC	11.29
	158	JHC	11.79
	158	JSP	11.49
	170	JHC	12.29
	170	FMJ Match	15.29
	180	FPJ Match	13.49
10mm	150	JHP	14.29
	165	JHP	14.99
	180	JHP	14.79
	190	FPJ	14.99
41	170	JHC	14.99
	210	JHC	14.99
	220	FPJ Match	15.99
44 Spl./	180	JHC	14.99
44 Mag.	210	JHC	15.29
	220	FPJ Match	15.99
	240	JHC	15.79
	250	FPJ Match	16.49
	300	JSP	9.29
45	185	JHP	14.79
	185	FPJ Match	15.49
	200	FPJ Match	15.79
	230	FMJ Match	16.29
	240	JHC	15.79
SINGLE SHOT PISTOL			
6mm	80	SPT	$12.29
7mm	130	SPT	13.99
30	135	SPT	14.49

BT = Boattail; SPT = Spitzer; SBT = Spitzer Boattail; HP = Hollowpoint; HPBT = Hollowpoint Boattail; JHP = Jacketed Hollowpoint; JSP = Jacketed Softpoint; JHC = Jacketed Hollow Cavity; FMJ = Full Metal Jacket; FPJ = Full Profile Jacket; FMJBT = Full Metal Jacket Boattail; FN = Flat Nose; RN = Round Nose; SMP = Semi-Pointed. *For rifles with twist of 1 in 7 to 1 in 10. **For rifles with twist of 1 in 7 or 8.

SIERRA
The Bulletsmiths®

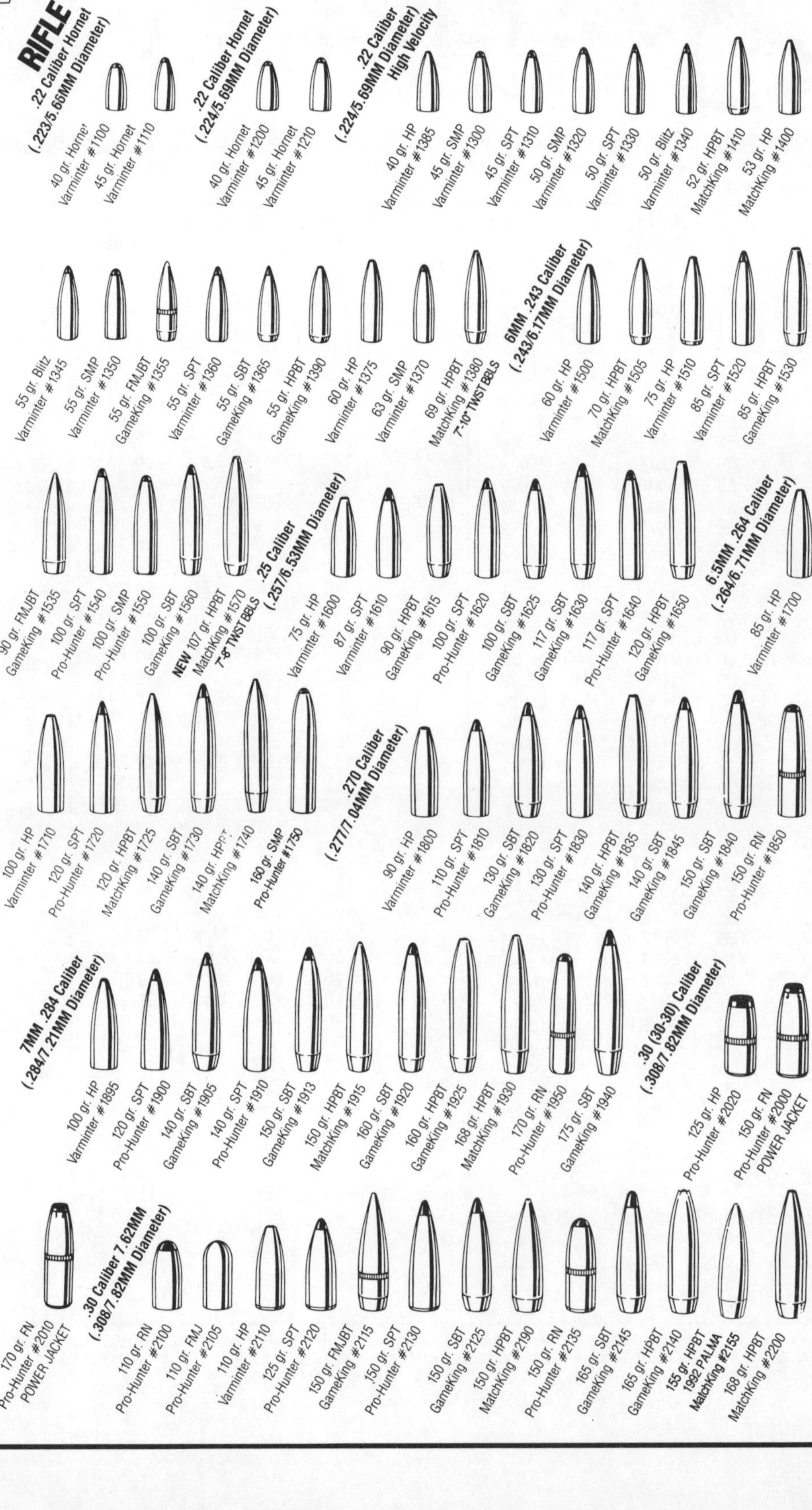

RIFLE
.22 Caliber Hornet (.223/5.66MM Diameter)
40 gr. Hornet Varminter #1100
45 gr. Hornet Varminter #1110
.22 Caliber Hornet (.224/5.69MM Diameter)
40 gr. Hornet Varminter #1200
45 gr. Hornet Varminter #1210
.22 Caliber High Velocity (.224/5.69MM Diameter)
40 gr. HP Varminter #1385
45 gr. SMP Varminter #1300
45 gr. SPT Varminter #1310
50 gr. SMP Varminter #1320
50 gr. SPT Varminter #1330
50 gr. Blitz Varminter #1340
52 gr. HPBT MatchKing #1410
53 gr. HP MatchKing #1400
55 gr. Blitz Varminter #1345
55 gr. SMP Varminter #1350
55 gr. FMJBT GameKing #1355
55 gr. SPT Varminter #1360
55 gr. SBT GameKing #1365
55 gr. HPBT GameKing #1390
60 gr. HP Varminter #1375
63 gr. SMP Varminter #1370
69 gr. HPBT MatchKing #1380 7"-10" TWST BBLS
6MM .243 Caliber (.243/6.17MM Diameter)
60 gr. HP Varminter #1500
70 gr. HPBT MatchKing #1505
75 gr. HP Varminter #1510
85 gr. SPT Varminter #1520
85 gr. HPBT GameKing #1530
90 gr. FMJBT GameKing #1535
100 gr. SPT Pro-Hunter #1540
100 gr. SMP Pro-Hunter #1550
100 gr. SBT GameKing #1560
NEW 107 gr. HPBT MatchKing #1570 7"-8" TWST BBLS
.25 Caliber (.257/6.53MM Diameter)
75 gr. HP Varminter #1600
87 gr. SPT Varminter #1610
90 gr. HPBT GameKing #1615
100 gr. SPT Pro-Hunter #1620
100 gr. SBT GameKing #1625
117 gr. SBT GameKing #1630
117 gr. SPT Pro-Hunter #1640
120 gr. HPBT GameKing #1650
6.5MM .264 Caliber (.264/6.71MM Diameter)
85 gr. HP Varminter #1700
100 gr. HP Varminter #1710
120 gr. SPT Pro-Hunter #1720
120 gr. HPBT MatchKing #1725
140 gr. SBT GameKing #1730
140 gr. HPBT MatchKing #1740
160 gr. SMP Pro-Hunter #1750
.270 Caliber (.277/7.04MM Diameter)
90 gr. HP Varminter #1800
110 gr. SPT Pro-Hunter #1810
130 gr. SBT GameKing #1820
130 gr. SPT Pro-Hunter #1830
140 gr. HPBT GameKing #1835
140 gr. SBT GameKing #1845
150 gr. SBT GameKing #1840
150 gr. RN Pro-Hunter #1850
7MM .284 Caliber (.284/7.21MM Diameter)
100 gr. HP Varminter #1895
120 gr. SPT Pro-Hunter #1900
140 gr. SBT GameKing #1905
140 gr. SPT Pro-Hunter #1910
150 gr. SBT GameKing #1913
150 gr. HPBT MatchKing #1915
160 gr. SBT GameKing #1920
160 gr. HPBT GameKing #1925
168 gr. HPBT MatchKing #1930
170 gr. RN Pro-Hunter #1950
175 gr. SBT GameKing #1940
.30 (30-30) Caliber (.308/7.82MM Diameter)
125 gr. HP Pro-Hunter #2020
150 gr. FN Pro-Hunter #2000 POWER JACKET
170 gr. FN Pro-Hunter #2010 POWER JACKET
.30 Caliber 7.62MM (.308/7.82MM Diameter)
110 gr. RN Pro-Hunter #2100
110 gr. FMJ Pro-Hunter #2105
110 gr. HP Varminter #2110
125 gr. SPT Pro-Hunter #2120
150 gr. FMJBT GameKing #2115
150 gr. SPT Pro-Hunter #2130
150 gr. SBT GameKing #2125
150 gr. HPBT MatchKing #2190
150 gr. RN Pro-Hunter #2135
165 gr. SBT GameKing #2145
165 gr. HPBT GameKing #2140
155 gr. HPBT 1992 PALMA MatchKing #2155
168 gr. HPBT MatchKing #2200

BULLETS/ Sierra

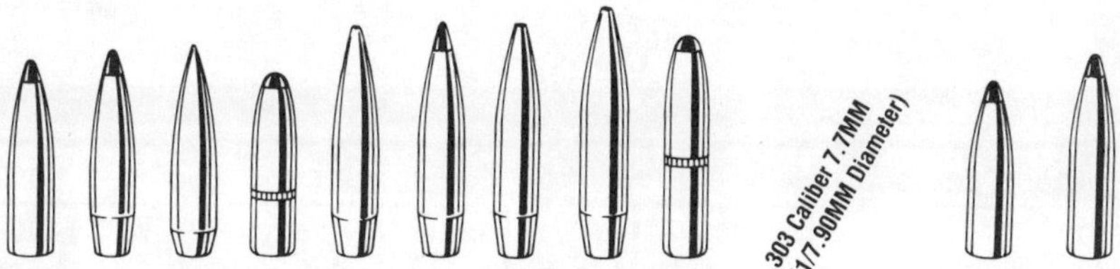

- 180 gr. SPT Pro-Hunter #2150
- 180 gr. SBT GameKing #2160
- 180 gr. HPBT MatchKing #2220
- 180 gr. RN Pro-Hunter #2170
- 190 gr. HPBT MatchKing #2210
- 200 gr. SBT GameKing #2165
- 200 gr. HPBT MatchKing #2230
- 220 gr. HPBT MatchKing #2240
- 220 gr. RN Pro-Hunter #2180

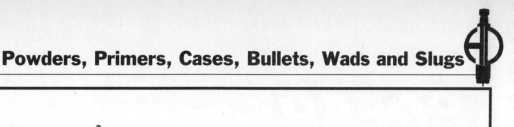

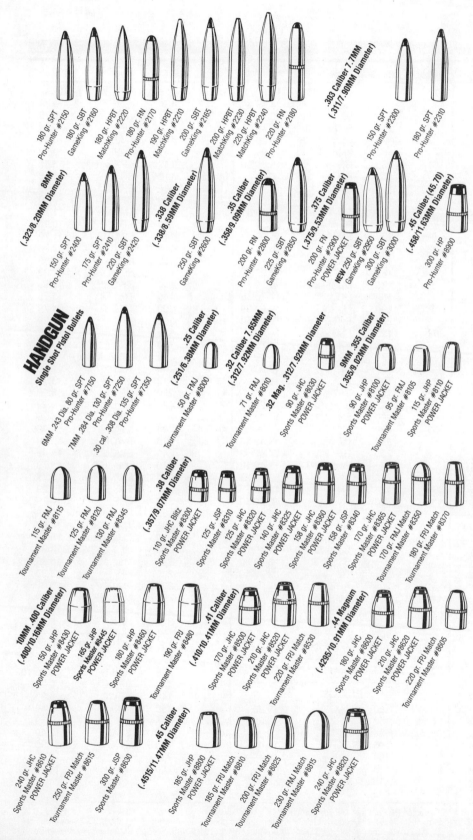

.303 Caliber 7.7MM (.311/7.90MM Diameter)

- 150 gr. SPT Pro-Hunter #2300
- 180 gr. SPT Pro-Hunter #2310

8MM (.323/8.20MM Diameter)

- 150 gr. SPT Pro-Hunter #2400
- 175 gr. SPT Pro-Hunter #2410
- 220 gr. SBT GameKing #2420

.338 Caliber (.338/8.59MM Diameter)

- 250 gr. SBT GameKing #2600

.35 Caliber (.358/9.09MM Diameter)

- 200 gr. RN Pro-Hunter #2800
- 225 gr. SBT GameKing #2850

.375 Caliber (.375/9.53MM Diameter)

- 200 gr. FN Pro-Hunter #2900 POWER JACKET
- **NEW** 250 gr. SBT GameKing #2950
- 300 gr. SBT GameKing #3000

.45 Caliber (45.70) (.458/11.63MM Diameter)

- 300 gr. HP Pro-Hunter #8900

HANDGUN

Single Shot Pistol Bullets

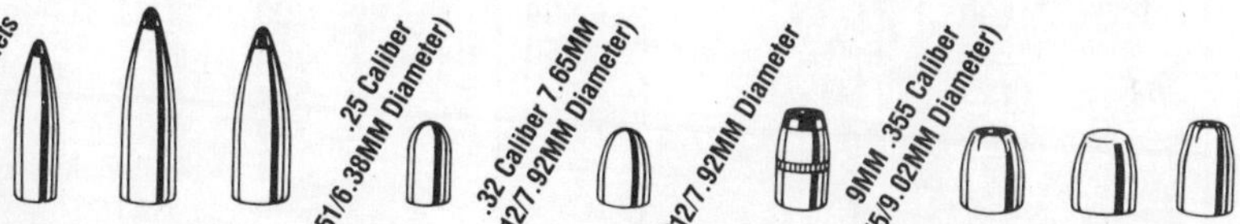

- 6MM .243 Dia. 80 gr. SPT Pro-Hunter #7150
- 7MM .284 Dia. 130 gr. SPT Pro-Hunter #7250
- 30 cal. .308 Dia. 135 gr. SPT Pro-Hunter #7350

.25 Caliber (.251/6.38MM Diameter)

- 50 gr. FMJ Tournament Master #8000

.32 Caliber 7.65MM (.312/7.92MM Diameter)

- 71 gr. FMJ Tournament Master #8010

.32 Mag. .312/7.92MM Diameter

- 90 gr. JHC Sports Master #8030 POWER JACKET

9MM .355 Caliber (.355/9.02MM Diameter)

- 90 gr. JHP Sports Master #8100 POWER JACKET
- 95 gr. FMJ Tournament Master #8105
- 115 gr. JHP Sports Master #8110 POWER JACKET

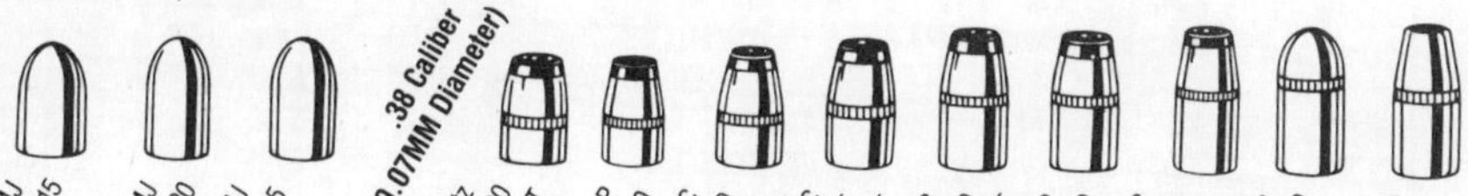

- 115 gr. FMJ Tournament Master #8115
- 125 gr. FMJ Tournament Master #8120
- 130 gr. FMJ Tournament Master #8345

.38 Caliber (.357/9.07MM Diameter)

- 110 gr. JHC Blitz Sports Master #8300 POWER JACKET
- 125 gr. JSP Sports Master #8310
- 125 gr. JHC Sports Master #8320 POWER JACKET
- 140 gr. JHC Sports Master #8325 POWER JACKET
- 158 gr. JHC Sports Master #8360 POWER JACKET
- 158 gr. JSP Sports Master #8340
- 170 gr. JHC Sports Master #8365 POWER JACKET
- 170 gr. FMJ Match Tournament Master #8350
- 180 gr. FPJ Match Tournament Master #8370

10MM .400 Caliber (.400/10.16MM Diameter)

- 150 gr. JHP Sports Master #8430 POWER JACKET
- 165 gr. JHP Sports Master #8445 POWER JACKET
- 180 gr. JHP Sports Master #8460 POWER JACKET
- 190 gr. FPJ Tournament Master #8480

.41 Caliber (.410/10.41MM Diameter)

- 170 gr. JHC Sports Master #8500 POWER JACKET
- 210 gr. JHC Sports Master #8520 POWER JACKET
- 220 gr. FPJ Match Tournament Master #8530

.44 Magnum (.4295/10.91MM Diameter)

- 180 gr. JHC Sports Master #8600 POWER JACKET
- 210 gr. JHC Sports Master #8620 POWER JACKET
- 220 gr. FPJ Match Tournament Master #8605

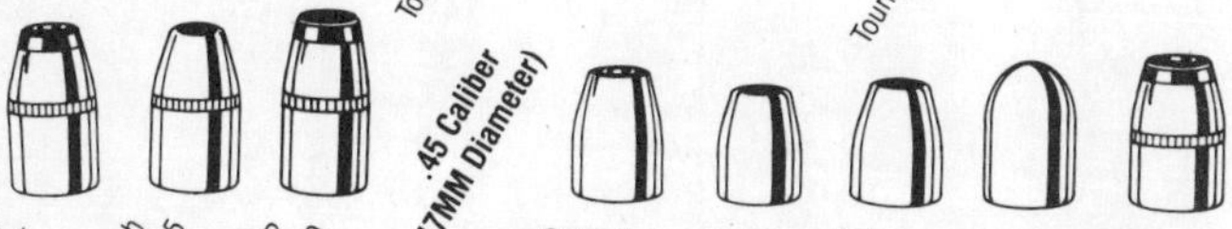

- 240 gr. JHC Sports Master #8610 POWER JACKET
- 250 gr. FPJ Match Tournament Master #8615
- 300 gr. JSP Sports Master #8630

.45 Caliber (.4515/11.47MM Diameter)

- 185 gr. JHP Sports Master #8800 POWER JACKET
- 185 gr. FPJ Match Tournament Master #8810
- 200 gr. FPJ Match Tournament Master #8825
- 230 gr. FMJ Match Tournament Master #8815
- 240 gr. JHC Sports Master #8820 POWER JACKET

SPEER

RIFLE

Caliber	Wgt. Grs.	Type	Price/100
22	40	SP (.223, .224)	$8.99
	45	SPTZ (.223, .224)	8.99
	40	SP	8.99
	45	SPTZ	8.99
	46	FN w/c	8.99
	50	HPTNT	9.49
	50	SPTZ	8.99
	52	HPBT Match	11.29
	52	HP	9.99
	55	SPTZ	9.29
	55	SPTZ w/c	9.79
	55	FMJBT	9.79
	70	Semi-SPTZ	12.79
243/6mm	75	HP	11.79
	80	SPTZ	11.79
	85	BTSPTZ	13.29
	90	SPTZ	12.29
	100	BTSPTZ	13.29
	105	RN	12.99
	105	SPTZ	12.99
25	75	FN w/c	11.99
	87	SPTZ	12.79
	100	SPTZ	12.99
	100	HP	13.79
	100	BTSPTZ	14.99
	120	BTSPTZ	15.49
	120	SPTZ	14.49
6.5mm	120	SPTZ	15.29
	140	SPTZ	15.49
270	100	HP	14.79
	100	SPTZ	13.99
	130	BTSPTZ	15.79
	130	SPTZ	13.79
	130	GS	15.79/50
	150	BTSPTZ	16.79
	150	SPTZ	14.99
	150	GS	16.79/50
7mm	115	HP	14.29
	120	SP	14.79
	130	SPTZ	14.99
	130	BTSPTZ	15.79
	145	BTSPTZ	16.79
	145	SPTZ	15.89
	145	BT Match	19.29
	145	GS	16.49/50
	160	BTSPTZ	17.79
	160	SPTZ	16.79
	160	Mag. Tip	17.79
	160	GS	18.49/50
	175	Mag. Tip	18.29
	175	GS	18.99/50
30	100	P	9.49
	110	HP	11.49
	110	RN	11.79
	110	FMJRN	11.79
	110	SP	13.29
	130	HP	14.99
	130	FN (30-30)	14.99
30	150	FN (30-30)	$14.69
	150	RN	14.49
	150	BTSPTZ	16.79
	150	SPTZ	14.49
	150	Mag. Tip	18.29
	150	FMJ/BT	15.99
	150	GS	16.59/50
	165	RN	16.39
	165	BTSPTZ	16.79
	165	SPTZ	15.99
	165	GS	17.19/50
	168	BT Match	18.99
	170	FN (30-30)	15.29
	180	RN	16.69
	180	BTSPTZ	18.79
	180	SPTZ	15.99
	180	Mag. Tip	20.59
	180	GS	17.79/50
	190	Match	9.99/50
	200	SPTZ	9.49/50
303	123	FMJ w/c	14.79
	125	SP w/c	14.79
	150	SPTZ	15.99
	180	RN	17.29
32	170	FN	16.49
8mm	150	SPTZ	15.79
	170	Semi-SPTZ	16.29
	200	SPTZ	10.29/50
338	200	SPTZ	9.99/50
	225	BTSP	15.49/50
	250	GS	24.99/50
	275	Semi-SPTZ	11.49/50
	275	AGS	85.99/25
35	180	FN	19.79
	220	FN	10.49/50
	250	SPTZ	11.49/50
	250	GS	20.99/50
9.3mm	270	Semi-SPTZ	11.79/50
375	235	Semi-SPTZ	11.49/50
	270	BTSP	18.79/50
	285	GS	32.79/50
	300	AGS Solid	87.99/25
416	400	AGS Solid	90.99/25
	400	AGS	72.99/25
45	350	FN	16.99/50
	400	FN	15.99/50
	500	AGS Solid	99.99/25
	500	AGS	83.99/25
50	647	FMJBT	24.99/20

PISTOL

Caliber	Wgt. Grs.	Type	Price/100
25 ACP	50	TMJ	$9.29
32	100	JHP	10.29
9mm	88	HP	9.99
	95	TMJ	10.49
	100	HP	10.49
	115	TMJ	10.49
	115	HP	9.49
	115	PHP	9.49
9mm	115	HP Gold Dot	$11.99
	124	JSP	10.79
	124	TMJ	10.79
	124	HP	10.99
	147	TMJ	10.99
	147	PHP	10.99
	147	HP Gold Dot	13.49
38/357	110	HP	10.49
	125	SP	10.49
	125	HP	10.49
	125	TMJ	11.29
	140	HP	10.99
	146	SWCHP	11.79
	158	TMJ	12.79
	158	HP	10.99
	158	SP	11.29
	160	SWCSP	11.99
	180	TMJ Sil.	13.79
	200	TMJ Sil.	14.79
10mm	155	HP	13.29
	180	TMJ	13.99
	180	PHP	13.79
	180	HP(Gold Dot)	17.49
	200	TMJ	14.99
41 AE	180	HP	13.79
41	200	HP	15.29
	220	SWCSP	16.29
	210	TMJ Sil.	16.29
44 Spl./	200	Mag. HP	14.49
44 Mag.	225	SWCHP	15.29
	240	SWCSP	15.49
	240	Mag. HP	15.79
	240	Mag. SP	15.79
	240	TMJ Sil.	16.29
	300	PSP	10.79/50
45	185	HP Gold Dot	17.99
	185	TMJ Match	14.99
	200	TMJ Match	15.49
	200	HP	14.99
	225	Mag. HP	16.29
	230	HP	13.99
	230	FMJ	15.29
	260	Mag. HP	17.79
	300	PSP	10.79/50
50 AE	325	HP	9.79/50

LEAD HANDGUN

Caliber	Wgt. Grs.	Type	Price/100
9mm	125	RN	$7.79
32	98	HBWC	48.99/1000
38	148	BBWC	8.29
	148	HBWC	8.29
	158	hpswc	8.49
	158	RN	7.79
44	240	SWC	12.49
45	200	SWC	11.99
	230	RN	12.29
	250	SWC	12.79

SP = Softpoint; SPTZ = Spitzer; BT = Boattail; HP = Hollowpoint; PHP = Plated Hollowpoint; HP TNT = Hollowpoint TNT; HPBT = Hollowpoint Boattail; FMJ/BT = Full Metal Jacket Boattail; TMJ = Totally Metal Jacketed; JHP = Jacketed Hollowpoint; JSP = Jacketed Softpoint; PSP = Plated Softpoint; Sil. = Silhouette; FN = Flat Nose; RN = Round Nose; P= Plinker; SWC = Semi Wad Cutter; BBWC = Bevel Base Wad Cutter; HBWC = Hollow Base Wad Cutter; w/c = with cannelure; AGS = African Grand Slam; GS = Grand Slam

SPEER

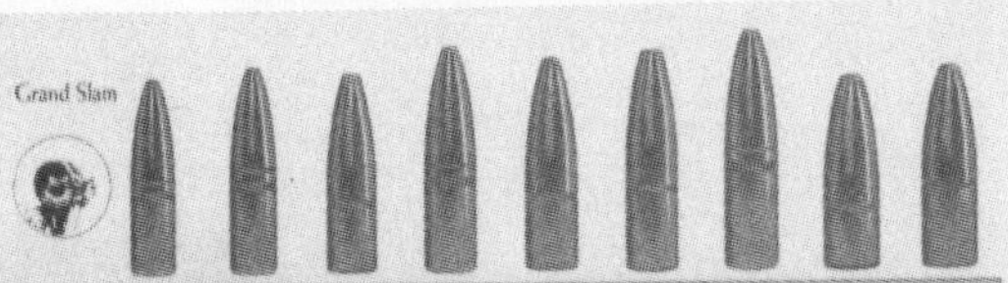

Bullet Caliber & Type	6mm GS Soft Point	25 GS Soft Point	270 GS Soft Point	270 GS Soft Point	7mm GS Soft Point	7mm GS Soft Point	7mm GS Soft Point	30 GS Soft Point	30 GS Soft Point
Diameter	.243"	.257"	.277"	.277"	.284"	.284"	.284"	.308"	.308"
Weight (grs.)	100	120	130	150	145	160	175	150	165
Ballist. Coef.	0.351	0.328	0.345	0.385	0.327	0.387	0.465	0.305	0.393
Part Number	1222	1415	1465	1608	1632	1638	1643	2026	2038
Box Count	50	50	50	50	50	50	50	50	50

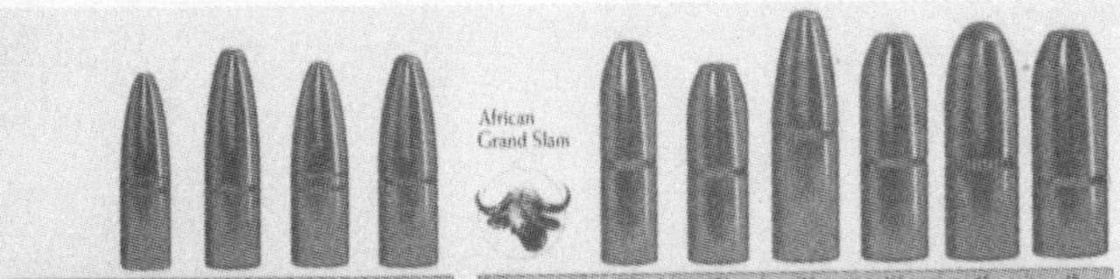

Bullet Caliber & Type	30 GS Soft Point	338 GS Soft Point	35 GS Soft Point	375 GS Soft Point
Diameter	.308"	.338"	.358"	.375"
Weight (grs.)	180	250	250	285
Ballist. Coef.	0.416	0.431	0.335	0.354
Part Number	2063	2408	2455	2473
Box Count	50	50	50	50

Bullet Caliber & Type	338 AGS Tungsten Solid	375 AGS Tungsten Solid	416 AGS Soft Point	416 AGS Tungsten Solid	45 AGS Soft Point	45 AGS Tungsten Solid
Diameter	.338"	.375"	.416"	.416"	.458"	.458"
Weight (grs.)	275	300	400	400	500	500
Ballist. Coef.	0.291	0.258	0.381	0.262	0.285	0.277
Part Number	2414	2478	2475	2476	2485	2486
Box Count	25	25	25	25	25	25

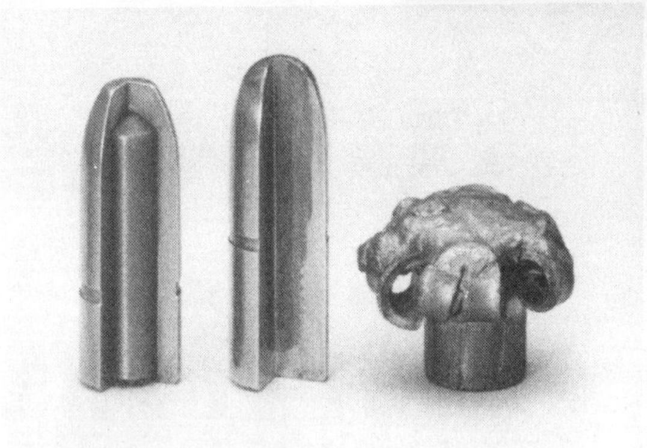

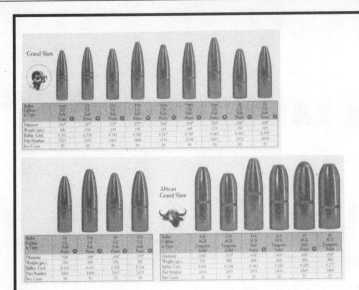

Speer African Grand Slam

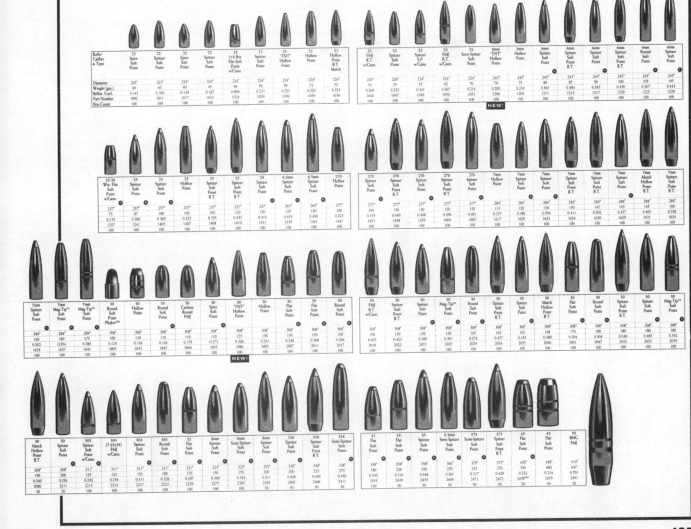

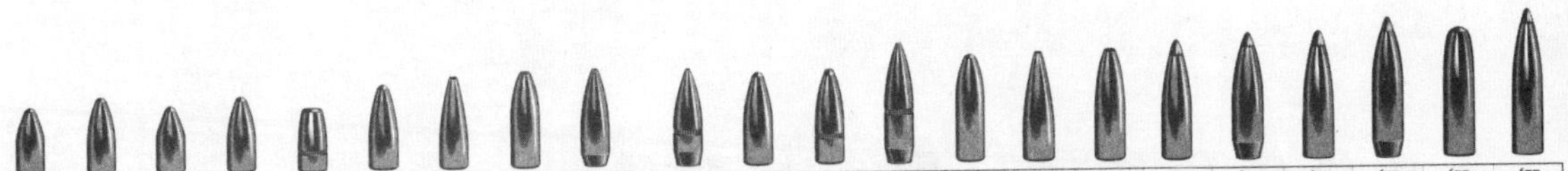

Bullet Caliber & Type	22 Spire Soft Point	22 Spitzer Soft Point	22 Spire Soft Point	22 Spitzer Soft Point	22 218 Bee Flat Soft Point w/Cann.	22 Spitzer Soft Point	22 "TNT" Hollow Point	22 Hollow Point	22 Hollow Point B.T. Match
Diameter	.223"	.223"	.224"	.224"	.224"	.224"	.224"	.224"	.224"
Weight (grs.)	40	45	40	45	46	50	50	52	52
Ballist. Coef.	0.145	0.166	0.144	0.167	0.094	0.231	0.223	0.225	0.253
Part Number	1005	1011	1017	1023	1024	1029	1030	1035	1036
Box Count	100	100	100	100	100	100	100	100	100

	22 FMJ B.T. w/Cann.	22 Spitzer Soft Point	22 Spitzer S.P. w/Cann.	22 FMJ B.T. w/Cann.	22 Semi-Spitzer Soft Point	6mm "TNT" Hollow Point	6mm Hollow Point	6mm Spitzer Soft Point	6mm Spitzer Soft Point B.T.	6mm Spitzer Soft Point	6mm Spitzer Soft Point B.T.	6mm Round Soft Point	6mm Spitzer Soft Point
Diameter	.224"	.224"	.224"	.224"	.224"	.243"	.243"	.243"	.243"	.243"	.243"	.243"	.243"
Weight (grs.)	55	55	55	62	70	70	75	80	85	90	100	105	105
Ballist. Coef.	0.269	0.255	0.241	0.307	0.214	0.282	0.234	0.365	0.404	0.385	0.430	0.207	0.443
Part Number	1044	1047	1049	1050	1053	1206	1205	1211	1213	1217	1220	1223	1229
Box Count	100	100	100	100	100	100	100	100	100	100	100	100	100

NEW!

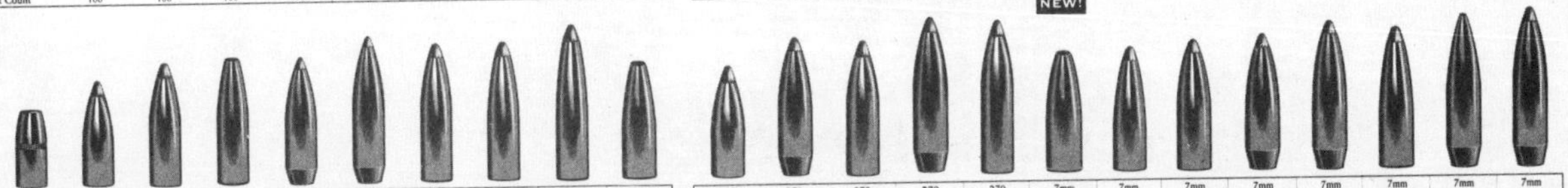

	25-20 Win. Flat Soft Point w/Cann.	25 Spitzer Soft Point	25 Spitzer Soft Point	25 Hollow Point	25 Spitzer Soft Point B.T.	25 Spitzer Soft Point B.T.	25 Spitzer Soft Point	6.5mm Spitzer Soft Point	6.5mm Spitzer Soft Point	270 Hollow Point
Diameter	.257"	.257"	.257"	.257"	.257"	.257"	.257"	.263"	.263"	.277"
Weight (grs.)	75	87	100	100	100	120	120	120	140	100
Ballist. Coef.	0.133	0.300	0.369	0.255	0.393	0.435	0.410	0.433	0.496	0.225
Part Number	1237	1241	1405	1407	1408	1410	1411	1435	1441	1447
Box Count	100	100	100	100	100	100	100	100	100	100

	270 Spitzer Soft Point	270 Spitzer Soft Point B.T.	270 Spitzer Soft Point	270 Spitzer Soft Point B.T.	270 Spitzer Soft Point	7mm Hollow Point	7mm Spitzer Soft Point	7mm Spitzer Soft Point	7mm Spitzer Soft Point B.T.	7mm Spitzer Soft Point B.T.	7mm Spitzer Soft Point	7mm Match Hollow Point B.T.	7mm Spitzer Soft Point B.T.
Diameter	.277"	.277"	.277"	.277"	.277"	.284"	.284"	.284"	.284"	.284"	.284"	.284"	.284"
Weight (grs.)	100	130	130	150	150	115	120	130	130	145	145	145	160
Ballist. Coef.	0.319	0.449	0.408	0.496	0.481	0.257	0.386	0.394	0.411	0.502	0.457	0.465	0.556
Part Number	1453	1458	1459	1604	1605	1617	1620	1623	1624	1628	1629	1631	1634
Box Count	100	100	100	100	100	100	100	100	100	100	100	100	100

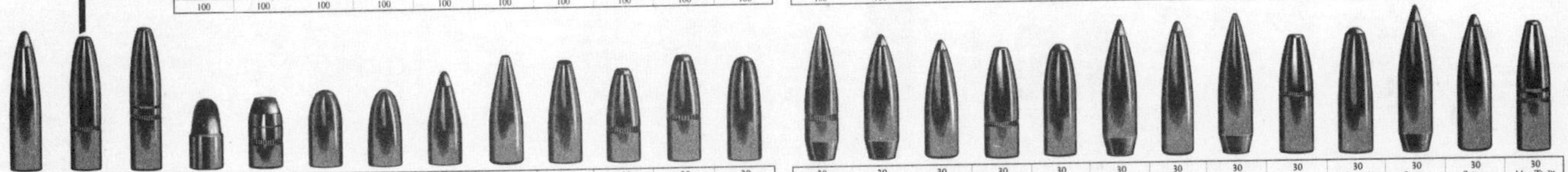

	7mm Spitzer Soft Point	7mm Mag-Tip™ Soft Point	7mm Mag-Tip™ Soft Point	30 Round Soft Point Plinker™	30 Hollow Point	30 Round Soft Point	30 Carbine Round FMJ	30 Spire Soft Point	30 "TNT" Hollow Point	30 Hollow Point	30 Flat Soft Point	30 Flat Soft Point	30 Round Soft Point
Diameter	.284"	.284"	.284"	.308"	.308"	.308"	.308"	.308"	.308"	.308"	.308"	.308"	.308"
Weight (grs.)	160	160	175	100	110	110	110	110	125	130	130	150	150
Ballist. Coef.	0.502	0.354	0.385	0.124	0.136	0.144	0.179	0.273	0.326	0.263	0.248	0.268	0.266
Part Number	1635	1637	1641	1805	1835	1845	1846	1855	1986	2005	2007	2011	2017
Box Count	100	100	100	100	100	100	100	100	100	100	100	100	100

NEW!

	30 FMJ B.T. w/Cann.	30 Spitzer Soft Point B.T.	30 Spitzer Soft Point	30 Mag-Tip™ Soft Point	30 Round Soft Point	30 Spitzer Soft Point B.T.	30 Spitzer Soft Point	30 Match Hollow Point B.T.	30 Flat Soft Point	30 Round Soft Point	30 Spitzer Soft Point B.T.	30 Spitzer Soft Point	30 Mag-Tip™ Soft Point
Diameter	.308"	.308"	.308"	.308"	.308"	.308"	.308"	.308"	.308"	.308"	.308"	.308"	.308"
Weight (grs.)	150	150	150	150	165	165	165	168	170	180	180	180	180
Ballist. Coef.	0.425	0.423	0.389	0.301	0.274	0.477	0.433	0.480	0.304	0.304	0.540	0.483	0.352
Part Number	2018	2022	2023	2025	2029	2034	2035	2040	2041	2047	2052	2053	2059
Box Count	100	100	100	100	100	100	100	100	100	100	100	100	100

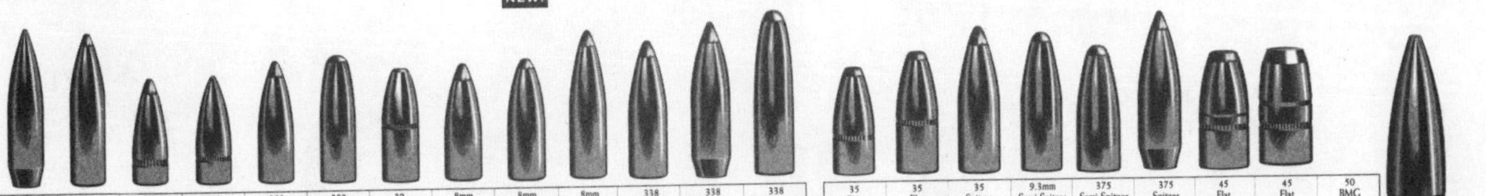

	30 Match Hollow Point B.T.	30 Spitzer Soft Point	303 Spitzer Soft Point w/Cann.	303 (7.62x39) FMJ w/Cann.	303 Spitzer Soft Point	303 Round Soft Point	32 Flat Soft Point	8mm Spitzer Soft Point	8mm Semi-Spitzer Soft Point	8mm Spitzer Soft Point	338 Spitzer Soft Point	338 Spitzer Soft Point B.T.	338 Semi-Spitzer Soft Point
Diameter	.308"	.308"	.311"	.311"	.311"	.311"	.321"	.323"	.323"	.323"	.338"	.338"	.338"
Weight (grs.)	190	200	125	123	150	180	170	150	170	200	200	225	275
Ballist. Coef.	0.540	0.556	0.292	0.256	0.411	0.328	0.297	0.369	0.354	0.411	0.448	0.484	0.456
Part Number	2080	2211	2213	2214	2217	2223	2259	2277	2283	2285	2405	2406	2411
Box Count	50	50	100	100	100	100	100	100	100	50	50	50	50

	35 Flat Soft Point	35 Flat Soft Point	35 Spitzer Soft Point	9.3mm Semi-Spitzer Soft Point	375 Semi-Spitzer Soft Point	375 Spitzer Soft Point B.T.	45 Flat Soft Point	45 Flat Soft Point	50 BMG FMJ
Diameter	.358"	.358"	.358"	.366"	.375"	.375"	.458"	.458"	.510"
Weight (grs.)	180	220	250	270	235	270	350	400	647
Ballist. Coef.	0.245	0.316	0.446	0.361	0.317	0.429	0.232	0.214	0.701
Part Number	2435	2439	2453	2459	2471	2472	2478***	2479	2491
Box Count	100	50	50	50	50	50	50	50	20

SPEER

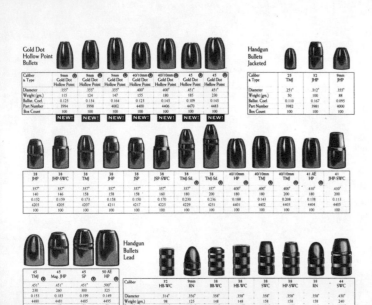

Gold Dot Hollow Point Bullets

Caliber & Type	9mm Gold Dot Hollow Point	9mm Gold Dot Hollow Point	9mm Gold Dot Hollow Point	40/10mm Gold Dot Hollow Point	40/10mm Gold Dot Hollow Point	45 Gold Dot Hollow Point	45 Gold Dot Hollow Point
Diameter	.355"	.355"	.355"	.400"	.400"	.451"	.451"
Weight (grs.)	115	124	147	155	180	185	230
Ballist. Coef.	0.125	0.134	0.164	0.123	0.143	0.109	0.143
Part Number	3994	3998	4002	4400	4406	4470	4483
Box Count	100	100	100	100	100	100	100
	NEW!	NEW!	NEW!	NEW!	NEW!	NEW!	NEW!

Handgun Bullets Jacketed

Caliber & Type	25 TMJ	32 JHP	9mm JHP
Diameter	.251"	.312"	.355"
Weight (grs.)	50	100	88
Ballist. Coef.	0.110	0.167	0.095
Part Number	3982	3981	4000
Box Count	100	100	100

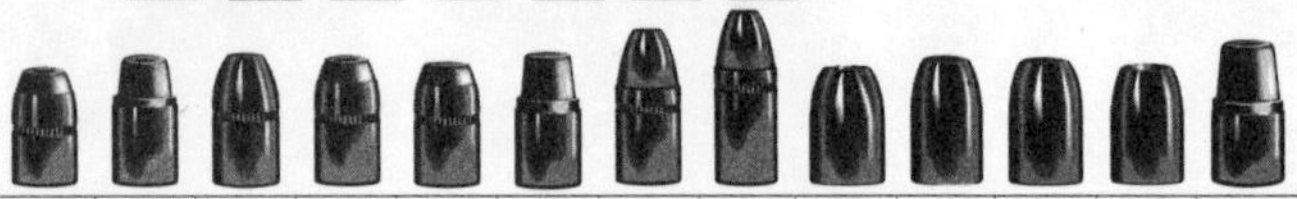

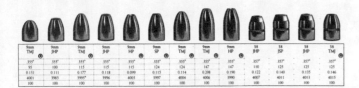

38 JHP	38 JHP-SWC	38 TMJ	38 JHP	38 JSP	38 JSP-SWC	38 TMJ-Sil.	38 TMJ-Sil.	40/10mm HP	40/10mm TMJ	40/10mm TMJ	41 AE HP	41 JHP-SWC
.357"	.357"	.357"	.357"	.357"	.357"	.357"	.357"	.400"	.400"	.400"	.410"	.410"
140	146	158	158	158	160	180	200	180	180	200	180	200
0.152	0.159	0.173	0.158	0.150	0.170	0.230	0.236	0.188	0.143	0.208	0.138	0.113
4203	4205	4207	4211	4217	4223	4229	4231	4401	4402	4403	4404	4405
100	100	100	100	100	100	100	100	100	100	100	100	100

45 TMJ	45 Mag. JHP	45 SP	50 AE HP
.451"	.451"	.451"	.500"
230	260	300	325
0.153	0.183	0.199	0.149
4480	4481	4485	4495
100	100	50	50

Handgun Bullets Lead

Caliber	32 HB-WC	9mm RN	38 BB-WC	38 HB-WC	38 SWC	38 HP-SWC	38 RN	44 SWC
Diameter	.314"	.356"	.358"	.358"	.358"	.358"	.358"	.430"
Weight (grs.)	98	125	148	148	158	158	158	240
Part Number	4600*	4601*	4605*	4617*	4623*	4627*	4647	4660*

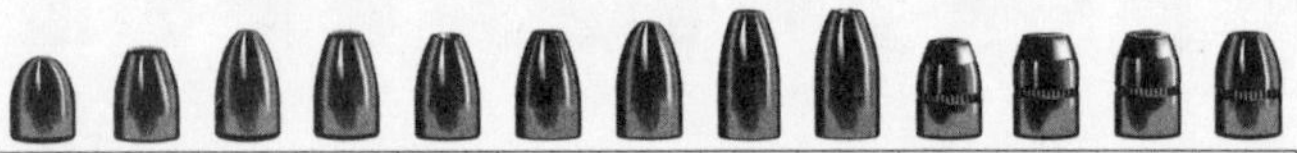

9mm TMJ	9mm JHP	9mm TMJ	9mm JHP	9mm HP	9mm SP	9mm TMJ	9mm TMJ	9mm HP	38 JHP	38 JSP	38 JHP	38 TMJ
.355"	.355"	.355"	.355"	.355"	.355"	.355"	.355"	.355"	.357"	.357"	.357"	.357"
95	100	115	115	115	124	124	147	147	110	125	125	125
0.131	0.111	0.177	0.118	0.099	0.115	0.114	0.208	0.190	0.122	0.140	0.135	0.146
4001	3983	3995*	3996	4003	3997	4004	4006	3990	4007	4011	4013	4015
100	100	100	100	100	100	100	100	100	100	100	100	100

41 JSP-SWC	41 TMJ-Sil.	44 Mag. JHP	44 JHP-SWC	44 JSP-SWC	44 Mag.JHP	44 Mag.JSP	44 TMJ-Sil.	44 Mag. SP	45 TMJ-Match	45 TMJ-Match	45 JHP	45 Mag. JHP
.410"	.410"	.429"	.429"	.429"	.429"	.429"	.429"	.429"	.451"	.451"	.451"	.451"
220	210	200	225	240	240	240	240	300	185	200	200	225
0.137	0.216	0.122	0.146	0.157	0.165	0.164	0.206	0.213	0.090	0.129	0.138	0.169
4417	4420	4425	4435	4447	4453	4457	4459	4463	4473	4475	4477	4479
100	100	100	100	100	100	100	100	50	100	100	100	100

45 SWC	45 RN	45 SWC
.452"	.452"	.452"
200	230	250
4677*	4690*	4683*

Plastic Indoor Ammo

		Bullets	Cases
No. Per Box		50	50
Part No.	38 Cal.	8510	8515
	44 Cal.	8520	8525
	45 Cal.	8530	See Note

Note: Shown are 38 bullet and 38 case. 45 bullet is used with regular brass case.

Shot Shell Capsules

Empty Capsules with Base Plugs		
No. Per Box		50
Part No.	38/357	8780
	44	8782

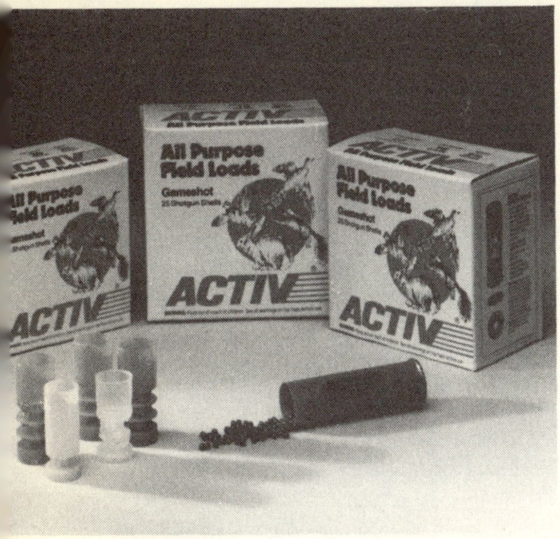

ACTIV Wads

ACTIV		*Wad Specifications*	
Model	**Gauge**	**Color**	**Load**
TG-30	12	Red	$1\frac{1}{8}$
TG-32	12	Yellow	$1\frac{1}{4}$
T-35	12	Blue	$1\frac{1}{4}$ & $1\frac{3}{8}$
T-42	12	Green	$1\frac{1}{2}$ & $1\frac{5}{8}$
G-28	16	White	1
W-28	20	White	$\frac{7}{8}$ & 1
W-32	20	Yellow	$1\frac{1}{8}$

Ballistic Products Steel Shot Wads

BALLISTIC PRODUCTS *Small Gauge Wads*

Gauge	Wad	Price/200	Price/1000	Price/5000
16	Dispersor-X	$5.95	$24.75	$99.75
16	Sporting 16	4.95	21.00	82.95
20	Sporting 20	4.95	21.00	82.95
24	Sporting 24	5.95	24.75	99.75
28	Brush	5.95	24.75	99.75
28	Sporting 28	5.50	23.50	92.95
410	Sporting 410	4.95	21.00	82.95

BALLISTIC PRODUCTS *European Sporting Wads**

Wad	Price/200	Price/1000	Price/5000
Competition Special	$3.95	$13.75	$63.75
Dispersor-X	5.95	24.75	99.50
Brush Wad	5.95	24.75	99.75
ITD Target Driver	5.95	24.75	99.50
Piston Skeet	5.50	23.50	92.75
Short Range Crusher	5.50	23.50	92.50
Ultra-Short Eurotarget	5.50	23.50	93.00
Compact Eurotarget	4.95	21.00	82.50

*12-Gauge G/BP

ACTIV

Plastic Wads

Straight wall design for tube resistance. Are color coded to avoid reloading accidents or confusion. Contact your dealer for prices. From ACTIV Industries, Inc.

Price: . . . . **Contact manufacturer.**

AMERICAN PRODUCTS

Plastic Wad

Black wad moulded with a deep, tapered powder cup to give efficient gas seal. The "X" mid-section design provides even pressure on the shot column. For the trap shooter using $1\frac{1}{8}$-oz. load, but also works well with 1- or $1\frac{1}{4}$-oz. loads. Will fit any standard shell. Load data available. From American Products, Inc.

Price: Per 1,000 . . . . **$14.80**

BALLISTIC PRODUCTS

A-Q Slugs

A 12-ga. $2\frac{3}{4}$" and 3" lead ball/nylon base 1-oz. slug. Outside base diameter of .740, slug diameter of .735. From Ballistic Products, Inc.

Price: Per 25 . . . . **$11.95**
Price: Per 100 . . . . **$39.95**

BP-12 Shotcup

Loads in both the $2\frac{3}{4}$" and 3" hulls. Ribbed construction allows barrel to act as specially modified "overbored" barrel. Has tapered base. Designed for use with the BPGS gas seal. Comes in bags of 250. From Ballistic Products, Inc.

Price: **$9.95**

BP12-Tuff Shotcup

For $\frac{7}{8}$- to 1-oz. steel shot or heavy buckshot loads. Designed for use with the BPGS gas seal. Comes in bags of 250. From Ballistic Products, Inc.

Price: **$9.95**

BPD-10 Shotcup

Designed for extended range shooting. One-piece construction for $1\frac{1}{2}$-oz. to $2\frac{1}{2}$-oz. loads. For lead shot, buck shot and slug loads. Bags of 100. From Ballistic Products, Inc.

Price: **$8.95**

BPGS Gas Seal

Designed for use with the BP12 and BP12-Tuff shotcups. Comes in bags of 250. From Ballistic Products, Inc.

Price: **$8.95**

BALLISTIC PRODUCTS

Cork Wads

Lighter, denser and more flexible than cardboard. Wads are $\frac{1}{2}$" thick. Available for 12- and 20-ga. in bags of 200. From Ballistic Products, Inc.

Price: **$5.95**

Dangerous Game Slugs

Works in either smoothbore or rifled slug barrels. Available in 10, 12, 16, 20 gauges and 410 bore. Come 25 per pack. From Ballistic Products, Inc.

Price: 10, 12, 16, 20 . . . . **$14.95**
Price: 410 . . . . **$9.95**

Felt Wads

Wool felt wads made to fit the BPD 12-ga. shotcup (20-ga. wad), BPD 10-ga. shotcup (20-ga. wad) and BPD-Tuff 10-ga. cup (12-ga. wad). Comes in $\frac{1}{4}$" and $\frac{1}{8}$" thicknesses in bags of 250. From Ballistic Products, Inc.

Price: $\frac{1}{4}$" **$7.95**
Price: $\frac{1}{8}$" **$7.50**

G/BP 8-Ga. Shotcup

One of the rarest of shotshell components. Comes in bags of 100. From Ballistic Products, Inc.

Price: **$12.95**

G/BP 12-Ga. Brush Wad

Traditional field wad with double ended gas seal with no shotcup. For short-range brush loads. Preferred applications: 10-25 yards; #$8\frac{1}{2}$-#10 magnum shot. From Ballistic Products, Inc.

Price: . . . . **See chart.**

G/BP 12 Short Range Crusher Wad

Designed for fast burn-rated powders. Underside of gas seal has 25 plastic teeth for even, extended-duration burn necessary for $3\frac{1}{4}$-dram, 1-oz. loads. Three-stage cage design. Preferred application: 15-35 yards; #$7\frac{1}{2}$-#9 magnum shot. From Ballistic Products, Inc.

Price: . . . . **See chart.**

G/BP 16 Wad

For 1-oz. 16-ga. loads. Preferred application: 20-45 yards; #6-#$8\frac{1}{2}$ copper-plated or magnum shot. From Ballistic Products, Inc.

Price: . . . . **See chart.**

G/BP 28-Ga. Brush Wad

Double-ended gas seal wad with no shotcup. Preferred application: #7 magnum or copper #11. From Ballistic Products, Inc.

Price: . . . . **See chart.**

BALLISTIC PRODUCTS

G/BP Compact Eurotarget 12 Wad
Conducive to loading $2^1/_4$ and $2^1/_2$ English cartridges. Designed for light framed double guns. Preferred applications: 15-35 yards; #6-#9 nickel- and copper-plated shot; #8-#9 magnum. From Ballistic Products, Inc.
Price: . . . . **See chart.**

G/BP Competition Special 12 Wad
For the competitive target shooter using $\#7^1/_2$ through #9 magnum shot. Will fit tapered or straight-wall hulls. From Ballistic Products, Inc.
Price: . . . . **See chart.**

G/BP Dispersor-X 12 Wad
One-piece plastic wad with integrated X spreader for quick spreading patterns. Preferred application: 5-25 yards; $\#8^1/_2$-#11 shot. From Ballistic Products, Inc.
Price: . . . . **See chart.**

G/BP Dispersor-X 16 Wad
One-piece plastic wad with integrated X spreader. Preferred application: 5-25 yards; $\#8^1/_2$-#11 shot. From Ballistic Products, Inc.
Price: . . . . **See chart.**

G/BP ITD 12 Wad
For International Trap shooters. Preferred application: 40-60 yards; #6-#8 magnum shot. From Ballistic Products, Inc.
Price: . . . . **See chart.**

G/BP Piston Skeet 12 Wad
Specialized for 1- and $^7/_8$-oz. European design load using compact, high burn-rate powders. "V" petals give dense pattern with short shot string. Preferred application: 20-40 yards; $\#7^1/_2$-$\#8^1/_2$ magnum shot. From Ballistic Products, Inc.
Price: . . . . **See chart.**

G/BP Sporting 20 Wad
For field and target high-velocity loads. Preferred application: #5-#7 plated shot for field loads; #8-#9 shot for target loads. From Ballistic Products, Inc.
Price: . . . . **See chart.**

G/BP Sporting 24 Wad
General target, light field usage with $\#7^1/_2$ plated shot. From Ballistic Products, Inc.
Price: . . . . **See chart.**

G/BP Sporting 28 Wad
A favorite of European field shooters. Preferred applications: 16-19.5 gram field loads; $\#8^1/_2$-#9 plated or magnum shot. From Ballistic Products, Inc.
Price: . . . . **See chart.**

BALLISTIC PRODUCTS

G/BP Sporting 410 Wad
For field/target loads. $\#8^1/_2$-#10 plated or magnum shot. From Ballistic Products, Inc.
Price: . . . . **See chart.**

G/BP Ultra-Short Eurotarget 12 Wad
For bulkier powders and English $2^1/_4$ and $2^1/_2$ English cartridges. Has same applications as Compact Eurotarget. From Ballistic Products, Inc.
Price: . . . . **See chart.**

Over-Shot Wads
Designed for use with buffered loads. Three sizes: .100 Nitro Cards; .030 Over-shot Cards; $^1/_2$ Fiber Cushion Wads. From Ballistic Products, Inc.
Price: **$6.95**

Ranger-Plus Wads
Designed for 12-ga. $2^3/_4$" and 3" lead or steel shot loads. Will hold up to $1^1/_4$ oz. steel shot up to BB size; or $1^5/_8$ oz. lead. Comes in bags of 100. From Ballistic Products, Inc.
Price: **$7.95**

Shot
BPI offers high antimony Super Buck Shot (3% antimony), nickle-plated lead shot manufactured in Italy, high antimony magnum lead shot, copper-plated lead shot and steel shot. From Ballistic Products, Inc.
Price: . . . . **See chart.**

Slugmaster
Hollowpoint slug with three moulded fracture lines. Available in 20 (275-gr., $^5/_8$-oz.); 16 (328-gr., $^3/_4$-oz.); 12 (410-gr., $^7/_8$-oz.) and 12 (437-gr., 1-oz.) gauges. Come in packs of 25. From Ballistic Products, Inc.
Price: **$6.95**

Spreader-X Wads
A two-piece cardboard wad that fits together to form four spread chambers. Sits on the base of the wad or atop the gas seal. Opens Full Choke to Improved Cylinder. Available in 10- through 20-ga. for 125 loads. From Ballistic Products, Inc.
Price: **$4.95**

Steel Shot Wads
Made for steel shot loads, the vented design of the 10-ga. Tuff BPD and BP-12 12-ga. wads allow bleed-off at peak pressures. Available in bags of 100 (10-ga.) and 250 (12-ga.) From Ballistic Products, Inc.
Price: **$9.95**

Turkey Ranger Wad
Heavy plastic wad designed for heavy magnum loads of plated lead shot. Load information provided with wads. Come in bags of 100. From Ballistic Products, Inc.
Price: **$7.95**

BALLISTIC PRODUCTS

Tyvex Over-Shot/Over-Cushion Wads
Designed for 10- and 12-gauge heavy magnum steel shot loads. The 12-ga. $^5/_8$-inch over-cushion wad prevents steel pellets imbedding in wad base. Over-shot wads, $^3/_4$ (10-ga.) and $^5/_8$ (12-ga.), contain steel pellets during firing. Come in bags of 500. From Ballistic Products, Inc.
Price: **$6.95**

Waxed Hard Wads
For buckshot, slug and special Skeet loads. $^1/_4$-inch thick waxed surface cardboard. Available in 10, 12, 16 and 20 gauges. Come 200 per bag. From Ballistic Products, Inc.
Price: **$5.98**

BALLISTIC PRODUCTS *Super Buck*

Shot	Size(in.)	Price/8 lb.	Price/32 lb.	Price/96 lb.
#F	.220	$13.45	$51.00	$140.00
#T	.200	13.45	51.00	140.00
#4	.240	13.45	51.00	140.00
#3	.250	13.45	51.00	140.00
#2	.270	13.45	51.00	140.00
#1	.300	13.45	51.00	140.00
#0	.320	13.45	51.00	140.00
#00	.340	13.45	51.00	140.00
#000	.360	13.45	51.00	140.00

BALLISTIC PRODUCTS *Steel Shot*

Shot	Size (in.)	Price/5 lb.	Price/50 lb.
F	.218	$10.93	$99.80
T	.200	10.93	99.80
BB	.188	10.93	99.80
#1	.170	11.43	104.00
#2	.156	10.93	99.80
#3	.140	11.43	104.00
#4	.125	10.93	99.80
#5	.120	10.51	95.64
#6	.110	9.55	86.90
#7	.100	8.68	78.99

BALLISTIC PRODUCTS *Copper-Plated Shot*

Shot	Size (in.)	Price/10 lb.	Price/50 lb.
BB	.180	$17.21	$81.00
#2	.150	15.96	75.00
#3	.130	15.96	75.00
#4	.120	15.96	75.00
#5	.110	15.96	75.00
$\#7^1/_2$		15.96	75.00

BALLISTIC PRODUCTS *Nickel-Plated Shot*

Shot	Size(in.)	Price/8 lb.	Price/24 lb.	Price/60 lb.
BB	.181	$15.99	$44.90	NA
#1	.161	15.99	44.90	NA
#2	.156	15.99	44.90	NA
#5	.140	15.17	42.78	$99.00
#7$^1/_2$		14.86	41.91	97.00

Ballistic Products Lead Shot Wads

BALLISTIC PRODUCTS *Magnum Lead Shot*

Shot	Size(in.)	Price/25 lb.	Price/100 lb.
#4	.150	$18.93	$71.00
#5	.130	18.93	71.00
#6	.110	18.93	71.00
#7	.100	18.93	71.00
#7$^1/_2$		18.93	71.00
#8	.090	18.93	71.00
#8$^1/_2$		18.93	71.00
#9	.080	18.93	71.00

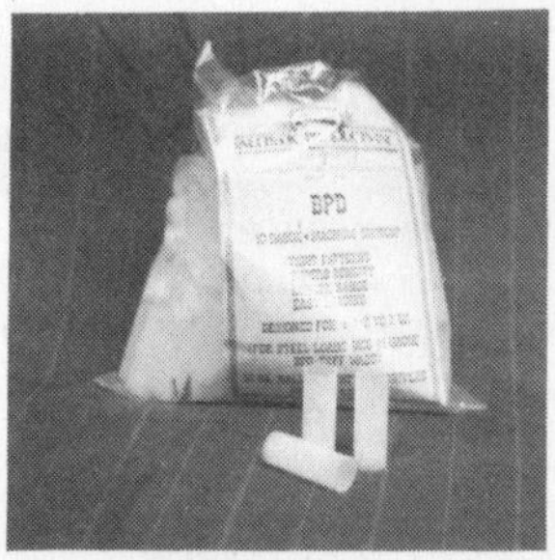
Ballistic Products 10-Ga. Wads

Ballistic Products Felt Wads

LAWRENCE BRAND

Shot

Copper-plated magnum shot or lead buckshot in 10-lb. bags. From Precision Reloading, Inc.

Price: **$15.95**

BRENNEKE

Slugs

Slugs available for 16- and 20-gauge. 16-gauge offered in 415-grain weight with wad; 20-gauge in 370-grain weight with wad. Come in boxes of 25. From The Old Western Scrounger.

Price: **$13.45**

C&D

Claybuster Wads

Straight-wall and tapered-wall target wads in 12-, 20-, 28-gauge and 410 bore. Copies of Winchester, Federal and Remington designs. From C&D Special Products.

Price: . . . . **Contact manufacturer.**

HORNADY

Buckshot

Cold-swaged buckshot using lead alloy hardened with 3% antimony. Strict roundness tolerance of +.002. Comes in 5-lb. bag. From Hornady Mfg. Co.

Price: **$9.40**

Versalite Wads

Compressible center section adjusts wad to correct column length. Available in 12- and 20-gauge. Flared shotcup to slip easily over wad seating punch. From Hornady Mfg. Co.

Price: 250 . . . . **$5.65**
Price: 1000 . . . . **$20.65**

Ballistic Products Slugs

FEDERAL *Shotshell Wads*

Plastic Wad Columns		
Type	Gauge	Number
Champion	12	12C1
Gold Medal	12	12SO
Gold Medal	12	12S3
Gold Medal	12	12S4
Gold Medal	20	20S1
Gold Medal	28	28S1
2$^1/_2$"	410	410SC

Hornady Versalite

Federal Wads

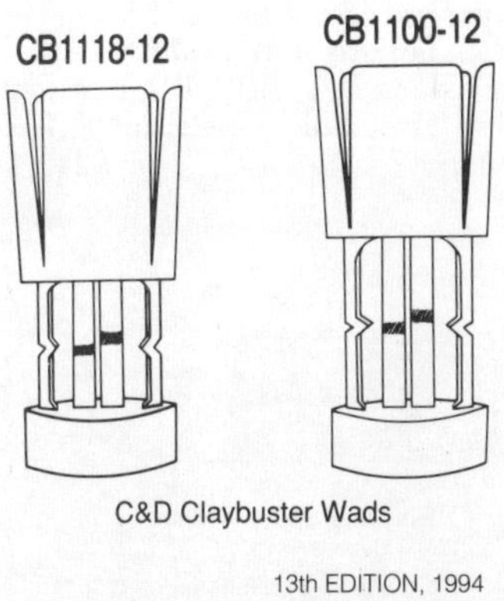

C&D Claybuster Wads

MEC

Steel Shot

Steel shot comes in 10-lb. containers and in sizes #7, #6, #5, #4, #3, #2, #1, B, BB, BBB, T, TT and F. From Mayville Engineering Company, Inc.

Price: . . . . **Contact manufacturer.**

Steel Shot Wads

Three wad sizes for 10- and 12-gauge. MEC #12 wads are for 12-ga. $2^3/_4$", $1^1/_8$-oz. loads. MEC #12 replaces MEC #12 TW and MEC #122. The MEC #312 wad is for 12-ga. 3", $1^1/_4$-oz. loads and the #105 wad for 10-ga. $1^5/_8$-oz. loads. All come 150 per bag. From Mayville Engineering Company, Inc.

Price: . . . . **Contact manufacturer.**

PATTERN CONTROL

Wads

Designed especially for Skeet, trap and field loads. Available in 12 ($1^1/_8$, 1 oz.), 20 ($^7/_8$-oz.), 28 ($^3/_4$-oz.) and 410 ($^1/_2$-oz.) in seven styles. Interchangeable with Winchester AA, ACTIV, Federal, Fiocchi and Remington Powder Piston wads. Come in bags of 1000. From Pattern Control.

Price: **$15.00**

POLYWAD

Spred-R Wad

Device to open patterns up from Full to Improved Cylinder. Can be used with any wad and size shot. Shaped like thumbtack, Spred-R is inserted into shotshell before crimp with post side down into shot. Installed manually or with rammer tube of shotshell press. Available in 12, 16, 20 or 28 gauges. From Polywad, Inc.

Price: 400 . . . . **$10.00**
Price: 1000 . . . . **$20.00**
Price: 2500 . . . . **$40.00**

PRECISION RELOADING

Nickel-Plated Shot

Nickel shot with 4% antimony in sizes BB, #2, #4, #6, #8, #9. Come in 10-lb. bags. From Precision Reloading, Inc.

Price: **$19.95**

Tin-Plated Steel Shot

Non-toxic tin-plated steel shot. Tin plating provides 40% less friction between pellets and prohibits rust. Available in F, T, BBB, BB, B, #1, #2 and #3. From Precision Reloading, Inc.

Price: 10 lbs. **$21.95**

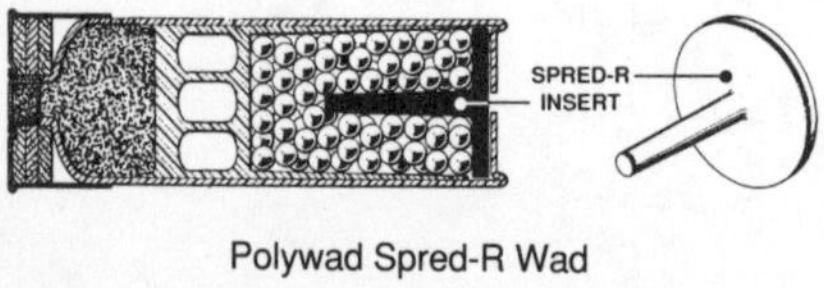

Polywad Spred-R Wad

Pattern Control Wads

U.S. Manufactured Steel Shot

90 DPH steel shot in sizes F, T, BBB, BB, B, #1, #2, #3, #4, #5, #6, #7 and #8. Available in 10- or 20-lb. bags. From Precision Reloading, Inc.

Price: 10 lbs., F, T, BBB, BB, B, #1, #2, #3, #4 . . . . **$16.95**
Price: 10 lbs., #5, #6, #7, #8 . . . . **$17.95**
Price: 20 lbs., F, T, BBB, BB, B, #3, #4 . . . . **$32.00**
Price: 20 lbs., #5, #6, #7, #8 . . . . **$34.00**

RELOADING SPECIALTIES

Sam I Wads

Steel shot wads for loading 12-ga. $2^3/_4$", 3" and $3^1/_2$"; 10-ga. $3^1/_2$"; 20-ga. 3". Unique patented design plus conical vaning, focal points and flexible base. Come 100 or 150 per bag. From Reloading Specialties, Inc.

Price: **$7.95**

Steel Shot

SAAMI-spec annealed steel shot. See chart for sizes. Available in 10-lb. bags. From Reloading Specialities, Inc.

Price: **$19.95**

Super Sam Felt Spacers

Allows all RS Sam wads to use various payloads. $^1/_8$" thick. Available in bags of 250. From Reloading Specialties, Inc.

Price: **$7.50**

Super Sam Over-Shot Cards

For steel shot loads where use of buffer and cards allow better crimp and ignition. Come 1000 per bag. From Reloading Specialties, Inc.

Price: **$7.50**

Reloading Specialties
Super Sam Overshot Cards

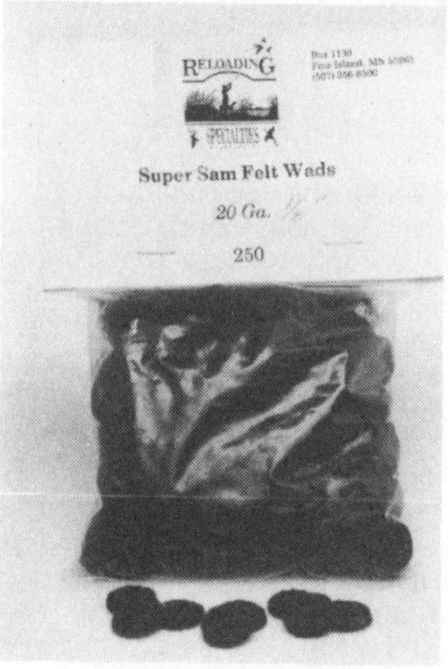

Reloading Specialties
Super Sam Felt Wads

RELOADING SPECIALTIES *STEEL SHOT*

		APPROXIMATE # PELLETS PER LOAD							
	Diameter	$^5/_8$	$^3/_4$	$^7/_8$	1	$1^1/_8$	$1^1/_4$	$1^3/_8$	$1^1/_2$
TTT	.220	24	29	34	39	44	49	54	59
TT	.210	28	34	40	46	51	57	62	69
T	.200	32	39	48	54	60	67	74	81
BBB	.190	40	48	53	61	69	76	85	91
BB	.180	44	54	62	70	79	87	91	99
B	.170	52	63	75	87	97	108	119	130
1	.160	63	76	90	102	116	129	141	153
2	.150	76	92	108	125	142	156	170	187
3	.140	95	115	139	163	183	203	225	244
4	.130	119	141	165	187	211	235	259	280
5	.120	150	184	215	244	275	307	336	366
6	.110	194	233	255	291	350	363	398	436

REMINGTON

Power Piston Wads

One-piece wads feature special compression sections to compensate for seating pressures for uniform crimp with different powder charges. Manufactured to factory standards to duplicate factory performance. From Remington Arms Company, Inc.

Price: . . . . **See chart.**

STEEL RELOADING COMPONENTS

Card Wads

Steel shot over-shot card wads for better crimp. Come 500 to a bag. From Steel Reloading Components Incorporated.

Price: **$4.99**

Steel Shot

SAAMI-approved steel shot in sizes #8, #$7\frac{1}{2}$, #7, #6, #5, #4, #3, #2, #1, B, BB, BBB, T, TT and F. Same shot sizes also available in both zinc or copper-plated versions. Come in 10-lb. bags. From Steel Reloading Components Incorporated.

Price: **$11.95**

Steel Shot Wads

Tapered and straight-walled wads in 12-ga. $2\frac{3}{4}$", 3", $3\frac{1}{2}$" and 10-ga. $3\frac{1}{2}$", strengthened to prevent pinholing. Come 150 wads to the bag. From Steel Reloading Components, Incorporated.

Price: **$9.95**

TRICO PLASTICS

Wads

Self-adjusting 12-ga. and 20-ga. wads can load any $2\frac{3}{4}$" shell with any inner base wad height. Three 410 wads also available for Winchester 296 powder and for Remington and Federal cases. Come 1000 to a bag. From Trico Plastics.

Price: **$12.75**

VITT/BOOS

Slugs

Slug with high, thin helical ribs to tightly fit bore. Weighs 580 grains. Comes in box of 25. From Vitt/Boos.

Price: **$15.00**

Vitt/Boos Slug

SHOT **BUCKSHOT**

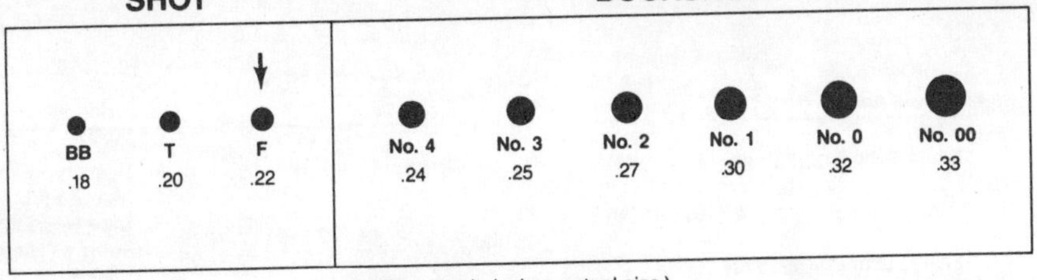

(Diameter in inches, actual size.)

REMINGTON *Shotshell Wads*

Wad	Gauge	Shot Oz.	Price/250
	PLASTIC TRAP AND SKEET		
FIG8	12	$1\frac{1}{8}$	$4.10
RXP12	12	$1\frac{1}{4}$	5.45
RXP20	20	$\frac{7}{8}$	5.45
PT28	28	$\frac{3}{4}$	5.45
SP410	410	$\frac{1}{2}$	5.45
	PLASTIC FIELD		
SP10	10	$1\frac{5}{8}$, 2	7.00
R12L	12	1	5.45
R12H	12	$1\frac{1}{8}$	5.45
RP12	12	$1\frac{1}{4}$	5.45
SP12	12	$1\frac{1}{4}$	5.45
SP16	16	$1\frac{1}{8}$	5.45
SP20	20	1	5.45

WINCHESTER *Shotshell Wads*

Wad	Gauge	# Oz.
WAA12	12	$1\text{-}1\frac{5}{8}$
WAA12R	12	$1\frac{1}{8}\text{-}1\frac{7}{8}$
WAA12F114	12	$1\frac{1}{4}\text{-}1\frac{3}{8}$
WAA12SL	12	$1\text{-}1\frac{1}{8}$
WAA16	16	$1\text{-}1\frac{1}{8}$
WAA20	20	$\frac{7}{8}\text{-}1\frac{1}{4}$
WAA20F1	20	$1\text{-}1\frac{1}{8}$
WAA28	28	All
WAA41	410	All

Remington Power Piston

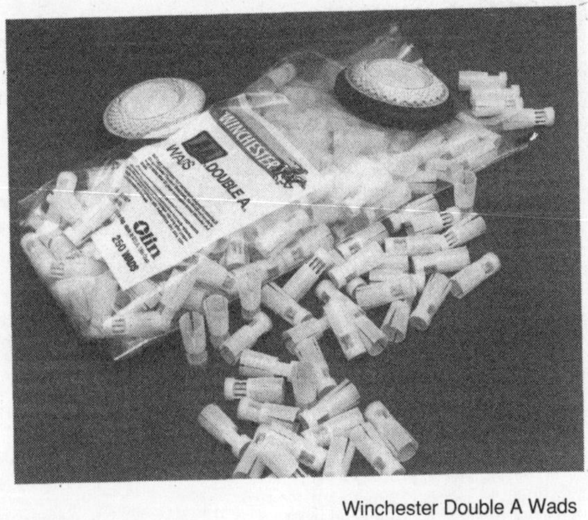

Winchester Double A Wads

Wozenitz Slug

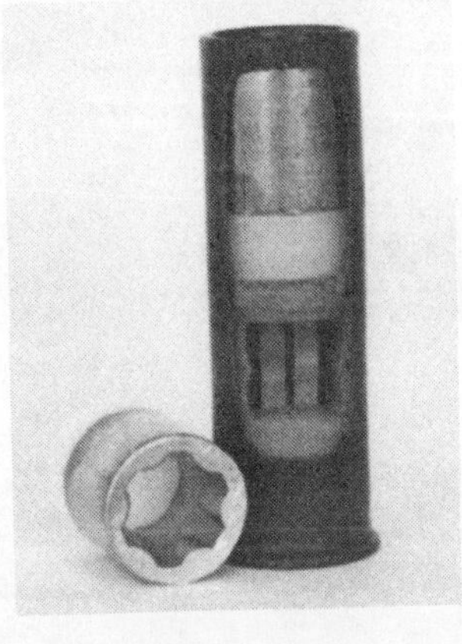

WINCHESTER

Shotshell Wads

Winchester AA wads for 12, 16, 20, 28 and 410. See chart for available loads. Available in bags of 1000. From Winchester.

Price: **$21.76**

WOZENITZ

Slugs

Tubular design 490-gr. slug with inside tapered in Venturi shape to cause vacuum as slug passes through air. On impact slug expands to donut shape $1\frac{1}{4}$" in diameter. Come in boxes of five. From Wosenitz VHP Inc.

Price: **$4.90**

OBSOLETE POWDERS

Make and name	Type	Remarks
DU PONT		
No. 1 Rifle Smokeless (1894-1926)	Irregular grains	Bulk type for low pressures (20,000-25,000 psi). For cartridges like .45-90.
Smokeless Rifle No. 2 (1894-1926)	"	Like No. 1 above, but for interchangeable rifle-revolver cartridges such as .44-40, etc.
Schuetzen (1908-1923)	"	Like Rifle Smokeless No. 1.
Schultz Shotgun (1900-1926)	"	Also light gallery charges in metallic cases.
Gallery Rifle No. 75 (1904-1928)	Irregular, smoothed	Previously called "Marksman," and widely used for reloading military rifle cartridges.
SR 80 (1913-1939)	Irregular grains	Bulk type for black powder cartridges.
MR 19 (1908-1909)	Tube	A double base type for full to medium loads in large to medium capacity cases.
MR 10 (1910-1915)	Tube	Designed for the .280 Ross.
MR 21 (1913-1926)	"	Full charges in medium cases.
IMR 15 (1914-1917)	"	For full loads with metal-jacketed bullets. The first IMR (progressive burning) powder.
IMR 13 (1917-1918)	"	IMR type. Made for special government use.
IMR 16 (1916-1927)	"	30,000-55,000-lb. pressures; a very flexible powder.
IMR 17 (1915-1925)	"	Military powder for .303 Lee-Enfield, .30-06, too.
IMR 18 (1915-1930)	"	Small to full rifle charges; a very flexible powder.
IMR 15½ (1919-1934)	"	For full loads in .30-06 size cartridges.
IMR 17½ (1923-1933)	"	Full and mid-range loads in large cartridges.
IMR 1147 (1923-1935)	Short tube	Full loads in military cases.
IMR 1204 (1925-1935)	Tube	For small capacity rifle cartridges.
Pyro Cal. .30, DG (1909-1927)	"	Military powder for the .30-06 not commercially offered. Also called MR 20 at one time.
IMR 1185 (1926-1938)	"	For 173-gr. Mark I bullet in .30-06. Never commercially available.
RSQ (Resque) (1909-1911)	Smooth, egg shaped	Pistol powder of bulk type.
Pistol No. 1 (1914-1915)	Disc	A nitroglycerine powder, never offered commercially, and like Bullseye.
Pistol No. 3 (1913-1921)	"	A dense gov't. pistol powder.
Pistol No. 5 (1920-1940)	Flake	Full and medium handgun charges.
Pistol No. 6 (1932-1953)	"	Reduced to medium handgun charges.
Ballistite (1909-1926)	"	A dense shotgun type, still a popular form in Europe.
MX Shotgun (1933-1953)	"	Designed for standard loads.
Oval Shotgun (1921-1942)	Disc	Maximum load shotshells.
HERCULES		
** E.C. Powder (1894-1931)	Irregular grains	Designed for shotguns, but useful also in light rifle loads.
308 (1915-1930)	Tube	Military powder for the .30-06 and like Pyro DG.
300 (1916-1932)	"	For full lodas with metal-jacketed bullets. A single base powder quite like Du Pont IMR 15.
Sharpshooter (No. 1 1897-1953; No. 2 1902-†)	Disc	Full or reduced loads in black powder cartridges. Fastest of the old double base powders.
W.A. .30 cal. (1898-1930)	"	Military powder for .30-40 Krag.
Lighting (No. 1 1899-1950; No. 2 1903-1917)	"	Full and reduced loads in medium to .30-06 size cartridges.
Pyro Pistol (1922-1928)	"	Dense .45 ACP (gov't.) powder.
HiVel No. 1 (1908-1915)	Tube	Military powder for .30-06.
HiVel No. 2 (1908-1964)	"	Full to medium loads in large to medium capacity cases.
HiVel No. 3 (1926-1940)	"	Full loads in medium capacity cases.
HiVel No. 5 (1929-1934)	"	Special for .30-06.
HiVel No. 6 (1933-1941)	"	High velocities with heavy bullets. Was not available to the public.
HiVel No. 6.5 (1937-1939)	"	High velocity .30-06.
1908 Bear (1908-†)	"	Not generally available to handloaders, this was intended for medium capacity cases.
1908 Stag (1908-1914)	"	Like 1908 Bear.
KINGS Semi-smokeless	Grain	Any and all black powder cartridges.

**Also manufactured by Du Pont previous to formation of Hercules.

†Still available to loading companies.

Most of the above powders were discontinued in the late 30's and early 40's. Kings Semi-smokeless powder, a bulk type, was manufactured and used from 1899 to about 1936. It was pouplar in small-bore match cartridges as it gave les smoke and fouling than black powder. Granulation range was similar to black powder, but there was also a size made called "Cg," for musket use, that was larger than Fg.

MR = Military Rifle   IMR = Improved Military Rifle

1994 HANDLOADER'S DIGEST

13th EDITION

PART

1 2 3 4 5 6

MISCELLANEOUS

Section 6: Miscellaneous

CHRONOTECH Chronograph

Reads from 75 to 9999 fps within .5% accuracy. Features LCD display, durable plastic casing and one-year warranty against defects in electronic circuitry. From Chronotech Ltd.

Price: U.S. **$89.99**
Price: Canada **$110.00**

COMPETITION ELECTRONICS Pro-Tach

Direct readouts from 75 to 4500 fps. Features large LCD display, diffuser hood, optional remote control, low battery indicator. Records number of shots, velocity from shot to shot and average velocity per shot string. Powered by 9-volt battery. Comes with skyscreens and targets. From Competition Electronics, Inc.

Price: **$149.95**
Price: Remote control **$30.00**
Price: Additional targets (8) **$7.50**

OEHLER 35P Carrying Case

Hard plastic case holds Model 35P, three skyscreens, 4-foot rail, pair of folding stands, and spare paper and batteries. From Oehler Research.

Price: **$25.00**

OEHLER BNC/BNC Signal Cable

30-foot signal cables to connect Model 55 screens to chronograph. From Oehler Research.

Price: Each **$15.00**

OEHLER Diffuser Assembly

Assembly includes rigid plastic diffuser with two side-rails for one Skyscreen III. From Oehler Research.

Price: **$10.00**

OEHLER Diffuser Assembly, Lighted

Clamps to hold tubular 120-volt incandescent bulb to add to diffuser assembly. Includes bulb, socket and cord. From Oehler Research.

Price: **$30.00**

OEHLER Model 35 Chronograph

Available with either two or three Skyscreen IIIs. Same features as 35P without printer and, in two skyscreen configuration, without proof channel. Comes with 2-foot mounting rail and battery. From Oehler Research.

Price: With 2 Skyscreen III **$195.00**
Price: With 3 Skyscreen III **$225.00**

OEHLER Model 35BNC Chronograph

Same unit as Model 35P retaining built-in printer and proof channel but requires Model 55 photoelectric screens and uses 120 vac power instead of battery. From Oehler Research.

Price: **$400.00**

OEHLER Model 35P Chronograph

Model 35P uses three Skyscreen III detectors to proof velocity readouts by taking two readings per shot and comparing the two for extreme differences. Includes built-in printer with plain paper printout to record each round as fired. At end of shot string a statistical summary of valid shots with high, low, extreme spread, mean and standard deviation with asterisk denoting possible shot error. Uses 4MHz clock for higher accuracy at short screen spacings. Comes with 2-foot mounting rail and battery. From Oehler Research.

Price: **$345.00**

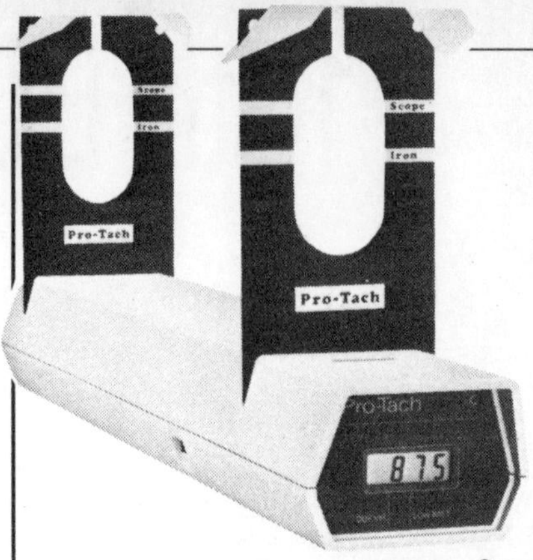

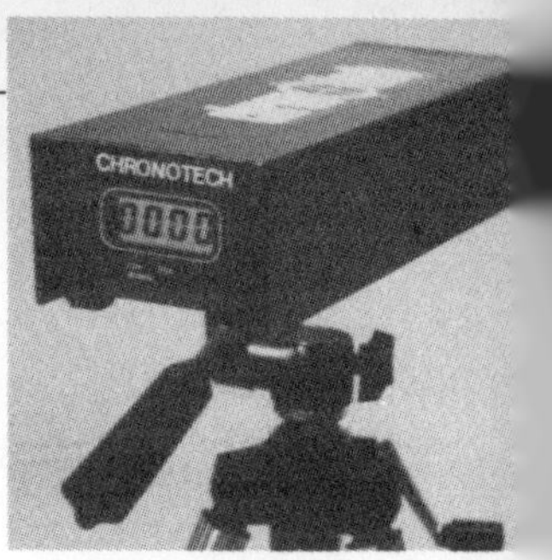

Chronotech Chronograph

Competition Electronics Pro-Tach

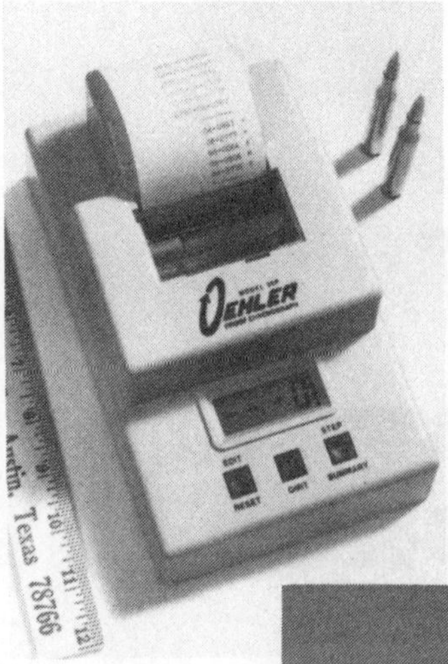

Oehler Model 35P

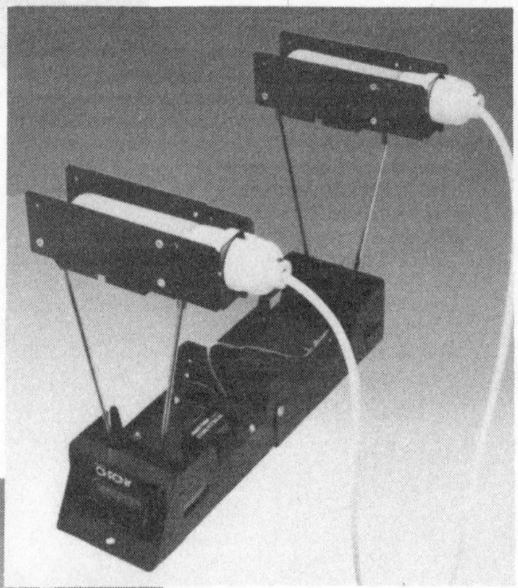

Shooting Chrony Indoor Light Fixture

Shooting Chrony Chronograph

OEHLER Model 43 Personal Ballistics Laboratory
IBM-compatible host computer Model 43 measures firearm pressure curves, muzzle velocity, time-of-flight and downrange velocity using integrated multi-channel electronics; graphically shows point of impact on target with use of Acoustic Target, measures it and makes permanent record. Consists of 9x11x1.4" metal case connecting to computer via serial port and powered by internal rechargeable battery. Uses one set of three skyscreens near muzzle and second set downrange. Both sets include proof channel. Host computer must be MS-DOS compatible and have CGA, EGA, VGA or Hercules graphics; a serial port; and minimum of 384K of free RAM. Optional equipment includes: Pressure strain gauge starter kit with five gauges, cables and connectors, cleaners and adhesives, soldering iron and other incidentals; Acoustic target with three acoustic sensors; downrange amplifier with 110-yard cable; Skyscreen mounting kit with 4-foot rail and two adjustable stands; set of three downrange Skyscreens. Comes with three Skycreen IIIs, cables, an AC adapter/charger and all software including Ballistic Explorer. From Oehler Research.

Price: Model 43 . . . . . . **$600.00**
Price: Pressure strain gauge **$170.00**
Price: Downrange skyscreens **$90.00**
Price: Acoustic Target **$600.00**
Price: Downrange amplifier **$140.00**
Price: Skyscreen mounting kit **$50.00**
Price: Extra strain gauges, 5 . . . . . . **$35.00**

OEHLER Model 55 Photoelectric Screens
Steel frame screen of 18"x36"x3" dimensions with shooting window of 16"x28". Built-in light source L60 Lumiline lamp. Output is +12; bolt pulse via BNC connector. 120 vac required. From Oehler Research.

Price: Two screens **$850.00**
Price: Three screens **$1,275.00**

OEHLER Printer Upgrade
To upgrade Model 35 to 35P by adding plain paper printer. From Oehler Research.

Price: **$145.00**

OEHLER Skyscreen III
For use with Oehler Model 12, 33 and 35 chronographs as replacement or spare. Complete with cable and moulded plastic diffuser assembly. From Oehler Research.

Price: **$30.00**

OEHLER Skyscreen III Plastic Shells
Four black outside pieces to repair damaged skyscreens. From Oehler Research.

Price: **$10.00**

PACT PC2

OEHLER Skyscreen III Plastic Shell with Lenses
Kit includes both lenses and two black outside pieces to repair one skyscreen. From Oehler Research.

Price: **$15.00**

PACT Model 1
Shot number and velocity alternate on four digit display. Provides statistical summary of average velocity, high and low velocities as well as standard deviation and average deviation. Holds up to 24 shots and recalls any one from memory. Optional infrared print driver allows communication with HP infrared printer. Comes with M5 skyscreens. From PACT

Price: **$179.95**
Price: Infrared print driver **$25.00**
Price: Infrared HP printer **$125.00**
Price: Skyscreen mounting bracket **$24.95**
Price: Carrying case **$16.95**

PACT PC2
Smaller version of PACT Professional chronograph. Maintains all basic features but with less memory, less powerful software and no printout capability. Optional serial port allows dumping of data to host computer; compatible with RCBS PC Bullet. Optional infrared print driver allows communication with HP battery powered printer. Comes with M5 skyscreens. From PACT.

Price: **$219.95**
Price: Infrared print driver **$25.00**
Price: Infrared HP printer **$125.00**
Price: Skyscreen mounting bracket **$24.95**
Price: Carrying case **$16.95**

PACT Professional Chronograph
Chronograph with ballistics computer built in. Records in memory and displays each shot, shot number and velocity to tenth of a foot per second at top of 32-character display and current average velocity on lower half of display. Recalculates current string statistics: extreme spread, standard deviation and average deviation. Features "hot key" control to allow user interface with stored data to review any aspect of shot string. Holds up to 300 shots in memory. Ballistics computer features trajectory function to calculate optimal 100-yard zero to tenth of an inch, correcting for altitude and temperature or cross wind; drop tables based on entered data; calculates recoil, ballistic co-efficient; and includes terminal ballistics functions such as kinetic energy, momentum, IPSC power factor, Taylor knock out and Wootters lethality index. Plain paper dot-matrix printer. Comes with M5 14"x12" skyscreens. Skyscreen mounting bracket and carrying case optional. From PACT.

Price: **$369.95**
Price: Skyscreen mounting bracket **$24.95**
Price: Carrying case **$16.95**
Price: Extra printing paper, 6 rolls **$12.00**

SHOOTING CHRONY Chronograph
Made of 20-gauge steel, measures $2^3/_4$x$4^1/_4$x$7^1/_2$ and weighs only 2.5 lbs. Set up on table top or tripod. Features velocity range from 70 fps to 9999 fps; accuracy to +99.5%; large LCD readout; individually calibrated. Readouts in fps or metric m/s. Indoor shooting light fixture also available. From Shooting Chrony, Inc.

Price: **$99.95**
Price: Indoor light fixture **$29.95**

BALLISTIC PRODUCTS 10-Ga. Shell Box

Plastic, moisture-proof shell box holds 25 $3^{1}/_{2}$" shells. From Ballistic Products, Inc.

Price: **$3.95**

BALLISTIC PRODUCTS Factory-Style Shell Box

Manila cardboard boxes available in 20-ga. $2^{3}/_{4}$" and 3"; 12-ga. $2^{3}/_{4}$" and 3"; and 10-ga. $3^{1}/_{2}$". Come in packs of 10. From Ballistic Products, Inc.

Price: **$3.49**
Price: 5 packs **$13.89**
Price: 10 packs **$23.99**

BALLISTIC PRODUCTS Shell Box

Plastic, snap-lid storage box for loaded shells. Capacity 25 shells, 28-ga. through 12-ga. 3". From Ballistic Products, Inc.

Price: **$3.50**

BALLISTIC PRODUCTS Shell Box Labels

Self-adhesive, enameled and water-proof labels. Come in packs of 20. From Ballistic Products, Inc.

Price: **$1.95**
Price: Two or more **$1.75**

DILLON AkroBins

Stackable bins to store and keep components separate. Made of heavy-duty polypropylene. Small bins measure $4^{3}/_{4}$ x $3^{7}/_{16}$ x $2^{13}/_{16}$; medium bins are $6^{3}/_{4}$ x $3^{7}/_{16}$ x $2^{13}/_{16}$; large bins, $10^{1}/_{4}$ x $4^{3}/_{8}$ x $4^{3}/_{4}$. Available 10, 24 and 48 packs. From Dillon Precision Products, Inc.

Price: Sm./Med., each **$2.50**
Price: Sm./Med., 10 pack **$19.95**
Price: Sm./Med., 24 pack **$34.95**
Price: Sm./Med., 48 pack **$59.90**
Price: Lrg., each **$5.00**
Price: Lrg., 10 pack **$23.95**
Price: Lrg., 24 pack **$43.95**

DILLON Pistol Ammunition Boxes

Heavy-duty, lightweight plastic ammo boxes. Available in 50- or 100-round sizes. The "38" series boxes can accommodate 38 Super, 32-20, 30 Carbine and 30 Mauser; "9" series hold 30 Luger, 9x21 and 380; "44" series also for 10mm and 40 S&W. From Dillon Precision Products, Inc.

Price: 38/357, 44, 45 ACP, 9mm 50-round **$1.75**
Price: 38/357, 44, 45 ACP, 9mm 100-round **$3.75**

DILLON Rifle Ammunition Boxes

Translucent, heavy-duty plastic. Available in small rifle, medium rifle, large rifle or extra-large rifle. Small rifle cases accommodate 222, 223 to 7.62x39; CBRM medium cases hold 7.62x39, 22-250 to 30-06; Medium rifle cases 22-250, 308 to 30-06 length; large boxes from 30-06, 8x57 to all belted cartridges; and extra large size holds large base/rim ammo such as 45-70. From Dillon Precision Products, Inc.

Price: Small, 50-rd. **$2.70**
Price: Medium, 20-rd. **$1.95**
Price: Medium, 50-rd. **$3.75**
Price: Large, 20-rd. **$1.95**
Price: Large, 50-rd. **$3.75**
Price: Extra large, 20-rd. **$3.45**

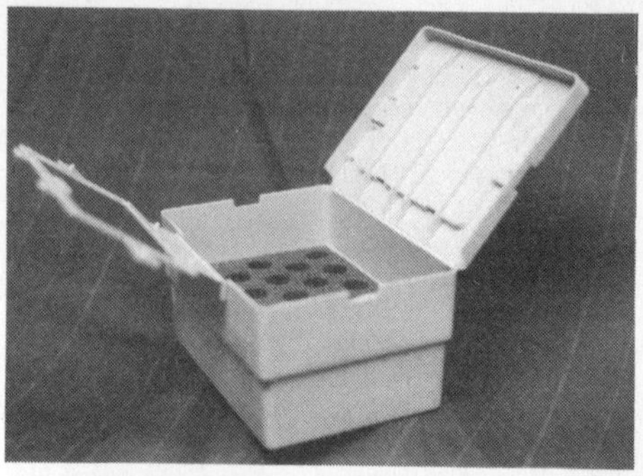

Ballistic Products Shotshell Boxes

Dillon AkroBins

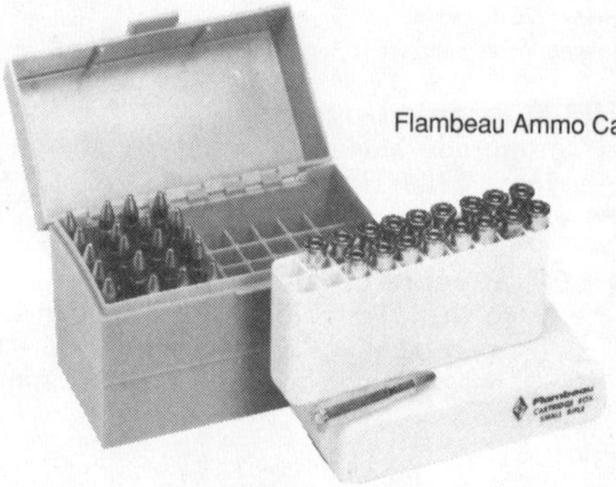

Flambeau Ammo Cases

FLAMBEAU 100-Round Shotgun Shell Box

Durable plastic 100-shell boxes. Three configurations available: 5254 has four adjustable 25-shell trays for 12, 16 and 20 gauge; 5255 has two 50-shell trays for 12 and 16 gauge; 5256 has two 50-shell trays for 20 gauge. From Flambeau Products Corporation.

Price: 5254 . . . . **Contact manufacturer.**

FLAMBEAU 20-Round Slip-Top Rifle Cartridge Box

Plastic 20-round box for calibers: 222, 243, 244, 264, 270, 7mm, 284, 30-30, 308, 30-06, 300 H&H, 35. From Flambeau Products Corporation.

Price: . . . . **Contact manufacturer.**

FLAMBEAU 25-Round Shotgun Shell Box

Slip-top 25-round plastic shell box for 12, 16 or 20 gauge. From Flambeau Products Corporation.

Price: . . . . **Contact manufacturer.**

J&J Ammo Boxes

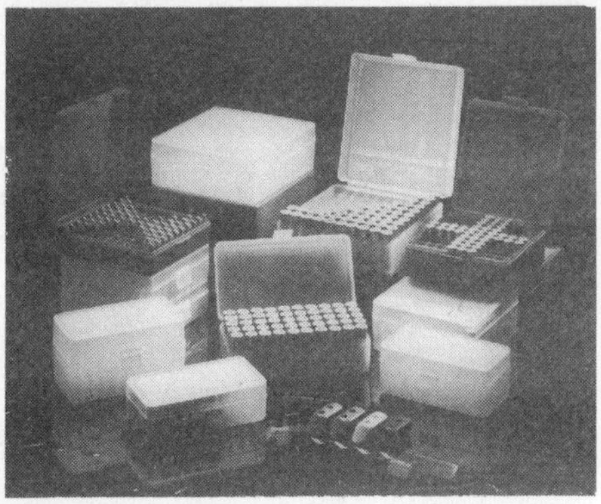

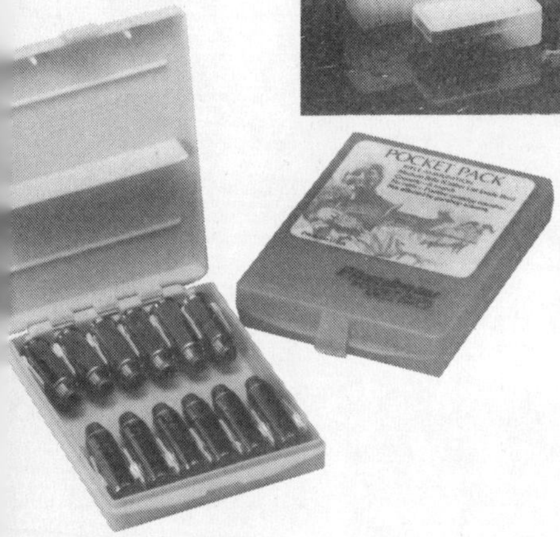

Flambeau Pocket Pack

Midway Plastic Ammo Boxes

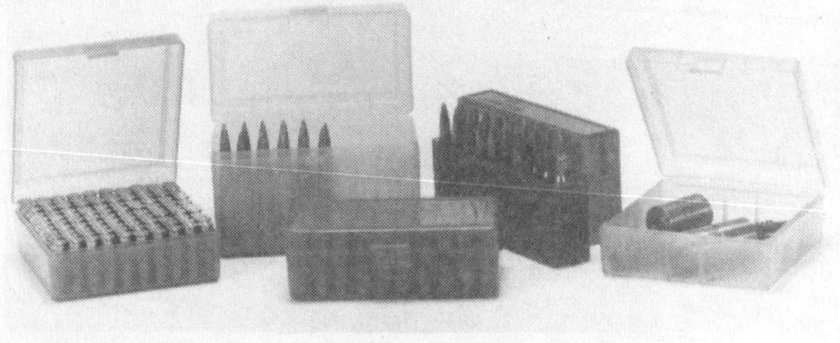

Hornady Shotshell Boxes

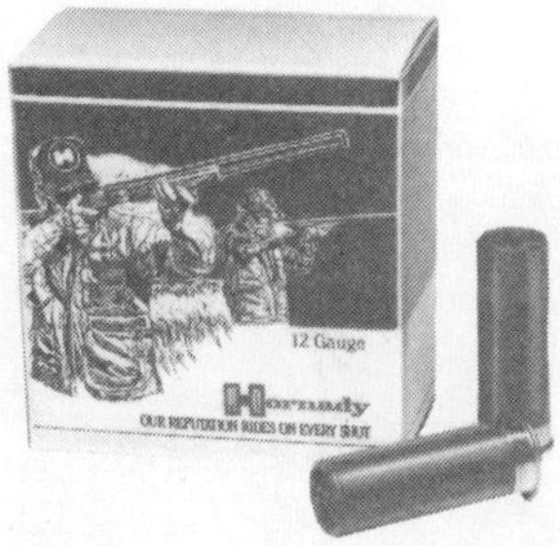

MIDWAY ARMS CB Ammo Boxes		
Caliber	Price/25	Price/100
380/9mm	$10.99	$32.99
38 SWC	10.99	32.99
38/357	10.99	32.99
222/223	11.99	39.99
44 Spl./44 Mag.	10.99	35.99
10mm/45 ACP	10.99	34.99
243/308	10.49	32.99
270/30-06	10.49	33.99

MIDWAY Plastic Ammo Boxes				
Caliber	#Rounds	Price/1	Price/10	Price/50
380/9mm	50	$1.79	$10.79	$37.99
38/357	50	1.79	10.79	37.99
221/30 M1	100	2.79	15.99	69.99
222/223	50	2.79	15.99	69.99
44 Spl./44 Mag.	50	1.79	10.99	42.99
	100	3.79	20.99	94.99
10mm/45	50	1.79	10.99	42.99
243/308	20	1.79	10.79	39.99
	50	3.29	17.99	79.99
270/30-06	20	1.99	12.99	49.99
	50	3.79	21.99	97.99

FLAMBEAU Flip-Top or Slip-Top Cartridge Box

Sturdy plastic 50-round boxes with either flip-top or standard slip-on lids for storing pistol or rifle cartridges. From Flambeau Products Corporation.

Price: . . . . **Contact manufacturer.**

FLAMBEAU Pocket Packs

Eight-round pocket packs for rifle cartridges. Made of sturdy plastic. For calibers 22-250, 38-357, 41 Magnum and 44 Magnum. From Flambeau Products Corporation.

Price: . . . . **Contact manufacturer.**

HORNADY Shotshell Boxes

Cardboard boxes for 12-gauge reloads. Each holds 25 shells. Come in packs of 10. From Hornady Mfg. Co.

Price: **$9.50**

J&J Ammo Boxes

Sturdy hinge- and slip-top plastic ammo boxes offered in various styles and sizes to accommodate most popular pistol and rifle cartridges as well as shotshell cases. Pistol cases come in either 50- or 100-round; rifle in 20-, 50- or 100-round; and shotshell in 50- to 100-round. From J&J Products Company.

Price: Pistol, 50-round hinge top or slip top **$1.20**
Price: Pistol, 100-round hinge top **$2.89**
Price: Rifle, 20-round, med. rifle, slip top **$1.20**
Price: Rifle, 20-round, lrg. rifle, slip top **$1.45**
Price: Rifle, 20-round, X-lrg. rifle, slip top **$2.89**
Price: Rifle, 50-round, sm. rifle, hinge top **$2.25**
Price: Rifle, 50-round, med. and lrg. rifle, hinge top **$2.89**
Price: Shotshell, 50-round, hinge top, 1 tray **$9.45**
Price: Shotshell, 100-round, hinge top, 2 trays **$14.50**

MIDWAY CB Ammo Boxes

Cardboard box with styrofoam tray. All sizes hold 50 rounds except for 243/308 and 270/30-06 which hold 20 rounds. Each size available in packs of 25 or 100 boxes. From Midway Arms, Inc.

Price: . . . . **See chart.**

MIDWAY Plastic Ammo Boxes

See-through plastic ammo boxes in ten sizes with hinged tops and two sizes with slip tops. Offered in three colors. Each available individually and in packs of 10 or 50 of one color. From Midway Arms, Inc.

Price: . . . . **See chart.**

MIDWAY Shotshell/Metallic Reloading Labels

Peel and stick 2"x2$^{1}/_{2}$" (handgun/rifle), 2"x2$^{1}/_{4}$" (shotshell) labels for ammo boxes to record pertinent reload data. 100 labels per roll. From Midway Arms, Inc.

Price: **$4.99**

Midway CB Ammo Boxes

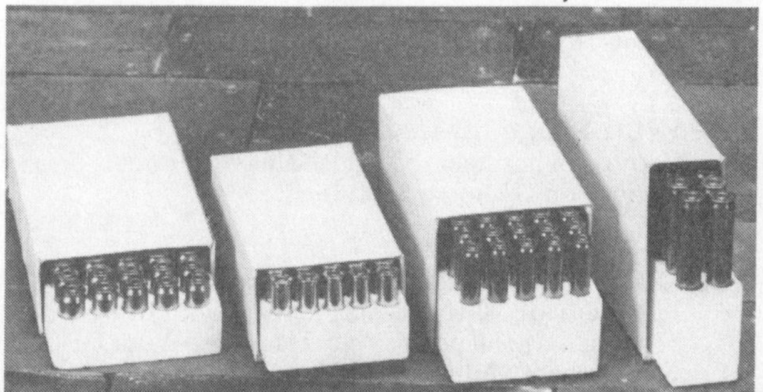

Section 6: Miscellaneous

MTM Handgun Ammo Cases

Sturdy, plastic ammo cases come in a variety of colors and types. 50- or 100-round cases are available in slip-top or flip-top styles. Fits from 32- to 45-caliber. From MTM Moulded Products Company.

Price: Case-Gard 50 Series **$1.51**
Price: Case-Gard E-50 Series Slip-Top Boxes **$1.40**
Price: Case-Gard J-50 Series Slip-Top Boxes **$2.34**
Price: P50 Series **$1.40**
Price: P-100 Series **$3.17**

MTM Rifle Ammo Cases

A wide variety of plastic ammo boxes for 10-, 20-, 50-, 60- and 100-rounds. Available in flip-top or slip-top styles, some with carrying handles, to accommodate calibers from 22 through 500 Nitro Express. From MTM Moulded Products Company.

Price: African Big Game Ammo Carrier **$5.17**
Price: Case-Gard Ammo Holster **$5.89**
Price: Case-Gard **$3.07**
Price: Case-Gard 50 Series **$3.17**
Price: Case-Gard 60 Series **$4.53**
Price: Case-Gard H-50 Series **$5.89**
Price: Case-Gard H-50-XL Series **$7.54**
Price: Case-Gard R-100 . . . . **$8.17**
Price: Case-Gard RS-100 . . . . **$5.63**
Price: J-20 Slip-Top Boxes **$1.67**

MTM Shotshell Ammo Carriers

Plastic shotshell holders, in various colors and styles, with capacities of 5, 10, 25, 50 and 100 rounds. In flip-top style, with or without handles, hold 10, 12 and 20 gauges. From MTM Moulded Products Company.

Price: Case-Gard S-5 . . . . **$2.59**
Price: Case-Gard S-10 . . . . **$2.94**
Price: Case-Gard S-25 . . . . **$3.31**
Price: Case-Gard S-100 . . . . **$16.49**
Price: Case-Gard SF-50 . . . . **$6.18**
Price: Case-Gard SF-50-10 . . . . **$12.24**
Price: Case-Gard SF-100 . . . . **$14.24**
Price: 50-Rd. Shotshell Trays **$3.68**

PATTERN CONTROL Shotshell Box

Clear plastic 25-shell capacity box with snap-on lid. From Pattern Control.

Price: **$2.00**

RCBS Ammo Boxes

Tough plastic boxes come in five sizes and feature flush exteriors with recessed latches, anti-rattle bullet tip next, empty case support and strong hinge. From RCBS.

Price: Small or medium rifle **$4.46**
Price: Large rifle **$4.94**
Price: Medium pistol **$2.70**
Price: Large pistol **$2.76**

SCHARCH Range Master Loose Pack

Loose pack carboard box holds 50 loaded rounds or 100 bullets. Price for 50. From Scharch Mfg., Inc.

Price: **$10.95**

SCHARCH Range Master Shotgun Box

Cardboard box holds 25 loaded shotshell rounds. Price for 25. From Scharch Mfg., Inc.

Price: **$13.95**

SCHARCH Range Master Styrofoam Boxes

Patented 50-, 20-round plastic trays with white cardboard boxes in all popular hand gun sizes. Price for 100. From Scharch Mfg., Inc.

Price: **$28.50**

MTM Case-Gard 100

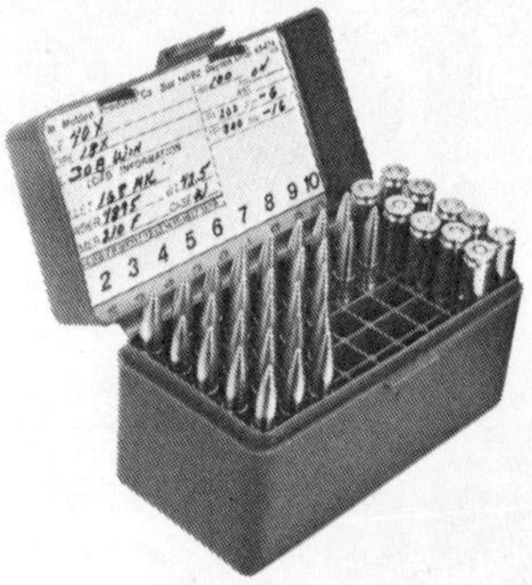

MTM Case-Gard 50

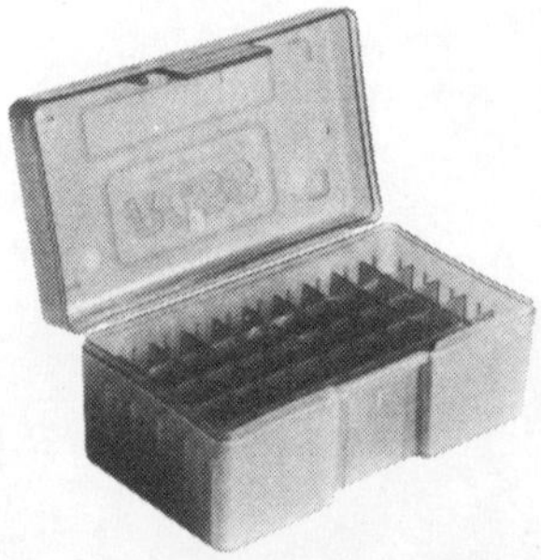

RCBS Cartridge Box

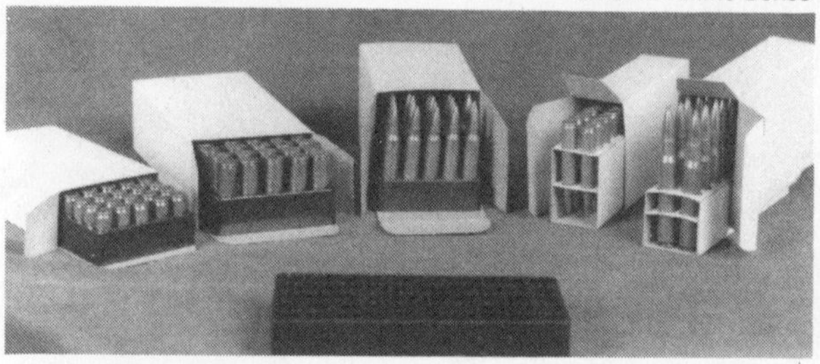

Scharch Ammo Boxes

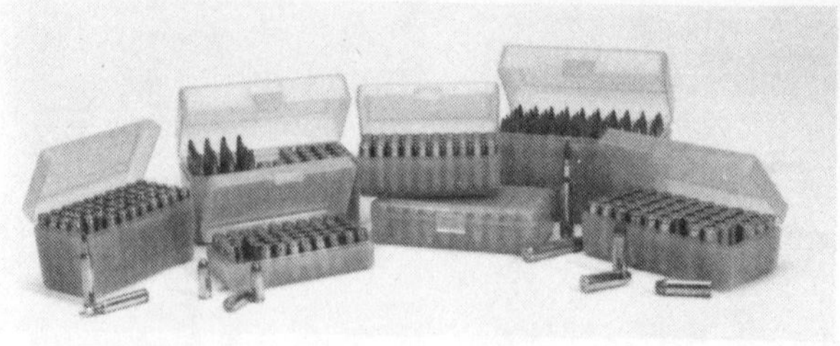

Midway Plastic Ammo Boxes

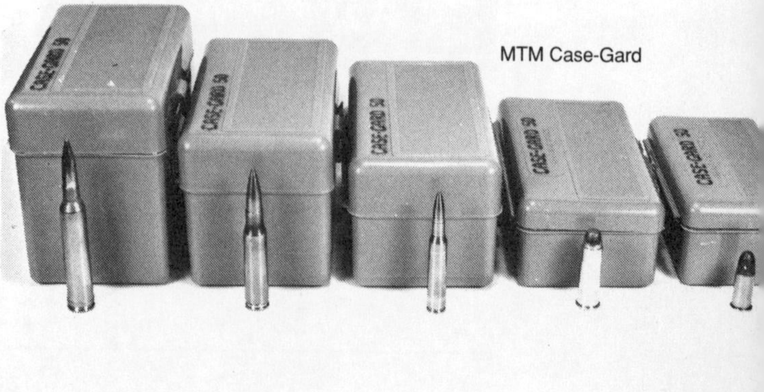

MTM Case-Gard

Birchwood Casey Target Spots

Birchwood Casey Precision Squares

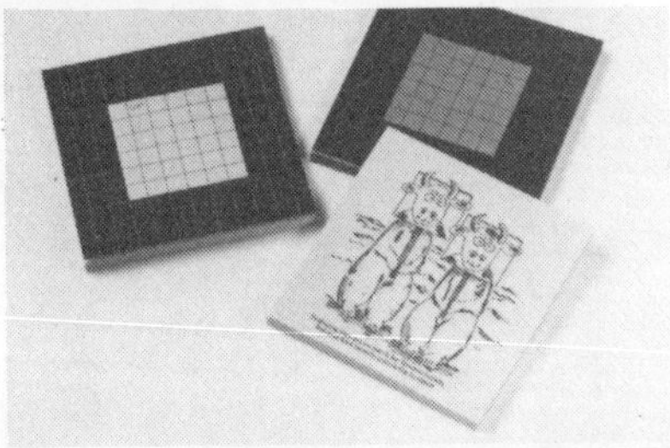

Hornady Target Squares

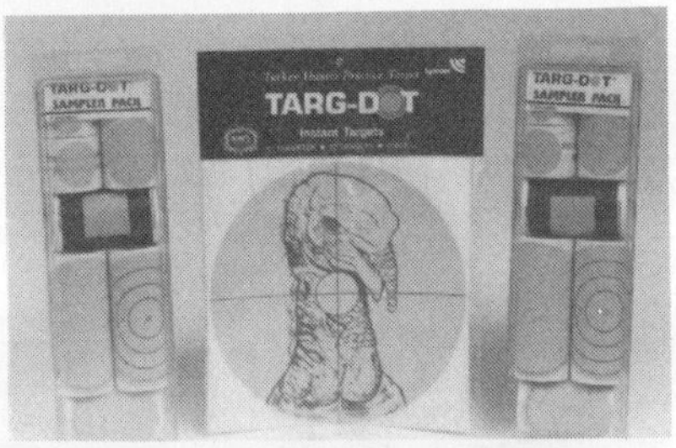

Lyman Targ-Dot

LYMAN Targ-Dots Product	Size	Targets*	Price
Targ-Dots	1/2"	110	$3.60
	1"	100	3.60
	1 1/2"	70	3.60
	2"	45	3.60
	3"	25	3.60
	6"	15	3.60
Accupoint	1"	100	3.60
	2"	45	3.60
	3"	25	3.60
50' Bullseye Slow Fire	3"	50	3.60
Rapid Fire	3"	50	3.60
Hot Bullseye	3"	25	3.60
Hot Squares	1"	50	3.60
	2"	40	3.60
	3"	20	3.60
Instant Benchrest Squares	1"	75	3.60
	2"	60	3.60
Instant Target Pasters	1"	200	3.60
Sampler Pack	1/2" to 3"	359	9.95**

*Per pack; **7 packs

BIRCHWOOD CASEY Precision Squares
Multiple-faced sight-in paper targets for the hunter, benchrester and varmint shooter. High contrast black, white and red for visibility and definition. Available in three sizes: 2", 4" and 8" squares. From Birchwood Casey.
Price: **$4.55**

BIRCHWOOD CASEY Target Spots
Self-adhesive flourescent red target spots in 1", 1 1/2", 2", 3" and 6" diameters. Available as individual packages: 105 1" spots; 70 1 1/2"; 35 2", 35 1"; 25 3"; and 15 6". Also available three sizes (1", 2", 3") in one 20-sheet package. From Birchwood Casey.
Price: 1", 1 1/2", 2", 3" **$3.55**
Price: 6" **$3.85**
Price: Package of three **$5.30**

BULL-X IPSC Targets
Official IPSC targets. Minimum order of 50. Come either plain or white backed. From Bull-X, Incorporated.
Price: 1-50, plain, each . . . . **$.50**
Price: 1-50, white, each . . . . **$.55**
Price: 51-100, plain, each . . . . **$.45**
Price: 51-100, white, each . . . . **$.50**
Price: 101-300, plain, each . . . . **$.43**
Price: 101-300, white, each . . . . **$.48**
Price: 301-500, plain, each . . . . **$.40**
Price: 301-500, white, each . . . . **$.45**

GOZON Sight On Target Patches
Self-adhesive 2" and 6" round target patches. Come 50 (2") or 20 (6") to a bag. From Gozon Corporation.
Price: **$3.75**

HORNADY Shotgun Patterning Kit
Lightweight, self-standing kit comes with five duck or turkey targets. Additional targets of pheasant, turkey, dove and duck also available. From Hornady Mfg. Co.
Price: **$12.20**
Price: Pack of 10 replacement targets **$12.20**

HORNADY Target Squares
Sight-in 3"-square targets printed on post-it note pads. Come 100 to a pack. From Hornady Mfg. Co.
Price: **$3.95**

INNOVISION Insta Range
Free-standing target and sight-in kit. Target folds out to self-supporting target stand. Includes five targets, bullet hole patches and sight-in instructions. From Innovision Enterprises.
Price: **$6.95**
Price: Extra targets, 10 . . . . **$4.95**

ED LEWIS Stik-It Target
Adhesive targets for the benchrester and casual shooter. Many styles and sizes to choose from. From Ed Lewis.
Price: . . . . **Contact manufacturer.**

LYMAN Targ-Dots
A variety of stick-on targets available separately or assortment sheets. From Lyman Products Company.
Price: . . . . **See chart.**

MIDWAY Notebook Targets
Three-hole punched targets to file in any 3-ring binder. Five target styles available. 100 targets per package. From Midway Arms, Inc.
Price: **$4.99**

MIDWAY Shooting Spots and Squares

Peel and stick flourescent red targets for adhesion to make a target or use to highlight target center. "B" Series available in three aiming patterns. "C" series squares have black borders. From Midway Arms, Inc.

Price: 1" squares or spots, 100 . . . . **$1.99**
Price: 2" squares or spots, 50 . . . . **$2.99**
Price: 3" squares or spots, 50 . . . . **$3.99**
Price: 3" "B" or "C" series square or spots, 50 . . . . **$4.99**
Price: 1" "C" series squares, 100 . . . . **$2.99**
Price: 2" "C" series squares, 50 . . . . **$3.99**

MIDWAY Target Pasters

Apply over bullet holes for target reuse. Come in four colors, white, off-white, brown and black. 500 $^3/_4$" square pasters to a roll. From Midway Arms, Inc.

Price: Each **$3.59**
Price: Combo pack (1 of each color) **$10.99**

OUTERS Official NRA Targets

Heavyweight, non-glare targets that conform to all NRA specifications for regulation matches. From Outers.

Price: . . . . **Contact manufacturer.**

OUTERS Scorekeeper Targets

Feature high-visibility orange bullseyes or traditional black with data area for recording firearm, bullet weight, cartridge length, etc. For rifles, pistols or airguns. From Outers.

Price: . . . . **Contact manufacturer.**

RAM-LINE Target

Features graduated reticle sight-in bars; circular pistol ring in 1" intervals; silhouette targets in $^1/_4$-minute, $^1/_2$-minute or 1-MOA at 100 yards. From Ram-Line, Inc.

Price: . . . . **Contact manufacturer.**

RED STAR Alpha and Omega

100-yard five in one target. Size, 17x22 with 1" grid. Come in packages of 5 targets. From Red Star Target Co.

Price: **$1.89**

RED STAR Global Sun

For iron sight or long distance scoped rifle shooting. Size, 17x22 with 1" grid size. Come in packages of 5 targets. From Red Star Target Co.

Price: **$1.89**

RED STAR Fine Tuner

For fine tuning scope and rifle up to 100 yards. Size, $8^1/_2$x11 with $^1/_2$" grid size. Come in packages of 10 targets. From Red Star Target Co.

Price: **$1.89**

RED STAR Marksman

Custom designed 50-yard five in one target for 22-caliber or flat shooting. Size, $8^1/_2$x11 with $^1/_2$" grid size. Come in packages of 10 targets. From Red Star Target Co.

Price: **$1.89**

RED STAR Official 100

Standard 100-yard, seven ring, sighting in, bilingual target. Size, 14x20 with 1" grid size. Come in packages of 5 targets. From Red Star Target Co.

Price: **$1.19**

Innovision Insta-Range

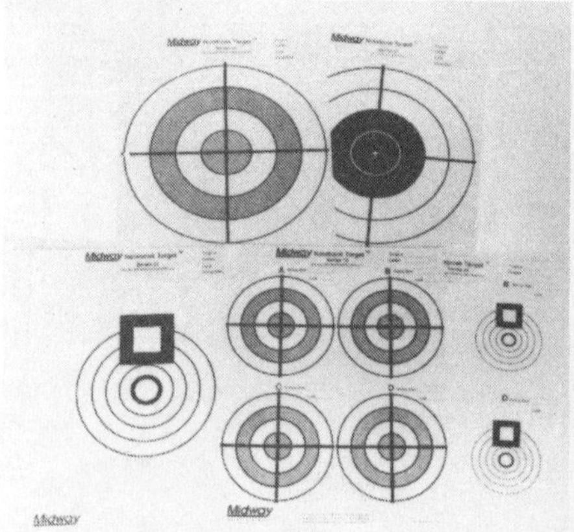

Midway Notebook Targets

Midway Shooting Spots and Squares

Outers Score Keeper Targets

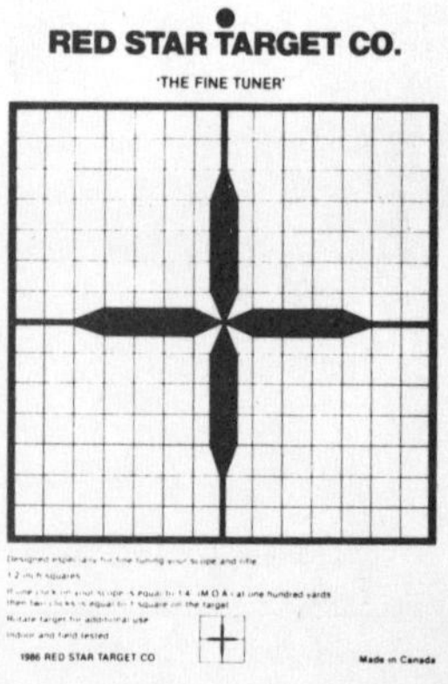

Red Star Targets

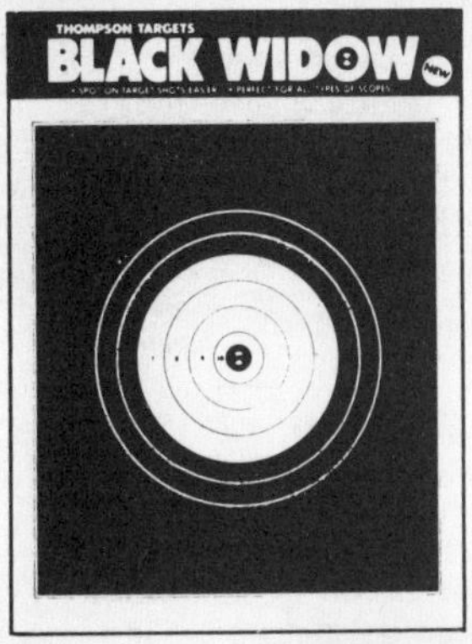

Thompson Target

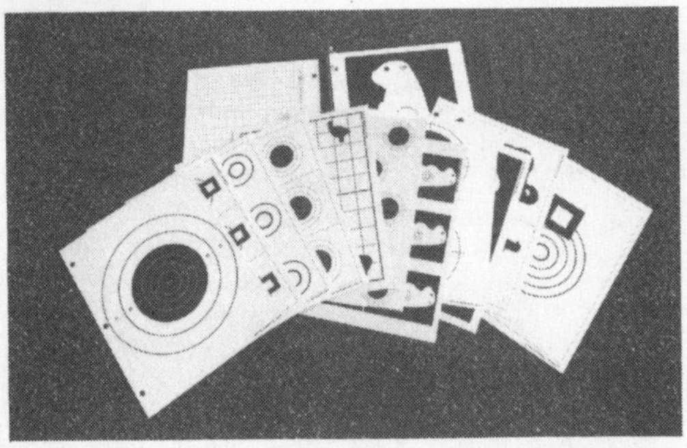

Sinclair Target Copier Kit

ROCKY MOUNTAIN TARGETS			
Target	Size	Price/100	Price/500
DATA-TARG			
R-100-LD	$8^1/_2$ x 11	$11.85	$55.65
R-100	$8^1/_2$ x 11	11.85	55.65
R-200-LD	$8^1/_2$ x 11	11.85	55.65
R-200	$8^1/_2$ x 11	11.85	55.65
R-100-LD-S	$8^1/_2$ x 11	11.85	55.65
R-200-LD-S	$8^1/_2$ x 11	11.85	55.65
R-100-S	$8^1/_2$ x 11	11.85	55.65
R-200-S	$8^1/_2$ x 11	11.85	55.65
SPECIAL PURPOSE			
Keith-50	11 x 17	22.40	79.85
Milek 25/300P	11 x 17	23.60	87.75
Skelton 50-100P	11 x 17	22.40	79.85
ZRO-100	11 x 17	23.60	79.85
TRAJECTORY ANALYSIS			
TRJ-123	17 x $22^1/_2$	69.00	310.00
MATCH COMPETITION PISTOL			
B-2	$10^1/_2$ x 12	42.00/500	73.90/1000
B-3	$10^1/_2$ x 12	42.00/500	73.90/1000
B-4	$10^1/_2$ x 12	42.00/500	73.90/1000
B-5	$10^1/_2$ x 12	42.00/500	73.90/1000
B-6(CP)	$10^1/_2$ x 12	26.90/500	45.90/1000
B-6(P)	$10^1/_2$ x 12	73.90	131.00
B-8(P)	21 x 24	73.90/500	131.00
TQ-6	6 x 7	23.50/500	42.00/1000
TQ-7	6 x 7	23.50/500	42.00/1000
TQ-1/1	7 x $9^1/_4$	17.35/500	30.80/1000
TQ-1/5	7 x $9^1/_4$	17.35/500	30.80/1000
TQ-1/5(T)	$7^3/_4$ x $9^1/_4$	28.55/500	49.85/1000
TQ-3/1	7 x $9^1/_4$	17.35/500	30.80/1000
TQ-3/2	9 x 14	31.35/500	54.30/1000
TQ-4	14 x 14	39.20/500	69.45/1000
A-17	$10^1/_2$ x 12	42.00/500	73.90/1000

SPEEDWELL DIVISION Benchrest/Hunter Targets				
Target	Yards	Color	Size	Price/100
BR	100	Black	8x$15^1/_2$	$7.50
BR	200	Black	8x$16^1/_2$	7.50
BR	300	Red	12x$33^1/_2$	22.75
HR	100	Black	12x19	11.25
HR	200	Black	13x21	11.25
HR	300	Black	13x26	26.50

RED STAR Official Bench Rest

100-yard and 200-yard targets with data entry space in lower right-hand corner. Come in packages of 10 targets. From Red Star Target Co.

Price: . . . . **$.99**

RED STAR Pistol Target

Designed specifically for pistol shooting with or without scope. Size, $8^1/_2$x11 with $^1/_2$" grid size. Come in packages of 10 targets. From Red Star Target Co.

Price: **$1,89**

RED STAR Shotgun Special

40-yard target with 30" circle divided into four segments and 2" aiming point. Size, 34x38. From Red Star Target Co.

Price: Each **$1.29**

RED STAR Triple Three

Nine shooting points for testing different loads without changing targets. Size, 17x22 with 1" grid size. Come in packages of five targets. From Red Star Target Co.

Price: **$1.99**

ROCKY MOUNTAIN

A variety of targets from Data-Targ load developement targets to NMLRA Muzzle-Loader. See chart for targets and prices. From Rocky Mountain Target Company.

Price: . . . . **See chart.**

SPEEDWELL DIVISION Targets

Benchrest and hunter 100-, 200- and 300-yard targets in three sizes. From Speedwell Division, Rockwood Corporation.

Price: . . . . **See chart.**

TARGOT MAN

High visibility self-adhesive targets for practice and benchrest. High contrast circecles with crosshairs and diamond in sizes: 1", $1^3/_8$", $2^7/_8$" and 6"; benchrest 100 and 200 yard competition practice targets; Bull's-eyes in $2^7/_8$" and 6" sizes. Come in packs of six targets. From Targot Man.

Price: 1" circle **$2.49**
Price: $1^3/_8$" circle **$2.89**
Price: $2^7/_8$" circle **$2.99**
Price: 6" circle **$3.99**
Price: 100-yard benchrest **$2.99**
Price: 200-yard benchrest **$3.99**
Price: $2^7/_8$" Bull's-eye **$2.99**
Price: $2^7/_8$" Bull's-eye **$3.99**

THOMPSON TARGET

Five 5-in-1 15"x16" or 9"x10" target configurations with 4" bulls. Scope Alignment provides lock-on center point for scopes at 50 to 300 yards or 50 to 100 yards. Black Widow for center-hold shooters at 25 to 100 yards. Yellow Jacket designed for target practice on bright days. White Lightning, black bulls on white background, for handgun and rifle at 25 to 100 yards. Hot Shot, white bulls on red background for handguns and rifles at 25 to 100 yards. Come 10 per pack larger target; 12 per pack smaller size target. From Thompson Target Technology.

Price: 15"x16" **$4.19**
Price: 9"x10" **$2.99**

Section 6: Miscellaneous

ARMS ARMSCalc

IBM-compatible version 4.01 ballistics software for calculating exterior ballistics, reoil, power factors and coefficients. Will compute, chart and graph eight separate functions: trajectory, up- and downhill trajectory, point of impact bullet drop, wind deflection, time in flight, remaining velocity and energy, maximum height above line of sight. Will compute an additional nine functions: velocity, energy and mass relationships, metallic cartridge recoil, shotgun recoil, USPSA/IPSC ratings, ballistic coefficients, corrected coefficients, point-blank range, corrected velocity due to wind direction and chronograph lag, sectional density and RSP. Pre-loaded with look up tables of over 600 bullets and most commercial ammunition. From ARMS-Peripheral Data Systems.

Price: **$49.95**

ARMS ARMSLoad

IBM-compatible version 4.01 ballistics software designed to track load performance of both shotshell and metallic cartridges, calculate cost comparisons, analyze chronograph and target data. Used in conjunction with ArmsCalc, load performance is estimated and input for the shooter. Loads may be printed in different formats and sorted by any combination of parameters. Labels may be printed for ammo identification. Database is preloaded with most commercial components. From ARMS-Peripheral Data Systems.

Price: **$49.95**

BALLISTIC PROGRAM The Ballistic Program

Compatible with IBM PC, PC-XT, AT and IBM clones running DOS 2.1 or higher, this 1.3 million byte software provides Interior, Exterior and Ballistic Coefficient menu-driven programs. Both Interior and Exterior modules have a database containing up to 75 cartridges from 17 Rem. to 460 Weatherby. **Interior** module computes powder charge weights, pressure (CUP), velocity, port pressure, point of peak pressure, specific volume and sectional density. Will also compute free recoil velocity and energy based on rifle weight and load. **Exterior** module computes altitude and temperature compensated range tables and ballistic data out to 1500 yards and rifle zero tables and point-blank range tables out to 1000 yards. Displays cartridge, range interval, remaining velocity and energy , drop from bore, mid-range ordinate, deflection, time of flight data. **Ballistic Coefficient** module computes ballistic coeffients, the "raw," instrumental velocity and instrumental velocity at two distances. Available in two versions, 4.55 and 5.15 on three 360K or two 720K disks. From The Ballistic Program Co., Inc.

Price: **$59.95**

BARNES BULLETS Ballistics Program

IBM-compatible, graphics capability, menu-driven ballistics software to calculate bullet trajectory, velocity, wind deflection, target lead, striking energy and point-blank maximum range. Displays up to five trajectories graphically on screen or to print; graphs velocity, energy and wind deflection results. Complete library of Barnes bullets, including ballistic coefficients and muzzle velocities. Available in 5¼" (360K) or 3½" 9720K disks. From Barnes Bullets, Inc.

Price: **$79.95**

BLACKWELL Ballistic Coefficients On A Disk

IBM-compatible single source software for up-to-date listing of bullet ballistic coefficients from ten major ammunition and bullet manufacturers in the U.S. from 17- to 60-caliber. Bullets are listed by manufacturer and caliber. Free with purchase of Load From A Disk I and II. From W.W. Blackwell.

Price: **$20.00**

BLACKWELL Handgun Internal Ballistics

IBM-compatible menu-driven software includes loading data for thirty handgun calibers from 22 Hornet to 454 Casull. Load data (3,000 loads) for all popular powders and load range from minimum to maximum. Program calculates muzzle velocity for any barrel length from 1 to 14 inches; load density, energy and stopping power for each change in powder charge. From W.W. Blackwell.

Price: **$75.00**

BLACKWELL Load From A Disk 7.3

IBM-compatible menu-driven software calculates internal and external ballistics for any rifle, commercial or wildcat up to 50-caliber and bullet weights up to 800 grains. Powder type (over 50 listed), charge weight, velocity, pressure, bullet drop, bullet energy, point-blank range, trajectory, recoil, uphill/downhill correction. Built-in database for 89 cartridges, their case capacities and lengths. From W.W. Blackwell.

Price: **$49.95**

BLACKWELL Load From A Disk II

IBM-compatible menu-driven software to calculate optimum rifle twist, muzzle velocity from trajectory, ballistic coefficient from velocity, ballistic coefficient from trajectory and from bullet shape. From W.W. Blackwell.

Price: **$25.00**

Price: Load From A Disk I and II **$74.95**

CORBIN Bullet Design

IBM-compatible for computing ballistic coefficients. Specify bullet type, weight, nose shape, caliber, bullet material and material to be fired into. Program calculates ballistic coefficient, volume of lead, minimum spin rate, amount of material in shank and ogive, weight of core and jacket and overall length of jacket. From Corbin Manufacturing & Supply, Inc.

CORBIN Bullet Design Engineer's Pak

Includes Corbin bullet and paper patch design programs as well as the handbook and plot programs. From Corbin Manufacturing & Supply, Inc

Price: **$72.00**

CORBIN Handbook of Bullet Swaging

A two-disk, IBM-compatible set. The disk version of Corbin's 200-page illustrated guide to the use of Corbin bullet making tools. From Corbin Manufacturing & Supply, Inc.

Price: **$12.00**

CORBIN Paper Patch Bullet Design

Four-section, IBM-compatible program that finds patch length, paper thickness, bullet length for various alloys, bullet diameter for four different bullet to barrel fit; calculates length and volume of material needed for given bullet caliber plus bullet jacket length for tubing. From Corbin Manufacturing & Supply, Inc.

Price: **$10.00**

CORBIN Plot Program
IBM-compatible terminal ballistics program calculates actual retardation due to skin effect, base drag, nose drag and graphs bullet drop and energies at various distances. From Corbin Manufacturing & Supply, Inc.
Price: **$25.00**

DATATECH Computer Marksman
Apple II Plus, IIc, IIe or IIGS compatible. Provides simulated field hunting conditions, simulated shot results utilizing user reload or 19 preprogrammed cartridges. Program offers 19 exterior ballistic calculations. Comes on single 5.25" disk. From Datatech Software Systems, Inc.
Price: **$39.50**

EXE External Ballistic Program
IBM-compatible software designed to calculate downrange velocity, energy, momentum, drop from bore, trajectory, crosswind drift, time of flight, up/downhill trajectory, ballistic coefficient, recoil energy and more based on actual shooting conditions input. From Exe, Inc.
Price: **$39.95**

HORNADY Video: Introduction To Reloading
Step-by-step instructional reloading video. From the case to a finished cartridge both rifle and pistol. 24 minutes. VHS. Weight: 8 oz. From Hornady Mfg. Co.
Price: **$29.95**

HORNADY Video: Joyce Hornady On Reloading And Bullet Accuracy
Twenty-five minute video for reloading pros and beginners. VHS. Weight: 12 oz. From Hornady Mfg. Co.
Price: **$29.95**

MAGMA Load Master
IBM-compatible with hard disk, VGA monitor and two megabites of disk space. Multimedia software database and graphics program containing more than 1,200 cast bullet loads for fifteen popular pistol cartridges. There are, for example, 174 loads for the 38 Special. The user can add, display, edit and delete up to two billion additional loads. Also included are more than fifty bullet and cartridge drawings complete with dimensional reference data. Available on 5.25 DSHD and 3.5 HD formats. From Magma Engineering Co.
Price: . . . . **Contact manufacturer.**

OEHLER Ballistic Explorer
IBM-compatible software calculates zeroed range, sight adjustment, path, maximum point-blank range, ballistic coefficient, velocity, drop, energy, wind drift, time of flight and momentum. Handles up to three loads simultaneously moving among the loads and 15 parameters or comparing two or three loads at same time on screen. Ballistic Explorer requires hard drive, a 3.5" floppy drive or high-density 5.25" drive; DOS 2.0 or higher; Hercules, CGA, VGA or EGA graphics; 432K of free RAM after DOS and memory resident programs are loaded; math co-processor speeds program operation. From Oehler Research.
Price: **$70.00**

PEJSA Ballistics Program
Apple II, Comodore, Macintosh and IBM-compatible. Measured velocity or drag data of any projectile matched by an adjustable modeled drag coifficient curve; resulting trajectory, velocity, time, etc. are computed. Other unique features include: impact, height at any sight-in range, or rise at mid-range, flight path, zeros etc. If ballistic coefficient not known, approximate value may be found based on size and shape or precise value computed, based on actual measurements of velocity loss. Effects of temperature, altitude, inclines or winds can be computed as well as recoil energy and retardation. Available on either 3.5" or 5.25" disk. From Pejsa Ballistics.
Price: **$29.95**

RCBS PC Bullet
IBM-compatible trajectory analysis menu-driven software. Allows viewing up to eight loads at once, displaying nine different plots and access to over 500 bullets, most powders and primers. Compatible with the PACT chronograph. Available in 3.5" or 5.5" floppy disk. From RCBS.
Price: **$69.95**

SIERRA High Power Rifle Reloading Video
Three-hour, two-volume high-power rifle video for advanced reloaders. G. David Tubb offers step-by-step instructions and techniques to improve precision and accuracy. From Sierra Bullets.
Price: **$39.95**

TIOGA ENGINEERING Baltec1
IBM-compatible ballistics software to calculate trajectory data for elongated bullets or round balls; recoil impulse, free-recoil velocity and energy; muzzle velocity from chronographed instrumental velocity; constructs charge/velocity table from chronograph data; analyzes strings of velocity data; compares accuracy data for two loads, guns or conditions; compares extreme spread for different numbers of shots/groups; checks target for true flyer; computes accuracy statistics from X, Y-coordinates; estimates ballistic coefficient; computes twist using Greenhill Formula; computes vertical trajectory and ballistic coefficient from down-range velocities. Available on 5.25 360K floppy or 3.5 720 floppy. From Tioga Engineering Company.
Price: **$24.00**

CARL VANCINI Bestload
IBM-compatible software to design loads. Computes bullet ballistic coefficient, gyroscopic stability factor, residual velocity at various ranges; terminal ballistics, wind deflection, pressure and velocity profiles in the bore; instrumental velocity and chamber pressure prediction, intrumental velocity at various barrel lengths, recoil, piezometric ratio, suggested powder charge and burn-out point. From Carl Vancini.
Price: **$43.00**

THE HANDLOADER'S LIBRARY

IMPORTANT NOTICE TO BOOK BUYERS

Books listed here may be bought from the publisher or Ray Riling Arms Books Co., 6844 Gorsten St., P.O. Box 18925, Philadelphia, PA 19119, phone 215-438-2456.

A full variety of books on the subject of handloading are also available from Rutgers Book Center, 127 Raritan Ave., Highland Park, NJ 08904.

***New Book**

The AA Hull, Revision IV, Ballistic Products, Corcoran, MN, 1989. 19 pp., paper covers, $4.00.
Informative manual about the AA hull and loads for it.

***ABC's of Reloading, 5th Edition,** by Dean A. Grennell, DBI Books, Inc., Northbrook, IL, 1993. 288 pp., illus. Paper covers. $18.95.
The definitive guide to every facet of cartridge and shotshell reloading.

The Accurate Varmint Rifle, by Boyd Mace, Precision Shooting, Inc., Whitehall, NY, 1991. 184 pp., illus. $22.95.
A long overdue and long needed work on what factors go into the selection of components for and the susequent assembly of...the accurate varmint rifle.

Advantages II, Ballistic Products, Corcoran, MN, 1987. 72 pp., paper covers, $7.00.
Comprehensive reloading guide for the hunter.

African Rifles & Cartridges, by John Taylor, The Gun Room Press, Highland Park, NJ, 1977. 431 pp., illus. $35.00.
Experiences and opinions of a professional ivory hunter in Africa describing his knowledge of numerous arms and cartridges for big game. A reprint.

The American Cartridge, by Charles R. Suydam, Borden Publishing Co., Alhambra, CA, 1986. 184 pp., illus. $12.50.
An illustrated study of the rimfire cartridge in the United States.

Ammunition Making, by George E. Frost, National Rifle Association of America, Washington, D.C., 1990. 160 pp., illus. Paper covers. $17.95.
Reflects the perspective of "an insider" with half a century's experience in successful management of ammunition manufacturing operations.

AQ-Slug Manual, Revision III, Ballistic Products, Corcoran, MN, 1991. 16 pp., paper covers, $4.00.
Special loads and information for the 12-gauge AQ slug.

Ballistic Science for the Law Enforcement Officer, by Charles G. Wilber, Ph.D., Charles C. Thomas, Springfield, IL, 1977. 309 pp., illus. $80.00.
A scientific study of the ballistics of civilian firearms.

***Barnes Reloading Manual,** Wolfe Publishing, Prescott, AZ, 1992. 356 pp., $24.95.
This bullet maker's new reloading manual, also containing loads for their X Bullets.

Basic Handloading, by George C. Nonte, Jr., Outdoor Life Books, New York, NY, 1982. 192 pp., illus. Paper covers. $6.95.
How to produce high-quality ammunition using the safest, most efficient methods known.

Big Bore Rifles And Cartridges, Wolfe Publishing Co., Prescott, AZ, 1991. Paper cover. $26.00.
This book covers cartridges from 8mm to .600 Nitro with over 60 chapters containing loading tables and commentary.

Black Powder Guide, 2nd Edition, by George C. Nonte, Jr., Stoeger Publishing Co., So. Hackensack, NJ, 1991. 288 pp., illus. Paper covers. $12.95.
How-to instructions for selection, repair and maintenance of muzzleloaders, making your own bullets, restoring and refinishing, shooting techniques.

Blue Dot Powder, Revision IV, Ballistic Products, Corcoran, MN, 1992. 24 pp., paper covers, $4.00.
A discussion of the characteristics of Blue Dot under various conditions.

Bob Pease Collection Revised Vol. 1, Bob Pease Accuracy, New Braunfels, TX, 1990. 40 pp., $6.00.
Covers bedding, turning, case sorting and preparation.

Bob Pease Collection Revised Vol. 2, Bob Pease Accuracy, New Braunfels, TX, 1990. 40 pp., $6.00.
Info on resting, aiming and sitting techniques, as well as accuracy loading.

Bob Pease Collection Revised Vol. 3, Bob Pease Accuracy, New Braunfels, TX, 1990. 40 pp., $6.00.
Answers shooters' questions on troubleshooting and case and rifle preparation.

Bob Pease Collection Revised Vol. 4, Bob Pease Accuracy, New Braunfels, TX, 1990. 40 pp., $6.00.
Explains the newest tools and equipment.

The Bullet Swage Manual. MDSU/I, by Ted Smith, Corbin Manufacturing and Supply Co., White City, OR, 1988. 45 pp., illus. Paper covers. $10.00.
A book that fills the need for information on bullet swaging.

Cartridge Case Measurements, by Dr. Arthur J. Mack, Amrex Enterprises, Vienna, VA, 1990. 300 pp., illus. Paper covers. $49.95.
Lists over 5000 cartridges of all kinds. Gives basic measurements (rim, head, shoulder, neck, length, plus bullet diameter) in both English and metric. Hundreds of experimental cartridges and wildcats.

Cartridges for Breechloading Rifles, by A. Mattenheimer, Armory Publications, Oceanside, CA, 1989. 90 pp. with two 15"x19" color lithos containing 163 drawings of cartridges and firearms mechanisms. $29.95.
Reprinting of this German work on cartridges. Text in German and English.

***Cartridges of the World, 7th Edition,** by Frank Barnes, edited by Mike Bussard, DBI Books, Inc., Northbrook, IL, 1993. 464 pp., illus. Paper covers. $21.95
Completely revised edition of the general purpose reference work for which collectors, police, scientists and laymen reach first for answers to cartridge identification questions. (September '93)

Cast Bullets, by Col. E. H. Harrison, A publication of the National Rifle Association of America, Washington, DC, 1979. 144 pp., illus. Paper covers. $12.95.
An authoritative guide to bullet casting techniques and ballistics.

The Complete Black Powder Handbook, Revised Edition, by Sam Fadala, DBI Books, Inc., Northbrook, IL, 1990. 320 pp., illus. Soft covers. $17.95.
Expanded and refreshed edition of the definitive book on the subject of blackpowder.

Complete Guide to Handloading, by Philip B. Sharpe, Wolfe Publishing, Prescott, AZ, 1988. 456 pp., (229 pp. supplement) $60.00.
His most sought-after classic including a supplement.

The Complete Handloader, by John Wootters, Stackpole Books, Harrisburg, PA, 1989. 224 pp., illus. $29.95.
One of the deans of gun writers shares a lifetime of experience and recommended procedures on handloading for rifles, handguns, and shotguns.

The Complete Handloader for Rifles, Handguns and Shotguns, by John Wootters, Stackpole Books, Harrisburg, PA, 1988. 214 pp., $29.95.
Loading-bench know-how.

Complete Reloading Manuals, Loadbooks, USA.

.22 Hornet, 1990. $7.95.
.22-250 Remington, 1990. 7.95.
.220 Swift, 1990. $7.95.
.222 Remington, 1990. $7.95.
.223 Remington, 1990. $7.95.
.243 Winchester, 1990. $7.95.
.25-06 Remington, 1990. $7.95.
.270 Winchester, 1990. $7.95.
.280 Remington (7mm Exp), 1990. $7.95.
.30 M1 Carbine, 1990. $7.95.
.30-06 Springfield, 1990. $7.95.
.30-30 Winchester, 1990. $7.95.
.300 Weatherby, 1990. $7.95.
.300 Winchester Magnum, 1990. $7.95.
.308 Winchester, 1990. $7.95.
.32 H&R, 1990. $7.95.
.338 Winchester, 1990. $7.95.
.357 Magnum, 1990. $7.95.
.38 Special, 1990. $7.95.
.38 Super, 1990. $7.95.
.380 ACP, 1990. $7.95.
.41 Magnum, 1990. $7.95.
.44 Magnum, 1990. $7.95.
.45 ACP, 1990. $7.95.
.45 Colt, 1990. $7.95.
.45-70 Gov't, 1990. $7.95.
10mm & .41 Handgun, 1990. $7.95.
12 Gauge Shotgun, 1990. $9.95.
20/28 Gauge/.410 Shotgun, 1990. $9.95.
6mm Remington (.244), 1990. $7.95.
6.5x55 Swedish, 1990. $7.95.
7mm Remington Magnum, 990. $7.95.
7x57 Mauser, 1990. $7.95.
7mm-08 Remington, 1990. $7.95.
7.62x39, 1990. $7.95.
8mm Mauser, 1990. $7.95.
9mm Luger, 1990. $7.95.
Remington XP-100, 1990. $10.95.
T/C Contender Pistol, 1990. $17.95.

Corbin Technical Bulletins, Vol. I, Corbin Manufacturing, White City, OR, 1977. 66 pp., $8.00.
Details basic operations and techniques concerning bullet swaging.

Corbin Technical Bulletins, Vol. II, Corbin Manufacturing, White City, OR, 1980. 92 pp., $8.00.
Deals with specific calibers, including the obsolete and experimental, detailing the various styles and weights.

Corbin Technical Bulletins, Vol. III, Corbin Manufacturing, White City, OR, 1983. 98 pp., $8.00.
Collection of papers describing experimental work on cores, shapes and jacket styles.

The Custom Government Model Pistol, by Layne Simpson, Wolfe Publishing, Prescott, AZ, 1992. 650 pp., illus., $24.50.
Includes handloading data and custom improvements for the one of the world's greatest handguns.

Discover Swaging, by David R. Corbin, Stackpole Books, Harrisburg, PA, 1979. 283 pp., illus. $18.95.

A guide to custom swaged bullet design and performance.

*__Elk Rifles, Cartridges and Hunting Tactics,__ by Wayne van Zwoll, Larsen's Outdoor Publishing, Lakeland, FL, 1992. 414 pp., illus. $24.95.

The definitive work on which rifles and cartridges are proper for hunting elk plus the tactics for hunting them.

Encyclopedia and Price Guide of American Paper Shotshells, compiled by Dick Iverson, prices by Bob Strauss, Circus Promotions Corp., Spring, TX, 1991. 436 pp., illus. Paper covers. $25.00.

Pages of headstamps, head types, dimensions, color listed, and 3,100 individual prices.

Experiments of a Handgunner, by Walter F. Roper, Wolfe Publishing, Prescott, AZ, 1989. 202 pp., illus., $37.00.

A limited edition reprint. A listing of experiments with functioning parts of handguns, with targets, stocks, rests, handloading, etc.

Extended Ballistics for the Advanced Rifleman, by Art Blatt, Pachmayr, Inc., Los Angeles, CA, 1986. 379 pp. Spiral bound. $15.95.

Enhanced data on all factory centerfire rifle loads from Federal, Hornady, Norma, Remington, Weatherby, and Winchester.

Federal Gold Medal, 12-Gauge 2³/₄", Ballistic Products, Corcoran, MN, 1990. 12 pp., paper covers, $4.00.

More than 23 loads, along with other information.

Federal Gold Medal 12-Gauge, 3" Hull, Revision IV, Ballistic Products, Corcoran, MN, 1991. 15 pp., paper covers, $4.00.

Hunting loads for different situations.

Fiocchi 12-Gauge 3" Hunting Loads, Ballistic Products, Corcoran, MN, 1985. 12 pp., paper covers, $4.00.

More than 16 loads for various conditions.

Fiocchi 12-Gauge 2³/₄" Hunting Loads, Revision IV, Ballistic Products, Corcoran, MN, 1989. 12 pp., paper covers, $4.00.

Specific loads for cold weather shooting, as well as slug loads.

Firearms Pressure Factors, by Dr. Lloyd Brownell, Wolfe Publishing Co., Prescott, AZ, 1990. 162 pp., illus. $14.00.

The only book available devoted entirely to firearms and pressure. Contains chapters on secondary explosion effect, modern pressure measuring techniques in revolvers and rifles, and Dr. Brownell's series on pressure factors.

Forty Years with the .45-70, by Paul Matthews, Wolfe Publishing, Prescott, AZ, 1989. 147 pp., illus., paper covers, $11.50.

The author's experience handloading this cartridge.

*__G/BP European Sporting Wads, Revised,__ Ballistic Products, Corcoran, MN, 1993. 50 pp., paper covers, $5.00.

High performance loads for use with Europe's finest sporting wads.

*__Game Loads and Practical Ballistics for the American Hunter,__ by Bob Hagel, Wolfe Publishing Co., Prescott, AZ, 1992. 310 pp., illus. $27.90.

Hagel's knowledge gained as a hunter, guide and gun enthusiast is gathered in this informative text.

Gibbs' Cartridges and Front Ignition Loading Technique, by Roger Stowers, Wolfe Publishing Co., Prescott, AZ, 1991. 64 pp., illus. Paper covers. $14.95.

The story of this innovative gunsmith who designed his own wildcat cartridges known for their flat trajectories, high velocity and accuracy.

*__Gun Digest, 1994, 48th Edition,__ edited by Ken Warner, DBI Books, Inc., Northbrook, IL, 1993. 544 pp., illus. Paper Covers. $21.95.

All-new edition of the world's best selling gun book; the only one to make the *USA Today* list of best-selling sports books.

The Gun Digest Black Powder Loading Manual, Revised Edition, by Sam Fadala, DBI Books, Inc., Northbrook, IL, 1991. 320 pp., illus. Paper covers. $16.95.

Revised and expanded edition of this landmark loading book first published in 1982. Covers 600 loads for 120 of the most popular blackpowder rifles, handguns and shotguns.

*__Guns Illustrated, 1994, 26th Edition,__ edited by Harold A. Murtz, DBI Books, Inc., Northbrook, IL, 1993. 320 pp., illus. Paper covers. $18.95.

Truly the Journal of Gun Buffs, this all-new edition consists of articles of interest to every shooter as well as a complete catalog of all U.S. and imported firearms with latest specs and prices.

Guns, Loads, and Hunting Tips, by Bob Hagel, Wolfe Publishing Co., Prescott, AZ, 1986. 509 pp., illus. $19.95.

A large hardcover book packed with shooting, hunting and handloading wisdom.

Handbook of Bullet Swaging No. 7, by David R. Corbin, Corbin Manufacturing and Supply Co., White City, OR, 1990. 200 pp., illus. Paper covers. $10.00.

This handbook explains the most precise method of making quality bullets.

The Handbook of Commercial Bullet Casting, Revised, by Paul B. Moore, Magma Engineering Co., Queen Creek, AZ, 1993. 169 pp., illus., paper covers. $19.95.

A how-to book outlining the field of commercial bullet casting.

Handbook for Shooters and Reloaders, Vol. I, by P.O. Ackley, Salt Lake City, UT, 1970, illus. 567 pp., $15.95.

Handbook for Shooters and Reloaders, Vol. II, by P.O. Ackley, Salt Lake City, UT, 1970, illus. 495 pp., $15.95

A new printing with specific new material.

Handbook of Metallic Cartridge Reloading, by Edward Matunas, Winchester Press, Piscataway, NJ, 1981. 272 pp., illus. $19.95.

Up-to-date, comprehensive loading tables prepared by four major powder manufacturers.

Handgun Reloading, The Gun Digest Book of by Dean A. Grennell and Wiley M. Clapp, DBI Books, Inc., Northbrook, IL, 1987. 256 pp., illus. Paper covers. $15.95.

Detailed discussions of all aspects of reloading for handguns, from basic to complex. New loading data.

Handloader's Bullet Making Annual Vol. I, Wolfe Publishing, Prescott, AZ, 1990. 120 pp., paper covers, $6.95.

Collection of articles from *Handloader's* magazine for the advanced handloader.

Handloader's Bullet Making Annual Vol. II, Wolfe Publishing, Prescott, AZ, 1991. 120 pp., paper covers, $6.95.

Collection of articles from *Handloader's* magazine for the advanced handloader.

Handloader's Bullet Making Annual Vol. III, Wolfe Publishing, Prescott, AZ, 1992. 120 pp., paper covers, $6.95.

Collection of articles from *Handloader's* magazine for the advanced handloader.

*__Handloader's Digest 1994, 13th Edition,__ edited by Bob Bell, DBI Books, Inc., Northbrook, IL, 1993. 464 pp., illus. Paper covers. $20.95

Top writers in the field contribute helpful information on techniques and components. Greatly expanded and fully indexed catalog of all currently available loading tools, accessories and components.

Handloader's Guide, by Stanley W. Trzoniec, Stoeger Publishing Co., So. Hackensack, NJ, 1985. 256 pp., illus. Paper covers. $14.95.

The complete step-by-step fully illustrated guide to handloading ammunition.

Handloader's Manual of Cartridge Conversions, by John J. Donnelly, Stoeger Publishing Co., So. Hackensack, NJ, 1986. Unpaginated. $34.95.

From 14 Jones to 70-150 Winchester in English and American cartridges, and from 4.85 U.K. to 15.2x28R Gevelot in metric cartridges. Over 900 cartridges described in detail.

Handloader's Shotgun Special Edition, Wolfe Publishing, Prescott, AZ, 1992. 96 pp., paper covers, $6.95.

Technical features on the latest in handloading and shotgunning techniques.

Handloading, by Bill Davis, Jr., NRA Books, Wash., D.C., 1980. 400 pp., illus. Paper covers. $15.95.

A complete update and expansion of the *NRA Handloader's Guide.*

Handloading for Hunters, by Don Zutz, Winchester Press, Piscataway, NJ, 1977. 288 pp., illus. $30.00.

Precise mixes and loads for different types of game and for various hunting situations with rifle and shotgun.

Hatcher's Notebook, by S. Julian Hatcher, Stackpole Books, Harrisburg, PA, 1992. 488 pp., illus. $29.95.

A reference work for shooters, gunsmiths, ballisticians, historians, hunters and collectors.

The History and Development of Small Arms Ammunition, Volume 1, by George A. Hoyem, Armory Publications, Oceanside, CA, 1991. 230 pp., illus. $75.00.

Military musket, rifle, carbine and primitive machine gun cartridges of the 18th and 19th centuries with the firearms that chambered them.

The History and Development of Small Arms Ammunition, Volume 2, by George A. Hoyem, Armory Publications, Oceanside, CA, 1991. 303 pp., illus. $65.00.

Covers the blackpowder military centerfire rifle, carbine, machine gun and volley gun ammunition used in 28 nations and dominions, together with the firearms that chambered them.

The History and Development of Small Arms Ammunition (British Sporting Rifle) Volume 3, by George A. Hoyem, Armory Publications, Oceanside, CA, 1991. 300 pp., illus. $60.00.

Concentrates on British sporting rifle cartridges that run from the 4-bore through the .600 Nitro to the .297/.230 Morris.

*__Hodgdon Number 26 Data Manual,__ Hodgdon Powder Co., Shawnee Mission, KS, 1993. 800 pp., illus. $19.95.

This company's latest publication on load data, cartridge cases and powder uses. Contains the most recent info and data available.

The Home Guide to Cartridge Conversions, by Maj. George C. Nonte Jr., The Gun Room Press, Highland Park, NJ, 1976. 404 pp., illus. $24.95.

Revised and updated version of Nonte's definitive work on the alteration of cartridge cases for use in guns for which they were not intended.

Hornady Handbook of Cartridge Reloading, Fourth Edition, Hornady Mfg. Co., Grand Island, NE, 1991. 1124 pp., illus., Two Volume Set, $27.95.

New edition of this reloading handbook. Latest loads, ballistic information, etc.

How to Load the 16-Gauge, Ballistic Products, Corcoran, MN, 1991. 14 pp., paper covers, $5.00.

Lead and steel loads for the Sweet Sixteen.

How to Reload Better for Upland Bird Hunting, Revised, Ballistic Products, Corcoran, MN, 1992. 32 pp., paper covers, $5.00.

More than 18 loads for various winged game under varying conditions.

How to Reload Great Hunting Shotgun Shells, Volume II, by Dave Fackler, Ballistic Products, Corcoran, MN, 1979. 56 pp., paper covers, $5.00.

A basic reloading shotgun manual with loads and ballistic information.

How to Use Decoys on Field and Water, Ballistic Products, Corcoran, MN, 1991. 24 pp., paper covers, $4.00.

Learn about the art of using decoys.

The Hunter's Shooting Guide, by Jack O'Connor, Outdoor Life Books, New York, NY, 1982. 176 pp., illus. Paper covers. $5.95.

A classic covering rifles, cartridges, shooting techniques for shotguns/rifles/handguns.

The Ideal Handbook of Useful Information for Shooters, No. 15, originally published by Ideal Manufacturing Co., reprinted by Wolfe Publishing Co., Prescott, AZ, 1991. 142 pp., illus. Paper covers. $10.95.

A facsimile reprint of one of the early Ideal Handbooks.

*__The Ideal Handbook, No. 5__, Facsimile reprint by Armory Publications, Oceanside, CA, 1993. 80 pp., illus. Paper covers. $12.95.
A limited reprinting of the rare 1893 edition of the handbook issues by the Ideal Manufacturing Co., of New Haven, CT.

Identification of Firearms and Forensic Ballistics, by Major Gerald Burrard, Wolfe Publishing, Prescott, AZ, 1964. 217 pp., illus., $38.00.
The fundamental essentials of firearms and ballistics of forensic importance.

The Illustrated Reference of Cartridge Dimensions, Wolfe Publishing, Prescott, AZ, 1993. 343 pp., illus., $19.00.
Comprehensive volume of dimensions for more than 300 cartridges, standard and metric.

IMR Handloader's Guide for Smokeless Powders, IMR Powder Co., Plattsburgh, NY, 1990. 52 pp., paper covers, Free.
Load data for shotshell, rifle and handgun using the various powders the company offers.

The Law Enforcement Book of Weapons, Ammunition and Training Procedures, Handguns, Rifles and Shotguns, by Mason Williams, Charles C. Thomas, Publisher, Springfield, IL, 1977. 496 pp., illus. $135.00.
Data on firearms, firearm training, and ballistics.

Load Log Book, Ballistic Products, Corcoran, MN, 1990. Paper covers, $14.95.
Helps you keep track of loads and results.

Loading Booklet for Accurate Smokeless Powders, Fourth Edition, Accurate Arms Co., McEwen, TN, 1989. 32 pp., paper covers, $1.00.
Load data using the company's powders for shotshell, handgun and rifle cartridges.

*__Loading the Black Powder Rifle Cartridge,__ by Paul A Matthews, Wolfe Publishing Co., Prescott, AZ, 1993. 121 pp., illus. Paper covers. $22.50.
Author Matthews brings the black powder cartridge shooter valuable information on the basics, including cartridge care, lubes and moulds, powder charges and developing and testing loads in his usual authoritative style.

Loads and Information Concerning the AA Winchester 12-Gauge 2$^3/_4$" Hull, Ballistic Products, Corcoran, MN, 1989. 16 pp., paper covers, $2.00.
Technical information and numerous loads.

Lyman Cast Bullet Handbook, 3rd Edition, edited by C. Kenneth Ramage, Lyman Publications, Middlefield, CT, 1980. 416 pp., illus. Paper covers. $18.95.
Information on more than 5000 tested cast bullet loads and 19 pages of trajectory and wind drift tables for cast bullets.

Lyman Black Powder Handbook, ed. by C. Kenneth Ramage, Lyman Products for Shooters, Middlefield, CT, 1975. 239 pp., illus. Paper covers. $14.95.
Comprehensive load information for the modern blackpowder shooter.

Lyman Pistol & Revolver Handbook, edited by C. Kenneth Ramage, Lyman Publications, Middlefield, CT, 1978. 280 pp., illus. Paper covers. $14.95.
An extensive reference of load and trajectory data for the handgun.

*__Lyman Reloading Handbook No. 47,__ edited by Edward A. Matunas, Lyman Publications, Middlefield, CT, 1992. 480 pp., illus. Paper covers. $19.95.
"The world's most comprehensive reloading manual." Complete "How to Reload" information. Expanded data section with all the newest rifle and pistol calibers.

Lyman Shotshell Handbook, 3rd Edition, edited by C. Kenneth Ramage, Lyman Publications, Middlefield, CT, 1984. 312 pp., illus. Paper covers. $18.95.
Has 2000 loads, including slugs and buckshot, plus feature articles and a full color I.D. section.

Making Loading Dies & Bullet Molds, by H. Hoffman, H&P Publishing, San Angelo, TX, 1991. 230 pp., $19.95.
A primer on how to design and make loading equipment.

Manual of Pistol and Revolver Cartridges, Volume 2, Centerfire U.S. and British Calibers, by Hans A. Erlmeier and Jakob H. Brandt, Journal-Verlag, Wiesbaden, Germany, 1981. 270 pp., illus. $34.95.
Catalog system allows cartridges to be traced by caliber or alphabetically.

Metallic Cartridge Reloading, 2nd Edition, by Edward A. Matunas, DBI Books, Inc., Northbrook, IL., 1988. 320 pp., illus. Paper covers. $17.95.
A true reloading manual with a wealth of invaluable technical data provided by a recognized expert.

The Mighty 10-Gauge, Revision IV, by Dave Fackler, Ballistic Products, Corcoran, MN, 1987. 64 pp., paper covers, $6.00.
Reloading manual and overview of this big bore.

Military Rifle & Machine Gun Cartridges, by Jean Huon, Paladin Press, Boulder, Co. 1990. 392 pp., illus., $34.95.
Describes the primary types of military cartridges and their principal loadings, as well as their characteristics, origins and use.

Modern Handloading, by Maj. Geo. C. Nonte, Winchester Press, Piscataway, NJ, 1972. 416 pp., illus. $15.00.
Covers all aspects of metallic and shotshell ammunition loading, plus more loads than any book in print.

Modern Practical Ballistics, by Art Pejsa, Pejsa Ballistics, Minneapolis, MN, 1990. 150 pp., illus. $24.95.
Covers all aspects of ballistics and new, simplified methods. Clear examples illustrate new, easy, but very accurate, formulas.

Modern Shotguns & Loads, by Charles Askins, Wolfe Publishing, Prescott, AZ, 1992. 432 pp., $30.00.
Shotgun history, ammunition, handloading, and the principles and terms of wingshooting are explained.

Nosler Reloading Manual No. 3, edited by Gail Root, Nosler Bullets, Inc., Bend, OR, 1989. 516 pp., illus. $21.95.
All-new book. New format including feature articles and cartridge introductions by well-known shooters, gun writers and editors.

NRA Firearms Fact Book, by the editors of NRA, National Rifle Association, Washington, DC, 1991. 330 pp., illus., paper covers, $10.95.
The second, revised edition of the classic *NRA Firearms and Ammunition Fact Book.* Covers gun collecting, firearms safety, ballistics and general references.

Outdoor Life Gun Data Book, by F. Philip Rice, Outdoor Life Books, New York, NY, 1987. 412 pp., illus. $27.95.
All the facts and figures that hunters, marksmen, handloaders and other gun enthusiasts need to know.

Pagoda Design Loads, Ballistic Products, Corcoran, MN, 1992. 20 pp., paper covers, $5.00.
Special loads using a second gas seal for better powder burning.

The Paper Jacket, by Paul A. Matthews, Wolfe Publishing, Prescott, AZ, 1991. 140 pp., illus., paper covers, $13.50.
Up-to-date and accurate information about paper-patched bullets.

Pet Loads, Third Edition, by Ken Waters, Wolfe Publishing, Prescott, AZ, 1986. Two Volumes, 636 pp., $29.50.
Comprehensive work on over 100 cartridges. Incorporates supplements 1-12.

Supplements to Pet Loads, Third Edition, by Ken Waters.
Supplement No. 13, 1989. 16 pp., $8.50.
Supplement No. 14, 1990. 16 pp., $8.50.
Supplement No. 15, 1990. 16 pp., $8.50.
Supplement No. 16, 1991. 36 pp., $8.50.
Supplement No. 17, 1992. 36 pp., $10.50.
*__Supplement No. 18,__ 1993. 36 pp., $10.50.

The Powder Manual, Ballistic Products, Corcoran, MN, 1991. 56 pp., paper covers, $6.00.
A guide to shotgun powders and when to use them.

Practical Dope on the .22, by F.C. Ness, Wolfe Publishing, Prescott, AZ, 1989. 313 pp., $39.00.
History, development, characteristics, ballistics and game killing power of this small bore.

Practical Handgun Ballistics, by Mason Williams, Charles C. Thomas, Publisher, Springfield, IL, 1980. 215 pp., illus. $55.00.
Factual information on the practical aspects of ammunition performance in revolvers and pistols.

Precision Handloading, by John Withers, Stoeger Publishing Co., So. Hackensack, NJ, 1985. 224 pp., illus. Paper covers. $12.95.
An entirely new approach to handloading ammunition.

*__Prices Paid for British Sporting Rifle Cartridges,__ by Bill Fleming, Armory Publications, Oceanside, CA, 1992. 31 pp. Paper covers. $15.00.
A list reflecting the relative scarcity of case types, particular load variations, and unusual headstamps of cartridges for British sporting rifles.

Propellant Profiles New and Expanded, 3rd Edition, Wolfe Publishing Co., Prescott, AZ, 1991. Paper covers. $16.95.
Convenient reference of powders available to American reloaders from 25 years of *Handloader* features.

Ranger-Plus Loads, Revision IV, Ballistic Products, Corcoran, MN, 1992. 34 pp., paper covers, $4.00.
Numerous loads for the Ranger-Plus wad.

*__RCBS Cartridge & Chamber Drawings,__ Oroville, CA, 1993. 120 pp., illus., $75.00.
A reference book including the SAAMI drawings for the most popular calibers.

RCBS Cast Bullet Manual, Omark Industries, Lewiston, ID, 1986. 172 pp., $9.95.
An introduction to the casting and loading of cast bullets for rifle and handgun.

Rediscover Swaging, by David R. Corbin, Corbin Manufacturing, White City, OR, 1989. 240 pp., illus. $24.50.
Covers the swaged bullet making process, along with a brief history.

Reloader's Guide, 3rd Edition, by R.A. Steindler, Stoeger Publishing Co., So. Hackensack, NJ, 1984. 224 pp., illus. Paper covers. $11.95.
Complete, fully illustrated step-by-step guide to handloading ammunition. The very latest in reloading information for the shotgunner.

Reloaders' Guide for Hercules Smokeless Powders, Hercules Inc., Wilmington, DE, 1991. 58 pp., paper covers. Free.
Load data using the company's powders for handguns, rifles and shotguns.

*__Reloading for Shotgunners, 3rd Edition,__ by Edward A. Matunas, DBI Books, Inc., Northbrook, IL, 1993. 288 pp., illus. Paper covers. $16.95. (October '93)
Expanded reloading tables with over 2,000 loads. Bushing charts for every major press and component maker. All new presentation on all aspects of shotshell reloading by one of the top experts in the field.

Reloading Tools, Sights and Telescopes for Single Shot Rifles, by Gerald O. Kelver, Brighton, CO, 1982. 163 pp., illus. Paper covers. $15.00.
A listing of most of the famous makers of reloading tools, sights and telescopes with a brief description of the products they manufactured.

Remington 12-Gauge 3" Hunting Loads, Revision IV, Ballistic Products, Corcoran, MN, 1989. 15 pp., paper covers, $4.00.
Loads to improve your game shooting.

Remington Type 5 SP12 12-Gauge 3" Hull Loads for Hunting, Revised, Ballistic Products, Corcoran, MN, 1989. 15 pp., paper covers, $2.00.
A wide spectrum of reloading tips and loads.

Rifleman's Handbook: A Shooter's Guide to Rifles, Reloading & Results, by Rick Jamison, NRA Publications, Washington, DC, 1990. 303 pp., illus. $21.95.

Helpful tips on precision reloading, how to squeeze incredible accuracy out of an "everyday" rifle, etc.

Roll Crimper's Manual, Ballistic Products, Corcoran, MN, 1992. 40 pp., paper covers, $5.00.

The complete loading and instructional manual for roll-crimped loads.

Scot Powder Co. Reloading Manual, Seventh Edition, Scot Powder Co. of Ohio, McArthur, OH, 1992. 52 pp., paper covers, Free.

Load data and general guidelines for reloading shotshell, handgun or rifle cartridges.

.17 Caliber Data Book, Saunders' Gun And Machine Shop, Manchester, IA 1993. $15.00

Load data for 31 different rifles, as well as a listing of .17 accessories.

The Shooter's Inventory Book, Wolfe Publ., Prescott, AZ, 1985. 32 pp., $3.95.

A record-keeping log allowing an owner to inventory his firearms equipment for insurance, tax or other purposes.

Shooting and Hunting Buyer's Guide, Wolfe Publishing, Prescott, AZ, 1992. 112 pp., paper covers, $6.95.

Critical and scientific evaluations of the year's new products.

Shot Shell Boxes: Prices Realized at Auction 1985-1990, compiled by Bob Strauss, Circus Promotions Corp., Spring, TX, 2nd edition, 1990. 148 pp., illus. Paper covers. $12.00.

Actual prices realized at all major auctions over the past five years.

Shotgun Stuff, by Don Zutz, Wolfe Publishing, Prescott, AZ, 1991. 172 pp., illus., soft covers, $19.95.

Collection of ideas covering the various aspects of smoothbore shooting.

The Shotshell in the United States, by Richard J. Iverson, Circus Promotions Corp., Jefferson, ME, 1988. 193 pp., illus. Paper covers. $35.00.

Lists manufacturers, distributors, trade brands, headstamps, gauges, shot sizes, colors and configurations.

Sierra Handgun Manual, 3rd Edition, edited by Kenneth Ramage, Sierra Bullets, Santa Fe Springs, CA, 1990. 704 pp., illus. 3-ring binder. $19.95.

New listings for XP-100 and Contender pistols and TCU cartridges...part of a new single shot section. Covers the latest loads for 10mm Auto, 455 Super Mag, and Accurate powders.

Sierra Rifle Manual, 3rd Edition, edited by Kenneth Ramage, Sierra Bullets, Santa Fe Springs, CA, 1990. 856 pp., illus. 3-ring binder. $24.95.

Updated load information with new powder listings and a helpful tips.

Sixguns, by Elmer Keith, Wolfe Publishing, Prescott, AZ, 1992. 336 pp., hardcover. $34.95.

The history, selection, repair, care, loading and use of this historic frontiersman's friend—the one-hand firearm.

Sixgun Cartridges and Loads, by Elmer Keith, The Gun Room Press, Highland Park, NJ, 1986. 151 pp., illus. $24.95.

A manual covering the selection, uses and loading of the most suitable and popular revolver cartridges. Originally published in 1936. Reprint.

Slug and Buckshot Manual, Ballistic Products, Corcoran, MN, 1983. 33 pp., paper covers, $5.00. Addendum $2.00.

A guide to slug reloading with many techniques and tips to improve shooting.

Small Arms Design and Ballistics, Volume 1, by Col. Townsend Whelen, Wolfe Publishing Co., Prescott, AZ, 1991. 352 pp., illus. $45.00.

Reprinting of this sought-after book dealing with small arms in general, barrels in general, breech actions, stocks and sights, ammunition, etc.

Small Arms Design and Ballistics, Volume 2, by Col. Townsend Whelen, Wolfe Publishing Co., Prescott, AZ, 1991. 314 pp., illus. $45.00.

Covers interior and exterior ballistics; trajectories; wounding effects; pressures and velocities; recoil, jump and vibration; shotgun ballistics; handloading ammunition, etc.

Speer Reloading Manual Number 11, edited by members of the Speer research staff, Omark Industries, Lewiston, ID, 1987. 621 pp., illus. $13.95.

Reloading manual for rifles and pistols.

SPG Black Powder Cartridge Reloading Primer, by Mike Venturino & Steve Garbe, Livingston, MT, 1992. 120 pp., $19.95.

Covers blackpowder reloading and gives individual reloading data.

The Sporting Ballistics Book, by Charles W. Matthews, Bill Matthews, Inc., Lakewood, CO, 1992. 182 pp. Wirebound. $19.95.

A useful book for those interested in doing their own exterior-ballistic calculations without the aid of a computer.

Sporting Clays, Loading and Shooting, Ballistic Products, Corcoran, MN, 1991. 44 pp., paper covers, $5.00.

Information to improve your loads and scores.

Status of Steel, Revision VI, Ballistic Products, Corcoran, MN, 1991. 78 pp., paper covers, $5.00.

Instructional guide to the use of steel shot.

Steel Shotshell Reloading Handbook, Reloading Specialties, Inc., Pine Island, MN, 1992. 65 pp., $3.99.

An instructional reference guide featuring the newest recipies for steel shot.

Subject Index to American Rifleman Magazine (1976-1990), Tioga Engineering Co., Wellsboro, PA, 1992. 68 pp., paper covers. $16.00.

Detailed subject listing of the articles published during that 14-year time span.

Tables of Bullet Performance, by Philip Mannes, Wolfe Publishing, Prescott, AZ, 1979. 420 pp., paper covers, $17.50.

Projectile ballistics for many different bullets and loads are covered in these tables.

The .30-'06, A Sourcebook for the Advanced Handloader, by W.L. Godfrey, Mountain South, Barnwell, SC, 1990. 400+ pp., illus. $24.95.

Source book on this cartridge's ballistics with eight different bullet weights and more than 50 powders, including blackpowder.

.38 Super Reprint, Wolfe Publishing, Prescott, AZ, 1978. 16 pp., $3.00.

The 1978 article describing the problems with headspacing and pressure in this cartridge.

28-Gauge Loading & Information, Ballistic Products, Corcoran, MN, 1989. 12 pp., paper covers, $4.00.

Specific load data information about this special gauge.

Twenty-Two Caliber Varmint Rifles, by Charles Landis, Wolfe Publishing, Prescott, AZ, 1991. 535 pp., $32.00.

An overview of .22 varmint rifles, cartridges, bullets and loads.

Ultimate in Rifle Accuracy, by Glenn Newick, Benchrest and Bucks, Houston, TX, 1989. 200 pp., illus., $34.95.

Getting the most out of your equipment and yourself.

***Varmints and Small Game Rifles and Cartridges,** Wolfe Publishing, Prescott, AZ, 1993. 250 pp., $26.00.

The definitive book on small caliber rifles and cartridges from .17 to 6mm.

VihtaVuori Oy Reloading Guide, VihtaVuori Oy, FINLAND, 1992. 19 pp., Free.

Load data for handgun and rifle cartridges, as well as an overview of the company's powders.

Why Not Load Your Own? by Col. T. Whelen, A.S. Barnes, New York, 1957, 4th ed., rev. 237 pp., illus. $10.95.

A basic reference on handloading, describing each step, materials and equipment. Loads for popular cartridges are given.

***Wildcat Cartridges, Volume I,** Wolfe Publishing Company, Prescott, AZ, 1992. 125 pp. Soft cover. $16.95.

From *Handloader* magazine, the more popular and famous wildcats are profiled.

***Wildcat Cartridges, Volume II,** compiled from *Handloader* and *Rifle* magazine articles written by featured authors, Wolfe Publishing Co., Prescott, AZ, 1992. 971 pp., illus. Paper covers. $34.95.

This volume details rifle and handgun cartridges from the 14-221 to the 460 Van Horn. A comprehensive work containing loading tables and commentary.

***Winchester Reloading Components Catalog, 13th Edition,** Winchester Technical Services Department, East Alton, IL, 1993. 52 pp., illus. Free.

Contains reloading data for shotshell, centerfire rifle and pistol ammunition, as well as detailing their component offerings.

***World Directory of Custom Bullet Makers,** Corbin Manufacturing, White City, OR, 1993, 200 pp., $24.50.

Commercial listing of the names and addresses and what they produce.

Yours Truly, Harvey Donaldson, by Harvey Donaldson, Wolfe Publ. Co., Inc., Prescott, AZ, 1980. 288 pp., illus. $19.50.

Reprint of the famous columns by Harvey Donaldson which appeared in "Handloader" from May 1966 through December 1972.

ORGANIZATIONS & PUBLICATIONS

ORGANIZATIONS

Amateur Trapshooting Assn.
601 W. National Rd., Vandalia, OH 45377

The Cast Bullet Assn., Inc.
Ralland J. Fortier, Membership Director, 4103 Foxcraft Dr., Traverse City, MI 49684

Fifty Caliber Shooters Assn.
11469 Olive St. Rd., Suite 50, St. Louis, MO 63141

International Benchrest Shooters
Joan Borden, RD 1, Box 244A, Tunkhannock, PA 18657

IHMSA (Intl. Handgun Metallic Silhouette Assn.)
Frank Scotto, 127 Winthrop Terr., Meriden, CT 06450

National Bench Rest Shooters Assn., Inc.
Pat Baggett, 2027 Buffalo, Levelland, TX 79336

National Muzzle Loading Rifle Assn.
Box 67, Friendship, IN 47021

National Reloading Manufacturers Assn.
One Centerpointe Dr., Suite 300, Lake Oswego, OR 97035

National Rifle Assn. of America
1600 Rhode Island Ave., NW, Washington, DC 20036

National Skeet Shooting Assn.
Mike Hampton, Exec. Director, P.O. Box 680007, San Antonio, TX 78268-0007

National Sporting Clays Association
P.O. Box 680007, San Antonio, TX 78268/800-877-5338

Sporting Arms & Ammunition Manufacturers Institute (SAAMI)
Flintlock Ridge Office Center, 11 Mile Hill Rd., Newtown, CT 06470-2359/203-426-1320; FAX: 203-426-1087

Sporting Clays of America (SCA)
Linda Fairchild, Director of Membership Services, 9 Mott Ave., Suite 103, Norwalk, CT 06850/203-831-8483; FAX: 203-831-8497

USPSA/IPSC
Dave Stanford, P.O. Box 811, Sedro Woolley, WA 98284/206-855-2245

The Varmint Hunters Assn., Inc.
Box 730, Lone Grove, OK 73443/405-657-3098

The Wildcatters
P.O. Box 170, Greenville, WI 54942

The Women's Shooting Sports Foundation (WSSF)
Glynne Moseley, 1505 Highway 6 South, Suite 103, Houston, TX 77077

PUBLICATIONS

American Firearms Industry
Nat'l. Assn. of Federally Licensed Firearms Dealers, 2455 E. Sunrise Blvd., Ft. Lauderdale, FL 33304. $25.00 yr. For firearms retailers, distributors and manufacturers.

American Handgunner*
591 Camino de la Reina, Suite 200, San Diego, CA 92108. $16.75 yr. Articles for handgun enthusiasts, competitors, police and hunters.

American Rifleman (M)
National Rifle Assn., 1600 Rhode Island Ave., NW, Washington, DC 20036. Publications Div., 470 Spring Park Pl., Suite 1000, Herndon, VA 22070. $25.00 yr. Firearms articles of all kinds.

The Cast Bullet*(M)
Official journal of The Cast Bullet Assn. Director of Membership, 4103 Foxcraft Dr., Traverse City, MI 49684. Annual membership dues $14, includes 6 issues.

Gun List
700 E. State St., Iola, WI 54990. $24.95 yr. (26 issues); $46.50 2 yrs. (52 issues). Indexed market publication for firearms collectors and active shooters; guns, supplies and services.

Gun Show Calendar (Q)
700 E. State St., Iola, WI 54990. $12.95 yr. (4 issues). Gun shows listed chronologically by date, and alphabetically by state.

Gun World
Gallant/Charger Publications, Inc., 34249 Camino Capistrano, Capistrano Beach, CA 92624. $20.00 yr. For the hunting, reloading and shooting enthusiast.

Guns & Ammo
Petersen Publishing Co., 6420 Wilshire Blvd., Los Angeles, CA 90048. $21.94 yr. Guns, shooting, and technical articles.

Guns
Guns Magazine, P.O. Box 85201, San Diego, CA 92138. $19.95 yr. In-depth articles on a wide range of guns, shooting equipment and related accessories for gun collectors, hunters and shooters.

Guns Review
Ravenhill Publishing Co. Ltd., Box 35, Standard House, Bonhill St., London EC 2A 4DA, England. £20.00 sterling (approx. U.S. $38 USA & Canada) yr. For collectors and shooters.

Handgunning (Q)
PJS Publications, News Plaza, P.O. Box 1790, Peoria, IL 61656. Cover price $3.95; subscriptions $19.95 for 6 issues. Various recreational uses of handguns; hunting, silhouette, practical pistol and target shooting.

Handloader*
Wolfe Publishing Co., 6471 Airpark Dr., Prescott, AZ 86301. $19.00 yr. The journal of ammunition reloading.

INSIGHTS*
NRA, 1600 Rhode Island Ave., NW, Washington, DC 20036. Editor, John E. Robbins. $10.00 yr., which includes NRA junior membership; $10.00 for adult subscriptions (12 issues). Plenty of details for the young hunter and target shooter; emphasizes gun safety, marksmanship training, hunting skills.

Muzzle Blasts (M)
National Muzzle Loading Rifle Assn., P.O. Box 67, Friendship, IN 47021. $30.00 yr. annual membership. For the blackpowder shooter.

Muzzleloader Magazine*
Rebel Publishing Co., Inc., Dept. Gun, Route 5, Box 347-M, Texarkana, TX 75501. $14.00 U.S.; $17.00 U.S. for foreign subscribers a yr. The publication for blackpowder shooters.

Precision Shooting
Precision Shooting, Inc., 37 Burnham St., East Hartford, CT 06108. $25.00 yr. Journal of the International Benchrest Shooters, and target shooting in general. Also considerable coverage of varmint shooting, as well as big bore, small bore, schuetzen, lead bullet and wildcats.

Rifle*
Wolfe Publishing Co., 6471 Airpark Dr., Prescott, AZ 86301. $19.00 yr. The sporting firearms journal.

Safari* (M)
Safari Magazine, 4800 W. Gates Pass Rd., Tucson, AZ 85745/602-620-1220. $30.00 (6 times). The journal of big game hunting, published by Safari Club International. Also publish *Safari Times*, a monthly newspaper, included in price of $30.00 field membership.

Second Amendment Reporter
Second Amendment Foundation, James Madison Bldg., 12500 NE 10th Pl., Bellevue, WA 98005. $15.00 yr. (non-contributors).

Shooting Times
PJS Publications, News Plaza, P.O. Box 1790, Peoria, IL 61656. $19.98 yr. Guns, shooting, reloading; articles on every gun activity.

The Shotgun News‡
Snell Publishing Co., Box 669, Hastings, NE 68902. $20.00 yr.; all other countries $100.00 yr. Sample copy $3.00. Gun ads of all kinds.

Shotgun Sports
P.O. Box 6810, Auburn, CA 95603/916-889-2220; FAX:916-889-9106. $26.00 yr. Trapshooting how-to's, shotshell reloading, shotgun patterning, shotgun tests and evaluations, Sporting Clays action, waterfowl/upland hunting.

The Skeet Shooting Review
National Skeet Shooting Assn., P.O. Box 680007, San Antonio, TX 78268. $15.00 yr. (Assn. membership of $20.00 includes mag.) Competition results, personality profiles of top Skeet shooters, how-to articles, technical, reloading information.

Sporting Clays Magazine*
5211 South Washington Ave., Titusville, FL 32780. $26.00 yr. (6 issues).

Sporting Gun
Bretton Court, Bretton, Peterborough PE3 8DZ, England. £24.00 (approx. U.S. $36.00), airmail £33.00 yr. For the game and clay enthusiasts.

Trap & Field
1200 Waterway Blvd., Indianapolis, IN 46202. $22.00 yr. Official publ. Amateur Trapshooting Assn. Scores, averages, trapshooting articles.

The Varmint Hunter Magazine (Q)
The Varmint Hunters Assn., Box 730, Lone Grove, OK 73443/405-657-3098. $24.00 yr.

DIRECTORY

OF THE HANDLOADER'S TRADE

The **Product Directory** contains a total of 57 handloading product categories. Each category lists manufacturers of that handloading product.

The **Manufacturers' Directory** lists the manufacturers alphabetically with their addresses, phone numbers and FAX numbers, if available.

DIRECTORY OF THE HANDLOADER'S TRADE INDEX

PRODUCT DIRECTORY

AMMUNITION COMPONENTS, BULLETS

A-Square Co., Inc.
Action Bullets, Inc.
Alaska Bullet Works
Allred Bullet Co.
Alpha LaFranck Enterprises
American Bullets
Armfield Custom Bullets
Ballard Built
Banaczkowski Bullets
Barnes Bullets, Inc.
Bell Reloading, Inc.
Berger Bullets, Ltd.
Berry's Bullets
Bitterroot Bullet Co.
Black Mountain Bullets
Blue Mountain Bullets
Blue Point Mfg. Co.
Brownells, Inc.
BRP, Inc. High Performance Cast Bullets
Bruno Shooters Supply
Buckeye Custom Bullets
Bull-X, Inc.
Bullet, Inc.
Bullseye Bullets
Burling Bullets
Calhoon Varmint Bullets, James
Canadian Custom Bullets
Carnahan Bullets
Carroll Bullets
Cartridges Unlimited
CheVron Bullets
Circle M Custom Bullets
Cook Bullets
Cor-Bon, Inc.
Creative Cartridge Co.
Cummings Bullets
Custom Bullets by Hoffman
Cutsinger Bench Rest Bullets
C.W. Cartridge Co.
D&J Bullet Co. & Custom Gun Shop, Inc.
Denver Bullets, Inc.
DKT, Inc.
Dohring Bullets
Eagle Flight Bullet co.
Ed's Custom Bullets
Eichelberger Bullets, Wm.
Elland Custom Bullets
Eureka Bullets
Fowler Bullets
Foy Custom Bullets
Freedom Arms, Inc.
Fusilier Bullets
G&C Bullet Co., Inc.
Gise Bullets
Gotz Bullets
Grand Falls Bullets, Inc.
Granite Custom Bullets
Green Bay Bullets
Grizzly Bullets
Group Tight Bullets
Gun City
Hammets VLD Bullets
Harrison Bullet Works
Hart & Son, Inc., Robert W.
Hawk Laboratories, Inc.
Heidenstrom Bullets
Higgs Bullets
High Country Custom Bullets
Hobson Precision Mfg. Co.
Hornady Mfg. Co.
HT Bullets
Huntington Die Specialties
Idaho Bullets
IMI
J&L Superior Bullets
Jensen Bullets
Jester Bullets
JLK Bullets
Kasmarsik Bullets
Kaswer Custom, Inc.
Keith's Bullets
Ken's Kustom Kartridges
Keystone Bullets
Kodiak Custom Bullets
Lachaussee, S.A.
Lane Bullets, Inc.
Lathrop's, Inc.
Lomont Precision Bullets
M&D Munitions Ltd.
Magnus Bullets
Maine Custom Bullets
Marchmon Bullets
Master Class Bullets
McKenzie, Lynton
Miller Enterprises, Inc.
Mitchell Bullets, R.F.
MoLoc Bullets
Montana Precision Swaging
Mulhern, Rick
Mushroom Express Bullet Co.
Nagel's Bullets
National Bullet Co.
Naval Ordnance Works
Northern Precision Custom Swaged Bullets
Nosler, Inc.
Old Wagon Bullets
Old Western Scrounger, Inc., The
Ordnance Works, The
Page Custom Bullets
Patrick Bullets
Phillippi Custom Bullets, Justin
Precision Bullet Co.
Precision Cast Bullets
Precision Reloading, Inc.
Prescott Projectile Co.
Price Bullets, Patrick W.
Rainier Ballistics Corp.
Redwood Bullet Works
Remington Arms Co., Inc.
Rencher Bullets
Renner Co., R.J.
Rubright Bullets
RWS
Schneider Bullets
Shappy Bullets
Sierra Bullets
Sioux Bullets
Small Group Bullets
Speer Products
Stanley Bullets
Star Custom Bullets
Stark's Bullet Mfg.
Swift Bullet Co.
3-D Ammunition & Bullets
TCCI
Trophy Bonded Bullets, Inc.
Tru-Flight Bullet Co.
USAC
Vann Custom Bullets
Vincent's Shop
Watson Trophy Match Bullets
Williams Bullet Co., J.R.
Winkle Bullets
Woodland Bullets
Woodleigh
Wyant Bullets
Wyoming Bonded Bullets
Wyoming Casting Co.
Wyoming Custom Bullets
Zero Ammunition Co., Inc.

AMMUNITION COMPONENTS, CASES

A-Square Co., Inc.
Bertram Bullet Co.
Brown Co., E. Arthur
Bruno Shooters Supply
Bull-X, Inc.
Buzztail Brass
Canyon Cartridge Corp.
Classic Brass
DKT, Inc.
Dynamit Nobel-RWS, Inc.
Eichelberger Bullets, Wm.
First Distributors, Inc., Jack
Freedom Arms, Inc.
Gehmann, Walter
Hardin Specialty Dist.
Huntington Die Specialties
Imperial Magnum Corp.
KJM Brass Group
Naval Ordnance Works
Norma
O'Connor Rifle Products Co., Ltd.
Old Western Scrounger, Inc., The
Pomeroy, Robert
Precision Reloading, Inc.
Red Willow Tool & Armory, Inc.
Remington Arms Co., Inc.
RWS
TCCI
Vom Hoffe
Weatherby, Inc.
Winchester Div., Olin Corp.

AMMUNITION COMPONENTS, POWDERS

Accurate Arms Co., Inc.
B-West Imports, Inc.
Hercules, Inc.
Hodgdon Powder Co., Inc.
IMR Powder Co.
Lathrop's, Inc.
Norma
Scot Powder Co.
TCCI
Vihtavuori Oy
Winchester Div., Olin Corp.

AMMUNITION COMPONENTS, PRIMERS

CCI
Dynamit Nobel-RWS, Inc.
Federal Cartridge Co.
Fiocchi of America, Inc.
M&D Munitions Ltd.
Remington Arms Co., Inc.
Winchester Div., Olin Corp.

AMMUNITION COMPONENTS, SHOTSHELL

ACTIV Industries, Inc.
American Products Co.
Ballistic Products, Inc.
Brenneke KG, Wilhelm
Bismuth Cartridge Co.
C&D Special Products
Federal Cartridge Co.
Hornady Mfg. Co.
Lage Uniwad, Inc.
Lawrence Brand Shot
MEC, Inc.
Murmur Corp.
Old Western Scrounger, Inc., The
Pattern Control
Polywad, Inc.
Precision Reloading, Inc.
Reloading Specialties, Inc.
Remington Arms Co., Inc.
Steel Reloading Components, Inc.
Trico Plastics
Vitt/Boos
Windjammer Tournament Wads, Inc.
Wosenitz VHP, Inc.

AMMUNITION, COMMERCIAL

Action Arms Ltd.
ACTIV Industries, Inc.
A-Square Co., Inc.
Black Hills Ammunition
Blammo Ammo
Blount, Inc. Sporting Equipment Division
Bottom Line Shooting Supplies
Buck Stix
Bull-X, Inc.
The BulletMakers Workshop
California Magnum
CBC
Century International Arms, Inc.
ChinaSports, Inc.
Cor-Bon, Inc.
Daisy Mfg. Co.
Diana
Denver Bullets, Inc.
Dynamit Nobel-RWS, Inc.
Eley Ltd.
Elite Ammunition
Enguix Import-Export
Estate Cartridge, Inc.
Federal Cartridge Co.
Fiocchi of America, Inc.
FN Herstal
Gamo
Garrett Cartridges, Inc.
GDL Enterprises
Glaser Safety Slug, Inc.
"Gramps" Antique Cartridges
Hansen Cartridge Co.
Hirtenberger Aktiengesellschaft
Hornady Mfg. Co.
ICI-America
IMI
Jones, J.D.
Kent Cartridge Mfg. Co. Ltd.
Lapua Ltd.
Lethal Force Institute
M&D Munitions Ltd.
Maionchi-L.M.I.
MAGTECH Recreational Products, Inc.
Markell, Inc.
Master Class Bullets
Men—Metallwerk Elisenhuette, GmbH
Midway Arms, Inc.
New England Ammunition Co.
Neutralizer Police Munitions
Old Western Scrounger, Inc., The
Omark Industries
Paragon Sales & Services, Inc.
PMC/Eldorado Cartridge Corp.
Police Bookshelf
Pony Express Reloaders
Precision Delta Corp.
Pro Load Ammunition, Inc.
Ravell Ltd.
Remington Arms Co., Inc.
Rocky Fork Enterprises
Rucker Ammunition Co.
RWS
Safari Gun Co.
Sherwood Intl. Export Corp.
SOS Products Co.
Speer Products
Star Reloading Co., Inc.
3-D Ammunition & Bullets
3-Ten Corp.
USAC
Valor Corp.
Weatherby, Inc.
Winchester Div., Olin Corp.
Wosenitz VHP, Inc.
Zero Ammunition Co., Inc.

AMMUNITION, CUSTOM

AFSCO Ammunition
All American Bullets
Ballistica Maximus North
Ballistica Maximus South
Bertram Bullet Co.
Bottom Line Shooting Supplies
Brynin, Milton
Buck Stix
The BulletMakers Workshop
Cartridges Unlimited
Country Armourer, The
Cubic Shot Shell Co., Inc.
Custom Hunting Ammo & Arms
Custom Tackle & Ammo
Dakota Arms
Deadeye Sport Center
DKT, Inc.
E.A.A. Corp.
Eagle Flight Bullet Co.
Elite Ammunition
Elko Arms, L. Kortz
Ellis Sport Shop, E.W.
Epps "Orillia" Ltd., Ellwood
Estate Cartridge, Inc.
Fitz Pistol Grip Co.
Freedom Arms, Inc.

Garrett Cartridges, Inc.
Gammog, Gregory B. Gally
GDL Enterprises
Glaser Safety Slug, Inc.
"Gramps" Antique Cartridges
Granite Custom Bullets
Hardin Specialty Dist.
Heidenstrom Bullets
Hindman, Ace
Hirtenberger Aktiengesellschaft
Horizons Unlimited
Jensen's Custom Ammunition
Jensen's Firearm Academy
Jett & Co., Inc.
Kaswer Custom, Inc.
Keeler, R.H.
Kent Cartridge Mfg. Co. Ltd.
KJM Brass Group
Lindsley Arms Cartridge Co.
Lomont Precision Bullets, Kent
MagSafe Ammo Co.
Marple & Associates, Dick
McMurdo, Lynn
M&D Munitions Ltd.
Monte Kristo Pistol Grip Co.
Mountain South
Mullins Ammo
Newman Gunshop
Old Western Scrounger, Inc., The
Personal Protection Systems Ltd.
Precision Cartridge
Precision Delta Corp.
Precision Munitions, Inc.
Sanders Custom Gun Service
Sandia Die & Cartridge Co.
SOS Products Co.
Specialty Gunsmithing
Spence, George W.
SSK Industries
Star Custom Bullets
State Arms Gun Co.
Stewart's Gunsmithing
3-D Ammunition & Bullets
Three-Ten Corp.
Vitt/Boos
Weaver Arms Corp.
Westley Richards & Co.
Worthy Products, Inc.
Wosenitz VHP, Inc.
Wyoming Armory, Inc.

AMMUNITION, FOREIGN

Action Arms Ltd.
AFSCO Ammunition
Bertram Bullet Co.
Bottom Line Shooting Supplies
Brenneke KG, Wilhelm
The BulletMakers Workshop
Cartridges Unlimited
CBC
Champion's Choice, Inc.
Cubic Shot Shell Co., Inc.
Diana
Dynamit Nobel-RWS, Inc.
Enguix Import-Export
Estate Cartridge, Inc.
Fiocchi of America, Inc.
FN Herstal
Gamo
"Gramps" Antique Cartridges
Hansen Cartridge Co.
Hirtenberger Aktiengesellschaft
IMI
K.B.I., Inc.
Lapua Ltd.
Maionchi-L.M.I.
MAGTECH Recreational Products, Inc.
Merkuria Ltd.
New England Arms Co.
Old Western Scrounger, Inc., The
Paragon Sales & Services, Inc.
PMC/Eldorado Cartridge Corp.
Precision Delta Corp.
R.E.T. Enterprises
Rocky Fork Enterprises
RWS
Safari Gun Co.
Sako, Ltd.
Samco Global Arms, Inc.
T.F.C. S.p.A.

BOOKS & MANUALS, PUBLISHERS

Accurate Arms Co., Inc.
ADC, Inc.
American Handgunner Magazine
Aplan Antiques & Art, James O.
Armory Publications
Arms & Armour Press, Ltd.
Blacksmith Corp.
Blacktail Mountain Books
Blue Book Publications, Inc.
Brownells, Inc.
Calibre Press, Inc.
Colorado Sutlers Arsenal
Corbin, Inc.
DBI Books, Inc.
Executive Protection Institute
Flores Publications, Inc., J.
Fortress Publications, Inc.
Golden Age Arms Co.
"Gramps" Antique Cartridges
Gun City
Guncraft Sports, Inc.
Gun Hunter Books
Gun Room Press, The
GUNS Magazine
Gunnerman Books
H&P Publishing
Handgun Press
Hercules, Inc.
Hodgdon Powder Co., Inc.
Hornady Mfg. Co.
Hungry Horse Books
IMR Powder Co.
Ironside International Publishers, Inc.
Jackson Arms
King & Co.
Krause Publications
Lane Publishing
LBT
Lyman Products Corp.
Madis, David
Magma Engineering Co.
Martin, J.
McKee Publications
Midway Arms, Inc.
Mountain South
MTM Molded Products Co., Inc.
NECO
New Win Publishing, Inc.
NgraveR Co., The
North Mountain Pine Training Center
Old Western Scrounger, Inc., The
Outdoorsman's Bookstore, The
Pease Accuracy, Bob
Pejsa Ballistics
Petersen Publishing Co.
Pettinger Books, Gerald
PFRB Co.
Pranger, Ed G.
Ravell Ltd.
R.G.-G., Inc.
Riling Arms Books Co., Ray
Rutgers Book Center
Rutgers Gun & Boat Center
Safari Press, Inc.
S.A.F.E.
Scot Powder Co.
Shootin' Accessories, Ltd.
Stackpole Books
Stoeger Publishing Co.
Survival Books/The Larder
Thomas, Charles C.
Threat Management Institute
Trafalgar Square
Trotman, Ken
Vihtavuori Oy
Vintage Industries, Inc.
VSP Publishers
Wahl Corp., Paul
Weisz Antique Gun Parts
Wilderness Sound Productions Ltd.
Winchester Press
Wolfe Publishing Co.

BULLETS, CASE & DIE LUBRICANTS

Armite Laboratories
Blackhawk East
Blackhawk Mountain
Blackhawk West
Blount, Inc. Sporting Equipment Division
Brown Co., E. Arthur
Bullet Swaging Supply, Inc.
CF Ventures
C-H Tool & Die Corp./4-D Custom Die Co.
Camp-Cap Products
Chem-Pak, Inc.
Cooper-Woodward
Corbin, Inc.
Dillon Precision Products, Inc.
Fitz Pistol Grip Co.
Forster Products
GAR
Gozon Corp.
Guardsman Products
Hollywood Engineering
Hornady Mfg. Co.
Huntington Die Specialties
INTEC International, Inc.
Javelina Products
Lane Bullets, Inc.
LBT
Lee Precision, Inc.
Lighthouse Mfg. Co., Inc.
Lithi Bee Bullet Lube
Lyman Products Corp.
M&N Bullet Lube
Magma Engineering Co.
Micro-Lube
Midway Arms, Inc.
Monte Kristo Pistol Grip Co.
Ponsness/Warren
Ravell Ltd.
RCBS
Reardon Products
Redding Reloading Equipment
Rooster Laboratories
Rorschach Precision Products
SAECO
Shay's Gunsmithing
Shooters Accessory Supply
Silver Eagle Machining
Slipshot MTS Group
Small Custom Mould & Bullet Co.
Tamarack Products, Inc.
Thompson Bullet Lube Co.
Thompson/Center Arms
VibraShine, Inc.
Watson Trophy Match Bullets
White Systems, Inc.

BULLET CASTING, FURNACES & POTS

Ballisti-Cast, Inc.
Lee Precision, Inc.
Lyman Products Corp.
Magma Engineering Co.
Necromancer Industries, Inc.
Rapine Bullet Mould Mfg. Co.
RCBS

BULLET CASTING, LEAD

Ames Metal Co.
Busch Metal Merchants, Roger
Essex Metals
Federated-Fry
Graphics Direct
Green, Arthur S.
Liberty Metals
Miller Enterprises, Inc.
Peerless Metals
RSR Corp. (CA)
RSR Corp. (TX)
Signet Metal Corp.
TCSR
Tejas Resource
Wheel Weights Corp.

BULLET CASTING, ACCESSORIES

Advance Car Mover Co., Inc.
Brownells, Inc.
GAR
LBT
Lee Precision, Inc.
Lyman Products Corp.
Magma Engineering Co.
Midway Arms, Inc.
RCBS
Redding Reloading Equipment

BULLET JACKETS & GAS CHECKS

Ballard Built
Berger Bullets
Bullet Swaging Supply, Inc.
C-H Tool & Die Corp./4-D Custom Die Co.
Corbin, Inc.
Hornady Mfg. Co.
J-4, Inc.
Lyman Products Corp.
Sport Flite Manufacturing Co.

BULLET PULLERS

C-H Tool & Die Corp./4-D Custom Die Co.
Forster Products
Hollywood Engineering
Hornady Mfg. Co.
Lyman Products Corp.
Midway Arms, Inc.
Old Western Scrounger, Inc., The
Ponsness/Warren
Quinetics Corp.
RCBS

BULLET TOOLS

C-H Tool & Die Corp./4-D Custom Die Co.
Corbin, Inc.
Eagan, Donald V.
Forster Products
Hart & Son, Inc., Robert W.
Sinclair International, Inc.
Wilson, Inc., L.E.

CARTRIDGES FOR COLLECTORS

Ad Hominem
Ammunition Consulting Services, Inc.
Baekgaard Ltd.
Cameron's
Campbell, Dick
Duffy, Chas. E.
Ed's Gun House
Eichelberger Bullets, Wm.
Epps "Orillia" Ltd., Ellwood
First Distributors, Inc., Jack
Forty Five Ranch Enterprises
Gun City
"Gramps" Antique Cartridges
Hansen & Co.
Idaho Ammunition Service
Kelley's
Lock's Philadelphia Gun Exchange
Montana Outfitters
Mountain Bear Rifle Works, Inc.
Muzzleloaders Etcetera, Inc.
Old Western Scrounger, Inc., The
Paragon Sales & Services, Inc.
Ranch Products
Ravell Ltd.
San Francisco Gun Exchange
Tillinghast, James C.
Ward & Van Valkenburg
Yearout, Lewis E.

CASE CLEANERS & POLISHING MEDIA

American Gas and Chemical Co., Ltd.
Birchwood Laboratories, Inc.
Davis Products, Mike
Dillon Precision Products, Inc.
Flitz International, Ltd.
Forster Products
Hart & Son, Inc., Robert W.
Hornady Mfg. Co.
Iosso Products
RCBS

CASE PREPARATION TOOLS

C-H Tool & Die Corp./4-D Custom Die Co.
Corbin, Inc.
Forster Products
Hart & Son, Inc., Robert W.
Haydon, Russ
Hoehn's Shooting Supply
Hornady Mfg. Co.
K&M Services
Lee Precision, Inc.
Lyman Products Corp.
Marquart Precision Co.
Midway Arms, Inc.
Miller Engineering
Precision Reloading, Inc.
RCBS
Redding Reloading Equipment
Scharch Mfg., Inc.
Sinclair International, Inc.
Synchronized Shooting Systems
Whitetail Design and Engineering Ltd.
Wilson, Inc., L.E.

CASE & AMMUNITION PROCESSORS, SEPARATORS,INSPECTORS, BOXERS

Ammo Load, Inc.
Ben's Machines
Camdex, Inc.
Scharch Mfg., Inc.

CASE TRIMMERS, TRIM DIES & ACCESSORIES

Blue Ridge Machinery and Tools, Inc.
C-H Tool & Die Corp./4-D Custom Die Co.
Dillon Precision Products, Inc.
Forster Products
Hollywood Engineering
Hornady Mfg. Co.
Lee Precision, Inc.
Lyman Products Corp.
OK Weber, Inc.
RCBS
Redding Reloading Equipment
Sinclair International, Inc.
Whitetail Design and Engineering Inc.
Wilson, Inc., L.E.

CASE TUMBLERS, VIBRATORS, MEDIA & ACCESSORIES

Brown Co., E. Arthur
C-H Tool & Die Corp./4-D Custom Die Co.
Corbin, Inc.
Davis Products, Mike
Dillon Precision Products, Inc.
GAR
Hornady Mfg. Co.
Lortone, Inc.
Lyman Products Corp.
Midway Arms, Inc.
Raytech
RCBS
Rooster Laboratories
Tru-Square Metal Prods., Inc.
Vibra-Tek Co.
VibraShine, Inc.
Wilcox All-Pro Tools & Supply

CHRONOGRAPHS & PRESSURE TOOLS

Canons Delcour
Chronotech
Competition Electronics, Inc.
Custom Chronograph, Inc.
D&H Precision Tooling
Dedicated Systems
Lachaussee, S.A.
Oehler Research, Inc.
P.A.C.T., Inc.
Shooting Chrony, Inc.
Stratco, Inc.
Tepeco

CLEANERS & DEGREASERS

American Gas & Chemical Co., Ltd.
Beeman Precision Airguns, Inc.
RIG Products

COMPUTER SOFTWARE/VIDEOS, BALLISTICS & RELOADING

ADC, Inc.
AmBr Software Group Ltd.
Arms, Peripheral Data Systems
Ballistic Program Co., Inc., The
Barnes Bullets, Inc.
Best Load
Blount, Inc. Sporting Equipment Division
Canons Delcour
Corbin Applied Technology
Corbin, Inc.
Country Armourer, The
Data Tech Software Systems
Destination North Software
Exe, Inc.
Ford, Jack
Hornady Mfg. Co.
J.I.T., Ltd.
Lachaussee, S.A.
Lee Precision, Inc.
Load From A Disk
Magma Engineering Co.
Maionchi-L.M.I.
Oehler Research, Inc.
P.A.C.T., Inc.
Pejsa Ballistics
Ravell Ltd.
RCBS
Regional Associates
Sierra Bullets
Tioga Engineering Co., Inc.
Vancini, Carl A./Bestload

DIE ACCESSORIES, METALLIC

Alex, Inc.
C-H Tool & Die Corp./4-D Custom Die Co.
Forster Products
Hornady Mfg. Co.
Lyman Products Corp.
MTM Moulded Products Co., Inc.
RCBS
Redding Reloading Equipment
Whitetail Design and Engineering Ltd.

DIES, METALLIC

A-Square Co., Inc.
Bald Eagle Precision Machine Co.
Bullet Swaging Supply, Inc.
C-H Tool & Die Corp./4-D Custom Die Co.
Carbide Die & Mfg. Co., Inc.
Dillon Precision Products, Inc.
First Distributors, Inc., Jack
Forster Products
Freedom Arms, Inc.
Fremont Tool Works
Hart & Son, Inc., Robert W.
Hollywood Engineering
Hornady Mfg. Co.
Jones Custom Products, Neil
King & Co.
Lee Precision, Inc.
Lyman Products Corp.
MCRW Associates
Niemi Engineering, W.B.
Old Western Scrounger, Inc., The
Ponsness/Warren
RCBS
Redding Reloading Equipment
Star Machine Works
Wilson, Inc., L.E.

DIES, SHOTSHELL

Hollywood Engineering
Hornady Mfg. Co.
Lee Precision, Inc.
MEC, Inc.
Ponsness/Warren
RCBS

DIES, SWAGE

Bullet Swaging Supply, Inc.
C-H Tool & Die Corp./4-D Custom Die Co.
Corbin, Inc.
Hollywood Engineering
Rorschach Precision Products
Sport Flite Manufacturing Co.

GAUGES, CALIPERS & MICROMETERS

Accuracy Components Co.
Accuracy Den, The
Blue Ridge Machinery and Tools, Inc.
C-H Tool & Die Corp./4-D Custom Die Co.
CP Specialties
Clymer Manufacturing Co., Inc.
Dillon Precision Products, Inc.
Forgreens Tool Mfg., Inc.
Forster Products
Hornady Mfg. Co.
K&M Services
Lyman Products Corp.
MEC, Inc.
McKillen & Heyer, Inc.
Midway Arms, Inc.
NECO
Pease Accuracy, Bob
Plum City Ballistic Range
Precision Reloading, Inc.
RCBS
Sinclair International, Inc.
Stoney Point Products, Inc.
Varner's Service
Wilson, Inc., L.E.

GUNS, CLEANING & REFINISHING SUPPLIES

Acculube II, Inc.
Accupro Gun Care
Accuracy Products, S.A.
ADCO International
American Gas & Chemical Co., Ltd.
Armoloy Co. of Ft. Worth
Belltown, Ltd.
Beretta, Dr. Franco
Big 45 Frontier Gun Shop
Bill's Gun Repair
Birchwood Laboratories, Inc.
Blount, Inc. Sporting Equipment Division
Break-Free
Bridgers Best
Brobst, Jim
Browning Arms Co.
Bruno Shooters Supply
Chopie Mfg., Inc.
Clenzoil Corp.
Corbin, Inc.
Crane & Crane Ltd.
Creedmoor Sports, Inc.
Crouse's Country Cover
Custom Products
Decker Shooting Products
Deepeeka Exports Pvt. Ltd.
Dewey Mfg. Co., Inc., J.
Dri-Slide, Inc.
Du-Lite Corp.
Dutchman's Firearms, Inc., The
Dykstra, Doug
Eezox, Inc.
Faith Associates, Inc.
Flitz International Ltd.
Flouramics, Inc.
Forster Products
Forty Five Ranch Enterprises
Frontier Products Co.
G96 Products Co., Inc.
Golden Age Arms Co.
Gozon Corp.
Graves Co.
Guardsman Products
Gun Works, The
Half Moon Rifle Shop
Heatbath Corp.
Hoppe's Div.
INTEC International, Inc.
Iosso Products
Jantz Supply
J-B Bore Cleaner
Johnson Gunsmithing, Inc., Neal G.
Johnston Bros.
Jonad Corp.
Kleen-Bore, Inc.
Kopp, Terry K.
Lee Supplies, Mark
LEM Gun Specialties, Inc.
LPS Laboratories, Inc.
LT Industries, Inc.
Marble Arms Corp.
Micro Sight Co.
Mountain View Sports, Inc.
MPC
Munger, Robert D.
Nesci Enterprises, Inc.
Northern Precision Custom Swaged Bullets
Old World Oil Products
Omark Industries
Ox-Yoke Originals, Inc.
Outers Laboratories
P&M Sales and Service
Parker Gun Finishes
Pendleton Royal
Pflumm Gun Mfg. Co.
Precision Sports
Prolix®
Pro-Shot Products, Inc.
Radiator Specialty Co.
Ravell Ltd.
R&S Industries Corp.
Rice, Keith
Richards Classic Oil Finish, John
Rickard, Inc., Pete
RIG Products
Robar Co.'s, Inc., The

Rusteprufe Laboratories
Rusty Duck Premium Gun Care Products
San Angelo Sports Products, Inc.
Scott, Inc., Tyler
Shooter's Choice
Shootin' Accessories, Ltd.
Slipshot MTS Group
Speer Products
Sports Support Systems, Inc.
Stoney Point Products, Inc.
Svon Corp.
TDP Industries, Inc.
TETRA Gun Lubricants
Texas Platers Supply Co.
T.F.C. S.p.A.
Treso, Inc.
United States Products Co.
Valor Corp.
Van Gorden & Son, Inc., C.S.
Verdemont Fieldsports
Watson Trophy Match Bullets
WD-40 Co.
White Rock Tool & Die
Williams Shootin' Iron Service
Young Country Arms
Z-Coat Industrial Coatings, Inc.

HEARING PROTECTORS

Bausch & Lomb, Inc.
Bilsom Intl., Inc.
Blount, Inc. Sporting Equipment Division
Champion's Choice, Inc.
Clark Co., Inc., David
Cobra Gunskin
E-A-R, Inc.
Fitz Pistol Grip Co.
Flents Products Co., Inc.
Johnson Gunsmithing, Inc., Neal G.
MCRW Associates
North Specialty Products
Paterson Gunsmithing
Peltor, Inc.
R.E.T. Enterprises
Rockwood Corp., Speedwell Div.
Safari Gun Co.
Safariland Ltd., Inc.
Safety Direct
Smith & Wesson
Valor Corp.
Willson Safety Prods. Div.

LABELS, BOXES, CARTRIDGE HOLDERS

Accuracy Products, S.A.
Anderson Manufacturing Co., Inc.
Arkfeld Mfg. & Dist. Co., Inc.
Ballistic Products, Inc.
Cabinet Mtn. Outfitter
Del Rey Products
Dillon Precision Products, Inc.
Fitz Pistol Grip Co.
Flambeau Products Corp.
Hornady Mfg. Co.
Huey Gun Cases, Marvin
J&J Products Co.
KLP, Inc.
Kolpin Mfg., Inc.
Lakewood Products, Inc.
Lyman Products Corp.
MTM Moulded Products Co., Inc.
Midway Arms, Inc.
Monte Kristo Pistol Grip Co.
Pattern Control
Peterson Instant Targets, Inc.
RCBS
Ravell Ltd.
Scharch Mfg., Inc.
Stalwart Corp.

LEAD WIRE & WIRE CUTTERS

Ballard Built
Berger Bullets, Ltd.
Bullet Swaging Supply, Inc.
C-H Tool & Die Corp./4-D Custom Die Co.
Corbin, Inc.
Eichelberger Bullets, Wm.
Hollywood Enginering
Sport Flite Manufacturing Co.

LOAD TESTING & PRODUCT TESTING, CHRONOGRAPHING & BALLISTIC STUDIES

ADC, Inc.
Ballistic Research
Bustani Appraisers, Leo
Clerke Co., J.A.
Corbin Applied Technology
D&H Precision Tooling
Farr Studio, Inc.
Jensen Bullets
Jones, J.D.
Jurras, L.E.
Lachaussee, S.A.
Lomont Precision Bullets
Maionchi-L.M.I.
McMurdo, Lynn
Neutralizer Police Munitions
Pejsa Ballistics
Rupert's Gun Shop
Russell's Rifle Shop
Schumakers Gun Shop, William
SSK Industries
Specialty Gunsmithing
Star Custom Bullets
White Laboratory, Inc., H.P.
Wildcatters, The

LOADING BLOCKS, METALLIC & SHOTSHELL

Ballistic Products, Inc.
Bruno Shooters Supply
C-H Tool & Die Corp./4-Die Custom Die Co.
Flambeau Products Corp.
Hornady Mfg. Co.
Lyman Products Corp.
MEC, Inc.
Midway Arms, Inc.
MTM Moulded Products Co., Inc.
RCBS
Redding Reloading Equipment
Stalwart Corp.
Trico Plastics

LUBRISIZERS, DIES & ACCESSORIES

Andela Tool & Machine, Inc.
Ballisti-Cast, Inc.
Ben's Machines
Camdex, Inc.
Eagan, Donald V.
GAR
LBT
Lee Precision, Inc.
Lyman Products Corp.
Magma Engineering Co.
Midway Arms, Inc.
MKL Service Co.
RCBS
Redding Reloading Equipment
Star Machine Works
Stillwell, Robert

MOULDS & MOULD ACCESSORIES

Andela Tool & Machine, Inc.
Brownells, Inc.
Bullet Swaging Supply, Inc.
C-H Tool & Die Corp./4-D Custom Die Co.
Colorado Shooter's Supply
Corbin, Inc.
Eagan, Donald V.
Hensley & Gibbs
LBT
Lee Precision, Inc.
Loweth, Richard
Lyman Products Corp.
Magma Engineering Co.
Old West Bullet Moulds
Rapine Bullet Mould Mfg. Co.
RCBS
Redding Reloading Equipment
Sport Flite Manufacturing Co.

POWDER MEASURES, SCALES, FUNNELS & ACCESSORIES

ASI
Brown Co., E. Arthur
C-H Tool & Die Corp./4-D Custom Die Co.
Dedicated Systems
Denver Instrument Co.
Dillon Precision Products, Inc.
Forster Products
Hollywood Engineering
Hornady Mfg. Co.
Jones Custom Products, Neil
Lee Precision, Inc.
Lyman Products Corp.
MCRW Associates
MTM Moulded Products Co., Inc.
Old Western Scrounger, Inc., The
Precision Reloading, Inc.
Quinetics Corp.
RCBS
Redding Reloading Equipment
Sinclair International Inc.
S.L.A.P. Industries
Vega Tool Co.
VibraShine, Inc.

PRESS ACCESSORIES, METALLIC

Ammo Load, Inc.
Bullet Swaging Supply, Inc.
C-H Tool & Die Corp./4-D Custom Die Co.
Dillon Precision Products, Inc.
Forster Products
Hollywood Engineering
Hornady Mfg. Co.
Huntington Die Specialties
Kapro Mfg. Co., Inc.
Lee Precision, Inc.
Lyman Products Corp.
MA Systems
Old Western Scrounger, Inc., The
Pease Accuracy, Bob
Ponsness/Warren
Quinetics Corp.
RCBS
Redding Reloading Equipment
S.L.A.P. Industries
Vega Tool Co.

PRESS ACCESSORIES, SHOTSHELL

Ballistic Products, Inc.
Hollywood Engineering
Hornady Mfg. Co.
Lee Precision, Inc.
MEC, Inc.
Multipax, Inc.
Multi-Scale Charge Ltd.
Pattern Control
Ponsness/Warren
Precision Reloading, Inc.

PRESSES, ARBOR

B-Square Co.
Bald Eagle Precision Machine Co.
Hart & Son, Inc., Robert W.
Jones Custom Products, Neil
Sinclair International, Inc.

PRESSES, METALLIC

Ammo Load, Inc.
C-H Tool & Die Corp./4-D Custom Die Co.
Camdex, Inc.
Dillon Precision Products, Inc.
Forster Products
Hollywood Engineering
Hornady Mfg. Co.
Huntington Die Specialties
Lee Precision, Inc.
Lyman Products Corp.
MCRW Associates
Old Western Scrounger, Inc., The
Ponsness/Warren
RCBS
Redding Reloading Equipment
Star Machine Works

PRESSES, SHOTSHELL

Hollywood Engineering
Hornady Mfg. Co.
Lee Precision, Inc.
MEC, Inc.
Ponsness/Warren

PRESSES, SWAGE

Bullet Swaging Supply, Inc.
Corbin, Inc.

PRIMING TOOLS & ACCESSORIES

C-H Tool & Die Corp./4-D Custom Die Co.
Dewey Mfg. Co., Inc., J.
Dillon Precision Products, Inc.
Flambeau Products Corp.
Forster Products
Hart & Son, Inc., Robert W.
Hornady Mfg. Co.
Huntington Die Specialties
Jones Custom Products, Neil
K&M Services
Lee Precision, Inc.
Lyman Products Corp.
MTM Moulded Products Co., Inc.
PEM'S Mfg. Co.
RCBS
Redding Reloading Equipment
Sinclair International, Inc.
Whitetail Design and Engineering Ltd.
Wilson, Inc., L.E.

REBORING & RERIFLING

Ackley Rifle Barrels, P.O.
Bellm Contenders
Chuck's Gun Shop
DKT, Inc.
H&S Liner Service
Ivanoff, Thomas G.
Jackalope Gun Shop
Jaeger, Inc., Paul/Dunn's
K-D, Inc.
Kopp, Terry K.
LaBounty Precision Reboring
Matco, Inc.
Mid-America Recreation, Inc.
Morrow, Bud
Ozark Gun Works
Pac-Nor Barreling
Pence Precision Barrels
Redman's Rifling & Reboring
Ridgetop Sporting Goods
Sharon Rifle Barrel Co.
Shaw, Inc., E.R.
Swift River Gunworks, Inc.
300 Gunsmith Service, Inc.
Tom's Gun Repair
Van Patten, J.W.
West, Robert G.

RESTS—BENCH, PORTABLE—AND ACCESSORIES

Adventure 16, Inc.
Armor Metal Products
Bald Eagle Precision Machine Co.
Blount, Inc. Sporting Equipment Division
B-Square Co.
Champion's Choice, Inc.
Clift Mfg., L.R.
Clifton Arms, Inc.
Cravener's Gun Shop
Davidson Products
Desert Mountain Mfg.
Forster Products
Greenwalt Rifles
Harris Engineering, Inc.
Hart & Son, Inc., Robert W.
Hidalgo, Tony
Holden Co., J.B.
Hoppe's Div.
Johnson Gunsmithing, Inc., Neal G.
MCRW Associates
Millett Sights
Newman Gunshop
Protektor Model Co.
Ransom International Corp
Sinclair International, Inc.
Sportsman Supply Co.
Sports Support Systems, Inc.
Sure Shot of LA, Inc.
Thompson Target Technology
Ultra Light Arms, Inc.
Verdemont Fieldsports
World of Targets

RIFLE BARREL MAKERS

Ackley Rifle Barrels, P.O.
American Bullets
Bellm Contenders
Borovnik KG, Ludwig
Bullberry Barrel Works, Ltd.
Bustani Appraisers, Leo
Carter's Gun Shop
Camas Hot Springs Mfg.
Cincinnati Swaging
Clark Custom Guns, Inc.
Clerke Co., J.A.
Competition Limited
DKT, Inc.
Donnelly, C.P.
Douglas Barrels, Inc.
Federal Ordnance, Inc.
Frank Custom Gun Service, Ron
Getz Barrel Co.
Graybill's Gun Shop
Green Mountain Rifle Barrel Co., Inc.
H-S Precision, Inc.
Half Moon Rifle Shop
Hart Rifle Barrels, Inc.
Hastings Barrels
K-D, Inc.
KOGOT
Kopp, Terry K.
Krieger Barrels, Inc.
LaBounty Precision Reboring
Lilja Precision Rifle Barrels
Lock's Philadelphia Gun Exchange
Marquart Precision Co., Inc.
Matco, Inc.
McGowen Rifle Barrels
McMillan Rifle Barrels
Mid-America Recreation, Inc.
Oakland Custom Arms, Inc.
Obermeyer Rifled Barrels
Olympic Arms, Inc.
Pell, John T.
Pence Precision Barrels
Ravell Ltd.
Robar Co.'s, Inc., The
Rocky Mountain Rifle Works Ltd.
Safari Arms, Inc./SGW
Schneider Rifle Barrels, Inc., Gary
Sharon Rifle Barrel Co.
Shaw, Inc., E.R.
Shilen Rifles, Inc.
Siskiyou Gun Works
Small Arms Mfg. Co.
Societa Armi Bresciane Srl
Springfield, Inc.
Strutz Rifle Barrels, Inc., W.C.
Unique/M.A.P.F.
Verney-Carron
White Systems, Inc.
Wilson Arms Co., The

SCOPES, MOUNTS & ACCESSORIES, OPTICAL EQUIPMENT

Ackley Rifle Barrels
Action Arms Ltd.
ADCO International
Adventurer's Outpost
Aimpoint, Inc.
Aimtech Mount Systems
Air Venture
Ajax Custom Grips, Inc.
Alley Supply Co.
Anderson Manufacturing Co., Inc.
Apel GmbH, Ernst
Applied Laser Systems, Inc.
A.R.M.S., Inc.
Armscorp USA, Inc.
Armurier Hiptmayer
Baumannize Custom
Bausch & Lomb, Inc.
Beaver Park Products, Inc.
Beeman Precision Airguns, Inc.
Bellm Contenders
Blount, Inc. Sporting Equipment Division
B.M.F. Activator, Inc.
Brownells, Inc.
Brunton U.S.A.
B-Square Co.
Buehler Scope Mounts
Burris Co., Inc.
Bushnell
Butler Creek Corp.
California Armory, Inc.
California Grip
Camp-Cap Products
Cape Outfitters
Celestron International
Clark Custom Guns, Inc.
Clearview Mfg. Co., Inc.
Combat Military Ordnance Ltd.
Compass Industries, Inc.
Conetrol Scope Mounts
Creedmoor Sports, Inc.
Del-Sports, Inc.
D&H Prods. Co., Inc.
E.A.A. Corp.
E&L Mfg., Inc.
Ednar, Inc.
Eggleston, Jere D.
Europtik Ltd.
Farr Studio, Inc.
Flaig's
Forster Products
Fujinon, Inc.
Galati International
Global Industries
Grace Tool, Inc.
Greenwalt Rifles
Griffin & Howe, Inc.
GSI, Inc.
G.U., Inc.
Hakko Co. Ltd.
Hermann Leather Co., H.J.
Hertel & Reuss
Hiptmayer, Klaus
Holden Co., J.B.
Imatronic, Inc.
Jaeger, Inc., Paul/Dunn's
Jason Empire, Inc.
Jeffredo Gunsight
Johnson Gunsmithing, Inc., Neal G.
Kahles USA
K-D, Inc.
Keng's Firearms Specialty, Inc.
KenPatable Ent., Inc.
Kesselring Gun Shop
Kilham & Co.
Kimber, Inc.
Kmount
Kowa Optimed, Inc.
Kris Mounts
KVH Industries, Inc.
Kwik Mount Corp.
Kwik-Site Co.
L&S Technologies, Inc.
Laseraim
Laser Devices, Inc.
Leatherwood-Meopta, Inc.
Lectro Science, Inc.
Lee Supplies, Mark
Lee Co., T.K.
Leica USA, Inc.
Leupold
Lite Tek International
Lohman Mfg. Co., Inc.
London Guns Ltd.
Mac-1 Distributors
Mac's .45 Shop
McKee, Arthur
McMillan Optical Gunsight Co.
Meier Works
Midway Arms, Inc.
Military Armament Corp.
Millett Sights
Mirador Optical Corp.
Muzzle-Nuzzle Co.
New Democracy, Inc.
Newman Gunshop
Nichols Sports Optics
Night Vision Equipment Co., Inc.
Nikon, Inc.
North American Specialties
Nygord Precision Products
Oakshore Electronic Sights, Inc.
Old Western Scrounger, Inc., The
Olympic Optical Co.
OMR Feinmechanik, Jagd-und Sportwaffen, GmbH
Optolyth-USA, Inc.
Orchard Park Enterprise
Outdoor Connection, Inc., The
Pace Marketing, Inc.
Pachmayr Ltd.
PECAR Herbert Schwarz, GmbH
PEM's Mfg. Co.
Pentax Corp.
Pilkington Gun Co.
Precise Metalsmithing Enterprises
Precision Sport Optics
Premier Reticles
Ram-Line, Inc.
Ranch Products
Randolph Engineering, Inc.
Ranging, Inc.
Ravell Ltd.
Redfield, Inc.
Robar Co.'s, Inc., The
Rocky Mountain High Sports Glasses
Sanders Custom Gun Service
Schmidt & Bender
Seattle Binocular & Scope Repair Co.
Selsi Co., Inc.
Shepherd Scope Ltd.
Sheridan USA, Inc., Austin
Shooters Supply
Simmons Enterprises, Ernie
Simmons Outdoor Corp.
S&K Mfg. Co.
Societa Armi Bresciane Srl.
Specialized Weapons, Inc.
Speer Products
Sportsmatch Ltd.
Springfield, Inc.
Sure Shot of LA, Inc.
Swift Instruments, Inc.
Tapco, Inc.
Tasco Sales, Inc.
Tele-Optics
Tele-Optics, Inc.
Thompson/Center Arms
Trijicon, Inc.
Unertl Optical Co., Inc., John
United Binocular Co.
United States Optics Technologies, Inc.
Valor Corp.
Warne Manufacturing Co.
WASP Shooting Systems
Weatherby, Inc.
Weaver Products
Weaver Scope Repair Service
Wells Custom Gunsmith, R.A.
Western Design
Westfield Engineering
White Systems, Inc.
Wideview Scope Mount Corp.
Williams Gun Sight Co.
York M-1 Conversions
Zeiss Optical, Inc., Carl

SHELLHOLDERS

C-H Tool & Die Corp./4-D Custom Die Co.
Forster Products
Hollywood Engineering
Hornady Mfg. Co.
Lee Precision, Inc.
Lyman Products Corp.
Old Western Scrounger, Inc., The
Quinetics Corp.
RCBS
Redding Reloading Equipment
Vega Tool Co.

SHOTSHELL MISCELLANY

Ballistic Products, Inc.
Hornady Mfg. Co.
Precision Reloading, Inc.

SIGHTS, METALLIC

Alley Supply Co.
All's, The Jim J. Tembelis Co., Inc.
Alpec Team, Inc.
Andela Tool & Machine, Inc.
Armurier Hiptmayer
Bo-Mar Tool & Mfg. Co.
Bradley Gunsight Co.
Burris Co., Inc.
Cape Outfitters
Carter's Gun Shop
Champion's Choice, Inc.
Colonial Repair
E.A.A. Corp.
Engineered Accessories
Fausti & Figlie s.n.c., Stefano
Fautheree, Andy
Francesca Stabilizer's, Inc.
Guardian Group International
Gun Doctor, The
Heinie Specialty Products
Hesco-Meprolight
Hiptmayer, Klaus
Imatronic, Inc.
Innovision Enterprises
Jaeger, Inc., Paul/Dunn's
J.O. Arms & Ammunition Co.
Johnson Gunsmithing, Inc., Neal G.
Kopp, Terry K.
Lofland, James W.
London Guns Ltd.
L.P.A. Snc
Lyman Products Corp.
Marble Arms Corp.
McKee, Arthur
MCS, Inc.
Meier Works
Meprolight
Merit Corp.
Mid-America Recreation, Inc.
Millett Sights
MMC
Newman Gunshop
Novak's .45 Shop, Wayne
OMR Feinmechanik, Jagd-und Sportwaffen, GmbH
Pachmayr Ltd.
PEM's Mfg. Co.
Peterson Instant Targets, Inc.
Ravell Ltd.
Robar Co.'s, Inc., The
RPM
Sheridan USA, Inc., Austin
Slug Site Co.
Tanfoglio S.r.l., Fratelli
T.F.C. S.p.A.
Trijicon, Inc.
Vintage Arms, Inc.
WASP Shooting Systems
Wichita Arms, Inc.
Williams Gun Sight Co.

STOCKS, COMMERCIAL & CUSTOM

Angelo & Little Custom Gun Stock Blanks
Apel, Dietrich
Arms Ingenuity Co.
Armurier Hiptmayer
Balickie, Joe
Barta's Gunsmithing
Bartlett, Don
Barton, Michael D.
Beeman Precision Airguns, Inc.
Belding's Custom Gun Shop
Benchmark Guns
Biesen, Al
Biesen, Roger
Billeb, Stephen L.
Bishop, E.C.
B.M.F. Activator, Inc.
Bob's Gun Shop
Boltin, John M.
Borovnik KG, Ludwig
Bowerly, Kent
Boyds' Gunstock Industries, Inc.
Brace, Larry D.
Brgoch, Frank
Brown Precision, Inc.
Buckhorn Gun Works
Bullberry Barrel Works, Ltd.
Burkhart Gunsmithing, Don
Burres, Jack
Butler Creek Corp.
Cali'co Hardwoods, Inc.
Camilli, Lou
Campbell, Dick
Cape Outfitters
Caywood, Shane J.
Chicasaw Gun Works
Churchill, Winston
Clifton Arms, Inc.
Clinton River Gun Serv., Inc.
Cloward's Gun Shop
Cochran, Oliver
Coffin, Charles H.
Coffin, Jim
Conrad, C.A.
Costa, David
Crane Sales Co., George S.
Creedmoor Sports, Inc.
Custom Checkering Service
Custom Gun Products
Custom Gun Stocks
D&D Gunsmiths, Ltd.
Dahl's Custom Stocks
Dangler, Homer L.
Desert Industries, Inc.
Dever Co., Jack
Devereaux, R.H. "Dick"
Dillon, Ed
Dowtin Gunworks
Dressel Jr., Paul G.
Duane Custom Stocks, Randy
Dutchman's Firearms, Inc., The
Duncan's Gunworks, Inc.
E.A.A. Corp.
Echols & Co., D'Arcy
Eggleston, Jere D.
Erhardt, Dennis
Eversull Co., Inc., K.
Fajen, Inc., Reinhart
Farmer-Dressel, Sharon
Fiberpro Rifle Stocks
Fibron Products, Inc.
Fisher, Jerry A.
Flaig's
Folks, Donald E.
Forster, Kathy
Forster, Larry L.
Frank Custom Gun Service, Ron
Game Haven Gunstocks
Garrett Accur-Lt. D.F.S. Co.
Gene's Custom Guns
Gentry Custom Gunmaker, David
Glaser Safety Slug, Inc.
Goens, Dale W.
Golden Age Arms Co.
Gordie's Gun Shop
Goudy Classic Stocks, Gary
Grace, Charles E.
Green, Roger M.
Greene, M.L.
Greenwalt Rifles
Griffin & Howe, Inc.
Gun Shop, The
Gunsmithing Ltd.
Halstead, Rick
Hank's Gun Shop
Hanson's Gun Center, Dick
Harper's Custom Stocks
Hecht, Hubert J.
Heilmann, Stephen
Hensley, Darwin
Heppler, Keith M.
Heydenberk, Warren R.
Hillmer Custom Gunstocks, Paul D.
Hiptmayer, Klaus
Hoenig & Rodman
H-S Precision, Inc.
Huebner, Corey O.
Hughes, Steven Dodd
Intermountain Arms & Tackle, Inc.
Ivanoff, Thomas G.
Jackalope Gun Shop
Jaeger, Inc., Paul/Dunn's
Jamison's Forge Works
Jarrett Rifles, Inc.
Johnson Gunsmithing, Inc., Neal G.
Johnson Wood Products
Keith's Custom Gunstocks
Ken's Rifle Blanks
Klein Custom Guns, Don
Klingler Woodcarving
Knippel, Richard
Kopp, Terry K.
Lawson Co., Harry
Lind Custom Guns, Al
Lynn's Custom Gunstocks
Makinson, Nicholas
Mandarino, Monte
Masen Co., John
McCullough, Ken
McCament, Jay
McDonald, Dennis
McFarland, Stan
McGuire, Bill
McMillan Fiberglass Stocks, Inc.
McMillan Rifle Barrels
Mercer Custom Stocks, R.M.
Mid-America Recreation, Inc.
Miller Gun Woods
Monell Custom Guns
Morrison Custom Rifles, J.W.
Morrow, Bud
MPI Stocks
Muzzlelite Corp.
Nettestad Gun Works
New England Custom Gun Service
Newman Gunshop
Nickels, Paul R.
Nicklas, Ted
Norman Custom Gunstocks, Jim
Oakland Custom Arms, Inc.
Old World Gunsmithing
One Of A Kind
Or-Un
Orvis Co., The
Ottmar, Maurice
Pachmayr Ltd.
Pasadena Gun Center
Paulsen Gunstocks
PEM's Mfg. Co.
Pentheny de Pentheny
Perazzi USA, Inc.
P&S Gun Service
Reiswig, Wallace E.
Richards Micro-Fit Stocks
R&J Gun Shop
RMS Custom Gunsmithing
Robar Co.'s, Inc., The
Robinson, Don
Robinson Firearms Mfg. Ltd.
Roto Carve
Royal Arms
Ryan, Chad L.
Schaefer, Roy V.
Schiffman, Curt
Schiffman, Mike
Schwartz Custom Guns, David W.
Shaw's Finest in Guns
Sherk, Dan A.
Shooting Gallery, The
Sile Distributors, Inc.
Six Enterprises
Skeoch, Brian R.
Snider Stocks, Walter S.
Speedfeed, Inc.
Speiser, Fred D.
Strawbridge, Victor W.
Swan, D.J.
Szweda, Robert
Talmage, William G.
Tecnolegno S.p.A.
T.F.C. S.p.A.
Tiger-Hunt
Tirelli
Tom's Gun Repair
Tom's Gunshop
Trevallion Gunstocks
Tucker, James C.
Vest, John
Vic's Gun Refinishing
Vintage Industries, Inc.
Waffen-Weber Custom Gunsmithing
Wallace's
Weatherby, Inc.
Weems, Cecil
Wenig Custom Gunstocks, Inc.
Werth, T.W.
West, Robert G.
Western Gunstock Mfg. Co.
Westminster Arms Ltd.
Windish, Jim
Winter, Robert M.
Wright's Hardwood Sawmill
Yee, Mike
York M-1 Conversions
Zeeryp, Russ

STUCK CASE REMOVERS

Alex, Inc.
C-H Tool & Die Corp./4-D Custom Die Co.
Forster Products
Hornady Mfg. Co.
RCBS
Redding Reloading Equipment

TARGETS

Abbott Industries
Action Target, Inc.
Aldis Gunsmithing & Shooting Supply
American Whitetail Target Systems
Applied Laser Systems, Inc.
Armor Metal Products
Aztec International Ltd.
Barsotti, Bruce
Birchwood Laboratories, Inc.
Blount, Inc. Sporting Equipment Division
Bull-X, Inc.
Caswell International Corp.
Champion's Choice, Inc.
Champion Target Co.
Clay Target Enterprises
Cummingham Co., Eaton
Dapkus Co., J.G.
Datumtech Corp.
Detroit-Armor Corp.
Diamond Mfg. Co.
Dutchman's Firearms, Inc., The
Epps "Orillia" Ltd., Ellwood
Federal Champion Target Co.
Freeman Animal Targets
G.H. Enterprises Ltd.
Gozon Corp.
Hiti-Schuch, Atelier Wilma
Hornady Mfg. Co.
Hunterjohn
Innovision Enterprises
Johnson Gunsmithing, Inc., Neal G.
Kennebec Journal
Kleen-Bore, Inc.
Lewis, Ed
Littler Sales Co.
Lyman Products Corp.
MTM Molded Products Co., Inc.
Maki Industries
Midway Arms, Inc.
National Target Co.
North American Shooting Systems
Nu-Teck
Outers Laboratories
Ox-Yoke Originals, Inc.
Primos Wild Game Calls, Inc.
Quack Decoy Corp.
Ram-Line, Inc.
Red Star Target Co.
Remington Arms Co., Inc.
Richards, John
River Road Sporting Clays
Rockwood Corp., Speedwell Div.
Rocky Mountain Target Co.
R-Tech Corp.
Schaefer Shooting Sports
Seligman Shooting Products
Shooting Arts Ltd
Shotgun Shop, The
Stoney Baroque Shooters Supply
Targot Man, Inc.
Thompson Target Technology
Verdemont Fieldsports
White Flyer
White Flyer Targets
World of Targets

TRIGGERS, RELATED EQUIPMENT

Boyds' Gunstock Industries, Inc.
Canjar Co., M.H.
Central Specialties Ltd.
Clark Custom Guns, Inc.
Custom Products
Cycle Dynamics, Inc.
Dayton Traister
E.A.A. Corp.
Electronic Trigger Systems, Inc.
Flaig's
Forster Products
Gentry Custom Gunmaker, David
Greenwalt Rifles
Hart & Son, Inc., Robert W.
Johnson Gunsmithing, Inc., Neal G.
Jones, Neil
Krieger Barrels, Inc.
Lee's Red Ramps
London Guns Ltd.
Mac's .45 Shop
Mahony, Philip Bruce
Mid-America Recreation, Inc.
Miller Single Trigger Mfg. Co.
Newman Gunshop
Pace Marketing, Inc.
Pachmayr Ltd.
Pease Accuracy, Bob
PEM's Mfg. Co.
Penrod Precision
Perazzi U.S.A., Inc.
Royal Arms
S&B Industries
Shilen Rifles, Inc.
Taurus, S.A., Forjas
Timney Mfg., Inc.
Tyler Mfg.-Dist., Melvin

MANUFACTURERS' DIRECTORY

A

Abbott Industries, 3368 Miller St., Philadelphia, PA 19134/215-426-3435; FAX: 215-426-1718
A.B.S. III, 9238 St. Morritz Dr., Fern Creek, KY 40291
Acadian Ballistic Specialties, Rt. 1, Box 1-D, Galliano, LA 70354
Acculube II, Inc., 22261 68th Ave. S., Kent, WA 98032-1914/206-395-7171
Accupro Gun Care, 15512-109 Ave., Surrey, BC U3R 7E8, CANADA/604-583-7807
Accuracy Components Co., P.O. Box 60034, Renton, WA 98058/206-255-4577
Accuracy Den, The, 25 Bitterbrush Rd., Reno, NV 89523/702-345-0225
Accuracy Products, S.A., 14 rue de Lawsanne, Brussels, 1060 BELGIUM/32-2-539-34-42; FAX: 32-2-539-39-60
Accuracy Unlimited, 16036 N. 49 Ave., Glendale, AZ 85306/602-978-9089
Accura-Site (See All's, The Jim Tembellis Co., Inc.)
Accurate Arms Co., Inc., Rt. 1, Box 167, McEwen, TN 37101/615-729-4207; FAX 615-729-4217
Ackley Rifle Barrels, P.O. (See Bellm Contenders)
Action Ammo Ltd. (See Action Arms Ltd.)
Action Arms Ltd., P.O. Box 9573, Philadelphia, PA 19124/215-744-0100; FAX: 215-533-2188
Action Bullets, Inc., 1811 W. 13th Ave., Denver, CO 80204/303-595-9636; FAX: 303-893-9161
Action Target, Inc., P.O. Box 636, Provo, UT 84603/801-377-8033; FAX: 801-377-8096
ACTIV Industries, Inc., 1000 Zigor Rd., P.O. Box 339, Kearneysville, WV 25430/304-725-0451; FAX: 304-725-2080
Ad Hominem, RR 3, Orillia, Ont. L3V 6H3, CANADA/705-689-5303
ADC, Inc., 32654 Coal Creek Rd., Scappoose, OR 97056-2601/503-543-5088
ADCO International, 1 Wyman St., Woburn, MA 01801-2341/617-935-1799; FAX: 617-932-4807
Advance Car Mover Co., Rowell Div., P.O. Box 1, 240 N. Depot St., Juneau, WI 53039/414-386-4464
Adventure 16, Inc., 4620 Alvarado Canyon Rd., San Diego, CA 92120/619-283-6314
Adventurer's Outpost, P.O. Box 70, Cottonwood, AZ 86326/800-762-7471; FAX: 602-634-8781
AFSCO Ammunition, 731 W. Third St., P.O. Box L, Owen, WI 54460/715-229-2516
Aimpoint, Inc., 580 Herndon Parkway, Suite 500, Herndon, VA 22070/703-471-6828; FAX: 703-689-0575
Aimtech Mount Systems, 101 Inwood Acres, Thomasville, GA 31792/912-226-4313; FAX: 912-227-0222
Air Venture, 9752 E. Flower St., Bellflower, CA 90706/213-867-6344
Ajax Custom Grips, Inc., Div. of A. Jack Rosenberg & Sons, 9130 Viscount Row, Dallas, TX 75247/214-630-8893
Alaska Bullet Works, P.O. Box 54, Douglas, AK 99824/907-789-3834
Aldis Gunsmithing & Shooting Supply, 502 S. Montezuma St., Prescott, AZ 86303/602-445-6723; FAX: 602-445-6763
Alex, Inc., Box 3034, Bozeman, MT 59772/406-282-7396; FAX: 406-282-7396
All American Bullets, 889 Beatty St., Medford, OR 97501/503-770-5649
All American Lead Shot Corp., P.O. Box 224566, Dallas, TX 75062
All's, The Jim J. Tembelis Co., Inc., 280 E. Fernau Ave., Oshkosh, WI 54901/414-426-1080; FAX: 414-426-1080
Alley Supply Co., P.O. Box 848, Gardnerville, NV 89410/702-782-3800
Allred Bullet Co., 932 Evergreen Drive, Logan, UT 84321/801-752-6983
American Target, 1328 S. Jason St., Denver, CO 80223/303-733-0433
Ames Metal Co., 4324 S. Western Blvd., Chicago, IL/312-523-3230
Alpec Team, Inc., 55 Oak Ct., Danville, CA 94526/510-820-1763; FAX: 510-820-8738
Alpha LaFranck Enterprises, P.O. Box 81072, Lincoln, NE 68501/402-466-3193
Alpine's Precision Gunsmithing & Indoor Shooting Range, 2401 Government Way, Coeur d'Alene, ID 83814/208-765-3559; FAX: 208-667-6401
AmBr Software Group Ltd., The, 2205 Maryland Ave., Baltimore, MD 21218/301-243-7717; FAX: 301-366-8742
American Bullets, 2190 C. Coffee Rd., Lithonia, GA 30058/404-482-4253
American Gas & Chemical Co., Ltd., 220 Pegasus Ave., Northvale, NJ 07647/201-767-7300
American Handgunner Magazine, 591 Camino de la Reina, Suite 200, San Diego, CA/92108 619-297-5350; FAX: 619-297-5353
American Products Co., 14729 Spring Valley Road, Morrison, IL 61270/815-772-3336; FAX: 815-772-7921
American Whitetail Target Systems, P.O. Box 41, 106 S. Church St., Tennyson, IN 47637/812-567-4527
Ammo Load, Inc., 1560 East Edinger, Suite G., Santa Ana, CA 92705/714-558-8858; FAX: 714-569-0319
Amm-O-Mart, Ltd., P.O. Box 125, Hawkesbury, Ont., K6A 2R8 CANADA/613-632-9300
Ammunition Consulting Services, Inc., P.O. Box 1303, St. Charles, IL 60174/708-377-4625; FAX: 708-377-4680
AMT, 6226 Santos Diaz St., Irwindale, CA 91702/818-334-6629; FAX: 818-969-5247
Analog Devices, Box 9106, Norwood, MA 02062
Andela Tool & Machine, Inc., RD3, Box 246, Richfield Springs, NY 13439
Anderson Manufacturing Co., Inc., P.O. Box 2640, 2741 N. Crosby Rd., Oak Harbor, WA 98277/206-675-7300; FAX: 206-675-3939
Angelo & Little Custom Gun Stock Blanks, Chaffin Creek Rd., Darby, MT 59829/406-821-4530
AO Safety Products, Div. of American Optical Corp. (See E-A-R, Inc.)
Apel GmbH, Ernst, Am Kirschberg 3, D-8708 Gerbrunn, GERMANY/0(9 31)-70 71 91; FAX: 0(9 31)70 71 92
Apel, Dietrich, New England Custom Gun Service, RR 2, Box 122W, Brook Rd., W. Lebanon, NH 03784/603-469-3565; FAX: 603-469-3471
Aplan Antiques & Art, James O., HC 80, Box 793-25, Piedmont, SD 57769/605-347-5016
Applied Laser Systems, Inc., 2160 NW Vine St., Grants Pass, OR 97526/503-479-0484; FAX: 503-476-5105
Arcadia Machine & Tool, Inc. (See AMT)
Arizona Ammo & Arms, 2611 Sierra Lane, Kingman, AZ 86401
Arkfeld Mfg. & Dist. Co., Inc., P.O. Box 54, Norfolk, NE 68702-0054/402-371-9430; 800-533-0676
Armfield Custom Bullets, 4775 Caroline Drive, San Diego, CA 92115/619-582-7188
Armite Laboratories, 1845 Randolph St., Los Angeles, CA 90001/213-587-7768; FAX: 213-587-5075
Armoloy Co. of Ft. Worth, 204 E. Daggett St., Fort Worth, TX 76104/817-332-5604; FAX: 817-335-6517
Armor Metal Products, P.O. Box 4609, Helena, MT 59604/406-442-5560
Armory Publications, P.O. Box 4206, Oceanside, CA 92052-4206/619-757-3930; FAX: 619-722-4108
A.R.M.S., Inc., 375 West St., West Bridgewater, MA 02379/508-584-7816; FAX: 508-588-8045
Arms, Peripheral Data Systems, 15110 SW Boones Ferry Rd., Suite 225, Lake Oswego, OR 97035/800-366-5559, 503-697-0533; FAX: 503-697-3337
Arms & Armour Press, Ltd., Villiers House, 41-47 Strand, London WC2N 5JE ENGLAND
Arms Ingenuity Co., P.O. Box 1, 51 Canal St., Weatogue, CT 06089/203-658-5624
Armscorp USA, Inc., 4424 John Ave., Baltimore, MD 21227/301-247-6200
Armurier Hiptmayer, RR 112 #750, P.O. Box 136, Eastman, Quebec JOE 1P0, CANADA/514-297-2492
ASI, 6226 Santos Dias St., Irwindale, CA 91706/818-334-6629
A-Square Co., Inc., RR2, Box 357D, Bedford, KY 40006-9667/502-255-7456; FAX: 502-255-7657
Atlanta Discount Ammo (See Bottom Line Shooting Supplies)
Atlantic Research Marketing Systems (See A.R.M.S., Inc.)
Audette, Creighton, 19 Highland Circle, Springfield, VT 05156/802-885-2331
Automatic Equipment Sales, 627 E. Railroad Ave., Salesburg, MD 21801
Aztec International Ltd., P.O. Box 1384, Clarkesville, GA 30523/404-754-8282

B

Baekgaard Ltd., 1855 Janke Dr., Northbrook, IL 60062/708-498-3040; FAX: 708-493-3106
Balaance Co., 340-39 Ave. S.E. Box 505, Calgary, AB, T2G 1X6 CANADA
Bald Eagle Precision Machine Co., 101 Allison St., Lock Haven, PA 17745/717-748-6772; FAX: 717-748-4443
Balickie, Joe, 408 Trelawney Lane, Apex, NC 27502/919-362-5185
Ballard Built, P.O. Box 1443, Kingsville, TX 78364/512-592-0853
Ballisti-Cast, Inc., Box 383, Parshall, ND 58770/701-862-3324
Ballistic Products, Inc., 20015 75th Ave. North, Corcoran, MN 55340/612-494-9237; FAX: 612-494-9236
Ballistic Program Co., Inc., The, 2417 N. Patterson St., Thomasville, GA 31792/912-228-5739, 800-368-0835
Ballistic Research, 1108 W. May Ave., McHenry, IL 60050/815-385-0037
Ballistica Maximus North, 107 College Park Plaza, Johnstown, PA 15904/814-266-8380
Ballistica Maximus South, 3242 Mary St., Suite S-318, Miami, FL 33133/305-446-5549
Banaczkowski Bullets, 56 Victoria Dr., Mount Barker, S.A. 5251 AUSTRALIA
Barnes Bullets, Inc., P.O. Box 215, American Fork, UT 84003/801-756-4222
Barlett, J., 6641 Kaiser Ave., Fontana, CA 92336-3265
Barsotti, Bruce (See River Road Sporting Clays)
Barta's Gunsmithing, 10231 US Hwy. 10, Cato, WI 54206/414-732-4472
Bartlett, Don, 3704 E. Pine Needle Ave., Colbert, WA 99005/509-467-5009
Barton, Michael D. (See Tiger-Hunt)
Baumannize Custom, 4784 Sunrise Hwy., Bohemia, NY 11716/800-472-4387; FAX: 516-567-0001
Baumgartner Bullets, 3011 S. Alane St., W. Valley City, UT 84120
Bausch & Lomb Sports Optics Div. (See Bushnell)
Bausch & Lomb, Inc., 42 East Ave., Rochester, NY 14603/800-828-5423
Bear Machine Co., 1108 Society Building, 159 S. Main, Akron, OH 44308/216-376-3747
Beaver Park Products, Inc., 840 J St., Penrose, CO 81240/719-372-6744
Beeman Precision Airguns, Inc., 3440 Airway Dr., Santa Rosa, CA 95403/707-578-7900; FAX: 707-578-4751
Belding's Custom Gun Shop, 10691 Sayers Rd., Munith, MI 49259/517-596-2388
Bell Reloading, Inc., 1725 Harlin Lane Rd., Villa Rica, GA 30180
Bell's Gun & Sport Shop, 3309-19 Mannheim Rd, Franklin Park, IL 60131
Bellm Contenders, P.O. Ackley Rifle Barrels, P.O. Box 459, Cleveland, UT 84518/801-653-2530
Belltown, Ltd., 11 Camps Rd., Kent, CT 06757/203-354-5750
Ben's Machines, 1151 S. Cedar Ridge, Duncanville, TX 75137/214-780-1807
Benchmark Guns, 12593 S. Ave. 5 East, Yuma, AZ 85365
Benchrest & Bucks, 6601 Kirby Drive #527, Houston, TX 77005/713-669-0925
Beretta, Dr. Franco, via Rossa, 4, Concesio (BC), Italy I-25062/030-2751955; FAX: 030-218-0414
Berger Bullets, Ltd., 4234 N. 63rd Ave., Phoenix, AZ 85033/602-846-5791; FAX: 602-848-0780
Bergman & Williams, 2450 Losee Rd., Suite F, Las Vegas, NV 89030/702-642-1901
Berry's Bullets, Div. of Berry's Mfg., Inc., Box 100, Bloomington, CA 92316/714-823-5222; FAX: 714-823-4715
Bertram Bullet Co., P.O. Box 313, Seymour, Victoria 3660, AUSTRALIA/61-57-922912; FAX: 61-47-991650
Best Load, P.O. Box 4354, Stamford, CT 06907
Biesen, Al, 5021 Rosewood, Spokane, WA 99208/509-328-9340
Biesen, Roger, 5021 W. Rosewood, Spokane, WA 99208/509-328-9340
Big 45 Frontier Gun Shop, 515 Cliff Ave., Valley Springs, SD 57068/605-757-6248; FAX: 605-757-6248
Bill's Gun Repair, 1007 Burlington St., Mendota, IL 61342/815-539-5786
Billeb, Stephen L., 1100 N. 7th St., Burlington, IA 52601/319-753-2110
Bilsom Intl., Inc., 109 Carpenter Dr., Sterling, VA 20164/703-834-1070
Birchwood Laboratories, Inc., 7900 Fuller Rd., Eden Prairie, MN 55344/612-937-7933; FAX: 612-937-7979
Bishop, E.C., P.O. Box 7, Warsaw, MO 65355/816-438-5121; FAX: 816-4387-2201
Bismuth Cartridge Co., 3500 Maple Ave., Suite 1650, Dallas, TX 75129/800-759-3333; 214-521-5882
Bitterroot Bullet Co., Box 412, Lewiston, ID 83501-0412/208-743-5635
Black Hills Ammunition, P.O. Box 3090, Rapid City, SD 57709/605-348-5150; FAX: 605-348-9827
Black Hills Shooters Supply, P.O. Box 4220, Rapid City, SD 57709
Blackhawk East, P.O. Box 2274, Loves Park, IL 61131
Blackhawk Mountain, P.O. Box 210, Conifer, CO 80433
Blackhawk West, P.O. Box 285, Hiawatha, KS 66434
Black Mountain Bullets, Rt. 7, Box 297, Warrenton, VA 22186/703-347-1199
Blacksmith Corp., 830 N. Road #1 E., Box 1752, Chino Valley, AZ 86323/602-636-4456; FAX: 602-636-4457
Blacktail Mountain Books, 42 First Ave. West, Kalispell, MT 59901/406-257-5573
Blammo Ammo, P.O. Box 1677, Seneca, SC 29679/803-882-1768
Blount, Inc., Sporting Equipment Div., 2299 Snake River Ave., P.O. Box 856, Lewiston, ID 83501/800-627-3640, 208-746-2351
Blue and Gray Products, Inc. (See Ox-Yoke Originals, Inc.)
Blue Book Publications, Inc., One Appletree Square, Minneapolis, MN 55425/800-877-4867; FAX: 612-853-1486
Blue Mountain Bullets, HCR 77, P.O. Box 231, John Day, OR 97845/503-820-4594
Blue Point Mfg. Co., P.O. Box 722, Massena, NY 13662
Blue Ridge Machinery & Tools, Inc., P.O. Box 536-GD, Hurricane, WV 25526/304-562-3538; FAX: 304-562-5311
Bluebonnet Specialty, P.O. Box 737, Palestine, TX 75802/214-723-2075

BMC Supply, Inc., 26051 - 179th Ave. S.E., Kent, WA 98042
B.M.F. Activator, Inc., 803 Mill Creek Run, Plantersville, TX 77363/409-894-2005, 800-527-2881
Bo-Mar Tool & Mfg. Co., Rt. 12, Box 405, Longview, TX 75605/903-759-4784; FAX: 903-759-9141
Bob's Gun Shop, P.O. Box 200, Royal, AR 71968/501-767-1970
Boltin, John M., P.O. Box 644, Estill, SC 29918/803-625-2185
Borovnik KG, Ludwig, 9170 Ferlach, Bahnhofstrasse 7, AUSTRIA
Bottom Line Shooting Supplies, P.O. Box 258, Clarkesville, GA 30523/706-754-9000; FAX: 706-754-7263
Bowerly, Kent, HCR Box 1903, Camp Sherman, OR 97730/503-595-6028
Bowlin, Gene, Rt. 1, Box 890, Snyder, TX 79549
Boyds' Gunstock Industries, Inc., 3rd & Main, Box 305, Geddes, SD 57342/605-337-2123; FAX: 605-337-3363
Brace, Larry D., 771 Blackfoot Ave., Eugene, OR 97404/503-688-1278
Bradley Gunsight Co., P.O. Box 140, Plymouth, VT 05056/203-589-0531; FAX: 203-582-6294
Break-Free, P.O. Box 25020, Santa Ana, CA 92799/714-953-1900
Brenneke KG, Wilhelm, Ilmenauweg 2, P.O. Box 16 46, D-3012 Langenhagen, GERMANY/511-772288
Brgoch, Frank, 1580 S. 1500 East, Bountiful, UT 84010/801-295-1885
Bricker Bullets, Box 509M RD3, Manheim, PA 17545/717-665-4332
Bridgers Best, P.O. Box 1410, Berthoud, CO 80513
Brobst, Jim, 299 Poplar St., Hamburg, PA 19526/215-562-2103
Brown Co., E. Arthur, 3404 Pawnee Dr., Alexandria, MN 56308/612-762-8847
Brown Precision, Inc., 7786 Molinos Ave., Los Molinos, CA 96055/916-384-2506; FAX: 916-384-1638
Brownells, Inc., 200 S. Front St., Montezuma, IA 50171/515-623-5401; FAX: 515-623-3896
Browning Arms Co. (Gen. Offices), 1 Browning Place, Morgan, UT 84050/801-876-2711; FAX: 801-876-3331
BRP, Inc. High Performance Cast Bullets, 1210 Alexander Rd., Colorado Springs, CO 80909/719-633-0658
Bruno Shooters Supply, 106 N. Wyoming St., Hazleton, PA 18201/717-455-2211; FAX: 717-455-2211
Brunton U.S.A., 620 E. Monroe Ave., Riverton, WY 82501/307-856-6559; FAX: 307-856-1840
Bryant, A.V., 72 Whiting Road, E. Hartford, CT 06118
Brynin, Milton, P.O. Box 383, Yonkers, NY 10710/914-779-4333
B-Square Co., P.O. Box 11281, 2708 St. Louis Ave., Ft. Worth, TX 76110/817-923-0964, 800-433-2909; FAX: 817-926-7012
Buck Stix—SOS Products Co., Box 3, Neenah, WI 54956
Buckeye Custom Bullets, 6490 Stewart Rd., Elida, OH 45807/419-641-4463
Buckhorn Gun Works, Rt. 6, Box 2230, Rapid City, SD 57702/605-787-6289
Buehler Scope Mounts, 17 Orinda Way, Orinda, CA 94563/510-254-3201; FAX: 510-254-9720
Buffalo Bullet Co., Inc., 12637 Los Nietos Rd. Unit A, Santa Fe Springs, CA 90670/310-944-0322; FAX: 310-944-5054
Buffalo Rock Shooters Supply, R.R. 1, Ottawa, IL 61350/815-433-2471
Bullberry Barrel Works, Ltd., 2430 W. Bullberry Ln. 67-5, Hurricane, UT 84737/801-635-9866
Bull-X, Inc., 520 N. Main St., Farmer City, IL 61842/309-928-2574, 800-248-3845 orders only
Bullet, Inc., 3745 Hiram Alworth Rd., Dallas, GA 30132
Bullet Swaging Supply, Inc., P.O. Box 1056, 303 McMillan Rd, West Monroe, LA 71291/318-387-7257; FAX: 318-387-7779
BulletMakers Workshop, The, RFD 1 Box 1755, Brooks, ME 04921
Bullseye Bullets, 1610 State Road 60, Suite 12, Valrico, FL 33594/813-654-6563
Burkhart Gunsmithing, Don, P.O. Box 852, Rawlins, WY 82301/307-324-6007
Burling Bullets, 306 Range St., Elizabethton, TN 37643/615-542-8162
Burres, Jack, 10333 San Fernando Rd., Pacoima, CA 91331/818-899-8000
Burris Co., Inc., P.O. Box 1747, Greeley, CO 80631/303-356-1670; FAX: 303-356-8702
Busch Metal Merchants, Roger, 48765 West Rd., Wixon, MI 48393/800-876-5337
Bushmann Hunters/Safaris, P.O. Box 110639, Aurora, CO 80011
Bushnell, Bausch & Lomb Sports Optics Div., 9200 Cody, Overland Park, KS 66214/913-888-0220
Bustani Appraisers, Leo, P.O. Box 8125, W. Palm Beach, FL 33407/305-622-2710
Butler Creek Corp., 290 Arden Dr., Belgrade, MT 59714/406-388-1356; FAX: 406-388-7204
Buzztail Brass, 5306 Bryant Ave., Klamath Falls, OR 97603/503-884-1072
B-West Imports, Inc., 5132 E. Pima St., Tucson, AZ 85712/602-881-3525; FAX: 602-322-5704

C

C&D Special Products (Claybuster), 309 Sequoya Dr., Hopkinsville, KY 42240/800-922-6287, 800-284-1746
Cabinet Mtn. Outfitter, P.O. Box 766, Plains, MT 59859/406-826-3970
Calhoon Varmint Bullets, James, 6035 Penworth Rd., S.E., Calgary, Alberta, T2A 4E9 CANADA/403-235-2959
Calibre Press, Inc., 666 Dundee Rd., Suite 1607, Northbrook, IL 60062-2760/800-323-0037; FAX: 708-498-6869
Cali'co Hardwoods, Inc., 1648 Airport Blvd., Windsor, CA 95492/707-546-4045; FAX: 707-546-4027
California Armory, Inc., 881 W. San Bruno Ave., San Bruno, CA 94066/415-871-4886; FAX: 415-871-0713
California Grip, 1323 Miami Ave., Clovis, CA 93612/209-299-1316
California Magnum, 20746 Dearborn St., Chatsworth, CA 91313/818-341-7302; FAX: 818-341-7304
Camas Hot Springs Mfg., P.O. Box 639, Hot Springs, MT 59845/406-741-3756
Camdex, Inc., 2330 Alger, Troy, MI 48083/313-528-2300
Cameron's, 16690 W. 11th Ave., Golden, CO 80401/303-279-7365; FAX: 303-628-5413
Camilli, Lou, 4700 Oahu Dr. NE, Albuquerque, NM 87111/505-293-5259
Camp-Cap Products, P.O. Box 173, Chesterfield, MO 63006/314-532-4340
Campbell, Dick, 20,000 Silver Ranch Rd., Conifer, CO 80433/303-697-0150
Canadian Custom Bullets, Box 52, Anola Man. R0E 0A0 CANADA
Canjar Co., M.H., 500 E. 45th Ave., Denver, CO 80216/303-295-2638
Canons Delcour, Rue J.B. Cools, B-4040 Herstal, BELGIUM/+32.(0)41.40.13.40; FAX: +32(0)412.40.22.88
Canyon Cartridge Corp., P.O. Box 152, Albertson, NY 11507/FAX: 516-294-8946
Cape Outfitters, Rt. 2, Box 437C, Cape Girardeau, MO 63701/314-335-4103; FAX: 314-335-1555
Carbide Die & Mfg. Co., Inc., 15615 E. Arrow Hwy., Irwindale, CA 91706/818-337-2518
Carnahan Bullets, 17645 110th Ave. SE, Renton, WA 98055
Carroll Bullets (See Precision Reloading, Inc.)
Carter's Gun Shop, 225 G St., Penrose, CO 81240/719-372-6240
Cartridges Unlimited, 190 Bull's Bridge Rd., South Kent, CT 06785/203-927-3053
Cascade Bullet Co., Inc., 413 Main St., Klamath Falls, OR 97601/503-884-9316
Cascade Shooters, 2155 N.W. 12th St., Redwood, OR 97756
Cast Bullet Assoc., Inc., The, 4103 Foxcraft Dr., Traverse City, MI 49684
Caswell International Corp., 1221 Marshall St. NE, Minneapolis, MN 55413/612-379-2000
Catco-Ambush, Inc., P.O.Box 300, Corte Madera, CA 94926
Caywood, Shane J., P.O. Box 321, Minocqua, WI 54548
CBC, Avenida Industrial, 3330, Santo Andre-SP-BRAZIL 09080/11-449-5600
CCI, Div. of Blount, Inc., 2299 Snake River Ave., P.O. Box 856, Lewiston, ID 83501/800-627-3640, 208-746-23511
Celestron International, P.O. Box 3578, Torrance, CA 90503
Central Specialties Ltd., 1122 Silver Lake Road, Cary, IL 60013/708-537-3300; FAX: 708-537-3615
Century International Arms, Inc., 48 Lower Newton St., St. Albans, VT 05478/802-527-1252; FAX: 802-527-0470
CF Ventures, 509 Harvey Dr., Bloomington, IN 47403-1715
C-H Tool & Die Corp. (See 4-D Custom Die Co.)
Champion Target Co., 232 Industrial Parkway, Richmond, IN 47374/800-441-4971
Champion's Choice, Inc., 223 Space Park South, Nashville, TN 37211/615-834-6666; FAX: 615-831-2753
Cheddite France, S.A., 99 Route de Lyon, F-26500 Bourg Les Valence, FRANCE/75 56 45 45; FAX: 75 56 98 89
Chem-Pak, Inc., 11 Oates Ave., P.O. Box 1685, Winchester, VA 22601/800-336-9828; FAX: 703-722-3993
Cherokee Gun Accessories (See Glaser Safety Slug, Inc.)
CheVron Bullets, RR1, Ottawa, IL 61350/815-433-2471
CheVron Case Master (See CheVron Bullets)
Chicasaw Gun Works (See Cochran, Oliver)
ChinaSports, Inc., 2010 S. Lynx Place, Ontario, CA 91761/714-923-1411; FAX: 714-923-0775
Chopie Mfg., Inc., 700 Copeland Ave., LaCrosse, WI 54603/608-784-0926
Chronotech, 1655 Siamet Rd. Unit 6, Mississauga, Ont. L4W 1Z4 CANADA/416-625-5200; FAX: 416-625-5190
Chuck's Gun Shop, P.O. Box 597, Waldo, FL 32694/904-468-2264
Churchill, Winston, Twenty Mile Stream Rd., RFD P.O. Box 29B, Proctorsville, VT 05153/802-226-7772
Chu Tani Ind., Inc., Box 3782, Chula Vista, CA 92011
Cincinnati Swaging, 2605 Marlington Ave., Cincinnati, OH 45208
Circle M Custom Bullets, 2718 Button Willow Parkway, Abilene, TX 97606/915-698-3106
Clark Co., Inc., David, P.O. Box 15054, Worcester, MA 01615-0054/508-756-6216; FAX: 508-753-5827
Clark Custom Guns, Inc., P.O. Box 530, 11462 Keatchie Rd., Keithville, LA 71047/318-925-0836; FAX: 318-925-9425
Classic Brass, 14 Grove St., Plympton, MA 02367/FAX: 617-585-5673
Clay Target Enterprises, 300 Railway Ave., Campbell, CA 95008/408-379-4829
Clearview Mfg. Co., Inc., 413 S. Oakley St., Fordyce, AR 71742/501-352-8557; FAX: 501-352-8557
Clenzoil Corp., P.O. Box 80226, Canton, OH 44708/216-833-9758
Clerke Co., J.A., P.O. Box 627, Pearblossom, CA 93553-0627/805-945-0713
Clift Mfg., L.R., 3821 Hammonton Rd., Marysville, CA 95901/916-755-3390; FAX: 916-755-3393
Clift Welding Supply & Cases, 1332-A Colusa Hwy., Yuba City, CA 95993/916-755-3390; FAX: 916-755-3393
Clifton Arms, Inc., P.O. Box 1471, Medina, TX 78055/210-589-2666; FAX: 210-589-2661
Clinton River Gun Serv., Inc., 30016 S. River Rd., Mt. Clemens, MI 48045/313-468-1090
Cloward's Gun Shop, 4023 Aurora Ave. N, Seattle, WA 98103/206-632-2072
Clymer Manufacturing Co., Inc., 1645 W. Hamlin Rd., Rochester Hills, MI 48309/313-853-5555; FAX: 313-853-1530
Coats, Mrs. Lester, 300 Luman Rd., Space 125, Phoenix, OR 97535/503-535-1611
Cobra Gunskin, 133-30 32nd Ave., Flushing, NY 11354/718-762-8181; FAX: 718-762-0890
Cochran, Oliver, Box 868, Shady Spring, WV 25918/304-763-3838
Coffin, Charles H., 3719 Scarlet Ave., Odessa, TX 79762/915-366-4729
Coffin, Jim, 250 Country Club Lane, Albany, OR 97321/503-928-4391
Colonial Repair, P.O. Box 372, Hyde Park, MA 02136-9998/617-469-4951
Colorado Shooter's Supply, 138 S. Plum, P.O. Box 132, Fruita, CO 81521/303-858-9191
Colorado Sutlers Arsenal, Box 991, Granby, CO 80446/303-887-3813
Combat Military Ordnance Ltd., 3900 Hopkins St., Savannah, GA 31405/912-238-1900; FAX: 912-236-7570
Companhia Brazileira de Cartuchos (See CBC)
Compass Industries, Inc., 104 East 25th St., New York, NY 10010/212-473-2614
Competition Electronics, Inc., 3469 Precision Dr., Rockford, IL 61109/815-874-8001; FAX: 815-874-8181
Competition Limited, 1664 S. Research Loop Rd., Tucson, AZ 85710/602-722-6455
Competitor Corp., Inc., P.O. Box 244, 293 Townsend Rd., West Groton, MA 01472/508-448-3521; FAX: 603-673-4540
Conetrol Scope Mounts, 10225 Hwy. 123 south, Seguin, TX 78155/210-379-3030, 800-CON-ETROL
CONKKO, P.O. Box 40, Broomall, PA 19008/215-356-0711
Conrad, C.A., 3964 Ebert St., Winston-Salem, NC 27127/919-788-5469
Continental Kite & Key (See CONKKO)
Cook Bullets, 1846 Rosemeade Parkway #188, Carrollton, TX 75007/214-394-8725
Cook Engineering Service, 891 Highbury Rd., Vermont VICT 3133 AUSTRALIA
Cooper-Woodward, P.O. Box 1788, East Helena, MT 59635/406-475-3321
Cor-Bon, Inc., 4828 Michigan Ave.,P.O. Box 10126, Detroit, MI 48210/313-894-2373
Corbin Applied Technology, P.O. Box 2171, White City, OR 97503/503-826-5211
Corbin, Inc., 600 Industrial Circle, P.O. Box 2659, White City, OR 97503/503-826-5211; FAX: 503-826-8669
Costa, David, P.O. Box 428, Island Pond, VT 05846
Country Armourer, The, P.O. Box 308, Ashby, MA 01431/508-386-7789
CP Specialties, 1814 Mearns Rd., Warminster, PA 18974
Crane & Crane Ltd., 105 N. Edison Way #6, Reno, NV 89502-2355/702-856-1516; FAX: 702-856-1616
Crane Sales Co., George S., P.O. Box 385, Van Nuys, CA 91409/818-505-8337
Cravener's Gun Shop, 1627-5th Ave., Ford City, PA 16226/412-763-8312
Crawford Co., Inc., R.M., P.O. Box 277, Everett, PA 15537/814-652-6536; FAX: 814-652-9526
Creative Cartridge Co., 56 Morgan Rd., Canton, CT 06019/203-693-2529
Creedmoor Sports, Inc., P.O. Box 1040, Oceanside, CA 92051/619-757-5529
Crouse's Country Cover, P.O. Box 160, Storrs, CT 06268/203-423-0702
CRW Products, Inc., Box 2123, Des Moines, IA 50310
Cubic Shot Shell Co., Inc., 98 Fatima Dr., Campbell, OH 44405/216-755-0349; FAX: 216-755-0349
Cumberland Arms, Rt. I, Box 1150 Shafer Rd., Blantons Chapel, Manchester, TN 37355
Cummings Bullets, 1417 Esperanza Way, Escondido, CA 92027
Cummingham Co., Eaton, Admiral Blvd. at Oak, Kansas City, MO 64106/816-842-2600
Cunard & Co., J., P.O. Box 755, Newark, OH 43058-0755/614-345-6646
Custom Bullets by Hoffman, 2604 Peconic Ave., Seaford, NY 11783
Custom Checkering Service, Kathy Forster, 2124 SE Yamhill St., Portland, OR 97214/503-236-5874
Custom Chronograph, Inc., 5305 Reese Hill Rd., Sumas, WA 98295/206-988-7801
Custom Gun Products, 5021 W. Rosewood, Spokane, WA 99208/509-328-9340
Custom Gun Stocks, Rt. 6, P.O. Box 177, McMinnville, TN 37110/615-668-3912
Custom Hunting Ammo & Arms, 2900 Fisk Rd., Howell, MI 48843/517-546-9498
Custom Products (See Jones Custom Products, Neil)
Custom Tackle and Ammo, P.O. Box 1886, Farmington, NM 87499/505-632-3539
Cutsinger Bench Rest Bullets, RR 8, Box 161-A, Shelbyville, IN 46176/317-729-5360
C.W. Cartridge Co., 242 Highland Ave., Kearney, NJ 07032/201-998-1030
C.W. Cartridge Co., 71 Hackensack St., Wood Ridge, NJ 07075
Cycle Dynamics, Inc., 74 Garden St., Feeding Hills, MA 01030/413-786-0141

D

D&D Gunsmiths, Ltd., 363 E. Elmwood, Troy, MI 48083/313-583-1512
D&H Precision Tooling, 7522 Barnard Mill Rd., Ringwood, IL 60072/815-653-4011
D&H Prods. Co., Inc., 465 Denny Rd., Valencia, PA 16059/412-898-2840
D&J Bullet Co. & Custom Gun Shop, Inc., Rt. 1, Box 223 A-1, Flatwoods, KY 41139/606-836-2663; FAX: 606-836-2663
D&R Distributing, 308 S.E. Valley St., Myrtle Creek, OR 97457/503-863-6850
Dahl's Custom Stocks, Rt. 4, P.O. Box 558, Lake Geneva, WI 53147/414-248-2464
Daisy Mfg. Co., P.O. Box 220, Rogers, AR 72756/501-636-1200; FAX: 501-636-1601
Dakota Arms, HC55, Box 326, Sturgis, SD 57785/605-347-4686; FAX: 605-347-4459
Dangler, Homer L., Box 254, Addison, MI 49220/517-547-6745
Dapkus Co., J.G., P.O. Box 293, Durham, CT 06422
Dara-Nes, Inc. (See Nesci Enterprises, Inc.)
Data Tech Software Systems, 19312 East Eldorado Drive, Aurora, CO 80013
Datumtech Corp., 2275 Wehrle Dr., Buffalo, NY 14221
Davidson Products, 2020 Huntington Dr., Las Cruces, NM 88801/505-522-5612
Davis Products, Mike, 643 Loop Dr., Moses Lake, WA 98837/509-765-6178, 800-765-6178 orders only
Dayton Traister, P.O. Box 593, Oak Harbor, WA 98277/206-679-4657; FAX:206-675-1114
DBASE Consultants (See Peripheral Data Systems)
DBI Books, Inc., 4092 Commercial Ave., Northbrook, IL 60062/708-272-6310; FAX: 708-272-2051
D.C.C. Enterprises, 259 Wynburn Ave., Athens, GA 30601
D.D. Custom Rifles, R.H. "Dick" Devereaux, 5240 Mule Deer Dr., Colorado Springs, CO 80919/719-548-8468
Deadeye Sport Center, RD 1, Box 147B, Shickshin, PA 18655/717-256-7432
Decker Shooting Products, 1729 Laguna Ave., Schofield, WI 54476/715-359-5873
Dedicated Systems, 105-B Cochrane Circle, Morgan Hill, CA 95037/408-779-2808; FAX: 408-779-2673
Deepeeka Exports Pvt. Ltd., D-78, Saket, Meerut-250-006, INDIA/0121-74483; FAX: 0121-74483
Del Rey Products, P.O. Box 91561, Los Angeles, CA 90009/213-823-0494
Del-Sports, Inc., Box 685, Main St., Margaretville, NY 12455/914-586-4103; FAX: 914-586-4105
Delta Co. Ammo Bunker, 1209 16th Place, Yuma, AZ 85364/602-783-4563
Delta Enterprises, 284 Hagemann Drive, Livermore, CA 94550
Denver Bullets, Inc., 1811 W. 13th Ave., Denver, CO 80204/303-893-3146
Denver Instrument Co., 6542 Fig St., Arvada, CO 80004/800-321-1135, 303-431-7255
Desert Industries, Inc., 3245 E. Patrick Ln., Suite H, Las Vegas, NV 89120/702-597-1066; FAX: 702-434-9495
Desert Mountain Mfg., P.O. Box 184, Coram, MT 59913/406-387-5381
Destination North Software, 804 Surry Road, Wenatchee, WA 98801/509-662-6602
Detroit-Armor Corp., 720 Industrial Dr. #112, Cary, IL 60013/708-639-7666
Dever Co., Jack, 8590 NW 90, Oklahoma City, OK 73132/405-721-6393
Devereaux, R.H. "Dick" (See D.D. Custom Rifles)
Dewey Mfg. Co., Inc., J., P.O. Box 2014, Southbury, CT 06488/203-598-7912; FAX: 203-598-3119
Diamond Mfg. Co., P.O. Box 174, Wyoming, PA 18644/800-233-9601
Diana (See U.S. importer—Dynamit Nobel-RWS, Inc.)
Dillon Precision Products, Inc., 7442 E. Butherus Dr., Scottsdale, AZ 85260/602-948-8009
Dillon, Ed, 1035 War Eagle Dr. N., Colorado Springs, CO 80919/719-598-4929; FAX: 719-598-4929
Division Lead Co., 7742 W. 61st Pl., Summit, IL 60502
DKT, Inc., 14623 Vera Drive, Union, MI 49130-9744/616-641-7120; FAX: 616-641-2015
Dohring Bullets, 100 W. 8 Mile Rd., Ferndale, MI 48220
Donnelly, C.P., 405 Kubli Rd., Grants Pass, OR 97527/503-846-6604
Douglas Barrels, Inc., 5504 Big Tyler Rd., Charleston, WV 25313-1398/304-776-1341; FAX: 304-776-8560
Dowtin Gunworks, Rt. 4, Box 930A, Flagstaff, AZ 86001/602-779-1898
Dressel Jr., Paul G., 209 N. 92nd Ave., Yakima, WA 98908/509-966-9233
Dri-Slide, Inc., 411 N. Darling, Fremont, MI 49412/616-924-3950
Du-Lite Corp., 171 River Rd., Middletown, CT 06457/203-347-2505
Duane Custom Stocks, Randy, 110 W. North Ave., Winchester, VA 22601/703-667-9461; FAX: 703-722-3993
Duffy, Charles E., Williams Lane, West Hurley, NY 12491/914-679-2997
Duncan's Gun Works, Inc., 1619 Grand Ave., San Marcos, CA 92069/619-727-0515
DuPont (See IMR Powder Co.)
Durward, John, 448 Belgreen Way, Waterloo, Ontario N2L 5X5 CANADA
Dutchman's Firearms, Inc., The, 4143 Taylor Blvd., Louisville, KY 40215/502-366-0555
Dybala Gun Shop, P.O. Box 1024, FM 3156, Bay City, TX 77414/409-245-0866
Dykstra, Doug, 411 N. Darling, Fremont, MI 49412/616-924-3950
Dynamit Nobel-RWS, Inc., 81 Ruckman Rd., Closter, NJ 07624/201-767-1995; FAX: 201-767-1589

E

E&L Mfg., Inc., 39042 N. School House Rd., Cave Creek, AZ 85331/602-488-2598; FAX: 602-488-0813
E.A.A. Corp., 4480 E. 11th Ave., Hialeah, FL 33013/305-688-4442; FAX: 305-688-5656
Eagan, Donald V., P.O. Box 196, Benton, PA 17814/717-925-6134
Eagle Flight Bullet Co., 925 Lakeville St., Suite 123, Petaluma, CA 94954/707-762-6955
Eagle Products Co., 1520 Adelia Ave., S. El Monte, CA 91733
E-A-R, Inc., Div. of Cabot Safety Corp., 5457 W. 79th St., Indianapolis, IN 46268/800-327-3431; FAX: 800-488-8007
Echols & Co., D'Arcy, 164 W. 580 S., Providence, UT 84332/801-753-2367
Ed's Gun House, Rt. 1, Box 62, Minnesota City, MN 55959/507-689-2925
Edmisten Co., P.O. Box 1293, Boone, NC 28607
Ednar, Inc., 2-4-8 Kayabacho, Nihonbashi, Chuo-ku, Tokyo, JAPAN/81(Japan)-3-3667-1651
Ed's Custom Bullets, 431 North 75 East, North Salt Lake, UT 84054/801-295-3960
Eezox, Inc., P.O. Box 772, Waterford, CT 06385-0772/203-447-8282; FAX: 203-447-3484
Efemes Enterprises, P.O. Box 691, Colchester, VT 05446
Eggleston, Jere D., 400 Saluda Ave., Columbia, SC 29205/803-799-3402
Eichelberger Bullets, Wm., 158 Crossfield Rd., King of Prussia, PA 19406
Eiland Custom Bullets, P.O. Box 688, Buena Vista, CO 81211/303-429-8850
Eldorado Cartridge Corp. (See PMC/Eldorado Cartridge Corp.)
Electronic Trigger Systems, Inc., 4124 Thrushwood Lane, Minnetonka, MN 55345/612-935-7829
Eley Ltd., P.O. Box 705, Witton, Birmingham, B6 7UT, ENGLAND/21-356-8899; FAX: 21-331-4173
Elite Ammunition, P.O. Box 3251, Oakbrook, IL 60522/708-366-9006
Elko Arms, Dr. L. Kortz, 28 rue Ecole Moderne, B-7060 Soignies, BELGIUM/(32)67-33-29-34
Ellis Sport Shop, E.W., RD 1, Route 9N, P.O. Box 315, Corinth, NY 12822/518-654-6444
Engineered Accessories, 1307 W. Wabash Ave., Effingham, IL 62401/217-347-7700; FAX: 217-347-7737
Enguix Import-Export, Alpujarras 58, Alzira, Valencia, SPAIN 46600/(96) 241 43 95; FAX: (96) 241 43 95
Ensign-Bickford Co., The, 660 Hopmeadow St., Simsbury, CT 06070
Epps "Orillia" Ltd., Ellwood, RR 3, Hwy. 11 North, Orillia, Ont. L3V 6H3, CANADA/705-689-5333
Erhardt, Dennis, 3280 Green Meadow Dr., Helena, MT 59601/406-442-4533
Essex Metals, 1000 Brighton St., Union, NJ 07083/800-282-8369
Estate Cartridge, Inc., 2778 FM 830, Willis, TX 77378/409-856-7277; FAX: 409-856-5486
Eureka Bullets, Hill House, Taylors Arm, NSW 2447 AUSTRALIA
European American Armory Corp. (See E.A.A. Corp.)
Europtik Ltd., P.O. Box 319, Dunmore, PA 18512/717-347-6049, 800-873-5362; FAX: 717-969-4330
Eversull Co., Inc., K., 1 Tracemont, Boyce, LA 71409/318-793-8728; FAX: 318-793-5483
Exe, Inc., 18830 Partridge Circle, Eden Prairie, MN 55346/612-944-7662
Executive Protection Institute, Rt. 2, Box 3645, Berryville, VA 22611/703-955-1128

F

4-D Custom Die Co., 711 N. Sandusky St., P.O. Box 889, Mt. Vernon, OH 43050-0889/614-397-7214; FAX: 614-397-6600
Faith Associates, Inc., 1139 S. Greenville Hwy., Hendersonville, NC 28792/704-692-1916; FAX: 704-697-6827
Fajen, Inc., Reinhart, 1000 Red Bud Dr., P.O. Box 338, Warsaw, MO 65355/816-438-5111; FAX: 816-438-5175
Farmer-Dressel, Sharon, 209 N. 92nd Ave., Yakima, WA 98908/509-966-9233
Far North Outfitters, Box 1252, Bethel, AK 99559
Farr Studio, Inc., 1231 Robinhood Rd., Greeneville, TN 37743/615-638-8825
Fausti & Figlie s.n.c., Stefano, Via Martini Zudipeudente, 70, Marcheno, ITALY 25060
Fautheree, Andy, P.O. Box 4607, Pagosa Springs, CO 81157/303-731-5003
Federal Cartridge Co., 900 Ehlen Dr., Anoka, MN 55303/612-422-2840
Federal Champion Target Co., 232 Industrial Parkway, Richmond, IN 47374/800-441-4971; FAX: 317-966-7747
Federal Ordnance, Inc., 1443 Potrero Ave., S. El Monte, CA 91733/818-350-4161; FAX: 818-444-3875
Federated-Fry, 6th Ave., 41st St., Altuna, PA 16602/814-946-1611
Ferguson, Bill, P.O. Box 1238, Sierra Vista, AZ 85636/602-452-0533; FAX: 602-458-9125
Fiberpro Rifle Stocks, Div. of Fibers West, 10977 San Diego Mission Rd., San Diego, CA 92108/619-282-4211; FAX: 619-282-0598
Fibron Products, Inc., 170 Florida St., Buffalo, NY 14208/716-886-2378; FAX: 716-886-2394
Finch Custom Bullets, 40204 La Rochelle, Prairieville, LA 70769
Fiocchi of America, Inc., Rt. 2, P.O. Box 90-8, Ozark, MO 65721/417-725-4118; FAX: 417-725-1039
First Distributors, Inc., Jack, 44633 Sierra Hwy., Lancaster, CA 93534/805-945-6981; FAX: 805-942-0844
Fisher Enterprises, 655 Main St. #305, Edmonds, WA 98020/206-776-4365
Fisher, Jerry A., 535 Crane Mt. Rd., Big Fork, MT 59911/406-837-1024
Fitz Pistol Grip Co., P.O. Box 610, Douglas City, CA 96024/916-623-4019
Flaig's, 2200 Evergreen Rd., Millvale, PA 15209/412-821-1717
Flambeau Products Corp., P.O. Box 97, Middlefield, OH 44062/216-632-1631; FAX: 216-632-1581
Flents Products Co., Inc., P.O. Box 2109, Norwalk, CT 06852/203-866-2581; FAX: 203-854-9322
Flitz International Ltd., 821 Mohr Ave., Waterford, WI 53185/414-534-5898; FAX: 414-534-2991
Flores Publications, Inc., J., P.O. Box 830131, Miami, FL 33283/305-559-4652
Flouramics, Inc., 103 Pleasant Ave., Upper Saddle River, NJ 07458/201-825-8110
FN Herstal, Voie de Liege 33, Herstal 4040, BELGIUM/(32)41.40.82.83; FAX: (32)40.86.79
Folks, Donald E., 205 W. Lincoln St., Pontiac, IL 61764/815-844-7901
Ford, Jack, 1430 Elkwood, Missouri City, TX 77489/713-499-9984
Forgreens Tool Mfg., Inc., P.O. Box 990, Robert Lee, TX 76945/915-453-2800
Forster, Kathy (See Custom Checkering Service)
Forster, Larry L., P.O. Box 212, 220 First St. NE, Gwinner, ND 58040-0212/701-678-2475
Forster Products, 82 E. Lanark Ave., Lanark, IL 61046/815-493-6360; FAX: 815-493-2371
Fortress Publications, Inc., P.O. Box 9241, Stoney Creek, Ont. L8G 3X9, CANADA/416-662-3505
Forty Five Ranch Enterprises, Box 1080, Miami, OK 74355-1080/918-542-5875
Fouling Shot, The, 6465 Parfet St., Arvada, CO 80004
Fowler Bullets, 4003 Linwood Rd., Gastonia, NC 28052/704-867-3259
Foy Custom Bullets, 104 Wells Ave., Daleville, AL 36322
Francesca Stabilizer's, Inc., 3115 Old Ranch Rd., San Antonio, TX 78217/512-826-2584
Frank Custom Gun Service, Ron, 7131 Richland Rd., Ft. Worth, TX 76118/817-284-4426
Freedom Arms, Inc., P.O. Box 1776, Freedom, WY 83120/307-883-2468; FAX: 307-883-2005
Freeman Animal Targets, 2559 W. Morris St., Plainsfield, IN 46168/317-271-5314; FAX: 317-271-9106
Fremont Tool Works, 1214 Prairie, Ford, KS 67842/316-369-2338
Frontier Products Co., 164 E. Longview Ave., Columbus, OH 43202/614-262-9357
Fujinon, Inc., 10 High Point Dr., Wayne, NJ 07470/201-633-5600
Fusilier Bullets, 10010 N. 6000 W., Highland, UT 84003/801-756-6813

G

G96 Products Co., Inc., 237 River St., Paterson, NJ 07524/201-684-4050; FAX: 201-684-3848
G&C Bullet Co., Inc., 8835 Thornton Rd., Stockton, CA 95209
Galati International, P.O. Box 326, Catawissa, MO 63015/314-257-4837; FAX: 314-257-2268
Game Haven Gunstocks, 13750 Shire Rd., Wolverine, MI 49799/616-525-8257
Gammog, Gregory B. Gally, 16009 Kenny Rd., Laurel, MD 20707/301-725-3838
GAR, 139 Park Lane, Wayne, NJ 07470/201-256-7641
Garrett Accur-Lt. D.F.S. Co., P.O. Box 8675, 1413B East Olive Ct., Ft. Collins, CO 80524/303-224-3067
Garrett Cartridges, Inc., P.O. Box 178, Chehalis, WA 98532/206-736-0702
GDL Enterprises, 409 Le Gardeur, Slidell, LA 70460/504-649-0693
Gehmann, Walter (See Huntington Die Specialties)
Genco, P.O. Box 5704, Asheville, NC 28803
Gene's Custom Guns, P.O. Box 10534, White Bear Lake, MN 55110/612-429-5105
Gentry Custom Gunmaker, David, 314 N. Hoffman, Belgrade, MT 59714/406-388-4867
George & Ray's Primer Sealant, 2950 NW 29th, Portland, OR 97210/800-553-3022
Getz Barrel Co., P.O. Box 88, Beavertown, PA 17813/717-658-7263
G.H. Enterprises Ltd., Bag 10, Okotoks, Alberta T0L 1T0 CANADA/403-938-6070
Gise Bullets, P.O. Box 772, Santa Clara, CA 95052
Glaser Safety Slug, Inc., P.O. Box 8223, Foster City, CA 94404/415-345-7677; FAX: 415-345-8217
Global Industries, 1501 E. Chapman Ave., #306, Fullerton, CA 92631/714-879-8922
Goens, Dale W., P.O. Box 224, Cedar Crest, NM 87008/505-281-5419
GOEX, Inc., 1002 Springbrook Ave., Moosic, PA 18507/717-457-6724; FAX: 717-457-1130
Golden Age Arms Co., 115 E. High St., Ashley, OH 43003/614-747-2488
Gonzalez Guns, Ramon B., P.O. Box 370, Monticello, NY 12701/914-794-4515
Gordie's Gun Shop, 1401 Fulton St., Streator, IL 61364/815-672-7202
Gotz Bullets, 7313 Rogers St., Rockford, IL 61111

Goudy Classic Stocks, Gary, 263 Hedge Rd., Menlo Park, CA 94025-1711/415-322-1338
Gozon Corp., P.O. Box 6278, Fulsom, CA 95763/916-983-1807; FAX: 916-983-9500
Grace, Charles E., 10144 Elk Lake Rd., Williamsburg, MI 49690/616-264-9483
Grace Tool, Inc., 3661 E. 44th St., Tucson, AZ 85713/602-747-0213
"Gramps" Antique Cartridges, Box 341, Washago, Ont. L0K 2B0 CANADA/705-689-5348
Grand Falls Bullets, Inc., 1120 Forest Dr., Blue Springs, MO 64015/816-229-0112
Granite Custom Bullets, Box 190, Philipsburg, MT 59858/406-859-3245
Graphics Direct, 18336 Gault St., Reseda, CA 91335/818-344-9002
Graves Co., 1800 Andrews Av., Pompano Beach, FL 33069/800-327-9103; FAX: 305-960-0301
Graybill's Gun Shop, 1035 Ironville Pike, Columbia, PA 17512/717-684-6220
Green, Arthur S., 485 S. Robertson Blvd., Beverly Hills, CA 90211/310-274-1283
Green Bay Bullets, 1860 Burns Ave., Green Bay, WI 54313/414-494-5166
Green Genie, Box 114, Cusseta, GA 31805
Green Mountain Rifle Barrel Co., Inc., RFD #2, Box 8 Center, Conway, NH 03813/603-356-2047; FAX: 603-356-2048
Green, Roger M., P.O. Box 984, 435 E. Birch, Glenrock, WY 82637/307-436-9804
Greene, M.L., 17200 W. 57th Ave., Golden, CO 80403/303-279-2383
Greenwalt Rifles, 102 Brandon Rd., Yonkers, NY 10704/914-776-1581
Greg's Superior Products, P.O. Box 46219, Seattle, WA 98146
Griffin & Howe, Inc., 33 Claremont Rd., Bernardsville, NJ 07924/908-766-2287; FAX: 908-766-1068
Grizzly Bullets, 2137 Hwy. 200, Trout Creek, MT 59874/406-847-2627
Group Tight Bullets, 482 Comerwood Court, San Francisco, CA 94080/415-583-1550
GSI, Inc., 108 Morrow Ave., P.O. Box 129, Trussville, AL 35173/205-655-8299; FAX: 205-655-7078
G.U., Inc., 4325 S. 120th St., Omaha, NE 68137/402-330-4492
Guardian Group International, 21 Warren St., Suite 3E, New York, NY 10007/212-619-3838
Guardsman Products, 411 N. Darling, Fremont, MI 49412/616-924-3950
Gun City, 212 W. Main Ave., Bismarck, ND 58501/701-223-2304
Gun Doctor, The, 435 East Maple, Roselle, IL 60172/708-894-0668
Gun Doctor, The, P.O. Box 39242, Downey, CA 90242
Gun Hunter Books, Div. of Gun Hunter Trading Co., 5075 Heisig St., Beaumont, TX 77705/409-835-3006
Gun List (See Krause Publications)
Gun Room, The, 1121 Burlington, Muncie, IN 47302/317-282-9073; FAX: 317-282-9073
Gun Room Press, The, 127 Raritan Ave., Highland Park, NJ 08904/908-545-4344; FAX: 908-545-6686
Gun Shop, The, 5550 S. 900 East, Salt Lake City, UT 84117/801-263-3633
Gun Shop, The, 62778 Spring Creek Rd., Montrose, CO 81401
Gun Shop, The, Shop 31 320 West St., Durban 4001 SOUTH AFRICA
Gun South, Inc. (See GSI, Inc.)
Gun Works, The, 236 Main St., Springfield, OR 97477/503-741-4118
Guncraft Sports, Inc., 10737 Dutchtown Rd., Knoxville, TN 37932/615-966-4545
Gunline Tools, P.O. Box 478, Placentia, CA 92670/714-528-5252; FAX: 714-572-4128
Gunnerman Books, P.O. Box 214292, Auburn Hills, MI 48321/313-879-2779
GUNS Magazine, 591 Camino de la Reina, Suite 200, San Diego, CA 92108/619-297-5350; FAX: 619-297-5353
Guns Unlimited, Inc. (See G.U., Inc.)
Gunsmith in Elk River, The, 14021 Victoria Lane, Elk River, MN 55330/612-441-7761
Gunsmithing Ltd., 57 Unquowa Rd., Fairfield, CT 06430/203-254-0436

H

H&H Engineering, Box 642, Narberty, PA 19072
H&P Publishing, 7174 Hoffman Rd., San Angelo, TX 76905/915-655-5953
H&S Liner Service, 515 E. 8th, Odessa, TX 79761/915-332-1021
Hakko Co. Ltd., 5F Daini-Tsunemi Bldg., 1-13-12, Narimasu, Itabashiku Tokyo 175, JAPAN/(03)5997-7870-2
Half Moon Rifle Shop, 490 Halfmoon Rd., Columbia Falls, MT 59912/406-892-4409
Halstead, Rick, P.O. Box 63, Grinnell, IA 50112/515-236-5904
Hammets VLD Bullets, P.O. Box 479, Rayville, LA 71269/318-728-2019
Handgun Press, P.O. Box 406, Glenview, IL 60025/708-657-6500
Handloader's Journal, 60 Cottage St. #11, Hughesville, PA 17737
Hank's Gun Shop, Box 370, 50 West 100 South, Monroe, UT 84754/801-527-4456
Hanned Line, The, P.O. Box 161565, Cupertino, CA 95016-1565/916-324-9089
Hanned Precision (See Hanned Line, The)
Hansen & Co. (See Hansen Cartridge Co.)
Hansen Cartridge Co., 244 Old Post Rd., Southport, CT 06490/203-789-7337
Hanson's Gun Center, Dick, 233 Everett Dr., Colorado Springs, CO 80911
Hardin Specialty Dist., P.O. Box 338, Radcliff, KY 40159-0338/502-351-6649
Harper's Custom Stocks, 928 Lombrano St., San Antonio, TX 78207/512-732-5780
Harris Engineering, Inc., Rt. 1, Barlow, KY 42024/502-334-3633; FAX: 502-334-3000
Harris Enterprises, P.O. Box 105, Bly, OR 97622/503-353-2625
Harrison Bullet Works, 6437 E. Hobart Street, Mesa, AZ 85205/602-985-7844
Hart & Son, Inc., Robert W., 401 Montgomery St., Nescopeck, PA 18635/717-752-3655; FAX: 717-752-1088
Hart Rifle Barrels, Inc., RD 2, Apulia Rd., P.O. Box 182, Lafayette, NY 13084/315-677-9841
Hastings Barrels, 320 Court St., Clay Center, KS 67432/913-632-3169; FAX: 913-632-6554
Hawk Co., P.O. Box 1843, Glenrock, WY 82637/307-436-5561
Hawk Laboratories, Inc., P.O. Box 1843, Glenrock, WY 82637/307-436-5561
Hawken Shop, The (See Dayton Traister)
Haydon, Russ, 15018 Goodrich Dr., Big Harbor, WA 98329/206-857-7557
Heatbath Corp., P.O. Box 2978, Springfield, MA 01101/413-543-3381
HEBB Resources, P.O. Box 999, Mead, WA 99021-09996/509-466-1292
Hecht, Hubert J., Waffen-Hecht, P.O. Box 2635, Fair Oaks, CA 95628/916-966-1020
Heidenstrom Bullets, Urds GT 1 Heroya, 3900 Porsgrunn, NORWAY
Heilmann, Stephen, P.O. Box 657, Grass Valley, CA 95945/916-272-8758
Heinie Specialty Products, 323 W. Franklin St., Havana, IL 62644/309-543-4535; FAX: 309-543-2521
Henry Customs, J., P.O. Box 3281, Texas City, TX 77592
Hensley & Gibbs, Box 10, Murphy, OR 97533/503-862-2341
Hensley, Darwin, P.O. Box 179, Brightwood, OR 97011/503-622-5411
Heppler, Keith M., Keith's Custom Gunstocks, 540 Banyan Circle, Walnut Creek, CA 94598/510-934-3509
Hercules, Inc., Hercules Plaza, 1313 N Market St., Wilmington, DE 19894/302-594-5000
Hermann Leather Co., H.J., Rt. 1, P.O. Box 525, Skiatook, OK 74070/918-396-1226
Hertel & Reuss, Werk für Optik und Feinmechanik GmbH, Quellhofstrabe 67, 3500 Kassel, GERMANY/0561-83006; FAX: 0561-893308
Hesco-Meprolight, 2821 Greenville Rd., LaGrange, GA 30240/706-884-7967; FAX: 706-882-4683
Heydenberk, Warren R., 1059 W. Sawmill Rd., Quakertown, PA 18951/215-538-2682
Hickman, Jaclyn, Box 1900, Glenrock, WY 82637
Hidalgo, Tony, 12701 SW 9th Pl., Davie, FL 33325/305-476-7645
Higgs Bullets, 403 E. Broadway, Denver City, TX 79323/806-592-8794
High Country Custom Bullets, 19822 NW Sauvie Island Rd., Portland, OR 97231/503-621-3721
Hillmer Custom Gunstocks, Paul D., 7251 Hudson Heights, Hudson, IA 50643/319-988-3941
Hindman, Ace, 1880 1/2 Upper Turtle Creek Rd., Kerrville, TX 78028/512-257-4290
Hiptmayer, Klaus, RR 112 #750, P.O. Box 136, Eastman, Quebec J0E 1P0, CANADA/514-297-2492
Hirtenberger Aktiengesellschaft, Leobersdorferstrasse 31, A-2552 Hirtenberg, AUSTRIA
Hiti-Schuch, Atelier Wilma, A-8863 Predlitz, Pirming Y1 AUSTRIA/0353418278
Hobson Precision Mfg. Co., Rt. 1, Box 220-C, Brent, AL 35034/205-926-4662
Hodgdon Powder Co., Inc., P.O. Box 2932, Shawnee Mission, KS 66201/913-362-9455; FAX: 913-362-1307
Hoehn's Shooting Supply, 75 Greensburg Ct., St. Charles, MO 63304/314-441-4231
Hoenig & Rodman, 6521 Morton Dr., Boise, ID 83704/208-375-1116
Hoffman New Ideas, 821 Northmoor Rd., Lake Forest, IL 60045/312-234-4075
Holden Co., J.B., P.O. Box 700320, 975 Arthur, Plymouth, MI 48170/313-455-4850; FAX: 313-455-4212
Hollywood Engineering, 10642 Arminta St., Sun Valley, CA 91352/818-842-8376
Hondo Ind., 510 S. 52nd St.,#I04, Tempe, AZ 85281
Hoppe's Div., Penguin Industries, Inc., Airport Industrial Mall, Coatesville, PA 19320/251-384-6000
Horizons Unlimited, 8351 Roswell Rd., Suite 168, Atlanta, GA 30350/404-683-1269; FAX: 404-993-9770
Hornady Mfg. Co., P.O. Box 1848, Grand Island, NE 68801/800-338-3220, 308-382-1390
Howell Machine, 815 1/2 D St., Lewiston, ID 83501/208-743-7418
H-S Precision, Inc., 1301 Turbine Dr., Rapid City, SD 57701/605-341-3006; FAX: 605-342-8964
HT Bullets, 244 Belleville Rd., New Bedford, MA 02745/508-999-3338
Huebner, Corey O., P.O. Box 2074, Missoula, MT 59804/406-721-9647
Huey Gun Cases, Marvin, P.O. Box 22456, Kansas City, MO 64113/816-444-1637
Hughes, Steven Dodd, P.O. Box 11455, Eugene, OR 97440/503-485-8869
Hungry Horse Books, 4605 Hwy. 93 South, Whitefish, MT 59937/406-862-7997
Hunterjohn, P.O. Box 477, St. Louis, MO 63166/314-531-7250
Huntington Die Specialties, 601 Oro Dam Blvd., Oroville, CA 95965/916-534-1210; FAX: 916-534-1212

I

ICI-America, P.O. Box 751, Wilmington, DE 19897/302-575-3000
Idaho Ammunition Service, 2816 Mayfair Dr., Lewiston, ID 83501/208-743-0270
Idaho Bullets, Box 2532, Orofino, ID 83544/208-476-5046
Illinois Lead Shop, 7742 W. 61st Place, Summit, IL 60501
Imatronic, Inc., 1275 Paramount Pkwy., P.O. Box 520, Batavia, IL 60510/708-406-1920; FAX: 708-879-6749
IMI, P.O. Box 1044, Ramat Hasharon 47100, ISRAEL/972-3-5485222
Imperial Magnum Corp., 1417 Main St., Oroville, WA 98844/604-495-3131; FAX: 604-495-2816
IMR Powder Co., Box 247E, Xplo Complex, RTS, Plattsburgh, NY 12901/518-561-9530; FAX: 518-563-0044
Independent Machine & Gun Shop, 1416 N. Hayes, Pocatello, ID 83201
Info-Arm, P.O. Box 1262, Champlain, NY 12919
Innovision Enterprises, 728 Skinner Dr., Kalamazoo, MI 49001/616-382-1681; FAX: 616-382-1830
INTEC International, Inc., P.O. Box 5828, Sparks, NV 89432-5828
Intermountain Arms & Tackle, Inc., 105 E. Idaho St., Meridian, ID 83642/208-888-4911; FAX: 208-888-4381
Iosso Products, 1485 Lively Blvd., Elk Grove Village, IL 60007/708-437-8400
Ironside International Publishers, Inc., P.O. Box 55, 800 Slaters Lane, Alexandria, VA 22313/703-684-6111; FAX: 703-683-5486
Israel Military Industries Ltd. (See IMI)
I.S.W., 106 E. Cairo Dr., Tempe, AZ 85282
Ivanoff, Thomas G. (See Tom's Gun Repair)

J

J-4, Inc., 1700 Via Burton, Anaheim, CA 92806
J&J Products Co., 9240 Whitmore, El Monte, CA 91731/818-571-5228; FAX: 818-571-8704
J&L Superior Bullets (See Huntington Die Specialties)
J&R Enterprises, 4550 Scotts Valley Rd., Lakeport, CA 95453
Jackalope Gun Shop, 1048 S. 5th St., Douglas, WY 82633/307-358-3441
Jackson Arms, 6209 Hillcrest Ave., Dallas, TX 75205
JACO Precision Co., 11803 Indian Head Dr., Austin, TX 78753/512-836-4418
Jaeger, Inc., Paul/Dunn's, P.O. Box 449, 1 Madison Ave., Grand Junction, TN 38039/800-223-8667; FAX: 901-764-6503
Jamison's Forge Works, 4527 Rd. 6.5 NE, Moses Lake, WA 98837/509-762-2659
Jantz Supply, P.O. Box 584-GD, Davis, OK 73030/405-369-2316; FAX: 405-369-3082
Jarrett Rifles, Inc., 383 Brown Rd., Jackson, SC 29831/803-471-3616
Jason Empire, Inc., 9200 Cody, Overland Park, KS 66214-3259/913-888-0220; FAX: 913-888-0222
Javelina Products, P.O. Box 337, San Bernardino, CA 92402/714-882-5847; FAX: 714-434-6937
J-B Bore Cleaner, 299 Poplar St., Hamburg, PA 19526/215-562-2103
Jeffredo Gunsight, P.O. Box 669, San Marcos, CA 92079/619-728-2695
Jensen Bullets, 86 North, 400 West, Blackfoot, ID 83221/208-785-5590
Jensen's Custom Ammunition, 5146 E. Pima, Tucson, AZ 85712/602-325-3346; FAX: 602-322-5704
Jensen's Firearms Academy, 1280 W. Prince, Tucson, AZ 85705/602-293-8516
Jerry's Sport Center, P.O. Box 121 Main St., Forest City, PA 18421
Jester Bullets, Rt. 1 Box 27, Orienta, OK 73737
Jett & Co., Inc., R.R. #3, Box 167-B, Litchfield, IL 62056/217-324-3779
JGS Precision Tool Mfg., 1141 S. Summer Rd., Coos Bay, OR 97420/503-267-4331; FAX:503-267-5996
J.I.T., Ltd., P.O. Box 749, Glenview, IL 60025/708-998-0937
JLK Bullets, RR1, Box 310C, Dover, AR 72837/501-331-4194
J.O. Arms & Ammunition Co., 5709 Hartsdale, Houston, TX 77036/713-789-0745; FAX: 713-789-7513
Johnson Gunsmithing, Inc., Neal G., 111 Marvin Dr., Hampton, VA 23666/804-838-8091; FAX: 804-838-8157
Johnson Wood Products, RR #1, Strawberry Point, IA 52076/319-933-4930
Johnston Bros., 1889 Rt. 9, Unit 22, Toms River, NJ 08755/800-257-2595; FAX: 800-257-2534
Jonad Corp., 2091 Lakeland Ave., Lakewood, OH 44107/216-226-3161
Jones Custom Products, Neil, RD 1, Box 483A, Saegertown, PA 16443/814-763-2769; FAX: 814-763-4228
Jones, J.D., 721 Woodvue Lane, Wintersville, OH 43952/614-264-0176
JP Sales, Box 307, Anderson, TX 77830
JRW, 2425 Taffy Ct., Nampa, ID 83687
Jurras, L.E., P.O. Box 680, Washington, IN 47501/812-254-7698

K

K&M Services, P.O. Box 363, 2525 Primrose Lane, York, PA 17404/717-764-1461
K&T Co., Div. of T&S Industries, Inc., 1027 Skyview Dr., W. Carrollton, OH 45449/513-859-8414
Kahles USA, P.O. Box 81071, Warwick, RI 02888/800-752-4537: FAX: 717-540-8567
Ka Pu Kapili, P.O. Box 745, Honokaa, HI 96727/808-776-1644; FAX: 808-776-1731
Kapro Mfg. Co., Inc., P.O. Box 88, Tallevast, FL 34270/813-755-0085
Kasmarsik Bullets, 152 Crstler Rd., Chehalis, WA 98532
Kaswer Custom, Inc., 13 Surrey Drive, Brookfield, CT 06804/203-775-0564; FAX: 203-775-6872
K.B.I., Inc., P.O. Box 6346, Harrisburg, PA 17112/717-540-8518; FAX: 717-540-8567
K-D, Inc., 665 W. 300 South, Price, UT 84501/801-653-2530
Keeler, R.H., 817 "N" St., Port Angeles, WA 98362/206-457-4702
Keith's Bullets, 942 Twisted Oak, Algonquin, IL 60102/708-658-3520
Keith's Custom Gunstocks (See Heppler, Keith M.)
Kelley's, P.O. Box 125, Woburn, MA 01801/617-935-3389
Ken's Kustom Kartridges, 331 Jacobs Rd., Hubbard, OH 44425/216-534-4595
McCullough, Ken, Ken's Rifle Blanks, Rt. 2, P.O. Box 85B, Weston, OR 97886/503-566-3879
Keng's Firearms Specialty, Inc., 875 Wharton Dr. SW, Atlanta, GA 30336/404-691-7611; FAX: 404-505-8445
Kennebec Journal, 274 Western Ave., Augusta, ME 04330/207-622-6288
KenPatable Ent., Inc., P.O. Box 19422, Louisville, KY 40219/502-239-5447
Kent Cartridge Mfg. Co. Ltd., Unit 16, Branbridges Industrial Estate, East Peckham, Tonbridge, Kent, TN12 5HF ENGLAND/622-872255; FAX: 622-873645
Kesselring Gun Shop, 400 Hwy. 99 North, Burlington, WA 98233/206-724-3113; FAX: 206-724-7003
Keystone Bullets, RD 1, Box 312, New Bloomfield, PA 17068/717-582-8347
Kilham & Co., Main St., P.O. Box 37, Lyme, NH 03768/603-795-4112
Kimber, Inc., 16709 NE Union Rd., Ridgefield, WA 98642/206-573-4783
King & Co., P.O. Box 1242, Bloomington, IL 61701/309-473-3964
KJM Brass Group, P.O. Box 162, Marietta, GA 30061
K.K. Arms Co., Star Route Box 671, Kerrville, TX 78028/512-257-4718
Kleen-Bore, Inc., 20 Ladd Ave., Northampton, MA 01060/413-586-7240; FAX: 413-586-0236
Klein Custom Guns, Don, 433 Murray Park Dr., Ripon, WI 54971/414-748-2931
Klingler Woodcarving, P.O. Box 141, Thistle Hill, Cabot, VT 05647/802-426-3811
KLP, Inc., 215 Charles Dr., Holland, MI 49424/616-396-2575; FAX: 616-396-1287
Kmount, P.O. Box 19422, Louisville, KY 40259/502-239-5447
Knippel, Richard, 5924 Carnwood, Riverbank, CA 95367/209-869-1469
Kodiak Custom Bullets, 8261 Henry Circle, Anchorage, AK 99507/907-349-2282
KOGOT, 410 College, Trinidad, CO 81082/719-846-9406
Kolbe Precision, Riccarton Farm, Newcastleton SCOTLAND U.K. T09 0SN
Kolpin Mfg., Inc., P.O. Box 107, 205 Depot St., Fox Lake, WI 53933/414-928-3118; FAX: 414-928-3687
Kopp, Terry K., 1301 Franklin, Lexington, MO 64067/816-259-2636
Kowa Optimed, Inc., 20001 S. Vermont Ave., Torrance, CA 90502/310-327-1913; FAX: 310-327-4177
Krause Publications, 700 E. State St., Iola, WI 54990/715-445-2214; FAX: 715-445-4087
Krieger Barrels, Inc., N114 W18697 Clinton Dr., Germantown, WI 53022/414-255-9593; FAX: 414-255-9586
Kris Mounts, 108 Lehigh St., Johnstown, PA 15905
Kustom Kast Bullets, 18533 Roscoe Blvd. S. 137, Northridge, CA 91324
KVH Industries, Inc., 110 Enterprise Center, Middletown, RI 02840/401-847-3327; FAX: 401-849-0045
Kwik Mount Corp., P.O. Box 19422, Louisville, KY 40259/502-239-5447
Kwik-Site Co., 5555 Treadwell, Wayne, MI 48184/313-326-1500; FAX: 313-326-4120

L

L&S Technologies, Inc. (See Aimtech Mount Systems)
LaBounty Precision Reboring, P.O. Box 186, 7968 Silver Lk. Rd., Maple Falls, WA 98266/206-599-2047
Lachaussee, S.A., 29 Rue Kerstenne, Ans, B-4430 BELGIUM/041-63 88 77
Lage Uniwad, Inc., P.O. Box 446, Victor, IA 52327/319-647-3232
Lake Center, P.O. Box 38, St. Charles, MO 63302/314-946-7500
Lakewood Products, Inc., P.O. Box 1527, 1445 Eagle St., Rhinelander, WI 54501/715-369-3445
Lane Bullets, Inc., 1011 S. 10th St., Kansas City, KS 66105/913-621-6113, 800-444-7468
Lane Publishing, P.O. Box 759, Hot Springs, AR 71902/501-623-4951; FAX: 501-623-9832
Lan Orchards, 3601 10th St. SE, Ewenatchee, WA 98801
Lapua Ltd., P.O. Box 5, Lapua, FINLAND SF-62101/64-310111
Laseraim (Emerging Technologies, Inc.), P.O. Box 3548, Little Rock, AR 72203/501-375-2227; FAX: 501-372-1445
Laser Devices, Inc., 2 Harris Ct. A-4, Monterey, CA 93940/408-373-0701; FAX: 408-373-0903
Lathrop's, Inc., 5146 E. Pima, Tucson, AZ 85712/602-881-0226, 800-875-4867
Lawrence Brand Shot (See Precision Reloading, Inc.)
Lawson Co., Harry, 3328 N. Richey Blvd., Tucson, AZ 85716/602-326-1117
LBT, HCR 62, Box 145, Moyie Springs, ID 83845/208-267-3588
Lead Bullets Technology (See LBT)
Leatherwood-Meopta, Inc., 719 Ryan Plaza, Suite 103, Arlington, TX 76011
Lectro Science, Inc., 6410 W. Ridge Rd., Erie, PA 16506/814-833-6487; FAX: 814-833-0447
Leding Loader, RR 1, Box 645, Ozark, AR 72949
Lee Precision, Inc., 4275 Hwy. U, Hartford, WI 53027/414-673-3075
Lee Supplies, Mark, 9901 France Ct., Lakeville, MN 55044/612-461-2114
Lee's Red Ramps, Box 291240, Phelan, CA 92329-1240/619-868-5731
Lee Co., T.K., One Independence Plaza, Suite 520, Birmingham, AL 35209
Leica USA, Inc., 156 Ludlow Ave., Northvale, NJ 07647/201-767-7500; FAX: 201-767-8666
LEM Gun Specialties, Inc., P.O. Box 87031, College Park, GA 30337
Lenahan Family Enterprise, P.O. Box 46, Manitou Springs, CO 80829
Lethal Force Institute (See Police Bookshelf)
Leupold, P.O. Box 688, Beaverton, OR 97075/503-526-1491
Lewis, Ed, P.O. Box 875, Rico Rivera, CA 90660
Liberty Metals, 2233 East 16th St., Los Angeles, CA 90021/213-581-9171; FAX: 213-581-9351
Lighthouse Mfg. Co., Inc., 443 Ashwood Place, Boca Raton, FL 33431/407-394-6011
Lilja Precision Rifle Barrels, P.O. Box 372, Plains, MT 59859/406-826-3084; FAX: 406-826-3083
Lincoln, Dean, Box 1886, Farmington, NM 87401
Lind Custom Guns, Al, 7821 76th Ave. SW, Tacoma, WA 98498/206-584-6361
Lindner Custom Bullets, 325 Bennetts Pond La., Mattituck, NY 11952
Lindsley Arms Ctg. Co., P.O. Box 757, 20 College Hill Rd., Henniker, NH 03242/603-428-3127
Lite Tek International, 133-30 32nd Ave., Flushing, NY 11354/718-463-0650; FAX: 718-762-0890
Lithi Bee Bullet Lube, 2161 Henry St., Muskegon, MI 49441/616-755-4707
Littler Sales Co., 20815 W. Chicago, Detroit, MI 48228/313-273-6888; FAX: 313-273-1099
Load From A Disk, 9826 Sagedale, Houston, TX 77089/713-484-0935
Lock's Philadelphia Gun Exchange, 6700 Rowland Ave., Philadelphia, PA 19149/215-332-6225; FAX: 215-332-4800
Lofland, James W., 2275 Larkin Rd., Boothwyn, PA 19061/215-485-0391
Lohman Mfg. Co., Inc., 4500 Doniphan Dr., P.O. Box 220, Neosho, MO 64850/417-451-4438; FAX: 417-451-2576
Lomont Precision Bullets, 4236 W. 700 South, Poneto, IN 46781/219-694-6792; FAX: 219-694-6797
London Guns Ltd., Box 3750, Santa Barbara, CA 93130/805-683-4141; FAX: 805-683-1712
Lortone, Inc., 2856 NW Market St., Seattle, WA 98107/206-789-3100
Loweth, Richard, 29 Hedgegrow Lane, Kirby Muxloe, Leics. LE9 9BN ENGLAND
L.P.A. Snc, Via V. Alfieri #26, Gardone V.T. BS, ITALY 25063/(30)8911481; FAX: (30)8910951
LPS Laboratories, Inc., 4647 Hugh Howell Rd., P.O. Box 3050, Tucker, GA 30084/404-934-7800
LT Industries, Inc., 20504 Hillgrove Ave., Maple Heights, OH 44137/216-587-5005
Lyman Products Corp., Rt. 147 West St., Middlefield, CT 06455/203-349-3421; FAX: 203-349-3586
Lynn's Custom Gunstocks, RR 1, Brandon, IA 52210/319-474-2453

M

M&D Munitions Ltd., 127 Verdi St., Farmingdale, NY 11735/516-752-1038; FAX: 516-752-1905
M&M Engineering (See Hollywood Engineering)
M&N Bullet Lube, P.O. Box 495, 151 NE Jefferson St., Madras, OR 97741/503-255-3750
MA Systems, P.O. Box 489, Chouteau, OK 74337/918-479-6378
Mac-1 Distributors, 13972 Van Ness Ave., Gardena, CA 90249/310-327-3582
Mac's .45 Shop, P.O. Box 2028, Seal Beach, CA 90740/310-438-5046
Macks Sport Shop, P.O. Box 1155, Kodiak, AK 99615/907-486-4276
Madis, David, 2453 West Five Mile Pkwy., Dallas, TX 75233/214-330-7169
Magma Engineering Co., P.O. Box 161, Queen Creek, AZ 85242/602-987-9008; FAX: 602-987-0148
Magnum Power Products, Inc., P.O. Box 17768, Fountain Hills, AZ 85268
Magnus Bullets, P.O.Box 239, Toney, AL 35773/205-828-5089
MagSafe Ammo Co., Box 5692, 2725 Friendly Grove Rd NE, Olympia, WA 98506/206-357-6383
MAGTECH Recreational Products, Inc., 5030 Paradise Rd., Suite C211, Las Vegas, NV 89119/702-795-7191, 800-460-7191; FAX: 702-795-2769
Mahony, Philip Bruce, 67 White Hollow Rd., Lime Rock, CT 06039-2418/203-435-9341
Maine Custom Bullets, RFD 1, Box 1755, Brooks, ME 04921
Maionchi-L.M.I., Via Di Coselli-Zona Industriale Di Guamo, Lucca, ITALY 55060/011 39-583 94291
Maki Industries, 26-10th St. SE, Medicine Hat, AB T1A 1P7 CANADA/403-526-7997
Makinson, Nicholas, RR 3, Komoka, Ont. N0L 1R0 CANADA/519-471-5462
Malcolm Enterprises, 1023 E. Prien Lake Rd., Lake Charles, LA 70601
Mandarino, Monte, 205 Fifth Ave. East, Kalispell, MT 59901/406-257-6208
Manufacture D'Armes Des Pyrenees Francaises (See Unique/M.A.P.F.)
Marble Arms Corp., 420 Industrial Park, P.O. Box 111, Gladstone, MI 49837/906-428-3710; FAX: 906-428-3711
Marchmon Bullets, 8191 Woodland Shore Dr., Brighton, MI 48116
Markell, Inc., 422 Larkfield Center 235, Santa Rosa, CA 95403/707-573-0792; FAX: 707-573-9867
Marple & Associates, Dick, 21 Dartmouth St., Hooksett, NH 03106/603-627-1837; FAX: 603-641-4837
Marquart Precision Co., Inc., Rear 136 Grove Ave., Box 1740, Prescott, AZ 86302/602-445-5646
Marshall Enterprises, 792 Canyon Rd., Redwood City, CA 94062
Martin Bookseller, J., P.O. Drawer AP, Beckley, WV 25802/304-255-4073; FAX: 304-255-4077
Masen Co., John, P.O. Box 5050, Suite 165, Lewisville, TX 75057/817-430-8732
Master Class Bullets, 4110 Alder St., Eugene, OR 97405/503-687-1263
Matco, Inc., 1003-2nd St., N. Manchester, IN 46962/219-982-8282
Mayville Engineering Co. (See MEC, Inc.)
McCament, Jay, 1730-134th St. Ct. S., Tacoma, WA 98444/206-531-8832
McDonald, Dennis, 8359 Brady St., Peosta, IA 52068/319-556-7940
McFarland, Stan, 2221 Idella Ct., Grand Junction, CO 81505/303-243-4704
McGowen Rifle Barrels, 5961 Spruce Lane, St. Anne, IL 60964/815-937-9816; FAX: 815-937-4024
McGuire, Bill, 1600 N. Eastmont Ave., East Wenatchee, WA 98802/509-884-6021
McKee Publications, 121 Eatons Neck Rd., Northport, NY 11768/516-575-8850
McKee, Arthur, 121 Eatons Neck Rd., Northport, NY 11768/516-757-8850
McKillen & Heyer, Inc., 35535 Euclid Ave. Suite 11, Willoughby, OH 44094/216-942-2044
McMillan Fiberglass Stocks, Inc., 21421 N. 14th Ave., Phoenix, AZ 85027/602-582-9635; FAX: 602-581-3825
McMillan Gunworks, Inc., 302 W. Melinda Lane, Phoenix, AZ 85027/602-582-9627; FAX: 602-582-5178
McMillan Optical Gunsight Co., 28638 N. 42nd St., Cave Creek, AZ 85331/602-585-7868; FAX: 602-585-7872
McMillan Rifle Barrels, Bill Wiseman & Co., Inc., P.O. Box 3427, Bryan, TX 77805/409-690-3456; FAX: 409-690-0156
McMurdo, Lynn (See Specialty Gunsmithing)
MCRW Associates, R.R. 1 Box 1425, Sweet Valley, PA 18656
MCS, Inc., 34 Delmar Dr., Brookfield, CT 06804/203-775-1013; FAX: 203-775-9462
Measurement Group, Inc., Box 27777, Raleigh, NC 27611
MEC, Inc., 715 South St., Mayville, WI 53050/414-387-4500
Meier Works, P.O. Box 423, Tijeras, NM 87059/505-281-3783
Men-Metallwerk Elisenhuette, GmbH, P.O. Box 1263, W-5408 Nassau, GERMANY/2604-7819
Meprolight (See Hesco-Meprolight)
Mercer Custom Stocks, R.M., 216 S. Whitewater Ave., Jefferson, WI 53549/414-674-3839
Merit Corp., Box 9044, Schenectady, NY 12309/518-346-1420
Merkuria Ltd., Argentinska 38, 17005 Praha 7, CZECH REPUBLIC/422-875117; FAX: 422-809152
Michael's Antiques, Box 591, Waldoboro, ME 04572
Micro Sight Co., 242 Harbor Blvd., Belmont, CA 94002/415-591-0769; FAX: 415-591-7531
Micro-Lube, Rt. 2, P.O. Box 201, Deming, NM 88030/505-546-9116
Mid-America Recreation, Inc., 1328 5th Ave., Moline, IA 52807/309-764-5089; FAX: 309-764-2722
Midway Arms, Inc., P.O. Box 1483, Columbia, MO 65205/314-445-6363; FAX: 314-446-1018
Military Armament Corp., P.O. Box 120, Mt. Zion Rd., Lingleville, TX 76461/817-965-3253
Millenium Safety Products, P.O. Box 9802-916, Austin, TX 78766/512-346-3876
Miller Engineering, R&D Engineering & Manufacturing, P.O. Box 6342, Virginia Beach, VA 23456/804-468-1402
Miller Enterprises, Inc., 1557 E. Main St., Brownsburg, IN 46112/317-852-8187
Miller Gun Woods, 1440 Peltier Dr., Point Roberts, WA 98281/206-945-7014
Miller Single Trigger Mfg. Co., R.D.1, P.O. Box 99, Millersburg, PA 17061/717-692-3704
Miller, Tom (See Huntington Die Specialties)
Millett Sights, 16131 Gothard St., Huntington Beach, CA 92647/714-842-5575, 714-847-5245; FAX: 714-843-5707
Miniature Machine Co. (See MMC)
Mirador Optical Corp., 4501 Glencoe Ave., Marina Del Rey, CA 90292/310-821-5587; FAX: 310-305-0386

Mitchell Bullets, R.F., 430 Walnut St., Westernport, MD 21562
MKL Service Co., 610 S. Troy St., P.O. Box D, Royal Oak, MI 48068/313-548-5453
MMC, 606 Grace Ave., Ft. Worth, TX 76111/817-831-0837
MMP, Rt. 6, Box 384, Harrison, AR 72601/501-741-5019; FAX: 501-741-3104
MoLoc Bullets, P.O. Box 2810, Turlock, CA 95381/209-632-1644
Monell Custom Guns, Red Mill Road, Pine Bush, NY 12566/914-744-3021
Montana Outfitters, Lewis E. Yearout, 308 Riverview Dr. E., Great Falls, MT 59404/406-761-0859
Montana Precision Swaging, P.O. Box 4746, Butte, MT 59702/406-782-7502
Monte Kristo Pistol Grip Co., P.O. Box 85, Whiskeytown, CA 96095/916-623-4019
Morrison Custom Rifles, J.W., 4015 W. Sharon, Phoenix, AZ 85029/602-978-3754
Morrow, Bud, 11 Hillside Lane, Sheridan, WY 82801-9729/307-674-8360
Mo's Competitor Supplies (See MCS, Inc.)
Mountain Bear Rifle Works, Inc., 100 B Ruritan Rd., Sterling, VA 20164/703-430-0420
Mountain South, P.O. Box 381, Barnwell, SC 29812/FAX: 803-259-3227
Mountain View Sports, Inc., Box 188, Troy, NH 03465/603-357-9690; FAX: 603-357-9691
MPC, 188 Freeport Rd., Butler, PA 16001/800-227-7049, 412-283-0567; FAX: 412-283-8310
MPI Stocks, P.O. Box 83266, Portland, OR 97283-0266/503-226-1215
MTM Molded Products Co., Inc., 3370 Obco Ct., Dayton, OH 45414/513-890-7461; FAX: 513-890-1747
Mulhern, Rick, Rt. 5, Box 152, Rayville, LA 71269/318-728-2688
Mullins Ammo, Rt. 2, Box 304K, Clintwood, VA 24228/703-926-6772
Multipax, Inc., 8086 S. Yale, Suite 286, Tulsa, OK 74136/918-496-1999; FAX: 918-492-7465
Multiplex International, 26 S. Main St., Concord, NH 03301/FAX: 603-796-2223
Multi-Scale Charge Ltd., P.O. Box 101 LP, Niagara Falls, NY 14303/416-566-1255; FAX: 416-276-6295
Mundy, Thomas A., 69 Robbins Road, Somerville, NJ 08876/201-722-2199
Munger, Robert D. (See Rusteprufe Laboratories)
Murmur Corp., 2823 N. Westmoreland Ave., Dallas, TX 75222/214-630-5400
Muscle Products Corp. (See MPC)
Mushroom Express Bullet Co., 601 W. 6th St., Greenfield, IN 46140/317-462-6332
Muzzle-Nuzzle Co., 609 N. Virginia Ave., Roswell, NM 88201/505-624-1260
Muzzlelite Corp., P.O. Box 987, DeLeon Springs, FL 32130
Muzzleload Magnum Products (See MMP)
Muzzleloaders Etcetera, Inc., 9901 Lyndale Ave. S., Bloomington, MN 55420/612-884-1161

N

Nagel's Bullets, 9 Wilburn, Baytown, TX 77520
National Bullet Co., 1585 E. 361 St., Eastlake, OH 44095/216-951-1854; FAX: 216-951-7761
National Target Co., 4690 Wyaconda Rd., Rockville, MD 20852/800-827-7060, 301-770-7060; FAX: 301-770-7892
Naval Ordnance Works, Rt. 2, Box 919, Sheperdstown, WV 25443/304-876-0998
NECO, 1316-67th St., Emeryville, CA 94608/510-450-0420
Necromancer Industries, Inc., 14 Communications Way, West Newton, PA 15089/412-872-8722
Nesci Enterprises, Inc., P.O. Box 119, Summit St., East Hampton, CT 06424/203-267-2588
Nettestad Gun Works, RR 1, Box 160, Pelican Rapids, MN 56572/218-863-4301
Neutralizer Police Munitions, 5029 Middle Rd., Horseheads, NY 14845-9568/607-739-8362; FAX: 607-594-3900
New Democracy, Inc., 719 Ryan Plaza, Suite 103, Arlington, TX 76011
New England Ammunition Co., 1771 Post Rd. East, Suite 223, Westport, CT 06880/203-254-8048
New England Arms Co., Box 278, Lawrence Lane, Kittery Point, ME 03905/207-439-0593; FAX: 207-439-6726
New England Custom Gun Service (See Apel, Dietrich)
New Win Publishing, Inc., Box 5159, Clinton, NJ 08809/201-735-9701; FAX: 201-735-9703
Newark Electronics, 4801 N. Ravenswood Ave., Chicago, IL 60640
Newman Gunshop, Rt. 1, Box 90F, Agency, IA 52530/515-937-5775
NgraveR Co., The, 67 Wawecus Hill Rd., Bozrah, CT 06334/203-823-1533
Nichols Sports Optics, P.O. Box 37669, Omaha, NE 68137/402-339-3530; FAX: 402-330-8029
Nickels, Paul R., 4789 Summerhill Rd., Las Vegas, NV 89121/702-435-5318
Nicklas, Ted, 5504 Hegel Rd., Goodrich, MI 48438/313-797-4493
Niemi Engineering, W.B., Box 126 Center Road, Greensboro, VT 05841/802-533-7180 days, 802-533-7141 evenings
Night Vision Equipment Co., Inc., P.O. Box 266, Emmaus, PA 18049/215-391-9101
Nikon, Inc., 1300 Walt Whitman Rd., Melville, NY 11747/516-547-4200
Norma (See U.S. importer—Paul Co., The)
Norman Custom Gunstocks, Jim, 14281 Cane Rd., Valley Center, CA 92082/619-749-6252
Normington Co., Box 6, Rathdrum, ID 83858
North American Arms, 1800 North 300 West, Spanish Fork, UT 84660/800-821-5783, 801-897-7401; FAX: 801-798-9418
North American Shooting Systems, P.O. Box 306, Osoyoos, B.C. V0H 1V0 CANADA
North American Specialties, 25442 Trabuco Rd., 105-328, El Torro, CA 92630/714-979-4867; FAX: 714-979-1520
North Mountain Pine Training Center (See Executive Protection Institute)
North Specialty Products, 2664-B Saturn St., Brea, CA 92621/714-524-1665
Northern Precision Custom Swaged Bullets, 337 S. James St., Carthage, NY 13619/315-493-3456
Nosler, Inc., P.O. Box 671, Bend, OR 97709/800-285-3701, 503-382-3921; FAX: 503-388-4667
Novak's .45 Shop, Wayne, 1206 1/2 30th St., P.O. Box 4045, Parkersburg, WV 26101/304-485-9295
Numrich Arms Corp., 203 Broadway, W. Hurley, NY 12491
Nu-Teck, 30 Industrial Park Rd., Box 37, Centerbrook, CT 06409/203-767-3573; FAX: 203-767-9137
NW Sinker and Tackle, P.O. Box 1931, Myrtle Creek, OR 97457
Nygord Precision Products, P.O. Box 8394, La Crescenta, CA 91224/818-352-3027; FAX: 818-352-3027

O

Oakland Custom Arms, Inc., 4690 W. Walton Blvd., Waterford, MI 48329/313-674-8261
Oakshore Electronic Sights, Inc., P.O. Box 4470, Ocala, FL 32678-4470/904-629-7112; FAX: 904-629-1433
Obermeyer Rifled Barrels, 23122 60th St., Bristol, WI 53104/414-843-3537; FAX: 414-843-2129
O'Connor Rifle Products Co., Ltd., 2008 Maybank Hwy., Charleston, SC 29412/803-795-8590
Oehler Research, Inc., P.O. Box 9135, Austin, TX 78766/512-327-6900
Oil Rod and Gun Shop, 69 Oak St., East Douglas, MA 01516/508-865-2005
OK Weber, Inc., P.O. Box 7485, Eugene, OR 97401/503-747-0458; FAX: 503-747-5927
Old Wagon Bullets, 32 Old Wagon Rd., Wilton, CT 06897
Old West Bullet Moulds, P.O. Box 519, Flora Vista, NM 87415
Old Western Scrounger, Inc., The, 12924 Hwy. A-12, Montague, CA 96064/916-459-5445
Old World Gunsmithing, 2901 SE 122nd St., Portland, OR 97236/503-760-7681
Old World Oil Products, 3827 Queen Ave. N., Minneapolis, MN 55412/612-522-5037
Olsen Development Lab, 111 Lakeview Ave., Blackwood, NJ 08012
Olympic Arms, Inc., 624 Old Pacific Hwy. SE, Olympia, WA 98503/206-456-3471; FAX: 206-491-3447
Olympic Optical Co., P.O. Box 752377, Memphis, TN 38175-2377/901-794-3890
Omark Industries, Div. of Blount, Inc., 2299 Snake River Ave., P.O. Box 856, Lewiston, ID 83501/800-627-3640, 208-746-2351
Omnishock, 2219 Verde Oak Drive, Hollywood, CA 90068
OMR Feinmechanik, Jagd-und Sportwaffen, GmbH, Postfach 1231, Schutzenstr. 20, D-5400 Koblenz, GERMANY/0261-31865-15351
One Of A Kind, 15610 Purple Sage, San Antonio, TX 78255/512-695-3364
On Target, P.O. Box 3648, University Park, NM 88003
Optolyth-USA, Inc., 18805 Melvista Lane, Hillsboro, OR 97123/503-628-0246; FAX: 503-628-0797
Orchard Park Enterprise, P.O. Box 563, Orchard Park, NY 14227/616-656-0356
Ordnance Works, The, 2969 Pidgeon Point Road, Eureka, CA 95501/707-443-3252
Or-Un, Tahtakale Menekse Han 18, Istanbul, TURKEY 34460/901-522-5912; FAX: 901-522-7973
Orvis Co., The, Rt. 7, Manchester, VT 05254/802-362-3622 ext. 283; FAX: 802-362-3525
Ottmar, Maurice, Box 657, 113 E. Fir, Coulee City, WA 99115/509-632-5717
Outdoor Connection, Inc., The, 201 Douglas, P.O. Box 7751, Waco, TX 76712/800-533-6076; 817-772-5575; FAX: 817-776-6076
Outdoorsman's Bookstore, The, Llangorse, Brecon, County Powys LD3 7UE, U.K./44-87484-660; FAX: 44-87484-650
Outers Laboratories, Div. of Blount, Inc., Route 2, Onalaska, WI 54650/608-781-5800
Ox-Yoke Originals, Inc., 34 Main St., Milo, ME 04463/800-231-8313; FAX: 207-943-2416
Ozark Gun Works, 335 Cemetary Rd., Rogers, AR 72756/FAX: 501-631-6944

P

P&M Sales and Service, 5724 Gainsborough Pl., Oak Forest, IL 60452/708-687-7149
P&P Tool Co., 125 W. Market St., Morrison, IL 61270/815-772-7618
P&S Gun Service, 2138 Old Shepardsville Rd., Louisville, KY 40218/502-456-9346
Pac-Nor Barreling, 99299 Overlook Rd., P.O. Box 6188, Brookings, OR 97415/503-469-7330; FAX: 503-469-7331
Pace Marketing, Inc., 9474 NW 48th St., Sunrise, FL 33351-5137/305-741-4361; FAX: 305-741-2901
Pachmayr Ltd., 1875 S. Mountain Ave., Monrovia, CA 91016/818-357-7771, 800-423-9704; FAX: 818-358-7251
Pacific Tool Co., P.O. Box 2048, Ordnance Plant Rd., Grand Island, NE 68801
Paco's (See Small Custom Mould & Bullet Co.)
P.A.C.T., Inc., P.O. Box 531525, Grand Prairie, TX 75053/214-641-0049
Page Custom Bullets, P.O. Box 25, Port Moresby Papua, NEW GUINEA
Palmer Manufacturing Co., Inc., C., P.O. Box 220, West Newton, PA 15089/412-872-8200; FAX: 412-872-8302
Paragon Sales & Services, Inc., P.O. Box 2022, Joliet, IL 60434/815-725-9212; FAX: 815-725-8974
Parker Gun Finishes, 9337 Smokey Row Rd., Strawberry Plains, TN 37871/615-933-3286
Pasadena Gun Center, 206 E. Shaw, Pasadena, TX 77506/713-472-0417; FAX: 713-472-1322
Patchbox & Museum of the Great Divide, The, 600 Farm Rd., Kalispell, MT 59901/406-756-8851
Paterson Gunsmithing, 438 Main St., Paterson, NJ 07502/201-345-4100
Patrick Bullets, P.O. Box 172, Warwick QSLD 4370 AUSTRALIA
Patriot Manufacturing, P.O. Box 50065, Lighthouse Point, FL 33074/305-783-4849
Pattern Control, 114 N. Third St., Garland, TX 75040/214-494-3551
Paul Co., The, Rt. 1, Box 177A, Wellsville, KS 66092/913-883-4444
Paulsen Gunstocks, Rt. 71, Box 11, Chinook, MT 59523/406-357-3403
Pease Accuracy, Bob, P.O. Box 310787, New Braunfels, TX 78131/210-625-1342
Peasley, David, P.O. Box 604, 2067 S. Hiway 17, Alamosa, CO 81101
PECAR Herbert Schwarz, GmbH, Kreuzbergstrasse 6, Berlin 61, 1000 GERMANY/004930-785-7383; FAX: 004930-785-1934
Peerless Metals, 1445 Osage St., Denver, CO 80204/303-825-6394
Pejsa Ballistics, 2120 Kenwood Pkwy., Minneapolis, MN 55405/612-374-3337; FAX: 612-374-3337
Pell, John T., 410 College, Trinidad, CO 81082/719-846-9406
Peltor, Inc., 63 Commercial Way, E. Providence, RI 02914/401-438-4800; FAX: 800-EAR-FAX1
PEM's Mfg. Co., 5063 Waterloo Rd., Atwater, OH 44201/216-947-3721
Pence Precision Barrels, 7567 E. 900 S., S. Whitley, IN 46787/219-839-4745
Pend Oreille Sport Shop, 3100 Hwy. 200 East, Sandpoint, ID 83864/208-263-2412
Pendleton Royal, 4/7 Highgate St., Birmingham, ENGLAND B12 0X5/44 21 440 3060; FAX: 44 21 446 4165
Penrod Precision, 312 College Ave., P.O. Box 307, N. Manchester, IN 46962/219-982-8385
Pentax Corp., 35 Inverness Dr. E., Englewood, CO 80112/303-799-8000
Pentheny de Pentheny, 2352 Baggett Ct., Santa Rosa, CA 95401/707-573-1390
Pepperbox Gun Shop, P.O. Box 922, E. Moline, IL 61244
Perazzi USA, Inc., 1207 S. Shamrock Ave., Monrovia, CA 91016/818-303-0068
Peripheral Data Systems (See Arms)
Professional Firearms Record Book Co. (See PFRB Co.)
Personal Protection Systems, RD 5, Box 5027-A, Moscow, PA 18444/717-842-1766
Petersen Publishing Co., 6420 Wilshire Blvd., Los Angeles, CA 90048
Peterson Instant Targets, Inc. (See Lyman Products Corp.)
Pettinger Books, Gerald, Rt. 2, Box 125, Russell, IA 50238/515-535-2239
Pflumm Gun Mfg. Co., 6139 Melrose Ln., Shawnee, KS 66203/800-888-4867
PFRB Co., P.O. Box 1242, Bloomington, IL 61701/309-473-3964
Phillippi Custom Bullets, Justin, P.O. Box 773, Ligonier, PA 15658/412-238-9671
Pilkington Gun Co., P.O. Box 1296, Muskogee, OK 74402/918-683-9418
Plum City Ballistic Range, N2162 80th St., Plum City, WI 54761-8622/715-647-2539
PMC/Eldorado Cartridge Corp., P.O. Box 62508, 12801 U.S. Hwy. 95 S., Boulder City, NV 89006-2508/702-294-0025; FAX: 702-294-0121
Police Bookshelf, P.O. Box 122, Concord, NH 03301/603-224-6814; FAX: 603-226-3554
Polywad, Inc., P.O. Box 7916, Macon, GA 31209/912-477-0669
Pomeroy, Robert, RR1, Box 50, E. Corinth, ME 04427/207-285-7721
Ponsness/Warren, P.O. Box 8, Rathdrum, ID 83858/208-687-2231; FAX: 208-687-2233
Pony Express Reloaders, 608 E. Co. Rd. D, Suite 3, St. Paul, MN 55117/612-483-9406
Powder Horn, Inc., The, P.O. Box 114 Patty Drive, Cusseta, GA 31805/404-989-3257
Power Plus Enterprises, P.O. Box 6070, Columbus, GA 31907-0058/404-561-1717
PPC Corp., 627 E. 24th St., Paterson, NJ 07514/201-278-5428
Pranger, Ed G., 1414 7th St., Anacortes, WA 98221/206-293-3488
Precise Metalsmithing Enterprises, 146 Curtis Hill Rd., Chehalis, WA 98532/206-748-3743; FAX: 206-748-8102
Precision Bullet Co., 5200 A. Florence Loop, Dunsmuir, CA 96025/916-235-0565
Precision Cartridge, 176 Eastside Rd., Deer Lodge, MT 59722/800-397-3901, 406-846-3900
Precision Cast Bullets, 101 Mud Creek Lane, Ronan, MT 59864/406-676-5135
Precision Castings & Equipment, Inc., P.O. Box 326, Jasper, IN 47547-0135/812-634-9167
Precision Components and Guns, Rt. 55, P.O. Box 337, Pawling, NY 12564/914-855-3040
Precision Delta Corp., P.O. Box 128, Ruleville, MS 38771/601-756-2810; FAX: 601-756-2590
Precision Munitions, Inc., P.O. Box 326, Jasper, IN 47547

Precision Ordnance, 1316 E. North St., Jackson, MI 49202
Precision Reloading, Inc., P.O. Box 122, Stafford Springs, CT 06076/203-684-7979; FAX: 203-684-6788
Precision Shooting, Inc., 5735 Sherwood Forest Dr., Akron, OH 44319
Precision Sport Optics, 15571 Producer Lane, Unit G, Huntington Beach, CA 92649/714-891-1309; FAX: 714-892-6920
Precision Sports, 3736 Kellogg Rd., P.O. Box 5588, Cortland, NY 13045-5588/607-756-2851, 800-847-6787; FAX: 607-753-8835
Premier Reticles, 920 Breckenridge Lane, Winchester, VA 22601-6707
Prescott Projectile Co., 1808 Meadowbrook Road, Prescott, AZ 86303
Price Bullets, Patrick W., 16520 Worthley Drive, San Lorenzo, CA 94580/415-278-1547
Primos Wild Game Calls, Inc., P.O. Box 12785, Jackson, MS 39236-2785/601-366-1288; FAX: 601-362-3274
Pro Load Ammunition, Inc., 5180 E. Seltice Way, Post Falls, ID 83854/208-773-9444; FAX: 208-773-9441
Pro-Shot Products, Inc., P.O. Box 763, Taylorville, IL 62568/217-824-9133; FAX: 217-824-8861
Professional Hunter Supplies (See Star Custom Bullets)
Prolix®, 15578 Mojave Dr. Unit D, Victorville, CA 92392/800-248-LUBE, 619-243-3129; FAX: 619-241-0148
Protektor Model Co., 7 Ash St., Galeton, PA 16922/814-435-2442
ProWare,Inc., 15847 NE Hancock St., Portland, OR 97230/503-239-0159

Q

Quack Decoy Corp., 4 Mill St., Cumberland, RI 02864/401-723-8202
Qualigraphics, Inc., 25 Ruta Ct., P.O. Box 2306, S. Hackensack, NJ 07606/201-440-9200
Quartz-Lok, 13137 N. 21st Lane, Phoenix, AZ 85029
Quinetics Corp., P.O. Box 13237, San Antonio, TX 78213/512-684-8561; FAX: 512-684-2912

R

R&J Gun Shop, 133 W. Main St., John Day, OR 97845/503-575-2130
R&S Industries Corp., 8255 Brentwood Industrial Dr., St. Louis, MO 63144/314-781-5400
Radiator Specialty Co., 1900 Wilkinson Blvd., P.O. Box 34689, Charlotte, NC 28234/800-438-6947; FAX: 800-421-9525
Radix Research & Mktg., Box 247, Woodland Park, CO 80863
Rainier Ballistics Corp., 4500 15th St. East, Tacoma, WA 98424/800-638-8722; FAX: 206-922-7854
Ram-Line, Inc., 10601 W. 48th Ave., Wheat Ridge, CO 80033/303-467-0300; FAX: 303-467-9833
Ranch Products, P.O. Box 145, Malinta, OH 43535/313-277-3118; FAX: 313-565-8536
Randolph Engineering, Inc., 275 Centre St., Unit 17, Holbrook MA 02343/617-961-6070, 800-541-1405; FAX: 617-767-5239
Ranging, Inc., Routes 5 & 20, East Bloomfield, NY 14443/716-657-6161
Ransom International Corp., P.O. Box 3845, 1040-A Sandretto Dr., Prescott, AZ 86302/602-778-7899; FAX: 602-778-7993
Rapine Bullet Mould Mfg. Co., P.O. Box 1119, East Greenville, PA 18041/215-679-5413
Ravell Ltd., 289 Diputacion St., 08009, Barcelona SPAIN
Raytech, Div. of Lyman Products Corp., Rt. 32 Stafford Ind. Park, Box 6, Stafford Springs, CT 06076/203-684-4273; FAX: 203-684-7938
RCBS, Div. of Blount, Inc., 605 Oro Dam Blvd., Oroville, CA 95965/800-533-5000, 916-533-5191
R.D.P. Tool Co., Inc., 49162 McCoy Ave., East Liverpool, OH 43920/216-385-5129
Reagent Chemical & Research, Inc. (See Cali'co Hardwoods, Inc.)
Reardon Products, P.O. Box 126, Morrison, IL 61270/815-772-3155
Rebec's Reloading, P.O. Box 30550, Santa Barbara, CA 93130
Red Diamond Dist. Co., 1304 Snowdon Dr., Knoxville, TN 37912
Red Star Target Co., 4519 Brisebois Dr. NW, Calgary AB T2L 2G3 CANADA/403-289-7939; FAX: 403-289-3275
Red Willow Tool & Armory, Inc., 4004 Hwy. 93 North, Stevensville, MT 59870/406-777-5401; FAX: 406-777-5402
Redding Reloading Equipment, 1089 Starr Rd., Cortland, NY 13045/607-753-3331; FAX: 607-756-8445
Redfield, Inc., 5800 E. Jewell Ave., Denver, CO 80224/303-757-6411; FAX: 303-756-2338
Redman's Rifling & Reboring, Rt. 3, Box 330A, Omak, WA 98841/509-826-5512
Redwood Bullet Works, 3559 Bay Rd., Redwood City, CA 94063/415-367-6741
Regional Associates, P.O. Box 9849, Alexandria, VA 22304/703-780-6189
Reiswig, Wallace E., Claro Walnut Gunstock Co., 1235 Stanley Ave., Chico, CA 95928/916-342-5188
Reloaders Equipment Co., 4680 High St., Ecorse, MI 48229
Reloading Specialties, Inc., 209 S.W. 2nd Ave. Box 1130, Pine Island, MN 55963/507-356-8500
Remington Arms Co., Inc., 1007 Market St., Wilmington, DE 19898/302-773-5291
Rencher Bullets, 5161 NE 5th St., Redmond, OR 97756
Renner Co., R.J./Radical Concepts, P.O. Box 10731, Canoga Park, CA 91309/818-700-8131
R.E.T. Enterprises, 2608 S. Chestnut, Broken Arrow, OK 74012/918-251-GUNS; FAX: 918-251-0587
R.G.-G., Inc., P.O. Box 1261, Conifer, CO 80433-1261
Rice, Keith (See White Rock Tool & Die)
Richards Classic Oil Finish, John, Rt. 2, Box 325, Bedford, KY 40006/502-255-7222
Richards Micro-Fit Stocks, 8331 N. San Fernando Rd., P.O. Box 1066, Sun Valley, CA 91352/818-767-6097
Pete Rickard, Inc., RD 1, Box 292, Cobleskill, NY 12043/800-282-5663; FAX: 518-234-2454
Ridgetop Sporting Goods, P.O. Box 306, 42907 Hilligoss Ln. East, Eatonville, WA 98328/206-832-6422
Riebe Co., W.J., 3434 Tucker Rd., Boise, ID 83703
RIG Products, 87 Coney Island Dr., Sparks, NV 89431-1990/702-331-5666; FAX: 702-331-5669
Riling Arms Books Co., Ray, 6844 Gorsten St., P.O. Box 18925, Philadelphia, PA 19119/215-438-2456
R.I.S. Co., Inc., 718 Timberlake Circle, Richardson, TX 75080/214-235-0933
River Road Sporting Clays, Bruce Barsotti, P.O. Box 3016, Gonzales, CA 93926/408-675-2473
RLCM Enterprises, 110 Hill Crest Drive, Burleson, TX 76028
RMS Custom Gunsmithing, 4120 N. Bitterwell, Prescott Valley, AZ 86314/602-772-7626
Robar Co.'s, Inc., The, 21438 N. 7th Ave., Suite B, Phoenix, AZ 85027/602-581-2648; FAX: 602-582-0059
Roberts Products, 25238 SE 32nd, Issaquah, WA 98027/206-392-8172
Robinson Firearms Mfg. Ltd., RR2, Suite 51, Comp. 24, Winfield, B.C. CANADA V0H 2C0/604-766-5353
Robinson, Don, Pennsylvania Hse., 36 Fairfax Crescent, Southowram, Halifax, W. Yorkshire HX3 9SQ, ENGLAND/0422-364458
Rochester Lead Works, 76 Anderson Ave., Rochester, NY 14607/716-442-8500
Rockwood Corp., Speedwell Division, 136 Lincoln Blvd., Middlesex, NJ 08846/908-560-7171
Rocky Fork Enterprises, P.O. Box 427, 878 Battle Rd., Nolensville, TN 37135/615-941-1307
Rocky Mountain High Sports Glasses, 8121 N. Central Park Ave., Skokie, IL 60076/708-679-1012; FAX: 708-679-0184
Rocky Mountain Rifle Works Ltd., 1707 14th St., Boulder, CO 80302/303-443-9189
Rocky Mountain Target Co., 3 Aloe Way, Leesburg, FL 34788/904-365-9598
Rolston Jr., Fred, 210 E. Cummins, Tecumseh, MI 49286/517-423-6002
Rooster Laboratories, P.O. Box 412514, Kansas City, MO 64141/816-474-1622; FAX: 816-474-1307
Rorschach Precision Products, P.O. Box 151613, Irving, TX 75015/214-790-3487
Rossi S.A. Metalurgica E Municoes, Amadeo, Rua Amadeo Rossi, 143, Sao Leopoldo, RS, BRAZIL 93 030/0512-92-5566
Roto Carve, 2754 Garden Ave., Janesville, IA 50647
Royal Arms, 5126 3rd Ave. N., Great Falls, MT 59401/406-453-1149
Royal Labs, Ltd., P.O. Box 2043, 710 Elm St., Truth or Consequences, NM 87901
RPM, 15481 N. Twin Lakes Dr., Tucson, AZ 85737/602-825-1233; FAX: 602-825-3333
RSR Corp., 1111 West Mockingbird Lane, Dallas, TX 75247/214-631-6070
RSR Corp., 720 S. 7th Ave., City of Industry, CA 91746-3124/818-330-2294
R-Tech Corp., P.O. Box 1281, Cottage Grove, OR 97424/503-942-5126; FAX: 503-942-8624
Rubright Bullets, 1008 S. Quince Rd., Walnutport, PA 18088/215-767-1339
Rucker Ammunition Co., P.O. Box 479, Terrell, TX 75160
Rupert's Gun Shop, 2202 Dick Rd., Suite B, Fenwick, MI 48834/517-248-3252
Russell's Rifle Shop, Rt. 5, P.O. Box 92, Georgetown, TX 78626/512-778-5338
Rusteprufe Laboratories, Robert D. Munger, 1319 Jefferson Ave., Sparta, WI 54656/608-269-4144
Rusty Duck Premium Gun Care Products, 7785 Founion Dr., Florence, KY 41042/606-342-5553
Rutgers Book Center, 127 Raritan Ave., Highland Park, NJ 08904/908-545-4344; FAX: 908-545-6686
Rutgers Gun & Boat Center, 127 Raritan Ave., Highland Park, NJ 08904/908-545-4344; FAX: 908-545-6686
RWS (See U.S. importer—Dynamit Nobel-RWS, Inc.)
Ryan, Chad L., RR 3, Box 72, Cresco, IA 52136/319-547-4384

S

S&B Industries, 11238 McKinley Rd., Montrose, MI 48457/313-639-5491
S&K Mfg. Co., P.O. Box 247, Pittsfield, PA 16340/814-563-7808; FAX: 814-563-7808
SAECO (See Redding Reloading Equipment)
Safari Gun Co., 6410 Brandon Ave., Springfield, VA 22150/703-569-1097
Safari Press, Inc., 15621 Chemical Lane B, Huntington Beach, CA 92649/714-894-9080; FAX: 714-894-4949
Safariland Ltd., Inc., 3120 E. Mission Blvd., P.O. Box 51478, Ontario, CA 91761/714-923-7300; FAX: 714-923-7400
S.A.F.E., P.O. Box 864, Post Falls, ID 83854/208-773-3624
Safety Direct, 56 Coney Island Dr., Sparks, NV 89431/702-354-4451
Sako Ltd., P.O. Box 149, SF-11101, Riihimaki, FINLAND
Samco Global Arms, Inc., 6995 NW 43rd St., Miami, FL 33166/305-593-9782
San Angelo Sports Products, Inc., 909 W. 14th St., San Angelo, TX 76903/915-655-7126; FAX: 915-653-6720
San Francisco Gun Exchange, 124 Second St., San Francisco, CA 94105/415-982-6097
Sanders Custom Gun Service, 2358 Tyler Ln., Louisville, KY 40205/502-454-3338
Sanders Gun and Machine Shop, 145 Delhi Road, Manchester, IA 52057
Sandia Die & Ctg. Co., 37 Atancacio Rd. NE, Albuquerque, NM 87123/505-298-5729
Saunders Gun & Machine Shop, R.R. 2, Delhi Road, Manchester, IA 52057
Schaefer Shooting Sports, 2280 Grand Ave., Baldwin, NY 11510/516-379-4900; FAX: 516-379-6701
Schaefer, Roy V., 101 Irving Rd., Eugene, OR 97404/503-688-4333
Scharch Mfg., Inc., 10325 Co. Rd. 120, Unit C, Salida, CO 81201/719-539-7242
Schiffman, Curt, 3017 Kevin Cr., Idaho Falls, ID 83402/208-524-4684
Schiffman, Mike, 8233 S. Crystal Springs, McCammon, ID 83250/208-254-9114
Schmidpke, Karl, P.O. Box 51692, New Berlin, WI 53151
Schmidt & Bender (See Jaeger, Inc., Paul/Dunn's)
Schmidtman Custom Ammunition, 6 Gilbert Court, Cotati, CA 94931
Schneider Bullets, 3655 West 214th St., Fairview Park, OH 44126
Schneider Rifle Barrels, Inc., Gary, 12202 N. 62nd Pl., Scottsdale, AZ 85254/602-948-2525
Schumakers Gun Shop, William, 512 Prouty Corner Lp. A, Colville, WA 99114/509-684-4848
Schwartz Custom Guns, David W., 2505 Waller St., Eau Claire, WI 54703/715-832-1735
Scot Powder Co., 1200 Talley Road, Wilmington, DE 19809/302-764-9779
Scot Powder Co. of Ohio, Inc., 430 Powder Plant Rd., McArthur, OH 45651/614-596-2706; FAX: 614-596-4050
Scott, Inc., Tyler, 313 Rugby Ave., Terrace Park, OH 45174/513-831-7603
Seattle Binocular & Scope Repair Co., P.O. Box 46094, Seattle, WA 98146/206-932-3733
Security Awareness & Firearms Education (See S.A.F.E.)
Seebeck Assoc., R.E., P.O. Box 59752, Dallas, TX 75229
Seligman Shooting Products, Box 133, Seligman, AZ 86337/602-422-3607
Selsi Co., Inc., 40 Veterans Blvd., Carlstadt, NJ 07072-0497/201-935-5851
Service Armament, 689 Bergen Blvd., Ridgefield, NJ 07657
Shappy Bullets, 76 Milldale Ave., Plantsville, CT 06479/203-621-3704
Sharon Rifle Barrel Co., 14396 D. Tuolumne Rd., Sonora, CA 95370/209-532-4139
Shaw's Finest in Guns, 1255 N. Broadway 351, Escondido, CA 92026-2858
Shaw, Inc., E.R. (See Small Arms Mfg. Co.)
Shay's Gunsmithing, 931 Marvin Ave., Lebanon, PA 17042
Shepherd Scope Ltd., Box 189, Waterloo, NE 68069/402-779-2424; FAX: 402-779-4010
Sheridan USA, Austin, Inc., P.O. Box 577, Durham, CT 06422
Sherk, Dan A., 1311-105 Ave., Dawson Creek, B.C. V1G 2L9, CANADA/604-782-3720
Sherwood Intl. Export Corp., 18714 Parthenia St., Northridge, CA 91324/818-349-7600
Shilen Rifles, Inc., P.O. Box 1300, 205 Metro Park Blvd., Ennis, TX 75119/214-875-5318; FAX: 214-875-1442
Shooter's Choice, 16770 Hilltop Park Place, Chagrin Falls, OH 44022/216-543-8808; FAX: 216-543-8811
Shooter's Edge, Inc., P.O.Box 769, Trinidad, CO 81082
Shooters Accessory Supply (See Corbin, Inc.)
Shooters Supply, 1120 Tieton Dr., Yakima, WA 98902/509-452-1181
Shootin' Accessories, Ltd., P.O. Box 6810, Auburn, CA 95604/916-889-2220
Shooting Arts Ltd., Box 621399, Littleton, CO 80162/303-933-2539
Shooting Chrony, Inc., P.O. Box 101 LP, Niagara Falls, NY 14304/416-276-6292; FAX: 416-276-6295
Shooting Gallery, The, 8070 Southern Blvd., Boardman, OH 44512/216-726-7788
Shotgun Shop, The, 14145 Proctor Ave., Suite 3, Industry, CA 91746/818-855-2737; FAX: 818-855-2735
Siegrist Gun Shop, 8754 Turtle Road, Whittemore, MI 48770
Sierra Bullets, 1400 W. Henry St., Sedalia, MO 65301/816-827-6300; FAX: 816-827-4999
Sierra Specialty Prod. Co., 1344 Oakhurst Ave., Los Altos, CA 94024
Signet Metal Corp., 551 Stewart Ave., Brooklyn, NY 11222/718-384-5400; FAX: 718-388-7488
Sile Distributors, Inc., 7 Centre Market Pl., New York, NY 10013/212-925-4389; FAX: 212-925-3149
Silencio (See Safety Direct)
Silver Eagle Machining, 18007 N. 69th Ave., Glendale, AZ 85308
Silver-Tip Corp., Rt. 1, Box 211-C, Liberty, MS 39645/601-384-5830

Simmons Enterprises, Ernie, 709 East Elizabethtown Rd., Manheim, PA 17545/717-664-4040
Simmons, Jerry, 715 Middlebury St., Goshen, IN 46526/219-533-8546
Simmons Outdoor Corp., 2571 Executive Ctr. Circle E, Tallahassee, FL 32301/904-878-5100; FAX: 904-878-0300
Sinclair, Fred, 2330 Wayne Haven St., Fort Wayne, IN 46803/219-493-1858
Sinclair International, Inc., 2330 Wayne Haven St., Fort Wayne, IN 46803/219-493-1858; FAX: 219-493-2530
Sioux Bullets, P.O. Box 3696, Midland, TX 79702
Siskiyou Gun Works (See Donnelly, C.P.)
Six Enterprises, 320-D Turtle Creek Ct., San Jose, CA 95125/408-999-0201; FAX: 408-999-0216
Skeoch, Brian R., P.O. Box 279, Glenrock, WY 82637/307-436-9804
Skip's Machine, 364 29 Road, Grand Junction, CO 81501/303-245-5417
SKR Industries, POB 1382, San Angelo, TX 76902/915-658-3133
S.L.A.P. Industries, P.O. Box 1121, Parklands 2121, SOUTH AFRICA
Slipshot MTS Group, P.O. Box 5, Postal Station D, Etobicoke, Ont., CANADA M9A 4X1/FAX: 416-762-0962
Slug Site Co., Ozark Wilds, Rt. 2, Box 158, Versailles, MO 65084/314-378-6430
Small Arms Mfg. Co., 611 Thoms Run Rd., Bridgeville, PA 15017/412-221-4343; FAX: 412-221-8443
Small Custom Mould & Bullet Co., Box 17211, Tucson, AZ 85731
Small Group Bullets, P.O. Box 20, Mertzon, TX 76941/915-835-4751
Smith & Wesson, 2100 Roosevelt Ave., Springfield, MA 01102/413-781-8300
Snider Stocks, Walter S., Rt. 2 P.O. Box 147, Denton, NC 27239
Societa Armi Bresciane Srl., Via Artigiani 93, Gardone Val Trompia, ITALY 25063/30-8911640, 30-8911648
SOS Products Co. (See Buck Stix—SOS Products Co.)
Southern Ammunition Co., Inc., Rt. 1, Box 6B, Latta, SC 29565/803-752-7751; FAX: 803-752-2022
Specialized Weapons, Inc. (See Tapco, Inc.)
Specialty Gunsmithing, Lynn McMurdo, P.O. Box 404, Afton, WY 83110/307-886-5535
Speedfeed, Inc., P.O. Box 258, Lafayette, CA 94549/510-284-2929; FAX: 510-284-2879
Speer Products, Div. of Blount, Inc., P.O. Box 856, Lewiston, ID 83501/208-746-2351
Speiser, Fred D., 2229 Dearborn, Missoula, MT 59801/406-549-8133
Spence, George W., 115 Locust St., Steele, MO 63877/314-695-4916
SPG Lubricants, Box 761-H, Livingston, MT 59047
SPI, 215 Poppleton St., Birmingham, MI 48009-5725
Sport Flite Manufacturing Co., P.O. Box 1082, Bloomfield Hills, MI 48303/313-647-3747
Sports Support Systems, Inc., 28416 Pacheco, Mission Viejo, CA 92692/714-367-0343
Sportsman Supply Co., 714 East Eastwood, P.O. Box 650, Marshall, MO 65340/816-886-9393
Sportsmatch Ltd., 16 Summer St., Leighton Buzzard, Bedfordshire, LU7 8HT ENGLAND/0525-381638; FAX: 0525-851236
Springfield, Inc., 25144 Ridge Rd., Colona, IL 61241/309-441-6002; FAX: 309-441-6003
SSK Co., 220 N. Belvidere Ave., York, PA 17404/717-854-2897
SSK Industries, 721 Woodvue Lane, Wintersville, OH 43952/614-264-0176; FAX: 614-264-2257
Stackpole Books, P.O. Box 1831, Harrisburg, PA 17105/717-234-5041; FAX: 717-234-1359
Stafford Bullets, 1920 Tustin Ave., Philadelphia, PA 19152
Stalwart Corp., P.O. Box 357, Pocatello, ID 83204/208-232-7899
Stanley Bullets, 2085 Heatheridge Ln., Reno, NV 89509
Star Custom Bullets, P.O. Box 608, 468 Main St., Ferndale, CA 95536/707-786-4040; FAX: 707-786-9117
Star Machine Works, 418 10th Ave., San Diego, CA 92101/619-232-3216
Star Reloading Co., Inc., 5520 Rock Hampton Ct., Indianapolis, IN 46268/317-872-5840
Stark's Bullet Mfg., 2580 Monroe St., Eugene, OR 97405
Starshot Holduxa, Bolognise 125, Miraflores, Lima PERU
State Arms Gun Co., 815 S. Division St., Waunakee, WI 53597/608-849-5800
Steel Reloading Components, Inc., P.O. Box 812, Washington, IN 47501/812-254-3775; FAX: 812-254-7269
Stegall, James B., 26 Forest Rd., Wallkill, NY 12589
Stevi Machine, Inc., 4004 Hwy. 93 North, Stevensville, MT 59870/406-777-5401
Stewart's Gunsmithing, P.O. Box 5854, Pietersburg North 0750, Transvaal, SOUTH AFRICA/01521-89401
Stillwell, Robert, 421 Judith Ann Dr., Schertz, TX 78154
Stoeger Industries, 55 Ruta Ct., S. Hackensack, NJ 07606/201-440-2700, 800-631-0722; FAX: 201-440-2707
Stoeger Publishing Co. (See Stoeger Industries)
Stoney Baroque Shooters Supply, John Richards, Rt. 2, Box 325, Bedford, KY 40006/502-255-7222
Stoney Point Products, Inc., 124 Stoney Point Rd., Courtland, MN 56021/507-354-3360; FAX: 507-354-7236
Stratco, Inc., 200 E. Center St., Kalispell, MT 59901/406-755-4034; FAX: 406-257-4753
Strawbridge, Victor W., 6 Pineview Dr., Dover, NH 03820/603-742-0013
Strutz Rifle Barrels, Inc., W.C., P.O. Box 611, Eagle River, WI 54521/715-479-4766
Sun Jammer Products, Inc., 9600 N. IH-35, Austin, TX 78753/512-837-8696
Super Vel, Hamilton Rd., Rt. 2, P.O. Box 1398, Fond du Lac, WI 54935
Sure Shot of LA, Inc., 103 Coachman Dr., Houma, LA 70360/504-876-6709
Survival Books/The Larder, 11106 Magnolia Blvd., North Hollywood, CA 91601/818-763-0804
Svon Corp., 280 Eliot St., Ashland, MA 01721/508-881-8852
Swann, D.J., 5 Orsova Close, Eltham North, Vic. 3095, AUSTRALIA/03-431-0323
Swift Bullet Co., P.O. Box 27, 201 Main St., Quinter, KS 67752/913-754-3959; FAX: 913-754-2359
Swift Instruments, Inc., 952 Dorchester Ave., Boston, MA 02125/617-436-2960; FAX: 617-436-3232
Swift River Gunworks, Inc., 450 State St., Belchertown, MA 01007/413-323-4052
Synchronized Shooting Systems, P.O. Box 52481, Knoxville, TN 37950-2481/800-952-8649
Szweda, Robert (See RMS Custom Gunsmithing)

T

3-D Ammunition & Bullets, 112 W. Plum St., P.O. Box J, Doniphan, NE 68832/402-845-2285; FAX: 402-845-6546
3-Ten Corp., P.O. Box 269, Feeding Hills, MA 01030/413-789-2086
300 Gunsmith Service, Inc., 6850 S. Yosemite Ct., Englewood, CO 80112/303-773-0300
Talmage, William G., RR16, Box 102A, Brazil, IN 47834/812-442-0804
Tamarack Products, Inc., P.O. Box 625, Wauconda, IL 60084/708-526-9333
Tanfoglio S.r.l., Fratelli, via Valtrompia 39, 41, 25068 Gardone V.T., Brescia, ITALY/30-8910361; FAX: 30-8910183
Tapco, Inc., P.O. Box 546, Smyrna, GA 30081/404-435-9782, 800-359-6195; FAX: 404-333-9798
Taracorp Industries, Inc., 16th & Cleveland Blvd., Granite City, IL 62040/618-451-4400
Targot Man, Inc., 49 Gerald Dr., Manchester, CT 06040/203-646-8335; FAX: 203-646-8335
Tasco Sales, Inc., 7600 NW 84th Ave., Miami, FL 33122/305-591-3670; FAX: 305-592-5895
Taurus, S.A., Forjas, Avenida Do Forte 511, Porto Alegre, BRAZIL 91360/55 512-40 22 44
TCCI, P.O. Box 302, Phoenix, AZ 85001/602-237-3823; FAX: 602-237-3858
TCSR, 3998 Hoffman Rd., White Bear Lake, MN 55110-4626/800-328-5323
TDP Industries, Inc., 603 Airport Blvd., Doylestown, PA 18901/215-345-8687
Tecnolegno S.p.A., Via A. Locatelli, 6, 10, 24019 Zogno, ITALY/0345-91114; FAX: 0345-93254
Tejas Resource, 104 Tejas Dr., Terrell, TX 75160/214-563-1220
Tele-Optics, 5514 W. Lawrence Ave., Chicago, IL 60630/312-283-7757
Tele-Optics, Inc., P.O. Box 176, 219 E. Higgins Rd., Gilberts, IL 60136/708-426-7444
Tepeco, P.O. Box 342, Friendswood, TX 77546/713-482-2702
Testing Systems, Inc., 220 Pegasus Ave., Northvale, NJ 07647
TETRA Gun Lubricants, 1812 Margaret Ave., Annapolis, MD 21401/410-268-6451; FAX: 410-268-8377
Texas Platers Supply Co., 2453 W. Five Mile Parkway, Dallas, TX 75233/214-330-7168
T.F.C. S.p.A., Via G. Marconi 118, B, Villa Carcina, Brescia 25069, ITALY/030-881271; FAX: 030-881826
Things Unlimited, 235 N. Kimbau, Casper, WY 82601/307-234-5277
Thomas, Charles C., 2600 S. First St., Springfield, IL 62794/217-789-8980; FAX: 217-789-9130
Thompson Bullet Lube Co., P.O. Box 472343, Garland, TX 75047/214-271-8063; FAX: 214-840-6743
Thompson Precision, 110 Mary St., P.O. Box 251, Warren, IL 61087/815-745-3625
Thompson Target Technology, 618 Roslyn Ave., SW, Canton, OH 44710/216-453-7707; FAX: 216-478-4723
Thompson/Center Arms, Farmington Rd., P.O. Box 5002, Rochester, NH 03867/603-332-2394
Threat Management Institute, 1 St. Francis Place 2801, San Francisco, CA 94107/415-777-0303
Thunderbird Cartridge Co., Inc. (See TCCI)
Tiger-Hunt, Michael D. Barton, Box 379, Beaverdale, PA 15921/814-472-5161
Tillinghast, James C., P.O. Box 405DG, Hancock, NH 03449/603-525-4049
Timber Heirloom Products, 618 Roslyn Ave. SW, Canton, OH 44710/216-453-7707; FAX: 216-478-4723
Timney Mfg., Inc., 3065 W. Fairmont Ave., Phoenix, AZ 85017/602-274-2999; FAX: 602-241-0361
Tioga Engineering Co., Inc., P.O. Box 913, 13 Cone St., Wellsboro, PA 16901/717-662-2730
Tirelli, Snc Di Tirelli Primo E.C., Via Matteotti No. 359, Gardone V.T., Brescia, ITALY 25063/030-8912819; FAX: 030-832240
TMI Products, 930 S. Plumer Ave., Tucson, AZ 85719/602-792-1075; FAX: 602-792-0093
Tom's Gun Repair, Thomas G. Ivanoff, 76-6 Rt. Southfork Rd., Cody, WY 82414/307-587-6949
Tom's Gunshop, 3601 Central Ave., Hot Springs, AR 71913/501-624-3856
Tooley, David, 516 Creek Meadow Dr., Gastonia, NC 28054
Totally Dependable Products (See TDP Industries, Inc.)
Trafalgar Square, P.O. Box 257, N. Pomfret, VT 05053/802-457-1911
Traft Gunshop, P.O. Box 1078, Buena Vista, CO 81211
Trammco, 839 Gold Run Rd., Boulder, CO 80302
Treso, Inc., P.O. Box 4640, Pagosa Springs, CO 81157/303-731-2295
Trevallion Gunstocks, 9 Old Mountain Rd., Cape Neddick, ME 03902/207-361-1130
Trico Plastics, 590 S. Vincent Ave., Azusa, CA 91702
Trijicon, Inc., P.O. Box 2130, Farmington Hills, MI 48333/313-553-4960; FAX: 313-553-6129
Trophy Bonded Bullets, Inc., 900 S. Loop W., Suite 190, Houston, TX 77054/713-645-4499; FAX: 713-741-6393
Trotman, Ken, 135 Ditton Walk, Unit 11, Cambridge CB5 8QD, ENGLAND/0223-211030; FAX: 0223-212317
Tru-Square Metal Prods., Inc., 640 First St. SW, P.O. Box 585, Auburn, WA 98001/206-833-2310
True Flight Bullet Co., 5581 Roosevelt St., Whitehall, PA 18052/800-875-3625; FAX: 215-262-7806
Tucker, James C., P.O. Box 38790, Sacramento, CA 95838/916-923-0571
Tyler Mfg.-Dist., Melvin, 1326 W. Britton Rd., Oklahoma City, OK 73114/405-842-8044

U

Ultra Light Arms, Inc., P.O. Box 1270, 214 Price St., Granville, WV 26534/304-599-5687
Unertl Optical Co., Inc., John, 308 Clay Ave., P.O. Box 818, Mars, PA 16046-0818/412-625-3810
Unique/M.A.P.F., 10, Les Allees, 64700 Hendaye, FRANCE 64700/33-59 20 71 93
United Binocular Co., 9043 S. Western Ave., Chicago, IL 60620
United States Ammunition Co. (See USAC)
United States Optics Technologies, Inc., 1501 E. Chapman Ave. 306, Fullerton, CA 92631/714-879-8922; FAX: 714-449-0941
United States Products Co., 518 Melwood Ave., Pittsburgh, PA 15213/412-621-2130
USAC, 4500-15th St. East, Tacoma, WA 98424/206-922-7589
Uvalde Machine & Tool, P.O. Box 1604, Uvalde, TX 78802

V

Valor Corp., 5555 NW 36th Ave., Miami, FL 33142/305-633-0127
Van Gorden & Son, Inc., C.S., 1815 Main St., Bloomer, WI 54724/715-568-2612
Van Patten, J.W., P.O. Box 145, Foster Hill, Milford, PA 18337/717-296-7069
Vancini, Carl A./Bestload, P.O. Box 4354, Stamford, CT 06907/FAX: 203-978-0796
Vann Custom Bullets, 330 Grandview Ave., Novato, CA 94947
Varner's Service, 102 Shaffer Rd., Antwerp, OH 45813/419-258-8631
Vega Tool Co., 1840 Commerce St. Unit H, Boulder, CO 80301/303-443-4750
Venco Industries, Inc. (See Shooter's Choice)
Verdemont Fieldsports, P.O. Box 9337, San Bernardino, CA 92427/714-880-8255; FAX: 714-880-8255
Verney-Carron, B.P. 72, 54 Boulevard Thiers, 42002 St. Etienne Cedex 1, FRANCE/33-77791500; FAX: 33-77790702
Vest, John, P.O. Box 1552, Susanville, CA 96130/916-257-7228
VibraShine, Inc., Rt. 1, P.O. Box 64, Mt. Olive, MS 39119/601-733-5614; FAX: 601-733-2226
Vibra-Tek Co., 1844 Arroya Rd., Colorado Springs, CO 80906/719-634-8611; FAX: 719-634-6886
Vic's Gun Refinishing, 6 Pineview Dr., Dover, NH 03820/603-742-0013
Vihtavuori Oy, SF-41330 VihtaVuori, FINLAND/358-41-779-211; FAX: 358-41-771643
Vihtavuori Oy/Kaltron-Pettibone, 1241 Ellis St., Bensenville, IL 60106/708-350-1116; FAX: 708-350-1606
Viking Video Productions, P.O. Box 251, Roseburg, OR 97470
Vincent's Shop, 210 Antoinette, Fairbanks, AK 99701
Vintage Industries, Inc., P.O. Box 872, Casselberry, FL 32718-0872/FAX: 407-699-4919; FAX: 407-699-8419
Vitt/Boos, 2178 Nichols Ave., Stratford, CT 06497/203-375-6859
Vom Hoffe (See Old Western Scrounger, Inc., The)
VSP Publishers, P.O. Box 887, McCall, ID 83638/208-634-4104

W

Waffen-Weber Custom Gunsmithing, 4-1691 Powick Rd., Kelowna, B.C. CANADA V1X 4L1/604-762-7575; FAX: 604-861-3655
Wahl Corp., Paul, P.O. Box 6, Bogota, NJ 07603-0006/201-342-9245; FAX: 201-487-9329
Walker Mfg., Inc., 8296 S. Channel, Harsen's Island, MI 48028
Wallace's, Star Rt.1, Box 76, Grandin, MO 63943/314-593-4773
Ward & Van Valkenburg, 114 32nd Ave. N., Fargo, ND 58102/701-232-2351
Warne Manufacturing Co., 9039 SE Jannsen Rd., Clackamas, OR 97015/503-657-5590; FAX: 503-657-5695
Warren Muzzleloading Co., Inc., Hwy. 21 North, Ozone, AR 72854/501-292-3268
WASP Shooting Systems, Rt. 1, Box 147, Lakeview, AR 72642/501-431-5606
Watson Trophy Match Bullets, 2404 Wade Hampton Blvd., Greenville, SC 29615/803-244-7948
Wayne Specialty Services, 260 Waterford Drive, Florissant, MO 63033/413-831-7083
WD-40 Co., P.O. Box 80607, San Diego, CA 92138/619-275-1400; FAX: 619-275-5823
Weatherby, Inc., 2781 Firestone Blvd., South Gate, CA 90280/213-569-7186, 800-227-2023; FAX: 213-569-5025
Weaver Arms Corp., P.O. Box 8, Dexter, MO 63841/314-568-3101
Weaver Products, Div. of Blount, Inc., P.O. Box 39, Onalaska, WI 54650/800-635-7656; FAX: 608-781-0368
Weaver Scope Repair Service, 1121 Larry Mahan Dr., Suite B, El Paso, TX 79925/915-593-1005
Webster Scale Mfg. Co., P.O. Box 188, Sebring, FL 33870/813-385-6362
Weems, Cecil, P.O. Box 657, Mineral Wells, TX 76067/817-325-1462
Weisz Antique Gun Parts, P.O. Box 311, Arlington, VA 22210/703-243-9161
Wells Custom Gunsmith, R.A., 3452 1st Ave., Racine, WI 53402/414-639-5223
Welsh, Bud, 80 New Road, E. Amherst, NY 14051/716-688-6344
Wenig Custom Gunstocks, Inc., 103 N. Market St., Lincoln, MO 65338/816-547-3334; FAX: 816-547-2881
Werth, T.W., 1203 Woodlawn Rd., Lincoln, IL 62656/217-732-1300
West, Robert G., 3973 Pam St., Eugene, OR 97402/503-344-3700
Western Design, 1629 Via Monserate, Fallbrook, CA 92028/619-723-9279
Western Gunstock Mfg. Co., 550 Valencia School Rd., Aptos, CA 95003/408-688-5884
Westfield Engineering, 6823 Watcher St., Commerce, CA 90040/FAX: 213-928-8270
Westley Richards & Co., 40 Grange Rd., Birmingham, ENGLAND B29 6AR/010-214722953
Westminster Arms Ltd., 9375 Freemont Way, Reno, NV 89506/916-827-2179
Wheel Weights Corp., 2611 Hwy. 40 East, Inglis, FL 34449
White Flyer Targets, 124 River Rd., Middlesex, NJ 08846/908-469-0100; FAX: 908-469-9692
White Flyer, Div. of Reagent Chemical & Research, Inc., 9139 W. Redfield Rd., Peoria, AZ 85381/800-647-2898
White Laboratory, Inc., H.P., 3114 Scarboro Rd., Street, MD 21154/410-838-6550; FAX: 410-838-2802
White Rock Tool & Die, 6400 N. Brighton Ave., Kansas City, MO 64119/816-454-047
White Systems, Inc., P.O. Box 190, Roosevelt, UT 84066/801-722-3085; FAX: 801-722-3054
Whitestone Lumber Corp., 148-02 14th Ave., Whitestone, NY 11357/718-746-4400; FAX: 718-767-1748
Whitetail Design & Engineering Ltd., 9421 E. Mannsiding Rd., Clare, MI 48617/517-386-3932
Whits Shooting Stuff, Box 1340, Cody, WY 82414
Wichita Arms, Inc., 923 E. Gilbert, P.O. Box 11371, Wichita, KS 67211/316-265-0661; FAX: 316-265-0760
Widener's Reloading & Shooting Supply, Inc., P.O. Box 3009 CRS, Johnson City, TN 37602/615-282-6786; FAX: 615-282-6651
Wideview Scope Mount Corp., 26110 Michigan Ave., Inkster, MI 48141/313-274-1238; FAX: 313-274-2814
Wilcox All-Pro Tools & Supply, RR 1, Montezuma, IA 50171/515-623-3138
Wildcatters, The, P.O. Box 170, Greenville, WI 54942
Wilderness Sound Products Ltd., 4015 Main St. A, Springfield, OR 97478/503-741-0263; FAX: 503-741-7648
William's Gun Shop, Ben, 1151 S. Cedar Ridge, Duncanville, TX 75137/214-780-1807
Williams Bullet Co., J.R., 2008 Tucker Rd., Perry, GA 31069/912-987-0274
Williams Gun Sight Co., 7389 Lapeer Rd., Box 329, Davison, MI 48423/313-653-2131, 800-530-9028; FAX: 313-658-2140
Williams Shootin' Iron Service, The Lynx-Line, 8857 Bennett Hill Rd., Central Lake, MI 49622/616-544-6615
Willson Safety Prods. Div., P.O. Box 622, Reading, PA 19603
Wilson Arms Co., The, 63 Leetes Island Rd., Branford, CT 06405/203-488-7297; FAx: 203-488-0135
Wilson, Inc., L.E., Box 324, 404 Pioneer Ave., Cashmere, WA 98815/509-782-1328
Winchester Div., Olin Corp., 427 N. Shamrock, E. Alton, IL 62024/618-258-3566; FAX: 618-258-3180
Winchester Press (See New Win Publishing, Inc.)
Windish, Jim, 2510 Dawn Dr., Alexandria, VA 22306/703-765-1994
Windjammer Tournament Wads, Inc., 750 W. Hampden Ave. Suite 170, Englewood, CO 80110/303-781-6329
Winkle Bullets, RR 1 Box 316, Heyworth, IL 61745
Winter, Robert M., RR 2, P.O. Box 484, Menno, SD 57045/605-387-5322
Wolfe Publishing Co., 6471 Airpark Dr., Prescott, AZ 86301/602-445-7810, 800-899-7810; FAX: 602-778-5124
Woodland Bullets, 638 Woodland Dr., Manheim, PA 17545/717-665-4332
Woodleigh (See Huntington Die Specialties)
World of Targets, Div. of Steidle Corp., 9200 Floral Ave., Cincinnati, OH 45242/513-791-0917; FAX: 513-792-0004
World of Targets (See Birchwood Laboratories, Inc.)
Worthy Products, Inc., RR 1, P.O. Box 213, Martville, NY 13111/315-324-5298
Wosenitz VHP, Inc., Box 741, Dania, FL 33004/305-923-3748; FAX: 305-925-2217
Wright's Hardwood Sawmill, 8540 SE Kane Rd., Gresham, OR 97080/503-666-1705
Wyant Bullets, Gen. Del., Swan Lake, MT 59911
Wyoming Armory, Inc., Box 28, Farson, WY 82932/307-273-5556
Wyoming Bonded Bullets, Box 91, Sheridan, WY 82801/307-674-8091
Wyoming Casting Co., 305 Commerce Dr. 10D, P.O. Box 1492, Gillette, WY 82717/307-687-7779, 800-821-2167
Wyoming Custom Bullets, 1626 21st St., Cody, WY 82414

Y

Yearout, Lewis E. (See Montana Outfitters)
Yee, Mike, 29927 56 Pl. S., Auburn, WA 98001/206-839-3991
York M-1 Conversions, 803 Mill Creek Run, Plantersville, TX 77363/800-527-2881, 713-477-8442
Young Country Arms, P.O. Box 3615, Simi Valley, CA 93093

Z

Z-Coat Industrial Coatings, Inc., 3375 U.S. Hwy. 98 S. No. A, Lakeland, FL 33803-8365/813-665-1734
Zeeryp, Russ, 1601 Foard Dr., Lynn Ross Manor, Morristown, TN 37814/615-586-2357
Zeiss Optical, Inc., Carl, 1015 Commerce St., Petersburg, VA 23803/804-861-0033; FAX: 804-862-3734
Zero Ammunition Co., Inc., 1601 22nd St. SE, P.O. Box 1188, Cullman, AL 35055-1188/800-545-9376; FAX: 205-739-4683
Zim's Inc., 4370 S. 3rd West, Salt Lake City, UT 84107/801-268-2505